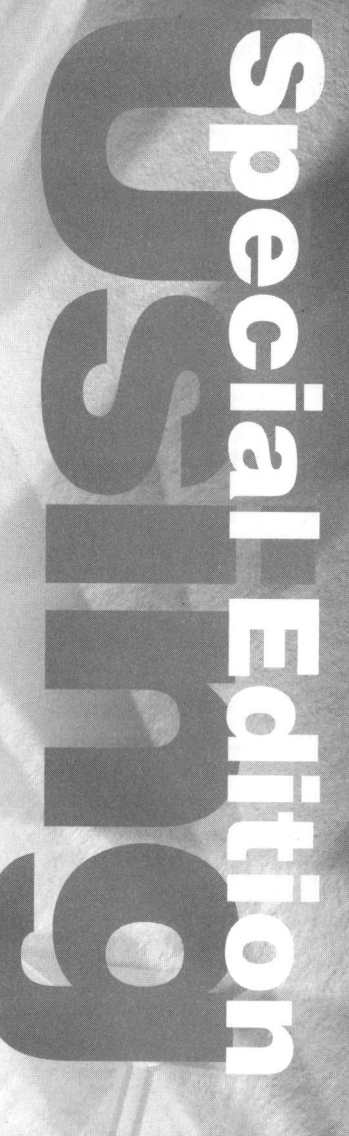

Using
Visual Basic® 6

Special Edition

que®

Special Edition

Using

Visual Basic® 6

que®

Brian Siler and Jeff Spotts

Special Edition Using Visual Basic® 6

Copyright© 1998 by Que

All rights reserved. No part of this book shall be reproduced, stored in a retrieval system, or transmitted by any means, electronic, mechanical, photocopying, recording, or otherwise, without written permission from the publisher. No patent liability is assumed with respect to the use of the information contained herein. Although every precaution has been taken in the preparation of this book, the publisher and author assume no responsibility for errors or omissions. Neither is any liability assumed for damages resulting from the use of the information contained herein.

International Standard Book Number: 0-7897-1542-2

Library of Congress Catalog Card Number: 98-84617

Printed in the United States of America

First Printing: September 1998

00 99 98   4 3 2

Trademarks

All terms mentioned in this book that are known to be trademarks or service marks have been appropriately capitalized. Que cannot attest to the accuracy of this information. Use of a term in this book should not be regarded as affecting the validity of any trademark or service mark.

Windows is a registered trademark of Microsoft Corporation.

Visual Basic is a registered trademark of Microsoft Corporation.

Warning and Disclaimer

Every effort has been made to make this book as complete and as accurate as possible, but no warranty or fitness is implied. The information provided is on an "as is" basis. The authors and the publisher shall have neither liability or responsibility to any person or entity with respect to any loss or damages arising from the information contained in this book.

Contents at a Glance

I | Getting Started with Visual Basic

1 Starting Out with Visual Basic 11
2 Creating Your First Program 17
3 Visual Basic Building Blocks 39
4 Using Visual Basic's Default Controls 59

II | Programming with Visual Basic

5 Responding to the User with Event Procedures 95
6 Giving More Control to the User: Menus and Toolbars 107
7 Using Dialog Boxes to Get Information 139
8 Using Variables to Store Information 159
9 Visual Basic Programming Fundamentals 173
10 Controlling the Flow of Your Program Code 203
11 Managing Your Project: Sub Procedures, Functions, and Multiple Forms 223

III | Visual Basic Program Components

12 Microsoft Common Controls 245
13 Working with Control Arrays 289
14 Creating ActiveX Controls 305
15 Extending ActiveX Controls 341
16 Classes: Resusable Components 359

IV | Visual Basic Interfaces

17 Multiple Document Interface Applications 381
18 Proper Interface Design 409
19 Using Visual Design Elements 425

V | Advanced Programming Topics

20 Accessing the Windows API 449
21 Working with Files 469
22 Using OLE to Control Other Applications 489
23 Master's Toolbox 501

VI | Visual Basic and Databases

24 Database Basics   527
25 The Data Control and Data-Bound Controls   545
26 Using Data Access Objects (DAO)   565
27 Using Remote Data Objects (RDO)   595
28 Using ActiveX Data Objects (ADO)   611
29 Creating Reports   641

VII | Visual Basic and the Internet

30 Using VBScript   665
31 Active Server Pages   687
32 ActiveX Documents   719
33 Visual Basic and Other Uses of the Internet   741

VIII | Appendixes

A Introduction to the Development Environment   759
B Packaging Your Applications   775
C SQL Summary   793

Index   829

Table of Contents

Introduction   1

Fundamental Visual Basic Programming   2

Working with Visual Basic Components   3

Creating Application Interfaces   4

Advanced Visual Basic Programming   4

Database Programming Techniques   5

Additional References   5

Source Code and Programs Used in This Book   6

Conventions and Special Elements Used in This Book   6

I Getting Started with Visual Basic   9

1 Starting Out with Visual Basic   11

What Is a Computer Program?   12

Computer Programs and Programming Languages   13

Visual Basic Is a Smart Language   14

The Importance of Designing Your Program   14
   How Design Fits into the Programming Process   15
   Program Design in a Nutshell   15

From Here...   16

2 Creating Your First Program   17

Creating Your Program's User Interface   18
   Getting Started   18
   Saving Your Work   20

Getting Information From the User   23
   Adding a TextBox Control   23
   Labeling Your Program's Controls   28
   Adding a Command Button   29

Changing a Form's Properties   30
   Saving Your Work—Again...   31

Coding Your Program's Actions   31
   Responding to Events   31
   Specifying Event Procedures   33
   Writing Program Code   34

Running Your Program   36

From Here...   38

3 Visual Basic Building Blocks   39

Forms   40
   Parts of a Form   40
   What Do Forms Do?   41

Using Controls   41
   What Are Controls?   41
   Control Functions   42

Exploring Properties   42
   Property Basics   43
   Common Properties   44
   Using Properties to Control an Object's Size   44
   Using Properties to Adjust an Object's Position   44
   Changing Properties at Runtime   45
   Using Properties to Control User Interaction   48
   Referencing Forms and Controls from Your Code   49

A First Look at Methods and Events   50
   Taking Action with Methods   50
   Responding to Actions with Events   51
   How Properties and Methods Are Related   51

Form Properties Revisited   52
   Displaying a Form   55

From Here...   57

4 Using Visual Basic's Default Controls   59

Introduction to the Intrinsic Controls   60

Working with Text   62
  Displaying Text with a Label Control   63
  Entering Text with a Text Box   65

Controls for Making Choices   66
  The Command Button   67
  Check Boxes   68
  Option Buttons   68
  The List Box   70
  The Combo Box   75

Special-Purpose Controls   78
  Scrollbars   78
  The Timer Control   81
  Frames   83

Working with Multiple Controls at Designtime   85
  Selecting Multiple Controls   86
  Using the Properties Window   87
  Using the Form Editor Toolbar   87
  Using the Format Menu   89
  Multiple Controls in a Frame   90

Working with the Controls Collection   90
  Changing All Controls   90
  Changing Selected Controls   91

From Here...   91

II Programming with Visual Basic   93

5 Responding to the User with Event Procedures   95

Introducing Events   96

Handling Events in Your Programs   97
  Determining When an Event Has Occurred   97
  Types of Events   98
  Writing Event Procedures   100
  Calling an Event Procedure from Code   101

Understanding Event Sequences   102
  Multiple Events for Each Action   102
  Determining the Order of Events   103

From Here...   106

6 Giving More Control to the User: Menus and Toolbars   107

Creating a Menu Bar   108
  Common Menus   109
  Setting Up the Main Items   110
  Multiple-Level Menus   112
  Grouping Menu Items   114
  Modifying the Menu   115
  Adding Access Keys and Shortcut Keys for Quick Access   116
  Writing Code for the Menu Items   119
  Optional Settings   119

Creating Pop-Up Menus   122
  Creating the Menu to Be Displayed   123
  Activating a Pop-Up Menu   124

Using Toolbars in Visual Basic   124
  Toolbar Basics   125
  Getting the Images for Your Toolbar   126
  Creating a Standard Toolbar   127
  Creating the Toolbar's Buttons   129
  Starting a Toolbar Example   131
  Enabling the Buttons with Code   132
  Creating a Toolbar with Code   133
  Allowing the User to Customize the Toolbar   135

Using the CoolBar Control   136

From Here...   137

7 Using Dialog Boxes to Get Information   139

Keeping the User Informed   140
  Understanding the Message Box   140
  Displaying a Message   141

Returning a Value from the *MsgBox* Function 143
Demonstrating the *MsgBox* Function 146

Getting Information from the User 146
Setting Up the *InputBox* Function 146
Values Returned by *InputBox* 147

Using Built-In Dialog Boxes 148
General Usage of the CommonDialog Control 148
Testing the CommonDialog Control 149
The File Dialog Boxes 150
The Font Dialog Box 152
The Color Dialog Box 154
The Print Dialog Box 155
The Help Dialog Box 157

Creating Your Own Dialog Boxes 157
Creating a Custom Dialog Box 157
Using Form Templates for Other Dialog Boxes 157

From Here... 158

8 Using Variables and Constants to Store Information 159

Introduction to Variables 160
Naming Variables 160
Types of Variables 161

Variable Declarations 163
Explicit Declaration 163
Implicit Declaration 164
Fixed-Length Strings 165

Variable Arrays 166

Determining Where a Variable Can Be Used 166
Creating Variables That Are Available Everywhere 167
Keeping a Variable Local 168
Using Static Variables 168

Using the *Option Explicit* Statement 169

What's Different About Constants 171
How to Use Constants 171
Constants That Visual Basic Supplies 171
Creating Your Own Constants 172

From Here... 172

9 Visual Basic Programming Fundamentals 173

Writing Statements 174

Using Assignment Statements 175

Using Math Operations 176
Addition and Subtraction 177
Multiplication and Division 178
Exponentiation 181
Operator Precedence 181

Working with Strings 182
String Concatenation 183
Determining the Length of the String 185
Changing the Case of a String 185
Searching a String 187
Extracting Pieces of a String 189
Getting Rid of Spaces 191
Replacing Characters in a String 191
Working with Specific Characters 193
Strings and Numbers 194

Formatting Results 195
Specific Formatting Functions 195
Using the *Format* Function 197
Manipulating Date Values 200

From Here... 202

10 Controlling the Flow of Your Program Code 203

Making Decisions in Your Program 204
Using the *If* Statement 204
Working with the *False* Condition 205
Working with Multiple If Statements 206
Using *Select Case* 207

Working with Loops 209
   For Loops 210
   Do Loops 211
   Enumeration Loops 214

Debugging Your Programs 214
   Stepping Through Your Code 216
   Working in the Immediate Window 217
   Tracking Variable Values 218

Error Trapping 219
   Using the *On Error* Statement 219
   Labeling Code Lines 219
   Controlling Program Flow After an Error 220
   Determining the Type of Error 221

From Here... 222

11 Managing Your Project: Sub Procedures, Functions, and Multiple Forms 223

Using Procedures and Functions 224
   Working with Procedures 224
   Working with Functions 231
   Determining the Scope of Procedures and Functions 232
   Reusing Functions and Procedures 233

Working with Multiple Forms 235
   Adding New Forms to Your Program 235
   Adding Code Modules to a Project 236
   Accessing the Forms and Modules of a Project 236

Managing Components in Your Project 237
   Managing Program References 238
   Controlling Your Controls 238
   Adding Forms, Modules, and Classes to the Project 238
   Removing Pieces 241

Controlling How Your Program Starts 241
   Setting the Startup Form 241
   Using *Sub Main* 241

From Here... 242

III Visual Basic Program Components 243

12 Microsoft Common Controls 245

Introduction to the Common Controls 246

The ImageList: A Fundamental Common Control 248
   Setting Up an ImageList at Designtime 248
   Setting Up an ImageList with Code 249

Organizing Your Data 250
   Using the ListView Control 251
   Using the TreeView Control 258
   Using the TabStrip Control 261

Accepting User Input 266
   Using an ImageCombo Control 266
   The UpDown Control 269
   Working with Dates 271
   Sliding into Numbers 275

Reporting Status and Progress 278
   Adding a Status Bar to Your Program 279
   Progress Bar 284
   Adding Video with the Animation Control 285

From Here... 287

13 Working with Control Arrays 289

Introducing Control Arrays 290
   Control Array Elements 290
   Understanding the Advantages of Control Arrays 290

Creating a Control Array 291
   Adding Control Arrays to a Form 291
   Writing Code for a Control Array 294
   Removing Elements from a Control Array 296

Working with Control Arrays 296
   Using a Control Array in Your Programs 296

Parallel Arrays 297

Creating a Menu Item Array 298

Loading and Unloading Controls at Runtime 299
  Creating the First Element of a Control Array 299
  Adding Controls at Runtime 300
  Removing Controls at Runtime 301

From Here... 303

14 Creating ActiveX Controls 305

ActiveX Basics 306
  Steps Involved in Building ActiveX Controls 306
  Development Strategies 307

Creating an ActiveX Control 307
  Starting the Address Control Project 307
  Adding Resize Code to the Control 309
  Adding a New Property to Your Control 310

Testing the ActiveX Control 311
  Testing with a Project Group 311
  Testing with Internet Explorer 313

Compiling Your Control 314
  Creating the OCX File 315
  Testing the Compiled Control 315
  Distributing the Control to Another Machine 315

Enhancing an ActiveX Control 317
  Setting Up the Base Control 318
  Enhancing the Base Control 319
  Testing the Limited Character Text Box 322
  Choosing a Toolbox Icon 323

Using the ActiveX Control Interface Wizard 323
  Adding the Wizard to Visual Basic 323
  Selecting and Creating Properties 324
  Mapping Properties 326
  Finishing the Code 327

Using the Property Pages Wizard 330
  Creating the Pages 330
  Adding Properties to the Pages 331
  Using the Property Pages in your Applications 332

Creating a User-Drawn ActiveX Control 332
  Starting the Project 333
  Creating the User Interface 333
  Creating the Properties of the Button 335
  Setting Up the Button's Events 337
  Creating Property Pages for the Button 337
  Testing the Color Button in a Program 338

From Here... 339

15 Extending ActiveX Controls 341

Using the *Ambient* Object to Maintain Uniformity 342
  Setting Up an *Ambient* Object Example 342
  Keeping Track of the *Ambient* Colors 343
  Properties of the *Ambient* Object 343

Introducing the *Extender* Object 344

Building the Calculator Control 345
  Creating the Control 345
  Creating the Interface 346
  Setting Up the *Operation* Property 347
  Coding Methods and Events 348
  Testing the Control 349

Creating Property Pages 350
  Creating Property Page Objects 350
  Placing Controls on the Property Pages 351
  Implementing the *SelectionChanged* Event Procedure 352
  Implementing the *Change Event* Procedures 352
  Implementing the *ApplyChanges* Event Procedure 353

Connecting the Property Page to the Control   353
Using Your Property Page   354
Handling Multiple Control Selections   355

Control Error Handling   355

From Here...   357

16 Classes: Reusable Components   359

Understanding Classes   360
Object-Oriented Programming   360
Classes in Visual Basic   361

Building Class Modules   361
Starting a New Class Module   362
Adding Properties to the Class   362
Adding Methods to the Class   365
Declaring and Using Objects   366
Adding Your Own Events   367

Creating an ActiveX DLL   368
Creating an ActiveX Project   368
Working with Multiple Projects   368
Setting the *Instancing* Property   371
Enums   372

Creating Classes That Contain Collections   373
Standard Collection Properties and Methods   373
Creating a New Collection for Grouped Actions   374

Using the Class Builder   376

From Here...   377

IV Visual Basic Interfaces   379

17 Multiple Document Interface Applications   381

Introducing MDI Applications   382
Characteristics of MDI Parent Forms   383
Characteristics of MDI Child Forms   384

Creating a Simple MDI Program   384
Setting Up a Parent Form   384
Setting Up a Child Form   386
Running the Program   387

Creating Multiple Instances of a Form   388
Setting Up the Basic Form   388
Creating Forms Using Object Variables   390
Using the Keywords *Me* and *ActiveForm*   390
Initializing an Instance of a Child Form   391

Working with Menus   391

Managing the Children   392
Using Automatic Organization   392
Maintaining a Window List   393

Creating a Sample Application—an MDI Contact Manager   395
Creating the MDI Form   396
Setting Up the Customer Child Form   397
Creating the Search Form   398
Creating the Heart of the Program   399
Running the Program   400

Optimizing Your MDI Application   400

Creating an MDI Application Framework   401
Creating the MDI Parent Template   402
The MDI Child   405

From Here...   407

18 Proper Interface Design   409

Designing Effective Forms   410
Keep Forms Neat and Uncluttered   410
Pay Special Attention to Data Entry Forms   411
Use the Right Control for the Job   412
Third-Party Controls   413
Multiple Forms   413

User PC Differences   415

Dealing with User Expectations 417
  The List Box 417
  Effective Menus 420
  Handling Multiple Instances of Your Application 420
  Perceived Speed 422

From Here... 423

19 Using Visual Design Elements 425

Using Graphics 426
  Graphics Controls 426
  Graphics Methods 432

Working with Text and Fonts 439
  Text Box Behavior 439
  Working with Fonts and Colors 441

From Here... 446

V Advanced Programming Topics 525

20 Accessing the Windows API 449

Understanding the Windows API 450

Using the Windows API in Visual Basic 452
  Using the API Viewer 452
  Creating a Wrapper Function 454
  Creating a Wrapper Class 455

Useful API Calls 457
  Fun API Calls 457
  Finding and Controlling Other Windows 458
  Waiting on a Program to Finish Running 461
  Callbacks and Subclassing 463

From Here... 467

21 Working with Files 469

File Functions in Visual Basic 470
  Using *Dir* to Find and List Files 470
  File-Manipulation Functions 473

Launching Other Programs with the Shell Function 475
Locating Files Relative to Your Application 475

Working with Text Files 477
  Sequential Text Files 477
  Reading from a Sequential Text File 478
  Writing to a Sequential Text File 480

Random Files—Creating Your Own File Format 482
  Creating a Record Type 482
  Opening a Random Access File 483
  Adding Records with *Put* 483
  Retrieving Records with *Get* 483
  Random Access with *Seek* 484

INI Files 484
  Understanding INI Files 484
  Using INI Files in Visual Basic 485

From Here... 487

22 Using OLE to Control Other Applications 489

Working with Word Objects 490
  The Microsoft Word Object Library 491
  Creating Application and Document Objects 492
  Saving, Opening, and Printing Documents 494
  Working with Text 494
  Other Useful Features 495
  Word.Basic 496

Working with Excel 496
  Creating Excel Objects 497
  Setting Cell and Range Values 497

Using the OLE Container Control 497
  Creating an Embedded Object at Designtime 498
  Creating an Embedded Object at Runtime 499
  Creating a Linked Object 499

From Here... 500

23 Master's Toolbox 501

Caller ID with Visual Basic 502
  Requirements for Using the Sample Program 502
  VB Techniques You'll Be Using 503
  Setting Up the Communications Control 505
  Checking for Calls 507

Building a Screen Saver in Visual Basic 509
  Setting Up the Main Form 510
  Adding Animation 511
  Interacting with Windows 512

SQL Server to Access Database Table Export Program 512
  Building the Sample Program 513
  Understanding the Sample Program 513

Using the Windows API to Create Transparent Images 519

From Here... 524

VI Visual Basic and Databases 525

24 Database Basics 527

Designing a Database 528
  Design Objectives 528
  Key Activities in Designing Your Database 529
  Organizing the Data 529
  Using Indexes 534
  Using Queries 536

Implementing Your Design 537

Using Visual Data Manager 537
  Creating the Database File 538
  Adding a New Table 539
  Making Changes to the Fields in Your Table 540
  Adding an Index to the Table 541
  Returning to the Visual Basic Design Window 542
  Viewing or Modifying the Structure of a Table 542
  Renaming or Deleting a Table 542
  Copying a Table 542

Creating a Database with Other Tools 543
  Using Microsoft Access 543
  Third-Party Database Designers 543

Why Use a Program Instead of Visual Data Manager? 543

From Here... 544

25 The Data Control and Data-Bound Controls 545

Understanding the Data Control 546
  What Is the Data Control? 546
  Adding a Data Control to Your Form 547
  The Two Required Properties 548

Getting Acquainted with Bound Controls 550
  What Do These Controls Do? 550
  Adding Controls to Your Forms 551
  Using a Bound Control to Display Data 552

Creating a Simple Application 553
  Setting Up the Form 553
  Navigating the Database 554
  Using Code with the Data Control 555
  Adding and Deleting Records 555

Creating Forms Automatically 557
  Setting Up the Data Form Wizard 557
  Getting to the Source of Your Data 559
  Choosing the Binding Type 560
  Choosing Fields with the Data Form Wizard 560
  Control Selection 561

From Here... 562

26 Using Data Access Objects (DAO) 565

Introduction to DAO 566

Setting Up a DAO Project 567

Opening an Existing Database 568

Deciding Which Recordset Type to Use 569
  Using Tables 570
  Using Dynasets 571
  Using Snapshots 573
  Using a Forward-Only Recordset 574

Placing Information Onscreen 575
  Accessing Information from Database Fields 575
  Displaying Data in the Sample Program 575

Positioning the Record Pointer 576
  Using the *Move* Methods 577
  Using the *Bookmark* Property 578
  Using the *Find* Methods 579
  Setting the Current Index in a Table 581
  Using the *Seek* Method 581
  Using the *PercentPosition* and *AbsolutePosition* Properties 584

Using Filters, Indexes, and Sorts 585
  Setting the *Filter* Property 585
  Setting the *Sort* Property 586
  Creating a New Index 586

Considering Programs That Modify Multiple Records 587
  Using Loops 587
  Using SQL Statements 589

Understanding Other Programming Commands 590
  Adding Records 590
  Editing Records 591
  Updating Records 591
  Deleting Records 592

Introducing Transaction Processing 592

From Here... 594

27 Using Remote Data Objects (RDO) 595

Database Access Philosophies 596

Working with ODBC 596
  Understanding ODBC Drivers 597
  Setting Up an ODBC Data Source 597

The Remote Data Objects 603
  Comparison of RDO to DAO 603
  Accessing a Database with RDO 605

Using the RemoteData Control 607
  Comparing the RDC and the Data Control 607
  Setting Up the RDC 608

From Here... 609

28 Using ActiveX Data Objects (ADO) 611

Introducing ADO 612
  Data Connection Methods 612
  Installation 612
  Setting Up a Data Source 613

Using the ADO Data Control 614
  Setting Up the ADO Data Control 615
  Connecting the ADO Data Control to a Data Source 616
  Displaying Data 618
  Changing the Record Source from Code 619

Using the DataGrid Control 619
  Getting Data into the Grid 620
  Setting Up the DataGrid 621
  Splitting Up the Grid 623
  Customizing the Grid's Layout 624
  Customizing the Grid with Code 626

Using ActiveX Data Objects 627
  Making the Connection with ADO 627
  Working with Recordsets 630
  The Command Object 636

Disconnected Recordsets 637
  Creating a Disconnected Recordset 637

Reconnecting a Recordset 638
Uses of a Disconnected Recordset 639

From Here... 640

29 Creating Reports 641

Creating a Simple Report 642
Setting Up the Data Source 642
Adding a Data Report to Your Project 643
Setting Up the Data Report 644
Displaying the Report 647

Enhancing Your Data Reports 648
Predefined Report Fields 648
Adding Graphics 649
Printing and Exporting 651
Function Fields 652

Using Crystal Reports 653
Creating a New Report 654
Customizing Your Report 657
Using the Crystal Reports Control 658

From Here... 661

VII Visual Basic and the Internet 663

30 Using VBScript 665

Introduction to VBScript 666
Enhancing the Internet with VBScript 666
VBScript on the Web Server 667
VBScript in the Browser 668

Tools Used with VBScript 671
The VB Scripting Engine 671
Host Application 671
Text Editor 672
Advanced Web Tools 672

The VBScript Language 673
Working with Variants Only 673
Using Objects for Added Power 674
Accessing the File System 675

Using VBScript in Internet Explorer 676
Events and Procedures 677
Forms 679
Using ActiveX Controls 681

The Windows Scripting Host 682
Running Scripts 683
Useful Objects and Methods 684

From Here... 685

31 Active Server Pages 687

Introduction to Active Server Pages 688
Active Server Pages Versus Standard HTML 688
Virtual Directories 690

Creating ASP Files 693
Creating a Simple ASP File 693
Using Server-Side Scripting Tags 693
Simple but Dynamic Web Pages 694
Using Include Files 696

Database Access with Active Server Pages 697
Querying a Database 698
Updating Information in a Database 701

The ASP Objects 704
Managing Security with the *Session* Object 705
Controlling Output with the *Response* Object 707
Retrieving Data with the *Request* Object 709
The *Server* Object 710
The *Application* Object and GLOBAL.ASA 710

Using Your Own ActiveX DLL with ASP 711

The IIS Application Project 711
Creating an IIS Application 712
Running an IIS Application 713
WebClass Instancing 714
Using an HTML Template WebItem 715
Using a Custom WebItem 717

From Here... 718

32 ActiveX Documents   719

Understanding ActiveX Documents   720
  What Is an ActiveX Document?   721
  What Are the Advantages of Using ActiveX Documents?   722

Creating Your First ActiveX Document   722
  Starting an ActiveX Document Project   723
  Creating the Interface of the Document   724
  Adding Code to the Document   726
  Testing Your ActiveX Document   726
  Compiling Your Document   729

Exploring the UserDocument Object   729
  Understanding the Key Events of a UserDocument   730
  Creating and Storing Properties for a UserDocument   730
  Working with the Methods of the UserDocument   731

Using the Hyperlink Object in Your Document   733

Using the ActiveX Document Migration Wizard   733
  Running the ActiveX Document Migration Wizard   734
  Looking at the Results of the Wizard's Work   736

Creating a More Complex Document   737
  Programming Additional Documents   737
  Using and Displaying Forms from the Document   738

From Here...   738

33 Visual Basic and Other Uses of the Internet   741

Adding Browser Functionality to Your Application   742
  Creating a Browser on a Form   742
  Launching the Browser from Your Application   744

Programming E-Mail   747
  Logging on to E-Mail   748
  Sending a Message   749
  Accessing the Contents of a Message   750

Using the Internet Transfer Control   751
  Retrieving HTML   751
  Transferring Files   753

From Here...   755

VIII Appendixes   759

A Introduction to the Development Environment   759

Understanding the Environment's Key Features   760

Starting Up   761

The Visual Basic Work Area   762
  Using the Menu Bar   763
  Accessing Functions with the Toolbars   764
  Organizing Visual Basic's Controls   766
  The Canvas of Your Programs   769
  Controlling Your Forms and Controls   770
  Using the Project Window   771
  Where Work Gets Done   772
  Customizing Your Environment   773

B Packaging Your Applications   775

Compiling Your Program   776
  Optimizing Your Code   776
  Setting the Project Name, Title, and Icon   777
  Preparing to Create a Setup Program   778

Packaging a Standard EXE Project   778
  Creating a Standard EXE Package   778
  A Closer Look at the Setup Process   785

Packaging ActiveX Components   788
  Internet Download   788

Scripting Options 789
Files Created for the Internet 790

From Here... 791

C SQL Summary 793

Defining SQL 794
What SQL Does 794
The Parts of the SQL Statement 795

Using *SELECT* Statements 796
Defining the Desired Fields 796
Specifying the Data Sources 801
Using *ALL*, *DISTINCT*, or *DISTINCTROW* Predicates 802
Setting Table Relationships 803
Setting the Filter Criteria 806
Setting the Sort Conditions 810
Using Aggregate Functions 811
Creating Record Groups 813
Creating a Table 815
Using Parameters 815

SQL Action Statements 816
Using the *DELETE* Statement 816
Using the *INSERT* Statement 817
Using the *UPDATE* Statement 818

Using Data-Definition-Language Statements 818
Defining Tables with DDL Statements 818
Defining Indexes with DDL Statements 819

Using SQL 820
Executing an Action Query 820
Creating a *QueryDef* 821
Creating Dynasets and Snapshots 821
Using SQL Statements with the Data Control 822

Creating SQL Statements 823
Using the Visual Data Manager 823
Using Microsoft Access 825

Optimizing SQL Performance 825
Using Indexes 826
Compiling Queries 826
Keeping Queries Simple 826

Passing SQL Statements to Other Database Engines 827

From Here... 827

Index 829

Credits

EXECUTIVE EDITOR
Brad Jones

ACQUISITIONS EDITOR
Kelly Marshall

DEVELOPMENT EDITOR
Christopher Nelson

MANAGING EDITOR
Jodi Jensen

PROJECT EDITOR
Maureen Schneeberger McDaniel

COPY EDITOR
Chuck Hutchison
Kelli Brooks

INDEXER
Bruce Clingaman

TECHNICAL EDITORS
Mark Hurst
Simon Mordzynski

PRODUCTION
Marcia Deboy
Jennifer Earhart
Cynthia Fields
Susan Geiselman

To Julia, Larry, Ben, and Brent for all of your loyal support.
　　　　　　　　　　　- Brian Siler

To my lovely wife Tina and our beautiful daughter Lauren, for making me smile every single day. You make me better at everything I do.
　　　　　　　　　　　- Jeff Spotts

About the Authors

Brian Siler works as a senior programmer analyst for a major hotel corporation, developing its executive information system in Visual Basic. Brian is a graduate of the University of Memphis with a B.S. in Computer Science. He has developed applications using Visual Basic, C, HTML, and SQL on a variety of platforms including PCs, AS/400, UNIX, and Vax. He was the co-author of Que's *Special Edition Using Visual Basic 5, Second Edition*, and Que's *Platinum Edition Using Visual Basic 5*. Brian may be contacted via e-mail at `bsiler@bigfoot.com`.

Jeff Spotts is a Senior Business Systems Analyst for Federal Express Corporation. By night, he teaches Visual Basic programming courses at State Technical Institute at Memphis. He also develops custom-designed software systems for individuals and businesses. His specialty is creating database applications using Visual Basic as a front-end interface to a variety of database engines. He has been involved with computer hardware and software since the late 1970s, and has been programming with Visual Basic since just after its introduction. Jeff was a co-author of *Special Edition Using Visual Basic 5, Second Edition*. He may be contacted via e-mail at `jspotts@bigfoot.com`.

Acknowledgments

The authors wish to acknowledge the steadying influence of our Acquisitions Editor, Kelly Marshall, and our Product Director, Chris Nelson, for helping to keep this project afloat and on track in occasionally stormy seas. We would also like to acknowledge our co-workers (both full-timers and the contractors who make the real money) for their continued advice and support.

Tell Us What You Think!

As the reader of this book, *you* are our most important critic and commentator. We value your opinion and want to know what we're doing right, what we could do better, what areas you'd like to see us publish in, and any other words of wisdom you're willing to pass our way.

As an Executive Editor for the Programming team at Macmillan Computer Publishing, I welcome your comments. You can fax, e-mail, or write me directly to let me know what you did or didn't like about this book—as well as what we can do to make our books stronger.

Please note that I cannot help you with technical problems related to the topic of this book, and that due to the high volume of mail I receive, I might not be able to reply to every message.

When you write, please be sure to include this book's title and author as well as your name and phone or fax number. I will carefully review your comments and share them with the author and editors who worked on the book.

Fax: 317-817-7070

E-mail: `adv_prog@mcp.com`

Mail: Executive Editor
Programming
Macmillan Computer Publishing
201 West 103rd Street
Indianapolis, IN 46290 USA

Introduction

In this chapter

Fundamental Visual Basic Programming   2

Working with Visual Basic Components   3

Creating Application Interfaces   4

Advanced Visual Basic Programming   4

Database Programming Techniques   5

Internet Programming   5

Additional References   5

Source Code and Programs Used in This Book   6

Conventions and Special Elements Used in This Book   6

Congratulations! You have decided to embark on learning Visual Basic.

This is an exciting time; there never has been a better time for Visual Basic programmers. While Visual Basic has always made it easy to develop Windows programs, through the years it has matured into a true professional development language and environment. You still can quickly create Windows programs with Visual Basic, but now you also can write enterprise-level client/server programs and robust database applications. In fact, the newest version contains several enhancements that greatly increase the power and flexibility that programmers have to write database-enabled applications. While this is enough to get you hyped up about programming in Visual Basic, there's even more available in Visual Basic version 6.

As you know, the Internet is revolutionizing computing. You also may have seen enough of Internet programming to think that it is reserved for only a select group of programmers. Visual Basic version 5 introduced several tools that let you work more easily with the Internet. Now, in version 6, these Internet tools are even more powerful and easy to use. There are tools that let you easily connect your programs to the Internet and include browser capabilities in your programs. In addition, over the past year or so, certain Web servers and browsers have added support for a special flavor of Visual Basic known as VBScript. The Visual Basic knowledge that you acquire will translate easily into the ability to create VBScript code as well.

With VBScript, you can create ActiveX documents and ActiveX controls from Visual Basic. Because ActiveX is a critically important part of Microsoft's Internet strategy, this puts you right in the middle of the action. And the really good news is that all of your ActiveX pieces can be used in non-Internet programs as well, extending the usefulness of any ActiveX components you create. The ActiveX components you create can even be used by programmers working with other languages, such as C++.

Microsoft also has integrated a special version of Visual Basic known as Visual Basic for Applications (VBA) into all the components of the Microsoft Office suite, Microsoft Project, and several other programs. Because VBA is the core language component of Visual Basic, this means that all your knowledge of Visual Basic can be applied to writing applications and macros for other products. And because Microsoft has licensed VBA to dozens of companies, you will soon be able to write applications and macros for those programs, as well. All this benefit comes from your Visual Basic knowledge.

Okay, so now you are excited about learning Visual Basic. Your next question is, "What will this book do for me?"

Fundamental Visual Basic Programming

Although this book presents a lot of material on advanced Visual Basic programming, you can't just jump into these topics and expect to understand them. You need a good foundation from which to work.

In Part I of the book, "Getting Started with Visual Basic," you are introduced to what Visual Basic can do and how to work in the development environment.

Chapter 1, "Starting Out with Visual Basic," discusses how Visual Basic works to create Windows-based computer programs and starts you out designing your first program.

In Chapter 2, "Creating Your First Program," you work step-by-step through the process of building a fully functional application in Visual Basic.

Chapter 3, "Visual Basic Building Blocks," takes you on a tour of forms and controls, which are the fundamental components of every program you will create in Visual Basic. You will see how you can manipulate forms and controls by modifying their properties and how you can perform tasks with their methods.

In Chapter 4, "Using Visual Basic's Default Controls," you learn how to work with the group of controls that is most commonly used when designing your applications.

Part II, "Programming with Visual Basic," covers the basics to get you started on your programming adventure.

Chapter 5, "Responding to the User with Event Procedures," discusses how Visual Basic programs become interactive. You'll learn how to make your programs react to the various actions your users can initiate.

In Chapter 6, "Giving More Control to the User: Menus and Toolbars," and Chapter 7, "Using Dialog Boxes to Get Information," you look at how you can enhance your programs by using menus, toolbars, and dialog boxes. These program components give your users an interface that is familiar because of their experience with other Windows programs. The proper use of menus, toolbars, and dialog boxes makes your programs more intuitive to the user. You also examine the Event model, which is the cornerstone of programming in a Windows environment.

In Chapter 8, "Using Variables to Store Information," and Chapter 9, "Visual Basic Programming Fundamentals," you are led into the world of programming commands, structures, and variables. Visual Basic is built upon the solid foundation of the BASIC language. The Visual Basic language is rich in features and functions that let you write programs to handle practically any task. You learn how to create and use variables, and how to perform math and string operations. Chapter 10, "Controlling the Flow of Your Program Code," explains how to control your program through the use of decisions and loops and through error handling.

Chapter 11, "Managing Your Project: Sub Procedures, Functions, and Multiple Forms," takes you even further into the programming concepts that will help you enhance your program code.

Working with Visual Basic Components

Part III, "Visual Basic Program Components," expands the fundamental knowledge that you have gained so far by exploring various types of components you can use to enhance your applications. Think of these components as building blocks that are more advanced than the basic ones you learned about in preceding chapters.

Chapter 12, "Microsoft Common Controls," introduces you to even more of the controls that Visual Basic provides for you to use when you build your programs.

In Chapter 13, "Working with Control Arrays," you learn more advanced techniques for using groups of variables to make your programs more efficient.

You learn much about ActiveX components in Chapter 14, "Creating ActiveX Controls," and Chapter 15, "Extending ActiveX Controls." These components can be used in Visual Basic programs, Internet applications, or other ActiveX-enabled programs. These chapters walk you through the process of creating, and then enhancing, your own ActiveX controls.

Chapter 16, "Classes: Reusable Components," teaches you how to create classes, which allow you to take advantage of a very powerful programming feature that simplifies your work when you have many programs that perform similar tasks.

Creating Application Interfaces

In Part IV, "Visual Basic Interfaces," you are introduced to some concepts of designing your programs' interfaces, which is what your users will interact with.

In Chapter 17, "Multiple Document Interface Applications," you learn how to create a Multiple Document Interface (MDI) program. This type of program enables your users to work with multiple windows contained within one main window. You'll see how MDI applications differ from those created with single forms.

Chapter 18, "Proper Interface Design," and Chapter 19, "Using Visual Design Elements," discuss reasons why it is important to design your program before you start writing code. You will also see some of the things that make a bad user interface and learn how to avoid some of the common design mistakes.

Advanced Visual Basic Programming

Part V, "Advanced Programming Topics," consists of several topics that that go beyond the concepts you have already learned to focus on some very specific programming techniques.

Chapter 20, "Accessing the Windows API," shows you how to access the multitude of predefined programming routines available in Windows' Applications Programming Interface. You will see how your programs can take advantage of a vast library of code that is available to any Windows application.

Chapter 21, "Working with Files," discusses how your programs can use different types of files for information storage and retrieval purposes.

Chapter 22, "Using OLE to Control Other Applications," shows you how to use OLE to have your programs interact with other programs, taking full advantage of the power of OLE.

Chapter 23, "Master's Toolbox," demonstrates several standalone Visual Basic applications that perform a variety of interesting tasks.

Database Programming Techniques

Database programs make up a large percentage of all programs in use in the business world today. These programs range in complexity from simple programs for managing mailing lists to complex programs handling reservations and billing for major corporations. Part VI, "Visual Basic and Databases," takes you through the process of building database applications to meet a variety of needs.

Chapter 24, "Database Basics," discusses how to create and manipulate a database. You continue in Chapter 25, "The Data Control and Data-Bound Controls," by learning how to quickly create applications using the Data control in conjunction with the controls that can be bound to it.

Chapter 26, "Using Data Access Objects (DAO)," and Chapter 27, "Using Remote Data Objects (RDO)," show you how to harness the programming power that is available for creating database applications.

Chapter 28, "Using ActiveX Data Objects (ADO)," introduces you to Microsoft's latest model for working with databases.

Finally, Chapter 29, "Creating Reports," shows you how to output data from your database applications using the new Data Report Designer and Crystal Reports, a third-party reporting tool.

Internet Programming

In Part VII, "Visual Basic and the Internet," you are exposed to the growing world of using variations of Visual Basic for Web-based applications.

Chapter 30, "Using VBScript," teaches you about this up-and-coming cousin of Visual Basic. You will apply much of this knowledge in Chapter 31, "Active Server Pages," where you learn how VBScript is processed by Web servers to provide flexibility in the information that is presented on the Internet.

Chapter 32, "ActiveX Documents," extends the ActiveX concepts that you learned earlier into the ability to create ActiveX components that can be shared in an advanced way.

Chapter 33, "Visual Basic and Other Uses of the Internet," shows you how to Web-enable your Visual Basic applications. Among other topics, you learn how to add Internet-browsing and e-mail capabilities to your programs.

Additional References

You can use Part VIII, "Appendixes," as a guide to some of the things you'll need to know as you develop your Visual Basic applications.

Appendix A, "Introduction to the Development Environment," gives you a tour of Visual Basic's interface. You can use this appendix as a guide while you explore the Visual Basic environment.

Appendix B, "Packaging Your Applications," shows you how to prepare the Visual Basic programs that you write for distribution.

Appendix C, "SQL Summary," presents the fundamentals of Structured Query Language (SQL), which is used to perform operations such as data retrieval on databases. This information will be of value to you as you read the chapters that deal with accessing databases from your Visual Basic programs.

Source Code and Programs Used in This Book

All the source code from the listings and programs included in this book is available via download from the Que—Macmillan Computer Publishing Web site. You can download the listings code to save typing time and errors as you follow examples in the book. You also can obtain all the programs built in the book and additional sample programs we've included.

To access this material, follow these steps:

1. Point your browser to the following URL:
   www.mcp.com/info
2. Enter the book's ISBN as directed:
   0-7897-1542-2
3. Follow the instructions to access and download the specific code or program you are looking for.

Conventions and Special Elements Used in This Book

This book includes various conventions and special elements to highlight specific things and make using the book easier. Familiarize yourself with these conventions and elements, and allow them to enhance your reading experience.

Conventions

The following list details conventions used in the book:

- *Italic type* is used to emphasize the author's points or to introduce new terms.
- Screen messages, code listings, and command samples appear in monospace type.
- URLs, newsgroups, Internet addresses, and anything you are asked to type also appear in monospace type.
- Keyboard hotkeys are indicated with underlining. For example, if you see the command Tools, Options, pressing Alt and T causes the Tools menu to open. You can then press O to select the Options menu item.

- Occasionally, a code sample or listing will show a portion of program code with certain lines set in **`bold monospace`** type. In such cases, the bold type signifies code you are to add to existing code. This approach enables you to see what you are supposed to add or change in context.
- Because of the space limitations of this book's pages, a few code lines in this book's examples cannot be printed exactly as you must enter them. In cases where breaking such a line is necessary to fit within the book's margins, the Visual Basic continuation character (_) will be used at the end of the line that is broken. You can leave these characters out and enter the code on a single line, or just enter the characters as they appear. Visual Basic will understand the code either way.

Special Elements

Certain types of information is set off in special book elements. The following explanations and examples indicate the kinds of elements you will encounter in the book.

Each chapter begins with a "road map," or list of the key topics covered in the chapter, along with a page number so you can easily find the relevant material. Then at the end of each chapter, a "From Here..." section summarizes briefly the topics discussed in the chapter and refers you to other chapters that cover related material or extend the topic you just read about.

▶ **See** cross-references within each chapter for directions to more information on a particular topic.

TIP Tips present short advice on a quick or often overlooked procedure.

NOTE Notes provide additional information that might help you avoid problems, or offer advice that relates to the topic. ■

CAUTION
Cautions warn you about potential problems that a procedure might cause, unexpected results, and mistakes to avoid.

Sidebar
Longer discussions not integral to the flow of the chapter are set aside as sidebars. Look for these sidebars to find out even more information.

PART I

Getting Started with Visual Basic

1 Starting Out with Visual Basic 11

2 Creating Your First Program 17

3 Visual Basic Building Blocks 39

4 Using Visual Basic's Default Controls 59

CHAPTER 1

Starting Out with Visual Basic

In this chapter

What is a Computer Program? 12

Computer Programs and Programming Languages 13

Visual Basic Is a Smart Language 14

The Importance of Designing Your Program 14

When people find out I know something about Visual Basic, I am often asked questions such as the following:

- What is Visual Basic?
- Is Visual Basic a program?
- What can you do with Visual Basic?
- Why should I learn Visual Basic?

Microsoft's Visual Basic product is defined as a *programming system*. Simply put this programming system is used to write Windows-based computer programs; it includes the Visual Basic language as well as a number of tools that help you write these programs. You don't use Visual Basic as a productivity tool; you use it to create customized productivity tools. By using Visual Basic to create your own customized programs, you (or your company) are not bound by the limitations of a particular "off-the shelf" computer program; rather, you can design applications to meet your own specific needs. A good computer program should be flexible enough to fit the task at hand, rather than having to modify your needs to fit the program.

This chapter introduces you to the concept of a computer program and discusses programming languages as they pertain to creating your own programs. The chapter concludes with some important considerations related to planning and designing a program. This material provides a bit of context for Chapter 2, "Creating Your First Program."

What Is a Computer Program?

With Visual Basic, you can design programs, also known as *applications*, to accomplish just about any task you can imagine. Computer programs generally fall into two very broad categories—packaged and custom.

Packaged programs are those that you can purchase in a software store, via mail order, direct from a manufacturer, and so on. Packaged programs are predesigned to accomplish some specific task. For example, you may purchase Microsoft Word to meet your word processing needs, Symantec's WinFax Pro to enable your computer to send and receive faxes, or McAfee's VirusScan to help prevent viruses from attacking your system. You may also be interested in game programs such as Broderbund's Myst or Microsoft Flight Simulator. All these programs are among the thousands upon thousands of software packages that are available for Windows-based PCs.

Custom programs are usually designed for a specific purpose within a particular organization. For example, a company may need an application that tracks product orders from the time they are placed until they are actually shipped. If there is no packaged program available that meets the company's specific needs, a custom program could be developed. One advantage of a custom program in this case is that the program can be continually modified as the company's needs change—packaged programs generally can't be modified by the user.

> **N O T E** Some computer programs fall in between our characterization of packaged and custom programs. A number of software developers offer customized versions of their programs that start off as packaged programs. This is quite common among *vertical-market* software developers—those who create programs that are used in a specific industry. For example, I have spent a number of years developing a software system that is used by exposition managers to manage flea markets, antique fairs, trade shows, and so on. All my clients use the same basic system, but many of them have asked for special customization features that apply to a specific situation.
>
> Another of these types of "hybrid" programs is actually meant to work as a customized interface to a packaged program, in effect enabling a user to customize a program that wasn't designed as customizable!

One thing that all computer programs have in common, however, is that they are developed using one or more programming languages such as Visual Basic.

Computer Programs and Programming Languages

A computer program is nothing more than a set of instructions that a computer follows to accomplish a specific task. A programming language such as Visual Basic is used to translate instructions as we humans understand them into the steps that the computer can comprehend and follow.

When you get down to a computer's most basic level, the microprocessor that is at the core of the computer's functionality doesn't understand anything other than numeric instructions. To make matters worse, the only instructions that the processor can understand are incredibly simplistic commands, most of which have to do with moving numbers around between memory locations. These commands that the processor understands are known as *machine language*, or the most basic language that the machine (the PC) can use.

Machine language is known as a *low-level* language, because it's all the way down at the processor's level of understanding. As you might imagine, writing programs in machine language is an incredibly daunting task. Fortunately, you don't have to get down to that level to create computer programs. Several higher-level programming languages have been developed to enable us to write programs. These programming languages allow programmers to write instructions in something resembling English; the instructions are then converted into a program containing machine-language instructions that the processor can understand.

Some examples of programming languages that have developed over the years include Fortran and COBOL, which are generally used with mainframe computers, as well as BASIC, Pascal, C, and C++, which are commonly used to write programs at the personal computer level.

Visual Basic is a descendant of BASIC, which has been around for a number of years. BASIC (Beginner's All-Purpose Symbolic Instruction Code) was originally developed, as the name implies, as a language for beginners. BASIC was often the first language that programmers learned in order to become familiar with programming basics before moving on to more powerful languages.

With the advent of Windows, Microsoft developed Visual Basic, which is a *visual* (graphical) version of BASIC. Since its introduction, Visual Basic has developed into an extremely powerful application development tool, leaving its reputation as a beginners' language far behind.

One very nice feature of Visual Basic is the fact that you can use it to create a solid application very quickly. As you'll see throughout this book, Visual Basic makes short work of what would normally be very time-consuming programming tasks. This frees up the programmer to spend his time developing the application's functionality, rather than spending time on mundane, repetitive programming tasks. Visual Basic is often referred to as a Rapid Application Development (RAD) tool.

Visual Basic Is a Smart Language

The main reason why Visual Basic is so popular and powerful is the same reason behind the success of Windows. Microsoft took a complex technology (writing computer programs) and made it easier to use through a graphical interface. Suppose you have to write a program for your company. In a visual programming environment, you can quickly design the windows that the user sees by drawing and arranging them just as you would lay out elements for a newspaper. In a text-based programming system, you control the user interface through program language commands. Common sense tells you that the visual programming method is easier for newcomers to learn and requires less time to maintain. In this case, the old adage "a picture is worth a thousand words" truly applies.

However, do not let me give you the impression that Visual Basic is just another pretty interface. Another key concept of Visual Basic is the ability to create and use self-contained components, or *objects*. One type of object that you learn about very shortly is a Visual Basic control.

Controls are elements you can use when designing a user interface, just like the real-life controls on a car dashboard. These controls can be used to display information (like a speedometer) or take action (like the ignition switch). The underlying operations of the car, such as the relationship between ignition, starter, and engine, are hidden from the driver; he "communicates" with the car through a clearly defined interface. In the same way, Visual Basic controls enable you to add features to your programs without you having to be involved in the details of how these features work. For example, receiving input from a user of your program is as simple as drawing a control that accepts input. This is a great advantage of visual programming languages—you can concentrate on what you want your program to do, not how to get the programming language to do it.

The Importance of Designing Your Program

A college English professor of mine was once describing different types of novelists: "A traditionalist author usually orders his story beginning-middle-end, a modernist might reverse that order, and a post-modernist would only include two of the three parts."

Unfortunately, authors of computer programs don't have that luxury. Due to the structured nature of computing, it's critically important to design your programs *before* beginning to code them. Many programmers tend to want to dive in and start coding right off the bat, but you should get into the habit of planning, even with small programs. If you do nothing else, sit down with a blank sheet of paper, make some notes about what you want the program to accomplish, and sketch out what the user interface should look like.

> **NOTE** Please keep in mind that the strategy presented in this chapter is by no means the only approach to programming, but rather one set of general guidelines. Your technique, of course, may be totally different.

How Design Fits into the Programming Process

When creating a computer program, it's important to take a structured approach. Certain steps need to be accomplished in a certain order, and you might as well get used to doing things the right way. It's always tempting to fire up Visual Basic and dive right in to designing and coding the program, but a little time spent with proper planning can save you a lot of headaches later in the process.

The key steps in creating a computer program are as follows:

1. Plan the program's tasks (how it should work).
2. Design the user interface (how it should look).
3. Write the program's code (implement steps 1 and 2).
4. Test and debug the program (including beta testing with users outside of the development team, if appropriate).
5. Document and distribute the program (put it in use).

These steps are very generalized and definitely not all-inclusive. As I discuss the sample program in this chapter, I'll list some steps specific to Visual Basic programming.

The first two steps listed define the core process of actually building the program. The sample program in Chapter 2 provides a context for explaining some of the specifics in designing and building a Visual Basic program. Although you run the sample program in Chapter 2, the last two steps aren't covered until later in the book.

> **NOTE** If you are tackling a large project, breaking it down into smaller pieces will make it much more manageable. Many of Visual Basic's features can be used to divide up a large project among members of a development team.

Program Design in a Nutshell

When starting a new project, it is tempting to just sit down and start hacking out code. After all, drawing the interface and writing the program code is the most fun and creative aspect of programming. However, a good program starts with a solid design. An in-depth flowchart might not be necessary for very small-scale projects, but on the other hand it is always a good idea to start with a plan.

The design process should produce the following results:

- A concise list of tasks to be performed by the program.
- Deadlines for when particular tasks need to be completed.
- Clarification of the dependence of one part of the program on another.
- The criteria for testing the program.

For a program like the example in Chapter 2, the design can be a simple statement of what the program should accomplish. For more complex programs, the design might include written criteria, data diagrams, flowcharts, a milestone document, and a test and acceptance plan. It is up to you and your client (the program's user) to determine the right level of documentation that is necessary for a given project. However, you should always make sure that the design is clearly spelled out, and you should always write it down.

From Here...

This chapter has exposed you to the fundamentals of writing Visual Basic programs. The following chapters will get you started in developing your own applications:

- To step through the process of developing a Visual Basic program, see Chapter 2, "Creating Your First Program."
- For an explanation of the fundamental pieces that comprise Visual Basic programs, see Chapter 3, "Visual Basic Building Blocks."
- For a more in-depth discussion of writing Visual Basic applications, see Chapter 9, "Visual Basic Programming Fundamentals."

CHAPTER 2

Creating Your First Program

In this chapter

Creating Your Program's User Interface   18

Getting Information From the User   23

Changing a Form's Properties   30

Coding Your Program's Actions   31

Running Your Program   36

It's common among programming texts to have the reader begin by creating a very basic first program along the lines of the classic `Hello, World` application. In this extremely simple example, the user is asked to initiate some action such as clicking a button or pressing a key, and the computer responds with a message such as "Hello, World!" A slightly more advanced variation asks for the user's name and responds with a customized greeting like "Hello, Lauren!"

Although these examples might be sufficient for demonstrating that you can indeed use a programming language to create a program, the resulting application isn't very useful. Our approach is to begin with a sample program that not only demonstrates the fundamentals of creating a Visual Basic application, but can also be used in the real world.

In this chapter, you'll create a Loan Calculator program that calculates the periodic payment needed to repay a loan, based on various factors such as the loan term and interest rate. Your users will be able to input and modify values for these and other variable factors, perform the calculation, and view the results. In addition, they will be able to view an amortization schedule for the entire life of the loan.

As you can see, the preceding paragraph specified what the program would do and what information was required to perform the task, and provided some information about how the interface should be designed. That wasn't so bad, was it?

NOTE The application you'll be creating was adapted from a shareware program I wrote named My Amortizer. With proper planning and design, Visual Basic can be used to create commercial-quality software applications.

Creating Your Program's User Interface

A program's *user interface* refers to the part(s) of the program that the user sees and interacts with. As you develop this application's interface, you'll see how to use some of the many tools provided in Visual Basic's Integrated Development Environment (IDE). As discussed in Chapter 1, "Starting out with Visual Basic," the Visual Basic IDE makes short work of interface design, which was once a daunting task at best.

Before you begin, take a look at what the final product will look like. Figure 2.1 shows the Loan Calculator's main screen as it's being used.

Getting Started

Let's begin by creating a new project. A *project* is simply a set of files that store information about the components that make up an application (program). To create a Visual Basic program, you customize your project's various components.

To get started with the Loan Calculator program, start Visual Basic; you will see the New Project dialog box shown in Figure 2.2. If Visual basic is already running, or if you don't see the New Project dialog, choose File, New Project (see Figure 2.3).

Creating Your Program's User Interface   19

FIGURE 2.1
The Loan Calculator program offers the user a variety of options.

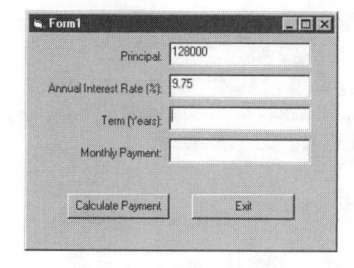

FIGURE 2.2
When Visual Basic starts, this version of the New Project dialog box is shown.

FIGURE 2.3
This version of the New Project dialog box is presented when a new project is begun after Visual Basic is already running.

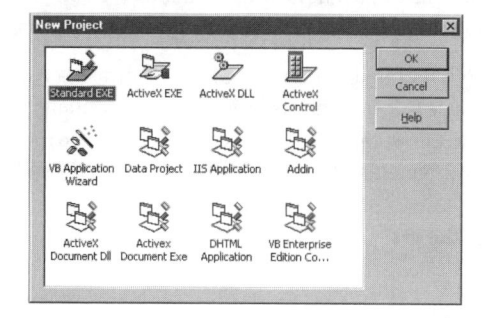

The New Project dialog box enables you to specify the type of project you want to create. For the Loan Calculator project, select the Standard EXE option and click OK. You will then be placed in Visual Basic's design environment, as illustrated in Figure 2.4.

NOTE Due to Visual Basic's many customization features, your screen may not look exactly like the one shown in Figure 2.4.

FIGURE 2.4
Visual Basic's design environment is the canvas for creating your application.

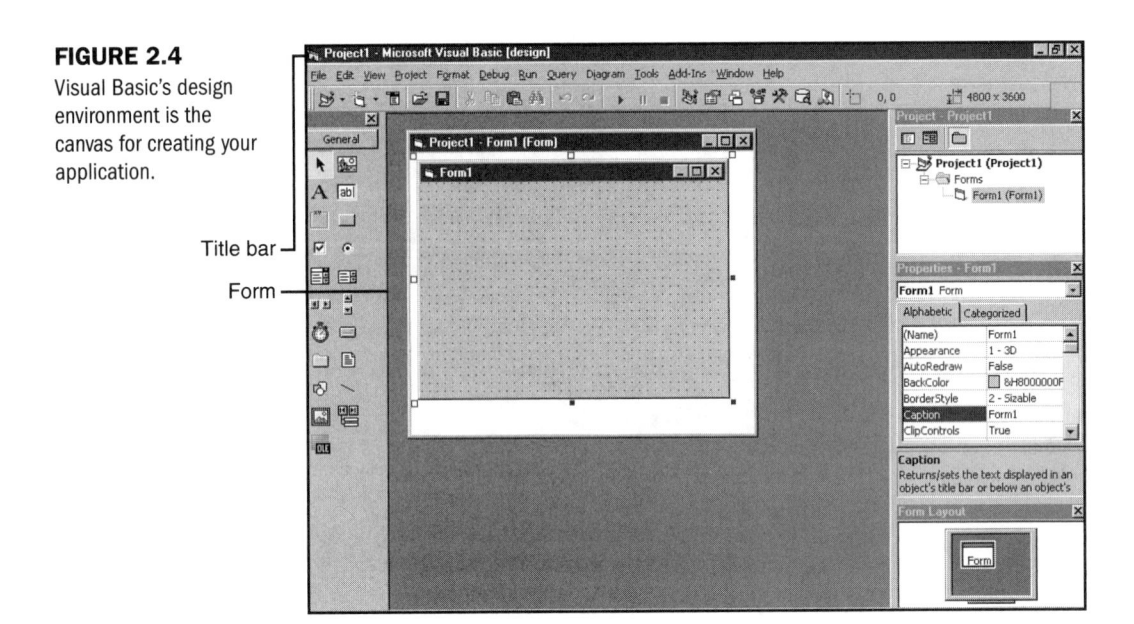

Title bar
Form

First off, notice Visual Basic's title bar—specifically, the word *design*. This means that you are in *Design mode*, also known as *designtime*, a name for the time you spend designing your program. Later, when you run your program, Visual Basic will be in *Run mode*.

As you see, a new Standard EXE project consists of one *form*, or window, which will usually be your program's main user interface. Visual Basic applications are comprised of one or more components, such as forms, code modules and classes, along with controls and other components.

Look at the *Project Explorer* (illustrated in Figure 2.5). It consists of a list of the contents of the current project. Because you've just begun this project, it only contains a single form named Form1, which is located in the Forms folder of the project (named Project1 by default). A project can grow to include many components; the Project Explorer helps keep them organized.

FIGURE 2.5
The Project Explorer lists all the components that make up a project.

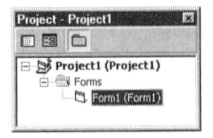

Saving Your Work

It's bound to happen eventually—your system crashes, the electricity goes out, or Fido kicks out your computer's power cord, and all your hard work is gone. To minimize your losses when something like this (inevitably) happens, you should get in the habit of saving your work to your hard disk as soon as you begin a new project, and then save it frequently as your application grows. At the very least, you should always save your application before running it. That way, if running your program causes the system to crash (yes, it can—and does—happen to the best of us), you won't lose your work.

Saving Visual Basic Projects   The process of saving a project is a little more complex than you might expect; however, with a little practice you'll have no problem. To save a project, you must save each component of your project (each form, code module, and so on) into its own file, and then save the project itself into its project file. Think of the project file as a list of the names and locations of the components that make up the project.

> **TIP**   It's a good idea to create a folder on your hard drive for each project that you work on. This makes it easy to keep all the files that make up a particular project organized in one place. If you follow this practice, you can also store non–Visual Basic files, such as documentation, project cost analysis spreadsheets, customized graphics, and so on, in the same folder.

To save a project, choose File, Save Project from the Visual Basic menu system, or simply click the Save Project button on the toolbar. The first time you save the project, (or after you subsequently add any files to the project) you'll be led through one or more of the Save File As dialog boxes (see Figure 2.6), one for each of the project components, and then a Save Project As dialog box for the project file. You specify the name and location of each file where the components (and project) are to be saved. Subsequent Save Project operations simply resave the components using the same filenames as before. Then you can easily execute frequent, quick saves of a previously saved project by clicking the Save Project button. If one or more components have been added to the project since it was last saved, the Save File As dialog box will be presented for each new component.

> **NOTE**   Visual Basic has an option that assists you in making sure your project is properly saved. Choose Tools, Options from Visual Basic's main menu, and then click the Options dialog's Environment tab. In the When a Program Starts frame, you can tell Visual Basic to automatically save any changes to your project when you run it, or to prompt you to decide if changes should be saved before running.

FIGURE 2.6
The Save File As dialog box enables you to specify the name and location of the files that store your application's components.

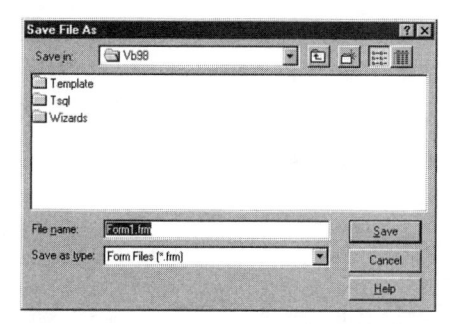

> **TIP** You can save a single project component individually by selecting the component in the Project Explorer and choosing File, Save *(component name)* in the menu system, or by right-clicking the component in the Project Explorer and choosing Save *(component name)* from the context menu that appears. You can also save a component with a different filename than it was originally saved under by using one of these methods and selecting the Save *(component name)* As option.

Saving the Loan Calculator Project Now let's save the sample Loan Calculator project. Choose File, Save Project, or click the Save Project button on the toolbar. You will first be prompted to save your application's one form (Form1). This displays the Save File As dialog box so you can specify the name and location of your application's files:

- The *File Name* text box is used to name the file where the component will be stored. In the example, the default filename of Form1.frm is presented. Change the filename to the more descriptive LoanCalcMain. You don't need to add the file extension .FRM; it will be automatically appended to the filename you enter.

- The *Save In* drop-down list box at the top of the dialog box enables you to specify the *location* where the component should be stored. If nothing has been saved during this Visual Basic session, a default folder (usually the folder where Visual Basic resides) will be presented. Use the Save In drop-down list box to navigate to the folder where you want to store the files that make up this application. If necessary, you can use the Create New Folder button to make a new folder for the project.

> **CAUTION**
> *Never* save your application's component files in the same folder as Visual Basic's program files. It's usually good practice for an application to have its own folder.

For the purposes of this example, navigate to the root of your hard drive, use the Create New Folder button to make a new folder, and change the folder's name from New Folder to LoanCalc. Then double-click the LoanCalc folder to make it current, and click Save to complete the operation.

After you've saved the form, you'll be presented with the Save Project As dialog box, where you can specify the name and location of the project file. The default location should now be the same location where you saved the form file. Change the suggested filename Project1.vbp to Loan Calculator (the extension .VBP, for Visual Basic Project, will be added for you). Click Save to finish.

Now that you've laid out the application's infrastructure and named and saved its files, you're ready to begin true development. Of course, in order for your program to process data, you need to plan how to get the necessary data from the user.

> **NOTE** Depending upon the options that were chosen when Visual Studio was installed, you may be presented with a dialog box asking if you want to add the project to SourceSafe.

SourceSafe is a system that helps ensure that project source files are properly protected and backed up, and it helps organize different versions of source files. For now, just answer No to this question. ■

Getting Information from the User

Most computer programs are interactive—they need to receive information from the user as well as provide information to the user. A Visual Basic program interacts with its user through controls that are placed on the program's form(s). A *control* is an object you place on a form that interacts with the user or the program. Many of Visual Basic's controls can be used to obtain input from the user.

The user interface for the Loan Calculator program will be responsible for accepting input, displaying output, and initiating the loan calculations. You use three of Visual Basic's most commonly used controls:

- *TextBox* controls to accept textual information needed from the user, and to display certain information back to the user.
- *Label* controls to act as captions, displaying information to the user. Labels are similar to TextBoxes, except that the user can't edit the information presented in them.
- *CommandButton* controls, which the user can click to initiate program actions.

All these controls are part of the basic set of controls found in Visual Basic's Toolbox (see Figure 2.7).

FIGURE 2.7
Visual Basic's Toolbox contains the controls needed to build applications.

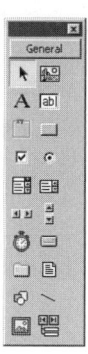

Adding a TextBox Control

The TextBox control, also known simply as a *text box*, is (as its name implies) a *box* that displays and accepts *text*. In a way, it's similar to a text box you might find on a survey form. It can accept input (from a pen or pencil) as well as display information. The TextBox control is one example of how far programming languages have advanced. Earlier programming environments required a lot of work to exchange information with the user. Visual Basic works in conjunction with Windows to take care of the mundane details of where the text is positioned on the screen, how it's retrieved from the user, and so on. Your Visual Basic program simply needs to be concerned with the text in the text box; the control itself takes care of the rest.

Adding a Control to a Form   In order for a Visual Basic program to use a control, that control must be placed on a form. For your Loan Calculator program, you begin by placing a TextBox control on the main form:

1. Click the tool for the TextBox control in the Toolbox. If you aren't sure which is the TextBox control, let your mouse pointer pause over each in turn to see a ToolTip.
2. Move the mouse pointer to the form. Note that the pointer changes to a crosshair, indicating that you're about to draw a control.
3. Move the pointer to one corner of the area where you want to draw the control.
4. Click and hold the left mouse button.
5. Drag the mouse to where you want the diagonally opposite corner of the control. As you drag the mouse, notice that a sizing box appears from the first corner of the control's location (where you first clicked the mouse button) to the current mouse pointer location. This box indicates where the control will eventually be (see Figure 2.8).

FIGURE 2.8
A ToolTip-type box appears showing the actual dimensions of the control in twips (a special unit of measurement that will be covered later in the book).

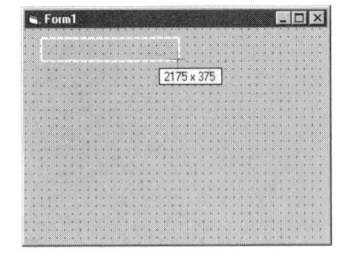

6. When you're satisfied with the size and shape of your control, release the mouse button. The control will be drawn on the form (see Figure 2.9).

FIGURE 2.9
The completed text box appears on the form and is selected (notice the sizing handles).

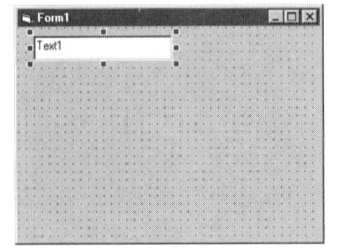

> **TIP** You can also add a control to a form by double-clicking the control's Toolbox icon. This places a control of a default size in the center of the form. You can then move and resize the control as desired with the sizing handles, as described in the upcoming section, "Moving and Resizing a Control."

The procedures used to draw the TextBox control are the same as those for drawing most controls on a form.

Setting a Control's Properties   After you have added a control to a form, you will usually want to set one or more of the control's properties. *Properties* are settings that control the appearance and behavior of an object. For the text box you just added, you want to set the Name and Text properties.

The Name property is very important. It is used in program code to identify the control. Because a program will likely have many controls of the same type, you can use the control's name property to identify the particular control for which a particular code statement is written.

Every control must have a name, which is represented by the value of its Name property. In addition, every control on a particular form must have a *unique* name, unless it's part of a control array. (*Control arrays* are covered in detail in Chapter 13, "Working with Control Arrays;" for now, just make sure all your controls on a given form have unique names.)

Visual Basic assigns a default name to every control placed on a form. Because this is the first text box you've placed on this form, its default name is Text1. Subsequently placed text boxes would be named Text2, Text3, and so on. It's very good programming practice to change the default control names to be more descriptive. Assume, for example, you have three text boxes on a form that are used to accept a customer's last name, first name, and address. If you change the default names of Text1, Text2, and Text3 to something more descriptive, such as txtLName, txtFName, and txtAddress, it will be much easier to remember what each control's purpose is when you (inevitably) must modify your program's code at some future date.

> **TIP** Note that the control names suggested begin with the prefix txt. It's common to begin a control name with a three-character lowercase prefix denoting the type of control; the rest of the name describes the control's purpose. Thus, when debugging program code, it is immediately clear that txtLName refers to a TextBox control that contains last name information. Other commonly used prefixes include lbl for Label controls and cmd for CommandButton controls.

To change the name of the first text box you placed on the form for the Loan Calculator project, you must first make sure the control is selected. The *selected* control is the one for which properties will be changed in the Properties window. As you'll see a little later, multiple controls can be selected at the same time. You can tell if a control is selected if it has a series of eight sizing handles around its borders. The selected control's name also appears in the Properties window's Object box, which is the drop-down list just below the Properties window's title bar. If the desired control isn't selected, simply click it one time to select it.

Now that the control is selected, look at the Properties window. The left column of the Properties window is a list of properties that apply to the selected object at design time. Each property's current value is denoted in the right side of the Properties window. Look for the Name property in the left column, which appears at the top of the list (because the Name property is so important, it appears before all the other properties, which are presented alphabetically. You can also sort the properties by Category by clicking the Categorized tab). Click the Name property, making it the current property (note that the property name is highlighted). Note the default value—Text1—of the Name property on the right side. At this point, you can simply type a new value for the Name property, or edit the existing value. Change the value of your TextBox control's Name property by typing a more descriptive name—let's use txtPrincipal—and pressing Enter. Figure 2.10 shows the Properties window after making this change.

A TextBox control's Text property represents the text that's entered in the box—that is, what is displayed inside the box on the screen. As the user types in a text box, Visual Basic constantly modifies the text box's Text property to reflect the current contents of the box. By default, a new text box contains its own name; your new text box contains Text1 in its Text property (recall that Text1 was the control's name when it was created). You don't want anything in the Text property when the program starts; in other words, you want the box to start off empty. To accomplish this, locate the TextBox control's Text property in the Properties window. Select the current value (Text1), and press the Delete key.

FIGURE 2.10
Use the Properties window to set values for your controls' properties.

Adding the Remaining Text Boxes Now that you've added one TextBox control to the form, it should be a simple matter to add the other text boxes that you need for your Loan Calculator program. Add three more text boxes to the form; name them txtIntRate, txtTerm, and txtPayment. Clear their Text properties as well. When you're done, your form should look similar to the one in Figure 2.11.

If your form doesn't look exactly like the one in Figure 2.11, don't worry. One nice thing about a visual design environment is that you can change the appearance of objects quite easily.

FIGURE 2.11
The interface of the Loan Calculator program has four text boxes.

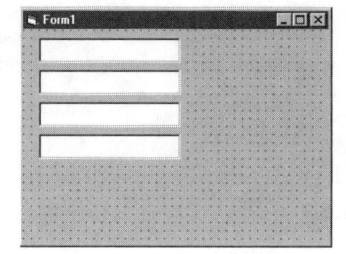

> **TIP** To draw multiple controls of the same type, hold down the Ctrl key when you select the control's tool in the Toolbox. That tool will remain selected in the Toolbox even after you've finished drawing a control. You can keep drawing multiple instances of that control without having to reselect the tool. When you're through drawing that control, select the Toolbox's pointer tool to return the mouse pointer to its normal state.

Moving and Resizing a Control   If you don't like where a control is positioned, use the mouse to drag it to a new location. If you pause while dragging it, note that the control's current position (relative to the form's top-left corner) is displayed as a ToolTip.

If you want to change the size of a control, you must first select it, which causes the sizing handles to appear. You can then use the mouse to change the control's size by dragging the sizing handles. The handles on the control's top and bottom edges change its height. The handles on the control's left and right edges change its width. The handles on the control's corners change its height and width simultaneously. Note how the sizing box described earlier appears as you're resizing the control to help you visualize the control's final size.

Now that you have created text boxes for the user's input, you should label them so that the user knows what to enter in each box. To make room for the labels, move the text boxes to the right. You could drag each text box individually; however, it is quicker to move them all together at the same time. You can easily select them all and move the entire group. To do this, click one of the text boxes to select it, and then hold down Ctrl while you click each of the others. Notice that each text box that you select in this manner gets its own set of sizing handles. After you've got them all selected, begin dragging one of them. As you drag, the entire group is dragged at once. Drop the controls on the right side of the form; when you're done, your form should look like Figure 2.12.

FIGURE 2.12
Selecting multiple controls enables you to move them together as a group.

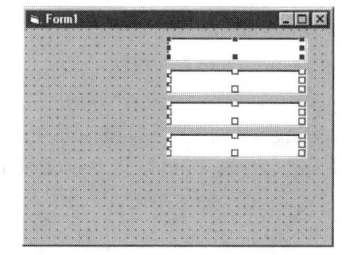

> **TIP** Instead of Ctrl+clicking multiple controls, you can select a group of controls by drawing a rectangle around them. Click and hold down the left mouse button in an empty area of the form. Note that a "rubber-band" box stretches as you move the mouse. Draw the box around all the controls you want to select.

Labeling Your Program's Controls

Obviously, the user needs to know which values are to be entered into each of the text boxes. The easiest way to do this is to add a Label control next to each text box. The label will then act as a caption for the text box, containing a brief description of what data is to be entered there.

Although the user perceives Label controls and TextBox controls to be quite different, they are very similar from a programmer's perspective. They can both contain the same types of text, although the text in a Label control can't be modified by the user. However, by setting various properties of a Label control, the *appearance* of the text contained in it can be altered in many ways. Figure 2.13 illustrates several Label controls demonstrating a variety of looks.

FIGURE 2.13
Labels can take on many different sizes and appearances.

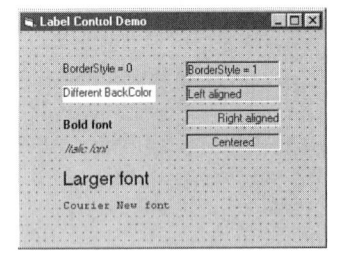

To continue your earlier analogy of a survey form, Label controls are like the words that are pre-printed on the form to identify the purpose of the text boxes. The key difference between a Label control and a TextBox control is that a Label control contains text that the user cannot change. The text contained in a Label control is stored in its Caption property (as opposed to a TextBox control's Text property).

To add a Label control to a form, follow these steps:

1. Select the Label control's tool in the Toolbox.
2. Draw a Label control to the left of the first TextBox control.
3. In the Properties window, change the Label control's Name property to lblPrincipal.
4. Change the Label control's Caption property to Principal:.
5. Change the Label control's Alignment property to 1 - Right Justify, using the drop-down arrow next to the property setting (see Figure 2.14). This makes the label align its caption along the right side, next to its corresponding text box, as is common with caption labels.

FIGURE 2.14
Clicking the drop-down arrow for the Alignment property allows you to select from predefined settings.

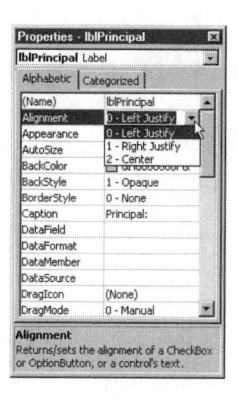

You should now be able to see how the Label control will aid the user in determining what to type in the first text box. Create three more Label controls, one for each of the remaining text boxes. Use the recommended values for the Name and Caption properties outlined in Table 2.1 (don't forget to set the Alignment property as well). When you're finished, your form should look like the one shown in Figure 2.15.

Table 2.1 Name and Caption Properties for the Loan Calculator Program's Label Controls

Name Property	Caption Property
lblPrincipal	Principal:
lblIntRate	Annual Interest Rate (%):
lblTerm	Term (Years):
lblPayment	Monthly Payment:

FIGURE 2.15
The Loan Calculator program's labels show the user what to enter in the text boxes.

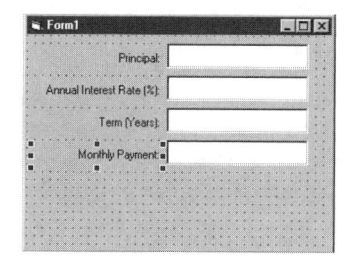

Adding a Command Button

So far, your sample application's form has a set of text boxes to accept the user's input, and a set of labels to identify those text boxes. You also need some way for the user to initiate actions—this is the purpose of CommandButton controls. A user can click a CommandButton control, also commonly known as a *command button* (or simply a *button*), to cause something to happen. You can add a command button to a form just like you add other controls—by using the mouse to draw it.

Like labels, command buttons have a Caption property that enables you to determine what text will appear on the button's face, so the user will know what the button does.

To complete the interface of the Loan Calculator program, add two command buttons near the bottom of the form. Set their Name and Caption properties according to Table 2.2. Figure 2.16 shows the completed Loan Calculator interface.

Table 2.2 Name and Caption Properties for the Loan Calculator Program's CommandButton Controls

Name Property	Caption Property
cmdCalculate	Calculate Payment
cmdExit	Exit

FIGURE 2.16
After you have added the CommandButton controls, the Loan Calculator's interface is complete.

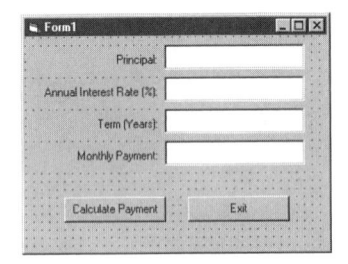

Changing a Form's Properties

Just as you define a control's appearance and behavior by setting its properties, you can also set a form's properties to govern its appearance and behavior.

Just like controls, forms have a Name property. The default name for a project's first form is Form1; subsequently added forms are named Form2, Form3, and so on. As with controls, it's a good idea to give forms a more descriptive name. Use the Properties window to change the Name property of the Loan Calculator project's one and only form to frmMain.

Follow these steps to change the form's Width property:

1. Click an empty area of the form to deselect any control(s) that may be selected. This has the effect of selecting the form itself. Note that the form's name appears in the Properties window's Object box.

2. Now that the form itself is selected, the properties presented in the Properties window are the *form's* properties. Scroll the Properties window until you find the Width property near the bottom of the list and note its value.

3. Change the form's width by using the mouse to click and drag the sizing handle in the center of the form's right edge (if you've changed your setup so that VB is running in SDI mode, you resize a form by simply dragging an edge or corner). Note that the value of the Width property in the Properties window has changed.

4. To change the Width property back to its original value, select the new value in the right side of the Properties window and replace it with its original value. When you press Enter, the form's width is changed.

Saving Your Work—Again...

Now that you've completed designing the Loan Calculator's interface, this would be an excellent time to save your work so far. Because you already saved your nearly empty project just as you started it, resaving it is very easy—and highly recommended. In fact, it makes sense to save your work at several stages of the interface development process. You never know when you'll have problems; a quick save only takes a few seconds, and could save you a lot of work when those problems do happen.

To resave your project, choose File, Save Project from the menu system, or simply click the Save Project button on the toolbar. Because you've already told Visual Basic where to save the files that make up your project, they're automatically saved in the same location, using the same filenames. If you have added new components (forms, modules, and so on) since the last save, you will be prompted for a filename and location for each of the newly added components.

Coding Your Program's Actions

As mentioned earlier, the user interface of the Loan Calculator program is now complete. However, it doesn't actually do anything at this point. In order for your program to become functional, you need to write some code. The term *code*—as it is used in this book—refers to one or more lines of programming commands, written in a particular programming language (Visual Basic, in your case).

Responding to Events

Visual Basic is an object-oriented, event-driven language. This means that a program's interface is comprised of *objects* (controls, forms, and so forth); the program is "taught" what actions to perform when *events* happen to those objects.

An event is usually initiated by the user. By anticipating the possible events that can (and should) occur to the various objects in your program, you can write code to respond to those events appropriately. For example, in the case of a command button labeled Exit, your code should respond to that button's Click event by ending the program. This code should execute whenever the Exit button's Click event occurs.

You cause a program to respond to events by placing code in *event procedures*. An event procedure is a segment of code that is executed when a particular event occurs to a particular object.

In the case of a user clicking an Exit button, you need to add code to the Exit button's Click event procedure. Let's illustrate this by writing code for the Click event procedure of your Loan Calculator program's Exit button.

Double-click the Exit button that you placed on the sample application's form. You'll see a new window called a Code window (see Figure 2.17). You can open a separate code window for each form (or other kind of module) in your project, and this is where you place code that relates to that form and the objects contained in it. Notice that the Code window contains a template, or shell, of a sub procedure, beginning with the words Private Sub and ending with the words End Sub. A *sub procedure* (also known simply as a *procedure*) is a discrete sequence of code statements that has a name and is executed as a unit.

FIGURE 2.17
The Code window is a full-featured editor for the code that relates to your program's objects.

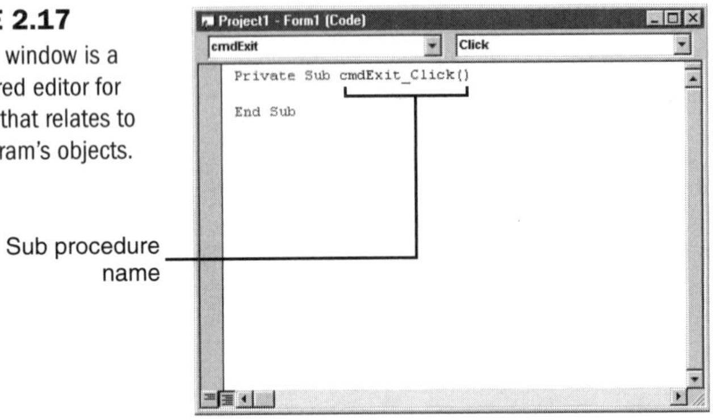

Sub procedure name

The part after the words Private Sub denotes the sub procedure's name. This particular sub procedure is named cmdExit_Click, a predefined name that denotes the Click event procedure for the control named cmdExit. Visual Basic will execute any code located within this sub procedure whenever the Click event occurs to this command button.

> **NOTE** Most controls can react to one of several different events; each type of control has a default event, which is the event that usually occurs to that type of control most often. For example, the Click event is the one that occurs most often to a CommandButton control. The default event is the one that is opened in the Code window when you double-click a new control.

To cause the program to end when the user clicks the Exit button, you simply need to add one line of code—Visual Basic's End statement—to the cmdExit_Click procedure. Your cursor should already be on the blank line between the Private Sub cmdExit_Click() and End Sub statements; if it's not, simply click there. Press Tab to indent the code (that makes it easier to read), and then type the word End. Press Enter to insert a new blank line into the procedure (this isn't necessary, but the extra blank line improves readability). When you're done, your complete sub procedure should look like this code:

```
Private Sub cmdExit_Click()
    End

End Sub
```

Congratulations! You just wrote your first Visual Basic code.

Specifying Event Procedures

Look at the two drop-down list boxes near the top of the Code window, as shown in Figure 2.18. The *Object box* (the one on the left) lists all the objects that have been placed on the current form, as well as the form itself. The *Procedure box* (on the right) lists all the events that apply to whichever object is currently selected in the Object box. Using these two drop-down list boxes enables you to navigate to any portion of the Code window. Think of the code for a particular form as one long text file; the Code window is a navigation tool that helps you quickly display a specific object/event combination.

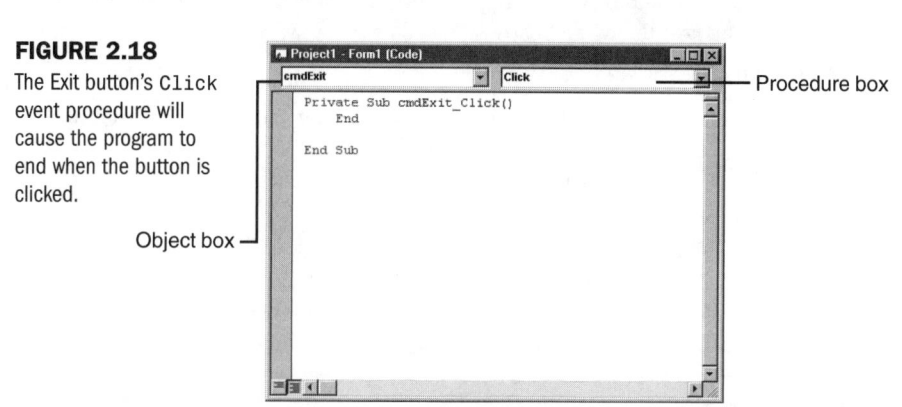

FIGURE 2.18
The Exit button's `Click` event procedure will cause the program to end when the button is clicked.

Object box

Procedure box

```
Private Sub cmdExit_Click()
    End
End Sub
```

When you double-click a control at design time, the Code window automatically opens to the default event for the control you clicked, unless some event other than the default already has code in its event procedure. In that case, the event procedure that contains code is selected, in case you want to edit that code. Of course, you can use the Object and Procedure boxes at any time to quickly locate the desired object/event combination.

> **TIP**
> In addition to double-clicking an object, you can also open the Code window by pressing F7, by clicking the View Code button in the Project window, or by selecting View, Code from the menu.

Now that you've properly coded the Exit button to end the application, all that remains is to code the Calculate Payment button. Its function is to calculate the monthly payment amount, based on the information the user has supplied. This code will be written as the `Click` event procedure for the command button `cmdCalculate`. You could display the `cmdCalculate` button's `Click` event procedure by bringing the form designer to the front and double-clicking `cmdCalculate`; however, because the Code window is already open, it would be more efficient to drop down the Code window's Object box and select `cmdCalculate`. This displays the procedure `cmdCalculate_Click` in the Code window.

Writing Program Code

The procedure that calculates the loan payment will be more complex than the `Exit` procedure. Obviously, the code that performs the payment calculation will be more involved than a simple `End` statement. In addition, you must do some additional housekeeping in this procedure, as you will be using variables.

A *variable* is a temporary storage location for information. Very often, your programs will need to remember information—such as calculation results, the user's name, order totals, and so on—as the program is running. Think of a variable like a white board that the program can use to remember information. Within certain guidelines, the program can write information on the white board, modify that information, even erase it completely. One important consideration is that when the program finishes, the white board is erased completely.

▶ **See** "Working with Variables," **p. 159**

Variable Declarations The first part of the Calculate sub procedure will be used to declare the variables you'll need. That means that you will tell Visual Basic the *names* of the variables that the procedure will be using, as well as what *type* of information each variable may contain. Although Visual Basic doesn't require you to declare your variables (by default), it's always good practice to do so.

> **TIP**
>
> *Always declare your variables!* In the Tools, Options menu, under the Editor tab, make sure Require Variable Declaration is checked. This causes Visual Basic to report an error if you attempt to run a program that uses a variable that hasn't been declared (for example, if you inadvertently misspell the variable's name).

Your `Calculate` procedure uses four variables—one each to hold the principal amount, the interest rate, the loan term, and the calculated monthly payment. Make sure the cursor is on the blank line between `Private Sub cmdCalculate_Click()` and `End Sub`. Press Tab to indent the code, and then type the following line of code:

```
Dim cPrincipal As Currency
```

Notice that when you press Enter after typing this code, the cursor doesn't go back to the left margin of the code window. Visual Basic assumes that you want to indent the next line of code to the same level as the preceding line. This aids in your code's readability. You can increase the level of indent by pressing Tab; Backspace will decrease the indent.

As you can tell from this code, the general format for declaring variables is the word `Dim`, followed by a variable name, the word `As`, and the variable's type. As with object names, you should follow a naming standard. Throughout this book, you'll use a very common variable naming standard that uses the first (lowercase) character of the variable name as a prefix designating its type; the remaining portion of the variable's name describes its purpose. The variable named `cPrincipal`, for example, is a Currency type variable that stores the principal amount. Some variable types and their common prefixes are outlined in Table 2.3.

Table 2.3 Prefixes Used in a Common Variable Naming Convention

Prefix	Variable Type
s	String
n	Integer
l	Long Integer
f	Single-precision Floating Point
d	Double-precision Floating Point
c	Currency
b	Boolean (True/False)
v	Variant

Add the following line of code for the next declaration:

```
Dim fIntRate As Single
```

This would be a good time to point out that multiple variables can be declared on the same line of code. If you do so, each variable must have its own type listed. Add the following line of code to declare two more variables:

```
Dim nTerm As Integer, cPayment As Currency
```

> **CAUTION**
>
> A common beginner mistake is to attempt to include multiple variable declarations in a statement like `Dim x, y, z As Integer`. Remember, however, that each variable must have its type explicitly mentioned. In this case, only z would be an Integer; x and y would be initialized as Variants. The Variant data type is a special type discussed later in the book. The correct syntax would be to place the words `As Integer` after each variable name.

Procedure Code   The procedure code is the remaining part of the procedure that does the actual work. In your Loan Calculator program, this part of the procedure will be responsible for retrieving the input values from the first three text boxes, calculating the monthly payment, and displaying the payment in the fourth text box.

Enter the following two lines into the Code window (after the variable declaration statements):

```
'Store the principal in the variable cPrincipal
cPrincipal = Val(txtPrincipal.Text)
```

The first line is a comment explaining what's going on. A comment is denoted by a single quotation mark ('), usually at the beginning of a line. When Visual Basic encounters a single quote on a line, the remainder of the line is ignored. Visual Basic then looks to the next line for the next instruction.

The second line in this code retrieves the information that the user entered into the `txtPrincipal` text box, placing the value into the variable `cPrincipal`. This is done with an assignment statement, much like an assignment statement in algebra—a variable appears on the left side of the equal sign, and the value to be placed in that variable appears on the right side. The `Val()` function is used to convert whatever is between the parentheses to a numeric type for subsequent calculation purposes. The actual value in the text box is retrieved by accessing its `Text` property (you refer to properties of an object in code using the notation `object.property`). Think of `txtPrincipal.Text` as being equivalent to the current value of the `Text` property of `txtPrincipal` (recall that the `Text` property of a TextBox control contains the current contents of the box on the screen).

> **TIP** As you enter the remaining code, you'll notice several more comments within the code statements. Again, a *comment* is a line of code that isn't executed; rather, it's used to explain the purpose or functionality of the executable portions of the code. Comments, which are a form of documentation, help a programmer to quickly understand the purpose of a section of code when she must edit it at some point in the future. It's usually a very good idea to include a lot of comments in your code. You may think you'll remember why you solved a problem a certain way, but when you look at code that you (or someone else) wrote a year earlier, comments will make the code's purpose much clearer.

Enter the remaining code presented in Listing 2.1 in the Code window. The comments should help you understand how the code works. Figure 2.19 shows the completed sub procedure in the Code window.

Listing 2.1 Code to Calculate the Monthly Payment

```
'Convert interest rate to its decimal equivalent
'  i.e. 12.75 becomes 0.1275
fIntrate = Val(txtIntRate.Text) / 100

'Convert annual interest rate to monthly
'  by dividing by 12 (months in a year)
fIntrate = fIntrate / 12

'Convert number of years to number of months
'  by multiplying by 12 (months in a year)
nTerm = Val(txtTerm.Text) * 12

'Calculate and display the monthly payment.
'  The Format function makes the displayed number look good.
cPayment = cPrincipal * (fIntrate / (1 - (1 + fIntrate) ^ -nTerm))
txtPayment.Text = Format(cPayment, "Fixed")
```

Running Your Program

I'll bet you're anxious to see your program in action! Before running it, however, make sure you save your work so far. To run the program, you need to execute Visual Basic's Start command using any of these methods:

- Click the Start button on the Visual Basic toolbar.
- Choose Run, Start.
- Press F5.

FIGURE 2.19
Entering the code to calculate the monthly payment completes the `Click` event procedure for `cmdCalculate`.

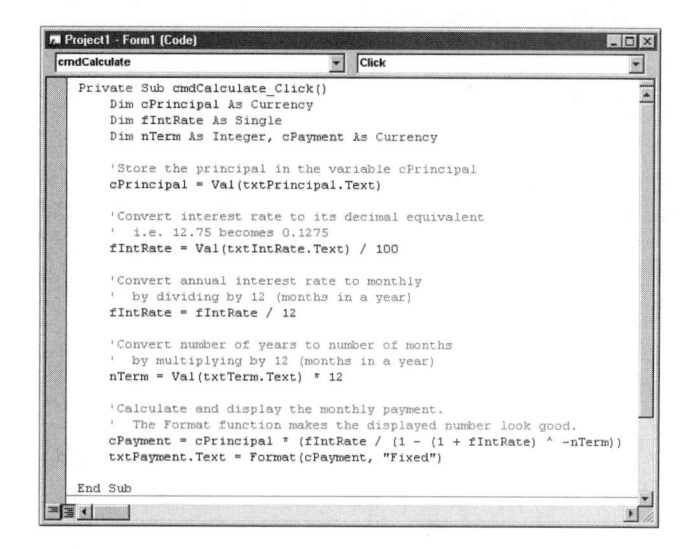

```
Private Sub cmdCalculate_Click()
    Dim cPrincipal As Currency
    Dim fIntRate As Single
    Dim nTerm As Integer, cPayment As Currency

    'Store the principal in the variable cPrincipal
    cPrincipal = Val(txtPrincipal.Text)

    'Convert interest rate to its decimal equivalent
    '  i.e. 12.75 becomes 0.1275
    fIntRate = Val(txtIntRate.Text) / 100

    'Convert annual interest rate to monthly
    '  by dividing by 12 (months in a year)
    fIntRate = fIntRate / 12

    'Convert number of years to number of months
    '  by multiplying by 12 (months in a year)
    nTerm = Val(txtTerm.Text) * 12

    'Calculate and display the monthly payment.
    '  The Format function makes the displayed number look good.
    cPayment = cPrincipal * (fIntRate / (1 - (1 + fIntRate) ^ -nTerm))
    txtPayment.Text = Format(cPayment, "Fixed")
End Sub
```

When you execute the Start command, Visual Basic compiles your program to check for certain types of errors. If none are found, the program will begin executing, and you'll see the main form. Notice in Visual Basic's title bar that you've gone from Design mode to Run mode, meaning that the program is actually running. Because the application is object-oriented and event-driven, it's waiting for you (the user) to cause an event to occur to an object, such as typing in a text box or clicking a button.

Test your program by entering values for the principal, term, and interest rate. Use these values for your first test:

Principal	128000
Interest Rate	9.75
Term	30

After entering these values, click the Calculate Payment button. The monthly payment displayed should be 1099.72 (see Figure 2.20).

> **NOTE** Because this program is a demonstration of basic programming techniques, its interface is quite simple, and very little effort has gone into making it error-proof. Numbers must be typed without thousands separators or dollar signs in order for the calculations to work properly. As you develop your programming skills later in the book, you'll see how to overcome these types of limitations.

FIGURE 2.20
The Loan Calculator program is now fully functional and can calculate loan payments.

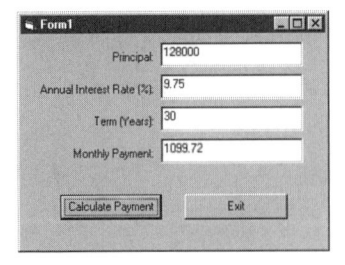

Test the program with other combinations of numbers. When you're through, end the program by clicking the Exit button, or by clicking the End button on Visual Basic's toolbar. This will return you to the design environment.

ON THE WEB

The completed Loan Calculator program is contained in the file LOANCALC.ZIP, which can be downloaded from www.mcp.com/info.

From Here...

The loan calculator program has enabled us to dive right in to writing a Visual Basic program from scratch. In this chapter, you learned how to do the following:

- Start Visual Basic
- Begin a new project
- Add controls to a form
- Set properties of your project's objects
- Write code to bring the program to life

Believe it or not, these steps comprise the core of Visual Basic programming. You've seen simple examples of all these steps, but most Visual Basic programming involves repetition of these steps over and over until the desired results are obtained.

As you start working with more complex applications, you'll see many ways to practice and enhance these fundamental Visual Basic programming skills. Refer to the following chapters for additional related information:

- To see how to use Visual Basic's fundamental components to create your own applications, see Chapter 3, "Visual Basic Building Blocks."
- To learn about the various controls that you can use when building programs, see Chapter 4, "Using Visual Basic's Default Controls."
- To learn more about writing Visual Basic code to interact with your program's users, see Chapter 5, "Responding to the User with Event Procedures."

CHAPTER 3

Visual Basic Building Blocks

In this chapter

Forms 40

Using Controls 41

Exploring Properties 42

A First Look at Methods and Events 50

Form Properties Revisited 52

You've already learned that objects such as forms and controls are the parts of a Visual Basic program with which users interact. Collectively, these objects that users see and use are known as a program's *visual component*. Compare this to a program's *code component*, which refers to the program code that the programmer has created.

In this chapter, you'll examine some of the fundamentals necessary to build a program's visual component. You'll see how you can define the appearance and behavior of an object by working with its *properties*, *methods*, and *events*. By knowing how to manage these components of your program's objects, you'll be well on your way to creating professional quality user interfaces.

NOTE The term *object* in this chapter refers to visual objects such as forms and controls. In later chapters, I'll further discuss these types of objects as well as some other objects and how they relate to Visual Basic program code.

Forms

So far, most of the examples have used the Form object. A form is a container that holds all the other controls (such as labels, text boxes, and pictures) that make up part of a program's user interface. Most of your programs will use a number of forms.

NOTE If you want, you can create a Visual Basic program that contains no forms at all! One example might be a command-line program that processes files and requires no user interface.

Parts of a Form

When you start a new Standard EXE project, you are presented with the default Visual Basic project, which normally includes a single standard form (see Figure 3.1). Because this form is the place where you start work on your user interface, take a brief look at the different parts of it now.

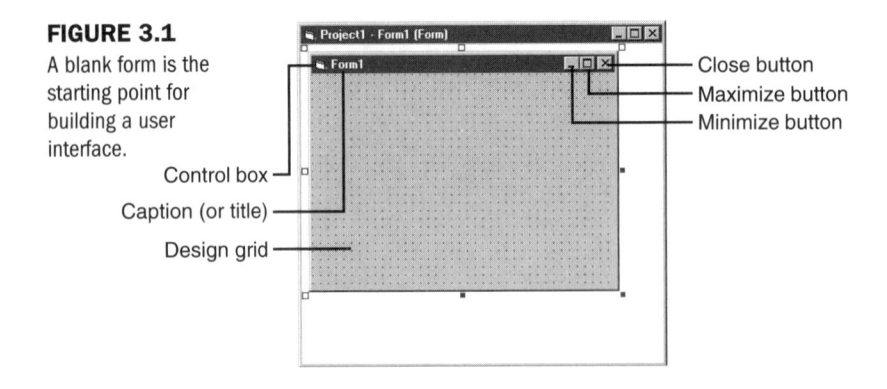

FIGURE 3.1
A blank form is the starting point for building a user interface.

Labels: Close button, Maximize button, Minimize button, Control box, Caption (or title), Design grid

As you can see in Figure 3.1, a Visual Basic form contains all the elements you would expect to find as part of a window in a program. It contains a title bar, a control menu, and a set of Minimize, Maximize/Restore, and Close buttons. Note that many of these elements, such as the Close button, are always present at design time even if the properties are set in such a way that they are not visible at runtime.

Another design-time feature is a grid of dots that allows you to line up controls easily as you are designing your interface. You can control the behavior of the design grid through the Options dialog box, which you can access by choosing Tools, Options from the menu system. In this dialog box, you can change the size of the grid or even turn it off completely. You can also choose whether controls are automatically aligned to the grid. If this option is on (the default setting), the upper-left corner of each control is aligned with the grid point that's closest to the corner. Using the default setting enables you to line up controls easily. In fact, I set the grid to be smaller than the default, which allows more precise control alignment.

What Do Forms Do?

As I mentioned earlier, forms represent your program's user interface. That is, forms are what your users see and interact with. All the controls that users work with, such as text boxes, command buttons, and so forth, are contained on one or more forms.

In addition to serving as containers for controls, forms act as a sort of overall "traffic cop" overseeing the use of the objects that make up the interface. You'll see many examples of using program code to respond to events that occur to various objects. All the program code that relates to the objects on a particular form is stored (and edited) as a part of the form itself. In other words, the form contains not only the objects the users *can* see, but it also contains the program code that the users *can't* see.

Using Controls

Although forms are an important part of your programs, you can't do very much without adding controls to them. Visual Basic controls let you perform a wide variety of tasks including editing text, displaying pictures, and interfacing with a database. The liberal use of controls has always been one of Visual Basic's strongest features.

What Are Controls?

In Visual Basic, controls are objects designed to perform specific tasks. Like form objects, controls have associated properties, events, and methods. For example, if you use a TextBox control, you can set properties to determine the size of the text box, the font for the text that it displays, and the color of the text and background.

Because of Visual Basic's design, you are not limited to using only the controls provided by Microsoft. The design allows easy integration of third-party controls—which has led to a thriving market for these custom controls. With this amount of third-party involvement, chances are that you can find a control to perform almost any task you want, from data acquisition to custom reporting to specialized graphics processing to game play, and everything in between.

Although controls have been around since the beginning of Visual Basic, the capability to create your own controls did not exist until version 5. Visual Basic now allows you to create your own ActiveX controls for use in your programs and in any other program that adheres to ActiveX standards.

Control Functions

You can think of a control as a miniature program in itself that performs certain tasks for you. For example, the text box correctly sizes and displays the text based on the property values that you assign. Also, a text box contains internal code that allows it to process keystrokes so that it knows, for example, to erase a character when you press the Backspace key. If you wrote programs in earlier languages, particularly in the DOS and mainframe environments, you know that you might have had to write a significant amount of code just to accept and process keystrokes that allowed the users to enter input. Now you can just drop a control on your form, and the rest is done for you. In other words, controls are prepackaged objects that perform specific tasks.

Visual Basic 6 comes with a standard set of controls that are available in all editions and that let you perform many types of programming tasks. These controls are illustrated in the Toolbox shown in Figure 3.2. The use and purpose of these standard controls are discussed in Chapter 4, "Using Visual Basic's Default Controls."

FIGURE 3.2
Visual Basic's Toolbox contains a standard set of controls.

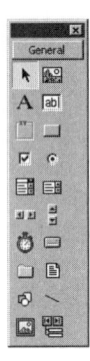

> **N O T E** The standard controls that automatically appear in the Toolbox shown in Figure 3.2 are not the only ones included with Visual Basic. To add other controls, such as the TreeView control or ImageList control, use the Components dialog box by choosing C̲omponents from the P̲roject menu.
>
> ▶ **See** "Using the `TreeView` Control," **p. 258**

Exploring Properties

In Chapter 2, "Creating Your First Program," you saw how to set an object's properties to modify its appearance when your program runs. Think of a property as an adjective that describes one specific thing about an object. By changing the value of one or more properties, you can easily customize an object's appearance to the task at hand. In the following sections, you learn about properties as they relate to a form object; the same concepts apply to properties of controls as well.

Property Basics

When you look at a form, you see a rectangular window on the screen, like the one shown in Figure 3.3. This window's appearance is defined by a set of properties. For example, the position of the form on the screen is denoted by its Left and Top properties, and its size is denoted by its Width and Height properties. The form's Caption property dictates what is shown in its title bar. You can even specify which (if any) control buttons appear on the form's title bar by setting a couple of properties.

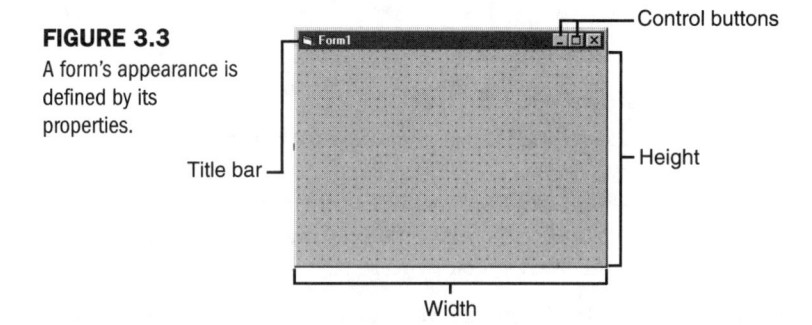

FIGURE 3.3
A form's appearance is defined by its properties.

When you save a form as part of a project, Visual Basic creates a text file with an .FRM extension. This file stores information about the form, its properties, the objects contained in the form, and the objects' properties, as well as any program code that may have been created for that form. Figure 3.4 shows part of the .FRM file for the form illustrated in Figure 3.3.

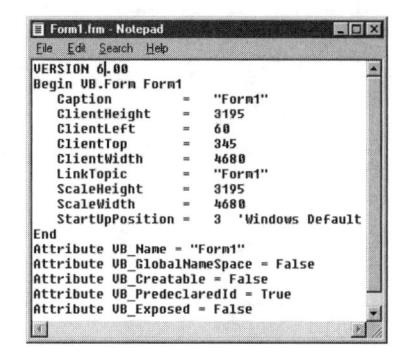

FIGURE 3.4
A form's .FRM file contains information about the properties that define the form and its objects.

> **CAUTION**
>
> For some forms, Visual Basic also creates a file with an .FRX extension. This file stores graphics and other binary elements that cannot be defined in a text file. If you copy a form from one folder to another, copying the associated .FRX file as well is very important.

Common Properties

All objects in Visual Basic do not have the same set of properties. However, several properties are common to many objects. Important common properties include the following:

- `Name`
- `Index`
- `Left`
- `Top`
- `Height`
- `Width`
- `Enabled`
- `Visible`

Using Properties to Control an Object's Size

The size of an object in Visual Basic is governed by its `Height` and `Width` properties. As you've seen, you can modify an object's size by selecting it and dragging a sizing handle at design-time, or by changing the values of its `Height` and `Width` properties at either design time or runtime. If you resize an object at design time, you see a corresponding change in the `Height` and `Width` properties in the Properties window, as you discovered in Chapter 2.

During program execution (in other words, at runtime), you can use code to initiate a change in an object's size. In some cases, the size of an object (such as a form) can be changed by the users, as when they drag the edge of the form. In the "Changing Properties at Runtime" section, you'll see an example that demonstrates this concept.

Figure 3.5 illustrates how a form's `Height` and `Width` properties relate to its size.

FIGURE 3.5
A form's size is determined by its `Height` and `Width` properties.

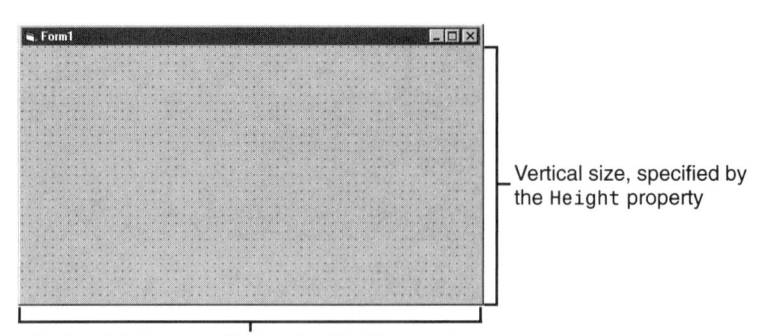

Vertical size, specified by the `Height` property

Horizontal size, specified by the `Width` property

Using Properties to Adjust an Object's Position

In addition to controlling an object's *size*, you can also control its *position* with the `Left` and `Top` properties (see Figure 3.6). The `Left` property specifies the distance of the left side of an object from the left side of the object's container. The `Top` property specifies the distance of the top edge of an object from the top edge of its container. In the case of a standard form, the container is the entire screen. If you draw a control on a form, the form is the control's container. I should also mention that some controls themselves, such as the PictureBox and Frame controls, can act as containers for other controls.

FIGURE 3.6
This TextBox control's position is measured relative to the form, which is its container.

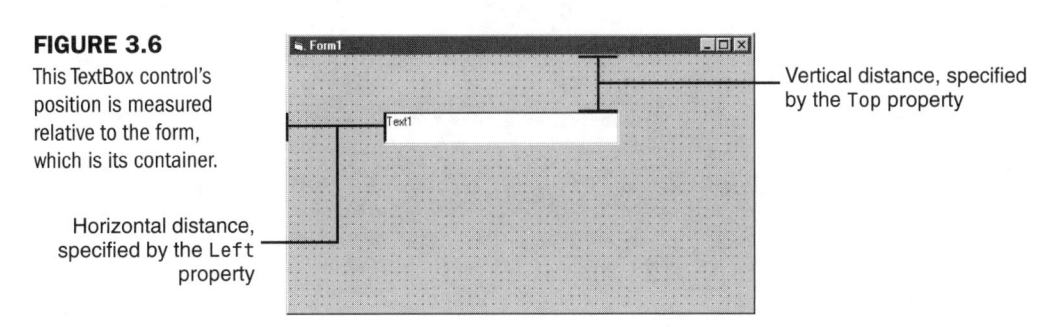

Vertical distance, specified by the `Top` property

Horizontal distance, specified by the `Left` property

NOTE An object's `Top` and `Left` properties can actually have a negative value. For example, a Label control whose `Left` property value is `-1440` is positioned so that its left edge is approximately one inch to the left of its container; therefore, some (or all) of it can't be seen.

Whereas the position of most forms is measured in relation to the upper-left corner of the screen, a form that is part of a Multiple Document Interface (MDI) application is positioned relative to the upper-left corner of the client area of the parent form (see Figure 3.7).

FIGURE 3.7
An MDI child form is positioned relative to its parent form.

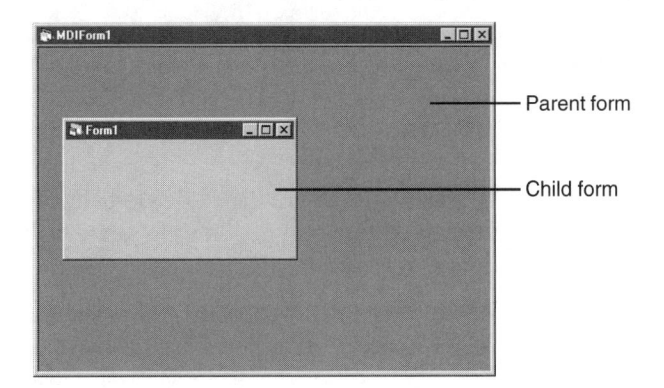

Parent form

Child form

Changing Properties at Runtime

As you've learned, objects' properties can be changed at runtime, either through user action or program code. At this point, you can work through an exercise that illustrates this concept. This sample project presents the users with a standard form. They can modify the form's size or position simply by using the mouse to drag the form or one of its edges. The form also has a command button that *programmatically* increases the form's width and another that programmatically lowers the form's position. Finally, a set of Label controls reports the form's Height, Width, Left, and Top properties.

Creating the Form Resize Program   When program code refers to properties of various objects, *dot notation* is used. As an example, the Caption property for a Label control named lblAddress on a particular form is referred to in code as lblAddress.Caption.

If you don't remember how to add objects to a form and set the objects' properties, you might want to review Chapter 2.

Figure 3.8 shows my completed sample form; you may want to refer to it as you build the project.

▶ **See** "Creating Your Program's User Interface," **p. 18**

FIGURE 3.8
This sample project demonstrates the use of code to set various properties of a form.

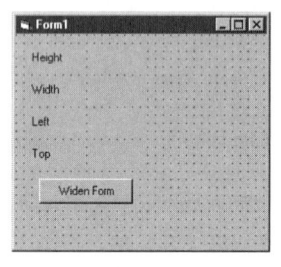

Perform the following steps to create your own version of this project:

1. Create a new Standard EXE project.
2. Add four Label controls to the form, aligned in a column at the left side of the form. These labels will be used as captions for other information; you generally don't need to modify the Name properties for labels used in this manner, as they won't be referred to in code. Change the four Label controls' Caption properties to Height, Width, Left, and Top (working from top to bottom).
3. Add another column of four Label controls just to the right of the first set. Change their Name properties to lblHeight, lblWidth, lblLeft, and lblTop. Change their Caption properties to nothing (clear out the default captions).
4. Add a CommandButton control near the bottom of the form. Change its Name property to cmdWiden, and change its Caption property to Widen Form.
5. Select the form and change its Width property to 4000 twips. (See the sidebar "Measurements in Visual Basic" for a definition of the term *twip*.)
6. Double-click the command button to bring up the Code window. You should see an empty cmdWiden_Click sub procedure.
7. Press the Tab button, and then type the code Form1.Width = Form1.Width + 100. This line of code causes the value of Form1's Width property to increase by 100 twips each time the command button is clicked.

8. Drop down the Code window's Object box and select Form. Drop down the Code window's Event box and select Resize. You are presented with the shell of the Form_Resize event procedure. The Resize event occurs whenever the width and/or height of the form is changed, either through user actions or program code.

9. Add the following lines of code to the Form_Resize event procedure:

```
lblWidth.Caption = Form1.Width
lblHeight.Caption = Form1.Height
lblLeft.Caption = Form1.Left
lblTop.Caption = Form1.Top
```

This code causes the current values of the form's Width, Height, Left, and Top properties to be displayed in the appropriate Label controls. Because this code is in the form's Resize event procedure, the labels will be updated whenever the size of the form changes, whether programmatically or by user action.

10. Save the form and project if you want; however, you probably don't need to bother because this is just a simple demonstration.

TIP Visual Basic provides a useful tool called *Auto List Members* that helps with properties. When you type the name of an object followed by a dot (period), Visual Basic attempts to help you complete the dot notation by providing a pop-up list of all properties that apply to that object (along with other things that apply, such as methods and events). Just type enough characters of the desired property name to highlight it in the pop-up list. You can then press Enter or Ctrl+Enter, and the dot notation is completed for you.

Measurements in Visual Basic

By default, all distances are measured in twips. A *twip* is a device-independent unit of measure equivalent to 1/20th of a printer's point, which means that there are 1440 twips per inch. The actual physical size of a twip varies depending on screen resolution. You can specify another unit of measure for positioning and sizing objects within a container using the container's ScaleMode property. However, the screen's scale mode cannot be changed, so a form's Left, Top, Height, and Width properties are always measured in twips.

Testing the Form Resize Program After you've completed this project, run it. Change the form's width and/or height by dragging its edges; notice how the form's labels report the modified Width and Height properties. This action illustrates how an object's properties can be changed at runtime by user action.

Next, click the Widen Form command button to cause the form's width to increase. The Width label is updated with the new property value. This example illustrates a programmatic modification of a property (even though a user initiated the action that led to the width change, the actual property change was performed by a code statement).

Finally, try moving the form (by dragging the form's title bar). By doing so, you (the user in this case) are modifying the form's Top and Left properties. One problem with this example is that the revised `Top` and `Left` properties aren't automatically displayed in the Label controls. This result is due to the fact that the code to update the labels is contained in the form's `Resize` event procedure, and the form wasn't resized when you moved it. Unfortunately, no event is similar to a `Resize` event that occurs when a form is repositioned. This problem can be overcome, of course; however, the solution is beyond the scope of this chapter. For now, you can "manually" update the labels by resizing the form just after you've moved it, allowing you to see the updated `Top` and `Left` properties.

Using Properties to Control User Interaction

Even if your application includes many forms and controls, you probably don't want the users to have access to all of them at the same time. For example, suppose you are writing a program that allows users to enter expense reports. You might have a command to allow the users to print the expense reports, but you would not want the command to be available unless the reports balance. Two properties, the `Visible` property and the `Enabled` property, help you to manage this process.

The `Visible` property determines whether an object can be seen on the screen. The `Enabled` property determines whether the users can interact with an object. You can set both properties to either `True` or `False`.

If the `Visible` property is set to `False`, the object is not shown, and the users will not know that the object is even there. If the `Enabled` property is set to `False`, the object is visible (provided that the `Visible` property is `True`), but the users cannot use it. Typically, if an object is disabled, it is shown on the screen in a grayed-out, or dimmed, mode. This mode provides a visual indication that the object is unavailable.

A good example of objects that are variably available and unavailable occurs in the wizard interface in some Windows programs. A wizard organizes a task into several logical steps, with three navigation buttons (typically labeled Back, Next, and Finish), which are used to move between steps. Depending on which step a user is currently working on, all these buttons may not be enabled, as in Figure 3.9.

FIGURE 3.9
Because the user of this wizard is on step 1, the `Enabled` property of the Back button is set to `False`, causing it to be grayed out.

TIP If you are implementing a wizard interface in Visual Basic, one option is to draw the controls for each step in a frame. Visual Basic's `Frame` control acts as a container, so setting its own `Visible` property relevant to the user's current step affects all the controls within it.

Referencing Forms and Controls from Your Code

One other key property of every Visual Basic object is the Name property. The Name property defines a unique identifier by which you can refer to the object in code. Each form, text box, label, and so on must have a unique name.

> **NOTE** All forms in a project must have different names. However, control names have to be unique only for the form on which they are located. That is, you can have a Text1 control on each form in your project, but you can't have two forms called Form1 in your project.

Visual Basic provides a default name when an object is first created. For example, Form1 is the name given to the first form created for your project, and Text1 is the name given to the first text box that you place on a form. However, the first thing you should usually do after drawing a control or form is to provide it with a name that has some meaning. For example, I often use frmMain as the name of the main interface form in my applications.

As mentioned in Chapter 2, following a standard when naming forms and other objects is good programming practice. It's common to use a three-letter contraction of the control's type as a lowercase prefix to identify the type of object to which the name refers; the remainder of the name describes the purpose of the object. In the frmMain form just discussed, the prefix frm indicates that the object is a form, and the suffix Main indicates that it's the main form in the program. Table 3.1 lists suggested prefixes for many of Visual Basic's objects (forms and controls).

Table 3.1 Visual Basic Object Types and Common Name Prefixes

Object Type	Name Prefix	Object Type	Name Prefix
CheckBox	chk	Horizontal ScrollBar	hsb
ComboBox	cbo	Image	img
Command Button	cmd	Label	lbl
Common Dialog	cdl	Line	lin
Data Control	dat	ListBox	lst
Data Bound ComboBox	dbc	Menu	mnu
Data Bound Grid	dbg	OLE Container	ole
Data Bound ListBox	dbl	Option Button	opt
Directory ListBox	dir	Picture Box	pic
Drive ListBox	drv	Shape	shp
File ListBox	fil	TextBox	txt
Form	frm	Timer	tmr
Frame	fra	Vertical ScrollBar	vsb
Grid	grd		

Remember that the names you assign will be used in code, so avoid carpal tunnel syndrome by keeping them short!

To set the Name property for an object, select the object, view the Properties window (by clicking the Properties button; by selecting View, Properties Window; or by pressing the F4 key), and click the Name property. You can then type a new value. Figure 3.10 shows the Name property in the Properties window.

FIGURE 3.10
The Name property is located at the top of the list on the Alphabetic page and is the first property listed under the Misc group on the Categorized page.

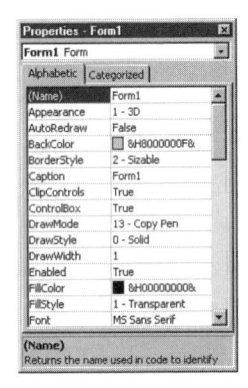

NOTE The Properties window displays in Visual Basic 6 by default, so you won't need to open it unless you have previously closed it.

A First Look at Methods and Events

So far, this chapter has concentrated on properties, showing how they can control an object's appearance. In addition to properties, an object can have *methods*, which define tasks that it can perform. The tasks can be simple, such as moving the object to another location, or they can be more complex, such as updating information in a database.

Taking Action with Methods

A method is really just a program function that is built into the object. Using its embedded methods, the object knows how to perform the task; you don't have to provide any additional instructions. For example, forms have a `PrintForm` method that prints an image of the form on the current printer. The statement `Form1.PrintForm` prints an exact duplicate of `Form1`. Because the low-level details for the `PrintForm` method are encapsulated within the form object, a Visual Basic programmer does not have to be concerned with them.

As you may have guessed, methods, like properties, are referenced using dot notation. Visual Basic uses the *Auto List Members* feature described earlier to list an object's methods, properties, and events when you type the object's name followed by a period. Although different objects have different methods, many objects have the following methods in common:

- **Drag.** Handles the operation of the users' dragging and dropping the object within its container
- **Move.** Changes the position of an object
- **SetFocus.** Gives focus to the specified control
- **Zorder.** Determines whether an object appears in front of or behind other objects in its container

> **NOTE** Focus refers to the current control that receives keystrokes. Only one control on any form can have the focus at any given time. Focus is usually indicated by the position of the edit cursor (for text boxes) or a dotted rectangle around the control (for check boxes, option buttons, and command buttons).

Responding to Actions with Events

In addition to performing tasks, the objects in your program can respond to actions, whether generated by the users or externally. Responses to actions are handled through the use of events. For example, when users click a command button, the button raises a `Click` event. Part of the definition of an object is the set of events it can raise and the user actions that trigger them.

Examples of user actions that trigger events are clicking a command button, selecting an item in a list box, or changing the contents of a text box. Events also occur when users exit a form or switch to another form. When an object raises an event, the object executes an event procedure for that specific event. To respond to events, you need to place program code in the appropriate event procedures. For example, in the Loan Calculator example in Chapter 2, you placed code in the `Click` event procedure of a command button.

Chapter 5, "Responding to the User with Event Procedures," delves into all the intricacies of events. In that chapter, you will learn how to write code to handle events and how multiple events are related.

How Properties and Methods Are Related

By now, you know that objects have properties to define their appearance, methods that let them perform tasks, and events that let them respond to user actions. You might think that all these things happen independently of one another, but that is not always the case. Sometimes, the properties and methods of an object are related. That is, as you invoke a method of an object, the properties of the object may be changed. Also, most times that you use the methods of an object or change its properties with code, you do so in response to an event.

> **NOTE** Some property changes can trigger events. For example, changing the `Height` or `Width` property of a form in code triggers the form's `Resize` event.

You can see one example of the interdependence of methods and properties of an object when the `Move` method is used and the `Left` and `Top` properties are set. You can cause an object to change position either by using the `Move` method or by setting the `Left` and `Top` properties to new values. For example, the following two code segments accomplish the same task of changing a TextBox control's position to 100 twips from the left and 200 twips from the top of its container:

```
'CODE SEGMENT 1 - Move the text box by setting its properties
txtName.Left = 100
txtName.Top = 200

'CODE SEGMENT 2 - Move the text box using the Move method
txtName.Move 100, 200
```

To see an example of the difference between using properties and methods, add code to move the command button in the previous example. With that project open, follow these steps:

1. Open the Code window to the `Form_Resize` event.

2. Add the following two lines of code to the end of the event procedure:
   ```
   cmdWiden.Left = 100
   cmdWiden.Top = Form1.ScaleHeight - cmdWiden.Height
   ```

3. Run the program and resize the form. The code repositions the command button near the bottom of the form as you resize it, always 100 twips from the left.

4. Stop the program and replace the two statements you just added with the following line of code:
   ```
   cmdWiden.Move 100, Form1.ScaleHeight - cmdWiden.Height
   ```

5. Run the program again. Notice that the code statements in both cases are slightly different, but they have the same end result. No matter whether you use the `Left` and `Top` properties or the `Move` method, the control itself handles the actual change in position for you.

If you type these code segments, you may notice that the `Move` method has two additional arguments available. These optional arguments can change the size of the object. Using this method has the same effect as setting the `Height` and `Width` properties to new values.

Similarly, the `Show` and `Hide` methods of a form have the same effect as changing the form's `Visible` property. When you invoke the form's `Hide` method, the effect is the same as setting its `Visible` property to `False`. (The effect, of course, is that the form disappears from the screen.) Likewise, the form's `Show` method produces the same effect as setting its `Visible` property to `True`.

Form Properties Revisited

Forms, like most of the objects used in Visual Basic, have a series of properties that control their behavior and appearance. In the earlier section "Exploring Properties," you learned about some of the properties that apply to forms. In this section, you'll learn several additional key properties of forms. You'll see how these properties can be controlled during program design and execution. Table 3.2 lists several of the key properties of a form and provides a brief description of each. The table also identifies whether the value of the property can be changed while the program is running.

Table 3.2 Key Form Properties

Property Name	Description	Changeable at Runtime
BorderStyle	Sets the type of border that is used for the form	No
ControlBox	Determines whether the control box (containing the Move and Close menus) is visible when the program is running	No
Font	Determines the font used to display text on the form	Yes
Icon	Determines the icon that is shown in the form's title bar and that appears when the form is minimized	Yes
MaxButton	Determines whether the Maximize button is displayed on the form when the program is running	No
MDIChild	Determines whether the form is a child form for an MDI application	No
MinButton	Determines whether the Minimize button is displayed on the form when the program is running	No
StartUpPosition	Determines the initial position of a form when it is first shown	No
WindowState	Determines whether the form is shown maximized, minimized, or in its normal state	Yes

Now you can take a closer look at some of these properties. The BorderStyle property has six possible settings that control the type of border displayed for the form (see Table 3.3). These settings control whether the form is sizable by clicking and dragging the border, they control the buttons that are shown on the form, and they even control the height of the form's title bar (see Figure 3.11).

Table 3.3 *BorderStyle* Property Settings

Setting	Effect
0 - None	No border is displayed for the form. The form also does not display the title bar or any control buttons.
1 - Fixed Single	A single-line border is used. The title bar and control buttons are displayed for the form. The user cannot resize the form.

continues

Table 3.3 Continued

Setting	Effect
2 - Sizable	The border appearance indicates that the form can be resized. The title bar and control buttons are displayed. The user can resize the form by clicking and dragging the border. This setting is the default.
3 - Fixed Dialog	The form shows a fixed border. The title bar, control box, and Close button are shown on the form. Minimize and Maximize buttons are not displayed. The form cannot be resized.
4 - Fixed ToolWindow	The form has a single-line border and displays only the title bar and Close button. They are shown in a reduced font size (approximately half height).
5 - Sizable ToolWindow	This is the same as the Fixed ToolWindow, except that the form has a sizable border.

FIGURE 3.11
Changing the BorderStyle property can give a form many different appearances.

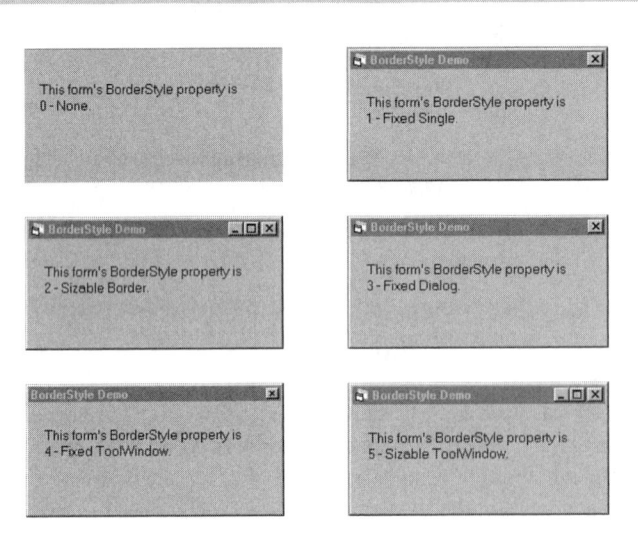

NOTE Setting the BorderStyle property to prevent resizing does not affect the form's appearance in the design environment; it does so only at runtime.

The default BorderStyle property setting provides a border that allows the users to resize the form while the program is running. You can find this type of form in a typical Windows application. However, you can change the BorderStyle setting to make the form look like almost any type of window that you would see in a program, including Toolboxes and dialog boxes. You can even remove the form's border altogether.

In Table 3.3, several of the BorderStyle definitions indicate that a control box and the Close, Minimize, and Maximize buttons would be displayed in the title bar of the form. This behavior is the default. But even with these border styles, you can individually control whether these elements appear on the form. The `ControlBox`, `MaxButton`, and `MinButton` properties each have a `True` or `False` setting that determines whether the particular element appears on the form. The default setting for each of these properties is `True`. If you set a property to `False`, the corresponding element is not displayed on the form. These properties can be changed only at design time.

The `Font` property lets you set the base font and font characteristics for any text displayed directly on the form by using the form's `Print` method.

> **NOTE** The `Font` property of a form is actually an object itself with its own properties. For example, to change the size of a form's font, you enter `Form1.Font.Size = 10` in a Code window (or the Immediate window, for that matter) to change the size to 10 points.

In addition, setting the form's `Font` property sets the font for all controls subsequently added to the form.

One final form property of note is the `StartupPosition` property. As you might guess, this property controls where the form is located when it is first displayed. The `StartupPosition` property has four possible settings, which are summarized in Table 3.4.

Table 3.4 *StartupPosition* **Property Settings**

Setting	Effect
0 - Manual	The initial position is set by the `Top` and `Left` properties of the form.
1 - CenterOwner	The form is centered in the Windows desktop unless it is an MDI child form, in which case it is centered within its parent window.
2 - CenterScreen	The form is centered in the Windows desktop.
3 - Windows Default	The form is placed in a position determined by Windows based on the number and position of other windows open at that time.

Although the `StartupPosition` property can center your form for you when the form first loads, it does not keep the form centered. For example, if you resize the form, it does not remain centered.

Displaying a Form

If you write a program with just a single form, you needn't worry about displaying the form or hiding it. This process is performed automatically for you as the program starts and exits. This single form is known as the Startup Object or Startup Form. When you run your program, Visual Basic loads your Startup Form into memory and displays it. As long as this form remains loaded, your program keeps running and responding to events. When you click the Close button on the form (or execute the `End` statement), the program stops.

> **NOTE** You can select a Startup Form in the Project Properties dialog box. You also can have a program start from a sub procedure named `Main` in a code module rather than from a form.

However, if you have multiple forms—as most programs do—you need to understand how to manage them. The state of a form is controlled by Visual Basic's `Load` and `Unload` statements as well as the form's `Show` and `Hide` methods.

The `Load` statement places a form in memory but does not display it. The following line of code shows how the statement is used:

```
Load frmApplication
```

By using this statement, you are explicitly loading the form. However, the form is loaded automatically if you access a property, method, or control on it. Because the load operation is performed automatically, using the `Load` statement with a form is not really necessary. However, being aware when a form is being loaded is important because the code in the `Form_Load` event will be executed at that time.

To display a form other than the Startup Form, you must use the `Show` method. The `Show` method works whether or not the form was loaded previously into memory. If the form was not loaded, the `Show` method implicitly loads the form and then displays it. The `Show` method is used as follows:

```
frmApplication.Show
```

The `Show` method also has an optional argument that determines whether the form is shown as a *modal* or *modeless* form. If a form is shown modally (a *modal* form), then program control doesn't return to the procedure that called the `Show` method until the modal form is closed. Think of the program code as being paused as long as a modal form is displayed. An example of a modal form is the Windows 95 Shutdown screen. You cannot put the focus on another window while the Shut Down Windows form is displayed.

If a form is shown *modeless*, your program's users can move at will between the current form and other forms in the program. The preceding statement displayed a form as modeless. To create a modal form, you simply set the optional argument of the `Show` method to `vbModal`, as shown here:

```
frmApplication.Show vbModal
```

> **NOTE** A modal form is typically used when you want the users to complete the actions on the form before working on any other part of the program. For example, if a critical error occurs, you do not want the users to switch to another form and ignore it.

After a form is displayed, you have two choices for getting rid of it programmatically. The `Hide` method removes the form from the screen but does not remove it from memory. Use `Hide` when you need to remove the form from view temporarily but still need information in it:

```
frmApplication.Hide
sUserName = frmApplication.txtUserName.Text
```

In this example, the second line of code is able to access information in a control on frmApplication, even though that form is not visible on the screen. The Hide method leaves a form in memory.

If you are finished with a form and the information contained on it, you can remove it from both the screen and memory by using the Unload statement. The Unload statement uses basically the same syntax as the Load statement, as shown here:

```
Unload frmApplication
```

> **TIP** If you are using the Unload statement from within the form you are removing, you can use the keyword Me to specify the form. By using this approach, you can prevent errors if you later rename your form. In this case, the statement would be the following:
>
> ```
> Unload Me
> ```

Using *Load* to Enhance Program Performance

Because the Show method automatically loads a form into memory, you typically do not need to use the Load statement in your program at all. However, some forms with a very large number of controls display slowly when they are shown. One way around this problem is to load the form into memory by using the Load statement when the program begins to run. With the form already in memory, subsequent Hide and Show methods appear to perform much more quickly. If you use this trick, be careful of two things. First, don't forget to unload the form at the end of your program. Second, be aware of possible memory limitations. If you load too many forms in memory at once, you might see a decline in the overall performance of your program.

Loading forms into memory does increase the amount of time required for your program to start, but you will save time whenever the form is shown. If you show a form only once during the program, no net time savings is gained by loading it at the beginning. However, if the form is shown more than once, usually an overall time savings is experienced. Also, users are typically more tolerant of time delays when a program loads (especially if they're busy looking at a splash screen) than later when they are performing a task.

From Here...

This chapter introduced you to the world of forms and controls. You began to see how to use forms and controls as the basic building blocks of user interface design. You learned how to manage the appearance of forms and controls by manipulating their properties, both at design-time and runtime. The basic concepts discussed here will carry over into the upcoming discussions of many of the controls that are available for you to use in designing your Visual Basic applications.

- Learn more about the standard controls by reading Chapter 4, "Using Visual Basic's Default Controls."

- To explore program events in more detail, see Chapter 5, "Responding to the User with Event Procedures."
- To discover more about the Visual Basic language, see Chapter 8, "Using Variables to Store Information," and Chapter 11, "Managing Your Project: Sub Procedures, Functions, and Multiple Forms."

CHAPTER 4

Using Visual Basic's Default Controls

In this chapter

Introduction to the Intrinsic Controls 60

Working with Text 62

Controls for Making Choices 66

Special-Purpose Controls 78

Working with Multiple Controls at Designtime 85

Working with the Controls Collection 90

By now, you are familiar with what a control is and how controls are used in a Visual Basic program. A great way to learn more about Visual Basic is to explore each of the available controls. Controls are discussed in almost every chapter in this book. The next three chapters focus on how to use specific controls.

In this chapter, you learn about the controls that are included by default with a new Visual Basic project. While there are very many controls that you can add to your projects—including controls provided by Microsoft as well as third-party companies—the controls discussed here are always available to use with no extra effort on your part.

Introduction to the Intrinsic Controls

Visual Basic comes with controls that let you perform many types of programming tasks. Some of these controls appear in the Toolbox automatically when you start Visual Basic. These standard controls are called the *intrinsic* controls. These controls, pictured in Figure 4.1, include some very general controls likely to be used by almost every VB programmer. They are summarized in Table 4.1.

FIGURE 4.1
The Toolbox contains tools that represent Visual Basic's intrinsic controls.

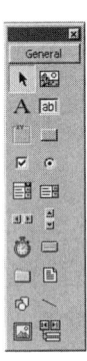

Table 4.1 Controls Contained in Visual Basic's Toolbox

Control Name	Function
PictureBox	Displays graphics. Can also serve as a container for other controls.
Label	Displays text that the users cannot edit.
TextBox	Displays text. Allows the users to enter and edit the text.
Frame	Serves as a container for other controls. Provides grouping of controls.
CommandButton	Allows the users to initiate actions by clicking the button.

Control Name	Function
CheckBox	Lets the users make a true/false choice.
OptionButton	Lets the users choose one option from a group of items.
ComboBox	Lets the users choose from a list of items or enter a new value.
ListBox	Lets the users choose from a list of items.
Horizontal ScrollBar	Lets the users choose a ScrollBar value based on the position of the button in the bar.
Vertical ScrollBar	Same as Horizontal ScrollBar.
Timer	Lets the program perform functions on a timed basis.
Drive List Box	Lets the users select a disk drive.
Directory List	Lets the users select a Box directory or folder.
File List Box	Lets the users select a file.
Shape	Displays a shape on the form.
Line	Displays a line on the form.
Image	Similar to a PictureBox control. Uses fewer system resources but doesn't support as many properties, events, and methods.
Data Control	Provides an interface between the program and a data source.
OLE	Provides a connection between the program and an OLE server.
Common Dialog	Allows use of Windows standard dialog boxes to retrieve information such as filenames, fonts, and colors.

NOTE The controls shown in Figure 4.1 and described in Table 4.1 are not the only ones included with Visual Basic. To add other controls such as the Microsoft CommonDialog control or Microsoft FlexGrid control to the Toolbox, use the Components dialog box by choosing Project, Components, or right-clicking an empty area of the Toolbox and selecting Components from the context menu.

Many of the controls listed in Table 4.1 are discussed in the following sections. Others are described in chapters more closely associated with their purposes. The controls covered in other chapters are as follows:

- The PictureBox, Image, Shape, and Line controls are covered in Chapter 19, "Using Visual Design Elements."
- The Data control is covered in Chapter 25, "The Data Control and Data-Bound Controls."
- The OLE control is covered in Chapter 22, "Using OLE to Control Other Applications."

Working with Text

In Chapter 2, "Creating Your First Program," you built a simple program that used the TextBox and Label controls. If you have not read that chapter, you may want to review it before continuing. From the examples, you learned that the TextBox and Label controls are designed to work with text. The term *text* here does not just mean paragraphs and sentences like those you handle with a word processor. When you deal with text in a program, you also might want to display or retrieve a single word, a number, or even a date. You also may have noticed the major difference between the text box and label: the text box can be used both to display and accept text input, whereas the label control is designed for display-only use. Figure 4.2 shows various examples of TextBox and Label controls in use.

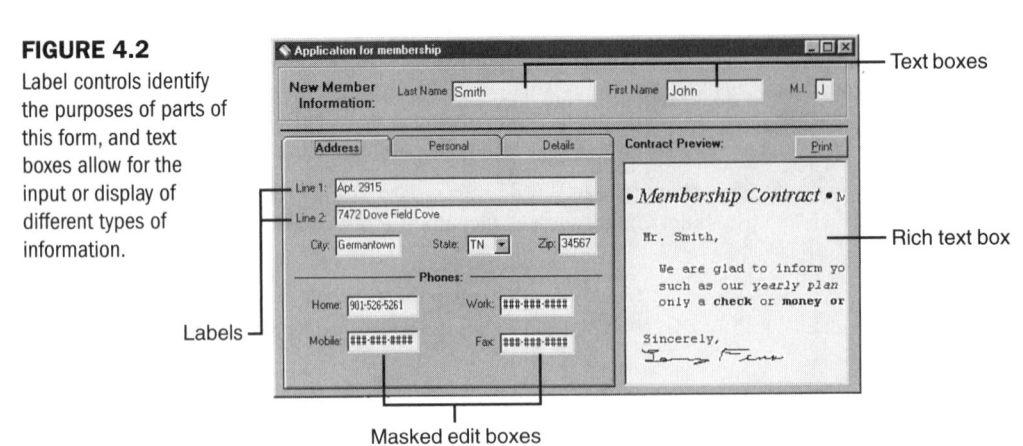

FIGURE 4.2
Label controls identify the purposes of parts of this form, and text boxes allow for the input or display of different types of information.

Displaying Text with a Label Control

The purpose of the Label control is to display text. It is most often used to identify items on a form to the users. The simplest way to use the Label control is to place it next to an input field and set its Caption property. Refer to Figure 4.2 and notice that the Label controls are used to inform the users what type of information is to be entered in the text boxes.

Although the Label control does not allow the users to enter text directly, it contains events and properties that allow the programmer to manipulate the text directly from code. To test this feature, create a new Standard EXE project and place a Label control on the form. Place the following code in the label's Click event:

```
Private Sub Label1_Click()
    Label1 = "The time is: " & Time$
End Sub
```

Run the program. Each time you click in the label using the mouse, the label displays the current time. Also, in the preceding code, notice that you do not specifically mention the Caption property because it is the default property of the Label control. As you may recall, to specify a property of an object, you use dot notation, as in the following line of code:

```
Label1.Caption = "The time is: " & Time$
```

However, you are not limited to using the label control to display small amounts of text. In fact, you can use the Label control to display multiple lines or even paragraphs of information. If you want to display a large amount of information in a label control, you need to pay particular attention to the AutoSize and WordWrap properties.

The *AutoSize* Property   If you know in advance what text is going to be displayed in a label's Caption property, you can set the size of the label to accommodate the text. However, if different text will be displayed in the label at different times (for example, in a database application), you may want the label to adjust to the length of its current contents. The AutoSize property of the Label control determines whether the size of the control automatically adjusts to fit the text being displayed. When AutoSize is False (the default), the label's size remains unchanged regardless of the length of its caption. If a caption is too long for the label, some of the caption is not visible because it's wider than the label, and it does not wrap to another line.

The *WordWrap* Property   Setting AutoSize to True causes a label to adjust its size automatically to fit its caption. If the caption is longer than the label's original size allows, the method of resizing depends on the value of the WordWrap property. If the WordWrap property is False (the default), the label expands horizontally to allow the caption to fit, even if the label grows so large that it runs past the right edge of the screen. If the WordWrap property is set to True, the label expands vertically to allow enough lines of text to accommodate the caption, even if the label runs off the bottom edge of the screen. (The words wrap to new lines—hence, the property name WordWrap.) In either case, the Caption property contains the entire caption, even if some of the text isn't visible on the form. The effects of the different settings of the AutoSize and WordWrap properties are shown in Figure 4.3.

FIGURE 4.3
These four labels have the same long caption; their `AutoSize` and `WordWrap` properties determine whether and how they resize to fit the caption.

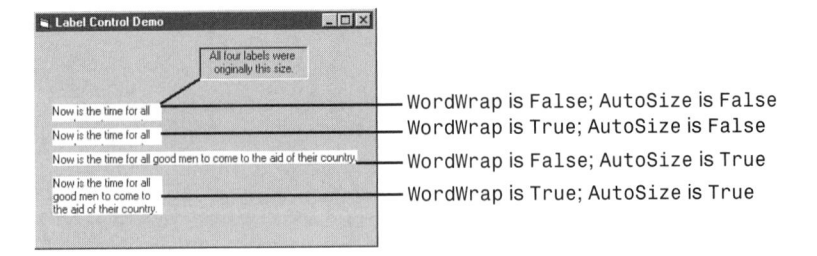

- WordWrap is False; AutoSize is False
- WordWrap is True; AutoSize is False
- WordWrap is False; AutoSize is True
- WordWrap is True; AutoSize is True

> **CAUTION**
> To preserve the original width of your label control, you must set the `WordWrap` property to `True` before setting the `AutoSize` property. Otherwise, when you set the `AutoSize` property to `True`, the label control adjusts horizontally to fit the current contents of the `Caption` property.

> **TIP**
> When assigning a label's `Caption` property, you can force a new line by including a carriage return and line feed combination. This technique, as well as its nomenclature, is a throwback to the ancient days of manual typewriters. When a manual typewriter user reached the end of a line, he or she had to move the paper up manually to the next line (a line feed) and return the carriage to the beginning of that line (a carriage return). In Visual Basic, you can insert a carriage return/line feed combination by inserting ASCII characters 13 and 10 into the caption at the point where the line should break. Visual Basic supplies a predefined constant, `vbCrLf`, to help you accomplish this task:
>
> `Label1.caption = "First Line" & vbCrLf & "Second Line"`

Controlling the Appearance of Text The `Caption` property contains the text to be displayed, but other properties control the appearance of the text. You have already looked at `AutoSize` and `WordWrap`; other properties are listed here:

- `Alignment`—Controls text justification (left, right, or centered)
- `Appearance`—Causes the label to look flat or three-dimensional
- `BorderStyle`—Determines whether the label control has a border
- `Font`—Makes the text boldface, underlined, italic, or changes the typeface
- `ForeColor` and `BackColor`—Control the color of the text and the label background
- `UseMnemonic`—Controls whether an ampersand (&) in the `Caption` property is treated like an access key indicator

> **NOTE** With `BorderStyle` set to `Fixed Single`, the label control takes on the appearance of a noneditable text box.

You can set these properties to provide any different number of visual effects to emphasize text in the label and other controls. The effects of setting some of these properties are shown in Figure 4.4.

FIGURE 4.4
The Alignment, Appearance, and BorderStyle properties can change the look of a label control.

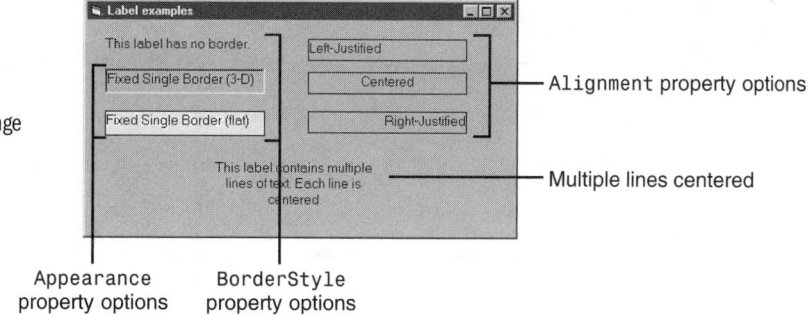

> **NOTE** The Alignment property also affects the text when the label is used to display multiple lines. The control aligns each line according to the setting of the Alignment property (refer to Figure 4.4).

Entering Text with a Text Box

Because much of what programs do is to retrieve, process, and display text, you might guess (and you would be correct) that the major workhorse of many programs is the TextBox control. The text box allows you to display text; more important, however, it also provides an easy way for your users to enter and edit text and for your program to retrieve the information that was entered.

Handling Multiple Lines of Text In most cases, you use the text box to handle a single piece of information, such as a name or address. But the text box can handle thousands of characters of text. A TextBox control's contents are stored in its Text property—the main property with which your programs interact. You can also limit the number of characters users can enter by using the MaxLength property.

By default, the text box is set up to handle a single line of information. This amount of information is adequate for most purposes, but occasionally your program needs to handle a larger amount of text. The text box has two properties that are useful for handling larger amounts of text: the MultiLine and ScrollBar properties.

The MultiLine property determines whether the information in a text box is displayed on a single line or wraps and scrolls to multiple lines. If the MultiLine property is set to True, information is displayed on multiple lines, and word wrapping is handled automatically. Users can press Enter to force a new line. The ScrollBar property determines whether scrollbars are displayed in a text box, and if so, what types of scrollbars (None, Horizontal, Vertical, or Both). The scrollbars are useful if more text is stored in the Text property than fits in the text box. The ScrollBar property has an effect on the text box only if its MultiLine property is set to True. Figure 4.5 shows the effects of the MultiLine and ScrollBar properties.

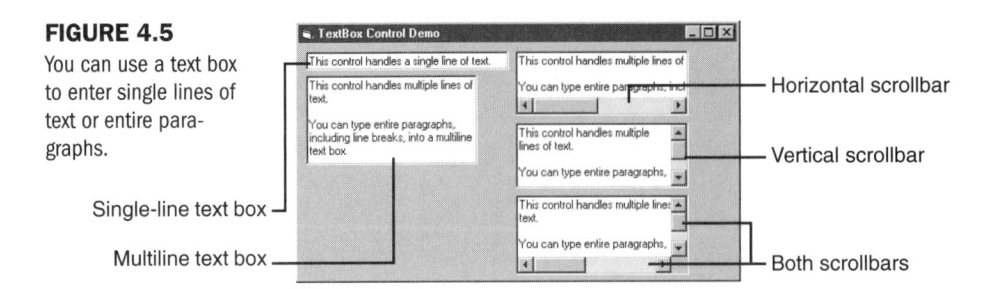

FIGURE 4.5
You can use a text box to enter single lines of text or entire paragraphs.

Single-line text box
Multiline text box
Horizontal scrollbar
Vertical scrollbar
Both scrollbars

> **TIP**
>
> When a text box is activated (known as *receiving the focus*) by the user tabbing to it or clicking in it, a common practice is for the contents to be selected (or highlighted). Although this feat cannot be accomplished automatically, it can be done pretty easily. Enter these lines of code in the text box's event procedure, replacing `Text1` with the text box's actual name:
>
> ```
> Text1.SelStart = 0
> Text1.SelLength = Len(Text1.Text)
> ```
>
> The `SendKeys` statement sends a string of characters to the active form at runtime just as if the users had typed them at the keyboard. In this case, you're acting as if the users had pressed the Home key and then a shifted End key (the plus sign before `{End}` represents Shift). This action causes the text to be highlighted, so the users can begin entering new text without having to delete what is already there.

Validating Input   When accepting free-form text input from the users, you often need to perform some data validation before proceeding. For example, if you have a text box for Phone Number, you can use code to check the length of the phone number or even to verify that the users entered any information at all.

A new feature in Visual Basic 6 is the `Validate` event of a text box. This event procedure can contain code that validates the information in the associated control. It is triggered by another control whose `CausesValidation` property is set to `True`. For example, the following line of code displays a message box if a text box does not contain numeric data:

```
If Not IsNumeric(Text1) Then MsgBox "please enter a number"
```

To test this event, create a new Standard EXE project. Place a command button and a text box on the form, and enter the preceding line of code in the text box's `Validate` event. As you use the Tab key to move away from the text box, the message is displayed unless you enter a number. Setting the `CausesValidation` property of the command button to `False` turns off the `Validate` event.

Controls for Making Choices

Previously, you learned how to acquire input from users through the use of a text box. This approach works well for a number of data-gathering needs. But what if you just want a simple piece of information, such as "Do you own a car?" or "What is your marital status?" In these cases, the choice of answers you want to provide is limited to two or, at most, a few fixed choices. If you set up a program to handle only the words *yes* and *no*, your program will have a problem if users type `Maybe` or if they mistype a word.

You can eliminate this problem, however, and make your programs easier to use by employing controls to display and accept choices. In the following sections, you will examine several controls used for making choices. You can offer these choices through the use of check boxes, option buttons, lists, and combo boxes:

- **Check Box.** Switches one or more options on or off
- **Option Button.** Selects a single choice from a group
- **List Box.** Displays a list of user-defined items
- **Combo Box.** Like a list box, but also displays selected item

The Command Button

A control important to practically every application that you will develop is the `CommandButton` control. Typically, this control lets users initiate actions by clicking the button. You can set up a `CommandButton` control by drawing the button on the form and then setting its `Caption` property to the text that you want displayed on the button's face. To activate the button, just place code in the button's `Click` event procedure. Like any other event procedure, this code can consist of any number of valid Visual Basic programming statements.

Although users most often use command buttons by clicking them, some users prefer accessing commands through the keyboard versus using the mouse. This is often the case for data-entry intensive programs. To accommodate these users, you can make your program trigger command button events when certain keys are pressed. You do so by assigning an access key to the command button. When an access key is defined, the user holds down the Alt key and presses the access key to trigger the `CommandButton` control's `Click` event.

You assign an access key when you set the `CommandButton` control's `Caption` property. Simply place an ampersand (&) in front of the letter of the key you want to use. For example, if you want the users to be able to press Alt+P to run a print command button, you set the `Caption` property to `&Print`. The ampersand does not show up on the button, but the letter for the access key is underlined. The caption P̲rint then appears on the command button.

> **NOTE** If, for some reason, you need to display an ampersand in a command button caption, simply use two of them in a row in the `Caption` property; for example, `Save && Exit` produces the caption `Save & Exit`.

One command button on a form can be designated as the *default button*. Therefore, the user can simply press Enter while the focus is on any control (except another command button or a text box whose `MultiLine` property is `True`) to trigger the default button. This action triggers the default button's `Click` event, just as if the users had clicked it with the mouse. To set up a button as the default button, set its `Default` property to `True`. Only one button on a form can be the default button.

You can also designate one button as the *cancel button*, which is similar to the default button but works with the Esc key. To make a command button into a cancel button, set its Cancel property to True. As with default buttons, only one button on a form can be a cancel button. As you set the value of the Default or Cancel property of one button to True, the same property of all other buttons on the form is set to False.

Check Boxes

You use Visual Basic's CheckBox control to get an answer of either "yes" or "no" from the user. This control works like a light switch. Either it is on or it is off; there is no in between. When a check box is on, a check mark (✓) is displayed in the box. It indicates that the answer to the check box's corresponding question is "yes." When the check box is off, or unchecked, the box is empty, indicating an answer of "no." Check boxes also have a third state, *grayed*, which is represented by a check mark with a gray background. This is usually used to indicate that a partial choice (some, but not all, of a number of sub-choices) has been made. A user can uncheck a grayed check box; if he rechecks it, it becomes fully checked. Figure 4.6 shows check boxes exhibiting all three possible states.

N O T E The check mark or empty box format is characteristic of the standard-form check box. If you set the check box's Style property to 1 - Graphical, pictures are used to indicate checked and unchecked. Graphical check boxes are illustrated in Figure 4.6 as well.

FIGURE 4.6
A check box can indicate a "yes" or "no" response to a question.

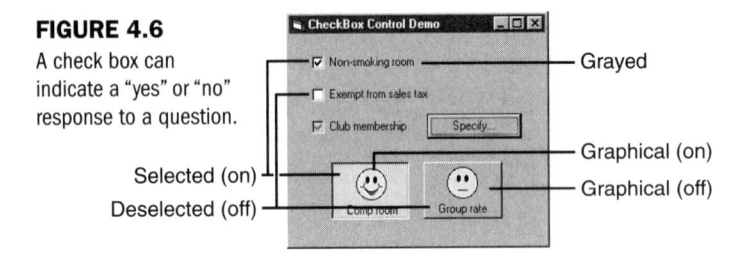

Selected (on)
Deselected (off)
Grayed
Graphical (on)
Graphical (off)

Figure 4.6 shows graphical check boxes as well as standard check boxes. Two properties, Picture and DownPicture, determine the pictures displayed by a graphical check box.

Option Buttons

Option buttons, also called *radio buttons*, are like the buttons on a car radio; they exist in a group, and only one of them can be "selected" at a time. They are useful for presenting a fixed list of mutually exclusive choices. Try it yourself: Draw several option buttons on a form. Initially, each option button has the default value of False. However, notice that if you set the value of any one of them to True, and then subsequently set the value of a different button in the group to True, the one that was True will automatically become False, as shown in Figure 4.7.

You can use option buttons in two basic ways in code:

FIGURE 4.7
Option buttons can be used to provide a list of fixed choices.

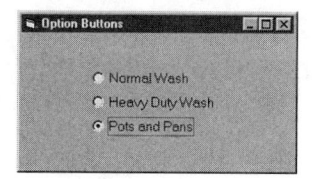

- Use the Click event if you want to take an action when users select an option. This method is useful when you are using option buttons that are in a control array, as in the following example:

```
Private Sub optWash_Click(Index As Integer)
    Select Case Index
        Case 0
            MsgBox "You selected: Normal"
        Case 1
            MsgBox "You selected: Heavy Duty"
        Case 2
            MsgBox "You selected: Pots and Pans"
    End Select
End Sub
```

- Do not write any code in the option button events. Instead, use an if statement to check their state, as shown here:

```
Private Sub cmdStartWash_Click()

    If optHeavy = True Then
        DoHeavyWash
    Else
        DoNormalWash
    End If

End Sub
```

This second method is useful if you do not want something to happen immediately when users select options.

You may be wondering whether it is ever possible to have multiple option buttons on a form selected at the same time. The answer is yes, but you have to separate the option buttons into groups by using container controls. Using a container, such as the Frame control discussed later in this chapter, allows you to group option buttons, as shown in Figure 4.8.

FIGURE 4.8
To create multiple groups of option buttons, place them in a container such as a frame or picture box.

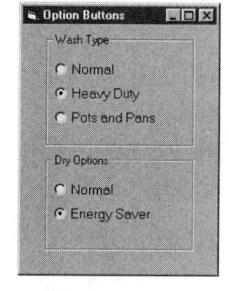

The List Box

You can use the ListBox control to present a list of choices. Figure 4.9 shows a simple list used to pick a state abbreviation for use on a mailing label. This list shows all the components that make up the list box.

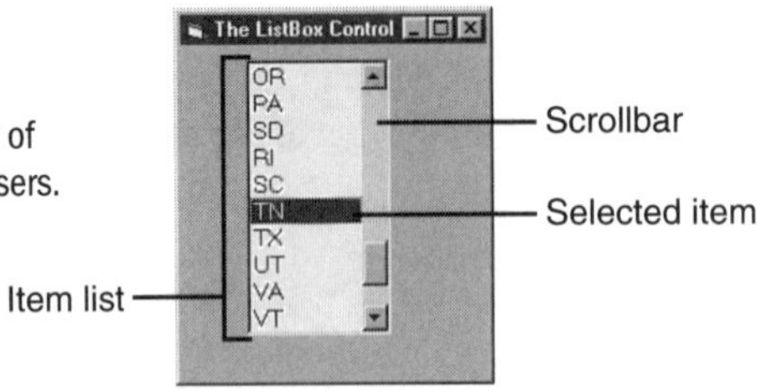

FIGURE 4.9
A simple list box contains a series of choices for the users.

The key parts of the list box are the following:

- **Item list.** This is the list of items from which the users can select. These items are added to the list in the design environment or by your program as it is running.
- **Selected item.** This item is chosen by the users. Depending on the style of list you choose, a selected item is indicated by a highlight bar or by a check in the box next to the item.
- **Scrollbar.** This part indicates that more items are available on the list than will fit in the box and provides the users with an easy way to view the additional items.

To the users, using the list box is similar to choosing channels on a TV. The cable company decides which channels to put on the selection list. The customers then can pick any of these channels but can't add one to the list if they don't like any of the choices provided. With the list box, the choices are set up by you, the programmer; the users can select only from the items you decide should be available.

When you first draw a list box on the form, it shows only the border of the box and the text List1 (the name of the list box). No scrollbar is present and, of course, no list items are available. A vertical scrollbar is added to the list box automatically when you list more items than fit in the box. Note that the list box doesn't have a horizontal scrollbar if the choices are too wide for the control, so you should make sure that the list box is wide enough to display all of its entries.

Basic Use of the List Box The simplest way to control the choices available in a list box is to use the AddItem method to add items to the list box. The only thing you need to specify is the text that you want to be placed in the list box. To try it out, start a new Standard EXE project, draw a list box on the form, and add the following lines of code to the form's Load event:

```
Private Sub Form_Load()
    Dim i As Integer

    For i = 1 To 100
        List1.AddItem "This is item " & i
    Next i

End Sub
```

NOTE Although this example uses code to add items, you can also create the list at designtime by typing the text that you want to appear in the `List` property of a list box. Each line in the property corresponds to a selection that is presented to the users. After you add an item to the list, press Ctrl+Enter to move to the next line of the list.

Run the project, and you'll notice that 100 lines of text appear in the list box. To clear all the items in a list box, use the `Clear` method, as in the following example:

```
List1.Clear
```

The items in a list box are stored in an array, which is accessible via the `List` property of the list box. The list array starts with a zero index, so to print the first item in the list, you can use the following statement:

```
Print List1.List(0)
```

You can test this statement by putting the sample program in break mode (press Ctrl+Break) and entering the `Print` statement in the Immediate window.

Two other properties are critical for using a list box: `ListCount` and `ListIndex`. `ListCount` represents the number of items in a list box. `ListIndex` represents the selected item.

CAUTION
When you are using `ListCount` in a loop to examine the contents of an unknown number of items, remember that the `List` array starts with zero, so your code should look like this:
```
For i = 0 To List1.ListCount - 1
     'Process List1.List(i)
Next i
```

NOTE Listindex is -1 if no item is selected.

To illustrate the `ListIndex` property in action, stop the sample program and add the following code to the `Click` event of the list box:

```
Msgbox List1.List(List1.ListIndex)
```

Run the program again, and when you click an item, it is displayed in a message box.

Another way to retrieve the value of the list box item selected by the user is to check the list box's `Text` property. The `Text` property contains the item from whichever line of the list box has the focus. If it's a simple list box, the line that the user clicked is returned in the `Text` property. If no list box item has yet been clicked, the `Text` property contains an empty string (" ").

To remove items from the list box, use the `RemoveItem` method, specifying the array index of the item you want removed from the list. To demonstrate, add the following line of code to the `KeyDown` event of the list box:

```
Private Sub List1_KeyDown(KeyCode As Integer, Shift As Integer)
If KeyCode = vbKeyDelete And List1.ListIndex <> -1 Then
    List1.RemoveItem List1.ListIndex
End If

End Sub
```

Run the program with the new modification, and you should be able to remove a specific item from the list by selecting it and pressing the Delete key.

Using the List Array   You already know how to use the AddItem method to add an item to the end of the list. An optional parameter, Index, can be used with the AddItem method. This parameter specifies the location within the list where you want the new item to appear. You specify the index value of the item in front of which you want to add your item. For example, if the list contains five items, and you want your item to appear ahead of the third item, you use code like the following:

```
lstAvailable.AddItem "Corvette", 2
```

Sorting Items   In the preceding section, you saw how to modify the list by adding and removing items. You also saw that you can add an item to a specific location by specifying an index. But what do you do if you want your entire list sorted in alphabetic order?

Fortunately, this task is simple. To sort the list, you simply set the Sorted property to True. Then, no matter in which order you enter your items, they appear in alphabetic order to the users. The indexes of the list items are adjusted as they are added so that they remain in order.

NOTE   Remember, in alphabetic order, *2* is listed after *11*.

This built-in sorting capability is a nice feature of the list box because you can use it to sort data quickly. However, you have to specify the Sorted property at designtime. If you want to have the users turn sorting on or off at runtime, you can use two list box controls and use the Visible properties so that only one is displayed at a time.

Setting the Appearance of a List Box   In addition to the "plain" list box in Figure 4.9, several additional styles are available. You can make your list look like a series of check boxes or include multiple columns of items.

You handle the selection of the list type by setting the Style property. The two settings of the property are 0 - Standard and 1 - Checkbox, as illustrated in Figure 4.10. You also can change this property at runtime by setting its value to one of the intrinsic constants vbListBoxStandard or vbListBoxCheckBox, respectively.

Another way to change the list's appearance is to use the Columns property. The default value of the property is 0. This value results in the standard list box previously discussed. Setting the property to 1 causes the list to be presented one column at a time, but to scroll horizontally instead of vertically. Setting the property to greater than 1 causes the list to display in the number of columns specified by the property (for example, a value of 2 displays the list in two col-

FIGURE 4.10
Checkbox-style list boxes provide the users with an intuitive way to select multiple items.

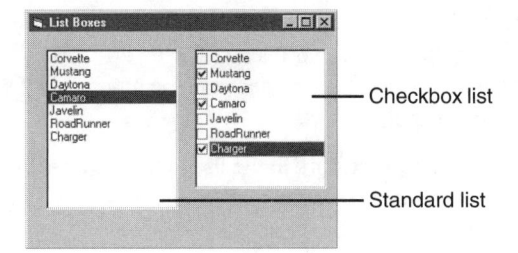

— Checkbox list

— Standard list

umns). When the list is displayed in multiple columns, the list scrolls horizontally. You can use the `Columns` property with either the Standard or Checkbox styles of lists. Figure 4.11 shows single-column and multicolumn lists. The list works the same way no matter how many columns you use.

FIGURE 4.11
You also can create multicolumn lists.

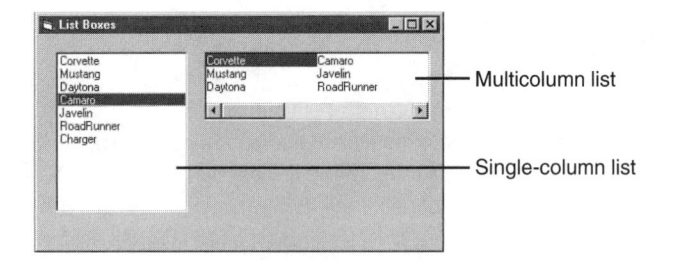

— Multicolumn list

— Single-column list

Working with Multiple Selections Sometimes you need to let the users select more than one item from a list. The list box supports this capability with the `MultiSelect` property. This property has three possible settings: `0 - None`, `1 - Simple`, and `2 - Extended`:

- The default setting, `0 - None`, means that multiple selections are not permitted, and the list box can accept only one selection at a time. The other two settings both permit multiple selections; the difference is in how they let the users make selections.
- With a setting of `1 - Simple`, users can click an item with the mouse to select it or click a selected item to deselect it. If they use the keyboard to make the selection, they can use the cursor keys to move the focus (the dotted line border) to an item and then press the Spacebar to select or deselect it.
- The other setting of the `MultiSelect` property, `2 - Extended`, is more complex. In this mode, users can use standard Windows techniques to quickly select multiple items. They can select a range of items by clicking the first item in the range and then, while holding down the Shift key, clicking the last item in the range; all items in between the first and last item are selected. To add or delete a single item to or from this selection, users hold down the Ctrl key while clicking the item.

Getting the selections from a multiple-selection list box is a little different than getting them for a single selection. Because the `ListIndex` property works only for a single selection, you can't use it. Instead, you have to examine each item in the list to determine whether it is selected.

Whether an item is selected is indicated by the list box's Selected property. Like the List property mentioned earlier, the Selected property is an array that has an element for each item in the list. The value of the Selected property for each item is either True (the item is selected) or False (the item is not selected).

You also need to know how many items are in the list so that you can set up the loop to check all the selections. This information is contained in the ListCount property. The following code prints onto the form the name of each list item that is selected:

```
numitm = Fruits.ListCount
For I = 0 to numitm - 1
    If Fruits.Selected(I) Then Form1.Print Fruits.List(I)
Next I
```

Keeping Other Data in the List What if you want the users to see a meaningful list, such as a list of names, but you also want to have the list remember a number that's associated with each name? The ItemData property of a list box is, in essence, an array of long integers, one for each item that has been added to the list box. No matter what position an item occupies in the list box, the ItemData array remembers the number associated with that particular element. This happens even if the list box's Sorted property is True, meaning that items aren't necessarily listed in the order that they're added. For example, the ItemData array element associated with the first item in a list box named List1 can be accessed as List1.ItemData(0). The array element for the currently selected list box entry can be accessed with List1.ItemData(List1.ListIndex) (recall that the ListIndex property reports which item is currently selected).

As items are added to a list box, an associated element is created in the ItemData array. Of course, it's your job to place the appropriate value into the proper position of the ItemData array. So how can your program know into which list box position a newly added item went, especially if the list box is sorted? Visual Basic makes this task easy. A list box's NewIndex property contains the index number of the most recently added item in the list. The following code adds a new customer to a sorted list box and then adds that customer's account number to the correct element of the associated ItemData array:

```
lstCustomers.AddItem "Thomas, June"
lstCustomers.ItemData(lstCustomers.NewIndex) = 21472301
```

Now, your programs can allow the users to select from a list box containing meaningful elements (names), but the background processing can be done with an associated number, which is easier for the computer. This approach is illustrated in the following Click event procedure of the list box:

```
Private Sub lstCustomers_Click()
    Dim lgThisCust As Long
    lgThisCust = lstCustomers.ItemData(lstCustomers.ListIndex)
    Call LookUpAccount(lgThisCust)
End Sub
```

The Combo Box

Another control that enables you to present lists to the users is the ComboBox control. The combo box can be used in three different forms:

- **The drop-down combo box.** Presents the users with a text box combined with a drop-down list (see Figure 4.12). The users can either select an item from the list portion or type an item in the text box portion.
- **The simple combo box.** Displays a text box and a list that doesn't drop down (see Figure 4.13). As with the drop-down combo box, the users can either select an item from the list portion or type an item in the text box portion.
- **The drop-down list.** Displays a drop-down list box from which the users can make a choice (see Figure 4.14). The users cannot enter items that are not in the list.

> **NOTE** A new type of combo box, the ImageCombo, was added in Visual Basic version 6.0. This control is discussed in Chapter 12, "Microsoft Common Controls."

FIGURE 4.12
With the drop-down combo box, you can select an item from the drop-down list or type an alternative item in the text box.

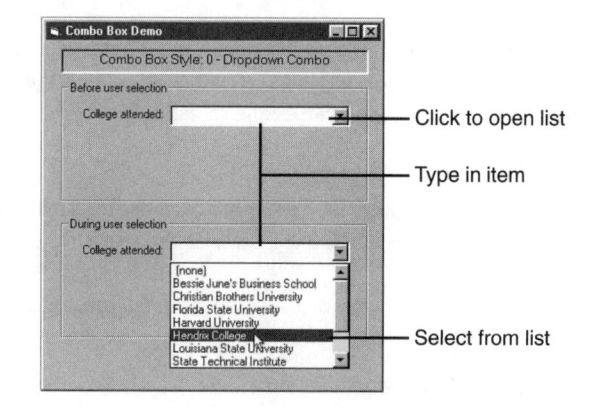

FIGURE 4.13
This simple combo box works like the drop-down combo box, except the list is always displayed.

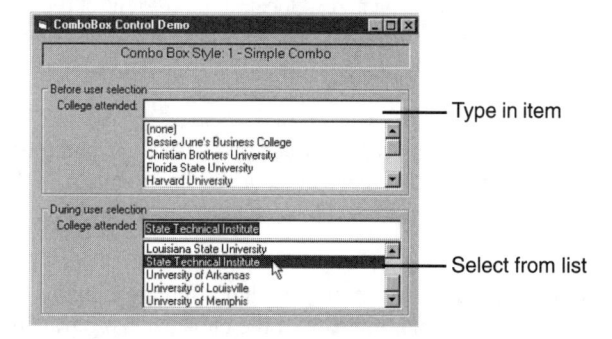

FIGURE 4.14
With the drop-down list, you cannot type an alternative item.

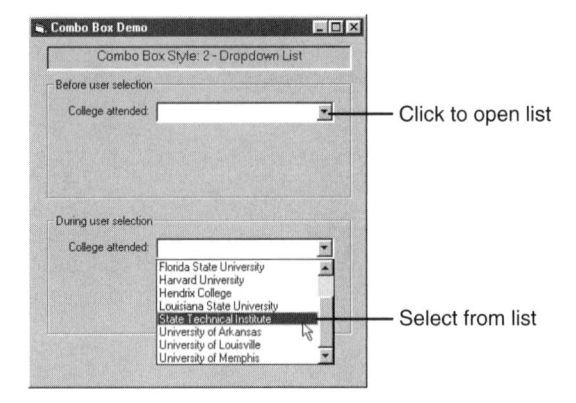

— Click to open list

— Select from list

The combo box has much in common with the list box. Both use the AddItem, RemoveItem, and Clear methods to modify the contents of the list. Both can present a sorted or an unsorted list. Both support the ItemData array and NewIndex property. However, one box can do some things that the other cannot.

The combo box mainly lacks support for multiple selections. The key advantage of the combo box, though, is that it allows the users to enter choices that are not on the list. This feature works like an election ballot, in which you can choose a candidate from the list of those running or write in your own.

NOTE The drop-down list does not support the users' entering choices that are not on the list. Its chief advantage over a simple list box is that it occupies less space.

The following sections explain how to use the different forms of the combo box. The drop-down list is examined first because it is the simplest of the combo box styles.

Creating a Drop-Down List A drop-down list functions exactly like a list box. The key difference is that the drop-down list takes up less room on your form. When users want to select an item from the list, they click the down arrow, located to the right of the box, to extend the list. After the drop-down list appears, they then make a selection by clicking the item they want to choose. After the selection is made, the list retracts like a window shade, and the selection appears in the box.

You create a drop-down list by drawing a combo box on the form and then setting the Style property to 2 - Dropdown List. You then can begin adding items to the list by using the List property, just like you did for the list box. However, keep in mind that the users can't add items that are not in the list.

Setting the Initial Choice Depending on your application, you might want to set the initial item for a combo box. For example, you can set the choice in a program that needs to know your citizenship. You can provide a list of choices but set the initial value to "U.S. Citizen" because that would be the selection of most people in this country.

You set the initial value by using the `ListIndex` property. For example, if "U.S. Citizen" is the fourth entry in the list, you can use the following code to cause that item to be pre-selected (recall that `ListIndex` begins its counting with zero):

```
Fruits.ListIndex = 3
```

This statement causes the fourth item in the list to be displayed when the combo box is first shown. (Remember, the list indexes start at 0.) You can set the initial choice with any of the three combo box styles. You also can set the initial choice of the combo box by setting the `Text` property to the value you want. If you do not set an initial choice by setting the index, the text contained in the `Text` property is displayed.

> **CAUTION**
> The initial value of the `Text` property is the name of the combo box. If you do not want this name to appear in your combo box on startup, set either the `ListIndex` property or the `Text` property in code.

> **TIP**
> If you want your combo box to be blank when the form is first shown, simply delete the contents of the `Text` property while you are in the design environment.

Working with Choices Not on the List The drop-down list is useful for presenting several choices in a small amount of space. However, the real power of the combo box is its capability to allow users to enter choices other than those on the list. This capability is available with the other two styles of combo boxes—the simple combo box and the drop-down combo box. Both styles provide a list of items from which you can select, and both allow you to enter other values. The difference between the two styles is the way in which you access items already in the list.

You set up a simple combo box by drawing the control on the form and then setting the `Style` property to `1 - Simple Combo`. With the simple combo box, the users can access the items in the list using the mouse or the arrow keys. If the users don't find what they want on the list, they can type new choices.

The drop-down combo box works like a combination of the drop-down list and the simple combo box. You select an item from the list the same way you would for a drop-down list, but you also can enter a value that is not on the list. You create the drop-down combo box by setting the `Style` property to `0 - Dropdown Combo`. The drop-down combo box is the default setting of the `Style` property.

As with the list box and the drop-down list, you can use the `List` property to add items to the list of selections. You also can modify the list for any of the combo box styles while your program is running. As with the list box control, you modify the list by using the `AddItem`, `RemoveItem`, and `Clear` methods.

Special-Purpose Controls

The last group of intrinsic controls is labeled "special purpose" because they really do not fit into a group with other controls. However, you will probably find that they still get a lot of use.

The following are the types of controls covered in this section:

- ScrollBar controls
- Timer control
- Frame control

Scrollbars

If you have used Windows, then you are already familiar with scrollbars. Scrollbars provide a graphical way for you to perform tasks such as control your position within a document or make adjustments to your sound card volume.

Scrollbars work just like the real-world volume control on your stereo system, which can be set to any point between certain maximum and minimum values. From the programmer's point of view, the Visual Basic scrollbar controls return a numeric value; it is the programmer's responsibility to use this value appropriately in an application.

Visual Basic provides two types of scrollbars for entering numerical data: the vertical scrollbar and the horizontal scrollbar. These two controls are shown in Figure 4.15. The two scrollbars are referred to in the documentation as the VScrollBar and HScrollBar controls, respectively.

FIGURE 4.15
The VScrollBar and HScrollBar controls can be used to enter and display a numeric value graphically.

The only difference between the two controls is the orientation of the bar on the form. The following section examines the HScrollBar control, but it applies equally to the VScrollBar control.

Setting Up the Scrollbar To use a scrollbar, you simply use properties to set and retrieve the range and value. The three most important properties, available at designtime and runtime, are as follows:

- Value—Retrieves or sets the current numeric value
- Min—Controls the minimum value of the Value property
- Max—Controls the maximum value of the Value property

To use these properties, set the `Min` and `Max` properties to values representing the range you want and then access the `Value` property to find the result. One typical range is from 0 to 100, where the users would enter a number as a percentage.

> **NOTE** The scrollbar can accept whole numbers (integers) anywhere in the range of –32,768 to 32,767. However, the valid values for the `Value` property depend on the values of the `Min` and `Max` properties. Remember this point when you are setting a scrollbar value from code, because a value outside the current range causes an error.

The `Change` event of the scrollbar fires when the `Value` property changes. To test a scrollbar, start a new Standard EXE project. Place a horizontal scrollbar and a text box on the form. Then enter the following code in the `Form_Load` event and `HScroll1_Change` events:

```
Private Sub Form_Load()
    HScroll1.Min = Me.Left
    HScroll1.Max = Me.ScaleWidth
End Sub
Private Sub HScroll1_Change()
    Text1.Left = HScroll1.Value
End Sub
```

Run the program and set the scrollbar to different values by dragging, clicking, and using the arrow, Home, and End keys. The text box should change positions on the form to match the current setting of the scrollbar.

Controlling the Size of the Value Changes If you have used a scrollbar in a word processor or other program, you know that clicking the arrow at either end of the bar moves you a short distance, and clicking between an arrow and the position button moves you a larger distance. The scrollbar controls work the same way, and you get to set how much the numbers change with each kind of move. The number entered in a scrollbar is contained in the `Value` property. This property changes every time you click the scrollbar or drag the position button, as indicated in Figure 4.16.

FIGURE 4.16
Clicking various parts of the scrollbar changes its value by different amounts.

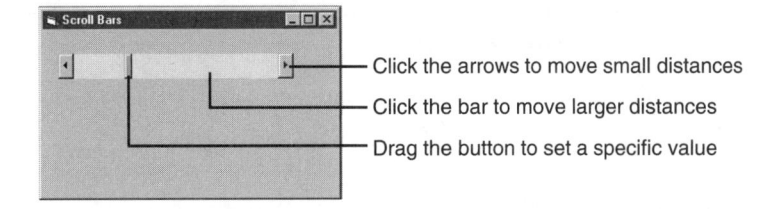

- Click the arrows to move small distances
- Click the bar to move larger distances
- Drag the button to set a specific value

The amount that the `Value` property increases or decreases when an arrow is clicked is controlled by the `SmallChange` property, unless such a change would exceed the bounds of the `Min` and `Max` properties. This property gives you very fine control over the numbers being entered. Its default value is 1, which is probably a good number to use for most purposes.

When you click between the arrow and the position button, the `Value` property can change by a different amount than if you click an arrow. The amount of this change is set by the

`LargeChange` property. The default setting of the `LargeChange` property is 1. The setting you use depends on your application. For example, a value of 10 is a good number if you are setting percentages.

> **TIP** A good rule of thumb is to set the `LargeChange` property to a number about five to ten percent of the total range (for example, a value of 50 for a 0 to 1000 range.)

Showing the User the Numbers   Although the visual representation is nice, users cannot tell what the range is or the exact numeric value. Sometimes you may need to write code to provide more detailed feedback. For example, suppose you are using a scrollbar to browse the letters of the alphabet for a database search. As users move the mouse, you can display the value they are scrolling through and then, when they release the mouse, perform the actual database search (see Figure 4.17).

FIGURE 4.17
Associating labels or text boxes with the scrollbar shows the users the range and actual value.

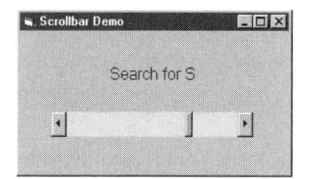

The tricky part is knowing where to put the code statements. To show the value at all times, you actually have to place this statement in three events:

- `Form_Load`—Use this event to display the initial value of the scrollbar after setting up the range.
- `Change`—The `Change` event is triggered when you release the mouse button after dragging the position button to a new location. The `Change` event is also triggered each time the user clicks one of the arrows or clicks the scrollbar.
- `Scroll`—The `Scroll` event fires while the scrollbar position button is being dragged. This event allows you to display the value or take action as the `Value` property changes but before the `Change` event fires.

To test this alphabet example, create a new Standard EXE project. Place a scrollbar and label on the form. Then enter the code in Listing 4.1.

Listing 4.1   SCRLDEMO.ZIP—Using the Scrollbar

```
Private Sub Form_Load()
    'Set Max, then Min properties to numeric values
    HScroll1.Max = Asc("Z")
    HScroll1.Min = Asc("A")

    'Display the Initial Value
    Label1.Caption = Chr$(HScroll1.Value)
End Sub
```

```
Private Sub HScroll1_Change()
    Label1.Caption = "Search for " & Chr$(HScroll1.Value)
    'Insert code here to actually perform the db search
End Sub
Private Sub HScroll1_Scroll()
    Label1.Caption = "Release to select " & Chr$(HScroll1.Value)
End Sub
```

Run the program and watch the text in the label change as you manipulate the scrollbar. By putting code in the appropriate events, as in the example in Listing 4.1, you can have your program always display the exact value of the scrollbar but take action only when appropriate.

The Timer Control

As you may guess from looking at its icon, the Timer control works like a stopwatch or an alarm clock. However, three major differences exist between a timer in the real world and one in Visual Basic:

- Instead of making a noise or beeping, the Timer control executes code (in its Timer event) when the interval is complete.
- The Timer control counts down repeatedly, as long as the Enabled property is set to True.
- The Timer control is designed to work with very small amounts of time; the maximum setting is just a little longer than a minute.

The Timer control has many uses, including scheduling and performing repeated operations.

Setting Up the Timer You set up a Timer control by first drawing it on the form, as shown in Figure 4.18. The Timer control always shows up as an icon at designtime, but it does not show up at all while your program is running.

FIGURE 4.18
The Timer control appears as an icon, no matter what size you draw it.

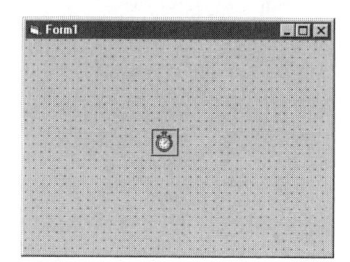

To make the control work, you must first place code in the Timer event and then set the following properties, either at designtime or runtime:

1. Set the Interval property.
2. Set the Enabled property to True.

The Enabled property acts like a switch that turns your timer on and off. If the Timer control is enabled, the code in the Timer event is executed at the end of the time specified in the Interval property. The `Interval` property can be set to any value between zero and 65,535. Setting the `Interval` property to zero disables the Timer control. Otherwise, the `Interval` property specifies the amount of time in milliseconds between firings of the `Timer` event. In other words, if you want 10 seconds to elapse, set the value to 10,000.

NOTE If the `Enabled` property is set to True at designtime, the timer begins countdown as soon as the form containing it is loaded.

Because the maximum value of the `Interval` corresponds to about a minute, how can you set up longer time intervals? You set up code within the `Timer` event that uses the system time to determine whether your interval has elapsed, as shown in Listing 4.2. The code in this listing causes the current time to be printed in the Immediate window every five minutes.

Listing 4.2 TIMEREX.ZIP—Using a Timer Control for Long Intervals

```
Option Explicit
Dim dtNextTime As Date

Private Sub Form_Load()
    'Set up the timer
    Timer1.Interval = 500
    Timer1.Enabled = True

    'We want to do something every 5 minutes
    dtNextTime = DateAdd("n", 5, Now)

End Sub

Private Sub Timer1_Timer()
    If Now >= dtNextTime Then
        Timer1.Enabled = False

        'Do what you want here then update dtNextTime
        Debug.Print "Timer Event at " & Now
        dtNextTime = DateAdd("n", 5, Now)

        Timer1.Enabled = True
    End If
End Sub
```

The code in Listing 4.2 does not use the Timer control to execute an event; instead, it uses the Timer control to check the system date to see whether it needs to execute an event. The key to this listing is the `DateAdd` function, which is used to compute a date five minutes in the future.

NOTE A code-only alternative to using the Timer control is the `Timer` function, which returns the number of seconds elapsed since midnight. You can subtract the current return value of this function from a stored value to find the number of elapsed seconds, as in the following example:

```
Dim sngStart As Single
sngStart = Timer
' (perform some action)
Debug.Print "Elasped time was " & CInt(Timer - sngStart) & " seconds."
```

Creating a Simple Animation To see how easily you can use the Timer control, create a simple animation now:

1. Start a new Standard EXE project in Visual Basic.
2. Place a Timer control and an Image control on the form.
3. From the Properties window on the Image control, select the ellipsis button next to the `Picture` property.
4. When the Load Picture dialog box appears, select an icon file from your Visual Basic \Graphics\Icons directory. For example, select the file FACE03.ICO from the Misc directory. The Image control should now contain an image of some type.
5. Enter the following code in the `Timer` event, `Form Load` event, and declarations section:

   ```
   Dim xChange As Integer
   Dim yChange As Integer

   Private Sub Form_Load()

       xChange = 100
       yChange = 100

   End Sub

   Private Sub Timer1_Timer()

       Image1.Left = Image1.Left + xChange
       Image1.Top = Image1.Top + yChange

       If Image1.Left > Me.ScaleWidth Then xChange = xChange * -1
       If Image1.Left < 0 Then xChange = xChange * -1
       If Image1.Top > Me.ScaleHeight Then yChange = yChange * -1
       If Image1.Top < 0 Then yChange = yChange * -1
   End Sub
   ```

6. Open the Properties window for the Timer control.
7. Set the `Interval` property to `200` and the `Enabled` property to `True`.

When you run the program, the image should move around your form, changing direction when it "hits" the side of the form.

Frames

The Frame control is special because it is a type of control called a *container*. Containers are controls in which you can draw other controls, much like a real picture frame visually encloses (or contains) an artist's picture. When you hide a container control (using the `Visible` property) or change its position on a form, the controls it contains are also affected. This feature is useful for creating multiple "pages" of controls on a single form.

> **NOTE** Container controls create a different visual relationship between the form and the controls they contain. The code events and scope of variables on the form remain unaffected.

As with all other controls, the first step in setting up the frame control is to draw it on your form in the size that you want. Then, of course, you need to set the `Name` property to a unique name. At this point, you can set several properties that control the appearance of the frame, the effects of which are shown in Figure 4.19:

- `Caption`—If you enter a value in the `Caption` property, the text you enter appears in the upper-left corner of the frame. This caption can be used to identify the contents of the frame or provide other descriptive information. If you don't want a caption and simply want an unbroken border around the frame, delete the text in the `Caption` property.

- `Appearance`—This property controls whether the border is shown as a single-line, single-color border, which gives the control a flat look, or is shown using lines that give the control a 3D effect.

- `BorderStyle`—This property determines whether the border around the frame is displayed. If the `BorderStyle` property is set to `None` (using a value of 0), no border is displayed, and the caption is not displayed because it is also part of the border.

> **TIP** To avoid having the lines of the border touch the text of the caption, insert a space before and after the text when you set the `Caption` property.

FIGURE 4.19
You control the frame's appearance through the Appearance, BorderStyle, and Caption properties.

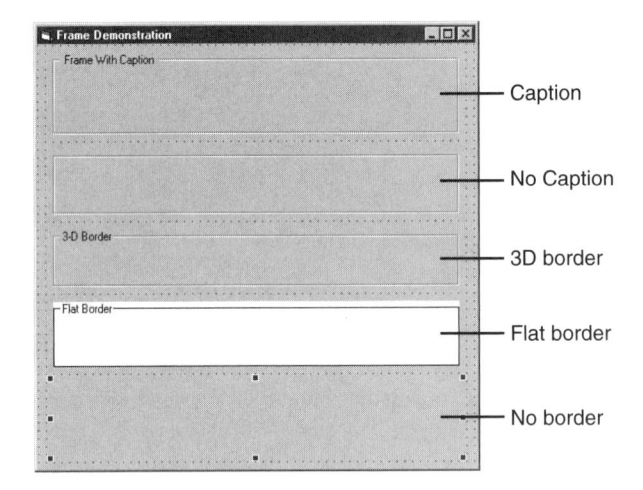

> **TIP** If you want the frame to appear without a border, leave the border turned on while you are in design mode and then set the `BorderStyle` property to 0 when your form loads. Having the border displayed in the design environment makes it easier to see the boundaries of the frame.

Working with Controls in the Frame After you draw a Frame control, you are ready to start placing other controls in it. You can place any controls you like in the frame (or any other container). You can even place containers within containers.

To place controls in a frame, simply draw them directly in the frame just like you would draw them on the form. (If you double-click a Toolbox tool to add a control, it's important that the frame is selected before adding the control.) Then draw controls in the frame just like you would draw them on the form. You need to make sure that the cursor is inside the frame when you start drawing the control. Otherwise, the control is not contained by the frame. Figure 4.20 shows several controls for a personnel application drawn on a frame.

FIGURE 4.20
Make sure your cursor is inside the frame before you start to draw a control.

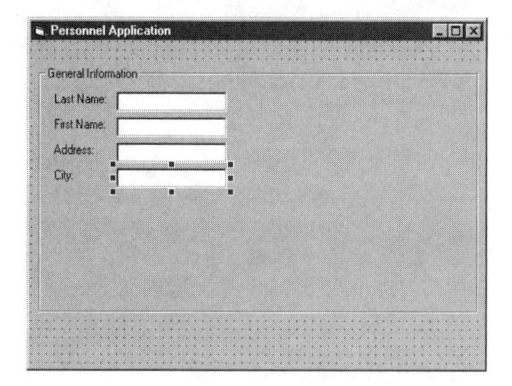

Here are a couple of points about controls and frames:

- First, if you already have controls on the form, they are not contained by the frame, even if you draw the frame over the control.
- Second, when you are moving a control on a frame, unlike moving controls around on a form, you cannot move a control into or out of the frame by dragging and dropping the control.

You can drag a control over the frame, and the control will look like it is contained within the frame, but it really isn't. The only way to move a control from other parts of the form into the frame is to cut and paste. Cut the control from the form, select the frame, and then paste the control in the frame. (You can also copy a control from another part of the form and paste it into the frame.) The control is initially placed in the upper-left corner of the frame, but after the control is in the frame, you can drag and drop the control within the frame. You can use the same technique to move a control out of the frame. You can, of course, move multiple controls at the same time.

> **TIP** If you want to make sure a control is in the frame, try moving the frame. If the control moves with it, the control is part of the frame. If the control does not move with the frame, you can cut and paste to move it into the frame.

Working with Multiple Controls at Designtime

So far, you have seen how to add controls to your forms and how to set the properties of a single control at a time. Sometimes, though, you need to be able to work with multiple controls at the same time. For example, if you have a bunch of Label controls on a form and decide to change their font, you don't want to have to select and change each Label control individually. Fortunately, you don't have to handle controls one at a time; you can work with them in groups.

Selecting Multiple Controls

The first step in working with multiple controls is to select all the controls that you need to move or modify. You can select a group of controls by clicking the mouse on your form and dragging it. As you drag the mouse, a dashed-line box appears on the form, as shown in Figure 4.21 (the designtime Form Grid has been disabled for clarity). Use this box to enclose the controls you want to select.

FIGURE 4.21
You can easily select multiple controls by using the mouse.

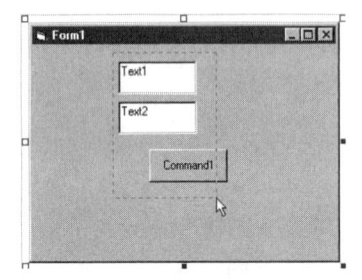

When you release the mouse button, any controls that are inside the box or touching it are selected. The selected controls are indicated by sizing handles at each corner and in the center of each side of the control, as you can see in Figure 4.22.

FIGURE 4.22
Sizing handles indicate that one or more controls are selected.

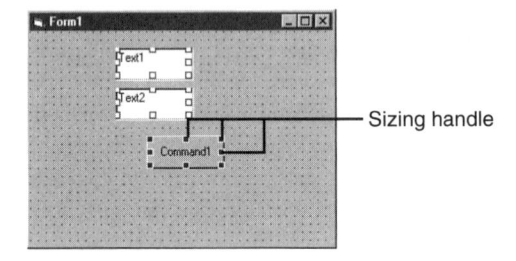

NOTE You can also select multiple controls by holding down the Ctrl key while you click them individually. If you need to select a group of controls that are contained within a frame or picture box, you must Ctrl+click them because the dashed-line box technique doesn't work.

You can add controls to a group or remove them by clicking the control while holding down the Shift or Ctrl key. You can even use this approach after making an initial selection with a mouse drag, so you can refine your selection to exactly the group of controls you want to work with.

After the group of controls has been selected, you can move the group as a whole by clicking one of the controls in the group and dragging the group to a new location. The controls retain their relative positions within the group as you move them. You can also use editing operations such as Delete, Cut, Copy, and Paste on the group as a whole.

Using the Properties Window

In addition to the ability to move, cut, copy, paste, and delete a group of controls, you can also work with their properties as a group. For example, if you want to change the font of a group of Label controls, simply select the group of controls and access the Font property in the Properties window. When you change the property, all the selected controls are affected. This technique is great for making changes to many controls at once.

Although this method obviously works for a group of controls of the same type (such as a group of labels or a group of text boxes), you might be wondering what happens when your group includes controls of several different types. In this case, Visual Basic displays the properties that are common to all the controls in the group. These properties typically include Top, Left, Height, Width, Font, ForeColor, Visible, and Enabled. You can edit only the properties that are common to all the controls. However, this capability is useful if you want to align the left or top edges of a group of controls. To do so, simply select the group and set the Left property of the group (or the Top property). Figure 4.23 shows a selected group of different controls and the Properties window containing their common properties.

FIGURE 4.23
Common properties of different controls can be modified as a group.

Using the Form Editor Toolbar

Editing common properties is not the only way to work with a group of controls. You can also use the *Form Editor toolbar* (see Figure 4.24). You access it by selecting View, Toolbars, Form Editor. Table 4.2 shows and explains each of the toolbar buttons.

FIGURE 4.24
The Form Editor toolbar makes aligning and sizing multiple controls easy.

Table 4.2 Form Editor Toolbar Buttons

Name	Function
Bring to Front	Moves the selected control in front of other controls on the form
Send to Back	Moves the selected control behind other controls on the form
Align	Lines up a group of controls
Center	Centers a group of controls
Make Same Size	Resizes a group of controls to match
Lock Controls Toggle	Prevents movement or resizing of controls with the mouse (however, the controls can still be modified with the Properties window)

Using the Form Editor toolbar, you can manipulate the position and size of a group of controls. The Align button allows you to align the left, right, top, or bottom edges of a group of controls. Although you can align the left and top edges of a group by setting the Left and Top properties directly, you cannot align the right or bottom edges directly. The Align button also allows you to line up the vertical or horizontal centers of the controls. You cannot make this change directly with the properties. To choose which type of alignment to use, click the arrow button to the right of the Align button. This action displays a menu from which you can pick the alignment. You can also choose to align all the selected controls to the grid. Aligning the controls this way causes the upper-left corner of each control to be moved so that it is touching the grid point nearest its current location.

Another task that was tedious in earlier versions of Visual Basic was centering controls on the form. This task has also been made easy using the Form Editor toolbar. Next to the Align button is the Center button. This button allows you to center the group of controls horizontally or vertically within the form. The entire group is centered as if it were a single control; the relative position of each control in the group remains the same. As with the alignment options, you select the type of centering you want from a pop-up menu that appears when you click the arrow button next to the Center button.

The Make Same Size button allows you to make the height and/or width of all the controls in the group the same. Although you can do so by setting the appropriate properties, the Form Editor makes this task much more convenient. Figure 4.25 shows a group of controls made the same size as well as centered horizontally within the form.

FIGURE 4.25
When you use the Form Editor toolbar, centering and resizing controls is a snap.

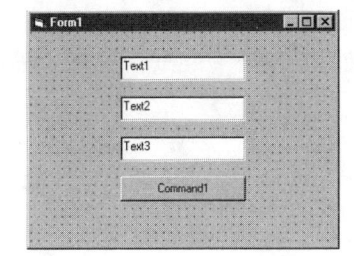

> **TIP** If you click the wrong button on the Form Editor toolbar, you can undo the changes by clicking the Standard toolbar's Undo button or by pressing Ctrl+Z.

Using the Format Menu

Visual Basic's Format menu is also useful when you are working with controls. The Format menu contains all the same functions as the Form Editor toolbar, but it also has three other options for working with multiple controls: Horizontal Spacing, Vertical Spacing, and Size to Grid (see Figure 4.26).

FIGURE 4.26
The Format menu offers a number of tools for fine-tuning the appearance of controls on your forms.

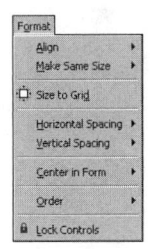

Using the Horizontal Spacing option, you can make the spacing between controls equal. Equal spacing gives you a clean look for groups of controls such as command buttons. If you think the controls are too close together, you can increase the spacing. The spacing is increased by one grid point. You can also decrease the spacing between controls or remove the spacing altogether. By choosing Vertical Spacing, you can perform the same tasks in the vertical direction. Figure 4.27 shows a "before" and "after" look at a group of command buttons. The "after" portion shows the effect of setting the horizontal spacing equal.

FIGURE 4.27
Equal horizontal spacing makes this group of buttons look orderly.

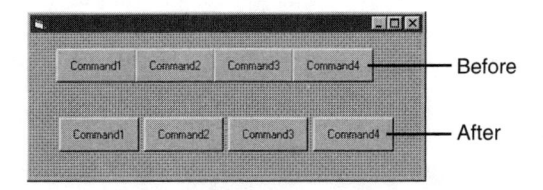

The final item on the F_ormat menu is the Size to Gri_d item. Selecting this option sets the `Height` and `Width` properties of each selected control so that it exactly matches the grid spacing.

Multiple Controls in a Frame

Now you know how to select multiple controls on a form to work with their common properties or to handle alignment and sizing tasks. You can use the same approach with controls inside a frame. The only difference is in the way that you select the controls. To select a group of controls, you first need to click the form so that no controls are selected. Then hold down the Shift or Ctrl key while you click, and drag the mouse around the controls in the frame. This action selects the group of controls. You can still select or deselect other controls by holding down the Ctrl key while you click the controls.

> **N O T E** When you are selecting a group of controls, all the controls must be inside or outside a container. Also, control selection cannot span containers.

After you select the multiple controls, you can work with their common properties or use the commands of the F_ormat menu to position and size the controls.

> **CAUTION**
> The C_enter in Form command of the Format menu still centers the controls in the form, not within the frame. This result may be undesirable.

Working with the Controls Collection

By now, you're probably thinking, "All this is great when I am in the design environment, but what about while my program is running?" Well, as you know, you can change the properties of any single control by specifying the control name, the property name, and the new property value. But does this mean that you have to set each control individually? No way!

Each form contains a *collection* called the `Controls` collection. This collection identifies each control on the form. Using this collection and a special form of the `For` loop, you can change a specific property of every control on your form.

Changing All Controls

As an example of changing controls, you might want to give your users a way to select the font they want to use for the controls on the form. Trying to set each form in code would be a real pain. But, with the `For Each` loop, you can set the font of every control on the form with just three lines of code:

```
For Each Control In Form1.Controls
    Control.Font = "Times New Roman"
Next Control
```

> **CAUTION**
> This code will only work if all controls on the form support the Font property. A few controls, such as the Timer control, don't have that property.

You can use the same approach with any other properties that are supported by all the controls on the form.

Changing Selected Controls

What if you want to set a property that is not supported by all the form's controls? For example, if you want to change the text color of your controls, the command button doesn't have a ForeColor property, although other types of controls do. For this problem, you use another code statement: the TypeOf statement. This statement allows you to determine the type of any object. This way, you can set up a routine that changes the ForeColor property of all controls that are not command buttons:

```
For Each Control In Form1.Controls
    If Not TypeOf Control Is CommandButton Then
        Control.ForeColor = &HFF
    End If
Next Control
```

From Here...

This chapter introduced you to the world of forms and controls. You learned how to control the appearance of forms and controls through their properties and how you can use the methods of forms to perform tasks. You also saw how to work with multiple controls in both the design environment and in your programs.

For more information on topics discussed in this chapter, see the following:

- To learn about some controls other than the standard controls, see Chapter 6, "Giving More Control to the User: Menus and Toolbars," and Chapter 12, "Microsoft Common Controls."
- To learn about using controls in an array, see Chapter 13, "Working with Control Arrays."
- To find out how to arrange controls in a manner that is visually pleasing, as well as learn about some graphics-related controls, see Chapter 19, "Using Visual Design Elements."

PART II

Programming with Visual Basic

- **5** Responding to the User with Event Procedures   95
- **6** Giving More Control to the User: Menus and Toolbars   107
- **7** Using Dialog Boxes to Get Information   139
- **8** Using Variables to Store Information   159
- **9** Visual Basic Programming Fundamentals   173
- **10** Controlling the Flow of Your Program Code   203
- **11** Managing Your Project: Sub Procedures, Functions, and Multiple Forms   223

CHAPTER 5

Responding to the User with Event Procedures

In this chapter

Introducing Events **96**

Handling Events in Your Programs **97**

Understanding Event Sequences **102**

With the advent of graphical, object-based operating systems such as Microsoft Windows and its successors, the way that users interact with programs has changed forever. Gone are the days when a character-based program ran from beginning to end with few user interactions. With Windows, you now have tremendous control over what functions a program performs, as well as the order in which these functions are performed. Although this concept made programs much easier to use, they can be much more difficult to develop. A program's developer is no longer in control of the entire program experience. Programmers of event-driven programs must plan for many possible user activities and, in many cases, must protect the users from themselves.

Windows applications are inherently *event-driven*, meaning that the flow of program execution is controlled by the events that occur as the program is running. As you'll see, most of these events are the direct result of actions initiated by the users; however, some events are invoked by other objects, including the program itself.

NOTE Although event-driven programs were around before Windows arrived on the scene (Macintosh programs and even a few DOS programs were event-driven), it was Windows that started the groundswell that has defined desktop computing today.

Introducing Events

The concept of an event-driven program might be fairly new to you, but the idea of responding to events should not be. Most of the world could be called *event-driven*. For example, consider your TV. You can change the channel whenever you feel like it, and with today's remote controls, you can go directly to your favorite channel instead of having to switch through all the channels on the TV. By the same token, you can change the volume of the TV whenever you want by as much as you want. You can probably also cut out the sound altogether by pressing the mute button. This type of control over how and when things happen correlates to event-driven programming. You (the user of your TV) initiate an event (by pressing a button) that causes the TV to take an action appropriate to the event that occurred. You also control when these events happen.

Windows programs work in a similar manner. In Microsoft Word, for example, you can easily change the font or style of a piece of text. You can also highlight a section of text and drag it to a new location. Each of these actions is made possible by the program's capability to take actions in response to user-initiated events.

As you create your own Windows programs, you will seek to model the program after the real-world tasks that the program is supposed to handle. Therefore, you should give the users command buttons or menu selections so that they can perform tasks when they want. Figure 5.1 shows an example of the interface for an event-driven program.

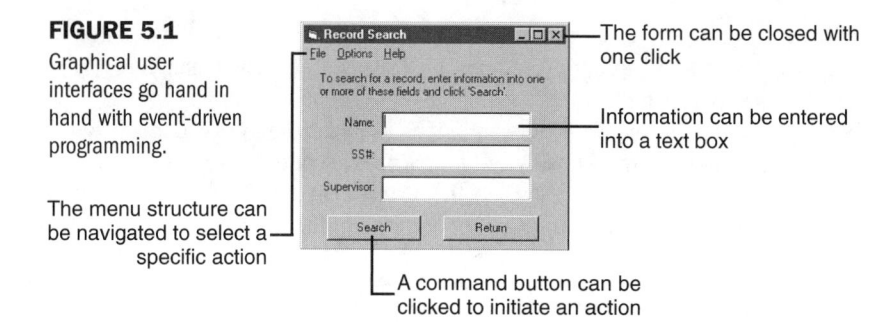

FIGURE 5.1
Graphical user interfaces go hand in hand with event-driven programming.

- The form can be closed with one click
- Information can be entered into a text box
- A command button can be clicked to initiate an action
- The menu structure can be navigated to select a specific action

Another advantage of event-driven programming is that you can use the events to provide immediate feedback to the user. For example, you can program an event to verify a user's entry as soon as the user finishes typing. Then, if a problem occurs with what the user entered, he or she knows immediately and can fix it. This type of feedback is handled by code, such as that shown in Listing 5.1, which ensures that the user has entered required information in the text box.

Listing 5.1 EVENTS.FRM—Code to Verify Entry of a Last Name

```
Private Sub txtLastName_LostFocus()
    If Trim(txtLastName.Text) = "" Then
        smsg = "You must enter your Last Name."
        MsgBox smsg, vbExclamation, "Warning"
        txtLastName.SetFocus
    End If

End Sub
```

Handling Events in Your Programs

In a typical program, many events can occur and many user actions can trigger these events. Program events can be triggered by actions such as the user clicking a mouse button, pressing a key, moving the mouse, changing the value of the information in a control, or switching to another window in the program. The program itself can cause events to occur. Windows events can also be triggered by system functions such as a timer, or even by external factors such as receiving an e-mail message. Hundreds—if not thousands—of events can occur in any given program. Your program should be able to isolate the events that are relative to the program's function. Visual Basic makes this task easy.

Determining When an Event Has Occurred

When Windows detects a user action destined for your program, it sends your program a message. The Visual Basic runtime kernel embedded in your program interprets the message and, if appropriate, raises a corresponding event. If you've written code to handle this event, Visual Basic invokes your code.

Each object in a Visual Basic program can raise a specific group of events, depending on the object's type (text box, form, command button, and so on). However, the key to handling events is to determine exactly which object/event combinations are appropriate to your program and then write code for those object/event combinations. You do so by creating an *event procedure* in a *Code window*. For example, if you want to write some code that will be executed whenever a command button named cmdExit is clicked, you write the Click event procedure for cmdExit. You can edit this procedure by opening a Code window on the form that contains cmdExit.

Recall from Chapter 2, "Creating Your First Program," that you use the drop-down boxes at the top of the Code window to select an event procedure. The object is selected in the Code window's upper-left drop-down list box (the *Object* box); the appropriate event procedure is selected in the upper-right drop-down list box (the *Procedure* box). When that object/event combination occurs at runtime, if code has been written for that combination, Visual Basic executes the code. If no code has been written for the combination, Visual Basic ignores the event. Figure 5.2 shows an example of an event procedure written for a specific control and event.

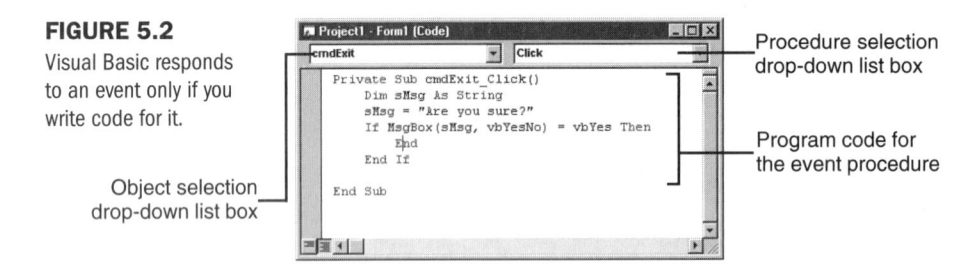

FIGURE 5.2
Visual Basic responds to an event only if you write code for it.

Object selection drop-down list box

Procedure selection drop-down list box

Program code for the event procedure

```
Private Sub cmdExit_Click()
    Dim sMsg As String
    sMsg = "Are you sure?"
    If MsgBox(sMsg, vbYesNo) = vbYes Then
        End
    End If
End Sub
```

Types of Events

Two basic types of events can occur in your Visual Basic program: user-initiated events and system-initiated events. Most often, you will write code for user-initiated events, which let your users control the flow of the program. That is, your users can take a specific action whenever they want (within the constraints imposed by the program), which gives them almost complete control.

> **NOTE** You can, of course, limit the actions that users can take by hiding or disabling controls when you don't want users to have access to them. This technique is discussed in Chapter 3, "Visual Basic Building Blocks."

▶ **See** "Using Properties to Control User Interaction," p. 48

User-Initiated Events User-initiated events are those that occur because of an action taken by the user. As you might guess, these events include keystrokes and mouse clicks, but other events are also caused by the user, either directly or indirectly. For example, when the user clicks a text box to start editing the information in the box, a Click event is fired for the text box. What you might not realize is that several other events are also fired.

One of these events is the `GotFocus` event for the text box. This event occurs every time the user moves to the text box, either by clicking the mouse or using the Tab key. Also, when the text box gets the program's focus, another control must lose the focus. This action causes a `LostFocus` event to fire for the other control. The `GotFocus` and `LostFocus` events are caused by the user's action, just as the `Click` event is. As you will see in the upcoming section "Understanding Event Sequences," multiple events can occur for each action a user takes. The order in which the events occur can be important.

The following are some of the main user actions that trigger events in a program:

- Starting the program
- Pressing a key
- Clicking the mouse
- Moving the mouse
- Closing the program

System Events Although forms and controls can respond to many different events, many controls have several events in common, as you can see in Table 5.1.

Table 5.1 Events Common to Many Controls

Event	Occurs When
Change	The user modifies the text in a text box or combo box.
Click	The user clicks an object with the primary mouse button (usually the left button).
DblClick	The user double-clicks an object with the primary mouse button.
DragDrop	The user drags a control to another location.
DragOver	An object is dragged over a control.
GotFocus	An object receives the focus.
KeyDown	A key is pressed while an object has the focus.
KeyPress	A key is pressed and released while an object has the focus.
KeyUp	A key is released while an object has the focus.
LostFocus	The focus has left an object.
MouseDown	A mouse button is pressed while the mouse pointer is over an object.
MouseMove	The mouse cursor is moved over an object.
MouseUp	A mouse button is released while the mouse pointer is over an object.

You might have noticed that several of the events seem to correspond to the same user action. For example, the `Click`, `MouseDown`, and `MouseUp` events all occur when the user clicks the mouse button. Although some of the differences between the events are obvious—for example, the MouseDown event occurs when you press the mouse button—other differences between the events do exist. In the case of pressing a mouse button, the Click event is fired only if the left mouse button is pressed; it does not respond to the click of any other mouse button. The MouseDown and MouseUp events not only respond to any mouse button, but the event also can report which button was pressed, so your program can take appropriate action.

The KeyDown, KeyPress, and KeyUp events work in a similar manner. The KeyPress event tells you only which key was pressed, not whether a Shift or Ctrl key was held down when the key was pressed. If you need that information, you need to use the KeyDown or KeyUp events.

Writing Event Procedures

With all these events going on, how do you make your code respond to them? And how do you filter out the events that you don't want? The answer to both questions is the same. To respond to any event for any object, you write program code specifically for that event happening to that object. Any object/event combination that has no code written for it is ignored. So the next question is, how do you write code for an event?

To write code, you first need to access a *Code window*. Do so by double-clicking a control on your form (or the form itself), by clicking the View Code button in the project window, by selecting Code from the View menu, or by pressing F7. Any of these actions presents you with the Code window for the current form (see Figure 5.3).

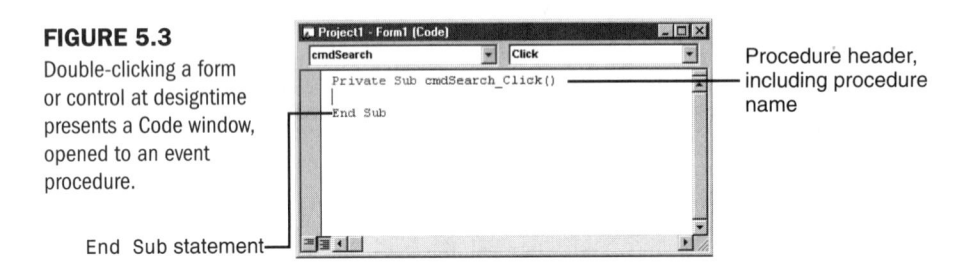

FIGURE 5.3
Double-clicking a form or control at designtime presents a Code window, opened to an event procedure.

End Sub statement

Procedure header, including procedure name

Follow these steps to write a simple example:

1. Start Visual Basic and choose a Standard EXE project.
2. Double-click the form to open the Code window. By default, if no other code exists for the form, you are placed in the form's Load event procedure.
3. From the Object box, select the Form object.
4. From the Procedure box, select the MouseMove event.

> **NOTE** Notice that when you make a selection, Visual Basic automatically sets up the skeleton of a procedure with the procedure's name and the End Sub statement (which denotes the end of the procedure).

The procedure name for an event procedure contains the name of the object and the name of the event. In this example, Form is the object and MouseMove is the event. Notice that the MouseMove event procedure also contains several parameters; for example, the parameters X and Y represent the coordinates of the mouse.

5. At this point, you can write program statements to take whatever action(s) should happen in response to an occurrence of the event. Add the following line of code to the event procedure:

```
Me.Caption = "Mouse Coordinates are (" & X & "," & Y & ")"
```

Your event procedure should now look like this:

```
Private Sub Form_MouseMove(Button As Integer,
Shift As Integer, X As Single, Y As Single)
    Me.Caption = "Mouse Coordinates are (" & X & "," & Y & ")"
End Sub
```

The preceding code displays the values of the X and Y parameters in the form's title bar by setting the Caption property of the form. Press Visual Basic's Start button, or F5, and move the mouse pointer over the form. You should see the form's caption (title) change as the mouse pointer moves.

> **TIP** If you enter a Code window by double-clicking an object, the Code window automatically selects that object's most commonly used event procedure. For example, if you double-click a command button at designtime, the Code window is opened to that command button's Click event procedure.

Calling an Event Procedure from Code

As you learn Visual Basic, you will be writing and calling many procedures. Event procedures are kind of special in that they are called by Visual Basic itself. In the MouseMove example in the preceding section, Visual Basic executed the code you wrote in response to an event. However, it is noteworthy to mention that you can execute event procedures yourself, just like any other procedure you would write. You might do so when you have written code in an event procedure that needs to be executed in multiple places.

Let me demonstrate this by example. If you still have the Standard EXE project open from the previous example, return to Design mode and draw a CommandButton control on the form. Double-click the command button and change the event procedure to display the current date and time, as follows:

```
Private Sub Command1_Click()
    MsgBox "The system time is " & Now
End Sub
```

The preceding code is easy to understand. It just displays a message box when the button Command1 is clicked. However, you can call the Command1_Click procedure from other parts of your code, including another event. Double-click the form itself, and from the Procedure box, select the Click event. Change the Form_Click event procedure to call the Command1_Click procedure:

```
Private Sub Form_Click()
    Command1_Click
End Sub
```

Run the program, and you will notice that whether you click the form or the command button, the same `MsgBox` statement is executed, just as if the user had clicked the command button itself.

> **NOTE** If the event procedure you are calling has parameters, such as the `MouseMove` event, you have to supply them when calling the event procedure.

Understanding Event Sequences

By now, you should have an understanding of what events are and how Visual Basic handles them. You have seen how to write code to take action when an event occurs. But you need to dive just a little deeper into the world of events.

As you learned earlier, a single user action or system event can trigger multiple events. This result can be good because you can use these different events to handle different situations, as in the case of the `MouseDown` and `Click` events. However, there is a flip side. (Isn't there always?) If you write code for multiple events that can occur, these procedures can interact in ways that you don't want. In the worst case, a sequence of events—each with its own event procedure—can put your system into an infinite loop. The following are several keys to avoiding these problems:

- Recognize that multiple events can occur.
- Determine which events occur for a user action.
- Understand the sequence in which the events occur.
- Test the interactions between multiple events in your code.

In the following sections, you examine some issues to be aware of when writing event procedures in Visual Basic.

Multiple Events for Each Action

One of the problems of handling multiple events is that the user can interact with your program in a very large number of ways. For example, did the user move to the text box with a mouse or with the Tab key? Prior to the move, was the focus on another text box or was it on a command button? And what happens when you move from one form to another? As you can see, the possibilities can be almost overwhelming.

The good news, though, is that you will not write code for most object/event combinations. Therefore, even though these events might occur, your program ignores them—and they do not cause you any problems.

Even though not writing this extra code simplifies the task of handling multiple events, it does not eliminate the task. To get a handle on this situation, take a look at some simple sets of events that occur when a user performs an action.

Consider, for example, the Logon dialog box that appears when you start Windows. If you imagine that this dialog box had been written in Visual Basic, as you enter your username and password, several events occur.

First, look at the simple keystroke. For each character that you type in your username, three events are fired: `KeyDown`, `KeyPress`, and `KeyUp` (in that order). When you move from the username field to the password field, you change the focus from one control to another, so two additional events are triggered: `LostFocus` for the current control and `GotFocus` for the new control.

Finally, as you click the OK button, the simple mouse click fires three events: `MouseDown`, `MouseUp`, and `Click`. If you double-click another object such as the form, two more events occur after the `Click` event: the `DblClick` event and another `MouseUp` event. That's five events for what would seem like a single user action. In addition, if the mouse click causes the focus to move from one control to another, `LostFocus` and `GotFocus` events would be triggered, for a total of seven events.

Another problem is that different actions to achieve the same purpose cause different event sequences. For example, consider the OK button on the Windows Logon dialog box. Did you know that you can either click it with the mouse or tab over to it and press the spacebar? Using the mouse triggers the `MouseDown`, `MouseUp`, and `Click` events. Using the spacebar triggers the `KeyDown`, `KeyPress`, `KeyUp`, and then the `Click` events. This process can be confusing, can't it?

However, you can determine what events will occur in your program and in what order they will occur.

Determining the Order of Events

The key to understanding the purposes of these events is knowing *when* they occur. If this information is still a bit unclear, try the simple tutorial that follows. In the tutorial, you create a program to monitor form events and then trigger those events to determine the firing order. You also preview the type of code you might want to put in each of these event procedures.

Creating a Sample Form Events Program   Five special events occur to each form, and you can place code in the associated event procedure for any of them:

- `Load`. Occurs when the form is loaded into memory
- `Activate`. Occurs when the form is displayed initially or when the user returns to the form from another form
- `Deactivate`. Occurs when the user moves to another form or the form is hidden
- `Unload`. Occurs when the form is unloaded from memory
- `Initialize`. Occurs when an instance of the form object is created
- `Terminate`. Occurs when an instance of the form object is destroyed

This sample program is very simple; it has only two forms with no controls. To create it, follow these steps:

1. Open Visual Basic and create a new Standard EXE project.
2. Double-click Form1 to bring up its Code window.
3. Make sure the Load event is selected in the drop-down Event box at the upper-right of the Code window.
4. Type the statement MsgBox "The Form Load Event occurred" into the event procedure so that the code looks like this:

```
Private Sub Form_Load()
    MsgBox "The Form Load Event occurred "
End Sub
```

5. Repeat steps 3 and 4 to place similar MsgBox statements in the Initialize and Unload event procedures.
6. Add a second form, Form2, to the project by choosing Project, Add Form.

Now that you have created the project, press F5 to run it. Notice that the Initialize event comes first, followed by the Load event. Click the form's Close button, and you should notice that the Unload and Terminate events occur before the program stops.

Testing Program Events Now start the program again and press Ctrl+Break to pause execution. Press Ctrl+G to bring up the Immediate window. Put the cursor in the Immediate window, and enter the following lines (pressing Enter after each), observing the messages that appear:

```
Load Form2
Unload Form1
Load Form1
```

(You load Form2 to prevent the program from ending when you unload Form1.) You should have noticed that the Initialize event did not occur when Form1 was loaded the second time. Now enter the following lines:

```
Unload Form1
Set Form1 = Nothing
```

Setting an instance of a form to Nothing when you're done with it is good practice. This way, you can ensure that all resources that were allocated to the form are properly released.

Now enter this line:

```
Load Form1
```

The Initialize event occurs again because the instance of Form1 that you created before was destroyed when it was set to Nothing.

Using Form Events You can use program code in these events to set the properties of the form or any of its controls, set up databases or recordsets needed for the form, or run any other code that you might find necessary. The Load and Unload events each occur only once in the life of a form—when the form is loaded and unloaded from memory, respectively. On the other hand, the Activate and Deactivate events can occur many times. Therefore, you need to be careful which code is placed in which event.

The following code segment shows you a couple of simple but useful things that you can do with code in the `Load` event procedure. One very common use of the Load event procedure is to "preset" the value of one or more properties of controls on your form (or the form itself). Listing 5.2 illustrates how to set the form's `Caption` property as the form loads to reflect the current user's name (which you can assume has been previously determined elsewhere in the program and stored in the string variable `sUserName`). You also see how to set the `Text` property of a text box to contain the current date.

Listing 5.2 TESTLOAD.FRM—Using the *Load Event* Procedure to Set Properties

```
Private Sub Form_Load()
    Me.Caption = "Expense Summary for " & sUserName
    txtDate.Text = Date
End Sub
```

Other common uses of the `Load` event include setting up connections to data stored in databases, initializing variables, and positioning the form relative to other forms that may be open.

Another form event that you will use often is the `Resize` event. This event is triggered any time the size of the form is changed, either by the user or by your program. It also occurs after the form's `Load` event, before the `Activate` event occurs. Typically, you use the `Resize` event to change the size of one or more controls on your form. Doing so gives the user more room to work when the size of the form is increased and prevents information from being hidden when the size of the form is decreased. Listing 5.3 shows how the size of a data-bound `Grid` control changes when the form's size is changed. The code also checks the `WindowState` property of the form and does not perform the operation when the form is minimized.

Listing 5.3 RESIZE.FRM—Changing the Size and Position of Objects When the Form's Size Changes

```
If Me.WindowState <> vbMinimized And AllowResize Then
    dbgResults.Width = Me.ScaleWidth - 180
    dbgResults.Height = Me.ScaleHeight - dbgResults.Top - 60
End If
```

The first step in determining the event interaction is to map the order of events in a program. You can easily write a simple program to familiarize yourself with when events occur. First, create a new standard EXE project and place a `TextBox` control and a command button on it. You can then place code in the control and form event procedures to notify you when an event occurs. The easiest way to do so is to use the `Debug.Print` statement, which causes text to be displayed in the Immediate window. Simply add `Debug.Print` statements to the event procedures, such as the following ones for the text box:

```
Private Sub Text1_Click()
    Debug.Print "Text1 Click Event"
End Sub

Private Sub Text1_GotFocus()
    Debug.Print "Text1 Got Focus Event"
End Sub

Private Sub Text1_KeyPress(KeyAscii As Integer)
    Debug.Print "Text1 Keypress Event"
End Sub
```

Whether you use a tool like this program, or some other method, understanding the sequence of events is critically important. Once you realize that one user action can lead to several events, you can use that information to plan for which events you want to write code. For example, you can use a text box's KeyDown event, which is the first event that occurs when the user presses a key while the text box has the focus, to determine whether the user has pressed Ctrl. That may be an indication within your program of some special action, such as opening a new record or saving initialization information. Whatever the case, you should test your applications thoroughly, using a variety of sequences of actions to your objects, to make sure that unexpected event sequences won't cause undesired results.

From Here...

This chapter focused on how Visual Basic handles events. However, events are useful only in the context of forms and controls because they are the objects capable of receiving events. Also, events can cause an action in your program only if some code has been written for the event. You can learn more about these related topics in the following chapters:

- See Chapter 3, "Visual Basic Building Blocks," for introductions to forms, controls, properties, methods, and events.
- For further fundamental information on using Visual Basic controls, see Chapter 4, "Using Visual Basic's Default Controls."
- Chapter 6, "Giving More Control to the User: Menus and Toolbars," covers menus and toolbars in Visual Basic programs.
- For information on the Common Dialog control, see Chapter 7, "Using Dialog Boxes to Get Information."
- To find out more about writing your own procedures, see Chapter 11, "Managing Your Project: Sub Procedures, Functions, and Multiple Forms."
- To learn about the many different events available in the custom controls, see Chapter 12, "Microsoft Common Controls."

CHAPTER 6

Giving More Control to the User: Menus and Toolbars

In this chapter

Creating a Menu Bar 108

Creating Pop-Up Menus 122

Using Toolbars in Visual Basic 124

Using the Coolbar Control 136

Many computer programs are interactive; that is, they perform functions in response to user actions. In Chapter 5, "Responding to the User with Event Procedures," you learned how to make the objects in your program react to user actions. In this chapter, you explore how to give more control to your users. You learn how to add menu structures to your programs, giving your users the capability to select from a number of program commands. You will then see how to add toolbars to give your users a shortcut to commonly-used program functions.

Creating a Menu Bar

One of the most important aspects in designing any program is providing the users with easy access to all the program's functions. Users are accustomed to accessing most functions with a mouse click or two. In addition, they want all the functions located conveniently in one place. To help facilitate this strategy, Visual Basic lets you quickly and easily create a menu system with the Menu Editor. You can use this editor to create a menu bar for each of your application's forms, as well as context-sensitive "pop-up" menus (see the section "Creating Pop-Up Menus" later in this chapter).

The menu bar for the main form of a custom-designed exposition management program is shown in Figure 6.1.

FIGURE 6.1
A well-designed menu system enables a program's users to locate and execute its functions easily.

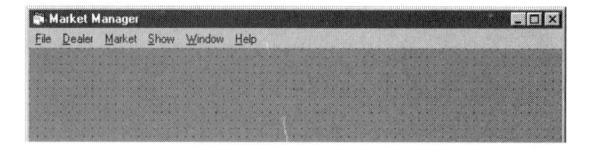

The first step in creating a menu is determining what program commands need to be on the menu and how these commands should be organized. Figure 6.2 shows Visual Basic's own main menu. As you can see, the commands are organized into functional groups (File, Edit, View, and so forth).

FIGURE 6.2
Visual Basic's main menu, shown here with its File menu opened, provides a convenient and intuitive way for users to select the various program functions.

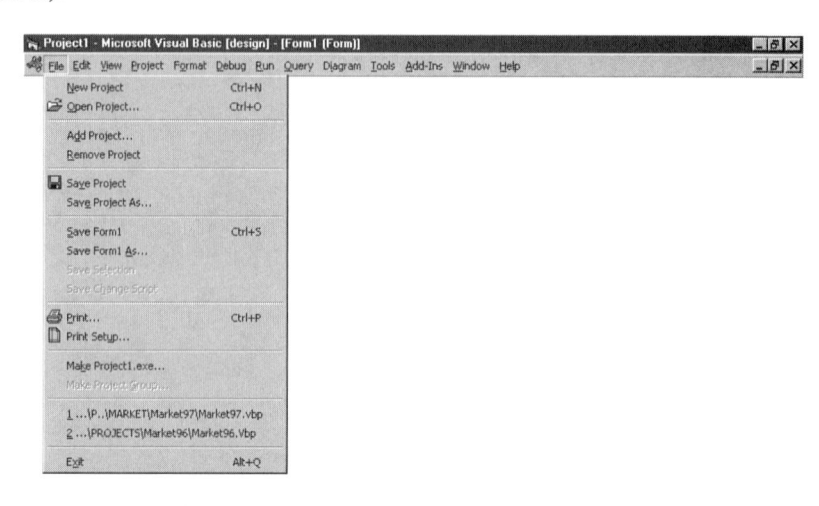

The following sections provide the details about menus and building and coding them.

Common Menus

When you create your program's menu, you should group similar items. In fact, if possible, you should use groups with which your users are already familiar. This way, users have some idea where to find particular menu items, even if they've never used your program. The following list describes some standard menus you will find on many menu bars:

- **File.** This menu contains any functions related to whole files used by your program. Some of the typical menu items are New, Open, Close, Save, Save As, and Print. If your program works extensively with different files, you might also want to include a quick access list of the most recently used files. If you include a File menu, the program's Exit command is usually located near the bottom of this menu.

- **Edit.** The Edit menu contains the functions related to editing of text and using the Windows Clipboard. Some typical Edit menu items are Undo, Cut, Copy, Paste, Clear, Find, and Replace.

- **View.** The View menu might be included if your program supports different looks for the same document. A word processor, for example, might include a normal view for editing text and a page-layout view for positioning document elements, as well as a variety of zoom options. Another use of the View menu is to allow the users to display or hide special forms in your program, like the Visual Basic View, Toolbox option.

- **Tools.** This menu is a catchall for your program's utilities or "helper" functions. For example, a spelling checker, grammar checker, or equation editor might be included for a word processor.

- **Window.** This menu typically is included if your program uses a Multiple Document Interface (MDI). MDI programs, like Microsoft Word, support the simultaneous editing of different documents, databases, or files. The Window menu lets users arrange open documents or switch rapidly between them.

- **Help.** The Help menu contains access to your program's Help system. Typically, it includes menu items for a Help Index (a table of contents for help), a Search option (to let the users quickly find a particular topic), and an About option (providing summary, authoring, and copyright information regarding your program).

You can use these six "standard" menus as a basis for creating your own menu system. Include any or all of them as needed by your program, and add other menu groups as needed. Plan well before adding a lot of new groups, though. Make sure your users can easily access all your program's functions through the menu system.

Setting Up the Main Items

After deciding what functions to include in your menu and how to group these functions, you can then build the menu. To create a menu, first open the form on which you want the menu located, and then start the Menu Editor in any of three ways: click the Menu Editor button on the toolbar; choose Tools, Menu Editor; or press Ctrl+E. The Menu Editor then appears, as shown in Figure 6.3.

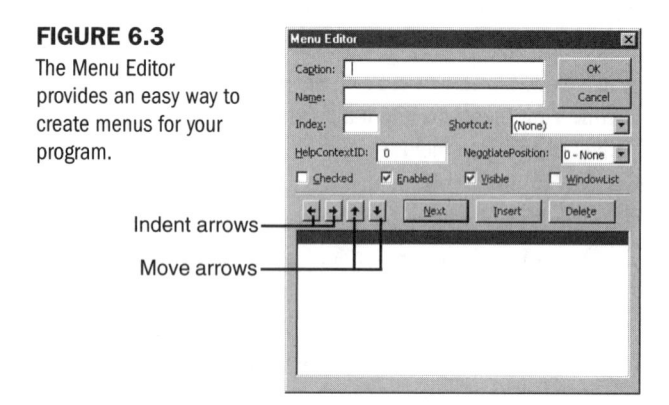

FIGURE 6.3
The Menu Editor provides an easy way to create menus for your program.

Indent arrows
Move arrows

Menu Controls Each line of text (menu item) in a menu is a *Menu control*, just as each command button that you place on a form is a `CommandButton` control. You use the Menu Editor to create Menu controls and to set the following properties for each control:

- **Caption.** The caption is the actual text that is displayed in the menu item. You can specify an access key, which allows the users to select the menu item with the keyboard instead of a mouse, by placing an ampersand (&) before the appropriate letter of the caption. For example, if a particular menu item's `Caption` property is set to `F&ormat`, the "o" is underlined, and the users can select that item by pressing *O* when the menu is active. The `Caption` property is required for all menu items.

- **Name.** This property is used to identify the menu item in code. The `Name` property is required for all menu items. Like all other controls, each Menu control must have a name that will be used to refer to it in code. With these controls, unlike other controls, however, Visual Basic does not give menu items a default name; therefore, you must set the `Name` property of all menu items before leaving the Menu Editor.

- **Index.** If this menu item is part of control array, the `Index` property uniquely identifies the particular control array element.

- **Shortcut.** With this property, you can define shortcut key combinations that allow your users to select a menu item with one keystroke, bypassing the menu system entirely. For example, many programs use Ctrl+P as a shortcut key, eliminating the need to choose File, Print from the menu system.

- **HelpContextID.** This property sets a context ID that can be used in conjunction with a custom help file to provide context-sensitive help for your application.
- **NegotiatePosition.** If your application has linked or embedded objects, this property determines if and how this menu item is displayed while the linked or embedded object is active.
- **Checked.** If this property is `True`, a check mark appears to the left of the menu item's caption to indicate, for example, that a user has selected a particular option. If this property is `False`, no check mark appears.
- **Enabled.** This property can be set to `False` if its associated action isn't appropriate at a particular time. For example, if no text is selected, an Edit menu's Copy command can be disabled by setting its `Enabled` property to `False`.
- **Visible.** This property determines whether the menu item can be seen. Your application may have menu items that should not be seen at certain times; for example, you may not want the users to be able to see the Window menu item if no windows are open.
- **WindowList.** If your menu is on an MDI (Multiple Document Interface) form, , setting this property for a top-level menu control appends a dynamically-updated list of any active MDI child windows to the menu automatically.

Creating a Simple Menu System   To illustrate the process of designing menus, you actually create a simple menu system now. You'll create a menu structure that includes some standard menu items. First, create a sample File menu:

1. Start Visual Basic, if necessary, and begin a Standard EXE project.
2. Make sure that the form for which you want to create the menu system is selected. `Form1` should already be selected; if not, click it.
3. Start the Menu Editor by selecting Tools, Menu Editor, or clicking the Menu Editor button on the toolbar.

   The cursor should be in the Caption field. In this field, you enter the text to be displayed by the menu item.
4. Type `&File` (remember, the ampersand indicates that the next character—*F*, in this case—is to be the access key). As you type, notice that the caption you are typing automatically appears in the box at the bottom of the Menu Editor. In this area, you can preview the layout of your menu. Note also that the top line of this box is highlighted.
5. Tab to the Name field and type `mnuFile`.

   The two properties you just set—`Caption` and `Name`—are all you need to set for now. The default values of the other properties work fine.
6. Click Next or press Enter to accept the properties you've set up for this Menu control. The property boxes are then cleared to prepare for a new control. Note that the highlight in the box at the bottom moves down to a new (blank) line.
7. Repeat steps 4 through 6 to create a second menu item. Use `&New` for the caption and `mnuFileNew` for the name.

8. Click OK to close the Menu Editor.

After following these steps, your form should have a menu bar like the one illustrated in Figure 6.4.

FIGURE 6.4
This menu bar, shown at designtime, was created with the Menu Editor.

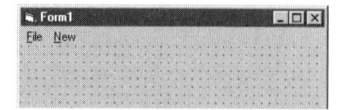

You may have expected the menu to look different than this, with the New menu being a sub-item within the File menu. Instead, both File and New are top-level menus. To fix this problem, you need to learn about the different levels that a menu can have. You learn more information about this topic in the following section, "Multiple-Level Menus."

You may also have tried clicking one of the menu items in the design environment. If you did, you were presented with a Code window. What you've done here is the equivalent of double-clicking an object on a form at designtime: You've opened the `Click` event procedure associated with the menu item that you clicked. Here, you can write code to be executed when that menu item is chosen at runtime. You learn about writing code for menu items later in the chapter in the section "Writing Code for the Menu Items"; for now, just close the Code window.

Multiple-Level Menus

Typical menus in Windows-based applications contain multiple levels of commands. Top-level menu items are the ones that are visible in the program's menu bar. Normally, clicking a top-level menu item opens that item's submenu. Each item in a submenu can represent either a program command or another submenu. In Visual Basic, your menus can have up to six levels of submenus.

TIP Although Visual Basic allows menus to have up to six levels, you should usually limit your program's menus to two or three levels. Too many levels can make navigating the menu system more difficult for your users.

Follow these steps to continue creating the File menu you started in the preceding section and to add the Edit and Options menus:

1. While Form1 is selected, open the Menu Editor.
2. In the box at the bottom of the Menu Editor, click the New item to select it.
3. Locate the four arrow buttons in the left-center area of the Menu Editor. Then click the right-facing arrow once. This action moves the selected menu item down a level. Notice in the box that the caption for this item becomes indented as a visual cue that it is a lower-level item. Clicking the left-facing arrow moves the item up a level.

4. Click Next to prepare the Menu Editor for another new item. Notice that in addition to clearing the property boxes, the new (blank) item in the Menu Editor's box is automatically indented to the level of the item preceding it.

5. Add new (indented) menu items with the following captions and names:

Caption	Name
&Open...	mnuFileOpen
&Print...	mnuFilePrint
&Save	mnuFileSave
Sen&d To	mnuFileSendTo

6. The Send To menu item will itself be a submenu. After you create it, indent the next blank menu item to another level by clicking the right-facing arrow, and add new (twice-indented) menu items with these captions and names:

Caption	Name
&Mail Recipient	mnuFileSendToMail
&Fax Recipient	mnuFileSendToFax

> **NOTE** When you create multiple menu levels, as in the Send To option of the sample menu, Windows automatically provides the arrow-like indicator that lets users know a submenu exists.

7. Click the left-facing arrow once to unindent the next blank menu item by one level. Set this item's caption to `E&xit` and its name to `mnuFileExit`.
8. Click Next or press Enter to create a new menu item.
9. Click the left-facing arrow to make this a top-level menu item (not indented at all). Set this new item's caption to `&Edit` and its name to `mnuEdit`.
10. Indent the next menu item so that it is subordinate to the Edit menu. Add new menu items with these captions and names:

Caption	Name
Cu&t	mnuEditCut
&Copy	mnuEditCopy
&Paste	mnuEditPaste

11. On your own, add a top-level menu item. Set its `Caption` property to `&Options` and its `Name` property to `mnuOptions`.
12. Add these indented (second-level) menu items under the Options menu:

Caption	Name
&Text Only	mnuOptionsText
&Uppercase	mnuOptionsUppercase

The Menu Editor should look like the one in Figure 6.5.

FIGURE 6.5
The Menu Editor enables you to create hierarchical menu systems quickly and easily.

13. Click OK to close the Menu Editor.

> **TIP**
> I typically use a hierarchical structure to assign the Name property of my menu items. Each menu item's name begins with the prefix mnu-, followed by words that describe the portion of the menu in which the item is located. For example, mnuFileSendToFax is used to represent the menu item with the caption Fax Recipient; I can tell from the name that this item is in the Send To submenu of the File menu.

> **NOTE** Occasionally, a menu item's caption ends with an ellipsis (...), as in the Open and Print items in the example. This ellipsis signifies to the users that more information, such as a filename and location, are needed to complete the requested command. After users select such a command, your program requests the appropriate information via a dialog box.

Now that you're back in the Visual Basic design environment, you can click Form1's File menu to see what it looks like. At this point, you may decide that you would like to group the commands that work with managing files—New, Open, and Save—together, as well as the Print and Send To commands. To do so, you need to move the Print menu down so that the file functions are together. You can then insert *separator bars* to group the related functions.

Grouping Menu Items

In addition to using menu levels to organize the items in your menu, you might want to further separate items in a particular level. Placing *separator bars* in the menu breaks up a long list of items and further groups the items, without your having to create a separate level. To place a separator bar in your menu, enter a hyphen (-) as the menu item's Caption property. It creates a separator bar that is the full width of the drop-down menu in which it appears. Remember, you must give each separator bar a unique value for its Name property, just as with any other menu item. I typically use incrementing numbers as part of the names of my separator menu items—mnuHyphen1, mnuHyphen2, and so on.

> **CAUTION**
> You cannot use a separator bar in the top level of the menu (the menu bar); separator bars must be part of a submenu. If you attempt to use a separator in the menu bar, Visual Basic informs you of the error as you try to save the menu.

Modifying the Menu

After creating your menu, you will probably find that you need to make some changes to the menu's structure. This task also is easily accomplished with the Menu Editor. Table 6.1 lists some common editing needs and how they are accomplished.

Table 6.1 Modifying Your Menu

Editing Function	How to Do It
Move an item	Select the item, and then click one of the Move arrows to move the item up or down in the list. The indentation level of the menu does not change as you move the item.
Add an item to the middle of the list	Select the item that should appear below the new item in the list, and then click the Insert button. A blank item appears; you can then enter the Caption and Name properties for the item. The new item is indented at the same level as the item below it.
Remove an item	Select the item, and then click the Delete button. The item is immediately deleted, without any confirmation. (There is no Undo feature available in the Menu Editor; whatever you delete is gone. However, if you wrote any program code for the menu control, that code is still present in the Code window.)

Now you can use these menu modification techniques to regroup the items and to insert the separator bars mentioned in the preceding section. To do so, follow these steps:

1. While Form1 is selected, open the Menu Editor.
2. Click the Print menu item once to select it.
3. Click the downward-facing arrow twice to move the item just above the Send To menu item. (If you need to move an item up, click the upward-facing arrow.)
4. With the Print menu item still selected, click the Insert button to create a blank menu item above the Print item.
5. Click in the Caption field, and type a single hyphen (-).
6. Tab to the Name field and type mnuHyphen1.

7. To insert another blank item before the Exit menu item, select the Exit item and then click Insert.
8. Enter a hyphen as the new item's Caption property and mnuHyphen2 as its Name property.
9. Click OK to close the Menu Editor.

Figure 6.6 depicts the Menu Editor after creating and modifying the sample File menu.

FIGURE 6.6
Multiple menu levels help organize your program's functions.

Adding Access Keys and Shortcut Keys for Quick Access

Many menu items in Windows programs can be accessed by using keystroke combinations. You can let users access your menu items in the same way. Two types of key combinations can be used this way: *access keys* and *shortcut keys*.

Access Keys Access keys offer users a way to navigate a menu system by using the keyboard instead of a mouse. If a menu item has an access key defined, the access key is indicated by an underscore beneath the letter in the item's caption (for example, the *F* in File). You create an access key by placing an ampersand (&) in front of the appropriate letter in the Caption property. For the File menu, the Caption property would be &File. You can create an access key for any or all of the items in your menu.

> **TIP** Where possible, use the first letter of the menu item as the access key, because typically the users expect it. On the other hand, you shouldn't use the first letter if that letter is already in use in that menu. For example, Visual Basic's Format menu uses the second letter as the access key to avoid conflict with the File menu. You can assign the same access key to multiple menu items. If you do so, Visual Basic just cycles through the items with each press of the access key. However, this approach is not standard practice because having to press an access key multiple times defeats its purpose. In addition, many users don't know that they can cycle through the items in this manner and become frustrated when they see no apparent way to select the desired choice.

When you have access keys defined for your menu items, the users can select a top-level menu item (in the menu bar) by holding down the Alt key and then pressing the access key. This action causes the submenu for that item to drop down, showing the items for that group. The users can then start the desired task by pressing the access key defined for the menu item. For example, for the New item of the File menu, users could press Alt+F and then press N.

To create an effective set of access keys, you must specify a different key for each of the top-level menu items. Then you need to specify a different key for each of the items in the submenu. Conceivably, you can have up to 36 access keys on the same menu, one for each letter of the alphabet and one for each of the 10 digits, but you may run out of screen space for the choices before running out of letters.

Shortcut Keys In addition to the access keys just discussed, you can assign shortcut keys to some of the more commonly used functions in your program. Shortcut keys provide direct access to a function through a single key (such as Delete) or key combination (such as Ctrl+S), bypassing the menu system entirely. Users can take advantage of shortcut keys to perform tasks quickly.

To assign a shortcut key to one of your functions, enter the Menu Editor, select the menu item for which you want a shortcut key, and then select the desired key from the Shortcut list. The key is assigned to that function, and the shortcut key information appears next to the menu item in the menu.

To illustrate this use, assign Ctrl+P as the shortcut key for the sample menu's File, Print function, as follows:

1. Make sure Form1 is selected, and then open the Menu Editor.
2. Click the Print menu item to select it.
3. Click the drop-down arrow next to the Shortcut list, and select Ctrl+P from the list.
4. On your own, assign the following shortcut keys:

Menu Item	Shortcut Key
File, New	Ctrl+N
File, Open	Ctrl+O
File, Save	Ctrl+S
Edit, Cut	Ctrl+X
Edit, Copy	Ctrl+C
Edit, Paste	Ctrl+V

5. Click OK to close the Menu Editor.

Now that you're back in the design environment, click the File menu to see how the shortcut key combinations are displayed. Figure 6.7 illustrates the results.

FIGURE 6.7
Shortcut keys have been assigned to several of the File menu's functions.

Ctrl+P shortcut

File, Print menu item

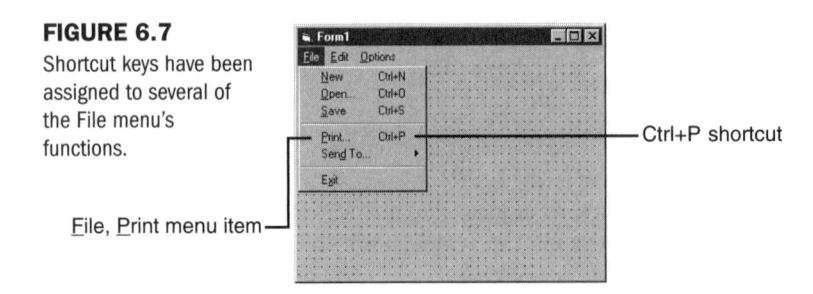

You can assign any unused shortcut key to any menu item, but you should try to make your program use the same "standard" keys that are used in many Windows programs. Some of these keys are listed in Table 6.2. As examples, the "Description" column explains what these keys do when you're working within Visual Basic itself.

Table 6.2 Commonly Used Shortcut Keys Speed Access to Program Tasks

Menu Item	Shortcut Key	Description
Edit, Cut	Ctrl+X	Removes selected text from its current location and copies it to the Clipboard.
Edit, Copy	Ctrl+C	Makes a copy of the selected text in the Clipboard.
Edit, Paste	Ctrl+V	Pastes the contents of the Clipboard to the active document.
Edit, Undo	Ctrl+Z	Undoes the last change.
Edit, Find	Ctrl+F	Opens the Find dialog box to allow the users to search for something (text, for example).
File, New	Ctrl+N	Creates a new document.
File, Open	Ctrl+O	Opens a dialog box to allow the users to select a document to open.
File, Save	Ctrl+S	Saves the current document.
File, Print	Ctrl+P	Opens the Print dialog box to allow selection of items to be printed.

> **TIP** As with access keys, you should try to make the shortcut key correspond to the first letter of the item name—for example, Ctrl+P for Print. Users can remember the shortcuts more easily this way. To avoid confusing your users, you should use the standard shortcut keys listed in Table 6.2 whenever possible.

Writing Code for the Menu Items

After creating the menu's structure, you need to write code to let the menu items actually perform tasks. As with a form or other controls, you do so by writing code in an event procedure. A menu item handles only one event: the Click event. This event is triggered when a user clicks the menu item, or when the user selects the item and presses Enter. Think of the user's action of selecting a menu item as being similar to clicking a command button.

> **NOTE** A menu item's Click event is also triggered when a user uses an access key or shortcut key to access an item.

To add code to a menu item's Click event procedure, first select the menu item on the form by clicking the item. This action opens a Code window and sets up the Event procedure for the selected item, in the same manner as if you had double-clicked some other object on your form. Then simply type in the code to handle the task.

Now you can enhance the menu example by coding the File, Exit function, as shown in the following steps:

1. In the design environment, click Form1's File menu to open it; then click Exit. You are presented with the Code window for the Click event procedure for your mnuFileExit menu item.

2. Type the following code into the event procedure:
   ```
   Dim nTemp As Integer, sTemp As String
   sTemp = "Are you sure you want to exit?"
   nTemp = MsgBox(sTemp, vbYesNo, "Menu Sample Program")
   If nTemp = vbYes Then
           End
   End if
   ```

3. Close the Code window.

Save and run your test application. When you choose File, Exit from the menu system, you should be presented with a message box asking you to verify your decision to exit the program. If you click the Yes button, your program ends.

Optional Settings

In addition to the required Caption and Name properties, each menu item has several optional properties that you can set either to control the behavior of the menu or to indicate the status of a program option. The most commonly used of these properties are the Visible, Enabled, and Checked properties.

The *Visible* and *Enabled* Properties   The menu item's Visible and Enabled properties work just like they do with any other object. When the Visible property is set to True, the menu item is visible to the users. If the Visible property is set to False, the item (and any associated submenus) are hidden from the users. You have probably seen the Enabled and Visible properties used in a word processing program (though you might not have been aware of how it was accomplished), where only the File and Help menus are visible until a document is selected for editing. After a document is open, the other menu items are shown.

Changing the setting of the Visible property allows you to control what menu items are available to the users at a given point in your program. Controlling the menu this way lets you restrict the users' access to menu items that might cause errors if certain conditions are not met. (You wouldn't want the users to access edit functions if no document was open to edit, right?)

The Enabled property serves a function similar to that of the Visible property. The key difference is that when the Enabled property is set to False, the menu item is *grayed out*. This means that the menu item still can be seen by the users but cannot be accessed. For example, the standard Edit, Cut and Edit, Copy functions should not be available if no text or object is selected, but nothing is wrong with letting the users see that these functions exist (see Figure 6.8).

FIGURE 6.8
Disabled menu items are visible to the users but are shown in gray tones, indicating that the items are currently unavailable.

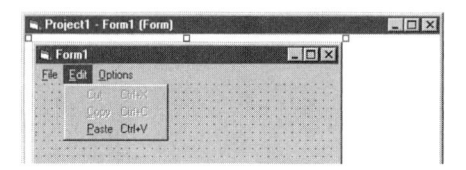

Although the Visible and Enabled properties of menu items can be set at designtime using the Menu Editor, they are typically set using code at runtime in response to changes in your program's status. Just as with other objects, you can set the value of a Menu control property in code by specifying the menu item's Name property, the name of the property to be changed, and the new value.

To continue with the running example, you can enhance the simple menu system. When the program starts, no document will be open. Therefore, the File menu's Save, Send To, and Print options should not be enabled. Also, you don't want the Edit menu to be visible at all unless a document has been opened. Follow these steps to ensure that the menu system is properly set up when the program starts:

1. Make sure Form1 is selected, and then open the Menu Editor.
2. Click the Save menu item to select it.
3. Click the check box next to the Enabled property to uncheck it. This action has the effect of setting the Enabled property to False.
4. Set the Enabled property for the Send To and Print menu items to False as well.
5. Click the Edit menu item to select it.
6. Click the check box next to the Visible property to uncheck it. This action has the effect of setting the Visible property to False.
7. Close the Menu Editor.

> **TIP** Notice that the Edit menu is no longer visible, even in the design environment. You can still access the menu item's `Click` event procedure by entering the form's Code window and selecting the appropriate menu item from the object box. If you prefer, you can also leave the menu item's `Visible` property set to `True` and use the form's `Load` event procedure to set it to `False`.

Follow these steps to enable the appropriate portions of the File menu and to make the Edit menu visible whenever a document is opened:

1. In the design environment, click the File menu, and then click the Open menu item. You are presented with `mnuFileOpen`'s `Click` event procedure.

2. In a fully functional application, your code for opening a file would be placed here. You can use a comment line to represent that portion of the code. Enter these lines of code into the `mnuFileOpen_Click` procedure:

   ```
   'Code for opening a file goes here
   mnuFileSave.Enabled = True
   mnuFileSendTo.Enabled = True
   mnuFilePrint.Enabled = True
   mnuEdit.Visible = True
   ```

3. Close the Menu Editor.

4. Save and run your application. Notice that the Edit menu can't be seen. Notice also that when you click the File menu, some of the items are grayed out.

5. Choose File, Open, which causes the Open menu item's `Click` event procedure to be executed. Choose the File menu again, and notice that all File menu items are now available. Notice also that the Edit menu is now visible.

6. Click the End button on the toolbar to end the program.

The `Checked` Property The `Checked` property of the menu item determines whether a check mark is displayed to the left of the item in the menu, as shown in Figure 6.9. The `Checked` property is typically used to indicate the status of a program option; for example, if a user has selected a particular option, a check mark appears next to that item in the menu. The menu item is then used to toggle back and forth between two program states.

FIGURE 6.9
The Checked property determines whether a check mark is placed to the left of a submenu item.

Enter the following code into the `Click` event procedure of the `mnuOptionsText` menu item in the sample menu:

`mnuOptionsText.Checked = Not mnuOptionsText.Checked`

Because the `Checked` property can only be `True` or `False`, the preceding code makes nice use of some Boolean logic with the `Not` keyword. `Not` represents the opposite of a Boolean value, so `Not mnuOptionsText.Checked` returns the opposite of the current value of the `Checked` property of `mnuOptions`. This process is known as "toggling" a Boolean value. At any point in the program code, the state of the `Checked` property indicates whether the user wants the document to be composed of plain text.

Of course, you can set a menu item's `Checked` property at designtime if you want that item to be checked when the program begins.

> **CAUTION**
> You cannot set the `Checked` property to `True` for an item on the menu bar (top menu level). Doing so results in an error.

Other Properties   You might have noticed two other items in the Menu Editor. These items specify the value of the `NegotiatePosition` and `WindowList` properties of the menu item. The `NegotiatePosition` property specifies whether and where the menu item of your application is displayed when an embedded object on a form is active and its menu is shown (for example, if your application has an instance of Word embedded for modifying a document). If the `NegotiatePosition` property is 0, your menu is not displayed while the object is active. If the property is not 0, your menu item is displayed to the left of, in the middle of, or to the right of the object's menu (property settings of 1, 2, or 3, respectively). The `WindowList` property specifies whether the current menu should maintain a list of active MDI child forms. When this property is `True`, items are automatically appended to the menu as child forms are opened, and removed when the corresponding child forms are closed. You learn about this topic in more detail in Chapter 17, "Multiple Document Interface Applications."

Creating Pop-Up Menus

So far, the discussion of menus has looked at the menu bar that appears along the top of the form. Visual Basic also supports *pop-up menus* in your programs. A pop-up menu is a small menu that appears somewhere on your form in response to a program event.

Pop-up menus often are used to handle operations or options related to a specific area of the form (see Figure 6.10)—for example, a format pop-up menu for a text field that lets you change the font or font attributes of the field. You can find such context-sensitive menus in many of the latest generation of Windows programs, including Visual Basic itself.

When a pop-up menu is invoked, usually by right-clicking an object with the mouse, the menu appears onscreen near the current mouse pointer location. The user then makes a selection from the menu. After the selection is made, the menu disappears from the screen.

FIGURE 6.10
This grid's pop-up menu provides a convenient way to initiate program functions specifically related to the grid.

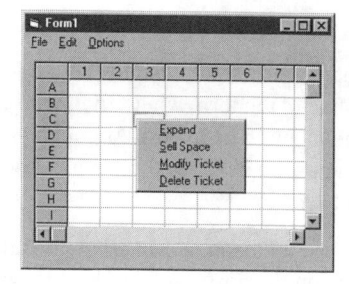

Creating the Menu to Be Displayed

You create a pop-up menu in the same way that you created the main menu for your program—with the Menu Editor. There is, however, one extra step. The pop-up menu should be hidden so that it does not appear on the menu bar. To hide the menu, you set the `Visible` property of the top-level menu item to `False`.

> **NOTE** Typically, you hide the menu item that is used as a pop-up menu, but you can use any of the top-level items of a menu bar as a pop-up menu. That is, a particular menu can appear both as a pop-up menu and as a part of the main menu of a form.

To illustrate the concept of a pop-up menu, add a simple one to the sample menu system, as follows:

1. Using the Menu Editor, add a new top-level menu item at the end of the list of menu items. Set its `Caption` property to `Format`, and its `Name` property to `mnuFormat`.
2. Set mnuFormat's `Visible` property to `False`.
3. Create these indented menu items under the Format menu:

Caption	Name
&Bold	mnuFormatBold
&Italic	mnuFormatItalic
&Underline	mnuFormatUnderline

4. Close the Menu Editor.

Notice that the Format menu does not appear on your form's menu bar. However, the menu is present and can be modified in the Menu Editor.

The technique you must use to add code to the `Click` event of the items in a pop-up menu is also a little different. Because the menu is not visible on the form, you cannot just click the item to bring up the Code window. Instead, you bring up the Code window by selecting the View Code button in the Project window or double-clicking the form. Then you can select the desired menu item in the Code window's Object list at the upper-left corner. This way, you can enter code for the hidden items.

Activating a Pop-Up Menu

To have the pop-up menu appear on your screen, you must invoke the form's PopUpMenu method. You do so by specifying the name of the form where the menu will be displayed, the PopUpMenu method, and the name of the menu to be shown. Although you can use this method from anywhere in your code, pop-up menus are used most often in response to mouse clicks, usually those using the right mouse button.

To illustrate this use, make the sample pop-up menu appear when the user right-clicks the form. Of course, in a fully coded application that formats text, the user would probably be right-clicking selected text; however, the following steps illustrate the concept:

1. Open the form's Code window by double-clicking the form.
2. Drop down the Code window's Object box, and select the mnuFormatBold menu item.
3. In mnuFormatBold's Click event procedure, enter the following line of code, which simply causes a message box to appear and report that the procedure was indeed executed:

   ```
   MsgBox "You just bolded some text!"
   ```
4. Drop down the Code window's Object box, and select Form.
5. Drop down the Code window's Procedure box, and select the MouseUp event.
6. Enter the following code into the form's MouseUp event procedure:

   ```
   If Button = vbRightButton Then
       Form1.PopupMenu mnuFormat
   End If
   ```
7. Save and run the program. Right-click the form to open the Format menu. Choose the Bold item.

In the code segment you just entered, the MouseUp event is used to take an action whenever a mouse button is pressed. The event passes a parameter, the Button parameter, that tells you which of the mouse buttons was pressed. Because you want the menu to appear in response to only a right button click, you check for the value of the Button parameter. If it is equal to vbRightButton (an intrinsic constant for the right mouse button), the pop-up menu is displayed.

NOTE You can create multiple pop-up menus and have them displayed in response to different mouse buttons or in different areas of the screen. The X and Y parameters passed to the MouseUp event procedure report the location of the mouse cursor at the time the event occurred.

Using Toolbars in Visual Basic

You have probably noticed that many Windows programs now have one or more toolbars in addition to the menu system. These toolbars provide the users with an easy way to access the most commonly used functions of the program. Some programs also use toolbars to help with specific tasks, such as the Drawing toolbar that is in Microsoft Word. Because toolbars are becoming so common, users have come to expect them in all programs.

Fortunately, you can easily set up a toolbar in Visual Basic. In fact, Visual Basic Version 6 now has two different styles of toolbars: the standard toolbar and the newer CoolBar control.

Toolbar Basics

Although these two types of toolbars (pictured in Figure 6.11) appear different to the user, they both are used for the same purpose: to provide a set of graphical buttons to access common program functions.

The ToolBar control enables you to create six different types of buttons:

- Pushbuttons that work like command buttons
- Check buttons that work in an on-off mode, like a check box
- Button groups that work like option buttons
- Separator buttons that create spaces in the toolbar
- Placeholder buttons that create empty space, allowing you to place other controls, such as combo boxes, on the toolbar
- Drop-down buttons that, when clicked, offer the user a drop-down menu of choices

FIGURE 6.11
The sleek-looking coolbar was first introduced in Microsoft Internet Explorer.

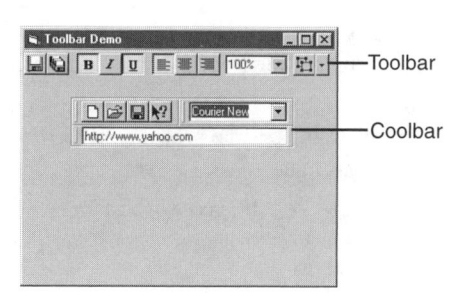

To create a toolbar, you need to use multiple controls: one or more of the ToolBar controls and the ImageList control. The ImageList control contains a collection of bitmaps for use by other controls. In this case, the ToolBar control displays images from the ImageList control on its buttons. The ImageList control is part of the Microsoft Windows Common Controls 6.0 Group, discussed in Chapter 12, "Microsoft Common Controls."

▶ **See** "The ImageList: A Fundamental Common Control," **p. 248**

To draw a ToolBar control on a form, you first need to add it to the Toolbox. To begin, right-click in an empty area of the Toolbox, and choose Components from the pop-up menu. When the Components dialog box appears, select the first group of Common controls—Microsoft Windows Common Controls 6.0—as shown in Figure 6.12. This group of controls contains the standard toolbar and the ImageList control. The CoolBar control is in the third group (Microsoft Windows Common Controls–3 6.0); select this group to add the coolbar to the Toolbox.

FIGURE 6.12
The CoolBar control is in a new group called Microsoft Windows Common Controls - 36.0.

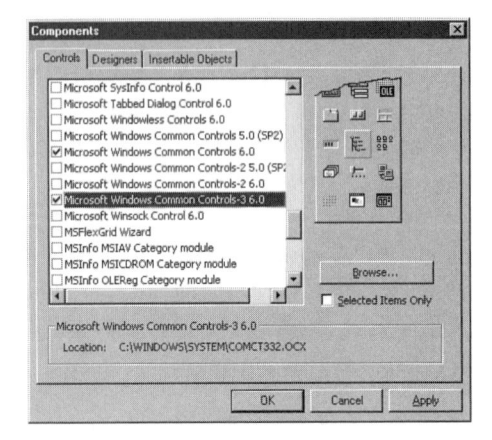

In the following sections, you discover how to include both types of toolbars in your program.

Getting the Images for Your Toolbar

The first step in creating any toolbar is adding the images that will be displayed on the toolbar to an ImageList control. Follow these steps to get those images:

1. Draw an ImageList control on your form, and give it a unique name. Because the ImageList control is not visible to the users, its size is set by Visual Basic. No matter what size you draw it on the form, it always appears as a little icon at designtime.

2. To add bitmap images to the control, open its Property Pages dialog box either by pressing the ellipsis (…) button of the Custom property in the Properties window, or by right-clicking the ImageList control and selecting Prope_r_ties.

   From this dialog box, shown in Figure 6.13, you can add images from graphics files (icons and bitmaps) stored on your hard drive.

FIGURE 6.13
At designtime, you can add images to the ImageList control by using the Images tab of the Property Pages dialog box.

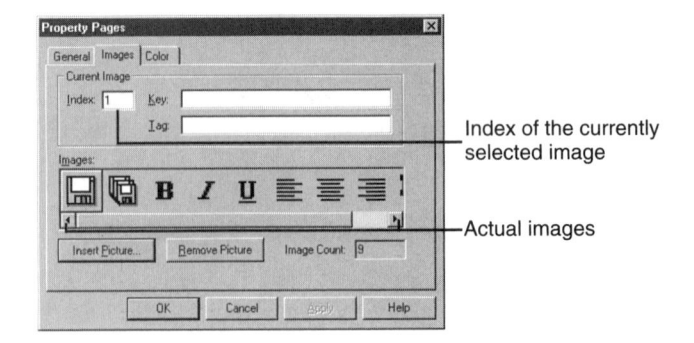

Index of the currently selected image

Actual images

3. To add an image to the ImageList control, click the Insert Picture button. This action presents you with the Select Picture dialog box, from which you can choose the bitmap or icon you want. As you select the picture, it is added to the control and displayed in the Images area.

4. After you add all the pictures you might need, click the OK button to close the dialog box.

> **NOTE** Many sample icons and bitmaps are included with Visual Basic. If you installed them, they are located in a subdirectory called Graphics (the location of this directory depends on which installation options you chose, and whether you installed just Visual Basic or the entire Visual Studio suite).

After you complete these steps, your ImageList control is ready to use for supplying images to your toolbar.

Creating a Standard Toolbar

To use the standard ToolBar control, you first need to position it on a form. To do so, follow these steps:

1. Draw the ToolBar control on your form. Visual Basic positions the toolbar at the top of the form, and the control spans the width of the form.

2. Set the toolbar's alignment. A toolbar can be aligned along any of the four edges of its form or float freely:

   - To position the toolbar along the top of your form, leave the Align property set at its 1 - vbAlignTop default setting.
   - To position it along the bottom of your form, set its Align property to 2 - vbAlignBottom.
   - To align it to the left or right edge of the form, set the Align property to 3 - vbAlignLeft or 4 - vbAlignRight, respectively. In these cases, you should adjust the Width property to keep it from filling the form completely.
   - To use a free-floating toolbar, set its Align property to 0 - vbAlignNone. You can adjust the toolbar's position and size by setting the Left, Top, Width, and Height properties.

3. Open the ToolBar control's Property Pages dialog box by right-clicking the control and choosing Properties. Figure 6.14 shows the first page of the ToolBar control's Property Pages.

4. Set the ToolBar control's ImageList property to the name of the ImageList control that you already set up to provide images. Clicking the arrow to the right of the ImageList property provides you with a list of all ImageList controls on the current form.

FIGURE 6.14
You can assign an ImageList control to your toolbar in the General tab of the toolbar's Property Pages dialog box.

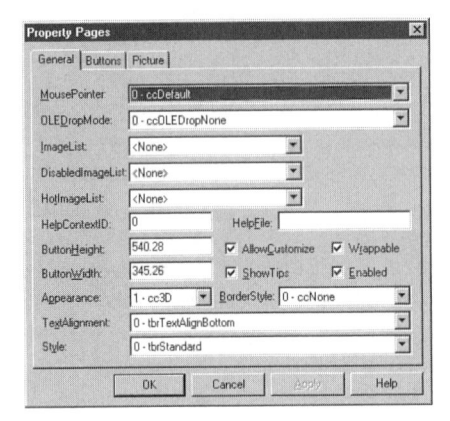

Several other properties on the Property Pages' General tab control the appearance and behavior of the toolbar. These properties are summarized in Table 6.3.

Table 6.3 Toolbar Properties That Control Its Appearance and Behavior

Property Name	Description
`BorderStyle`	Determines whether a single-line border is displayed around the toolbar or no border is used.
`ButtonHeight`	Specifies the height (in twips) of the buttons in the toolbar.
`ButtonWidth`	Specifies the width (in twips) of the buttons in the toolbar.
`AllowCustomize`	Determines whether the user is allowed to customize the toolbar by adding, deleting, or moving buttons.
`ShowTips`	Determines whether ToolTips are shown if the mouse pointer is rested on one of the buttons.
`Wrappable`	Determines whether the toolbar wraps around to a second row of buttons if the toolbar has more buttons than fit on a single row.
`HotImageList`	Specifies a different ImageList control to provide images for drop-down and check-style buttons when they are activated. An alternate image will also be displayed when the mouse pointer hovers over any button if the toolbar's `Style` property is set to `1 - tbrFlat`. To use this property, make sure the desired image in the ImageList control referenced by this property has the same index as the image in the primary image list.
`DisabledImageList`	Specifies a different ImageList control to provide images for toolbar buttons whose `Enabled` property is set to `False`. To use this property, make sure the desired image in the ImageList control referenced by this property has the same index as the image in the primary image list.
`Style`	Determines whether the toolbar is drawn with a three-dimensional effect or whether it appears flat on the form.

Creating the Toolbar's Buttons

The next step in creating your toolbar is to create the buttons that will be placed on the toolbar. For this task, you move to the Buttons tab of the Property Pages (see Figure 6.15).

FIGURE 6.15
You can assign images, captions, identifiers, and even menus to toolbar buttons in the Buttons tab.

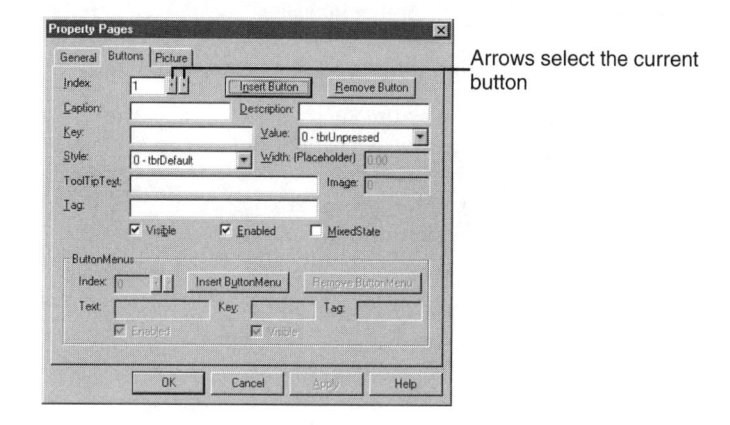

Arrows select the current button

Adding a Standard Button to the Toolbar To add a button to the toolbar, click Insert Button. If other buttons already exist on the toolbar, a new button appears after the currently selected button. For each button that you add, you should specify several properties—the Key property, the Style property, and the Image property.

The Key property specifies a string that is used to identify the button in code. You will see how it is used in the upcoming section "Enabling the Buttons with Code." The Key property for each button must be unique, and you should assign a string that is meaningful to you. This way, you can remember it more easily when you are writing your code.

The Image property specifies the index of the picture that you want to appear on the face of the button. The index corresponds to the index of the picture in the ImageList control. You can specify a value of zero for the Image property if you do not want a picture to appear on the button.

The Style property determines the type of button that you create. Table 6.4 summarizes the various settings of the Style property. Each of the button styles is shown in Figure 6.16.

Table 6.4 Style Property Settings That Control the Behavior of Toolbar Buttons

Setting Example	VB Constant	Description of Behavior
0 - tbrDefault	The button is a standard pushbutton.	The Save Project button in Visual Basic

continues

Table 6.4 Continued

Setting Example	VB Constant	Description of Behavior	
1 -	tbrCheck	The button indicates that an option is on or off by its state.	The Bold button in Word
2 -	tbrButtonGroup	The button is part of a group. Only one button of the group can be pressed at a time.	The alignment buttons in Word
3 -	tbrSeparator	The button is used to provide space between other buttons. The button has a width of eight pixels.	N/A
4 -	tbrPlaceHolder	This button is used to hold a space in the toolbar for other controls such as a combo box.	The font combo box in Word
5 -	tbrDropDown	Used with a `ButtonMenu` to create a drop-down menu on the toolbar button.	The Add Form button in Visual Basic

FIGURE 6.16
Examples of the different toolbar button styles are shown here. Note that the placeholder and separators are not really buttons.

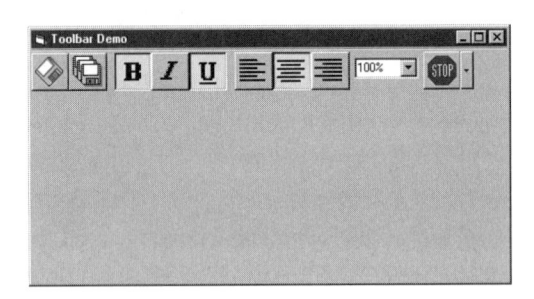

In addition to these three key properties, you can set several other properties for each button on the toolbar (see Table 6.5).

Table 6.5 Optional Properties That Provide Further Control over Toolbar Buttons

Property	Description
Caption	This text is displayed beneath the picture on a button.
Description	This text describes the button to the users when they invoke the Customize Toolbar dialog box.
ToolTipText	This text appears when the mouse pointer rests on the button. This text is displayed only if the ShowTips property of the toolbar is set to True (which is the default).
Value	This property sets or returns the current state of the button. A value of 0 indicates that the button is not pressed. A value of 1 indicates that the button is pressed. This property is typically used to pre-select a check-style button, or one button in a group.

> **TIP** Unless the images on your buttons are self-explanatory, you should include ToolTips. A *ToolTip* is a text message describing a button that appears when the users move the mouse pointer over the button. Depending on your application, you may be able to include ToolTips instead of captions to save some screen real estate. Without some text indication the users cannot know what the button does unless they click it. ToolTips give your program a professional appearance and are easy to add.

After setting up the buttons on the toolbar, you can exit the Property Pages dialog box by clicking the OK button.

Adding a Drop-Down Toolbar Button   A new feature in Visual Basic 6 is the tbrDropDown style button. This button combines a normal toolbar button with a drop-down menu for an effect that is similar to a combo box. The following example illustrates how to create such a button and program its events.

Starting a Toolbar Example

To illustrate the use of toolbars, this section walks you through the creation of a sample program containing a standard toolbar button and a drop-down toolbar button, with a separator button providing blank space between them. Follow these steps:

1. Create a new Standard EXE project. Add a ToolBar control and an ImageList control to the form as described in the preceding sections.

2. Set the toolbar's Name property to tbrDemo. Leave the ImageList control's Name property set to the default of ImageList1.

3. On the Images tab of the Property Pages dialog box for ImageList1, add two appropriate icons to the ImageList control (click the Insert Picture button and browse to the picture files). These icons will eventually be the pictures displayed on two toolbar buttons.

4. Right-click the ToolBar control and choose P<u>r</u>operties. In the toolbar's Property Pages dialog box, set the `ImageList` property of the toolbar to `ImageList1`, the name of your image list.

5. On the Buttons tab, click I<u>n</u>sert button. The `Style` property should already be set to the default, `0 - tbrNormal`. Set the button's `Key` value to `newfile`.

6. Set the `Image` property of the button to the index of the appropriate icon in the ImageList control (which should be `1` if you've followed these steps).

7. Click the I<u>n</u>sert button again to add a second button. Set the `Style` property of this button to `3 - tbrSeparator`. This separator button will be seen as blank space between the first and third buttons.

8. Click the I<u>n</u>sert button again to add a third button. Set the `Style` property of this button to `5 - tbrDropdown`. Set its `Key` value to `report` and its `Image` property to the index of the other icon from the ImageList control (2). Set its `Caption` property to `REGION`.

6. To add items to the button menu for this drop-down button, click the Insert B<u>u</u>ttonmenu button. Enter `East` for the button menu item's `Text` property.

7. Repeat step 6 for West, South, and Central regions.

8. Click OK to close the Property Pages dialog box. Your drop-down button should now appear on the toolbar.

Enabling the Buttons with Code

You have seen how to set up the toolbar, but until you add code to the toolbar's events, it cannot perform any functions. The buttons of the toolbar do not have events of their own. Instead, you actually write your code for the `ButtonClick` and `ButtonMenuClick` events of the toolbar itself. These events pass a `Button` or `ButtonMenu` object reference as a parameter to the event procedure. In your code, you use the value of the `Button` object's `Key` property to determine which button was actually pressed.

By completing the steps outlined in the preceding sections, you have created a toolbar with buttons that look good and can be clicked, but that don't actually do anything. You need to add code to make them functional. Writing an event procedure for a button on a toolbar is a little different than writing a procedure for a standard command button. Rather than have a separate event procedure for each button and menu, your code must look at object properties to determine which button or button menu item was selected.

Enter the code presented in Listing 6.1 into the form's Code window.

Listing 6.1 TBRDEMO.TXT—Using Code to Activate a Toolbar

```
Option Explicit
Dim sCurrentRegion As String

Private Sub tbrDemo_ButtonClick(ByVal Button As ComctlLib.Button)
    Select Case UCase(Button.Key)
        Case "NEWFILE"
```

```
            'Code to create a new file goes here
            MsgBox "Creating a new file..."
        Case "REPORT"
            'Create a report with the current region
            Call MakeReport
    End Select

End Sub

Private Sub tbrDemo_ButtonMenuClick(ByVal ButtonMenu As ComctlLib.ButtonMenu)
    'Create a report using the newly selected region
    sCurrentRegion = UCase(ButtonMenu.Text)
    ButtonMenu.Parent.Caption = sCurrentRegion
    Call MakeReport

End Sub

Sub MakeReport()
    Dim sTemp As String
    'If no region selected, use WEST as default
    If Trim(sCurrentRegion) = "" Then
        sCurrentRegion = "WEST"
    End If
    sTemp = "Creating report for " & sCurrentRegion
    sTemp = sTemp & " Region..."
    MsgBox sTemp
    'Actual report-creating lines go here...

End Sub
```

Once you have entered this code, run the program and examine the behavior of the toolbar buttons.

The procedures being called are actually the Click event procedures of menu items. With these procedures being called, you can code an action once and then call it from either the menu or the toolbar. Doing so makes it easier to maintain your code because changes or corrections have to be made in only a single location. Also, note the introduction of the Select Case statement, which is more readable than a nested If statement. You learn about it in more detail in a later chapter.

▶ **See** "Using Select Case," **p. 207**

Creating a Toolbar with Code

Although you can set up a toolbar in the design environment, you can also set up and change a toolbar at runtime with program code. To use the Toolbar and other common controls successfully, you need to understand the concept of *collections*.

Understanding Collections A collection is a group of objects. In the case of the ImageList control, you will find a collection called ListImages. The objects stored in this particular collection are the images in the ImageList control. By manipulating the ListImages collection from code, you can add, remove, and change images.

Think of a collection as being similar to, but not exactly like, an array. You can access it like an array, as in the following line of code, which sets a form's picture to the first image in an ImageList control:

```
Set form1.Picture = ImageList1.ListImages(1).Picture
```

Notice that a specific object is referred to with its *index*—in this case, 1. Remember, a collection stores objects, unlike an array, which stores values. These objects have their own set of properties.

Objects in a Buttons collection have a special property: the Key property. A Button object's key is a text string that can be used in the same manner as an index:

```
Set form1.Picture = ImageList1.ListImages("Smiley Face").Picture
```

Generally, the Button object's Key property is set when the object is added to the Buttons collection through the key parameter of the Buttons collection's Add method.

Setting Up the Toolbar   To set up a ToolBar control in code, you have to first set up an ImageList control (either in design mode or with code), including populating it with images. Then you can assign the ImageList control to the toolbar with a statement like the following:

```
Set tbrMain.ImageList = ImageList1
```

Next, you manipulate the toolbar's Buttons collection to create toolbar buttons. In the following example, a separator and standard button are added to a toolbar control, tbrMain:

```
tbrMain.Buttons.Add 1, "Sep1",, tbrSeparator, 0
tbrMain.Buttons.Add 2, "open","Open File" , tbrDefault, 1
```

In this example, two additional Button objects are created in the Buttons collection by using the Add method. The first two parameters are the button's index and key, each of which must be unique. The third parameter is the button caption. The fourth parameter (tbrSeparator and tbrDefault) is a constant representing the type of button. Finally, an index value from the associated image list tells the toolbar which picture to use.

The Add method can also work as a function. If used in this manner, it returns a reference to the Button object just created. You could rewrite the preceding code like this:

```
Dim btn As Button

Set btn = tbrMain.Buttons.Add(, "Sep1", , tbrSeparator, 0)

Set btn = tbrMain.Buttons.Add(,"open", , tbrDefault)
btn.ToolTipText = "Click to open a file"
btn.Caption = "Open File"
btn.Image = 1
```

Note that the ToolTipText property must be added to the Button object because it is not in the Add method's parameters. Also, in the preceding example, the Index properties are defined automatically because they are not specified. This approach is generally the preferred way of coding because, as objects are added and deleted from a collection, the index of a particular object will change. The Key, however, is always associated with a specific object.

Your code can use the button parameter's Key property to determine which button was pressed. For example, consider the following code in the toolbar's ButtonClick event:

```
Private Sub Toolbar1_ButtonClick(ByVal Button As ComctlLib.Button)

    Select Case Button.Key
        Case "open"
            'Insert open file code here
        Case "save"
            'Insert save file code here
        Case "exit"
            'Insert code to end the program
    End Select

End Sub
```

The preceding code works great for buttons of type tbrDefault. However, if you have any tbrCheck buttons, you should have your code also check the Value property to see what the state of the button is:

```
Case "boldface"
    If Button.value = tbrUnpressed then
        'Button is "Up" - Turn bold off
    Else
        'Button is "down" - Turn bold on
    End If
```

If you set the MixedState property of a button to True, it always looks grayed out—no matter what the value.

Allowing the User to Customize the Toolbar

One of the really great features of the ToolBar control is that you can allow your users to customize the toolbar to their liking. When the AllowCustomize property of the toolbar is set to True, users can access the Customize Toolbar dialog box by double-clicking the toolbar. This dialog box, shown in Figure 6.17, allows the user to add buttons to the toolbar, remove buttons, or move the buttons to a different location.

FIGURE 6.17
The AllowCustomize property lets users customize the toolbar to their liking, without the need for additional code.

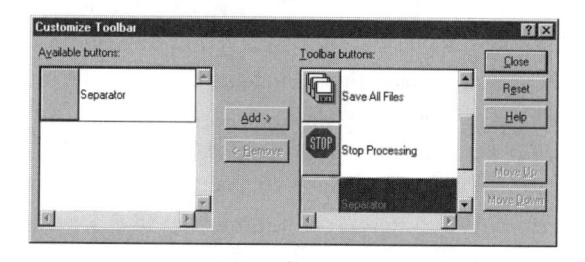

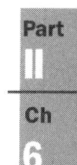

Using the CoolBar Control

The CoolBar control, pictured earlier in Figure 6.11, is a special control that acts as a container for other controls but looks like a toolbar. The CoolBar control itself does not have "built-in" Button objects like a toolbar does. However, since the coolbar is a container control, it can contain objects such as command buttons and even toolbars.

The CoolBar control contains a collection of Band objects, each of which is a mini-container that the user can resize at runtime.

To illustrate how the CoolBar control can contain other controls, let's extend the example from the earlier part of the chapter. Follow these steps:

1. If you haven't done so already, add the CoolBar control to the Toolbox by selecting Microsoft Windows Common Controls – 3 6.0 from the Components dialog box.
2. Change the `Align` property of the toolbar you created earlier to `0 - vbAlignNone`. Drag it to an open area of the form and adjust its width so it is just wide enough to display the buttons you added earlier.
3. Double-click the coolbar icon in the Toolbox to add a CoolBar control to your form.
4. Click the CoolBar control to select it. Click the CommandButton icon and draw a command button directly on the coolbar.
5. Create a simple `Click` event procedure for the command button, adding a line of code like `MsgBox "You clicked Command1"`.
6. Right-click the toolbar and select Cut to remove it from the form, placing it on the Windows Clipboard.
7. Right-click the CoolBar control and select Paste. The toolbar from the Clipboard is pasted into the coolbar container.
8. Right-click a blank area of the CoolBar control (don't click the contained toolbar or command button). Select Properties to display the coolbar's Property Pages dialog box.
9. The Bands tab of the Property Pages dialog box contains properties for each of the CoolBar control's bands. Band 1 should be selected in the Index box at the top. Drop down the Child list and select `tbrDemo`. This action instructs the coolbar to display `tbrDemo` in the Band 1 mini-container.
10. Change the index to 2 to select the second band. Set its Child property to `Command1` (the command button you added earlier).
11. Click OK to close the Property Pages dialog box. While the CoolBar control is still selected, go to the Properties window and change its `Align` property to `1 - vbAlignTop`.

When you have completed these steps, run the program and observe the behavior of the objects on the CoolBar control. You can experiment with placing different types of objects on a CoolBar control in your applications.

From Here...

This chapter showed you the advantages of creating menus and toolbars for your programs. Hopefully, you have seen how easy it is to create these items. You were also exposed to several other topics in this chapter. To learn more about them, refer to the following chapters:

- To review using forms to build your applications, see Chapter 3, "Visual Basic Building Blocks."
- To learn about another way that your programs interact with your users, see Chapter 7, "Using Dialog Boxes to Get Information."
- For more information about using variables to remember information throughout your programs, see Chapter 8, "Using Variables to Store Information."

CHAPTER 7

Using Dialog Boxes to Get Information

In this chapter

Keeping the User Informed   140

Getting Information from the User   146

Using Built-In Dialog Boxes   148

Creating Your Own Dialog Boxes   157

A dialog box is a window used to display and/or accept information. Its name comes from the fact that it is, in essence, a *dialog* (or conversation) with the user. A dialog box is usually shown *modally*, which means the user must close it (or "answer the dialog") before continuing with any other part of the program. In this chapter, you'll look at two dialog boxes built in to Visual Basic: the message box and the input box. Next, you'll use the CommonDialog custom control, which allows you to place four types of standard dialog boxes in your program. Finally, you'll review some guidelines for creating your own form-based dialog box.

Keeping the User Informed

A big part of any programming project is providing information to the users about the program's progress and status. Although the forms and controls of your program provide the main interface to the users, they are not necessarily the best vehicles for providing bits of information that require immediate attention, such as warnings or error messages. For providing this type of information, the message box is the way to go.

Understanding the Message Box

The *message box* is a simple form that displays a message and at least one command button. The button is used to acknowledge the message and close the form. Because message boxes are built in to the Visual Basic language, you do not have to worry about creating or showing a form. To see a simple message box, type the following line of code into Visual Basic's Immediate window (choose <u>V</u>iew, <u>I</u>mmediate Window to open the window) and press Enter:

```
MsgBox "I love Visual Basic!"
```

Optionally, the message box can display an icon or use multiple buttons to let the user make a decision. This is done with the use of optional parameters. For example, the following code line produces the message box shown in Figure 7.1:

```
MsgBox "Delete record?", vbYesNo + vbExclamation, "Confirm Delete"
```

> **N O T E** You can try this example yourself. Just type the code in the Immediate window and press Enter. This action has the same effect as if the statement were executed at runtime.

FIGURE 7.1
A message box communicates with the user.

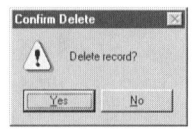

Message boxes can be used in either of two ways, depending on your needs. You can use the message box to simply display information, or you can use it to get a decision from the user. In either case, you will use some form of the MsgBox function.

NOTE Although this chapter refers to functions and statements interchangeably, a conceptual difference does exist between using `MsgBox` as a function and as a statement. By definition, a *function* returns a value, whereas a *statement* does not. Also, the syntax for parameters is slightly different; a function's parameters must be enclosed in parentheses. For example, if you want to see the return value from the `MsgBox` function, you could type the following line in the Immediate window:

```
Print MsgBox ("Delete record?", vbYesNo + vbExclamation, "Confirm Delete")
```

Although the message box is useful, it does have a few limitations:

- The message box cannot accept text input from the user. It can only display information and handle the selection of a limited number of choices.
- You can use only one of four predefined icons and one of six predefined command button sets in the message box. You cannot define your own icons or buttons.
- By design, the message box requires a user to respond to a message before any part of the program can continue. This means that the message box cannot be used to provide continuous status monitoring of the program because no other part of the program can be executing while the message box is waiting for the user's response.

Displaying a Message

The simplest way to create a message box in your program is to use the `MsgBox` function as if it were a statement, without returning a value. Using the `MsgBox` function this way, you simply specify the message text that you want to appear in the message box and then call the function. The message box displays an OK button to allow the user to acknowledge the message.

```
MsgBox "Record processing is complete."
```

When you specify the message text, you can use a *string constant* (a string of text enclosed in quotation marks, as shown in the preceding line) or a string *variable*, as in this example:

```
Dim sMyText as String

sMyText = "Hello," & vbCrLf & "World"
MsgBox sMyText
```

Note the use of the intrinsic (predefined) constant `vbCrLf`, representing a carriage return/line feed combination, to make `"Hello"` and `"World"` appear on separate lines.

The default message box uses the project's title (which can be set in the Project, Properties dialog) for its caption and only has an OK button. You can dress up your messages somewhat by using two optional parameters: the `buttons` argument and the `title` argument. The `buttons` argument is an integer number that can specify the icon to display in the message box, the command button set to display, and which of the command buttons is the default. The `title` argument is a text string that specifies custom text to be shown in the title bar of the message box. The full syntax of the `MsgBox` function is as follows:

```
MsgBox(prompt[, buttons] [, title] [, helpfile, context])
```

If you choose to display an icon in the message box, you have a choice of four icons. These icons and their purposes are summarized in Table 7.1.

Table 7.1 Icons Indicate the Type of Message Being Shown

Icon Name	Typical Purpose
Critical Message	Indicates that a severe error has occurred. Often a program is shut down after this message.
Warning Message	Indicates that a program error has occurred; this error may require user correction or may lead to undesirable results.
Query	Indicates that the program requires additional information from the user before processing can continue.
Information Message	Informs the user of the status of the program. This message is often used to notify the users of the completion of a task.

To tell Visual Basic that you want to use a particular icon in the message box, you set a value for the `buttons` argument of the `MsgBox` function. The `buttons` argument can be set to one of four values, as defined in the following table. You can use either the numerical value or the constant from the following table:

Message Type	Argument Value	Constant
Critical	16	`vbCritical`
Query	32	`vbQuestion`
Warning	48	`vbExclamation`
Information	64	`vbInformation`

> **TIP** Good programming practice dictates that you use the appropriate constant to represent the integer value. Using the correct constant makes your programs more readable and will not require any conversion should Microsoft change the arguments' values.

> **NOTE** The constants listed in the preceding table not only affect the icon that is displayed, but also the sound produced by Windows when a message appears. You can set sounds for different message types in the Windows Control Panel.

To illustrate how icons and titles can be used in your message boxes, enter the following code, which produces the message box shown in Figure 7.2:

```
MsgBox "This message box contains an icon.", vbInformation, "Icon Demo"
```

FIGURE 7.2
Use titles and icons to give the user visual cues to the nature of the message.

Returning a Value from the *MsgBox* Function

The MsgBox function, as described previously, works fine for informing users of a problem or prompting them to take an action. However, to get a decision from the users, you need to use the MsgBox function's return value. There are two key differences to using the MsgBox function this way—you must deal with the function's return value, possibly by assigning it to a variable, and you must enclose the arguments of the function in parentheses. This value reports which command button a user clicked. The following line of code shows how the value returned by the function can be assigned to a variable for further processing:

```
nResult = MsgBox("The printer is not responding", _
    vbRetryCancel,"Printer Error!")
```

Additional statements after the preceding code could check the value of the variable nResult with, for example, an If statement and take appropriate action.

Choosing Among the Command Button Sets The following six sets of command buttons can be used in the MsgBox function:

- **OK.** Displays a single button with the caption OK. This button simply directs the user to acknowledge receipt of the message before continuing.
- **OK, Cancel.** Displays two buttons in the message box, letting the user choose between accepting the message and requesting a cancellation of the operation.
- **Abort, Retry, Ignore.** Displays three buttons, usually along with an error message. The user can choose to abort the operation, retry it, or ignore the error and attempt to continue with program execution.
- **Yes, No, Cancel.** Displays three buttons, typically with a question. The user can answer yes or no to the question, or choose to cancel the operation.
- **Yes, No.** Displays two buttons for a simple yes or no choice.
- **Retry, Cancel.** Displays the two buttons that allow the user to retry the operation or cancel it. A typical use is reporting that the printer is not responding. The user can either retry after fixing the printer or cancel the printout.

To specify the command buttons you want to appear in the message box, you need to specify a value for the buttons argument of the MsgBox function. The values for each of the command button sets are listed in Table 7.2.

Table 7.2 Set the *buttons* Argument to One of the Following Values to Specify Which Set of Buttons to Use

Button Set	Value	Constant
OK	0	vbOKOnly
OK, Cancel	1	vbOKCancel
Abort, Retry, Ignore	2	VBAbortRetryIgnore
Yes, No, Cancel	3	vbYesNoCancel
Yes, No	4	vbYesNo
Retry, Cancel	5	vbRetryCancel

Because the `buttons` argument controls both the icon and the command button(s) used for a message box, you might wonder how you can specify both at the same time. You do so by adding the values of the constants together. The `MsgBox` function is designed so that any combination of the icon constant and the command button constant creates a unique value. This value is then broken down by the function, to specify the individual pieces. The following code combines an icon constant and command button constant to create a warning message that allows the user to choose an action. The results of the code are illustrated in Figure 7.3:

```
nOptVal = vbExclamation + vbAbortRetryIgnore
nRetVal = MsgBox("File does not exist.", nOptVal, "My Application")
```

N O T E If you want your message box to display a Help button, add the constant `vbMsgBoxHelpButton`, which has a value of 16384, to whichever button set constant you choose.

FIGURE 7.3
The `buttons` argument controls both the icon and the command buttons displayed by the `MsgBox` function.

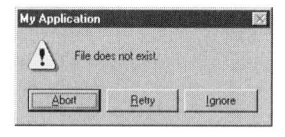

Setting the Default Button   If you are using more than one command button in the message box, you can also specify which button is the default. The *default button* is the one that has focus when the message box is displayed. This button is the one that the user is most likely to choose so that he or she can just press the Enter key. For example, if you display a message box to have the user confirm the deletion of the record, you probably should set up the default button so that the record would not be deleted. This way, the user must make a conscious choice to delete the record.

To specify which button is the default, you need to add another constant to the `buttons` argument of the `MsgBox` function. You can choose from four possible default button values, which are identified in the following table:

Default Button	Value	Constant
First	0	vbDefaultButton1
Second	256	vbDefaultButton2
Third	512	vbDefaultButton3
Fourth	768	vbDefaultButton4

A user might choose from seven buttons, with the selection depending on the button set used in the message box. Each of these buttons returns a different value to identify the button to your program (see Table 8.3).

Table 7.3 Return Values Indicate the User's Choice

Button	Value	Constant
OK	1	vbOK
Cancel	2	vbCancel
Abort	3	vbAbort
Retry	4	vbRetry
Ignore	5	vbIgnore
Yes	6	vbYes
No	7	vbNo

As always, using the constant in your code rather than the actual integer value is preferable. After you know which button the user selected, you can use that information in your program.

Making a Message Box Modal For completeness, you can apply one final setting to the `buttons` argument of the `MsgBox` function. You can choose to have the message box be modal for your application or for the entire system. Remember from earlier chapters that when a *modal* window is shown, it must be closed before continuing with the program. If you specify that the message box is modal to the system, the user must respond to the message box before he or she can do any further work on the computer at all. The system modal option should be used with extreme care. The default behavior is application modal, which means the users can continue to work in other applications.

To use the default, application modal, you do not have to add anything to the `buttons` argument, or you can add the `vbApplicationModal` constant, which has a value of 0. To make the message box system modal, you need to add the constant `vbSystemModal`, which has a value of 4096, to the `buttons` argument.

Demonstrating the *MsgBox* Function

To see the message box in action, create a simple program that utilizes it. You'll use a message box to confirm that a user who is attempting to exit the program is sure he or she wants to exit. Follow these steps:

1. Start Visual Basic, if necessary, and begin a new Standard EXE project.
2. Add a single command button to Form1. Set the command button's Name property to cmdExit and its Caption property to Exit.
3. Enter the following code into cmdExit's Click event procedure:

   ```
   Dim sMsg As String
   Dim nButtons As Integer
   Dim nResult As Integer
   sMsg = "Are you sure you want to exit?"
   nButtons = vbYesNo + vbQuestion
   nResult = MsgBox(sMsg, nButtons, "My Program")
   If nResult = vbYes Then
         End
   End If
   ```

4. Run the program and click the Exit button. You are asked whether you are sure you want to exit the program. Click the No button, and notice that the program does not close.

Getting Information from the User

Many times in a program, you need to get a single piece of information from the user. You might need the user to enter a name, the name of a file, or a number for various purposes. Although the message box lets your user make choices, it does not allow him or her to enter any information in response to the message. Therefore, you have to use some other means to get the information. Visual Basic provides a built-in dialog box for exactly this purpose: the *input box*.

The input box displays a message to tell the user what to enter, a text box where the user can enter the requested information, and two command buttons—OK and Cancel—that can be used to either accept or abort the input data. A sample input box is shown in Figure 7.4.

FIGURE 7.4
An input box lets the user enter a single piece of data in response to a message.

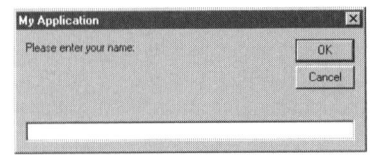

Setting Up the *InputBox* Function

Programmatically, the input box works very much like the message box with a return value. You can specify a variable to receive the information returned from the input box and then supply the input box's message (prompt) and, optionally, a title and default value. An example of the `InputBox` function is the following:

```
Dim sMsg as String, sUserName As String
sMsg = "Please type your name below:"
sUserName = InputBox(sMsg, "Enter user name", "Anonymous")
```

In this statement, the information returned by the `InputBox` function is stored in the variable `sUserName`. The first argument, the `prompt` parameter, represents the message that is displayed to the user to indicate what should be entered in the box. Like the message in the message box, the prompt can display up to approximately 1,024 characters before it is truncated. Word-wrapping is automatically performed on the text in the prompt so that it fits inside the box. Also, as with the message box, you can insert a carriage return/line feed combination (`vbCrLf`) to force the prompt to show multiple lines or to separate lines for emphasis.

After the prompt comes the `title` argument, which specifies the text in the input box's title bar. The other argument in the preceding example is the `default` argument. If included, it appears as an initial value in the input box. The user can accept this value, modify it, or erase it and enter a completely new value.

The minimum requirement for the `InputBox` function is a prompt parameter, as in this statement:

```
sReturnVal = InputBox("How's the weather?")
```

In addition to the input box's optional parameters to specify a window title and default value, other optional parameters allow you to set its initial screen position, as well as the help file to be used if the user needs assistance. Refer to the complete syntax of the `InputBox` function in Visual Basic's help system.

NOTE Unlike the `MsgBox` function, no option in the `InputBox` function specifies any command buttons other than the defaults of OK and Cancel.

Values Returned by *InputBox*

When the input box is used, the user can enter up to 255 characters of text in the input box's entry area, which resembles a text box. If the user types more text than will fit in the displayed entry area, the text he or she has already typed scrolls to the left. After the user is done, he or she can choose the OK or Cancel button. If the user chooses the OK button, the input box returns whatever is in the text box, whether it is new text or the default text. If the user chooses the Cancel button, the input box returns an empty string, regardless of what is in the text box.

To be able to use the information entered by the user, you must determine if the data meets your needs. First, you probably should make sure that the user actually entered some information and chose the OK button. You can do so by using the `Len` function to determine the length of the returned string. If the length is zero, the user clicked the Cancel button or left the input field blank. If the length of the string is greater than zero, you know that the user entered something. To see how the `Len` function works, enter each of these lines in the Immediate window and note the different results:

```
Print Len("Hello")

Print Len("")
```

You may also need to check the returned value to make sure it is of the proper type. If you are expecting a number that will subsequently be compared to another number in an `If` statement, your program should present an error message if the user enters letters. To make sure that you have a numerical value with which to work, you can use the `Val` function. The `Val` function's purpose is to return the numerical value of a string. If the string contains or starts with numbers, the function returns the number. If the string does not start with a number, the function returns zero. To understand the `Val` function, enter these lines in the Immediate window to see what each returns:

```
Print Val("Hello")

Print Val("50 ways to leave your lover")

Print Val("100 and 1 make 101")
```

The following code illustrates additional processing of the returned value of the input box with `Val` and `Len`:

```
Dim stInputVal As String
stInputVal = InputBox("Enter your age")
If Len(stInputVal) = 0 Then
    MsgBox "No age was selected"
Else
   If Val(stInputVal) = 0 Then
        MsgBox "You entered an invalid age."
   Else
        MsgBox "Congratulations for surviving this long!"
   End If
End If
```

Using Built-In Dialog Boxes

In earlier sections, you learned what a dialog box is and how to use two simple dialog boxes. In the following sections, you'll learn about the Microsoft CommonDialog control, which allows you to use standard Windows dialog boxes to specify filenames, select fonts and colors, and control the printer. And although the ease of setup is a great benefit, an even bigger bonus is that these dialog boxes are already familiar to the user because they are the same dialog boxes used by Windows itself.

General Usage of the CommonDialog Control

Using a single CommonDialog control, you have access to the following standard Windows dialog boxes:

- **Open.** Lets the user select the name and location of a file to open.

- **Save As.** Lets the user specify a filename and location in which to save information.
- **Font.** Lets the user choose a base font and set any font attributes that are desired.
- **Color.** Lets the user choose from a standard color or create a custom color for use in the program.
- **Print.** Lets the user select a printer and set some of the printer parameters.
- **Help.** Takes the user into the Windows Help system.

Although the CommonDialog control is included with Visual Basic, it's not one of the controls included in the Toolbox by default. To access the CommonDialog control, you might first have to add it to your project (and to the Toolbox) by selecting it from the Components dialog box. You can access this dialog box by choosing Project, Components. From there, select Microsoft Common Dialog Control 6.0 in the Controls list and click OK.

After you add the CommonDialog control to the Toolbox, you can add the control to a form by clicking the control and drawing it on the form just like any other control. The CommonDialog control appears on your form as an icon, as the control itself is not visible when your application is running.

The following sections describe each type of dialog box that can be created with the CommonDialog control. For each of these dialog boxes, you need to set some of the control's properties. You can do so through the Properties window, or you can use the CommonDialog control's Property Pages dialog box. The Property Pages dialog box provides you with easy access to the specific properties that are necessary for each of the common dialog box types (see Figure 7.5). You can access the Property Pages dialog box by clicking the ellipsis (...) button in the Custom property of the CommonDialog control, or by right-clicking the control and selecting Properties.

FIGURE 7.5
The Property Pages dialog box enables you to set up the `CommonDialog` control easily.

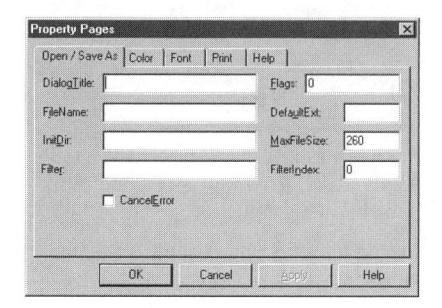

Testing the CommonDialog Control

Throughout this section, you'll want to try each of the styles of common dialog boxes. To get ready to test them, follow these steps:

1. Start Visual Basic, if necessary, and begin a new Standard EXE project.
2. Select Project, Components from the menu system.

3. Click the check box next to the control named *Microsoft Common Dialog Control 6.0*, making sure a check mark appears in the box.
4. Click OK to close the Components dialog box.
5. When you see the CommonDialog tool in the Toolbox, double-click it to add a common dialog control to Form1.
6. Set the CommonDialog control's Name property to cdlTest.
7. Add a command button to Form1. Set its Name property to cmdTest and its Caption property to Test Common Dialog.

You'll use this shell program to see how the various flavors of the CommonDialog control work. When instructed, enter code into cmdTest's Click event procedure.

The File Dialog Boxes

One of the key uses of the CommonDialog control is to obtain file names from the user. The CommonDialog control's File dialog box can be used in either of two modes: Open and Save As. Open mode lets the user specify the name and location of a file to be retrieved and used by your program. Save As mode lets the user specify the name and location of a file to be saved.

Open and Save As Dialog Boxes The dialog boxes for the Open and Save As functions are similar. Figure 7.6 shows the Open dialog box.

FIGURE 7.6
The Open and Save dialog boxes share many components.

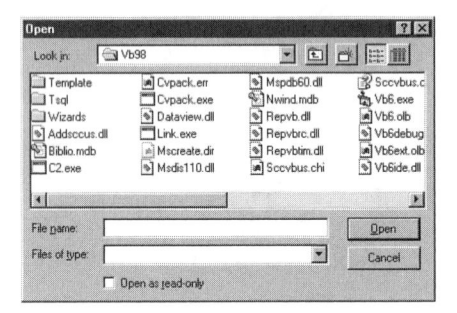

The dialog box's major components are as follows:

- **Drive/Folder list.** The current folder is listed here. If the current folder is the root (\), the current drive is listed here. You can use the combo box and navigation buttons to move up folder levels, similar to the way you would in the Windows Explorer.
- **File/Folder selection list.** The names indicated in this area are the folders and files one level beneath the item in the Drive/Folder list. An item in this area can be opened either by double-clicking it, or by highlighting it and pressing Enter. If the item you open is a folder, the display is updated to show the contents of the new current folder. If the item you open is a file, the dialog box closes.
- **File Name text box.** The user can use this text box for manual filename entry and folder navigation. If the user enters a filename, the dialog box closes. If he or she enters

a path such as C:\Data\Word and presses Enter, the dialog box is updated to show that folder. Also, if the user single-clicks a filename in the file/folder selection area, it appears here.

- **File Type list box.** Here, the user selects the types of files to display. These types are determined by the extension portion of the filename; the available types are controlled by the `Filter` property of the CommonDialog control.

- **Toolbar buttons and Command buttons.** The buttons in the upper-right corner let the user move up one folder level, create a new folder, or switch the file display area between the list mode and the file details mode. The buttons at the lower-right corner let the user process the selection or cancel the dialog box.

Opening and Saving Files   To open an existing file, use the `ShowOpen` method of the CommonDialog control. (This method displays the dialog box in Figure 7.6.) You use this method by specifying the name of the CommonDialog control and the method name. To try it, type this code into the `Click` event procedure of the command button `cmdTest` in the sample project:

```
cdlTest.ShowOpen
Msgbox "You Selected " & cdlTest.FileName & " to be opened."
```

After the preceding code is executed, the name of the file selected is available to your code through the CommonDialog control's `FileName` property.

Using the CommonDialog control for saving and opening involves essentially the same steps. The name of the method used to invoke the Save As dialog box is `ShowSave`. You will find a few subtle differences between the dialog boxes shown for the `Open` and `Save` functions, such as the title of the dialog box and the captions on the command buttons.

To test the CommonDialog control's `ShowSave` method, replace the code in the sample project's `cmdTest_Click` procedure with these lines:

```
cdlTest.ShowSave
Msgbox "You Selected " & cdlTest.FileName & " to be saved."
```

> **NOTE** The Open and Save As dialog boxes don't actually open or save files; they simply get information from the user as to the names and locations of the files to be opened or saved. Your program must take whatever steps are necessary to complete the operation.

Specifying File Types with the *Filter* Property   When using the CommonDialog control, you might need to specify that only certain file types are listed. If your program reads Microsoft Excel (.XLS) files, for example, you would not want the user to attempt to open batch (.BAT) files. You can restrict (or "filter") the files shown in the dialog box by using the `Filter` property.

You set the `Filter` property at designtime from either the Properties window or the Property Pages dialog box, or at runtime with an assignment statement in code. The `Filter` property is a string value that includes a file type description followed by the file extension. It requires a special format, as shown here:

```
cldTest.Filter = "Word Documents (*.doc)¦*.doc"
```

The vertical line in the preceding code line is known as the *pipe symbol.* This symbol must be present in the filter. Preceding the pipe symbol is a short description of the file type, in this case Word Documents (*.doc). Following the pipe symbol is the actual filter for the files. You typically express the filter as an asterisk followed by a period and the extension of the files that you want to display. Some examples are *.txt, *.doc, and *.*.

If you specify the Filter property with an assignment statement, you must enclose the filter in double quotation marks, as with any string. The quotes are omitted if you specify the filter from the Properties dialog box.

You can specify multiple description¦filter pairs within the Filter property. Each pair must be separated from the other pairs by the pipe symbol, as shown in the following example:

```
cdlTest.Filter = "Text Files¦*.txt¦All Files¦*.*"
```

To see the Filter property in action, replace the code in the test project's cmdTest_Click event procedure with these lines, and then run the program:

```
cdlTest.Filter = "Text Files (*.txt)¦*.txt¦All Files (*.*)¦*.*"
cdlTest.ShowOpen
```

When you test this code, note that the CommonDialog control's Filter property causes only text files to be displayed, unless the user selects another filter by dropping down the Files of type drop-down list.

Customizing the File Dialog Boxes with the *Flags* Property   Another important property is the Flags property. The Flags property is set using a constant or combination of constants, similar to the MsgBox function's Options parameter. A complete list of constants is listed in Visual Basic's Help system. For example, if the Open as Read Only check box doesn't make any sense in your program, you can set a flag to hide it, like this:

```
cdlTest.Flags = cdlOFNHideReadOnly
cdlTest.InitDir = "C:\Windows"
cdlTest.ShowOpen
```

Note also the use of the InitDir property, which starts the dialog box in a specific folder.

> **CAUTION**
> Flags, Filters, and other properties that affect the CommonDialog control must be set before displaying it.

The Font Dialog Box

Setting up the CommonDialog control to show the Font dialog box is just as easy as setting it up for file functions. In fact, you can use the same CommonDialog control on a form to handle file, font, color, and printer functions, just by resetting the properties and invoking the appropriate method.

The first step in using the CommonDialog control to handle font selection is to set a value for the `Flags` property. Among other things, this property tells the CommonDialog control whether you want to show screen fonts, printer fonts, or both. This setting is required; the constants are listed in the following table:

Font Set	Constant	Value
Screen fonts	cdlCFScreenFonts	1
Printer fonts	cdlCFPrinterFonts	2
Both sets	cdlCFBoth	3

> **CAUTION**
> If you do not set a value for the `Flags` property, you get an error message stating that no fonts are installed.

You can set the value of the `Flags` property from the design environment by using the Properties window or the Property Pages dialog box, or you can set it from your program by using an assignment statement. After the `Flags` property has been set, you can invoke the Font dialog box from your code, using the CommonDialog's `ShowFont` method. After the dialog box is closed, information about the font that the user selected is contained in the CommonDialog's properties.

To see this process in action, follow these steps to modify the sample program you created earlier in this chapter:

1. If the program is still running from an earlier test, stop it.
2. Add a `Label` control to Form1. Set the `Label` control's `Name` property to `lblTest` and its `Caption` property to `This is a test`.
3. Set `lblTest`'s `AutoSize` property to `True`.
4. Replace the code in `cmdTest`'s `Click` event procedure with the following:

   ```
   cdlTest.Flags = cdlCFBoth + cdlCFEffects
   cdlTest.ShowFont
   lblTest.Font.Name = cdlTest.FontName
   lblTest.Font.Size = cdlTest.FontSize
   lblTest.Font.Bold = cdlTest.FontBold
   ```

5. Run the application. When you click `cmdTest`, a Font dialog box should appear. Change the font to something totally different than the default. When you click OK, `lblTest`'s font should match what you selected in the dialog box.

Note two things in the preceding code. First, an extra flag, `cdlCFEffects`, allows the user to select additional font "effects" such as bold, color, and underline. Second, note the slight difference in syntax between the Label control's `Font` properties and the CommonDialog's `Font` properties. The `Font` property of a Label control (or of other objects, such as a `TextBox` control) is an object itself (a `Font` object), and the CommonDialog box stores each attribute about a font (`Name`, `Size`, `Bold`, and so on) in a separate property. The text box has the older, separate properties for compatibility, but you should avoid them. If you have to set the font for two text boxes, for example, you can set one directly from the CommonDialog control's properties and the other one simply by assigning the first text box's Font property:

```
Set txtAddress.Font = txtName.Font
```

Figure 7.7 shows the Font dialog box that is presented to the user. This particular dialog box contains both screen and printer fonts.

FIGURE 7.7
The Font dialog box can be programmed to display screen fonts, printer fonts, or both.

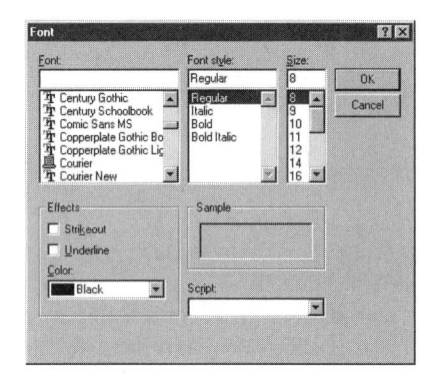

Table 7.4 shows the control's properties and the font attributes that each manipulates.

Table 7.4 CommonDialog Control Properties That Store Font Attributes

Property	Attribute
FontName	The name of the base font
FontSize	The height of the font in points
FontBold	Whether boldface is selected
FontItalic	Whether italic is selected
FontUnderline	Whether the font is underlined
FontStrikethru	Whether the font has a line through it

The font information can be used to set the font of any object in your program or even to set the font for the Printer object. Be sure to peruse the Help system for a complete list of Flags property constants.

The Color Dialog Box

The CommonDialog control's Color dialog box lets the user select colors that can be used for the foreground or background colors of your forms or controls (see Figure 7.8). The user has the option of choosing one of the standard colors, or creating and selecting a custom color.

FIGURE 7.8
The Color dialog box lets the user select a color graphically and then returns it to your program as a hex value.

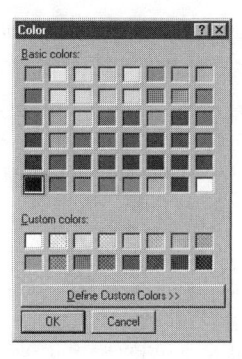

Setting up the CommonDialog control for colors is basically the same as for fonts. You set the `Flags` property to the constant `cdlCCRGBInit` and then invoke the control's `ShowColor` method.

When the user selects a color from the dialog box, a hexadecimal number representing that color is stored in the `Color` property of the control. To see how the Color dialog box works, replace the code in the test project's `cmdTest_Click` event procedure with the following:

```
cdlTest.Flags = cdlCCRGBInit
cdlTest.ShowColor
Form1.BackColor = cdlTest.Color
```

As with the other dialog boxes, you can alter the behavior of the Color dialog box by using the `Flags` property. For example, if you want only default colors available, use the `cdlCCPreventFullOpen` flag so that the user cannot open the Define Custom Colors window. Check the Color Dialog Box/Flags Property (Color dialog) topic in the Visual Basic Help system for a full listing of the flags and properties that affect the Color dialog box.

The Print Dialog Box

Another type of dialog box that the CommonDialog control can display is the Print dialog box. A Print dialog box is usually displayed just before your application initiates a printing process. It lets the user select which printer to use and specify options for the print process (see Figure 7.9). These options include specifying which pages to print and the number of copies, as well as an option of printing to a file.

FIGURE 7.9
The Print dialog box provides a consistent way for your users to set printer options.

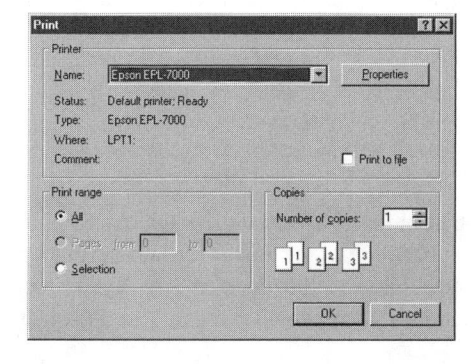

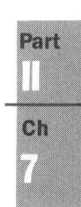

To invoke the Print dialog box, just call the CommonDialog control's `ShowPrinter` method. There are no required flags to set prior to the call.

After the Print dialog box is displayed, the user can select the printer from the Name list at the top of the dialog box. This list contains all the printers installed in the user's operating system. Just below the Name list is the Status line, which tells you the current status of the selected printer.

If a user wants to change any printer-specific parameters (such as paper size and margins), he or she can click the Properties button on the Print dialog box. This action brings up the Properties dialog box for the selected printer, as shown in Figure 7.10. This dialog box lets the user control all the settings of the printer, just as with the Windows Control Panel.

FIGURE 7.10
The Properties dialog box for the printer lets you control paper size, margins, and other printer attributes.

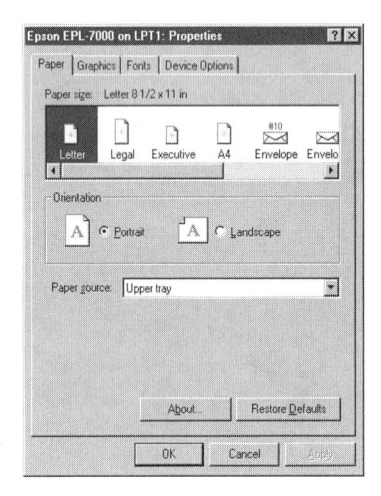

The Print dialog box returns the information provided by the user in the dialog box's properties. The `FromPage` and `ToPage` properties tell you the starting and ending pages of the printout as selected by the user. The `Copies` property tells you how many copies the user wants printed. These details are provided only as information. The Print dialog box does not automatically create the desired printout.

To see how the Printer dialog box works, replace the code in the test project's `cmdTest_Click` event procedure with the following:

```
cdlTest.Flags = cdlPDDisablePrintToFile
cdlTest.Copies = 3
cdlTest.PrinterDefault = True
cdlTest.ShowPrinter
MsgBox "The default printer is:" & Printer.DeviceName
```

In this sample code, properties and flags are used to disable the Print to File option and set the default number of copies to 3. In addition, the `PrinterDefault` property means that the dialog box will use the control's properties to modify the default system printer. The Printer dialog box has quite a few useful options that are detailed in the Visual Basic help system.

The Help Dialog Box

This use of the CommonDialog control invokes the Windows Help engine by running WINHLP32.EXE. To use the Help dialog box, you must set the CommonDialog control's `HelpFile` property to the name and location of a properly formatted Windows help (.HLP) file and set the `HelpCommand` property to tell the Help engine what type of help to offer. After you set these properties, use the CommonDialog control's `ShowHelp` method to initiate the Help system. The user can then navigate the Help system using your program's Help file.

Creating Your Own Dialog Boxes

Although the CommonDialog control provides you with several types of dialog boxes to use in your programs, sometimes you just can't accomplish some tasks with these built-in tools. For example, if you want to set your own captions for the command buttons in a dialog box, you can't use the message box; nor can the message box handle more than three buttons (not including the Help button). Also, consider the built-in input box. This dialog box cannot display an icon, nor can it handle more than one input item. If your program needs dialog box capabilities that the CommonDialog control can't offer, you can simply use a standard Visual Basic form to create your own custom dialog box.

Creating a Custom Dialog Box

You need only follow a few simple guidelines if you decide to create a custom dialog box:

- Set the form's `BorderStyle` property to `3 - Fixed Dialog`. Standard dialog boxes can't be resized. This property setting also removes the form's Maximize/Restore and Minimize buttons.
- Remove the form's icon by deleting the setting for its `Icon` property.
- Set the form's `StartUpPosition` property to `1 - CenterOwner` so that the dialog box is centered on the parent application.
- Add controls as necessary to obtain the required information from the user. Use Label controls as captions for text boxes.
- Use Frame controls to group other controls where appropriate (see the Print range area of the Printer dialog control for an example).
- Include an OK button that accepts the user's choices.
- Include a Cancel button that allows the user to abort the action.
- When you show the dialog box, show it modally (`frmDialog.Show vbModal`).

Feel free to look to some of the standard Windows dialog boxes or to other programs' custom dialog boxes for design ideas.

Using Form Templates for Other Dialog Boxes

Microsoft has included several form templates with Visual Basic representing custom dialog boxes that can be handy to use in your programs. You can quickly add one of these form templates to your project by selecting the appropriate type when you add a new form; you can then customize it to suit your needs. The available templates include the following:

- **About Dialog.** Used to provide the user with information about your program.
- **Log In Dialog.** Allows the user to enter a user ID and password.
- **Options Dialog.** Creates a dialog box similar to Property Pages or the Options dialog box of Visual Basic.
- **Tip Dialog.** Can provide a Tip of the Day function for your program.

You can add these forms based on these dialog box templates to your program by choosing Project, Add Form, or by clicking the Add Form button. You then see the Add Form dialog box shown in Figure 7.11. You can choose the desired dialog box from the templates available and then customize it to suit your needs.

FIGURE 7.11
Several custom dialog boxes are available as form templates.

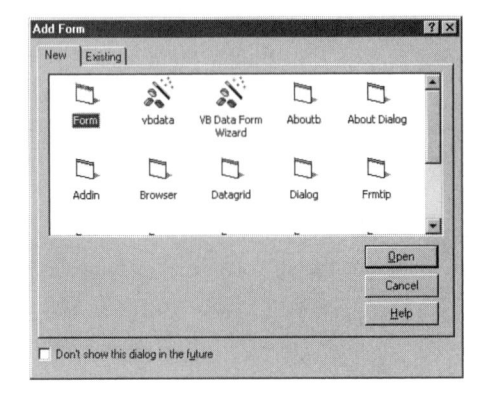

From Here...

In this chapter, you learned how dialog boxes can be used to help the user select files, printers, and fonts in your programs. You also learned how the message box and input box are used to inform the user and to get decisions or single pieces of information. You even saw how to design your own dialog boxes when the built-in ones are insufficient for the task. To learn more about using some of the concepts presented here, take a look at the following chapters:

- To learn more about desigining the forms you use in your applications, see Chapter 3, "Visual Basic Building Blocks."
- For an introduction to writing the code that enables your forms to react to your users' actions, see Chapter 5, "Responding to the User with Event Procedures."
- For a more complete discussion of writing Visual Basic code, see Chapter 9, "Visual Basic Programming Fundamentals."

CHAPTER 8

Using Variables to Store Information

In this chapter

Introduction to Variables   160

Variable Declarations   163

Variable Arrays   166

Determining Where a Variable Can Be Used   166

Using the `Option Explicit` Statement   169

What's Different About Constants   171

To make Visual Basic programs truly functional, they must be able to store information temporarily. With Visual Basic, as with any programming language, there is a need to remember information as the program runs. Visual Basic allows you to store information using variables and constants.

This chapter examines the types of variables and constants available to Visual Basic programmers and explores how to use them to allow the necessary retention of information.

Introduction to Variables

Simply stated, you use variables to store information in the computer's memory while your programs are running. Three components define a variable:

- The variable's name (which correlates to its location in memory)
- The type of information being stored
- The actual information itself

Suppose you are given this assignment: "Go count all the cars in the parking lot." As you count each car, you are storing information in a variable. Your location in memory is either a notepad or your brain. The type of information being stored is a number. And the actual information you are storing is the current number of cars.

As the name *variable* suggests, the information stored in a variable can change (vary) over time. In the example of counting cars, the count will be increased periodically. With any variable, there are two basic functions you can perform: storing information (writing on the notepad) and retrieving information (reading what is written on the notepad).

Naming Variables

A variable must have a name for you to be able to assign values to it. You might have noticed statements like the following in earlier examples:

```
Dim X As Integer
```

This example illustrates a `Dim`, or *Dimension*, statement, used for *dimensioning* (or *declaring*) variables (see the section "Variable Declarations" later in this chapter). When your program declares a variable, it is, in essence, telling Visual Basic, "Set aside a memory location that will be used to store variable information; call it *X*." The last two words in the `Dim` statement tell Visual Basic what type of information you plan to store—in this case, integer numbers. This information helps determine how much memory is to be set aside for the variable.

In naming a variable, you have a tremendous amount of flexibility. Variable names can be simple, or they can be descriptive of the information they contain. In the preceding example, *X* is a perfectly legal name but not very descriptive to the readers. Although you are allowed great latitude in naming variables, you must adhere to a few restrictions:

- The name must start with a letter, not a number or other character.

- The remainder of the name can contain letters, numbers, and/or underscore characters. No spaces, periods, or other punctuation characters are allowed.
- The name must be unique within the variable's scope. (Scope refers to the context in which the variable is defined, as we will see shortly.)
- The name can be no longer than 255 characters.
- The name cannot be one of Visual Basic's reserved words.

Make your variable names descriptive of the task to make your code easy to read, but also keep the names as short as possible to make the code easy to type. Many programmers also use prefixes in their variable names to indicate the type of data stored; usually, these conventions are variations of the Hungarian Naming Convention. These prefixes usually consist of one or two lowercase characters at the beginning of the variable; the next letter is usually capitalized.

For example, a prefix of s, as in sCity, indicates a variable that stores a String value. Table 8.1 lists some of the common prefixes that you should use when naming variables. This convention, which is recommended in a Microsoft Knowledge Base article, is used for many of the original code samples in this book. You might prefer a two-character prefix or some other convention altogether.

Table 8.1 Variable Naming Prefixes

Variable Type	Prefix	Example
String	s	sFirstName
Integer	n	nAge
Long Integer	l	lPopulation
Single (Floating Point)	f	fAverageGrade
Double	d	dThrustRatio
Currency	c	cPayRate
Boolean	b	bTaxable

For integers, the prefix n is used rather than the seemingly more obvious i because the prefix i is used to represent indexes.

Types of Variables

Okay, you know what a variable does and how to name it. But what can you store in a variable? The simple answer is: *almost anything*. A variable can hold a number; a string of text; or a reference to an object, such as a form, control, or database. This chapter looks specifically at using variables to store numbers, strings, and logical values. Using variables to represent objects and databases is covered later in Chapters 16, "Classes: Reusable Components," and 26, "Using Data Access Objects (DAO)," respectively.

Each type of variable has its own memory requirements and is designed to work efficiently with different types of information. Therefore, you cannot store a string like `"Hello"` in a variable that you declare as an integer.

Table 8.2 shows some of the standard variable types that are available in Visual Basic. The table also shows the range of values that the variable can hold and the amount of memory required. Variables with smaller memory requirements should be used wherever possible to conserve system resources.

Table 8.2 Variables Store Many Types of Information

Type	Stores	Memory Requirement	Range of Values
Integer	Whole numbers	Two bytes	−32,768 to +32,767
Long	Whole numbers	Four bytes	(approximately) +/− 2 billion
Single	Decimal numbers	Four bytes	+/− 1E-45 to 3E38
Double	Decimal numbers	Eight bytes	+/− 5E-324 to 1.8E308
Currency	Numbers with up to 15 digits left of the decimal and four digits right of the decimal	Eight bytes	+/− 9E14
String	Text information	One byte per character	Up to 65,400 characters for fixed-length string and up to 2 billion characters for dynamic strings
Byte	Whole numbers	One byte	0 to 255
Boolean	Logical values	Two bytes	`True` or `False`
Date	Date and time information	Eight bytes	1/1/100 to 12/31/9999
Object	Instances of classes; OLE objects	Four bytes	N/A
Variant	Any of the preceding data types	16 bytes + 1 byte per character	N/A

In addition to the preceding variable types, you also can create *user-defined types* to meet your needs. Consider the following code segment, which demonstrates the declaration and use of a user-defined type:

```
Private Type Point
        x As Integer
        y As Integer
```

```
End Type
Private Sub Command1_Click()
        Dim MyPoint As Point
        MyPoint.x = 3
        MyPoint.y = 5
End Sub
```

As you can see from the sample, you declare a new type by using the `Type` statement. Note that types must be defined in the general declarations section; in this case, we have defined a private type called `Point` within a form. To create a variable of the new type, you use the `Dim` statement just as you would with any other type. The parts of a type are accessed via dot notation.

As you know, there are some specialized types to deal with databases (such as `Database`, `Field`, and `Recordset`). Visual Basic knows about these other data types when you add a reference to a *type library*. A type library is a DLL or other file that makes these types available to your program. A good example of using a type library is discussed in Chapter 22, "Using OLE to Control Other Applications."

▶ **See** "The Microsoft Word Object Library" **p. 489**

Variable Declarations

Earlier, in the section "Naming Variables," you saw an example of the `Dim` statement, which is used to tell Visual Basic the name and type of your variable. However, Visual Basic does not require you to specifically declare a variable before it is used. If a variable is not declared, Visual Basic creates the variable by using a default data type – usually a *variant*. A variant can contain any type of information. Using a variant for general information has two major drawbacks—it can waste memory resources, and the variable type might be invalid for use with functions that expect a specific variable type.

Always declaring your variables before they are used is good programming practice. Therefore, you should now take a look at the two ways to declare a variable in Visual Basic—*explicit* and *implicit* declarations—and the special case of *fixed-length strings*.

Explicit Declaration

Explicit declaration means that you use statements to define the names and types of your program's variables. These statements do not assign values to the variables but merely tell Visual Basic what the variables should be called and what type of data they can contain.

You can use each of the following statements to explicitly declare a variable's type:

```
Dim varname [As vartype][, varname2 [As vartype2]]

Private varname [As vartype][, varname2 [As vartype2]]

Static varname [As vartype][, varname2 [As vartype2]]

Public varname [As vartype][, varname2 [As vartype2]]
```

`Dim`, `Private`, `Static`, and `Public` are Visual Basic keywords that define how and where the variable can be used. (You learn more about where these keywords can be used in upcoming sections.) *varname* and *varname2* represent the names of two variables that you want to declare. As indicated in the syntax, you can specify multiple variables in the same statement as long as you separate the variables with commas. Note that the syntax shows only two variables on one line, but you can specify several. In fact, over a thousand characters can fit on one line in the Code window. From a practical standpoint, however, you should refrain from writing lines of code that are wider than the displayed Code window. This way, you make your code much easier to read because you don't have to scroll left and right when looking at it.

vartype and *vartype2* represent the data types of the respective variables. A *data type* is a keyword that tells Visual Basic what kind of information is stored in the variable. As indicated, the variable type is an optional property. If you include the variable type, you must include the keyword `As`. If you do not include a variable type, the default type (usually Variant type) is used.

The following code shows the use of these declaration statements for actual variables:

```
Private nNumVal As Integer
Private nAvgVal As Integer, vInptVal As Variant
Static fClcAverage As Single
Dim sFirstName As String
```

Implicit Declaration

Declaring your variables using the `Dim` or other statements shown in the preceding section is best, but in many cases you can also assign a type to a variable using an *implicit declaration*. With this type of declaration, a special character is used at the end of the variable name when the variable is first assigned a value. The characters for each variable type are shown in Table 8.3.

Table 8.3 Special Variable Type Characters

Variable Type	Character
Integer	%
Long	&
Single	!
Double	#
Currency	@
String	$
Byte	None
Boolean	None
Date	None
Object	None
Variant	None

Visual Basic automatically sets aside space for implicitly declared variables the first time each variable is encountered. The variables that were declared using the code in the preceding section could have been used as implicitly declared variables, as follows:

```
nNumVal% = 0
nAvgVal% = 1
vInptVal = 5
fClcAverage! = 10.1
sFirstName$ = "Lauren"
```

Notice that the variable vInptVal doesn't have a declaration character. This means that vInptVal will be of the Variant type.

Fixed-Length Strings

Most strings that you use in your programs will be of the type known as *variable-length strings*. These strings can contain any amount of text, up to approximately 2 billion characters. As information is stored in the variable, the size of the variable adjusts to accommodate the length of the string. Both the implicit and explicit declarations shown earlier created variable-length strings. Visual Basic, however, does have a second type of string: the *fixed-length string*.

As the name implies, a fixed-length string remains the same size, regardless of the information assigned to it. If a fixed-length string variable is assigned an expression shorter than the defined length of the variable, the remaining length of the variable is filled with spaces. If the expression is longer than the variable, only as many characters as will fit in the variable are stored; the rest are truncated.

A fixed-length string variable can only be declared using an explicit declaration like the following:

```
Dim varname As String * strlength
```

Notice that this declaration is slightly different from the previous declaration of a string variable. The declaration of a fixed-length string variable contains an asterisk (*) to tell Visual Basic that the string will be of a fixed length. The final parameter, strlength, tells the program the maximum number of characters that the variable can contain.

One example of a fixed-length string is to aid in building a column-delimited text file. Suppose 25 characters of the file are used to represent a person's name. The following code would automatically cut the string off at 25 characters:

```
Dim sName As String * 25
sName = "This text is too long for the string variable."
```

Assigning a value less than 25 characters in length to sName would make the remaining characters spaces.

> **NOTE** Another common use of fixed-length strings is to receive information from a Windows API function, as discussed in Chapter 20, "Accessing the Windows API."

Variable Arrays

All the variables discussed so far have been single-instance variables. Often, however, you may find it very useful to work with *arrays*. An array is a group of variables of the same type, sharing the same name. In this way, processing groups of related areas is easy. For example, you might want to have a group of variables that tracks the sales in each of your company's four regions. You can declare a currency variable for each region, plus one for the total sales across all regions, like this:

```
Dim cRegSales1 As Currency, cRegSales2 As Currency
Dim cRegSales3 As Currency, cRegSales4 As Currency
Dim cTotalSales As Currency
```

Then, if you want to calculate the total sales for all regions, you might use this code:

```
cTotalSales = cRegSales1 + cRegSales2 + cRegSales3 + cRegSales4
```

This approach isn't all that cumbersome. However, what if you have 20 regions? Or several hundred? You can see how working with large numbers of related variables could get messy very quickly.

You can greatly simplify this example by using an array. Here, create an array of variables named cRegSales; the array can contain as many elements (instances of variables) as you have regions. You can rewrite the previous example for 20 regions like this:

```
Dim cRegSales(1 To 20) As Currency
Dim cTotalSales As Currency
Dim nCounter As Integer
Dim sTemp As String

    cTotalSales = 0
    For nCounter = 1 To 20
        cTotalSales = cTotalSales + cRegSales(nCounter)
    Next nCounter
    sTemp = "Total sales for all regions = "
    sTemp = sTemp & Format(cTotalSales, "currency")
MsgBox sTemp, vbInformation, "Sales Analysis"
```

Note this example's use of a *loop*. The block of code beginning with the For instruction and ending with the Next instruction defines a group of program statements that will be repeated a certain number of times (in this case 20). Using loops makes short work of processing variable arrays.

As you progress through this book, you'll see several cases in which arrays can make your coding much simpler.

Determining Where a Variable Can Be Used

In addition to telling Visual Basic what you want to be able to store in a variable, a declaration statement tells Visual Basic where the variable can be used. This area of usage is called the *scope* of the variable. This is analogous to the coverage area of a paging system. When you purchase a pager, you make a decision whether you want local service, regional service, or nationwide service. This information is then programmed into your pager when you buy it. If you go outside the service area, your pager does not work. In a similar manner, you can declare variables to work in only one procedure, work in any procedure of a form, or work throughout your program.

By default, a variable that is implicitly declared is local to the procedure in which it is created. If you don't specify any kind of declaration, explicit or implicit, you create a local variable. Therefore, to create variables that have a scope other than local, you must use a declaration statement.

> **NOTE** The scope of a variable is determined not only by the type of declaration, but also by the location of the declaration. For example, the `Dim` and `Private` keywords assume different meanings in different parts of a form's code.

Creating Variables That Are Available Everywhere

In most programs, unless you have only one form and no code modules, you will find that you need some variables that can be accessed from anywhere in the code. These variables are called `Public` variables. (Other languages, as well as earlier versions of Visual Basic, might refer to them as `Global` variables. In fact, Visual Basic still recognizes the `Global` keyword.) These variables are typically used to hold information such as the name of the program's user, or to reference a database that is used throughout the program. They might also be used as flags to indicate various conditions in the program.

To create a `Public` variable, you simply place a declaration statement with the `Public` keyword in the General Declarations section of a module (.BAS file) of your program. The following line shows the `Public` declaration of a variable used for storing the program user's name:

```
Public sUserName As String
```

In a form or a class module, the `Public` keyword has a special meaning. Variables defined as `Public` act like a property of the form or class that is available anywhere in the program. These properties are referenced like the built-in properties of a form or control instead of like a variable. The `Public` properties are used to pass information between forms and other parts of your program. For example, suppose the previous declaration for `sUserName` existed in a form. The following lines of code could be used to set and retrieve the user name from the form:

```
frmLogin.sUserName = "CKRAMER"
frmLogin.Show vbModal
MsgBox "The name entered was " & frmLogin.sUserName
```

The first line of code sets the contents of the public variable (and loads `frmLogin` if it is not already loaded) as if it were a property of the form. The second line of code shows the form modally, so that the third line of code is not executed until the form is hidden. If a user of the form changes the value of `sUserName` from within the form itself and then hides the form, the third line of code displays a message box with the new value.

Keeping a Variable Local

If you do not need to access a variable from everywhere in your program, you should not use the `Public` keyword in a declaration. Instead, you should use the `Dim` or `Private` keywords, which tell Visual Basic to define the variable within the scope of the current procedure or form, respectively. With these declarations, the location of the statement determines the actual scope of the variable. If the variable is defined in the General Declarations section of a form or module, the variable is available to every procedure in that form or module. This type is known as a *form-level* or *module-level variable*. If the variable is declared inside a procedure, it can be used only within that procedure. This type is typically known as a *local variable*.

You may be wondering the reasons behind wanting to keep a variable as local as possible. The answer is two-fold:

- **Good Programming Practice**. Having code that relies on a public variable is harder to debug and maintain. For example, consider the following implementations of a simple procedure, `CalcArea`:

```
Sub CalcArea()
            MsgBox "The Answer is " & nHeight * nWidth
End Sub

Sub CalcArea(nHeight As Integer, nWidth As Integer)
            MsgBox "The Answer is " & nHeight * nWidth
End Sub
```

  If you are tasked with debugging the `CalcArea` procedure, the first example is the most difficult. The calculation depends on two public variables (`nHeight` and `nWidth`) being set correctly. The second implementation improves on this problem slightly by making `nHeight` and `nWidth` function parameters, allowing the programmer to easily call the function from the Immediate window without having to preset many variables. Of course, to make `CalcArea` as modular and reusable as possible, you would probably want to turn it into a function.

- **Use of Resources**. The second reason for keeping variables as local as possible should be almost common sense. If you declare a variable as `Public`, Visual Basic has to make that variable available to all forms and modules in your application. The limited scope of local variables does not require as many resources and will make your programs more efficient.

Using Static Variables

Most variables that are created inside a procedure are discarded by Visual Basic when the procedure is finished. Sometimes, however, you might want to preserve the value of a variable even after the procedure has run. This is often the case when you call the procedure multiple times, and the value of a variable for one call to the procedure is dependent on the value left over from previous calls. As an example, you may have a procedure that prints a header at the top of each page of a report, and the procedure needs to remember the page number from the previous time it was called so that it can be incremented.

To create a variable that retains its value, you use the `Static` keyword in the variable declaration. It tells Visual Basic that the variable can be referenced only within the procedure but to remember the value because it might be needed again. Here's an example of a variable declared using the `Static` keyword:

```
Static nPageNumber As Integer
```

NOTE If you use the `Static` keyword in front of a Function or Sub header (such as `Static Sub MySub()`), all variables in that procedure are treated as static. The following example subroutine demonstrates this concept:

```
Static Sub Test()
     Dim x As Integer
     Debug.Print "Value of x before assignment statement = " & x
     x = 1234
     Debug.Print "Value of x after assignment statement = " & x
End Sub
```

In this example, the variable x would be treated as a static variable. The first time you called the Test function, the output would be 0 and 1234. The next call would print 1234 for both the before and after values.

Using the *Option Explicit* Statement

Earlier, in the section "Variable Declarations," you learned that declaring your program's variables before they are used is good programming practice. You can have Visual Basic "force" you to declare variables by setting one of its environment options. To do so, access Visual Basic's Options dialog box by choosing Tools, Options. On this dialog box's Editor tab is the Require Variable Declaration option (see Figure 8.1). Selecting this box requires you to declare each variable before you use it.

FIGURE 8.1
The Require Variable Declaration option helps prevent you from mistyping variable names.

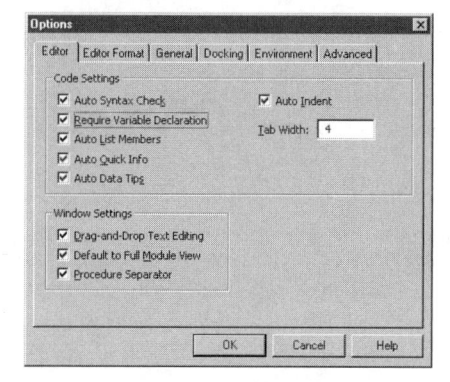

Setting the Require Variable Declaration option causes the `Option Explicit` statement to be placed in the General Declarations section of all new modules and forms that are added to your project, as shown in Figure 8.2.

FIGURE 8.2
The `Option Explicit` statement is added to your program.

If a form or module contains the `Option Explicit` statement and you fail to declare a variable, you receive the error message `Variable not defined` when you try to run your code. The integrated debugger highlights the offending variable and aborts the compilation of your program. The benefit of this message is that it helps you avoid errors in your code that might be caused by typographical errors. For example, you might declare a variable using the following statement:

```
Dim sMyName As String
```

If, in a later statement, you mistype the variable name, Visual Basic catches the error for you rather than continues with unpredictable results. For example, the following statement causes an error if `Option Explicit` is used; otherwise, the program continues without having set the value of the intended variable:

```
sMyNme = "Tina Marie"
```

Without the `Option Explicit` statement, the previous line of code would create an additional variable. In other words, you would have two string variables: `sMyName` and `sMyNme`.

> **CAUTION**
> If you set the Require Variable Declaration option after starting to create a program, the option has no effect on any forms or modules that have already been created. In this case, you can add the `Option Explicit` statement as the first line of code in the General Declarations section of any existing forms or modules.

> **TIP**
> If you use some capital letters in your variable declarations, enter your code in all lowercase letters. Visual Basic automatically sets the capitalization of your variables to match the declarations. This convention gives you an immediate visual indication that you typed the name correctly.

What's Different About Constants

Using variables is just one way of storing information in the memory of a computer. Another way is to use *constants*. Constants in a program are treated a special way. After you define them (or they are defined for you by Visual Basic), you cannot modify them later in the program. If you try, Visual Basic generates an error when you run your program. It may help you to think of a constant as a variable whose value cannot change.

How to Use Constants

Constants are most often used to replace a value that is hard to remember or to type, such as the color value for the Windows title bar. Remembering the constant vbActiveTitleBar is easier than remembering the value -2147483646. You can also use a constant to avoid typing long strings if they are used in a number of places. For example, you can set a constant such as FileErrMsg containing the string "The requested file was not found."

Constants are also used frequently for conversion factors, such as 12 inches per foot or 3.3 feet per meter. The following code example shows how constants and variables are used:

```
Const MetersToFeet = 3.3
nDistMeters = InputBox("Enter a distance in meters")
nDistFeet = nDistMeters * MetersToFeet
MsgBox "The distance in feet is: " & CStr(nDistFeet)
```

Another common use for constants is to minimize changes to your code for reasons such as changing your program's name, version number, and so forth. You can define constants at the beginning of your program and use the predefined constants throughout the program. Then, when a version number changes, all you need to do is change the declaration of the constant. The following example illustrates this technique:

```
Public Const ProgTitle = "My Application Name"
Public Const ProgVersion = "3.1"
```

Note the use of the Public keyword, which makes these constants available throughout the application (assuming that their declaration is in a module).

Constants That Visual Basic Supplies

Visual Basic supplies a number of built-in constants for various activities. They are known as *intrinsic constants*. Color-definition constants, data-access constants, keycode constants, and shape constants, among many others, are available. Especially useful are constants correlating to a command's parameter information, such as the vbExclamation constant used for a MessageBox statement in previous chapters.

The constants that you need for most functions are described in the help system's topic for the function. If you want to know the value of a particular constant, you can use the Object Browser (see Figure 8.3). Access the Object Browser by clicking its icon in the Visual Basic toolbar, by selecting View, Object Browser from the menu system, or simply by pressingF2. You can use the list to find the constant that you want. When you select it, its value and function are displayed in the text area at the bottom of the dialog box.

FIGURE 8.3
The Object Browser shows you the value and function of most of Visual Basic's internal constants.

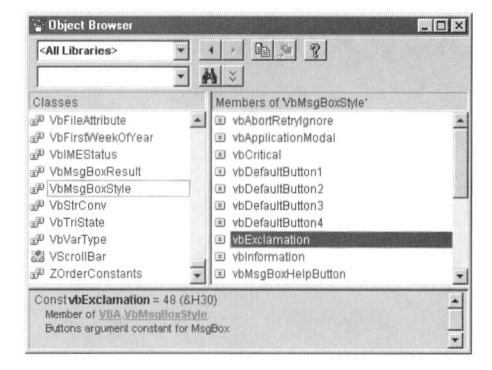

Creating Your Own Constants

Although Visual Basic defines a large number of constants for many activities, sometimes you need to define your own constants. Constants are defined using the `Const` statement to give the constant a name and a value, as illustrated in the following syntax:

[Public | Private] Const *constantname* [As *constanttype*] = *value*

If you think this statement looks similar to the declaration of a variable, you're right. As with declaring a variable, you provide a name for the constant and, optionally, specify the type of data it should hold. The `Const` keyword at the beginning of the statement tells Visual Basic that this statement defines a constant. This keyword distinguishes the statement from one that just assigns a value to a variable. In declaring the type of a constant, you use the same intrinsic types as you do for defining variables. (These types are defined in Table 8.2.) Finally, to define a constant, you must include the equal sign (=) and the value to be assigned. If you are defining a string constant or date constant, remember to enclose the value in either quotation marks (") or the pound sign (#), respectively.

A constant's scope is also important. The same rules for the scope of variables, which were discussed in the earlier section "Determining Where a Variable Can Be Used," apply to constants as well.

From Here...

This chapter provided you with an overview of using variables and constants in Visual Basic. In Chapter 11, "Managing Your Project: Sub Procedures, Functions, and Multiple Forms" you learn the fundamentals of writing the code that comprises the gist of your Visual Basic applications. For some more material on programming, refer to the following chapters:

- Read Chapter 9, "Visual Basic Programming Fundamentals" to learn more about the Visual Basic Language.
- To learn about the many different events available in the custom controls, see Chapter 12, "Microsoft Common Controls."

CHAPTER 9

Visual Basic Programming Fundamentals

In this chapter

Writing Statements   174

Using Assignment Statements   175

Using Math Operations   176

Working with Strings   182

Formatting Results   195

Although designing your program's user interface with forms and controls is important, most of the actual work is done with code. By code, I mean the sections of the program where you type statements and functions. You already know that forms can contain code, and you have seen how to access the code "below the surface" of a form's visual interface. As a reminder, consider all the parts of a Visual Basic program that can contain code:

- Forms
- Code modules
- Class modules
- User controls

The great thing about Visual Basic is that the language you write code in is both powerful and relatively easy to use. It is a direct descendant of the BASIC programming language, which has been around for many years. BASIC was designed as a language for beginning programmers, hence the name, which is an abbreviation for *Beginner's All-Purpose Symbolic Instruction Code*.

Don't let the "Basic" part of the name fool you, however. Visual Basic is a far more powerful language than the BASIC you may have already learned. The more recent releases have extended the language far beyond its primitive ancestry. Visual Basic has grown into a robust programming environment that can solve a wide variety of application needs.

This chapter looks at some of the fundamental concepts of programming in Visual Basic: writing program code, working with and formatting information, and so on. Chapter 10, "Controlling the Flow of Your Program Code," continues this discussion by examining how to control your program with loops and conditional statements.

Writing Statements

In the preceding chapter, "Using Variables to Store Information," you learned a little about variables and constants. You know what type of data they can store and how to declare them. But that is just the beginning of working with information in a program. You also need to be able to assign information to variables, manipulate that information, and use the contents of variables in other Visual Basic code.

To perform these tasks, you use code *statements*. Simply put, a statement is a line of code that makes the computer do something. Here are a few examples of the things you can do with statements:

Statement Type	Example
Assign a value to a variable	`sName = "Lauren"`
Call a predefined function	`MsgBox "Good morning!"`
Call your own function	`bSuccess = BuildBudgetReport("12/31/99")`
Assign object properties	`frmMain.Visible = False`
Make decisions	`If nTideHeight > 1000 then MoveOn`

The next several sections discuss basic assignment statements, mathematical operations, and strings. Later in the chapter, in the section "Formatting Results," you learn how to format numbers and other information manipulated by your program code.

Using Assignment Statements

After you declare a variable, the first thing you often need to do is to store information in the variable. This is the job of the *assignment statement*. The assignment statement is quite simple; you specify a variable whose value you want to set, place an equal sign after the variable name, and then follow it with the expression that represents the value you want stored. For example, the following line of code is the most basic type of assignment statement:

```
x = 5
```

The assignment statement tells Visual Basic to assign the integer value 5 to the space in memory represented by the variable x. Of course, you are not limited to assigning integer numbers. The expression following the equal sign can be a literal value, an expression or equation using some combination of other variables and constants, or even a function that returns a value. There is no limit on the complexity of the expression you can use. The only restriction is that the expression must yield a value of the same type as the variable to which it is assigned.

Table 9.1 illustrates several assignment statements.

Table 9.1 Types of Assignment Statements

Assignment Statement	Type of Expression
nNumStudents = 25	Numeric literal
sTopStudent = "June Thomas"	String literal
fAvgScore = nTotScore / nNumStudents	Mathematical expression
sSpouseName = "Mrs. " & "Tina Fortner"	String expression
sCapitalName = UCase$("Chris Cawein")	Return value of a function

You might have noticed that these statements look similar to the ones used to set the properties of forms and controls in the section "Referencing Forms and Controls from Your Code" in Chapter 3, "Visual Basic Building Blocks." Actually, they are the same. Most properties of forms and controls act like variables. They can be set at design time but can also be changed at runtime using an assignment statement.

You use a control property on the right side of a statement to assign its value to a variable for further processing or on the left side to change the value of the property. For example, suppose you have three text boxes on a form: txtLastname, txtFirstName, and txtEntireName. As a user types in the first or last name, automatically populating the txtEntireName box would be nice. One way to accomplish this feat would be to first store the information from each text box in a variable, as follows:

```
Dim sFName As String
Dim sLName As String
sFName = txtFirstname
sLName = txtLastName
```

You can then store the combination of the last name and first name values in another variable and use it to update the `txtEntireName` box, like this:

```
Dim sName As String
sName = txtFirstName & " " & txtLastName
txtEntireName = sName
```

Of course, because text boxes themselves can be treated as variables (via the control's default property), you can achieve the same result without having to declare any variables, as in this line:

```
txtEntireName = txtFirstname & " " & txtlastName
```

The preceding line of code is more efficient because it does not require dimensioning variables. However, when you are dealing with code that repeatedly accesses a property of a control (such as a `For` loop), sometimes storing a property in a temporary variable is more efficient.

Using Math Operations

Processing numerical data is one of the key activities of many computer programs. Mathematical operations determine customer bills, interest due on savings or credit card balances, average scores for class tests, and many other bits of information. Visual Basic supports a number of different math operators that you can use in program statements. These operations and the Visual Basic symbol for each operation are summarized in Table 9.2. The operations are then described in detail in the following sections.

Table 9.2 Math Operations and the Corresponding Visual Basic Symbol

Operation	Operator
Addition	+
Subtraction	-
Multiplication	*
Division	/
Integer division	\
Modulus	mod
Exponentiation	^

In Visual Basic, you use mathematical operations to create equations. These equations can include multiple operators, variables, and expressions, as in the following example:

```
(115 + txtAmount.Text) / 69 * 1.0825
```

Note that although the sample expression is valid, the preceding line of code does not do anything by itself. While you're reading, keep in mind that when you use these operators, the result will be going somewhere; for example, it may be assigned to a variable or displayed on the screen.

Addition and Subtraction

The two simplest math operations are addition and subtraction. If you have ever used a calculator to do addition and subtraction, you already have a good idea how these operations are performed in a line of computer code.

A computer program, however, gives you greater flexibility in the operations you can perform than a calculator does. Your programs are not limited to working with literal numbers (for example, 1, 15, 37.63, –105.2). Your program can add or subtract two or more literal numbers, numeric variables, or any functions that return a numeric value. Also, as with a calculator, you can perform addition and subtraction operations in any combination. Now take a look at exactly how you perform these operations in your program.

Using the Addition Operator   The operator for addition in Visual Basic is the plus sign (+). The general use of this operator is shown in the following syntax line:

```
result = number1 + number2 [+ number3]
```

`result` is a variable (or control property) that contains the sum of the numbers. The equal sign indicates the assignment of a value to the variable. `number1`, `number2`, and `number3` are the literal numbers, numeric variables, or functions that are to be added together. You can add as many numbers together as you like, but each number pair must be separated by a plus sign.

Using the Subtraction Operator   The operator for subtraction is the minus sign (-). The syntax is basically the same as for addition:

```
result = number1 - number2 [- number3]
```

Although the order does not matter in addition, in subtraction, the number to the right of the minus sign is subtracted from the number to the left of the sign. If you have multiple numbers, the second number is subtracted from the first, then the third number is subtracted from that result, and so on, moving from left to right. For example, consider the following equation:

```
result = 15 - 6 - 3
```

The computer first subtracts 6 from 15 to yield 9. It then subtracts 3 from 9 to yield 6, which is the final answer stored in the variable `result`.

> **TIP** You can control the order of operations by using parentheses. For example, the following line of code assigns 12 to the variable `result`:
>
> `result = 15 - (6 - 3)`

You can create assignment statements that consist solely of addition operators or solely of subtraction operators. You can also use the operators in combination with one another or other math operators. The following code lines show a few valid math operations:

```
val1 = 1.25 + 3.17
val2 = 3.21 - 1
val3 = val2 + val1
val4 = val3 + 3.75 - 2.1 + 12 - 3
val4 = val4 + 1
```

If you are not familiar with computer programming, the last line (in which the same variable name appears both on the right and left of the equal sign) might look a little strange to you. In fact, that line is not allowed in some programming languages. However, in Visual Basic, you can enter a line of code that tells the program to take the current value of a variable, add another number to it, and then store the resulting value back in the same variable.

Multiplication and Division

Two other major mathematical operations with which you should be familiar are multiplication and division. Like addition and subtraction, these operations are used frequently in everyday life.

Using the Multiplication Operator   Multiplication in Visual Basic is straightforward, just like addition and subtraction. You simply use the multiplication operator—the asterisk (*) operator—to multiply two or more numbers. The syntax of a multiplication statement, which follows, is almost identical to the ones for addition and subtraction:

`result = number1 * number2 [* number3]`

As before, `result` is the name of a variable used to contain the product of the numbers being multiplied, and `number1`, `number2`, and `number3` are the literal numbers, numeric variables, or functions.

Using the Division Operators   Division in Visual Basic is a little more complicated than multiplication. In Listing 9.1, you see how one type of division is used. This division is what you are most familiar with and what you will find on your calculator. This type of division returns a number with its decimal portion, if one is present.

However, this type is only one of three different types of division supported by Visual Basic. They are known as *floating-point division* (the normal type of division, with which you are familiar); *integer division*; and *modulus*, or *remainder*, *division*.

Floating-point division is the typical division that you learned in school. You divide one number by another, and the result is a decimal number. The floating-point division operator is the forward slash (/):

```
result = number1 / number2 [/ number3]
'The following line returns 1.333333
Print 4 / 3
```

Integer division divides one number into another and then returns only the integer portion of the result. The operator for integer division is the backward slash (\):

```
result = number1 \ number2 [\ number3]
'The following line returns 1
Print 4 \ 3
```

Modulus, or remainder, division divides one number into another and returns what is left over after you have obtained the largest integer quotient possible. The modulus operator is the word mod:

```
result = number1 mod number2 [mod number3]
'The following line returns 2, the remainder when dividing 20 by 3
Print 20 mod 3
```

As with the case of addition, subtraction, and multiplication, if you divide more than two numbers, each number pair must be separated by a division operator. Also, like the other operations, multiple operators are handled by reading the equation from left to right.

Figure 9.1 shows a simple form that is used to illustrate the differences between the various division operators. The code for the command button of the form is shown as follows:

```
inpt1 = Text1.Text
inpt2 = Text2.Text
Text3.Text = inpt1 / inpt2
Text4.Text = inpt1 \ inpt2
Text5.Text = inpt1 Mod inpt2
```

FIGURE 9.1
This program demonstrates the difference between Visual Basic's three types of division operators.

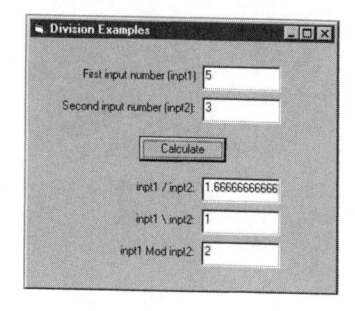

After you set up the form, run the program, enter 5 in the first text box and 3 in the second text box, and then click the command button. Notice that different numbers appear in each of the text boxes used to display the results. You can try this example with other number combinations as well.

Using Multiplication and Division in a Program As a demonstration of how multiplication and division might be used in a program, consider the example of a program to determine the amount of paint needed to paint a room. Such a program can contain a form that allows the painter to enter the length and width of the room, the height of the ceiling, and the coverage and cost of a single can of paint. Your program can then calculate the number of gallons of paint required and the cost of the paint. An example of the form for such a program is shown in Figure 9.2. The actual code to perform the calculations is shown in Listing 9.1.

FIGURE 9.2
Multiplication and division are used to determine the amount of paint needed for a room.

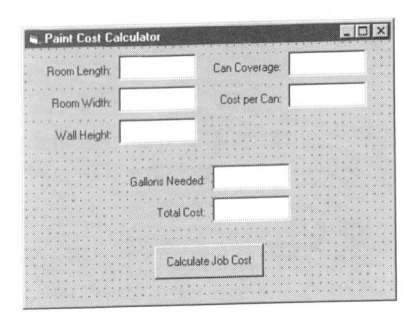

Listing 9.1 MATHEX.ZIP—Painting Cost Estimate Using Multiplication and Division Operators

```
Private Sub cmdCalculate_Click()
    Dim fRoomLength As Single
    Dim fRoomWidth As Single
    Dim fRoomHeight As Single
    Dim fCanCoverage As Single
    Dim cCanCost As Currency
    Dim fRoomPerimeter As Single
    Dim fWallArea As Single
    Dim fNumGallons As Single
    Dim cProjCost As Currency

    fRoomLength = Val(txtLength.Text)
    fRoomWidth = Val(txtWidth.Text)
    fRoomHeight = Val(txtHeight.Text)
    fCanCoverage = Val(txtCoverage.Text)
    cCanCost = Val(txtCost.Text)
    fRoomPerimeter = 2 * fRoomLength + 2 * fRoomWidth
    fWallArea = fRoomPerimeter * fRoomHeight
    fNumGallons = fWallArea / fCanCoverage
    cProjCost = fNumGallons * cCanCost
    txtGallons.Text = fNumGallons
    txtTotalCost.Text = cProjCost

End Sub
```

To test this code, start by creating a new EXE project in Visual Basic. Add seven text boxes to the form; set their Name properties to txtLength, txtWidth, txtHeight, txtCoverage, txtCost, txtGallons, and txtTotalCost. The first five are to accept information from the user; the last two will report information back to the user. You may want to add descriptive Label controls beside each text box.

Next, add a command button to the form. Change its `Name` property to `cmdCalculate` and its `Caption` property to `Calculate Job Cost`. Enter the lines of code in Listing 9.1 into the command button's `Click` event procedure. Save and run the program to see it in action.

ON THE WEB

This example is available on the Que Web site at www.quebooks.com.

Exponentiation

Exponents are also known as *powers* of a number. For example, 2 raised to the third power (2^3) is equivalent to 2×2×2, or 8. Exponents are used quite a lot in computer operations, where many things are represented as powers of two. Exponents are also used extensively in scientific and engineering work, where mathematical terms are often represented as powers of 10 or as natural logarithms. Simpler exponents are used in statistics, where many calculations depend on the squares and the square roots of numbers.

To raise a number to a power, you use the *exponential operator*, which is a caret (^). Exponents greater than one indicate a number raised to a power. Fractional exponents indicate a root, and negative exponents indicate a fraction. The following is the syntax for using the exponential operator:

```
answer = number1 ^ exponent
```

The equations in the following table show several common uses of exponents. The operation performed by each equation is also indicated.

Sample Exponent	Function Performed
3 ^ 2 = 9	This is the square of the number.
9 ^ 0.5 = 3	This is the square root of the number.
2 ^ -2 = 0.25	A fraction is obtained by using a negative exponent.

Operator Precedence

Many expressions contain some combination of the operators just discussed. In such cases, knowing in what order Visual Basic processes the various types of operators is important. For example, what's the value of the expression 4 * 3 + 6 / 2? You might think that the calculations would be performed from left to right. In this case, 4 * 3 is 12; 12 + 6 is 18; 18 / 2 is 9. However, Visual Basic doesn't necessarily process expressions straight through from left to right. It follows a distinct order of processing known as *operator precedence*.

Simply put, Visual Basic performs subsets of a complex expression according to the operators involved, in this order:

- Exponentiation (^)
- Negation (-)
- Multiplication and division (*, /)

- Integer division (\)
- Modulus arithmetic (Mod)
- Addition and subtraction (+, -)

Within a subset of an expression, the components are processed from left to right. When all subset groups have been calculated, the remainder of the expression is calculated from left to right.

In the previous example (4 * 3 + 6 / 2), the multiplication and division portions (4 * 3, which is 12, and 6 / 2, which is 3) would be calculated first, leaving a simpler expression of 12 + 3, for a total of 15.

An important note is that you can override normal operator precedence by using parentheses to group subexpressions that you want to be evaluated first. You can use multiple nested levels of parentheses. Visual Basic calculates subexpressions within parentheses first, innermost set to outermost set, and then applies the normal operator precedence.

> **CAUTION**
>
> Understanding operator precedence is crucial to making sure your programs evaluate expressions the way that you expect. For example, if you want to calculate the average of two test scores, you might write this line of code:
>
> fAvgScore = nTest1 + nTest2 / 2
>
> This line of code might look right, but Visual Basic's calculation won't be correct. Because the division operator has a higher precedence than the addition operator, the subexpression nTest2 / 2 is calculated first and then added to nTest1. This order is obviously incorrect. You can avoid this problem by using parentheses to control the flow of evaluation:
>
> fAvgScore = (nTest1 + nTest2) / 2
>
> This expression will be calculated properly by evaluating the sum of nTest1 + nTest2 first and then dividing the sum by 2. If value of nTest1 is 97 and the value of nTest2 is 85, the expression is evaluated as (97 + 88) / 2, or 185 / 2, which stores the correct result of 92.5 in fAvgScore. Leaving out the parentheses would have resulted in an undesired answer (following the rules of operator precedence) of 97 + 88 / 2, or 97 + 44, or 141.

Visual Basic's *Operator Precedence* Help screen has a good discussion of the topic, including how the precedence extends to comparison operators and logical operators.

Working with Strings

As you develop your applications, you use strings for many purposes. The better you manipulate the strings that you use, the more professional your programs appear. Visual Basic allows you to be quite flexible as you work with the strings in your programs.

Visual Basic supports only one string operator, the *concatenation* operator. However, several string functions are built in to the Visual Basic language, and you can use them to manipulate strings. Some of these functions are as follows:

- `UCase` and `LCase`—Change the case of text to all uppercase or all lowercase, respectively
- `InStr` and `InStrRev`—Find the location of one string contained within another
- `Left` and `Right`—Retrieve a selected number of characters from one end of a string
- `Mid`—Retrieves or replaces a selected number of characters in a string
- `LTrim`, `RTrim`, and `Trim`—Remove spaces from one or both end(s) of a string
- `Len`—Returns the length of a string
- `Chr` and `Asc`—Work with a single character's ASCII code
- `Str`, `CStr`, and `Val`—Convert a number or expression to a string, and vice versa
- `Len`—Finds and replaces within a string
- `StrReverse`—Reverses the order of characters in a string

NOTE Some of the functions in this list (such as `UCase`) return a `Variant` data type. For each of them, an identical function with a dollar sign ($) at the end of the function's name indicates a `String` type return value. I recommend using the $ versions (such as `Left$`) whenever possible because they are more efficient.

In this section, you examine how you can manipulate strings to give your programs a professional appearance.

String Concatenation

As stated previously, Visual Basic supports only one string operator, the *concatenation operator*. This operator, which is the ampersand symbol (&), combines two or more strings of text, similar to the way the addition operator combines two or more numbers. When you combine two strings with the concatenation operator, the second string is added directly to the end of the first string. The result is a longer string containing the full contents of both source strings.

The concatenation operator is used in an assignment statement as follows:

```
newstring = stringexpr1 & stringexpr2 [& stringexpr3]
```

In this syntax, `newstring` represents the variable that contains the result of the concatenation operation. `stringexpr1`, `stringexpr2`, and `stringexpr3` all represent string expressions. They can be any valid strings, including string variables, literal expressions (enclosed in quotation marks), or functions that return a string. The ampersand between a pair of string expressions tells Visual Basic to concatenate the two expressions. The ampersand must be preceded and followed by a space. The syntax shows an optional second ampersand and a third string expression. You can combine any number of strings with a single statement. Just remember to separate each pair of expressions with an ampersand.

N O T E If you are working on converting programs from an older version of Visual Basic, you might find strings combined using the plus sign operator (+). This usage was prevalent in earlier versions of Visual Basic, as well as in older BASIC languages. Although Visual Basic still supports using the plus sign operator to concatenate strings (in case this operator is present in older code that you are modifying), I recommend that you use the ampersand for this purpose. This operator helps to avoid confusion with the mathematical addition operation.

Listing 9.2 shows how to concatenate strings in a simple program to generate an address label. The fields from the different text boxes are combined to create the different lines of the address label.

Listing 9.2 MAILING.ZIP—String Concatenation Used in Address Labels

```
Private Sub cmdPrintAddr_Click()
    Dim sFName As String, sLName As String
    Dim sAddr As String, sCity As String
    Dim sState As String, sZIP As String
    Dim sTitle As String
    Dim sName As String, sCSZ As String

    sFName = txtFirst.Text
    sLName = txtLast.Text
    sAddr = txtAddress.Text
    sCity = txtCity.Text
    sState = txtState.Text
    sZIP = txtZIP.Text
    If optMr.Value Then sTitle = "Mr. "
    If optMrs.Value Then sTitle = "Mrs. "
    If optMiss.Value Then sTitle = "Miss "
    If optMs.Value Then sTitle = "Ms. "
    sName = sTitle & sFName & " " & sLName
    sCSZ = sCity & ", " & sState & "   " & sZIP
    Printer.Print sName
    Printer.Print sAddr
    Printer.Print sCSZ

End Sub
```

The form for this program is shown in Figure 9.3.

FIGURE 9.3
The address label application shows how strings can be combined for display or printing.

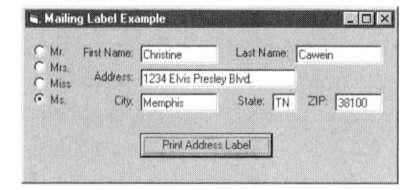

Determining the Length of the String

For many operations, you may need to know how many characters are in a string. You might need this information to know whether the string with which you are working will fit in a fixed-length database field. Or, if you are working with big strings, you may want to make sure that the combined size of the two strings does not exceed the capacity of the string variable. In any case, to determine the length of any string, you use the Len function, as illustrated in the following code line:

```
result = Len(inputstr)
```

You can use the Len function in a number of applications. In many cases, it is used to determine whether any characters appear in a string. If no characters exist, you might want to issue an error message or at least bypass any further processing.

Changing the Case of a String

Two functions can modify the case of letters in a string: UCase and LCase. The UCase function returns a string with all the letters converted to uppercase (capital) letters. The LCase function does just the opposite, converting the entire string to lowercase letters.

Although these functions may appear to be somewhat trivial, they actually are quite useful for a number of tasks. First, you can use the functions to properly capitalize names or other words that a user may enter. The code in Listing 9.3 capitalizes the first letter of a word and makes the rest of the word lowercase.

Listing 9.3 CASECONV.ZIP—Using *UCase* and *LCase* to Capitalize a Word Properly

```
Dim sWord as String, sProperWord as String
sWord="mIxEd CaSe"
sProperWord = UCase$(Left$(sWord, 1))
sProperWord = sProperWord & LCase$(Mid$(sWord,2))
```

NOTE The string functions return values, but they do not modify the input. Consider the following example with the UCase function:

```
Dim s1 As String
Dim s2 As String
s1 = "which case am i"
s2 = UCase$(s1)
```

After this code is executed, the variable s2 appears in all uppercase letters, whereas s1 remains unchanged, unless you put s1 on both sides of the assignment statement, like this:

```
s1 = UCase$(s1)
```

The case functions are useful, for example, when you are comparing user input to a predefined value or a range of values. If you convert the user's input to uppercase, you can compare it to an uppercase test string, as in the following example:

```
Select Case UCase(txtOperation.Text)

    Case "WASH"
      ' Do Something
    Case "RINSE"
      ' Do Something Else
    Case "SPIN"
      ' Do Something Else Yet
    Case Else
       MsgBox "Invalid Entry!"

End Select
```

In the preceding code, if the UCase function had not been used, the user would receive the Invalid Entry message even if he or she had entered a "correct" choice in lowercase or mixed case (Rinse, for example).

> **TIP** A common practice is to nest string functions within statements rather than use an extra variable to store each intermediate step. For example, consider the following Select Case statement, which uses a bunch of nested string functions to help with input validation. Users can come up with any capitalization they want to, but it will be handled by the code.
>
> ```
> stUserInput = InputBox$("Type Yes or No, please!")
> Select Case Left$(Trim$(UCase$(stUserInput)),1)
>    Case "Y"
>      MsgBox "Yes"
>    Case "N"
>      MsgBox "No"
>    Case Else
>      MsgBox "type YES or NO please!"
> End Select
> ```

Another Visual Basic function, StrConv, performs special conversions of strings. Most of the conversions it can perform are either redundant (converting to all uppercase or all lowercase, for example) or beyond the scope of this book (converting between different types of Japanese characters), but one of its conversion types is worth mentioning here. StrConv can convert a string to *proper case*, in which the first letter of each word is capitalized. The following code sample demonstrates this technique:

```
lblHeadline = StrConv(stHeadline, vbProperCase)
```

Examples of using UCase and LCase, as well as StrConv, are illustrated in Figure 9.4.

FIGURE 9.4
You can use LCase, UCase, and StrConv to modify the case of the letters in a string of text.

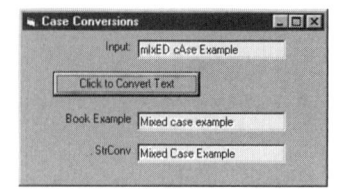

Searching a String

For many string-related tasks, the first programming requirement is to determine whether a word, phrase, or other group of characters exists in a string and, if so, where. The capability to find one string within another enables you to perform word searches within text. You can do these searches to perform a global replacement of a string, such as replacing the word *text* with the word *string* throughout a word processing document.

Another, more common, reason for searching within a string is *parsing* the string. For example, suppose you have an input string that contains a person's name in this format: "Dr. Stirling P. Williams, Jr." If you have a file of a hundred such strings, putting this information into a database with separate first and last name fields would be a little difficult. However, you can use a string search function along with a little program logic to parse the string into smaller pieces.

The function that enables you to search a string for a character or group of characters is the `InStr` function. This function has two required and two optional parameters. The required parameters are the string to be searched and the text to search for. If the search text appears in the string being searched, `InStr` returns the index of the character where the search string starts. If the search text is not present, `InStr` returns 0. The simple syntax of the `InStr` function is shown here:

```
chrpos = InStr(sourcestr, searchstr)
```

For example, the function call

```
Print Instr("I'll see you next Tuesday.","you")
```

prints a result of 10 because that is the position where the word *you* begins.

The first optional parameter of the `InStr` function tells the function the character position from which to start the search. This position must be a positive integer. If the starting position is greater than the length of the string, `InStr` returns 0. The syntax of the `InStr` function is as follows:

```
chrpos = InStr(StartPos, sourcestr, searchstr)
```

For example, the function call

```
Print Instr(7,"Pride cometh before a fall","e")
```

returns the value of 10, even though the first *e* in the string is at position 5, because the search starts from position 7.

The other optional parameter determines whether the search to be performed is case-sensitive (uppercase and lowercase letters do not match) or not case-sensitive. Setting the value of the comparison parameter to 0, its default value, performs a case-sensitive search. Setting the value to 1 performs a search that is not case-sensitive. This syntax is shown here:

```
chrpos = InStr(StartPos, sourcestr, searchstr, 1)
```

Note that with the optional parameters, you can write code that finds each successive search string in your text. The code in Listing 9.4 prints the words in a string that are separated by spaces. It works by taking the result of the `Instr` function and passing it back in to the `StartPos` parameter.

Listing 9.4 INSTREX.ZIP—Using the *InStr* Function to Divide a String into Words

```
Sub PrintWords(stInput As String)
    Dim inCounter As Integer
    Dim inFoundPos As Integer

    Const PARSECHAR = " "   'Space

    'If string is blank then do nothing
    If Len(stInput) = 0 Then Exit Sub

    'Start at the first character
    inCounter = 1

    'Search for a space
    inFoundPos = InStr(inCounter, stInput, PARSECHAR)

    'If a space is found print the word and keep searching
    While inFoundPos <> 0
      Debug.Print Mid$(stInput, inCounter, inFoundPos - inCounter)
      inCounter = inFoundPos + 1
      inFoundPos = InStr(inCounter, stInput, PARSECHAR)
    Wend

    'Print the remainder of the string
    If inCounter < Len(stInput) Then
        Debug.Print Mid$(stInput, inCounter)
    End If
End Sub
```

The input and results of this code appear in Figure 9.5.

FIGURE 9.5
Use InStr to find all the spaces in a string.

In Listing 9.4, notice that the InStr function searches from the first position in the string to the last. Visual Basic now includes a similar function called InstrRev to perform the search in the opposite direction. InstrRev works the same way as InStr, but the syntax is slightly different:

```
InstrRev(string1, string2[, start[, compare]])
```

The main difference is that the start parameter is located *after* the strings, not before. Using `InstrRev`, you can modify the code in Listing 9.4 slightly to come up with a new sub procedure, `PrintWordsReverse`.

```
Sub PrintWordsReverse(stInput As String)
    Dim inCounter As Integer
    Dim inFoundPos As Integer

    Const PARSECHAR = " "   'Space

    'If string is blank then do nothing
    If Len(stInput) = 0 Then Exit Sub

    'Start at the last character
    inCounter = Len(stInput)

    'Search for a space
    inFoundPos = InStrRev(stInput, PARSECHAR, inCounter)

    'If a space is found print the word and keep searching
    While inFoundPos <> 0
      Debug.Print Mid$(stInput, inFoundPos + 1, inCounter - inFoundPos)
      inCounter = inFoundPos - 1
      inFoundPos = InStrRev(stInput, PARSECHAR, inCounter)
    Wend

    'Print the remainder of the string
    If inCounter > 0 Then
        Debug.Print Left$(stInput, inCounter)
    End If
End Sub
```

Extracting Pieces of a String

Look at the code from Listing 9.3 again. In addition to using just the `UCase` and `LCase` functions, it also uses several functions to extract pieces of text from the original string.

You will find many situations in which you need to work with only part of a string. Perhaps you need to extract the first name of a person from the full name, or maybe you need to make sure that the information you're working with fits in the database field in which it needs to be stored. You can easily accomplish this task by using one of the following Visual Basic functions:

- `Left`—Retrieves a specified number of characters from the left end of a string
- `Right`—Retrieves a specified number of characters from the right end of a string
- `Mid`—Retrieves characters from the middle of a string

First, look at the `Left` and `Right` functions, as they are slightly easier to use. (By the way, none of these functions is hard to use.) To use these functions, you specify the input string and the number of characters to be retrieved. The syntax of these two statements is shown in the following lines:

```
OutStr = Left$(InptStr, NumChars)
OutStr = Right$(InptStr, NumChars)
```

When you use these functions, the number of characters specified must be a number greater than or equal to zero. If you enter 0, a zero-length string is returned. If the number of characters is greater than the length of the input string, the entire string is returned.

You will find, as you write programs that manipulate strings, that the Left and Right functions are often used in conjunction with the other string functions. This is illustrated in Listing 9.5, which retrieves the first name of a person from the full name. This function is used to print name tags for an organization's events. The function assumes that the person's first and last names are separated by a space. The function then looks for a space in the input text, and upon finding the space, it extracts the characters preceding the space and supplies those characters as the first name. If no spaces appear in the input string, the function assumes that only a first name was entered.

Listing 9.5   INSTREX.ZIP—Using the *InStr* and *Left* Functions to Extract a Person's First Name

```
Dim sName As String
Dim sFirstName As String
Dim nSpacePos As Integer

sName = Trim$(txtName.Text)
nSpacePos = InStr(sName, " ")

If nSpacePos > 0 Then
    sFirstName = Left$(sName, nSpacePos - 1)

    lblname = "Hello, my name is " & sFirstName

End If
```

Mid is another function that is used to retrieve a substring from a string, and it works in a similar manner to the Left and Right functions, but it has one additional argument. You can use the Mid function to retrieve a letter, word, or phrase from the middle of a string.

The Mid function contains two required arguments and one optional argument, as shown in the following syntax:

```
newstr = Mid(sourcestr, startpos[, numchars])
```

Startpos represents the character position at which the retrieved string begins. If startpos is greater than the length of the string, an empty string is returned. The optional argument numchars represents the number of characters to be returned from the sourcestr. If numchars is omitted, the function returns all characters in the source string, from the starting position, on to the end. The following are some examples of the Mid function:

```
Print Mid("Robert Allen",8)     'Returns "Allen"

Print Mid("Robert Allen",8,2)   'Returns "Al"
```

Getting Rid of Spaces

In Listing 9.5, you used `InStr` to find the first space in a person's name, assuming that it was the space between the first and middle name. Most long strings contain spaces in the middle of the string, which are necessary for proper spacing of words, paragraphs, and so on. However, you also may end up with spaces at the beginning or end of your strings, which often are unwanted spaces. These spaces typically occur when the user accidentally types a space at the beginning or end of a text field. They also show up when you are using a fixed-length string and the number of characters in the string do not fill the available space.

For example, the following calls to the `Len()` function each return a different number:

```
Print Len("Hello, world!")

Print Len("   Hello, world!")

Print Len("Hello, world!    ")
```

Most of the time, spaces don't do any harm except take up a little memory. However, when you combine strings or try to take action based on their content, unwanted spaces can cause all kinds of problems. For example, suppose you have two 30-character text boxes for first and last names. A user could inadvertently type three characters of text and then a bunch of spaces. If you need to concatenate the first and last name for a mailing label, the extra spaces are included. However, Visual Basic provides some string "trimming" functions to eliminate the trailing spaces.

To get rid of the spaces at the end of a string, you can use one of these Visual Basic functions:

- `LTrim`—Removes the spaces from the beginning of a string
- `RTrim`—Removes the spaces from the end of string
- `Trim`—Removes the spaces from both the beginning and end of a string

Each of these functions uses a similar syntax; you've already seen an example in Listing 9.5. The code in the following lines shows how to use the `Trim` function to remove the spaces in a mailing label example:

```
picMail.Print Trim(FirstName) & " " & Trim(LastName)
picMail.Print Trim(Address)
picMail.Print Trim(City) & ", " & Trim(State) & "  " & Trim(Zip)
```

Replacing Characters in a String

Now let me add a little confusion to your life. You just saw how the `Mid` function retrieves a piece of a string from the middle of a source string. The same keyword, `Mid`, is used to replace a part of a string. However, the syntax is quite different, in that you use the function on the left-hand side of an assignment statement in this case. When it is used to replace characters in a string, it is referred to as the `Mid` statement.

The `Mid` statement replaces part of one string with another string by using the following syntax:

```
Mid(sourcestr, startpos[, numchars]) = replstr
```

The `sourcestr` in this case is the string that receives the replacement characters. `sourcestr` must be a string variable; it cannot be a literal string or string function. `startpos` is the character position at which the replacement starts. This position must be an integer number greater than zero. `numchars` is an optional argument that specifies the number of characters from the replacement string being used by the function. `replstr` represents the string containing the replacement characters. This string can be a string variable, a literal string, or a string function.

The `Mid` statement preserves the original length of the string. In other words, if the space remaining between the starting position and the end of the string is less than the length of the replacement string, only the leftmost characters are used from the replacement string.

You will find a number of uses for the `Mid` statement in your programs. Remember the capitalization example in Listing 9.3? Using the `Mid` statement, you can perform the same function with the following code:

```
Dim sWord as String, sProperWord as String
sWord="mIxEd CaSe"
sProperWord = LCase$(sWord)
Mid(sProperWord,1) = UCase$(Left$(sWord,1))
```

In another program, I needed to eliminate any carriage return or line feed characters that were embedded in a string to keep them from causing printing problems. I used the `Mid` statement to replace these characters with a space. This example is shown in Listing 9.6.

Listing 9.6 REPLACE.ZIP—Using the *Mid* Statement to Eliminate Specific Characters in a String

```
'Replace Line feeds with spaces
    nFindPos = 0
    Do
       nFindPos = InStr(sInput, Chr$(10))
       If nFindPos > 0 Then Mid(sInput, nFindPos) = " "
    Loop Until nFindPos = 0

'Replace Carriage returns with spaces
    nFindPos = 0
    Do
       nFindPos = InStr(sInput, Chr$(13))
       If nFindPos > 0 Then Mid(sInput, nFindPos) = " "
    Loop Until nFindPos = 0
```

Note that the code in Listing 9.6 modifies the source string; that is, it actually changes characters in the string `sInput`. Visual Basic now includes the `Replace` function, which returns a string with the characters replaced. The syntax is

```
outString = Replace(inString, searchString, _
replacewith[, start[, count[, compare]]])
```

This function acts like a combination of the Mid statement and the Instr function. You simply pass a string, the characters you want to search for, and what you want them replaced with. Using the Replace function, you can rewrite the code in Listing 9.6 as follows:

```
'Replace Line feeds with spaces
sInput = Replace(sInput, vbCr, " ")
'Replace carriage returns with spaces
sInput = Replace(sInput, vbLf, " ")
```

One possible use of the Replace function would be to remove quotation marks from a text entry field before placing the field value into a database.

Working with Specific Characters

A string is made up of individual characters. Each of these characters has a numeric code, known as the ASCII code. You can use ASCII codes with numeric operations on characters, or you can use them to add untypeable characters to a string, as shown in Listing 9.6. You use the Chr function to return a character that corresponds to a specific ASCII code. For example, the following two statements both print HELLO:

```
Print "HELLO"
```

```
Print Chr$(65) & Chr$(69) & Chr$(76) & Chr$(76) & chr$(79)
```

> **NOTE** As with other functions mentioned earlier in this chapter, Chr has two forms: Chr() returns a Variant; Chr$() returns a string. ■

In the preceding example, typing HELLO is a lot simpler. However, you can't type some characters, such as line feeds and carriage returns, so you have to use the Chr function, as follows:

```
Print "Line 1" & Chr$(13) & Chr$(10) & "Line 2"
```

The carriage return/line feed combination deserves special mention. Frequently, you may find yourself using this combination to force a new line in a string, text box, or message box. For this purpose, Visual Basic has included an intrinsic constant, vbCrLf, so that the preceding line of code can be rewritten as follows:

```
Print "Line 1" & vbCrLf & "Line 2"
```

You also can use the Chr function to include quotation marks:

```
Print Chr$(34) & "This will be printed with quotes" & Chr$(34)
Print "this will not have quotes"
```

You can also use the Chr function to return any letter or number character. Table 9.3 lists some commonly used ASCII character codes.

Table 9.3 ASCII Codes for Some Commonly Used Characters

Code	Represents
8	Backspace
9	Tab
10	Line feed
13	Carriage return
32	Space
34	Double quotation mark (")
48	0 (the character for zero)
65	A
97	a

Asc is the companion function to the Chr function. Asc returns the ASCII code of the input character. The following code shows how Asc is used:

```
Print Asc("A") 'Returns 65
```

Strings and Numbers

A string value can actually contain numeric digits, as you can see here:

```
Dim sStringVal As String
Dim nNumber As Integer
nNumber = 99      'A number that can be used with math expressions
sStringVal = "16 candles" 'A string that cannot be used with math expressions
```

You may already know that some numbers are often treated as character strings. Zip codes and phone numbers are two such examples. However, sometimes you need to convert a number to a string variable to use it in a string function or to print it in combination with another string. Likewise, you sometimes need to use numbers contained in a string variable in a mathematical equation or a numeric function.

Visual Basic provides the Str function to convert a number to a string and the Val function to convert a string to a number. To convert a number to a string, you can do the following:

```
numstr = Str(inptnum)
```

numstr represents a string variable that contains the output of the function. inptnum represents the number to be converted. It can be a number, a numeric variable, or a numeric function. If inptnum is a positive number, Str returns a space in front of the number because Str reserves one character to contain a negative sign, if necessary.

To convert a string to a number, you can use the Val function, as follows:

```
numvar = Val(inptstr)
```

`numvar` represents a numeric variable that stores the output of the function. `inptstr` can be a literal string, a string variable, or a string function. The `Val` function first strips out any spaces from the string and then starts reading the numbers in the string. If the first character in the string is not a number (or minus sign), `Val` returns `0`. Otherwise, `Val` reads the string until it encounters a nonnumeric character. At this point, it stops reading and converts the digits it has read into a number.

> **NOTE** When building a string for display with concatenation, you can implicitly convert a number to a string, as follows:

```
Dim sOutput As String
Dim nWeight As Integer
nWeight = 145
sOutput = "The answer is " & nWeight & " pounds."
```

Formatting Results

When information, such as a number, is stored in a variable, it is stored in a format that you need in order to manipulate it with program code. However, often you need to change the format of information before displaying it or printing it on a report. Suppose, for example, you have several numbers stored in variables that represent dollar amounts. If the numbers are the result of a division, they may contain extra decimal places, and if you print them as is, they will probably not be aligned the way you want them.

In this section, you'll look at a few functions designed to help you format numbers and other information. In particular, you'll look at the `Format` function, which has been around a long time, and some more specific formatting functions introduced in Visual Basic 6.

Specific Formatting Functions

Visual Basic provides a number of formatting functions to format specific types of information. These functions are listed in Table 9.4.

Table 9.4 New Formatting Functions Introduced in Visual Basic 6

Function	Used For	Input	One Possible Output
`FormatCurrency`	Money	8675.309	$8,675.31
`FormatNumber`	Numbers	-5000	(5,000.00)
`FormatPercent`	Percents	0.1234	12.34%
`FormatDateTime`	Date/Time	"12-31 13:34"	12/31/98 1:34:00 PM
`Round`	Numbers	123.6	124

All the functions listed in Table 9.4 return string values. Simply pass the function an expression (which may or may not be a string value) and some optional parameters that control the output.

For example, `FormatCurrency` formats a number in currency (money) style. You can test the `FormatCurrency` function by opening Visual Basic's Immediate window (a project does not have to be running). Type the following line into the Immediate window, and press Enter:

```
Print FormatCurrency(1234)
```

The output looks something like this:

```
$1,234.00
```

Notice the dollar ($) signs, comma separators (,), and the appropriate number of decimal places associated with money. You can control these settings in the Currency tab of the Regional Settings screen in the Control Panel.

Optional Parameters   All the functions listed in Table 9.4, except for `FormatDateTime`, have the following optional parameters:

- `NumDigitsAfterDecimal`—Determines the number of decimal places in the output
- `IncludeLeadingDigit`—Determines whether a zero is displayed for fractional values (for example, 0.567 or .567)
- `UseParensForNegativeNumbers`—Determines whether negative numbers are returned with parentheses around them instead of the negative sign
- `GroupDigits`—Determines whether a grouping symbol (that is, the comma) is used in the return value (for example, 1,234 or 1234)

Many of these optional parameters, such as the `IncludeLeadingDigit` parameter, are known as *Tristate* parameters. A Tristate parameter has three settings, or states: `vbTrue`, `vbFalse`, and `vbUseDefault`. Well, really there are only two valid values: `True` or `False`. When you choose a setting of `vbUseDefault`, the function determines the `True` or `False` setting based on the Regional Settings in the Control Panel.

New Date Format Functions   The `FormatDateTime` function does not have any of the optional parameters listed in the preceding section. It simply accepts an expression representing a date or time, and a constant that represents one of the named date formats. The named date formats are listed later in the chapter in Table 9.7. Visual Basic displays a list of the constants as you type the function in the Code window. For example, type the following statement in the Immediate window:

```
Print FormatDateTime("20:10",vbLongTime)
```

The `FormatDateTime` function converts the military time value to the AM/PM time, 8:10. Notice that a string value is used for the first parameter. The expressions used by `FormatDateTime` must be able to be converted into a valid date or time; otherwise, an error occurs.

Two other functions added to Visual Basic version 6 allow you to retrieve the printed name of the month or weekday from any date expression. These functions are `MonthName` and `WeekDayName`, respectively. They both accept a numeric value and return a string. Optional parameters allow you to specify whether to abbreviate the output:

```
Print MonthName(12)        'Returns December
Print MonthName(12,True)   'Returns Dec
```

The `WeekDayName` function also has an optional parameter that allows you to specify the starting day of the week:

```
Print WeekDayName(1)       'Returns Sunday only if it is set to be
                           'the first day in Control Panel
Print WeekDayName(1,False,vbSunday) 'Always Returns Sunday
```

One point to keep in mind about these functions is that they accept only numeric values. To find out the weekday or month for a specific date, you first have to use other Visual Basic functions to determine the numeric values. For example, suppose you want to find out the day of the week for February 18, 1991. You can use the `WeekDay` function to return the day number and then pass it to the `WeekDayName` function, as follows:

```
Print WeekDayName(WeekDay("2/18/91"))
```

Rounding Numbers   A new function, the `Round` function, allows you to round a numeric expression to a specified number of decimal places. It has two parameters: the expression and the number of digits used in rounding. Test this function by typing the following statements in the Immediate window:

```
Print Round(202.5)_      'Returns 202
Print Round(202.56)      'Returns 203
Print Round(202.56,1)    'Returns 202.6
Print Round(202.56,2)    'Returns 202.56
```

As you can see, the `Round` function is easy to use. The only thing you need to remember is that your results may still need additional formatting if you always want to display digits after a decimal. In other words, no digits are printed after the decimal if you execute this line of code:

```
Print Round(202,4)_      'Returns 202 - no decimal places
```

Using the *Format* Function

The `Format` function is more versatile than the previously discussed functions. `Format` is a single function that can handle and return dates, numbers, and strings. Rather than relying on a bunch of optional parameters, the `Format` function uses a control string, which can represent either a user-defined or named (system-defined) format.

Formatting Numbers   The most common use of the `Format` function is to place numbers in a particular format to make them easier for users to read. To use the `Format` function, you specify the input value and the format, as shown in the following lines of code:

```
Printer.Print Format(GrossSales, "Currency")
Printer.Print Format(GrossSales, "$####.00")
```

To work with numbers, you can use several named formats. In all cases, you must enclose the name of the format in double quotation marks. Table 9.5 shows the named formats for numbers that are available with the `Format` function. Figure 9.6 shows how each named format displays several different numbers.

Table 9.5 Named Formats to Make Displaying Numbers Easy

Named Format	Description
General Number	Prints the number with no special formatting
Currency	Prints the number with a thousands separator, and prints two digits to the right of the decimal
Fixed	Prints at least one digit to the left and two digits to the right of the decimal
Standard	Prints the number with the thousands separator, and prints at least one digit to the left and two digits to the right of the decimal
Percent	Multiplies the number by 100 and displays the number followed by the percent (%) sign
Scientific	Displays the number in standard scientific notation
Yes/No	Displays Yes for a nonzero value and No for zero
True/False	Displays True for a nonzero value and False for zero
On/Off	Displays On for a nonzero value and Off for zero

FIGURE 9.6
You can display numbers in a variety of ways by using the Format function.

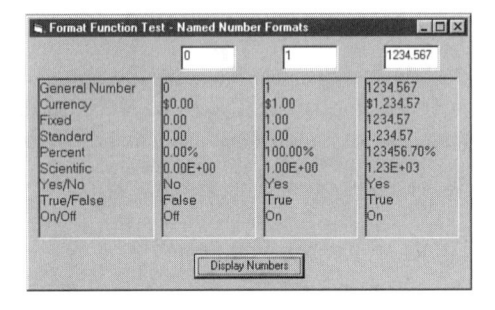

If the named formats in Visual Basic don't meet your needs, you can define your own formats. You specify a format by indicating where the digits of the number should be placed, if thousands and decimal separators are used, and by listing any special characters that you want printed. For example, the following line of code prints a number with four decimal places and a thousands separator:

```
Printer.Print Format(TotalDistance, "##,##0.0000")
```

The codes you use in specifying the format are defined in Table 9.6.

Table 9.6 Codes for Defining Numeric Formats

Symbol	Purpose	Meaning
0	Digit placeholder	Displays the digit or displays 0 if no digit appears in that location.
#	Digit placeholder	Displays the digit or displays nothing if no digit appears in that location. This causes leading and trailing zeros to be omitted.
.	Decimal separator	Indicates where the decimal point is displayed.
,	Thousands separator	Indicates where the separators are displayed.
%	Percentage indicator	Indicates where a percent sign is displayed. Also causes the number to be multiplied by 100.
E-, E+, e-, e+	Scientific Notation	Using E- or e- displays a minus sign next to negative exponents but displays no sign for positive exponents. Using E+ or e+ displays a sign for any exponent.

Formatting Dates Another form of data that is often a chore to print is dates. If you specify the Print method with a date, it is displayed in the default format for your system—typically something like 7/5/98. If you want to display the date in another manner (for example, July 5, 1998), you need to use the Format function. Table 9.7 lists some predefined date and time formats (see Figure 9.7).

Table 9.7 Named Date and Time Formats

Named Format	Description
General Date	Shows the date and time if the expression contains both portions. Otherwise, displays either the date or the time.
Long Date	Prints the day of the week, the day of the month, the month, and the year.
Medium Date	Prints the day of the month, a three-letter abbreviation for the month, and the year.
Short Date	Prints the day, month, and year—for example, 7/5/98.
Long Time	Print hours, minutes, and seconds along with the AM/PM indication.
Medium Time	Prints hours and minutes along with AM or PM.
Short Time	Prints hours and minutes in military time.

In addition to the named values in Table 9.7, there are many codes available that you can use to create your own date and time formats. For example, the following line of code prints today's date on the form:

```
Form1.print Format(Now,"mm/dd/yyyy")
```

FIGURE 9.7
Using named formats enhances the appearance of date information.

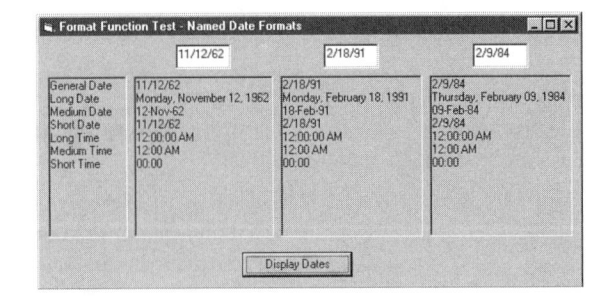

The Format function uses the output of the Now function and prints only the part represented by the letter codes. A complete listing of codes is available in the Help system, under the topic "User-defined date formats."

Manipulating Date Values

You just learned how to format dates. Visual Basic also includes several functions used for working with dates as values, similar to the way you work with numbers in an equation. This capability is possible because of the Visual Basic Date data type, which stores a date (and time) in a format that can be used by the various functions. As you may have noticed, the Format function and many other functions accept a date parameter that is of the type String or Date. However, some functions accept only a variable that is actually a date. To convert a string to a date, you can use the CDate function. However, be careful because an invalid string causes an error:

```
Print CDate("November 23, 1963") 'Works - returns 11/23/63
Print CDate("oops") 'Causes an error message!
```

To determine whether a string can be converted to a valid date, use the IsDate function. In the preceding example, this function would return True and False, respectively.

Extracting Parts of a Date   If you need to work with dates in an automated fashion, you might want to extract part of a date. Suppose, for example, you need to schedule a process to run every Wednesday. In previous sections, you saw that you can determine the weekday number by using the WeekDay function and determine the current date and time by using the Now function. As with many things in Visual Basic, you can perform this task in several additional ways. For example, you can use the Format function to retrieve the weekday number, as follows:

```
If Format(Now, "w") = 4 Then RunTheProcess
```

Visual Basic also includes functions to retrieve the day, month, and year. They, of course, are called Day, Month, and Year.

Working with Date Intervals   Two other useful functions for working with dates are DateAdd and DateDiff. You can use the DateAdd function to add any type of interval to a date. It returns the resulting date. For example, if you have a program that must always print a report for yesterday's date, use DateAdd to determine what that day is:

```
Dim dtYesterday As Date
dtYesterday = DateAdd("d",-1,Now)
```

The code simply tells the `DateAdd` function to add an interval of minus one days to the current system date. The same codes (d, w, m, and so on) you use with the `Format` function can be used to specify an interval type.

Whereas `DateAdd` allows you to add an interval to a date, `DateDiff` allows you to determine the interval between two dates. This capability is useful in scheduling programs, for example, running a process every hour, like this one:

```
Dim dtLastRun As Date
Dim dtNextRun As Date
Dim nMinRemain As Integer

dtLastRun = Now
dtNextRun = DateAdd("n", 60, Now)

nMinRemain = DateDiff("n", Now, dtNextRun)
While nMinRemain > 0
    Debug.Print "Start in " & nMinRemain & " minutes."
    nMinRemain = DateDiff("n", Now, dtNextRun)
    DoEvents
Wend

MsgBox "OK Done waiting!"
```

The `While` loop in the preceding code example causes the loop to continue as long as the interval between the current time and the next scheduled time is greater than zero.

The Year 2000 Much has been said in the news media about "the year 2000 problem" and how it will wreak havoc on computer systems. The problem is that many programs (and people) use two digits to represent the year, which could cause confusion. Does 2/18/00 mean 2/18/2000 or 2/18/1900? This question has no simple solution. You can't assume that 2/18/00 refers to February 18, 2000 if it really represents the birthday of a 100-year-old person.

In addition, many programs have files and calculations based on a two-digit year. Consider the following lines from a database table:

```
Date       amount
960101     123.45
960102     432.34
.
.
991231     442.00
```

In this file, dates are stored as integer numbers, making it easy to find a certain range of numbers. For example, to sum all amounts from 1997 forward, select rows in which the date is greater than or equal to the number 970101. However, suppose a date following the year 2000 is added: 000101. In this case, the program would fail.

Luckily, most of these problems can be taken care of fairly easily in the PC world. The issues in Visual Basic will probably not be with dates stored in a database, but rather with dates being entered by users who still in some cases prefer the two-digit year.

Consider the following code:

```
Dim dt As Date
dt = "01/01/00"
Debug.Print "Date is " & FormatDateTime(dt, vbLongDate)
```

The actual date stored in the variable is for the year 2000. From a programmer's standpoint, a decision must be made as to whether it is appropriate to continue to allow users to enter two digits for the year. If so, your program must include appropriate logic to convert the two digits to the correct year. In some cases, acceptance of two-digit years may no longer be acceptable, and users must learn to accept that fact.

In any case, with a little planning and added logic in your programs, you should be able to proudly state that your own Visual Basic applications are year-2000 compliant.

From Here...

This chapter provided you with an overview of programming in Visual Basic. You learned the fundamentals of creating code statements, as well as how to handle and format various types of information. For some more material on programming, refer to the following chapters:

- To learn how to control the flow of your program code and how it can make decisions, see Chapter 10, "Controlling the Flow of Your Program Code."
- To learn how to create your own functions, see Chapter 11, "Managing Your Project: Sub Procedures, and Functions, and Multiple Forms."
- To find out how to write a sharp-looking interface, see Chapter 18, "Proper Interface Design."

CHAPTER 10

Controlling the Flow of Your Program Code

In this chapter

Making Decisions in Your Program **204**

Working with Loops **209**

Debugging Your Programs **214**

Error Trapping **219**

In Chapter 9, "Visual Basic Programming Fundamentals," you learned how to create a number of programming code statements. Now, you will see how to enhance this knowledge by controlling the order in which parts of your program code are executed.

Two of the fundamental strengths of computers are their capabilities to execute instructions quickly and to make decisions precisely. In this chapter, you will learn how to take advantage of these capabilities in two very important ways: through the use of decision-making techniques and the use of loops, which allow portions of code to run a controlled number of times. Also, you will learn how to make your code react to errors that may occur during program execution.

Making Decisions in Your Program

In Chapter 9, you learned about a class of code statements known as assignment statements, which are used to set and modify the values of variables. Another group of statements is important for handling more complex tasks. These statements are known collectively as *control statements*. Without control statements, your program would start at the first line of code and proceed line by line until the last line was reached, at which point the program would stop.

One type of control statement is the *decision statement*. This statement is used to control the execution of parts of your program, based on conditions that exist at the time the statement is encountered. The two basic types of decision statements are If statements and Select Case statements. Each is covered in the following sections.

Using the *If* Statement

For many decisions, you may want to execute a statement (or group of statements) only if a particular condition is True. Two forms of the If statement handle True conditions: the *single-line* If statement and the *multiple-line* If statement. Each uses the If statement to check a condition. If the condition is True, the program runs the commands associated with the If statement. For example, the following two If statements perform the same function:

```
'Single-Line IF
If x > 5 then x = 0

'Multiple-Line IF
If x > 5 Then
    x = 0
End If
```

Note that indenting lines of code in a multiple-line If statement is a customary formatting practice. This indentation makes the code more readable when you use nested Ifs.

If the condition is False (in the preceding example, if x is *not* greater than 5), the commands on the If line (single-line If) or between the If and End If statements (multiple-line If) are skipped, and the next line of code is executed.

The Single-Line *If* Statement You use the single-line If statement to perform a single task when the condition in the statement is True. The task can be a single command, or you can perform multiple commands by calling a procedure. The following is the syntax of the single-line If statement:

```
If condition Then command
```

The argument *condition* represents any type of logical condition, which can be any of the following:

- Comparison of a variable to a literal, another variable, or a function
- A variable or database field that contains a True or False value
- Any function or expression that returns a True or False value

The argument *command* represents the task to be performed if the condition is True. This task can be any valid Visual Basic statement, including a procedure call. The following code shows how an If statement is used to print an employee's name only if his or her salary is greater than a predefined maximum value:

```
If cSalary > cMaxSalary Then Printer.Print sEmpName
```

Multiple Commands for a Condition If you need to execute more than one command in response to a condition, you can use the multiple-line form of the If statement. It is also known as a *block* If statement. This construct bounds a range of statements between the If statement and an End If statement. If the condition in the If statement is True, all the commands between the If and End If statements are executed. If the condition is False, the program skips to the first line after the End If statement. The following example shows how a block If statement is used in processing a market exhibitor's payments. If the exhibitor has a deposit on file, the deposit amount is moved to the total amount paid, and a procedure that processes a reservation is called.

```
If cDepositAmt > 0 Then
    cTotalPaid = cTotalPaid + cDepositAmt
    cDepositAmt = 0
    Call UpdateReservation
End If
```

Working with the *False* Condition

Of course, if a condition can be True, it can also be False; and sometimes you might want code to execute only on a False condition. Other times, you might want to take one action if a condition is True and another action if the condition is False. The following sections look at handling the False side of a condition.

Using the *Not* Operator One way to execute a statement, or group of statements, for a False condition is to use the Not operator. The Not operator inverts the actual condition that follows it. If the condition is True, the Not operator makes the overall expression False, and vice versa. The following code uses the Not operator to invert the value of the Boolean variable bTaxable, which reports an exhibitor's sales and use tax status. bTaxable is True if the exhibitor is to pay sales and use taxes, and False if he or she is not. The code tests for the condition Not bTaxable; if this condition evaluates to True, the exhibitor is not taxable.

```
If Not bTaxable Then
    cSalesTax = 0
    cUseTax = 0
End If
```

Handling *True* and *False* Conditions The other way of handling `False` conditions allows you to process different sets of instructions for the `True` or `False` condition. You can handle this "fork in the road" in Visual Basic with the `Else` part of the `If` statement block.

To handle both the `True` and `False` conditions, you start with the block `If` statement and add the `Else` statement, as follows:

```
If condition Then
    statements to process when condition is True
Else
    statements to process when condition is False
End If
```

The `If` and `End If` statements of this block are the same as before. The condition is still any logical expression or variable that yields a `True` or `False` value. The key element of this set of statements is the `Else` statement. This statement is placed after the last statement to be executed if the condition is `True`, and before the first statement to be executed if the condition is `False`. For a `True` condition, the program processes the statements up to the `Else` statement and then skips to the first statement after the `End If`. If the condition is `False`, the program skips the statements prior to the `Else` statement and starts processing with the first statement after the `Else`.

NOTE If you want to execute code for only the `False` portion of the statement, you can just place code statements between the `Else` and `End If` statements. You are not required to place any statements between the `If` and `Else` statements.

TIP If you have several commands between the `If` and `End If` statements, you might want to repeat the condition as a comment in the `End If` statement, as in this example:

```
If cTotalSales > cProjectedSales Then
    '
    ' A bunch of lines of code
    '
    Else
        '
        ' Another bunch of lines of code
        '
    End If 'cTotalSales > cProjectedSales
```
Adding this comment makes your code easier to read.

Working with Multiple *If* Statements

In the preceding sections, you saw the simple block `If` statements, which evaluate one condition and can execute commands for either a `True` or a `False` condition. You can also evaluate multiple conditions with an additional statement in the block `If`. The `ElseIf` statement allows you to specify another condition to evaluate whether the first condition is `False`. Using the `ElseIf` statement, you can evaluate any number of conditions with one `If` statement block. The following lines of code demonstrate how you can use `ElseIf` to test for three possibilities—whether the contents of the variable `fTest` are negative, zero, or positive:

```
If fTest < 0 Then
    lblResult.Caption = "Negative"
ElseIf fTest = 0 Then
    lblResult.Caption = "Zero"
Else
    lblResult.Caption = "Positive"
End If
```

The preceding code works by first evaluating the condition in the `If` statement. If the condition is `True`, the statement (or statements) immediately following the `If` statement is executed; then the program skips to the first statement after the `End If` statement.

If the first condition is `False`, the program skips to the first `ElseIf` statement and evaluates its condition. If this condition is `True`, the statements following the `ElseIf` are executed, and control again passes to the statement after the `End If`. This process continues for as many `ElseIf` statements as are in the block.

If all the conditions are `False`, the program skips to the `Else` statement and processes the commands between the `Else` and the `End If` statements. The `Else` statement is not required.

Using *Select Case*

Another way to handle decisions in a program is to use the `Select Case` statement. It allows you to conditionally execute any of a series of statement groups based on the value of a test expression, which can be a single variable or a complex expression. The `Select Case` statement is divided into two parts: a test expression to be evaluated and a series of `Case` statements listing the possible values.

How *Select Case* Works   The `Select Case` structure is similar to a series of `If/Then/ElseIf` statements. The following lines of code show the syntax of the `Select Case` block:

```
Select Case testvalue
   Case value1
      statement group 1
   Case value2
      statement group 2
End Select
```

The first statement of the `Select Case` block is the `Select Case` statement itself. This statement identifies the value to be tested against possible results. This value, represented by the *testvalue* argument, can be any valid numeric or string expression, including literals, variables, or functions.

Each conditional group of commands (those that are run if the condition is met) is started by a `Case` statement. The `Case` statement identifies the expression to which the *testvalue* is compared. If the *testvalue* is equal to the expression, the commands after the `Case` statement are run. The program runs the commands between the current Case statement and the next Case statement or the End Select statement. If the *testvalue* is not equal to the value expression, the program proceeds to compare the expression against the next Case statement.

The End Select statement identifies the end of the Select Case block.

NOTE Only one case in the Select Case block is executed for a given value of *testvalue*, even if more than one of the Case statements matches the value of the test expression.

> **CAUTION**
>
> The *testvalue* and *value* expressions should represent the same data type. For example, if the *testvalue* is a number, the values tested in the Case statements also must be numbers.

Case statements within a Select Case structure can also handle *lists*, *ranges*, and *comparisons* of values in addition to discrete values. Note the use of Case Is < 0, Case 1 to 9, and Case Is > 50 in this example:

```
nQtyOrdered = Val(txtQuantity)
Select Case nQtyOrdered
    Case Is < 0 'note use of comparison
        MsgBox "Order quantity cannot be negative!", vbExclamation
        Exit Sub
    Case 1, 2, 3 'note use of list
        fDiscount = 0
    Case 4 To 9 'note use of range
        fDiscount = 0.03
    Case 10 To 49
        fDiscount = 0.08
    Case Is > 50
        fDiscount = 0.1
End Select
```

Handling Other Values The preceding examples work fine if your test variable matches one of the conditions in a Case statement. But how do you handle other values that are outside the ones for which you tested? You can have your code do something for all other possible values of the test expression by adding a Case Else statement to your program. The Case Else statement follows the last command of the last Case statement in the block. You then place the commands that you want executed between the Case Else and the End Select statements.

You can use the Case Else statement to perform calculations for values not specifically called out in the Case statements. Alternatively, you can use the Case Else statement to let users know that they entered an invalid value.

Consider a simple form used to enter three test scores for a student into three text boxes. A Calculate button computes the average of the test scores and uses a Select Case block to determine the student's letter grade based on the average test score. Listing 10.1 shows the code behind the Calculate button's Click event.

Listing 10.1 SELCASE.ZIP—Using *Select Case* to Determine a Student's Letter Grade

```
Private Sub cmdCalc_Click()
    Dim nSum As Integer
    Dim fAvg As Single
    nSum = Val(txtTest1) + Val(txtTest2) + Val(txtTest3)
    fAvg = nSum / 3
    lblAverage = FormatNumber(fAvg, 1)
    Select Case Round(fAvg)
        Case Is = 100
            lblGrade = "A+"
        Case 93 To 99
            lblGrade = "A"
        Case 83 To 92
            lblGrade = "B"
        Case 73 To 82
            lblGrade = "C"
        Case 63 To 72
            lblGrade = "D"
        Case Is < 63
            lblGrade = "F"
    End Select
End Sub
```

To test this code, follow these steps:

1. Add three text boxes named `txtTest1`, `txtTest2`, and `txtTest3` to a form.

2. Add a command button named `cmdCalc`.

3. As with any form, you should add Label controls as appropriate. In this case, you are using two labels to display the results: `lblAverage` and `lblGrade`. Add each label to the form and set the `Caption` property to an empty string.

4. Enter the code from Listing 10.1 into the `Click` event procedure of `cmdCalc`.

5. Click the VB Start button.

Working with Loops

The other major type of control statement is the *loop*. You use loops to perform repetitive tasks in your program. The three main types of loops supported by Visual Basic are counter loops, conditional loops, and enumerator loops. Counter, or `For`, loops perform a task a set number of times. Conditional, or `Do`, loops perform a task while a specified condition exists or until a specified condition exists. Enumerator loops are used to perform an action on each item in a group of objects. Each of these types of loops is discussed in the following sections.

For Loops

A counter loop is also known as a `For` loop, or a `For/Next` loop, because the ends of the loop are defined by the `For` statement and the `Next` statement. At the beginning of a `For` loop, you define a counter variable, as well as the beginning and end points of the variable's value, and optionally the `Step` value, or the amount it is to be increased or decreased after each pass through the loop. The first time the loop is run, the counter variable is set to the value of the beginning point. Then, after each time the program runs through the loop, the value of the counter is incremented by the `Step` value and checked against the value of the endpoint. If the counter is larger than the end point, the program skips to the first statement following the loop's `Next` statement

> **CAUTION**
> If the beginning value of the loop is greater than the ending value, the loop does not execute at all. The exception is if you set up the loop to count backward, by setting the `Step` value to a negative number. In this case, the loop executes until the counter variable is less than the end point.

> **TIP**
> For ease of reading your program, including the variable name in the `Next` statement is good practice. Adding the name is especially important in nested loops.

> **CAUTION**
> Although you can use any numeric variable for the counter, you need to be aware of the limits of variable types. For example, trying to run a loop 40,000 times using an integer variable causes an error during execution because an integer has a maximum value of 32,767. The limits of each variable type are documented in the Help file in a topic titled "Data Type Summary."

The following code illustrates using a `For/Next` loop to print on the printer the numbers 1 through 10 and their squares:

```
For i = 1 To 10
    sTemp = i & " squared is " & (i * i)
    Printer.Print sTemp
Next i
```

The next example shows the use of a `For/Next` loop to reset the elements of three variable arrays to zero. Iterative processing allows these few lines of code to take the place of many. Using `For/Next` loops in conjunction with arrays in this manner is quite common:

```
For i = 1 To 12
    fMonthSales(i) = 0
    fMonthExpenses(i) = 0
    fMonthProfit(i) = 0
Next i
```

> **NOTE** As you can see in this example and in others in the book, arrays and For loops are often used together. A For loop provides an easy way of looking at or processing each element of an array because the counter variable can be used as the array index.

> **CAUTION**
> Never reset the value of the counter variable inside a For loop. Doing so can cause an infinite loop.

Typically, you will want your For loop to run through all the values of the counter variable. However, sometimes you might want the loop to terminate early. To do so, simply place an Exit For statement at the point in your loop where you want the loop to stop. The Exit For statement is typically associated with an If statement that determines whether the loop needs to be exited. In the following sample code from a trivia game, the player's score is examined after each question. If the score dips below zero, no more questions are asked.

```
For i = 1 To nNumQuestions
    Call AskAQuestion
    If bPlayerWasRight Then
        nScore = nScore + nQValue
    Else
        nScore = nScore - nQValue
    End If
    If nScore <= 0 Then Exit For
Next i
```

Do Loops

The key feature of a conditional loop is, of course, the *condition*. The condition is any expression that can return either a True or a False value. It can be a function, such as EOF; the value of a property, such as the Value property of an Option button; or an expression, such as numval < 15. The two basic types of conditional loops are the Do While loop, which repeats *while* the condition is True, and a Do Until loop, which repeats *until* the condition is True.

> **NOTE** EOF stands for End-Of-File. The EOF function returns True if you have reached the end of a file or recordset.

Using *Do While* Statements The keyword While in the Do While statement tells the program that the loop will be repeated while the condition expression is True. When the condition in a Do While loop becomes false, the program moves on to the next statement after the Loop statement.

You can use two forms of the Do While loop. The difference between the two is the placement of the condition. You can place the condition either at the beginning of the loop or at the end.

The first form of the Do While loop places the condition at the beginning of the loop, as shown in the following example. This code repeats the steps while records are available in the recordset.

```
'This code assumes the following:
        ' db is an open database with data
        ' rs is an open recordset with data
        ' lstdata is a listbox
        ' lblcount is a label

    Do While Not rs.EOF
        lstData.AddItem rs.Fields(0)
        lblCount = lstData.ListCount
        DoEvents
        rs.MoveNext
    Loop
```

By placing the `While` condition clause in the `Do` statement, you tell the program that you want to evaluate the condition *before* you run any statements inside the loop. If the condition is `True`, the repetitive statements between the `Do` statement and the `Loop` statement are run. Then the program returns to the `Do` statement to evaluate the condition again. As soon as the condition is `False`, the program moves to the statement following the `Loop` statement. Both the `Do` and the `Loop` statements must be present.

With this form of the loop, the statements inside the loop might never be run. If the condition is `False` before the loop is run the first time, the program just proceeds to the statements after the loop.

To run the `Do While` loop at least once, you must use the second form of the `Do While` loop. This form of the loop places the condition in the `Loop` statement. This placement tells the program that you want the loop to run at least once and then evaluate the condition to determine whether to repeat the loop:

```
Do
        lstData.AddItem rs.Fields(0)
        lblCount = lstData.ListCount
        DoEvents
        rs.MoveNext
Loop While Not rs.EOF
```

Be careful when using the loop in such a manner because statements between the `Do` and `Loop` statements will be executed without first checking the loop condition. For example, if the `EOF` function already returns `True` before entering the loop, an error would occur when trying to access the current record.

> **CAUTION**
> Do not put the `While` condition clause in both the `Do` and the `Loop` statements because doing so causes an error when you try to run your program.

NOTE If you are working on code that was developed by someone else, you might find a loop that starts with a `While` statement and ends with a `Wend` statement (Wend stands for "While-End," or the End of the `While` loop). This type of loop, left over from earlier versions of BASIC, works the same as a `Do While` loop with the `While` clause in the `Do` statement. Visual Basic still supports a `While...Wend` loop, but I recommend that you use the `Do While` type of loop because it is more flexible.

Using a *Do Until* Statement The `Do Until` loop is basically the same as the `Do While` loop except that the statements inside a `Do Until` loop are run only as long as the condition is `False`. When the condition becomes `True`, the loop terminates. As with the `Do While` loop, the `Do Until` loop has two forms: one with the condition in the `Do` statement and one with the condition in the `Loop` statement. If you place the condition in the `Do` statement, it is evaluated before the statements in the loop are executed. If you place the condition in the `Loop` statement, the loop is run at least once before the condition is evaluated.

A frequent use of the `Do Until` statement is in reading and processing data files. A loop starts with the first record of the file and processes each record until the end of file is reached. The following lines of code use a `Do Until` loop to load all the authors from the sample database BIBLIO.MDB into a list box:

```
Dim dbTest As Database
Dim rsTest As Recordset
Set dbTest = OpenDatabase("biblio.mdb")
Set rsTest = dbTest.OpenRecordset("authors")
Do Until rsTest.EOF
    List1.AddItem rsTest("author")
    rsTest.MoveNext
Loop
```

The loop does not execute at all if the condition `rsTest.EOF` (which signifies that the recordset is at its end) is `True` before the loop begins; this is an advantage of testing the condition at the beginning of the loop.

TIP Indenting your code inside a loop or other structure (such as an `If/Then/Else` block or `Select Case/End Select` block) makes the code easier to read. To indent a line of code, press Tab at the beginning of the line. When you press Enter at the end of the line, the indention remains at the same point. Try to match up beginning and ending points of code blocks, as has been done in many of this book's code examples.

As with the `Do While` loop, the `Do Until` loop can be written so that it always executes at least once. Consider the following example:

```
Dim I As Integer
I = 0

Do
    I = InputBox("Enter 0 to exit the loop!")
Loop Until I = 0
```

Even though the variable I is initialized to the value 0, the loop executes before the Until condition is encountered. Executing this example causes the input box to be displayed repeatedly until the user enters 0.

Enumeration Loops

Another type of loop supported by Visual Basic is the For Each loop. The For Each loop is considered to be an enumeration loop because it is used for processing (or enumerating) each member of a set of objects. As you will see in Chapter 16, "Classes: Reusable Components," a group of objects can be stored in a *collection*.

▶ **See** "Creating Classes That Contain Collections," **p. 373**

One example of a collection is the Printers collection, a built-in collection which represents each attached printer as an object. The following code uses a For Each loop to print the DeviceName property of all of the printers:

```
Dim objPrinter As Printer

For Each objPrinter In Printers

    Debug.Print objPrinter.DeviceName

Next objPrinter
```

The object variable objPrinter acts similar to the counter variable in a For Next loop in that it contains the current item being processed.

The For Each loop can also be used with an array, as in the following example:

```
Dim nNumber As Variant
    Dim MyArray As Variant

    MyArray = Array(3, 6, 9, 9, 5, 2, 3, 9)

    For Each nNumber In MyArray
        If nNumber > 5 Then Debug.Print nNumber
    Next nNumber
```

The code first creates a variant array containing eight integers and then uses the enumeration loop to list each integer with a value greater than 5.

Debugging Your Programs

As you write code and add objects to your VB programs, you should test them for bugs. A typical example of a bug occurs in a program that appears normal but does not work under all conditions. As a test, introduce an error now and debug it. Suppose that you want to use a While loop to print the numbers from 1 to 100 in the Immediate window. Start a new Standard EXE project, and enter the following code in the Form_Load event procedure:

```
Dim i As Integer
i=1
While i <= 100
    Debug.Print "Count=" & i
Wend
End
```

Run the program, and you should immediately spot the bug, which causes the same value to be printed over and over again. As a matter of fact, the erroneous `While` loop will never stop.

When you are working in Visual Basic's IDE, you know that you can click the Stop button to end the program, fix the code, and then restart the application. However, often you might want to debug your programs while they are executing. To do so, you need to use the Break button on Visual Basic's Debug toolbar, or press Ctrl+Break. If you are still running the sample program, press Ctrl+Break now. Notice that code execution stops (the numbers in the Immediate window are no longer printing), but your program is not completely stopped. The forms are still loaded, and the variables still contain their contents. You can press F5 or click the VB Start button to resume execution. If you display the Code window while the program is paused, Visual Basic highlights the next statement and places an arrow indicator in the margin of the Code window.

This paused state of execution is known as *break mode*. While you are in break mode, you can view or change variable values in the Immediate window. In some cases, you can even modify the code and continue execution.

TIP The easiest way to know if you are in break mode is to look at Visual Basic's caption, which will have the word [break] in it. You can also look at the buttons on the toolbar, or try to type in the Immediate window.

NOTE Correcting errors like this one *before* compiling the program is best. Because users are running outside the Visual Basic IDE, they have no way of pausing or ending an infinite loop other than killing the task from the Windows Task Manager.

In the example, you obviously "forgot" a statement to increment the counter variable `i`. Because the value of `i` never changes, the `While` condition will never become `False`. To fix this error, while you are still in break mode, modify the code as follows to include the missing line:

```
Dim i As Integer
i=1
While i <= 100
    Debug.Print "Count=" & i
    i = i + 1
Wend
```

Next, press F5 or click the VB Start button after adding the statement, and the program should count up to 100 and then stop.

NOTE You can't add some types of statements while your program is running. In these cases, Visual Basic informs you that you must stop and restart the application.

Stepping Through Your Code

Once you are in break mode, you have more options besides restarting execution. You can step through code line by line or skip statements entirely. Visual Basic has three methods of stepping through code, each of which can be performed from the Debug toolbar:

- Step Over, which steps through lines in the current procedure but not through lines in any called procedures (the shortcut key is Shift+F8).
- Step Into, which steps through lines in the current procedure and into any called procedures (Shortcut key: F8).
- Step Out, which runs until the end of the current procedure (the shortcut key is Ctrl+Shift+F8).

To demonstrate stepping through code, end the sample project, and then press F8 several times. Notice that the program executes a line every time you press the function key. It also highlights the next statement in the Code window, as shown in Figure 10.1.

FIGURE 10.1
When you are debugging, Visual Basic allows you to set the next statement by dragging the arrow in the margin.

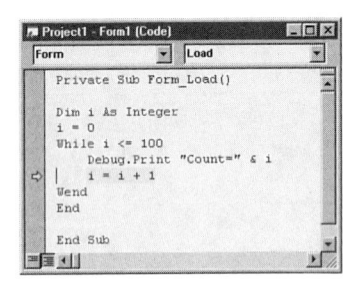

If you want to skip statements or execute them again, you can use the Set Next Statement feature. Simply put the cursor on the statement you want, and then press Ctrl+F9 or choose Debug, Set Next Statement. You can also drag the arrow in the left margin so that it points to the next statement you want to execute.

Try it now: Step through the sample program until the arrow is pointing to the line of code that increments the variable i. Next, drag the arrow back to the previous Print statement, and step through it again by pressing F8. Notice that you have caused the same value of i to be printed twice.

In the code example, you have been stepping through a While loop. Suppose that you don't care about debugging the While loop, but what happens before and after it. Stepping through the While loop would be a real pain if you did not have to, especially if it was to execute 1,000 times. In this case, you would need to use breakpoints.

Breakpoints are lines of code designated to put Visual Basic in break mode before they execute. By using breakpoints, you can run the program normally and then stop execution and begin stepping through code at the desired location.

To set a breakpoint, highlight the line of code you want in design mode, and then press F9 or choose Debug, Toggle Breakpoint. Visual Basic highlights the breakpoint, and a circle appears in the margin, as shown in Figure 10.2.

FIGURE 10.2
Breakpoints allow you to execute a program up to a certain line; you can then examine a variable value and continue running to the next breakpoint.

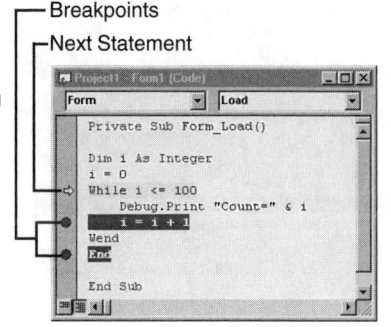

Now, test a breakpoint with the sample code. Set a breakpoint on the End statement by clicking it and pressing F9. Next, click the VB Start button (or press F5) like you are running the program normally. It should execute the While loop and then automatically enter break mode. Print the value of i (it should be 101) to verify that the While loop did indeed execute. Then press F5 to continue execution, and the End statement should stop the program.

Working in the Immediate Window

The Immediate window, also known as the Debug window, provides a way for you to enter code statements while a program is in break mode. To display the window, make sure that the program is in break mode, and press Ctrl+G. To restart the program, simply press F5 or step to the next line of code.

Some common uses of the Immediate window are demonstrated in Figure 10.3.

FIGURE 10.3
You can copy and paste statements from the Code window to the Immediate window to execute them manually.

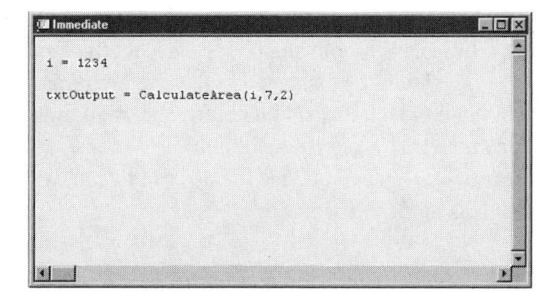

Figure 10.3 demonstrates assigning a variable to a value and calling a program function manually. You can also end the program prematurely by typing End into the Immediate window.

Tracking Variable Values

While you are in break mode, printing out variable values in the Immediate window is common practice. However, Visual Basic includes two special features for keeping track of variables during program execution. One of them is simple; just hover the mouse pointer over the variable name, and the value appears in a ToolTip. The other, more advanced method is to use the Watches window, as shown in Figure 10.4.

FIGURE 10.4
In the Watches window, you can watch and change variable values.

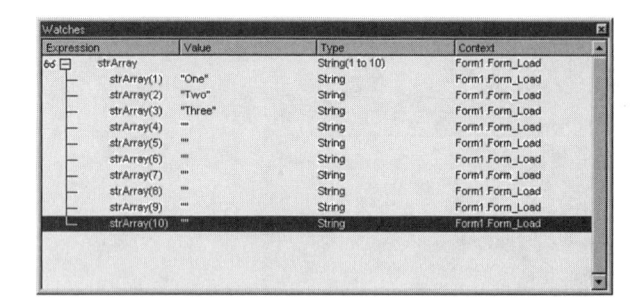

To monitor a variable in the Watches window, simply right-click the variable, and choose <u>A</u>dd Watch from the context menu. Try it now: Start a new Standard EXE project, and enter the following code in the `Form_Load` event:

```
Private Sub Form_Load()

    Dim strArray(1 To 10) As String

    strArray(1) = "One"
    strArray(2) = "Two"
    strArray(3) = "Three"

End Sub
```

While you are still in design mode, right-click `strArray` and select <u>A</u>dd Watch. The Add Watch dialog box appears, as shown in Figure 10.5. Click the OK button, and the Watches window includes an entry for `strArray`. Notice that the Value column displays <Out of context>, because the program has not started yet, and the array doesn't exist. Press F8 once to start the program, and make sure that the Watches window is visible. If it is not, choose <u>V</u>iew, Watc<u>h</u> Window. Press F8 several times, each time stopping to inspect the Watches window. The values for each element of `strArray` should be displayed in the window. You can even double-click a variable and enter a new value (which is just like entering an assignment statement in the Immediate window). Also note that variables with multiple dimensions (such as arrays or objects) are displayed in a tree-like hierarchy. This feature can be handy when you are dealing with complex objects such as an ADO recordset.

FIGURE 10.5
You set up watches in the Add Watch dialog box.

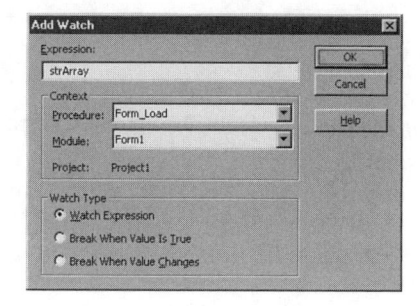

Error Trapping

As you are writing code, Visual Basic informs you of syntactical errors. However, once the program is running, you may encounter unexpected runtime errors in many circumstances. For example, suppose you try to open a text file that the user has deleted. When a compiled program has an error like this, an error message is displayed, as shown in Figure 10.6, and the program ends.

FIGURE 10.6
You can avoid cryptic error messages and ungraceful exits by adding error handling to your application.

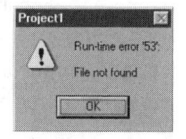

Although you cannot predict and write code for every possible type of error, `File Not Found` errors, such as the one in Figure 10.6, are fairly easy to handle. If you do not write code to work around the error, you can at least provide a message that makes more sense before ending the program.

Using the *On Error* Statement

The most common way to handle error conditions is to use Visual Basic's `On Error` statement. The `On Error` statement interrupts the normal flow of your program when an error occurs and begins executing your error handling code. A typical use is as follows:

```
On Error Goto FileOpenError
```

When this statement is executed, any errors that occur in subsequent statements cause Visual Basic to stop the normal line-by-line execution and jump to the statement labeled as `FileOpenError`.

Labeling Code Lines

This discussion brings up another new concept: line labels. If you have used an early version of BASIC, you may remember statements with line numbers, like this:

```
10 Print "hello"
20 Goto 10
```

Line labels in Visual Basic are similar to the line numbers of early BASIC. In Visual Basic, line labels can include text if you want, but each label must be unique. They are followed by a colon (:), as in the following example:

```
Private Sub Form_Load()
On Error GoTo FileOpenError
    Open "C:\NOFILE.TXT" For Input As #1
    Line Input #1, sData
    Exit Sub

FileOpenError:
    MsgBox "There was a problem opening the file. Call the Help Desk!"
    End

End Sub
```

In the preceding sample code, if the `Open` or `Line Input` statements cause an error, the statements starting at the label `FileOpenError` are executed, causing the message to be displayed and ending the program.

You should note a few points about the sample code. First, note the location and style of the error handling routine. It is usually placed near the end of the subroutine, with the label not indented to indicate a special section of code. Second, and more important, notice the `Exit Sub` statement after the `Open` statement. It is necessary to prevent the error handling routine from executing even when the `Open` statement is successful.

Controlling Program Flow After an Error

In the preceding code example, you simply end the program if an error occurs. However, you can handle the error in several (better) ways:

- Exit the subroutine after informing the user of the error, and allow the program to continue running with limited functionality.
- Resume execution with the next statement following the error.
- Provide a way for the user to correct the error and retry the offending statement.

You can also have multiple labels within a procedure and set the current error handler multiple times. For example, you can add a line to the code sample after the `Open` statement that specifies a new label, `FileInputError`. You can also turn off error handling with the following statement:

```
On Error Goto 0
```

The `On Error` statement goes hand in hand with the `Resume` statement. For example, this statement causes errors to be ignored and the program to proceed through each line of code anyway:

```
On Error Resume Next
```

You should use the preceding line of code sparingly because it really just ignores errors rather than handles them. A better use of `Resume` is to go to another section of code, as in the following example:

```
Private Sub Form_Load()

    On Error GoTo FileOpenError
RetryHere:
    Open "C:\NOFILE.TXT" For Input As #1
    Line Input #1, sData
    Exit Sub

FileOpenError:
    Dim sMessage As String

    sMessage = "There was a problem opening the file. " & vbCrLf
    sMessage = sMessage & "Press Retry to try again, or Cancel to quit."

    If MsgBox(sMessage, vbRetryCancel + vbCritical, "Error!") = vbRetry Then
        Resume RetryHere
    Else
        End
    End If

End Sub
```

The preceding example displays a message box with Retry and Cancel buttons. If the user clicks Retry, the code resumes executing at the label `RetryHere`, causing the `Open` statement to be executed again.

Determining the Type of Error

After an error has occurred, your code can find out more information about the error in several ways:

- `Err`—Contains a number that represents the error.
- `Error`—Contains a string describing the error.
- `Err Object`—Contains error number, description, and additional information. Also used to raise your own custom errors.

If you know how to recover from certain errors that may occur, you can use these objects to respond intelligently to a specific error. In the previous example, you received a `File Not Found` error, which is number 53. You can easily add code in the error handler to take appropriate action (that is, check another file) if the value of `Err` is equal to 53.

> **TIP** When you are writing an error handling routine with a message box, display the error number and description in your message box to make troubleshooting easier.

From Here...

This chapter provided you with an overview of programming in Visual Basic. You learned how to handle string manipulations, decisions, and loops in your code. For some more material on programming, refer to the following chapters:

- For more information about the Visual Basic language, see Chapter 9, "Visual Basic Programming Fundamentals."
- To learn how to create your own functions, see Chapter 11, "Managing Your Project: Sub Procedures, Functions, and Multiple Forms."
- To find out how to write a sharp-looking interface, see Chapter 18, "Proper Interface Design."

CHAPTER 11

Managing Your Project: Sub Procedures, Functions, and Multiple Forms

In this chapter

Using Procedures and Functions 224

Working with Multiple Forms 235

Managing Components in Your Project 237

Controlling How Your Program Starts 241

In Chapter 9, "Visual Basic Programming Fundamentals," you learned about writing code to make your computer programs accomplish various tasks. You saw how you can manipulate data and how control statements allow you to execute repetitive tasks and to execute statements selectively. However, creating a good, maintainable program involves more details than just writing code.

One of the tasks you need to be able to perform is to create reusable pieces of code and reusable program pieces so that you are not constantly reinventing the wheel (or the program, in this case). Another important skill is the ability to manage those various pieces of code and forms effectively. This chapter deals with both of these aspects of project management. First, you learn how you can use *procedures* to eliminate repetitive code in your programs. Then you learn how those procedures and other program components are added to your project. Finally, this chapter gives you a brief look at compiling and distributing your programs for others to use.

Using Procedures and Functions

As you create more and larger programs, you will often find yourself using the same block of code over and over in several places throughout your program and in multiple programs. Surely, there must be a better way to handle repetitive code than to just place it in multiple locations in your program, right? Of course, there is. The solution is to use *procedures* and *functions*. Procedures and functions are segments of code that perform a particular task and then return processing to the area of the code from which they were called. This means that a single procedure (or function) can be called from multiple places in your code and, if managed properly, can be used with multiple programs.

You have already been exposed to working with procedures even if you didn't know it. Each time you entered code to be executed by a command button (or other control) in response to an event, you were building an event procedure. Event procedures are called by the program when an event is triggered. As you might already know, you can also create your own procedures and call them when you need them. The procedures that you build are referred to as user-defined sub procedures (or subroutines). Although the code in earlier examples was entirely contained in event procedures, a "real" program might contain more code in user-defined sub procedures.

Working with Procedures

The key idea behind working with procedures is to break down your program into a series of smaller tasks. Each of these tasks can then be encapsulated in a procedure, function, or possibly a class. (Classes are discussed in Chapter 16, "Classes: Reusable Components.") Programming in this manner presents several advantages:

- You can test each task individually. The smaller amount of code in a procedure makes debugging easier and makes working on the same project with other developers easier.
- You can eliminate redundant code by calling a procedure each time a task needs to be performed instead of repeating the program code.

- You can create a library of procedures that can be used in more than one program, saving yourself development time in new projects.
- Program maintenance is easier for a couple of reasons. First, if code is not repeated, you have to edit it only once. In addition, separating key components (for example, the user interface and the database functions) allows you to make major changes in one part of the program without recoding the whole thing.

> **TIP** To make your code reusable, use comments often. This extra detail allows another programmer (or yourself after a long period of time) to see quickly the purpose of each procedure and how it accomplishes its task.

Creating the Procedure As with your program as a whole, the process of creating a procedure starts with design. You need to determine the task to be performed, what information will be needed by the procedure, and what information will be returned by the procedure. After you complete this task, you can start the actual coding of the procedure. You can start building a procedure in Visual Basic in two ways: starting from scratch or using the Add Procedure dialog box. Both methods are relatively easy, and the one you use is a matter of personal preference. Also, both methods require you to be in the Code window before you can build a procedure.

To create a procedure from scratch, place your cursor in the Code window in a location that is not within a currently defined function or procedure. For example, you might place the cursor after the End Sub statement of a procedure, before the Sub statement of another procedure, or at the top of the Code window. Figure 11.1 shows where you can start.

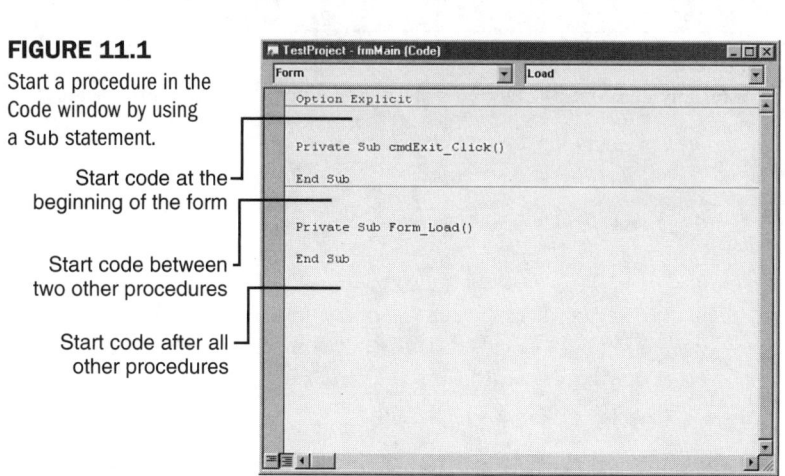

FIGURE 11.1
Start a procedure in the Code window by using a Sub statement.

Start code at the beginning of the form

Start code between two other procedures

Start code after all other procedures

> **TIP** Placing your procedures in alphabetical order makes finding them easier when you page through the Code window. However, they will always be in alphabetical order in the Code window's drop-down Procedure box.

You can create a new procedure in the Code window by following these steps:

1. Open the code for Form1 by clicking the View Code button.
2. Type the keyword **Sub**, followed by a space.
3. Type the name of your new procedure—**FirstProc** in this example.
4. Press the Enter key to create the procedure.

When you press Enter, three things happen: a set of parentheses is added at the end of the **Sub** statement, an **End Sub** statement is placed in the Code window, and the current object in the Procedure drop-down list of the code editing window becomes your new procedure name. Figure 11.2 shows these changes for a procedure named **FirstProc**.

FIGURE 11.2
The End Sub statement is automatically added when you define a new procedure.

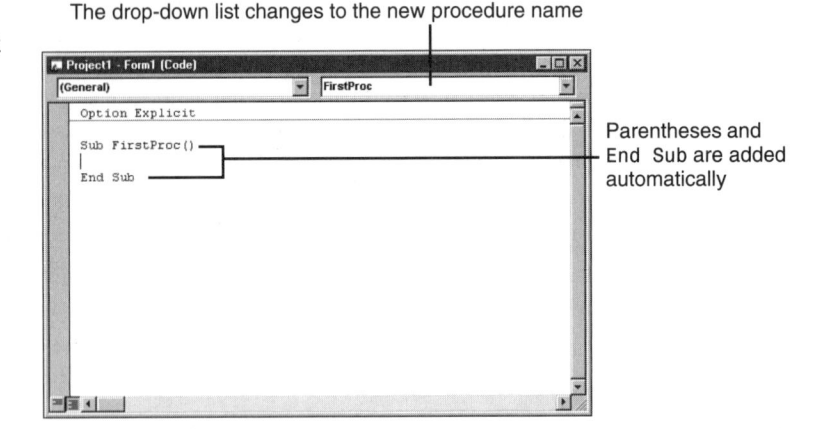

You are now ready to enter any commands that you want to run when the procedure is called.

The full syntax of a **Sub** procedure includes the **Sub** statement, the **End Sub** statement, and the procedure commands:

```
[Public | Private] [Static] Sub procname([arguments])
statements_to_be_run
End Sub
```

The **Public**, **Private**, and **Static** keywords in the **Sub** statement are optional and affect the locations from which the procedure might be called. These keywords indicate the scope of the procedure in the same way that they indicate the scope of a variable.

▶ **See** "Determining Where a Variable Can Be Used," **p. 166**

The other method of creating a procedure is to use the Add Procedure dialog box (see Figure 11.3). You access this dialog box by choosing Tools, Add Procedure.

FIGURE 11.3
Although typing a procedure by hand is faster, you can also create a new procedure in the current module or form by using the Add Procedure dialog box.

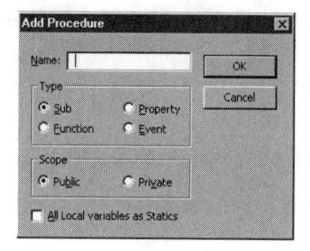

In the Add Procedure dialog box, perform the following steps to create the shell of your procedure:

1. Enter the name of the procedure in the Name text box.
2. Choose the type of procedure (Sub, Function, Property, or Event).
3. Choose the scope of the procedure (Public or Private).
4. Check the All Local Variables as Statics check box if necessary.

To create a procedure, you need to choose the sub procedure type. You are presented with four choices. A *function type of procedure* returns a specific value. These procedures are covered later in this chapter. A *property procedure* sets or retrieves the value of a property in a form or class module. An *event procedure* responds to an event in a form or class module; choosing Event in this dialog box inserts a forward declaration to a user-defined event that you will create. The Property and Event procedures are described in Chapter 16, "Classes: Reusable Components."

▶ See "Property Procedures," **p. 359**

After you enter the necessary information, click OK. Visual Basic then creates the framework of a procedure in the Code window.

Running the Procedure   After you develop a procedure, you need a way to run it from other parts of your program. You can choose from two methods for running a procedure: use the Call statement or use just the procedure name. With either method, you simply specify the procedure name and any arguments that are required by the procedure. (The arguments are the ones specified in the Sub statement when you defined the procedure.)

The syntax for running a procedure is as follows:

Call *procname*([*arguments*])

or

procname arguments

In either syntax, *procname* refers to the name of the procedure. This name is specified in the Sub statement that defined the procedure. *Arguments* refers to the parameters passed to the procedure. In the calling statement, the arguments can be literal values, variables, or functions that return the proper data type. This is different from the Sub statement in which all the arguments have to be variable names. Parameters, if present, must be separated by commas.

Now look at a brief example of a procedure that uses parameters. Suppose your program needs to log all its operations and errors to a text file. A procedure that handles writing messages to the log file, along with a date and time, could be very useful:

```
Sub LogPrint(sMessage As String)
    Dim nFileNum As Integer
    nFileNum = FreeFile
    Open "C:\EVENTLOG.TXT" for append as #nFileNum
    Print #nFileNum, Now & " - " & sMessage
    Close #nFileNum
End Sub
```

The following line of code calls the procedure. When calling a procedure, you can supply values for its arguments using either a variable, a literal string, or a combination of the two:

```
LogPrint "Error Opening file " & sUserFile
```

The `LogPrint` procedure is simple, yet it saves a lot of time in the long run. It makes the calling code shorter and more readable. In addition, if you ever want to change the format of the output file or change the destination of the log information from a text file to a database, printer, or pager, you have to modify only the `LogPrint` function itself.

> **CAUTION**
>
> Typically, you must include the same number of parameters in the calling statement as are present in the definition of the procedure. Also, the values supplied by the calling statement must match the data types expected by the procedure. Violating either of these conditions results in an error when you run your program.

At the start of this section, I listed two methods of calling a procedure. The following line of code calls the `LogPrint` procedure using the other syntax:

```
Call LogPrint ("The server was rebooted")
```

As you can see, the `Call` keyword itself is optional when calling the procedure. If you use the `Call` keyword, you must include the parameters in a set of parentheses. I recommend using the syntax that does not use `Call`. As you will see after looking at the examples in the next section, this approach makes distinguishing between procedure calls and function calls easier.

Passing Data to a Procedure   You can get information into a procedure for processing in two ways: you can define the variables as public variables that are available everywhere in your program, or you can pass the variables directly to the procedure in the calling statement.

For example, you could add a second argument to the `LogPrint` procedure that allows it to work with multiple files:

```
Sub LogPrint(sLogFile As String, sMessage As String)
    Dim nFileNum As Integer
    nFileNum = FreeFile
    Open sLogFile for Append as #nFileNum
    Print #nFileNum, Now & " - " & sMessage
    Close #nFileNum
End Sub
```

However, this approach means that if your program uses only one log file, you still have to pass the filename to the procedure each time you call it:

```
LogPrint "C:\LOGFILE.TXT", "Error Opening the file " & sUserFile
```

For this particular procedure, the `sLogFile` argument probably does not change much throughout the program. However, hard-coding it into the `LogPrint` procedure does not make much sense either, so a public variable would be the logical choice:

```
Public sLogFileName As String

Sub LogPrint(sMessage As String)
    Dim nFileNum As Integer
    nFileNum = FreeFile
    Open sLogFileName for Append as #nFileNum
    Print #nFileNum, Now & " - " & sMessage
    Close #nFileNum
End Sub
```

Before calling the procedure, your program needs to set the value of `sLogFileName`. The `Public` keyword makes it visible to all the other procedures in your program. The variable `nFileNum`, on the other hand, can be used only within the `LogPrint` procedure, as it should be.

If you are going to use the variables in a number of procedures and the procedure is specific to the current program, setting up the variables as public variables is the better approach. However, for the sake of reusability among projects, keeping procedures as independent as possible is a good idea. To do so, you should define all the necessary parameters to be passed to the procedure in the `Sub` statement and pass the parameters in the calling statement. Additionally, all variables used by the procedure should be `Private` (local) variables that are declared within the procedure itself.

The parameters used by a procedure can provide two-way communication between the procedure and the calling program. The procedure can use information in the parameters to perform a calculation and then pass the results back to the calling program in another parameter.

For example, the following procedure gets the height and width of a rectangle from the parameters list and then calculates the area and perimeter of the rectangle. These values are returned through the parameters list:

```
Sub CalcRectangle(nWidth as Integer, nHeight as Integer, _
                  nArea as Integer, nPerimeter as Integer)
    nArea = nWidth * nHeight
    nPerimeter = 2 * (nWidth + nHeight)
End Sub
```

The procedure can be called by using variables for both the input and output parameters, as follows:

```
nWid = 5
nHgt = 5
nArea = 0
nPerm = 0
CalcRectangle nWid, nHgt, nArea, nPerm
```

It can also be called by using literal values for the input parameters and variables for the output parameters:

```
nArea = 0
nPerm = 0
CalcRectangle 4, 10, nArea, nPerm
```

Passing parameters to a procedure in this way is known as *passing by reference*. In this case, the variable name passed to the procedure and the variable name used in the procedure both refer to (reference) the same location in memory. When entering a function or procedure declaration, you can explicitly indicate "by reference" parameters with the ByRef keyword, as in the following example:

```
Sub ChangeString(ByRef AnyString As String)
    AnyString = "After"
End Sub

Dim sSampleString As String
sSampleString = "Before"
ChangeString sSampleString
```

The first three lines of code define a simple subroutine that changes the contents of a string passed as a parameter. The ByRef keyword indicates that any changes made to the parameter will be reflected in the variable passed to the procedure. In other words, changing the value of AnyString within the procedure causes the value of sSampleString to be changed as well. This capability enables the procedure to modify the value that is then passed back to the calling code.

You can also pass a parameter to a procedure *by value*. This approach causes the procedure to use a *copy* of the information that was passed to it, which prevents the procedure code from modifying the value used by the calling program. By default, when you declare a parameter for a procedure, the passing by reference approach is used. To modify this behavior, you must explicitly tell Visual Basic to pass the parameter by value. Do so by placing the ByVal keyword in the parameter list before each variable that is to be passed by value, as illustrated in the following code:

```
Sub CalcRectangle(ByVal nWidth As Integer, ByVal nHeight As Integer, _
        _nArea, nPerimeter As Integer)
```

> **CAUTION**
> If you are passing parameters by reference, you need to explicitly declare the variable in the calling program and in the procedure, and you need to be sure that the variable types are the same.

Exiting a Procedure Early   As your programs, and therefore your procedures, grow in complexity, sometimes you might not need to execute all the commands in the procedure. If you need to exit the procedure before all the commands have been executed, you can use the Exit Sub statement.

One way to use the Exit Sub statement is in the beginning of the procedure in a routine that checks parameters for proper values. If any of the parameters passed to procedure are the wrong type or have values that could cause a problem for the procedure, use Exit Sub to terminate the procedure before the error occurs. Using the statement this way is a type of *data validation*. The following code modifies the previous area calculation code to perform this check:

```
Sub CalcRectangle(nWidth as Integer, nHeight as Integer, nArea as Integer, _
                  nPerimeter as Integer)
If nWidth <= 0 Or nHeight <= 0 Then
    Exit Sub
    End If
    nArea = nWidth * nHeight
    nPerimeter = 2 * (nWidth + nHeight)
End Sub
```

Working with Functions

Functions are similar to procedures, with one key difference: they return a value. This value can be assigned to a variable or used in expressions. Visual Basic offers a number of built-in functions that you can use, such as Abs, which returns the absolute value of a number, or Left, which returns a specified number of characters from the left end of a string. You can build your own functions as well.

To build a function, you have the same two choices you had in building a procedure—starting from scratch or using the Add Procedure dialog box. To start from scratch, select the place in the Code window where you want the function to start and then enter the keyword Function followed by the name of the function. The naming conventions for functions are the same as those for procedures. To use the Add Procedure dialog box, just select the Function Type option button in the dialog box. Either method creates the shell of a function just as it does for a procedure. An example of this shell is shown in the following lines of code:

```
Public Function NumAverage()

End Function
```

Although the first line is an acceptable function declaration, most of the time you will define the type of value that will be returned by the function. You define this function type like you define variable types in a Dim statement—by using the As keyword followed by the variable type. This function type declaration follows the parentheses that enclose the parameter declaration. In addition, you will typically declare the parameters that are passed to the function in the declaration statement. A more complete declaration statement is shown in the following line:

```
Public Function NumAverage(inpt1 As Single, inpt2 As Single) As Single
```

The other key difference between building a function and a procedure is that you assign a value to the function name somewhere within the code of the function. This value must be of the same type as specified in the function declaration. This is shown in the second line of the following code:

```
Public Function NumAverage(inpt1 As Single, inpt2 As Single) As Single
    NumAverage = (inpt1 + inpt2) / 2
End Function
```

> **NOTE** Although your function code can assign a value to the function multiple times, only the last value assigned before the end (or exit) of the function is returned.

When you call a function, you typically assign its return value to a variable in your program, or use the value in a conditional statement as shown here:

```
'Assigning a function to a variable
fAvgNum = NumAverage(25, 15)

'Using a function in a conditional expression
If NumAverage(num1, num2) > 20 Then MsgBox "What an average!"
```

> **NOTE** If you need your function to simply perform a task (opening a database, for example), you can call the function the same way that you would call a procedure, throwing away the return value.

ON THE WEB
There are a number of functions built and demonstrated in the FUNCDEMO.VBP project, which you can download from www.mcp.com/info.

Determining the Scope of Procedures and Functions

When you create a procedure (or function), you might want to limit where it can be used and how resources are allocated to make its code available to other parts of your program. Where a procedure can be called from is referred to as the *scope* of the procedure.

Procedures can be defined in either of two ways: as *public procedures* or as *private procedures*. Which of these keywords you use in the Sub statement determines which other procedures or programs have access to your procedure.

> **NOTE** The scope of procedures and functions is related to the scope of variables, which is discussed in the section titled "Determining Where a Variable Can Be Used" in Chapter 9, "Using Variables to Store Information."

▶ See "Determining Where a Variable Can Be Used," **p. 166**

Going Public   If you want to have your procedure or function available throughout your program, you need to use the Public keyword when you define the procedure. Using the Public keyword allows a procedure defined in one form or module to be called from another form or module. However, you have to be careful with the names of public procedures because each public procedure must have a name that is unique throughout the current scope.

If you omit the keywords Public and Private from the Sub statement, the procedure is set up by default as a public procedure.

Keeping the Procedure Private   Using the `Private` keyword in the `Sub` statement lets the procedure be accessed from only the form or module in which it is defined. This approach, of course, poses advantages and disadvantages. One advantage is that a private procedure is resident in memory only while the module in which it is stored is loaded, conserving system resources. A disadvantage is that the procedure is not accessible from other modules.

When working with event procedures in other chapters, you might have noticed that they are, by default, private procedures. They are private because, typically, controls are not accessed outside the form on which they reside. This is an example of *information hiding*, or *encapsulation*, a technique used in object-oriented programming. If you are sharing a module with a team of developers, you could define the functions they call as public, while the internal procedures they don't need to know about remain private.

Preserving Variables   Typically, when a procedure is executed, the variables it uses are created, used in the procedure, and then destroyed when the procedure is terminated. However, sometimes you might want to preserve the values of the variables for future calls to the procedure. You can handle this task by using the `Static` keyword. This keyword can be applied to the declaration of the variables in the procedure or in the declaration of the procedure itself.

When `Static` is used in a variable declaration, only the variables included in the `Static` statement are preserved. If you use the `Static` keyword in the procedure declaration, all the variables in the procedure are preserved. For example, a procedure that prints a report header on the printer may keep track of the current page number. In the following code example, the value of the static variable `nPageNum` is retained each time the procedure is run:

```
Public Sub PrintHeader()
    Static nPageNum As Integer
    nPageNum = nPageNum + 1
    Printer.Print "FORTNER MASONRY ANNUAL EARNINGS REPORT"
    Printer.Print Date
    Printer.Print "Page " & nPageNum
    Printer.Print
End Sub
```

> **TIP**   For efficiency's sake, it's important to place your procedures in the appropriate scope. Giving a procedure a scope that is too broad (for example, making a procedure public when it only needs to be private) wastes valuable system resources. If you create a public procedure, Visual Basic must allocate appropriate resources to make it available to all parts of your program. Using the `Static` keyword to force a procedure to "remember" its local variables causes an extra allocation of resources as well. In general, you should make procedures private if possible, and avoid the use of static variables as well. If you use this approach, Visual Basic can manage memory more efficiently because it is free to unload the various sections of code as needed.

Reusing Functions and Procedures

You can create a procedure in either of two places: a form or a module. Where you place the procedure depends on where you need to use it and what its purpose is. If the procedure is specific to a form or modifies the properties of the form or its associated controls, you should probably place the procedure in the form itself.

If, on the other hand, you are using the procedure with multiple forms in your program or have a generic procedure used by multiple programs, you should place it in a module. The storage location of your procedure is determined by where you create it. If you want, you can move a procedure from a form to a module or vice versa using cut-and-paste editing or even drag-and-drop editing.

Storing a Procedure in a Form File   To create a procedure in a form file, you just need to choose the form from the Project window and then access the code for the form. You do so either by double-clicking the form itself (or any control) or choosing the View Code button in the Project window (see Figure 11.4). After the Code window appears, you create a procedure as described in the earlier section "Creating the Procedure."

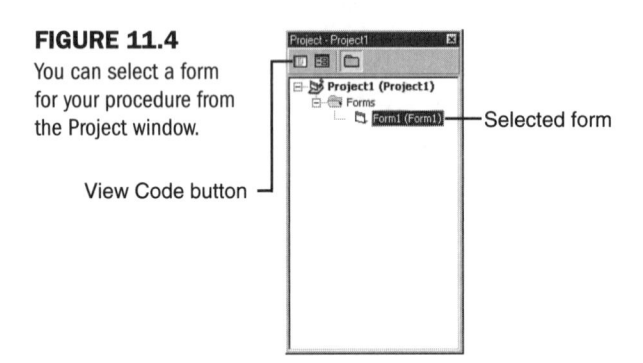

FIGURE 11.4
You can select a form for your procedure from the Project window.

View Code button

Selected form

Using a Module File for Procedures   A module file contains only code—no form elements or events. If you already have a module file in your project, you can create a new procedure by selecting the file, opening the Code window, and then using the steps listed earlier to build the procedure.

> **TIP**   Double-clicking the module name in the Project window automatically opens the Code window for the module.

If you don't have a module file in your project, or if you want to use a new module, you can create a module by selecting Project, Add Module. You can also create a new module by clicking the arrow on the Add Form button in the toolbar and then choosing Module from the drop-down menu. Either way, you are presented with the Add Module dialog box; select the Module icon and click Open. A new module is created, and the Code window appears for you to begin editing. When you save your project or exit Visual Basic, you are asked for a filename for the module file.

> **NOTE** The toolbar button for adding new forms and modules is a drop-down button, which means clicking on the arrow gives you a list of items. After an item has been selected, the icon on the button changes.

Working with Multiple Forms

Although some programs you write will be simple enough that you can use a single form, most will be made up of multiple forms. One reason for this is the limitation of the amount of space on a single form. Another, more important, reason is that you will want to use multiple forms in your program to separate program tasks logically. For example, if you have a task in your program that is not performed often, putting it onto a separate form makes more sense than trying to squeeze it onto a single form with everything else. Also, by loading and unloading forms as you need them, you can save system resources. In other words, your program takes up as little space as possible while running.

Adding New Forms to Your Program

When Visual Basic first starts a new project, typically it loads one blank form, as shown in Figure 11.5. As you design your program, you add controls to this form and write code to handle events that occur on the form.

FIGURE 11.5
Visual Basic starts a new project with a single blank form.

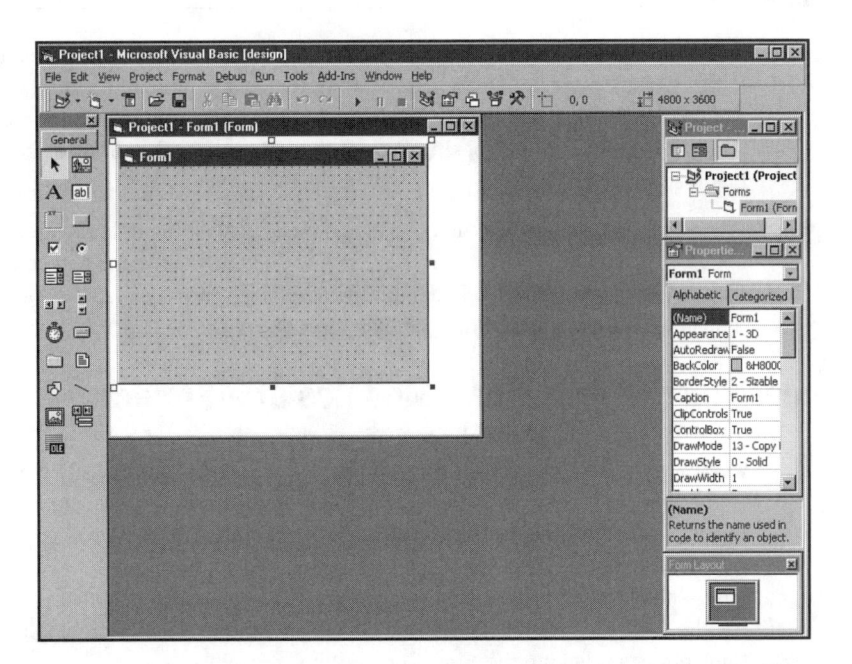

At some point in your design, you may decide that you need one or more additional forms to handle a new task or provide space to relieve the crowding on the initial form. Adding a new form is simple. You can either click the Add Form button or select Project, Add Form. This action places a new blank form on the screen. This form looks just like your first form initially did. If you did not rename your first form from the default of Form1, the new form is named Form2 (or Form3, Form4, and so on). Otherwise, the new form is named Form1.

> **TIP** You can add files, forms, or modules from a pop-up menu by right-clicking within the Project window.

After you add a new form, you can place controls on it and write code for its events, just like for the initial form. You also need to be able to access the new form from other forms in your program. Access is handled through the Load and Unload statements and the Show and Hide methods of the form object.

▶ See "Displaying a Form," **p. 55**

Adding Code Modules to a Project

As you write more code to handle more events and more tasks, you may often find that you need to access the same procedure from a number of different places on a form or from multiple forms. If this is the case, storing the procedure in a module file makes sense.

> **TIP** If you have a library of common functions, such as printing routines, keep them in a separate module file so that you can easily add the library to different projects.

Again, a module file contains only Visual Basic code; it does not contain any controls, graphics, or other visual information. When you want to add a module file to hold your procedures, you can do so either by clicking the arrow on the Add Form button and choosing Module from the drop-down menu, or by choosing Project, Add Module. Either of these actions adds a new module to your project and places you in the Code window for the module (see Figure 11.6).

When you first open a new module, Visual Basic gives it the default name of Module1 (or Module2 for a second module, and so on). As you do with your forms and controls, you should give the module a unique name. The module has a Name property, just as a form does. To change the name of the module, simply change the value of the Name property in the Property window.

Accessing the Forms and Modules of a Project

As you add forms and modules to your program, they are added to the Project window. This window allows you to access any of the pieces of your program easily (see Figure 11.7). You simply select a form or module by clicking its name in the Project window. For a form, you can then click the View Object button to work on the design of the form, or you can click the View Code button to edit the code associated with the form. For a module, only the View Code button is enabled because a module has no visual elements. Double-clicking the name of a form has the same effect as clicking the View Object button. Double-clicking a module name has the same effect as clicking the View Code button.

FIGURE 11.6
You can open the Code window by double-clicking the module name in the Project window.

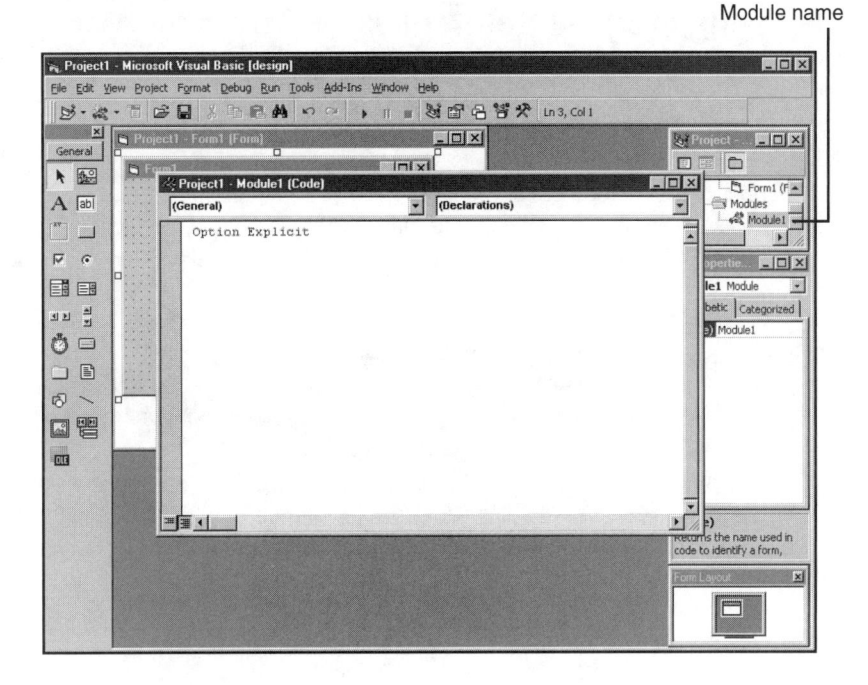

FIGURE 11.7
The Project window gives you easy access to all your forms and modules.

View Code button
View Object button

Managing Components in Your Project

Forms and modules are just two of the types of components that you can add to your project. In addition, you can also add *custom controls* and *class modules*. Some of these components, such as forms and modules, are editable code. Others, such as third-party controls and DLLs, are usually already compiled. Although these types of items are part of your project, they do not show up in the Project window and are added by means of some special dialog boxes.

Managing Program References

One of the elements that you have to manage is your program's *references*. The references point to different library routines that enable your code to perform specific tasks. For example, if you plan to access databases with your programs, you need to specify the Data Access Objects library as one that is used by your code. Controlling references is quite easy in Visual Basic. The References dialog box lets you select the references required by your program; to do so, mark the check box to the side of the reference (see Figure 11.8). Mark the ones you need and unmark the ones you don't need. You access the References dialog box by selecting Project, References.

FIGURE 11.8
The References dialog box lets you choose which libraries are used by your program.

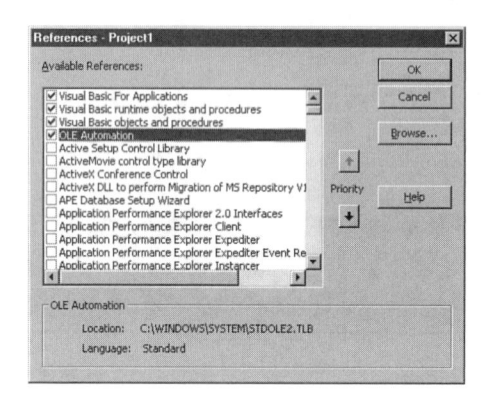

> **TIP**
> After you add a reference to your project, you can view its public constants and functions in the Object Browser, which you display by clicking the Object Browser button or by pressing F2.

Controlling Your Controls

In a manner similar to library references, you can add and remove custom controls from your project. When you loaded Visual Basic, a number of custom controls were loaded into the Toolbox window automatically. However, you usually need controls designed to perform specific tasks that are beyond the capabilities of the standard controls. You can manage the custom controls in your project by using the Components dialog box (see Figure 11.9). Select Project, Components to access this dialog box. Here, as in the References dialog box, you choose the custom controls to add to your program by marking the check box next to the control name. After you exit the dialog box, your control toolbox is modified to display the new controls.

Adding Forms, Modules, and Classes to the Project

As you develop more programs, you might find that you have standard procedures or forms that can be used in many of your projects. You also might have developed custom procedures for getting the names and passwords of users, for opening files, or for any number of other tasks that are used in almost every program.

Managing Components in Your Project | 239

FIGURE 11.9
The Components dialog box lets you add controls to your project.

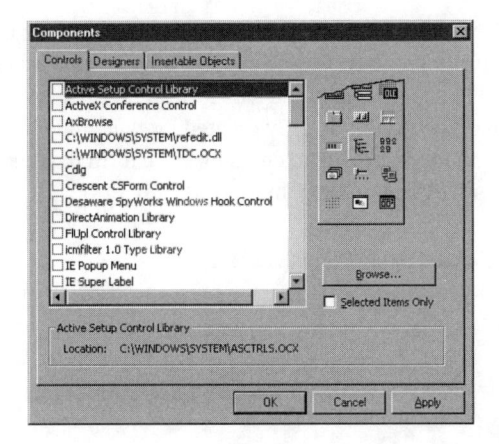

You could rebuild the form or rewrite the procedure for each program, but that would be a very inefficient way to do your program development. A better way is to reuse modules and forms that have been previously developed and fully tested.

Getting these modules and forms into your current project is a simple process. By selecting Project, Add File, you bring up the Add File dialog box (see Figure 11.10). This dialog box lets you locate and select files to be added to your current project. Unfortunately, the Add File dialog box lets you add only a single file at a time. Therefore, if you have multiple files to add, you must repeat the operation several times.

> **CAUTION**
> If you add the same form or module to separate projects, remember that changing functions in the module affects all projects that use it. If you are about to change a shared module radically, use the Save *modulename* As option in the File menu or copy the module to another subdirectory first.

FIGURE 11.10
The Add File dialog box can be accessed from the menu system, standard toolbar, by right-clicking in the Project window, or by pressing Ctrl+D.

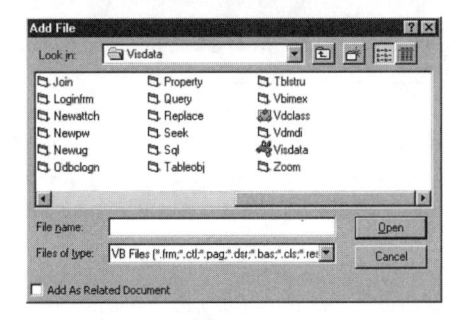

N O T E Files with the .FRM and .FRX extensions are form files. Files with the .BAS extension are module files. ▪

You also might want to use one of Visual Basic's form templates in your project. These templates are predefined forms that are set up for a specific function, such as an About Box, a Splash Screen, a DataGrid form, or a Tip of the Day form. The advantage of using these templates is that the skeleton of the form is already created for you. You simply add your own graphics, label captions, and minimal code to customize the form to your needs. As an example, Figure 11.11 shows the About Box form template.

FIGURE 11.11
Form templates make developing common pieces of a program easy.

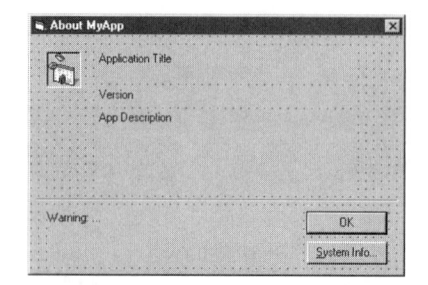

To access one of the form templates, bring up the Add Form dialog box by clicking the Add Form button on the toolbar or selecting Project, Add Form. You can then choose one of the form types from the New tab of the dialog box (see Figure 11.12).

FIGURE 11.12
Form templates can be quickly customized and used in your project.

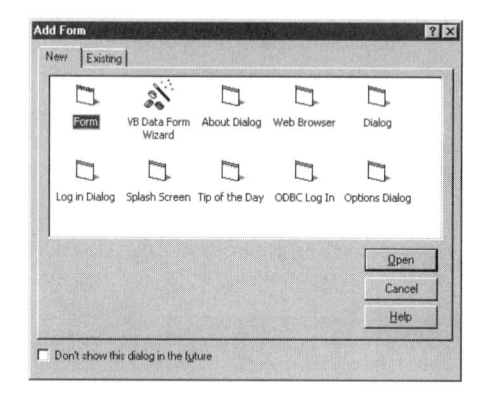

If you create a form that you think you will use in a number of programs, you can make a template out of it as well. Simply save the form in the form template folder of Visual Basic. Then the next time you want to add a new form, your template will appear in the Add Form dialog box as well.

> **NOTE** If you let Visual Basic install to the default directory, the forms templates are stored in the Visual Basic \Template\Forms folder.

Removing Pieces

To remove a module or form from your project, simply select the form or module in the Project window and choose Project, Remove. Visual Basic asks you to confirm that you want to remove the file and then removes it from your project.

Controlling How Your Program Starts

When you first start a programming project, Visual Basic assumes that the first form created is the one that will be displayed as soon as the program starts. Although this will be the case for many programs, for others you may want to start with one of the forms you create later in the development process. For some programs, you might not want to start with a form at all.

Setting the Startup Form

If the first form is not the one you want to use to start your program, Visual Basic lets you choose which of your forms is shown initially by the program. This selection is made in the Project Properties dialog box, as shown in Figure 11.13. You access this dialog box by selecting Project, Project Properties.

FIGURE 11.13
The Startup Object list lets you choose which form is loaded when your program starts.

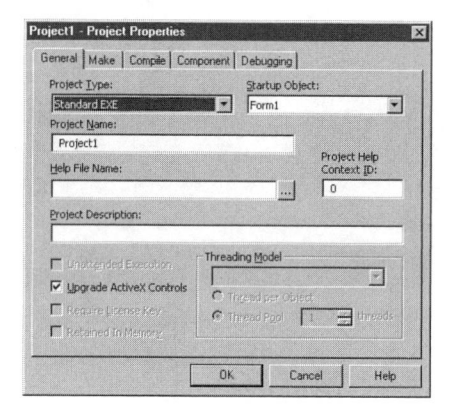

Using *Sub Main*

You might have noticed that, in addition to listing all the forms contained in your project, the Startup Object list includes the entry `Sub Main`. This reserved procedure name lets your program start without an initial form. If you choose this option, one of your module files must include a procedure called `Main`.

One reason to start your program with the `Sub Main` option might be that you need to perform some initialization routines before loading any forms. Another reason might be that you are developing a command-line utility that requires no user interaction.

From Here...

This chapter gave you a look at how you manage the various parts of your programs. You saw several techniques for making your programming more efficient. You also were exposed to many of the assorted components that comprise a complete program. For more information on creating and using the various parts, see the following chapters:

- For a basic discussion of how to write Visual Basic code, see Chapter 9, "Visual Basic Programming Fundamentals."
- To learn about how to make your code more efficient, see Chapter 10, "Controlling the Flow of Your Program Code."

PART III

Visual Basic Program Components

- **12** Microsoft Common Controls 245
- **13** Working with Control Arrays 289
- **14** Creating ActiveX Controls 305
- **15** Extending ActiveX Controls 341
- **16** Creating Classes: Reusable Components 359

CHAPTER 12

Microsoft Common Controls

In this chapter

Introduction to the Common Controls   246

The ImageList: A Fundamental Common Control   248

Organizing Your Data   250

Accepting User Input   266

Reporting Status and Progress   278

Visual Basic ships with a group of common controls that enable you to develop programs with many of the same features as programs from Microsoft and other vendors. These controls let you create toolbars and status bars, and allow you to display data in various ways. This chapter continues the earlier discussions of controls by covering the capabilities of the Microsoft common controls.

Introduction to the Common Controls

The Windows common controls are a group of controls that let you add some of the same features to your program that Windows uses—hence, the name "common" controls. In Visual Basic 6.0, some of the existing common controls have been updated with new features, and several entirely new controls have been added.

The complete list of common controls is detailed in Table 12.1, including the control buttons that appear in the Toolbox.

Table 12.1 The Microsoft Common Controls

Control Name	Description
ImageList	Stores groups of pictures for use with the other controls.
TabStrip	Allows you to include property-page-style tabs on a form.
Toolbar	Displays a graphical application toolbar. (This control is discussed in Chapter 6, "Giving More Control to the User: Menus and Toolbars.")
StatusBar	Displays status information that can be divided into panels.
ProgressBar	Provides a graphical progress gauge.
TreeView	Organizes information in a collapsible tree.
ListView	Provides an advanced list control with several views.
Slider	Displays a slider bar, much like a stereo equalizer control.
ImageCombo	Provides an enhancement to the standard combo box discussed in Chapter 4, "Using Visual Basic's Default Controls." (New to Visual Basic 6)
Animation	Allows you to add silent video clips to your forms.

Introduction to the Common Controls

Control Name	Description
UpDown	Provides arrow buttons for incrementing and decrementing values.
MonthView	Provides a calendar control, similar to the one used in Microsoft Project 98.
DTPicker	Allows you to enter a date by hand or use the MonthView control to pick it.
CoolBar	Provides a sliding toolbar container with vertical separators, much like those used in Visual Basic's IDE.

Before you can use any of the controls discussed in this chapter, you have to add them to your Toolbox, as follows:

1. Choose Project, Components. The Components dialog box opens.
2. Select the Microsoft Windows Common Controls 6.0 groups you want installed (see Figure 12.1). The three groups contain the following controls:
   - **Microsoft Windows Common Controls 6.0.** All the controls in Table 12.1 up to and including the ImageCombo control
   - **Microsoft Windows Common Controls-2 6.0.** The rest of the controls in Table 12.1 except for the CoolBar control
   - **Microsoft Windows Common Controls-3 6.0.** The CoolBar control
3. Click OK to add the Common controls to the Toolbox (see Figure 12.2).

FIGURE 12.1
All three Common control groups are selected and will be added to the Toolbox when you click OK.

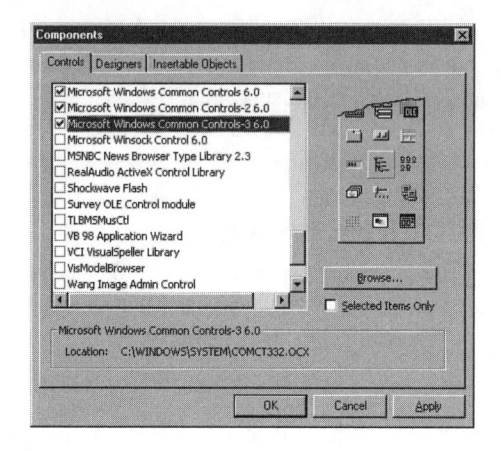

FIGURE 12.2
This Toolbox contains the Common controls from all three groups.

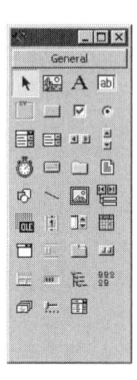

If you want to use the Common controls in a new project, you will need to add them to the Toolbox. You also need to perform2 these steps whenever you want to use one of the Common controls in an existing project where you have not used them before. After you add them to the Toolbox and save your project, the Common controls appear in the Toolbox automatically the next time the project is loaded.

The ImageList: A Fundamental Common Control

The ImageList control is just what it sounds like: a list of images. It is like a picture box or Image control, but instead of storing only a single picture, the ImageList stores a collection of pictures. Also, the ImageList does not contain anything visible at runtime; it is merely a storage area for images. If you want to view one of the images contained in an ImageList, you have to use an additional control.

The ImageList is a very important control for you to understand because many of the other Windows Common controls depend on it to display pictures. As a matter of fact, the ImageList control's most common use is to store pictures that another control needs; rarely is it used by itself.

Setting Up an ImageList at Designtime

The most common way to set up an ImageList control is to add pictures manually at designtime. In this case, the pictures are stored in the form itself. The actual image files do not need to be distributed with the application.

> **NOTE** In this chapter, you will fill image lists with images that are included with Visual Basic. You'll find these graphis in your Visual Basic Graphics directory. You can access these same images (if you chose to install them) by finding the corresponding directory on your PC. Icons are ideal for use with the ImageList because they are small, and you can preview them in the File, Open dialog box.

Follow these steps to set up an ImageList control at designtime:

1. Draw an ImageList control on your form, and give it a unique name.
2. Open the control's Property Pages dialog box by right-clicking the control and selecting Properties.
3. Select the Images tab from the Property Pages dialog box (see Figure 12.3). Here you can load graphics files and assign each graphic a unique identifier.
4. To add an image, click the Insert Picture button. The Select Picture dialog box then appears. In this dialog box, you can select a bitmap, icon, cursor, GIF, or JPEG file to add to the list.

   As you add images, they are automatically given indexes (again, see Figure 12.3). You can also give them your own unique string identifiers by typing them in the Key field. Using a key is recommended because it allows you to refer to a specific image by name, no matter what the order of the images.
5. When you finish adding images, press OK to close the Property Pages.

FIGURE 12.3
If you set up an ImageList control at designtime, the images are stored with the form and compiled into the executable program.

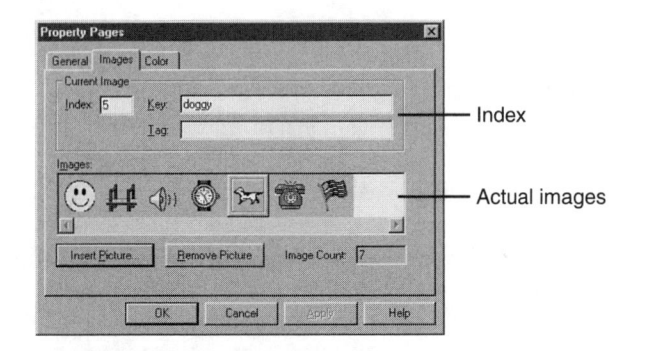

Setting Up an ImageList with Code

You can also set up and change an ImageList at runtime by using program code. When you access an ImageList from code, each image is part of a *collection*.

NOTE Collections are a fundamental concept used in many areas of Visual Basic besides the ImageList control. If you are new to the topic, keep reading. Collections are discussed throughout the chapter.

A collection is a group of objects. In the case of the ImageList control, there is a collection called `ListImages`. The objects stored in this particular collection are the images in the ImageList control. By manipulating the `ListImages` collection in code, you can add, remove, and change images. For example, the following line of code adds an image to an imagelist called `ImageList1`:

```
ImageList1.Add ,,LoadPicture("D:\MYDIR\MYPIC.BMP")
```

You can call the Add method of the `ListImages` collection repeatedly to add multiple images at designtime. Think of a collection as being similar to, but not exactly like, an array. You can access it like an array, as in the following line of code, which sets a form's picture to the first image in an ImageList control:

```
Set form1.Picture = ImageList1.ListImages(1).Picture
```

Notice that a specific object is referred to with its *index*—in this case, 1. Remember, a collection stores objects, unlike an array, which stores values. These objects, in turn, have their own set of properties.

One special property that objects in a collection have is the Key property. An object's key is a text string that can be used in the same manner as an index:

```
Set form1.Picture = ImageList1.ListImages("Smiley Face").Picture
```

To use a key to look up an object in a collection, you have to specify it when the object is added to the collection. Each type of collection has defined Add and Remove methods, which include Key and Index as parameters. If the index is omitted, it is supplied by Visual Basic. The key, however, is optional.

Organizing Your Data

The ListView and TreeView controls allow you to organize data for viewing in a manner similar to that used by the Windows Explorer (see Figure 12.4). The great thing about these controls is that they effectively separate the controls' appearance from the data contained in the controls. For example, consider a list of 100 items. Using the ListView, you can sort these items and change the way they are viewed by simply setting properties of the control. This is a great improvement over a standard list box, in which rearranging items means reloading the list box.

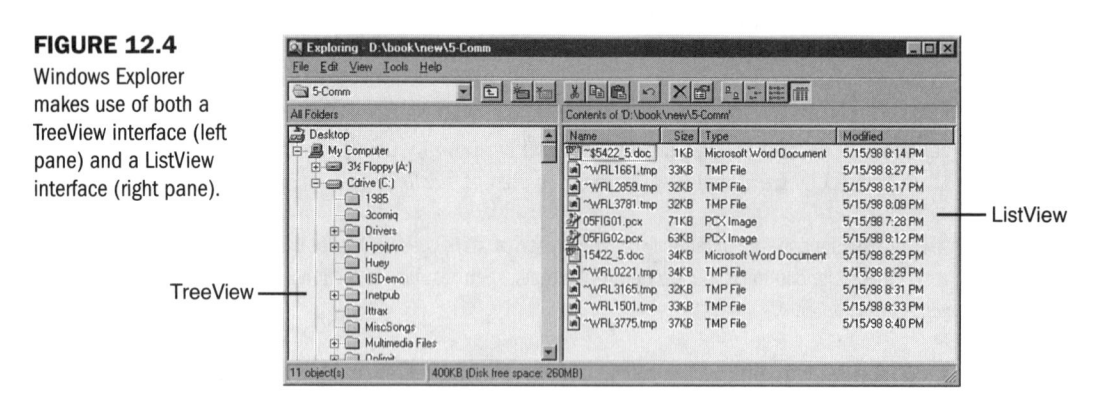

FIGURE 12.4
Windows Explorer makes use of both a TreeView interface (left pane) and a ListView interface (right pane).

In the following section, you create sample ListView and TreeView projects. Keep in mind that they are tricky controls to master. You might want to spend a little time going over the online help files to get a good grounding in their use. Your time will be well spent.

Using the ListView Control

The ListView control is similar to the ListBox but is enhanced in a number of ways. The ListView control can display information in one of a variety of modes: icon lists that are arranged from left to right, a columnar list, or a "report" view. These options correspond to the options in the Windows Explorer's View menu (Large Icons, Small Icons, List, or Details). After the items are stored in the `ListItems` collection, you can simply set the `View` property to switch to any of the modes you want.

The report-style list is special because it shows more information than the other modes. When using the Windows Explorer, you may have noticed that the Details option displays more information than just the filename. In this case, the filename is the main item, and the size, type, and date modified are "sub-items" associated with each filename.

In your programs, you control sub-items with the `SubItems` property, which is an array of strings associated with each item in the list. A `ColumnHeaders` collection supplies the headings at the top of the report.

Recall from earlier in this chapter that the ImageList control supplies pictures for other Common controls. The ListView control can use up to three ImageLists because it can display both large and small icons, as well as pictures in the column headers. You can set these ImageLists in the Property Pages dialog box or in code, as follows:

```
Set lViewMain.Icons = ImageList1
Set lViewMain.SmallIcons = ImageList2
Set lViewMain.ColumnHeaderIcons = ImageList3
```

The ability to add Column Header images is a new feature in the Common controls included with Visual Basic 6.0.

If you don't set the `SmallIcons`, `Icons`, and `ColumnHeaderIcons` properties of the ListView control, no images will appear. Also, using the smaller ImageList dimension (16×16) is a good idea when you are filling the image list that you plan to use for small icons.

Recall that the ListBox control's items are stored in an array. All the items in a ListView control are in a collection called `ListItems`, and each item has several properties, including an index to the icon images and a caption. As with most collections, the `ListItems` collection has an `Add` method, which is defined as follows:

```
listview1.ListItems.Add ,"mykey","My Item",1,1
```

You will learn more details about each parameter of the ListView's `Add` method as you build the sample project.

Starting the Sample Project The sample program will display a list of baseball teams and their win/loss statistics. To begin the project, follow these steps:

1. Start a new Standard EXE project in Visual Basic.
2. As described earlier in the chapter, add the Microsoft Windows Common Controls 6.0 to your Toolbox.

3. Add a ListView control to the form, and name it `lvMain`.

4. Add three ImageList controls to the form, and name them `ilNormal`, `ilSmall`, and `ilHeader`.

5. Add appropriate images to the ImageList controls. The sample code assumes that the `ilNormal` and `ilSmall` ImageLists contain only one image, and the `ilHeader` list contains three images.

Setting Properties of the ListView Control As with most controls, you can set up the ListView control in two ways: by using the Properties window and Property Pages or by using code. If you want to set up the ListView while you are in the design environment, you can use the Property Pages, shown in Figure 12.5. For the sample project, you need to set four properties: `View`, `Icons`, `SmallIcons`, and `ColumnHeaderIcons`. You will learn how to set these properties at designtime, as well as examine sample code that does the job.

FIGURE 12.5
Property Pages let you set the properties of the ListView control.

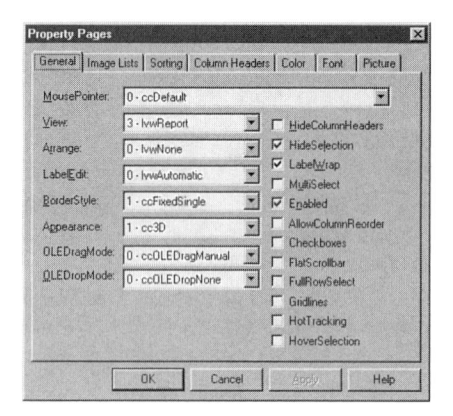

First, you need to set the `View` property, which determines how the list presents information to the users. The `View` property has the following four possible values:

- `lvwIcon`—Displays each item in the list using a large icon and a simple text description.
- `lvwSmallIcon`—Displays each item in the list using a small icon and a simple text description. The items are ordered horizontally.
- `lvwList`—Displays icons similarly to the small icon view, except that items are arranged in a single vertical column.
- `lvwReport`—Displays each item with a small icon, a text description, and detailed information, if it is provided. As with the list view, items are arranged in vertical columns.

For the ListView control, you also need to set the names of the ImageList controls that contain the normal, small, and column heading icons that are shown in the list. If you are using the Property Pages, you can select the ImageList controls from drop-down lists on the Image Lists page. These lists contain the names of all the ImageList controls on your form. In the sample project, you set the `View` property from code.

Organizing Your Data

Adding Items to the List The next step is to write some code to add items to the ListView. You can use the sample code in Listing 12.1 to add objects to the `ListItems` collection. Run the program, and you should see the results pictured in Figure 12.6.

Listing 12.1 LISTVIEW.ZIP—Using the *Load* Event to Set Up the ListView Control

```
Private Sub Form_Load()

    'Set up the icons from the image List
    lvMain.Icons = ilNormal
    lvMain.SmallIcons = ilSmall
    lvMain.ColumnHeaderIcons = ilHeader

    ' Add ColumnHeaders.  The width of the columns is the width
    ' of the control divided by the number of ColumnHeader objects.
    Dim clmX As ColumnHeader
    Set clmX = lvMain.ColumnHeaders.Add(, , "Team", , , 1)
    Set clmX = lvMain.ColumnHeaders.Add(, , "Wins", , , 2)
    Set clmX = lvMain.ColumnHeaders.Add(, , "Losses", , , 3)

    'Create a ListItem object.
    Dim itmX As ListItem

    'Add some data setting to the ListItem:

    'Red Sox Stats:
    Set itmX = lvMain.ListItems.Add(, , "Red Sox", 1, 1)    ' Team
    itmX.SubItems(1) = "64"                                 ' Wins
    itmX.SubItems(2) = "65"                                 ' Losses

    ' You can duplicate the above 3 lines of code
    ' to add information for more teams...

    lvMain.View = lvwReport   ' Set View property to Report.

End Sub
```

FIGURE 12.6
The ListView looks like this after being set up with your code.

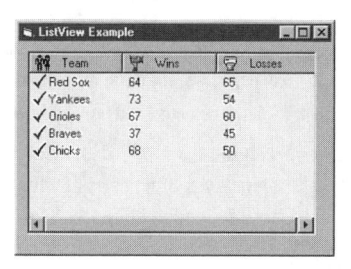

In Listing 12.1, notice that temporary object variables are used to set up the `ColumnHeaders` and `ListItems` collections. You first call the `Add` method, which returns you to a reference to the object it just added. For the code that sets up the column headings, this was not really necessary because you do not refer to the temporary value `clmX` beyond the initial call to the `Add` method.

However, when you add team information, you do not supply your own key. Remember, a key is a string that uniquely identifies an object in a collection. If you don't supply your own key, Visual Basic makes one up. Therefore, the object itmX is needed to set the two sub-items. If a key were supplied, you also could have written the code as follows:

```
lvMain.ListItems.Add , "RSox", "Red Sox", 1, 1
lvMain.ListItems("RSox").SubItems(1) = "64"
lvMain.ListItems("RSox").SubItems(2) = "65"
```

Adding a *ListItem* Object to a ListView Control

The examples in this section introduce the ListItems collection, which stores ListItem objects that are created using the Add method. The syntax for a ListItem's Add method is as follows:

object.Add(index, key, text, icon, smallIcon)

Here's what the different pieces are and what they do:

- object—For all intents and purposes, you can use *ListViewName*.ListItems. This element is required.

- index—You can use this number to position the ListItem object within the ListItems collection. If you don't assign a number to this argument, the ListItem is added to the end of the collection. This parameter is optional. Remember that the index of an item can change as other items are added or deleted.

- key—You can use a string to give a unique, friendly name to the ListItem. This parameter is optional.

- text—This parameter contains the string that you want the ListItem to display in the ListView window. It is optional. However, for novice users of this control, I recommend that you use it. This argument should not be confused with the key argument.

- icon—This parameter contains the index number or key of the image within the ImageList that has been assigned to the Icons property of the ListView control. Use this parameter to select the image you want. This argument is optional. Be careful; if you forget to fill in a value, no large icon appears in the ListView lvwIcons view.

- smallIcon—Similar to the previous argument, icon, this parameter contains the index number of the image within the ImageList that has been assigned to the SmallIcons property of the ListView control. It is optional. If you do not fill in a value, no small icon appears in the ListView's lvwSmallIcons, lvwList, or lvwReport views.

If you want to add additional information, as done with the team win/loss information, to the created ListItem object, MyListItem, you manipulate the object's SubItems(Index) property. See your online Visual Basic documentation for additional information on the SubItems property.

Changing the View After you have data in the ListView, you can display it in several different views by setting the View property in code. To see what the different views look like, you can add a View menu to the sample program.

To create the menu, use Visual Basic's Menu Editor (by clicking the Menu Editor button or by choosing Tools, Menu Editor), and create the menu items, as shown in Figure 12.7.

Organizing Your Data | 255

FIGURE 12.7
The Menu Editor shows the menu for the sample program.

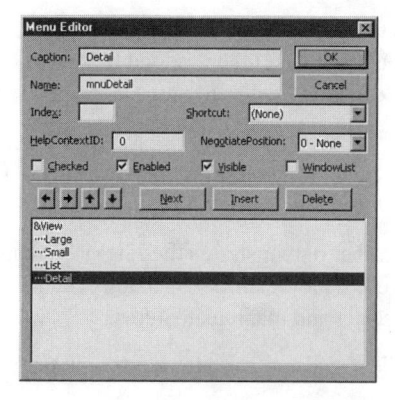

After exiting the Menu Editor, you need to add code to each menu item to make it perform a task. The code for each of these items is contained in Listing 12.2.

Listing 12.2 LISTVIEW.ZIP—Using Menu *Click* events for the Sample Project

```
Private Sub mnuDetail_Click()
    lvMain.View = lvwReport
End Sub

Private Sub mnuLarge_Click()
    lvMain.View = lvwIcon
End Sub

Private Sub mnuList_Click()
    lvMain.View = lvwList
End Sub

Private Sub mnuSmall_Click()
    lvMain.View = lvwSmallIcon
End Sub
```

You now can run the program and use the menu to display each different view. Figure 12.8 shows the Large Icon view.

FIGURE 12.8
Whereas the Report view displays detailed information with column headings, the Large Icon view simply shows a picture above the item text.

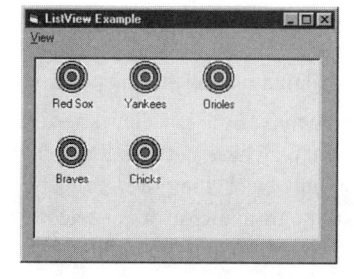

In the `Form_Load` event, the `ListItem` objects (baseball teams) for the ListView's `ListItem` collection are created and added. As each `ListItem` is added to the `ListItems` collection, values are assigned to `SubItems(1)`, (the "Win" column) and `SubItems(2)` (the "Loss" column) of the `ListItem, itmX`.

The `Click` event procedures of the menu items set the `View` property of the ListView control. The views are `lvwIcons`, `lvwSmallIcons`, `lvwList`, and `lvwReport`, respectively.

You have just seen a sample project that demonstrates the ListView's capability to display items. Like the ListBox control, the ListView control has many events and properties, such as the `ItemClick` event, designed to select and manipulate items.

The `ItemClick` event passes an object to your program, so you can take appropriate action:

```
Private Sub ListView1_ItemClick(ByVal Item As ComctlLib.ListItem)
    If Item.Text = "Magic Item" Then MsgBox "You clicked the magic item!"
End Sub
```

The ListView control also has properties to sort the report view based on a column header. By using the `ColumnClick` event, you can easily change the sort order to the selected column, as shown here:

```
Private Sub lvMain_ColumnClick(ByVal ColumnHeader As ComctlLib.ColumnHeader)
    lvMain.SortKey = ColumnHeader.Index - 1
    lvMain.Sorted = True
End Sub
```

As you may have noticed, you can rename items in a ListView by single-clicking the text. Two events, `BeforeLabelEdit` and `AfterLabelEdit`, let your program know which item the users are changing.

As you can see, the ListView is a fairly complex control. To discover all the features, you might try creating several sample programs to test all the properties and methods.

New Features of the ListView Control   If you have used the ListView control in prior versions of Visual Basic, you will be happy to know that it has been greatly enhanced for version 6. You have already seen one improvement—the `ColumnHeaderIcons` collection, which allows pictures to be displayed in the report view headings. Several additional features, which allow you to further improve the appearance of the ListView control, are listed here:

- `AllowColumnReorder`—This property allows users to rearrange the column order in a `lvwReport` view. For example, set it to `True` on the sample project, and you should be able to click and drag the "Wins" column to the leftmost position in the report.
- `FullRowSelect`—This new property makes the ListView an excellent candidate to replace the standard list box. As you may have noticed, the default behavior of the ListView is to allow item selection only by clicking the leftmost column. Setting the `FullRowSelect` property to `True` not only allows users to select by clicking any column, but also provides a visual indicator by extending the highlight bar across all columns.
- `GridLines`—This property controls whether gridlines are drawn on the report, which makes it look similar to an Excel spreadsheet.

- **FlatScrollBars**—This property changes the scrollbars to the newer flat-style control.
- **HoverSelection**—Normally, you have to click an item in the ListView to select it. If you set HoverSelection to True, the item is selected (and the ItemClick event fired) when you hover the mouse pointer on the item's icon for a few seconds.
- **HotTracking**—The name of this property sounds like a dating service, but it is actually a mouse pointer enhancement to bring the look and feel of the ListView more in line with the new Microsoft Active Desktop user interface.
- **CheckBoxes**—The CheckBoxes property controls whether a check box control is displayed beside each item in the ListView. You can determine or set the state of the check box with the Checked property of the item. An ItemCheck event also fires when users click the check box.

Also new to the VB6 ListView is the capability to display a picture behind the items. This feature works much like the background of a Web page. You can load the picture by setting the Picture property of the ListView, as in the following example:

```
ivMain.Picture=LoadPicture("D:\Pictures\Test.JPG")
```

In addition, these two properties control the behavior of the picture and its interaction with the list items:

- The TextBackGround property controls whether the text has an opaque or transparent background.
- The PictureAlignment property controls how the picture is painted on the ListView. You can start at the center or any corner of the picture and display as much as possible, or if the picture is smaller than the list view, you can have it displayed over and over in tiled format.

Examples of some of the new display options are shown in Figure 12.9.

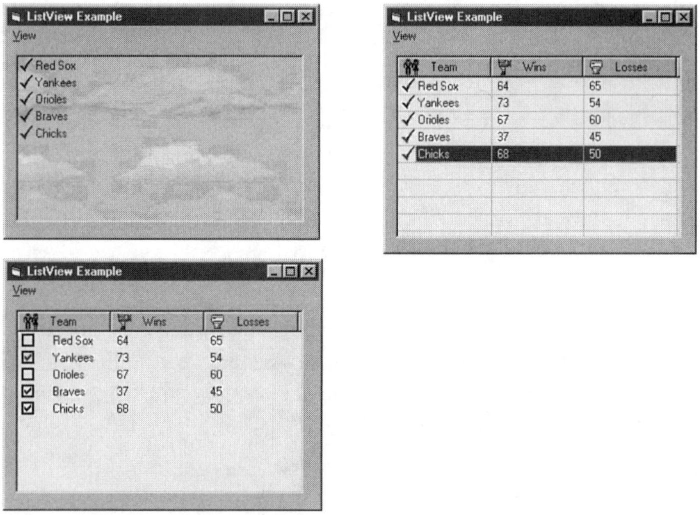

FIGURE 12.9
These examples of ListView configurations were not possible in previous versions of Visual Basic.

Using the TreeView Control

The TreeView control is similar to a ListView in that it can display items with a combination of text and graphics. However, the TreeView does so by showing items within a tree hierarchy. If you have ever taken a math or computer science class, you already may know about the "tree hierarchy." Figure 12.10 shows an example of a tree you might have seen before.

FIGURE 12.10
A true structure defines a relationship between objects (represented by the circles).

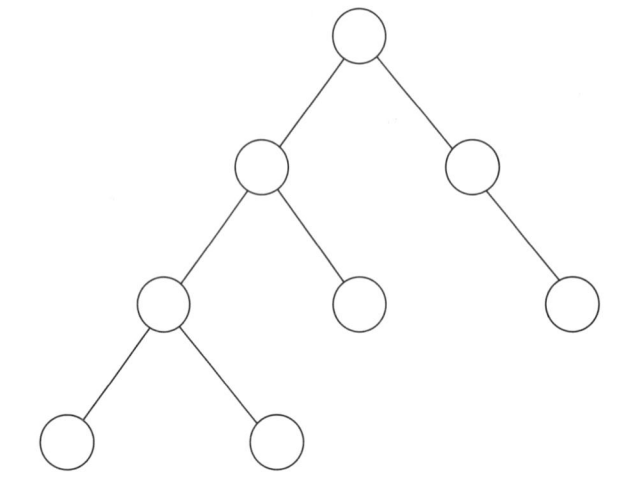

Given the hierarchical nature of the TreeView control, *root, parent,* and *child* are fundamental concepts that you must understand so that you can work effectively with the control. Also, the TreeView uses the Node object extensively. Therefore, mastery of the Node object is also a requirement for effective use of the TreeView. The most common example of the TreeView is shown in the left pane of the Windows Explorer (refer to Figure 12.4).

Understanding Nodes   A *hierarchy* is an organization in which each part has a defined relationship with the other parts. For example, consider your family tree. Your parents are "above" you in the hierarchy, and your children are "below" you.

In the family tree example, each person is considered to be a *node* on the tree. Relationships between nodes are indicated by *branches.* A node's branches can connect it to other nodes (that is, lines on the family tree connect you to your ancestors), although a node does not necessarily have to have any descendants.

Like the family tree or a real-life tree, all TreeView controls have nodes. The Nodes property of a TreeView control is itself a collection of Node objects. If you have followed the discussion up to now regarding collections, this concept probably makes some sense to you. (If you're unclear about collections, review the ListView section, earlier in this chapter.) Like the ListView's ListItems collection, the TreeView's Nodes collection has properties and methods, including an Add method used to create new nodes:

```
tv1.Nodes.Add , , "mykey", "Test Node", 1, 2
```

Like the other `Add` methods discussed so far, it can return a reference to the object just created, as shown here:

```
Dim tempNode As Node
Set tempNode = tv1.Nodes.Add(, , "mykey", "Test Node")
tempNode.Image = 1
tempNode.SelectedImage = 2
tempNode.ExpandedImage = 3
```

The TreeView control presents a "collapsible" view of the tree structure, as shown in Figure 12.11.

FIGURE 12.11
This simple tree structure was created using the TreeView control.

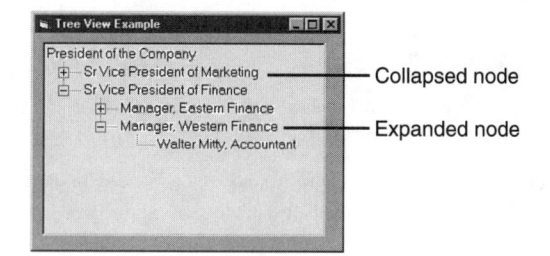

In Figure 12.11, notice the use of plus, minus, lines, and images to indicate which parts of the tree are "expanded" and which are "collapsed." Users can manipulate the tree with the mouse, expanding and collapsing its branches as desired. For the programmer, the key to getting the items to appear where you want them is understanding the relationships between them.

By using the `SingleSel` property, you can make the tree automatically expand a node when users select it.

Understanding the *Root* Property At the very top of a tree structure is its root. A root is the node from which all other nodes descend. A tree has only one root node. The tree pictured in Figure 12.11 is a simple organizational chart for a small company. The node called "President of the Company" is the root node, simply because it was the first one added to the TreeView control.

Part of what defines any node in a tree is its root. Therefore, each node in the `Nodes` collection has a `Root` property that refers to the tree's root node. For the tree pictured in Figure 12.11, you can use the following code to verify that every node has the same root:

```
Dim tempNode As Node
For Each tempNode in tv1.Nodes
        Print tempNode.Text & "'s root is " & tempnode.Root.Text
Next tempNode
```

Note that `Root` is both a property of a node and a node itself.

Working with the *Parent* Property You have just seen that every node in the `Nodes` collection can access the root. However, just knowing the root of a node is not enough to define a position in the tree hierarchy.

If you want to know where you are in the sample company structure in Figure 12.11, you need to know more than just where the root (President) is. Now you're ready to examine the first of several tree relationships, the *parent relationship*. To be a parent, a node must have children. In Figure 12.11, the president of the company is a parent to both of the vice president nodes. Both managers shown in the figure also have the same parent, the VP of Finance.

Suppose you were an ambitious little node trying to climb the corporate ladder. You could use this code to check your progress:

```
Dim MyNode As Node

Set MyNode = tv1.Nodes("Me")

If MyNode Is MyNode.Root Then
    MsgBox "You're the boss!"
Else
    MsgBox "Try getting promoted to " & MyNode.Parent.Text
End If
```

As you can see from the example, each node object has a `Parent` property that refers to its parent node. The only exception is the root node, whose `Parent` property does not refer to anything (it has the special value `Nothing`).

Working with the *Children* Property   To find out whether a node is a parent, you can query the `Children` property by using code like this:

```
Private Sub TreeView1_NodeClick(ByVal MyNode As Node)
    If MyNode.Children = 0 Then
        MsgBox "I am not a parent"
    End If
End Sub
```

As you can see, the `Children` property returns an integer value that represents the number of children the given node has. To be considered a child, a node must have a direct connection. In other words, as shown in Figure 12.11, the president of the company has two children—the two senior vice presidents.

Working with the *Child* property   Whereas the `Children` property simply returns the count of child nodes, the `Child` property returns an actual node (just like the `Root` and `Parent` properties). However, even if a parent has multiple children, the `Child` property returns only the first of the given parent node's descendants. If a given node doesn't have a child, then its `Child` property contains the value `Nothing`. Therefore, you should not try to access it if the `Children` property is `0`. In the example shown in Figure 12.11, the second manager's `Child` property refers to the accountant, Walter Mitty.

The immediate problem that comes to mind is how to access child nodes other than the first one. Each node has several properties that are used to determine who its "brothers and sisters" are, as demonstrated in the following code:

```
Sub PrintAllChildren()

    Dim anyNode As Node
    Dim kidNode As Node
```

```
    Dim inCounter As Integer

    For Each anyNode In tv1.Nodes

       If anyNode.Children <> 0 Then 'this node is a parent

          Print anyNode.Text & "'s children are: "
          Set kidNode = anyNode.child
          Print kidNode.Text

          inCounter = kidNode.FirstSibling.Index
          While inCounter <> kidNode.LastSibling.Index
             Print tv1.Nodes(inCounter).Next.Text
             inCounter = tv1.Nodes(inCounter).Next.Index
          Wend

       End If

    Next anyNode
End Sub
```

Remember, a given node has only one `Child`. All the other nodes that share the `Child`'s parent are considered `"Next"` or `"Previous"` nodes. However, among all the nodes that share the same value for the `Parent` property, you can find a `FirstSibling` and a `LastSibling`.

> **NOTE** Nodes are tricky; there's no question about it. One of the best ways to get a grasp of the concept of nodes is to see the node code (no poetry intended) in action. The online help file examples that Microsoft provides with your version of VB are pretty good once you have a basic understanding of the hierarchy concepts. I suggest that you create several test programs until you are comfortable using the TreeView control.

To learn more about the TreeView control, keep reading. This section focused on accessing nodes already in the TreeView control. In the next section, you will add nodes to a TreeView control as part of a sample project.

Using the TabStrip Control

The TabStrip, shown in Figure 12.12, is a control widely used in the Windows interface arsenal. It allows you to divide a form visually into several tabs, creating the appearance of a set of organized folders.

The TabStrip shown in the figure is the sample project you'll create in this section. In this sample project, the purpose of the TabStrip control is to switch between two lists of information; the lists are baseball teams displayed in a TreeView control. The TabStrip enables you to select which league to display.

Starting the Sample Project   To begin the TreeTab project, start a new Standard EXE project in Visual Basic. Then follow these steps:

1. Add a TabStrip control, and name it something short and meaningful, like `tsMain`.
2. Add a TreeView control to the form, and name it `tv1`. Now you are ready to start setting the properties of the controls.

FIGURE 12.12
The sample project uses TabStrip and TreeView controls.

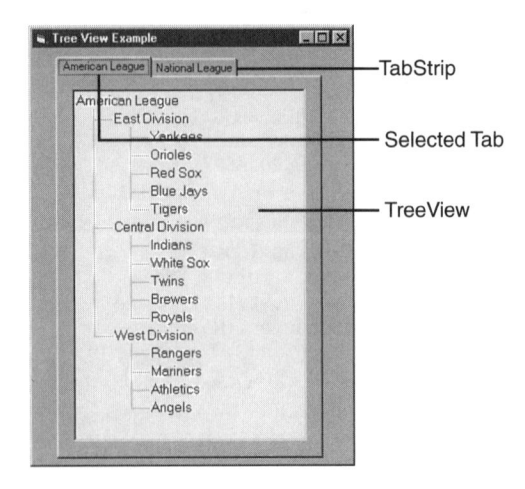

(Screenshot of Tree View Example window showing TabStrip with "American League" and "National League" tabs, Selected Tab, and TreeView displaying American League organized into East Division (Yankees, Orioles, Red Sox, Blue Jays, Tigers), Central Division (Indians, White Sox, Twins, Brewers, Royals), and West Division (Rangers, Mariners, Athletics, Angels).)

> **CAUTION**
>
> The TabStrip control is *not* a container. This means that controls placed in a TabStrip control do not assume the `Visible`, `Enabled`, and relative `Top` and `Left` properties of the TabStrip, as they would if you were to draw a control into a selected Frame control. Thus, clicking a TabStrip brings it to the front, covering other controls that are before it.
>
> To manipulate how controls appear in relation to a TabStrip, pay particular attention to the `ZOrder` method of the TabStrip and the affected controls. While you're working in design mode, you may need to right-click the TabStrip control and choose Send to Back.

Setting Up the TabStrip The next step in creating the project is to create the tabs in the TabStrip. Because you need to show two leagues, you need two tabs in the TabStrip. To set up the TabStrip control, follow these steps:

1. Start by right-clicking `tsMain` to bring up the TabStrip context menu.
2. Click the Properties menu item at the bottom of the context menu to display the Property Pages dialog box for `tsMain`.
3. Click the Tabs tab, and type `American League` in the Caption field (see Figure 12.13).
4. Click the Insert Tab button to add a tab.
5. In the Caption field, type `National League`.
6. Click OK. The captions then appear in the TabStrip control.

Setting Up the TreeView Control As was the case in the ListView project, you will set up the TreeView control by adding objects to a collection with code. You use the TreeView control to display a hierarchical organization of a selected baseball league. Each league has three divisions: East, West, and Central. The divisions have five, five, and four teams, respectively.

Organizing Your Data

FIGURE 12.13
Using the Property Pages dialog box (which uses a TabStrip itself), you can easily insert tabs into a TabStrip control.

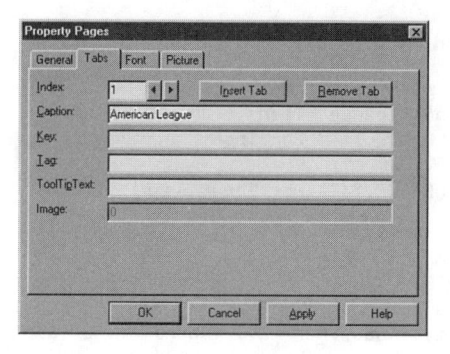

You can take advantage of this common structure by putting the data into two text files, ALEAGUE.TXT and NLEAGUE.TXT. These files contain lists of the 14 teams in each league. You can create them in Notepad or any other text editor, as shown in Figure 12.14.

FIGURE 12.14
In the sample program, the TreeView is filled with items from the two text files pictured here.

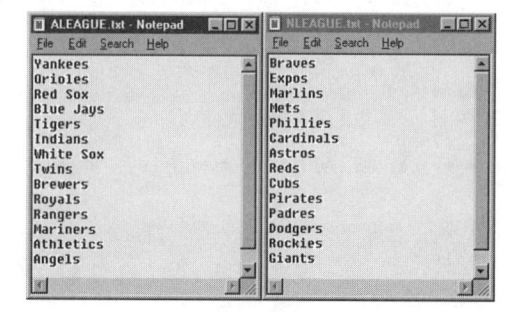

Create the subroutine shown in Listing 12.3 to load information from the text files into the TreeView control.

Listing 12.3 TREEVIEW.ZIP—Using the *DisplayLeague* Procedure to Load the Selected Information into the TreeView

```
Public Sub DisplayLeague(sLeague As String)

    Dim tempNode As Node
    Dim nCounter As Integer
    Dim sTemp As String

    tv1.Nodes.Clear

    'Add the League
    Set tempNode = tv1.Nodes.Add(, , "R", sLeague)

    'Add the Divisions
    Set tempNode = tv1.Nodes.Add("R", tvwChild, "E", "East Division")
    Set tempNode = tv1.Nodes.Add("R", tvwChild, "C", "Central Division")
    Set tempNode = tv1.Nodes.Add("R", tvwChild, "W", "West Division")
```

continues

Listing 12.3 Continued

```
'Open the text file with team names
If sLeague = "National League" Then
Open App Path & "\NLEAGUE.TXT" For Input As #1
Else
Open App Path & "\ALEAGUE.TXT" For Input As #1
End If

'Add the 5 EAST teams
For nCounter = 1 To 5
    Line Input #1, sTemp
    Set tempNode = tv1.Nodes.Add("E", tvwChild, "E" & nCounter, sTemp)
Next nCounter
tempNode.EnsureVisible

'Add the 5 CENTRAL teams
For nCounter = 1 To 5
    Line Input #1, sTemp
    Set tempNode = tv1.Nodes.Add("C", tvwChild, "C" & nCounter, sTemp)
Next nCounter
tempNode.EnsureVisible

'Add the 4 WEST teams
For nCounter = 1 To 4
    Line Input #1, sTemp
    Set tempNode = tv1.Nodes.Add("W", tvwChild, "W" & nCounter, sTemp)
Next nCounter
tempNode.EnsureVisible

'Close the Input file
Close #1

'Set the Desired style
tv1.Style = tvwTreelinesText
tv1.BorderStyle = vbFixedSingle

'Set the TreeView control on top
tv1.ZOrder 0
End Sub
```

Notice that the relationships in the tree view are defined as a node is added. The Add method's first parameter lists a "relative" node and the second parameter lists the relationship to that relative. The constant tvwChild indicates that the new node is a child of the relative node.

Taking Action in the Program Now, you are ready to return to the topic of the TabStrip control and set up the form's Load event. When the form first appears, you probably want it to show something, so you can call the DisplayLeague procedure to display the American League teams. The code for the Load event is shown in Listing 12.4. At this point, you can run your program, and the American League teams are displayed. However, clicking the TabStrip has no effect on the TreeView because you have not yet added the necessary code to the TabStrip's Click event. This code, also shown in Listing 12.4, calls the DisplayLeague procedure with the name of the desired league.

Listing 12.4 TREEVIEW.ZIP—Working with the *Load* and *Click* Events

```
Private Sub Form_Load()

    'Put the tree view on top of the tab
    tv1.ZOrder 0

    'Call our procedure
    DisplayLeague "American League"
End Sub

Private Sub tsMain_Click()
    Dim nTemp As Integer

    nTemp = tsMain.SelectedItem.Index
    DisplayLeague tsMain.Tabs(nTemp).Caption

End Sub
```

Now your sample program is done. Figure 12.15 shows how the program looks.

FIGURE 12.15
The sample application displays a list of baseball teams when a tab is clicked.

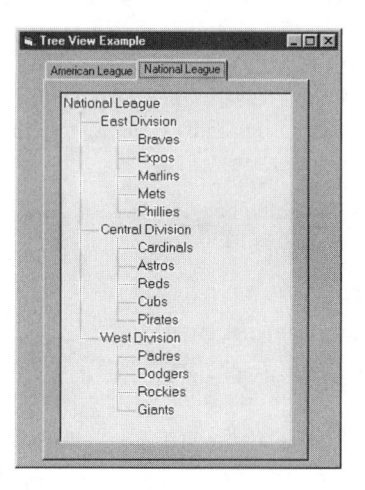

The crux of the project is the `DisplayLeague` procedure. First, this procedure creates a node for the League divisions:

```
Set tempNode = tv1.Nodes.Add("R", tvwChild, "E", "East Division")
```

The constant `tvwChild` tells the application to make this new node a child of the node `"R"`.

Then, to each Division node, several team nodes are added:

```
Set tempNode = tv1.Nodes.Add("E", tvwChild, "E" & nCounter, sTemp)
```

Notice that the first argument in the `Add` method is now `"E"`, which is the unique key of the node of the Eastern Division. The `"E1"` node (which displays Yankees) knows that it is a child of the Eastern Division because of this key.

Next, you tell the entire Division node and its children to remain expanded (TreeView nodes can be expanded and collapsed) in this line:

```
MyNode.EnsureVisible
```

(You also could have set each Division node's Expanded property to True.)

The last thing that deserves attention is the way the TabStrip reports back which tab has been clicked. In the TabStrip control, tabs are an array of tabs. So, when you click a tab, you are actually selecting a tab, like selecting a ListIndex in a ListBox control. In light of this knowledge, if you want to find out which tab is being clicked, the following line should make a bit more sense to you:

```
nTemp = tsMain.SelectedItem.Index
```

In this example, you simply get the index of the selected tab and store it in the variable nTemp.

Accepting User Input

Several of the Windows Common controls offer different ways to accept user input. For example, displaying a calendar when users want to input dates is not necessary, but it makes your program look very professional. One of the great benefits of Visual Basic's many controls is that you can quickly create a sharp-looking program by bringing together prebuilt objects. In this section, you will review the following controls:

- ImageCombo, which is a graphical combo box
- MonthView, which is a calendar control
- DTPicker, which is a date combo box
- UpDown, which is used to enhance numeric input.
- Slider, which is used to input numbers graphically

Using an ImageCombo Control

One of the new controls in Visual Basic 6.0 is the ImageCombo control. From a user interface standpoint, the ImageControl serves the same purpose as the standard ComboBox control discussed in Chapter 4, "Using Visual Basic's Default Controls." However, the image combo box allows you to add pictures beside each item in the combo box's drop-down list, as pictured in Figure 12.16.

FIGURE 12.16
An ImageCombo looks sharper than a standard combo box.

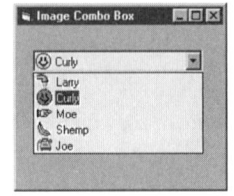

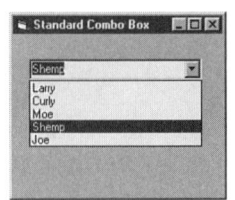

NOTE Another difference is that the ImageCombo control supports only one style of combo box: the drop-down list. As you may recall, a standard ComboBox control has several other styles available.

▶ See "The Combo Box," **p. 75**

Setting Up an ImageCombo Box Like many of the other Windows Common controls, an ImageCombo uses an ImageList control to store the pictures to be displayed in the combo box. For each Item in the ImageCombo's ComboItems collection, you can actually specify the index of these two images:

- Image—Set this property to the index of the image that you want to appear to the left of each item.
- SelImage—This property is optional. If you supply a value for this property, the image beside an item changes when the item is selected or highlighted with the mouse. If you do not supply a value for the SelImage property, the control uses the image from the Image property.

To learn how users interact with the two types of images, follow these steps:

1. Start a new Standard EXE project, and add an ImageList control.

2. Set the size of the images in the list to 16×16, and insert two pictures. For the example, I used a smiley face and an arrow.

3. Add an ImageCombo control to the form, and add the following code to the form's Load event:

    ```
    ImageCombo1.ImageList = ImageList1
    ImageCombo1.ComboItems.Add , , "Moe", 1, 2
    ImageCombo1.ComboItems.Add , , "Larry", 1, 2
    ImageCombo1.ComboItems.Add , , "Curly", 1, 2
    ImageCombo1.ComboItems.Add , , "Shemp", 1, 2
    ImageCombo1.ComboItems.Add , , "Joe", 1, 2
    ```

    Notice that the Add statements use the same Image and SelImage image indexes for each item.

4. Run the program, and drag the mouse pointer over each item the item list. As you highlight an item, the image should change. In addition, if you have an item selected, the image represented by SelItem is displayed beside both the selected item and the highlighted item, as shown in Figure 12.17.

FIGURE 12.17
You can use the SelImage property to set apart the highlighted and selected items.

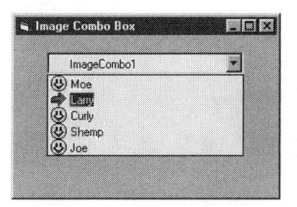

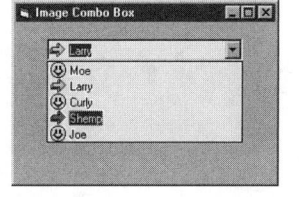

Working with the Selected Item   Each item displayed in the ImageCombo is a member of the `ComboItems` collection. To determine whether users have selected items, check the `SelectedItem` property for a reference to the items, as in the following lines of code:

```
If ImageCombo1.SelectedItem Is Nothing Then
        ' No Item is Selected!
Else
        MsgBox "You selected: " & ImageCombo1.SelectedItem.Text
End If
```

NOTE   You can also select an item from code by setting the item's `Selected` property to `True`, as in the following example:

`ImageCombo1.ComboItems(1).Selected = True`

Why do you need to check the `SelectedItem` property to see whether it is `Nothing`? As you may recall from using the standard combo box control, users can not only select items from the item list, but they also can enter text in the combo box's input area. The ImageCombo control also exhibits this behavior. If the information in the input area does not represent an item in the list, attempting to access properties of the `SelectedItem` object causes an error.

NOTE   You can force the users to select one of your items from the list by setting the `Locked` property of the ImageCombo to `True`, which disables free-form text input.

As with the standard combo box, the text for the selected or entered item is available via the `Text` property.

Organizing Combo Box Items   Another feature of the ImageCombo control is that you can specify a level of indentation for each item in the `ComboItems` collection. By indenting certain items, you can give your list a sense of organization.

To set an item's indentation, you assign the `Indentation` property an integer value. The `Indentation` property can also be specified as the final optional parameter in the `Add` method, as in the following example:

`cmbMain.ComboItems.Add , "mykey", "mytext", 1, 2, 1`

Each indentation level represents 10 pixels. A sample ImageCombo that makes use of the `Indentation` property is shown in Figure 12.18.

FIGURE 12.18
You can use the Indentation property to organize an ImageCombo list.

The UpDown Control

The UpDown control is another Common control used to accept input from users. However, the UpDown control is unique in that it is not designed to be a standalone control. Instead, it works with another "buddy" control to allow users to modify its numeric values easily. In other words, if you have a text field that requires a numeric value, you can link an UpDown control to it so that users can run up and down through numbers without typing anything.

The UpDown control, shown in Figure 12.19 with a text box, consists of a pair of arrow buttons. These buttons let users increment or decrement the value of a number. The UpDown control can be used with any other control that can handle numbers, including text boxes, labels, scrollbars, and sliders.

FIGURE 12.19
The UpDown control allows users to adjust the value of a number.

UpDown control

TextBox control

Setting Up the UpDown Control   To set up the UpDown control, follow these steps:

1. On your form, draw a control that can handle numbers, such as the TextBox control.
2. Draw the UpDown control on your form.
3. Set the `BuddyControl` property of the UpDown control to the name of the control that displays the numeric values. Note that you have to type the name of the control (such as `Text1`) or use the `AutoBuddy` property.
4. Set the `BuddyProperty` of the UpDown control to `Default`. This action causes the UpDown control to update the default property of its Buddy control, such as the `Text` property of a text box. You can also set it to another property, as long as the property you select is numeric.

After completing the basic setup of the UpDown control, you can set other properties to control its appearance and behavior. For controlling the appearance of the UpDown control, the two key properties are as follow:

- `Alignment`—Controls whether the UpDown control appears to the left or the right of the Buddy control
- `Orientation`—Controls whether the UpDown control's buttons are oriented horizontally or vertically

The effects of the `Alignment` and `Orientation` properties are shown in Figure 12.20.

FIGURE 12.20
The UpDown control can be arranged many different ways.

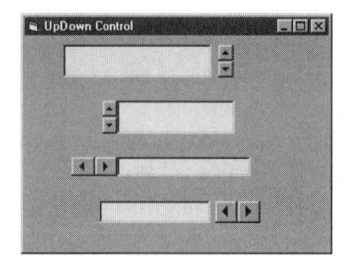

Probably of greater importance to the programmer and users are the properties that determine the behavior of the UpDown control. These properties are as follows:

- `Increment`—Sets the amount that a value changes each time a button is clicked.
- `Max`—Sets the maximum value the control can contain.
- `Min`—Sets the minimum value the control can contain.
- `SyncBuddy`—Causes the UpDown control to update the Buddy control. You might want this property set to `False` only if you are using the UpDown control without a Buddy control. For example, you might use the UpDown control by itself to allow users to move between pages in a report.
- `Wrap`—Determines whether the control starts over with the minimum value if users click the up button after the maximum value is reached (or vice versa).

Working with Values and Events When you use the UpDown control, you can obtain the number selected by the users in two ways: by retrieving the `Value` property of the UpDown control or retrieving the appropriate property of the Buddy control. For almost all cases, either value will do. You might want to use the property of the Buddy control only if the users are allowed to enter a value that is outside the range of the UpDown control.

> **CAUTION**
> Keep in mind that the `SyncBuddy` property previously mentioned updates the Buddy control with its values, not the other way around. In the sample figures, if users were to type numbers in the text box, the UpDown control's `Value` property would not be updated. One way to remedy this situation would be to assign the `Value` property in the text box's `Change` event.

In addition to the usual events that are present for most controls, the UpDown control has three key events of interest:

- `Change`—Occurs any time the `Value` property of the control is changed
- `DownClick`—Occurs when users click the down arrow of the control
- `UpClick`—Occurs when users click the up arrow of the control

Working with Dates

In Visual Basic 6.0, two controls that greatly simplify your ability to enter dates were added to the second Windows Common controls group. These controls are the MonthView control and the DTPicker control. The MonthView control, pictured in Figure 12.21, is a versatile calendar control that lets users select dates visually rather than enter dates with the keyboard.

FIGURE 12.21
A MonthView control allows your users to select a date value by looking at a calendar rather than having to type it.

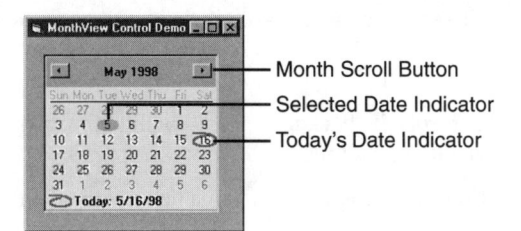

- Month Scroll Button
- Selected Date Indicator
- Today's Date Indicator

Changing the Appearance of the MonthView   Figure 12.21 shows the MonthView control as it appears by default. You can use several additional properties to change the initial appearance and behavior of the control, however. Some of them are listed in Tables 12.2 and 12.3.

Table 12.2   Appearance Properties of the MonthView Control

Name	Default Value	Description
ShowToday	True	Controls whether a line appears at the bottom of the calendar indicating the current date.
ShowWeekNumbers	False	Controls whether a column displaying the week number appears to the left of each month.
ScrollRate	1	Controls how many months the calendar advances or moves back when users click the scroll buttons. Note that even if this property is set to a value higher than 1, users can still move through the months one at a time by clicking the trailing dates at the corners of the MonthView control.
DayBold()	False	Controls whether the specified date is displayed in bold type. This property is useful if you want to indicate special days on the calendar, such as holidays. To use the property, you must specify a date, as in the following example: `MonthView1.DayBold(#7/4/1998#) = True`

The MonthView control allows you to specify colors for each of its individual sections.

Table 12.3 Color Properties of the MonthView

Name	Description
ForeColor	Controls the color of the days of the month and the horizontal line beneath the week labels.
TrailingForeColor	Determines the color of the days that are outside the months currently being displayed but still visible on the screen. Trailing days on a normal calendar often appear as empty space at the end of the month.
MonthBackColor	Controls the background area behind the days of the month, but not including the title.
TitleBackColor	Controls the color of the area behind the month name.
TitleForeColor	Sets the color of the text used to display the month name.

Displaying Multiple Months If you want to display more than one month at a time using the MonthView control, you can set the MonthRows and MonthCols properties. For example, Figure 12.22 shows a MonthView control with both of these properties set to a value of 2, creating a grid.

FIGURE 12.22
The MonthView control is not limited to displaying a single month at a time.

> **CAUTION**
> You cannot display more than 12 months on the screen at one time. Attempting to do so causes an error.

For even more flexibility, you can set the MonthRows and MonthCols properties at runtime, allowing the users to choose dynamically how much of the calendar they want to view. Note that the size of the MonthView control is not user scalable. In other words, the 2×2 grid shown in Figure 12.22 always has a fixed size. If you change the size of the grid at runtime, the MonthView control automatically expands and contracts to the new size. Therefore, knowing the new size beforehand would be nice. Fortunately, the MonthView control offers a method called `ComputeControlSize` that returns the size of a MonthView with the specified number of rows and columns, as shown in the following example:

```
Dim sngWidth As Single, sngHeight As Single
MonthView1.ComputeControlSize 4, 2, sngWidth, sngHeight
Debug.Print "New control dimensions: " & sngWidth, sngHeight
```

N O T E The numbers returned by `ComputeControlSize` are in the units of the form's `ScaleMode` property (twips by default).

The preceding code sample calls the `ComputeControlSize` method to determine the size of a 4×2 MonthView control. The resulting height and width are returned via output parameters to the variables `sngWidth` and `sngHeight`.

Working with Values So far, you have seen how to control the display behavior of the MonthView control. However, to do anything useful with the control, you need a way to determine and set the current date. The main property that you use to do so is the `Value` property. You can use the `Value` property to return or set the current date of a month view, as in the following examples:

```
MonthView1.Value = #01/03/1943#
MonthView1.Value = "7/19/75 2:34:00 PM"
MonthView1.Value = Now
Debug.Print "The Selected date is " & MonthView1.Value
```

N O T E You can control the range of valid dates by setting the `MinDate` and `MaxDate` properties of the control.

Although the `Value` property always uses the Visual Basic Date data type, the MonthView control includes several additional properties that represent different parts of the current date value:

- `Month`—The selected month of the year (1 through 12)
- `Day`—The day of the selected month (1 through 31)
- `Year`—The selected year (for example, 1998)
- `Week`—The selected week of the year (1 through 52)

Each of the preceding properties is automatically updated when the `Value` property changes, and vice versa. You can assign or read integer values to these properties to work with just the information you want.

Although the MonthView control's `Value` property always has only one value, you can set some properties that allow users to select multiple consecutive days on the calendar. By setting the `MultiSelect` property to `True`, the users can click and drag to select a range of days, as shown in Figure 12.23.

If you set the `MultiSelect` property to `True`, use the `SelStart` and `SelEnd` properties to determine the selected date range.

FIGURE 12.23
The MultiSelect property allows the selection of a range of days.

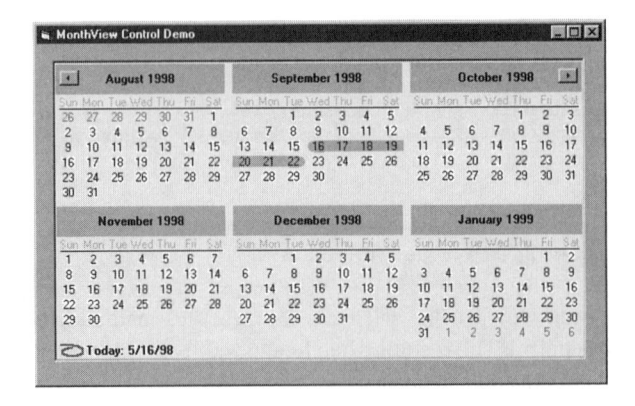

The DTPicker Control The DTPicker (or DateTimePicker) control combines the calendar functionality of the MonthView control with the ability to type a date manually. This control allows users who know the exact date to enter it quickly, and at the same time, it makes a calendar available for those people who need it. The DTPicker looks like a combo box, but when you click the drop-down arrow, a MonthView control appears. Both states of the DTPicker control are shown in Figure 12.24.

FIGURE 12.24
The DTPicker control allows both graphical and text input of dates.

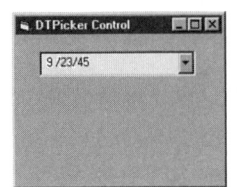

Many of the same properties available in the MonthView control are available in the DTPicker control. However, unlike the MonthView, the DTPicker cannot display multiple months at the same time.

Because the DTPicker control allows manual entry of dates, a few parameters are used to determine their format. You can set the Format parameter to any of the following values:

- 0 - dtpLongDate—Displays the Long Date format, as defined in Control Panel.
- 1 - dtpShortDate—(default) Displays the Short Date format, as defined in Control Panel—usually M/D/YY.
- 2 - dtpTime—Displays only the time portion of the date value. When this setting is selected, the drop-down button is replaced by up/down arrows, and the calendar does not appear.
- 3 - dtpCustom—Displays a custom date format.

When you set this control to 3 -dtpCustom, you can supply your own format string in the Custom property. Several formats are shown in Figure 12.25.

FIGURE 12.25
You can display dates in several formats with the DTPicker control.

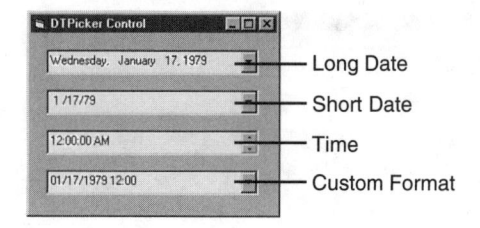

- Long Date
- Short Date
- Time
- Custom Format

Sliding into Numbers

Another of the Windows common controls is the Slider control. The Slider control provides a means for users to enter numeric data into a program. The slider works like the slider switches you might find on your stereo system's graphic equalizer or in a manner similar to the scrollbars that you have in the standard control set of Visual Basic.

▶ See "Scrollbars," **p. 78**

You create the slider by drawing it on your form. You then can set four main properties that control the appearance of the slider. These properties are summarized in Table 12.4. The effects of these properties are shown in Figure 12.26.

Table 12.4 Properties of the Slider Control

Property	Settings
BorderStyle	Determines the type of border. Set to 0 for no border or 1 for a single-line border.
Orientation	Determines the orientation of the sliders. Set this property to 0 for a horizontal slider or 1 for a vertical slider.
TickStyle	Controls the placement of the tick marks on the slider. Set this property to 0 to display tick marks below or to the right of the slider, set it to 1 to place tick marks above or to the left of the slider, set it to 2 to place tick marks on both sides, or set it to 3 to show no tick marks.
TickFrequency	Determines how many tick marks are displayed. This property can be set to any positive number.

After you set up the appearance of the slider, you need to set several properties that control its operation. The first two properties are the Min and Max properties, which control the range of values that can be handled by the Slider control. The other two properties are the LargeChange and SmallChange properties. The LargeChange property controls how much the value of the slider changes if users press the PageUp or PageDown keys or click the mouse on either side of the slider bar. The SmallChange property controls how much the value of the slider changes if users press the right or left arrow keys. SelectRange is the final property affecting the operation of the slider. This property determines whether the slider can select only a single value or possibly select a range of values.

FIGURE 12.26
The Slider lets you graphically enter numeric information.

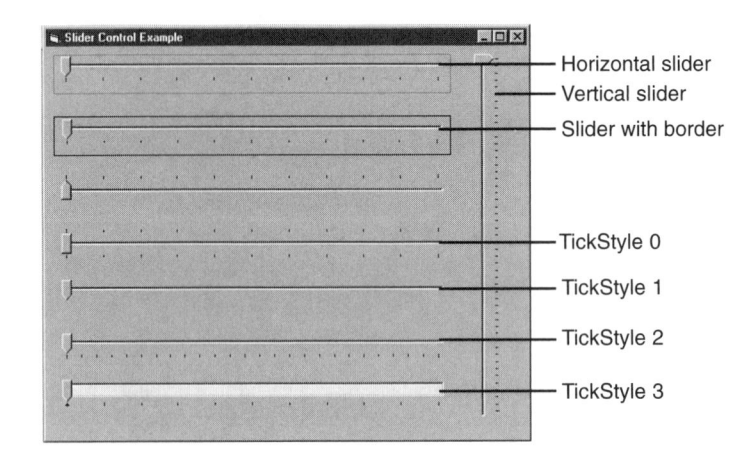

- Horizontal slider
- Vertical slider
- Slider with border
- TickStyle 0
- TickStyle 1
- TickStyle 2
- TickStyle 3

Using the Slider Control When your users encounter the Slider control in your program, they can click the slider bar and drag it to set a value. They can also use the PageUp, PageDown, and right and left arrow keys to change the value. The information entered by the users is contained in the Value property of the slider.

N O T E The keyboard keys only work on a Slider if it has the focus.

If the SelectRange property is set to True, the users also can select a range of values by holding down the Shift key while clicking and dragging the slider bar. Unfortunately, this technique is not automatic; it must be managed by your code. You need to add code to the slider's MouseDown event procedure to determine whether users have held down Shift while dragging the slider. If so, your code can set the slider's SelStart property, which defines the starting value of the range, and the SelLength property, which defines the extent of the range. Visual Basic's help system contains a good example under the help topic for the Slider Control.

The Color Blender Project To demonstrate the use of the Slider control, you will now build a "color blender" sample project. As you know, Visual Basic forms have a BackColor property, which contains a numeric value representing the form's background color. This sample project uses an array of Slider controls to set the BackColor property.

Follow these steps to create the color blender project and add the controls for the project:

1. Create a new Standard EXE project.
2. Place a check box on the form, name it ckGray, and set the Caption property to Only Shades Of Gray.
3. Place a Slider control on the form, and name it sldColor.
4. Place a label on the form to the left of the slider, and name it lblColor.

5. Make a set of control arrays for lblColor and sldColor. To do so, hold down the Ctrl key and click both lblColor and sldColor. Choose Edit, Copy. Then choose Edit, Paste to paste the copied controls onto the form. You then are presented with a dialog box asking whether you want to create a control array. Click Yes. (Control arrays are covered in detail in Chapter 13, "Working with Control Arrays.")
6. Add a third element to each control array by choosing Paste again.
7. Using the Properties window, set the caption of lblColor(0) to Red:, the caption of lblColor(1) to Green:, and lblColor(2) to Blue:.
8. Arrange the lblColor() and sldColor() control arrays on the form as shown in Figure 12.27.

FIGURE 12.27
The main form of the color blender project contains an array of slider controls.

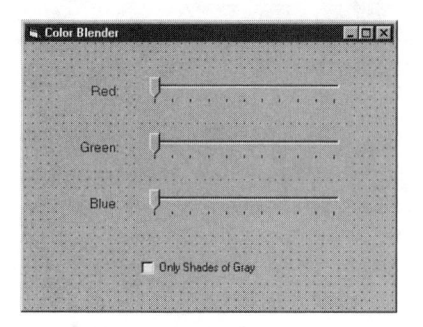

After you set up the interface of the program, you need to add some code to a couple of events to make the program work. The first event is the Load event of the form, as shown in Listing 12.5. This event sets the initial condition of the program.

Listing 12.5 SLIDERS.ZIP—Initializing the Program in the *Load* Event of the Form

```
Private Sub Form_Load()

    Dim nCount As Integer
    Dim lRed As Long, lGreen As Long, lBlue As Long

'Set up the sliders
    For  nCount = 0 To 2
        sldColor(nCount ).Min = 0
        sldColor(nCount ).Max = 255

        sldColor(nCount ).TickFrequency = 4
    Next  nCount

    'Initialize the color of the form
    'control. (This will set the color to black. RGB(0,0,0))
    Me.BackColor = RGB(lRed, lGreen, lBlue)

End Sub
```

Next, you need to add the code that actually changes the colors in response to movements of the Slider control. You place this code, shown in Listing 12.6, in the `Scroll` event of the Slider controls.

Listing 12.6 SLIDERS.ZIP—Moving the Slider to Change the Color of the Form

```
Private Sub sldColor_Scroll(Index As Integer)

    Dim nCount As Integer
    Dim lRed As Long, lGreen As Long, lBlue As Long

    'Gray is equal values of Red, Green and Blue
    If ckGray.Value = vbChecked Then
        'move all the sliders
            For nCount = 0 to 2
            sldColor(nCount).Value = sldColor(Index).Value
        Next nCount
    End If

    'Set the RGB value
    lRed = sldColor(0).Value
    lGreen = sldColor(1).Value
    lBlue = sldColor(2).Value

    'Assign the resultant RGB value to the backcolor
    Me.BackColor = RGB(lRed, lGreen, lBlue)
End Sub
```

Running the Project   After you enter the code, press F5 to compile and run the program. Then try setting different combinations of the color sliders to see the effect on the color blender.

The Color Blender project works like this: After an initialization process in the `Form_Load` event, most of the work takes place in the `sldColor_Scroll` event. As a user moves a slider from the array of Slider controls, the moved slider's index is passed into the `sldColor_Scroll` event. The application checks the value of the `ckGray` check box. If it is checked (`Value = vbChecked`), the value of the moved slider is assigned to all the controls in the slider control array. This causes all the sliders to move to the same position before any other code is executed.

The application then assigns the value from the `Value` property of each Slider in the `sldColor` control array to their respective color variables—`lRed`, `lGreen`, `lBlue`. The color variables are then passed as parameters to the `RGB()` function. The return of the `RGB()` function sets the `BackColor` property of the form.

Reporting Status and Progress

One of the most important aspects of any program is keeping the users informed about what is going on in the program at any given time. For a program such as a word processor, the users like to know what's the current page and what's the current position on that page. This type of information, called *status information*, is usually displayed onscreen all the time rather than in a message box. In addition, users want to know how long a given task will take to accomplish and what part of the task is occurring at any given point in time. This type of information can be called *progress information*. In this section, you look at three of the common controls used for these purposes:

- StatusBar, which displays status messages
- ProgressBar, which provides a graphical representation of progress toward a goal
- Animation, which allows you to display a "movie" to let the users know your program is doing something

Before you can use any of these controls, you must add them to the Visual Basic Toolbox. For information on how to add controls, see the first section of this chapter, "Introduction to the Common Controls."

Adding a Status Bar to Your Program

Before the advent of the StatusBar control, Visual Basic programmers often used "fake" status bars made from panels and Label controls. They worked quite well (and still do today). However, the StatusBar control provides a simpler alternative. If you are already using one of the other Common controls from the same group, you don't have to worry about the extra overhead of distributing another because all of the controls in the group are included in the same OCX file, which you have to distribute anyway.

Figure 12.28 shows a typical status bar from a Visual Basic program.

FIGURE 12.28
Status bars are usually positioned at the bottom of a form.

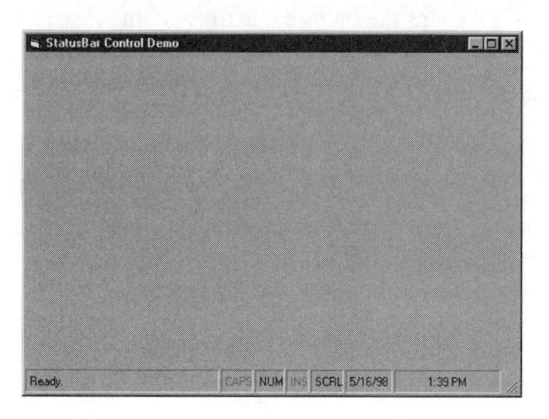

Creating a Status Bar You create a status bar by first selecting the control and drawing it on your form. When it is first drawn, the status bar spans the width of its parent form and contains a single panel, as shown in Figure 12.29. Notice that no matter where on your form you draw the status bar, it automatically moves to the bottom of the form. This position is the typical location for a program's status bar.

FIGURE 12.29
When you place a status bar on a form, it is configured automatically.

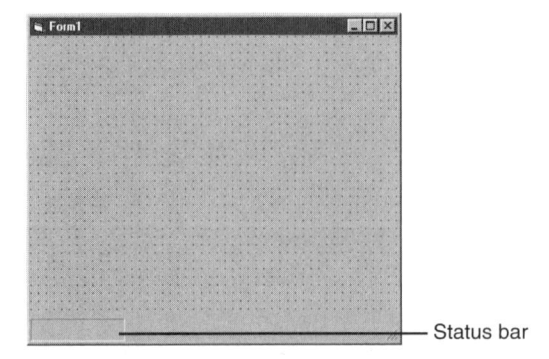

— Status bar

After you draw the status bar, you can start setting the properties to control its appearance and to create any additional panels that you need to display information. As you saw when you first drew the status bar control, it sizes itself to fit across the entire form. You can, however, control the height of the status bar either by setting its Height property or by clicking and dragging one of its sizing handles.

Two other properties control the basic appearance of the entire status bar: the Align property and the Style property.

The Align property of the status bar controls which edge of the form, if any, the status bar is "docked" against. The Align property has five possible settings:

- vbAlignNone—Allows you to position the status bar anywhere on your form.
- vbAlignTop—Positions the status bar at the top of the form.
- vbAlignBottom—Positions the status bar at the bottom of the form. This is the default setting of the property and the position where users probably expect to find the status bar.
- vbAlignLeft—Places the status bar at the left edge of the form.
- vbAlignRight—Places the status bar at the right edge of the form.

NOTE Unless you have a specific reason for using a different alignment, sticking with the default, bottom alignment is best. Although another alignment might be a novel approach, it would probably confuse users who are accustomed to the standard alignment.

As you can see in Figure 12.28, the StatusBar control allows you to display a number of different messages at the same time. Each section of the status bar is known as a *panel*. The following two settings of the Style property of the status bar determine whether the status bar displays a single panel or multiple panels:

- sbrNormal—Allows multiple panels to be displayed
- sbrSimple—Allows only a single panel to be displayed

If you set the `Style` to `sbrSimple`, then the StatusBar acts like a simple label control, whose single panel caption is controlled via the `SimpleText` property. However, more features are available when you create a multiple panel status bar.

Working with the Panels of the Status Bar The real work of the status bar is handled by its panels. Each panel is a separate object with its own properties that control its appearance and behavior. Each panel is part of the status bar's `Panels` collection. After you draw the status bar on your form and set its basic properties, you can begin adding panels to the bar. You do so through the Property Pages of the status bar, shown in Figure 12.30.

FIGURE 12.30
You can manage your status bar by clicking the ellipsis button to the right of the `Custom` property in the Properties window.

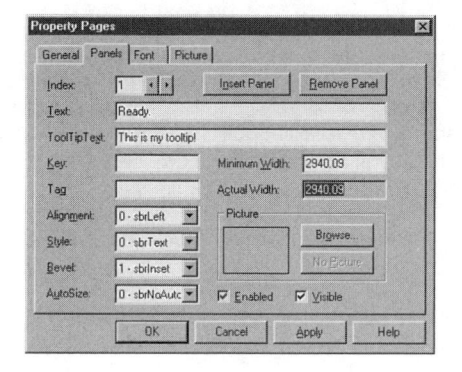

To set up an individual panel, use the Property Pages dialog box to set these eight main properties that control the appearance and behavior of the panel:

- `Text`—Determines the text to be displayed in a text style panel. (Usually you set this property at runtime.)
- `ToolTipText`—Sets the text that is displayed when users rest the mouse pointer over the panel.
- `Alignment`—Determines whether the text in the panel is left-justified, right-justified, or centered in the panel.
- `Style`—Determines the type of panel created.
- `Bevel`—Sets the type of shadowing used for the 3D look of the panel.
- `AutoSize`—Determines how the size of the panel is handled by the program.
- `MinWidth`—Sets the minimum size of the panel.
- `Picture`—Determines what, if any, picture is displayed in the panel.

Although most of these properties are self-explanatory, the `Style` and `AutoSize` properties merit further attention.

You can create seven different styles of panels for your status bar. Although one of the styles (`sbrText`) is designed for you to display your own text, most of the other styles are predefined status items. These styles display the settings of the lock keys (such as Caps Lock, Num Lock, and so on) or the system date and time. These styles are handled by the control itself, so you can set them up in design mode; this way, you don't have to do anything while the program is running. The styles of panels are summarized in Table 12.5. Each of these styles is also displayed in Figure 12.28.

Table 12.5 Panel Styles Available to Your Programs

Setting	Description
sbrText	Displays text or a bitmap. The text displayed is contained in the `Text` property of the panel, whereas the bitmap is contained in the `Picture` property.
sbrCaps	Handles the status of the Caps Lock key. This panel displays CAPS in bold letters when the key is on and displays the letters dimmed when the key is off.
sbrNum	Handles the status of the Num Lock key. This panel displays NUM in bold letters when the key is on and displays the letters dimmed when the key is off.
sbrIns	Handles the status of the Insert key. This panel displays INS in bold letters when the key is on and displays the letters dimmed when the key is off.
sbrScrl	Handles the status of the Scroll Lock key. This panel displays SCRL in bold letters when the key is on and displays the letters dimmed when the key is off.
sbrTime	Displays the current time.
sbrDate	Displays the current date

NOTE An eighth setting, sbrKana, is also associated with the Scroll Lock key. It displays KANA in bold letters when the key is on and displays dimmed letters when the key is off. The KANA indicator is a special setting for Japanese programs.

The `AutoSize` property of each panel has three settings that help determine the size of the panel. The default setting, `NoAutoSize`, sets the size of the panel to the dimension specified in the `MinWidth` property; this size does not change as other panels are added and removed. The `sbrContents` setting sets the size of the panel to fit the text that the panel contains, whether this is text you enter or the text used for the key status and date/time panels. The final setting, `sbrSpring`, allows panels to stretch to fit the width of the status bar. This setting prevents any empty space from being present in the bar.

NOTE No matter which setting you choose for the `AutoSize` property, a panel is not made smaller than the dimension set by the `MinWidth` property.

One final property of note is the `Bevel` property. As stated previously, this property determines whether and how the 3D effects of the panel are displayed. This property has three settings: sbrNoBevel, which produces a flat panel; sbrInset (the default), which produces a panel that looks embedded in the status bar; and sbrRaised, which produces a raised panel. These three bevel styles are shown in Figure 12.31.

FIGURE 12.31
You can create flat, inset, or raised panels.

Managing Panels with Code You have seen how to set the properties of an individual panel, but you also need to know how to add and remove panels. Within the Property Pages, you can simply use the Insert Panel and Remove Panel buttons. However, the status bar also enables you to add and remove panels from code. This task is handled by the three methods of the Panels collection:

- Add—Creates a new panel for the status bar
- Remove—Deletes a specific panel from the status bar
- Clear—Removes all the panels of the status bar

N O T E Unlike most other built-in collection types, the Panels collection starts with an index of 1, and the index values run up to the Count property.

You have seen that the key status and date/time panels handle their tasks automatically. These things are great, but the real power of the status bar is its capability to change the text that appears in the text-style panel(s) as your program is running. These text panels tell the users the actual status of operations in your program.

To update the status of an item in your program, you assign a text string to the Text property of the Panel object, as shown in the following line of code:

```
StatusBar1.Panels(1).Text = "Viewing record 1 of 10"
```

You can, of course, set other properties of the panels the same way. You can even set up your entire status bar in code by using the methods of the Panels collection and the properties of the Panel objects. As an example, Listing 12.7 shows how to set up the status bar shown in Figure 12.32. This listing also uses the Count property of the Panels collection, which tells you how many panels are present in the status bar.

Listing 12.7 STATUS.ZIP—Setting Up a Status Bar in Code

```
Private Sub Form_Load()

    With StatusBar1

        'Remove the default panel
        .Panels.Remove 1

        'Add a Text panel at the left
        .Panels.Add 1, "mykey", "This is the status text", sbrText
```

continues

Listing 12.7 STATUS.ZIP—Setting Up a Status Bar in Code

```
        .Panels(1).AutoSize = sbrSpring
        'Add the current time display
        .Panels.Add , , , sbrTime
    End With

End Sub
```

FIGURE 12.32
You can control your status bar by setting properties of the Panel objects.

Progress Bar

The status bar is not the only control that you can use to monitor progress in your program. Many programs have some tasks that take a relatively long time, so you'll want the capability to provide users with a dynamic indication of the operation's progress. The ProgressBar control is ideal for this situation. For example, Microsoft Internet Explorer uses a progress bar to indicate the percentage completed of a file transfer operation. In this case, the progress bar lets you know two things: First, as long as the bar is changing, you know that the file transfer is progressing. Second, by looking at the progress bar, you have some idea how much time is left in the transfer operation.

Setting Up the Progress Bar You can easily set up and use the ProgressBar control. As with other controls, you first draw the bar on your form. Then you need to set the bar's properties. Among the several properties that can influence the look of the progress bar, Height and Width are the key properties. A progress bar typically is many times wider than it is tall. In fact, Microsoft recommends (in the Help system) that you make the width of the bar at least 12 times the height. Figure 12.33 shows a typical progress bar.

The Value property of the progress bar sets or retrieves how much of the progress bar appears filled in. If you compare a ProgressBar control to a thermometer, the Value property is like the temperature. Everything below the current temperature is filled with mercury, and the remaining area is blank.

FIGURE 12.33
Progress bars provide a visual indication of how much of an operation has been completed.

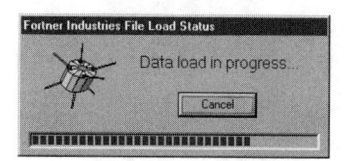

Max and Min are the other properties that you need to set for the progress bar. They represent the maximum and minimum values allowed for the Value property. In the case of the thermometer, they represent the top and bottom of the temperature scale. For example, if you set the Min property to 0 and the Max property to 100, setting the Value property to 50 causes the progress bar to look half full.

The setting of the Max and Min properties can be any valid integer, though the Max property must always be greater than the Min property. You can set these properties to any values that make sense for your applications. Some examples are as follows:

- In processing a database, set Min to 0 and Max to the number of records to be processed. As each record is processed, incrementing the Value property informs the users of the processing progress.

- For a file download operation, you might set Max to the number of kilobytes or number of blocks in the file. One typical setting is a Min of 0 and a Max of 100 to represent the percentage of the file that has been transferred.

Updating the Progress Bar as Your Code Runs The key to displaying the progress of an operation in the progress bar is setting the Value property. As your code runs through an operation, you periodically update the setting of the Value property. As you might expect, you often do so in a loop that performs a repetitive operation, as in the following code sample:

```
'In the following code, "rsMain" is a recordset
'that has already been opened and populated.
'"pbr" is the ProgressBar control.

pbr.Min = 0
rsMain.MoveLast
pbr.Max = rsMain.RecordCount
rsMain.MoveFirst
inCounter = 0

While Not rsMain.EOF
'Insert code to process record here
    inCounter = inCounter + 1
    pbr.Value = inCounter
    rsMain.MoveNext
Wend
```

Adding Video with the Animation Control

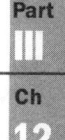

The Animation control provides you with an easy way to add animation to your programs. You use this control to play silent Audio Video Interleaved (AVI) clips. The AVI file format is basically a series of bitmaps that are shown in sequence to create the animation effect, similar to the individual drawings in a cartoon. You typically use the Animation control to indicate that a task is in progress, such as the File, Copy routine of Windows, shown in Figure 12.34. These animations run in the background while other tasks are performed.

FIGURE 12.34
A copy in progress is indicated by a simple animation.

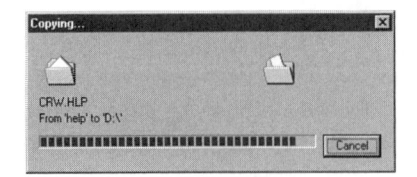

> **NOTE** Another way to create simple animation effects might be to use a Timer control to change the position of an Image control at a specified interval. Although this method requires a little more coding than is necessary with the Animation control, you do not need to have your animation already saved in an AVI file. The Timer control is covered in Chapter 4, "Using Visual Basic's Default Controls."

Setting Up the Animation Control   To set up an Animation control, first add an instance of the control by drawing it on the form. Figure 12.35 shows the initial appearance of the Animation control.

FIGURE 12.35
The Animation control initially looks like a picture box with a reel of film in the middle.

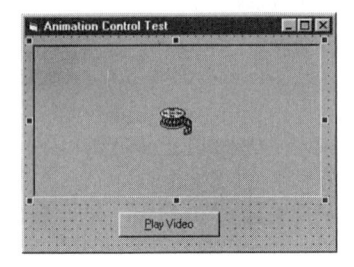

Drawing the Animation control on the form provides the container for the animation sequence. However, to run an animation, you need to open a file and start playback.

You can do this by adding a command button to your form and writing code in the `Click` event to open and play a video file.

To open a file, use the `Open` method of the Animation control, specifying the path to the desired AVI file. (Several AVI videos are included in the \Graphics\Videos directory, if you chose to install them.) After you open an AVI file, execute the `Play` method to start the animation. The following two lines of code play an AVI file:

```
Animation1.Open "C:\Progra~1\Micros~1\Common\Graphics\Videos\FileNuke.Avi"
Animation1.Play
```

Figure 12.36 shows the control during playback. To stop the animation, simply use the `Stop` method of the control.

FIGURE 12.36
Calling the `Play` method causes the video to play repeatedly.

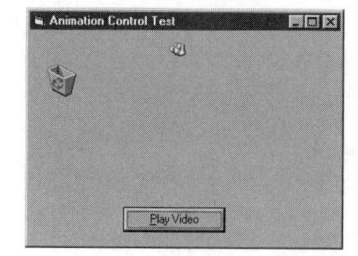

> **TIP** Create a form that you can use in all your Visual Basic projects to display status information. The form could include an Animation control and progress bar. You can set the Animation control's `AutoPlay` property to `True` to start the video automatically, without executing the `Play` method.

Optional Parameters of the *Play* Method   The default behavior of the Animation control is to "loop" the video playback. In other words, the animation is played over and over from start to finish until the `Stop` method executes. The following three optional parameters to the `Play` method allow you to change this behavior, however:

- `Repeat`—Specifies the number of times to play the video segment.
- `Start`—Specifies the frame where playback should begin.
- `Stop`—Specifies the frame where playback should end. You can use the Windows Media Player (MPLAYER.EXE) to find frame numbers.

These optional parameters are used in the following line of code, which repeats frames 5 through 15 of an animation two times:

```
anmAviPlayer.Play 2, 5, 15
```

You can specify any or all the optional parameters. Any parameters that are omitted use their default values. The parameters must be specified in the order `Repeat`, `Start`, and `Stop`. If you omit one of the earlier parameters, you must use a comma as a placeholder.

From Here...

This chapter introduced you to the group of controls known as the Windows Common controls. Several of the controls covered here are new to Visual Basic 6.0. You can use these controls to enhance your projects in many ways. The best way to learn about them is to test them in your programs. To find out more about related topics, see the following chapters:

- If you have not yet studied the controls that are available in your toolbox by default, see Chapter 4, "Using Visual Basic's Default Controls."
- To learn about using the Toolbar control (which was not covered in this chapter) and creating menus, see Chapter 6, "Giving More Control to the User: Menus and Toolbars."
- For a discussion of using controls in an array, see Chapter 13, "Working with Control Arrays."

CHAPTER 13

Working with Control Arrays

In this chapter

Introducing Control Arrays   290

Creating a Control Array   291

Working with Control Arrays   296

Creating a Menu Item Array   298

Loading and Unloading Controls at Runtime   299

By now, you've learned how to use controls to allow your programs to interact with your users. The controls you've added to forms so far have been independent controls, with no particular relationship to other controls on your forms. As you design more complex user interfaces, however, you will often find it convenient to work with controls as a group.

In Chapter 4, "Using Visual Basic's Default Controls," you learned how to select multiple controls in the design environment and manipulate their properties as a group. Although this type of manipulation is convenient at design time, it does nothing to allow your program to work with groups of controls at runtime. Using control arrays can make runtime manipulation of multiple controls easy.

Introducing Control Arrays

A *control array* is a group of controls, all of the same type, that have the same name and are identified by an index. If you are familiar with arrays, you will find that control arrays are similar.

Control Array Elements

Each individual control in the array is referred to as an *element* of the array. Each element of a control array must meet several criteria:

- Each control must be of the same type. For example, a control array can contain either labels or text boxes, but cannot contain both.
- Each control must have the same value for the Name property.
- Each control is identified by having a unique value for its Index property. The Index property is an Integer type; therefore, its maximum possible value is 32767.

Often, a control array's elements share the same values for appearance-related properties such as Font and BorderStyle, but only the Name property is required to be the same. All other properties can be different for each element of the array.

Understanding the Advantages of Control Arrays

Working with control arrays instead of a group of individual controls presents a number of advantages; they help you in designing the interface of your program and in handling the program code. The following are some of the advantages of control arrays:

- Adding an element to a control array requires fewer system resources than adding an individual control of the same type. For example, three independent text boxes (Text1, Text2, and Text3) use more resources than a three-element text box array.
- The elements of a control array share a common set of event procedures. This means you have to write program code in only one place to handle the same event for all controls in the array.
- Control arrays provide the only means of adding controls to a form while your program is running.

- Using control arrays, you can avoid hitting the limit of 254 control names per form. Because a control array uses only one name, you can have as many elements of the array as you need. This capability allows you to place more controls on a form.

> **CAUTION**
> Don't get control-happy! Placing too many controls on a form makes your forms load slowly and can exhaust your system resources.

Creating a Control Array

You must create a control array at designtime. Although you can add elements to a control array at runtime, at least the first element of the array must be created in the design environment.

You can create a control array in three ways:

- Add a control to a form and then use the design environment's Copy and Paste capabilities to duplicate the control on the form.
- Add individual controls to a form and then change the Name properties of all the controls to the same value.
- After adding a control to your form, set its Index property to a number between 0 and 32767.

In the following sections, you'll work through the steps of creating a control array using the first method described.

Adding Control Arrays to a Form

Here, you'll add a four-element array of text boxes and another four-element array of labels to a form. Follow these steps to create the two control arrays:

1. Start a new project, if necessary. Add a new TextBox control to the form, as shown in Figure 13.1.

FIGURE 13.1
Although this text box will be part of a control array, it is initially created by normal means.

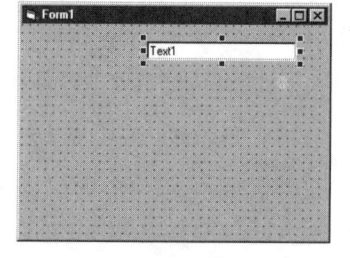

2. Set the text box's properties as follows:
   - Set the Name property to txtArray (or any other valid name).
   - Clear the Text property.
   - Set the Font property to Courier New, 10 point.

   Note that the Index property is empty (has no value).

3. Click the text box to ensure that it is still selected, and press Ctrl+C or choose Copy from the Edit menu to copy it to the Clipboard.

4. Click the form to make sure it (and not the Properties window, for example) is the active window. Press Ctrl+V, or choose Paste from the Edit menu to place a copy of the text box on the form.

5. At this point, a dialog box asks you to confirm that it is your intention to create a control array (see Figure 13.2). Choose Yes to create a control array.

FIGURE 13.2
The easiest way to create a control array is to copy and paste an existing control.

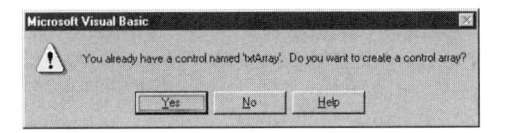

Look at the properties of the new (pasted) control. The Properties window shows that you are setting properties for txtArray(1), which specifically refers to the new element of the control array that is currently selected. Notice that its Font and Text properties match those of the text box that was copied. Notice also that the new control's Index property is set to 1.

6. Drag the new text box to a position directly below the original.

7. Click the original text box to select it. Notice that its Index property has changed from having no value to a value of 0.

8. The text box that you copied in step 3 is still on the Clipboard, so you don't need to copy it again. Paste another copy of the text box onto the form, and drag it to a position below the other two.

   Note that the new control's relevant properties match the others, and that its Index property is 2. As each control is added to the control array, its Index property is assigned a value that is one greater than the Index of the previous element. The indexes of a control array start at 0.

NOTE You don't see the control array confirmation box again, as it appears only when you attempt to make the first copy of the control.

9. Add a fourth TextBox control in the same manner, drag it to a position below the others, and set its Width property to 495 twips.

Creating a Control Array 293

10. Add a Label control named `lblArray` to the left of the first text box. Set its `Caption` property to `First Name:` and its `Alignment` property to `1 - Right Justify`.

11. Copy the Label control to the Clipboard, and paste a copy of it on the form. Answer Yes when asked whether you want to create a control array. Set the copy's `Caption` property to `Last Name:`, and drag it to the left of the second text box. (Note that you can set properties of individual control array elements just as if they were independent controls.)

12. Paste two more copies of the Label control on the form. Drag them to the left of the third and fourth text boxes, and set their `Caption` properties to `City:` and `State:`, respectively.

Figure 13.3 shows the form after completing the design steps. The figure also points out the `Index` property of a control. The non-empty value of the `Index` property indicates that the control is part of a control array.

FIGURE 13.3
This form contains two control arrays.

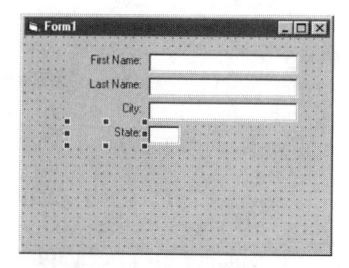

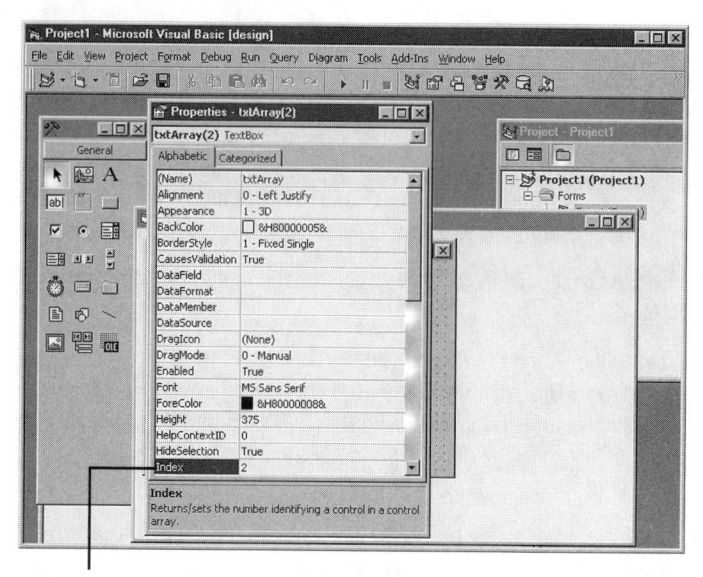

Non-empty `Index` property

Writing Code for a Control Array

After you create a control array, you can write a single piece of code to handle a particular event for all the controls in the array. For each event, Visual Basic passes the Index property of the control that triggered the event to the event procedure as an argument. This process is illustrated in Figure 13.4.

FIGURE 13.4
Control array event procedures can use the Index parameter to act according to which element caused the event to occur.

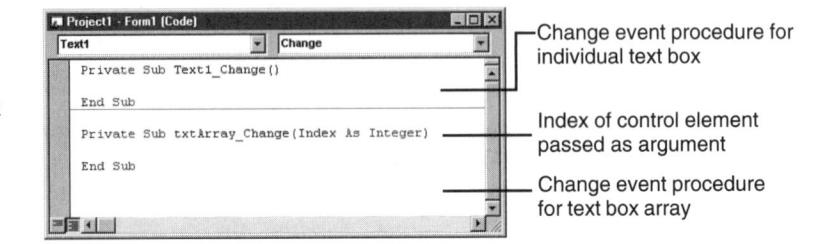

— Change event procedure for individual text box
— Index of control element passed as argument
— Change event procedure for text box array

Handling the Control Array's Events To write code for each of the elements of a control array, you simply enter the code in the Code window just as you would for any other control. Then, whenever that event is fired by any of the controls in the array, the code is executed.

Now you can enhance the sample project with an event procedure. Whenever users complete an entry in any of the three text boxes, you want to convert the text that they typed into *proper case* (only the first letter of each word is to be capitalized). You can do so by using Visual Basic's StrConv function.

But where do you put this code? Controls that can receive the form's focus have a LostFocus event that occurs just before the focus moves from that control to another one. This gives you an excellent opportunity for programmatic validation and formatting of the contents of text boxes. You can add code to the LostFocus event procedure of the text box control array. This code is executed whenever any text box loses the focus, meaning a user has most likely just entered something in the text box.

To code the LostFocus event procedure for the test application's text box control array, follow these steps:

1. Double-click any of the text boxes that make up the text box control array. The Code window is then displayed, open to the txtArray_Change event procedure. Notice that the parameter Index as Integer is available inside the procedure.

2. Because you don't want to write code for the Change event, change the event displayed in the Event drop-down box to LostFocus.

3. You should now see the txtArray_LostFocus event procedure, which also has the parameter Index as Integer available. Enter the following line of code into this event procedure:

    ```
    txtArray(Index) = StrConv(txtArray(Index), vbProperCase)
    ```

The left side of this assignment statement, txtArray(Index), refers to a specific element of the txtArray control array. Which element? The array subscript Index, which is passed into the event procedure as a parameter, allows you to determine which element of the control array just lost the focus (causing this event to fire). Therefore, this line of code assigns to that specific control array element the value of the expression on the right side of the assignment statement—in this case, the contents of that array element's default property (Text), converted to proper case via the StrConv function.

After you close the Code window, double-click one of the other elements of the text box control array. Notice that the Code window opens to the *exact same event procedure*. Remember, control array elements share event procedures.

Now try your sample application. Start by running the program; then type TINA MARIE in uppercase letters in the first text box (next to the First Name label). When you press Tab to move to the next text box, the LostFocus event fires and the text that you typed is converted to proper case. Type jones (all lowercase) in the Last Name text box. Press Tab again, and notice that this text is also converted to proper case. The LostFocus event procedure that you wrote is executed whenever the LostFocus event occurs to any of the controls in the array.

Isolating Control Array Elements with the *Index* Property   If you need to execute code only for one or more specific members of the array, your code can use the Index argument to determine which array element fired the event. Then you can, for example, place the necessary code within an If block or Select Case block.

Examine this use with the sample project. The code that converts the users' entries into proper case is working fine, but state abbreviations should be all uppercase. Therefore, you should modify the txtArray_LostFocus event procedure to isolate the state text box (array element number 3) and perform a different action for it.

Modify the code in the txtArray_LostFocus event procedure to match the following:

```
If Index = 3 Then
    txtArray(Index) = UCase(txtArray(Index))
Else
    txtArray(Index) = StrConv(txtArray(Index), vbProperCase)
End If
```

Try this new event procedure by running the program and using all lowercase letters to type your first and last name, city, and state in the appropriate text boxes. Notice how the event procedure modifies the text in the State text box differently than the others.

Manipulating Multiple Controls in Code   Another benefit of using a control array is that you can set properties for each element in an array at runtime by using a For...Next loop. This way, your program can easily work with all the controls in a control array. For example, the following lines of code convert the text in all the members of a text box control array into uppercase:

```
Dim i As Integer
For i = 0 To 3
    txtArray(i) = UCase(txtArray(i))
Next i
```

Note that the `For...Next` loop counts from 0 to 3, not 1 to 4 because the array elements, by default, are numbered beginning with 0.

Removing Elements from a Control Array

While you are in the design environment, you can remove control array elements from a form in several ways:

- By selecting the control element and pressing the Delete key
- By selecting it and choosing Edit, Delete from the menu system
- By right-clicking it and selecting Delete from the context menu

This way, you can clear the control from the form and reduce the number of elements of the control array. If, for some reason, you want to return the elements of the control array to individual controls that are not part of the array, you need to specify new `Name` property values for all but one of the controls and then delete the `Index` property values of the controls to return them to null values.

> **CAUTION**
>
> When you remove a control from a control array, the rest of the controls are not automatically renumbered. Therefore, deleting controls can leave gaps in the `Index` values of the array's remaining elements. These gaps can cause problems if, for example, you have code that uses a `For` loop to work with the elements of the control array. In this particular case, an error occurs when the loop tries to access a control array element via an `Index` property value that has been deleted.

Working with Control Arrays

Now that you understand the mechanics behind creating control arrays, you will learn some ways that they are commonly used. In general, you group controls into an array when you need to use similar code to process each control, such as four text boxes representing lines in a street address. Simplifying the programming of event procedures is another reason to use a control array. For example, if you have 26 command buttons that represent the letters of the alphabet, it is easier to deal with them as an array than as separate controls.

Using a Control Array in Your Programs

There are a number of uses for control arrays in your programs. The example of simultaneously converting the contents of all text boxes to uppercase is one.

Another common use of control arrays is to find which option button in an array is selected. Because only one option button in a group can be selected at any one time, you can use a `For` loop to determine the value, as illustrated in Listing 13.1.

Listing 13.1 OPTIONARRAY.TXT—Using *LBound* and *UBound* to Determine the Range of a Control Array

```
Dim I As Integer, nChosen As Integer
For I = optArray.Lbound To optArray.Ubound
    If optArray(I).Value Then
        nChosen = I
        Exit Sub
    End If
Next I
```

In Listing 13.1, you might notice that, instead of specifying exact values for the start and end of the For loop, the code uses the LBound and UBound properties. These properties return the lower and upper boundaries of the control array indexes, respectively. Using these properties allows your code to handle additions or deletions in the control array automatically. Lbound and Ubound are properties of the control array itself, not of individual members of the control array.

> **NOTE** Although LBound and UBound provide the maximum and minimum values of the array indices, this does not mean that the elements of the array are numbered contiguously.

Parallel Arrays

One handy technique when working with control arrays involves the use of two (or more) different control arrays whose elements match with each other in some way. They are known as *parallel arrays*.

Consider the two control arrays in the sample program. One is a group of text boxes into which the users can enter information; the other is a group of label controls, each of which matches one of the text boxes. Suppose that you want the label that identifies whichever control has the focus to appear in boldface as a visual cue to the users to help spot the current control. You could accomplish this task by adding some code to the GotFocus event procedure for the TextBox control array elements; this code should set the Font.Bold property for the Label control that matches the TextBox control that has the focus. That is, when a given text box receives the focus, you want its associated label to become bold. You also should add some code to the TextBox control array's LostFocus event procedure to set the appropriate Label control's font back to normal.

To accomplish this enhancement, follow these steps:

1. Enter the following line of code into txtArray's GotFocus event procedure:

   lblArray(Index).Font.Bold = True

   Note that this code, although it is placed in an event procedure of the TextBox control array, actually acts on a member of the parallel Label control array. The Index parameter is used to determine which element of the Label control array to act on.

2. Add the following line of code to the end of the existing `txtArray_LostFocus` event procedure:

   ```
   lblArray(Index).Font.Bold = False
   ```

3. Run the application. When you tab through the text boxes, notice that the associated Label control for the currently selected text box appears bold.

Creating a Menu Item Array

In addition to arrays of controls, you can also create an array of menu items. Like other control arrays, menu item arrays provide the only means to add items to the menu at runtime. You might use a menu item array to keep a list of the files most recently used by your program. This feature is found in many commercial programs.

To create a menu item array, you need to be in the Menu Editor (click the Menu Editor button or choose Tools, Menu Editor). You then create menu items by entering the `Caption` and `Name` properties of each item. When you create the menu item array, you also specify a value for the `Index` property of the item. Figure 13.5 shows the Menu Editor with these properties set for the first of what may be multiple menu items listing recently used files.

FIGURE 13.5
You can set a Menu control's `Index` property in the Menu Editor to create an array of Menu controls.

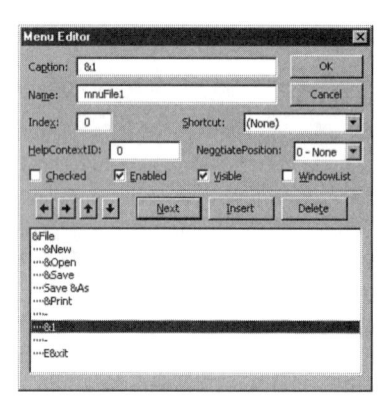

Like control arrays, the elements of a menu item array must meet certain requirements:

- All elements must have the same value for the `Name` property.
- All elements must be at the same indentation level in the menu.
- All elements must be contiguous in the menu. If you need a separator bar in the menu, it must also be part of the array.
- Each element of the menu array must have a unique index number.

Loading and Unloading Controls at Runtime

In other chapters, you learned how to add controls to forms while you are in the design environment. In the preceding section, you even learned how you can create control arrays to handle processing of multiple controls easily in code. However, nothing you have seen yet shows you how to add and remove controls at runtime.

> **TIP** If you plan to add menu items at runtime, place the menu item array at the bottom of a menu. By doing this, you cause the menu to expand after the fixed items so that the user is not confused by items changing positions within the menu.

> **NOTE** You can hide and show controls at runtime by setting the `Visible` property appropriately. However, you must create these controls before you can use them. Showing and hiding controls is not the same as adding new controls.

The only way to add controls at runtime is to add elements of a control array. You cannot add a new individual control because you wouldn't have any event code to handle any events triggered by the users. Because event code has already been defined for a control array at designtime, new elements of the array are automatically handled.

> **CAUTION**
> If you use `If` or `Select` statements to process code for different index values, you should make sure that your code works for all array elements, even new ones that might have been added at runtime. `LBound` and `UBound` help you accomplish this task; however, keep in mind that the indices in a control array may not be numbered sequentially.

Creating the First Element of a Control Array

Because any new control that you add at runtime must be part of a control array, you must create the array, or at least its first element, at designtime. For many arrays, you will want only a single element to be created at design time. This gives you the maximum flexibility to add and remove controls during program execution. To create the first element of a control array, follow these steps:

1. Draw the control on your form.
2. Set the `Name` property of the control.
3. Set the `Index` property of the control to an integer value (usually `0`).

Note that setting the `Index` property to something other than an empty value creates a control array. If you copy and paste a control, Visual Basic sets the `Index` property for you.

Adding Controls at Runtime

After you create the first element of the array, you can use code to add other elements in response to events. For many applications, you add the controls during form load. One application of this technique would be to create a generic data entry form. By using control arrays, you could pass a recordset to the form and then create the number of controls you need to handle however many fields are in the recordset. (Recordsets represent data in a database and are discussed in Chapter 24, "Database Basics.")

To add a control at runtime, you use the Load statement. It is the same statement that you can use to bring a form into memory. With the Load statement, you must specify the name of the control to be loaded and its index. To avoid an error, you must ensure that the index is unique. Note that the new control's Visible property is set to False. The complete process for adding a new control is detailed in the following steps:

1. Use the Load statement to create the new control and bring it into memory.
2. The new control is shown in the same position as the original control because it inherits the properties of the original control. Therefore, you need to move the new control using the Move method or by setting its Top and Left properties.
3. Set the new control's Visible property to True to display it on the form.
4. Set any other necessary properties of the new control. (All other properties are inherited from the original designtime control.)

TIP Setting the index of the new element to one greater than the UBound property of the array ensures that you will have a unique index.

Now examine this technique by adding it to the sample program. Add a test command button that will be responsible for adding a new element to the txtArray control array. To do so, follow these steps:

1. At designtime, set the main form's Height property to 6000. This setting allows plenty of room for the new controls that will be added when the program is running.
2. Add a command button in an empty area of the form. Set its Name property to cmdAdd and its Caption property to Add a text box.
3. Enter the following code into cmdAdd's Click event procedure:

```
Dim i As Integer
i = txtArray.UBound
Load txtArray(i + 1)
txtArray(i + 1).Visible = True
txtArray(i + 1).Top = txtArray(i).Top + txtArray(i).Height + 120
txtArray(i + 1).Left = txtArray(i).Left
```

The preceding code sets the position of the new control array element to a position 120 twips below the most recently added control (taking into account the control's height as well). Run the program and click the command button to give it a try. Figure 13.6 shows how the form looks after several clicks.

FIGURE 13.6
Control array elements can be added at runtime.

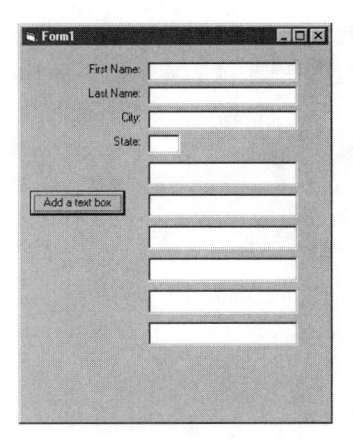

Removing Controls at Runtime

Just as you may need to add one or more controls at runtime, you might also need to remove one or more controls at runtime as well. To remove a control, use the `Unload` statement. As with the `Load` statement, you need to specify the name of the control and its index, as shown here:

```
Unload txtArray(5)
```

> **CAUTION**
> You can use `Unload` only with controls that were created at runtime. You cannot use `Unload` with any control array elements that were created at design time.

You discovered earlier that you could use control arrays to create a generic data entry form. This form would examine the structure of the recordset and then create controls to handle all the fields in the recordset. In this section, you learn how such a form would work.

To keep it simple, the form will have two arrays—one for the labels describing the fields and one for text boxes to hold the field values. To start the setup of the form, add a label array and a text box array to a form, as shown in Figure 13.7.

> **N O T E** To create array elements rather than separate controls, set the `Index` property of your label and text box to 0.

You also need to add a Data control to the form to provide the recordset for the form to use. You learn about the Data control and related data-bound controls in Chapter 25, "The Data Control and Data-Bound Controls."

FIGURE 13.7
At designtime, the generic data entry form contains the beginnings of two control arrays.

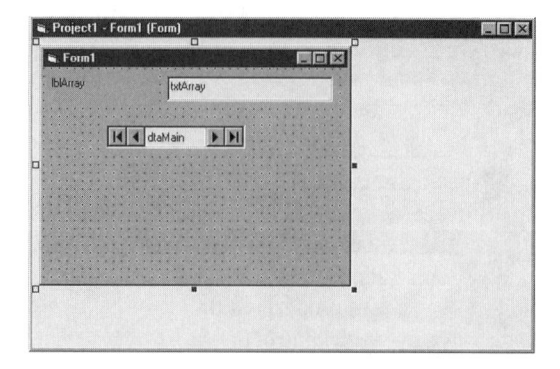

For the Data control, you will need to set the DatabaseName and RecordSource properties of the control to access a recordset. After setting up the Data control, assign the control to the DataSource property of the text box. This property will be inherited by each of the text boxes you add to the form. Next, place the code in Listing 13.2 in the form.

Listing 13.2 GENDATA.FRM—Using the Fields Collection to Drive the Code for Creating Controls

```
Option Explicit

Dim bFirstLoad As Boolean

Private Sub Form_Activate()
    Dim i As Integer
    Dim nFields As Integer
    Dim sName As String

    If Not bFirstLoad Then Exit Sub

    With dtaMain.Recordset
        nFields = .Fields.Count
        For i = 0 To nFields - 1
            sName = .Fields(i).Name
            If i > 0 Then
                Load lblArray(i)
                Load txtArray(i)
                txtArray(i).Top = txtArray(i - 1).Top + txtArray(i - 1).Height + 120
                txtArray(i).Left = txtArray(i - 1).Left
                lblArray(i).Top = txtArray(i).Top
                lblArray(i).Left = lblArray(i - 1).Left
                txtArray(i).Visible = True
                lblArray(i).Visible = True
            End If
            lblArray(i).Caption = sName
            txtArray(i).DataField = sName
        Next i
    End With
    i = txtArray.UBound
    dtaMain.Top = txtArray(i).Top + txtArray(i).Height + 120
```

```
        Me.Height = dtaMain.Top + dtaMain.Height + 525
        bFirstLoad = False
End Sub

Private Sub Form_Load()
    bFirstLoad = True
End Sub
```

This code adds a new label and text box for each field after the first one. New controls are positioned directly below the last set of controls. Next, the code assigns the `Caption` property of the Label control and the `DataField` property of the TextBox control. After all the fields have been added, the code positions the Data control below the other controls and resizes the form to accommodate all the controls. A runtime example of the form is shown in Figure 13.8.

FIGURE 13.8
The generic data form can handle almost any recordset.

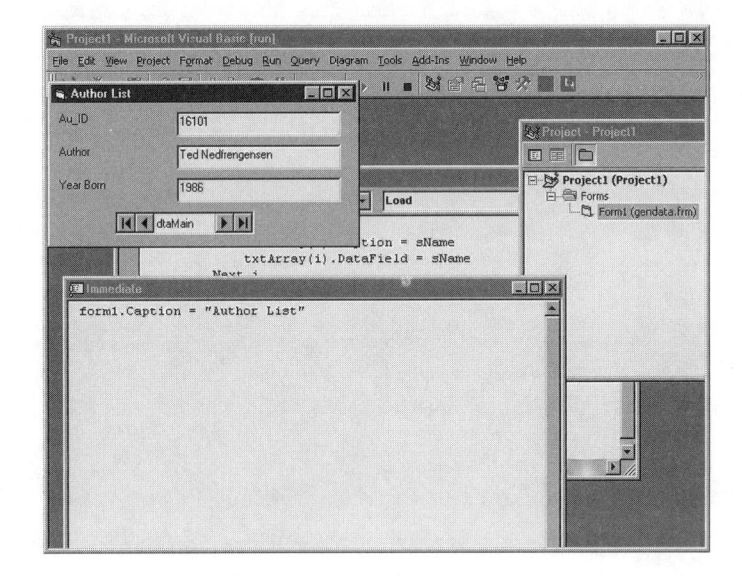

From Here...

In this chapter, you learned some of the techniques you can use to make your programs do more with your controls. You learned how to use control arrays to enhance your ability to work with similar controls as a group. You also saw how to add controls dynamically while your program is running.

For more information on some of the topics presented here, see the following chapters:

- To learn more about controls in general, see Chapter 4, "Using Visual Basic's Default Controls," and Chapter 12, "Microsoft Common Controls."
- Databases and recordsets are introduced in Chapter 24, "Database Basics," and discussed further in Chapter 26, "Using Data Access Objects (DAO)."

CHAPTER 14

Creating ActiveX Controls

In this chapter

ActiveX Basics   306

Creating an ActiveX Control   307

Testing the ActiveX Control   311

Compiling Your Control   314

Enhancing an ActiveX Control   317

Using the ActiveX Control Interface Wizard   323

Using the Property Pages Wizard   330

Creating a User-Drawn ActiveX Control   332

As you learned in earlier chapters, you can combine the controls included with Visual Basic to build a powerful application quickly. One of the most exciting features of Visual Basic is the ability to create your own controls. These programmer-built controls, also known as ActiveX controls, can then be used in Visual Basic applications like any other control. (*ActiveX* is a Microsoft term that refers to a group of components that include controls, DLLs, and ActiveX documents.) In addition to the obvious advantage of reusing code, ActiveX controls can be used on a Web page to deliver program-like functionality over the Internet.

In this chapter, you take a look at the various approaches you can take and some of the issues that you need to consider when creating ActiveX controls. The information contained in this chapter is then further expanded in the following chapter, "Extending ActiveX Controls," which teaches you how to build more robust ActiveX controls.

ActiveX Basics

You are familiar with controls such as the TextBox and Label controls. To use these controls, you draw them on a form and control their behavior through properties, methods, and events. When you create your own ActiveX control, you are creating a similar object, except you are determining the properties, methods, and events. After you create your own ActiveX control, you and others can use it in other Visual Basic projects, just like a TextBox control. You can use your controls in any application or development tool that can use ActiveX controls, including other Visual Basic projects or Microsoft Internet Explorer. In fact, using ActiveX controls is an ideal way to create a reusable component that can be used both inside a traditional client/server EXE and on the Internet.

Steps Involved in Building ActiveX Controls

Creating an ActiveX control in Visual Basic is different from creating a Standard EXE application. Therefore, a brief overview of the steps involved is useful:

1. Create a high-level design to determine what you want your ActiveX control to do. An ActiveX control is like a standalone object, so you need to ask yourself what purpose does the object serve? What appearance do you want it have onscreen? What properties, methods, and events need to be made available to the program using the control?
2. Determine whether you will be using other controls as building blocks for your control. For example, you might want to create an ActiveX control that includes a third-party grid. When you are using other controls within your control, consider licensing and distribution issues.
3. Start a new Visual Basic ActiveX control project, and draw the interface for your control.
4. Add code to enable all the properties, methods, and events you want your control to have.
5. Build a test project, and test your control from within Visual Basic. Make sure to use all the properties, methods, and events that you give your control.
6. Compile your control into an OCX file, and perform testing on the compiled version of your control. If you are developing for the Internet, test your control on a Web page.

7. Use the Package and Deployment Wizard or another utility to build a distributable version of the control that includes all the supporting files.

Development Strategies

Building an ActiveX control in Visual Basic can be as easy or difficult as you choose. The level of difficulty depends on whether you use existing controls in your design, how sophisticated the interface will be, and of course, how much code you have to write to make it work. In any case, you can go about building an ActiveX control in three basic ways:

- **Assemble the control from existing controls.** This approach is also known as building a control from *constituent controls*. It is the easiest way to build an ActiveX control because you are just bringing existing controls together. For example, you can package a combo box and a text box together and write minimal code that causes them to interact in the desired manner.
- **Enhance an existing control.** You can use an existing control as a starting point for your own creative efforts by modifying the control properties. For example, you can take a text box and add a custom property called TextCaps that causes the text to always be displayed in capital letters. This approach is a good way to get the exact functionality that you need in a control.
- **Create a user-drawn control.** You can draw the interface yourself with graphics methods, creating a totally original control that does not include any existing controls. Drawing your own control requires a little more work than the other two strategies but can be done to provide an original or different user interface.

This chapter introduces you to the world of creating ActiveX controls. You'll learn about each of the preceding development strategies through sample projects, as well as learn about distributing and compiling the finished control. Chapter 15, "Extending ActiveX Controls," looks at some of the more advanced topics relating to ActiveX controls.

Creating an ActiveX Control

Assembling an ActiveX control from other existing controls provides many advantages. First, when you add an existing control to your new custom control, you get the existing control's complete functionality—an important consideration when you think about how many event procedures, methods, and properties are supported by an average control. Second, combining a number of controls into one allows them to be treated as a single unit, which may make things easier from an application architecture standpoint; this approach also allows them to be drawn on the form all at once. An additional advantage is that the users can easily understand a control made up of controls they already know.

Starting the Address Control Project

Now that you have some background information on ActiveX controls, you can get started by creating your first ActiveX control. The control that you'll build in this section is the AddressCtl control, which is simply text box fields that allow the users to enter their names and addresses.

Chapter 14 Creating ActiveX Controls

This example will give you a hands-on understanding of the issues involved in developing ActiveX controls in the Visual Basic IDE. The AddressCtl control will be built entirely of existing Label and TextBox controls. First, you will draw the user interface of the control and then add minimal code to make it work in the VB design environment.

To build the Address control, follow these steps:

1. Start Visual Basic 6.0. If it is already running, choose File, New Project.
2. From the New Project dialog box, select ActiveX Control. A new project is created with a UserControl object named UserControl1, as shown in Figure 14.1.

FIGURE 14.1
A UserControl object is similar to a form but has no borders or standard window elements.

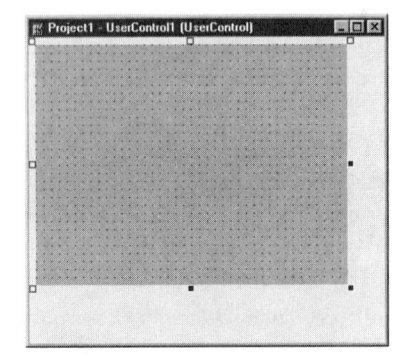

3. Change the name of the UserControl object to AddressCtl in the Properties window.
4. Choose Project, Project1 Properties. The Project1 Properties dialog box appears.
5. In the Project Name text box, change the name of the project (Project1) to something meaningful, such as Address.
6. Add five TextBox controls to the form. Set the values of their Text properties to empty strings, and give them the following names:
   - txtName
   - txtStreet
   - txtCity
   - txtState
   - txtZip
7. Add five Label controls to the form and give them the following properties:

Name **Property**	Caption **Property**
lblName	Name:
lblStreet	Street:
lblCity	City:
lblState	State:
lblZip	Zip:

8. Arrange the labels next to the appropriate text boxes. Click the UserControl object, and resize it so that the constituent controls fit neatly inside. You can resize your control by using the sizing handles or changing the `Height` and `Width` properties in the Properties window. The sample control should be around 4395 twips wide by 3600 twips high and look like the one in Figure 14.2.

FIGURE 14.2
The full set of constituent controls is drawn on the UserControl object.

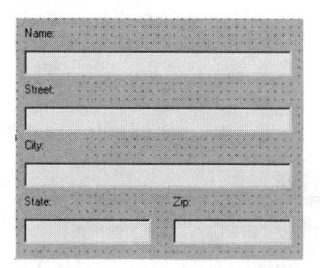

9. As with all VB projects, saving your work is important. Do so now before continuing.

Adding Resize Code to the Control

As you know from using standard controls such as a text box, you can adjust the size of a control in design mode by using the mouse or by setting its `Height` and `Width` properties. A TextBox control responds appropriately by automatically redrawing itself at the new size. When you are designing your own ActiveX control, especially one that is made up of existing controls, resizing is an important consideration. As you resize your control, you need to take action to make sure that the constituent controls are not hidden from the user or arranged in a way that prevents useful operation of the control.

To handle this control, you need to add code that responds to the `Resize` event of the UserControl object. This code will be executed whenever someone is drawing your control in a Visual Basic project. To add the necessary code for the Address control, take the following steps:

1. Double-click the UserControl object, as you would a standard form. The Code window opens.
2. From the Procedures box of the Code window, select the `Resize` event.
3. Add the following lines of code to the `UserControl_Resize` event:

```
Private Sub UserControl_Resize()
    With UserControl

        'Enforce minimum dimensions
        If .Height < 3615 Then .Height = 3615
        If .Width < 2175 Then .Width = 2175

        'Resize objects on the control
        txtName.Width = .ScaleWidth - 500
        txtStreet.Width = .ScaleWidth - 500
        txtCity.Width = .ScaleWidth - 500
        txtZip.Width = .ScaleWidth / 2 - 500
```

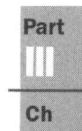

```
                txtState.Width = .ScaleWidth / 2 - 500
                'Move the Zipcode text box
                txtZip.Left = .ScaleWidth / 2 + 160
                lblZip.Left = .ScaleWidth / 2 + 160
        End With
    End Sub
```

4. Save the changes to your project.

NOTE The size numbers in the sample `Resize` event code are arbitrary. Their purpose is to keep the control's interface looking okay when the developer sizes it.

As the user changes the dimensions of the Address control, the `Resize` event procedure is executed. The first two lines in the preceding code sample prevent the user from making the control instance too small. The remaining lines resize all the constituent controls based on the size of the UserControl object.

Adding a New Property to Your Control

Including multiple text boxes within a single ActiveX control groups them visually and allows you to draw all the text boxes on the form at once. However, for an ActiveX control to be useful, you also need to be able to access its properties, methods, and events as a single control. In other words, if you intend to treat all the constituent controls separately from code, you really have not gained anything by combining them into one control. In the case of the Address control, the purpose of the control is to provide a way to enter address information. For this reason, you will create an `AddressText` property on the Address control that is much like the `Text` property of a text box. The difference here is that the `AddressText` property returns text from *all* the text boxes on the form in a single string.

For simplicity's sake, the property will be read-only, using the `Get` property procedure. (Property procedures are discussed in Chapter 16, "Classes: Reusable Components.")

▶ **See** "Property Procedures," **p. 363**

To set up this property, open the Code window for the UserControl, and add the following procedure code:

```
Public Property Get AddressText() As String
    Dim s As String

    s = txtName & vbCrLf
    s = s & txtStreet & vbCrLf
    s = s & txtCity & vbCrLf
    s = s & txtState & vbCrLf
    s = s & txtZip
    AddressText = s

End Property
```

The `Property Get` procedure code is not complex; it just combines the contents of the constituent controls and returns a single string to the calling application. However, the creation of this custom property illustrates the concept of taking a programming task (combining the address fields into a string) and encapsulating it in an object (your ActiveX control). The advantage is that other programmers can use this property without having to understand the details of its implementation.

Testing the ActiveX Control

An ActiveX control eventually ends up as a compiled OCX. An OCX file, when registered on another user's machine, can be added to a Visual Basic project or displayed on a Web page in Internet Explorer. However, during the development process, you need a way to test and debug your ActiveX controls within the Visual Basic design environment. This process is slightly more complicated than debugging a Standard EXE project because you have to deal with two separate sets of running code: the ActiveX control itself and the project using the ActiveX control.

Testing with a Project Group

The easiest way to test an ActiveX component is to use a project group. Throughout most of the samples in this book, you will open projects one at a time; that is, when you choose New Project or Open Project from Visual Basic's File menu, any projects already loaded close. However, the Visual Basic development environment allows you to have multiple projects loaded simultaneously. This arrangement is known as a project group and is useful for testing ActiveX components. A typical project group consists of the ActiveX component itself plus a test project (usually a Standard EXE project).

Adding a Test Project to the Group To begin testing the AddressCtl component, you need to add a Standard EXE project to the design environment, creating a project group. Just choose File, Add Project and then select a Standard EXE project type from the Add Project dialog box. The Project Explorer window is updated to show both projects, as shown in Figure 14.3.

> **TIP** You can quickly add a Standard EXE project by simply clicking the Add Project button.

FIGURE 14.3
You can open another project at the same time as an ActiveX component for testing purposes.

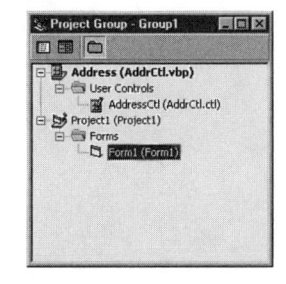

Setting Up the Test Project When you added the Standard EXE project to the group, you may have noticed that a grayed-out (dimmed) icon was added to your Toolbox. This icon represents your user control, and it remains disabled as long as you have the UserControl form open.

Close the UserControl window, and open the window for the default form from Project1. The Toolbox icon for your user control should be available, and hovering the mouse pointer over it displays the name of the sample control, AddressCtl, as shown in Figure 14.4.

FIGURE 14.4
To make your ActiveX control available to the project group, close the UserControl window.

Now your custom ActiveX control is available. Go ahead and draw an instance on the form, just as you would with any other control. Notice that it appears just as you drew it on the UserControl, but it acts like a single control; all the text boxes within the control move together and cannot be selected individually.

At this point, your ActiveX control object is loaded and running, so try resizing the Address control on your form. As you change its size with the mouse, the code in the Resize event of the UserControl keeps the text boxes sized appropriately. If you try to reduce the height of the Address control too much, the control springs back to its minimum size, as pictured in Figure 14.5. You can, however, enlarge the control as much as you like.

FIGURE 14.5
The test application shows the Address control set to its minimum width.

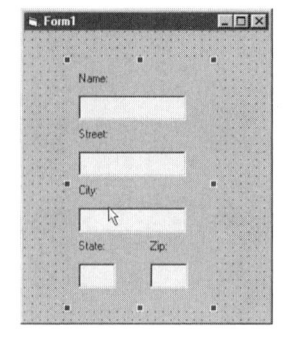

Setting the Startup Project Now that you have drawn an instance of your control on the form, you can start the test project. When you are using a project group, you must first specify which project is the *startup project*. Visual Basic gives that project the focus, starting the other projects automatically. Because the ActiveX control is designed to be used within another project, you need to set the startup project to be the test project, `Project1`. To do so, right-click `Project1` in the Project Explorer window, and select Set as Start Up from the context menu that appears, as shown in Figure 14.6. The `Project1` project should change to boldface to indicate that it is the startup project.

FIGURE 14.6
Set the startup project to be the test Standard EXE project. The ActiveX project starts automatically.

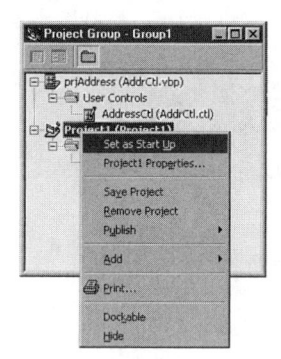

Running the Test Program To start the test project, press F5 or click Visual Basic's Start button. The form should load, and the text boxes on the Address control become active.

Enter some text in each field. Next, press Ctrl+Break to put the project in Break mode. Open the Immediate window by pressing Ctrl+G, and print the value of the `AddressText` property by entering the following statement:

```
Print AddressCtl1.AddressText
```

If you see a list of the values you entered in the control, then the control is working properly. Notice also that as you enter the `Print` command, Visual Basic displays all the properties of your control in a pop-up list, and the `AddressText` property is included.

If you cannot print the value of the `AddressText` property successfully, make sure that the code in the `Property Get` procedure is entered correctly. If you want to learn more about debugging a program, see Chapter 10, "Controlling the Flow of Your Program Code." You can use the methods described there to step through the code in the `AddressText` property procedure, examining the contents of the variables to verify that they are correct.

▶ **See** "Debugging Your Programs," **p. 214**

Testing with Internet Explorer

You have just seen how to use the Address control in a Visual Basic project group. As you already know, a compiled ActiveX control can be used in Internet Explorer on a Web page. However, in previous versions of Visual Basic, testing with Internet Explorer was difficult; you first had to create a test HTML file outside the Visual Basic IDE and then launch Internet Explorer manually. Fortunately, Visual Basic 6.0 has improved this process. You can now automatically launch Internet Explorer and debug your ActiveX control code from within the Visual Basic IDE.

If you still have the project group open, remove the Standard EXE project from the group. Simply right-click Project1 in the Project Explorer window, and choose Remove Project from the context menu. The only remaining project should be the Address control.

Start the Address control project by pressing F5 or clicking the Visual Basic Start button. If you have Internet Explorer installed, it should be automatically launched, as shown in Figure 14.7.

FIGURE 14.7
Visual Basic 6.0 makes testing controls a snap by automatically launching the browser.

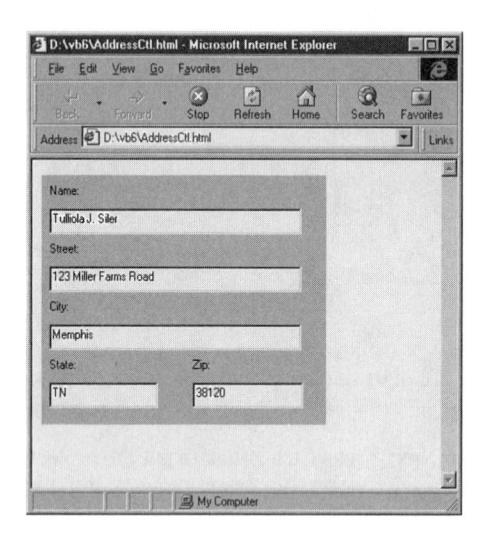

After you finish testing the control in Internet Explorer, close the browser and stop the Visual Basic project.

NOTE The Debugging tab of the Project Properties dialog box determines how ActiveX components are launched when you press F5. For more information about it, see Chapter 16, "Classes: Reusable Components." ■

▶ **See** "Working with Multiple Projects," **p. 235**

Compiling Your Control

So far, you learned how to test the control project running as code in the design environment. However, to use the control outside the design environment (that is, on a user's PC), you must compile your source code into an OCX file and package it for distribution. Others can then install the OCX file on their systems and use your control in their own projects, regardless of whether they are working with a programming language, a Web page, or some other development tool.

Creating the OCX File

The steps for compiling an ActiveX control project are similar to those for compiling a Standard EXE project. However, the end result of compiling an ActiveX control project is an OCX file rather than an EXE program file.

To create an OCX file for the Address control, perform the following steps:

1. Choose Make from Visual Basic's File menu.
2. When the Make Project dialog box appears, enter a filename, such as ADDRESS.OCX. (You might also need to set the directory where you want the file saved.)
3. Click OK. Visual Basic compiles the control and writes the OCX file to disk.

After the ActiveX control is compiled, you should be able to test the compiled control. Keep in mind that an ActiveX control is different from a Standard EXE application in that it does not run on its own. To test your compiled control, you need to use a container application.

Testing the Compiled Control

After you compile your control, it should work just like any other control. Start a new Standard EXE project in Visual Basic, removing the loaded project or project group. Next, display the Components dialog box by pressing Ctrl+T or choosing Project, Components. Click the Browse button, and select your OCX file. When you close the Components dialog box, a new icon should appear in the Toolbox. You should then be able to draw your control on the form as you did earlier when testing with a project group; this time, however, you can use compiled code. (See the earlier section "Setting Up the Test Project.")

> **NOTE** When working with a compiled control in Visual Basic, you cannot debug within the control or view its code.

Distributing the Control to Another Machine

Your ActiveX controls can run on another user's or developer's PC. However, just copying the OCX file to the other computer is not a sufficient way to distribute it. For your control to run on any given PC, the appropriate support files must be installed. The reason for this requirement is that Visual Basic code is a fairly high-level language and thus depends on other runtime libraries (that is, DLL files). For example, one of the most basic requirements to run any Visual Basic program is the file MSVBVM60.DLL (Microsoft Visual Basic Virtual Machine 6.0). Without this file, none of your Visual Basic programs can run.

> **NOTE** Other users who already have Visual Basic (and the support files) installed on their machines may be able to use your control by simply copying your file to their machines and registering it with the `REGSVR32` command, as in the following example:

`REGSVR32 C:\WINDOWS\SYSTEM\ADDRESS.OCX`

The bottom line is, for your control to work, it must be properly installed. You can install in two ways, depending on the control's intended use:

- **Standard installation.** If your custom ActiveX control is part of another VB project, it is installed and registered on the user's machine when the application files are installed.
- **Internet installation.** If your control is part of a Web page, you must place the correct <OBJECT> tag in the HTML code. The OCX and supporting files, which must placed in CAB files on the Web server, are downloaded and installed by Internet Explorer.

Installing Your Control in a Setup Program   A standard installation is the easiest way to install your control on a PC. In a typical Standard EXE installation, a user runs a SETUP.EXE program, which installs and registers all the appropriate files. When you create the installation files for your Standard EXE project, use the Package and Deployment Wizard. The Wizard knows to include your OCX. However, if you think your OCX requires some support files that your application does not, you need to create a Dependency File by using the wizard. Using the Packaging and Deployment Wizard is described in detail in Appendix B, "Packaging Your Applications."

▶ **See** "Packaging ActiveX Components," **p. 788**

Installing Your Control over the Internet   As you already know, for your ActiveX control to work on any given PC, the OCX file and other supporting files must be installed. If you intend to use your ActiveX control in a Web page, Microsoft Internet Explorer can automatically download and install the ActiveX control. However, deploying an ActiveX control in this manner is different from the traditional, interactive setup method. When a user accesses a Web page containing an ActiveX control, Internet Explorer downloads the required CAB (cabinet) files from the Web server and then installs the ActiveX components. This is one of the advantages of using Internet Explorer; you can quickly publish your latest ActiveX controls from a central Web server. However, for this process to work, you must provide all the necessary information to Internet Explorer.

First, you need to create CAB files for your ActiveX control. A CAB file is a special type of file that contains one or more compressed files; for example, a single CAB file might contain your compiled OCX and some Visual Basic runtime DLL files. The files contained within a CAB cannot be used until they are extracted to their original size on the client machine. You can create a CAB file with the Package and Deployment Wizard, as discussed in Appendix B, "Packaging Your Applications." However, occasionally you may need to work with a CAB file manually. The Internet Client SDK, available on Microsoft's Web site, provides some tools that you can use to manipulate CAB files from the command prompt.

Another (optional) step is to sign your CAB files digitally. You can buy a digital signature file, which verifies your identity to someone downloading your control. This file is intended as a security feature because an ActiveX control has full access to the machine on which it runs. If you do not sign your CAB files, an Internet Explorer user who wants to use your control has to lower the security settings in Internet Explorer to allow unsigned controls to execute on his or her PC.

A command-line utility included with the Internet Client SDK, SIGNCODE, allows you to sign your files. When you compile your ActiveX control into an OCX file, it is given a *global unique identifier*, or *GUID*. This identifier is necessary to add the control to a Web page. To determine this GUID, you can look at the sample HTM file generated by the Package and Deployment Wizard. For an example use of the <OBJECT> tag, see Appendix B. After you determine the GUID, use it to embed the control in your Web page.

▶ **See** "Files Created for the Internet," **p. 790**

The final step is to place the CAB and HTML files on the Web server. Make sure that the previously mentioned <OBJECT> tag contains the name of the CAB file, as described in Appendix C.

After all the files are in place, other users should be able to use your control on their machines. To verify that the page works, try hitting your Web page on a machine that does not have your control installed. If the control fails to load, check the following:

- From the Security tab in the Internet Explorer Internet Options dialog box (accessed from the View menu), add your Web server to the trusted sites zone. Restart the browser and reload the page.

- Install and register the ActiveX control with a standard setup program. This way, you can verify that the problem is in the CAB file.

While troubleshooting control problems in Internet Explorer, you may want to delete the cached files and objects so that you get a "fresh" copy when you reload the page. You can delete the temporary files by clicking the Delete Files button on the General tab of the Internet Options dialog box. You then can remove your ActiveX control by selecting it in the \Windows\Downloaded Program Files directory and choosing File, Remove Program File.

Enhancing an ActiveX Control

The preceding section introduced the concepts involved in creating an ActiveX control by arranging existing controls on a UserControl object. However, you can also create "new" controls simply by adding capabilities to an existing control. This means that you are working with a single base control but adding properties, methods, and events to provide additional capabilities to the user. For example, you might want to create a special scrollbar control that uses letters instead of numbers or a text box that accepts only certain characters.

Placing the code that performs these tasks into a separate ActiveX control makes it easier to use the code in future programs. For example, rather than add special code to every TextBox control in your program, you can simply use your "enhanced" control in place of the text box. To create these enhanced controls, you use many of the same techniques that you learned in the previous sections:

1. Start a new ActiveX control project.
2. Add the base control to the UserControl window.
3. Add code for properties, methods, and events.

The following sections walk you through these steps, using a text box as the base control. Your "enhanced" text box will be known as a "Limited Character Text Box." It will have a user-defined property that allows the programmer to choose a set of acceptable characters that the user can enter. This additional property, `CharAccept`, will allow the user to restrict text entry to only letters, only numbers, or allow both.

Setting Up the Base Control

The steps for creating the enhanced text control are similar to the steps you used to create the Address control. For the enhanced text control, the steps are as follows:

1. Start a new ActiveX Control project.
2. Add a text box to the UserControl window, with the upper-left corner of the text box in position 0, 0.
3. Name the text box `txtCharSet`, and clear its `Text` property.
4. Set the properties of the ActiveX project and the UserControl to the values specified in Table 14.1.

Table 14.1 Settings for the Limited Character TextBox Control

Item	Setting
Project Type	ActiveX Control
Project Name	TextLimited
Project Description	Text Box for Limited Character Set
User control `Name` property	`TxtCharLimit`
User control `Public` property	`True`

To set the first three values in the table, use the Properties dialog box (which you access by choosing <u>P</u>roject, Prop<u>e</u>rties). To set the remaining values, highlight the UserControl object, and press F4 to show the Properties window. After you set up the user interface of the enhanced text control, it should look like the one in Figure 14.8.

FIGURE 14.8
The base control, pictured here, will be enhanced with additional capabilities.

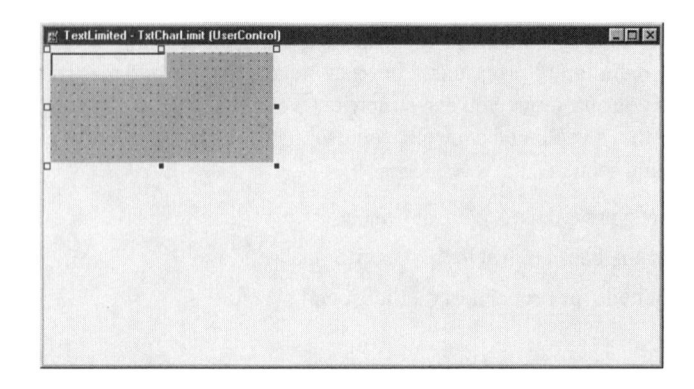

5. Set up the `Resize` event procedure of the UserControl to make the text box fit the space that is drawn by the developer when using your control. This `Resize` event procedure is shown in Listing 14.1.

Listing 14.1 LIMITED.ZIP—Using the *Resize* Event to Make Sure the Control Fills the Space

```
Private Sub UserControl_Resize()
  txtCharSet.Height = UserControl.ScaleHeight
  txtCharSet.Width = UserControl.ScaleWidth
End Sub
```

The simple two-line `Resize` event procedure is all the code necessary for the user interface of the sample control. Its purpose is to keep the text box the same size as the UserControl object.

6. Save your project.

Before moving on, test the `Resize` event procedure by performing the following steps:

1. Close the UserControl window. If you have the Toolbox open, notice that a new icon appears for your control.
2. Choose File, Add Project. Then add a Standard EXE project.
3. Draw your control on Form1, and try resizing it.

The purpose of jumping the gun by using the control so quickly is to get you used to the idea that the code in your ActiveX control does not have to be executed explicitly. Remember, when you are developing an ActiveX control, the code you write is used at design time in the host program.

For now, remove the Standard EXE project by right-clicking it in the Project Explorer window and choosing Remove Project1. Now, it is time to work on the enhancements to the control.

Enhancing the Base Control

The enhancement you are going to make to the TextBox control is to tell it whether it should accept any characters, just letters, or just numbers. You can do so by adding your own property, called `CharAccept`, which can have one of the following three values:

- 0—Accepts any character
- 1—Accepts only numbers
- 2—Accepts only letters

Creating the *CharAccept* Property To create the `CharAccept` property, you first need to add a private variable to store the property value internally. To do so, create it in the General Declarations section of the UserControl object, as follows:

```
Private mCharAccept As Integer
```

Next, you need to create the new property, called CharAccept. You can do so either by entering the Get and Let procedures by hand, or by choosing Tools, Add Procedure, Property. The code for the CharAccept property is fairly easy to understand. When the developer needs the value of the CharAccept property, the Property Get procedure simply passes what is stored in the private variable. When the value of the CharAccept property is set, the Property Let procedure assigns one of the valid values to the private variable. The following is the code for both Property procedures:

```
Public Property Get CharAccept() As Integer
    CharAccept = mCharAccept
End Property

Public Property Let CharAccept(ByVal nNewValue As Integer)

    Select Case nNewValue
      Case 1 To 2
        mCharAccept = nNewValue
      Case Else
        mCharAccept = 0
    End Select

    PropertyChanged "CharAccept"

End Property
```

Notice the use of the PropertyChanged method. This method works in conjunction with the ReadProperties and WriteProperties events, which is discussed in the next few paragraphs.

You now need to use the InitProperties event of the user control to specify an initial value of the property:

```
Private Sub UserControl_InitProperties()
   mCharAccept = 0
End Sub
```

This code ensures that a value is set, even if the developer does not set it.

Using the *PropertyBag* Object   You also need to create the code for the WriteProperties and ReadProperties events to preserve the designtime settings of CharAccept. These two events use the PropertyBag object to save and retrieve the value of the CharAccept property. The PropertyBag object enables you to maintain the design environment value of CharAccept. The code for these two events, shown in Listing 14.2, is not hard to understand. What is important, however, is why the code is needed.

Listing 14.2   LIMITED.ZIP—Maintaining the Property Value

```
Private Sub UserControl_ReadProperties(PropBag As PropertyBag)
   mCharAccept = PropBag.ReadProperty("CharAccept", 0)
End Sub

Private Sub UserControl_WriteProperties(PropBag As PropertyBag)
   PropBag.WriteProperty "CharAccept", mCharAccept, 0
End Sub
```

Remember that an ActiveX control's code starts executing the moment you draw it on a form. Suppose you set the value of a property during designtime. In the sample control, assume that you set the value of CharAccept to 1. You also can change it several times while your program is running. The normal behavior for a control is to revert to its original designtime values when the program ends, thus adding the requirement of maintaining two separate *states* of the property.

More simply put, if you change a property at designtime, the control has to know to get this new value rather than use the default. Conversely, if the property's value is changed during program execution, the control has to retrieve the value when it returns to the design state.

The PropertyBag object allows your ActiveX control to store properties about itself, making this behavior possible. The PropertyChanged method provides notification that the user has changed a property. By knowing the state of the program and whether the PropertyChange method has been invoked, VB can fire the WriteProperties and ReadProperties events.

NOTE As you may have noticed, you have to add a lot of code just to create a single property. The next section introduces you to the ActiveX Control Interface Wizard, a Visual Basic Add-in that makes adding property and event procedure code easy. After you finish creating the basic TxtCharLimit control, keep reading to learn how to use the wizard.

Changing the Text Box's Behavior The next step in this sample project is to create the code that makes the limited character text box do something different than a normal text box. In this case, you can use the text box's KeyPress event to scan each character as it is entered. Visual Basic will pass the ASCII code of the characters through the event's KeyAscii parameter. Depending on the ASCII code and setting of the CharAccept property, you can either accept the character or set KeyAscii to 0, which causes the text box not to display the character.

In addition to not displaying the character, you should inform the host program that the user has entered an invalid character. You do so by creating an event called UserError. To create this event, add the following line of code to the General Declarations section of the UserControl object:

```
Public Event UserError()
```

This event works like an event in any other control. Someone using your control can place code in it. The only thing you have to do is fire the event by using the RaiseEvent method.

Because three sets of acceptable characters are available, you can use a Select statement to handle the choices. Here's one other item of note: You need to allow the use of the Backspace key (ASCII code 8) in any of the character sets that you use. Otherwise, the user cannot delete the previous character. The code for the KeyPress event is shown in Listing 14.3.

Listing 14.3 LIMITED.ZIP—Programming the *KeyPress* Event to Screen User Input

```
Private Sub txtCharSet_KeyPress(KeyAscii As Integer)
    If KeyAscii = 8 Then Exit Sub

    Select Case mCharAccept
        Case 0 'Any character is acceptable
            Exit Sub
        Case 1 'Only numbers may be entered
            If KeyAscii >= 48 And KeyAscii <= 57 Then
                Exit Sub
            Else
                KeyAscii = 0
                Beep
                RaiseEvent UserError
            End If
        Case 2 'Only letters may be entered
            If KeyAscii >= 65 And KeyAscii <= 90 Then
                Exit Sub
            ElseIf KeyAscii >= 97 And KeyAscii <= 122 Then
                Exit Sub
            Else
                KeyAscii = 0
                Beep
                RaiseEvent UserError
            End If
    End Select

End Sub
```

The code in Listing 14.3 is fairly simple. `KeyAscii` represents the typed character, which is checked for validity by `Select Case` and `If` statements. If the character falls outside an acceptable range, the control beeps and raises the `UserError` event.

Testing the Limited Character Text Box

After you enter all the code for the control, you can test the TxtCharLimit control by following these steps:

1. Save your code.
2. Add a Standard EXE project to the project group. (You may have already taken this step.)
3. Close the design and Code windows for the user control. Notice that an icon for your control appears in the Toolbox.
4. Add an instance of the TxtCharLimit control to the form in the test application.
5. Set the properties of the control.
6. Run the test program, and try out the control. Try setting the `CharAccept` property to different values to verify that it accepts only the keystrokes you want.

If you have problems with the control, you can use the same debugging techniques to find the problems in a control as you do to find problems in standard programs. You can set breakpoints and step through the code line by line, whether in the ActiveX Control project or in the Standard EXE project. (See Chapter 10, "Controlling the Flow of Your Program Code," for more information on debugging your code.)

▶ **See** "Debugging Your Programs," **p. 214**

Choosing a Toolbox Icon

You may have noticed by now that all the custom controls you create have the same symbol in the Toolbox. This feature can cause a lot of confusion if you are working with multiple controls. Although the ToolTips provide descriptions of the controls, having custom icons to identify each control is better. You can have this custom icon by setting the value of the `ToolboxBitmap` property of the user control. This property determines what is displayed in the Toolbox for your control. If the property is set to `None`, the default icon is used. You can set the property to any bitmap, but be aware that the Toolbox icon is only 16×15 pixels. Therefore, you should use custom bitmaps that are created in that size.

ON THE WEB
Many free icons and other graphics are available for download from the World Wide Web. For example, visit www.yahoo.com and search for "icons" to find a large list of sites.

Using the ActiveX Control Interface Wizard

When you created the `CharAccept` property of the enhanced text box, you created one piece of the public interface of the control. However, your users will probably also want to be able to access most of the standard properties, methods, and events of the text box. For example, you may have noticed that the `Text` property was not accessible for your custom control. This makes sense because no code was added for it; the TextBox control itself is merely an internal element of your own control. Previously, you created the `CharAccept` property by hand. However, as you can imagine, manually creating the dozens of properties of a control could get very tedious.

Fortunately, Visual Basic provides a tool to make this process much easier: the ActiveX Control Interface Wizard. First, you tell the wizard the names of all the properties that you want to have for your control. The wizard then allows you to "bind" the properties of your control to the properties of a component of your control. In other words, it can write the procedure and event code for you to make the `Text` property of your UserControl update the `Text` property of the TextBox.

Adding the Wizard to Visual Basic

To use the ActiveX Control Interface Wizard, you first add it to your design environment. For this purpose, Visual Basic includes the Add-In Manager. To start the Add-In Manager, choose Add-Ins, Add-In Manager to open the Add-In Manager dialog box.

To add the VB ActiveX Control Interface Wizard, click the box next to the name of the wizard. This action places a check mark in the box, indicating that the wizard will be included in the Add-Ins menu. Next, click OK to exit the Add-In Manager and add the wizard to Visual Basic.

Now, to demonstrate how to use the wizard, re-create the Limited Character TextBox control:

1. Start a new ActiveX Control project, and draw a text box on the UserControl window.
2. Set up the names and sizes the same way you did in the earlier example (refer to the section "Setting Up the Base Control").
3. Start the wizard by choosing the ActiveX Control Interface Wizard item from the Add-Ins menu. The wizard starts by displaying the initial screen shown in Figure 14.9.

TIP For the wizard to work most effectively, you must add all the required components to the user control before starting the wizard.

4. Click the Next button to start the actual work of setting up your properties.

FIGURE 14.9
The ActiveX Control Interface Wizard simplifies the process of creating properties by generating much of the code for you.

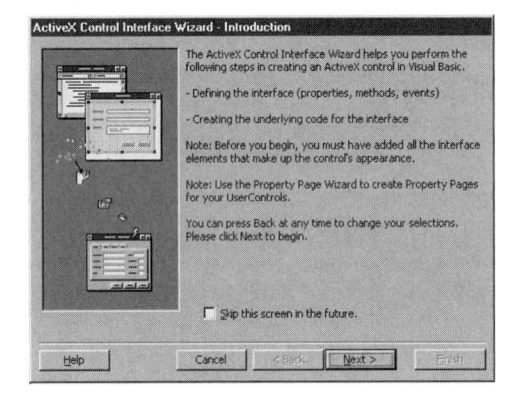

Selecting and Creating Properties

The next step in using the ActiveX Control Interface Wizard is to select the properties, methods, and events that you want to have available to your control. Collectively, properties, methods, and events are known as *members*. In the Select Interface Members dialog box, shown in Figure 14.10, the wizard contains a list of the names of just about every item that you could find in any control in Visual Basic. To select a property or method to create, highlight the name of the item in the Available Names list, and then click the right-arrow button to select the item. For the sample control, highlight the Text property on the left side, and click the right-arrow button.

TIP You also can select an item by double-clicking it in the list.

FIGURE 14.10
The first step in creating properties, methods, and events for your control is to add procedures for the commonly used member names.

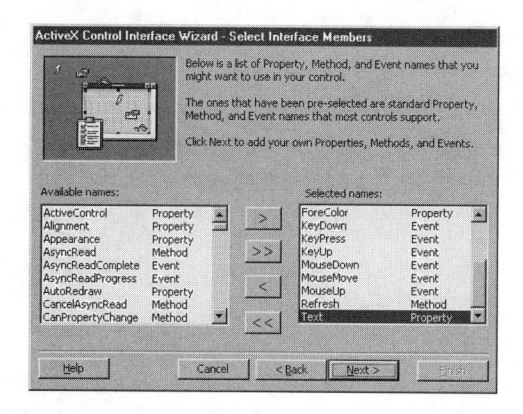

After you add the Text property to the Selected Names list, click the Next button to move to the next page of the wizard.

After selecting the predefined properties, methods, and events for your control, you move to the page of the wizard where you can enter the new custom items for your control. The Create Custom Interface Members dialog box contains a list of all the custom members that will be created for your control (see Figure 14.11).

FIGURE 14.11
The wizard also provides a dialog box to enter member names not listed in the Select Interface Members dialog box.

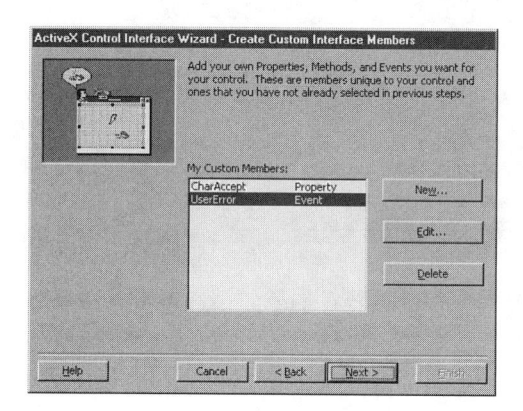

If you have previously defined public properties or other members, they appear in this list when you first access the dialog box. From this dialog box, you can add new members, and edit or delete existing ones. To add a new member, click the New button of the wizard to open the Add Custom Member dialog box. In this dialog box, you specify the name of the member and its type. Create the CharAccept property by typing CharAccept in the Name field, and click OK. After you return to the Add Custom Member dialog box, create the UserError event by following the same procedure. Finally, click the Next button to move on.

> **CAUTION**
>
> You should not edit or delete members of the control that you previously defined with code alone because the ActiveX Control Interface Wizard works by analyzing comments it places in the code. The wizard may or may not be able to interpret your hand-typed code correctly.

Mapping Properties

The next step in the ActiveX Control Interface Wizard is to assign the public members of the custom control to members of the constituent controls. This process is called *mapping the members*. For example, rather than create your own Text property, you can simply map the Text property of your custom control to the Text property of txtCharSet. The Set Mapping dialog box, shown in Figure 14.12, contains a list of all the properties, methods, and events that you identified as being part of the public interface of the custom control.

FIGURE 14.12
Mapping the public members of the control links them to members in the constituent controls.

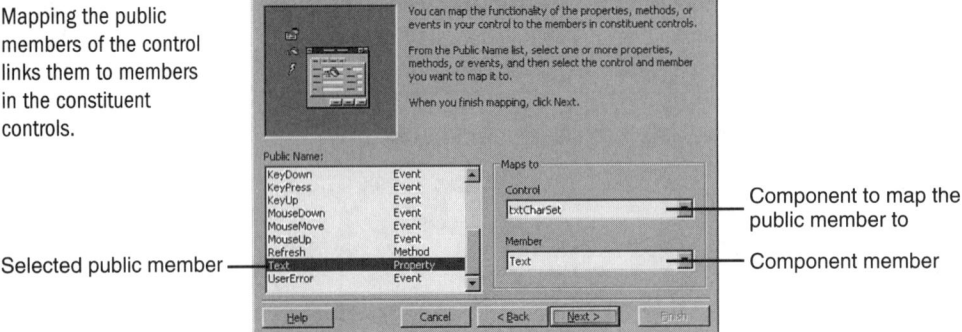

Selected public member

Component to map the public member to

Component member

The Set Mapping dialog box contains two combo boxes to identify the control and the control's member to which a public member should be mapped. To map a single public member of the custom control, follow these steps:

1. Select the member in the Public Name list. For this example, highlight the Text property on the left.

2. Select txtCharSet from the Control drop-down list. (This list contains the names of all the standard controls in your custom control.)

3. Select the member of that control from the Member drop-down list. In this case, the Text property is selected automatically for you. This process is illustrated in Figure 14.12 for the Text property of the TxtCharLimit control.

> **NOTE** In the Set Mapping dialog box, notice that you can map more than one public member at a time. The list of public names supports multiple selections. You can select multiple members from the list and then select a component to which to map the members. Each public

member is mapped to the property or method of the component that bears the same name. For example, the Text property of the custom control is automatically mapped to the Text property of a text or combo box.

4. Click the Next button to proceed to the wizard's final dialog box. This dialog box, shown in Figure 14.13, lets you set the attributes of each public member that is not mapped to a constituent control.

FIGURE 14.13
You can set the attributes for properties and methods before completing the code for the control.

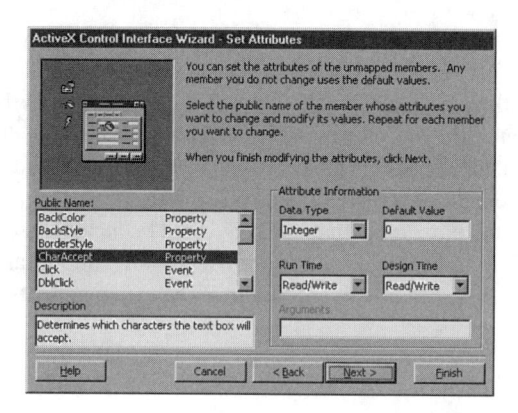

Depending on the type of member you are creating, the wizard enables you to specify different attributes. For a property, you can specify the type of data the property can hold, the default value of the property, and what type of access the user has to the property at designtime and runtime. The access type determines whether a Property Let, Property Get, or both procedures are created for the property. For runtime access, you can choose Read/Write, Read Only, Write Only, or none. For designtime access, you can choose Read/Write, Read Only, or none.

For the sample control, set the data type of the CharAccept property to Integer, and set the default value to 0. You can also type an optional description in the Description box. Property descriptions appear at the bottom of the Properties window during designtime. Because this is the final step of the wizard, you are now ready to click the Finish button.

Finishing the Code

After you click the Finish button, the ActiveX Control Interface Wizard creates a number of code modules in your control. The wizard also displays a summary page, providing details of the steps remaining to finish your control. A sample of this summary page is shown in Figure 14.14.

After reviewing the information on the summary page, you can take a look at the code that was generated by the wizard. You can view the code by clicking the user control in the Project window and then clicking the View Code button.

FIGURE 14.14
Refer to the summary page for tips on finishing your control.

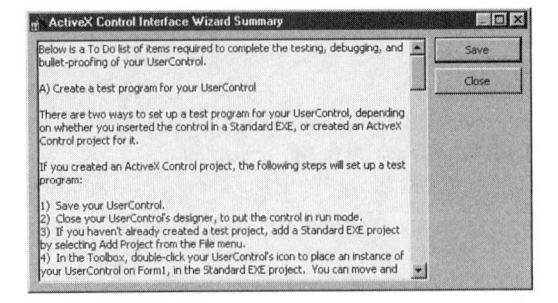

Take a look at some of the pieces of the code that is generated. First, in the General Declarations section, you will find that the wizard has created constants for the default values of any unmapped properties. The CharAccept property has been given a default value of 0. In addition, the wizard has automatically created the private property variable mCharAccept. It is followed by the declaration of any events that you requested be included in the control. A sample of this code is shown here. If you mapped any events, you will notice that the wizard places comments in the code to indicate how events are mapped to constituent control events:

```
Option Explicit

'Default Property Values:
Const m_def_BackColor = 0
Const m_def_ForeColor = 0
Const m_def_CharAccept = 0

'Property Variables:
Dim m_BackColor As Long
Dim m_ForeColor As Long
Dim m_CharAccept As Integer

'Event Declarations:
Event Click() 'MappingInfo=txtCharset,txtCharset,-1,Click
Event DblClick()
Event UserError()
Event KeyPress(KeyAscii As Integer)
```

The declarations of variables and events are followed by the property procedures. These procedures are created for properties that are mapped to a component property and those that are custom properties. As you can see in the following code segment, the code for the Text property is complete, whereas the CharAccept property has a skeleton function ready to be finished:

```
'WARNING! DO NOT REMOVE OR MODIFY THE FOLLOWING COMMENTED LINES!
'MappingInfo=txtCharset,txtCharset,-1,Text
Public Property Get Text() As String
    Text = txtCharset.Text
End Property

Public Property Let Text(ByVal New_Text As String)
    txtCharset.Text() = New_Text
    PropertyChanged "Text"
End Property
```

```
Public Property Get CharAccept() As Integer
    CharAccept = m_CharAccept
End Property

Public Property Let CharAccept(ByVal New_CharAccept As Integer)
    m_CharAccept = New_CharAccept
    PropertyChanged "CharAccept"
End Property
```

Note that if you request any methods, the wizard creates them as functions instead of sub procedures.

Finally, the code to read and write property values to the `PropertyBag` object is generated automatically. This code is as follows:

```
'Load property values from storage
Private Sub UserControl_ReadProperties(PropBag As PropertyBag)

    m_BackColor = PropBag.ReadProperty("BackColor", m_def_BackColor)
    m_ForeColor = PropBag.ReadProperty("ForeColor", m_def_ForeColor)
    txtCharset.Text = PropBag.ReadProperty("Text", "")
    m_CharAccept = PropBag.ReadProperty("CharAccept", m_def_CharAccept)
End Sub

'Write property values to storage
Private Sub UserControl_WriteProperties(PropBag As PropertyBag)

    Call PropBag.WriteProperty("BackColor", m_BackColor, m_def_BackColor)
    Call PropBag.WriteProperty("ForeColor", m_ForeColor, m_def_ForeColor)
    Call PropBag.WriteProperty("Text", txtCharset.Text, "")
    Call PropBag.WriteProperty("CharAccept", m_CharAccept, m_def_CharAccept)
End Sub
```

To complete the coding of your control, you need to add the custom code that is required for the `CharAccept` property and `KeyPress` event, shown in Listing 14.4.

Listing 14.4 LIMITED.ZIP—Changes to the Code Generated by the Wizard

```
Public Property Get CharAccept() As Integer
    CharAccept = mCharAccept
End Property

Public Property Let CharAccept(ByVal nNewValue As Integer)

      Select Case nNewValue
        Case 1 To 2
            mCharAccept = nNewValue
        Case Else
            mCharAccept = 0
      End Select

      PropertyChanged "CharAccept"

End Property
Private Sub txtCharSet_KeyPress(KeyAscii As Integer)
    If KeyAscii = 8 Then Exit Sub
```

continues

Listing 14.4 Continued

```
Select Case mCharAccept
    Case 0 'Any character is acceptable
        Exit Sub
    Case 1 'Only numbers may be entered
        If KeyAscii >= 48 And KeyAscii <= 57 Then
            Exit Sub
        Else
            KeyAscii = 0
            Beep
            RaiseEvent UserError
        End If
    Case 2 'Only letters may be entered
        If KeyAscii >= 65 And KeyAscii <= 90 Then
            Exit Sub
        ElseIf KeyAscii >= 97 And KeyAscii <= 122 Then
            Exit Sub
        Else
            KeyAscii = 0
            Beep
            RaiseEvent UserError
        End If
End Select

End Sub
```

Adding the custom code is necessary because the wizard creates a only "skeleton" for these items. After all, if the wizard could do everything, then you would be out of a job!

Using the Property Pages Wizard

You have seen Property Pages used for some of the controls that come with Visual Basic. These dialog boxes make it easy for you to set the properties of a control by organizing them into groups. You can create Property Pages for your own custom controls by using the Property Pages Wizard. As with the ActiveX Control Interface Wizard, you have to add the Property Pages Wizard to the desktop through the use of the Add-In Manager. After you take this step, you can access the Property Pages Wizard from the Add-Ins menu of Visual Basic. Upon starting the Property Pages Wizard, you see an introductory screen that explains the purpose of the wizard. Clicking the Next button on this page takes you to the first dialog box, where the real work is done.

Creating the Pages

The Select the Property Pages dialog box lets you define the pages of the Property Pages dialog box (see Figure 14.15). If you have included Font and Color properties in your control, the wizard starts with two default pages: StandardColor and StandardFont. If you do not need these pages, just click the boxes next to the names to remove them from the Property Pages.

FIGURE 14.15
You can create new pages or rename old ones in the Property Page Wizard.

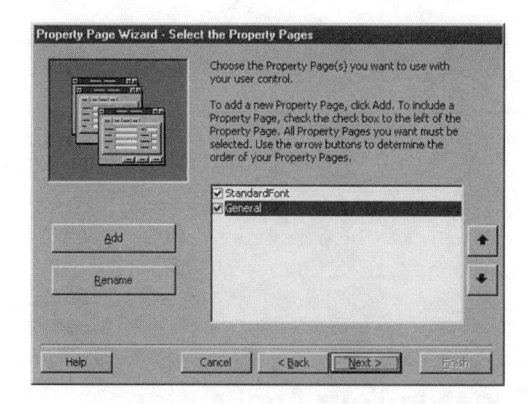

In addition to the default pages, you can add new pages to the dialog box. Clicking the Add button brings up the Property Page Name dialog box, which is an input box in which you can enter the name of the page to create. As you add a page name, it is placed in the list of available pages and is automatically checked. The order of the page names in the list is the order in which the tabs will appear in your Property Pages dialog box. You can change the order by selecting a page and using the arrow keys to move it within the list.

After you finish adding pages to the dialog box, click the Next button to move to the next dialog box.

Adding Properties to the Pages

The next step in creating your Property Pages is to add the appropriate properties to each page of the dialog box. The Add Properties dialog box is shown in Figure 14.16.

FIGURE 14.16
The Add Properties dialog box displays a list of available properties and shows the defined pages of the dialog box.

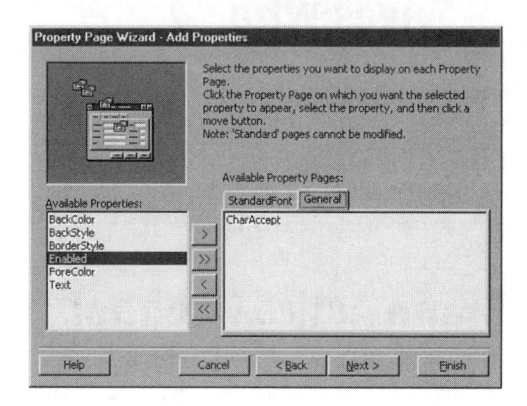

To add a property to a page, click the tab corresponding to the page where you want the property placed, and then select the property from the Available Properties list and click the right-arrow button. In Figure 14.16, notice the addition of a General Property Page and the inclusion of the `CharAccept` property. In addition, if you have the default pages of StandardColor and

StandardFont, you will notice that the appropriate properties have already been added to these pages.

> **TIP** You can drag and drop a property onto a tab to place it on the corresponding page of the Property Pages.

After you finish adding properties to the pages, click the Finish button to complete the creation of your Property Pages. Like the ActiveX Control Interface Wizard, the Property Pages Wizard shows a summary page that provides additional information for you to complete your custom control.

Using the Property Pages in Your Applications

To use the Property Pages you created, you need to add an instance of your custom control to a project. Then, in the Properties window, click the ellipsis (...) button next to the Custom property. Then, just like the Property Pages of other controls, your Property Pages dialog box presents itself to allow the user to customize the control. A sample of a custom control's Property Pages is shown in Figure 14.17.

FIGURE 14.17
Your Property Pages help the users set up your ActiveX control.

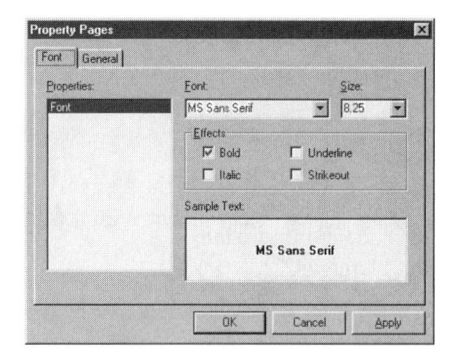

> **TIP** You also can access the Property Pages by right-clicking the control and selecting the Properties item from the context menu.

Creating a User-Drawn ActiveX Control

The previous two examples have demonstrated how to create ActiveX controls from other controls. The following sections will demonstrate how to create a control totally from scratch by drawing the interface with graphics methods and by creating the properties, methods, and events of the control. The control you create in this chapter is a command button with different foreground and background color settings, which is something you cannot do with a regular command button. Although a command button is a relatively simple example, it introduces you to the process of drawing your own control.

Starting the Project

To begin creating the Color Button control, you need to start a new ActiveX Control project. After creating the project, set the properties of the project and the user control, as shown in Table 14.2.

Table 14.2 Properties of the Project and Control

Item	Setting
Project Name	ColorButton
Project Description	Color Enhanced Command Button
User control Name property	ColorBtn
User control Public property	True

Creating the User Interface

In previous examples, you drew the user interface on the UserControl object by using existing controls. However, in this user-drawn control, you can create the interface entirely with code in the UserControl's event procedures. You need to place the code to draw the shape of the Color Button in the Paint event of the UserControl. The Paint event is fired whenever the container (such as a form) that holds your control is redrawn. You can also force the Paint event by issuing the Refresh method of the control. Keep in mind that your command button is really just a picture. You will be using graphics methods, such as the Line method, to draw what the user sees. For example, when a user clicks your control, you will use lines to redraw the button so that it looks like it has been pressed. For more information about graphics methods, refer to Chapter 19, "Using Visual Design Elements."

▶ **See** "Using the Line and Shape Controls," **p. 426**

To draw a rectangular command button, you need only the Line and Print methods. In this case, the button fills the entire space of the UserControl area. The code for drawing a colored button involves three steps:

1. Use the Line method of the UserControl object to draw a filled rectangular box the full size of the control. To create a box at the appropriate size, use the Height and Width of the control as parameters in the Line method.
2. To simulate the "raised" state of the button, change the colors of the lines that form the rectangular box. This action involves additional calls to the Line method that draw a white line along the top and left edges of the control and a black line along the bottom and right edges of the control. These lines give the button the standard "raised" appearance. (When the button is "pressed," you reverse the appearance by swapping the white and black lines.)
3. Using the Print method, draw a caption on the button.

The code for creating the body of the button, which should be placed in the UserControl's Paint event, is shown in Listing 14.5.

Listing 14.5 COLORBTN.ZIP—Using the *Line* Method to Draw the Color Button

```
Private Sub UserControl_Paint()
    Dim nHeight As Integer
    Dim nWidth  As Integer

    With UserControl

        'Leave some room for the border
        nHeight = .Height - 10
        nWidth = .Width - 10

        'Set UserControl's BackColor, draw a colored box
        .DrawWidth = 1
        .FillColor = lngBackColor
        .FillStyle = 0
        UserControl.Line (0, 0)-(nWidth, nHeight), , B

        'Draw lower right lines
        .DrawWidth = 3
        If bMouseDown = False Then
            .ForeColor = vbBlack
        Else
            .ForeColor = vbWhite
        End If
        UserControl.Line (0, nHeight)-(nWidth, nHeight)
        UserControl.Line (nWidth, 0)-(nWidth, nHeight)

        'Draw upper-left lines
        If bMouseDown = False Then
            .ForeColor = vbWhite
        Else
            .ForeColor = vbBlack
        End If
        UserControl.Line (0, 0)-(nWidth, 0)
        UserControl.Line (0, 0)-(0, nHeight)

        'Calculate and move to the the caption position
        .CurrentX = (.Width - .TextWidth(m_Caption)) / 2
        If .CurrentX < 5 Then .CurrentX = 5
        .CurrentY = (.Height - .TextHeight(m_Caption)) / 2
        If .CurrentY < 5 Then .CurrentY = 5

        'Draw the Caption
        .ForeColor = lngForeColor
        UserControl.Print m_Caption

    End With

End Sub
```

The code in Listing 14.5 should be fairly easy to follow. First, several calls to the Line method are used to draw a box and some lines to represent the command button. Next, the button caption is drawn in the center of the control. Note that several module-level variables are referenced in the `Paint` event; for example, the button's color is determined by the variable `lngBackcolor`, which holds the contents of the `BackColor` property. The following variables should be declared in the General Declarations section of the `UserControl` object:

```
Dim lngForeColor As Long     'Button Foreground
Dim lngBackColor As Long     'Button Background
Dim bMouseDown As Boolean    'Is the mouse pressed?
```

The module-level variables are necessary so that their values can be set from the property procedures of the control. The Boolean variable `bMouseDown` determines whether the button is drawn "raised" or "pressed."

Figure 14.18 shows how the basic Color Button control looks on the form of a test project.

FIGURE 14.18
Code in the `Paint` event draws the user interface for the custom command button.

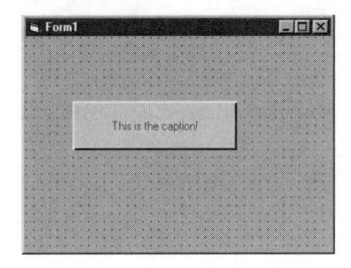

The final step in creating the user interface is to set initial values for the button colors. To do so, place a few assignment statements in the `Initialize` event of the control, as follows:

```
Private Sub UserControl_Initialize()
    lngBackColor = vbCyan
    lngForeColor = vbBlue
End Sub
```

The preceding lines of code provide initial settings for the `Paint` event.

Creating the Properties of the Button

As stated previously, you can keep the design of the command button simple. The four key properties of the button are the `BackColor`, `Caption`, `Font`, and `ForeColor` properties. Three of these properties—`BackColor`, `Font`, and `ForeColor`—will be tied to the corresponding properties of the user control. In addition, the `BackColor` and `ForeColor` properties will be stored as variables for use in the code.

Using the ActiveX Control Interface Wizard, you can easily create the properties that you need. You have to add the `Caption` property as a Custom Member, as well as map the `BackColor`, `Font`, and `ForeColor` properties to those of the `UserControl` object. The wizard creates the `Property Let` and `Property Get` procedures for the four properties. Consider, for example, the `Property Get` procedure for the control's `BackColor` property:

```
Public Property Get BackColor() As OLE_COLOR
    BackColor = UserControl.BackColor
End Property
```

This procedure simply returns the background color of the user control and can be used as is. However, you need to add an extra line to the `Property Let` procedure, as shown here:

```
Public Property Let BackColor(ByVal New_BackColor As OLE_COLOR)
    UserControl.BackColor() = New_BackColor
    lngBackColor = UserControl.BackColor
    PropertyChanged "BackColor"
End Property
```

In this code, notice that a line was added to store the color in the variable `lngBackColor`. This variable, declared in the General Declarations section, is used by code in the `Paint` event. The other properties, shown in Listing 14.6, are coded in a similar fashion.

Listing 14.6 COLORBTN.ZIP—Most of the Property Procedures Were Created by the Wizard

```
Public Property Get Font() As Font
    Set Font = UserControl.Font
End Property

Public Property Set Font(ByVal New_Font As Font)
    Set UserControl.Font = New_Font
    PropertyChanged "Font"
End Property

Public Property Get ForeColor() As OLE_COLOR
    ForeColor = UserControl.ForeColor
End Property

Public Property Let ForeColor(ByVal New_ForeColor As OLE_COLOR)
    UserControl.ForeColor() = New_ForeColor
    lngForeColor = UserControl.ForeColor
    PropertyChanged "ForeColor"
End Property

Public Property Get Caption() As Variant
    Caption = m_Caption
End Property

Public Property Let Caption(ByVal New_Caption As Variant)
    m_Caption = New_Caption
    UserControl_Paint
    PropertyChanged "Caption"
End Property
```

Although you need to declare the variables `lngForeColor` and `lngBackColor`, the ActiveX Control Interface Wizard declares `m_Caption` for you automatically. The reason for this difference is that the `Caption` property is not mapped to the `UserControl` object. You also might want to set the constant for the default caption name, `m_def_Caption`, to something other than 0. `ColorBtn` would be an appropriate choice.

N O T E The wizard also creates the code for the `WriteProperties` and `ReadProperties` events so that the property values can be saved in the `PropertyBag` object.

Setting Up the Button's Events

You also can use the ActiveX Control Interface Wizard to create the events for the Color Button control. You can do so at the same time you create the properties, or you can run the wizard again. Remember to map the `Click`, `GotFocus`, `MouseDown`, and `MouseUp` events to the corresponding events in the UserControl. (Refer to the section "Mapping Properties" earlier in the chapter.)

After the wizard creates the skeleton code, make an addition to the code for the `MouseDown` and `MouseUp` events. Because you want your custom button to behave similarly to a standard command button, change the appearance of the button as it is "pressed." You do so by drawing black lines along the top and left edges of the button when the `MouseDown` event is fired and by redrawing the white lines along those edges when the `MouseUp` event is fired. This is coded by setting the Boolean variable `bMouseDown` and then running the code in the UserControl's `Paint` event. After you make the additions to these two events, the event code for the ColorBtn control should look like the code in Listing 14.7.

Listing 14.7 COLORBTN.ZIP—Event Code Defined by the Wizard and Enhanced by You

```
Private Sub UserControl_MouseDown(Button As Integer, _
Shift As Integer, X As Single, Y As Single)
    bMouseDown = True
    UserControl_Paint
    RaiseEvent MouseDown(Button, Shift, X, Y)
End Sub

Private Sub UserControl_MouseUp(Button As Integer, _
Shift As Integer, X As Single, Y As Single)
    bMouseDown = False
    UserControl_Paint
    RaiseEvent MouseUp(Button, Shift, X, Y)
End Sub
```

> **NOTE** Do not confuse the events discussed here with the events of the ColorBtn control, as seen from the user's perspective. The code in Listing 14.7 executes when the `UserControl` object receives mouse events. The last statement, `RaiseEvent`, fires the corresponding event in the ColorBtn control, executing any code the user may have placed there.

Figure 14.19 shows the pressed state of the ColorBtn control.

Creating Property Pages for the Button

The final task you will perform for the design of the Color Button control is to create the Property Pages so that the user can set the properties of the control easily. Use the Property Page Wizard to create the pages (refer to the section "Using the Property Pages Wizard" earlier in the chapter), and follow these steps:

FIGURE 14.19
Black lines give the indication of a pressed button.

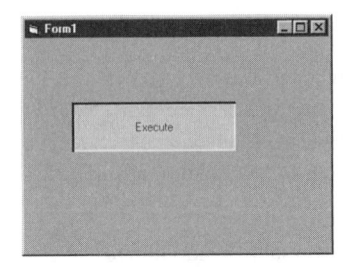

1. Add a General page to the pages.
2. Place the Caption property on the General page.
3. Verify that the BackColor and ForeColor properties are on the StandardColor page.
4. Verify that the Font property is on the StandardFont page.

Testing the Color Button in a Program

At this point, the design of the ActiveX control is complete. You now are ready to test it in a program. You first need to add a Standard EXE project to the project group containing the ColorBtn. You then need to close the ColorBtn design window to make the control available to your project.

Next, you can draw the control on your form just like any other control. As you draw the button, you will see the typical rubber band box indicating the size of the control. When you release the mouse button, the control will be drawn using the default colors and caption (refer to Figure 14.18 to see how the control looks).

Setting the Button's Properties   After the button is placed on the form, set the values of the properties. You can, of course, set the properties from the Properties window. One point to notice is that if you placed a description in the Caption property when you defined it in the wizard, this description shows up in the area below the properties list when the Caption property is selected. This description is another way to help your users work with your custom control.

Another way to set the properties of your control is to use the Property Pages you created. The dialog box shown in Figure 14.20 enables you to set the Caption, BackColor, ForeColor, and Font properties of the control. The Paint event is fired whenever you close the Property Pages. At this time, the effects of the new properties are shown.

Writing Code for the Events   Writing code for an event procedure of the custom control is like writing code for any other event procedure. You can double-click the control to access the Code window in your test project and then begin typing code. Just to make sure the Click event of the ColorBtn control works, place a message box in the event procedure to announce that the button has been clicked. This code is shown in the following line:

```
MsgBox "You clicked the ColorBtn control."
```

FIGURE 14.20
Property Pages provide an organized way for users to set properties of a control.

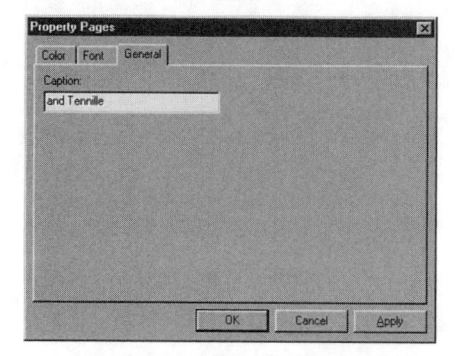

After you add the `MsgBox` statement, test the `Click` event by running the project. When you click the ColorBtn control, the message should be displayed. If you want to test any other events, follow the same steps.

From Here...

This chapter showed you how to create ActiveX controls, as an enhancement to existing controls as well as entirely from scratch. You also looked at two wizards that Visual Basic provides to aid in control creation. To learn more about the topics related to those in this chapter, see the following:

- To learn more about creating ActiveX controls, see Chapter 15, "Extending ActiveX Controls."
- To learn about ActiveX documents, see Chapter 32, "ActiveX Documents."

CHAPTER 15

Extending ActiveX Controls

In this chapter

Using the Ambient Object to Maintain Uniformity   342

Introducing the Extender Object   344

Building the Calculator Control   345

Creating Property Pages   350

Control Error Handling   355

In Chapter 14, "Creating ActiveX Controls," you learned the basics of creating an ActiveX control project in Visual Basic. You also used two add-in wizards to aid in control development. This chapter continues the discussion of ActiveX controls, with some additional topics that will help you build better controls. The following sections cover these topics:

- Using objects that enhance control integration with their containers
- Creating Property Pages for added flexibility without using a wizard
- Handling errors in your ActiveX controls

You'll also build a slightly more involved ActiveX control, the Calculator control.

Using the *Ambient* Object to Maintain Uniformity

With a Standard EXE project, you have a great amount of control over what the user sees, such as the color and layout of the forms. However, ActiveX controls can be placed in a number of containers, determined by the user. In order for the control to behave in a consistent and desired manner in each type of container, it is necessary for the control to have access to information about its container. Fortunately, programmers can write code in a UserControl object that uses the Ambient object to determine information about its surroundings.

Setting Up an *Ambient* Object Example

To demonstrate a use of the Ambient object, start a new Standard EXE project, and then add an ActiveX Control project to create a project group. Resize the UserControl object so that it is fairly small (about 1605×1050 twips), and close the UserControl window. Next, set the BackColor property of Form1 to purple, and draw an instance of the user control on the form. The results should look similar to Figure 15.1.

FIGURE 15.1
User controls will not automatically respond to color changes in the container.

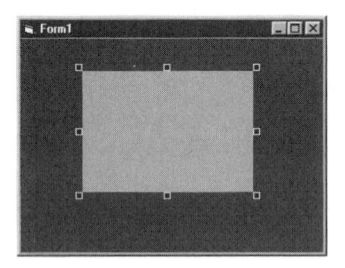

Notice that the control's background color does not match that of the form. Most likely, the control would work properly, but the color difference would be a distraction to the users. For the control to match the background automatically, code within the UserControl object needs a way to retrieve the BackColor property of its container. Fortunately, the Ambient object makes this and other information available.

Keeping Track of the Ambient Colors

To fix this potential problem, you have to set the control's colors to match those of its container. First, delete the instance of the sample control you just created, and return to the UserControl window. Next, add the following lines of code to the `InitProperties()` event procedure:

```
UserControl.BackColor = Ambient.BackColor
UserControl.ForeColor = Ambient.ForeColor
```

Your control should now be able to match itself to the container's colors. To verify this fact, close the UserControl window so that the control becomes available in the Toolbox. Then draw an instance of the user control on the form. When the new control instance appears, it should be the same color as the form (see Figure 15.2).

FIGURE 15.2
The `Ambient` object can retrieve information about the control's container, such as the color properties.

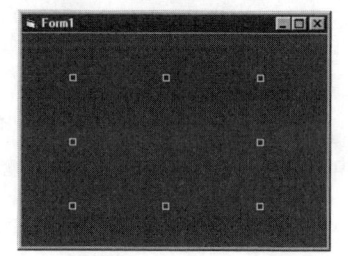

What happens, though, if the users of the control change the background color again? Go ahead and set the `BackColor` property of the form to another color. When you do, the form immediately changes to match your selection, but the control remains purple. You get this result because you placed code in the `InitProperties` event but not in the all-important `AmbientChanged` event.

To demonstrate, add code for this event to the user control now:

```
Private Sub UserControl_AmbientChanged(PropertyName As String)
    UserControl.BackColor = Ambient.BackColor
    UserControl.ForeColor = Ambient.ForeColor
End Sub
```

Now, close the UserControl window, and draw an instance of the control on the form. Change the `BackColor` property values, and this time the control's background color changes as well.

Properties of the *Ambient* Object

As you have probably guessed, the `AmbientChanged` event fires when the properties of the `Ambient` object are changed. The example updates the `ForeColor` and `BackColor` properties every time the event is fired, but the `PropertyName` parameter allows you to determine which property changed.

In addition to the color properties, the `Ambient` object contains several others. Some of the more important ones are listed in Table 15.1.

Table 15.1 Important *Ambient* Properties

Property	Description
`BackColor`	Holds the container's background color.
`DisplayAsDefault`	Indicates whether a user-drawn control is the default control in the container.
`DisplayName`	Holds the name of the control instance. You can use the `DisplayName` property to identify the messages presented to the developer at designtime.
`Font`	Represents the font of the container.
`ForeColor`	Holds the foreground color of the container.
`LocaleID`	Indicates the locale in which the control is running. In international programs, this property is useful for changing the language or date formats.
`TextAlign`	Represents the container's text alignment setting.
`UserMode`	Indicates whether the control is running at designtime or runtime. A `UserMode` value of `False` indicates designtime; `True` indicates runtime. Another property, `UIDead`, indicates break mode.

You can access each of the properties in Table 15.1 from within the control by using the `Ambient` object.

Introducing the *Extender* Object

In addition to the properties provided by the `Ambient` object, there is a separate object known as the `Extender` object, which provides some other useful properties. These properties, called *extender properties*, at first glance appear to be part of a control instance. For example, when you place a control on a form, the `Left` and `Top` properties look like they are part of that control. However, in reality, these properties and several others are part of the `Extender` object.

Although the `Ambient` and `Extender` objects both provide information about a control in relation to its container, the `Extender` object is not available until the control has been sited (placed) on its container. Because each container is different, you cannot determine in advance what the container is or which properties it will support. For this reason, you can't access the `Extender` object in a control's `Initialize` event procedure, which is called before the control is completely sited on its container. However, you can access the `Extender` object in the `InitProperties` and `ReadProperties` events.

To view the extender properties, draw an instance of the sample control on a form, and press F4 to display the Properties window. Notice that even though you have not added any properties to the user control, several are already listed. They are the properties of the `Extender` object.

To demonstrate, add the following code to the user control's `InitProperties` event:

```
UserControl.Extender.ToolTipText = "Testing the Extender object"
```

Next, draw an instance of the control on the form. The `ToolTipText` property should automatically appear after the control instance is drawn. You can verify this fact by hovering the mouse pointer over the control, as shown in Figure 15.3.

FIGURE 15.3
The `Extender` object allows the control to change properties set by its container.

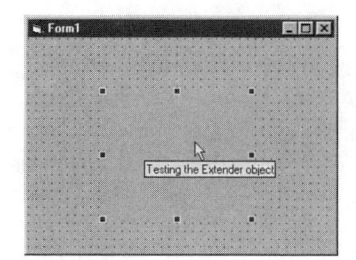

Building the Calculator Control

In this section, you build a sample Calculator control to be used as the basis for the topics presented in the remainder of this chapter. The Calculator control is a simple ActiveX control that allows users to provide two input values and perform a mathematical operation on them: multiply, add, subtract, or divide. The mathematical operation is controlled by the `Operation` property and performed when the users click a button. The sample control is shown in Figure 15.4.

FIGURE 15.4
This Calculator control has its constituent controls in place.

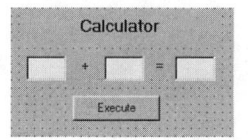

Creating the Control

To create the Calculator control, start a new ActiveX Control project. Then arrange the following constituent controls on the new UserControl designer:

- `lblCaption`—A label that the users will access through the `Caption` property of the control.

- `txtNum1` and `txtNum2`—Text boxes that hold input from the users.

- `lblOperation`—A label between the text boxes indicating which operation is to be performed.

- `lblEquals`—A label that displays the equal sign (=) to indicate a mathematical equation visually.

- `txtResult`—A text box used to hold the result of the calculation.
- `cmdExecute`—A command button used to perform the calculation. The users can change the button's caption through the `ButtonCaption` property of the control.

After you finish placing the controls, your control should look similar to the one shown in Figure 15.4.

Creating the Interface

The next step in creating the Calculator control is to write code for the properties. As you may recall from the preceding chapter, the ActiveX Control Interface Wizard enables you to expose properties, methods, and events of your control. The sample Calculator control includes a number of properties that can be exposed through the wizard. Follow these steps:

▶ **See** "Using the ActiveX Control Interface Wizard," **p. 323**

1. Start the Wizard by choosing the ActiveX Control Interface Wizard item from the Add-Ins menu. Then click Next.
2. In the Select Interface Members dialog box, add `Caption` property to the control.
3. In the Create Custom Interface Members dialog box, add two new properties, a method, and an event, as shown in Figure 15.5. These custom members are as follows:
    - `Operation` property—Determines whether the control adds, subtracts, multiplies, or divides
    - `ButtonCaption` property—Determines the caption of the command button
    - `ValidateEntries` method—Validates user input into the text boxes
    - `BadEntries` event—Fires when erroneous input is encountered

FIGURE 15.5
The Calculator control needs four new control members.

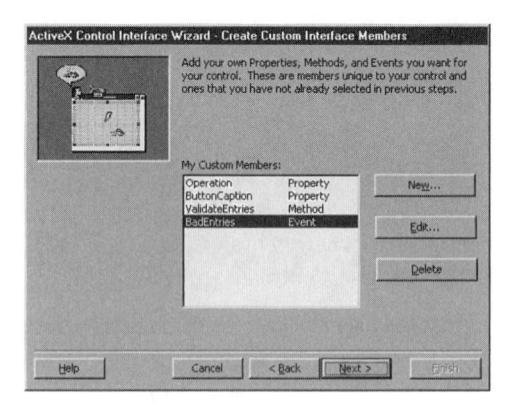

4. In the Set Mapping dialog box, map the `ButtonCaption` property to the `Caption` property of `cmdExecute`. Also, map the `Caption` property of the control to the `Caption` property of `lblCaption`.

You can also map the `BackColor`, `ForeColor`, and `BorderStyle` properties to the corresponding properties of the UserControl object, if you want.

5. Click Finish, and the wizard creates additional source code in your UserControl object.

Now all you have to do is write the program code for the properties, methods, and events.

Setting Up the *Operation* Property

By default, the ActiveX Control Interface Wizard creates the `Operation` property as a Variant and includes a private variable `m_Operation` to hold the property's value. However, you will use an integer value to represent the operation: 0 for addition, 1 for multiplication, 2 for subtraction, and 3 for division.

To make the control easy to use, you shouldn't require the users to memorize these arbitrary integer values. Therefore, you can use an `Enum` to provide the integer values. To allow your control to provide these values, you must first add the `Enum` declaration to the General Declarations section of the UserControl object, as shown in Listing 15.1.

Listing 15.1 CALC.ZIP—Declaring an Enum for the *Operation* Property

```
Public Enum OpType
    Add = 0
    Multiply = 1
    Subtract = 2
    Divide = 3
End Enum

Dim m_Operation As OpType      <--- Change this line
```

In Listing 15.1, you add a new type, `OpType`, as well as change the type of the `m_Operation` variable from Variant to `OpType`. Next, you need to modify the `Operation` Property's `Get` and `Let` procedures, as shown in Listing 15.2.

Listing 15.2 CALC.ZIP—Changing the Property Procedures to Use the *OpType* Type

```
Public Property Get Operation() As OpType
    Operation = m_Operation
End Property

Public Property Let Operation(ByVal New_Operation As OpType)
    m_Operation = New_Operation
    PropertyChanged "Operation"

    Select Case m_Operation
        Case Add
            lblOperation = "+"
        Case Subtract
            lblOperation = "-"
```

continues

Listing 15.2 Continued

```
            Case Multiply
                lblOperation = "X"
            Case Divide
                lblOperation = "/"
        End Select
        txtResult = ""
    End Property
```

In Listing 15.2, in addition to changing the property procedures to use the `OpType` type, you also add code to update `lblCaption` and clear `txtResult` when the operation type changes. Using `Enums` in this manner is just one way to make your control more robust. Figure 15.6 shows how the `Operation` property looks in the Properties window for a control instance.

FIGURE 15.6
The `Operation` property provides a list of valid values rather than requiring the users to know them.

Coding Methods and Events

The `ValidateEntries` method determines whether users have typed valid numeric data into the two text boxes. It is a simple function that returns `True` or `False`. The code for this function is shown in Listing 15.3.

Listing 15.3 CALC.ZIP—The *ValidateEntries* Method

```
Public Function ValidateEntries() As Boolean

    'Assume entries are invalid
    ValidateEntries = False

    'Check for Empty Strings
    If Trim$(txtNum1) = "" Or Trim$(txtNum2) = "" Then Exit Function

    'Check for Numeric values
    If Not IsNumeric(txtNum1) Then Exit Function
    If Not IsNumeric(txtNum2) Then Exit Function
```

```
        'If you made it this far, then they are valid!
        ValidateEntries = True

End Function
```

The `Click` event of the `cmdExecute` button contains the code that actually performs the calculation and displays the result. To create this event procedure, use the code from Listing 15.4.

Listing 15.4   CALC.ZIP—The *Click* Event of *cmdExecute*

```
Private Sub cmdExecute_Click()
    Dim nVal1 As Integer
    Dim nVal2 As Integer
    Dim nResult As Integer

    If ValidateEntries() = False Then
        RaiseEvent BadEntries
        txtResult = "???"
        Exit Sub
    End If

    nVal1 = Val(txtNum1)
    nVal2 = Val(txtNum2)

    Select Case m_Operation
        Case Add
            nResult = nVal1 + nVal2
        Case Multiply
            nResult = nVal1 * nVal2
        Case Subtract
            nResult = nVal1 - nVal2
        Case Divide
            nResult = nVal1 / nVal2
    End Select

    txtResult = nResult

End Sub
```

Testing the Control

To see the control from the developer's point of view, close the user control designer. You can create a project group with a Standard EXE test project by selecting File, Add Project. Open the form in the Standard EXE project. Draw an instance of the user control on the form, and display the Properties window. You can set the `ButtonCaption`, `Caption`, and `Operation` properties from this window. Double-click the control, and enter your own code in the `BadEntries` event:

```
Private Sub CalcControl1_BadEntries()
    MsgBox "You have entered invalid numbers!"
End Sub
```

Finally, run the test program, and verify that the calculator fires this event when invalid data is entered.

Creating Property Pages

Chapter 14 included a brief overview of Property Pages, which are tabbed dialog boxes designed to make it easy for users to set design-time properties. As you know, Property Pages can be displayed by pressing the ellipsis button in the Custom property of the Properties window, or by right-clicking a control and choosing Properties. In addition to being a neat way to organize the properties of your control, Property Pages included with your control can be used in a development environment other than Visual Basic.

Chapter 14 showed how to create Property Pages by using the Property Pages Wizard. The wizard is designed to provide you with a quick way of creating a property sheet, but it does not provide all the possible options. In this section, you learn how to create Property Pages manually, which allows you to make design and feature choices that are unavailable through the Property Pages Wizard.

▶ **See** "Using the Property Pages Wizard," **p. 330**

The following list describes the general steps involved in creating Property Pages, and the subsequent sections explain these steps in more detail:

1. Create Property Page objects for each group of properties.
2. On the Property Page objects, place controls that the developer can use to edit the properties.
3. Implement the SelectionChanged event procedure for each Property Page. This event procedure is responsible for reading in the current values of each control's properties.
4. Implement the Change event procedure (or sometimes the Click event procedure) for each control on each Property Page.
5. Implement the ApplyChanges event procedure for each Property Page. Its task is to copy the new property values from the Property Page controls to the corresponding properties on the user control.
6. Connect the Property Pages to the custom control.

Creating Property Page Objects

The first step in creating the Property Pages dialog box for your control is to create Property Page objects for each group of properties you want to include. How you organize these groups is entirely up to you, although you should use common sense. If your control has only a few properties, you may need only a single Property Page. However, if the control has many properties, you should group related properties on their own Property Pages.

For the sample Calculator control, you'll create only a single Property Page called General. Follow these steps to add the General Property Page object to the user control project:

1. Make sure that ActiveX Control project is selected in the Project Explorer and choose Project, Add Property Page. The Add PropertyPage dialog box appears.

2. Double-click the Property Page icon, and a new Property Page object appears. Notice that it looks similar to a form designer.
3. Bring up the Properties window of the Property Page by pressing F4.
4. Change the Name property of the Property Page to `CalcGeneral`.
5. Change the Caption property of the Property Page to `General`. (The caption appears in the tab of the Property Page, which is not displayed in the design environment.)

After you create the new Property Page objects, they should appear in your Project Explorer window, as shown in Figure 15.7.

FIGURE 15.7
Property Pages are separate objects in an ActiveX control project.

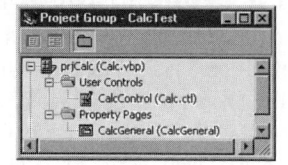

Placing Controls on the Property Pages

Now that you have created the Property Page objects, you can add the controls you need to edit the properties of custom controls to which the Property Page objects will be attached. The types of controls to use are up to you. Usually, though, you'll use text boxes to represent text properties, check boxes to represent Boolean (true/false) properties, list boxes to represent properties with multiple settings, and so on. Follow these steps to add controls to the Property Pages you have created for the Calculator control:

1. Double-click the `CalcGeneral` object in the Project Explorer window to display the General Property Page.
2. Add three Label controls to the Property Page, using the following properties:

Name	Caption
lblCaption	Caption
lblBCaption	Button Caption
lblOperation	Operation

3. Add two TextBox controls, `txtCaption` and `txtButtonCaption`, to hold the control captions.
4. Add a ComboBox control, `cmbOperation`, to hold the operation types.

After adding all these controls, your General Property Page should look like the one shown in Figure 15.8.

FIGURE 15.8
Here's the `CalcGeneral` Property Page with all its controls.

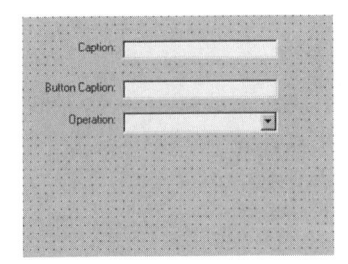

Implementing the *SelectionChanged* Event Procedure

Imagine for a moment that a developer is using the Calculator control as part of an application. The developer has placed two Calculator controls on a form, one for addition and the other for multiplication. When the developer displays the Property Pages dialog box for one or more of these user controls, the `SelectionChanged` event of the Property Page object fires so that each user control's current property settings can be displayed on the Property Page. To write code to load properties into the text box and combo box, open the code window for the `CalcGeneral` Property Page by double-clicking the Property Page object. Next, enter the lines of code from Listing 15.5 in the `SelectionChanged` event procedure.

Listing 15.5 CALC.ZIP—The *SelectionChanged* Event Procedure

```
Private Sub PropertyPage_SelectionChanged()

    txtCaption.Text = SelectedControls(0).Caption
    txtButtonCaption.Text = SelectedControls(0).ButtonCaption

    cmbOperation.Clear
    cmbOperation.AddItem "0 - Add"
    cmbOperation.AddItem "1 - Multiply"
    cmbOperation.AddItem "2 - Subtract"
    cmbOperation.AddItem "3 - Divide"
    cmbOperation.ListIndex = SelectedControls(0).Operation
    Changed = False
End Sub
```

Notice that each control on the Property Page is assigned a value from a property of a control in the `SelectedControls` collection. As you will see, Property Pages can modify the properties of several controls simultaneously. Currently, you've created a Property Page that can handle only a single control selection.

Implementing the *Change* Event Procedures

When a developer changes the value of a control on a form, the control's `Change` event is fired. For a Property Page, you use this event to notify Visual Basic that the contents of a property have changed.

> **NOTE** Some controls, such as the CheckBox and ComboBox, use the Click event instead of the Change event to handle the change notification.

All you have to do is set the Changed property of the Property Page object to True, which tells Visual Basic to enable the Apply button. The code for the Change and Click events of the CalcGeneral page is shown in Listing 15.6.

Listing 15.6 CALC.ZIP—Activating the Apply Button with the *Changed* Property

```
Private Sub cmbOperation_Click()
    Changed = True
End Sub
Private Sub txtButtonCaption_Change()
    Changed = True
End Sub

Private Sub txtCaption_Change()
    Changed = True
End Sub
```

Implementing the *ApplyChanges* Event Procedure

The ApplyChanges event is the opposite of the SelectionChanged event. Whereas the SelectionChanged event procedure loads information into the Property Page, the ApplyChanges event procedure saves new values back to the control. This event fires when the developer closes the Property Page or clicks the Apply button. For the Calculator control, you simply need to take the properties from the Property Page's controls and assign them to the custom control, as shown in Listing 15.7.

Listing 15.7 CALC.ZIP—The *ApplyChanges* Event Procedure

```
Private Sub PropertyPage_ApplyChanges()
    SelectedControls(0).Caption = txtCaption
    SelectedControls(0).ButtonCaption = txtButtonCaption
    SelectedControls(0).Operation = cmbOperation.ListIndex
End Sub
```

Connecting the Property Page to the Control

The Property Page you have been building is now complete. To use the CalcGeneral Property Page with your control, however, you must first connect the Property Page to the control. (Remember, the Property Page is a separate object or file that can be used with several controls.) To perform this final task, follow these steps:

1. Display the user control designer window for the Calculator control.

2. In the control's Properties window, double-click the PropertyPages property. The Connect Property Pages dialog box appears.

3. Place a check mark in the `CalcGeneral` check box, as shown in Figure 15.9.

FIGURE 15.9
The checked Property Pages will be attached to the control.

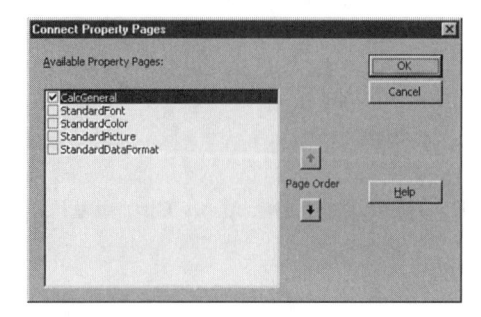

4. Click OK in the Connect Property Pages dialog box to associate the selected pages with the Calculator control.

Using Your Property Page

Now you have completed the property sheet for the Calculator control. When you are working on an application that contains the control, you can set the control's properties from either the Properties window or the Property Pages. To test the sample Property Page, first close all the control project's designers. Next, open the form from the test project. Draw an instance of the Calculator control on the form, and open its Properties window by pressing F4. If you look closely, you'll notice a new property called `Custom`.

To view the Property Page, double-click the `Custom` property, or click the ellipsis button. When you do, the property sheet appears, as shown in Figure 15.10.

FIGURE 15.10
Here, you see the completed Property Pages for the Calculator control.

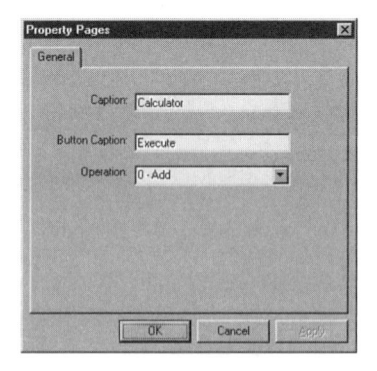

Notice that as soon as you change a control on a Property Page, the Apply button becomes enabled.

NOTE Remember to save the changes you have made to the Calculator project. Notice that when you do save changes, Property Page files are stored with .PAG extensions.

Handling Multiple Control Selections

As you may recall from the "Implementing the SelectionChanged Event Procedure" section, the SelectedControls collection object represents all the controls that the developer has selected when he or she displays the Property Pages. You use the SelectedControls object in the SelectionChanged and ApplyChanges event procedures to access the properties of each selected control. For example, if the developer has two Calculator controls selected, SelectedControls(0).Caption represents the first control's caption, and SelectedControls(1).Caption represents the caption of the second control. If you write the code appropriately, the developer can apply the same caption to both selected Calculator controls.

You might not want to apply some properties, such as the Operation property, to multiple selected controls. In this case, you can use the Count property of the SelectedControls collection to see whether you should ignore the change or even set the Visible property of a control on the Property Page to False.

Another way to handle this situation would be to apply only certain changes to all controls and others to only the first control. A sample ApplyChanges event that handles multiple controls is shown in Listing 15.8.

Listing 15.8 CALC.ZIP—Applying Changes to Multiple Controls

```
Private Sub PropertyPage_ApplyChanges()

    Dim control As CalcControl

    'Set Captions for every control
    For Each control In SelectedControls
        control.Caption = txtCaption
        control.ButtonCaption = txtButtonCaption
    Next control

    'Set only the first control's Operation property
    SelectedControls(0).Operation = cmbOperation.ListIndex

End Sub
```

To test this procedure, first open the Property Pages dialog box. Next, highlight multiple instances of the Calculator control, and change their properties.

Control Error Handling

The importance of controls running correctly cannot be overstated. Developers and users are depending on using the control as a self-contained, robust object that does not crash under unusual conditions. The developer is, of course, responsible for testing that the application runs correctly with your control, but you can take several precautions to help ensure your controls don't present developers and users with any nasty surprises.

▶ **See** "Packaging ActiveX Components," **p. 788**

First, use plenty of error handling in event procedures. If an error occurs, and you do not handle it with code, the control stops running, bringing down its container as well. Typically, all events that have any code attached to them should be error handled. Some key areas, however, need special attention:

- **File handling.** What if a file does not exist or is write-protected?
- **Input/Output connectivity.** What if the network times out or is unavailable, for example?
- **Interaction with other controls and the container.** Can you successfully use property values from other controls as input to your control?
- **Boundary conditions.** What happens with extreme or incorrect input values (such as, –99999)?

In Chapter 9, "Visual Basic Programming Fundamentals," you learned about using the On Error statement to control program flow after an error occurs.

▶ **See** "Controlling Program Flow After an Error," **p. 220**

Adding error handling to your procedures takes only a few lines of code, especially if you create a global error handling routine like the following:

```
Sub ErrorTrap(err as Integer)

Select Case err
     Case 3021
          sMessage = "Database problem!"
     Case 13
          sMessage = "A System Error has occurred"
'... (more error handling code here)

     Case Else
          sMessage = "An unknown Error has occurred"
End Select

End Sub
```

The ErrorTrap procedure can be called from every event in your control, in the following manner:

1. Use the On Error statement at the beginning of the procedure:

   ```
   On Error Goto Errhandler
   ```

2. In the procedure's Error handler, pass the error number to the ErrorTrap function, as follows:

   ```
   Errhandler:
   ErrorTrap err
   ```

Another way to avoid errors is to always use Get and Let procedures for a control's properties, so you can validate property values when they are set. If you create properties by declaring public variables, you have less control over their values. Using property procedures allows you to raise errors immediately if the users try to assign invalid values.

From Here...

In this chapter, you learned how to enhance ActiveX Controls by creating Property Pages. You also looked at the `Ambient` and `Extender` objects and built a sample control to perform calculations. For additional coverage on related topics, see the following chapters:

- Chapter 14, "Creating ActiveX Controls," provides a basic understanding of ActiveX controls and how to create them.
- Chapter 32, "ActiveX Documents," describes how to transform a standard application quickly for use on the Web.
- Appendix B, "Packaging Your Applications," provides information about deploying ActiveX controls.

CHAPTER 16

Classes: Reusable Components

In this chapter

Understanding Classes   360

Building Class Modules   361

Creating an ActiveX DLL   368

Creating Classes That Contain Collections   373

Using the Class Builder   376

Object-oriented programming techniques are useful because they allow you to reuse your code efficiently. This chapter discusses how to create classes in Visual Basic. Classes allow you to create objects and take advantage of object-oriented programming techniques in Visual Basic. When working on a large project, for example, each team member can create a specific class and compile it into an ActiveX DLL for others to use.

Understanding Classes

If you have used custom controls in a Visual Basic program, you have already used classes and objects. For example, when you draw a text box on a form, you are actually creating a specific *instance* of the text box class. For example, if you draw five text boxes on your form, you have created five instances of the text box class. Even though each instance is a distinct entity, they were all created from the same template.

Instances of a class are known as *objects*. Each different class is a template from which a specific type of object is created. In this example, the text box class defines that a text box has a Text property. However, the class definition itself does not contain information about the values of the properties. Instead, an object you create from the class, for example, txtLastName, actually contains information.

Object-Oriented Programming

You probably have heard the term *object-oriented programming* (*OOP*) or read about it in programming books and magazines. A key element of OOP is its use of reusable objects to build programs.

OOP begins in the design stage, when you determine the objects in an application. For example, suppose you have to write a system to manage paychecks for employees. A traditional design plan would be to determine each program function, such as "Adding an employee to the database" or "Printing an employee paycheck." An object-oriented design would instead try to separate programming tasks along the lines of the objects in the program (employees, database, paycheck, and so on). In order for a design to be considered object-oriented, several facts must be true about the objects. These fundamental concepts of OOP are summarized in the following list:

- **Encapsulation.** Encapsulation, or information hiding, refers to the fact that objects hide the details of how they work. For example, when you set the Text property of a text box, you do not know (or care) how the text box internally repaints the characters. Information hiding allows the programmer of an object to change how an object works without affecting the users of the object.

- **Inheritance.** A new object can be defined based on an existing object, and it can contain all the same properties and methods. For example, you can create a new object that contains all the standard properties and methods of an existing object plus a few of your own. You can just add your own extra properties and "inherit" the existing ones. Visual Basic, strictly speaking, does not support inheritance.

- **Polymorphism.** Although many objects can have methods bearing the same name, the method can perform differently for each of the objects. Through polymorphism, the program runs the method appropriate for the current object. For example, the + operator can be used with both strings and integers. Even though the same symbol is used for both data types, Visual Basic knows to perform different operations.

An important consequence of an OOP approach is reusable code. Part of what makes an object reusable is its interface, or the methods and properties the object uses to communicate with the outside world. If you build objects with well-defined interfaces, it is easy to change the object internally or even add new interfaces without affecting programs that use the object.

Classes in Visual Basic

You create your own classes in Visual Basic with a *class module*. Class modules can contain several types of elements:

- **Properties.** These elements are used to assign and retrieve values from the class.
- **Methods.** These are public functions or subroutines that are defined in the class.
- **Events.** Just as a control can raise events in the form that contains it, an object created from your class can also raise events in its containing object.

Class modules also contain two special events of their own, `Initialize` and `Terminate`. The `Initialize` event is triggered when a new instance of the class is created, and the `Terminate` event occurs when the object is destroyed.

Object definitions are created in a class module. A class module is like a standard code module in that it contains only variable declarations and procedure code. There is no user interface component of a class module. However, a class can take action using a form that is in the program, just like a normal code module. Class modules can be used in several ways, such as the following:

- In a Visual Basic project, a class module provides a way to create multiple instances of objects anywhere in your program, without using global variables.
- You can create ActiveX objects and compile them into a DLL or EXE that other programmers can use in their code. For example, you can put all of your business financial rules in a class and compile it as an ActiveX DLL. Other programmers can reference the DLL and use the financial rules in their applications.
- You can build an Add-In to Visual Basic, to enhance the functions of the Visual Basic IDE.

Building Class Modules

The easiest way to learn is by doing, so let's create a simple class module. This sample class module will contain employee information. After you create the class module, you learn how to use the employee object in your program.

Starting a New Class Module

First, create a new Standard EXE project in Visual Basic. Then, select Add Class Module from the Project menu. This action creates a new class module with the default name of `Class1` and opens the class module's Code window, as shown in Figure 16.1.

FIGURE 16.1
By using class modules in your VB applications, you can create your own custom program objects.

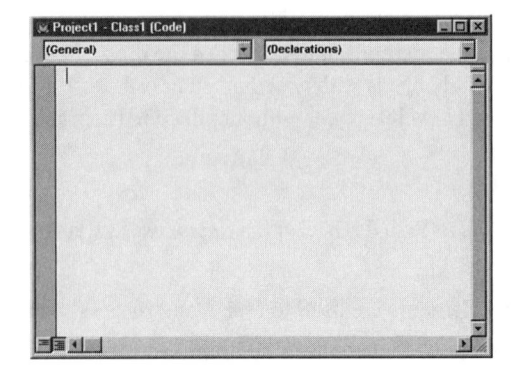

After creating the new class module, you should give the class a unique and descriptive name. The name of a class module is much more significant than the name of a standard code module because you actually use the class name within program code. Many developers like to use the letter c or cls to indicate a class name. This simple class example will be an employee class, so name the class module `clsEmployee`.

To name a class, bring up the Properties window for the class module. Press F4 while the Code window is open, or right-click the class module in the Project Explorer and choose Properties from the context menu.

Adding Properties to the Class

After the class module has been created, you can add your own properties. Properties in your own classes are used in the same way as those of controls, for storing and retrieving information. You can add properties to your class in two ways: by using public variables and property procedures.

Public Variables   Using public variables is the easiest way to create properties. You just enter them in the declarations section of the class module. For the sample `clsEmployee`, you can add a few simple properties with the following code:

```
Public FirstName As String
Public LastName As String
Public Salary As Currency
Public DateHired As Date
```

N O T E Your classes will also usually have several private variables, but only the public variables will be visible to the rest of your application when the object is created.

After you create an object from your class (you will see how shortly), you can use these properties just like those in a custom control:

```
MyObject.FirstName = "Joe"
MyObject.LastName = "Smith"
Msgbox "Hello, " & MyObject.FirstName
```

The drawback of using public variables for object properties is that no validation is performed on them. In the example, you can assign any values to the `FirstName`, `LastName`, and `DateHired` properties, as long as the value is of the correct type.

Property Procedures   Property procedures are more flexible than public variables because they offer the advantage of being able to execute code when someone accesses a property. Property procedures are written like functions, but to users of an object, they behave just like properties. The three types of property procedures are as follows:

- `Property Get`—A function executed when the user reads the property value.
- `Property Let`—A sub executed when the user writes the property value.
- `Property Set`—A special case of `Property Let`, in which the value being passed to the subroutine is itself an object.

You enter property procedures in the class module's Code window. To have Visual Basic create the skeleton of the property procedures, display the Add Procedure dialog box, shown in Figure 16.2, by selecting Add Procedure from the Tools menu. Suppose you want to add another property to the class, the `Department` property. In the Add Procedure dialog box, enter `Department` in the Name field, select Property for the procedure type, and click OK.

FIGURE 16.2
You can use the Add Procedure dialog box, accessible from the Tools menu, to create many different procedure types, including property procedures.

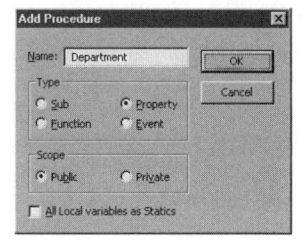

Using the Add Procedure dialog box causes Visual Basic to add the framework for the `Property Let` and `Property Get` procedures. By default, VB assumes that your property is a variant. For the `Department` property, use a `String` data type, so you can just change the procedure definitions. The new skeleton procedures are pictured in Figure 16.3.

FIGURE 16.3
Although property procedures look like regular functions, application code sees them as a property of the object.

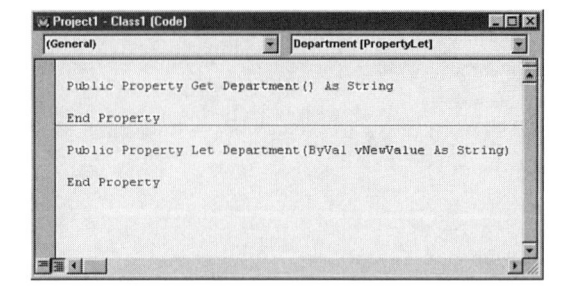

```
Public Property Get Department() As String
End Property

Public Property Let Department(ByVal vNewValue As String)
End Property
```

When users access the Department property, the appropriate property procedure is executed. Usually, a good action to take is to somehow store the value, as in the following example, which uses a private variable:

```
Public FirstName As String
Public LastName As String
Public DateHired As Date
Public Salary As Currency
Private nDeptNum As Integer

Public Property Get Department() As String
    Select Case nDeptNum
        Case 1
            Department = "Marketing"
        Case 2
            Department = "Accounting"
        Case Else
            Department = ""
    End Select
End Property

Public Property Let Department(ByVal sNewValue As String)
    Select Case Trim$(UCase$(sNewValue))
        Case "MARKETING"
            nDeptNum = 1
        Case "ACCOUNTING"
            nDeptNum = 2
        Case Else
            nDeptNum = 0
    End Select
End Property
```

In the preceding code, the property procedure actually stores the value representing the employee's department in a private integer variable. However, users of the object always assign and return a string. In a real program, the property procedures might do all sorts of things to the value, including storing it in a database.

NOTE To make a property Read-Only, omit the Property Set or Property Let procedure.

Using *Property Get* with Objects If you understand the code in the preceding section, then you know that the `Property Get` procedure is used to return values from the object and the `Property Let` procedure is used to accept values from the calling program. However, the `Property Let` procedure does not work with objects. For this reason, if the parameter is an object, you need to substitute the `Property Set` procedure, as in the following code:

```
Private objSupervisor As clsEmployee

Public Property Get Supervisor() As clsEmployee
    Set Supervisor = objSupervisor
End Property

Public Property Set Supervisor(objBoss As clsEmployee)
    Set objSupervisor = objBoss
End Property
```

Notice the `Set` statement, which is used to set the value of an object. `Set` also has to be used by the calling code that accesses the property procedures:

```
Dim objEmployee As New clsEmployee
Dim objBoss As New clsEmployee

objEmployee.FirstName = "George"
objEmployee.LastName = "Jetson"
objBoss.FirstName = "Mr."
objBoss.LastName = "Spacely"

Set objEmployee.Supervisor = objBoss

Msgbox "George's Boss is " & objEmployee.Supervisor.LastName
```

Adding Methods to the Class

As you may have noticed, objects can have methods, such as the `Print` method of the PictureBox control. You can create methods in your own class by adding *public procedures* to the class module. Public procedures work just like regular subroutines and functions, but the `Public` keyword indicates that they will be visible to users of your object. For example, the following `CalcRaise` procedure could be added to the employee object:

```
Public Function CalcRaise() As Currency
    Dim sgPercentRaise As Single

    Select Case DateDiff("yyyy", Me.DateHired, Now)
        Case Is > 1
            sgPercentRaise = 0.06
        Case Is <= 1
            sgPercentRaise = 0.02
    End Select

    CalcRaise = Me.Salary * sgPercentRaise + Me.Salary

End Function
```

The CalcRaise procedure uses the length of time from the DateHired property to determine whether to give the employee a 6 percent raise or a 2 percent raise. This example shows how to encapsulate a business rule within a class. Taking this idea a step further, you could have several different types of employee classes (for example, clsEmployeePartTime and clsEmployeeFullTime), each with its own CalcRaise method.

Declaring and Using Objects

After you have created your own class, you can create new objects in your program by referring to the class module's name:

```
Dim objX As New clsEmployee
```

The New keyword causes an instance of the class clsEmployee to be created and stored in the object variable objX. However, sometimes you may want to delay creation of the instance until later in the program. In this case, use New with the Set statement when you are ready:

```
Dim objX As clsMyClass
'
'Later...
Set objX = New clsMyClass
```

In the preceding code, the actual object instance is not created until the Set statement is executed. In the first example, the object instance is created the first time a property or method of the object is referenced.

> **NOTE** When you are accessing classes in other loaded VB projects or ActiveX DLLs, you can also include the project name in front of the class name. This is the only way to distinguish between classes with the same name from different projects, for example AS400Agent.clsFileTransfer versus SQLObject.clsFileTransfer.

> **TIP** Always use the Set statement with New rather than create the object with the Dim statement; you can debug your code more easily this way.

Early Versus Late Binding   All the declarations so far in this chapter have used *early binding*, meaning the object type is explicitly spelled out in the code. However, late binding is also an option, as in the following example:

```
Dim objX As Object
Set objX = CreateObject("MyObj.MyClass")
```

Late binding uses the CreateObject function and a string identifier. The disadvantage of late binding is that because objX is declared of a generic type Object, the properties and methods cannot be viewed in the Object Browser, and the intelligent typing features are not available. However, sometimes you do want to use late binding because it allows you to change the object without recompiling the program that uses it.

NOTE The `CreateObject` function is not necessary to use late binding. You can also write code to use late binding as follows:

```
Dim objX As Object
Set objX = New MyObj.MyClass
```

One example of when you might want to use late binding is when creating an instance of an object on a remote machine.

Destroying the Object   Assigning `Nothing` to an object variable frees up resources associated with the object and causes the code in the class module's `Terminate` to be executed. You accomplish this feat by using a `Set` statement:

```
Set objTemp = Nothing
```

TIP Even though the contents of objects are no longer available when a form or module containing them is destroyed, it is good programming practice to set objects equal to `Nothing` when you are finished with them. This ensures that all memory resources are freed and the object is destroyed.

Creating Objects from Other Projects   When you are accessing classes in other loaded VB projects or ActiveX DLLs, you can also include the project name:

```
Dim objX As New MyProject.clsMyClass
```

Remember, to access classes in other projects or DLLs, you have to add them to the Project References list.

Adding Your Own Events

Visual Basic objects can raise events, such as the `Load` event of a form. Events provide a way for an object to execute code written by the user of an object. The object triggers the event by way of an *event procedure*. You have already learned how to place code in event procedures. To create an event in your own class, you need to do two things:

1. Declare the event in the class.
2. Use the `RaiseEvent` statement to trigger the event when appropriate.

Now you can create a sample event in the employee class. Suppose you want to add a way to return errors to the user of an object. First, declare an event called `DataError` in the General Declarations section of `clsEmployee`, by adding a single line of code:

```
Public Event DataError(ByVal sMessageText As String)
```

Next, you need to add code to trigger the event. Recall the earlier method `CalcRaise`, which relies on the `Salary` property of the object. If the user does not assign a value to `Salary` property, then a raise cannot be properly calculated. You can modify `CalcRaise` to send this information to the user via the `DataError` event by adding a simple `If` statement:

```
If Me.Salary = 0 Then RaiseEvent DataError("SALARY UNSPECIFIED!!")
```

As you can see, adding an event is really easy. To access your events, the calling code must declare objects using the `WithEvents` keyword and have an event procedure written that the object can call. For example, placing the following code in the General Declarations section of a form or module would trap the `DataError` event:

```
Dim WithEvents objBoss As clsEmployee
Private Sub objBoss_DataError(ByVal sMessageText As String)
    MsgBox sMessageText, vbCritical, "Error!!!"
End Sub
```

The `WithEvents` keyword causes the name of the object to be added to the object drop-down box so that Visual Basic can create the skeleton event procedure for you.

To test this with the sample, create the `DataError` event in the class module and add code to trap the event as described above. You should then be able to cause the object to fire the event by calling the `CalcRaise` method when the `Salary` property is equal to zero.

Creating an ActiveX DLL

Although including classes in Standard EXE projects is useful, compiling them into a separate ActiveX DLL or ActiveX EXE component is even more useful. These ActiveX components can be installed and registered on another machine so that applications on that computer can access your classes. For example, you could create a database access DLL and install it on the Web server for use with Active Server Pages. The following sections describe some of the steps involved in creating an ActiveX project.

Creating an ActiveX Project

To create an ActiveX DLL, you need to add your class to an ActiveX DLL project. The easiest way to create a project of this type is to choose ActiveX DLL from the New Project dialog box. As you may recall, when you select a new Standard EXE project, you are given a project with a form named Form1. Similarly, creating a new ActiveX DLL or EXE project causes VB to create a project with a class module called Class1. If you are starting a new class, just rename Class1 to a better name and begin entering code. If you want to add class modules to the project that you have already written, right-click in the Project Explorer window and choose Add File.

NOTE ActiveX DLL and EXE projects can contain multiple class modules, code modules, and forms. Only the objects designated as public are visible to other applications.

Working with Multiple Projects

In the first part of this chapter, you added a class module to a Standard EXE project. Although the class module was fairly self-contained, it was still a part of the same project as the form. However, when working with an ActiveX DLL project, you will more than likely need an additional Standard EXE project to test your classes because an ActiveX DLL is intended for use from an outside application. In other words, the application's user interface might be one

Visual Basic project and the Data Access class would be another, separate project. In order to effectively develop and test such an application, you have to simulate this interaction between projects. Fortunately, you can do so in several ways, as described here:

- **Use a project group.** Add multiple projects to the Project Explorer window.
- **Use separate instances of Visual Basic.** Launch Visual Basic again and load your ActiveX DLL in the second VB IDE.
- **Use the compiled program.** Use this method to share your classes with other developers.

While you are reading through this section, consider a two-project situation: an ActiveX DLL project that contains a class and a Standard EXE project that uses the class.

NOTE When accessing an ActiveX DLL from an ActiveX EXE project in any of the ways described in the preceding list, you always have to add a reference to the DLL by using the References dialog box. See the section "Referencing and Using the DLL" later in this chapter.

Using a Project Group You can create a project group in Visual Basic by choosing Add Project from the File menu. Each project in a group appears in the Project Explorer window, as shown in Figure 16.4.

NOTE Creating a project group is different from the usual way you deal with multiple Visual Basic projects. Typically you would use the Open Project menu option, which causes the selected project to replace any currently open projects. When you create a project group, multiple projects are loaded in the development environment *at the same time*.

FIGURE 16.4
Project groups allow you to test and debug ActiveX components in a single instance of Visual Basic.

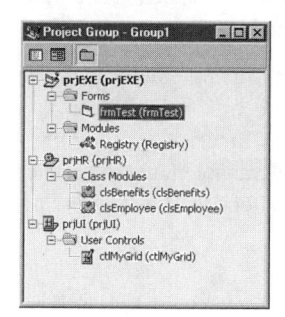

The typical way you use project groups is to first create an ActiveX component and then add a Standard EXE project to test it. You can use Visual Basic's debugging features such as stepping into code and using breakpoints in all projects in the group.

However, before you press Visual Basic's Start button, you may need to designate a Startup Project for the project group. By default, the first opened project is the Startup Project, and its name appears in boldface in the Project Explorer window. To set a different Startup Project, right-click the project's name and choose Set As Start Up.

NOTE Most of the time, you need to make the EXE project the Startup Project. Other controls and DLLs are started also, but only the Startup Project receives the focus. ■

Using Multiple Instances of VB   Sometimes using multiple instances of VB is more convenient than using a project group. If you have very complex EXE and DLL projects, using multiple instances may be a better option because you can look at each project in its own environment. The main difference is that with a project group, Visual Basic handles starting and stopping all the projects. With multiple instances of Visual Basic, you manually have to start the projects needed by a given project. In other words, you first start the ActiveX DLL project and then start the Standard EXE project.

All the debugging features are still available between multiple instances of VB. In other words, you can set breakpoints and step back and forth between code in both projects. However, since additional inter-process communication is involved between multiple instances of Visual Basic, you may have to restart projects more often than you would when using a project group.

Using the Compiled DLL   Using a compiled ActiveX DLL requires only a single open instance of Visual Basic. This is not a method for testing code within a class because you cannot use any of the debugging features. However, another developer can use a compiled DLL on his or her machine without having to copy your project and code. Using a compiled DLL involves a few simple steps:

1. **Installation.** Copy the DLL and any components or files it needs to the developer's PC.
2. **Register the DLL.** Use the REGSVR32 program to register the DLL in the Windows registry.
3. **Reference the DLL.** After the DLL is installed and registered on a machine, it should appear in the References Dialog in Visual Basic.

Referencing and Using the DLL   No matter which method you use to load an ActiveX DLL project (project group, multiple VB instances, compiled DLL), you always must *reference* the DLL in your Standard EXE project. Display the References dialog box by choosing Refere<u>n</u>ces from Visual Basic's <u>P</u>roject menu. The list of <u>A</u>vailable References should contain the project name of your ActiveX DLL. After you place a check mark in the box next to the ActiveX DLL name, it is available to the current project.

NOTE When using multiple instances of VB, you may have to rereference a DLL after you make changes to it. Also, the ActiveX DLL project does not show up in the References dialog box until the project is started. ■

Accessing the Class   In the earlier example, you created a new instance of the employee object by simply naming the class:

```
Dim objBoss As New clsEmployee
```

However, when the class is defined in another compiled ActiveX component, you also have to include the project name:

```
Dim objBoss As New EmployeeDLL.clsEmployee
```

If you have multiple public classes defined in a DLL, you can access all of them:

```
Dim objCEO As New EmployeeDLL.clsExecutive
Dim objDilbert As New EmployeeDLL.clsEngineer
```

Note that as you write code that uses these external classes, all the same editor features (such as parameter lists) are available in the Visual Basic editing window.

Setting the Instancing Property

In ActiveX DLL and ActiveX EXE projects, the Properties window for a class module has an extra property, the Instancing property, which is not available in a Standard EXE project. This property determines how instances of a class are created; the options vary for different project types. While learning the basics of classes and OOP, you can forget about this property and experiment with a Standard EXE project. However, this property is usually set during the creation of a class, so I mention it here. Table 16.1 describes the settings of the Instancing property.

Table 16.1 Using the *Instancing* Property

Value	Name	Components	Description
1	Private	EXE and DLL	The class cannot be accessed from outside the current project.
2	PublicNotCreatable	EXE and DLL	Instances of the class can be created only within the project that defines the class. However, other applications can access instances after they are created.
3	SingleUse	EXE only	Each time a new instance of a class is created, a new copy of the EXE containing the class is started.
4	GlobalSingleUse	EXE only	Like SingleUse, but it makes the properties and methods appear as global variables and preocedures in the client program.
5	MultiUse	EXE and DLL	Other applications can create any number of instances of the class, and only one copy of the program containing the class is started. ActiveX DLL projects generally use this setting.
6	GlobalMultiUse	EXE and DLL	Like MultiUse, but it makes the properties and methods appear as global variables and procedures in the client program.

Another way to look at the information in the preceding table is to think of EXE files versus DLL files. An ActiveX DLL file is intended to be a shared component, meaning the same instance of the ActiveX component is accessed by multiple clients, whereas an EXE runs in its own memory space. In addition, with an ActiveX EXE users can run the program, and at the same time other programs can reference and use classes within it.

Enums

One great feature of Visual Basic is the way it displays information and lists as you are entering code. For example, if you are using the Employee class, Visual Basic can display a list of available properties and methods, as shown in Figure 16.5.

FIGURE 16.5
Features such as Auto List Member and the Object Browser work with classes that you create.

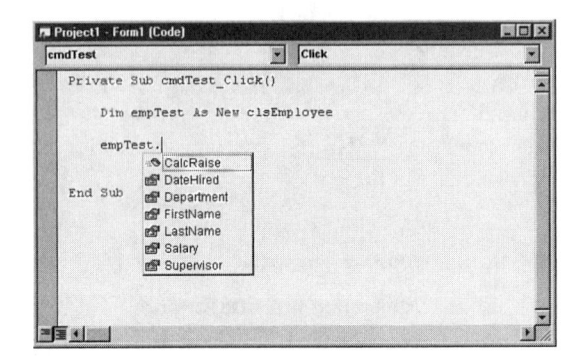

However, if you have written a method in the class, you often need a way to know valid parameter values. One example of this is the Message Box constants (for example, vbCritical) that are listed as you type a MsgBox statement. Consider the earlier example of the Department property in clsEmployee. Although you allow the users to enter some string values, you are really storing the employee's department as an integer. In addition, unless the users of the class know a list of valid departments, they will not know that MARKETING is an acceptable value.

One way to get around this problem is to use an enumeration, or in Visual Basic, an *enum*. Enumerations allow you to define a group of constants as a data type. You can then use this data type in function parameters.

For example, you could define an Enum for employee departments and then redefine the Department property of clsEmployee:

```
Public Enum Departments
Marketing = 101
Accounting = 102
InformationTech =103
Unknown=104
End Enum

Dim nDeptNum As Integer

Public Property Get Department() As Departments
Department = nDeptNum
End Property
```

```
Public Property Let Department(ByVal NewDept As Departments)
nDeptNum = NewDept
End Property
```

You could then access the Department property from code as follows:

```
objEmployee.Department = InformationTech
If objEmployee.Department = InformationTech Then MsgBox "IT department"
```

You can test this out by adding the Enum to the sample project you created earlier. Notice that as you type the equals sign to assign or read the value of the Department property, a list of valid values is displaed in a drop-down list.

Creating Classes That Contain Collections

A *collection* is a group of items that is itself a type of object. Visual Basic has some built-in collection objects, such as the Forms collection and the Controls collection. You can use collections with the For Each...Next statement to perform actions on all the items they contain. The MinimizeAll procedure, shown in Listing 16.1, minimizes each loaded form in an application.

Listing 16.1 COLLECT.ZIP—Using the *For Each* Structure to Handle All the Items in a Collection

```
' Minimizes all loaded forms.
Sub MinimizeAll()
    Dim frmElement As Form
    ' For each loaded form.
    For Each frmElement In Forms
        ' Minimize the form.
        frmElement.WindowState = vbMinimized
    Next frmElement
End Sub
```

Collections solve three problems faced by most programmers when working with objects:

- They provide a standardized way to create and track multiple instances of an object.
- They group similar objects for fixed tasks, such as changing color properties or dragging to a new location.
- Unlike an array, a collection can be used to contain members of different types.
- They organize large systems of objects into a hierarchy.

The following sections describe each of these aspects of using collections when you are creating object-based applications in Visual Basic.

Standard Collection Properties and Methods

User-defined collections share a common set of properties and methods. Some collections may have additional properties and methods, but all collections that you create in Visual Basic have at least the set described in Table 16.2.

> **N O T E** Built-in collections may not necessarily contain all of the following properties and methods. ■

Table 16.2 Properties and Methods Common to All Collections

Item	Use To
`Count` property	Report the number of objects in a collection
`Item` method	Get a single object from a collection

In addition to the items in Table 16.2, collections usually provide two more methods. The methods in Table 16.3 are common to most collections.

Table 16.3 Methods Common to Most Collections

Method	Purpose
`Add`	Add an object to a collection
`Remove`	Delete an object from a collection

The `Add` and `Remove` methods provide programmers a standard way to create and delete items in a collection. The Visual Basic `Forms` and `Controls` collections are maintained by Visual Basic, so they don't support these methods. The `Add` method usually includes key and index parameters, used to identify an object in a collection. However, `Add` and `Remove` may be implemented differently for different types of collections. For example, compare the `Add` syntax for the `ListView` control's `ListItems` collection and the `ListImages` collection of an image list:

```
ListView1.ListItems.Add index,key,text,IconNumber,smallIconNumber
```

```
ImageList1.ListImages.Add index,key,picture
```

Creating a New Collection for Grouped Actions

You can create collections to contain forms, controls, and objects. Use the `Collection` object data type when creating a new collection. The following declaration creates a new collection named `colSelected`:

```
Dim colSelected As New Collection
```

Declaring a variable as a `Collection` object gives you four built-in properties and methods, as shown in Table 16.4.

Table 16.4 *Collection* Object Built-In Properties and Methods

Item	Task
Count property	Returns the number of items in the collection
Add method	Adds an object to the collection
Item method	Gets a single object from the collection
Remove method	Deletes an object from the collection

The code in Listing 16.2 creates a new collection named colTextBoxes and adds all the text boxes on a form to the new collection.

Listing 16.2 COLLECT.ZIP—Creating a Collection with This Code

```
Option Explicit

' Create a new collection to contain all the
' text boxes on a form
Dim colTextBoxes As New Collection

Private Sub Form_Initialize()
    ' Variable used in For Each to get controls.
    Dim cntrlItem As Control
    ' Loop through the controls on the form.
    For Each cntrlItem In Me.Controls
        ' If the control is a text box, add it to the
        ' collection of text boxes.
        If TypeName(cntrlItem) = "TextBox" Then
            colTextBoxes.Add cntrlItem
        End If
    Next cntrlItem
End Sub
```

The code in Listing 16.3 uses the collection colTextBoxes to clear all the text entered on the form.

Listing 16.3 Using *For Each* to Handle the Collection.

```
Sub cmdClear_Click()
    ' Variable used in For Each to get controls.
    Dim cntrlItem As Control
    ' Clear each of the text boxes in the collection.
    For Each cntrlItem In colTextBoxes
        cntrlItem.Text = ""
    Next cntrlItem
End Sub
```

▶ **See** "Using the ListView Control," **p. 251**

Using the Class Builder

When you create a new class, Visual Basic presents the option of creating an empty class or starting the Class Builder (see Figure 16.6).

NOTE If you do not see the Class Builder as shown in Figure 16.6, use Add-In Manager (available in the Add-Ins menu) to make it available in Visual Basic.

FIGURE 16.6
Double-clicking Class Builder starts a tool to help you organize classes in your application.

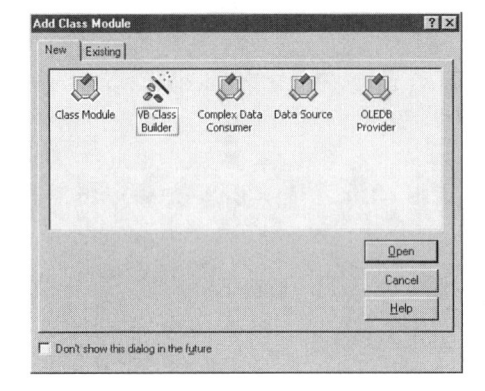

The Class Builder can be used to generate outlines for new classes or modify and reorganize existing classes. Figure 16.7 shows the Class Builder with the `clsEmployee` class loaded.

FIGURE 16.7
The Class Builder provides a graphic interface to the classes, properties, methods, constants, and events in your application.

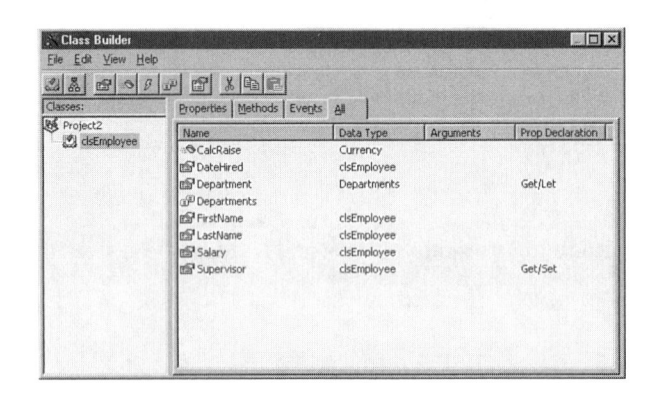

To add an item to your project, click one of the toolbar buttons; the Class Builder displays a dialog box where you can enter all the attributes of the new item. Figure 16.8 shows the dialog box presented for a new method.

FIGURE 16.8
The Method Builder dialog box presents all options available for a method.

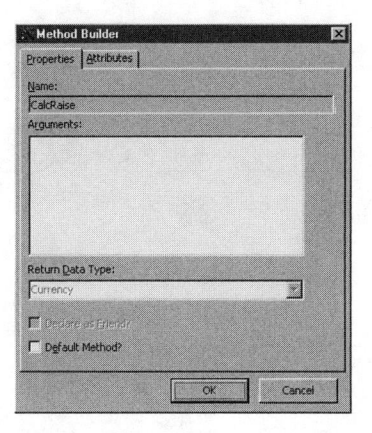

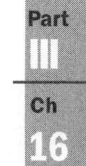

When you close the Class Builder, it updates your project with any changes or additions that you entered. You still have to fill in the working code, but the Class Builder generates the appropriate declarations and supporting code.

From Here...

This chapter provided you with an introduction to the creation of class modules and the objects that can be created from them. To learn more about some of the topics covered in this chapter, see the following chapters:

- To see how collections are used with controls, see Chapter 12, "Microsoft Common Controls."
- You can learn how the techniques applied to classes can be used in creating your own ActiveX controls by referring to Chapter 14, "Creating ActiveX Controls."
- To learn about accessing objects and collections in other applications such as Word and Excel, see Chapter 22, "Using OLE to Control Other Applications."
- Collections are also used with the Internet, as described in Chapter 31, "Active Server Pages."

PART IV

Visual Basic Interfaces

17 Multiple Document Interface Applications   381

18 Proper Interface Design   409

19 Using Visual Design Elements   425

CHAPTER 17

Multiple Document Interface Applications

In this chapter

Introducing MDI Applications   **382**

Creating a Simple MDI Program   **384**

Creating Multiple Instances of a Form   **388**

Working with Menus   **391**

Managing the Children   **392**

Creating a Sample Application—an MDI Contact Manager   **395**

Optimizing Your MDI Application   **400**

Creating an MDI Application Framework   **401**

As you begin to write more advanced Visual Basic applications, at some point you will probably want to utilize the Windows Multiple Document Interface (MDI). The MDI allows your programs to work with multiple forms contained within a parent form. Using the MDI makes your interface cleaner than one that has forms scattered about the screen.

The MDI standard can enhance your programs in two ways. First, you can have one container form that acts as the background for your overall application. If a user moves the container form, the child forms contained inside move as well, which helps keep your application's interface organized and self-contained. Second, and perhaps even more powerful, your users can work on multiple documents at one time. MDI applications allow the use of multiple instances of the same form, which can add a great deal of power and flexibility to your programs.

Introducing MDI Applications

Many of the applications that you create in Visual Basic consist of a series of independent forms, like the ones shown in Figure 17.1. Each of these forms is displayed separately on the screen and is moved, maximized, or minimized separately from any other form. With this type of interface, you cannot easily organize the forms or deal with them as a group. Even with this limitation, this interface is a good one to use for many programs and is probably the most prevalent interface design.

FIGURE 17.1
This program's user interface consists of two forms that appear to have no visual relationship to each other.

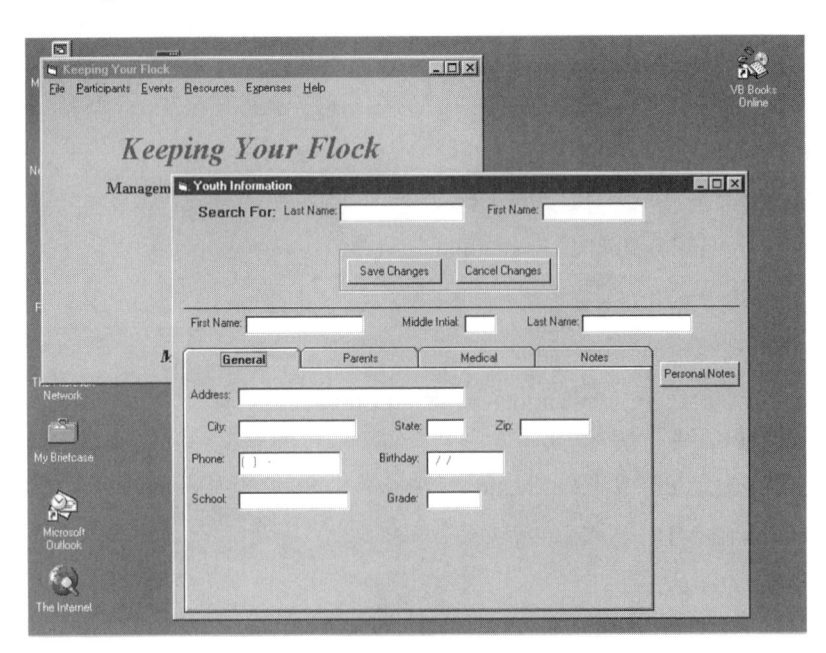

An alternative to this standard interface is the Multiple Document Interface, or MDI. This type of application has one *parent form* that contains most of the other forms in the program. Other forms can be *child forms*, which are contained within the parent, or standard forms, which are not. With an MDI application, you can easily organize all the child forms or minimize the entire group of forms just by minimizing the parent form. Programs such as Microsoft Word and Excel are examples of MDI applications. If you have worked with these programs, you know that you can open multiple windows in the program, access them easily from the menu, and minimize the whole thing with a single click of the mouse. In version 5, even Visual Basic itself went to a true MDI interface style. Figure 17.2 shows three blank workbooks opened simultaneously in Excel as an example of a typical MDI application.

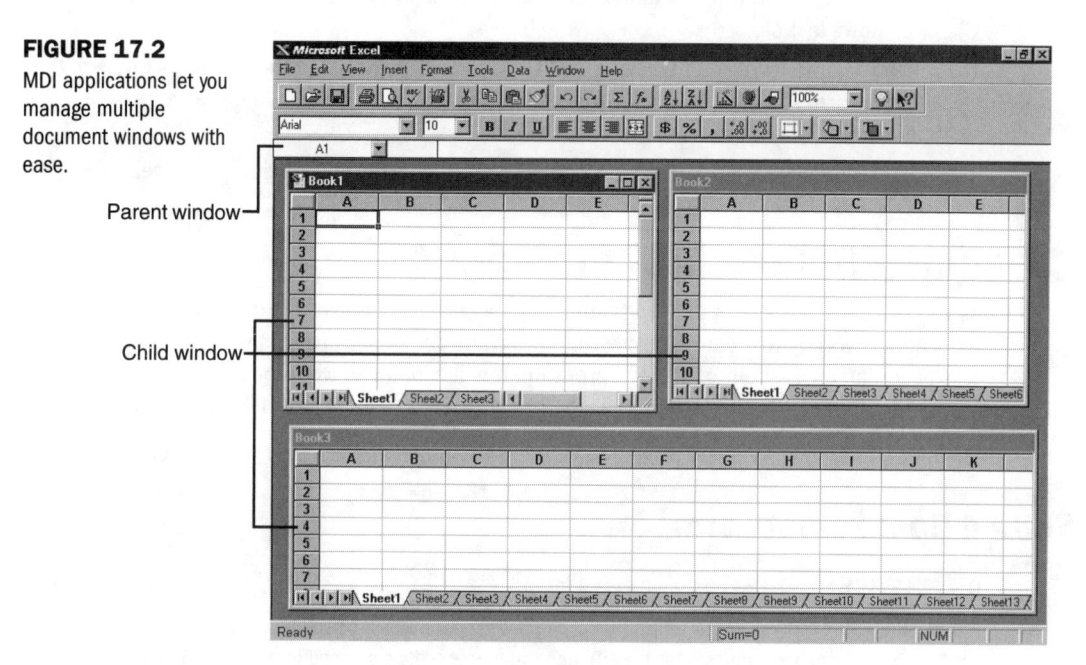

FIGURE 17.2
MDI applications let you manage multiple document windows with ease.

Parent window
Child window

Characteristics of MDI Parent Forms

The MDI form, also known as the parent form, is the container for all the child forms of the application. The MDI form has a number of characteristics that define its behavior:

- An application can have only one MDI form.
- The MDI form can contain only those controls that support the Align property, such as the PictureBox or Toolbar controls. You cannot place other controls on the MDI form.
- You cannot use the Print method or any of the graphics methods to display information on the MDI form.
- The MDI parent window and all child windows are represented by a single icon on the Windows taskbar. If the parent form is minimized and then restored, all the child forms are returned to the same layout as they had before the application was minimized.
- If a menu is defined for a child form, the menu is displayed in the parent form's menu bar. If a menu is defined for the parent form, it is not shown at all if a child form that has its own menu is the active form.

Characteristics of MDI Child Forms

Just as the MDI form has characteristics of its behavior, the MDI child forms also behave in a certain way. The characteristics of an MDI child form are as follows:

- Each child form is displayed within the confines of the parent form. A child form cannot be moved outside the boundaries of the MDI parent form.
- When a child window is minimized, its icon is displayed in the parent window, not on the Windows taskbar.
- When a child form is maximized, it fills the entire inner area of the parent form. Also, the parent form's title bar contains both the name of the parent form and the name of the maximized child form.
- When one child form is maximized, all other child forms are maximized as well.

Creating a Simple MDI Program

As you will discover with many programming concepts, the best way to understand how MDI applications work is to create a simple MDI program. This section walks you through the process of setting up a "shell" of an MDI program. It will contain an MDI form and a single child form. You can then use this program as the basis for a fully functional MDI application.

The first step is to start a new project in Visual Basic by choosing File, New Project.

Setting Up a Parent Form

ON THE WEB

The sample project MDITest is available on the Web (www.mcp.com/info) as the zipped file MDITEST.ZIP. This project demonstrates the MDI application concepts discussed in this chapter. The project's code is fully commented to explain each step.

After you start the new project, the next step is to create the MDI parent form. To create the MDI form for your project, select Project, Add MDI Form, or choose MDI Form from the Add Object button's drop-down menu. Then, from the Add MDI Form dialog box, select the MDI Form icon and click Open. When the MDI form is added to your project, it should look like the one in Figure 17.3.

FIGURE 17.3
The MDI form has a darker background than a standard form.

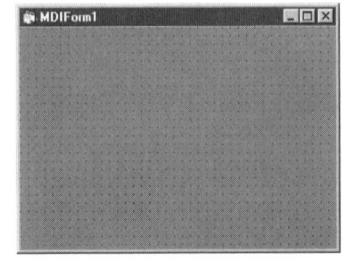

The MDI form is added to the Forms folder in the Project Explorer window. However, if you look closely, you might notice that the MDI form's icon in the Project window is different from the icon used for a standard form. By examining these icons, you can easily identify the type of each form. Figure 17.4 illustrates the difference between normal and MDI form icons.

FIGURE 17.4
Icons show the form type in the Project window.

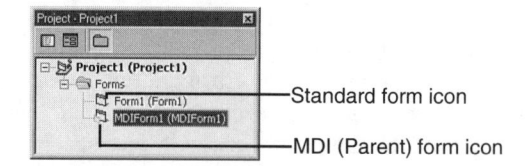

After you add the form to your project, you should specify a descriptive name for the form and set any of the other properties that you need. Most of the properties of the MDI form are the same ones that you set to control the appearance of a standard form.

▶ See "Parts of a Form," **p. 40**

Two properties are unique to the MDI form and deserve special note: the AutoShowChildren property and the ScrollBars property. The AutoShowChildren property determines whether child forms are shown automatically as they are loaded. If the AutoShowChildren property is set to True (the default value), then child forms are shown as soon as they are loaded. Therefore, the Load statement and the Show method have the same effect on the form.

The ScrollBars property determines whether the MDI form shows scrollbars when necessary. When this property is set to True (the default value), scrollbars are shown on the MDI form if one or more of the child forms extends beyond the boundary of the MDI form, as shown in Figure 17.5. If the property is set to False, scrollbars are not shown under any conditions.

FIGURE 17.5
Scrollbars let you view portions of child forms that extend beyond the boundary of the parent form.

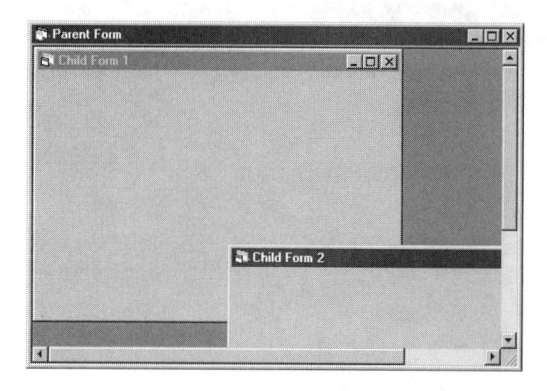

One other property of note is the Picture property. Although the MDI form does not support the Print method and graphics methods like a standard form does, you can still include a picture as the background of the form.

Setting Up a Child Form

Setting up a child form in an MDI application is even easier than setting up the parent form. A child form is basically a standard form that has the MDIChild property set to True. Therefore, everything you know about creating standard forms applies to creating the child forms of an MDI application.

For the sample application, all you need to do is set the MDIChild property of the form that was first created for the project. To do so, select the form in the Project window, select the MDIChild property in the Properties window, and change its value to True. You might notice that the icon for the form in the Project window changes from a standard icon to an MDI Child icon. This is the only change that you will notice while you are in the design window (see Figure 17.6).

FIGURE 17.6
Notice how the two child form icons differ from those for standard and parent forms.

Child form icons

> **TIP**
> As with other properties with predefined values, you can double-click the MDIChild property in the Properties window to toggle back and forth between the True and False values.

After you set the MDIChild property, all that is left to complete the form is to add the controls you need for your program. You can, of course, design the form first and change the MDIChild property later. The order of the operation has no effect on the behavior of the form. A typical MDI child form is shown in Figure 17.7.

FIGURE 17.7
MDI child forms look just like standard forms.

Running the Program

After you finish setting up both the parent and child forms, you are ready to run the program to see how a child form behaves inside the parent form. First, as always, you should save your work. Then click the Start button on the toolbar, or press F5 to run the program. When the program runs, the form layout should resemble Figure 17.8.

FIGURE 17.8
This simple MDI application shows a parent form and two child forms. Note that the child forms are instances of the same form.

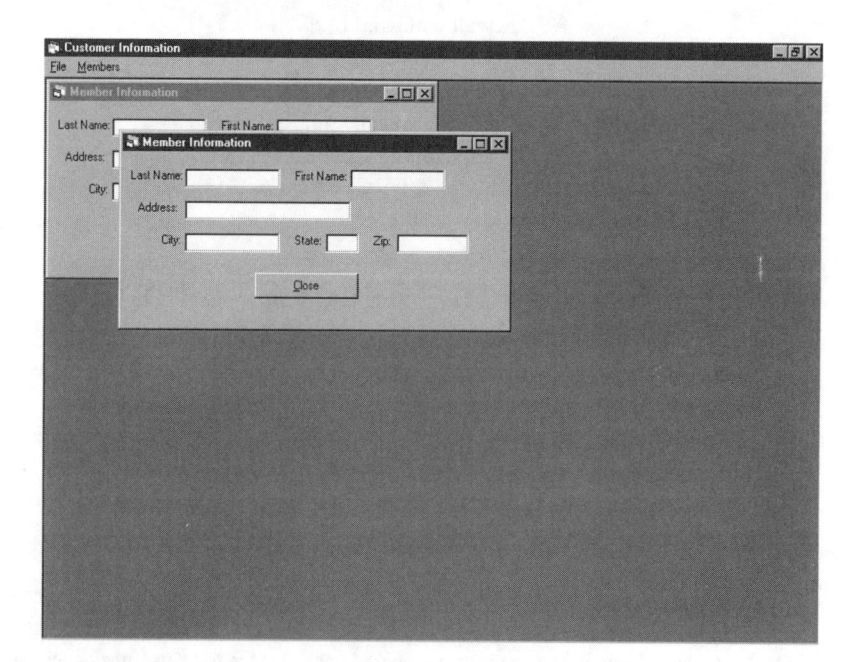

You should try the following tasks so that you fully understand the behavior of the parent and child forms:

- Minimize the child form, and note the location of its icon.
- Move the child form around. It does not move beyond the parent form's boundaries.
- Maximize the child form.
- Minimize and maximize the parent form.

When you started the program, you might have noticed that the child form was shown automatically. In the simple example, you get this result because the child form (the one first created when you started the project) was designated as the project's startup form by default. If you want to have the empty MDI parent form shown when you start the program, you need to change the Startup Object setting in the Project Properties dialog box, as shown in Figure 17.9. You access the project properties by choosing Project, Project Properties.

FIGURE 17.9
Set the startup form and other properties of the project in this dialog box.

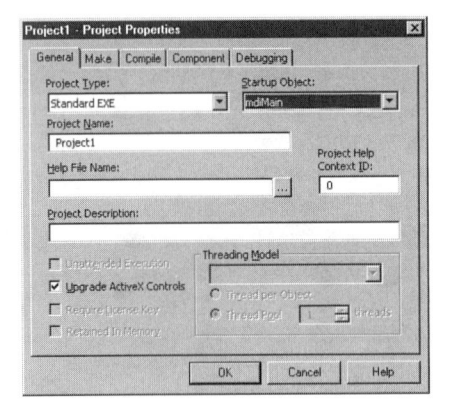

Creating Multiple Instances of a Form

You can use the MDI form just to make your application neater and its forms easier to manage. However, if that's all you use MDI forms for, you're missing out on the real power of MDI applications. The most powerful feature of an MDI application is its capability to create and handle multiple instances of a form at the same time. For example, if you are working in Microsoft Word, each document you open or each new document that you create is a new instance of the same basic form. In fact, many MDI applications are made up of only two forms: the MDI parent form and the template form for all the child forms in the application.

> **N O T E** You can have more than one type of template child form in your application. For example, Visual Basic itself has two basic types of MDI child forms: the Form design child form and the Code child form. You can create as many of each of these types of forms as you need, within the constraints of your system.

Creating an MDI application of this type requires a little more work than was required in the sample application. You first have to define the basic MDI child form at designtime and then use object variables to create instances of the form at runtime.

To start the process of creating an MDI application with multiple instances of a form, you need to start a new project and then add an MDI form to the project as described in the section "Creating a Simple MDI Program." Next, be sure to set up the MDI form as the startup object using the Project Properties dialog box.

Setting Up the Basic Form

As was the case in the earlier section "Creating a Simple MDI Program," creating the form template is the same as creating a standard form. You add to the form all the controls that you need for the user interface. Also, you need to write any code necessary for the controls to perform their intended functions. You also need to set the MDIChild property of the form to True.

One thing you might notice as you first create an MDI application is that the child form, when first shown at runtime, is probably sized differently than it was when you created it (see Figure 17.10). The reason is that Windows, by default, assigns a certain size and position to each MDI child form that is shown.

FIGURE 17.10
MDI applications automatically size and position their child forms.

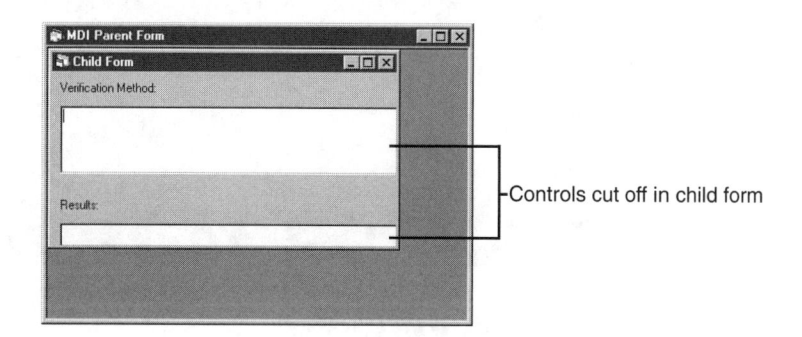

If the default size and position are not acceptable to you, you need to place code in the Load event procedure of the child form to position and size it the way you want. To determine the desired size of the child form, check the Height and Width properties of the form while you are in design mode, and then add code to the form's Load event procedure to set the Height and Width properties to their original values. The same concept applies to the position of the form. You can set the Top and Left properties of the child form to set its position. The code in Listing 17.1 shows how to set the size of a child form and center it within the parent form.

> **NOTE** If a child window's size becomes too large for its parent, whether by user action or through code, the parent's size is not changed automatically. The parent does, however, automatically show scrollbars when needed (assuming the ScrollBars property is True), as mentioned in the section "Setting Up a Parent Form" earlier in this chapter.

Listing 17.1 MDIDEMO2.FRM—Use Code to Size and Position the Child Form

```
Private Sub Form_Load()
    Me.Height = 2745
    Me.Width = 3690
    Me.Top = (mdiMain.ScaleHeight - Me.Height) / 2
    Me.Left = (mdiMain.ScaleWidth - Me.Width) / 2
End Sub
```

Figure 17.11 shows the effect of this code.

> **NOTE** You cannot use the StartUpPosition property to set the initial position of a child form in an MDI window. In fact, you cannot change the setting of the property for an MDI child form from its default value of 0 - Manual.

FIGURE 17.11
You can use code to override the default size and position of an MDI child form.

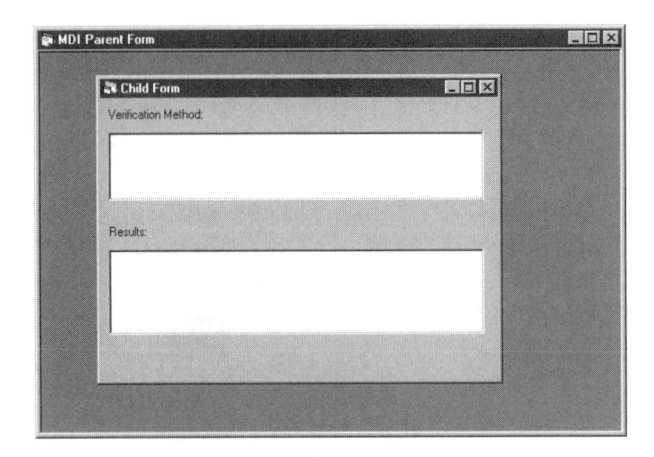

Creating Forms Using Object Variables

After you create the basic child form, you need a means to create an instance of the form (at runtime) and display it in the MDI application. Doing so requires all of two code lines. First, you use a Dim statement to create an *object variable* (a variable of Object type) that will contain an instance of the form. In the Dim statement, you need to use the New keyword to tell Visual Basic to create a *new instance* of the form. Otherwise, the statement just creates a new handle to the existing form. After you create the object variable, you use the Show method to display the form. However, instead of using the form name, you specify the name of the variable. The two required lines of code are shown here:

```
Dim NewFrm As New frmText
NewFrm.Show
```

To see how this code works, place the lines of code in the Click event procedure of the MDI form, and then run the program. Each time you click the MDI form, a new instance of the child form is displayed.

Using the Keywords *Me* and *ActiveForm*

Because all the child forms are the same, and you use the same variable to create each of them, how can you know which form to specify when running code—especially code that is generic and can work with any of the forms?

You will use two particular keywords extensively in working with MDI applications: Me and ActiveForm. These two keywords let you create generic code routines that work with any child form that you create.

Me is a keyword that can be used in any form to refer to itself, just as you can use the word *me* to refer to yourself without having to use your name. You saw how this keyword was used in Listing 17.1 to size and position the child form on startup. If you write all code in the child form using Me to refer to the form name, your code will work for whichever instance of the form is active at the time.

`ActiveForm` is actually a property of the MDI (parent) form. Its purpose is similar to the `Me` keyword. `ActiveForm` refers to whichever MDI child form is currently active. By using the `ActiveForm` property in all code that resides in the MDI form, the code operates only on the active form and on no other. The following line of code provides a simple example of the `ActiveForm` property:

```
mdiMain.ActiveForm.Print "This form is currently active."
```

To test this code, place it in the `Click` event procedure of the MDI (parent) form. Make sure more than one child form is loaded. When an empty area of the parent is clicked, the text previously mentioned prints on whichever form is active.

> **NOTE** Notice, here and in Listing 17.1, the use of the prefix `mdi` that was used when naming the MDI parent form.

Using the `ActiveForm` property, you can reference any property, method, or event of the currently active child form without having to know its name.

Initializing an Instance of a Child Form

If you need to write code that will be run when an instance of a child form is first created, you can place the code in the child form's `Activate` event procedure. The `Activate` event occurs as each new instance of the form is created, before the `Load` event occurs.

For example, you may want to set a child form's `Caption` property as the form is created. The sample project MDITest, available on the Web, contains code in the child form's `Activate` event procedure that increments a public variable to keep track of how many child form instances have been created and then sets the new form's `Caption` property to reflect that number.

Working with Menus

In Chapter 6, "Giving More Control to the User: Menus and Toolbars," you learned how to create a menu for your application. You also found out that you can have a different menu for each form in your program, if you so desire. MDI forms can also have menus. You create a menu for your MDI form the same way that you create a menu for a standard form, using the Menu Editor. The menu for the MDI form is usually the primary means by which you access the capabilities of an MDI application.

▶ **See** "Creating a Menu Bar," **p. 108**

In an MDI application, the child forms can also have menus. As you do with the menu for the MDI form itself, you create child form menus by using the Menu Editor. However, when a child form that has a menu is displayed, its menu is not displayed as part of the child form but is displayed on the menu bar of the MDI form. This behavior presents a problem in your MDI applications because the MDI child form's menu actually replaces the MDI parent form's menu when the child is active. You cannot access the parent form's menu functions while the child form is active.

You can take advantage of two solutions to the problems associated with the replacement of menus. First, you can duplicate all the necessary parent form functions on each child form. Unfortunately, this approach can lead to a bloated and hard-to-maintain program if you have several child forms with menus.

An alternative solution is to include in the parent window's menu all the menus that are necessary for all child windows. Then you can place code in the child form's `GotFocus` and `LostFocus` events to show (and hide) the parent's menus that are applicable to that child form when that child form has the focus. For example, in a word processing program, you want the File and Help menus to be available all the time, but you want the Edit and Format menus available only when you are working on a document. To make the Edit and Format menus visible, you can place code like the following in the appropriate child form's `GotFocus` event procedure:

```
mnuEdit.Visible = True
mnuFormat.Visible = True
```

The following code, placed in the child form's `LostFocus` event procedure, takes care of making the Edit and Format menus invisible again:

```
mnuEdit.Visible = False
mnuFormat.Visible = False
```

To make sure that any menu code in the parent form acts on the proper child form, use the parent form's `ActiveForm` property as described in the preceding section.

Managing the Children

One of the other benefits of working with MDI applications is that you can easily manage all the child forms. Visual Basic offers a number of tools that make it easy for your users to access the multiple forms that are open inside the MDI form. Your program can provide the users with the means to arrange the child windows automatically. You can even provide a menu item that keeps up with all the open child windows and lets the users access one of them by selecting it from the menu. These capabilities are particularly useful if the users will be switching back and forth between multiple tasks or multiple files in the application.

Using Automatic Organization

One way that users can access multiple forms is by displaying each form on the screen in a particular organizational style. This capability provides the users with access to each form with just a click of a mouse button. The key to this functionality is the MDI form's `Arrange` method. The `Arrange` method organizes all the child forms of the application in a particular pattern. Each of these patterns results in at least a portion of each form's being visible to the users, and they are commonly used by MDI-compliant Windows applications.

To use the `Arrange` method, you specify the name of the MDI form, the method itself, and a constant representing the pattern that you want to use for the arrangement of the forms. The following line of code illustrates the use of the method:

```
mdiMain.Arrange vbCascade
```

You can create four possible window arrangement patterns with the `Arrange` method. Each of these patterns is represented by an intrinsic constant. Table 17.1 summarizes the patterns, and they are illustrated in Figures 17.12 through 17.15.

Table 17.1 Arrangements of MDI Child Windows

Constant	Description
vbCascade	The nonminimized forms are arranged in a pattern in which each form is offset slightly from the others.
vbTileVertical	Each nonminimized child form occupies the full height of the parent form, and the child forms are displayed side by side. If you have many child forms, they can occupy multiple rows when tiled.
vbTileHorizontal	Each nonminimized child form occupies the full width of the parent form, and the child forms are displayed on top of one another. If you have many child forms, they can occupy multiple columns when tiled.
vbArrangeIcons	The icons of all minimized child forms are arranged near the bottom of the parent form.

FIGURE 17.12
These child forms have been arranged in a cascade pattern.

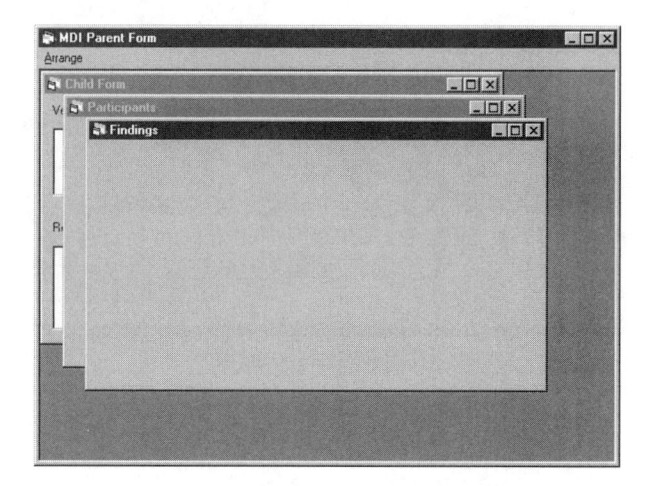

Typically, you place the arrangement options in a Window menu on the MDI form. Each arrangement option that you want to support is a separate menu item.

Maintaining a Window List

The other way of providing easy access to the child forms of your application is to maintain a list of the open child forms. Fortunately, this task is easy. You create a window list while you are creating the menu for the MDI parent form. You determine which menu will contain the list and then set that menu item's `WindowList` property to `True` in the Menu Editor, as shown in Figure 17.16.

Chapter 17 Multiple Document Interface Applications

FIGURE 17.13
These child forms have been arranged in a vertically tiled pattern.

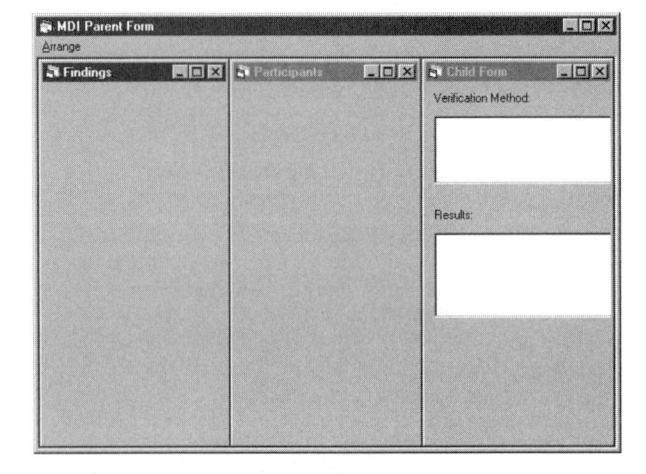

FIGURE 17.14
These child forms have been arranged in a horizontally tiled pattern.

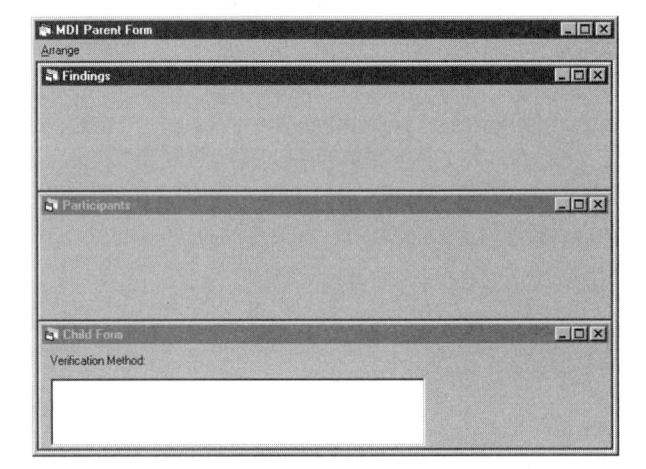

FIGURE 17.15
Minimized child forms are represented by icons arranged at the bottom of the MDI form.

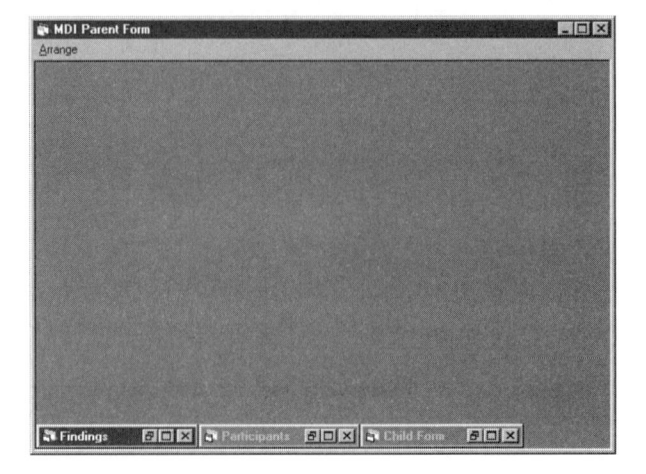

> **NOTE** You also can change the setting of the `WindowList` property from code.

FIGURE 17.16
Check the WindowList box to create a list of open child windows in your MDI menu.

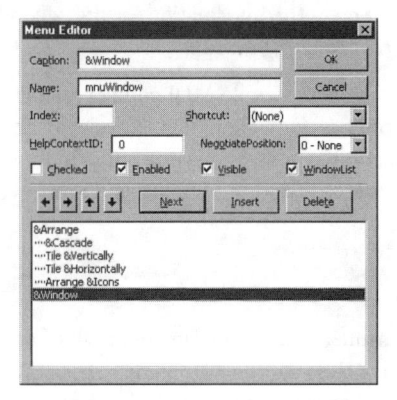

As you add child forms to the application, the window list menu item is automatically updated to include the new form. The caption of the menu item is the caption that is given to the form that you create. The active form in the window list is indicated by a check mark. Figure 17.17 shows a window list for an MDI application.

FIGURE 17.17
The window list lets the users select the form with which to work.

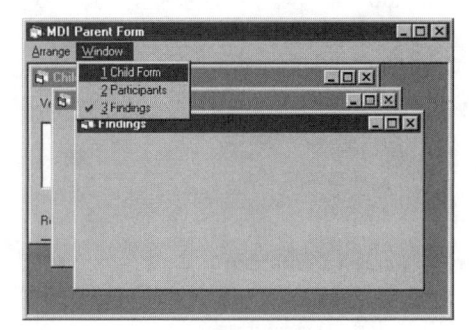

Creating a Sample Application—an MDI Contact Manager

Obviously, the best way to demonstrate the techniques of MDI applications is to build an application that you might actually use. This program uses multiple instances of a template form to become an MDI application.

If part of your job is keeping up with customer contacts, you probably use some kind of contact manager. These programs let you keep up with information about each of your customers, such as their name, address, phone numbers, the date you last contacted them, and so forth. One of the disadvantages of some contact managers is that you can only work with a single contact at a time. This can be very inconvenient if you are working on an order for one customer and another telephones to discuss a new service. In this case, you have to close the client information for the current customer and open the information for the second customer. Wouldn't it be great if you could just open the information for the second customer in a new window? Well, with an MDI contact manager, you can.

This section shows you how to build a very simple MDI contact manager. The program displays only name and address information for a client and is basically an illustration of the concept. To create a full-fledged contact manager, you have to add additional database code. The program uses a Microsoft Access database and the Jet engine to retrieve the data.

▶ **See** "Using Tables," **p. 570**

Creating the MDI Form

The setup of the MDI form is the same as you have seen in previous sections. You first need to add an MDI form to your project and then set the `AutoShowChildren` property to `False`. You also should set the `Name` and `Caption` properties of the MDI form to something other than the defaults.

After setting the properties of the form, you need to create a menu that displays the customer information in the appropriate child form. The menu items that you need to add are shown in Figure 17.18.

▶ **See** "Creating a Menu Bar," **p. 108**

FIG. 17.18
The sample MDI Contact Manager application has these menu items.

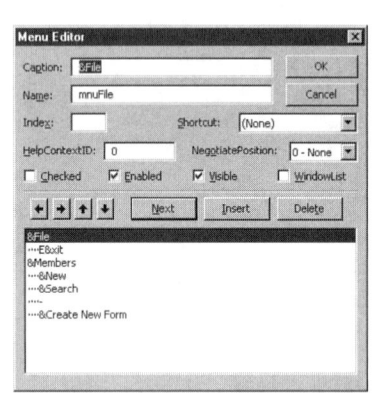

One menu item of note is the Create New Form item. The user can use this option to tell the program whether to display a selected customer in the existing child form or to create a new form for each new customer. The Checked property of the item is set to show the status of the user choice.

Of course, after you create the menu, you need to add code to make the menu options work. Listing 17.2 shows the code for the menu items shown in Figure 17.18.

Listing 17.2 MAINMDI.TXT—Use Menu Code to Handle the Tasks of the Contact Manager

```
Private Sub filExit_Click()
    Unload Me
End Sub

Private Sub MDIForm_Load()
    Me.WindowState = vbMaximized
End Sub

Private Sub MDIForm_Unload(Cancel As Integer)
    CustDb.Close
End Sub

Private Sub memCreate_Click()
Dim CheckSet As Boolean
    CheckSet = Not memCreate.Checked
    memCreate.Checked = CheckSet
    CreateForm = CheckSet
End Sub

Private Sub memNew_Click()
    If CreateForm Then
        Dim frmMem As New frmMember
        frmMem.Show
    End If
    ClearCust
End Sub

Private Sub memSearch_Click()
    frmSearch.Show vbModal
    If CreateForm Then
        Dim frmMem As New frmMember
        frmMem.Show
    End If
    ShowCust
End Sub
```

Setting Up the Customer Child Form

The next step in creating the contact manager is setting up the child form that displays a customer's information. To set up the customer form, add a form to your project (or use the initial form that was created) and then set its MDIChild property to True. You probably also need to change the Name and Caption properties of the form. (Set the name of the form to frmMember to match the code in the menu items.) After setting the properties of the form, you need to add controls to the form to display the data. The completed form is shown in Figure 17.19.

FIG. 17.19
Customer information is displayed in a child form.

Creating the Search Form

As you look up customer records, you need a search form to allow the user to enter a name to find. The search form can be very simple, consisting of a label, a text box to enter the name, and two command buttons to perform or cancel the search. The code for the form is also very simple. If you proceed with the search, the code uses the `FindFirst` method of the recordset that contains the contact information to locate the first name corresponding to the desired search information. The complete search form is shown in Figure 17.20, and the code for the form is shown in Listing 17.3.

> **N O T E** A *recordset* is a special type of object that acts as a link between a Visual Basic program and information stored in a database. You learn about recordsets in Chapter 26, "Using Data Access Objects (DAO)."

▶ **See** "Deciding Which Recordset Type to Use," **p. 569**

FIG. 17.20
You can make the search form more complex by adding a First Name search as well.

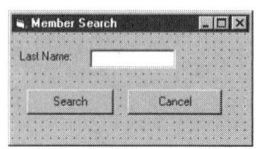

Listing 17.3 SEARCH.TXT—Use the *FindFirst* Method to Locate the Desired Customer

```
Private Sub cmdCancel_Click()
    Unload Me
End Sub

Private Sub cmdSearch_Click()
Dim SrchStr As String
    SrchStr = txtSearch.Text
    CustRset.FindFirst "LastName = '" & SrchStr & "'"
    Unload Me
End Sub
```

Creating the Heart of the Program

The forms provide the interface of the program, but the real heart of the program is a group of procedures that actually display the data and set the program up. To create the procedures, you first need to add a module to your program. You can do this by choosing Project, Add, or by selecting Module from the Add Object button's drop-down menu.

▶ **See** "Determining the Scope of Procedures and Functions," **p. 232**

After the module is added to the project, you need to define a couple of Public variables and create the procedure that sets up the program. The public variables are used to provide your entire program with access to the database object. Once you define the variables, you need to create a Sub Main procedure to set up the database information and display the MDI parent form. The Public variable declarations and the Sub Main procedure are shown in Listing 17.4.

Listing 17.4 MDIPROCS.TXT—Use *Sub Main* to Set Up the Database and Load the Main Form

```
Public CustDb As Database, CustRset As Recordset
Public CreateForm As Boolean

Sub Main()
    Set CustDb = DBEngine.Workspaces(0).OpenDatabase("D:\VB6Book\NewDb.mdb")
    Set CustRset = CustDb.OpenRecordset("Customers", dbOpenDynaset)
    mdiMain.Show
    CreateForm = True
End Sub
```

After you create the Sub Main procedure, you need to change the project options to make Sub Main the startup object of the program.

The next two procedures are the ones which either display information about a current customer or set up the information form for you to enter a new customer. These procedures are called by the appropriate menu items of the MDI form. The key feature to note in these procedures is that the ActiveForm property of the MDI form is used to designate which child form will receive the data being sent. The ClearCust and ShowCust procedures are shown in Listing 17.5.

Listing 17.5 MDIPROCS2.TXT—Use the *ActiveForm* Property to Send the Output of the Procedure to the Proper Location

```
Public Sub ClearCust()
Dim I As Integer
    For I = 0 To 5
        mdiMain.ActiveForm.txtMember(I).Text = ""
    Next I
End Sub
```

continues

Listing 17.5 Continued

```
Public Sub ShowCust()
    With mdiMain.ActiveForm
        .txtMember(0).Text = CustRset!LastName & ""
        .txtMember(1).Text = CustRset!FirstName & ""
        .txtMember(2).Text = CustRset!Address1 & ""
        .txtMember(3).Text = CustRset!City & ""
        .txtMember(4).Text = CustRset!State & ""
        .txtMember(5).Text = CustRset!Zip & ""
    End With
End Sub
```

Running the Program

As you run the program, you can create new windows for each customer that you add, or change the status of the Create New Form menu item to display each customer in the same window. As stated previously, this example is merely is an illustration of the concept, so feel free to add your own enhancements to the program. The MDI contact manager is shown in Figure 17.21.

FIG. 17.21
You can display multiple clients at the same time.

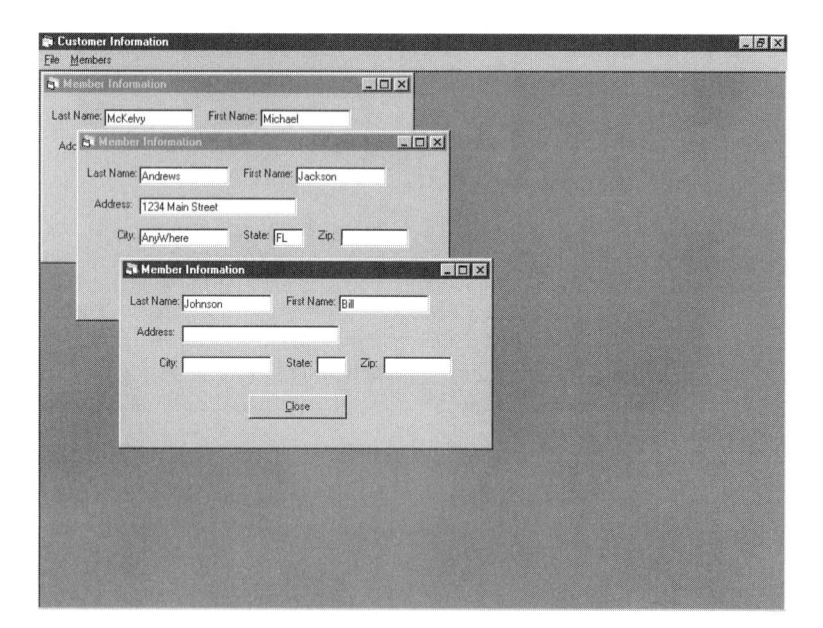

Optimizing Your MDI Application

This chapter demonstrated a number of techniques that you can use to create MDI applications. As you can see, the MDI form can be a powerful tool for creating programs. However, there are several considerations to keep in mind to optimize your MDI applications. These considerations help keep the performance of your programs as crisp as possible and help keep your users from running into problems:

- Each new child window that is loaded consumes memory. Having memory-intensive child windows causes your application to drain memory quickly, so keep the amount of code and the number of controls in your child windows to a minimum.
- If your child and parent windows have the same menu commands (such as File, Open or File, Exit), keep the code in the parent. This means your child form's menu Click event procedures should simply call the parent menu's Click event procedure for all shared code.
- Change all of your menu Click event procedures from Private to Public so your child and parent windows can share these events.
- Avoid using the Name property of your child form. Instead, your child forms should use Me (or nothing at all), and your parent form should use ActiveForm.
- Put *all* invisible controls (such as a common dialog control or image list) on the MDI parent form. This allows all of your child windows to share these controls, without consuming extra memory.

Adhering to these concepts both simplifies your code and improves the performance of your MDI application.

Creating an MDI Application Framework

The code shown in this section is designed to provide a basic skeleton for any MDI applications that you create. The skeleton code can be modified to suit your specific needs. Then you can use the skeleton project as a template for your other MDI applications. The completed application is shown in Figure 17.22.

FIG. 17.22
Creating a template project can simplify your future MDI work.

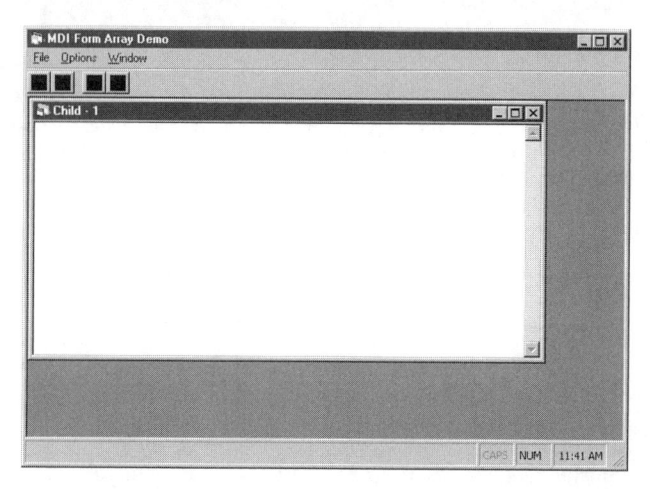

Creating the MDI Parent Template

The MDI parent form is the keeper (or container) of the child windows, so it is responsible for creating new children. With this duty, it is common for the parent to also keep track of the number of child windows it has created. In addition, the parent usually holds shared user interface elements like a toolbar, status bar, and so on.

The code in Listing 17.6 shows the code used to maintain and expose the window count. `WindowCreate` and `WindowDestroyed` are called by the child windows in their `Form_Load` and `Form_Unload` event procedures, respectively. `ChildWindowCount` is a `Public` property that allows the child windows to find out how many children are loaded.

Listing 17.6 MDIPARENT.TXT—Use the Parent to Contain Common Code for All the Child Forms

```
'**********************************************************************
' MDIParent.frm - Demonstrates some basic concepts on how a MDI parent
'   form should behave in an MDI application.
'**********************************************************************
Option Explicit
Private mintChildWinCount As Integer
'**********************************************************************
' Returns how many child windows have been created
'**********************************************************************
Public Property Get ChildWindowCount() As Integer
    ChildWindowCount = mintChildWinCount
End Property
'**********************************************************************
' Called when a window is created to increment the window counter
'**********************************************************************
Public Sub WindowCreated()
    mintChildWinCount = mintChildWinCount + 1
    UpdateButtons True
End Sub
'**********************************************************************
' Called when a window is created to decrement the window counter
'**********************************************************************
Public Sub WindowDestroyed()
    mintChildWinCount = mintChildWinCount - 1
    UpdateButtons mintChildWinCount
End Sub
```

You also might notice a call to `UpdateButtons` in Listing 17.6. This private helper routine enables and disables toolbar buttons. If children exist, then the toolbar buttons are enabled. When the last child is unloaded, `WindowDestroyed` decrements the variable `mintChildWinCount` to 0, which causes `UpdateButtons` to disable the toolbar buttons.

The most important code in MDIPARENT.FRM is the File menu's Click event procedure. This code is responsible for creating windows, opening files, and terminating the application.

Because all of these actions on the MDI parent file menu are also on the child form's file menu, you make this event public (see Listing 17.7).

Listing 17.7 MDIPARENT2.TXT—Handling Menu *Click* Events

```
'*******************************************************************
' File menu handler for the MDI form when no windows are displayed.
' In this demo the child windows will have a menu just like this,
' so we will make this Public so the children can call this event.
'*******************************************************************
Public Sub mnuFileItems_Click(Index As Integer)
    Select Case Index
        '*******************************************************************
        ' File New - Create a new child form, then display it.
        '*******************************************************************
        Case 1
            Dim frmNew As New frmChild
            frmNew.Visible = True
        '*******************************************************************
        ' File Open - Prompt the user for a filename, then load
        '             it into the child window (in OpenFile) if the user didn't
        '             press cancel in the dialog.
        '*******************************************************************
        Case 2
            On Error Resume Next
            With cdlg
                .Flags = cdlOFNFileMustExist
                .Filter = "Text Files (*.txt)|*.txt|All Files (*.*)|*.*"
                .ShowOpen
            End With
            If Err <> cdlg.cdlCancel Then OpenFile cdlg.filename
        '*******************************************************************
        ' Index 3 is the separator, so don't do anything.
        '*******************************************************************
        'Case 3
        '*******************************************************************
        ' File Exit - Terminate the application
        '*******************************************************************
        Case 4
            Unload Me
    End Select
End Sub
```

When the File, New menu is clicked (Index = 1), the Dim frmNew As New frmChild line creates a new instance of your child form. However, this doesn't really create the new form. The form is actually created as soon as you access one if its properties or methods. This means that the frmNew.Visible = True line is the line of code that creates the form. After the form is created, the Visible property is set to True, which displays your form.

> **TIP** Forms created using New are hidden by default, so remember to display them by setting Visible = True.

The File, Open (Index = 2) code in Listing 17.8 simply displays an Open dialog box so the user can supply a file name. If the user doesn't click Cancel, then the file is opened using the OpenFile routine, as presented in Listing 17.8. The last item in the select statement is Index 4, which represents the File, Exit case. This is an easy one because the proper way to terminate an MDI application is to unload the MDI form.

As mentioned earlier, the OpenFile code is responsible for opening a text file and loading it into a text box on your child form. This code is very simplistic and includes no basic error handling for such cases as testing for files greater than 44K under Windows 95. However, it does provide a basic example of how to load a file into a text box, which is sufficient for this example.

> **CAUTION**
>
> Avoid using the End statement to terminate your applications. End terminates your application immediately, which prevents your Form_Unload events from being executed. The best way to end an MDI application is to unload the MDI form.

Listing 17.8 MDIPARENT3.TXT—Shared Code

```
'**********************************************************************
' Code shared among the child windows should be put in either a
' module or the MDI parent form.  This OpenFile code will be used
' by all of the children, so we will keep it in the MDI parent form.
'**********************************************************************
Public Sub OpenFile(strFileName As String)
    Dim strFileContents As String
    Dim intFileNum As Integer
    '**********************************************************************
    ' Get a free file handle
    '**********************************************************************
    intFileNum = FreeFile
    '**********************************************************************
    ' Open the file
    '**********************************************************************
    Open strFileName For Input As intFileNum
        '**********************************************************************
        ' Put the contents of the file into the txtData control of
        ' the child form. This code will fail if the file is too
        ' large to fit in the textbox, so you should include
        ' additional error handling in your own code.
        '**********************************************************************
        With ActiveForm
            .txtData.Text = Input$(LOF(intFileNum), intFileNum)
            '**********************************************************************
            ' Set the caption of the child form to the filename
            '**********************************************************************
            .Caption = strFileName
        End With
        '**********************************************************************
        ' Always close files you open as soon as you are done with them
```

```
        '*****************************************************************
            Close intFileNum
        End Sub
```

You might notice that the `OpenFile` routine simply loads the file into the text box on the active window by referencing the `ActiveForm` property. This is a valid assumption to make, because the active menu will always refer to the active form. Because the user can open a file via the menu (even if he or she is using the toolbar), you can always assume that any actions you perform in your menu event handlers should be applied to the active form.

The MDI Child

Now that you have had a chance to understand what your MDI parent form is responsible for, let's take a look at how the child should behave in this parent/child relationship.

As mentioned earlier, child forms are responsible for calling the `WindowCreated` and `WindowDestroyed` methods of the MDI parent form. Listing 17.9 demonstrates how this is done from the `Form_Load` and `Form_Unload` events. In addition, your child window sets its initial caption based on the MDI parent `ChildWindowCount` property. Although this technique is good for this sample, you might want to make your algorithm for setting your initial caption a little more complex. What do you think would happen if you had three windows, closed the second window, and then created a new window? How could you avoid this problem?

Listing 17.9 MDICHILD.TXT—Use the Child Form for Code Specific to Each Child

```
'*****************************************************************
' MDIChild.frm - Demonstrates some basic techniques on how a MDI child
'    window should behave.
'*****************************************************************
Option Explicit
'*****************************************************************
' When a new form is created it should call the WindowCreated function
' in the MDI parent form (which increments the window count in this
' case). It should also set its caption to distinguish it from other
' child windows.
'*****************************************************************
Private Sub Form_Load()
    MDIParent.WindowCreated
    '*****************************************************************
    ' This works, but it has a fatal flaw.
    '*****************************************************************
    Caption = Caption & " - " & MDIParent.ChildWindowCount
End Sub
'*****************************************************************
' Make sure txtData always fills the client area of the form.
'*****************************************************************
```

continues

Listing 17.9 Continued

```
Private Sub Form_Resize()
    txtData.Move 0, 0, ScaleWidth, ScaleHeight
End Sub
'************************************************************************
' Let the MDI parent know that this window is being destroyed.
'************************************************************************
Private Sub Form_Unload(Cancel As Integer)
    MDIParent.WindowDestroyed
End Sub
```

One other minor detail you might have noticed in this code is the `Form_Resize` event. This code makes sure your TextBox control always covers the entire client area of the form. This code works with any control, so keep this in mind for your own applications.

Another important concept mentioned previously was that your child forms should use event handlers of the parent menu whenever possible (and vice versa). Listing 17.10 contains the event handlers for all of the menus used by MDICHILD.FRM.

Listing 17.10 MDICHILD2.TXT—Handling the Menu Code for the Application

```
'************************************************************************
' Since the child File menu is identical to the MDI parent File menu,
' we should avoid duplicate code by calling the parent's mnuFileItems
' click event.
'************************************************************************
Private Sub mnuFileItems_Click(Index As Integer)
    MDIParent.mnuFileItems_Click Index
End Sub
'************************************************************************
' The options menu is unique to the child forms, so the code should
' be in the child form or separate BAS module.
'************************************************************************
Public Sub mnuOptionsItems_Click(Index As Integer)
    '********************************************************************
    ' Don't stop for errors
    '********************************************************************
    On Error Resume Next
    '********************************************************************
    ' Show the color dialog (since all menu items here need it)
    '********************************************************************
    MDIParent.cdlg.ShowColor
    '********************************************************************
    ' If the use selected cancel, then exit
    '********************************************************************
    If Err = cdlCancel Then Exit Sub
    '********************************************************************
    ' Otherwise set the color based on the value returned from the dlg
    '********************************************************************
    Select Case Index
        Case 1 'Backcolor...
```

```
                txtData.BackColor = MDIParent.cdlg.Color
            Case 2 'Forecolor...
                txtData.ForeColor = MDIParent.cdlg.Color
        End Select
End Sub
'**********************************************************************
' If you set your indexes of your Window menu properly, you can save
' yourself some code. I was careful to make sure my Window menu items
' indices were equivalent to the possible values for the Arrange
' method.
'**********************************************************************
Private Sub mnuWindowItems_Click(Index As Integer)
    MDIParent.Arrange Index
End Sub
```

The first menu is the File menu, which is identical to the parent form, so you simply call the `mnuFileItems_Click` event in the parent for default processing. The second menu is the Options menu, which only appears in the child form, so you write your implementation code here. However, you make this event handler public so it could be accessed by your Toolbar control, which resides on the parent form. In addition, you use the CommonDialog control on the parent for your code, which displays the color dialog box.

> **TIP** If any menu item on your child form requires greater than 12 lines or so of code (excluding `Dims`, comments, and white space), you should move that code to a shared module or into the parent form. That prevents this code from consuming too much free memory every time a new form is added.

Finally, you have your Window menu that only applies to child forms (although it is the parent form that is responsible for this menu). By carefully creating your menu control array indices, you are able to write the implementation code for this menu using only one line of code.

ON THE WEB

From the Macmillan Web site, you can download another complete project that makes full use of the MDI concepts covered in this chapter. A text editor application named MDI Text Editor, it is similar in functionality to Windows Notepad, but it allows for multiple document windows to be open simultaneously. You can open this project from within Visual Basic; comments throughout the code explain how it works.

From Here...

This chapter provided you with an introduction to creating MDI applications using Visual Basic. For more information about some of the related topics covered in this chapter, see the following chapters:

- To learn more about setting up forms, see Chapter 3, "Visual Basic Building Blocks."
- To learn more about creating database programs like the example in this chapter, see Chapter 26, "Using Data Access Objects (DAO)."

CHAPTER 18

Proper Interface Design

In this chapter

Designing Effective Forms   410

User PC Differences   415

Dealing with User Expectations   417

In this chapter, you learn about the part of the program that everyone sees: the user interface. Some programmers are inclined to leave user interface design as an afterthought, thinking the code is the real "guts" of an application and therefore deserves the most attention. However, gripes about fonts, screens, and speed of execution should be taken very seriously. Your users cannot see the code, but the user interface (good or bad) is always right in front of them. Windows offers many opportunities to build an interface that will help get the job done easier. This chapter describes a series of guidelines and examples that will help you make the most of these opportunities.

Designing Effective Forms

Forms are the building blocks of your user interface. Although designing a form in Visual Basic is simple, doing it well is not very easy. Good form design involves more than just inserting controls and programming events. To make a well-designed form, you should understand the form's purpose, how it is going to be used, when it is going to be used, and its relationship with the rest of the program. In addition, within your application, you may have several open forms, each of which must be displayed when appropriate. Some users take advantage of the multitasking freedom offered by Windows, whereas others tend to use only one application at a time. Keep this point in mind when you're designing a user interface (UI): You must manage the flexibility Windows offers to the programmer so that users with any skill level can effectively use the application.

Keep Forms Neat and Uncluttered

The more controls you have on a form, the more important it is to keep them organized. Consider the form shown in Figure 18.1. It looks as though the controls have been placed on the form haphazardly. They are not labeled, lined up, or sized consistently. A better approach is shown in Figure 18.2. Notice that frames, lines, and labels have been added to group related controls. Both illustrations show "working" applications, but the second form has a more visually pleasing appearance, which makes it easier to use.

Visual Basic provides several excellent controls to help you organize a form. One of these controls is the TabStrip control, shown in Figure 18.3, which can be used to segregate controls so that only a few of them are displayed at any given time. This way, you can hide infrequently used options from the average users while still making them available if necessary.

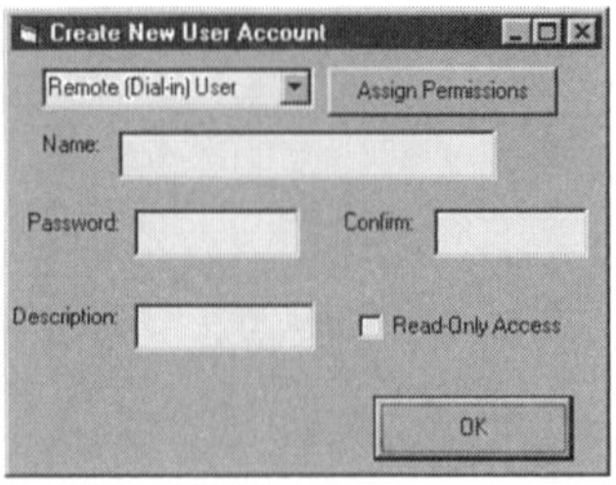

FIGURE 18.1
A messy form can prevent users from finding the information they need.

FIGURE 18.2
In a much better design than the form in Figure 18.1, frames and label controls are used to organize the form.

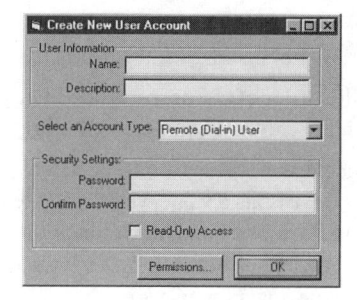

> **N O T E** The Tabbed Dialog control is similar to the TabStrip; the major difference is that it can act as a container for other controls. ■

▶ See "Using the TabStrip Control," **p. 261**

FIGURE 18.3
Use the TabStrip control, and keep your form a reasonable size.

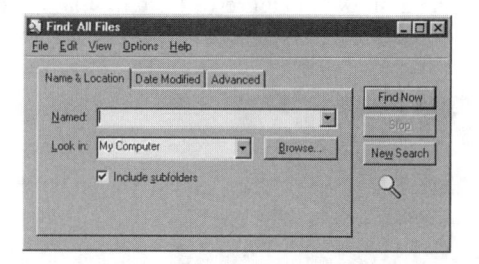

To keep from going overboard with too many controls on a form, you should always keep the form's purpose in mind. Consider the form in Figure 18.3. Everything on the form could fall under the general realm of "program options," but each separate category of options is in a different section of the TabStrip control. If you do find that you need a separate form, make sure logic dictates which controls you put on it.

In addition, make sure to set the appropriate form properties so that the form acts according to its intended purpose. For example, a modal form probably should not have a sizeable border or show up in the Windows taskbar.

▶ See "Form Properties Revisited," **p. 52**

Pay Special Attention to Data Entry Forms

Data entry forms are a special breed. They should allow users to work at their own pace, not the programmer's. Common sense is the main rule here: If users have to enter 10,000 records into your database, they don't want to answer a yes/no confirmation dialog for each record.

The preceding section emphasized separating and hiding certain controls. However, a data entry form should maximize the use of form space because showing and hiding forms slows down the process. Speed should definitely be one of your main goals when designing a data entry form. To make the data entry process faster, follow these guidelines:

- Always provide keyboard shortcuts; never require the use of a mouse. (This is good advice for all forms in your program, not just data entry forms.)
- Keep the layout consistent with the order of the users' tasks. In other words, don't make them jump from one section to another unnecessarily to enter information.
- Do not require the users to perform unnecessary work. In other words, if fields 2 through 10 require a value only if field 1 has a value, you don't need to make the users always tab through every field. On the other hand, don't make the behavior of your forms too field dependent; if a form works differently for every possible combination of required fields, you may actually slow down the users.
- Use noticeable but unobtrusive visual cues to provide feedback to the users. The way the VB code editor capitalizes correctly spelled variables and constants is a good example.
- If possible, perform adds and edits on the same form so that the users do not have to learn multiple methods of accessing the same data.

An example of a data entry form is shown in Figure 18.4. Notice that when a data validation error occurs, the offending field is highlighted, and an explanation is provided in the status bar.

FIGURE 18.4
In this sample data entry form, ease of use is of prime importance.

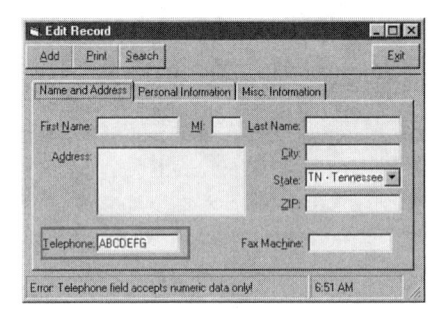

Use the Right Control for the Job

Visual Basic provides several custom controls that can be placed on a form. However, keep in mind that some controls work better in certain situations than others. The purpose of the form should help guide you in choosing the appropriate controls. For example, both the ListBox and ComboBox controls can be used to select from a list of choices. However, the combo box allows you to save form real estate by hiding the list of choices, as illustrated in Figure 18.5.

FIGURE 18.5
The amount of space available on a form may influence your choice of custom controls.

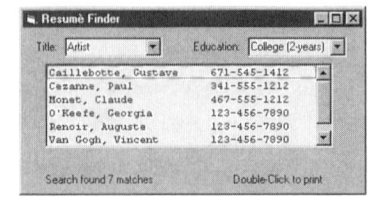

In Figure 18.5, list boxes could have just as easily been used for the selection criteria. However, using a combo box is more appropriate because it saves space while still accomplishing the intended task.

▶ **See** "The Combo Box," **p. 75**

Third-Party Controls

Third-party custom controls are useful; however, you should not use them unless doing so is really necessary. Picking a control included with VB over a third-party control offers several advantages:

- The chances are better that the control will be supported in future versions of VB.
- Distributing the control to users is easier.
- Many "native" VB controls, such as the Windows Common Controls, provide the users an interface with which they are already familiar.

Multiple Forms

If your user interface will contain multiple forms, a major decision you have to make is whether to use a single-document interface (SDI) or a multiple-document interface (MDI). MDI applications, discussed in Chapter 17, "Multiple Document Interface Applications," handle multiple forms by enclosing them visually within a "parent" window.

▶ **See** "Introducing MDI Applications," **p. 382**

Forms in an SDI application appear as totally independent windows. Whether you use SDI or MDI, user interaction with forms initiates many program actions through form and control events. If you have multiple forms, you need to code the program so that the users are not allowed to disrupt the intended program flow—for example, show a data form that has not been populated yet.

As an example of a potential problem with multiple forms, consider the two forms shown in Figure 18.6.

FIGURE 18.6
Forms that your code treats as independent when they really are not can cause unexpected errors.

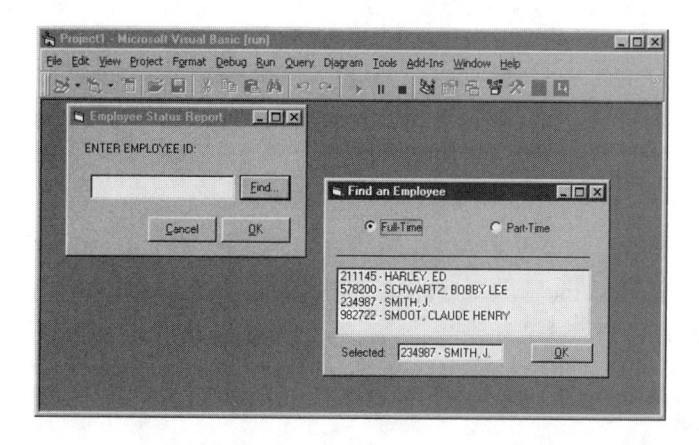

In the example shown in Figure 18.6, the main form, `frmMain`, is used to retrieve information from the database. If users do not know a valid value for the Employee ID field, they can click the Search button next to the field to display the second form, `frmSearch`. The second form comes up with a valid ID value and returns it to the main form. At first glance, the code to manage the transition between forms is easy to understand.

The Search button on the first form simply shows the second form:

```
Sub cmdSearch_OnClick()
    frmSearch.Show
End Sub
```

The second form, after performing the search function, places the valid value in a text box on the first form and then unloads itself:

```
Sub cmdOK_OnClick()
    frmMain.txtID = sSearchResult
    Unload Me
End Sub
```

Although the simple code listed here would get the job done, it has a couple of basic design problems. First, it treats `frmSearch` like a totally independent form. The users could return to `frmMain` without closing `frmSearch`, either on purpose or by accident, and an orphan form would be left open. If `frmMain` was later unloaded and `frmSearch` tried to access it, an error would occur. The second problem with this arrangement is that the code is hard-wired to these two specific forms, so reusing `frmSearch` in other parts of the application would be difficult. You can solve both of these problems by showing `frmSearch` modally.

Modal forms, as you may recall, keep the application focus until you hide them. In other words, you cannot switch from a modal form to another form without first closing the modal form. In addition, any code that would have been executed after the `Show` method is suspended until the modal form is hidden.

▶ **See** "Form Properties Revisited," **p. 52**

Showing `frmSearch` modally prevents the users from switching back to `frmMain` without first closing `frmSearch`. It also stops code execution in other modules while `frmSearch` is visible. You can use this capability to your advantage and consolidate some of the code. Consider the following search function that returns the value to the calling procedure rather than to any specific form:

```
Function sGetValidValue() As String
    frmSearch.Show vbModal
    sGetValidValue = frmSearch.sSearchResult
    Unload frmSearch
End Function
```

You can now call the preceding function from `frmMain` (or any other form) to display `frmSearch` and retrieve a valid search value:

```
Sub cmdSearch_OnClick()
    frmMain.txtID = sGetValidValue()
End Sub
```

> **TIP** If your project is very large, use modules, subroutines, and even custom DLLs to keep the "guts" of your program separate from the UI and thus easier to maintain.

User PC Differences

From a user interface standpoint, extra thought is required when you're writing a program that is designed to run on a PC other than your own. Visual Basic programs run on Windows 95, Windows 98, or Windows NT (not to mention Windows CE). Each of these operating systems is different, and each PC running them can be set up differently.

> **NOTE** If you want to know programmatically which operating system your user is running, check out the GetVersionEx API call or the SysInfo custom control. Instructions for using API calls are discussed in Chapter 20, "Accessing the Windows API."

In addition, the Windows operating system leaves a lot of room for user customization. One of the most noticeable differences may be screen resolution. If you go into the Windows Display Control Panel, you may notice that several options for screen size are available. As a developer and owner of a 21-inch monitor, I like to leave my PC at 1280×1024, which allows me to place a lot on the screen at once. However, most of your end users are likely to be operating at a lower resolution, say 640×480. The easiest solution to this problem is to design your forms for the minimum 640×480 resolution. The users at that resolution will see your application fill up the whole screen, while users at higher resolutions will have extra desktop space to open other windows. But what happens when the user adjusts the size of your form with the mouse? If you do not write code to handle this situation, users at higher resolutions could get unpleasant results, as in Figure 18.7.

FIGURE 18.7
If you do not respond to users resizing your form, wasted space appears.

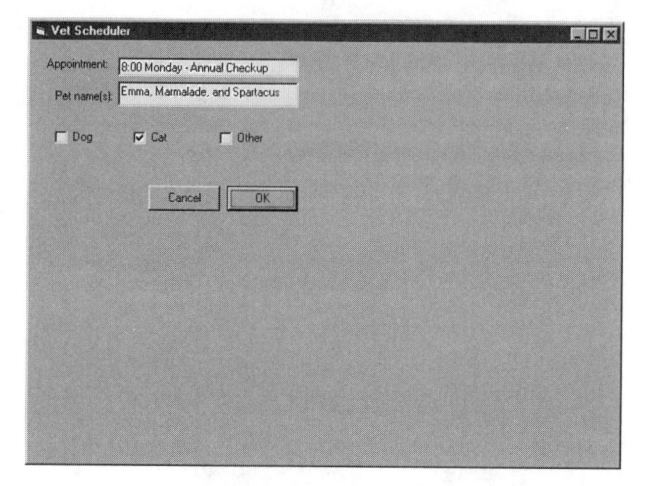

In addition, a user can make a form smaller, obscuring some controls. However, if your form is simple enough, you may be able to add some code to the form's `Resize` event to make it resolution independent. By looking at the `Height` and `Width` properties of each control and comparing them to the form's height and width, you can easily add code so that controls will maintain their relative positions when users resize your form. The following code adjusts the sizes of a list box and two command buttons so that their sizes will change with the form:

```
Private Sub Form_Resize()

    If Me.Height <= 1365 Then Exit Sub

    lstMain.Height = Me.Height - 1365
    lstMain.Width = Me.Width - 420

    cmdOK.Top = lstMain.Height + 360
    cmdOK.Left = lstMain.Width - cmdOK.Width

    cmdCancel.Top = cmdOK.Top
    cmdCancel.Left = cmdOK.Left - cmdCancel.Width - 120

End Sub
```

TIP For an even better form, change the font size of your controls as the form size changes.

Note that the first line of code in the Resize event exits the event procedure if the form height becomes too small because an error would occur if a negative value were assigned.

NOTE You also can find third-party controls that can be used to add resolution independence to your applications.

Another customization that can adversely affect your program is the Regional Settings Control Panel, pictured in Figure 18.8. This screen allows users to set their own currency and date format, among other things. If you use these predefined formats in your program, make sure that your variables, database fields, and calculations can handle them.

▶ See "Formatting Results," **p. 195**

FIGURE 18.8
Make sure your program is prepared to handle changes users make in the Regional Settings Control Panel.

Dealing with User Expectations

Users tend to have ideas about how they think Windows applications should behave. Some of these ideas make sense, and some do not. Most likely, these notions are derived from features they have seen in commercial programs. Of course, users will then expect every simple VB program you write to behave in exactly the same way.

For example, even though your program may have an Exit button, you can count on users to click the Close button in the upper-right corner. If you forget to add code to the `Form_Unload` event to handle this situation, your application could keep running when you don't want it to. The following sections describe several things about which you can count on users having expectations.

The List Box

Many users expect list boxes to behave a certain way. Suppose a list box is set up in a dialog box to select a single item. Some users may prefer to just double-click the item, whereas others single-click it and then press Enter or click OK. These alternative methods are easy to include in your program; simply remember to add code to the list box's `DblClick` event.

> **TIP** In the example described here of selecting items from a list box, both single-clicking and double-clicking are appropriate. However, there are users who do not understand when to use a single-click versus a double-click. You can easily spot these people because they tend to double-click everything, including hyperlinks, command buttons, and even menus. Help teach them the correct procedure by using the hourglass mouse pointer and providing instructions that say specifically whether to single- or double-click.

▶ See "The List Box" p. 70

Another list box feature available in commercial programs is the ability to enter letters on the keyboard to jump to a specific list item. By default, the list box accepts only a single character. However, you can easily add this "type-ahead" feature to your list box. Simply accumulate the entered characters from the `KeyPress` event in a string, and then move to the matching item in the list. The code in Listing 18.1 does this, plus provides the additional feature of a Timer control that gradually fills the list box. This capability allows users to begin using the type-ahead feature before the list is completely filled.

Listing 18.1 LISTBOX.ZIP—Adding Keyboard Search to a List Box

```
Option Explicit

Dim sLstSearch As String        'The search string
Dim CurrentLetter As String     'Letter being loaded into the list
Dim sWaitForLetter As String    'Letter not yet loaded but selected
Dim dbBiblio As Database        'The sample VB "biblio" database

Private Sub Form_Load()
```

continues

Listing 18.1 Continued

```
        sWaitForLetter = ""
        CurrentLetter = ""

        lblLoaded = "Loading the list . . ."
        Set dbBiblio = OpenDatabase("d:\vb6\biblio.mdb")
        DoEvents

        tmrLoad.Enabled = True
End Sub
Function SearchListBox(lstX As Control, KeyAscii As Integer)
    Dim nSearchPos As Integer
    Dim nSearchLen As Integer
    Dim nResult As Integer

    nSearchPos = lstX.ListIndex
    nSearchLen = Len(sLstSearch)
    sWaitForLetter = ""

    'CHECK FOR BACKSPACE KEY
    If KeyAscii = vbKeyBack Then
        nSearchPos = 0
        If nSearchLen > 0 Then sLstSearch = Left$(sLstSearch, nSearchLen - 1)
    End If

    'CAPTIALIZE THE NEW CHARACTER
    KeyAscii = Asc(UCase$(Chr$(KeyAscii)))

    'IF YOU PRESS 'X' AND DATA IS ONLY LOADED TO 'C' THEN WAIT....
    If nSearchLen = 0 And KeyAscii > Asc(CurrentLetter) Then
        lstX.ListIndex = lstX.ListCount - 1
        sWaitForLetter = Chr$(KeyAscii)
        DoEvents
        Exit Function
    End If

    'ADD NEW LETTER TO SEARCH STRING
    If KeyAscii >= Asc("A") And KeyAscii <= Asc("Z") Then
        sLstSearch = sLstSearch & Chr$(KeyAscii)
    End If

    'DISPLAY SEARCH STRING
    lblSrchtext = sLstSearch

    'RE-CALCULATE LENGTH
    nSearchLen = Len(sLstSearch)

    'SIMPLE SEARCH - COMPARES EACH ITEM TO SEARCH STRING
    While nSearchPos < lstX.ListCount
        nResult = StrComp(sLstSearch, UCase$(Left$(lstX.List(nSearchPos),_\
nSearchLen)))
        If nResult <= 0 Then
            lstX.ListIndex = nSearchPos
            SearchListBox = 0
            Exit Function
        End If
```

```
            nSearchPos = nSearchPos + 1
    Wend

    'IF ITEM WAS NOT FOUND THEN MOVE TO END OF LIST
    lstX.ListIndex = lstX.ListCount - 1
    SearchListBox = 0

End Function

Private Sub lstSearch_KeyPress(KeyAscii As Integer)

    If KeyAscii = 13 Then Exit Sub

    KeyAscii = SearchListBox(Me.ActiveControl, KeyAscii)

End Sub

Private Sub tmrLoad_Timer()
    Dim sSQL As String
    Dim nTemp As Integer
    Dim rs As Recordset

    'MOVE TO THE NEXT LETTER IN THE ALPHABET
    If CurrentLetter = "" Then CurrentLetter = "A" Else CurrentLetter = _
                        Chr(Asc(CurrentLetter) + 1)

    'IF 'Z' ITEMS HAVE BEEN LOADED THEN STOP THE TIMER
    If CurrentLetter > "Z" Then
            tmrLoad.Enabled = False
            lblLoaded = CStr(lstSearch.ListCount) & " records "
            dbBiblio.Close
            Screen.MousePointer = vbDefault
            lstSearch.SetFocus
            Exit Sub
    End If

    'QUERY THE DATABASE AND ADD RECORDS TO THE LIST BOX
    sSQL = "SELECT Name From Publishers where Name Like '" & CurrentLetter & _
            "*' order by Name"
    Set rs = dbBiblio.OpenRecordset(sSQL)
    While Not rs.EOF
        lstSearch.AddItem CStr(rs.Fields("Name"))
        rs.MoveNext
    Wend
    rs.Close
    lblLoaded = "Loading " & lstSearch.ListCount & " records ..."
    lstSearch.SetFocus
    DoEvents

    'DISPLAY HOURGLASS IF WAITING ON DATA
    If sWaitForLetter = "" Then
        Screen.MousePointer = vbDefault
        Exit Sub
    Else
        Screen.MousePointer = vbHourglass
        nTemp = SearchListBox(lstSearch, Asc(Trim$(sWaitForLetter)))
    End If

End Sub
```

Effective Menus

Another important part of form design is creating consistent, effective menus. Here are some important guidelines:

- Follow standard Windows layout convention: File, Edit, View, and so on.
- Group menu items logically and concisely.
- Use separator bars to group related items in a drop-down menu.
- Avoid redundant menu entries.
- Avoid top-level menu bar items without drop-down menus.
- Don't forget to use the ellipsis (...) to denote menu entries that activate dialog boxes.
- Use standard shortcuts and hotkeys whenever possible.
- Put frequently used menu items in a toolbar.

The steps involved in using the Menu Editor and creating a pop-up menu are discussed in Chapter 6, "Giving More Control to the User: Menus and Toolbars."

▶ **See** "Creating Pop-Up Menus," **p. 122**

Handling Multiple Instances of Your Application

Most Windows programs are started when users double-click a shortcut icon or menu. If users have 10 programs open, they can switch among them by using the taskbar or pressing Alt+Tab. However, many users like to double-click the shortcut icon again, even if the program is already open. Some shortcuts, such as the My Computer icon in Windows 95, simply bring up the existing window, whereas others launch a new instance of the program. For example, you can open multiple instances of Microsoft Word by selecting it from the Start menu, but double-clicking an associated document's icon uses an existing copy of Word. To further complicate matters, the Microsoft Office toolbar checks for an active copy of Word and shows it before launching a new one.

If you provide a desktop or toolbar shortcut to your application, users may expect the shortcut to activate an existing application rather than start a new one. This is especially true if users fill out a form and then minimize it to the taskbar. They may click the shortcut expecting the form to reappear, but if you have not coded for this occurrence, another instance of your application is launched, and the users see an empty form.

For certain applications, allowing multiple instances running at the same time may be desirable. However, if you do not design this capability into your application, errors will surely occur. For example, multiple copies of your application might try to write to the same database at the same time. Fortunately, preventing users from accidentally launching extra copies of your application is easy. The following lines of code in the `Form_Load` event or `Sub Main` do the job:

```
If App.PrevInstance = True Then
    MsgBox "Application already running!"
    End
End If
```

The preceding lines of code check the `PrevInstance` property of the `App` object and end the program if another instance is already running. Although this code prevents conflicts and errors, it does not help the users because they still have to find the other application window manually. With a few additional API calls, you can have your program show the previous application before exiting. Listing 18.2 shows a simple routine to display the previous instance before exiting.

Listing 18.2 PREVINST.ZIP—Handling Multiple Application Instances

```
Option Explicit
Private Declare Function FindWindow Lib "user32" Alias "FindWindowA" _
                    (ByVal lpClassName As String, ByVal lpWindowName _
                    As String) As Long
Private Declare Function ShowWindow Lib "user32" (ByVal hwnd As Long, _
                    ByVal nCmdShow As Long) As Long
Private Declare Function SetForegroundWindow Lib "user32" (ByVal hwnd As Long) _
                    As Long
Private Const SW_RESTORE = 9

Private Sub Form_Load()
    Dim sTitle As String
    Dim hwnd As Long
    Dim lRetVal As Long

    If App.PrevInstance Then
        sTitle = Me.Caption

        App.Title = "newcopy"
        Me.Caption = "newcopy"

        hwnd = FindWindow(vbNullString, sTitle)
        If hwnd <> 0 Then
            lRetVal = ShowWindow(hwnd, SW_RESTORE)
            lRetVal = SetForegroundWindow(hwnd)
        End If
        End
    End If

End Sub
```

In the preceding code, you first rename the current application's title and form caption properties so that the `FindWindow` API function cannot find it. Then you use three API calls to find the window belonging to the previous application, restore it, and move it to the foreground. The Windows API functions are discussed in more detail in Chapter 20, "Accessing the Windows API."

> **N O T E** The methods for dealing with multiple instances described here pertain to a Standard EXE project. ActiveX DLLs are discussed in Chapter 16, "Classes: Reusable Components."

▶ **See** "Setting the Instancing Property," **p. 371**

Perceived Speed

Perception is reality. I am referring here to how users' *observations* can influence their like or dislike of your program. Application speed is a prime example. You may have written the fastest VB code ever, but it matters little if users think it runs slowly. VB programmers tend to get defensive when users complain about speed because "the users don't know what the program is doing." However, you can incorporate a few tricks to make your program seem faster.

The key to a program's perceived speed is that something needs to happen when a user clicks an icon. Users are more willing to wait if they think the computer is working as fast as it can. Booting Windows is a good example; it usually takes quite a long time. However, all the graphics, beeps, and hard drive noise keep you distracted enough to make the wait acceptable. The techniques discussed in the following sections give you suggestions for creating "faster" VB applications.

Program Startup Time   At the beginning of your program, you probably will have some initialization to perform—for example, opening a network database. The `Sub Main` subroutine is an excellent place for all the initialization code required at startup time. If your program has only a few forms (two to five), you can load all of them during `Sub Main` so that they appear quickly when the application needs to show them. Although loading all these forms slows the application's performance at startup, the application's runtime performance is much faster. The `Load` method places the forms in memory, but they remain invisible to the users until the `Show` method is executed.

However, this technique may cause program startup time to get a bit lengthy, so displaying a *splash screen* during load time is a good idea. A splash screen (see Figure 18.9) displays information about the program and its designer, as well as indicates to the users that some action is happening.

FIGURE 18.9
This splash screen gives the users something to look at while program initialization takes place.

> **TIP**   If you are updating a label's caption on a splash or status screen, make sure to call `DoEvents` or the label's `Refresh` method so that program initialization does not prevent the label from being updated.

Inform the Users of Progress   When your application looks like it is doing something, users tend to be more forgiving of long wait times. One way to keep them informed is to use a ProgressBar control on your form. If you are updating records in a database, you can use a progress bar to indicate the number of records processed so far. To do so, simply add an extra line of code or two to update the progress bar as you move to the next record.

▶ **See** "Adding a Status Bar to Your Program," **p. 279**

However, sometimes the progress bar is not an option. For example, Visual Basic's `FileCopy` command might take some time depending on the size of the file. However, `FileCopy` is a self-contained statement, so you have no place to insert the progress bar update code. In this case, a video would be an easy alternative. Before starting the file copy, display a video with the animation control. Windows 95 uses this trick when copying files and emptying the Recycle Bin. The users see the video and think that it is linked to the file copy in progress when, in fact, it is a separate process running by itself.

▶ **See** "Setting Up the Animation Control," **p. 285**

From Here...

Although no steps guarantee a successful user interface, a bad user interface will certainly guarantee that no one will use the program. However, with the rapid pace of advances in computing, the definition of what is a "good" interface will surely keep changing. Consider, for example, the process of setting a VCR clock. Early VCR clocks were programmed with buttons and switches, but this method was soon replaced with onscreen displays. Now an over-the-air radio signal makes the whole process automatic in some models. Like the VCR example, your Visual Basic user interfaces will evolve over time, as the industry sets knew standards and you learn how to best meet your users' expectations.

For more information on the topics dicussed in this chapter, check out the following chapters:

- If you want to learn about the different types of controls that are available, see Chapter 4, "Using Visual Basic's Default Controls."
- For more details on creating menus and other UI elements, see Chapter 6, "Giving More Control to the User: Menus and Toolbars."
- To find out additional information on creating your own ActiveX components with class modules, see Chapter 16, "Classes: Reusable Components."
- To understand how to develop an MDI application, see Chapter 17, "Multiple Document Interface Applications."
- To learn more details about designing user interfaces, see Chapter 19, "Using Visual Design Elements."

CHAPTER 19

Using Visual Design Elements

In this chapter

Using Graphics 426

Working with Text and Fonts 439

In Chapter 18, "Proper Interface Design," you learned how to design the visual portion of your program in order to provide an appropriately usable and aesthetically pleasing interface for the users. This chapter continues that discussion to explore some of the design elements that you can use to give your programs a professional appearance.

Using Graphics

A typical user interface for an application consists of a menu, labels, text boxes, command buttons, and perhaps a few controls for specific pieces of data. However, without graphics, an otherwise functional interface can be quite boring and unintuitive. Graphics can be used to enhance the user interface in the following ways:

- Highlighting specific information on the screen
- Providing a different view of the information, such as using a graph
- Providing a more intuitive link to the application's functions

The subject of design and use of graphics is large and complex. Obviously, then, this single chapter cannot cover all the bases. However, it provides you with enough information so that you can begin building a more visually pleasing user interface.

You can use graphics in two basic ways in VB: *controls* and *methods*. For example, you can draw a line on a form either by placing a Line control on the form or by using the `Line` method.

N O T E The Windows API also contains many graphics-related functions. See Chapter 20, "Accessing the Windows API," for information on accessing these functions.

Graphics controls work just like any other custom controls in that they have events and properties and can be drawn at designtime with the mouse. Graphics methods are functions you can call from within the VB language at runtime. Although you can think of graphics controls as objects *placed* on the form, graphics methods draw on the form itself.

Graphics Controls

Visual Basic's Toolbox includes several graphics controls. Some of these controls, such as the Line control, are simple controls intended to act as visual enhancements by themselves. Others, such as the PictureBox control, include a variety of properties and methods to allow extended functionality. Each of the VB graphics controls is discussed in the following sections.

Using the Line and Shape Controls The Line and Shape controls provide the easiest means to add a graphic element to a form. You can draw the controls on the form at designtime and place them where you need them. During the execution of a program, these controls can be hidden or moved. Setting the appropriate property values in your code can change their colors.

As you would guess by its name, the Line control places a line on the form. You can control the width of the line, the line style, the color, and the position of the terminal points of the line through the control's properties. For example, start a new Standard EXE project and place a Line control on the form. Then enter the following code in the form's `Resize` event:

```
Private Sub Form_Resize()
    'A FORM'S (0,0) COORDINATES
    'ARE IN ITS UPPER-LEFT CORNER

    Line1.Y1 = Form1.ScaleHeight / 2
    Line1.X1 = 0

    Line1.X2 = Form1.ScaleWidth
    Line1.Y2 = Line1.Y1

End Sub
```

The code in the Resize event adjusts the size and position of the line so that it remains a horizontal line in the center of the form. By default, a Line control creates a solid line, but you can create dashed or other line styles by setting the BorderStyle property. Figure 19.1 shows several Line controls drawn on a form using the various styles and the BorderStyle property options for the Line control.

FIGURE 19.1
The Line control enables you to place lines of various styles on a form.

NOTE The BorderStyle property does not have any effect when the BorderWidth property is greater than one.

The Shape control provides another simple means of placing graphics elements on a form. You can use the Shape control to create any of the six shapes shown in Figure 19.2. As with the Line control, the BorderStyle property can be used to change the style of the line used to draw a shape.

FIGURE 19.2
You can change the Shape property of the Shape control to create any of the shapes pictured.

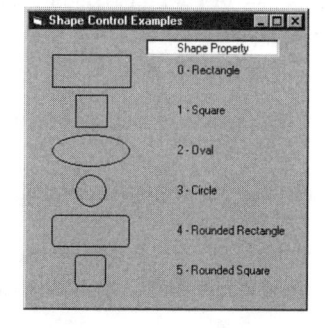

> **NOTE** Although a Shape control placed behind a set of controls can appear to visually enclose other controls, it cannot act as a *container* for those controls.

▶ See "Using Containers," **p. 66**

Although you can set the Shape control to several different types of shapes, it does not use mathematical coordinates as the Line control does. Instead, you use the `Height` and `Width` properties to set the size of a shape.

Pictures and Images   Another way to enhance your user interface with graphics is to place actual pictures on your form. These pictures can be loaded into the Image and PictureBox controls or on the form itself. Some possible sources for pictures are drawings you have created in a paint program or 35mm photos converted to files by your scanner. The types of files you can display are listed in Table 19.1.

Table 19.1 Graphics File Formats Compatible with Visual Basic

File Extension	Type of File
.BMP	Windows bitmap file
.DIB	Device Independent Bitmap file
.ICO, .CUR	Icon
.WMF	Windows metafile
.EMF	Enhanced Windows metafile
.GIF	Graphics Interchange Format; a file format originally developed by CompuServe and used on Internet Web pages
.JPG	JPEG images, named after the Joint Photographic Experts Group; similar to GIF but uses compression to reduce file size; used extensively on Internet Web pages

Using the *Picture* Property   The PictureBox control, Image control, and form all have a `Picture` property that can be set either at designtime or runtime. Loading an image file at designtime is easy. Try a simple example by placing an image on a form, as shown here:

1. Start a new project, and bring up the Properties window for the form.
2. Click the ellipsis button at the far right of the line to call up the Load Picture dialog box, shown in Figure 19.3.
3. From the Load Picture dialog box, select a picture file. The selected picture then appears on your form.

> **NOTE** Files loaded at designtime are stored saved with your form, which can increase program size and form load time.

FIGURE 19.3
To place a picture in a form, PictureBox, or Image control at designtime, use the Load Picture dialog box. Pictures can also be loaded during program execution.

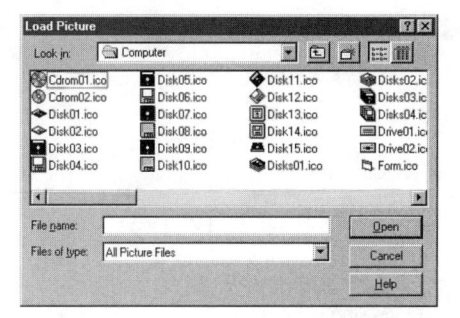

While your program is running, pictures can be moved from one control to another by assigning the `Picture` property or can be loaded from a file type listed in Table 19.1. To set the `Picture` property from a file, use the `LoadPicture` method. The following code sample shows you how to load pictures on a form, Image control, and PictureBox control at runtime:

```
'Examples of Loading pictures
Form1.Picture = LoadPicture("C:\MYPIC.BMP")
Image1.Picture = LoadPicture("D:\PAMELA.JPG")
Picture1.Picture = image1.PicturePicture1.Picture = LoadPicture("")
```

Note that passing an empty string to the `LoadPicture` function clears the current picture. Visual Basic also has a `SavePicture` statement, which is used to save pictures from the `Picture` property to a disk file. However, some limitations do exist on the file formats that can be saved. Although the `LoadPicture` function works with GIF or JPG files, the `SavePicture` function does not save in those formats. Pictures saved from the `Image` control are always saved in BMP format. For a complete list of restrictions, look up `SavePicture` in the Help index.

Loading Pictures on a Form A picture loaded on a form has a relatively fixed behavior, much like background wallpaper in Windows. The picture starts in the upper-left corner and is not sized or scaled in any way to match the size of the form. If the picture is smaller than the form, space is left below and to the right of the picture. If the picture is larger than the form, the entire picture is still loaded, but only part of it is visible. As the form is resized, the amount of the picture shown changes.

With the exception of the Label and Shape controls, the picture does not show through the background of the controls on the form. The Label and Shape controls allow the picture to show through if the `BackStyle` property of the control is set to `Transparent`. Figure 19.4 illustrates controls placed on a form containing a picture. Note how the background picture shows through the Label control just above the text box.

> **TIP**
> You cannot resize a picture that is placed directly on a form. If you want the picture to be a different size, you need to resize the original graphic file using a graphics utility.

The key advantage to placing your picture directly on the form is that this method uses fewer system resources than placing the picture in a Picture or Image control. Another benefit of placing the picture on the form is that you can use drawing methods to annotate the picture.

FIGURE 19.4
Some controls placed on a form do not allow the picture to show through.

For example, you can display a product's picture and then, by using the Print method, overlay the price or other database information on top of the picture. This capability is available with the PictureBox control as well but is not available with the Image control.

> **TIP** Placing a graphic image directly on a form is an excellent way to provide a texture or background image behind the rest of the form's objects.

Placing the picture directly on the form does, however, have several drawbacks, including the following:

- You cannot hide the picture; it can only be loaded or unloaded.
- You cannot control the placement of the picture on the form.
- You can place only one picture at a time on the form.
- You cannot resize the picture. It's placed on the form in its original (saved) size.

You can overcome these drawbacks by using the Picture or Image control.

Using the Image Control Using an Image control to display pictures provides a frame for the picture, allowing you to position it anywhere on the form. Another advantage is that the Image control can not only display pictures, but it also can resize them. The Stretch property determines whether the Image control is sized to fit the picture or the picture is sized to fit the control as drawn. If the Stretch property is set to False (the default), the Image control is automatically resized to fit the picture you assign to it. If the Stretch property is set to True, the picture is automatically resized so that the entire picture fits within the current boundaries of the Image control.

You can test this behavior at designtime by assigning a picture to an Image control, setting the `Stretch` property to `True`, and resizing the control. Figure 19.5 shows the same picture in several Image controls. The one with the `Stretch` property set to `False` shows the image at its original size, and others show some possible effects of resizing the Image control if the `Stretch` property is set to `True`.

FIGURE 19.5
The `Stretch` property of the Image control allows you to resize a picture.

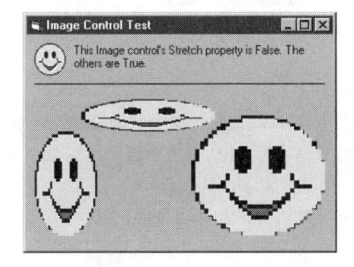

> **TIP** If you are loading pictures of different sizes into an Image control in your application, you should set the `Stretch` property to `True`. Otherwise, the size of the Image control changes with each picture. If the appearance of the pictures is unsuitable due to stretching, consider using the PictureBox control. It may be more desirable in some circumstances, such as a displaying a person's photograph, to hide some of the picture rather than show it all distorted.

Using the PictureBox Control Although the PictureBox control uses more system resources than the Image control, it has some added features. First, it can be used as a container for other controls, allowing you to treat controls drawn within it as a group. In addition, you can use drawing methods (for example, `Line` and `Print`) to draw on the picture box.

To use the picture box as a container, first draw a picture box on your form. Next, select a control from the toolbox, and draw the control within the boundaries of the picture box. When you move the picture box or set its `Visible` property, the controls contained within it are also affected.

The most striking difference between the Image and PictureBox is that the PictureBox does not allow resizing of the picture. The default behavior of the PictureBox control is to show only as much of a picture as can fit in its current boundaries. If the picture is larger than the PictureBox control, the upper-left corner of the picture is shown. If the picture is smaller than the PictureBox control, space is left around the edges of the picture. In either case, the entire picture, displayed or not, is loaded in the PictureBox control and available if the control is resized. Setting the `AutoSize` property to `True` changes this default behavior, causing the PictureBox control to resize itself to fit the current picture. As with the Image control, the top-left corner of the control is anchored in place, and resizing of the control occurs to the right and down. However, don't confuse the `AutoSize` property with the Image control's `Stretch` property; the PictureBox control always preserves the aspect ratio of the picture being shown, regardless of the dimensions of the PictureBox control. Figure 19.6 shows the same picture in each of two PictureBox controls—one with the `AutoSize` property set to `False` and the other with the `AutoSize` property set to `True`.

FIGURE 19.6

The `AutoSize` property determines whether the PictureBox control changes to fit the size of the picture being displayed. Note that the size of the picture itself does not change.

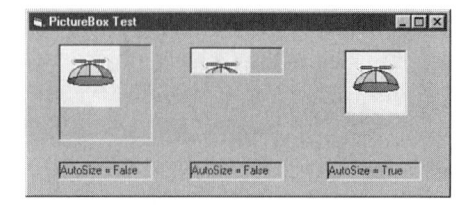

The easiest way to understand how the `AutoSize` property works is to create a simple test application. First, create a standard project with a file list box and a picture box. Then place the following code in the form:

```
Private Sub Form_Load()
    Picture1.AutoSize = True
    File1.Path = "C:\Windows"
    File1.Pattern = "*.BMP"
End Sub

Private Sub File1_Click()
    Picture1.Picture = LoadPicture(File1.Path & "\" & File1.filename)
End Sub
```

As you click a filename in the file list box, notice that the size of the picture box adjusts itself to the size of the loaded picture. Often this type of behavior would be undesirable because the picture box might cover other controls. In that case, you can use an image control or display the picture on a separate form.

Graphics Methods

Using controls is not the only way to add graphics to your application. Visual Basic also provides several methods that you can use to draw on a form or in a PictureBox control. You also can use them with the `Printer` object to send the output to the printer. If no object is specified with the method, the form that currently has focus receives the output of the methods.

You can use the following methods to create many types of graphics images:

- `Line`. This method draws a line or a box.
- `Circle`. This method draws a circle or oval.
- `PSet`. This method places a single point on the target object.
- `Point`. This method returns the color of a specific point.
- `PaintPicture`. This method draws an image stored in another control onto the target object.
- `Cls`. This method clears the output area of the target object.
- `Print`. This method places text on the target object.

You can use each of the preceding methods to draw on an object. Before I cover each method in more detail, though, I should mention that certain properties of the object being drawn on affect the way these methods work. These properties are listed in Table 19.2.

Table 19.2 Drawing Properties That Affect the Appearance of Graphics

Property Name	Purpose
DrawMode	Determines how the drawing color interacts with the colors already present on the object
DrawStyle	Sets a drawing pattern
DrawWidth	Sets the border width of lines and circles
FillColor	Determines the color used to fill a rectangle or circle
FillStyle	Determines the pattern used to fill a rectangle or circle
ForeColor	Determines the primary color used to draw with the graphics methods, if no color is specified in the method call
AutoRedraw	Determines whether the output of the graphics methods is automatically refreshed when the window has been obscured (Form and PictureBox only)

Lines and Circles You use the Line method to draw lines and boxes. To draw lines, supply the starting and ending points of the line on a coordinate system whose origin is in the upper-left corner. The following statements, for example, draw a green line from the upper-left corner of a form to the lower-right corner:

```
Dim x2 As Single, y2 As Single
x2 = Form1.ScaleWidth
y2 = Form1.ScaleHeight
Line (0, 0)-(x2, y2),vbGreen
```

If you omit the starting point of the line, the current position becomes the starting point. The current position is the ending point of the last line, or you can set it with the object's CurrentX and CurrentY properties. For example, the following code uses the Line method to draw a triangle on a form. In each call to the Line method, note that the first set of coordinates is omitted.

```
Private Sub Form_Click()
    Form1.CurrentX = 1500
    Form1.CurrentY = 750
    Line -(2000, 750), vbRed
    Line -(2000, 1250), vbBlue
    Line -(1500, 750)
End Sub
```

In the last of the preceding code segment statements, the optional parameter for the color of the line is omitted. If no color is specified, the line is drawn in the color specified in the object's

ForeColor property. You can add the optional parameter B or BF after the color parameter to draw boxes and filled boxes, respectively. For example, the following statements draw two boxes on a form:

```
Line (100, 850)-(500, 1800), vbBlue, B
Line -(900, 2450), , BF
```

When you're drawing a box, the coordinates passed to the Line method represent the upper-left and lower-right corners of the box.

The Circle method also has many optional parameters. The simplest form of the method is the following:

```
Circle (X,Y),R
```

This command draws a circle of radius R with a center at the position specified by X and Y. As with the Line method, the pattern and color of the circle's border and fill are determined by the settings of the object's properties. The full syntax of the Circle method is as follows:

```
Object.Circle [Step] (x,y), radius, [color, start, end, aspect]
```

The *start* and *end* arguments are used to draw an arc rather than a full circle. The values of *start* and *end* are the angles from horizontal expressed in radians. (The value of an angle in radians is determined by multiplying the angle in degrees by /180.) The values of *start* and *end* can range from zero to 2, or zero to –2. If you use a negative value for *start* and *end*, the lines are drawn from the center of the circle to both ends of the arc. The following code produces an arc that appears to move around a circle, much like a radar screen:

```
Private Sub Form_Click()
    Const PI = 3.14159
    Const ARCSIZE = 45
    Dim x As Integer, y As Integer, r As Integer
    Dim arcstart As Single, arcend As Single
    Dim nCount As Integer

    'Draw a circle in the middle of the form
    x = Me.ScaleWidth / 2
    y = Me.ScaleHeight / 2
    r = x / 2
    Me.DrawMode = vbCopyPen
    Me.FillStyle = vbFSTransparent
    Me.Circle (x, y), r

    'Draw the sweeping radar arc
    Me.DrawMode = vbXorPen
    Me.FillColor = vbRed
    Me.FillStyle = vbSolid

    For nCount = 0 To 360
        arcstart = nCount
        arcend = nCount + ARCSIZE
        If arcend > 360 Then arcend = arcend - 360
        Me.Caption = "Arc of " & ARCSIZE & " degrees starting at " _
                     & nCount
        Circle (x, y), r, , -arcstart * PI / 180, -arcend * PI / 180
        DoEvents
```

```
        Circle (x, y), r, , -arcstart * PI / 180, -arcend * PI / 180
    Next nCount

        Me.Caption = "Done"
End Sub
```

The *Print* Method   Although you might not traditionally associate the `Print` method with graphics because it produces text, it is a graphics method in that it "draws" the text on your object like any other graphics method. You can use the `Print` method in conjunction with other graphics methods to create charts or drawings or to annotate existing bitmaps. The `Print` method itself is quite simple. The following code displays a single line of text at the current position on the form:

```
Print "This is a one-line test."
```

The output of the `Print` method is controlled by the properties of the object being printed on. These properties are as follow:

- `CurrentX`. This property sets the horizontal position for the starting point of the text.
- `CurrentY`. This property sets the vertical position for the starting point of the text.
- `Font`. This property determines the font type and size used for the text.
- `ForeColor`. This property determines the color of the text.
- `FontTransparent`. On a form or picture, this property determines whether the background behind the text shows through the spaces in the text.

You can experiment with printing and other graphics methods by using Visual Basic's Immediate window. Follow these steps:

1. Create a new project and add a PictureBox control.
2. Set the form and picture box's `AutoRedraw` properties to `True`.
3. Run your project and then press Ctrl+Break.
4. Enter code statements that use graphics methods in the Immediate window:

```
form1.print "Hey"
picture1.Print "Now"
```

The *PSet* Method   You can use the `PSet` method to draw a single point on the form using the color specified by the `ForeColor` property. The size of the point drawn is dependent on the setting of the `DrawWidth` property. A larger `DrawWidth` setting produces a larger point. The `PSet` method draws the point at the coordinates specified in the argument of the method. The following code draws 100 points at random positions on the current form:

```
Dim i As Integer, x As Integer, y As Integer

    Me.DrawWidth = 5

    For i = 1 To 100
        'Choose random x and y
        x = Int(Me.ScaleWidth + 1) * Rnd
        y = Int(Me.ScaleHeight + 1) * Rnd
        PSet (x, y)
    Next i
```

The *PaintPicture* Method The `PaintPicture` method works exactly like it sounds; it paints a picture from one object onto another. By carefully setting the `height` and `width` arguments for the source and target objects, you can enlarge or reduce the size of the source picture. The following code paints part of a picture from a PictureBox control onto a form:

```
frmdest.PaintPicture picSource.Picture, 50, 50, 750, 750, 0, 0, 500, 500
```

The code in the preceding line takes a piece of a picture from the PictureBox control `picSource`, enlarges it, and places it on the form `frmDest`. As you can see, the `PaintPicture` method contains several arguments:

- **Source Picture.** All or part of this source picture is drawn in a "target region" on the destination object.
- **Target X and Y.** These two numerical arguments specify the coordinates of the upper-left corner of the target region. In the preceding line of code, drawing occurs on `frmDest` 50 scale units (in this case twips) from the left edge and 50 scale units from the top edge.
- **Target Size.** This argument specifies the horizontal and vertical size of the target region. If this size is different from the source picture or region, the picture is stretched or compressed to fit the target region.
- **Source X and Y.** The third pair of numbers in the command specifies the upper-left corner of the source region—that is, the part of the picture being copied.
- **Source Size.** This argument specifies the height and width of the source region.

These first three arguments are the only ones that are required for the `PaintPicture` method. All other arguments are optional. If only the three required arguments are specified, the entire source picture is copied to the target at full size.

The following are some uses of the `PaintPicture` method in creating graphics:

- To provide a zoom feature for looking more closely at specific regions of a picture. This capability would be useful for implementing print preview in your application.
- To copy or clear a specified region of a picture.
- To move the contents of a PictureBox control to the `Printer` object—for example, to put a company logo on your report.

For an example that uses `PaintPicture` and some of the other methods discussed so far, see the application in Figure 19.7.

This application captures song title and artist information from a satellite TV music service. Here's how it works:

1. Code in a Timer control activates the "Snappy" video capture device to capture the current picture on the TV screen. The result of the video capture is stored in the `Picture` property of the Snappy custom control.
2. The `PaintPicture` method is used to copy the bottom section with the displayed song information from the Snappy control to the larger PictureBox control at the right of the form.

FIGURE 19.7
You can use the `PaintPicture` method to combine parts from several images into a single composite image.

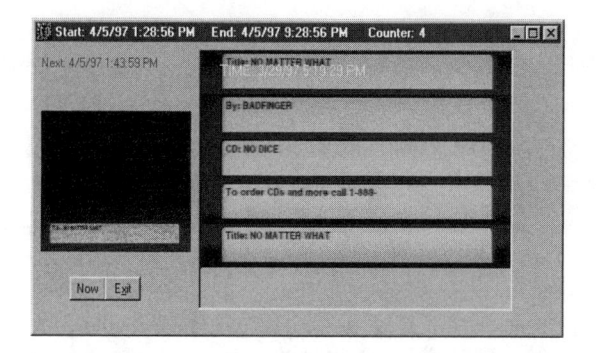

3. The process is repeated several times so that all the information is captured in a composite picture in the PictureBox control.
4. The tape counter information is added to the PictureBox control with the `Print` method, and the `SavePicture` method saves the image to disk. The entire process repeats itself in a few minutes for the next song.
5. The resulting bitmap files provide a means to locate your favorite songs on tape.

Other Graphics Methods Two other methods mentioned in the list in the earlier section "Graphics Methods" are the `Cls` method and the `Point` method. The `Cls` method, which stands for *Clear Screen* like the DOS command, clears all graphics drawn with graphics methods from a form or PictureBox control. The `Point` method returns the RGB color setting of a specified point, as in the following example:

```
Private Sub Form_Load()
    'Draw a red box
    Me.AutoRedraw = True
    Line (0, 0)-(500, 500), vbRed, BF

End Sub

Private Sub Form_MouseDown(Button As Integer,_
       Shift As Integer, X As Single, Y As Single)
    If Point(X, Y) = vbRed Then
        MsgBox "The point (" & X & "," & Y & ") is in the box"
    Else
        MsgBox "The point is not in the box"
    End If

End Sub
```

The code in the `MouseDown` event uses the `Point` method to determine whether the location clicked by the user is within the red box drawn during the form load.

Finally, although coverage of graphics API in detail is beyond the scope of this chapter, you should note that some graphics API calls allow you to do things that ordinary graphics methods do not. For example, consider the ListView control, which works like the far right pane of the Windows Explorer. In the report view (or detail mode in Explorer), selecting an item highlights only the left column, making it difficult to read one row all the way across. However, you can use the graphics API to draw your own lines across the columns. The example in Listing 19.1 uses a few API calls to do just that.

Listing 19.1 DRAWAPI.ZIP—Using the Graphics API to Enhance a *ListView* Control

```
Private Declare Function GetDC Lib "user32" (ByVal hwnd As Long) _
                    As Long
Private Declare Function ReleaseDC Lib "user32" (ByVal hwnd As Long, _
                    ByVal hdc As Long) As Long
Private Declare Function LineTo Lib "gdi32" (ByVal hdc As Long, _
                    ByVal X As Long, ByVal Y As Long) As Long
Private Declare Function MoveToEx Lib "gdi32" (ByVal hdc As Long, _
                    ByVal X As Long, ByVal Y As Long, _
                    lpPoint As POINTAPI) As Long

Private Type POINTAPI
        X As Long
        Y As Long
End Type

Private Sub Form_Load()

    'This code adds 100 items to a listview control

    Dim objTemp As ListItem
    Dim i As Integer
    Me.ScaleMode = 3

    With Me.ListView1
        .View = lvwReport
        .ColumnHeaders.Add , , "Column1"
        .ColumnHeaders.Add , , "Column2"
        For i = 1 To 100
                Set objTemp = .ListItems.Add(, , "Item " & i)
                objTemp.SubItems(1) = "Top " & objTemp.Top
                .Refresh
        Next i
    End With

End Sub

Private Sub ListView1_ItemClick(ByVal Item As ComctlLib.ListItem)
    Dim hdc As Long
    Dim pointx As POINTAPI
    Dim lRetVal As Long
    Dim nHeight As Integer
    Dim lTemp As Long

    'The form's ScaleMode property MUST be
    'set to pixels for this to work properly.

    nHeight = Me.TextHeight("X")

    With ListView1
        .Refresh
        hdc = GetDC(.hwnd)
```

```
            lTemp = MoveToEx(hdc, 0, Item.Top, pointx)
            lTemp = LineTo(hdc, .Width, Item.Top)
            lTemp = MoveToEx(hdc, 0, Item.Top + nHeight, pointx)
            lTemp = LineTo(hdc, .Width, Item.Top + nHeight)
            lTemp = ReleaseDC(.hwnd, hdc)
    End With

End Sub
```

The code in Listing 19.1 demonstrates one of the basic concepts of using graphics API calls: the device context. A device context can be used by other graphics API calls to draw on an object. The example uses the `GetDC` API call to determine the device context for the ListView control and then uses the `LineTo` API call to draw on the ListView control.

Working with Text and Fonts

To write almost any program in Visual Basic, you need to know how to work with text. In earlier chapters, you learned something about displaying text in labels and text boxes. You also learned about string functions used to manipulate text in code. This chapter will expand on that knowledge by showing you how to display text in a way that is most intuitive to the users of your programs.

Text Box Behavior

In Chapter 4, "Using Visual Basic's Default Controls," you were introduced to the text box. You already know that the `Text` property is used to store and retrieve information. In addition to the standard properties discussed in that chapter, several other properties make the TextBox control even more versatile:

- `Locked`. This property prevents the users from entering information in the text box.
- `MaxLength`. This property limits the number of characters that the text box can accept.
- `PasswordChar`. This property causes the text box to hide the information typed by the users.
- `SelLength`, `SelStart`, and `SelText`. These properties allow the users to manipulate only the selected (highlighted) part of the text in the text box.

Locking Out Users First, take a look at the `Locked` property, which allows you to use a text box for display only. The obvious question is why would you want to do that instead of just using a Label control? The answer is that although a locked text box does not allow users to update it, they still can scroll, select, and copy text. Of course, program code can always modify text in a text box whether or not it is locked. To lock a text box, simply set the `Locked` property to `True`, as in the following examples:

```
'LOCKS A SINGLE TEXT BOX
txtTest.Locked = True
txtTest.Text = "You can't edit this!"
```

```
'LOCKS EVERY TEXT BOX ON THE FORM
Dim objControl As Control

For Each objControl In Me.Controls
    If TypeOf objControl Is TextBox Then objControl.Locked = True
Next objControl
```

From a user interface standpoint, the Locked property allows you to use the same screen for data entry and lookup. Locking text boxes prevents unauthorized personnel from changing information, as shown in Figure 19.8.

FIGURE 19.8
Using the Locked property prevents inadvertent editing of text. In the pop-up menu (automatically implemented by Windows), notice that only the Copy option is available for a locked text box.

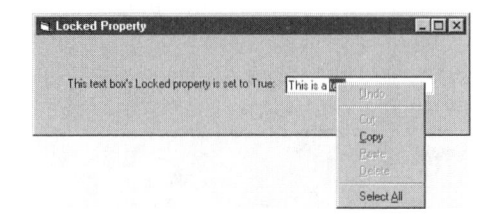

NOTE Do not confuse the Locked property with the Enabled property. The Locked property does not create the grayed-out effect. Additionally, it allows the users to select and copy text from the text box, but the Enabled property does not.

The *MaxLength* Property When you're designing a data entry form, one of the tasks you must perform is *data validation*. One type of data validation is making sure the data entered will fit in the designated database field. For example, Social Security numbers are by definition nine digits. Although this check can be performed in VB code with the Len statement, you can avoid the extra code by using the TextBox control's MaxLength property. The MaxLength property allows you to specify the maximum number of characters that can be entered in a text box, regardless of its size on the form.

The *PasswordChar* Property If you are using a text box as part of a login form, you will want to be able to hide the passwords entered by the users. To do so, simply enter a character in the PasswordChar property of the text box. This property changes the text box's display behavior so that the password character is displayed in place of each character in the Text property. You may have seen this effect many times when logging in to Windows.

Note that the contents of the Text property still reflect what was actually typed by the users, and your code always sees the "real" text. Although you can enter any character, using the asterisk (*) character for hiding text is customary.

Editing Text in a Text Box A standard text box allows the users to highlight text with the mouse or by using Ctrl+Shift with the cursor keys. Your code can then manipulate the selected text with the SelText, SelLength, and SelStart properties. You can use these properties to work with a selected piece of text in your program. Look at the example in Figure 19.9. In this case, the `SelText` property would contain just the phrase "jumped over the lazy dog." The `SelLength` property would contain the integer value 25, which is the length of that string. And the `SelStart` property would contain the integer value 20, which means the selected phrase starts with the 20th character in the text box.

FIGURE 19.9
Your users can copy text from one text box and paste it into another.

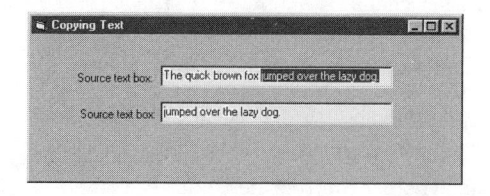

In addition to determining what has been selected, you can also set the properties from code to alter the selection. Every time you set the `SelStart` property, you must set the `SelLength` property to highlight some characters. To select the first three characters, you could use this code:

```
txtTest.SelStart = 0
txtTest.SelLength = 3
```

The `SelLength` property can be changed multiple times. This causes the selection to increase or decrease in size, automatically updating the `SelText` property. Setting the `SelText` property from code causes the currently selected text to be replaced with a new string—for example:

```
txtTest.SelText = "jumped into oncoming traffic."
```

One use of these properties is to highlight the entire contents of a text box. Suppose, for example, you have populated some text boxes for users to edit. When they press the Tab key to move to a text box, you might want to highlight whatever is in the text box automatically. This way, the user can start typing immediately, without deleting the existing text. This example is illustrated in the following code for a text box's `GotFocus` event:

```
Private Sub txtSelect_GotFocus()
  txtSelect.SelStart = 0
  txtSelect.SelLength = Len(txtSelect.Text)
End Sub
```

This same feature can be added by using the `SendKeys` statement to send the keystrokes for highlighting the entire text box:

```
Private Sub txtSelect_GotFocus()
  SendKeys ("{HOME}+{END}")
End Sub
```

Working with Fonts and Colors

Although drawings and pictures add a definite visual impact to your applications, the heart and soul of most of your programs will likely be the text fields for data entry and information display. Often, adding an image to enhance onscreen text is not possible or even useful. Instead, you must make sure that you use appropriate fonts and colors to get your point across.

Using the *Font* Object If you have used a word processor program, then you are already familiar with fonts. At designtime, you assign fonts to controls and forms by using the Properties window. If you set the font of a form, any controls subsequently drawn on the form will use the same font.

You may remember from earlier chapters that the `Font` property of an object is actually an object that has its own properties. The following `Font` object properties can be used to control the appearance of fonts in your program:

- `Name`. String identifier for one of the fonts installed on your system—for example, `"Arial"` or `"Times New Roman"`.
- `Bold`. True/False property that controls the boldface attribute of the font. The bold letters appear darker and heavier than nonbold characters.
- `Italic`. True/False property that determines whether letters are *italicized*.
- `Underline`. True/False property that controls whether the text is displayed with a thin line under each character.
- `Size`. Controls the point size of a font. One point is 1/72 of an inch; therefore, capital letters in a 72-point font are about one inch high.
- `Strikethrough`. True/False property that controls whether a thin line is drawn through the middle of the text.
- `Weight`. Controls the width of the line used to draw text. The two settings for `Weight` are 400 and 700. These settings correspond to normal and bold text, respectively.
- `Charset`. Controls the character set (standard, extended DOS, Japanese). This property is explained in more detail in the Help file.

As you may have already noticed, before you can set a particular font, you have to know its name. Not all systems have the same fonts installed. The `Screen` and `Printer` objects have a `Fonts` collection that lists the available fonts. You can write a quick program to list the available fonts on your system. Start a new project now and place the following code in the form's `Click` event. Clicking the form causes the name of each installed font to be printed on the form:

```
Dim nCount As Integer
Me.AutoRedraw = True
For nCount = 0 To Screen.FontCount - 1
  Me.Font.Name = Screen.Fonts(nCount)
  Me.Print Screen.Fonts(nCount)
Next nCount
```

Also, note that most fonts contain extra characters, beyond those that you can type on the keyboard. For example, the MS Sans Serif font contains special characters for fractions and accented letters. These characters can be displayed by using the `Chr$` function. The following code displays all 256 available characters (many of which are unprintable) on the form:

```
Dim i As Integer

For i = 0 To 255
    Me.Print Chr$(i); " ";
    If Me.CurrentX >= Me.Width Then Me.Print
Next i
```

Adding a Splash of Color A form designed with totally battleship gray components is dull and plain. However, you can easily assign color to the form and controls on it by using the `ForeColor` and `BackColor` properties. To set these properties at designtime, you can use either a Color list or a Color Palette. To view the Color list, bring up the Properties window for a control or form and click on the `ForeColor` or `BackColor` property. The Color list is shown in Figure 19.10.

FIGURE 19.10
You can set the `ForeColor` and `BackColor` properties from the Color list.

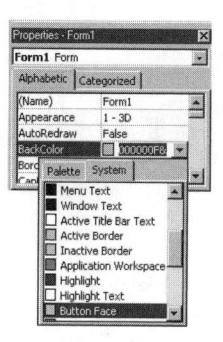

Notice that the Color list has two sections: Palette and System. Palette allows you to pick specific colors, whereas System lists the colors in the current Windows color scheme. If you use System colors, changing the Windows system colors in the Display control panel makes the colors in your program change, too. Considering this point is important when you're distributing a program.

The Color Palette, shown in Figure 19.11, allows you to change foreground and background colors at the same time. To view the Color Palette, select a control or form and then choose Color Palette from the View menu.

FIGURE 19.11
The Color Palette box is another means of changing colors at designtime.

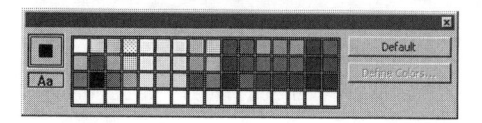

Change colors at designtime and then look at the `ForeColor` or `BackColor` properties. Notice that they are actually represented as numbers; for example, blue is represented by &HFF0000& in hexadecimal or decimal 16711680. VB also has built-in constants for some colors, listed in Table 19.3. To set colors of objects within your program code, simply assign numbers to the `ForeColor` and `BackColor` properties, as in the following code:

```
Form1.ForeColor = vbYellow
Form1.BackColor = vbBlue
```

Table 19.3 Visual Basic's Built-In Color Constants

Constant	Numeric Value (Decimal)
vbBlack	0
vbRed	255
vbGreen	65280
vbYellow	65535
vbBlue	16711680
vbMagenta	16711935
vbCyan	16776960
vbWhite	16777215

NOTE System color constants are also available. For example, the following statement sets the color of a form to the same color as the Windows desktop:

```
Form1.BackColor = vbDesktop n
```

The color constants use such unusual numbers because each number represents the levels of red, green, and blue in a given color. If you want to create a custom color and know how much of each primary color to include, you can find out the color number by using the RGB function. Each primary color can have a setting between 0 and 255. For example, the following code determines the number for the color gray (equal parts red, green, and blue):

```
Dim lNewColor As Long
lNewColor = RGB(192,192,192)
Form1.BackColor = lNewColor
```

NOTE An easy way to find out a color number for use in code is to select the color from the Color list and make a note of the number displayed in the Properties window.

Another useful color function is the QBColor function. In earlier versions of BASIC, such as QuickBasic and GWBasic for MS-DOS, consecutive integer numbers represented colors. The QBColor function returns the hexadecimal RGB equivalent color. This capability is useful if you want to generate random colors, as in the following example:

```
Private Sub Form_Click()

    Dim lRGBColor As Long
    Dim nIntColor As Integer

    'Choose random number between 0 and 15
    nIntColor = Int(16 * Rnd)
    lRGBColor = QBColor(nIntColor)
    Me.BackColor = lRGBColor

End Sub
```

The preceding code example, when placed in the Load event of a form, causes the form's background color to change every time you click it.

Using Fonts and Colors with a RichTextBox Control   The text box is great for general use, but the RichTextBox control allows even greater control over how text is displayed. The strength of the RichTextBox control, introduced in Chapter 6, "Giving More Control to the User: Menus and Toolbars," is that it can display multiple formats and colors within the same text area.

▶ See "Rich Text Boxes," **p. 445**

One use of this control can be to display database detail information in a neatly formatted manner, as in the application in Figure 19.12. When a user clicks an employee's name, the title and other information are displayed in the rich text box on the right of the form.

Although the information is displayed in a fancy format, the programming effort behind it is minimal. The first step is to use WordPad or Microsoft Word to create a template for your detail display. Enter what you want the data to look like, but use placeholders instead of actual data. A sample template is shown in Figure 19.12. Note that the # characters are used to surround each placeholder so that it is not confused with actual data.

FIGURE 19.12
The formatted RTF template file has to be created only once, and then it can be easily used to display data.

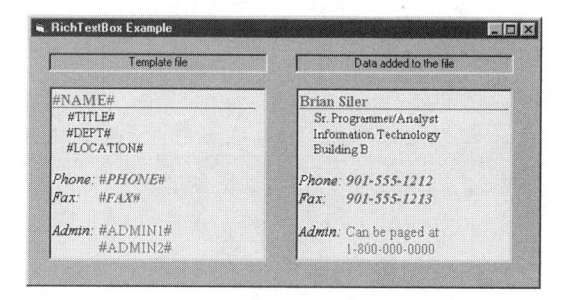

To display information in the rich text box, you must first load the template and then find and replace each placeholder. The following sample code uses a user-defined function, ReplRTBfield, to search for a placeholder and then replace it with data:

```
Sub ReplRTBfield(sField As String, sValue As String)
    rtbInfo.Find "#" & sField & "#"
    rtbInfo.SelText = sValue

End Sub

Private Sub cmdDisplay_Click()

   rtbInfo.LoadFile (App.Path & "\info.rtf")
   ReplRTBfield "NAME", "Brian Siler"
   ReplRTBfield "DEPT", "Accounting"
   ReplRTBfield "TITLE", "CIA"

End Sub
```

Although the code in this example is simple, you could easily expand it into a powerful formatting tool. The Find method of the rich text box allows you to replace your own codes in an RTF template instead of selecting and formatting each individual piece of text with VB code.

From Here...

Although I cannot suggest any steps that guarantee a successful user interface, a bad user interface certainly guarantees that no one will use your program. However, with the rapid pace of advances in computing, the definition of what is a good interface will surely keep changing. Consider, for example, the process of setting a VCR clock. Early VCR clocks were programmed with buttons and switches, but this method was soon replaced with onscreen displays. Now an over-the-air radio signal makes the whole process automatic in some models. Like the VCR example, your Visual Basic user interfaces will evolve over time, as the industry sets new standards and you learn how to best meet your users' expectations.

To learn more about the visual aspects of user interface design, see the following chapters:

- To find out about the controls that can be used in designing VB programs, see Chapter 4, "Using Visual Basic's Default Controls," and Chapter 12, "Microsoft Common Controls."
- For general interface design tips, see Chapter 18, "Proper Interface Design."
- To learn how to design an application for the Internet, see Chapter 32, "ActiveX Documents."

PART V

Advanced Programming Topics

- **20** Accessing the Windows API 449
- **21** Working with Files 469
- **22** Using OLE to Control Other Applications 489
- **23** Master's Toolbox 501

CHAPTER 20

Accessing the Windows API

In this chapter

Understanding the Windows API 450

Using the Windows API in Visual Basic 452

Useful API Calls 457

Chapter 20 Accessing the Windows API

The Windows API, or *Application Programming Interface*, is a set of functions that Windows exposes to programmers. These Windows operating system functions can be called from Visual Basic to perform tasks that cannot be programmed with standard VB code. For example, standard Visual Basic does not have a function to reboot the computer. However, rebooting can be accomplished through a Windows API call. You can think of many of the functions included with Visual Basic as "wrappers" around the underlying Windows API routines. Using Windows API functions is a bit more complicated than using standard user-defined functions, so writing your own wrapper functions is common. Although by no means an exhaustive guide, this chapter provides a solid foundation for common uses of the Windows API.

Understanding the Windows API

From the point of view of the Visual Basic programmer, Windows API functions can be thought of as similar to "normal" VB functions. They contain input and output parameters and sometimes a return value. However, API functions are already compiled in a separate file, known as a dynamic link library (or DLL).

To use these functions, you have to add a few lines of code that define the external function for Visual Basic. In other words, to use an API function, you must first *declare* it. API declarations are entered in the General Declarations section of a module. Just as you declare variables, you also must declare API functions so that your code can access them; and, as a declared variable provides a link to a memory location, an API declaration provides a link to an external DLL.

> **NOTE** The usual place for API declarations is in a module, but you can add them to forms and classes as well by adding the `Private` keyword in front of the declaration.

The `Declare` statement lists all the parameters of the API function, the DLL in which it is located, and the data type of the return value. Unlike a normal VB function, an API declaration has no function code. Instead, the single-line statement merely points to the DLL file containing the function. This relationship is illustrated in Figure 20.1.

FIGURE 20.1
API functions are stored in system DLLs. The API declaration makes these functions visible to your VB code.

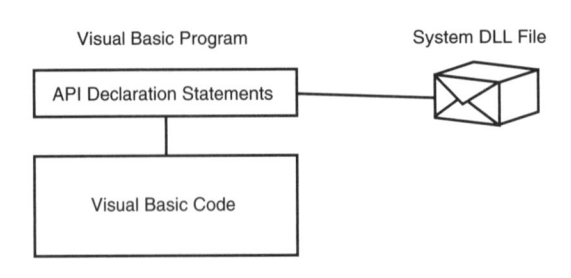

> **NOTE** Many `Declare` statements include the use of the `Alias` parameter. An *alias* specifies the "real" name of an API function as it is stored in the DLL, which may not match the name you want to give the function in your program. For example, a function named _lopen appears in the kernel32 DLL, but _lopen is not a valid function name within Visual Basic. In this case, the proper API declaration is as follows:

```
Declare Function lopen Lib "kernel32" Alias "_lopen" -
(ByVal lpPathName As String, ByVal iReadWrite As Long) As Long.
```

Visual Basic sees the function internally as `lopen` but knows from the `Declare` statement's `Alias` parameter to pass the call to the function named `_lopen` inside the kernel32 DLL.

Let me demonstrate the use of a Windows API function with the example mentioned earlier, rebooting the system. First, start a Standard EXE project, and add a new module by choosing Add Module from the Project menu. Next, go to the declarations section of the module, and enter the following `Declare` statement on a single line:

```
Declare Function ExitWindowsEx Lib "user32" (ByVal uFlags As Long,_
              ByVal dwReserved As Long) As Long
```

NOTE Notice the underscore at the end of the first code line. `Declare` statements can be entered on multiple lines if the line continuation character (_) is used.

Notice that the `Declare` statement contains the name of the function (`ExitWindowsEx`), the name of the library (`user32`), and a list of parameters. After you enter the `Declare` statement, the `ExitWindowsEx` function is visible within Visual Basic and can be called from other code.

However, before calling the API function, you need to set up some valid values for the two parameters. The following constants are acceptable values for the first parameter, `uFlags`:

```
Public Const EWX_FORCE = 4
Public Const EWX_LOGOFF = 0
Public Const EWX_REBOOT = 2
Public Const EWX_SHUTDOWN = 1
```

If you look at the constants in the preceding list, you may notice that they roughly correspond to the choices available when you're closing Windows. Each constant passed to the `uFlags` parameter causes the function to behave differently, much like the `Flags` property of a `CommonDialog` control.

The second parameter, `dwReserved`, is typical of many Windows API functions. It is a reserved parameter not intended for general use, so you can just use 0 for its value.

NOTE Constants used with the Windows API are just like normal Visual Basic constants. For the sake of readability, I suggest placing these constants in the same module as the function declaration.

After you have entered the declaration statements and constants, calling the API function from code is easy. For example, place the following lines of Visual Basic code in the `Form_Load` procedure to reboot your computer:

```
Dim lRetVal As Long
lRetVal = ExitWindowsEx(EWX_REBOOT, 0)
```

Executing the preceding code causes Windows to attempt to shut down, prompting you to save open documents.

Using the Windows API in Visual Basic

The Windows API is sometimes called the *Win32* API, in reference to the use of 32-bit functions. The 16-bit API was used in Windows 3.11 and earlier versions of Visual Basic. Although Windows 95 and NT provide backward compatibility for applications compiled using 16-bit calls, you cannot declare a 16-bit API function in Visual Basic 6.0. This point is important to remember when you're upgrading old projects.

Using the API Viewer

Windows API function declarations and the constants and types used with them are listed in the file WIN32API.TXT. This file is installed in the WINAPI subdirectory of the Visual Basic program directory. To use an API function in your program, simply copy and paste the information you need from this file. Comments are also included in the file to help you make some sense of the function's purpose.

Visual Basic comes with a tool called the API Text Viewer, which is designed to make adding API functions quick. The API Text Viewer, shown in Figure 20.2, organizes the Windows API functions alphabetically and allows you to copy multiple API functions to the Windows Clipboard.

To use the API Viewer, click the API Text Viewer icon in your Visual Basic program group. Next, from the File menu, choose Load Text File and select WIN32API.TXT. (Note that you are given the option of converting WIN32API.TXT to a database file for faster loading.) After the API Viewer parses the text file, you are presented with a list of available API declarations in the Available Items box.

FIGURE 20.2
The API Viewer lets you copy any combination of types, declares, and constants to the Windows Clipboard.

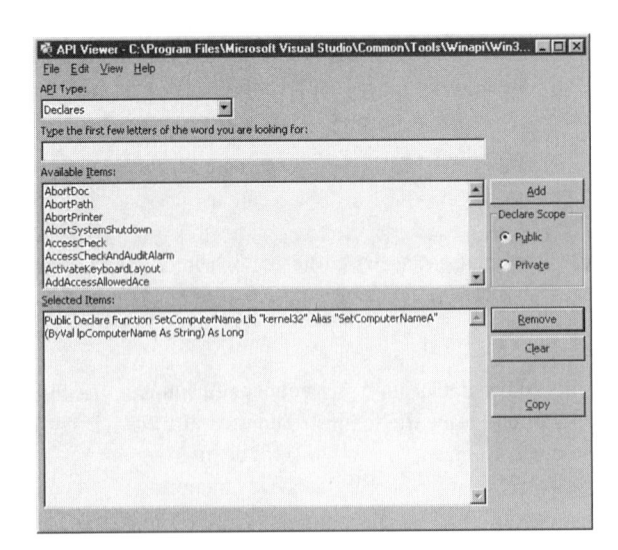

Test it yourself by copying the `GetDiskFreeSpace` function to the Clipboard. The quickest way to locate a specific function is to enter the first few letters to jump to it in the list.

Before continuing, note a new feature in the API Viewer: the ability to choose Public or Private declarations. All this feature really does is include the word *Private* or *Public* for you; you can still edit the API declaration later if desired. Public API declarations can be placed in a code module and accessed from other forms and modules in the project. On the other hand, if you want to place an API declaration in a form, it must be declared as Private. Since our example uses a form, go ahead and click the Private radio button.

Double-click `GetDiskFreeSpace`, and you will notice that it appears in the Selected Items box. Note that you can double-click additional function names to add them to the Selected Items box. Constants and types used by the API can be displayed if you set the API Type drop-down box, although it is up to you to know which constants go with the selected functions.

When you're finished browsing the list, click the Copy button. This action places any selected items on the Windows Clipboard. Next, start a new Visual Basic Standard EXE project and add a module. Open the Code window for the new module, and choose Paste from the Edit menu. The declaration for `GetDiskFreeSpace` should appear in your Code window:

```
Private Declare Function GetDiskFreeSpace Lib "kernel32" Alias
"GetDiskFreeSpaceA" _
              (ByVal lpRootPathName As String, lpSectorsPerCluster As Long, _
              lpBytesPerSector As Long, lpNumberOfFreeClusters As Long, _
              lpTtoalNumberOfClusters As Long) As Long
```

Now that the declaration is available to your program, you can write code that calls the `GetDiskFreeSpace` API function. Add a command button to the form, and add code to the Click event to call the `GetDiskFreeSpace` function, as in the following example:

```
Private Sub Command1_Click()
    Dim lSecPerClust As Long
    Dim lBytesPerSec As Long
    Dim lFreeClust As Long
    Dim lTotalClust As Long
    Dim lReturn As Long

    lReturn = GetDiskFreeSpace("C:\", lSecPerClust, lBytesPerSec, _
              lFreeClust, lTotalClust)

    Msgbox "Free Clusters on drive C = " & lFreeClust
End Sub
```

The preceding example calls the `GetDiskFreeSpace` API function with the appropriate parameters and displays one of the returned values in a message box. However, the example is not really practically useful; more than likely, you will be interested in the number of free bytes rather than clusters. Also, if you intend to use this function multiple times within your program, a lot of overhead is required to get back the results. You will solve both of these problems in the next section by creating a wrapper function.

Creating a Wrapper Function

Often programmers create a "wrapper" function around one or more Windows API calls. A wrapper function is a standard VB function that handles calls between the rest of your program and the API function. Although using this type of function sounds like an extra step, one of its purposes is actually to eliminate extra steps associated with calling the API function. For example, suppose you are writing an installation program and need to check for the amount of free storage space on a given disk drive. The Windows API function GetDiskFreeSpace returns free space information, but not in the exact format you need. A simple user-defined function such as dblFreeBytes, shown in Listing 20.1, calls the API but returns only the required information.

Listing 20.1 APIWRAP.ZIP—The Wrapper Function Returns Only the Information Needed by the Rest of the Program

```
Declare Function GetDiskFreeSpace Lib "kernel32" Alias "GetDiskFreeSpaceA" _
            (ByVal lpRootPathName As String, lpSectorsPerCluster As Long, _
            lpBytesPerSector As Long, lpNumberOfFreeClusters As Long, _
            lpTtoalNumberOfClusters As Long) As Long

Function dblFreeBytes(sPath As String) As Double
    Dim sDrive As String
    Dim lReturn As Long
    Dim l1 As Long      'l1 = Sectors Per Cluster
    Dim l2 As Long      'l2 = Bytes Per Sector
    Dim l3 As Long      'l3 = Number Of Free Clusters
    Dim l4 As Long      'l4 = Total Number Of Clusters

    sDrive = Left$(sPath, 1) & ":\" 'Get drive letter from path

    lReturn = GetDiskFreeSpace(sDrive, l1, l2, l3, l4)

    dblFreeBytes = l1 * l2 * l3

End Function
```

As you can see from the preceding listing, GetDiskFreeSpace actually returns four values. If you called this function directly several times throughout your program, you would have to add four Dim statements and know the purpose of each parameter. However, using dblFreeBytes, which automates the mundane work of the API call for you, is much easier:

```
If dblFreeBytes(app.path) < REQUIRED_BYTES Then
  Msgbox "Error: Not Enough Disk Space!"
End If
```

Wrapper functions can also be used to eliminate the extra string manipulation required by many API functions. Typically, API functions that modify a string passed to them require you to supply the length of the string and fill the string with spaces. An example of using a wrapper function to get around this step is demonstrated in Chapter 21, "Working with Files."

▶ **See** "Using INI Files in Visual Basic," **p. 485**

Creating a Wrapper Class

In the spirit of object-oriented programming, you can take the idea of a wrapper function one step further and create a wrapper class. You can use the sample class, `ComputerInfo`, to manipulate the Windows computer name. You can manually change the computer name from the Network Control Panel, shown in Figure 20.3.

FIGURE 20.3
The API calls in the `ComputerInfo` class can set your computer name.

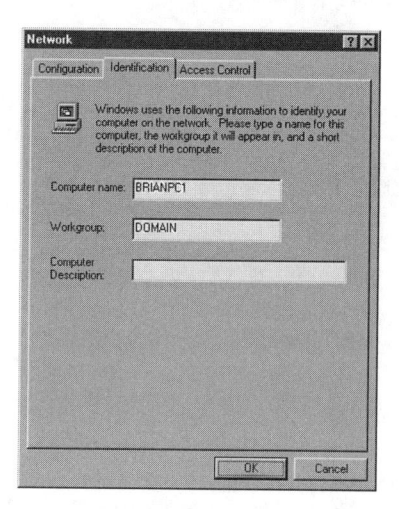

Two API calls are used to retrieve and set the computer name: `GetComputerName` and `SetComputerName`. Your class will encapsulate these functions into a single property that is easier to deal with from Visual Basic. Listing 20.2 shows the code for the `ComputerInfo` class, which includes one property and one event.

Listing 20.2   COMPNAME.ZIP—The *ComputerInfo* Class Sets the Windows Computer Name

```
Option Explicit

'Notice these API declarations are private - we don't want them accessed di-
rectly
Private Declare Function GetComputerName Lib "kernel32" Alias "GetComputerNameA" _
                (ByVal lpBuffer As String, nSize As Long) As Long
Private Declare Function SetComputerName Lib "kernel32" Alias "SetComputerNameA" _
                (ByVal lpComputerName As String) As Long

Public Event RebootNeeded()

Public Property Get ComputerName() As String
    Dim sName As String
    Dim lRetVal As Long
    Dim iPos As Integer
```

continues

Listing 20.2 Continued

```
    'API's generally require fixed-length strings, which means
    'pre-filling them with spaces, nulls, or Dim sName As String * 255
    sName = Space$(255)

    'Actually call the API
    lRetVal = GetComputerName(sName, 255&)

    'If the API returns 0 then it didn't work, so exit
    If lRetVal = 0 Then Exit Property

    'GetComputerName puts a null character, Chr$(0), on the end of the
    'string, so we need to remove it before returning the computer name.
    iPos = InStr(sName, Chr$(0))
    ComputerName = Left$(sName, iPos - 1)

End Property

Public Property Let ComputerName(ByVal sNewName As String)

    Dim lRetVal As Long
    lRetVal = SetComputerName(sNewName)
    RaiseEvent RebootNeeded

End Property
```

In this specific example, the reason that you create the `RebootNeeded` event is two-fold: First, although the new computer name can be verified in the Control Panel, the `GetComputerName` API will continue to return the old computer name until you reboot. Second, if you are on a network, you probably will need to reboot to register the new name. In any case, a custom event was used so that the calling program can take the appropriate action. A sample section of code used to test the `ComputerInfo` class is shown in Listing 20.3.

Listing 20.3 COMPNAME.ZIP—Testing the *ComputerInfo* Class from a Form

```
Dim WithEvents clsCompName As ComputerInfo

Sub TestComputerInfoClass()

    Dim sName As String

    'Create a new instance of the class
    Set clsCompName = New ComputerInfo

    'Display the computer name
    sName = clsCompName.ComputerName
    MsgBox "The current computer name is: " & sName

    'Set a new Computer name
    sName = InputBox$("Enter new computer name")
    clsCompName.ComputerName = sName

End Sub

Private Sub clsCompName_RebootNeeded()
    MsgBox "You need to reboot to make the changes effective!"
End Sub
```

The `ComputerInfo` class is a good example of using Visual Basic's object-oriented capabilities to your advantage. Not only does it make using the `ComputerName` APIs easier, but it is also very easy to include in multiple projects. You can also continue to add properties and events to the `ComputerInfo` class as needed.

Useful API Calls

The best way to learn about the Windows API is to practice. If you look at the WIN32API.TXT file, you'll notice that quite a few API calls are available. The following sections will introduce some of the most interesting ones.

Fun API Calls

The next two API calls you will explore on your tour are both easy to use and fun. The first function, `sndPlaySound`, allows you to play waveform (.WAV) sound files on the sound card. They have two parameters: the name of the sound file and flags to control how the sound is played. Listing 20.4 shows an example.

Listing 20.4 APIDEMO.ZIP—Playing WAV Files with *sndPlaySound*

```
Declare Function sndPlaySound Lib "winmm.dll" Alias "sndPlaySoundA" (ByVal _
                lpszSoundName As String, ByVal uFlags As Long) As Long

Public Const SND_ALIAS = &H10000      ' name is in WIN.INI or the Registry
Public Const SND_ASYNC = &H1          ' play asynchronously
Public Const SND_SYNC = &H0           ' play synchronously (default)
Public Const SND_NOWAIT = &H2000      ' don't wait if the driver is busy
Public Const SND_LOOP = &H8           ' loop the sound until next sndPlaySound

Sub SoundCheck()
    Dim lRetVal As Long

    lRetVal = sndPlaySound("C:\WINDOWS\MEDIA\CHIMES.WAV", SND_SYNC)
    lRetVal = sndPlaySound("SystemStart", SND_ALIAS + SND_ASYNC + SND_NOWAIT)

'The alias names of system sounds are listed in the registry together,
'to find them search for SystemStart

End Sub
```

All the constants that begin with the prefix SND are listed together and commented in the API text file. The two of most concern are SND_ASYNC and SND_SYNC, which control whether the program will wait until the sound is finished before continuing.

Another API function, `SystemParametersInfo`, can be used to set the Windows background wallpaper. I used this function with a video capture camera to create a "virtual window office" at work. An example with `SystemParametersInfo` is shown in Listing 20.5.

Listing 20.5 APIDEMO.ZIP—*SystemParametersInfo* Can Set the Windows Background

```
Public Const SPIF_UPDATEINIFILE = &H1
Public Const SPIF_SENDWININICHANGE = &H2
Public Const SPI_SETDESKWALLPAPER = 20
Declare Function SystemParametersInfo Lib "user32" Alias "SystemParametersInfoA" _
            (ByVal uAction As Long, ByVal uParam As Long, ByVal lpvParam _
            As Any, ByVal fuWinIni As Long) As Long

Sub ClearWallpaper()

    Dim lRetVal As Long
    lRetVal = SystemParametersInfo(SPI_SETDESKWALLPAPER, 0&, "(None)", _
            SPIF_UPDATEINIFILE Or SPIF_SENDWININICHANGE)

End Sub

Sub SetWallPaper(sBitmapFile As String)

    Dim lRetVal As Long
    lRetVal = SystemParametersInfo(SPI_SETDESKWALLPAPER, 0&, sBitmapFile, _
            SPIF_UPDATEINIFILE Or SPIF_SENDWININICHANGE)

End Sub
```

The `SetWallpaper` and `ClearWallpaper` functions cause the Windows wallpaper bitmap to change immediately. The constants in the last parameter of the API call, although not necessary, cause any changes to be reflected in the Control Panel. If you peruse the API text file, you'll notice that you can control many additional display options with the `SystemParametersInfo` function.

Finding and Controlling Other Windows

You can control window behavior and find out information about other windows with several API calls. Most of these API calls use the *window handle* to identify the window to which you are referring. A window handle is simply a unique number assigned to each window currently running on your system. In Visual Basic programs, the window handle is available to the hwnd property of a form. However, if you want to manipulate a window outside your Visual Basic program, you have to first use API calls to obtain its handle.

> **N O T E** In this section, I break temporarily from my l prefix naming convention for long variables. Window handles are understood to be long, and the API declarations typically refer to them as hwnd. ■

Finding Window Handles   To find the handle of a window, you can use the `FindWindow` API function. It has two parameters: the Window Name and the Window Class name. You can supply one or both parameters to `FindWindow`, and it will return the window handle or zero if no matching window exists.

For example, run Notepad and you will see that the initial caption of the Notepad window is Untitled - Notepad. To find this window, you could call FindWindow as follows:

```
hwndNotepad = FindWindow(vbNullString, "Untitled - Notepad")
```

Notice that here you use only the window caption, sending the class name parameter a null string. However, suppose you saved or opened a file. Notepad's caption would change to reflect the new filename, so the preceding line of code would no longer successfully find the window. However, I happen to know that the name of the Windows Notepad class is Notepad, so I could use that instead:

```
hwndNotepad = FindWindow("Notepad", vbNullString)
```

> **TIP** Windows class names are not always this obvious; for example, one of the early Visual Basic form class names was ThunderForm. However, a Windows class spy utility, such as the one included with Visual C++, makes finding class names easy.

The preceding line of code can find the handle of the Notepad window no matter what the caption. This example works fine with one instance of Notepad, but what if multiple copies are running? The answer is to introduce a few more API calls: GetWindow, GetWindowText, and GetWindowClass.

Like FindWindow, GetWindow is used to return a window handle. However, rather than search by name, GetWindow finds windows based on their relationships to other windows. GetWindow can be used in a loop to browse through the entire window list, as shown in Listing 20.6. The code in this listing counts the number of instances of Notepad and prints the caption of each.

Listing 20.6 APIDEMO.ZIP—Finding All the Notepad Windows

```
Public Const GW_HWNDFIRST = 0
Public Const GW_HWNDLAST = 1
Public Const GW_HWNDNEXT = 2
Public Const GW_HWNDPREV = 3
Public Const GW_OWNER = 4
Public Const GW_CHILD = 5
Public Const GW_MAX = 5

Declare Function GetWindow Lib "user32" (ByVal hwnd As Long, ByVal wCmd As Long) _
                 As Long
Declare Function FindWindow Lib "user32" Alias "FindWindowA" (ByVal lpClassName _
                 As String, ByVal lpWindowName As String) As Long
Declare Function GetClassName Lib "user32" Alias "GetClassNameA" (ByVal hwnd _
                 As Long, ByVal lpClassName As String, ByVal nMaxCount As Long) _
                 As Long
Declare Function GetWindowText Lib "user32" Alias "GetWindowTextA" (ByVal hwnd _
                 As Long, ByVal lpString As String, ByVal cch As Long) As Long
```

continues

Listing 20.6 Continued

```
Sub TestFindWindow()

    Const MAX_TEXT_SIZE = 50

    Dim hwndCurrent As Long
    Dim iCount As Integer
    Dim sClass As String
    Dim sCaption As String
    Dim lRetVal As Long

    iCount = 0
    hwndCurrent = FindWindow("Notepad", vbNullString)

    While hwndCurrent <> 0

        'Get the class name of the current Window
        sClass = Space$(MAX_TEXT_SIZE + 1)
        lRetVal = GetClassName(hwndCurrent, sClass, MAX_TEXT_SIZE)

        'If the Window is Notepad then increment count, print caption
        If Trim$(sClass) = "Notepad" & Chr$(0) Then
            iCount = iCount + 1
            sCaption = Space$(MAX_TEXT_SIZE + 1)
            lRetVal = GetWindowText(hwndCurrent, sCaption, MAX_TEXT_SIZE)
            Debug.Print Left$(sCaption, lRetVal)
        End If

        hwndCurrent = GetWindow(hwndCurrent, GW_HWNDNEXT)

    Wend

    Debug.Print "Number of open Notepad windows: " & iCount

End Sub
```

> **CAUTION**
>
> Take care to understand the role of null characters in API calls. In Listing 20.6, the GetClassName and GetWindowText API functions both put a Null on the end of the returned string. For this reason, I added a Null to the end of the word Notepad in the If statement so that the comparison would work. The Trim function removes spaces but not the ending Null. Another way to handle this dilemma is to use the return value of the GetClassName API with Left$ as follows:
>
> If Left$(sClass,lRetVal) = "Notepad" Then ... etc
>
> In any case, it would probably behoove you to write a quick function to remove extra null values and trailing spaces from a given string.

Using the Window Handle So now that you have gone to all the trouble of finding a window handle, what can you do with it? The answer is quite a bit. For starters, you can control the state of the window with the ShowWindow API:

```
lRetVal = ShowWindow(hwndNotepad, SW_SHOWMINIMIZED)
```

You can also use the `SendMessage` and `PostMessage` API calls to send Windows messages to a window. For example, the following line would cause Notepad to close as if you had ended it from the Windows Task Manager:

```
lRetVal = SendMessage(hwndNotepad, WM_CLOSE, 0&, 0&)
```

The preceding line of code causes Windows to send the `WM_CLOSE` message to the specified window. Upon receiving the message, Notepad exits, possibly prompting the user to save an open document. The `PostMessage` API has the same syntax as `SendMessage`, with the important distinction that it works *asynchronously*, meaning it does not wait until the message has been processed before continuing.

In the example, notice that the last two parameters are zeros because they are specific to an individual message and `WM_CLOSE` does not use them. For example, if you use a `WM_CHAR` message to send a character, these last two parameters are used to specify the character. Remember that you can send literally hundreds of messages, each with its own purpose.

> **CAUTION**
>
> Although the examples shown here are relatively safe when used with Notepad, other programs may react undesirably, causing errors. For the best results when using the Windows API with other windows, (1) read and understand the documentation for the API and/or Windows message, (2) make sure you are working with the right window, and (3) be prepared to reboot a lot.

Waiting on a Program to Finish Running

Sometimes you may need to launch other programs from within VB. Visual Basic has a built-in function to do so, `Shell`, which is covered in Chapter 21, "Working with Files."

▶ See "Launching Other Programs with the `Shell` Function," **p. 475**

However, the drawback of using `Shell` is that *it* does not wait for the shelled program to finish running before executing the next line of code:

```
'THIS DOES NOT WORK!!!
dRetVal = Shell("MyBat.Bat")
MsgBox "Batch file complete!"
```

The preceding lines of code do not have the intended result. The message box appears as soon as the `Shell` function is executed, whether the batch file is finished or not. In the 16-bit world of Windows 3.11 and Visual Basic 3.0, this problem was easy to get around with a few lines of code and two API calls. However, in the 32-bit world, things are a lot more complicated. In-depth coverage of 32-bit processes and threads would probably require half a book. Rather than go into that much detail, I will briefly describe a function to accomplish this task, from Microsoft Knowledge Base article Q129796. A function adapted from this example is shown in Listing 20.7.

Listing 20.7 SHELLWAIT.ZIP—Microsoft's Method of Waiting on a Program to Finish Executing

```vb
Private Type STARTUPINFO
        cb As Long
        lpReserved As String
        lpDesktop As String
        lpTitle As String
        dwX As Long
        dwY As Long
        dwXSize As Long
        dwYSize As Long
        dwXCountChars As Long
        dwYCountChars As Long
        dwFillAttribute As Long
        dwFlags As Long
        wShowWindow As Integer
        cbReserved2 As Integer
        lpReserved2 As Long
        hStdInput As Long
        hStdOutput As Long
        hStdError As Long
    End Type

    Private Type PROCESS_INFORMATION
       hProcess As Long
       hThread As Long
       dwProcessID As Long
       dwThreadID As Long
    End Type

    Private Declare Function WaitForSingleObject Lib "kernel32" (ByVal _
       hHandle As Long, ByVal dwMilliseconds As Long) As Long

    Private Declare Function CreateProcessA Lib "kernel32" (ByVal _
       lpApplicationName As Long, ByVal lpCommandLine As String, ByVal _
       lpProcessAttributes As Long, ByVal lpThreadAttributes As Long, _
       ByVal bInheritHandles As Long, ByVal dwCreationFlags As Long, _
       ByVal lpEnvironment As Long, ByVal lpCurrentDirectory As Long, _
       lpStartupInfo As STARTUPINFO, lpProcessInformation As _
       PROCESS_INFORMATION) As Long

    Private Declare Function CloseHandle Lib "kernel32" (ByVal _
       hObject As Long) As Long

    Private Const NORMAL_PRIORITY_CLASS = &H20&
    Private Const INFINITE = -1&

    Public Sub ExecCmd(cmdline$)
       Dim proc As PROCESS_INFORMATION
       Dim start As STARTUPINFO

       ' Initialize the STARTUPINFO structure:
       start.cb = Len(start)

       ' Start the shelled application:
       ret& = CreateProcessA(0&, cmdline$, 0&, 0&, 1&, _
```

```
            NORMAL_PRIORITY_CLASS, 0&, 0&, start, proc)
    ' Wait for the shelled application to finish:
    ret& = WaitForSingleObject(proc.hProcess, INFINITE)
    ret& = CloseHandle(proc.hProcess)
End Sub
```

By using the `ExecCmd` function from Listing 20.7, you can rewrite the example from the beginning of this section as follows:

```
'THIS WORKS AS INTENDED
ExecCmd "MyBat.Bat"
MsgBox "Batch file complete!"
```

Note that actually performing this task requires a fairly involved set of API declarations, but the `ExecCmd` function makes them easy to use.

Callbacks and Subclassing

API calls allow you to interact with the Windows operating system at a lower level than with standard VB code alone. When you write programs in standard VB, you are essentially using VB code as a wrapper for the Windows API. Although most of your programs will not be required to use complex API calls, at times you must use the API if the task you are trying to accomplish has not been implemented in the VB language directly. One area in which you may need the API is in processing Windows messages, which can be handled by callbacks and subclassing. These techniques are discussed in the following sections.

Callbacks   A callback is a function in your Visual Basic program that is called by Windows. Consider, for example, the declaration for the `EnumWindows` API function:

```
Declare Function EnumWindows lib "user32" (ByVal lpEnumFunc as Long, _
                                           lParam as Any) As Long
```

Notice that the first parameter of `EnumWindows` is a pointer to a function. The function pointed to is one you write in a Visual Basic module—your callback function. The `EnumWindows` function iterates through the Windows task list, executing your callback function each time. To pass a pointer to `EnumWindows`, you use the `AddressOf` keyword and the name of your callback function, as in the following example:

```
lRetVal = EnumWindows(AddressOf MyCallBackFunc, 12345&)
```

Executing the preceding line of code (only a single time) causes `EnumWindows` to call `MyCallBackFunc` repeatedly for each window in the task list. When `EnumWindows` calls `MyCallBackFunc`, it passes two parameters: a window handle and the second parameter originally passed to `EnumWindows`. (The second parameter can be used by your callback function however you see fit, much like the `SendMessage` parameters.) For this reason, callback functions are written specifically for the API that calls them. In other words, a valid callback function for `EnumWindows` needs to be declared according to certain rules. Specifically, it must have two parameters and return a `Long` value. The return value is used to stop `EnumWindows` before it finishes enumerating all the windows.

Listing 20.8 shows a sample version of `MyCallBackFunc`, used with `EnumWindows`. The use for the second parameter in this case is a form name. Each time `MyCallBackFunc` is called, it prints some information about the window handle passed to it on the specified form.

Listing 20.8 CALLBACK.ZIP—Callback Function Demo

```
Declare Function EnumWindows Lib "user32" (ByVal lpEnumFunc As Long, _
                  lParam As Any) As Long

Function MyCallBackFunc(ByVal hwnd As Long, lParam As Form) As Long

    Dim sInfo As String

    'sGetWindowInfo is a wrapper
    'for GetClassName and GetWindowText.

    sInfo = sGetWindowInfo(hwnd)

    lParam.Print "hwnd=" & hwnd & vbTab & sInfo

    'Returning False causes EnumWindows to stop
    'moving through the window list
    MyCallBackFunc = True

End Function

Sub InitiateCallback()
    'This code is called from the form's command button

    Dim lRetVal As Long
    Form1.Cls
    lRetVal = EnumWindows(AddressOf MyCallBackFunc, Form1)

End Sub
```

A sample run is shown in Figure 20.4.

FIGURE 20.4
EnumWindows passes your callback function the handle of each window in the task list.

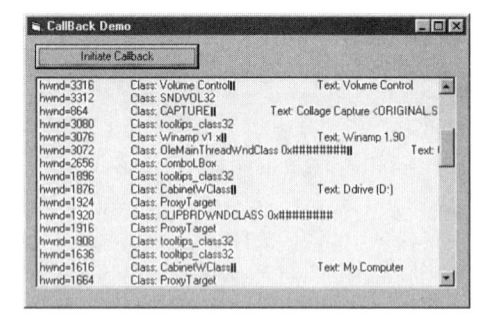

Subclassing   Now that you have examined callbacks, you're ready to look at a closely related concept called *subclassing*. To understand subclassing, you should first think of a standard Visual Basic form. You can think of the form as a special type (or class) of window. This class of window has been programmed to intercept specific events, such as the `MouseMove` event. The Visual Basic form "knows" to run the `MouseMove` event procedure because that is what it has been programmed to do. But what about all the Windows messages that the form is ignoring? And what if you want to change the way Windows handles the existing messages?

To intercept and react to messages, you must change the way the form class handles events. You do so through a technique known as subclassing, which, prior to VB version 5.0, could only be accomplished with a custom control. However, now that callbacks are possible, you can use a callback function with the `SetWindowLong` API function to intercept Windows messages.

Creating an Event Handler with Subclassing   A good example of subclassing is in the article "Passing Function Pointers to DLL Procedures and Type Libraries," which is included in the Visual Basic help files. The code for that example is shown in Listings 20.9 and 20.10, followed by a step-by-step explanation.

Listing 20.9   SUBCLASS.ZIP—Subclassing Example

```
Declare Function CallWindowProc Lib "user32" Alias "CallWindowProcA" _
                (ByVal lpPrevWndFunc As Long, ByVal hwnd As Long, ByVal Msg _
                As Long, ByVal wParam As Long, ByVal lParam As Long) As Long
Declare Function SetWindowLong Lib "user32" Alias "SetWindowLongA" (ByVal hwnd _
                As Long, ByVal nIndex As Long, ByVal dwNewLong As Long) As Long

Global Const GWL_WNDPROC = -4
Public lpPrevWndProc As Long
Public gHW As Long

Function WindowProc(ByVal hw As Long, ByVal uMsg As Long, ByVal wParam As Long, _
          ByVal lParam As Long) As Long
    Debug.Print "Message: "; hw, uMsg, wParam, lParam
    WindowProc = CallWindowProc(lpPrevWndProc, hw, uMsg, wParam, lParam)
End Function

Public Sub Hook()
    lpPrevWndProc = SetWindowLong(gHW, GWL_WNDPROC, _
        AddressOf WindowProc)
End Sub

Public Sub Unhook()
    Dim temp As Long
    temp = SetWindowLong(gHW, GWL_WNDPROC, _
        lpPrevWndProc)
End Sub
```

Although the code in Listing 20.9 is used to intercept messages sent to a form, a rule for callbacks is that they must be located in a module, so that is the place where the guts of the sample code resides. The form-level code is shown in Listing 20.10.

Listing 20.10 SUBCLASS.ZIP—Form-Level Code for the Subclass Example

```
Private Sub cmdHook_Click()
    Hook
End Sub

Private Sub cmdUnhook_Click()
    Unhook
End Sub

Private Sub Form_Load()
    gHW = Me.hwnd
End Sub
```

To look at these listings step by step, start with the Hook subroutine in Listing 20.9. Hook passes the address of the callback function, WindowProc, to the SetWindowLong API. SetWindowLong makes WindowProc the message handler for the form, replacing whatever VB message handler was already in place. The address of the VB message handler being replaced is returned and stored in lpPrevWndProc. UnHook calls SetWindowLong again with this variable to return control to the standard message handler. The Hook and Unhook subroutines act as a kind of switch that controls where Windows messages are sent. When Hook is called, all Windows messages are routed to WindowProc.

WindowProc accepts four parameters: the window handle of the form and the three parameters associated with each message. The first line of code in WindowProc simply prints all this information in the Immediate window. The second line calls yet another API function, CallWindowProc. CallWindowProc passes the message information on to the standard Windows message handler, whose address is available in the lpPrevWndProc variable.

So, in effect, the "custom" message handler WindowProc really doesn't do anything but print the message and call the message handler that would have been called anyway. A sample run is shown in Figure 20.5.

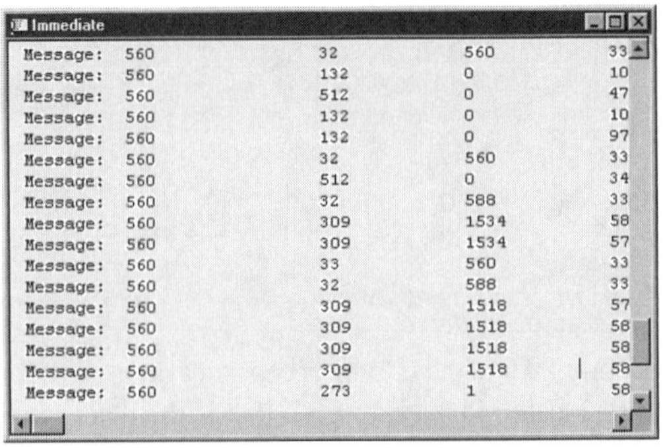

FIGURE 20.5
A sample program uses subclassing techniques to install its own Windows message handler.

To really prove that you are actually intercepting messages, you need to make WindowProc do something special, like throw away a message. Go back to the MouseMove event example. Place the following line of code in the form's MouseMove event procedure:

```
Debug.Print "THE VB MOUSE MOVE EVENT HAS FIRED!"
```

Run the sample program again, and notice that the Immediate window lists the output from the preceding `Print` statement, as well as the one in `WindowProc`. However, by modifying `WindowProc`, you can turn off the VB `MouseMove` event:

```
Function WindowProc(ByVal hw As Long, ByVal uMsg As Long, ByVal wParam As Long, _
        ByVal lParam As Long) As Long
    Debug.Print "Message: "; hw, uMsg, wParam, lParam
    If uMsg <> 512 Then WindowProc = CallWindowProc(lpPrevWndProc, hw, uMsg, _
        wParam, lParam)
    '(Decimal 512 is 200 hex which is WM_MOUSEMOVE in the API text file.)
End Function
```

From Here...

This chapter is by no means a complete API reference; rather, its intention is to introduce you to some of the issues involved when using the Windows API. Keep in mind that the Windows APIs are not the only APIs around. You can purchase third-party DLLs that perform a variety of functions, such as ZIP file creation or custom reporting. In this case, the documentation and `Declare` statements would be included with the product.

The Windows API documentation for Visual Basic is severely lacking. To use the Windows API effectively, you will almost certainly have to find another source. The standard API reference for Visual Basic programmers is Daniel Appleman's *Visual Basic Programmer's Guide to the Win32 API*, which has thorough and in-depth coverage. Another source is the Microsoft Developer Network Online, available at `http://www.microsoft.com/msdn/`.

For more detail on the informatin found in this chapter, refer to the following chapters:

- To learn about some graphics-related API calls, see the section "Other Graphics Methods" in Chapter 19, "Using Visual Design Elements."
- To use API calls to access INI files, see Chapter 21, "Working with Files."
- To see how API calls can be used to alter how bitmaps are painted on the screen, see Chapter 23, "Master's Toolbox."

CHAPTER 21

Working with Files

In this chapter

File Functions in Visual Basic   470

Working with Text Files   477

Random Files—Creating Your Own File Format   482

INI Files   484

No matter what development language and platform you use, at some point you will probably need to write code that interacts with underlying operating system files. For example, you might need to copy files or launch another program. You can do all this interactively by using Windows Explorer or an MS-DOS prompt window. As you will see in this chapter, you can accomplish these same file operations easily by using Visual Basic code.

Another use for files is the storage and retrieval of information. In other chapters, you learned how to use databases to store information. However, sometimes the power of the Visual Basic database engine may not be necessary or even appropriate. For example, you may want to create a simple activity log or process a comma-delimited text file. In this chapter, you will examine a couple of options that allow you to store and access information in three types of text files: sequential files, random access files, and initialization (.INI) files.

File Functions in Visual Basic

Files are the basic organizational unit of an operating system. There are many different types of files, from user-created documents to games to operating system commands. This section discusses some of the functions used to work with files from Visual Basic. Another method of accessing files, using the `FileSystemObject` interface, is discussed in Chapter 30, "Using VBScript." (This object interface was originally a part of VBScript but is now available in Visual Basic starting with version 6.) The functions discussed in this section have been around for a long time and are considered to be the "traditional" Visual Basic file functions.

▶ **See** "Accessing the File System" **p. 675**

Using *Dir* to Find and List Files

One useful file function is the `Dir$` function. This function works like the `Dir` command at an MS-DOS command prompt. You can use the `Dir$` function to retrieve a list of one or more operating system files that match a file specification or path. A path can include the name of a directory, a specific filename, or both. For example, C:*.BAT is the path to all the files in the root directory of drive C having a BAT extension. The syntax of the `Dir$` function is as follows:

```
stringvar = Dir$(path[,attributes])
```

Finding Files   One use of `Dir$` is to determine whether a file exists. If you try to open a database or access a file that does not exist, an error occurs. However, you can use `Dir$` first to check for a file's existence before opening it, as in the following example:

```
If Dir$("C:\MYFILE.TXT") = "" Then
Msgbox "The file was not found. Please try again!"
End If
```

The `Dir$` function returns the filename without the full path if the specified file is found, or it returns an empty string if no files were found. The preceding line of code displays a message box if MYFILE.TXT does not exist in the root directory of drive C. If the file does exist, the string `myfile.txt` is returned. To make things even simpler, you can create a generic function that returns a Boolean value `True` if the given file exists:

```
Public Function bFileExists(sFile As String) As Boolean
    If Dir$(sFile) <> "" Then bFileExists = True Else bFileExists = False
End Function
```

This function could then be used to check any filenames passed to the program by the user, as in the following example:

```
Dim sUserFile As String

sUserFile = InputBox$("Enter the file name:")

If Not bFileExists(sUserFile) Then
        MsgBox "The file does not exist. Please try again."
        End

End If
```

Notice that the code sample ends the program if the file does not exist, to prevent any errors that might occur later. Another way to handle this situation would be to keep asking the user for a filename until a valid filename is entered.

Listing Files and Folders   Another use of the Dir$ function is to return a list of files in the specified path. If you use the Dir command at an MS-DOS prompt, each matching file is listed on the screen. However, because the Dir$ function is designed to return only a single string variable, you have to use a loop and retrieve one filename at a time. (You also can display a list of files with a file list box, which is one of Visual Basic's default controls. These controls are covered extensively in Chapter 4, "Using Visual Basic's Default Controls.")

Suppose that your C:\DATA directory contains several picture files with a BMP (bitmap) extension. The path used to retrieve these files with the Dir$ function would be C:\DATA*.BMP. You can use the following lines of code to retrieve the filenames and add them to a list box:

```
Dim sNextFile As String

sNextFile = Dir$("C:\Data\*.BMP")

While sNextFile <> ""
    lstPictureList.AddItem sNextFile
    sNextFile = Dir$
Wend
```

In the preceding example, notice that only the file path to Dir$ is supplied on the first call. Each subsequent call to Dir$ has no arguments, indicating that you want to use the previous file path and move to the next filename in the list. When no more files match, Dir$ returns an empty string and the While loop terminates.

> **CAUTION**
> When you use Dir$ in a loop, always exit the loop after an empty string is returned. If you try to make another call to Dir$ with no arguments, a runtime error occurs.

The second, optional parameter of the Dir$ function is used to provide additional conditions (beyond the specified path) with which to select files. For example, using the constant vbDirectory returns only the subdirectories (or folders) in the specified path. The constant vbVolume causes Dir$ to return the specified drive's volume label. The available constants are summarized in Table 21.1. (You also can display a list of folders with a directory list box.)

Table 21.1 Constants Control the Behavior of the *Dir$* Function

Constant	Value	Purpose
vbNormal	0	(Default value)
vbHidden	2	Include hidden files
vbSystem	4	Include system files
vbVolume	8	Return drive volume label
vbDirectory	16	Display subdirectories
vbReadOnly	1	Include read-only files

NOTE Constants can be added together if you want to use more than one. For example, the following code finds the system, hidden, and read-only file IO.SYS on a Windows 95 machine:

```
Debug.Print Dir$("C:\IO.SYS",vbHidden+vbSystem+vbReadOnly)
```

Note that the vbHidden constant refers to a file's attributes and not the Windows Explorer option that hides certain file types. You can view the attributes of a file by right-clicking the file's name and choosing P<u>r</u>operties, as depicted in Figure 21.1, or by using the MS-DOS ATTRIB command.

FIGURE 21.1
File attributes, shown in the Windows Explorer, can determine whether the Dir$ function returns a specific filename.

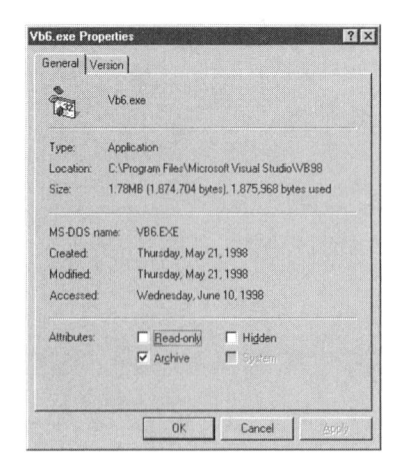

File-Manipulation Functions

As with the `Dir$` function, most of the file-manipulation commands in Visual Basic are as straightforward as their MS-DOS equivalents, although with a few limitations. These commands are summarized in Table 21.2.

Table 21.2 Summary of File Functions

Action	Syntax
Copy a file	`FileCopy source, dest`
Delete one or more files	`Kill path`
Rename a file	`Name oldname As newname`
Create a new folder	`MkDir pathname`
Remove an empty folder	`RmDir pathname`
Change current directory	`ChDir pathname`
Change current drive	`ChDrive drive`

Several of these system functions are described in the following sections.

Copying Files   The `FileCopy` command has the limitation that you cannot use wildcards to specify multiple files. `FileCopy` can copy files locally or over a network, as shown in the following examples:

```
'The following line copies a file while changing its name:
FileCopy "D:\My Documents\Hey Now.txt",  "C:\DATA\TEST.TXT"

'The following lines of code use a network path for the source file:
Dim sDest As String
Dim sSource As String

 SSource = "\\myserver\deptfiles\budget98.XLS"
SDest = "C:\DATA\BUDGET.XLS"

FileCopy sSouce, sDest
```

The `FileCopy` statement automatically overwrites an existing file, unless the file is read-only or locked open by another application.

> **NOTE**   When you copy files over a network or dial-up connection, using the `On Error` statement to trap errors is a good idea. For example, if the network is down or another user has the file exclusively locked, your program could bomb unexpectedly. You can easily provide an error trap and retry dialog, as described in Chapter 9, "Visual Basic Programming Fundamentals."

▶ **See** "Using the On Error Statement" **p. 219**

> **TIP**
>
> When you are performing file operations that take a long time (more than a few seconds), display an AVI file like Windows does. This capability is discussed in the section "Adding Video with the Animation Control" in Chapter 12, "Microsoft Common Controls."

Deleting Files Visual Basic also allows you to delete files by using the Kill statement. Kill can use wildcards to specify multiple files, as in the following example:

```
Kill "D:\NewDir\*.doc"
```

Renaming Files The Name statement is like MS-DOS's RENAME command but can be used on only one file at a time:

```
Name oldname As newname
```

You also can use Name like the MOVE command in MS-DOS if the specified paths are different:

```
'Moves the file to a new directory
MkDir "D:\NewDir"
Name "C:\Windows\Desktop\TEST1.TXT" AS "D:\NewDir\TEST2.TXT"
```

In the preceding example, note the MkDir statement, which you probably have guessed is used to create a new directory. The MkDir and RmDir statements add and remove directories, just like their MD and RD counterparts in MS-DOS.

Setting the Current Directory In the examples discussed so far, the path has always included the drive and directory. However, as you may recall from using MS-DOS, during the context of your MS-DOS session, you are always "in" a certain directory, which is usually displayed to the left of the MS-DOS cursor. For example, if you type CD \WINDOWS, you can rename, copy, or delete files within the WINDOWS directory without specifying C:\WINDOWS in the pathname. The same concept of a *current directory* applies to Visual Basic. By using the ChDir and ChDrive statements, you can set the current working directory on each drive and switch between current drives, eliminating the need to specify the full path for each file operation:

```
'Change to the desired directory and drive and rename a file
chdir "C:\Windows\Desktop"
chdrive "C:"
Name "TEST1.TXT" As "TEST2.TXT"

'Delete a file in the current directory
ChDrive "D:"
ChDir "D:\DATA"
Kill "OLDDATA.DAT"
```

Performing deletes can be dangerous if you don't know the current directory. Fortunately, Visual Basic offers a function that provides this value: the CurDir$ function. The syntax of CurDir$ is

```
stringvar = CurDir$([Drive])
```

> **NOTE** You can use the Left$ function to get the current drive, as in the following example:
> ```
> sDriveLetter = Left$(CurDir$(),1)
> ```

Launching Other Programs with the *Shell* Function

From time to time, you may need to launch another Windows program from your Visual Basic code. For example, you could use Visual Basic to schedule a data transfer or file cleanup. You could easily do so by checking the current system time and then running the secondary program when appropriate. You can run other programs by using the Shell function. The syntax for Shell is as follows:

```
DoubleVar = Shell(pathname[,windowstyle])
```

The following lines of Visual Basic code use Shell to run Notepad and bring up a text file called README.TXT:

```
Dim dTaskID As Double
dTaskID = Shell("Notepad D:\readme.txt", vbNormalFocus)
```

The first parameter of Shell is the command to be executed and the second, optional parameter is the window style. In the preceding example, the constant vbNormalFocus tells the Shell statement to run Notepad in a normal window with focus. The constant specifies two attributes of the new window: style and focus. Style describes how the window will be displayed (normal, minimized, maximized or hidden), and the focus describes whether the application will become the foreground application (only one running application can have the focus). The default window style is minimized with focus. This means the shelled application does not obscure another application's window, but the shelled program has the focus.

Launching another application with Shell is easy. If you need to wait for it to complete before your Visual Basic code continues, you need to use slightly more complex code with some additional Windows API calls. This specific API example is discussed in Chapter 20, "Accessing the Windows API."

▶ **See** "Waiting on a Program to Finish Running," **p. 461**

Locating Files Relative to Your Application

When you work with files in Visual Basic, "hard-coding" a file or folder name within your program is never a good idea. A commercial application such as Microsoft Office lets you change the default installation directory to anything you want. Even if you install the application in an off-the-wall location like D:\JUNK123\, it still can find all its other files (such as templates and clip art) and function normally.

Likewise, your applications will be more successful and professional if they can survive on any drive or installation path. If you include files beyond the actual program EXE (like a database), you can add some minor coding so that your program can locate these files in a manner that is transparent to the user.

Figure 21.2 shows an album selection screen. This program allows the user to click an album image to play the album. The program is designed to run from a CD-ROM drive. This means the path to the program might be D:\TUNES\TUNES.EXE if your CD-ROM drive letter is D. The album cover pictures and database information are also stored in the \TUNES subdirectory on the CD-ROM.

FIGURE 21.2
When your program is running from an unknown location, such as a mapped network drive or CD-ROM, use App.Path to locate the necessary supporting files.

For the program to always find the images, no matter what the CD-ROM drive letter, it uses the Path property of the App object (App.Path), as in the following example:

```
'Open database
Set db = OpenDatabase(App.Path & "\albums.mdb")

'Load image
Set picture1 = LoadPicture(App.Path & "\Picture1.GIF")
```

App.Path returns the directory in which the application is running. In the preceding example, the returned value is D:\TUNES or whatever directory the TUNES.EXE file is located in.

NOTE After you have saved your project and are working in the Visual Basic IDE, App.Path returns the path to your project's directory (with the .VBP file). If the project hasn't yet been saved, App.Path returns the current directory.

In the preceding examples, notice that you have to add a backslash before specifying the filename. App.Path doesn't add the final backslash unless it returns the root directory. You can use the Right$ function to check for this at the beginning of your program:

```
'Sets sAppPath (assumed to be a public variable) for use later in the program
sAppPath = App.Path
If Right$(sAppPath,1) <> "\" then sAppPath = sAppPath & "\"

'Later in the program:
Dim sDBLocation As String
sDBLocation = sAppPath & "finance.mdb"
```

Some programmers use the ChDir command (discussed earlier) to change the current directory to App.Path at the beginning of the program. I tend to stay away from this command because it also may affect other Windows programs.

TIP If your application uses many files spread across several directories and drives, you should take the next step and keep file locations in an INI file or database. (See "Understanding INI Files" later in the chapter.)

Working with Text Files

Sometimes you may need to store and retrieve information but not need the power of a database (not to mention the extra coding, configuration, and support files that go along with it). In these cases, a text file may be just the thing you need. In this section, you will learn about a simple type of file: a free-form, sequential text file. *Sequential* means that the file is accessed one byte after the other in sequence, rather than jumping to a specific location. *Free form* means that the file has no predefined structure; it is entirely up to the programmer.

Sequential Text Files

Suppose you have a form in which the user must choose salespersons from a list, as shown in Figure 21.3. Your mission is to load the names of each salesperson into a list box so that the user can select these names. You could just put a bunch of AddItem statements in the Form_Load event. However, doing so would be a poor solution because you have hard-coded information in the program. Any time the sales force changed, the program would have to be recompiled. A better solution is to use a text file with the salespersons' names in it. The program then reads the names from the text file and populates the list box.

FIGURE 21.3
The list box is populated with the contents of a text file.

To create the file itself, you can use a text editor such as Notepad, placing each salesperson's name on a separate line, as shown in Figure 21.4.

FIGURE 21.4
Data stored in sequential text files can be easily edited.

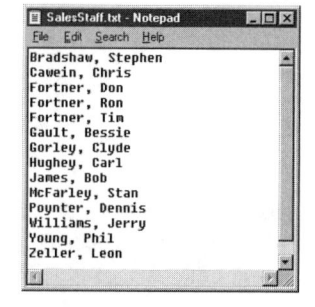

This process is simple, and the file can be edited by anyone—even if that person doesn't have a database tool. For example, a secretary could maintain this file on a network server, and the application could copy the most recent version at startup. Of course, if you are using a database anyway, you might want to go ahead and place the names of the sales force in a table. However, a standard text file could still be used for importing into the table.

> **NOTE** The concept of a shared network file also applies to databases and other documents, which may be useful if everyone on your network uses the same desktop application programs.

Reading from a Sequential Text File

Now that you know how easily you can create a sequential text file, you're ready to write some code to read information from the file. One easy way to process a sequential text file is to read it a line at a time. For the salesperson example described in the preceding section, the steps used for filling up the list box are very straightforward:

1. Open the file for input.
2. Read a line from the file and store it in a variable.
3. Add the contents of the variable to the list box.
4. Repeat steps 2 and 3 for each line in the file.
5. Close the file.

The code for filling up the list box, which is discussed in the following sections, is shown in Listing 21.1.

Listing 21.1 LISTFILL.ZIP—Filling a List Box from a Text File

```
Sub FillListBox()
   Dim sTemp As String
   lstPeople.Clear

   Open "C:\DATA\PEOPLE.TXT" For Input As #1
   While Not EOF(1)
  Line Input #1, sTemp
       LstPeople.AddItem sTemp
   Wend
   Close #1
End Sub
```

Now, examine the code a little closer. First, before you read or write information, you must open the file with the Open statement. The Open statement associates the actual filename (PEOPLE.TXT in the example) with a *file number*. A file number is an integer value used to identify the file to other Visual Basic code:

```
Open "C:\DATA\PEOPLE.TXT" For Input As #1
```

> **NOTE** In the preceding example, 1 is the file number. However, if you open and close multiple files throughout your program, using this number might not be a good idea. In that case, you should use the `FreeFile` function, which returns the next available file number, as in the following example:
>
> ```
> Dim nFile As Integer
> nFile = FreeFile
> Open "C:\MYFILE.TXT" for Input As #nFile
> ```

After you finish using a file, you should close it with the `Close` statement (refer to Listing 21.1). This way, you can free up the file number for use with other files.

In addition to providing the filename and number association, the `Open` statement tells Visual Basic how you intend to use the specified file. (Many different options are available with the `Open` statement, as discussed in the Help file.)

> **TIP** Before you open a file for input, use the `Dir$` function to see whether it actually exists.

The keyword `Input` indicates that the file will be opened for Sequential Input, which means that you can only move forward through the file in sequence. The act of reading information from the file automatically moves an internal file pointer forward for the next read. The code in Listing 21.1 uses a `Line Input` statement in a `While` loop to read information. The first `Line Input` statement reads the first line, the second `Line Input` reads the second line, and so on. A line in a file is delimited by an end of line marker, which in Windows is the carriage return character followed by the line feed character. The syntax of the `Line Input` statement is

```
Line Input #filenumber,variablename
```

where `filenumber` is an open file number and `variablename` is a string or variant variable. If you try to read more lines of text than are in the file, an error occurs. Therefore, you should use the `EOF` (end-of-file) function to check whether you have reached the end of file before attempting to read again.

After you open the file, you can choose from several methods of reading information from it. In the example, each name is the only piece of information on each line, so no further processing on the string variable is necessary. However, sometimes you may want to read less than a whole line or store more than one piece of information on a single line. In these cases, you can use the `Input #` statement or the `Input` function.

The `Input #` statement is designed to read information stored in a delimited fashion. For example, the following line of a text file contains three distinct pieces of information: a string, a number, and a date. Commas, quotation marks, and the `#` symbol are used to delimit the information.

```
"Test",100,#1998-01-01#
```

The following line of code correctly reads each item from the file into the appropriate variables:

```
Input #1, stringvar, intvar, datevar
```

Remember that the `Input #` statement looks for those delimiters, so make sure that your `Input #` statements match the format of the file.

Another method of reading information is the `Input` function. The `Input` function allows you to specify the number of characters to read from the file, as in the following example:

```
'Reads five Character from file number 1
s = Input(5,#1)
```

Now, compare how each of the methods just discussed would process the same line in a file:

```
'Assume our file has the following line repeated in it:
"This is a test string."

Dim s As String

Line Input #1, s
's contains the entire string including quotes

Input #1, s
's contains the string without quotes

s = Input(5,#1)
's Contains the first 5 characters ("This)
```

Writing to a Sequential Text File

One good use of a sequential text file is a log file. For example, I have a scheduler application that runs programs and database updates. I rarely work at the machine on which the scheduler application is running, but I can connect over the network and view the log file to see whether the updates have completed.

> **TIP** You can create batch files, FTP scripts, and many other simple file formats on-the-fly by using sequential text files.

Listing 21.2 is a subroutine called `LogPrint`, which can be added to your program to log error messages. It writes the error message and date to a sequential text file.

Listing 21.2 LOGPRINT.ZIP—Using a Sequential Output File to Build an Application Log

```
Sub LogPrint(sMessage As String)
   Dim nFile As Integer
   nFile = FreeFile
   Open App.Path & "\ErrorLog.TXT" for Append Shared as #nFile
   Print #nFile,format$(Now,"mm-dd hh:mm:ss") & " - " & sMessage
   Close #nFile
End Sub
```

The function can be called from an error routine or to inform you of a program event:

```
LogPrint "The database was successfully opened."
```

Working with Text Files

The output of the log file can be viewed with a text editor, as shown in Figure 21.5.

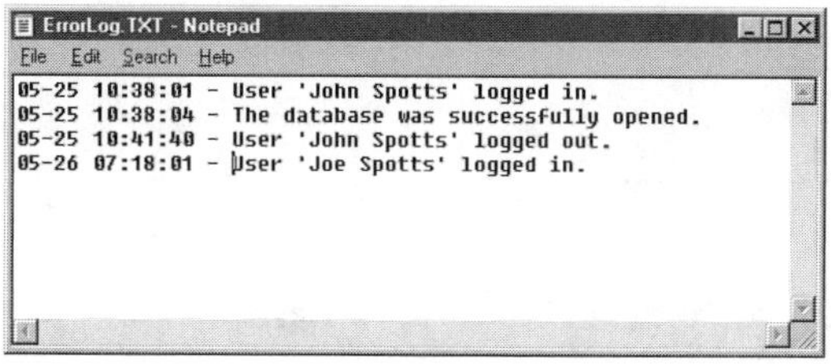

FIGURE 21.5
With a few lines of code, you can add a log file to your application.

```
ErrorLog.TXT - Notepad
File Edit Search Help
05-25 10:38:01 - User 'John Spotts' logged in.
05-25 10:38:04 - The database was successfully opened.
05-25 10:41:40 - User 'John Spotts' logged out.
05-26 07:18:01 - User 'Joe Spotts' logged in.
```

Recall from Listing 21.1 (in the preceding section) that you opened the file in input mode by using the keyword `Input`. To write data, you open the file for sequential output. However, instead of using the keyword `Output`, you use `Append`. Compare the following two lines of code, each of which opens a file for output:

```
'Append mode - adds to an existing file or creates a new one
Open "ErrorLog.TXT" for Append as #1

'Output Mode - always creates a new file, erases any existing information
Open "ErrorLog.TXT" for Output as #1
```

Append mode means data written to the file is added to the end of any existing data. This is perfect for the log file application because you want to keep adding to the log file. Opening a file for `Output` means that any existing data will be erased. In either case, the `Open` statement automatically creates the file if it does not exist. After a file has been opened for `Output`, you can use a couple of different statements to write information to it. The `Print#` and `Write#` statements, described in the next section, provide different formatting options for sequential files.

Using *Print* and *Write* The `Print#` statement works almost exactly like the `Print` method described in Chapter 20, "Accessing the Windows API," except instead of going to an onscreen object, the output is routed to the open file. Unless a semicolon or other separator is at the end of the list of things to be printed, a new line is automatically inserted into the file after each print. The syntax of the `Print#` statement is

```
Print #filenum,expressions
```

Another statement, the `Write#` statement, works like the `Print#` statement but automatically adds separators and delimiters. The syntax of the `Write#` statement is

```
Write #filenum,expressions
```

The `Write` statement is intended for use with the `Input#` statement, described earlier in the "Reading from a Sequential Text File" section. Some examples of both statements are listed here, and the resulting file is shown in Figure 21.6.

```
Print #1, "This is an example of Print# and Write#"
Print #1, "Siler","Brian"
Write #1, "Siler","Brian"
Print #1, "Really?", 2*3;Spc(5);"Good.";
Write #1,"Date",1/1/1998,1000*5;
Print #1, vbCrLf & "Bye!"
```

FIGURE 21.6
Whereas `Print#` gives you more control over output format, `Write#` adds delimiters for easy retrieval of information.

```
This is an example of Print# and Write#
Siler          Brian
"Siler","Brian"
Really?     6      Good."Date",5.00500500500501E-04,5000,
Bye!
```

Random Files—Creating Your Own File Format

Sequential files do not have any structure. As a matter of fact, the structure is defined by the code that reads the file rather than in the file itself. As you learned in the previous section, this feature is advantageous from a readability standpoint but limits the functions that a programmer can use to search through the file. For example, Visual Basic does not contain a function to jump to a specific record in a sequential file because Visual Basic does not know the file's structure. One way to move some structure into the file itself is to store user-defined record types rather than just string data. You can then open them in Random mode and are not limited to sequential access.

Creating a Record Type

Custom record types are really just user-defined data types. You create user-defined data types by using the `Type` statement. Type declarations are entered in the general declarations section of a Code window. The following code uses the `Type` statement to declare an `Employee` record type:

```
Private Type Employee
    EmpID As Integer
    LName As String * 30
    Fname As String * 20
    Title As String * 20
End Type
```

The custom record type can then be accessed from code by using dot notation, as in the following example:

```
Dim emp1 As Employee
Emp1.Fname= "Joe"
Emp1.Lname= "Smith"
Emp1.Title= "Chicken Plucker"
Emp1.EmpID = 12345
```

Notice that accessing fields in a custom data type is similar to accessing an object's properties, as discussed in Chapter 4, "Using Visual Basic's Default Controls."

Opening a Random Access File

The main difference between opening a random access file and a sequential file is that you must specify the record length in the Open statement. The record length for a user-defined data type can be obtained by using the Len statement on a variable of that type, as in the following example:

```
Dim emp1 As Employee
Open "D:\EMPINFO.DAT" for Random As #1 Len = Len(emp1)
```

The preceding line of code opens the file EMPINFO.DAT for random access. The Len= part of the Open statement tells Visual Basic that subsequent reads and writes to the file will assume that the file contains only records the length of emp1.

Adding Records with *Put*

After you open a file for random access, use the Put statement to store records in the file. The syntax of the Put statement is as follows:

```
Put filenumber,[recnumber],variablename
```

The following code uses the Put statement in a For loop to write five records of type Employee to file #1:

```
For i = 1 To 5
    emp1.LName = InputBox$("Enter Last Name")
    emp1.Fname = InputBox$("Enter First Name")
    emp1.Title = InputBox$("Enter Title")
    emp1.EmpID = i
    Put #1, , emp1
Next i
```

Notice the omission of the *recnumber* parameter, which specifies the location in the file where the new record should be written. This approach is useful for altering existing records in a file. If you do not specify this parameter, the record is written to the current file pointer location.

Retrieving Records with *Get*

To retrieve records from a random file, use the Get statement. The Get statement can be used to read information back into your record type, as in the following example that reads record number 4 in the file into the variable emp1 and then displays the Title field:

```
Get #1, 4, emp1
MsgBox "Employee title is " & emp1.Title
```

The syntax of the Get statement is similar to Put:

```
Get filenumber,[recnumber],variablename
```

If you omit the *recnumber* parameter, Get behaves like the sequential Line Input statement; that is, each subsequent Get reads the next record.

Random Access with *Seek*

To move from record to record, use the `Seek` statement. The `Seek` statement has two parameters, the file number and record number, as shown here:

```
Seek #1,3
```

The preceding line of code causes the next `Put` or `Get` to access record number 3.

INI Files

INI files (pronounced "any files" by us southerners) are useful for storing program information and user settings. An INI file is basically a text file with a simple structure that allows you to save and retrieve specific pieces of information; its filename extension is INI, short for *initialization*. By storing information in an INI file, you can avoid hard-coding values in your program. This way, you can easily change values without recompiling the program. In the following sections, you will look at some possible uses for INI files and discover what you need to do to use them in a program.

Understanding INI Files

The structure of INI files is simple. INI files can be viewed and edited with Notepad, or any other text editor. A sample INI file is shown in Figure 21.7.

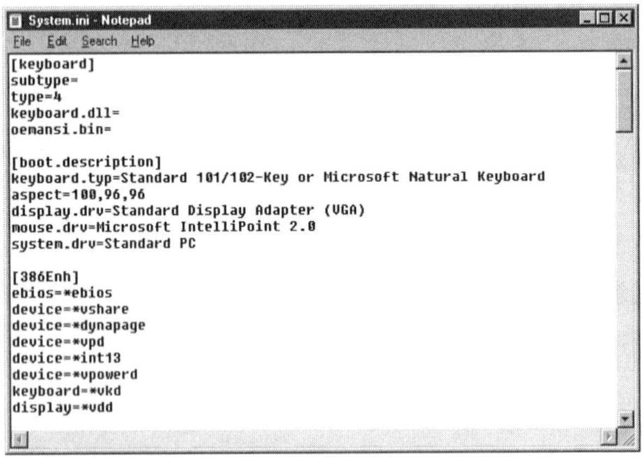

FIGURE 21.7
INI files can be used to store user settings and other information in an organized manner.

The three elements to an INI file are *sections*, *keys*, and *values*. (Microsoft calls a section an *application*; the reason for this involves the history of INI files when an application stored its own settings in WIN.INI.) The parts of an INI file are summarized in Table 21.3.

Table 21.3 Parts of an INI File

Element	Description
Section	A name enclosed in brackets ([ ]) that groups a set of values and keys together.
Key	A unique string. The key will be followed by an equal sign (=) and a value. A key needs to be unique only within a specific section.
Value	The actual information of a particular key in the INI file. A section and key together are used to read or write a value.

The order of sections and keys within the file is not important because the section and key names (should) point to only one value. One final note on the structure of an INI file: A semicolon (;) is used to indicate a comment; any keys or values following a semicolon are ignored. For example, look at this INI section:

```
[Settings]
DBLocation=P:\USERINFO.MDB
;DBLocation=D:\CODE\TEST.MDB
```

In the preceding section, switching from a local development database to a production database is easy. You can simply "comment out" the line you don't want.

Using INI Files in Visual Basic

One reason INI files are easy to use is that you do not have to worry about creating the file, opening the file, or finding the correct line. Before you can use INI files, however, you have to declare two Windows API functions and write a couple of "wrapper" functions around them. (To learn more about API calls, see Chapter 20, "Accessing the Windows API.") Simply add a new module to your program, and enter the code from Listing 21.3 in the General Declarations section.

> **TIP** Build a library of useful functions like these in a separate module (for example, UTILITY.BAS) that can easily be added to multiple projects.

Listing 21.3 INIFUNC.BAS—Using INI Files in Your Program

```
'API DECLARATIONS
Declare Function GetPrivateProfileString Lib "kernel32" Alias _
                 "GetPrivateProfileStringA" (ByVal lpApplicationName _
                 As String, ByVal lpKeyName As Any, ByVal lpDefault _
                 As String, ByVal lpReturnedString As String, ByVal _
                 nSize As Long, ByVal lpFileName As String) As Long
Declare Function WritePrivateProfileString Lib "kernel32" Alias _
                 "WritePrivateProfileStringA" (ByVal lpApplicationName _
                 As String, ByVal lpKeyName As Any, ByVal lpString As Any, _
                 ByVal lpFileName As String) As Long
```

continues

Listing 21.3 Continued

```
Public Function sGetINI(sINIFile As String, sSection As String, sKey _
            As String, sDefault As String) As String

    Dim sTemp As String * 256
    Dim nLength As Integer

    sTemp = Space$(256)
    nLength = GetPrivateProfileString(sSection, sKey, sDefault, sTemp, _
            255, sINIFile)
    sGetINI = Left$(sTemp, nLength)

End Function

Public Sub writeINI(sINIFile As String, sSection As String, sKey _
        As String, sValue As String)

    Dim n As Integer
    Dim sTemp As String

    sTemp = sValue

    'Replace any CR/LF characters with spaces
    For n = 1 To Len(sValue)
        If Mid$(sValue, n, 1) = vbCr Or Mid$(sValue, n, 1) = vbLf _
            Then Mid$(sValue, n) = " "
    Next n

    n = WritePrivateProfileString(sSection, sKey, sTemp, sINIFile)

End Sub
```

After the code in Listing 21.3 has been entered, you can now use the function sGetINI and the subroutine writeINI to easily read and write to an INI file. The following example shows how you can retrieve settings from an INI file for use at program startup.

Listing 21.4 INIEXAMPLE.ZIP—Using an INI File for Program Settings

```
Sub InitProgram()

Dim sINIFile As String
Dim sUserName As String
Dim nCount As Integer
Dim i As Integer

'Store the location of the INI file
sINIFile = App.Path & "\MYAPP.INI"

'Read the user name from the INI file
sUserName = sGetINI(sINIFile, "Settings", "UserName", "?")

If sUsername = "?" Then
    'No user name was present - ask for it and save for next time
    sUserName = InputBox$("Enter your name please:")
    writeini sINIFile, "Settings","UserName",sUserName
End If
```

```
'Fill up combo box list from INI file and select the user's
'last chosen item
nCount = Cint(sGetINI(sINIFile, "Regions", "Count", 0) )
For i = 1 to nCount
cmbRegn.AddItem sGetINI(sINIFile, "Regions", "Region" & i,"?")
Next i

cmbRegn.Text = sGetINI(sINIFile, "Regions", _
                "LastRegion",cmbRegions.List(0))

End Sub
```

The code in Listing 21.4 first checks the INI file for a username. By providing the default value ?, you know whether the username already exists in the INI file and can prompt for it. The default value is a great feature because it does not matter whether the INI file even exists.

The next part of the code sample reads the number of regions from the INI file and uses that value to place each region in a combo box. The final statement sets the Text property of the combo box to a value from the INI file, using the first item in the list as a default.

> **NOTE** Remember that writeINI is a subroutine, so it does not require parentheses.

Driving your program from INI files, as demonstrated in Listing 21.4, allows you to make minor changes to the program quickly and easily without even recompiling it.

From Here...

In this chapter, you looked at some of the file functions built in to the VB language, as well as examined how to use INI files in your application. From Visual Basic, you can copy, delete, and rename files, as well as store information in a variety of formats. Although the methods discussed in this chapter do not have the power of a database engine, they are well suited to simple tasks in which you cannot have a lot of extra overhead.

For more information about the topics discussed in this chapter, see the following chapters:

- If you want to learn about more advanced methods of information storage, see Chapter 24, "Database Basics."
- To find out additional information about API functions, see Chapter 20, "Accessing the Windows API."
- To learn more about text file access from a Web browser, see Chapter 30, "Using VBScript."

CHAPTER 22

Using OLE to Control Other Applications

In this chapter

Working with Word Obects 490

Working with Excel 496

Using the OLE Container Control 497

OLE, which stands for *object linking and embedding*, was introduced as a way to integrate the Microsoft Office family of products. Applications that support OLE allow users to use one application from within another without leaving the context of the original program's interface. The Microsoft Office suite is a stellar example of a group of individual programs that use OLE to work together. This capability makes a software suite much more than just a group of programs that are packaged together.

For example, by using OLE, you can embed an Excel spreadsheet in a Word document. A user working on that Word document can edit the spreadsheet by simply double-clicking it. This action opens Excel functionality while still working in Word.

The benefits to users include the ability to edit different types from a single, unified user interface. A benefit for programmers is that the Office applications contain a great set of exposed OLE (or ActiveX) objects that you can access from Visual Basic. Visual Basic also provides you with a very nice OLE Container control, which makes it very easy to give your users access to OLE-compliant applications from within your VB programs.

When you use Office's OLE objects in Visual Basic, you are essentially "remote controlling" Word or Excel. This means that not only must the applications be installed on a user's machine, but your application acts just as though a user were entering and typing the commands. The application loads, and depending on how you write your VB code, users may be able to watch or interact with it. For these reasons, OLE automation may be slow, but it is still useful in some circumstances.

The following are some advantages of using OLE automation:

- **Professional-looking reports.** Word and Excel can produce some nice printed reports. By driving Word and Excel remotely from VB, you can easily print reports using these programs' advanced formatting capabilities.
- **Automated document creation.** You can create documents and spreadsheets from VB code. For example, you can create a weekly summary of available job openings from a database and email it to prospective applicants.
- **Information retrieval.** You can use OLE objects in Visual Basic to extract information from an Excel spreadsheet and store it in a database.

In this chapter, you examine some of the ways to use Word and Excel from Visual Basic. Although the examples in this chapter will use standard Visual Basic, note that Office applications now practically have Visual Basic built in, so much of the same code described here can be included as VBA code in the document or worksheet itself.

Working with Word Objects

The capability of controlling an instance of Microsoft Word from within a Visual Basic program can lead to some powerful added value for your applications. Users will appreciate being able to edit a Word document without having to leave a specialized program. In this section, you learn how to add Word functionality to your programs.

The Microsoft Word Object Library

To use Word objects from Visual Basic, you must have Word installed on your computer. After Word has been installed, you should see the Microsoft Word Object Library available in Visual Basic's References dialog box, as shown in Figure 22.1.

FIGURE 22.1
To use Word objects in Visual Basic, add a reference to the Word Object Library. (The Word reference from Office 97 is shown here.)

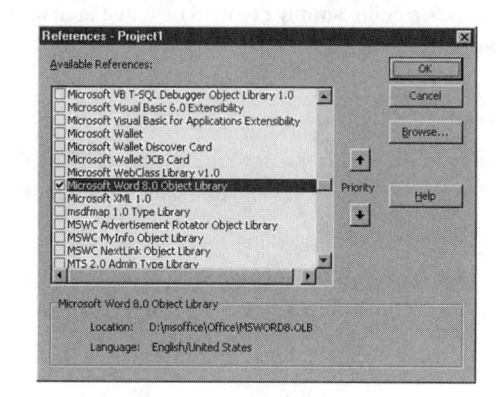

To add the reference, choose Refere<u>n</u>ces from the <u>P</u>roject menu, and place a check mark next to the Microsoft Word Object Library. After referencing the Word Object Library, you can press F2, or choose <u>V</u>iew, <u>O</u>bject Browser to see the objects Word makes available to your program, as in Figure 22.2.

FIGURE 22.2
The Object Browser is a useful tool for discovering what you can do with Word and Excel from Visual Basic.

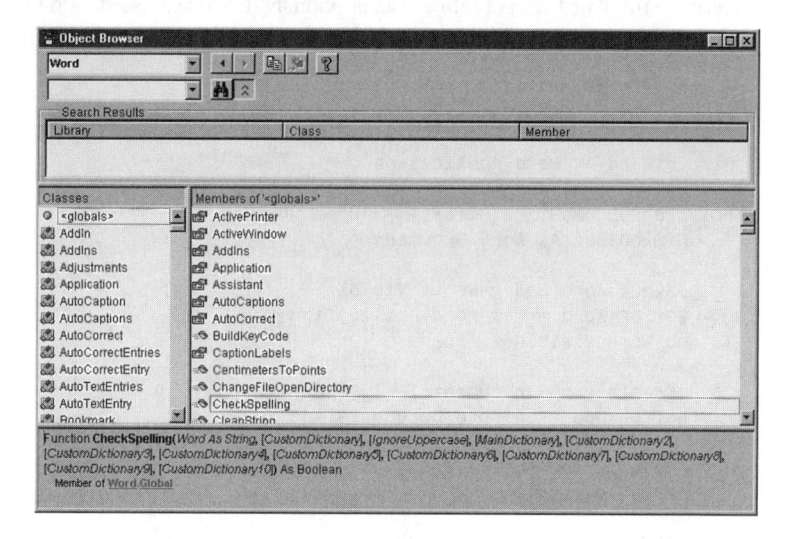

In the following sections, you explore how to manipulate Microsoft Word from Visual Basic by using the Microsoft Word Object Library.

Creating Application and Document Objects

The two most important Word objects you need to know about are the `Word.Application` and `Word.Document` objects, which provide access to instances of the Word application and Word documents, respectively.

To launch Word from Visual Basic code, simply create a new instance of the `Word.Application` object, as you would with any other object:

```
Dim objWord As Word.Application
Set objWord = New Word.Application
```

Here, notice that early binding is used with the `Set` statement, which makes programming with objects easier, as discussed in Chapter 16, "Classes: Reusable Components."

▶ **See** "Declaring and Using Objects," **p. 366**

The preceding two lines of code launch Word on your PC. Word then appears on the task list, but it remains invisible until you set the object's `Visible` property to `True`, as in the following example:

```
objWord.Visible = True
```

You can also create `Word.Document` objects from the application object. The `Word.Application` object contains a `Documents` collection. Recall from Chapter 13 that you can use the `Add` method of a collection to add new objects.

Now you can try a simple example. First, start a new Standard EXE project in Visual Basic and reference the Word Object Library as previously described. Next, add two command buttons, `cmdStart` and `cmdClose`, and enter the code from Listing 22.1 in the form.

Listing 22.1 WORDDEMO.TXT—Using Word from Visual Basic

```
Dim objWord As Word.Application

Private Sub cmdStart_Click()
    Dim objDoc As Word.Document

    'Start Word and make it visible
    Set objWord = New Word.Application
    objWord.Visible = True

    'Create a new document
    Set objDoc = objWord.Documents.Add

    'Make it the active document
    objDoc.Activate

    'Add some text to the document
    objDoc.ActiveWindow.Selection.InsertAfter "This is some text"
    objDoc.ActiveWindow.Selection.InsertParagraphAfter
    objDoc.ActiveWindow.Selection.InsertAfter "This is some more text."
    objDoc.ActiveWindow.Selection.InsertParagraphAfter
```

```
    'Make selected text bold face
    objDoc.ActiveWindow.Selection.Font.Bold = True

    'Unselect text
    objDoc.ActiveWindow.Selection.EndOf

End Sub

Private Sub cmdClose_Click()

    'Close word without saving changes
    objWord.Quit False

    'Destroy object reference
    Set objWord = Nothing

End Sub
```

When you execute the preceding program and click the `cmdStart` button, a new Word document is created. The code in the `Click` event procedure uses the `Selection` object of the document to enter some text and make it boldface.

NOTE In Listing 22.1, a form-level variable for the `Word.Application` object is used so that it can be referenced from multiple subroutines.

In Listing 22.1, you created a document object from the application object. You also can just create the document object directly, as in the following example:

```
Dim objDoc As Word.Document
Set objDoc = New Word.Document
objDoc.ActiveWindow.Selection.TypeText "Hello!"
```

The preceding code creates a new Word document, although unlike the code in Listing 22.1, it uses an existing instance of Word. In other words, if the user already has Word open, a new document is created in the existing copy of Word; whereas the first example creates a new instance of Word regardless.

When you are finished with document or application objects, you can close a document by using the `Close` method and close Word by using the `Quit` method:

```
objDoc.Close False
objWord.Quit False
```

The optional parameter `False` tells Word not to save changes. Omitting this parameter causes Word to prompt the user if a document has not been saved. Depending on your application, you may want to leave Word open for the user to edit a document. In this case, just omit the `Close` and `Quit` methods.

Saving, Opening, and Printing Documents

After creating a Word document in Visual Basic, you can use the `Save` and `SaveAs` methods of the document object to save it to disk. You should first use the `SaveAs` method to specify a filename:

```
objDoc.SaveAs "C:\Temp\MyDoc.Doc"
```

The `Save` method has no parameters; it is intended for saving a document after you have already specified a filename:

```
If objDoc.Saved = False then objDoc.Save
```

Note that you can use the `Saved` property to check whether a document has been saved since any changes were made.

> **NOTE** If you use the `Save` method without first calling `SaveAs`, Word prompts the user for a filename.

To open an existing document, create an instance of the `Word.Application` object and use the `Set` statement with the `Open` of the `Documents` collection:

```
Set objDoc = objWord.Documents.Open ("C:\Temp\Junk.Doc")
```

In the preceding line of code, if the file JUNK.DOC does not exist, Word displays an error message. You can handle this situation yourself in Visual Basic by using an `On Error` statement and checking the document object to see whether the document was actually opened:

```
On Error Resume Next
Set objDoc = objWord.Documents.Open("C:\Temp\Junk.Doc")
If objDoc Is Nothing Then MsgBox "Open was not successful!"
```

To print in Word, use the `PrintOut` and `PrintPreview` methods. The following line of code causes Word to print a document:

```
objdoc.PrintOut
```

If you are creating a report in Word, you might want to use the `PrintPreview` method instead so that the user can view the report and decide whether to print it.

Working with Text

In Listing 22.1, you used the `InsertAfter` and `InsertParagraphAfter` methods to add text to a Word document. However, many additional ways are available for you to work with text in Word.

For example, you can use the `Words` collection to retrieve text a word at a time. The following code sample adds the words in a `Word.Document` object to a list box:

```
For nWord = 1 to objDoc.Words.Count
    lstWords.AddItem "Word " & nWord & " is " & objDoc.Words(nWord).Text
Next nWord
```

You can also replace words in a document by assigning a value to the Text property, although you should keep in mind that replacing a single word with multiple words changes the number of words.

> **NOTE** The Word.Document object also contains Sentences and Paragraphs collections.

An easy way to insert text at a specific location is to use bookmarks. In Microsoft Word, you can place the cursor at a certain location and choose Bookmark from the Insert menu to create a named bookmark. From code, you can use the Bookmarks collection to identify a bookmark:

```
Set objDoc = objWord.Documents.Add("D:\DATA\MyTemplate.DOT")
objDoc.Bookmarks("Name").Range.Text = "John Smith"
objDoc.Bookmarks("Address").Range.Text = "123 Fourth Street"
objdoc.SaveAs "D:\DATA\JSMITH.DOC"
```

In this example, you create a new document from a custom template, add some data at the bookmark locations, and save the document and data to a new filename. Note that this code assumes that the document template MyTemplate contains predefined bookmarks.

Other Useful Features

If you want to create a report using Word, you need to call methods and set properties to control the formatting of the report. One way to make your report look neat is to add tables to the document's Tables collection, as in the following code sample:

```
Dim objTable As Word.Table
Set objTable = objDoc.Tables.Add(objDoc.Range(), 10, 2)
objTable.Cell(1, 1).Range.Text = "Hello"
objTable.Cell(1, 2).Range.Text = "Dolly"
objTable.Columns(2).AutoFit
```

The preceding code inserts a 10-row, 2-column table in the document and adds some text. Finally, the Autofit method is called on the second column to size it to the text in the column.

Another interesting feature is the ability to add your own variables to open documents. This feature is useful, for example, if you have several documents open and need a way to identify them. To add a variable, make up a name and use the Add method of the Variables collection:

```
objDoc.Variables.Add "EMPLOYEEID", "8675309"
```

You can then use your variable to identify a document:

```
For Each objDocTemp In objWord.Documents
        If objDocTemp.Variables("EMPLOYEEID") = "8675309" Then
            Set objDoc = objDocTemp
        End If
Next objDocTemp
```

For the preceding code to work, you must set objDoc to Nothing if it was used previously.

Word.Basic

Throughout the preceding sections, you explored how to use the Microsoft Word Object Library. You used early binding, meaning that objects are declared as a specific type rather than the more generic Object data type. However, if you have to maintain older Visual Basic applications, you may find a different library, the WordBasic library. Applications that use this object generally declare them as late bound, as in the following example:

```
Dim objWord As Object

Set objWord = CreateObject("Word.Basic")
```

The commands also differ slightly:

```
objWord.FileNew
objWord.StartOfDocument
objWord.FontSize 24
objWord.Insert "Some Big Text"
objWord.FontSize 12
objWord.InsertPara
objWord.Insert "Some Smaller Text"

objWord.FileSaveAS "C:\TEST.DOC"
Set objWord = Nothing
```

Using the preceding example is definitely not the preferred way to access Word from VB, but it is mentioned here so that you are not confused if you run into some old code.

Working with Excel

You can also control Excel from your Visual Basic applications by using the same techniques that you use with Microsoft Word. Like Word, Excel has its own object library, which must be referenced in your Visual Basic project. By using OLE automation with Excel, you can create some neat-looking reports, such as the one shown in Figure 22.3. The layout and formatting of the report was created in Excel, and Visual Basic was used to supply the data.

FIGURE 22.3
This report, which includes a graph and several columns of numbers, would be very difficult to create with Visual Basic's built-in printing functions.

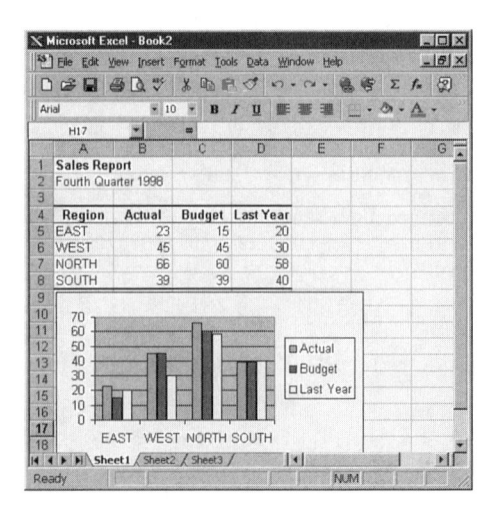

Creating Excel Objects

To start an instance of Excel, use the `Workbook` and `Worksheet` objects. The following code starts Excel and creates a new workbook containing one worksheet:

```
Dim objExcel As Excel.Application
Set objExcel = New Excel.Application
objExcel.Visible = True
objExcel.SheetsInNewWorkbook = 1
objExcel.Workbooks.Add
```

Setting Cell and Range Values

To set the values of individual cells in a worksheet, you can use the `Cells` collection or the `Range` property of the `Worksheet` object:

```
With objExcel.ActiveSheet
    .Cells(1,2).Value = "10"
    .Cells(2,2).Value = "20"
    .Cells(3,2).Value = "=SUM(B1:B2)"
    .Range("A3") = "Total"
End With
```

> **NOTE** Range also works with named ranges of one or more cells:
> ```
> objExcel.ActiveSheet.Range("myrange").Font.Color = vbRed
> ```

Notice that a `With` statement is used so that the object name is not repeated. In Excel, you may find that the object you need to reference is several levels deep in a collection:

```
ObjExcel.Workbooks(1).Sheets("Portfolio").Range(2,4).Font.Bold = True
```

Although this approach may seem confusing, it is a good way to organize a large number of classes. When you're programming Excel and Word, you can employ several methods to make working with collections easier:

- Create an intermediate object variable.
- Use the dot notation, as in the preceding line of code.
- Use a `With` statement to avoid extra typing.

Using the OLE Container Control

The OLE Container control allows you to embed or link OLE objects in your program. In preceding sections, you learned about using OLE objects to control another application. Using the OLE control is different in that the external object appears on a form in your program rather than as a separate application. In other words, you can have a form with buttons, labels, and an OLE control that contains a Word document. You can create the embedded object either at designtime or runtime, as long as the OLE control has been placed on your form.

Creating an Embedded Object at Designtime

As an example, create an embedded Windows Paintbrush object now. First, start a new Standard EXE project and draw the OLE Container control on the form. As soon as you draw the OLE Container control, the Insert Object dialog box, shown in Figure 22.4, appears.

FIGURE 22.4
The Insert Object dialog box lets you specify an embedded object at designtime.

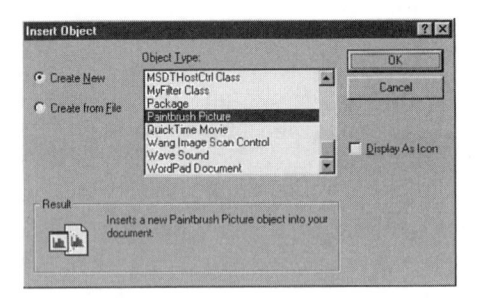

The Insert Object dialog box lists all the available objects that can be used with the OLE control. If you do not select an object, the OLE control becomes a placeholder for an object, which can be created at runtime. For the example, choose Paintbrush Picture and click OK.

States of an Object After choosing an object type and clicking OK, you may have noticed that Visual Basic's toolbars and menus changed. This change happened because the OLE object in the control was *activated*. When an object is active, you can interact with it. In the sample project, because you created a Paintbrush picture object, you can now draw in the control with the mouse and perform all the drawing operations you normally could in Paintbrush.

Draw some lines in the box, and deactivate the object by clicking outside the control on the form. Notice that you can still see your drawing in the inactive object, but the Visual Basic environment has returned to "normal." When an object is inactive, you cannot interact with it. The `DisplayType` property of the OLE control determines whether inactive objects are displayed as icons or as the actual contents (that is, the drawing).

Run your program by pressing F5, and notice that the object's behavior remains the same. Double-clicking the object activates Paintbrush so that you can edit the object, as shown in Figure 22.5.

Saving an Embedded Object to a File Now you can add saving and loading capability to the sample application. Add two command buttons, `cmdSave` and `cmdLoad`, to the form and enter the following code:

```
Private Sub cmdSave_Click()
    Open "C:\OBJECT.DAT" For Binary As #1
    OLE1.SaveToFile 1
    Close #1
End Sub
Private Sub cmdLoad_Click()
    Open "C:\OBJECT.DAT" For Binary As #1
    OLE1.ReadFromFile 1
    Close #1
End Sub
```

FIGURE 22.5
Notice that an active OLE object's File menu does not automatically appear because saving the file is up to the programmer.

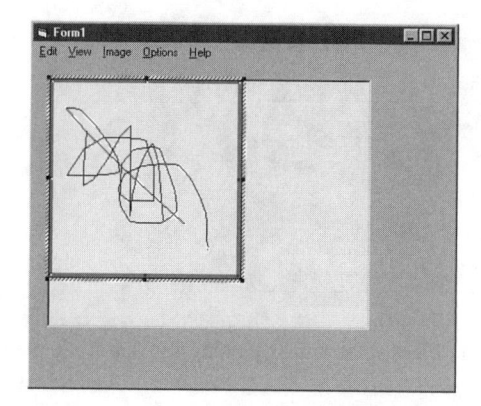

Notice that even though you are using methods of the OLE control to save and load the file, you still have to open the file yourself by using the Open statement. You can test the code by saving the drawing, making some changes to it, and then loading the original drawing back into the control.

Creating an Embedded Object at Runtime

In the preceding example, you created an embedded Paintbrush picture object at designtime. You can also create an "empty" OLE Container control at designtime and load the embedded object at runtime.

To create an empty OLE Container control, just choose Cancel when the Insert Object dialog box appears, or right-click the control and choose Delete Embedded Object if one already exists.

Create an embedded object at runtime by using the OLE control's CreateEmbed method. The CreateEmbed method takes two parameters: a source document and the class name of the object. You can leave the source document parameter empty if you want a blank object. The following line of code creates a Paintbrush picture object in an OLE control named OLE1:

```
OLE1.CreateEmbed "","Paint.Picture"
```

Notice that you have to specify the class name to create the object. You can view a list of valid class names by clicking the ellipses (...) in the Properties window by the Class property of the OLE control.

Creating a Linked Object

The OLE control is also capable of creating linked objects. A linked object is linked to an external file rather than embedded in your application. When you activate a linked object, the application window appears for editing the object.

To create a linked document, you must specify a source document name. For a Paintbrush picture object, you specify the location of a bitmap file, as shown in Figure 22.6.

FIGURE 22.6
To create a linked object at designtime, choose a filename and select the Link check box.

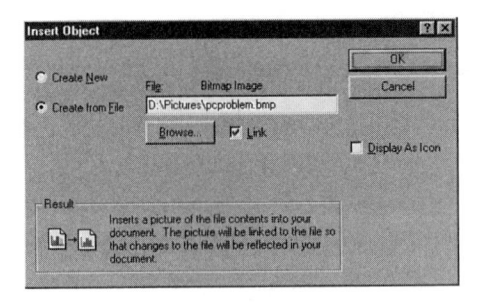

You can also create a linked object at runtime by using the `CreateLink` method, as in the following example:

```
OLE1.CreateLink "C:\Windows\Pinstripe.BMP"
```

When you're using linked objects, changes you make to the object's file are reflected in your program. Also, if you edit the linked object in the program, changes are made to the source file. How the object is updated is controlled by the `UpdateOptions` property, which has the following values:

Constant	Description
vbOLEAutomatic	The object is updated automatically when changes are made to the source file (default).
vbOLEFrozen	The object is updated when the source file is saved from the source application.
vbOLEManual	The object is updated when the `Update` method is called.

In the example from the previous section, changing the `UpdateOptions` property determines when the changes made to the Paintbrush drawing are reflected in the OLE control.

From Here...

In this chapter, you learned about using OLE to control other applications and embed objects in a program. Although the focus was on specific products, keep in mind that you may have other non-Microsoft products with their own type libraries installed on your system. To build on the material discussed in this chapter, refer to the following chapters:

- To learn more about classes and collections, see Chapter 16, "Classes: Reusable Components."
- To find out how to include data in your reports, see Chapter 24, "Database Basics."

CHAPTER 23

Master's Toolbox

In this chapter

Caller ID with Visual Basic 502

Building a Screen Saver with Visual Basic 509

SQL Server to Access Database Table Export Program 512

Using the Windows API to Create Transparent Images 519

This chapter is for people who learn by example. After the previous edition, many readers wanted even more examples, so based on their suggestions, this chapter includes a hodgepodge of various projects built with Visual Basic. In addition, the projects in this chapter bring together practical applications of information from the other chapters. After you are comfortable with Visual Basic, try some of these things; most of them are even fun!

Caller ID with Visual Basic

Caller ID is a service provided by the telephone company that lets you know the caller's name and/or number on a display screen, much like an office phone system. The information is transmitted between rings so that you can see the information before picking up the phone.

In this age of unsolicited telemarketing calls, Caller ID is a great invention, but of course there's a catch: To screen calls, you have to be near the display unit when the phone rings—that is, unless you write the Visual Basic program described in this section (see Figure 23.1). This program simulates the standard Caller ID display box with one addition—sound. When the phone rings, this program plays a sound file that you assign to a specific caller. For example, you can have the computer sound card scream "Don't answer it!" when the telemarketers make their rounds.

Although this application is fairly specific, in building it you learn a way to communicate with a modem from Visual Basic, a technique which can be applied to other areas.

FIGURE 23.1
The Caller ID program alerts you by playing a sound file.

Requirements for Using the Sample Program

Because this program interacts with the "real world" to some degree, you must follow some basic requirements to use it:

- You have to subscribe to a Caller ID service.
- You must have a modem that supports Caller ID data attached to the phone line.
- You have to know the commands to get your modem to display the data and the exact format in which it will be displayed.

Before you even get into Visual Basic, you should determine the commands necessary to use Caller ID with your modem and test it in a terminal program such as HyperTerminal. For example, issuing the command AT#CID=1 to my modem causes it to activate Caller ID display. Then, whenever the phone rings, the information is presented in the terminal session as follows:

```
RING

DATE = 0417
TIME = 2005
NMBR = 9015551212
NAME = SILER BRIAN

RING
```

NOTE The format and Caller ID implementation vary from modem to modem. For example, my ISDN modem returns the information in an entirely different manner. Although you can easily modify this program to suit your modem, being familiar with your modem's Caller ID format is imperative. ■

After you have determined how to get the Caller ID information from your modem using a terminal session, the next step is to write a Visual Basic application that talks to the modem, receives this information, and takes action based on it. The sample application described in this section issues the command to turn on Caller ID display, and then it repeatedly polls the modem to check for Caller ID data. If any data appears, the program plays the appropriate WAV file. The heart of this program is the Microsoft Communications (MS Comm) Control, which is the component that allows you to talk to the modem from VB.

VB Techniques You'll Be Using

In addition to the newly covered MS Comm Control, this program brings together some material covered in other chapters of the book: INI files, the Timer control, and API calls. In order to successfully complete this example, you should have a good understanding of each of these concepts.

Playing Sounds   An API call is used to play sounds on the computer's sound card. This specific example is covered in Chapter 20, "Accessing the Windows API." Refer to that chapter if you need help using the sndPlaySound API call.

▶ **See** "Useful API Calls," **p. 457**

Using Intervals   The Timer control, covered in Chapter 4, "Using Visual Basic's Default Controls," is used to initiate the process of checking for Caller ID data. In the sample program, the Timer event is coded with only a single line as follows:

```
Private Sub tmrMain_Timer()

    CheckForCall

End Sub
```

CheckForCall is a custom function you will write that checks the modem for new information.

▶ **See** "Special-Purpose Controls," **p. 78**

The INI Configuration File An INI file stores the information about each call as well as the path to the WAV file you want to play for each caller. You could, of course, store this information in a database or other file, but I picked an INI file because it has low overhead and is easy to edit. A sample INI file is shown here:

```
[General]
ComPort=3
InitString="AT#CID=1"
CallCount=3

[XREF]
VANDELAY INDUST=Dad at Work
PIERCE JAMES J=Nelda and Jerry Pierce
TAYLOR TECHNOLOG=This is a sales call, don't answer!
MEMPHIS, TN=Cellular phone in Memphis

[Sounds]
PAY PHONE=D:\wav\Dad.wav
VANDELAY INDUST=D:\wav\Hello.Wav

[Call1]
Time=05/25 03:05 p
Number=901-362-6030
Name=LAZENBY N D

[Call2]
Time=05/25 09:31 p
Number=901-555-1212
Name=PRENTICE BRUCE

[Call3]
Time=05/26 12:43 p
Number=901-754-7222
Name=FRIDAY JOE
```

The INI file is divided into a few basic sections:

- [SOUNDS]. This section contains the path to the WAV file for each caller name.
- [XREF]. This section contains a "friendly name" to display for the caller instead of the phone company name.
- [CALL##]. The program creates a new section as each call is received.
- [GENERAL]. This section contains the current number of [CALL] sections as well as some initialization information.

The program uses the INI wrapper functions sGetINIString and writeINIString described in Chapter 21, "Working with Files," to manipulate the INI file.

▶ **See** "Understanding INI Files," **p. 484**

Starting Out with the Program The next section will focus on the new material related to the communications control. However, if you are following along, complete the following steps to get started:

1. Start a new Standard EXE project.
2. Add a module to the project.
3. Add the code from Chapter 21 necessary to access INI files.
4. Add the code for the `sndPlaySound` API call from Chapter 20.
5. Draw a `Timer` control on the form, `tmrMain`, and set the `Interval` property to 900.
6. Make `Sub Main` the Startup object for the project.
7. You can also begin creating your INI file, using the sample in the preceding section as a model.

Setting Up the Communications Control

The Microsoft Communications (MS Comm) Control allows your Visual Basic programs to transmit and receive data across a serial port or modem (also known as a COM port), much like a terminal emulation application. Before you can use the control in a program, you must add it to the Toolbox. To do so, right-click in an empty area of the Toolbox and select Components from the menu. From the Components dialog box, place a check in the box next to Microsoft Comm Control 6.0 and click OK. The control should then appear in your Toolbox.

Next, draw an instance of the control on your form. Note that it always appears as an icon no matter how large you attempt to draw it.

To set up the MS Comm Control for use with your modem, you need to set these properties:

- `CommPort`. An integer that specifies the COM port to which your modem is attached—for example, 2 for COM2.
- `Settings`. A string that specifies the baud rate and parity settings.

These two properties can be set at design time or at the beginning of your program in the `Load` event or `Sub Main` procedure. If you have a modem on COM3, for example, the statements read as follow:

```
Form1.MSComm1.CommPort = 3
Form1.MScomm1.Settings = "9600,N,8,1"
```

Even if you set the `CommPort` and `Settings` properties at designtime, you still must perform several activities at program startup, namely initializing the communications control and sending the modem a command to turn on Caller ID display. The complete `Sub Main` procedure from the sample application is shown in Listing 23.1.

Listing 23.1 CALLID.ZIP—Initialization Routine for the Caller ID Program

```
Sub Main()
    Dim nComPort As Integer
    Dim sInit As String
    Dim sTemp As String
    Dim bStop As Boolean
```

continues

Listing 23.1 Continued

```
    sINIfile = App.Path & "\CALLID.INI"
    nComPort = CInt(sGetINIString(sINIfile, "General", "ComPort", "2"))
    sInit = sGetINIString(sINIfile, "General", "InitString", "AT#CID=1")

    With frmMain
        'SET UP THE COM PORT
        .MSComm1.CommPort = nComPort
        .MSComm1.Settings = "9600,N,8,1"
        .MSComm1.InputLen = 0

        'OPEN THE CONNECTION AND SEND THE INIT STRING
        .MSComm1.PortOpen = True
        .MSComm1.Output = sInit + Chr$(13)

        'WAIT A FEW SECONDS FOR MODEM RESPONSE
        nTemp = 0
        bStop = False
        While nTemp < 32000 And bStop = False
            nTemp = nTemp + 1
            If .MSComm1.InBufferCount >= 2 Then
                sTemp = .MSComm1.Input
                If InStr(sTemp, sInit) = 0 Then bStop = True
            End If
        Wend

        'IF THE MODEM DIDN'T SAY OK THEN END
        If InStr(sTemp, "OK") = 0 Then
            MsgBox "Modem did not respond with OK.", vbOK + vbCritical, "Error"
            End
        End If
        DoEvents

        'CLEAR REMAINING BUFFER INPUT
        sTemp = .MSComm1.Input

        'START THE TIMER
        .tmrMain.Enabled = True

    End With

    'DISPLAY CALLER INFORMATION FROM LAST TIME
    nCount = CInt(sGetINIString(sINIfile, "General", "CallCount", "0"))
    DisplayList nCount
    frmMain.Show

End Sub
```

The code in Listing 23.1, which executes only at program startup, demonstrates how to send and receive commands with the modem. Commands are sent to the modem using the MS Comm Control's Output property. (Note that the carriage return is added, just as you would type it.) In other words, if you want to dial a number using the ATDT command, you simply assign the command to the Output property. In Listing 23.1, this property is used to send the initialization string from the INI file to the modem.

If you think back to the process of sending commands to a modem by hand, you may remember that the modem responds with status messages such as `OK` or informational messages such as the Caller ID data or a register setting. The MS Comm Control captures these messages and stores them in a buffer. You use the control's `Input` property to pull information from this buffer into your program, typically by assigning it to a variable. In Listing 23.1, you check the `InputBufferLen` property to determine whether the control has any data waiting in the buffer. If data is present, you check the data with the `Instr` function to see whether the modem has responded to the initialization string with `OK`.

> **NOTE** The `InputLen` property controls the number of characters removed from the buffer when you access the `Input` property. Setting it to zero, as done here, causes every character in the buffer to be returned. ■

If the modem responds with `OK`, then you have successfully established communications with it and are ready to begin the process of checking for Caller ID information. To do so, you set the `Enabled` property of the timer to `True`, which starts the process. The only remaining item in the `Main` function is to display the last caller (stored in the INI file) on the form. The procedure `DisplayList` simply reads the values from the `[Call##]` section of the INI file and populates the labels on the form.

Checking for Calls

The most important routines in the sample Caller ID program are `CheckForCall` and `WriteCIDData`, shown in Listing 23.2. `CheckForCall` takes care of handling the input from the modem, and `WriteCIDData` actually parses the Caller ID information into the INI file.

Listing 23.2 CALLID.ZIP—Procedures That Parse the Information from the MS Comm Control

```
Sub CheckForCall()
    Dim nPrevCount As Integer
    Dim l As Long
    Dim sFile As String
    
    With frmMain
        If .MSComm1.InBufferCount >= 2 Then
            
            'STOP TIMER AND GET INPUT FROM COM PORT
            .tmrMain.Enabled = False
            sTemp = .MSComm1.Input
            
            'If input is a small string then ignore
            'It is just the first 'RING' response.
            If Len(sTemp) < 10 Then
                .tmrMain.Enabled = True
                Exit Sub
            End If
```

continues

Listing 23.2 Continued

```
                'STORE CALL COUNTER, ADD INFO TO INI FILE
                nPrevCount = nCount
                WriteCIDData (sTemp)

                'IF NO DATA WAS FOUND THEN EXIT
                If nCount = nPrevCount Then
                    ClearStuff
                    .lbldbName = "No Data Sent " & Now
                    Exit Sub
                End If

                'DISPLAY CALLER INFORMATION ON THE FORM,
                'PLAY THE SOUND FILE A COUPLE OF TIMES
                DisplayList nCount

                sTemp = sGetINIString(sINIfile, "Call" & nCount, "Name", "Unknown")
                sFile = sGetINIString(sINIfile, "Sounds", sTemp, "?")
                If sFile <> "?" Then
                    l = sndPlaySound(sFile, SND_SYNC)
                    l = sndPlaySound(sFile, SND_ASYNC)
                End If
            End If

            'CLEAR ANY EXTRA INPUT FROM THE COMM CONTROL
            sTemp = .MSComm1.Input

            'RESTART TIMER FOR NEXT CALL
            .tmrMain.Enabled = True

        End With

End Sub
Sub WriteCIDData(sInput As String)
    Dim sName As String
    Dim sNumber As String
    Dim sTime As String
    Dim sDate As String
    Dim sSection As String

    'PARSE EACH PIECE OF INFORMATION FROM THE INPUT STRING
    'THIS WILL VARY FROM MODEM TO MODEM (MINE IS A CARDINAL 33.6)

    sNumber = "?"

    If InStr(sInput, "MESG =") Then
        nTemp = InStr(sInput, "MESG =")
        sName = Mid(sInput, nTemp + 7)
        sNumber = "NO NUMBER SENT"
    Else
        nTemp = InStr(sInput, "NMBR =")
        If nTemp <> 0 Then sNumber = Mid(sInput, nTemp + 7, 10)

        nTemp = InStr(sInput, "NAME =")
        If nTemp <> 0 Then sName = Mid(sInput, nTemp + 7)
```

```
            nTemp = InStr(sInput, "DATE =")
            If nTemp <> 0 Then sDate = Mid(sInput, nTemp + 7, 4)

            nTemp = InStr(sInput, "TIME =")
            If nTemp <> 0 Then sTime = Mid(sInput, nTemp + 7, 4)

            sTemp = Left$(sNumber, 3) & "-" & Mid$(sNumber, 4, 3) _
                    & "-" & Right$(sNumber, 4)
            sNumber = sTemp
        End If

        If sNumber = "?" Then Exit Sub

        'WRITE INFORMATION TO THE INI FILE

        nCount = nCount + 1
        writeINIString sINIfile, "General", "CallCount", CStr(nCount)

        sSection = "Call" & nCount
        writeINIString sINIfile, sSection, "Time", Format$(Now, "mm/dd hh:mm a/p")
        writeINIString sINIfile, sSection, "Number", sNumber
        writeINIString sINIfile, sSection, "Name", sName

End Sub
```

The reason you need so many `Instr` calls is that when you receive information using the MS Comm Control, it comes across as one long string, with embedded carriage returns and line feeds. Notice that `WriteCIDData` sends the information to the INI file, and then it is read back as separate fields by the `CheckForCall` function.

ON THE WEB

This project is available at the Web site www.mcp.com/info. The project files are contained in the file CALLID.ZIP.

Building a Screen Saver in Visual Basic

Windows comes with programs known as screen savers, which are executed automatically after a period of inactivity. The theory behind a screen saver is that it will "save" your monitor from having information permanently burned on the picture tube. This burning was particularly a problem with older text-only terminals, which could have the same menu sitting on them for hours at a time. (It is also the reason that owners' manuals for televisions warn against using video games.) You can set the screen saver in the Screen Saver tab of the Display Properties dialog box, as shown in Figure 23.2.

FIGURE 23.2
You can write a VB program to act as a screen saver.

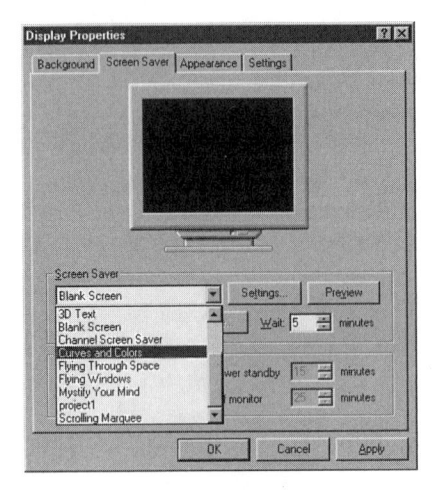

In recent years, the screen saver has almost become an art form, with everything from 3D pipes to flying toasters. However, if you want to be really creative, you can create your own screen saver. In Visual Basic, this task is actually very easy. You write the screen saver just like a normal program, but you program the events differently. For example, mouse movement stops the program. In the next section, you create a simple screen saver.

Setting Up the Main Form

Your screen saver will actually be a Standard EXE project. To begin, start a new Standard EXE project, and modify the form's designtime properties as follows:

1. Set the WindowState property to Maximized.
2. Set the BorderStyle property to None.
3. Set the BackColor property to the color black.

As you know, a screen saver ends when a user moves the mouse or presses keys on the keyboard. Add End statements to the form's MouseMove and KeyPress events as follows:

```
Dim nMouseCount As Integer
Private Sub Form_KeyPress(KeyAscii As Integer)
    End
End Sub

Private Sub Form_MouseMove(Button As Integer, Shift As Integer, _
  X As Single, Y As Single)
    nMouseCount = nMouseCount + 1
    If nMouseCount > 5 Then End
End Sub
```

Note that you use a counter so that the program does not end on the first MouseMove event. You need this counter because Windows sends a couple of MouseMove events to the program when it starts.

Adding Animation

Run the screen saver program in the Visual Basic IDE, and you see a blank screen until you press a key or move the mouse. This screen saver is not very exciting; it needs some animation, which can be added with the Timer control and some Image controls. The Timer control is covered in Chapter 4, "Using Visual Basic's Default Controls." Go ahead and add a simple animation now. For my screen saver, I created a car chase, as you can see in Figure 23.3.

▶ **See** *"Creating a Simple Animation"* **p. 83**

FIGURE 23.3
This screen saver form is shown in design mode, with all the animation elements.

The code for such an animation is simple; just be sure to include a `DoEvents` statement so that the `MouseMove` event can be processed:

```
Dim CarX As Integer, CarY As Integer

Private Sub Form_Load()
If App.PrevInstance Then End
CheckCommandLine
CarX = Me.Width + 1000
CarY = 0
End Sub

Private Sub tmrMain_Timer()
    CarX = CarX - 35
    CarY = CarY + 13

    If CarX < LeftBorder - 1000 Then Form_Load

    imgCar.Top = CarY
    imgCar.Left = CarX
    imgBronco.Top = CarY + 230
    imgBronco.Left = CarX - 7000

    DoEvents
End Sub
```

Also, note that the program ends in the `Load` event if a previous instance occurs. This code is very important because Windows sometimes launches multiple instances of a running screen saver.

Interacting with Windows

Now that you have the screen saver animation completed, you just need to add a few lines of code so that your program works properly as a screen saver. As you may know, the Screen Saver tab of the Display Properties dialog box allows you to configure and preview a screen saver. In each case, Windows sends a different command line to your program. Add the `CheckCommandLine` function to your form so that it acts appropriately:

```
Sub CheckCommandLine()
    Dim sCmdLine As String
    sCmdLine = Trim$(LCase$(Command$))

    'RUNNING AS A SCREEN SAVER
    If sCmdLine = "/s" Or sCmdLine = "" Then
        Exit Sub
    End If

    'RUNNING IN SETUP (CONFIG) MODE
    If sCmdLine = "/c" Then
        MsgBox "Config Screen Not Available"
        End
    End If

    'RUNNING IN PREVIEW MODE
    If Left$(sCmdLine, 2) = "/p" Then
        'parameter can be retrieved with Val(Mid$(sCmdLine,3))
End
    End If

End Sub
```

Finally, all you need to do is compile your project, change the filename extension from .EXE to .SCR, and copy the program to the Windows directory. It should then automatically show up in the list of available screen savers in the Screen Saver tab of the Display Properties dialog box.

SQL Server to Access Database Table Export Program

Large companies tend to rely on all different types of databases, ranging in scale from a mainframe all the way down to a single-user database on an employee's PC. Frequently, new applications that require access to these databases appear, creating a complex web of dependencies between them. For example, a consultant may be hired to write an application that needs to read some data from an established SQL Server database. With ODBC, you can simply allow the consultant's application to attach to the database. However, in certain situations this setup might pose a problem:

- The SQL Server administrator now has to maintain additional login information for the new application.
- SQL Server performance may be negatively affected by the extra application.

- Changing the SQL Server tables accessed by the new application may require changing the application code, which will be difficult after the consultant is long gone.

An easy answer to these problems is to build an export file on an automated basis for the new program to use. An Access database is an ideal format for this export file because the program can use it just as it would the SQL Server.

Building the Sample Program

In case you have not noticed, I like to rely on INI files a lot. There's a reason for this: They can make your program more useful. This result should be especially apparent in this example because the INI file contains all the information the program needs to perform the export operation. You can compile the program once and use several INI files for different exports. It is intended to be a command-line utility and is executed like this:

```
MDBMAKE C:\Data\REVENUE.INI
MDBMAKE C:\Data\Employee.INI
```

The INI files themselves contain information that the program needs to connect to the SQL Server and create the Access tables. For example, entries specify the Access database (destination database) and the SQL Server connect string (source database):

```
DBFile=\\MYSERVER\PUBLIC\HRDATA\HRDATA.MDB
SQLConnect="ODBC:DATABASE=personnel:uid=fred:pwd=garvin:DSN=MYSQLDB"
```

Next, the [Tables] section specifies the name and number of tables you want to create:

```
[Tables]
Tables=4
Table1SQL=hrinfo
Table1MDB=hrinfo
Table1INI=hrinfo
```

Each table also contains a section that specifies the number and type of the fields in the table. For example, the hrinfo section might look like this:

```
[hrinfo]
Fields=2
Fd1Name="EmployeeID"
Fd1Type=DOUBLE
Fd2Name="Name"
Fd2Type=TEXT
Fd2Size=40
```

While executing, the program uses For loops to browse through each section in the INI file as it needs the field information. For example, the hrinfo table created by the program has two fields: EmployeeID, which is of type Double, and Name, which is a 40-character text field.

Understanding the Sample Program

The SQL export program has just a few generic functions and no real user interface (other than a progress screen). The important functions are as follows:

- `CreateLocalFile`. Creates the database (MDB) file.
- `CreateTable`. Creates an empty table in the database.
- `TransferTable`. Transfers data from the SQL Server table to the new database.
- `Main`. Controls the flow of the program.

These functions are shown in Listing 23.3. Following the listing is an explanation of what happens during a sample program run.

Listing 23.3 SQLXPORT.ZIP—Transferring Information from SQL to Access

```
'Important variables:
Dim dbLocal As Database      'Destination database (Access)
Dim dbSQL As Database        'Source database (MS SQL Server)
Dim sDBLocalPath As String   'Path to destination database
Dim sINIPath As String       'Path to INI File

Sub Main()
    Dim sConnect As String       'SQL Server Connect String
    Dim nTables As Integer       'Number of tables to transfer
    Dim nCurTable As Integer     'Counter for current table
    Dim sSQLTable As String      'Name of the SQL table
    Dim sMDBTable As String      'Name of the Access table
    Dim sSection As String       'INI file [Section]
    Dim nCommand As Integer      'Commands can be run on the
    Dim sCommand As String       'Access database (i.e. create index)

    'GET INI FILE NAME
    sINIPath = App.Path & "\SQLXPORT.ini"
    If Trim$(Command$) <> "" Then sINIPath = Command$

    'READ INFO FROM THE INI FILE
    sDBLocalPath = sGetINIString(sINIPath, "General", "DBFile", "test.mdb")
    sConnect = sGetINIString(sINIPath, "General", "SQLConnect", "ODBC;")
    nTables = CInt(sGetINIString(sINIPath, "Tables", "Tables", "0"))

    'SHOW FORM AND CONNECT TO SQL SERVER
    frmWait.Show
    frmWait.lblWait = "Connecting to SQL Server..."
    DoEvents
    On Error GoTo MainError
    Set dbSQL = OpenDatabase("", False, True, sConnect)

    'CALL FUNCTION TO CREATE MDB FILE
    frmWait.lblWait = "Creating MDB file..."
    DoEvents
    CreateLocalFile
    DoEvents

    'CREATE TABLES IN THE NEW MDB FILE
    For nCurTable = 1 To nTables
        sSQLTable = sGetINIString(sINIPath, "tables", "table" & nCurTable & _
                         "SQL", "none")
        sMDBTable = sGetINIString(sINIPath, "tables", "table" & nCurTable & _
```

```
                         "MDB", "none")
        sSection = sGetINIString(sINIPath, "tables", "table" & nCurTable & _
                         "INI", "none")
        frmWait.lblWait = "Transferring " & sMDBTable
        TransferTable sSQLTable, sMDBTable, sSection
    Next nCurTable

    'THE DATABASE HAS BEEN CREATED, RUN COMMANDS ON IT IF NECESSARY
    nCommand = 0
    sCommand = ""
    While sCommand <> "?"
        If nCommand <> 0 Then dbLocal.Execute sCommand
        nCommand = nCommand + 1
        sCommand = sGetINIString(sINIPath, "General", "Command" & nCommand, "?")
    Wend

    'CLOSE EVERYTHING DOWN AND END
    frmWait.lblWait = "Disconnecting..."
    dbLocal.Close
    dbSQL.Close
    Unload frmWait
    DoEvents
    End

MainError:
    frmWait.Hide
    Screen.MousePointer = vbDefault
    WriteErrMsg "Main - Error " & Err & ": " & Error
    End
    Exit Sub

End Sub
Sub TransferTable(sSQLTable As String, sLocalTable As String, sSection As _
            String)

'This function transfers data from SQL server to an Access table

    Dim rstemp As Recordset    'SQL recordset
    Dim aTable As Recordset    'Access table
    Dim nTemp As Integer       '  Counter
    Dim nFields As Integer     '  variables
    Dim nCount As Integer      '
    Dim sSQL As String         'SQL statement
    Dim sTemp As String


On Error GoTo TRTError:

    frmWait.ProgressBar1.Visible = True
    nCount = 0
    frmWait.ProgressBar1.Min = 0

    'The user can either transfer a SQL table as-is,
    'or the results of a query involving multiple tables.
```

continues

Listing 23.3 Continued

```
    'This next IF statement determines which and sets up the
    'SQL statement- either "Select * from table" or the
    'user-defined SQL statement.

    sSQL = sGetINIString(sINIPath, sSection, "SQL", "")
    If sSQL = "" Then
        Set rstemp = dbSQL.OpenRecordset("Select Count(*) from " & sSQLTable, _
                    dbOpenSnapshot, dbForwardOnly)
        frmWait.ProgressBar1.Max = CInt(Trim$(" 0" & rstemp.Fields(0)))
        rstemp.Close
        DoEvents
    Else
        nTemp = 2
        sTemp = sGetINIString(sINIPath, sSection, "SQL" & nTemp, "")
        While sTemp <> ""
            If sTemp <> "" Then sSQL = sSQL & sTemp
            nTemp = nTemp + 1
            sTemp = sGetINIString(sINIPath, sSection, "SQL" & nTemp, "")
        Wend
        frmWait.ProgressBar1.Max = 2000 'Set arbitary value on progress bar
    End If


    'Actually open the recordset
    If sSQL = "" Then
        Set rstemp = dbSQL.OpenRecordset("Select * from " & sSQLTable, _
                    dbOpenSnapshot, dbForwardOnly)
    Else
        Set rstemp = dbSQL.OpenRecordset(sSQL, dbOpenSnapshot, dbForwardOnly + _
                    dbSQLPassThrough)
    End If

    'Open Local table
    Set aTable = dbLocal.OpenRecordset(sLocalTable, dbOpenTable)
    nFields = rstemp.Fields.Count - 1

    'Transfer each record
    While Not rstemp.EOF
        aTable.AddNew
        For nTemp = 0 To nFields
            aTable.Fields(nTemp) = rstemp.Fields(nTemp)
        Next nTemp
        rstemp.MoveNext
        nCount = nCount + 1
        frmWait.ProgressBar1.Value = nCount
        aTable.Update
    Wend
    rstemp.Close
    aTable.Close
    Exit Sub

TRTError:
    WriteErrMsg "TRT-Error " & Err & ": " & Error
```

```
            End
        Exit Sub

End Sub
Sub CreateTable(ByRef tbl As TableDef, sTableName As String, sINISection As _
            String)
'This function creates an empty table in an Access database

        Dim nFields As Integer      'Number of Fields
        Dim Fd() As New Field       'Array of fields
        Dim nCurField As Integer    'Counter for current field
        Dim sTemp As String

    On Error GoTo CRTError:

        nFields = CInt(sGetINIString(sINIPath, sINISection, "Fields", "0"))
        If nFields = 0 Then Exit Sub
        ReDim Fd(1 To nFields)

        tbl.Name = sTableName

        For nCurField = 1 To nFields
            Fd(nCurField).Name = sGetINIString_
                (sINIPath, sINISection, "Fd" & nCurField & "Name", "ERROR" & _
                    nCurField)
            sTemp = sGetINIString(sINIPath, sINISection, "Fd" & nCurField & "Type", _
                    "TEXT")
            Select Case sTemp
                Case "DOUBLE"
                    Fd(nCurField).Type = dbDouble
                Case "MEMO"
                    Fd(nCurField).Type = dbMemo
                    'VB4/5 only
                    Fd(nCurField).AllowZeroLength = True
                Case "BYTE"
                    Fd(nCurField).Type = dbByte
                Case "INTEGER"
                    Fd(nCurField).Type = dbInteger
                Case "DATE"
                    Fd(nCurField).Type = dbDate
                    Fd(nCurField).Required = False

                Case Else 'Text
                    Fd(nCurField).Type = dbText
                    Fd(nCurField).Size = CInt(sGetINIString_
                        (sINIPath, sINISection, "Fd" & nCurField & "Size", "50"))
                    Fd(nCurField).AllowZeroLength = True
            End Select

            tbl.Fields.Append Fd(nCurField)
        Next nCurField
        Exit Sub
```

continues

Listing 23.3 Continued

```
CRTError:
    WriteErrMsg "CRT-Error " & Err & ": " & Error
    End
    Exit Sub
End Sub
Sub CreateLocalFile()
'This procedure creates the MDB file itself
    Dim MainTable() As New TableDef
    Dim sTemp As String
    Dim nTables As Integer
    Dim nCurTable As Integer
    Dim sSQLTable As String
    Dim sMDBTable As String
    Dim sSection As String

On Error GoTo CRLError

    If bFileExists(sDBLocalPath) Then Kill sDBLocalPath
    Set dbLocal = CreateDatabase(sDBLocalPath, dbLangGeneral)

    nTables = CInt(sGetINIString(sINIPath, "Tables", "Tables", "0"))
    ReDim MainTable(1 To nTables)

    For nCurTable = 1 To nTables
        sSQLTable = sGetINIString(sINIPath, "tables", "table" & nCurTable & _
                    "SQL", "none")
        sMDBTable = sGetINIString(sINIPath, "tables", "table" & nCurTable & _
                    "MDB", "none")
        sSection = sGetINIString(sINIPath, "tables", "table" & nCurTable & _
                    "INI", "none")
        CreateTable MainTable(nCurTable), sMDBTable, sSection
        dbLocal.TableDefs.Append MainTable(nCurTable)
    Next nCurTable
    Exit Sub

CRLError:
    WriteErrMsg "CRL-Error " & Err & ": " & Error
    End
    Exit Sub
End Sub
Private Sub WriteErrMsg(sMessage As String)
    'Should an error occur, this function writes it to
    'another INI file. I did it this way because the
    'program runs as a scheduled process on a remote
    'machine, so no one would be there to answer an error
    'dialog. There is a second VB program that continuously
    'checks the Error.ini file and pages me with the error message.

    Dim sErrorINI As String
    sErrorINI = sGetINIString(sINIPath, "General", "ErrorINI", "error.ini")
    writeINIString sErrorINI, "Error", "Message", sMessage
    writeINIString sErrorINI, "Error", "Error", "True"
End Sub
```

First, the `CreateLocalFile` function gets the filename from the `Dbpath=` INI entry and uses Visual Basic's `CreateDatabase` function to create the new (and empty) MDB file. Next, the program uses a `For` loop to read through each table in the `[Tables]` section, repeatedly calling the `CreateTable` procedure. The `CreateTable` procedure, in turn, loops through the fields in the `[tablename]` section of the INI file, creating fields in the new table.

After a table is created, the `TransferTable` procedure takes care of transferring the data from an SQL Server table to one of the new tables. The procedure first creates a recordset from the SQL Server table and then loops through each record in the recordset, transferring the value for each field to the new table. During this process, users see a progress bar, as shown in Figure 23.4, to let them know something is happening.

FIGURE 23.4
The SQL data export program displays a progress bar while in action.

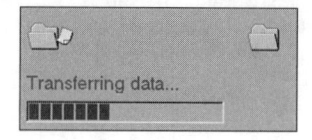

Using the Windows API to Create Transparent Images

One of the most complex features in the Win32 API is the Graphics Device Interface (GDI) APIs. Because these APIs are very complicated, tedious, and GPF prone, Microsoft played it safe and excluded most of them from VB. Although leaving out the APIs shelters you from the complexity and makes your programs more robust, it severely limits your ability to do the "cool" things that many users expect. VB4 helped to relieve this problem to some extent by providing new features such as the `PaintPicture` function and the `ImageList` control, but it still fell short. This means that sometime in the near future you are going to find yourself calling the GDI APIs from your application. To demonstrate some of the more common GDI APIs, you'll write a cool function called `TransparentPaint` in this section.

> **NOTE** The version of the `TransparentPaint` routine you see in this chapter is a Win32 version of the `TransparentBlt` code (written by Mike Bond) that originally appeared in the Microsoft KnowledgeBase KB article number Q94961. This version contains many modifications to the code and includes a wealth of new comments. ■

`TransparentPaint`, shown in Listing 23.4, is designed to treat a bitmap like an icon when you paint it on a surface. You can designate a part of the icons to be transparent, but you cannot do the same with bitmaps. `TransparentPaint` overcomes this limitation by allowing you to make all of a single color on a bitmap transparent. To accomplish this difficult feat, you need to create a series of temporary bitmaps and do some painting in memory only. Although this abstract concept can be complicated, the comments in `TransparentPaint` help explain what is happening at each step.

Listing 23.4 TRANSPAR.ZIP—Code for the *TransparentPaint* Procedure

```
'**********************************************************************
' Paints a bitmap on a given surface using the surface backcolor
' everywhere lngMaskColor appears on the picSource bitmap
'**********************************************************************
Sub TransparentPaint(objDest As Object, picSource As StdPicture, _
    lngX As Long, lngY As Long, ByVal lngMaskColor As Long)
    '**********************************************************************
    ' This sub uses a bunch of variables, so let's declare and explain
    ' them in advance...
    '**********************************************************************
    Dim lngSrcDC As Long        'Source bitmap
    Dim lngSaveDC As Long       'Copy of Source bitmap
    Dim lngMaskDC As Long       'Monochrome Mask bitmap
    Dim lngInvDC As Long        'Monochrome Inverse of Mask bitmap
    Dim lngNewPicDC As Long     'Combination of Source & Background bmps

    Dim bmpSource As BITMAP     'Description of the Source bitmap

    Dim hResultBmp As Long      'Combination of source & background
    Dim hSaveBmp As Long        'Copy of Source bitmap
    Dim hMaskBmp As Long        'Monochrome Mask bitmap
    Dim hInvBmp As Long         'Monochrome Inverse of Mask bitmap

    Dim hSrcPrevBmp As Long     'Holds prev bitmap in source DC
    Dim hSavePrevBmp As Long    'Holds prev bitmap in saved DC
    Dim hDestPrevBmp As Long    'Holds prev bitmap in destination DC
    Dim hMaskPrevBmp As Long    'Holds prev bitmap in the mask DC
    Dim hInvPrevBmp As Long     'Holds prev bitmap in inverted mask DC

    Dim lngOrigScaleMode&       'Holds the original ScaleMode
    Dim lngOrigColor&           'Holds original backcolor from source DC
    '**********************************************************************
    ' Set ScaleMode to pixels for Windows GDI
    '**********************************************************************
    lngOrigScaleMode = objDest.ScaleMode
    objDest.ScaleMode = vbPixels
    '**********************************************************************
    ' Load the source bitmap to get its width (bmpSource.bmWidth)
    ' and height (bmpSource.bmHeight)
    '**********************************************************************
    GetObject picSource, Len(bmpSource), bmpSource
    '**********************************************************************
    ' Create compatible device contexts (DCs) to hold the temporary
    ' bitmaps used by this sub
    '**********************************************************************
    lngSrcDC = CreateCompatibleDC(objDest.hdc)
    lngSaveDC = CreateCompatibleDC(objDest.hdc)
    lngMaskDC = CreateCompatibleDC(objDest.hdc)
    lngInvDC = CreateCompatibleDC(objDest.hdc)
    lngNewPicDC = CreateCompatibleDC(objDest.hdc)
    '**********************************************************************
    ' Create monochrome bitmaps for the mask-related bitmaps
    '**********************************************************************
```

```
hMaskBmp = CreateBitmap(bmpSource.bmWidth, bmpSource.bmHeight, _
    1, 1, ByVal 0&)
hInvBmp = CreateBitmap(bmpSource.bmWidth, bmpSource.bmHeight, _
    1, 1, ByVal 0&)
'*****************************************************************
' Create color bitmaps for the final result and the backup copy
' of the source bitmap
'*****************************************************************
hResultBmp = CreateCompatibleBitmap(objDest.hdc, _
    bmpSource.bmWidth, bmpSource.bmHeight)
hSaveBmp = CreateCompatibleBitmap(objDest.hdc, _
    bmpSource.bmWidth, bmpSource.bmHeight)
'*****************************************************************
' Select bitmap into the device context (DC)
'*****************************************************************
hSrcPrevBmp = SelectObject(lngSrcDC, picSource)
hSavePrevBmp = SelectObject(lngSaveDC, hSaveBmp)
hMaskPrevBmp = SelectObject(lngMaskDC, hMaskBmp)
hInvPrevBmp = SelectObject(lngInvDC, hInvBmp)
hDestPrevBmp = SelectObject(lngNewPicDC, hResultBmp)
'*****************************************************************
' Make a backup of source bitmap to restore later
'*****************************************************************
BitBlt lngSaveDC, 0, 0, bmpSource.bmWidth, bmpSource.bmHeight, _
    lngSrcDC, 0, 0, vbSrcCopy
'*****************************************************************
' Create the mask by setting the background color of source to
' transparent color, then BitBlt'ing that bitmap into the mask
' device context
'*****************************************************************
lngOrigColor = SetBkColor(lngSrcDC, lngMaskColor)
BitBlt lngMaskDC, 0, 0, bmpSource.bmWidth, bmpSource.bmHeight, _
    lngSrcDC, 0, 0, vbSrcCopy
'*****************************************************************
' Restore the original backcolor in the device context
'*****************************************************************
SetBkColor lngSrcDC, lngOrigColor
'*****************************************************************
' Create an inverse of the mask to AND with the source and combine
' it with the background
'*****************************************************************
BitBlt lngInvDC, 0, 0, bmpSource.bmWidth, bmpSource.bmHeight, _
    lngMaskDC, 0, 0, vbNotSrcCopy
'*****************************************************************
' Copy the background bitmap to the new picture device context
' to begin creating the final transparent bitmap
'*****************************************************************
BitBlt lngNewPicDC, 0, 0, bmpSource.bmWidth, bmpSource.bmHeight, _
    objDest.hdc, lngX, lngY, vbSrcCopy
'*****************************************************************
' AND the mask bitmap with the result device context to create
' a cookie cutter effect in the background by painting the black
' area for the non-transparent portion of the source bitmap
'*****************************************************************
```

continues

Listing 23.4 Continued

```
    BitBlt lngNewPicDC, 0, 0, bmpSource.bmWidth, bmpSource.bmHeight, _
        lngMaskDC, 0, 0, vbSrcAnd
    '**********************************************************************
    ' AND the inverse mask with the source bitmap to turn off the bits
    ' associated with transparent area of source bitmap by making it
    ' black
    '**********************************************************************
    BitBlt lngSrcDC, 0, 0, bmpSource.bmWidth, bmpSource.bmHeight, _
        lngInvDC, 0, 0, vbSrcAnd
    '**********************************************************************
    ' XOR the result with the source bitmap to replace the mask color
    ' with the background color
    '**********************************************************************
    BitBlt lngNewPicDC, 0, 0, bmpSource.bmWidth, bmpSource.bmHeight, _
        lngSrcDC, 0, 0, vbSrcPaint
    '**********************************************************************
    ' Paint the transparent bitmap on source surface
    '**********************************************************************
    BitBlt objDest.hdc, lngX, lngY, bmpSource.bmWidth, _
        bmpSource.bmHeight, lngNewPicDC, 0, 0, vbSrcCopy
    '**********************************************************************
    ' Restore backup of bitmap
    '**********************************************************************
    BitBlt lngSrcDC, 0, 0, bmpSource.bmWidth, bmpSource.bmHeight, _
        lngSaveDC, 0, 0, vbSrcCopy
    '**********************************************************************
    ' Restore the original objects by selecting their original values
    '**********************************************************************
    SelectObject lngSrcDC, hSrcPrevBmp
    SelectObject lngSaveDC, hSavePrevBmp
    SelectObject lngNewPicDC, hDestPrevBmp
    SelectObject lngMaskDC, hMaskPrevBmp
    SelectObject lngInvDC, hInvPrevBmp
    '**********************************************************************
    ' Free system resources created by this sub
    '**********************************************************************
    DeleteObject hSaveBmp
    DeleteObject hMaskBmp
    DeleteObject hInvBmp
    DeleteObject hResultBmp
    DeleteDC lngSrcDC
    DeleteDC lngSaveDC
    DeleteDC lngInvDC
    DeleteDC lngMaskDC
    DeleteDC lngNewPicDC
    '**********************************************************************
    ' Restores the ScaleMode to its original value
    '**********************************************************************
    objDest.ScaleMode = lngOrigScaleMode
End Sub
```

For simplicity's sake, I have omitted the API declarations from Listing 23.4. I could go on for pages explaining exactly what is happening during each step of TransparentPaint, but I won't because this sub contains the same comments I've made in this listing. Also, following this listing would be more difficult if it were broken into several smaller blocks. After you read the comments for this sub, I encourage you to single-step through the TRANSPARENT.VBP project, which you can get from Macmillan's Web site at www.mcp.com/info. Reading this project will help you to visualize what is happening at each step.

Although TransparentPaint is a difficult procedure to follow, using it is easy. Listing 23.5 loads a bitmap from a resource and paints it on the upper-left corner of the form using TransparentPaint. Next, it paints the picture using PaintPicture. The last parameter, vbGreen, tells TransparentPaint to replace any bits in the bitmap that are green, with the background color of the form. The result is shown in Figure 23.5.

Listing 23.5 TRANSPAR.ZIP—Using the TransparentPaint Procedure

```
'***********************************************************************
' Transparent.frm - Demonstrates how to use basTransparent's
'    TransparentPaint using a bitmap from a resource file.
'***********************************************************************
Option Explicit
'***********************************************************************
' Gets a StdPicture handle by loading a bitmap from a resource file
' and paints it transparently on the form by using Gray as the mask
' color.
'***********************************************************************
Private Sub cmdPaintTransBmp_Click()
    TransparentPaint Me, LoadResPicture(103, 0), 0, 0, QBColor(7)
End Sub
```

FIGURE 23.5
TransparentPaint is a must for your multimedia applications.

Try replacing the resource file in this project with your own resource file to see how TransparentPaint works. Also, try using different mask colors as well as the images from picture boxes. Now you never have to write an application that appears to be of inferior quality because it doesn't use transparent bitmaps.

From Here...

In this chapter, you explored a variety of specific projects. If you need more information on any of the topics discussed, see the following chapters:

- To learn about API calls, see Chapter 20, "Accessing the Windows API."
- For more information on INI files, see Chapter 21, "Working with Files."

PART **VI**

Visual Basic and Databases

24 Database Basics   527

25 The Data Control and Data-Bound Controls   545

26 Using Data Access Objects (DAO)   565

27 Using Remote Data Objects (RDO)   595

28 Using ActiveX Data Objects (ADO)   611

29 Creating Reports   641

CHAPTER 24

Database Basics

In this chapter

Designing a Database **528**

Implementing Your Design **537**

Using Visual Data Manager **537**

Creating a Database with Other Tools **543**

Why Use a Program Instead of Visual Data Manager? **543**

It's probably fair to say that most business-oriented computer applications work with data in one form or another. This data often is stored in one or more databases. Visual Basic can create powerful data management programs with a little planning and effort. The most fundamental part of that planning is in how the data is structured. A poorly designed database can doom even the most well-intentioned program from the start. On the other hand, a well-designed database can make a programmer's life much easier.

Creating an organized data structure requires you to learn about two separate tasks. First, you must learn about how to design a database. In the design, you decide what data goes in the database and how it will be organized. Second, you must learn how to translate the design into the actual database. You can do so in a variety of ways. In this chapter, you examine many of the considerations involved in designing databases and their structures. You can apply these concepts to any type of database, not just those that you may be designing to use in your Visual Basic applications.

Designing a Database

Like most tasks, building a database starts with a design. After all, you wouldn't try to build a house without a blueprint, and most people wouldn't attempt to prepare a new dish without a recipe. Like these other tasks, having a good design for your database is a major first step in creating a successful project.

In designing a database application, you must set up not only the program's routines for maximum performance, but you must pay attention also to the physical and logical layout of the data storage. A good database design does the following:

- Provides minimum search times when locating specific records
- Stores data in the most efficient manner possible to keep the database from growing too large
- Makes data updates as easy as possible
- Is flexible enough to allow inclusion of new functions required of the program

Design Objectives

When you're creating the design for your database, you must keep several objectives in mind. Although meeting all these design objectives is desirable, sometimes they are mutually exclusive. The primary design objectives are as follows:

- Eliminate redundant data
- Be able to locate individual records quickly
- Make enhancements to the database easy to implement
- Keep the database easy to maintain

Key Activities in Designing Your Database

Creating a good database design involves the following seven key activities:

- Modeling the application
- Determining the data required for the application
- Organizing the data into tables
- Establishing the relationships between tables
- Setting index and validation requirements for the data
- Creating and storing any necessary queries for the application
- Reviewing the design

Now, look briefly at the initial two activities in the list. First, take a look at modeling the application. When you model an application, you first should determine the tasks that the application is to perform. For example, if you're maintaining a membership list, you know that you want to create phone directories and mailing lists of the members. As you're determining the tasks to be performed by the application, you are creating what is called the *functional specification*. For a project that you are creating, you probably know all the tasks that you want to perform, but writing down these tasks in a specification document is a good idea. This document can help you keep focused on what you want your program to do. If you're creating the program for another person, a functional specification becomes an agreement of what the application will contain. This specification also can show milestones that need to be achieved on a set schedule.

When you're creating the program for other people, the best way to learn what task must be performed is to talk to the people requesting the work. As a first step, you can determine if they already have a system that they are looking to replace, or if they have reports that they want to produce. Then you can ask a lot of questions until you understand the users' objectives for the program.

After you determine the functional specifications for the program, you can start determining what data the program needs. In the case of a membership application, knowing that you have to produce directories and mailing lists tells you that the database needs to contain the address and phone number of each of the members. Taking this situation a little further, you know that, by presorting mail by ZIP code, you can take advantage of reduced rate postage. Therefore, you need an index or query that places the mailing list information in zip code order. So, you can see that the model not only tells you the data needed but also defines other components of the database.

Organizing the Data

One of the key aspects of good database design is determining how the data will be organized in the database. To have a good design, you should organize the data in a way that makes the information easy to retrieve and makes maintenance of the database easy. Within a database, data is stored in one or more *tables*. For many database applications, you can accomplish efficient data management by storing data in multiple tables and by establishing relationships between these tables. In the following sections, you learn how to determine what data belongs in each table of your database.

Tables as Topics   A *table* is a collection of information related to a particular topic. By thinking of a key topic for the table, you can determine whether a particular piece of data fits into the table. For example, if a country club wants to track information about members and employees, the club management might be tempted to put both in the same table (because both groups refer to people). However, look at the data required for each group. Although both groups require information about a person's name, address, and phone number, the employee group also requires information about the person's Social Security number, job category, payroll, and tax status. If you were to create just one table, many of the entries would be blank for the members. You also would have to add a field to distinguish between a member and an employee. Clearly, this technique would result in a lot of wasted space. It also could result in slower processing of employee transactions or member transactions because the program would have to skip a number of records in the table. Figure 24.1 shows a database table with the two groups combined. Figure 24.2 shows the reduction in the number of fields in a member-only database table.

FIGURE 24.1
Combining the employee and member tables wastes a lot of space.

LastName	FirstName	Address	City	State	ZIP	Employee	SSN	Title	Payrate
Sparks	Lauren	4302 Brooks Barre	Memphis	TN	38101	Yes	111-22-3456	Game Tester	$15.42
Layton	Michael	123 Tina Marie Pky	Collierville	TN	38017	No			
Cawein	Chris	409 Jackie Road	Boland	MS	10934	No			
Thomas	June	29 Windsor	Philbert	AR	72300	Yes	222-33-4567	Pastry Chef	$21.00
Sparks	Jeffrey	9534 SS North	Memphis	TN	38101	No			
McFarland	Stan	9326 Masonry Lane	Eads	TN	38910	No			
Thomas	John	102 Chrysler Ave	Detroit	MI	65100	Yes	333-44-5678	Engineer	$24.54
Ellis	Gene	127 Dop Road	Memphis	TN	38101	No			
Fortner	Bessie	316 Yaya Place	Germantown	TN	38139	Yes	444-55-6789	Gardener	$21.00
Bradshaw	Stephen	809 W Barton	Dumas	AR	72313	No			
						No			$0.00

FIGURE 24.2
A separate database table for members has only the relevant fields and is more efficient.

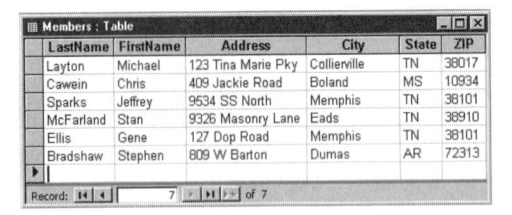

LastName	FirstName	Address	City	State	ZIP
Layton	Michael	123 Tina Marie Pky	Collierville	TN	38017
Cawein	Chris	409 Jackie Road	Boland	MS	10934
Sparks	Jeffrey	9534 SS North	Memphis	TN	38101
McFarland	Stan	9326 Masonry Lane	Eads	TN	38910
Ellis	Gene	127 Dop Road	Memphis	TN	38101
Bradshaw	Stephen	809 W Barton	Dumas	AR	72313

By thinking of the topic to which a table relates, you can determine more easily whether a particular piece of information belongs in the table. If the information results in wasted space for many records, the data belongs in a different table.

Data Normalization   *Data normalization* is the process of eliminating redundant data within a database. Taking data normalization to its fullest extent results in each piece of information in a database appearing only once, although that's not always practical.

Consider the example of order processing. For each item a person orders, you need the item's number, description, price, order number, and order date, as well as the customer's name, address, and phone number. If you place all this information in one table, the result looks like the table shown in Figure 24.3.

FIGURE 24.3
Nonnormalized data produces a large, inefficient data table.

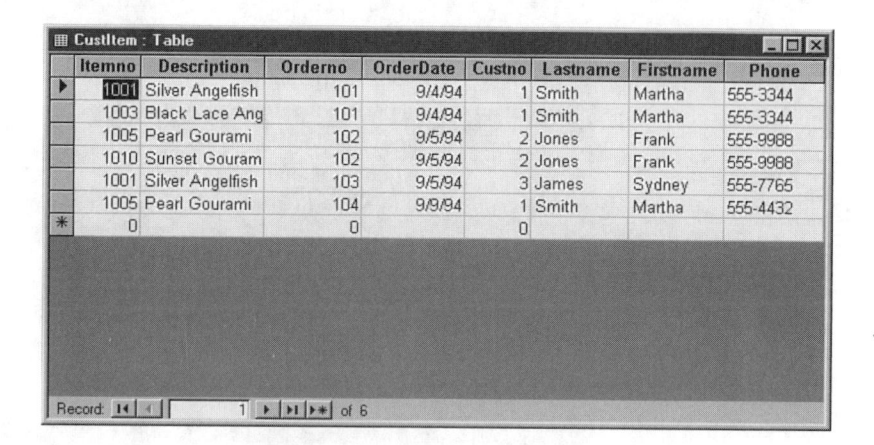

Itemno	Description	Orderno	OrderDate	Custno	Lastname	Firstname	Phone
1001	Silver Angelfish	101	9/4/94	1	Smith	Martha	555-3344
1003	Black Lace Ang	101	9/4/94	1	Smith	Martha	555-3344
1005	Pearl Gourami	102	9/5/94	2	Jones	Frank	555-9988
1010	Sunset Gouram	102	9/5/94	2	Jones	Frank	555-9988
1001	Silver Angelfish	103	9/5/94	3	James	Sydney	555-7765
1005	Pearl Gourami	104	9/9/94	1	Smith	Martha	555-4432
0		0		0			

As you can see, much of the data in the table is repeated. This repetition introduces two problems. The first problem is wasted space, because you repeat information. The second problem is one of data accuracy or currency. If, for example, a customer changes his or her phone number, you have to change it for all the records that apply to that customer—with the possibility that you will miss one of the entries. In the table in Figure 24.3, notice that Martha Smith's phone number was changed in the latest entry but not in the two earlier entries. If an employee looks up Martha Smith and uses an earlier entry, that employee would not find Martha's updated phone number.

A better solution for handling the data is to put the customer information in one table and the sales order information in another table. You can assign each customer a unique ID and include that ID in the sales order table to identify the customer. This arrangement yields two tables with the data structure shown in Figure 24.4.

With this type of arrangement, the customer information appears in only one place. Now, if a customer changes his or her phone number, you have to change only one record.

You can do the same thing to the items sold and order information. This leads to the development of four tables, but the organization of the tables is much more efficient. You can be sure that when information must be changed, it will change in only one place. This arrangement is shown in Figure 24.5. With the four-table arrangement, the Orders table and the Items Ordered table provide the links between the customers and the retail items they purchased. The Items Ordered table contains one record for each item of a given order. The Orders table relates the items to the date of purchase and the customer making the purchase.

FIGURE 24.4
Normalized customer and order tables eliminate data redundancy.

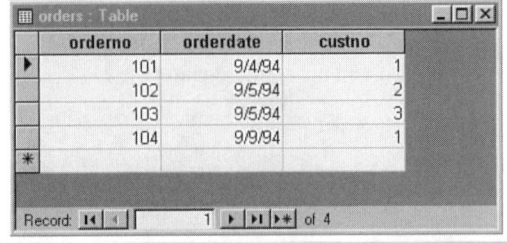

FIGURE 24.5
Complete normalization of the tables provides the greatest efficiency.

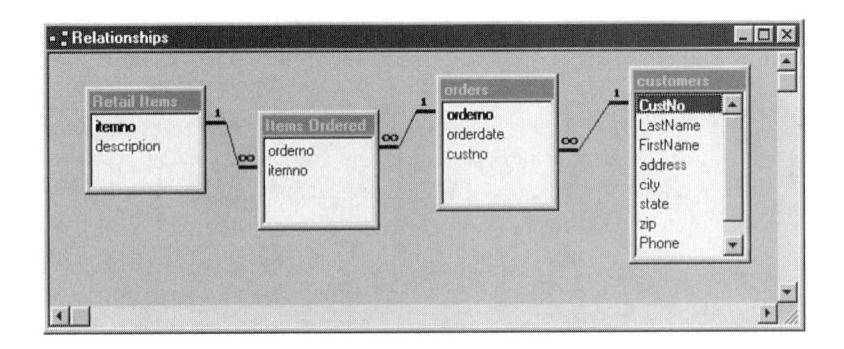

When information is moved out of one table and into another, you must have a way of keeping track of the *relationships* between the tables. You can do so through the use of data keys. For example, your Customers table has a field called CustNo. The Orders table also has a field called CustNo. These tables are *linked* through that field. If a program needs to obtain information about the customer who made a particular order, that customer's record can be located quickly in the Customers table via the common CustNo field.

Child and Lookup Tables Another way to handle data normalization is to create what is known as a child table. A *child table* is a table in which all the entries share common information that is stored in another table. A simple example is a membership directory; the family shares a common last name, address, and phone number, but each family member has a different first name. The table containing the common information is called the *parent table,* and the table containing the members' first names is the *child table*. Figure 24.6 shows a parent table and its related child table.

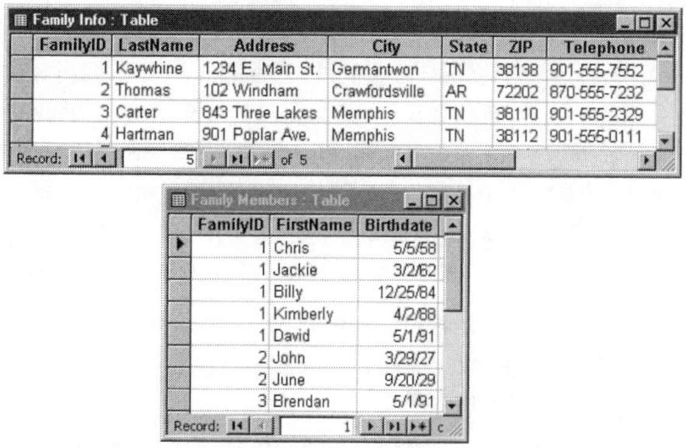

FIGURE 24.6
Parent and child tables are a form of data normalization.

Family Info : Table						
FamilyID	LastName	Address	City	State	ZIP	Telephone
1	Kaywhine	1234 E. Main St.	Germantwon	TN	38138	901-555-7552
2	Thomas	102 Windham	Crawfordsville	AR	72202	870-555-7232
3	Carter	843 Three Lakes	Memphis	TN	38110	901-555-2329
4	Hartman	901 Poplar Ave.	Memphis	TN	38112	901-555-0111

Family Members : Table		
FamilyID	FirstName	Birthdate
1	Chris	5/5/58
1	Jackie	3/2/62
1	Billy	12/25/84
1	Kimberly	4/2/88
1	David	5/1/91
2	John	3/29/27
2	June	9/20/29
3	Brendan	5/1/91

A *lookup table* is another way to store information to prevent data redundancy and to increase the accuracy of data entry functions. Typically, a lookup table is used to store valid data entries (for example, a state abbreviations table). When a person enters the state code in an application, the program looks in the abbreviations table to make sure that the code exists.

You also can use a lookup table in data normalization. If you have a large mailing list, many of the entries use the same city and state information. In this case, you can use a zip code table as a related table to store the city and state by zip code (remember that each zip code corresponds to a single city and state combination). Using the zip code table requires that the mailing list use only the zip code of the address, and not the city and state. During data entry, you can have the program check an entered zip code against the valid entries.

Rules for Organizing Tables Although no absolute rules exist for defining what data goes into which tables, here are some general guidelines to follow for efficient database design:

- Determine a topic for each table, and make sure that all data in the table relates to the topic.
- If several of the records in a table have fields intentionally left blank, split the table into two similar tables. (Remember the example of the employee and member tables.)
- If information is repeated in a number of records, move that information to another table and set up a relationship between the tables.
- Repeated fields indicate the need for a child table. For example, if you have Item1, Item2, Item3, and so on in a table, move the items to a child table that relates back to the parent table.
- Use lookup tables to reduce data volume and to increase the accuracy of data entry.
- Do not store information in a table if it can be calculated from data in other tables.

NOTE As stated previously, the guidelines for defining tables are not hard-and-fast rules. Sometimes, deviating from the guidelines makes sense.

Performance Considerations

One of the most frequent reasons for deviating from the guidelines just given is to improve performance. If obtaining a total sales figure for a given salesperson requires summing several thousand records, for example, you might find it worthwhile to include a Total Sales field in the salesperson table that is updated each time a sale is made. This way, when reports are generated, the application doesn't have to do large numbers of calculations, and the report process is dramatically faster. However, your program must ensure that the Total Sales field is consistently and accurately updated.

Another reason to deviate from the guidelines is to avoid opening a large number of tables at the same time. Because each open table uses precious resources and takes up memory, having too many open tables can slow down your application.

Deviating from the guidelines results in two major consequences. The first is increasing the size of the database because of redundant data. The second is the possibility of having incorrect data in some of the records because a piece of data was changed and not all the affected records were updated.

There are trade-offs between application performance and data storage efficiency. For each design, you must look at the trade-offs and decide on the optimum design.

Using Indexes

When information is entered into a table, records usually are stored in the order in which they are added. This order is the *physical order* or *natural order* of the data. However, you usually want to view or process data in an order different from the order of entry; that is, you want to define a *logical order*. You also frequently need to find a specific record in a table. Doing so by scanning the table in its physical order can be quite time-consuming.

An index provides a method of showing a table in a specific order. An *index* is a special table that contains a key value (usually derived from the values of one or more fields) for each record in the data table; the index itself is stored in a specific logical order. The index also contains pointers that tell the database engine where the actual record is located. This type of index is similar to the index in the back of this book. By using the book's index, you easily can look up key words or topics, because it contains pointers (page numbers) to tell you where to find the information.

Why Use an Index?   The structure of an index allows for rapid data search and retrieval. If you have a table of names indexed alphabetically, you rapidly can retrieve the record for a specific name by searching the index. To get an idea of the value of such an index, imagine a phone book that lists the customer names in the order in which they signed up for phone service. If you live in a large city, finding a person's number could take forever, because you have to look at each line until you find the one you want.

A table can have a number of different indexes associated with it to provide different organizations of the data. For example, an employee table can have indexes on last name, date of birth, date of hire, and pay scale. Each index shows the same data in a different order, for a different purpose.

Designing a Database

> **CAUTION**
> Although having many different views of the data may be desirable, keeping multiple indexes can take a toll on performance, because all indexes must be updated each time data changes. Once again, you must consider the trade-offs in the database design.

> **NOTE** You also can create different views of the information in a table by sorting the records or by specifying an order using the ORDER BY clause of a Structured Query Language (SQL) statement. Even though indexes aren't used directly by the SQL engine, their presence speeds up the sorting process when an ORDER BY clause is present. You learn about this topic in detail in Appendix C, "SQL Summary."

▶ See "Setting the Sort Conditions," **p. 810**

Single-Key Expressions The most common type of index is the *single-key index*, which is based on the value of a single field in a table. Examples of this type of index are Social Security number, zip code, employee ID, and last name. If multiple records exist with the same index key, those records are presented in physical order within the sort order imposed by the single-key index. Figure 24.7 shows the physical order of a Names table and how the table appears after being indexed on the last name field.

FIGURE 24.7
The physical and logical order of a table can be different. Logical order depends on an index.

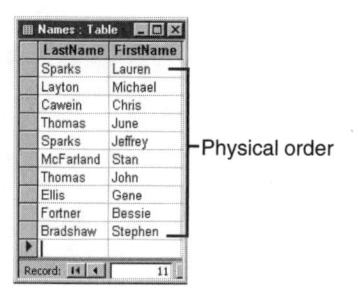

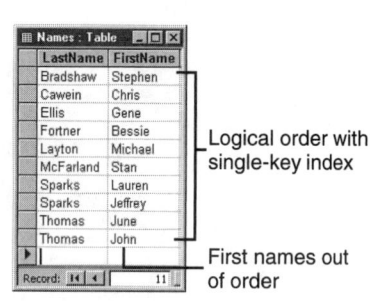

Multiple-Key Expressions Although single-key expressions are valuable in presenting data in a specific order, imposing an even more detailed order on the table is often necessary. You can do so by using multiple-key indexes. As you can infer from the name, a *multiple-key index* is based on the values of two or more fields in a table. A prime example is to use last name and first name when indexing a membership list. Figure 24.8 updates the view of the table shown in Figure 24.7 to show how using the first name field to help sort the records changes the order of the table. As with single-key indexes, if the key values of several records are the same, the records are presented in physical order within the index order.

FIGURE 24.8
Multiple-key indexes further refine the logical order of a table.

First names now in order

> **CAUTION**
>
> Although this point might be obvious, I must stress that the order of the fields in the index expression has a dramatic impact on the order of the records in the table. Indexing on first name and then last name produces different results than indexing on last name and then first name. Figure 24.9 shows the undesirable results of using a first name/last name index on the table used in Figure 24.7.

FIGURE 24.9
An improper index field order yields undesirable results.

Using Queries

When you normalize data, you typically are placing related information in multiple tables. However, when you need to access the data, you want to see the information from all the tables in one place. To do so, you need to create recordsets that consolidate the related information from the multiple tables. You create a recordset from multiple tables by using an SQL statement that specifies the desired fields, the location of the fields, and the relation between the tables. One way of using an SQL statement is to place it in the `Database` object's `OpenRecordset` method, which you use to create the recordset. However, you also can store the SQL statement as a query in the database.

Using stored queries presents several advantages:

- You can use the SQL statement more easily in multiple locations in your program or in multiple programs.
- Making changes to the SQL statement in a single location is easier.

- Stored queries run faster than those that are handled by parsing the statement from code.
- Moving your application up to a client/server environment is easier.

▶ See "Defining SQL," **p. 794**

Implementing Your Design

The first step in implementing the database design is to create the database itself. One consideration, of course, is the type of database to be used. Visual Basic's native database environment is the Microsoft Jet database engine. Jet databases are commonly known as Access databases, as Microsoft Access also uses the Jet database engine. You can choose from three main methods of creating an Access database for use with Visual Basic. You can use any of the following:

- Programmatically, using Visual Basic's Data Access Objects (DAO)
- Using the Visual Data Manager application provided with Visual Basic
- Using Microsoft Access itself
- Using other third-party database management programs

Creating a database programmatically using Data Access Objects gives your program complete control over how the database is created and structured. This topic is discussed in detail in Chapter 26, "Using Data Access Objects (DAO)."

The other methods of creating a Jet database are explained in the following list and discussed in the subsequent sections:

- **Visual Data Manager.** Using this Visual Basic add-in, you can create databases, as well as create, modify, and delete tables, indexes, and relations within a database.
- **Microsoft Access.** This tool is probably the most widely used to create Jet databases. It provides the added advantage of enabling you to create queries and relations using a visual drag-and-drop interface.
- **Third-party programs.** Many other programs, both commercial and shareware, are available to manage Jet and other types of databases. Some are highly specialized, whereas others are general-purpose utilities much like Visual Data Manager.

Using Visual Data Manager

The Visual Data Manager application that comes with Visual Basic provides you with an interactive way of creating and modifying databases. You can run this application by selecting the Visual Data Manager item from Visual Basic's Add-Ins menu.

> **NOTE** Visual Data Manager can work with Access (Jet), dBASE, FoxPro, Paradox, and ODBC databases, as well as text files. Typically, in Visual Basic applications, you use it to manipulate Access databases.

> **TIP** Visual Data Manager is also one of the sample applications that can be found in the Visual Basic Samples. Examining this project can provide you with a tremendous education in creating database applications in Visual Basic.

Creating the Database File

The first step in creating a new database is to create the database file itself. This file provides a physical location for the rest of your work. To create this file in Visual Data Manager, perform the following steps:

1. Choose File, New to bring up a submenu that allows you to specify the type of database to create.
2. For the purpose of this discussion, create an Access (Jet) database by choosing the Microsoft Access item. This action brings up another submenu from which you can choose the version of Access database to create.
3. If you plan to share data with users on a Windows 3.1 system, you should choose the 2.0 version; otherwise, choose the 7.0 version. Figure 24.10 shows the different menu levels for creating a database.

   After you choose the type of database, you are presented with the Select Microsoft Access Database to Create dialog box. This dialog box allows you to choose a name and folder for your database.

FIGURE 24.10
The menus allow you to choose the type and version of database to create.

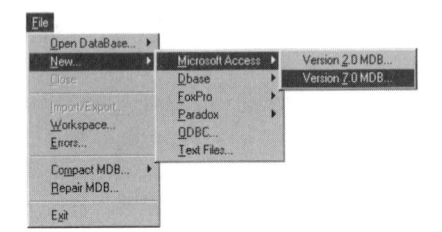

4. Enter a name and select a folder for your database, and then click the Save button. This action takes you to the design mode shown in Figure 24.11.

The Visual Data Manager presents the database information in a tree-like view. This type of view allows you to see the tables and queries quickly in the database. It also allows you to open the view further to see the fields and indexes of a table as well as its properties. Finally, you can open the view all the way to see the properties of the individual fields.

FIGURE 24.11
The Visual Data Manager Database window provides access to the design functions for tables, fields, and indexes.

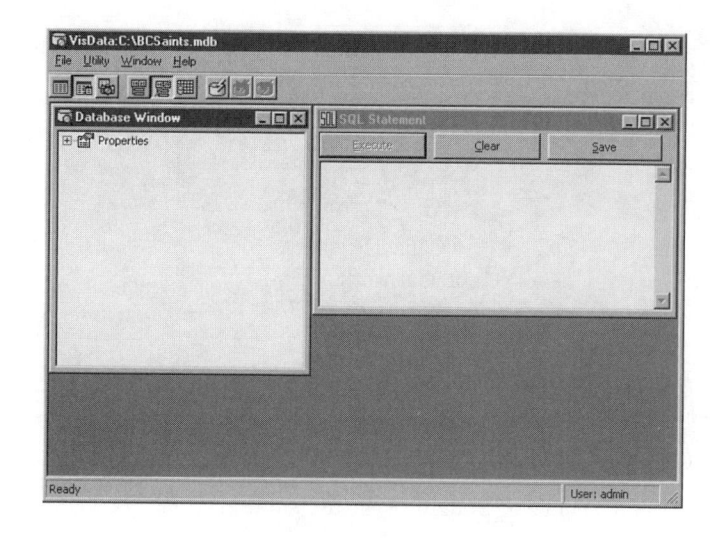

Adding a New Table

After you create the database, you can create tables. To create a new table, right-click anywhere in the Database window. Select the New Table item to bring up the Table Structure dialog box, as shown in Figure 24.12. This dialog box shows you information about the table itself, as well as a list of fields and indexes in the table. You also see buttons in the dialog box to add and remove fields and indexes. To add fields to the table, click the Add Field button to bring up the Add Field dialog box, as shown in Figure 24.13.

FIGURE 24.12
In the Table Structure dialog box, you can specify a table name.

FIGURE 24.13
In the Add Field dialog box, you can specify the properties of the fields for a table.

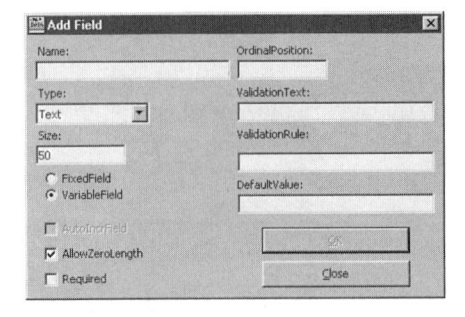

To continue our example database, first enter a name for the table in the Table Name text box. Then follow these steps for each field you want to add:

1. Click the Add Field button in the Table Structure dialog box.
2. Select the field type from the Type drop-down list.
3. Enter the size of the field (if necessary).
4. Enter any optional parameters, such as validation rules.
5. Click the OK button to add the field to the table.

After you enter all the fields for your table, click the Close button in the Add Field dialog box to return to the Table Structure dialog box.

If you want to remove a field from the table, select the field name in the dialog box's field list, and then click the Remove Field button. When you are satisfied with the fields in the table, click the Build the Table button to create the table.

Making Changes to the Fields in Your Table

After you create the fields in the table, you can set or change a number of the field properties from the Table Structure dialog box. To modify the properties, select the field name in the Field List. The properties of the field that can be modified appear in the dialog box as enabled text or check boxes. All other properties appear as disabled controls.

> **TIP** You also can edit the properties of a field from the Database window of the Visual Data Manager. Simply expand the database view to show field properties, and right-click the property to be edited. You then can select Edit from the pop-up menu to change the property.

> **NOTE** In Visual Basic, you cannot edit or delete any field that is part of an index expression or a relation. If you need to delete such a field, you must delete the index or relation containing the field and then make the changes to the field.

Adding an Index to the Table

In the Table Structure dialog box, you also can add, modify, or remove indexes in the table. Any indexes currently in the table appear in the Index List at the bottom of the dialog box, as shown in Figure 24.14.

FIGURE 24.14
You can add, edit, or delete indexes for a table from the Table Structure dialog box.

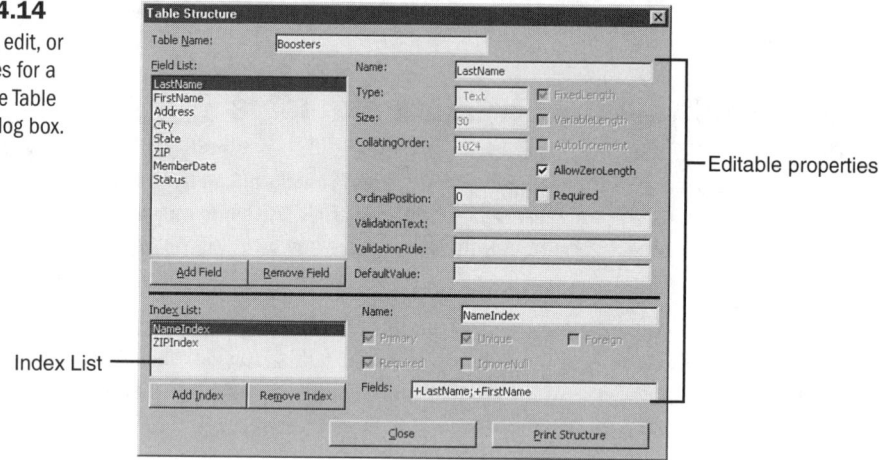

Index List

Editable properties

To add a new index, click the Add Index button; the Add Index dialog box then appears, as shown in Figure 24.15. In this dialog box, first enter an index name. Next, select the fields to be included in the index by clicking the fields in the Available Fields list. As you select each field, it is added to the Indexed Fields list in the order in which it was selected. By default, all fields are indexed in ascending order. To change the order to descending, precede the field name in the Indexed Fields list with a minus sign (–).

FIGURE 24.15
The Add Index dialog box provides a visual means of creating the indexes for a table.

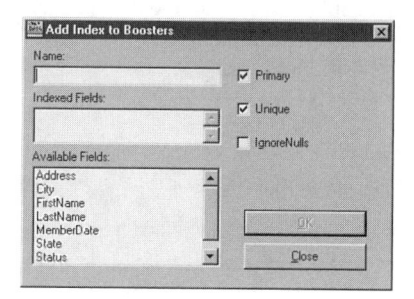

After you define the fields for the index, you can choose to require the index to be unique or to be the primary index (assuming that you do not already have a primary index) by selecting the appropriate check box in the window. When the index is completed to your liking, save it by clicking OK. The index you have just created is added to the index list on the Table Structure dialog box. To delete an index, simply select it in the list box and click Remove Index.

Returning to the Visual Basic Design Window

Closing the Visual Data Manager window or selecting File, Exit takes you back to Visual Basic's main design window. (You also can switch back and forth between the Data Manager and the Visual Basic design environment.) Since Visual Data Manager is a complete application, you may want to compile it and add a shortcut to its EXE file to your Windows desktop or Start menu. This will save having to load Visual Basic each time you want to run Visual Data Manager.

Viewing or Modifying the Structure of a Table

After you create a table, you can view its structure and even modify it to a certain extent. Right-click the table's name in the Database window, and select Design from the context menu that appears. The Table Structure dialog box that appears is the same one that you worked with in the preceding sections. From here, you can view the structure of the fields and indexes that comprise the table.

After a table has been created, you can't modify a field's type or size from within Visual Data Manager. You can, however, add, delete, or rename fields. You can also change some of the properties of the fields. As with fields, you can't modify the structure of your table's indexes, although you can add, delete, and rename indexes.

Renaming or Deleting a Table

Right-clicking a table name in the Database window also presents you with the opportunity either to rename or delete a table.

Selecting Rename from the context menu places the table's name in an editing box; you can simply type the new name into the box and press Enter. Press Escape if you decide not to change the table's name.

Selecting Delete presents you with a confirmation dialog box. If you click Yes in this dialog box, the table is irrevocably removed from the database.

Copying a Table

If you want to make a copy of a table, you can choose Copy Structure from the context menu presented after you right-click the table's name in the Database window.

In the Copy Structure dialog box, select the name of the table to be copied. The Target Database text box contains the name of the current database; if you want to copy the table into a different database, you can specify the desired destination here. The Copy Indexes check box is checked by default; clear it if you don't want the new table to contain the same indexes as the old one. The Copy Data check box, which is clear by default, allows you to copy the records contained in the table to the new table. If you leave this check box clear, your new table will have the same structure as the original table but will contain no data. After you make your selections, click OK to create the new table.

Creating a Database with Other Tools

Of course, Visual Data Manager is not the only way to create a database. It is simply a sample application provided with Visual Basic that happens to perform a very handy function. Many other tools that are available allow you and your users to create and maintain databases.

Using Microsoft Access

One option for creating a Jet database for use with a Visual Basic application is to use Microsoft Access. Access has a good visual design interface for setting up tables, indexes, queries, and table relationships. Obviously, this option is available only if you own a copy of Access. Note that Visual Basic can work with databases created with any version of Access; however, to exploit the power of 32-bit databases, you must use Access 95 or later.

Third-Party Database Designers

In addition to Visual Data Manager and Access, many third-party programs enable you to create and maintain Jet databases. Some of them provide you with advanced data modeling capabilities. These modeling capabilities enable you to determine easily what information goes in which table and to set up the relations easily between the tables. Then, after your data model is complete, the program can automatically generate the database for you.

However, you should be wary, or at least cautious, of third-party database management solutions. Some of them are focused on a very specific purpose; others offer more generalized capabilities. Usually, Access itself is far more powerful than a general-purpose third-party application. However, if you have a specific need that can be addressed by a more-focused application, by all means consider it. A vendor or author should be able to allow you to test the system to make sure that it meets your specific needs.

Why Use a Program Instead of Visual Data Manager?

In this chapter, you have learned that the Visual Data Manager application and Microsoft Access can create, modify, and load data into a database. So, you might be asking, "Why do I ever need to bother with the Visual Basic program commands for these functions?" The answer is that, in many cases, you don't. If you have direct control over the database (that is, you are the only user or you can access the database at any time), you may never need to use program commands to create or change a database.

If, however, you have an application with many users—either throughout your company or across the country—using a program for data management offers several benefits. One benefit is in initial installation. If the database creation routines are in the program itself, you don't have to include empty database files on your setup disks. Leaving out these files can reduce the number of disks required, and it certainly reduces the possibility that a key file is left out.

Along the same lines, a user accidentally may delete a database file, leading to the necessity to create a new one.

Another benefit occurs when you distribute updates to the program. With changes embedded in a program, your user merely can run the update program to change the file structure. He or she doesn't need to reload data into a new, blank file. Also, by modifying the file in place, you can preserve most structure changes in the database made by the end user.

Another reason for putting database creation and maintenance commands in a program is for performance considerations. Sometimes it is desirable, from a performance standpoint, to create a temporary table to speed up a program or to store intermediate results, and then delete the table at the completion of the program. You also might want to create a temporary index that creates a specific order or speeds up a search.

From Here...

In this chapter, you learned how to design and create a database for use in an application. To use the database, however, you must write a database access application. This topic is covered in other chapters of the book. For further information, refer to the following chapters:

- To learn how to use Visual Basic's Data control in conjunction with other controls to quickly create applications to work with databases, see Chapter 25, "The Data Control and Data-Bound Controls."
- For more advanced database programming techniques, see Chaper 26, " Using Data Access Objects (DAO)," and Chapter 27, " Using Remote Data Objects (RDO)."
- For a discussion of Microsoft's newest way of connecting your programs to databases, see Chapter 28, "Using ActiveX Data Objects (ADO)."

CHAPTER 25

The Data Control and Data-Bound Controls

In this chapter

Understanding the Data Control **546**

Getting Acquainted with Bound Controls **550**

Creating a Simple Application **553**

Creating Forms Automatically **557**

Visual Basic is designed to enable developers to create Windows-based applications quickly and easily. This ease-of-use extends to the creation of database programs as well. If you have an existing database that you want to access, Visual Basic makes it easy for you to write a complete data management application with almost no programming. You just drop a few controls on a form and set the properties. In fact, Visual Basic makes the task so easy that it can even create the data entry forms for you.

The components that make these capabilities possible are the Data control and data-bound controls. With just these few tools, you can create a wide variety of applications. However, before you get too excited, realize that as you progress to more complex applications, you need to do more of the programming yourself. However, if you are new to Visual Basic, these tools provide a good first step in the database-programming arena and enable you to create application prototypes rapidly.

Understanding the Data Control

The centerpiece of easy database applications is the Data control. The Data control is one of the controls available in Visual Basic's Toolbox. Setting up the Data control requires only four simple steps:

1. Select the Data control from the Toolbox.
2. Draw the control on your form.
3. Set the `DatabaseName` property of the control.
4. Set the `RecordSource` property of the control.

NOTE Following these four steps is the minimum required to set up the Data control for use with an Access database. The Jet engine allows you to use several types of databases (they are listed in the `Connect` property). If you want to access non-Jet databases, such as Microsoft SQL Server, you need to set additional properties.

A new Data control, the ActiveX Data Control, is discussed in Chapter 28, "Using ActiveX Data Objects (ADO)."

What Is the Data Control?

Basically, the Data control is a link between information in your database and the bound controls that you use to display the information. As you set the properties of the Data control, you tell it which database to connect to and what part of that database to access. The Data control makes data from your database available to your program in the form of a *recordset*. A recordset is just like it sounds, a set of records in the database. By default, the Data control creates a Dynaset-type recordset from one or more of the tables in your database.

> **NOTE** You can use several different types of recordsets. A dynaset (*dynamic recordset*) is a set of records that changes dynamically as the data in the underlying database is modified. A snapshot represents a "picture" of a set of records at the time the recordset is created; subsequent changes to the underlying data are not reflected in the recordset.

In addition to making data available to your program, the Data control also provides record navigation functions. With the buttons indicated in Figure 25.1, users can move to the first or last record in the recordset, or to a record prior to or following the current record. The design of the buttons makes their use intuitive; they are similar to the buttons you would find on a VCR or a CD player.

FIGURE 25.1
The VCR-like buttons on the Data control provide navigation capabilities.

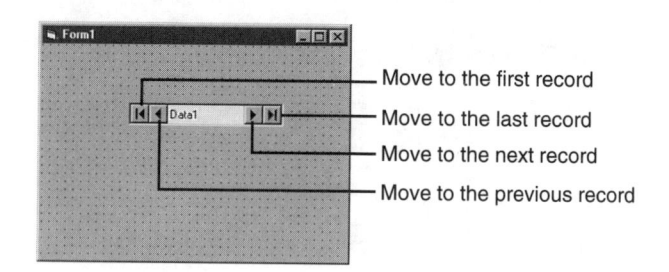

— Move to the first record
— Move to the last record
— Move to the next record
— Move to the previous record

The recordset created by the Data control is determined by the settings of the `DatabaseName` and `RecordSource` properties. If you set these two properties at designtime, then the recordset is created as the form containing the Data control loads. This recordset is normally active until the form is unloaded, at which time the recordset is released.

> **NOTE** A *recordset* by itself is not data; it is an object that represents (or points to) the data in a physical database. Even after a recordset is released or closed, the data in the underlying table(s) remains in the database.

Adding a Data Control to Your Form

The first step in using a Data control is to add the control to your application's form. Select the Data control tool from the Toolbox. Next, place and size the Data control just as you do any other control. After you set the desired size and placement of the Data control on your form, you can set its `Name` and `Caption` properties.

The `Name` property sets the control name, which you will be using later to identify the control to the data-bound controls. The default name for the first Data control added to a form is `Data1`. To change the name of a Data control, select its `Name` property from the Properties window and type the name you want.

The `Caption` property specifies the text that appears on the Data control. You usually want the caption to be descriptive of the data the control accesses. The default for the `Caption` property is the initial setting of the `Name` property (for example, `Data1` for the first Data control). You can change the `Caption` property the same way you change the `Name` property.

The Data control discussion in this chapter walks you through an example that you can follow along with. You'll create a simple application that allows you to browse the names of book authors stored in BIBLIO.MDB, which is a sample database provided with Visual Basic. To begin the sample project, start a new Visual Basic Standard EXE project and add a Data control to the form. Set the Data control's Name property to dtaMain and its Caption property to Authors. Also, make sure it is wide enough to display its caption. Figure 25.2 shows the form with this control added.

> **TIP** You also can add code to your program to change the Data control's caption to reflect information in the current record, such as a person's name.

FIGURE 25.2
Draw the Data control on your form, and set its caption appropriately.

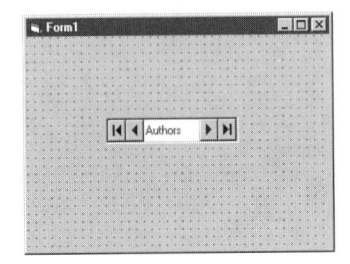

The Two Required Properties

After you place the Data control on your form, you need to make the connection between the Data control and the actual database. You do so by setting some of the Data control's properties. Although several properties can affect the way a Data control interacts with the database, only two properties are required to establish the link to a Jet database: the DatabaseName and RecordSource properties. Specifying these two properties tells the Data control what information to retrieve from the database and causes the Data control to create a recordset that allows nonexclusive, read/write access to the data.

> **NOTE** The DatabaseName property is not the same as the Name property mentioned earlier. The Name property specifies the name of the Data control object. This name references the object in code. The DatabaseName property specifies the path name of the physical database that the Data control is accessing.

Selecting a Database   Data controls can be set up to work with many different types of databases. This example, however, will concentrate on connecting to Microsoft Jet databases. For Jet databases, the DatabaseName property is the name of the database file. To enter the name, select the DatabaseName property from the Properties window, and type the database's fully qualified pathname.

The easiest way to locate a database is by browsing. Just click the ellipsis button (…) at the right of the DatabaseName property input line to display the DatabaseName dialog box, as shown in Figure 25.3. Browse to the appropriate database file and click OK. The selected filename and path are automatically entered into the `DatabaseName` property.

FIGURE 25.3
You can enter a database name in the Database property input line or choose it from the DatabaseName dialog box.

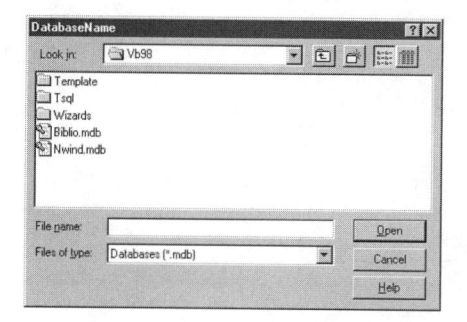

> **CAUTION**
>
> If you browse to the `DatabaseName` property at design time using the dialog box, the property includes a fully qualified path to the database's filename—for example, C:\MyData\LMS\TMS1112.MDB. This may be dangerous because the database will be expected to be in the same exact location at runtime. Allowing some flexibility in the location of the database would be better. For that reason, set the `DatabaseName` property using no path (TMS1112.MDB), in which case, your program would expect to find it in the program's current directory; then use a relative path from the current directory (LMS\TMS1112.MDB). Of course, an even better solution would be to set the property from code, based on user input or some type of program initialization parameters, as in the following example:
>
> ```
> Dim sDBLocation As String
> sDBLocation = App.Path & "\MYDB.MDB"
> Data1.DatabaseName = sDBLocation
> ```

Selecting a Recordset After you set the `DatabaseName` property, you can specify the information you want from that database with the `RecordSource` property. If you intend for your Data control to work with a single table within a database, you can enter the table name or select it from the list of tables, as shown in Figure 25.4.

If you want to use only selected information from a table or to use information from multiple tables, you can use a SQL (Structured Query Language) statement in the `RecordSource` property. To do so, you can either set the `RecordSource` property to the name of a QueryDef in the database that contains a SQL statement, or enter a valid SQL statement as the value of the `RecordSource` property. You can use any SQL statement that creates a recordset. (You can also include functions in your SQL statement.) If you're using a QueryDef, it must have already been defined and stored in the database.

> **TIP** To make sure that your SQL statements work correctly, you can test them in Visual Data Manager. Then copy and paste to place the statements in the `RecordSource` property.

▶ See "The Parts of the SQL Statement," **p. 795**

FIGURE 25.4
You can select the `RecordSource` property from a list of tables available in the database.

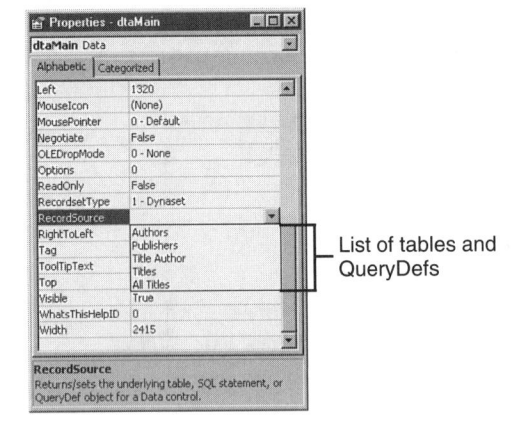

List of tables and QueryDefs

Getting Acquainted with Bound Controls

You have now completed the process of connecting to a database and specifying a recordset by setting the properties of a Data control. However, to use that data, you must take one more step: set up some bound controls. Bound controls in Visual Basic are controls that are set up to work with a Data control to create database applications; hence, the controls are "bound" to information in the database. Most of the bound controls in Visual Basic are simply standard controls that have additional properties allowing them to perform data access functions. A few custom controls are designed specifically to work with the Data controls.

Some of the controls that you use as bound controls are ones with which you are already familiar:

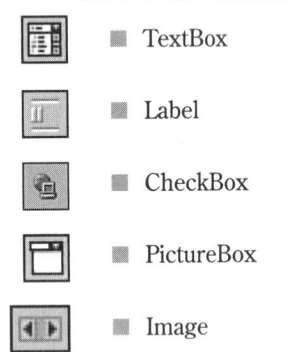

- TextBox

- Label

- CheckBox

- PictureBox

- Image

What Do These Controls Do?

Each bound control is tied to a Data control and, more specifically, to a particular field in the recordset attached to the Data control. The bound control automatically displays the information in the specified field for the current record. As the users move from one record to another using the navigation buttons of the Data control, the information in bound controls is updated to reflect the current record.

The bound controls are not limited, however, to just displaying the information in the record. Most can also be used to modify the information. To do so, the users just need to edit the contents of the control. Then, when the current record is changed or the form is closed, the information in the database is automatically updated to reflect the changed values.

> **NOTE** Because the Label control has no editable portion, the data displayed in the Label cannot be changed. Also, if a control is locked, or editing is otherwise prevented, the users cannot change the information.

You use each of the basic bound controls to edit and/or display different types of data. With the bound controls, you can handle strings, numbers, dates, logical values, and even pictures and memos. Table 25.1 lists the five basic bound controls and the types of database fields that they can handle. The table also lists the property of the control that contains the data.

Table 25.1 Controls Used to Handle Different Types of Data

Control Name	Data Type	Control Property
Label	Text, Numeric, Date	`Caption`
TextBox	Text, Memo, Numeric, Date	`Text`
CheckBox	Logical, True/False	`Value`
PictureBox	Long Binary	`Picture`
Image	Long Binary	`Picture`

Adding Controls to Your Forms

To add a bound control to your form, select the control from the Toolbox and draw it on the form. Figure 25.5 shows a text box added to the form that contains the Data control. Note that the Data control's `Caption` property has been modified as well.

FIGURE 25.5
You draw bound controls on your form just as you draw any other control.

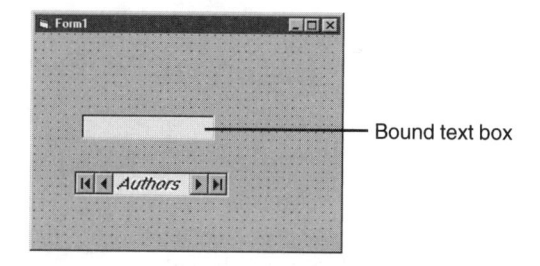

— Bound text box

> **TIP** If you hold down the Ctrl key when you click a control in the Toolbox, you can add multiple controls of that type to your form. This way, you don't have to click the control's Toolbox button repeatedly. When you're done, click the mouse pointer button in the Toolbox.

Of course, just drawing a text box or other control does notbind it to the database. You first have to set two more properties.

Using a Bound Control to Display Data

For a bound control to work with the data from a recordset, you must bind the control to the Data control that represents the recordset (recall that you've already read how to bind the Data control to data) and to a specific field within that recordset. The first step is to set the bound control's `DataSource` property. Setting this property establishes a connection between the bound control (that is, a text box) and the Data control. The next step is to set the `DataField` property of the bound control, which links it to a field in the recordset to be displayed. As you continue working through the BIBLIO example that you began earlier, you'll learn how many of these bound controls work.

Setting the *DataSource* Property   To set the `DataSource` property, select it from the Properties window for your control. Click the arrow to the right of the input area to see a list of all the Data controls on the current form. To set the `DataSource` property, select one of the controls from the list. Figure 25.6 shows this procedure.

> **TIP** Instead of dropping down the list, double-click the `DataSource` property to step through the available Data controls.

FIGURE 25.6
The DataSource property sets up the binding between a data-aware control and a Data control.

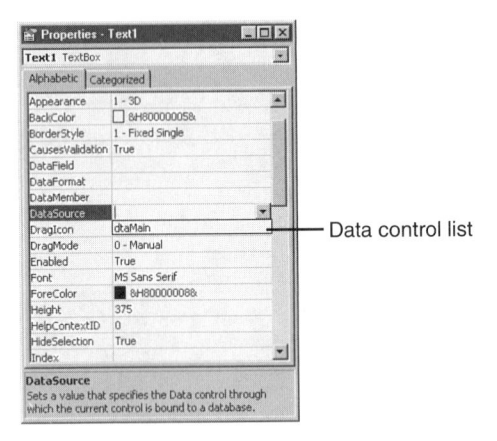

Setting the *DataField* Property   Although the `DataSource` property tells the bound control from which Data control to retrieve data, you still need to tell the bound control what specific data to retrieve. You do so by setting the `DataField` property. This property tells the control which field of the recordset will be handled by this bound control.

To set the `DataField` property of the control, select the `DataField` property from the Properties window, click the arrow to the right of the input area, and select one of the fields from the displayed list. The list includes all available fields from the recordset defined in the specified `DataSource` (see Figure 25.7).

FIGURE 25.7
Select the `DataField` property for the bound control from the list of fields in the selected Data control.

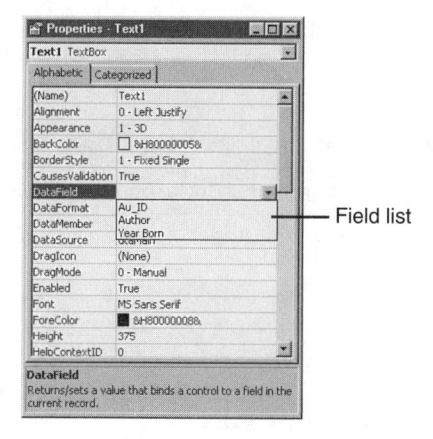

Field list

> **TIP**
> Instead of dropping down the list, double-click the `DataField` property to scroll through the available fields.

> **CAUTION**
> You cannot select a field for the `DataField` property from a list until the `DataSource` property has been set.

Creating a Simple Application

Earlier in this chapter, you began a simple test application that will allow you to browse and modify the names of authors stored in the sample BIBLIO database. Continue with that example now.

Setting Up the Form

You should have already set up a Data control that is bound to the BIBLIO database through its `DatabaseName` property. You are now ready to set the Data control's `RecordSource` property. From the Property window's selection list, select the Authors table. The Data control is now ready for use.

The next step in creating the data access form is to add the bound controls. To make the example easy, just use text boxes for each of the fields. Also, for each field, place a normal unbound Label control on the form to identify the information in the text box. For the sample case, you need three text boxes and three corresponding labels. Set the `DataSource` property of all the text boxes to `dtaMain`, which is the name of the Data control you have already created. For each text box, you also need to specify a `DataField` property. Remember that the `DataField` property ties the control to a specific field in the database. Table 25.2 lists the

DataField settings for each text box and the suggested captions for the corresponding label controls. The table uses the default names for the text boxes.

Table 25.2 *DataField* and *Caption* Settings for the Data Access Form

TextBox Name	DataField	Caption for Corresponding Label
Text1	Au_ID	Author ID:
Text2	Author	Name:
Text3	Year Born	Year Born:

After you add the bound controls and set their properties, your form should look like the one shown in Figure 25.8.

FIGURE 25.8
You can create a simple data entry form by using just the Data control and bound text boxes.

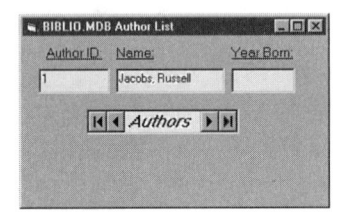

The DataSource property cannot be set at runtime using the standard Data control. However, if you use the new ADO Data control (discussed in Chapter 28, "Using ActiveX Data Objects (ADO)"), you can set this property.

▶ **See** "Using the ADO Data Control," **p. 614**

Navigating the Database

Now that you have created the data entry form, try it out by running the program. As the program first starts, you should see the form load, and the information for the first record should appear in the text boxes. Now you can see how the Data control is used to navigate through the records of the database. You can move to the first record, the previous record, the next record, or the last record by clicking the appropriate button on the Data control.

With this simple program, you can even update and edit the database. Try typing a year in the Year Born text box and moving to another record. By doing so, you are modifying a record in the physical database that is bound to the Data control. Even if you turn off the power on your PC, the record remains changed in the BIBLIO.MDB file.

Random Records

You look at your database and notice that the records of the database seem to be in random order, not alphabetical order. You have not created an error or done anything wrong in setting up the form. You are seeing the records presented in the physical order of the table, the order in which the records were entered. If you want to see the records in alphabetical order, place the following string in the RecordSource property of the Data control:

SELECT * FROM authors ORDER BY author

The string that you used to set the Data control's RecordSource property is an example of a SQL statement.

Using Code with the Data Control

In real life, your applications will be more dynamic than the sample you have just created. For that reason, it is important to understand that setting SQL statements and other nonpermanent items in code is generally better programming practice. Fortunately, the Data control allows you to manipulate most of the underlying objects from code.

To illustrate, continue with the sample project in Visual Basic. Place two command buttons named cmdSortAuthor and cmdSortYear on the form. Enter the following lines of code for their Click event procedures:

```
Private Sub cmdSortAuthor_Click()
  dtaMain.RecordSource = "SELECT * FROM authors ORDER BY author"
  dtaMain.Refresh
End Sub
Private Sub cmdSortYear_Click()
  dtaMain.RecordSource = "SELECT * FROM authors ORDER BY [Year Born] DESC"
  dtaMain.Refresh
End Sub
```

Run the program, and you should be able to change the sort order by clicking either of the buttons. Notice how setting the RecordSource property in code allows your program to be more flexible than when you simply set it at designtime.

NOTE You can control many additional aspects of the Data control with code. For example, you do not even need bound controls to display data. You can simply access the Recordset property of the Data control directly:

Msgbox "Current Author is " & dtaMain.Recordset.Fields("Author")

Chapter 26, "Using Data Access Objects (DAO)," discusses accessing databases entirely with code. ■

Adding and Deleting Records

As you can see, the Data control is quick and easy, but it lacks a few capabilities that are necessary for most data entry applications—specifically, adding and deleting records. The sample application allows you to edit existing records, but you cannot add a totally new record without a couple of modifications.

To add this functionality to the sample application, place two command buttons named `cmdAddRec` and `cmdDelRec` on the form. To make the buttons functional, add the code segments shown in Listing 25.1 to the `Click` event procedure of the appropriate button.

Listing 25.1 DATACNTL.ZIP—Enhancing the Sample Program

```
Private Sub cmdAddRec_Click()
    dtaMain.Recordset.AddNew
End Sub

Private Sub cmdDelRec_Click()
    dtaMain.Recordset.Delete
    If Not dtaMain.RecordSet.EOF Then
        dtaMain.Recordset.MoveNext
    Else
        dtaMain.Recordset.MoveLast
    End If
End Sub
```

As you'll learn in Chapter 26, when you are adding or editing a record, Visual Basic actually goes through a few stages:

1. **Add**. If you are adding a new record, a blank record is prepared in the *copy buffer*, which is a special place where records are edited before actually being entered into the database. You then proceed to edit the new record.
2. **Edit mode**. While you are changing the information in a record, you are in edit mode. At this point, the record has been copied to the copy buffer and may be modified by the program, but it has not yet been updated in the underlying database.
3. **Update**. After you finish editing field values, the data in the copy buffer is committed to the database, either when you change the current record or invoke the `Update` method.

As you can see, Listing 25.1 does not enter a command to invoke the `Update` method. (Updates are performed automatically by the Data control whenever you move to a new record or close the form.)

NOTE You add the `MoveNext` and `MoveLast` commands to the Delete button to force a move to a new record. After a record is deleted, it is no longer accessible but still shows on-screen until a move is executed. If you do not force a move and try to access the deleted record, an error occurs. ■

Your data entry form should now look like the one shown in Figure 25.9.

In addition to supplementing the functionality provided by the Data control buttons, you can replace them entirely. Just set the `Visible` property of the Data control to `False`, and add command buttons to perform `MoveNext` and other navigation methods on the Data control.

FIGURE 25.9
You can add new capabilities to the data entry screen by assigning program commands to command buttons.

Creating Forms Automatically

Using the bound controls, you can easily create data entry forms with a minimum of effort. You just draw the controls on your form, set a few properties, and you're done. What could be easier?

Well, actually you can create data entry forms in an even easier way—by using the Data Form Wizard (DFW). The DFW is one of the add-ins that comes with Visual Basic. Using this add-in, you can select a database and a record source; then it creates your data entry form automatically. Of course, the form might not be exactly like you want it, but you can easily change the default design and then save the changes. Using the DFW is a great way to create a series of data entry forms rapidly for a prototype or for a simple application.

Setting Up the Data Form Wizard

Again, the DFW is one of the add-ins that comes with Visual Basic. If, however, you choose the Add-Ins menu in Visual Basic, you don't see this option initially. You have to first tell Visual Basic that you want access to the form designer. You do so by choosing Add-Ins, Add-In Manager. The Add In Manager dialog box, shown in Figure 25.10, then appears.

FIGURE 25.10
By using the Add-In Manager, you can add capabilities to your Visual Basic design environment.

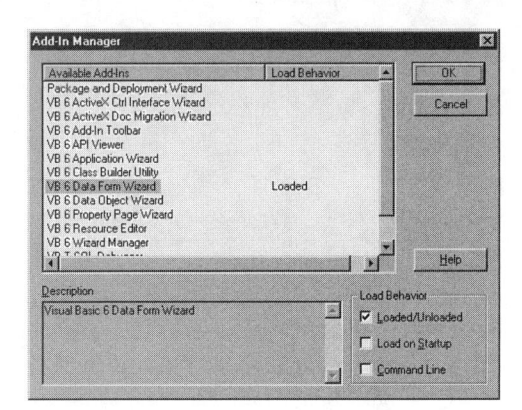

To access the DFW, highlight the VB 6 Data Form Wizard item in the list, and then click the Loaded/Unloaded check box. The word *Loaded* should appear in the rightmost column of the Add-In list. Next, click OK and you're set. Now, when you select the Add-Ins menu, you see the DFW as one of the items. Selecting the DFW opens the wizard's Introduction dialog box, which you can see in Figure 25.11. This screen tells you a little about the Data Form Wizard, as well as enables you to load settings from a previous DFW session.

FIGURE 25.11
The Data Form Wizard automatically creates data entry forms for you.

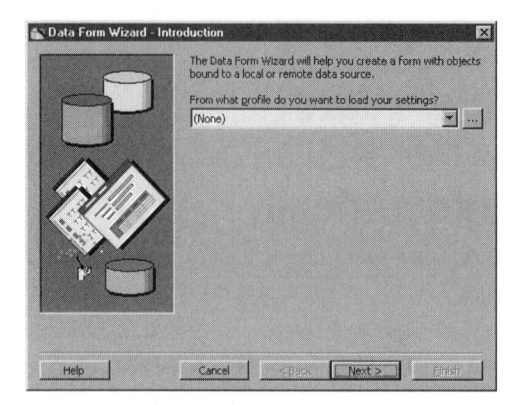

Clicking the Next button on the initial form takes you to the Data Form Wizard's Database Type screen. This screen, shown in Figure 25.12, enables you to choose the type of database that your form will be accessing. To choose a database type, simply click the type name in the list, and then click the Next button to continue creating your form. If you are following along with the example illustrated here, make sure Access is selected and click Next.

FIGURE 25.12
You can choose to create a form from common database source types.

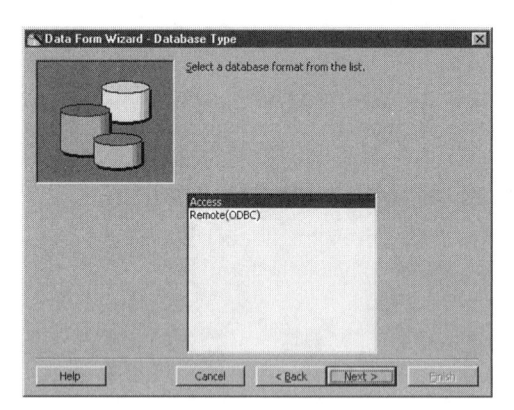

After you choose the type of database to use, you need to choose the actual database and record source that you will be working with. This is done in the Data Form Wizard's Database screen. If you choose ODBC, you are prompted for all the information necessary to connect to an ODBC data source (see Figure 25.13). If you choose Access, as you would to use the BIBLIO database, you are asked for the database filename (see Figure 25.14). For our example, use the Browse button to locate the BIBLIO.MDB database, which is in the main Visual Basic folder.

FIGURE 25.13
Complete all the information for your ODBC connection.

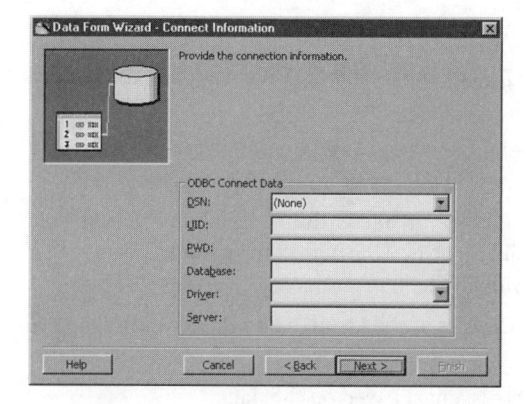

FIGURE 25.14
Using an Access database, all you need to indicate is the database path and filename.

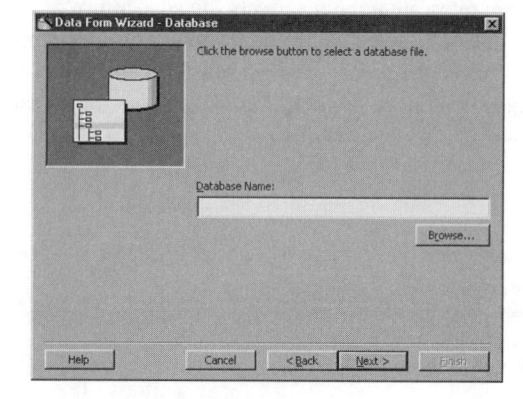

Getting to the Source of Your Data

After selecting the database, you move to the Form screen of the Data Form Wizard (see Figure 25.15). This screen allows you to name the form, as well as choose the way you want the information to be displayed.

FIGURE 25.15
The Form screen allows you to specify how you want the form to be set up.

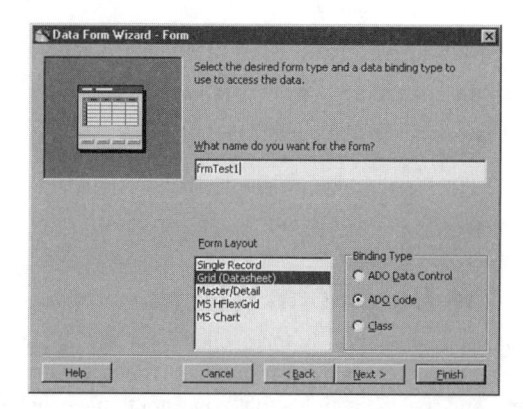

You can choose from among five types of data entry forms:

- **Single Record.** Allows you to edit the information in the recordset one record at a time. This is the classic data entry type of form.
- **Grid (DataSheet).** Allows you to edit multiple records at a time. This screen is similar to the recordset view in Access or an Excel spreadsheet.
- **Master/Detail.** Allows you to edit the information of a single parent record along with its associated child records. This type of form might be used to show information about an order along with all the items ordered.
- **MS HflexGrid.** Creates a grid layout using the new Microsoft Hierarchical FlexGrid control.
- **MS Chart.** Creates a chart based on the data.

Choosing the type of form to create not only affects the appearance of the form, but also determines what recordset(s) must be selected for the form. For a single record or grid form, you need to select only a single record source. For the Master/Detail form, you need to select two record sources. You really don't have to worry too much about this because the wizard guides you through this process. That's what wizards are for, right?

> **CAUTION**
> If you are creating a Master/Detail form, you first need to establish a relation between the tables you select. The relation information is used to keep the information synchronized.

For the sample project, name the form `frmTest1`. Select Grid (Datasheet) for the Form Layout.

Choosing the Binding Type

The standard Jet Data control, which has been around for a long time, uses Data Access Objects (DAOs). However, DAOs are on the way out and will eventually be replaced by the newer ActiveX Data Objects (ADOs). Evidence of this is the fact that in Visual Basic 6, the DFW creates only forms that use ADO. The Binding Type setting on the Form screen in Figure 25.15 allows three options for creating the data form:

- **ADO Data Control.** Creates a form with an ADO data control.
- **ADO Code.** Uses only code to access the database.
- **Class.** Creates a Class module that performs data access.

Any one of these methods you select uses the newer ActiveX Data Objects.

For our sample project, select ADO Code as the Binding Type.

Choosing Fields with the Data Form Wizard

After you select the database and the type of form, click Next and you see the Record Source screen, as shown in Figure 25.16. This screen provides a "friendly" way to choose the table or query to use for the form and the actual fields that you want to have included on the form.

FIGURE 25.16
You choose the record source and fields using simple combo boxes and lists.

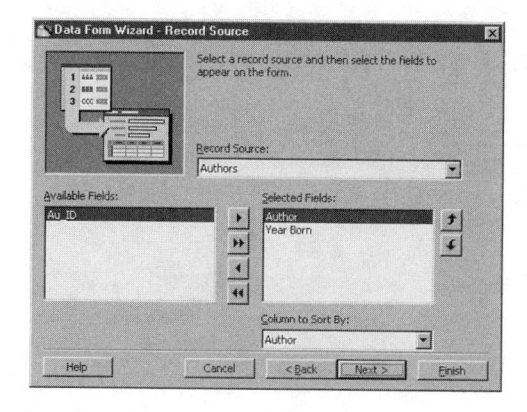

To set up the fields for the form, you need to follow these steps:

1. Select a record source (table or query name) from the combo box.
2. Select the fields to include by clicking the field names in the Available Fields list. You can double-click a field to select it, or highlight the field and click the selection button (>).
3. Place the fields in the order you want by moving them in the Selected Fields list. You move a field by highlighting it and then clicking the up or down buttons. (This step is optional.)
4. Select the column on which to sort the recordset by choosing it from the Column to Sort By combo box. (This step is optional.)
5. Click the Next button to move to the next screen.

For our sample project, use the drop-down list box to select the Authors table. Use the technique described here to include the Author and Year Born fields in the Data form.

Control Selection

After selecting all the fields that you want on the form, you have some more choices to make—about how your form will look. Depending on the type of form you chose in the Form screen, several dialog boxes may appear. One such dialog box allows you to choose the buttons that you want to appear on your form; it is the Control Selection screen of the DFW, shown in Figure 25.17.

Table 25.3 lists the buttons that you can elect to have appear on your data form. Not all of these buttons are available on all types of forms.

After you answer the dialogs concerning form design, click the Next button, and you have the option of saving all your settings in a profile. You can later load this profile without having to go through all the previous screens.

FIGURE 25.17
You can choose a number of command buttons to appear on your form.

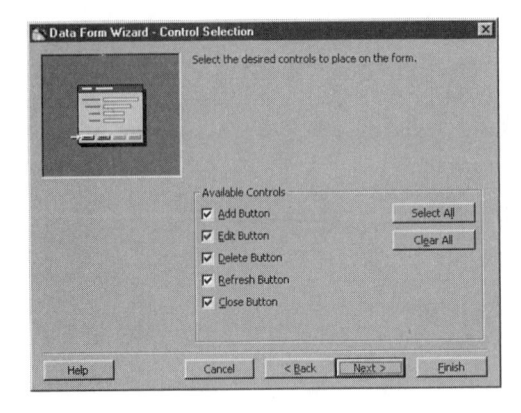

Table 25.3 Command Button Controls and Their Functions

Available Controls	Function
Add	Adds a new record to the recordset and clears the data entry fields.
Edit	Allows the user to modify the currently selected record.
Update	Stores any changes made to the data entry fields to the database for the current record.
Delete	Deletes the current record.
Refresh	Causes the Data control to reexecute the query used to create it. This process is necessary only in a multiuser environment.
Close	Closes and unloads the data entry form.
Show Data Control	If you selected the Grid (Datasheet) form type and ADO Data Control Binding Type, this option includes a button that allows the user to see the underlying ADO Data control.

You are now ready for the final step of the DFW—actually creating your form. Click the Finish button to start the creation process. At this point, you can sit back and relax for a minute while the DFW does the work. When it is finished, your program has a new data form, and all you did was answer a few questions and make a few selections. Figures 26.18 through 26.20 show you several types of data forms that you can create with the DFW.

FIGURE 25.18
This standard grid data form was created by the Data Form Wizard.

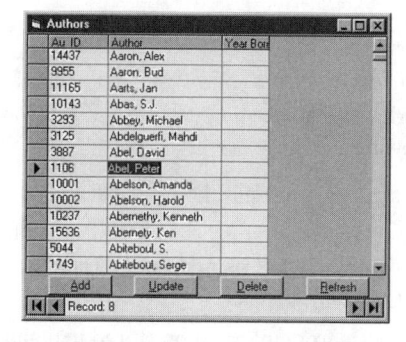

FIGURE 25.19
This more elegant FlexGrid data form also was created by the Data Form Wizard.

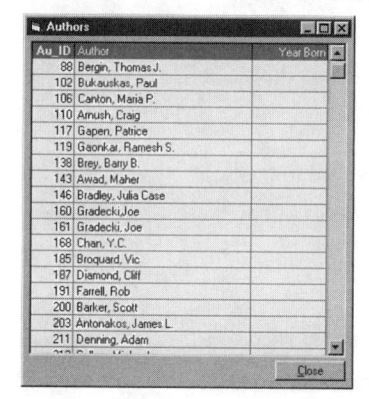

FIGURE 25.20
This Master/Detail data form was also created by the Data Form Wizard.

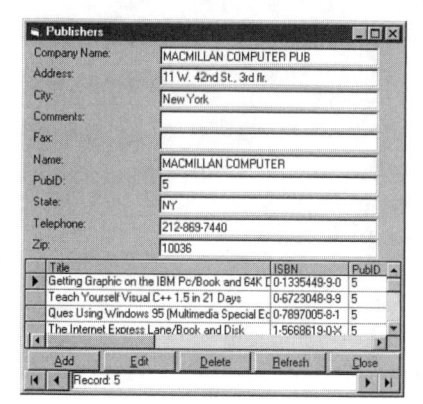

From Here...

In this chapter, you learned how to use the Data control and data-bound controls to quickly set up a database application that works with an existing database. If you want to learn more about related topics, check out the following:

- To learn about database design and normalization, see Chapter 24, "Database Basics."
- For more advanced ways that your programs can connect to databases, see Chapters 26, "Using Data Access Objects (DAO)," 27, "Using Remote Data Objects (RDO)," and 28, "Using ActiveX Data Objects (ADO)."
- To learn how to generate reports from information stored in databases, see Chapter 29, "Creating Reports."

CHAPTER 26

Using Data Access Objects (DAO)

In this chapter

Introduction to DAO 566

Setting Up a DAO Project 567

Opening an Existing Database 568

Deciding Which Recordset Type to Use 569

Placing Information Onscreen 575

Positioning the Record Pointer 576

Using Filters, Indexes, and Sorts 585

Considering Programs That Modify Multiple Records 587

Understanding Other Programming Commands 590

Introducing Transaction Processing 592

In Chapter 25, "The Data Control and Data-Bound Controls," you learned how you can write a database application quickly by using the Data control and data-bound controls that come with Visual Basic. This chapter shows you that, by setting a few properties, you can create a nearly complete data entry screen. I say *nearly* complete because the Data control by itself cannot handle some additional functions of a database application without additional coding—for example, adding or deleting records or finding a specific record.

These additional functions introduce you to some of the programming that you can do in a database application. However, you can write an entire database application with just program commands and not use the Data control at all. When you use just the program commands, you work with Visual Basic's *Data Access Objects* (*DAO*).

In this chapter, you learn how you can use Visual Basic's Data Access Objects to create complete, robust data management applications. Data Access Objects act as a Visual Basic program's internal representation of *physical data* data stored in some type of database or data management engine. Think of the Data Access Objects as special types of variables. These "variables," however, represent data stored *outside* the program rather than information stored in the computer's memory while the program is running.

Introduction to DAO

Using the Data Access Objects and their associated program commands is more complex than using the Data control and bound controls but does offer greater programming flexibility for many applications. The Data Access Objects and programming commands also provide the basis for many of the actions of the Data control and the bound controls. Therefore, they help you understand the concepts behind the controls. As you saw in Chapter 24, even if you use the Data control, you may also need to write some programming code to augment its capabilities.

To demonstrate the similarities and differences between Data Access Objects and the Data control, this chapter teaches you how to build a data entry screen that works with the BIBLIO.MDB sample database (included with Visual Basic). Figure 26.1 shows the data entry screen that you will build in this chapter.

FIGURE 26.1
You can create this data entry screen by following this chapter's instructions.

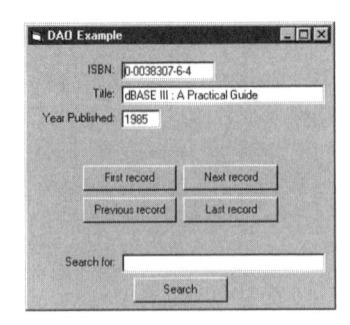

A key reason for using program commands is the flexibility they give you beyond what is available with the Data control. You can perform more detailed input validation than is possible with built-in database engine rules because program commands do not directly access the database. You also can cancel changes to your edited data without using transactions. In other words, your program can examine the input data *before* an attempt is made to enter the data into the database. The use of program commands also provides an efficient way to handle data input and searches that do not require user interaction. Examples are receiving data from lab equipment or across a modem, or looking up the price of an item in a table. Program commands enable you to perform transaction processing as well.

Setting Up a DAO Project

Before you can use any database capabilities (beyond the Data control and bound controls) in your program, you must specify one of the Data Access Object libraries in your program's references.

To set the program references, choose Project, References and then select one of the Microsoft DAO libraries from the References - ProjectName dialog box (see Figure 26.2).

FIGURE 26.2
Adding a reference to the DAO library makes these objects available to your program.

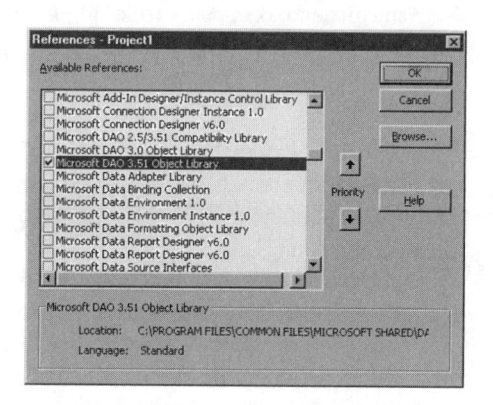

> **NOTE** Visual Basic can include two basic Jet DAO libraries in an application. These external libraries are the Microsoft DAO 3.51 Object Library and the Microsoft DAO 2.5/3.51 Compatibility Library. If you plan to program for 32-bit clients only and use 32-bit Jet (Access 95/97) databases, select the 3.51 library. If you need to exchange data with 16-bit systems or Access 2.0 applications, use the 2.5/3.51 compatibility library.

Within a program, a database is opened as part of a *session* with the *database engine*. The database engine is represented within a Visual Basic program by the DBEngine object; you define sessions by creating one or more Workspace objects within the DBEngine object. By default, once a project contains a reference to a DAO library, the DBEngine object and a single Workspace object, known as Workspaces(0) (because it is the first member of the zero-based Workspaces collection), are automatically created. These default objects are sufficient for most DAO projects.

After the DAO reference has been set up, you can then open a database by using the Workspace object's `OpenDatabase` method. The terminology gets a little confusing here: To *create* a *Database object* in your program, you *open* an existing *database*. The `OpenDatabase` method is technically a method of a Workspace object, but the default Workspace object `DBEngine.Workspaces(0)` is assumed and can be omitted. Therefore, assuming a project contains only one Workspace object, these lines of code are equivalent:

```
Set dbTest = DBEngine.Workspaces(0).OpenDatabase("BIBLIO.MDB")
Set dbTest = OpenDatabase("BIBLIO.MDB")
```

Throughout this chapter, you'll work on a application that opens the sample database BIBLIO.MDB, which is included with Visual Basic. Follow these steps to begin the sample application:

1. Start Visual Basic, if necessary, and create a new Standard EXE project.
2. Change the name of `Form1` to `frmDAOTest`, and save the project.
3. To add a reference to the proper DAO library to the project, choose Project, References. The References – ProjectName dialog box appears (refer to Figure 26.2).
4. Scroll down to Microsoft DAO 3.51 Object Library and select the check box next to it.
5. Click OK to close the dialog box.

Once you have completed these steps, your project contains a reference to the Data Access Objects library. You therefore can use DAO in the application.

Opening an Existing Database

The first step in writing many data access programs is to set up a link to the database with which you want to work. If your application will work with a database that already exists, you need to create a Database object within the program and then use that object to create a link to the existing database. In effect, you are "opening the database" for use in your program. Most of the other Data Access Objects flow from that Database object.

Think of the Database object as your Visual Basic program's internal *representation* of a physical database, not the database itself. The Database object within the program is simply a window into the database.

Continuing the sample application, the following steps use the `OpenDatabase` method to create a Database object and set it up to work with the BIBLIO.MDB database:

1. In the form's General Declarations section, add this code to declare a form-level Database object variable:

   ```
   Dim dbTest As Database
   ```

2. Add the following lines of code to the form's `Load` event procedure. This code, which executes as the form loads, creates the Database object `dbTest` by opening the BIBLIO.MDB database:

```
Dim sDBLocation As String
sDBLocation = "c:\Program Files\Microsoft Visual Studio\VB98\biblio.mdb"
Set dbTest = OpenDatabase(sDBLocation)
```

These commands open a Jet database with the default options of read/write data access and shared access. The full syntax of the `OpenDatabase` method lets you specify whether the database should be opened exclusively (no other users or programs can access it at the same time), whether it should be opened in read-only mode (no updates are allowed), or, if you are connecting to a non-Access database, you can specify the database type.

You might, for example, want to use read-only mode for a lookup database (for example, a zip code database or a state abbreviations database that you include with your application but do not want the users to be able to modify). To open the database as read-only, change the `Set` statement to the form shown in the following line of code. The first parameter after the database name indicates whether the database is opened for exclusive access; the second parameter indicates whether read-only mode is to be used:

```
Set OldDb = OldWs.OpenDatabase("C:\ZIPCODE.MDB",False,True)
```

After you open the database, you have only created a link from your program to the database file itself. You still do not have access to the information in the database. To gain access to the information, you must create and open a Recordset object that links to data stored in one or more of the tables in the database.

Deciding Which Recordset Type to Use

When you create a recordset object to open a recordset in your program, you can access any entire table, specific fields and records from the table, or a combination of records and fields from multiple tables. Three types of recordsets are available in Visual Basic:

Recordset Type	Type of Data Contained
Table	All records in an entire physical table in a database.
Dynaset	Sets of pointers that provide access to fields and records in one or more tables of a database.
Snapshot	Read-only copies of data from one or more tables. They are stored in memory.

> **NOTE** This chapter refers to tables, dynasets, and snapshots, but you should remember that they are all recordsets and can be accessed only by using the Recordset object. Specifically, all mentions of tables, dynasets, and snapshots actually refer to table-type recordsets, dynaset-type recordsets, and snapshot-type recordsets, respectively. Previous versions of Visual Basic supported objects that are now outdated: table objects, dynaset objects, and snapshot objects. ■

The following sections describe each type of recordset, point out some of the advantages and disadvantages of each, and demonstrate the commands used to access the recordset.

Using Tables

A *table* (table-type recordset) is a direct link to one of the physical tables stored in the database. Because all data in a database is stored in tables, using this type of recordset provides the most direct link to the data. Tables are also the only form of recordset that supports indexes; therefore, searching a table for a specific record can be quicker than searching a dynaset or snapshot.

When you are using tables, data is addressed or modified one table at a time, one record at a time. This arrangement provides very fine control over the manipulation of data. However, it does not give you the convenience of changing records in multiple tables with a single command, such as an action query.

Advantages of Using Tables   The use of tables in your programs gives you several advantages:

- You can use or create indexes to change the presentation order of the data in the table during program execution.
- You can perform rapid searches for an individual record using an appropriate index and the `Seek` command.
- Changes made to the table by other concurrent users or programs are immediately available. You do not need to "refresh" the table to gain access to these records.

Disadvantages of Using Tables   Of course, using tables in your programs also poses disadvantages:

- You can't set filters on a table to limit the records being processed to those that meet certain criteria.
- You can't use the `Find` commands on a table; the `Seek` command finds only the first record that meets its criteria. This implies that, to process a series of records in a range, you, the programmer, must provide a means to find the additional records.

You can usually overcome these disadvantages with programming, but the solutions are often less than elegant. This chapter discusses some of the workarounds in its coverage of the various methods for moving through a recordset and for finding specific records. These topics are covered later in this chapter.

▶ See "Positioning the Record Pointer," **p. 576**

Opening a Table for Use   To open a table for the program to use, define a Recordset object and then use your Database object's `OpenRecordset` method to access the table. To specify that a table-type recordset is to be created, use the `dbOpenTable` constant in the method's parameters.

Follow these steps to create a table-type recordset named `rsTitles` in the sample application:

1. Add the declaration `Dim rsTitles as Recordset` to the General Declarations section.
2. Add the following line of code to the end of the form's `Load` event procedure:

    ```
    Set rsTitles = dbTest.OpenRecordset("titles", dbOpenTable)
    ```

This command opens a table in a Jet database, with the default parameters of shared use and read/write mode. You can include optional parameters in the `OpenRecordset` method to open the table for exclusive use or to open the table in read-only mode. These options are summarized in Table 26.1.

> **NOTE** When you specify the name of an existing table in the `OpenRecordset` method, the Jet engine creates a table-type recordset by default.

Table 26.1 Options Used to Modify the Access Mode of Tables

Option	Action
dbDenyWrite	Prevents others in a multiuser environment from writing to the table while you have it open
dbDenyRead	Prevents others in a multiuser environment from reading the table while you have it open
dbReadOnly	Prevents you from making changes to the table

Using Dynasets

A *dynaset* is a grouping of information from one or more tables in a database. This information is composed of selected fields from the tables, often presented in a specific order and filtered by a specific condition. Dynasets address the records present in the base tables at the time the dynaset was created. Dynasets are updateable recordsets, so any changes made by the users are stored in the database. However, dynasets do not automatically reflect additions or deletions of records made by other users or programs after the dynaset was created. Therefore, dynasets are less useful for some types of multiuser applications.

A dynaset is actually a set of record pointers that point to the specified data as it existed when the dynaset was created. Changes made to information in the dynaset are reflected in the base tables from which the information was derived, as well as in the dynaset itself. These changes include additions, edits, and deletions of records.

Advantages of Using Dynasets   Some of the advantages provided by dynasets are as follows:

- Dynasets enable you to join information from multiple tables.
- You can use `Find` methods to locate or process every record meeting specified criteria.
- Dynasets enable you to limit the number of fields or records that you retrieve into the recordset.
- Dynasets make use of filters and sort order properties to change the view of data.

Disadvantages of Using Dynasets   Dynasets do have some limitations:

- You can't use indexes with dynasets; therefore, you can't change the presentation order of a dynaset by changing the index or by creating a new one.

- A dynaset does not automatically reflect additions or deletions made to the data by other users or other programs. A dynaset must be explicitly refreshed or re-created to show the changes.

Setting Up a Dynaset To set up a dynaset for use within a program, you must define the Recordset object with the `Dim` statement and then generate the dynaset using the `OpenRecordset` method with the `dbOpenDynaset` parameter. When you are creating a dynaset, the key part of the `OpenRecordset` method is the SQL statement that defines the records to be included, the filter condition, the sort condition, and any join conditions for linking data from multiple tables.

The following code example illustrates how to create a dynaset by using a SQL statement that selects only specific records and that sorts the records in a specific order. These statements provide you access to the same information as you had by accessing the table directly with the previous code. The only difference is the type of recordset created.

```
Dim MyDB As Database
Dim MyRS As Recordset
Dim sSQL As String
Set MyDB = OpenDatabase("biblio.mdb")
sSQL = "SELECT * FROM titles WHERE title <= 'B' ORDER BY title"
Set MyRS = MyDB.OpenRecordset(sSQL, dbOpenDynaset)
```

If you want to include all records from one table in a dynaset in no particular order, you can omit the SQL statement and simply use the table name as follows:

```
Set rsTitles = dbTest.OpenDatabase("titles")
```

NOTE However, using a SQL statement is a good idea in case you want to modify the record selection criteria later.

When you create a dynaset, you can use any valid SQL statement that selects records. You can also specify options that affect the dynaset's behavior. Table 26.2 lists these options.

Table 26.2   Options Used to Modify the Access Mode of a Dynaset

Option	Action
`dbDenyWrite`	Prevents others in a multiuser environment from writing to the dynaset while you have it open
`dbReadOnly`	Prevents you from making changes to the dynaset
`dbAppendOnly`	Enables you to add new records but prevents you from reading or modifying existing records
`dbSQLPassThrough`	Passes the SQL statement used to create the dynaset to an ODBC database server to be processed

For example, the following code shows how to create a dynaset-type recordset that allows the users to read the information in the database only:

```
Set rsTitles = dbTest.OpenRecordset("SELECT * FROM titles",_
    dbOpenDynaset, dbReadOnly)
```

▶ See "Using SELECT Statements," **p. 796**

> **NOTE** An *ODBC server* is a database engine, such as Microsoft SQL Server or Oracle, that conforms to the Open Database Connectivity (ODBC) standards. The purpose of a server is to handle query processing at the server level and return to the client machine only the results of the query. ODBC drivers, which are usually written by the vendor of the database engine, handle the connection between Visual Basic and the database server. An advantage of using ODBC is that you can connect to the information on the database servers without having to know the inner workings of the engine.

You can also create a dynaset from another dynaset. One reason for doing so is that you can use the `Filter` and `Sort` properties of the first dynaset to specify the scope of records and the presentation order of the second dynaset. By creating a second dynaset, you can create a subset of your initial data. The second dynaset is usually much smaller than the first, which allows faster processing of the desired records. In the following code, a dynaset is created from a customer table to result in a national mailing list. A second dynaset is then created, which includes only the customers living in Tennessee and sorts them by zip code for further processing.

```
Dim dbMarket As Database
Dim rsCustomers As Recordset
Dim rsTNCust As Recordset
Set dbMarket = OpenDatabase(sDBLocation)
Set rsCustomers = dbMarket.OpenRecordset("customers", dbOpenDynaset)
rsCustomers.Filter = "state = 'TN'"
rsCustomers.Sort = "ZIP5"
Set rsTNCust = rsCustomers.OpenRecordset(dbOpenDynaset)
```

You might wonder why, if you need the results in the second dynaset, you can't just create it from the base tables in the first place. The answer is that you can do so if your application needs only the second table. However, consider a member tracking system in which you want access to all your members (the creation of the first dynaset), and one of the functions of the system is to generate a mailing list for a particular region (the creation of the second dynaset). Because the pointers to all the required information are already present in the first dynaset, the creation of the second dynaset is faster than if it were created from scratch.

Using Snapshots

A *snapshot,* as the name implies, is a "picture," or copy, of the data in a recordset at a particular point in time. A snapshot is similar to a dynaset in that it is created from base tables, using a SQL statement, or from a QueryDef, dynaset, or another snapshot. A snapshot differs from a dynaset in that it is not updateable. The following line of code illustrates the creation of a snapshot-type recordset:

```
Set MyRS = MyDB.OpenRecordset(sSQL, dbOpenSnapshot)
```

As a general rule, use a snapshot whenever you want a set of data that isn't time sensitive; that is, it doesn't matter whether records in the underlying database are modified after the snapshot is created. The most frequent use of snapshots in a program is to generate reports or informational screens in which the data is static.

Advantages of Using Snapshots   Snapshots provide you with the following advantages:

- You can join information from multiple tables.
- You can use the Find methods to locate records.
- Record navigation and recordset creation can be faster for a snapshot than for a read-only dynaset because a snapshot is a copy of the data, not a set of pointers to the data.

Disadvantages of Using Snapshots   The primary disadvantage of using a snapshot is that it is not an updateable recordset. In addition, you can't use an index with a snapshot to help set the order of the data or locate specific records.

> **CAUTION**
> To avoid memory constraints, make sure that a snapshot returns only a small set of records.

Setting Up a Snapshot   You can create a snapshot by defining a Recordset object with the Dim statement and then using the OpenRecordset method with the dbOpenSnapshot parameter to assign the records to the object. As with a dynaset, you can specify optional parameters in the OpenRecordset method. Table 26.3 summarizes these parameters.

Table 26.3 Options Used to Modify the Access Mode of a Snapshot

Option	Action
dbDenyWrite	Prevents others in a multiuser environment from writing to the snapshot while you have it open
dbForwardOnly	Enables only forward scrolling through the snapshot
dbSQLPassThrough	Passes the SQL statement used to create the snapshot to an ODBC database to be processed

Using a Forward-Only Recordset

A forward-only recordset is a special type of snapshot that allows only forward scrolling through its records. This means that the MoveFirst, MovePrevious, and Find methods do not work on the recordset. The advantage of using this type of recordset is that it is faster than a snapshot. However, the forward-only recordset should be used only in situations in which a single pass through the recordset is needed, such as in report generation routines.

To set up a forward-only recordset, you use the OpenRecordset method and specify the dbOpenForwardOnly constant as shown in the following line of code:

```
Set MyRS = MyDB.OpenRecordset(sSQL, dbOpenForwardOnly)
```

Placing Information Onscreen

Suppose that you have written a data entry screen using the Data control and bound controls. To display information onscreen, you simply draw bound controls and then set the appropriate data fields for the controls. The display of the information is automatic. If you use Data Access Objects, the process is only slightly more involved. You still use control objects (text boxes, labels, check boxes, and so on) to display the information, but you have to assign the data fields to the correct control properties with each record displayed.

For example, you must assign the contents of a field to a text box's `Text` property or a Label control's `Caption` property. When used in this manner, the control objects are typically referred to as *unbound controls*. One advantage of using unbound controls is that you can use any control to display data, not just the bound controls specifically designated for use with the Data control.

Accessing Information from Database Fields

Information in fields can be accessed through a recordset's `Fields` collection in one of several ways. For example, any of the following techniques would suffice for retrieving the contents of a field named `ThisField` in a recordset named `rsTest` and placing it into a text box named `Text1`:

- Use the field's ordinal position in the `Fields` collection: `Text1.Text = rsTest.Fields(0)` (assuming `ThisField` is the first field in the recordset)
- Use the field's name to retrieve it from the `Fields` collection: `Text1.Text = rsTest.Fields("ThisField")`
- Take advantage of the fact that the `Fields` collection is the default collection of a recordset: `Text1.Text = rsTest("ThisField")`
- Use the shorthand version of the preceding technique: `Text1.Text = rsTest!ThisField`

> **NOTE** If a field's name contains spaces, you can enclose the entire name in square brackets, as in `Text1.Text = rsTest![longer field name]`.

Displaying Data in the Sample Program

Now you can enhance the sample program by having it actually display the data in the database. If you have followed the instructions so far, your program creates a Database object and a Recordset object by opening the BIBLIO.MDB database and its Titles table. Continue by writing a user-defined sub procedure that displays the ISBN, title, and year published of the current record, as shown in the following steps:

1. Add three text boxes named `txtISBN`, `txtTitle`, and `txtYear`.
2. Add associated Label controls to identify the text boxes.
3. Set the labels' `Caption` properties appropriately:

- ISBN:
- Title:
- Year Published:

Figure 26.3 shows the form with the text boxes in place.

FIGURE 26.3
Use unbound controls in conjunction with Data Access Objects to display data in a database.

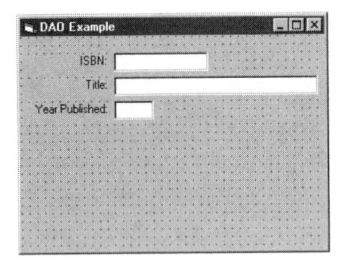

4. Create the following user-defined sub procedure in frmDAOTest's Code window:

```
Sub ShowFields()
    TxtTitle.Text = rsTitles!Title
    TxtISBN.Text = rsTitles!ISBN
    TxtYear.Text = rsTitles![Year Published]
End Sub
```

5. Add the following lines of code to the end of the form's Load event procedure:

```
rsTitles.MoveFirst
Call ShowFields
```

NOTE Because the Text property is the default property of a text box, you do not have to include the property name in the assignment statement. My personal preference is to include the name for readability.

Positioning the Record Pointer

Because a database with only one record is fairly useless, a database engine must provide ways to move from one record to another within recordsets. Visual Basic provides six such techniques:

Technique	Description
Move methods	Changes the position of the record pointer from the current record to another record.
Find methods	Locates the next record that meets the find condition. Find methods work on dynasets and snapshots.
Seek method	Finds the first record in a table that meets the requested condition.

Technique	Description
`Bookmark` property	Identifies the location of a specific record.
`AbsolutePosition`	Moves the record pointer to a specific record position in the recordset.
`PercentPosition`	Moves the record pointer to the record property nearest the indicated percentage position in the recordset.

Each of these techniques has benefits and limitations, as described in the following sections.

Using the *Move* Methods

You can use the five different `Move` methods on any recordsets available in Visual Basic:

Move Method	Action
`MoveFirst`	Moves the record pointer from the current record to the first record in the opened recordset.
`MoveNext`	Moves the record pointer from the current record to the next record (the record following the current record) in the opened recordset. If no next record exists (that is, if you are already at the last record), the end-of-file (EOF) flag is set, and there will be no current record.
`MovePrevious`	Moves the record pointer from the current record to the preceding record in the opened recordset. If no previous record exists (that is, if you are at the first record), the beginning-of-file (BOF) flag is set, and there will be no current record.
`MoveLast`	Moves the record pointer from the current record to the last record in the opened recordset.
`Move n`	Moves the record pointer from the current record *n* records down (if *n* is positive) or up (if *n* is negative) in the opened recordset. If the move would place the record pointer beyond the end of the recordset (either BOF or EOF), an error occurs.

These commands move the record pointer to the record indicated based on the current order of the recordset. The current order of the recordset is the physical order, unless an index was set for a table, or a dynaset or snapshot was created with a particular order specified.

To enhance the sample project to show the use of the `MoveFirst`, `MovePrevious`, `MoveNext`, and `MoveLast` methods, follow these steps:

▶ **See** "Setting the Current Index in a Table," **p.581**

1. Add four command buttons named `cmdFirst`, `cmdPrevious`, `cmdNext`, and `cmdLast`.
2. Set their `Caption` properties as follows:
   - `First record`
   - `Next record`
   - `Previous record`
   - `Last record`

Figure 26.4 shows the form with the command buttons in place.

FIGURE 26.4
Add command buttons to enable the users to navigate through the recordset.

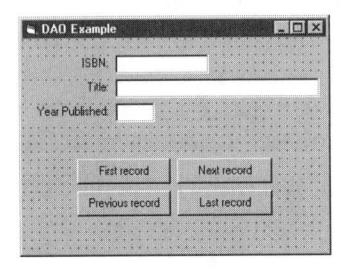

3. Add this code to the `Click` event procedure of `cmdFirst`:

   ```
   rsTitles.MoveFirst
   Call ShowFields
   ```

4. Add this code to the `Click` event procedure of `cmdPrevious`:

   ```
   rsTitles.MovePrevious
   Call ShowFields
   ```

5. Add this code to the `Click` event procedure of `cmdNext`:

   ```
   rsTitles.MoveNext
   Call ShowFields
   ```

6. Add this code to the `Click` event procedure of `cmdLast`:

   ```
   rsTitles.MoveLast
   Call ShowFields
   ```

When you run the project, you should be able to use the four command buttons to navigate the recordset.

The last `Move` method, `Move n`, lets you move more than one record from the current position. The value of *n* is the number of records to move in the recordset. This value can be either positive or negative to indicate movement either forward or backward in the recordset. The following line of code shows the use of this method to move two records forward from the current record:

```
rsTitles.Move 2
```

Using the *Bookmark* Property

Being able to return to a specific record after the record pointer moves or new records are added is often desirable. You can do so by using the `Bookmark` property of the recordset. The bookmark is a system-assigned string variable that is correlated to the record and is unique for each record in a recordset. To use a bookmark, simply create a string variable to "remember" the bookmark and set that variable to the value of the recordset's `Bookmark` property before the record pointer moves. When you need to move the record pointer back to that record, set the recordset's `Bookmark` property to the value of your bookmark variable. The following section demonstrates this technique while using the `Find` methods.

> **CAUTION**
> If you're working with a database type other than Jet, check the `Bookmarkable` property of the recordset you are using to see whether bookmarks are supported before you execute any methods that depend on the bookmarks.

Using the *Find* Methods

You can use the `Find` methods on dynasets and snapshots only. You can't use `Find` methods on table-type recordsets. (Because the sample program was created with a table-type recordset, you can't use the `Find` methods in the example.) The `Find` methods are used to locate records that meet specified criteria. You express the criteria in the same way that you specify the `Where` clause of a SQL command—except without the `Where` keyword. The four `Find` methods are as follows:

Find Method	Action
`FindFirst`	Starting at the *top* of the recordset, finds the first record in the recordset with the specified criteria
`FindNext`	Starting at the *current location* in the recordset, finds the next record down with the specified criteria
`FindPrevious`	Starting at the *current location* in the recordset, finds the next record up with the specified criteria
`FindLast`	Starting at the *bottom* of the recordset, finds the last record in the database with the specified criteria

After the `Find` method is executed, check the status of the recordset's `NoMatch` property. If `NoMatch` is `True`, the method failed to find a record that matched the requested criteria. If `NoMatch` is `False`, the record pointer is positioned at the desired record.

> **TIP**
> You might want to set a bookmark prior to invoking one of the `Find` methods. Then, if a matching record is not found, you can return to the record that was current before the `Find` was attempted.

The `Find` methods work by scanning each record to locate the appropriate record that matches the specified criteria. The starting record and direction searched depend on which of the four `Find` methods you use. Depending on the size of the recordset and the criteria specified, this search operation can be somewhat lengthy. The Jet engine can optimize searches if an index is available for the search expression. If you are going to perform many searches, consider creating an index for the field or fields in the base table.

When a `Find` method is successful, the record pointer moves to the new record. If a `Find` method is not successful, the recordset's `NoMatch` property is set to `True` and the record pointer does not move. One way to use the `NoMatch` property is to write an `If` condition that checks the value.

Listing 26.1 shows the use of the `FindFirst` method to look for records based on user-defined criteria.

Listing 26.1 FINDTEST.TXT—Using *FindFirst* to Look for a Record

```
Private Sub cmdFindFirst_Click()
    Dim sCriteria As String
    Dim sBkmark As String

    'Build the criteria string
    sCriteria = "title like '*" & txtFind.Text & "*'"

    'Remember where we were in case Find fails
    sBkmark = rsTitles.Bookmark

    'Execute the Find
    rsTitles.FindFirst sCriteria

    'Check for success
    If rsTitles.NoMatch Then
        MsgBox "Record not found!"
        'If failed, return to last good record
        rsTitles.Bookmark = sBkmark
    End If

    'Fill the text boxes
    ShowFields

End Sub
```

> **TIP** In many cases, re-creating a dynaset using the search criteria is faster than using the `Find` methods to process all matching records. You can also create a second filtered dynaset from the first dynaset by using the search criteria as the filter condition. The best technique depends on the amount of data, size of each record, as well as other factors. Try different approaches with your data to see what's best for a given situation.

Cannot bind... Error

When you use variables as the value to be compared to, you might encounter the error `Cannot bind name` *item* when you run the program. When the field and the variable you are comparing are string (or text) variables, surround the variable name with single quotation marks (`'`), as shown in the following sample code:

```
Dim sFindCrit As String, sFindStr As String
sFindStr = "Smith"
sFindCrit = "Lastname = '" & FindStr & "'"
rsTest.FindFirst FindCrit
```

For the sake of readability, you can also assign the single quotation mark to a constant and use that constant in your code.

In the same manner, surround a date variable with the pound symbol (#) to compare it to a date field. You don't need to include any additional symbols when comparing numbers.

Setting the Current Index in a Table

You can use an index with a table to establish a specific order for the records or to work with the Seek method to find specific records quickly. For an index to be in effect, the Index property of the table must be set to the name of an existing index for the table. An example of how to use a program command to set the current index follows:

```
rsTest.Index = "NameIndex"
```

The index specified for the table must be one that has already been created and is part of the indexes collection for the given table. If the index does not exist, an error occurs. The index is not created for you. To learn about creating a new index, see the section "Creating a New Index" later in this chapter.

> **NOTE** An index does not change the actual order of records in a table; it simply changes the order in which they are retrieved from the table and the order in which the table's records are searched.

Using the *Seek* Method

Using the Seek method is the fastest way to locate an individual record in a table; however, it is also the most limiting of the record-positioning methods. The following list outlines the limitations of the Seek method:

- This method can be performed only on a table; you can't use it with a dynaset or snapshot.
- This method can be used only with an active index; the parameters of the Seek method must match the fields of the index in use.
- This method finds only the first record that matches the specified index values; subsequent uses do not find additional matching records.

How the *Seek* Method Works The Seek method consists of the method call, the comparison operator, and the values of the key fields. The comparison operator can be <, <=, =, >=, >, or <>. The key values being compared must be of the same data type as the fields in the controlling index. Although you are not required to include the same number of key values as there are fields in the index, you do have to include a key value for each field you want to search. These values must appear in the same order as the fields in the index and be separated by commas. Listing 26.2 illustrates the use of the Seek method twice. The first part of the listing shows how to use Seek with an index based on one field; the second part uses an index based on two fields.

Listing 26.2 SEEKTEST.TXT—Using the *Seek* Method to Find a Specific Record in a Table

```
Dim dbTest As Database, rsDealers As Recordset

Set dbTest = OpenDatabase("C:\MARKET\MARKET.MDB")
Set rsDealers = dbTest.OpenRecordset("Dealers", dbOpenTable)
```

continues

Listing 26.2 Continued

```
'***********************
'* SEEKING A DEALER ID *
'***********************
'   The IDIndex index is based on the DealerID field.

'Set the recordset's index to the ID index
rsDealers.Index = "IDIndex"

'Look for dealer number 9534
rsDealers.Seek "=", 9534

'Display information or "Not Found" message as appropriate
If rsDealers.NoMatch Then
    MsgBox "Not Found"
Else
    MsgBox rsDealers!LastName & ", " & rsDealers!FirstName
End If


'*************************
'* SEEKING A DEALER NAME *
'*************************
'   The NameIndex index is based on the
'       LastName and FirstName fields.

'Set the recordset's index to the name index
rsDealers.Index = "NameIndex"

'Look for dealer named "Barbara Austin"
rsDealers.Seek "=", "Austin", "Barbara"

'Display information or "Not Found" message as appropriate
If rsDealers.NoMatch Then
    MsgBox "Not Found"
Else
    MsgBox rsDealers!LastName & ", " & rsDealers!FirstName
End If
```

You must carefully plan for one behavior of the Seek method. When the Seek method uses the comparison operators =, >=, >, or <>, Seek starts with the first record for the current index and scans forward through the index to find the first matching occurrence. If the comparison operator is < or <=, Seek starts with the last record in the table and scans backward through the table. If the index has unique values for each record, this search order presents no problem. However, if duplicate index values exist for the key fields being specified, the record found depends on the comparison operator and the sort order of the index. Figure 26.5 shows a table of first and last names indexed on last name and then first name. The table on the left is indexed in ascending order; the table on the right is indexed in descending order. Table 26.4 shows the results of different Seek operations that can be performed on this table.

Positioning the Record Pointer

FIGURE 26.5
These tables show the difference between using ascending and descending order in an index.

Ascending index order —

— Descending index order

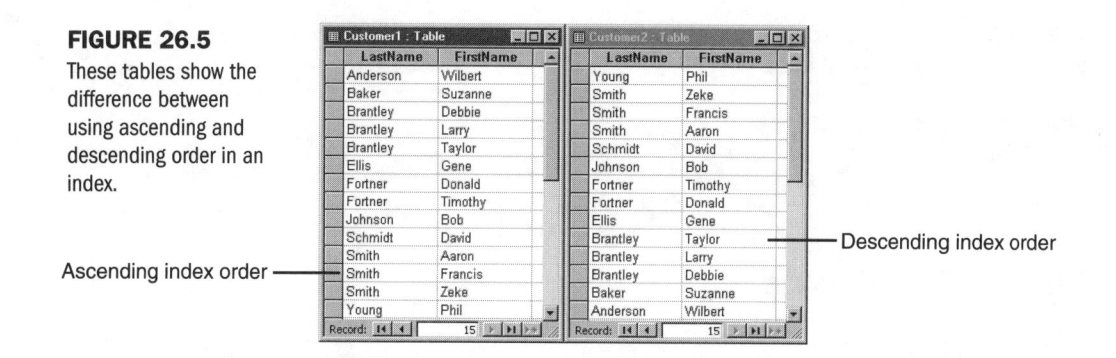

Table 26.4 Different *Seek* Comparison Operators and *Index* Sort Orders Yield Different Results

Seek Comparison Operator	*Index* Order	Resulting Record
">=", "Smith, A"	Ascending	Smith, Aaron
"<=", "Smith, Z"	Ascending	Smith, Francis
">=", "Smith, A"	Descending	Schmidt, David
"<=", "Smith, Z"	Descending	Smith, Zeke

Notice that you must also be careful when using the > ,< , >=, or <= operator on a descending index. The > (and >=) operator finds the record that occurs later in the index than the specified key value. For that reason, the ">=", "Smith" search on a descending index returns the record Schmidt, David. Similar behavior is exhibited by the < and <= operators. As you can see from the preceding example, you must use care when choosing both the index sort order and the comparison operator with the Seek method to ensure that the desired results are achieved.

As with the Find methods, if a Seek is successful, the record pointer moves. Otherwise, the recordset's NoMatch property is set to True, and the record pointer does not change.

Enabling a Sample *Seek* Now you can enhance the sample project to perform a Seek. Because the users shouldn't be expected to type an entire book title to find a match, you can use >= as the seek comparison. This means that even if NoMatch is false, indicating a successful Seek, you need to look at the current record to make sure it meets the users' criteria. Follow these steps:

1. Add a text box named txtSearch to the form.
2. Add a label to identify the text box, and set its Caption property to Search for:.
3. Add a command button named cmdSeek, and set its Caption property to Search.
   Figure 26.6 shows the form with the new controls added.

FIGURE 26.6
The Search button presents the users with an opportunity to enter search conditions.

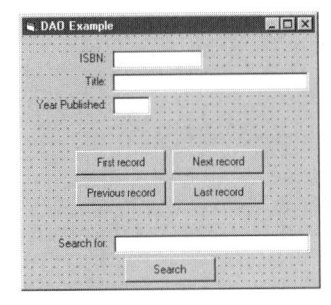

4. Add the following code to the `Click` event procedure of `cmdSeek`:

```
Dim sBkmark As Variant, sSeek As String
rsTitles.Index = "Title"
sBkmark = rsTitles.Bookmark
sSeek = UCase(txtSearch.Text)
rsTitles.Seek ">=", sSeek
If rsTitles.NoMatch Then
    MsgBox "No match!"
    rsTitles.Bookmark = sBkmark
Else
    If UCase(Left(rsTitles!Title, Len(sSeek))) <> sSeek Then
        MsgBox "No match!"
        rsTitles.Bookmark = sBkmark
    End If
End If
ShowFields
```

Using the *PercentPosition* and *AbsolutePosition* Properties

In addition to the `Bookmark` property, the Recordset object has two other properties that you can set to establish the position of the record pointer. These properties are `PercentPosition` and `AbsolutePosition`.

The `PercentPosition` property specifies the approximate position in a recordset where a record is located. By setting this property to a value between 0 and 100, you cause the pointer to move to the record closest to that location. Setting the property to a value outside the range causes an error to occur. You can use the `PercentPosition` property with all three types of recordsets.

The `AbsolutePosition` property enables you to tell the recordset to move to a specific record. The value of the property can range from 0 for the first record in the recordset to 1 less than the number of records. Setting a value outside that range causes an error. Therefore, including error checking in the code used to set the `AbsolutePosition` property is a good idea. The `AbsolutePosition` property can be used only with dynasets and snapshots. The following code shows how you can use the `AbsolutePosition` and `PercentPosition` properties. Note the validation of the requested position; it is used to prevent errors:

```
'Move to the percent position specified
If fPct > 100 Then fPct = 100
If fPct < 0 Then fPct = 0
NewDyn.PercentPosition = fPct
 'Move to the absolute position specified
If lAbs > rsTest.RecordCount Then lAbs = NewDyn.RecordCount
If lAbs < 0 Then lAbs = 0
NewDyn.AbsolutePosition = lAbs
```

Using Filters, Indexes, and Sorts

Filters, indexes, and sorts are properties of the recordset object. You can set these properties using an assignment statement such as this one:

```
rsTest.Filter = "LastName = 'Smith'"
```

Filters, indexes, and sorts enable you to control the scope of records being processed and the order in which records are processed. *Filters* (which are available only for dynasets and snapshots) limit the scope of records by specifying that they meet certain criteria, such as "last name starts with *M*." *Indexes* (available only for tables) and *sorts* (available only for dynasets and snapshots) specify the order of a recordset based on the value of one or more fields in the recordset. For sorts and indexes, you can also specify ascending or descending sort order.

Setting the *Filter* Property

The `Filter` property is available only for dynasets and snapshots. Although the following discussion refers only to dynasets, the same statements hold true for snapshots. When set, the `Filter` property does not affect the current dynaset, but filters records that are copied to a second dynaset or snapshot created from the first.

You can specify the `Filter` property of a dynaset the same way you specify the `Where` clause of a SQL statement, but without the `Where` keyword. The filter can be a simple statement, such as `State = 'TN'`, or one that uses multiple conditions, such as `State = 'AR' AND Lastname = 'Smith'`. You can also use an expression, such as `Lastname LIKE 'S*'`, to find people whose last names begin with *S*. See the section "Setting Up a Dynaset" earlier in this chapter for an example of creating a new recordset by using the `Filter` property.

You can include added flexibility in your `Filter` conditions by using functions in the condition. For example, if you want to filter a dynaset of all states with the second letter of the state code equal to *L,* use the `Mid` function, as shown here:

```
rsTest.Filter = "Mid(State,2,1) = 'L'"
```

Using functions does work, but it is an inefficient way to filter a dynaset. A better approach is to include the condition in the query used to create the dynaset in the first place.

> **More About Filters**
>
> The `Filter` condition of the dynaset has no effect on the current dynaset—only on secondary dynasets created from the current one. The only way to "filter" the existing recordset is to move through the recordset with the `Find` methods. By setting the `Find` condition to your `Filter` condition, you process only the records you want.
>
> If you work with only the filtered dynaset, creating the required dynaset using the appropriate SQL clause in the `OpenRecordset` method is more efficient.

Setting the *Sort* Property

As with the `Filter` property, the `Sort` property is available only for dynasets and snapshots. Although the following discussion refers only to dynasets, the same statements apply to snapshots. You can specify the `Sort` property by providing the field names and order (ascending or descending) for the fields on which the dynaset is to be sorted. You can specify any field or combination of fields in the current dynaset. The `Sort` condition is similar to the ORDER BY clause of a SQL statement. You can use the `Sort` property to create a recordset much like you used the `Filter` property in the preceding section. For example, the following statement specifies a sort order of last name followed by the birthdate:

```
rsTest.Sort = "LastName, Birthday"
```

> **CAUTION**
>
> When you are specifying a multiple field sort, the order of the fields is important. A sort on first name and then last name yields different results than a sort on last name and then first name.

You can also achieve the same results of a sorted dynaset in a more efficient manner by specifying the ORDER BY clause of the SQL statement used to create the dynaset.

Creating a New Index

In the earlier section "Setting the Current Index in a Table," you learned how to specify the index used in a database search. If the index you want does not exist, you can create it by using a few lines of code.

First, use the `CreateIndex` function of a `Table` object to create the new index object. Then add fields to the index object with its `Append` method, as in the following lines of code:

```
Dim Idx1 As Index
Dim Fld1 As Field
Set Idx1 = NewTbl.CreateIndex("Zip_Code")
Set Fld1 = Idx1.CreateField("Zip")
Idx1.Fields.Append Fld1
```

The preceeding lines of code set up a new index called "Zip Code." In order to use this index, you need to append it to the `Indexes` collection of the table and set the table object's `Index` property to the name of the index:

```
NewTbl.Indexes.Append Idx1
NewTbl.Index = "Zip_Code"
```

If your program needs an index, why not just create it at designtime so you don't have to worry about creating it at runtime? There are several reasons for not doing this:

- It takes time for the data engine to update indexes after records are added, deleted, or changed. If there are a large number of indexes, this process can be quite time-consuming. It may be better to create the index only when it is needed. Also, indexes take up additional disk resources; so many indexes on a large table can cause your application to exceed available resources.
- You are limited to 32 indexes for a table. Although this is a fairly large number, if you need more than 32, you must create some indexes as they are needed and then delete them.
- You may not be able to anticipate all the ways a user of your application wants to view data. By providing a method for creating indexes, specified by the user at runtime, you add flexibility to your application.

Of these reasons, the performance issue of updating multiple indexes is the one most often considered. To determine whether it is better to add the index at designtime or to create it only when you need it, set up the application both ways and test the performance of each.

NOTE Although it is desirable to limit the number of indexes your table has to keep current, it is advisable to have an index for each field that is commonly used in SQL queries. This is because the Jet engine (starting with version 2.0) employs query optimization that uses any available indexes to speed up queries. ■

Considering Programs That Modify Multiple Records

Some programs, or program functions, are meant to find one specific piece of information in a database. However, the vast majority of programs and functions work with multiple records as a group. There are two basic methods of working with multiple records:

Method	Definition
Program loops	Groups of commands contained inside a Do...While, Do...Until, or For...Next programming structure. The commands are repeated until the exit condition of the loop is met.
SQL statements	Commands written in Structured Query Language that tell the database engine to process records. SQL is covered in detail in Appendix C, "SQL Summary."

Using Loops

Most programmers are familiar with the use of Do...While and For...Next loops. When you are working with recordsets, all the programming principles for loops still apply. That is, you can perform a loop *while* a specific condition exists or *for* a specific number of records.

Another way of working with multiple records forms an *implied loop.* Most data entry or data viewing programs include command buttons on the form to move to the next record or previous record. When users repeatedly click these buttons, they execute a type of program loop by repeating the move events. Special considerations for this type of loop are what to do when you are at the first record, the last record, or if you have an empty recordset. The problem is that if you move backward from the first record, forward from the last record, or try to move anywhere in an empty recordset, an error occurs. Fortunately, the Jet database engine provides some help in this area. Some properties of the recordset can tell you when these conditions exist, as described in the following section.

You can use four main recordset properties to control the processing of multiple records in a recordset. Table 26.5 gives the definitions of these properties.

Table 26.5 Properties Used to Control Loop Processing

Property	Description
BOF	Beginning-of-file flag, indicates whether the record pointer is positioned before the first record (BOF = True) or not (BOF = False).
EOF	End-of-file flag, indicates whether the record pointer is positioned past the last record (EOF = True) or not (EOF = False).
RecordCount	Indicates the number of records in the recordset that have been accessed. This number gives a count of the total records in the recordset only after the last record is accessed (for example, by using MoveLast), unless the recordset in question is a table-type recordset.
NoMatch	Indicates that the last Find method or Seek method was unsuccessful in locating a record that matched the desired criteria.

You can use these properties to terminate loops or prevent errors. Consider the data entry form in Figure 26.3. To prevent an error from occurring when users clicks the Next Record button, use code that allows the move only if the recordset is not at the end of the file. The following code takes this possibility into account:

```
If Not rsTitles.EOF Then
      rsTitles.MoveFirst
      If rsTitles.EOF Then
          rsTitles.MoveLast
      End If
   End If
   Call ShowFields chuck
```

Alternatively, you can disable the Next button when you reach the end of the file. You can apply one of these principles to the Previous button and the BOF condition. You might also want to check the RecordCount property of a recordset and enable only the Add Record button if the count is zero.

After the `MoveNext` method is executed, the pointer may now be at the end of the file (EOF). If so, no current record exists. Therefore, if the end of the file is encountered, a `MoveLast` method is used to make sure the record pointer is positioned at the last record in the recordset. ■

Using SQL Statements

In addition to processing records with a program loop, you can use SQL statements to handle a number of functions that apply to multiple records. The following sections discuss two main types of functions:

- Calculation queries, which provide cumulative information about the requested group of records.
- Action queries that insert, delete, or modify groups of records in a recordset.

For a more in-depth discussion of the SQL language, see Appendix C, "SQL Summary."

Calculation Queries   Calculation queries allow you to determine cumulative information about a group of records such as the total; average, minimum, and maximum values; and the number of records. They work by specifying calculation functions built-in to the SQL language. You can also specify the filter criteria for the records using the standard WHERE clause. For example, you can extract total sales for all salesmen in the Southeast region or the maximum price of a stock on a given day (assuming, of course, that the base data is in your tables).

Suppose you have a database table that contains records for fish sales. Each record has a code to identify the amount of the sale and the type of fish. Consider the following lines of VB code:

```
sSQL = "SELECT SUM([Price]) As GrandTotal FROM FishSales WHERE Fishcode = 1001"
Set rsTotal = dbFish.OpenRecordset(sSQL)
Msgbox "Grand Total = " & rsTotal("GrandTotal")
```

The key to understanding the example SQL statement is the SUM function, which adds each value of the `Price` field together. The returned recordset has a single field called `GrandTotal`, which contains the result.

In addition to SUM, there are several other SQL functions which return calculated values. For example, the following SQL statement could be used to calculate the minimum, maximum, and average price of fish from the table:

```
SELECT MIN(Price) As MinPrice, AVG(Price) As AvgPrice, MAX(Price) As MaxPrice
FROM FishSales
```

The calculation query produces a dynaset with a single record containing the results. Using a calculation query can replace many lines of program code that would be required to produce the same results. In addition, a query is usually faster than the equivalent program code because the calculation is performed by the database engine rather than your own Visual Basic code.

Action Queries   Action queries operate directly on a recordset to insert, delete, or modify groups of records based on specific criteria. As with calculation queries, action queries perform the same work that would require several lines of program code. The following lists several types of action queries:

- **Updating a field value**—The SQL UPDATE statement can be used to change the value of multiple fields and multiple records, as in the following example:

  ```
  UPDATE FishSales SET Price=Price*2 WHERE FishCode=1001
  ```

  The sample UPDATE statement causes the value of the Price field to be doubled for each record where the value of the FishCode field is equal to 1001.

- **Deleting records**—The DELETE statement allows you to remove records from a table:

  ```
  DELETE From FishSales WHERE FishCode=1001 AND Price > 100
  ```

  Be careful when using the DELETE statement—if you leave out the WHERE clause, every record will be deleted!

- **Adding new records**—The INSERT statement allows you to specify the field values for a new record. The following example lists the new fields in a Values() clause in the same order as the destination table:

  ```
  INSERT INTO FishSales Values(1002,19.95)
  ```

  Note that if your table contains an AutoNumber field you do not specify a value in the INSERT statement.

In order to use an action query, you can just use the SQL statement as a parameter to the Database object's Execute method, as in the following example:

```
dbFish.Execute "INSERT INTO FishSales Values(1003,299.00)"
```

If your query will be executed repeatedly or contains parameters, you may want to create a QueryDef object containing the SQL statement:

```
Dim NewQry As QueryDef
Set NewQry = dbFish.CreateQueryDef("MyQueryDef","DELETE FROM FishSales")
NewQry.Execute
dbFish.DeleteQueryDef("MyQueryDef")
```

Notice that action queries do not return records, so you do not need any recordset objects in your code. Although the types of actions performed by such queries could be achieved by retrieving a recordset from the database and using methods such as AddNew and Delete, an action query is usually more efficient because it is handled by the database engine.

Understanding Other Programming Commands

So far in this chapter, you have learned how to find specific records and how to move through a group of records. However, in most programs, you also must add, modify, and delete records. The commands covered in the following sections apply only to tables and dynasets (remember that snapshots are not updateable).

Adding Records

To add a new record to a recordset, use the AddNew method. AddNew does not actually add the record to the recordset; it clears the copy buffer to allow information for the new record to be input. After invoking `AddNew`, your program can populate the fields by treating them like variables. Finally, to add the record physically after you put data into the record's fields, use the `Update` method. The following lines of code illustrate this technique:

```
'Prepare a new record in the copy buffer
rsTest.AddNew

'Populate the new record's fields
rsTest!FirstName = "Casey"
rsTest!LastName = "Jones"

'"Save" the changes with Update
rsTest.Update
```

> **CAUTION**
>
> Because `AddNew` places information only in the copy buffer, reusing the `AddNew` method or moving the record pointer with any `Move` or `Find` method (before using the `Update` method) clears the copy buffer. Any information entered in the new record up to that point is therefore lost.

Editing Records

In a manner similar to adding a record, you use the `Edit` method to make changes to a record. The `Edit` method places a copy of the current record's contents into the copy buffer so that information can be changed. As with `AddNew`, the changes take effect only when the `Update` method is executed.

To edit a record, first provide a way for the users to locate the record that they want to modify. You can use one or more of the techniques described earlier in this chapter to accomplish this task. After you locate the record you want (and make it the current record), invoke the `Edit` method. Then you can populate the fields (most likely obtaining the new information from the users) and finally invoke the `Update` method. This technique is illustrated in the following lines of code:

```
rsTest.Edit
rsTest!FirstName = txtFirstName.Text
rsTest!LastName = txtLastName.Text
rsTest.Update
```

> **CAUTION**
>
> Because `Edit` only places information in the copy buffer, reusing the `Edit` method or moving the record pointer with any `Move` or `Find` method (before using the `Update` method) clears the copy buffer. Any information entered in the record is therefore lost.

Updating Records

As you learned in the previous two sections, you use the `Update` method in conjunction with the `AddNew` and `Edit` methods to make changes to the recordsets. The `Update` method writes the information from the copy buffer to the recordset. In the case of `AddNew`, `Update` also creates a blank record in the recordset to which the information is written. In a multiuser environment, the `Update` method also clears the record locks associated with the pending `Add` or `Edit` method.

> **NOTE** If you use Data controls to work with recordsets, the use of the `Update` method is not required. An update is automatically performed when a move is executed by the Data control.

Deleting Records

Deleting a record requires the use of the `Delete` method. After you locate the appropriate record (and make it current), invoking the recordset's `Delete` method permanently removes the record from the table. This method removes the record from the recordset and sets the record pointer to a null value. The `Delete` method is illustrated in this line of code:

```
RsTest.Delete
```

> **CAUTION**
> After you delete a record, it is gone without warning. You can recover the record only if you issued a `BeginTrans` command before you deleted the record, in which case you can use `RollBack` to recover the transaction. Otherwise, the only way to get the information back into the database is to re-create the record by using the `AddNew` method.

> **NOTE** Deletions and changes to the database are made without confirmation by the users. If you want your program to have confirmation built in, you have to provide it in your code. The easiest way to do so is through the `MsgBox` function. With this function, you can provide a warning to the users and ask for confirmation.

Introducing Transaction Processing

Transaction processing enables you to treat a group of changes, additions, or deletions to a database as a single entity. This capability is useful when one change to a database depends on another change, and you want to make sure that all changes are made before any of the changes become permanent. For example, you have a point-of-sale application that updates inventory levels as sales are made. As each item is entered for the sales transaction, a change is made to the inventory database. However, you want to keep only the inventory changes if the sale is completed. If the sale is aborted, you want to return the inventory database to its initial state before the sale was started. Transaction processing is a function of the Workspace object and, therefore, affects all databases open in a particular workspace.

Visual Basic provides three methods for transaction processing. These methods perform the following functions:

Transaction Method	Function
BeginTrans	Starts a transaction and sets the initial state of the database.
RollBack	Returns the database to its initial state before the BeginTrans statement was issued. When RollBack is executed, all changes made after the last BeginTrans statement are discarded.
CommitTrans	Permanently saves all changes to the database made since the last BeginTrans statement. After the CommitTrans statement is issued, the transactions cannot be undone.

Listing 26.3 shows the BeginTrans, RollBack, and CommitTrans methods as they are used in an order entry application. The transactions are used in case a customer cancels an order prior to the completion of the order processing.

Listing 26.3 TRANSACT.TXT—Using Transaction Processing to Handle Multiple Changes to a Database as One Group

```
OldWs.BeginTrans
'*************************************************
'Perform loop until user ends sales transaction
'*************************************************
Do While Sales
'*************************************************
'Get item number and sales quantity from form
' Input Itemno,SalesQty
' Find item number in inventory
'*************************************************
    Inv.FindFirst "ItemNum = " & Itemno
'*************************************
'Update inventory quantity
'*************************************
    Inv.Edit
    Inv("Quantity") = Inv("Quantity") - SalesQty
    Inv.Update
Loop
'*******************************************
'User either completes or cancels the sale
'*******************************************
If SaleComp Then
    OldWs.CommitTrans
Else
    OldWs.Rollback
End If
```

From Here...

This chapter introduced you to Database Access Objects, which provide a way to work with databases from Visual Basic. Understanding DAO provides a good foundation for other data access technologies, such as RDO and ADO. The best way to learn more about DAO is to try some of the ideas discussed on the sample databases included with VB, such as the BIBLIO database. For newcomers, I suggest you make a backup copy of the sample database so you do not have to worry about destroying it.

Some of the topics mentioned in this chapter are covered in greater detail in other portions of the book. Refer to these chapters:

- For a recap of more fundamental database concepts, see Chapter 24, "Database Basics."
- To learn about a data access interface designed for client/server databases, see Chapter 27, "Using Remote Data Objects (RDO)."
- To find out about the method of data access that will eventually replace DAO and RDO, see Chapter 28, "Using ActiveX Data Objects (ADO)."
- The SQL language is discussed in more detail in Appendix C, "SQL Summary."

CHAPTER 27

Using Remote Data Objects (RDO)

In this chapter

Database Access Philosophies   596

Working with ODBC   596

The Remote Data Objects   603

Using the Remote Data Control   607

So far in the discussions of accessing databases, the focus has been on using PC-based databases. These types of databases include Access, FoxPro, dBase, and Paradox. However, Visual Basic is also a great tool for creating front ends for client/server applications. These types of applications are used to access data stored in database servers such as SQL Server and Oracle. Most of your front-end work—such as designing forms and writing code to process information—will be the same whether you are writing an application for a PC database or a client/server database. The key difference is in how you make the connection to the data.

This chapter discusses how your Visual Basic programs can easily access data stored in a variety of remote locations through the use of Remote Data Objects (RDO). You'll see how the addition of RDO to Visual Basic's repertoire makes short work of writing applications that need to work with remote data.

Database Access Philosophies

Before delving further into actually setting up applications that access client/server databases, you'll take a look at the difference in the philosophy of the two types of database access. In the PCdatabase world, information is accessed through the *database engine*, which is part of the application. For Visual Basic, the Jet engine is a part of your database applications. As you issue commands to retrieve information from the database, the commands are interpreted by the Jet engine and the processing of the commands is done locally on your PC. Regardless of whether the database file actually resides on your PC or is located on a file server, the database engine remains on your PC. The application itself contains the logic to directly access the database file. In the client/server world, this is not the case. Your application issues a request for information, usually in the form of a SQL statement. This request is passed to the database server, which processes the request and returns the results. This is true client/server computing, in which a database server does the actual processing of the request.

Client/server systems have a number of advantages over just sharing a database file. First, database logic is removed to a central, more maintainable location. For example, suppose you have a program that calculates sales tax based on your company's rules. In a client/server environment, the logic for this calculation process would be located on the database server. This means you can make changes to it in one place, without having to rewrite the client application. Other advantages include being able to distribute processing and separating the user interface design from the business logic.

Working with ODBC

One method used by Visual Basic to communicate with client/server databases is called *Open Database Connectivity*, or ODBC. ODBC is a component of Microsoft's *Windows Open System Architecture* (WOSA). ODBC provides a set of *application program interface* (API) functions, which makes it easier for a developer to connect to a wide range of database formats. Because of the use of ODBC standards, you can use the same set of functions and commands to access information in a SQL Server, Oracle, or Interbase server, even though the actual data-storage systems are quite different. You can even access a number of PC databases using ODBC functions.

Understanding ODBC Drivers

ODBC drivers are the DLLs containing the functions that let you connect to various databases. There are separate drivers for each database type. For many standard formats, such as PC databases and SQL Servers, these drivers are provided with Visual Basic. For other databases, the ODBC driver is provided by the server manufacturer.

> **NOTE** If you use ODBC in your application, make sure the appropriate drivers are distributed with your application. If you selected the Redistributable ODBC option when installing VB, an ODBC subdirectory should have been created in the Visual Basic program directory. Running SETUP.EXE installs ODBC drivers, although you still have to set up your data sources.

ODBC drivers can be one of two types: *single-tier* or *multiple-tier*. A single-tier driver is used to connect to PC-based database systems that may reside on either the local machine or a file server. Multiple-tier drivers are used to connect to client/server databases where the SQL statement is processed by the server, not the local machine.

Each ODBC driver you encounter must contain a basic set of functions, known as the *core-level capabilities*. These basic functions are as follows:

- Providing database connections
- Preparing and executing SQL statements
- Processing transactions
- Returning result sets
- Informing the application of errors

Setting Up an ODBC Data Source

Before you can use ODBC to connect to a database, you must make sure of two things:

- The ODBC drivers are installed on your system.
- You have set up the ODBC data source.

Both of these functions can be accomplished by using the ODBC Manager application. Also, the second function can be accomplished from code, by using the data access objects. Remember, an ODBC driver is used to connect to a *type* of database, for example, SQL Server. An ODBC Data Source is a configuration of an ODBC driver used to connect to a *specific database*, for example, Accounting Department Database.

> **NOTE** On Microsoft Windows 95 and 98 systems, you will find the ODBC manager in the Control Panel, under the Settings item on the Start menu. The icon you are looking for is labeled "32-bit ODBC." You might also have an icon called "ODBC" if you have some older 16-bit programs.

NOTE To ensure that all readers can use the information presented here, the Access ODBC driver is used in all examples. Although this is a PC database, the methods used can also be applied to server databases. It is important to remember that connecting to an Access .MDB file via ODBC is different than connecting directly through the Jet engine.

Gaining Access to ODBC Drivers To set up the ODBC Data Sources on your system, you need to use the Windows ODBC Data Source Administrator. You will find this in the Control Panel, which is accessible by choosing the Control Panel item from the Settings submenu on the Start menu. The Control Panel is illustrated in Figure 27.1.

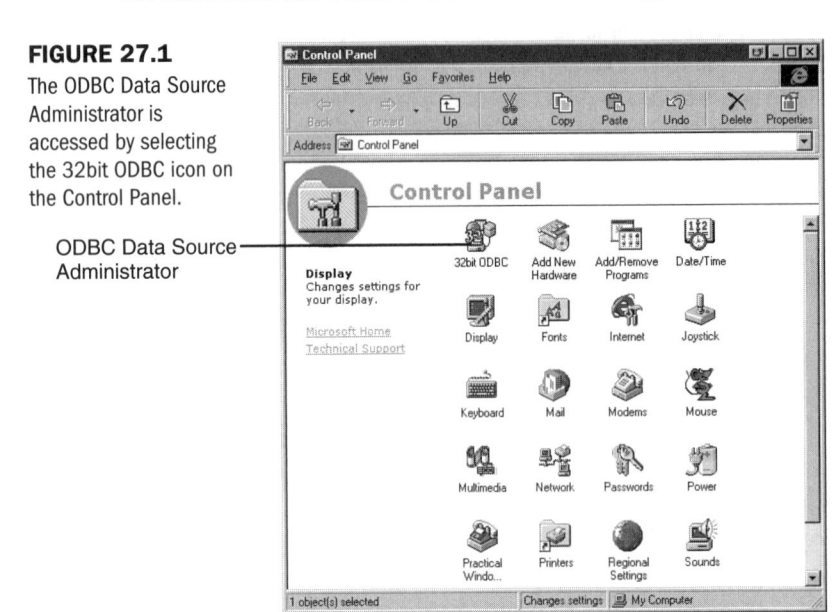

FIGURE 27.1
The ODBC Data Source Administrator is accessed by selecting the 32bit ODBC icon on the Control Panel.

ODBC Data Source Administrator

The ODBC Administrator Dialog Box

If you see different dialog boxes than the ones pictured here when you click the 32-bit ODBC icon, don't panic. As with any product, Microsoft has produced several versions of ODBC. ODBC is included with many of its products, including Office and Visual Basic. Depending on the installation options you chose, you may or may not have the latest version. Older versions of ODBC do not have the tabbed dialog box style. Fortunately, ODBC is included with VB so you can install it during setup.

When you open the ODBC Manager, you see the ODBC Data Source Administrator dialog box, as shown in Figure 27.2. The Data Source administrator includes several tabs used to add data sources as well as new ODBC drivers.

As you might notice, the titles of the first three tabs in the dialog box end in the letters *DSN*. DSN is an abbreviation for *Data Source Name*. The DSN is the key that your program uses to identify an ODBC Data Source. ODBC takes care of mapping the DSN to the actual driver, server, and database file.

FIGURE 27.2
The Data Source Administrator dialog box allows you to configure ODBC data sources.

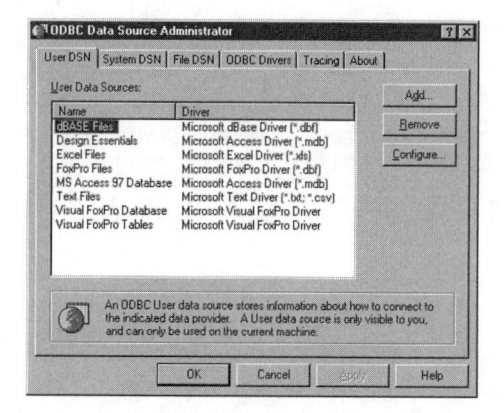

The ODBC Data Sources are divided into three types: user, system, and file. Although the purpose of all DSNs is essentially the same—to provide information about a specific data source—there are differences in where and when you can use each type:

- A System DSN, more applicable in Windows NT than Windows 95/98, is not associated with a particular user profile. This means that after the DSN has been set up, all programs and services running on the machine can access it. For example, if you are using Internet Information Server to connect to a database, you will probably be setting up a System DSN for the database.

- A File DSN stores DSN information in a text file. The text file is an INI file containing information about the database driver and location. It is not associated with a particular machine, so it can be on a network drive.

- A User DSN is the type you will probably use most often. User DSN information is stored in the Registry of the local machine. In Windows NT, each user DSN is associated with a specific user profile and invisible outside of it.

The remaining three tabs in the ODBC Data Source Administrator dialog box are used for informational and debugging purposes. The ODBC Drivers tab, shown in Figure 27.3, displays a list of the ODBC drivers installed on your machine.

The last tab, the About tab, is very similar to the ODBC Drivers tab. It lists the versions and files used by ODBC itself. You might find these two screens helpful in determining whether or not your users have the correct drivers installed.

Before moving on, notice the Tracing tab, pictured in Figure 27.4. This tab allows you to trace each call made by the ODBC Manager to the ODBC Drivers. Remember that ODBC is a means to connect to various databases via some common API functions. The Tracing options allow you to view those API calls. This is something you probably won't do very often, but it is nice to know about.

FIGURE 27.3
The ODBC Drivers tab tells you which drivers are installed on your system.

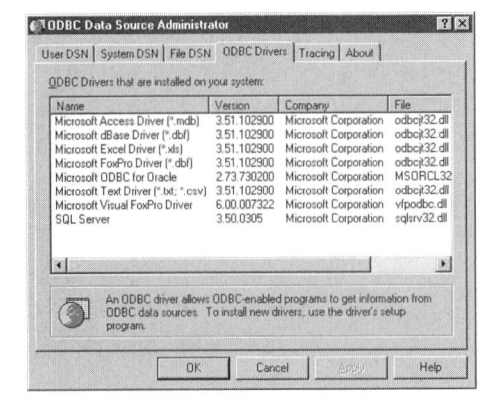

FIGURE 27.4
The Tracing tab of the ODBC Administrator is a low-level debugging aid.

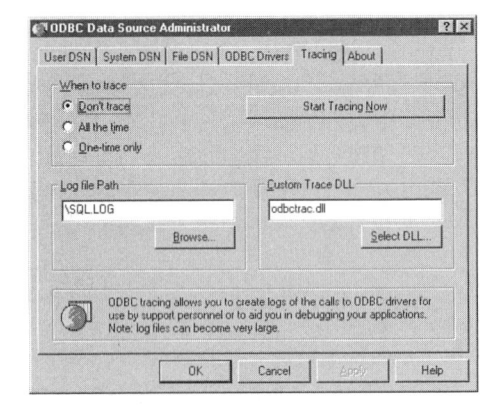

Creating an ODBC Source with the ODBC Manager   To set up a data source for use in your application, you need to know which driver to use and how to configure it. For example, you need to know the name of the SQL server or Access MDB file the data resides in. You also need to come up with a unique name to identify the data source.

Set up a sample data source now. Go to the User DSN screen and click the Add button to create a new data source. This presents you with the Create New Data Source dialog box, shown in Figure 27.5. In this first dialog box, you choose the ODBC driver that will be used to access the data.

After choosing the driver and clicking the OK button, you are presented with the Setup dialog box for the particular database type associated with the driver. Choose the Microsoft Access Driver and press the Finish button. You are presented with a dialog box like that in Figure 27.6.

In this dialog box, you provide a name in the Data Source Name box. This is the name you will use in your applications to refer to the data source. You can also choose to include a Description of the data source.

Database Access Philosophies

FIGURE 27.5
Selecting the ODBC driver is the first step to setting up a data source.

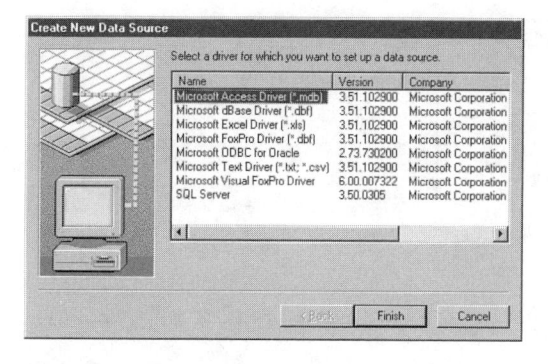

FIGURE 27.6
A Setup dialog box lets you specify the information necessary to connect to an ODBC data source.

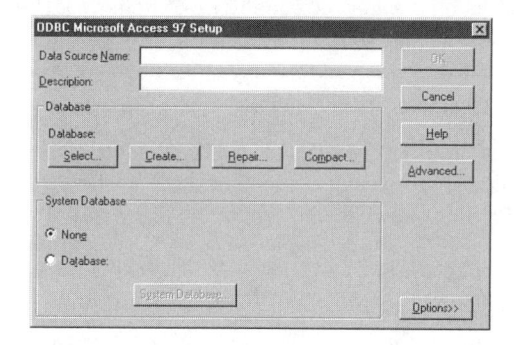

After setting the name, you need to choose the actual database file or server you want to use with your program. For the Access driver, this is done by clicking the Select button of the dialog box. You are then presented with a Select Database dialog box (which is basically an open-file dialog box). Try it by choosing an MDB file on your PC. Figure 27.7 shows a data source called MyDSN linked to the biblio database that comes with Visual Basic.

FIGURE 27.7
The Access dialog box allows you to select which MDB file you are going to be working with.

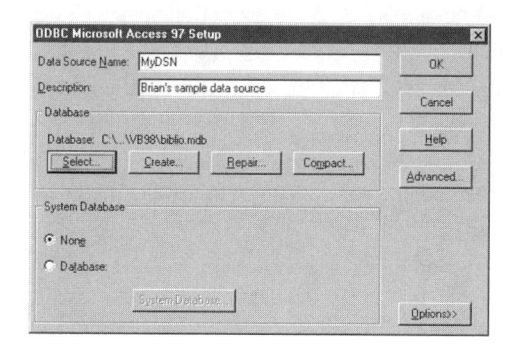

Keep in mind that the setup dialog boxes are driver dependent. In each case, however, you specify both a data-source name and the location of the data. Figure 27.8 shows the dialog box for Microsoft SQL Server.

FIGURE 27.8
The SQL Server dialog box requires you to specify the server where the information is located.

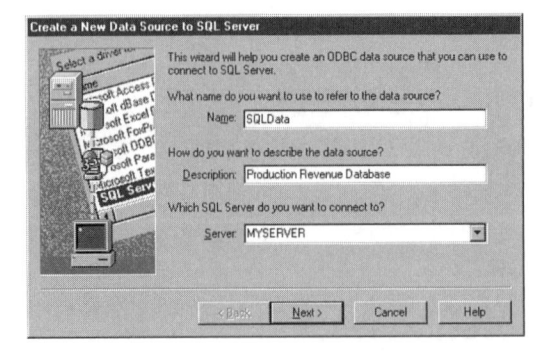

The DSN screens also give you the ability to Configure or Remove ODBC data sources. To modify a data source, select the data source and then click the Configure button. This presents you with the same dialog box that you used initially to set up the data source. To delete a data source, select it and then click the Remove button.

Using the DAOs to Create an ODBC Source You are not limited to setting up data sources interactively. There are times, such as application installation, where you might want to add a data source with code. For this purpose, you can use the `RegisterDatabase` method of the `DBEngine` object.

Here is the syntax of the `RegisterDatabase` method:

`DBEngine.RegisterDatabase` *dbname, driver, silent, attributes*

Table 27.1 defines the parameters used in the `RegisterDatabase` method.

Table 27.1 Parameters of the *RegisterDatabase* Method

Parameter	Definition
dbName	A user-definable string expression that specifies the data source name (for example, "MyDatabase").
driver	A string expression that indicates the installed driver's name (for example, ORACLE) as listed in the ODBC Drivers tab of the ODBC Administrator.
silent	True specifies that the next parameter (*attributes*) indicates all connection information. False specifies to display the Driver Setup dialog box and ignore the contents of the *attributes* parameter.
attributes	All connection information for using the ODBC driver. This parameter is ignored if *silent* is set to False.

The following code sample illustrates how the `RegisterDatabase` method is used to create a link to an Access database. Before attempting to use the Data Access Objects, remember to add the appropriate reference:

```
Dim sAttrib As String
    Dim sDriver As String

    sAttrib = "DBQ=D:\VB5\BIBLIO.mdb"
    sDriver = "Microsoft Access Driver (*.mdb)"
  DBEngine.RegisterDatabase "MyDSN", sDriver, True, sAttrib
```

After executing the preceding code, you can go back to the Data Source Administrator window and verify that a new User DSN has been added.

> **NOTE** You can also use the `rdoRegisterDataSource` method of the `rdoEngine` to perform the registration task for Remote Data Objects.

Notice that, for the Access driver, the `DBQ` parameter indicates the name of the database file. To determine all the parameters required for a particular ODBC driver, you should create a connection with the ODBC Manager and then examine the settings in the Registry. You can find these under HKEY_USERS\Default\Software\ODBC\ODBC.INI. (To view the Registry, use Windows' REGEDIT utility.) To specify multiple parameters with the `RegisterDatabase` method, separate them with a semicolon.

The Remote Data Objects

Data access objects (DAO) are a layer on top of the ODBC API. Before the advent of *Remote Data Objects* (RDO) in Visual Basic, programmers would sometimes skip this layer by calling the ODBC API directly. The reason, of course, was to make their applications run faster. However, the ODBC API calls are much harder to use than the Data Access Objects. Remote data objects changed this by providing an interface to the ODBC API that uses the familiar operations of setting properties and calling methods. Because properties and methods are used in all Visual Basic programs, this made the access of ODBC databases much easier for developers to understand and accomplish.

Comparison of RDO to DAO

The remote data objects, or RDO, are very similar to the data access objects (DAO), which were covered in Chapter 26, "Using Data Access Objects (DAO)." This similarity not only makes RDO easier to understand, but it also makes the conversion of programs from PC databases to client/server databases much easier. In fact, after the connection to the data source is made, the same code statements that were used for DAO can be used to access the data using RDO. To give you a feel for the similarities between the RDO and DAO models, Table 27.2 lists a number of RDO objects and their corresponding DAO objects.

In addition, the `rdoResultset` object supports several types of returned sets of records, similar to the recordset types of the `Recordset` object. Table 27.3 summarizes these similarities.

Table 27.2 Some RDO Objects and Their DAO Counterparts

RDO Object	DAO Object
rdoEngine	DBEngine
rdoEnvironment	Workspace
rdoConnection	Database
rdoTable	TableDef
rdoResultset	Recordset
rdoColumn	Field
rdoQuery	QueryDef
rdoParameter	Parameter

Table 27.3 *rdoResultset* Types and the Corresponding *Recordset* Types

rdoResultset Types	Recordset Types	Definition
Keyset	Dynaset	Updatable set of records in which movement is unrestricted.
Static	Snapshot	Non-updatable set of records that were present when the set was created. Updates by other users are not reflected.
Dynamic	N/A	Similar to a keyset.
Forward-only	Forward-only	Similar to a static resultset or snapshot, but you can move forward only through the set of records. This is the default resultset type.

Notice that the remote data objects do not support any rdoResultset type that returns a table. This is because the remote data objects are geared to using SQL statements to retrieve subsets of information from one or more tables. You must set the order of the rdoResultset with the Order By clause of the SQL statement used to create the set. Also, because there is no table equivalent, RDO does not support indexes.

As you might expect with the similarity of the objects, there are methods of the RDO that are similar to the methods of the DAO. These methods and their respective objects are summarized in Table 27.4.

Table 27.4 RDO Objects Methods and Related DAO Methods

RDO Method	RDO Object	DAO Method	DAO Object
rdoCreateEnvironment	rdoEngine	CreateWorkspace	DBEngine
BeginTrans	rdoConnection	BeginTrans	Workspace
CommitTrans	rdoConnection	CommitTrans	Workspace
OpenConnection	rdoEnvironment	OpenDatabase	Workspace
RollbackTrans	rdoConnection	Rollback	Workspace
CreateQuery	rdoConnection	CreateQueryDef	Database
Execute	rdoConnection	Execute	Database
OpenResultset	rdoConnection	OpenRecordset	Database

Finally, the `rdoResultset` object and the `Recordset` object have the following methods in common:

- AddNew—Adds a new row (record) to the set.
- Delete—Removes the current row (record) from the set.
- Edit—Prepares the current row for changing the information in the row.
- MoveFirst—Moves to the first row of the set.
- MoveLast—Moves to the last row of the set.
- MoveNext—Moves to the next row of the set.
- MovePrevious—Moves to the previous row of the set.
- Update—Commits the changes made to the copy buffer to the actual record. The copy buffer is a memory location that contains the values of the record with which the user is working.

Accessing a Database with RDO

To further illustrate the similarities between the RDO and DAO models, the code in Listings 27.1 and 27.2 perform the same function on the "biblio" database. The difference between the two listings is simply the objects and methods used to create returned records. After the recordset or resultset is established, the remaining statements simply print each entry in the first field. In the RDO example, the ODBC data source MyDSN was created previously with the ODBC Manager.

> **NOTE** To use the Remote Data Objects, you need to add a reference to the Microsoft Remote Data Object from the Project References menu.

Listing 27.1 RDOSAMPL.TXT—Accessing Information in an ODBC Data Source Using the RDO Methods

```
Dim db As rdoConnection
Dim rs As rdoResultset
Dim sSQL As String

Set db = rdoEngine.rdoEnvironments(0).OpenConnection("MyDSN")

sSQL = "Select * From Titles"
Set rs = db.OpenResultset(sSQL, rdOpenKeyset)

rs.MoveFirst
While Not rs.EOF
    Print rs.rdoColumns(0)
    rs.MoveNext
Wend

rs.Close
db.Close
```

Listing 27.2 DAOSAMPL.TXT—Accessing the Same Information Using the DAO Methods

```
Dim db As Database
Dim rs As Recordset
Dim sSQL As String

Set db = DBEngine.Workspaces(0).OpenDatabase("D:\VB5\BIBLIO.MDB")

sSQL = "Select * From Titles"
Set rs = db.OpenRecordset(sSQL, dbOpenDynaset)

rs.MoveFirst
While Not rs.EOF
    Print rs.Fields(0)
    rs.MoveNext
Wend

rs.Close
db.Close
```

Another thing you might want to explore with RDO is asynchronous execution of database operations. This means control is returned to your program *before* the database operation completes, as in the following example:

```
Set db = rdoEngine.rdoEnvironments(0).[ic:ccc]
   OpenConnection("MyDSN", , , , rdAsyncEnable)
While db.StillConnecting = True
      Print "Connecting..."
Wend
```

The constant rdAsyncEnable indicates asynchronous operation. The while loop keeps running until the connection is made and the StillConnecting property becomes False.

Using the RemoteData Control

If you want a faster way to create applications using ODBC data sources, you can use the *RemoteData control* (RDC). The RDC lets you set a few properties of the control, and then the RDC handles all the tasks of making the connections to the ODBC data source for you. In this way, the RDC automates the methods of the remote data objects in the same way that the data control automates the methods of the data access objects.

After setting up the RemoteData control, you can use the bound controls to display and edit information that is in the resultset created by the data control. The bound controls are set up the same way they are for use with the Data control—which was discussed in Chapter 25, "The Data Control and Data-Bound Controls"—except that the DataSource property of the bound controls points to a RemoteData control. After they are set up, the bound controls are updated with new information each time a new row is accessed by the remote data control.

Comparing the RDC and the Data Control

The remote data objects were compared to the data access objects in the earlier section "The Remote Data Objects"; now take a look at the similarities of the Data control and the RDC. As you might expect, many of the properties of the RDC have counterparts in the Data control. These properties and their functions are summarized in Table 27.5.

Table 27.5 Remote Data Control Properties Compared to Data Control Properties

RDC Property	Data Control Property	Purpose
BOFAction	BOFAction	Determines whether the beginning of file flag is set when the user invokes the MovePrevious method while on the first record.
DataSourceName	DatabaseName	Specifies the database containing the desired information.
EOFAction	EOFAction	Determines whether the end of file flag is set or if a new row (record) is added when the user invokes the MoveNext method while on the last record.
ResultsetType	RecordsetType	Determines the type of dataset created by the control.
SQL	RecordSource	The SQL statement that identifies the specific information to be retrieved.

Setting Up the RDC

Setting up the RDC for use in your program is also very similar to setting up the Data control. Before you can use the RDC, you must first add it to your project. You do this by using the Components dialog box, which you access by choosing the Components item from the Project menu. After you close the dialog box, the RemoteData control is added to your toolbox.

NOTE The RemoteData control is available only in the Enterprise Edition of Visual Basic. Also, if you did a custom installation of the Enterprise Edition and opted not to install the RemoteData control, it does not appear as one of the available controls in the Custom Controls dialog box. In this case, you need to reinstall that portion of the Visual Basic.

To set up the RemoteData control, follow these steps:

1. Draw the RemoteData control on your form.
2. Set the Name and Caption properties of the RDC to values that have meaning to you.
3. Set the DataSourceName property. You can enter a value or choose one from the drop-down list.
4. Set the SQL property to a valid SQL statement that specifies the information you need.

As stated in step 3, you can choose the DataSourceName value from a drop-down list. This list contains every registered ODBC data source on your system. An example of this list is shown in Figure 27.9.

FIGURE 27.9
You can choose from a list of available ODBC data sources when setting the DataSourceName.

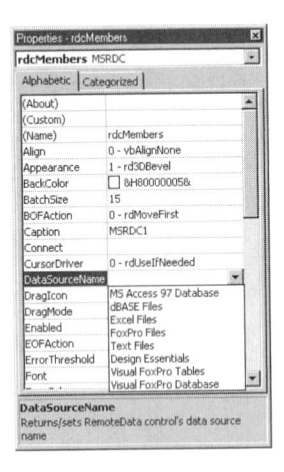

After you have set up the remote data control, you then can attach bound controls to it by setting the DataSource property. As shown in Figure 27.10, a drop-down list in the DataSource property contains the names of any remote data controls or data controls on the current form. After the DataSource property has been set, you can select the DataField property from a list, just as you did for the controls bound to a data control.

FIGURE 27.10
The `DataSource` property list contains all available data controls, remote or not.

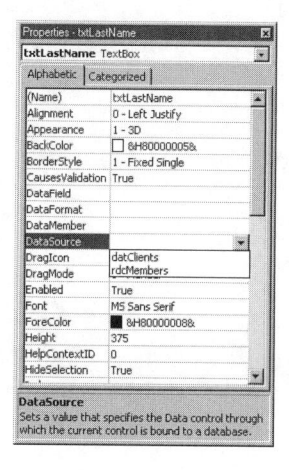

From Here...

This chapter has given you a basic understanding of client/server applications. The chapter has also shown you how the Remote Data Objects and RemoteData control make it easier to access the ODBC databases that are part of many client/server programs. For more information on the topics touched on in this chapter, see the following:

- For a discussion of fundamental database concepts, see Chapter 24, "Database Basics."
- To learn about the data access method that will eventually replace DAO and RDO, see Chapter 28, "Using ActiveX Data Objects (ADO)."
- The SQL language is discussed in more detail in Appendix C, "SQL Summary."

CHAPTER 28

Using ActiveX Data Objects (ADO)

In this chapter

Introducing ADO **612**

Using the ADO Data Control **614**

Using the DataGrid Control **619**

Using ActiveX Data Objects **627**

Disconnected Recordsets **637**

Version 2.0 of ActiveX Data Objects (ADO) is the latest entry in to the VB data access arena. It provides a way for you to interact with various types of databases from your Visual Basic programs, ActiveX components, and Active Server Pages. This chapter introduces ADO and demonstrates some of its key features.

Introducing ADO

ActiveX Data Objects, or *ADO*, is the most recent method of data access that Microsoft has introduced. ADO is intended to replace DAO (Data Access Objects), the original method of Visual Basic database access, and RDO (Remote Data Objects), a fast alternative to DAO. As with either of these object models, ADO provides several options for accessing your data. In this section, you briefly look at the steps and strategies necessary to set up a connection to data using ADO.

Data Connection Methods

ADO provides the means by which your program code accesses a database. But how does ADO itself connect to a database? The answer is through an *OLE DB provider*. OLE DB is Microsoft's new lower-level database interface that provides access to many different kinds of data. There are OLE DB providers for both traditional databases (such as SQL server) as well as other sources like an e-mail server. The OLE DB provider exposes these databases to ADO, which in turn allows you to connect to the data in the following ways:

- **Data controls.** A Data control is a custom control that handles communication with the database. You simply set a few properties and "bind" some other controls to the Data control to display information.
- **Object interface.** When you add a reference to ADO, a new set of objects becomes available to your program. You can manipulate data directly from code without any controls or combine the use of objects with a Data control.

The Data control is quick and easy to set up, but using the object interface provides more power and flexibility. In this chapter, you examine both methods as they relate to ADO.

Installation

If the past is any indicator, by the time you read this chapter, Microsoft will have come out with patches and service packs for many of its products. Before you start using ADO, it is worth your while to download and install the latest version. At the time of this writing, Visual Basic 6.0 includes ADO 2.0, and Visual Basic 5.0 users can download version 1.5c. The Microsoft Data Access Components (MSDAC) package includes ADO files and documentation, the latest version of ODBC, and Remote Data Services. You can find the Web site at http://www.microsoft/com/data/ado.

> **TIP** When you are installing the updated Data Access Components, select Custom Installation and make sure that you choose to install ADO documentation and the Access database driver.

In the References dialog box of Visual Basic, two entries are used with ADO: Microsoft ActiveX Data Objects 2.0 Library and Microsoft ActiveX Data Objects Recordset 2.0 Library. To use the ADO object examples in this chapter, make sure that you include the appropriate references, as pictured in Figure 28.1.

FIGURE 28.1
Choose Project, References to add references for ADO to your program.

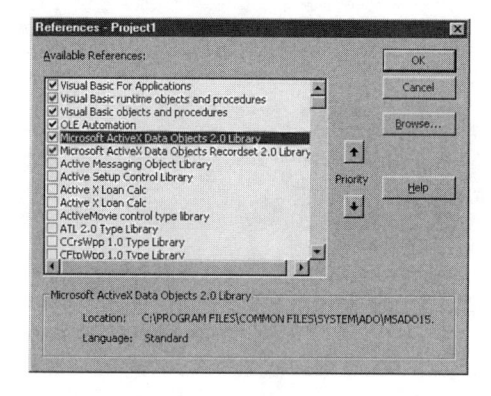

The reference titled Microsoft ActiveX Data Objects 2.0 Library contains the full-featured ADO objects discussed throughout most of this chapter. The other reference contains only the Recordset object, intended for use with remote disconnected recordsets.

Setting Up a Data Source

When you use data in your program, that data has to come from a *data source*. A data source is a database that can be anything from a small Microsoft Access database to an IBM AS/400. Many different types of database products are available, and you can connect to almost all of them. Open Database Connectivity, or ODBC, is one vehicle that allows you to connect to a variety of data sources. You set up the ODBC database driver in Windows and then use it to access the database from Visual Basic.

To use the examples in this chapter, you have to create a data source for the database BIBLIO.MDB, which is included with Visual Basic. Start by clicking the icon labeled 32-bit ODBC in the Windows Control Panel. You then see the ODBC Data Source Administrator, as shown in Figure 28.2.

> **NOTE** You also can create DSN-less connections. See the section "Making the Connection with ADO" later in this chapter.

To create a new data source, first click the Add button. BIBLIO.MDB is an Access database, so select Microsoft Access Driver and click Finish. A dialog box for the Access ODBC driver then appears. Click the Select button, and locate BIBLIO.MDB (usually in the Visual Basic application directory). Name the data source BIBLIO, and enter a description if you want. The completed configuration screen should look similar to Figure 28.3.

FIGURE 28.2
Using the ODBC Data Source Administrator, you can configure data source names (DSNs) that point to specific databases.

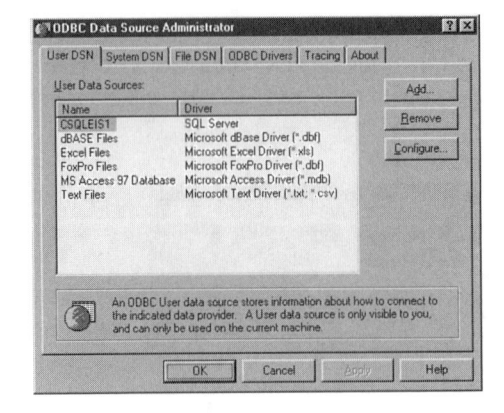

FIGURE 28.3
Using ODBC to connect to an Access database is somewhat different than using Jet, as discussed in Chapter 26, "Using Data Access Objects (DAO)."

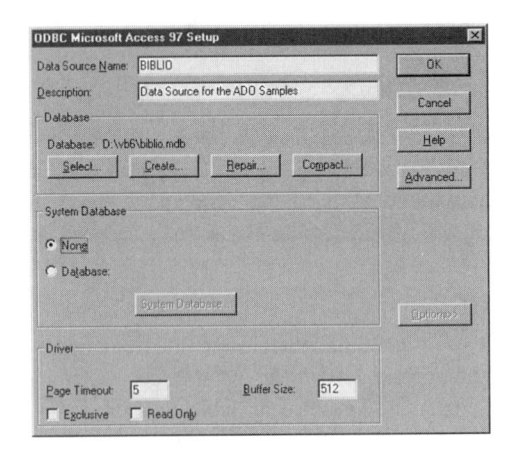

Click OK to close the ODBC Data Source Administrator. Now that the ODBC data source has been configured, you can work with data in the BIBLIO data source by using ADO.

> **NOTE** Although ODBC provides an easy way to set up a data source, you do not have to use ODBC to use ADO. There is also an ADO data provider for Jet databases that does not use ODBC.

Using the ADO Data Control

Visual Basic 6.0 includes a new Data control: the ADO Data control. This control serves the same purpose as the standard Data control that has been around for years, but it works with ADO.

As mentioned earlier, ADO can be used with controls, code, or both. ADO is a lot more flexible than DAO in this regard. Although a Data control can be used by itself, the most common use of a Data control is to provide data to other controls on the form. You can take a standard control, such as a text box, and "bind" it to a Data control. The text box is then referred to as a *bound control*. Bound controls are linked to the database, and their contents reflect the current database record provided by the Data control.

> **NOTE** If you have not read Chapter 25, "The Data Control and Data-Bound Controls," you may want to do so now. That chapter discusses the standard Data control as well as the concept of bound controls.

Setting Up the ADO Data Control

The easiest way to learn how to use a Data control is to create a sample project. In this section, you'll do just that as you learn about the ADO Data control. Begin by opening Visual Basic and starting a new Standard EXE project.

To use the ADO Data control, you must add it to the Visual Basic Toolbox. To do so, right-click in an empty area of the toolbox, select C<u>o</u>mponents from the context menu, and add the Microsoft ADO Data Control 6.0 control.

Next, draw an instance of the ADO Data control on the form. If you have seen the standard

FIGURE 28.4
The ADO Data control links your program to an ADO data source.

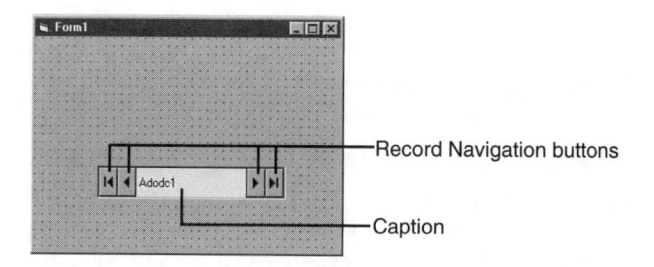

Data control, the ADO Data control should look similar, as pictured in Figure 28.4.

Before you continue setting up the Data control, notice its initial appearance. The four arrow buttons, which look similar to those you might find on an audio CD player, are used to change the current database record. The caption, set by the `Caption` property, is for informational purposes and should be changed to something meaningful. The initial setting, ADODC1, is the default name of the first ADO Data control.

To connect to a database and retrieve data, you need to set several properties of the ADO Data control. Most of these properties are controlled through the Property Pages dialog box, as shown in Figure 28.5. To display this dialog box, right-click the ADO Data control and choose ADODC Properties from the context menu.

FIGURE 28.5
To set up the ADO Data control at designtime, use its Property Pages.

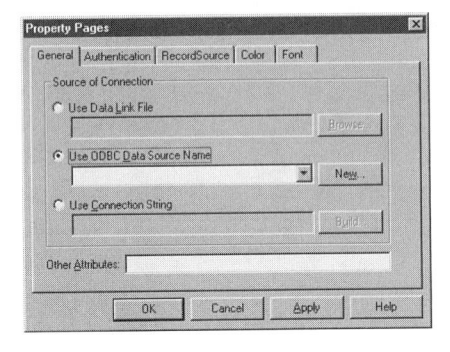

The Property Pages dialog box for the ADO Data control is divided into the following tabs:

- **General.** Specifies how the ADO Data control connects to the database.
- **Authentication.** Allows you to supply a username and password that the ADO Data control can use to connect to the database, if required.
- **RecordSource.** Defines what recordset the ADO Data control retrieves from the data source. Here, you can specify a table or stored procedure name, or an SQL query.
- **Color and Font.** Change the look of the ADO Data control.

Many of the options in these tabs can also be set from code. By setting the appropriate properties, you can link the ADO Data control to your database and use data-bound controls on your form to display the data.

Connecting the ADO Data Control to a Data Source

You already know that databases are made up of multiple tables and can contain a great deal of data. For example, the BIBLIO database includes one table that contains author information and another that contains a list of books written by those authors. When you think about working with data in a Visual Basic program, you generally do not plan to use every record in the database, but rather some smaller subset of the data that represents the information you want.

This subset of database information (or recordset) is defined by a *record source*, which is just a set of criteria that you specify. For example, suppose you want to query the database for the authors whose last name is *Smith*. In this example, the data source is the BIBLIO database, and the record source is the query that returns the set of records containing all the Smiths.

Anyway, the point of this discussion is to clarify what the ADO Data control represents to the rest of your program: a set of records resulting from a query against a database.

Making the Connection For the ADO Data control to access data, it has to first be able to connect to a database. You must set up the ConnectionString property of the ADO Data control to provide the necessary information. You can do so at runtime or designtime. The General tab of the Property Pages, shown earlier in Figure 28.5, provides three methods of building the connection string:

- **Use Data Link File.** This option allows you to load saved connection information from an MDL (Microsoft Data Link) file.
- **Use ODBC Data Source Name.** Here, you can select from one of the ODBC DSNs set up on your system. You can also click the New button to create a new DSN, just as you would from the Control Panel.
- **Use Connection String.** This option allows you to specify a connection string directly. Clicking the Build button brings up a wizard that helps you build the connection string.

Because you have already set up the BIBLIO data source, choose the Use ODBC Data Source Name option, and select BIBLIO from the drop-down list.

Setting Up the Record Source   Now that you have told the Data control that it needs to connect to the BIBLIO data source, you need to tell it what specific data to bring back from that data source. At designtime, you do so by selecting the RecordSource tab of the Property Pages dialog box, as shown in Figure 28.6.

FIGURE 28.6
The RecordSource property tells the ADO Data control exactly what data to retrieve.

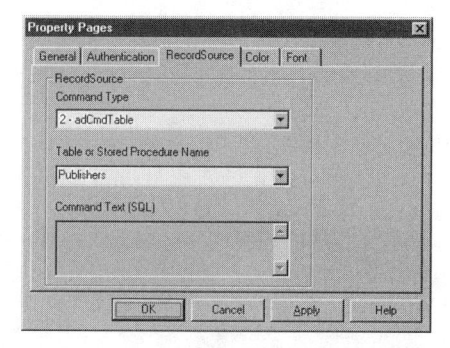

The ADO Data control acts like an ADO Command object, which you'll learn about in the upcoming section "The Command Object." You can use four types of commands to retrieve data:

- adCmdText—Runs an SQL query on the data source
- adCmdStoredProc—Calls a stored procedure on a database server
- adCmdTable—Specifies the name of a database table; used to return the entire table
- adCmdUnknown—Unknown command type

Depending on which command type you select, the appropriate text box becomes enabled, and you can enter the command. For the sample program that uses the BIBLIO database, select the entire Publishers table.

To select this table, first set the CommandType property to adCmdTable by selecting it from the drop-down list. The second drop-down box, Table or Stored Procedure Name, should then become enabled. Select the Publishers table from the list so that your settings look like those in Figure 28.6. Finally, click OK to close the dialog box and commit the changes.

Displaying Data

You have given the ADO Data control everything it needs to bring data into your program. However, most likely you'll want to display that data somehow so that the user can view, browse, and even edit it. You learned how to use a bound control in Chapter 25, "The Data Control and Data-Bound Controls." For the sample project, draw five text boxes on the form, as shown in Figure 28.7. These text boxes will display the publisher's name, address, city, state, and ZIP code.

FIGURE 28.7
You can bind text boxes to specific recordset fields.

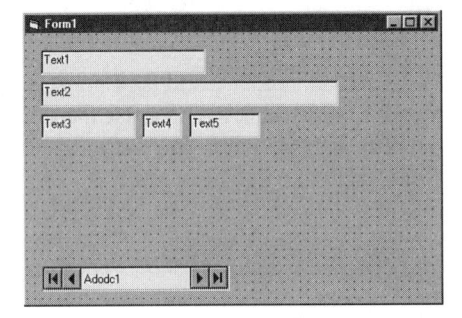

Next, you need to bind each control to a data field. To do so, set the `DataSource` property of each text box to the name of the ADO Data control, `ADODC1`, and the `DataField` property to the appropriate field name. After you finish setting the `DataSource` and `DataField` properties for each text box, run the sample project. You should be able to browse through the database and view or edit information, as shown in Figure 28.8.

FIGURE 28.8
Although the completed sample project is somewhat crude looking, it is fully functional and requires no code.

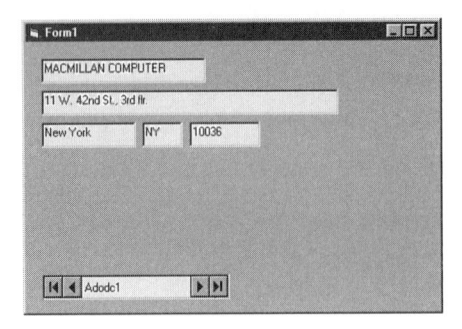

As you navigate through the recordset using the buttons on the ADO Data control, each bound text box is automatically updated to display the contents of the current record. If you want to use bound controls to display more than one record at a time, you need to use a specialized control such as the DataGrid control, discussed later in the "Using the DataGrid Control" section.

Changing the Record Source from Code

As you have just seen, you can easily set up the Data control while in design mode. However, even in the simplest project, you usually need to use the Data control in a more dynamic fashion. Fortunately, you can set it up from code by following a few simple steps:

1. Set the `ConnectionString` property.
2. Set the `CommandType` and `RecordSource` properties.
3. Execute the `Refresh` method of the ADO Data control to retrieve the data.

As it is now, the ADO Data control in the sample application retrieves every record in the Publishers table. However, you can easily add code that changes the RecordSource property so that a new recordset is displayed.

Suppose, for example, you want to display only information on publishers whose address is in a certain state. You can write a simple SQL query to display these addresses, as in the following example:

```
Select * from Publishers where State='NY'
```

Rather than set up the query at designtime, though, add some code to the sample project so that it can occur during program execution. First, add a command button to the form. Change the caption to State Lookup and the name of the command button to cmdState. Place the following lines of code in the Click event of cmdState:

```
Dim sState As String
Dim sSQL As String

'BUILD SQL QUERY
sSQL = "Select * from Publishers"
sState = InputBox$("Enter State abbreviation:")
If sState <> "" Then sSQL = sSQL & " WHERE State ='" & sState & "'"

'UPDATE THE ADO DATA CONTROL
Adodc1.CommandType = adCmdText
Adodc1.RecordSource = sSQL
Adodc1.Refresh
```

Run the sample project again, and click the button. Enter NY and available records should change to include only those publishers in New York. You can verify this information by clicking the navigation buttons on the ADO Data control.

Using the DataGrid Control

Much of the information that computer programs deal with is presented in the form of a grid of columns and rows, like you would find on a spreadsheet. In fact, for many people, and many types of data, this "grid" is the preferred method of viewing information. The DataGrid control, a new control in Visual Basic 6.0, allows you to display data from a database in grid format. Depending on how the DataGrid is set up, the user can even edit the cells of the grid directly and change the underlying data.

You may be familiar with the DBGrid control from previous versions of Visual Basic. Unlike that control, the DataGrid control is designed for use with the newer ActiveX Data Objects (ADO). Instead of the older Data control, the DataGrid is bound to the new ADO Data control, discussed earlier in this chapter.

A sample use of the data grid is shown in Figure 28.9. This grid is set up to display a view of the `Titles` table of the `BIBLIO` sample database included with Visual Basic.

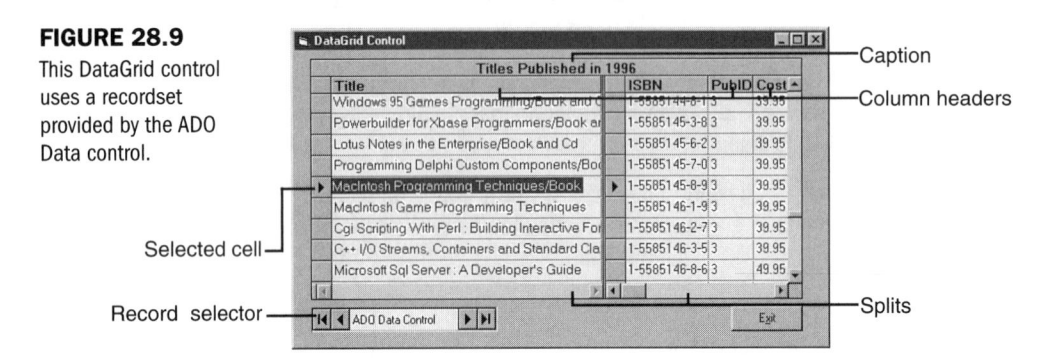

FIGURE 28.9
This DataGrid control uses a recordset provided by the ADO Data control.

The data grid is a fairly easy control to use, despite the fact that you not only have to understand how it works, but you also have to attach it to a database. Before you can use the DataGrid, however, you must add it to Visual Basic Toolbox. To do so, right-click in an empty area of the Toolbox, select Components from the context menu, and add the control called Microsoft DataGrid Control 6.0. Click OK to close the Components dialog box.

Getting Data into the Grid

To use the DataGrid, you have set up the grid to look the way you want and bind it to a data source. Binding the DataGrid is similar to working with other bound controls, as you can see in these steps:

1. Draw an ADO Data control on the form with the DataGrid, and set it up as described earlier in the section "Using the ADO Data Control."

2. Display the Properties window for the DataGrid, and set the `DataSource` property to the name of the ADO Data control. (Notice that no `DataField` property exists, because unlike other controls, the DataGrid displays multiple fields.)

3. The DataGrid can configure its columns automatically based on the data source. Simply right-click the control, and choose Retrieve Fields from the context menu. The layout of the grid changes to include fields from the ADO Data control.

4. Customize the layout of the grid, and perform any desired manual configuration.

▶ **See** "Getting Acquainted with Bound Controls," **p. 550**

Setting Up the DataGrid

The DataGrid is a fairly complicated control and has many properties that control its behavior. As with many other controls, Property Pages provide an organized way to access these properties. To access a control's Property Pages, right-click the control, and choose Properties from the context menu. The Property Pages dialog box for the DataGrid is shown in Figure 28.10.

FIGURE 28.10
Most aspects of the DataGrid control are set up via the Property Pages.

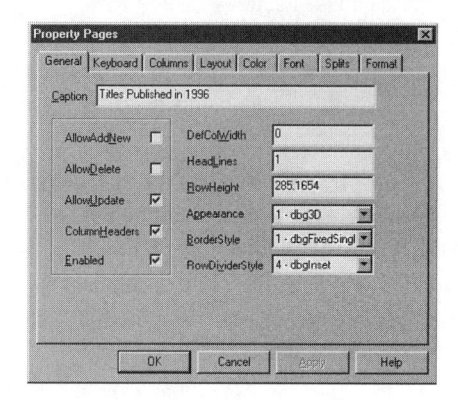

In the following sections, you explore how you use each of the Property Pages to control the grid and examine the issues involved with interacting with a data source.

General Options The General Property Pages tab, shown in Figure 28.10, contains some options that control overall grid behavior. Other tabs, such as Columns and Layout, allow you to adjust properties of individual grid elements.

> **NOTE** Look ahead to the section "Customizing the Grid's Layout" for information on the Columns and Layout tabs. "Customizing the Grid with Code" and "Splitting Up the Grid" cover other approaches to customizing the DataGrid control.

Some of the properties that affect the grid's appearance are listed here:

- The Caption property controls the title that appears at the top of the grid. Set it to an empty string if you do not want the title heading to appear at all.
- The ColumnHeaders property turns on or off the header row at the top of the grid. By default, the heading of a given column is the name of the database field displayed in that column, but as you will see, you can change the headings to suit your needs. The height of the column header row is controlled by the HeadLines property. Simply set HeadLines to an integer representing the desired height in number of rows.
- You can control the overall look of the DataGrid with the Appearance property. It has two settings, dbgFlat and dbg3d (the default), which cause the grid to be drawn with a flat or three-dimensional look, respectively.

- Use the `RowDividerStyle` to determine what type of line is drawn between each row of data. You can choose from several options, including turning off the row dividers completely. Note that the `RowDividerStyle` property does not affect the dividers of the record selectors.

- The `Enabled` property controls whether user interaction with the grid is allowed. If this property is set to `False`, the user cannot scroll, select cells, or modify data. However, the grid and some data still are visible on the screen.

In addition to the properties that control how the DataGrid control looks, the following three Boolean properties in the General tab control which data operations are allowed:

- `AllowAddNew`—Controls whether the user can add a new record to the recordset displayed in the data grid (`False` by default). If this property is set to `True`, a blank row is added to the end of the data so that the user can enter a new record. The record selector for the `AddNew` row is marked with an asterisk (*).

- `AllowDelete`—Controls whether the user can delete a record from the underlying recordset. To delete a row, use the record selector to highlight it, and then press the Delete key. This property is `False` by default.

- `AllowUpdate`—Controls whether the user can edit an existing record (`True` by default). Setting this property to `False` makes each cell in the grid act like a locked text box: You can select text using the mouse and copy it to the Clipboard, but you cannot change it.

Each of these three properties can be set at runtime or designtime. Setting all of them to `False` means that your grid will be read-only.

Keyboard Options Although you can select cells using the mouse, you might prefer using the keyboard because it allows you to perform operations much faster. The DataGrid has several properties that control keyboard behavior. You can set these properties in the Keyboard tab of the Property Pages or at runtime with code.

For example, the `AllowArrows` property determines whether the arrow keys can be used to navigate between cells on the DataGrid. If you set this property to `False`, the user has to use the Tab key or the mouse to put the cursor in a specific cell.

NOTE When you are editing a cell, the arrow key moves within the current cell. To put the grid in move mode, single-click a cell so that it is highlighted. You should then be able to use the arrow keys to move from cell to cell.

Handling the Tab key on any type of grid control presents a minor dilemma for programmers because the standard behavior is for the Tab key to cause the focus to move to the next control on the form. Fortunately, the DataGrid's `TabAction` property allows you to set up the Tab key for your specific needs. This property has three settings:

- `0 - dbgControlNavigation`—Pressing the Tab key while in the DataGrid moves the focus off the DataGrid to the next control in the form's tab order. In this case, the DataGrid acts like a standard control as far as Visual Basic is concerned.

- 1 - dbgColumnNavigation—Pressing the Tab key moves to the next cell in the current row of the DataGrid. Pressing Shift+Tab moves to the previous cell. When you reach the last cell in the row, Tab moves out of the grid to the next control on the form. To move to a different row, you must use the arrow keys or mouse.
- 2 - dbgGridNavigation—This setting by itself is not very different from dboColumnNavigation, but it allows you to set two other properties to further control the behavior of the Tab key: TabAcrossSplits and WrapCellPointer. Setting WrapCellPointer to True allows you to use the Tab key to move between rows on the grid. If TabAcrossSplits is set to True, then you can use the Tab or arrow keys to move between splits (sections) on the grid.

Splitting Up the Grid

Although a DataGrid generally has only one underlying set of data, you can split the grid into several sections. These sections, which are known as *splits*, behave much like sub-grids within a single DataGrid control. Refer to Figure 28.9 for an example of splits. The Title field is in a separate split from the other fields, allowing it to remain locked while you scroll horizontally through the other splits.

> **NOTE** Even if a DataGrid contains multiple splits, you still have only one current record. Splits are not as complicated as they sound; just think of them as areas of the grid that can be formatted individually.

Editing the Grid at Designtime To add or remove splits at designtime, you must go into the grid's design-environment editing mode. To do so, right-click the DataGrid control as you would to bring up the Property Pages. However, instead of selecting Properties, choose Edit from the context menu. Nothing appears to happen, but if you right-click again in the DataGrid, you will notice that the items on the context menu change from Visual Basic's to those provided by the DataGrid. While you're in this design-environment editing mode, you can perform the following operations from the context menu:

- Insert and delete columns
- Resize columns
- Retrieve the field layout from the data source
- Clear the existing field layout
- Add and remove splits

Creating a New Split By default, the DataGrid has only a single split, Split0, as pictured in Figure 28.11. To add a split, right-click the DataGrid while in the previously described editing mode, and choose Split from the context menu. An additional section is then added to the grid (also shown in Figure 28.11).

After creating a new split, you can continue to use the context menu to delete and add columns to the splits on the DataGrid.

FIGURE 28.11
Here, you can see the DataGrid control before and after adding a new split.

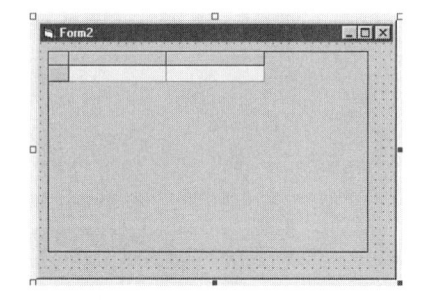

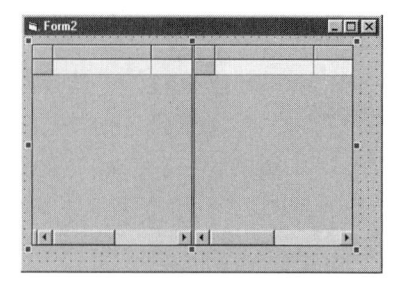

Working with Split Properties Every time you add a split to a DataGrid, it is also added to the Split drop-down list on the Property Pages, as shown in Figure 28.12.

FIGURE 28.12
Using the Splits tab of the Property Pages, you can set properties for a specific section of the DataGrid.

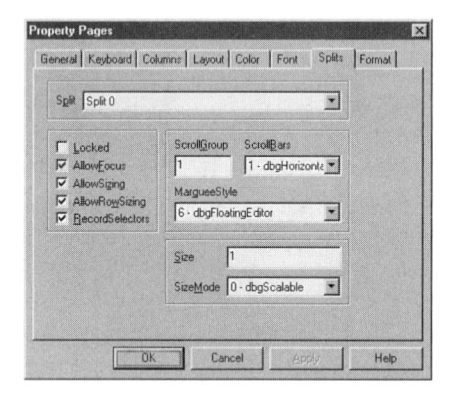

As you create new splits, they are named consecutively: Split0, Split1, Split2, and so on. To specify settings for a split, select it from the Split drop-down list, and set the appropriate properties. Several of these properties are described here:

- Locked—When this property is selected, the user cannot enter text.
- AllowFocus—When this property is set to False, the selected split cannot receive the program focus.
- AllowSizing—This property allows the user to resize the width of a split during program execution.
- AllowRowSizing—This property can prevent the user from resizing rows at runtime.
- RecordSelectors—This property turns record selectors on or off for the specified split. If you also set the RecordSelectors property of the DataGrid, the most recent setting takes effect.

Customizing the Grid's Layout

Although having the grid configure itself automatically is a nice feature, most times you will want to change the default configuration. For example, you might want to set up two splits with different columns. To do so, you need to set up the splits and then use the Column and Layout tabs of the Property Pages to customize the grid. The Columns tab controls the order of the data columns in the grid (see Figure 28.13).

FIGURE 28.13
You can reorder the columns manually if desired.

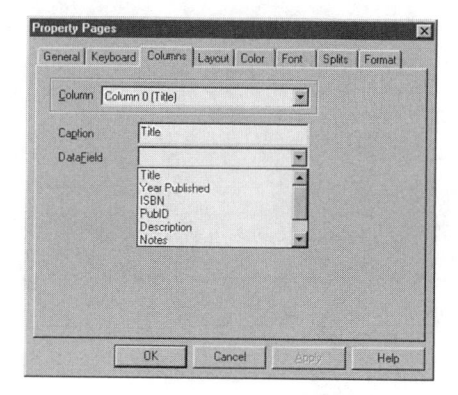

Working with the Columns tab is simple; just pick a column, and choose the Caption (column header) and the name of the data field.

NOTE If you do not enter a valid expression for the DataField, the column appears blank.

Whereas the Columns tab controls the data displayed, the Layout tab controls formatting of an individual column. To use the Layout tab, pictured in Figure 24.14, first select a column and split you want to work with. Then adjust the following properties:

- Locked—When this property is set to True, it prevents editing a column, even if the grid's General properties allow it.
- AllowSizing—This property, which is True by default, allows the user to resize a column at designtime.
- Visible—This property controls whether a column is seen on the grid. (However, if you don't need to display a column, the most efficient way to accomplish that is to eliminate it from your data source.)
- WrapText—This property determines whether the text in a column is displayed in multiple lines if it is longer than the column width. An example of the WrapText property in action is shown in Figure 28.15.
- Button—This property determines whether a drop-down button is displayed in the selected column for a highlighted field.
- DividerStyle—This property is similar to the RowDividerStyle property of the General tab, but it can be set for each column.

- **Alignment**—This property controls how values in a given column are aligned.
- **Width**—This property sets the width of the specified column. (An easier way to set column widths is to use the editing mode described earlier and resize them using the mouse.)

FIGURE 28.14
Here is the Layout tab of the DataGrid's Property Pages.

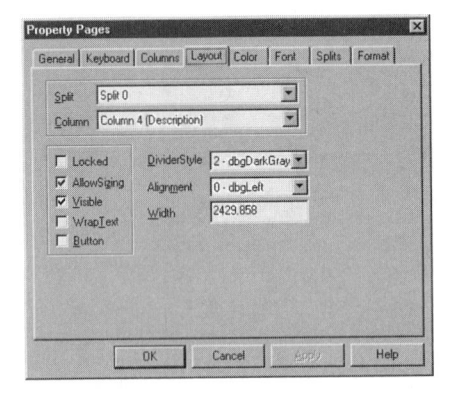

FIGURE 28.15
The leftmost split has the `WrapText` property set to True.

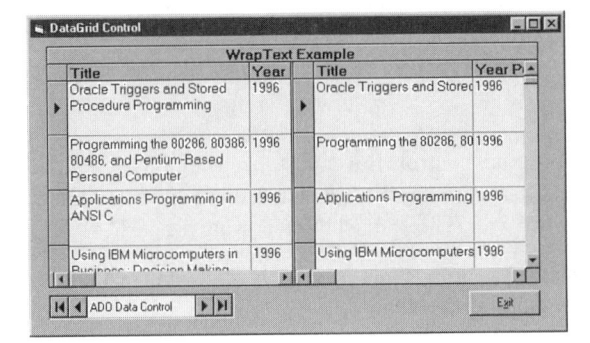

Customizing the Grid with Code

In learning about the DataGrid, you have concentrated on setting properties in the design environment. However, almost everything you have learned about the properties of the DataGrid can also be applied to the runtime environment. For example, if you want to set the `WrapText` property of the first column in the first split, use the following line of code:

```
datagrid1.Splits(0).Columns(0).WrapText = True
```

Although you may have to navigate through a few levels of collections to get to the property you want, you will find that most properties can be changed with code.

Using ActiveX Data Objects

Working with the ADO Data control is useful to a point, but the real power comes into play when you use ADO objects in your Visual Basic code. The objects that make up the ADO object model are listed in Table 28.1.

Table 28.1 ActiveX Data Objects

Object	Description
Recordset	Contains the records that make up the results of a query
Connection	Allows control over the connection to the data source
Command	Executes database commands and queries with parameterized queries
Error	Retrieves errors from ADO
Field	Represents a piece of data in a recordset
Parameter	Works with the Command object to set up a parameter in a query or stored procedure
Property	Allows you access to ADO object properties

To use these ADO objects, you must add a reference to your project. To do so, choose Project, References. Place a check mark next to Microsoft ActiveX Data Objects 2.0 library and click the OK button. After referencing the object library, you can use the following prefixes to declare ADO objects:

- ADODB—This object library contains all the objects listed in Table 28.1.
- ADOR—This object library contains only the objects associated with a recordset (RecordSet, Field, Property). ADOR is included with IE 4.01, allowing developers to pass disconnected recordsets across the Internet.

In the following sections, you'll explore some of the properties, methods, and events of the ADO objects. A complete list of these elements is available in the Visual Basic Object Browser, which you can display by pressing F2.

Making the Connection with ADO

The Connection object is used to establish a connection to a data source. Its most important property is the ConnectionString property, which contains the information used to connect to a database. You control the state of the database connection with the Open and Close methods.

Opening and Closing a Connection   The first step in opening a connection is to create a new instance of the ADODB.Connection object, as follows:

```
Dim cn As ADODB.Connection
Set cn = New ADODB.Connection
```

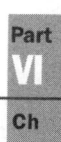

After the object instance is created, all you have to do to establish a connection is provide the connection string and call the `Open` method. You can set the connection string in two ways, the first being to assign it to the `ConnectionString` property:

```
cn.ConnectionString = "DSN=BIBLIO"
cn.Open
```

You can also pass the connection string as part of the call to the `Open` method:

```
cn.Open "DSN=BIBLIO"
```

> **NOTE** The connection string shown here is simple. For other data sources, your connection string may be longer and include additional information.

After you finish using a connection, call the `Close` method. As with most object variables, it is also a good idea to set them to `Nothing` to free up any used resources:

```
cn.Close
Set cn = Nothing
```

Using the *Execute* Method In ADO, you can accomplish the same goal in many different ways. Retrieving information is a perfect example. You can take your pick from the `Recordset`, `Command`, or `Connection` objects; they all have a method used to pull data into a recordset. The `Connection` object's `Execute` method allows you to run an SQL statement against a data source. If the SQL statement returns records, you can access them simply by assigning the return value of the `Execute` method to an ADO `Recordset` object.

Test the `Execute` method with a simple example. Start a new Standard EXE project, and add a reference to ADO. Then add a list box control to the form, and name it `lstAuthors`. Finally, place the following lines of code in the form's `Load` event:

```
Dim cn As ADODB.Connection
Dim rs As ADODB.Recordset

Set cn = New ADODB.Connection
cn.Open "DSN=BIBLIO"

Set rs = cn.Execute("Select * from Authors Where [Year Born] > 1943")

While Not rs.EOF
    lstAuthors.AddItem "Year Born: " & rs.Fields("Year Born") & vbTab _
                & "Name: " & rs.Fields("Author")
    rs.MoveNext
Wend

rs.Close
cn.Close
Set rs = Nothing
Set cn = Nothing
```

Run the program, and you should see results similar to those pictured in Figure 24.16.

FIGURE 28.16
The results of a simple query were created with the `Execute` method of the `ADODB.Connection` object.

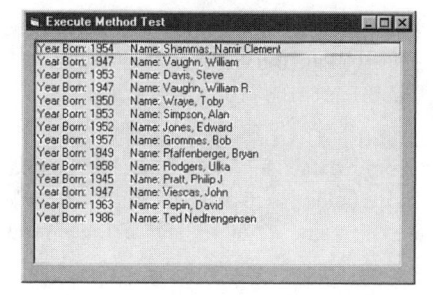

```
Execute Method Test
Year Born: 1954    Name: Shammas, Namir Clement
Year Born: 1947    Name: Vaughn, William
Year Born: 1953    Name: Davis, Steve
Year Born: 1947    Name: Vaughn, William R.
Year Born: 1950    Name: Wraye, Toby
Year Born: 1953    Name: Simpson, Alan
Year Born: 1952    Name: Jones, Edward
Year Born: 1957    Name: Grommes, Bob
Year Born: 1949    Name: Pfaffenberger, Bryan
Year Born: 1958    Name: Rodgers, Ulka
Year Born: 1945    Name: Pratt, Philip J
Year Born: 1947    Name: Viescas, John
Year Born: 1963    Name: Pepin, David
Year Born: 1986    Name: Ted Nedfrengensen
```

The `Execute` method of the `Connection` object returns a `Recordset` object, which is stored in the variable `rs`. Next, a `While` loop is used to move through the recordset, adding each author's name and birth year to the list box.

You can also use the `Execute` method to run SQL statements that do not return a recordset against the database, as in the following examples:

```
cn.Execute "Delete from Authors where Author = 'Jones, Amanda'"

cn.Execute _
"INSERT INTO AUTHORS ([Author],[Year Born]) Select 'Siler, Brian',1972"
```

The first statement deletes a record from the `Authors` table, and the second statement inserts a new record. (Remember, these examples were written for Access; in another database, the SQL syntax might be slightly different.)

Connecting Without a DSN   So far in this chapter, you have used a simple connection string that specifies the BIBLIO data source name, which was set up previously in the ODBC Data Source Manager. If you do not want to depend on a DSN's being set up, you can establish a DSN-less connection by giving ADO more information in the `ConnectionString` property, as in the following examples for a Microsoft Access database:

```
cn.ConnectionString = _
"Provider=Microsoft.Jet.OLEDB.3.51;Data Source=d:\vb6\biblio.mdb"

cn.ConnectionString = _
"Driver=Microsoft Access Driver (*.mdb);DBQ=D:\VB6\biblio.mdb"
```

> **NOTE** Even if you use a DSN-less connection, the appropriate drivers and support files still must be installed on the user's PC.

The preceding connection string names the driver rather than the DSN. For the Access driver, the DBQ parameter points to the database name. You can also specify other OLE DB providers, such as the following string used to connect to a Microsoft SQL Server:

```
"Provider=SQLOLEDB.1;Password=groovy:User ID=apowers:Location=SQLSRV1; _
database=employee"
```

As you can see from the preceding example, a connection string can contain many different types of information, including user ID, password, and default database name.

Working with Recordsets

Recordsets represent actual data from a database. A recordset has fields (such as Name and Phone Number) and values for those fields (such as John Smith and 555-1212). Each set of field values that go together makes up a single record, and all these records together make up a recordset.

An easy way to visualize a recordset is as a spreadsheet or grid: Fields are like column names, and the rows are the records. Recordsets are usually created as the result of a query on the database. You use recordsets in your program to retrieve and update data.

In ADO, a recordset is stored in a Recordset object. After a Recordset object is populated with data, you can perform the following operations on the data:

- Add new records
- Edit existing records
- Delete records
- Navigate the recordset (change the current record)

Creating a Recordset   You have already learned how to create and populate a Recordset by using the Execute method of the Connection object. However, a Recordset object has its own methods and properties that can be used to retrieve data. As with all objects, to use these properties, you need to create a new instance of the Recordset object first:

```
Dim rs As ADODB.Recordset
Set rs = New ADODB.Recordset
```

Next, you can use properties of the object to specify the connection, record source, and recordset type.

To specify a data source for a Recordset object, set the ActiveConnection property equal to an ADO Connection object:

```
rs.ActiveConnection = cn
```

The line of code assumes that cn represents an open connection that points to a data source, as discussed earlier. Another way to select a connection is to set the ActiveConnection property to the connection string:

```
rs.ActiveConnection = "DSN=BIBLIO"
```

If you use a string value instead of a Connection object, the Recordset object opens its own connection to the database.

A Recordset's Open method causes the recordset to be populated with data. To use the Open method, you must first set the Source property, which corresponds roughly to the RecordSource property of the ADO Data control. The code in Listing 28.1 creates a new Recordset object and then prints the data it contains.

Listing 28.1 ADOTEST.ZIP—Creating an ADO Recordset

```
Const sSQL = "SELECT * FROM Authors Where [Author] Like 'Q%'"
Dim cn As ADODB.Connection
Dim rs As ADODB.Recordset

'OPEN A CONNECTION
Set cn = New ADODB.Connection
cn.Open "DSN=BIBLIO"

'OPEN A RECORDSET
Set rs = New ADODB.Recordset
rs.ActiveConnection = cn
rs.Source = sSQL
rs.Open

'PRINT THE AUTHORS' NAMES
rs.MoveFirst
While Not rs.EOF
    Debug.Print "author = " & rs.Fields("Author")
    rs.MoveNext
Wend

'CLOSE EVERYTHING
rs.Close
Set rs = Nothing
cn.Close
Set cn = Nothing
```

The code in Listing 28.1 runs a SQL query that selects all the authors who have last names beginning with the letter Q.

NOTE The Like syntax of the SQL query in Listing 28.1 is specific to a Microsoft Access database. In a SQL Server environment, you might write the same statement as follows:

```
Select * from Authors where Author like "Q*"
```

Displaying Field Values To access data in the Recordset object, use the Fields collection. Table 28.2 lists the options you can use to refer to an individual field.

Table 28.2 Working with Field Values

Syntax	Example
Recordset.fields(field name)	rsPeople.Fields("LastName")
Recordset.fields(index)	rsPeople.Fields(2)
Recordset!field name	rsPeople!LastName

In the sample code, the `Recordset.Fields(field name)` syntax is used. However, for some purposes (such as when you do not know the field name), using the field index is more appropriate. Field indexes start at zero and end at one less than the number of fields in the recordset. The number of fields in a recordset is available through the `Count` property of the `Fields` collection. The following code sample prints each field name and then scrolls through the recordset printing each field value:

```
'PRINT THE FIELD NAMES
For i = 0 To rs.Fields.Count - 1
    Debug.Print rs.Fields(i).Name,
Next i
Debug.Print

'PRINT CONTENTS OF ALL FIELDS IN EACH RECORD
rs.MoveFirst
While Not rs.EOF
    For i = 0 To rs.Fields.Count - 1
        Debug.Print rs.Fields(i),
    Next i
    Debug.Print
    rs.MoveNext
Wend
```

This sample code uses two properties of the `Field` object: the `Name` and the `Value` properties. Notice that you do not have to explicitly specify the `Value` property because it is the default property.

Recordset Navigation   After data has been retrieved into a `Recordset` object, you can access and update the values of fields in the current record. Think of the recordset as a long sequential file. At any given time, the current record is a pointer to a location within that file. To work with different records, you can use the following navigation methods to change the current record:

- `MoveFirst`—Moves to the first record, just after the beginning-of-file marker (`BOF`)
- `MoveLast`—Moves to the last record, just before the end-of-file marker (`EOF`)
- `MoveNext`—Moves to the next record after the current record (toward `EOF`)
- `MovePrevious`—Moves back to the record before the current record (toward `BOF`)
- `Move`—Moves forward or backward a specified number of records

`BOF` and `EOF` are properties that indicate the beginning and ending points of a recordset, respectively.

Navigation and the CursorType Property   In the examples up to this point, you have seen only two methods used to navigate within a recordset: the `MoveFirst` and `MoveNext` methods. In Listing 28.1, you used a `While` loop to move forward through the records in an open recordset.

As a matter of fact, attempting to use `MovePrevious` or `MoveLast` with Listing 28.1 would cause an error, because it is invalid for the selected *cursor type*. A cursor in a recordset is like a cursor on a computer screen; it is a pointer to a current position.

Because you did not specify a value for the Recordset object's CursorType property, it was set to the default value of adOpenForwardOnly. The ramifications of the CursorType property are discussed shortly; but for now just remember that a "forward only" cursor does not support MovePrevious and MoveLast navigation methods.

Using Navigation Methods As an example of recordset navigation, you will create a project that uses the navigation methods. To get started, create a new Standard EXE project with a list box named lstData, three command buttons (cmdPrevious, cmdNext, and cmdJump), and a text box named txtJump.

The sample program runs a query against the BIBLIO database and then allows the user to execute the navigation methods to browse the recordset, much like you did with the Data control. The code for the sample project is shown in Listing 28.2.

Listing 28.2 ADONAV.ZIP—Using Recordset Navigation Methods

```
Option Explicit
Dim rs As ADODB.Recordset
Private Sub Form_Load()

    'FILL THE RECORDSET OBJECT RS
    Set rs = New ADODB.Recordset
    rs.CursorType = adOpenStatic
    rs.Source = "Select * from Publishers"
    rs.Open , "DSN=BIBLIO"
    DisplayCurrentRecord

End Sub
Sub DisplayCurrentRecord()
    Dim i As Integer
    Dim s As String

    If rs.BOF Then rs.MoveFirst
    If rs.EOF Then rs.MoveLast

    lstData.Clear
    For i = 0 To rs.Fields.Count - 1
        s = rs.Fields(i).Name & ": " & rs.Fields(i)
        lstData.AddItem s
    Next i
End Sub
Private Sub cmdJump_Click()
    rs.Move Val(txtJump)
    DisplayCurrentRecord
End Sub

Private Sub cmdNext_Click()
    rs.MoveNext
    DisplayCurrentRecord
End Sub

Private Sub cmdPrevious_Click()
    rs.MovePrevious
    DisplayCurrentRecord
End Sub
```

The use of the navigation methods in the sample project is straightforward. The only part that merits further explanation is the `DisplayCurrentRecord` function. Notice that it checks for `BOF` or `EOF` conditions before displaying the field names and values for the current record. This step is necessary because attempting to access the `Field` object without a current record would cause an error. The working project is pictured in Figure 28.17.

FIGURE 28.17
A sample program allows the user to browse a recordset.

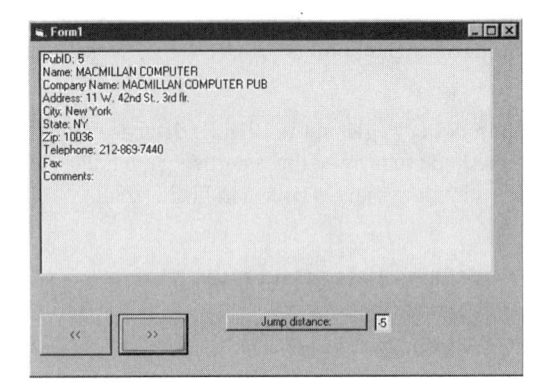

Updating Data Now that you know how to get information into a `Recordset` object and display it, you can take the next step and change (or update) the information in the database. If your recordset has been set up appropriately, you can change database information easily. Simply navigate to the appropriate record, assign a new value to each field you want to change, and finally call the `Update` method, as follows:

```
rs.Fields("Author")="Simpson, Bart"
rs.Update
```

> **NOTE** In DAO, you call the `Edit` method before changing the value of a field. In ADO, changing the field's value automatically turns on edit mode; there is no `Edit` method. You can query the `EditMode` property to determine whether the current record is being edited. ■

Setting the LockType Property By default, ADO recordsets are read only. Attempting to change a field value in a read-only recordset causes an error. To add, change, or delete records in an ADO recordset, you must set the `LockType` property to a different value than the read-only default. For example, setting the `CursorType` and `LockType` properties as follows creates an updateable Access recordset:

```
rs.CursorType = adOpenKeyset
rs.LockType = adLockOptimistic
```

You might wonder why the `LockType` property is important. The answer is that if you are editing records in a multiuser database, you have to be concerned with *record locking*. Record locking means preventing other users from trying to edit the same database record at the same time. Record locking is controlled with the `LockType` property, which has the following values:

- `adLockReadOnly`—Sets data in the recordset as read only
- `adLockPessimistic`—Provides pessimistic record locking, which means the record is locked while you are editing it
- `adLockOptimisitc`—Provides optimistic record locking, which means records are locked only when you call the `Update` method
- `adLockBatchOptimisitc`—Updates multiple records at a time with the `UpdateBatch` method

Why are the parameters named after attitudes (optimistic and pessimistic)? Because attempting to update a locked record causes an error in your program. You can be optimistic that a record will be available when you need to update it, or pessimistic and lock it for as long as you need it.

Viewing Others' Changes Another concern with multiuser databases is making sure the data in your recordset is as accurate as it needs to be. If you recall an earlier section, you know that the `CursorType` property can restrict recordset navigation. However, the main point of the different cursor types, listed in Table 28.3, is to control how your recordset is linked to the underlying data.

Table 28.3   The *CursorType* Property

Constant	Description
`adOpenForwardOnly`	This property is fast but allows only forward movement.
`adOpenKeySet`	Your program can see some of the data changes made by other users.
`adOpenDynamic`	Your program can see all the data changes made by other users.
`adOpenStatic`	This property provides a static picture of the database; you cannot see others' changes.

As you will find out from using ADO, not all cursor types are supported by all databases. For Access databases, the default `adOpenForwardOnly` cursor is intended for a quick read-only pass through the database, whereas the `adOpenKeySet` cursor is better suited for updates and more complex operations.

Adding New Data Adding new records to a `Recordset` object is similar to changing the content of existing records, but with one extra step:

1. Call the `AddNew` method.
2. Assign values to the fields.
3. Call the `Update` method.

The code in Listing 28.3 adds a new record to the Authors table in the BIBLIO database.

Listing 28.3 ADOTEST.ZIP—Adding a Record to an ADO Recordset

```
Dim cn As New ADODB.Connection
Dim rs As ADODB.Recordset

cn.Open "DSN=BIBLIO"

'OPEN A RECORDSET
Set rs = New ADODB.Recordset
rs.CursorType = adOpenKeyset
rs.LockType = adLockOptimistic
rs.Source = "Authors"
rs.ActiveConnection = cn
rs.Open

'ADD A NEW RECORD
rs.AddNew
rs.Fields("Author") = "King, Stevie"
rs.Fields("Year Born") = 1945
rs.Update
'NOTE: THE Au_ID field is an autonumber field,
'      it will be created automatically.

'DESTROY THE OBJECTS
rs.Close
cn.Close
Set rs = Nothing
Set cn = Nothing
```

The Command Object

When you are working with a set of data, most of the time you are working with properties and methods of the Recordset object. However, to retrieve that data, you will find that the ADO Command object is indispensable. It allows you to encapsulate a query or SQL stored procedure into a reusable object, which is especially ideal if you need to perform the operation multiple times. You can even store the parameters from your query or stored procedure in the object's Parameters collection, which means you don't have to worry about building an appropriate SQL string with code. After you set up a command object, you can change the parameters of the object and call it repeatedly.

For example, recall the SQL statement from Listing 28.1, which was used to select authors whose last names begin with the letter *Q*. Using Microsoft Access, you can create a generic query called LetterLookup by using the following SQL syntax:

```
PARAMETERS Letter Text;
SELECT *
FROM Authors
WHERE Author Like Letter+'*';
```

Running this query in Access prompts you for the Letter parameter and then displays the matching records. To run this Access query from VB code, you can use a Command object, as follows:

```
Dim cmd As New ADODB.Command
Dim parmTemp As ADODB.Parameter

Set cmd.ActiveConnection = cn
cmd.CommandText = "LetterLookup"
cmd.CommandType = adCmdStoredProc
Set parmTemp = cmd.CreateParameter("Letter", adChar, adParamInput, 1)
cmd.Parameters.Append parmTemp
cmd("Letter") = "Q"
Set rs = cmd.Execute
```

To use the Command object, you have to decide on the type of command it is (these types are listed earlier in the chapter) and specify the actual command. If any parameters are required, you can add them to the Parameters collection of the object. After you set up the Command object, simply call the Execute method to perform the command.

Disconnected Recordsets

If you have worked with DAO in the past, then you will find that ADO has new features that allow you to manipulate recordsets in ways that were never before possible. One new feature is the ability to create *disconnected recordsets*. This term means that you can have a recordset in memory that is independent of a database connection. While disconnected, the recordset acts as a standalone object, with all the usual methods and properties. What is even more amazing is that you can later reconnect the recordset and commit any changes made while the recordset was disconnected. As you will see shortly, disconnected recordsets are most useful on the Internet, because you do not always have a continuous connection to the database. In the following sections, you see how to handle these recordsets.

Creating a Disconnected Recordset

The key to creating a disconnected recordset is setting the CursorLocation property. It has two settings: adUseClient and adUseServer. To create a disconnected recordset (or *client-side cursor*), perform the following steps:

1. Set the CursorLocation property to adUseClient.
2. Populate the Recordset object.
3. Set the ActiveConnection property to Nothing.

Recall the example from Listing 28.2, which displayed publisher information in a list box. You can easily change it to use a disconnected recordset by changing the Form_Load event procedure, as follows:

```
Private Sub Form_Load()

    Set rs = New ADODB.Recordset
    rs.CursorLocation = adUseClient
    rs.CursorType = adOpenStatic
    rs.Source = "Select * from Publishers"
    rs.Open , "DSN=BIBLIO"
    Set rs.ActiveConnection = Nothing
    DisplayCurrentRecord

End Sub
```

The only changes from Listing 28.2 were to add two lines of code. You set the `CursorLocation` property so that records are stored on the client, and you disconnect the recordset by destroying its `ActiveConnection` object. However, I would bet that some skeptics in the audience need even more evidence that the recordset is indeed disconnected from the database. To prove this theory, run the sample project with the modification to create a disconnected recordset. When the first record is displayed on the screen, open Windows Explorer and temporarily rename the file BIBLIO.MDB to another name. Return to Visual Basic, and you will find that the program still functions normally. However, you cannot start the program a second time unless the database file exists.

Reconnecting a Recordset

Earlier, you learned how records are locked to prevent multiple users from "fighting" over the same record. Record locking takes on a different meaning when you use disconnected recordsets. If you are not connected to a database, then you are, in a sense, "checking out" the records, like you would check out books from a library. If you edit or change the data in the recordset, the changes are not reflected until you "check in" the records, or in database terms, perform a batch update to the database. Therefore, the type of record locking you have to use is known as *batch optimistic*.

Batch updates allow you to make multiple changes to a recordset and apply them to the underlying database at once with the `UpdateBatch` method. You can even make a change to a disconnected recordset, reestablish the connection, and update the database.

First, to use `UpdateBatch`, you must change the `Recordset` object's `LockType` property to use the `adLockBatchOptimisitc` record-locking method:

```
rs.LockType = adLockBatchOptimistic
```

After you retrieve a disconnected recordset, as in the preceding section of code, change one or more of the records by setting a new field value:

```
rs.Fields(0)= "Edited Field Value"
rs.MoveNext
rs.Fields(0)= "Another Edited Field Value"
```

Next, reestablish the connection by setting the recordset's `ActiveConnection` property to a new `Connection` object, as shown here:

```
Set cn = New ADODB.Connection
cn.ConnectionString = "DSN=BIBLIO"
cn.Open
Set rs.ActiveConnection = cn
```

Finally, execute the code that actually performs the database update:

```
rs.MarshalOptions = adMarshalModifiedOnly
rs.UpdateBatch
```

I hope you were watching closely because I just introduced a new property, `MarshallOptions`. This property determines whether the whole recordset is returned for updating or just the changed records, for the most efficient use of resources. The second line of code actually performs the update with the `UpdateBatch` method.

Uses of a Disconnected Recordset

Now that you know what a disconnected recordset is, you may be wondering why you would ever want to use one. In a traditional client/server environment, it might never be necessary. However, disconnected recordsets bring a whole new level of power to your Internet applications. Imagine being able to run a Visual Basic program inside a browser that communicates with your database server just as you would over a LAN. To build such a heavy-duty application, you need to break it up into the following components:

- **Internet client.** An ActiveX OCX or ActiveX Document that runs in Internet Explorer
- **Internet Server.** An ActiveX DLL component running on the Internet server

Creating an application that works in this manner involves understanding several fairly complex Microsoft products—coverage of which is beyond the scope of this chapter. However, if you understand a few key concepts (ADO and ActiveX components), you should be successful.

Microsoft offers a product called Remote Data Services (RDS), which acts as a link between Internet Information Server and Internet Explorer. The key to using RDS is its `DataSpace` object. You can create an instance of the RDS Data Space on the Internet client, as follows:

```
Set objRDS = CreateObject("RDS.DataSpace")
```

You can then use the RDS Data Space to create remote objects on a Web server:

```
Set objTest = objRDS.CreateObject("MyDLL.MyClass", _
   "http://server.somewhere.com")
```

Notice the difference in the two calls to `CreateObject`. The first line of code creates a local object. The second line of code creates a remote object, `objTest`. This process is somewhat similar (but not exactly like) using DCOM to create an instance of an object on a remote machine, but then using the features of that object on a local machine.

The sample object `objTest` is an instance of an ActiveX DLL that runs on the Web server. After you create this instance, you can make method calls and pass data to and from it. The ADOR object library mentioned earlier is a minimal implementation of an ADO Recordset (the *R* stands for remote) designed for this type of use. You can create functions in your ActiveX DLL to pass ADOR recordsets to the Internet client, which can then return the changed records to the server.

From Here...

This chapter provided an introduction to ActiveX Data Objects (ADO), which Microsoft is positioning to replace older data access methodologies such as DAO and RDO. ADO allows you to not only perform the standard database operations (such as adds and deletes), but also add a wide range of new database capabilities to your programs. In addition to a powerful object interface, there are several ADO-enabled controls including the DataGrid and the ADO Data control. For related information, see the following chapters:

- To apply what you have learned to the Internet, see Chapters 31, "Active Server Pages," and 33, "Visual Basic and Other Uses of the Internet."
- To learn how to build reports based on your data, see Chapter 29, "Creating Reports."
- For more information on data binding, see Chapter 25, "The Data Control and Data-Bound Controls."

CHAPTER 29

Creating Reports

In this chapter

Creating a Simple Report 642

Enhancing Your Data Reports 648

Using Crystal Reports 653

Despite the fact that online information systems always promise a "paperless" office, everyone likes to have printed reports. For some Visual Basic programmers, reporting has always been the most frustrating part of developing an application. If you create your own reporting functions using `Print` and other graphics methods, you tend to spend a lot of time and effort that could be better spent in other areas. At the other extreme is using a third-party reporting add-in, which is quicker to implement but raises a whole bunch of other issues, including additional cost and DLL distribution requirements.

In Visual Basic 6.0, Microsoft has added a new way to include reporting in your application: the Data Report. Data Reports enable you to easily display a print preview screen, with print and export buttons, from an ADO data source. All you have to do is provide the data and report layout. In addition to this new reporting tool, Visual Basic also supports Crystal Reports, a popular reporting tool that has been packaged with Visual Basic for quite some time now. Crystal Reports, a product of Seagate software, provides an easy way to graphically design and distribute reports.

In this chapter, you examine both of these reporting tools and learn how to use them in your applications.

Creating a Simple Report

The Data Report is known as an ActiveX Designer, meaning that it is a specialized ActiveX object that integrates into the VB environment. You saw another example of an ActiveX Designer, the IIS application, in Chapter 28, "Using ActiveX Data Objects (ADO)."

In this section, you'll create a sample Data Report based on a query of the BIBLIO database. To create this report, perform the following steps:

1. Set up the ADO recordset to be used by the report.
2. Add a `DataReport` object to the Visual Basic project.
3. Design the report by placing fields on the `DataReport` designer form.
4. Write code to display the report in the program.

Setting Up the Data Source

To begin the sample project, open Visual Basic and start a new Standard EXE project. The next step in creating the sample report has nothing to do with the report itself, but rather the data that goes into the report. Before you can design a report, you have to know what you are reporting. Therefore, you can build on the ADO knowledge you acquired from Chapter 28 and create a simple query that can be used for the `DataSource` property of the report.

▶ See "Setting up a Data Source," **p. 613**

Refer to Chapter 28 if necessary to perform these steps to create the query:

1. Add the reference for Microsoft ActiveX Data Objects to your project.
2. If you have not already set up the BIBLIO ODBC data source, do so now.

3. Declare form-level variables, cn and rs, to represent ADO connection and recordset objects.
4. Draw a command button, cmdFill, on the form and label it Fill Recordset.
5. Add code to the form's Load and Unload events to open and close a connection to the BIBLIO data source.
6. Add code to the button's Click event to populate the recordset with the following SQL query:

   ```
   "Select * from Titles where [Year Published] >= 1996"
   ```

The complete code for the form up to this point is shown in Listing 29.1.

Listing 29.1 RPTDEMO.ZIP—Getting Some Sample Data for the Report

```
Dim cn As ADODB.Connection
Dim rs As ADODB.Recordset

Private Sub cmdFill_Click()
    Set rs = cn.Execute("Select * from Titles where [Year Published] >= 1996")
    MsgBox "Recordset populated."
End Sub

Private Sub Form_Load()
    Set cn = New ADODB.Connection
    cn.Open "DSN=BIBLIO"
End Sub

Private Sub Form_Unload(Cancel As Integer)
    rs.Close
    cn.Close
End Sub
```

The preceding query creates a recordset containing some records from the Titles table of the BIBLIO sample database. The records were limited to those titles published in or after 1996 to make things quicker because the table has a lot of records in it. When you click the command button, the recordset object rs is populated with the fields from the Titles table. Next, you add a DataReport object to the project and learn how to create a report from the sample recordset.

Adding a Data Report to Your Project

Now that you have data, the next step is to determine how to display that data on a report. First, you need to add a new DataReport object to your Visual Basic project. To do so, choose Project, Add Data Report. You should notice that several things happen immediately:

- A new DataReport object called DataReport1 is added to the Project Explorer window.
- A new DataReport area is added to the Toolbox.
- The Report Designer window appears, as shown in Figure 29.1

> **NOTE** In general, each DataReport object in your program represents a separate report. However, depending on the complexity of your reports, you might be able to manipulate the report enough from code to use a single DataReport object for multiple reports.

FIGURE 29.1
The Data Report allows you to manage the report layout visually.

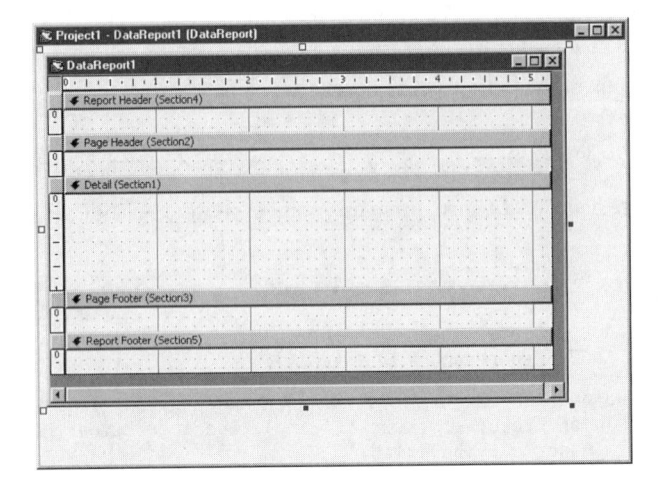

Notice that a Data Report is divided into several sections, much like reports in Microsoft Access. These sections display the following types of information:

- **Report Header.** Information displayed once, at the top of the report
- **Page Header.** Information displayed at the top of every page
- **Detail Section.** The part of the report that is repeated for each record in the ADO data source
- **Page Footer.** Information displayed at the bottom of every page
- **Report Footer.** Information displayed at the end of the report

> **NOTE** You can also add your own Group header/footer sections to a report so that you can display or calculate certain fields periodically throughout the report.

Note that each of these sections also has a section name (for example, Section1) so that you can access it from program code. To display the properties for an individual section in the Properties window, click the section's gray title bar. To display the properties for the DataReport object, click the square in the upper-left corner.

Setting Up the Data Report

While you are in design mode, use the Data Report Designer window to arrange report controls on the report, just as you would arrange custom controls on a form. The types of fields that you can place on a Data Report become available in your Toolbox when the DataReport object has focus. These fields are shown in Figure 29.2.

FIGURE 29.2
The elements that you can add to a Data Report are in a separate section of the Toolbox.

To add information to your report, you first draw the report control in the appropriate section of the report and then set its properties, just as you would with any other control. The controls that can be placed on a Data Report are shown in Table 29.1.

Table 29.1   Data Report Controls

Control Icon	Control Name	Description
	RptLabel	Specifies a label used to display text that is not data-bound, such as a column name or date printed
	RptTextBox	Displays the contents of a database field
	RptImage	Contains a picture or other graphic image, such as a company logo
	RptLine	Enables you to draw lines on the report—for example, to separate the different sections of the report
	RptShape	Enables you to draw a variety of shapes on the control to highlight information or provide other visual effects
	RptFunction	Allows you to place a field in the header or footer that contains one of several simple math functions, such as a total of all the values in a particular data field

Adding Fields to the Detail Section   Continue with the sample project by placing some fields on the report. Draw a `RptTextBox` object in the Detail section of `DataReport1`, just as you would draw a normal text box on a form. Notice that it appears with the word `Unbound` in it, meaning that it has not yet been assigned a data field to display.

Press F4 to bring up the Properties window for the new text box. Change the name to something meaningful. For the example, rename the box `txtTitle`, because you will use the text box to display book titles. Next, enter the word `Title` in the `DataField` property to bind the control to a data field. Close the Properties window. Notice that `Title` now appears on the text box.

Next, add two additional text fields named `txtDesc` and `txtYear` to the Detail section of the report using `Description` and `Year Published` for their `DataField` properties. Finally, resize the Detail section so that you don't have a lot of wasted space beneath the three text fields. The resulting form is pictured in Figure 29.3.

FIGURE 29.3
Setting up a report field is as easy as setting up a bound control.

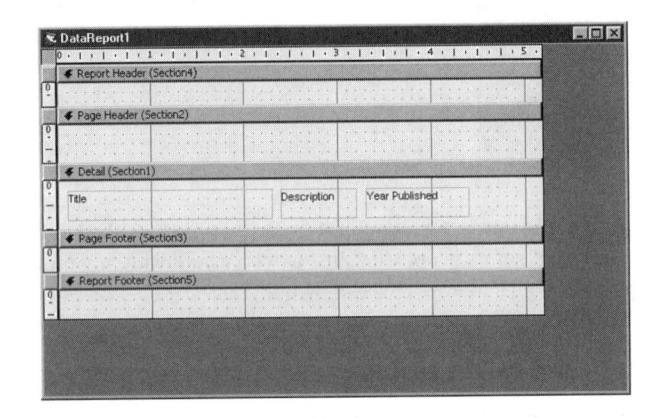

Adding Header Information   The three text box controls you just added appear in the Detail section of the report; they therefore will display information from the database. However, you also should add some fixed information in the header of the report to label these fields. To do so, you can simply add RptLabel controls to the appropriate sections of the report and set their `Caption` properties.

For the sample report, add three labels to the Page Header section. Make their captions `Title`, `Cost`, and `Year Published`. Arrange each label so that it describes the field below it in the Detail section.

Next, add a fourth RptLabel control to the report in the Report Header section. This field will display the name of the person who created the report, which will be set from Visual Basic code. Because you need to access this label control from code, the names of the section and the label control should be set to something meaningful. To change the `Name` properties of these two objects, do the following:

1. Select the RptLabel control, and change its `Name` property to `lblPerson` just as you would with a standard Label control. Also, change the `Caption` property to an empty string.
2. Click the gray bar at the top of the Report Header section, and press F4 to display the Properties window for this section.
3. Change the `Name` property of the section to `rptHeader`.

After you finish these steps, your Data Report should look like Figure 29.4. You are now finished with the report design.

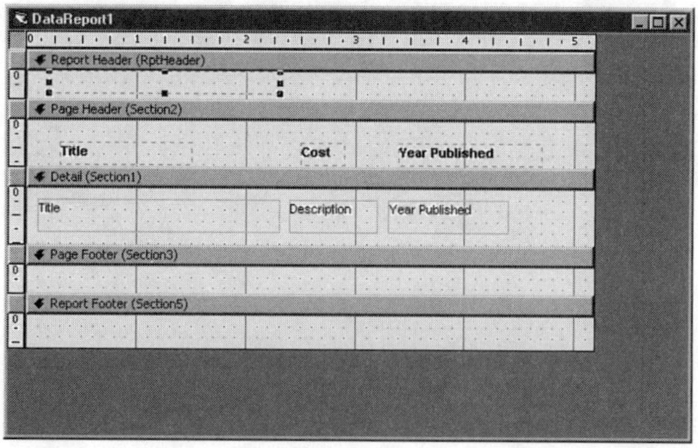

FIGURE 29.4
Here, you can see the report layout for the sample project, after adding the header fields.

Displaying the Report

Now that you have determined how you want the report to look, you have to add a few lines of code to display the report. Add a second command button, cmdReport, to the form. Make the caption Display Report. Enter the code from Listing 29.2 in the command button's Click event procedure.

Listing 29.2 RPTDEMO—Showing the Report to the Users

```
Private Sub cmdReport_Click()
    Dim s As String
    s = "Prepared by Abe Froman"

    Set DataReport1.DataSource = rs
    DataReport1.Sections("rptHeader").Controls("lblPerson").Caption = s
    DataReport1.Show

End Sub
```

The code in Listing 29.2 sets the DataSource property of the DataReport object to the ADO recordset rs.

NOTE In this example, you use an ADO recordset as the data source. However, you can also use other types of data sources, such as a Data Environment, in which case you can set the DataSource property at designtime.

Next, the code sets the Caption property of the label control in the report header. Finally, the Show method is invoked, causing the report to be displayed.

To test the sample report, run the project and click the Fill Recordset button. After you see the message box stating that the recordset has been filled, click the Display Report button. The Data Report should appear on a separate form in Print Preview mode, as pictured in Figure 29.5.

FIGURE 29.5
The completed sample Data Report is shown here.

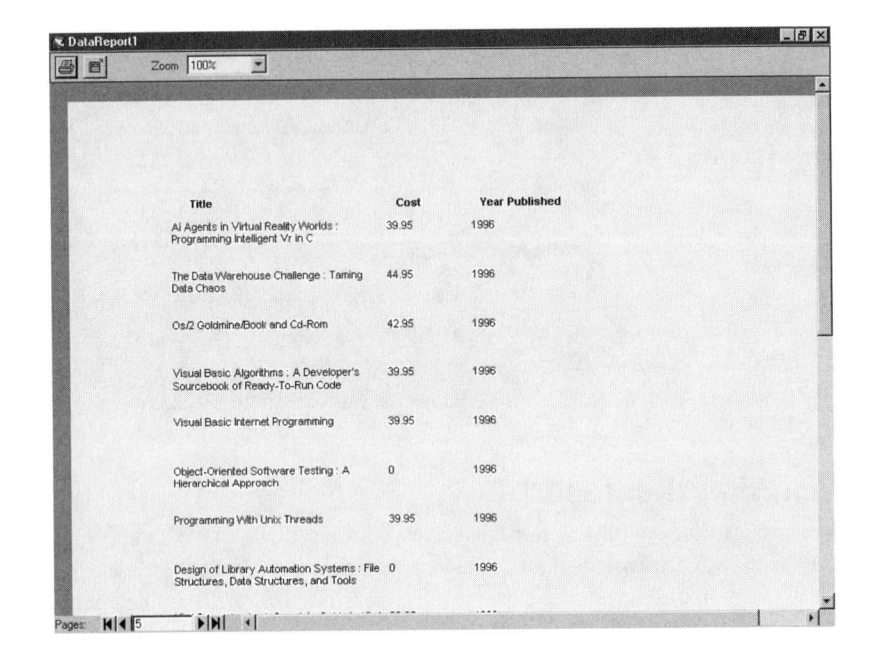

Enhancing Your Data Reports

In the preceding section, you learned how easily you can create a report using the Data Report Designer. The sample report ended up looking rather rudimentary, but it got the job done. As you may have noticed while building the sample, you can make many changes to the report fields, such as the Font property, that require no additional explanation. These options work just as they would in any other custom control. Simply apply your best artistic talents to make the report look like you want. However, the Data Report also has a few special features, some of which will be covered in the following sections.

Predefined Report Fields

As you saw in the example, the `DataReport` object enables you to programmatically access properties of report controls from code. For example, if you want to add a field that displays the date the report was created, you can set a label's caption to Now before displaying the report. However, you can achieve the same result in a much simpler way. The Data Report includes some predefined placeholders, which allow you to include several dynamic elements on a report. These items are listed in Table 29.2.

> **NOTE** The Title property is also used to identify the report to printer dialogs.

Table 29.2 Predefined Placeholders on a Data Report

Code	Description
%p	Current page number
%P	Total number of pages
%d	Current date (short format); for example, 5/24/98
%D	Current date (long format); for example, Sunday, May 24, 1998
%t	Current time (short format); for example, 16:10
%T	Current time (long format); for example, 4:10:00 PM
%i	Report title (string stored in the Title property of the DataReport object)

To use one of these fields, simply place a RptLabel control on the report and set its Caption property to include the placeholder you want. For example, if you want to add a page number to the bottom of the page, draw a label in the Page Footer section and set its caption to the following string:

Page %p of %P

Run the report, and the Data Report automatically replaces the placeholders with the proper information, as shown in Figure 29.6.

FIGURE 29.6
A page counter has been added to the sample report.

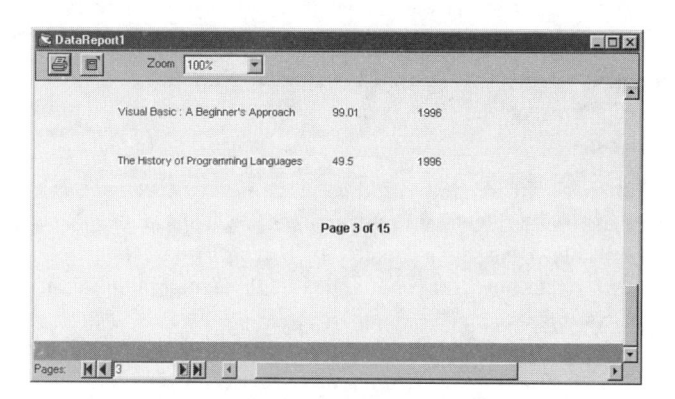

If you just want to use one of the placeholders by itself, without any of your own text, there is a quick way to add it to the report. Simply right-click the report, and choose Insert Control from the context-sensitive menu that appears. You can select from any of the predefined fields, as well as the other available report controls.

Adding Graphics

Graphical shapes and images do not add any functionality to your report, but they make it look nicer, so you can use them to highlight or visually organize certain information. Three controls allow you to add these elements: the RptImage, RptLine, and RptShape controls.

Pictures To add a picture to a report, first draw a RptImage control on the Report Designer window. Next, load a picture into the control by displaying the Properties window and clicking the ellipsis button next to the `Picture` property. Select a picture file just as you would for a standard Image or PictureBox control. Figure 29.7 shows a corporate logo in a report header that was added using the RptImage control.

FIGURE 29.7
You can add pictures to a Data Report by using the RptImage control.

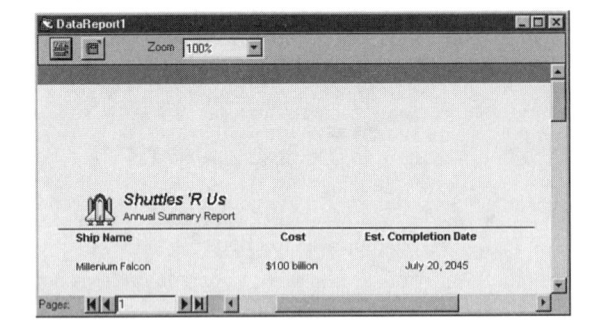

Although the RptImage control is similar to the standard Image control, it is a different control with its own set of properties. Some of the more notable differences are as follows:

- The `PictureAlignment` property allows you to position an image within the image control, similar to the way you can align text within the label control.
- More choices are available for the `BorderStyle` property in the RptImage control than with a standard Image control.
- The `SizeMode` property is more versatile than the Image control's `Stretch` property; it also allows a zoom setting in which the picture is magnified until it reaches the borders of the control.

Lines and Shapes In addition to adding pictures to a report, you can add lines and other shapes by using the RptLine and RptShape controls. These controls work similarly to the Line and Shape controls discussed in Chapter 19, "Using Visual Design Elements." Figure 29.8 shows a report that uses several lines and rectangles to highlight information.

▶ **See** "Using the Line and Shape Controls," **p. 426**

FIGURE 29.8
Adding shapes to the Detail section causes them to be repeated for each record.

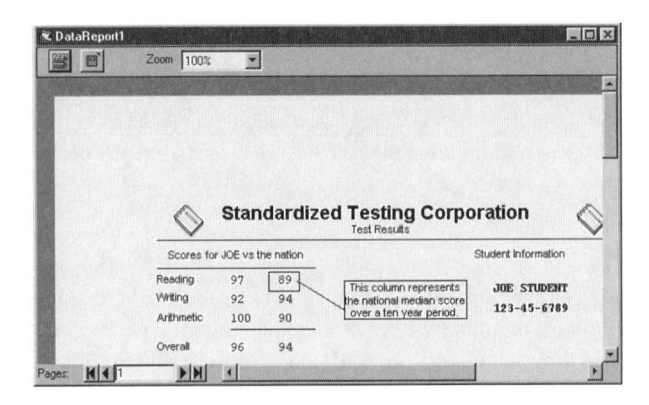

Printing and Exporting

As you have seen, designing a report involves setting up the report data source and page layout. After you create a report, you have basically three ways to get the report to the users:

- Call the Show method to display a report onscreen in a print preview window. The users can browse the information and print a copy if desired.
- Execute the PrintReport method to bypass the preview screen and print directly to the printer. This method is useful if you are automating reports, or your program already displays the data and therefore a preview is not necessary.
- Use the ExportReport method to save the contents of the report to a file. This function can be used to create a Web page from your reports.

In an earlier example, you learned how to use the Show method to display the report on the screen. Calling one of the other two methods to choose a different option is just as easy.

Using the *PrintReport* Method   In its simplest form, a call to the PrintReport method might look like this:

```
DataReport1.PrintReport
```

However, you can use several optional parameters to achieve more control over printing:

- ShowDialog—This parameter determines whether the Windows printer dialog box is shown, allowing users to cancel the operation or adjust printer settings. (This parameter is False by default.)
- Range—This parameter controls whether every page of the report is printed or just the pages you specify. The default setting is rptRangeAllPages, which causes every page to be printed.
- PageFrom and PageTo—If the Range parameter is set to rptRangeFromTo, these two parameters determine the starting and ending pages of the printed report.

The following line of code uses all the optional parameters so that only page 5 is printed:

```
datareport1.PrintReport True,rptRangeFromTo,5,5
```

Note that if the ShowDialog property is set to True, users can modify the page range or cancel the print job.

Using the *ExportReport* Method   To export a report to an HTML or text file, use the ExportReport method. For example, the following line of code creates an HTML page containing your report:

```
datareport1.ExportReport "key_def_HTML","D:\Temp\MyReport.HTM",True,False
```

As with PrintReport, ExportReport has several optional parameters:

- FormatIndexOrKey—Identifies the format of the export file. Four available formats are stored in the ExportFormats collection, but the choice is basically between text or HTML.

- `FileName`—Indicates the full pathname of the file you want to create.
- `Overwrite`—Specifies a Boolean parameter (`True` by default) indicating whether to overwrite an existing export file. If this parameter's value is `False`, attempting to overwrite an existing file causes an error.
- `ShowDialog`—Determines whether the Export dialog box is shown to the users.
- `Range`, `PageFrom`, `PageTo`—Determine which pages in the report are exported. They work exactly like the corresponding parameters in the `PrintReport` method.

Note that in addition to being able to print and export with Visual Basic code, users can do so manually by using the buttons at the top of the print preview screen.

Function Fields

You have already seen how to add fields to a Data Report to display static information or values from a database. The Data Report also can include fields whose values are the result of performing a simple function on the data displayed in the report. These fields, known as function fields, are created using the rptFunction control in the Toolbox.

The data displayed in a Function control is determined by the setting of two properties: the `DataField` property, which is the field on which the function will be performed, and the `FunctionType` property, which may be set to the following values:

- rptFuncSum—Sum
- rptFuncAve—Average
- rptFuncMin—Minimum value
- rptFuncMax—Maximum value
- rptFuncRCnt—Row count
- rptFuncVCnt—Value count, or the number of rows that have a value
- rptFuncSDEV—Standard deviation
- rptFuncSERR—Standard error

The Function control performs one of the listed functions on multiple rows of data from a given column of the recordset and displays the result. For this reason, you must place a Function control in the Report Footer section, because all the report data must be processed before the function control can calculate its value.

> **NOTE** You also can use Function controls in Group Footer sections, thus enabling you to create subtotals periodically throughout the report. For instructions on using Group Headers and Footers with the VB Data Environment Designer, see the Visual Basic Help file.

To demonstrate the Function control in action, consider a simple table that has only two columns: `SalesPerson` and `Revenue`. Figure 29.9 shows a report that uses the Function control to display the overall amount and average sales.

FIGURE 29.9
You can use the Function control to display averages, sums, and counts.

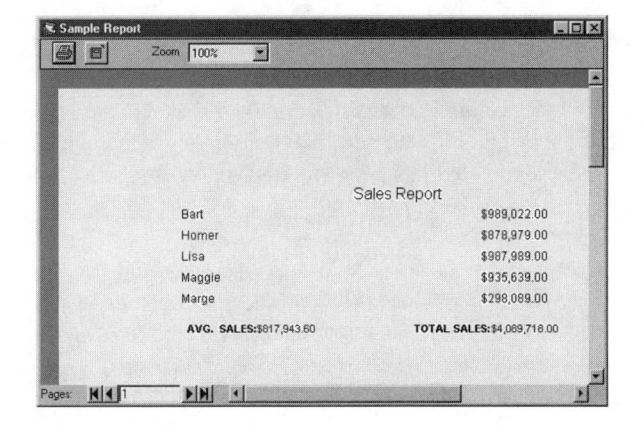

The Average and Sum functions were used on the Revenue field to create the two amounts at the bottom of the report in this figure.

Using Crystal Reports

Crystal Reports, a third-party reporting package included with Visual Basic, allows you to create reports from many different types of data sources. You can design and test reports graphically by using the Crystal Reports Designer. The report layout and other information are stored in a custom Crystal Reports file format with an .RPT extension. After you create a Crystal Report file, you can use any of the following methods to display your report for the user:

- The Crystal Reports control provides an easy way to integrate the finished reports into your Visual Basic program.
- Crystal Reports API calls allow you to access the Crystal Reports engine without using a custom control. All the API calls for Crystal Reports are located in a file called GLOBAL32.BAS, which should have been installed in your Crystal Reports program directory.
- The Crystal Reports Web Server, available in Crystal Reports Professional Edition, works with your Web server to deliver reports to an Internet client.

NOTE At the time of this writing, the latest version of Crystal Reports was Crystal Reports version 6.0. Visual Basic, however, includes an older version (4.6). To use this version of Crystal Reports, you must first install it. To install Crystal Reports, double click the executable Crystl32.exe in the folder \Common\Tools\Crysrept on Visual Studio CD 3.

In the next few sections, you are introduced to the basic operation of Crystal Reports, and you step through the process of displaying a report with the Crystal Reports control.

Creating a New Report

Assuming that Crystal Reports was installed correctly, you should be able to access the Crystal Reports Designer by selecting Report Designer from Visual Basic's Add-Ins menu. The Crystal Reports Designer, shown in Figure 29.10, is a development environment for report files. Here, you can design new reports, edit existing reports, and even preview what the finished report will look like.

> **NOTE** The executable to run the Crystal Reports Designer is CRW32.EXE. At the time of this writing, the install included with Visual Basic does not create an icon for the Crystal Reports Designer, so you will have to locate this file on your hard drive and manually create a shortcut if you want to open the Crystal Reports Designer from outside VB. (The default location is \Program Files\MS Visual Studio\Common\Tools\Reports.) If you have Crystal Reports version 6.0, a Start menu group and shortcut icon should have been automatically created.

FIGURE 29.10
The Crystal Report Designer is a separate application from Visual Basic. Use it to determine the layout of the fields on your report.

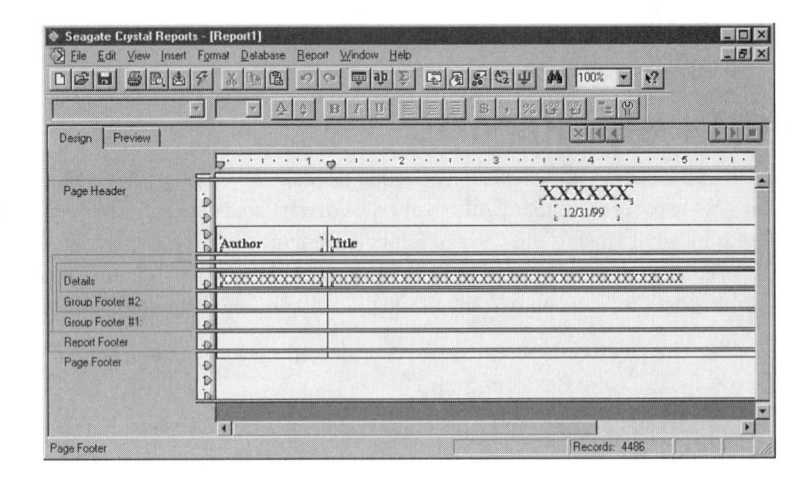

In Figure 24.10, notice the two tabs that control your view of the report: Design and Preview. While you are in Design mode, you can draw and arrange fields on the report. This process works just like drawing controls on a form; you place a report field on the page, setting the appropriate field name and other properties. If you switch to the Preview tab, Crystal Reports connects to the data source and populates the report with data.

To test this product, create a sample report from the BIBLIO database. First, open the Crystal Reports Designer and choose to create a new report by choosing New from the File menu. The Create New Report dialog box then appears, as shown in Figure 29.11.

As you can see, you can choose from several different types of reports. If you select one of the predefined report types, you use the Create Report Expert to create your report. The Create Report Expert organizes the report creation process into a series of steps, much like a wizard. You can also choose to create a custom report from scratch by clicking the Custom command button and making two selections from the bottom section of the dialog box: the report type and data source.

FIGURE 29.11
Crystal Reports allows you to design a report from scratch or with the help of an "expert." The data for your report can be retrieved through ODBC or one of the included drivers.

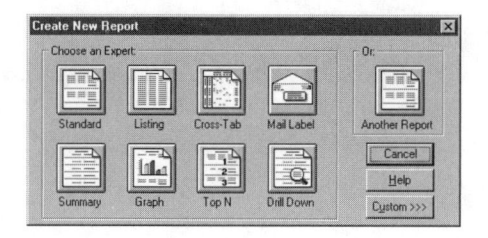

Creating a Report from Scratch   To continue with the sample report from the BIBLIO database, click the Custom button to display the Choose Report Type and Data Type dialog box. Make sure that the Custom Report button is selected and click the Data File button. Next, specify the location of the BIBLIO.MDB Access database (it's usually in the Visual Basic program directory).

After you select the database file, the Insert Database Field dialog box, shown in Figure 29.12, should automatically appear. This dialog box, which is also available from the Insert menu, allows you to determine which fields are placed on the report.

FIGURE 29.12
To highlight multiple items in this dialog box, hold down the Ctrl key while clicking the field names.

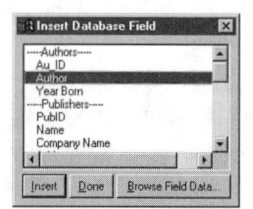

For the example, select the Author field from the Authors table, and the Title field from the Titles table. (The BIBLIO database already contains appropriate links between the various tables.) Position the Insert Fields dialog box so that you can also see the main Crystal Reports Designer window. Then drag the selected fields from the Insert Fields dialog box to the Details section of the report. Position the fields so that your report looks like the one shown in Figure 29.13. Click Done to close the Insert Database Field dialog box.

Finally, test your report by clicking the lightning bolt button in the toolbar. Clicking this button activates preview mode, allowing you to see how the report will look with database records. To save the finished report, click the Save button or choose File, Save.

> **TIP** Turn off the Save Data with Report option if you intend to programmatically display this report with new data every time. You can access this option by selecting File, Options and clicking the Reporting tab.

Creating a Report with the Create Report Expert   Using the Create Report Expert is another way to create your report. From the Create New Report dialog box, simply click the type of report you want. The available selections are described here:

FIGURE 29.13
When you drag a database field to the Details section, Crystal Reports automatically adds a corresponding header label.

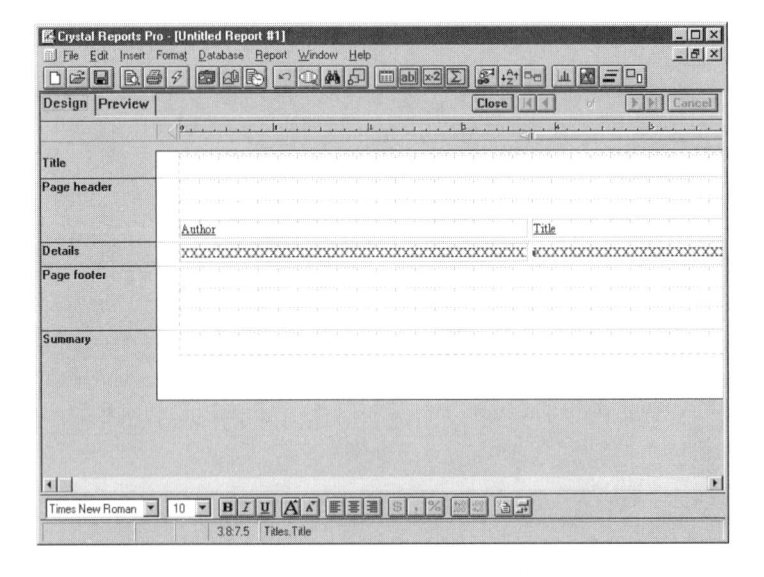

- **Standard.** This type of report is a standard report format of rows and columns. It often has summary information at the bottom of the columns. In the report, you also can group information according to certain criteria.
- **Listing.** This is a standard type of report in which data is presented in a list format. For example, an Employee List or a Customer List report would look best in this format.
- **Cross Tab.** A cross-tab report basically inverts the order of a standard columnar report. The columns of a cross-tab report are the records of a particular recordset. These reports are often used to obtain a quick summary view of a more complex set of data.
- **Mail Label.** You use these reports to create items such as mailing labels or name tags from the information in your database.
- **Summary.** This type of report summarizes data without showing the underlying details. Typically, data is broken into groups and the values in each group are summarized, but only the group totals—not the individual values in each group—are shown.
- **Graph.** This choice leads you through the creation of a Graph with step-by-step help from the Create Report Expert.
- **Top N.** This type of report shows only a specified number of the top records in the recordset. It can be used to show the top five salespeople in the company, for example.
- **Drill Down.** This type of report shows the supporting information or detail information for each record.

Figure 29.14 shows the first screen of the Create Report Expert, where you specify a data source. After completing this step, you are asked for each additional piece of information necessary to create the report.

When you are finished creating the report, you can still add or change report elements just as you would with a custom report.

FIGURE 29.14
The Create Report Expert has several tabs, each of which represents a step in the report-creation process.

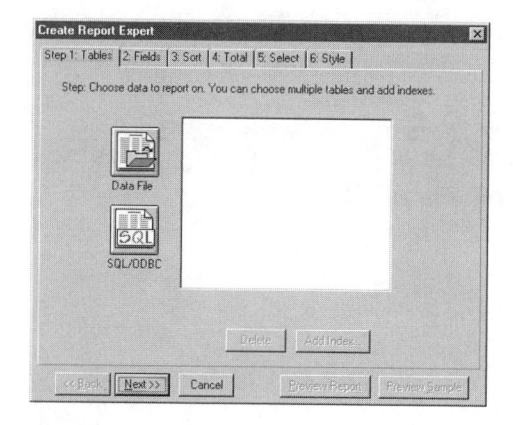

Customizing Your Report

Even if you use the Report Expert to build your initial report layout, most likely you will want to make additional changes. Fortunately, Crystal Reports provides a myriad of options that allow you to customize a report to suit your individual needs. Although coverage of every feature of Crystal Reports is beyond the scope of this book, this chapter introduces two important concepts: adding a new field and controlling selection criteria.

Field Types As mentioned earlier, fields are arranged on the report just as custom controls are drawn on a form. From the Insert menu, you can choose from several different types:

- **Database Field.** Links contents to fields in the data source, much like bound controls.
- **Text Object.** Provides fixed text information, such as a report title.
- **Formula Field.** Displays the results of a formula (expression). This may be the result of performing an operation on one or more database fields.
- **Parameter Field.** Allows you to specify parameters that can be passed into the report, either programmatically or manually. These parameter fields can then be used in selection criteria and other formulas.
- **Special Field.** Automatically shows the current page, the date and time, and other useful information.

To add a field to your report, you simply select it from the menu and provide the necessary information to create the field. If you want to remove an existing field, select it and then press Delete. You can also right-click to open a context-sensitive menu, from which you can choose options to control field properties, such as content and formatting.

Adding a Selection Formula From the Report menu, you can change the selection formula for your report. A selection formula allows you to filter the displayed records from within Crystal Reports. It works much like the WHERE clause of a SQL statement but is in a slightly different format. The Record Selection Formula dialog box allows you to filter records by selecting applicable fields and their respective selection criteria. The criteria statement is automatically generated by the dialog box. Figure 29.15 shows how the selection criteria have been changed to include only authors born during or after 1950.

FIGURE 29.15
Using the Formula Editor window, you can build expressions involving fields, functions, and operators.

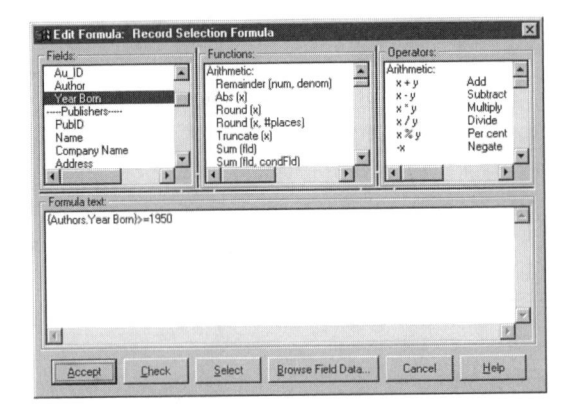

Note that changing the selection criteria within a report to limit records is far less efficient than changing the source recordset. If you modify the selection criteria, the report's underlying recordset still contains as many records as it did originally; the selection filter(s) only limits how many records are presented to the user in the report. In the example, the report would still contain all authors, even though it displays only the ones born since 1950.

Using the Crystal Reports Control

Once you complete the design of your report, you should have an RPT file saved on your hard drive. You can use this file in conjunction with the Crystal Reports control to display your report from within a Visual Basic application.

> **NOTE** If you use a Crystal Report in your application, you have to distribute the report file plus all the support files required to run the report on another user's machine.

Because the Crystal Reports control is a third-party control, it is not available in Visual Basic's Toolbox by default. To add the control to your Toolbox, choose Project, Components or press Ctrl+T. Then select the Crystal Reports Control check box and click OK.

To demonstrate how the control works, use it to display the sample report created in the preceding section. First, start a new Standard EXE project, and add the Crystal Reports control to your Toolbox. Draw an instance of the Crystal Reports control on the form. Notice that it appears icon-sized, as pictured in Figure 29.16.

Specifying the Report File   The key property that you need to specify is the `ReportFileName` property, which is the path to the RPT file you created in the Report Designer. If you plan to use the Crystal Reports control to display multiple reports, you probably should set this property at runtime, as in the following example:

```
CrystalReport1.ReportFileName = App.Path & "\Test.Rpt"
```

FIGURE 29.16
The Crystal Reports control is invisible while your program is running; reports are viewed in an independent window.

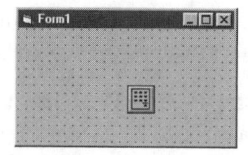

However, for the sample report, setting the ReportFileName property at designtime is sufficient. To do so, right-click the control and select Properties to display the Property Pages dialog box. On the General tab, shown in Figure 29.17, you can specify the location of the RPT file. You can also choose whether the report should go to the printer, a preview window, a file, or to an e-mail message.

FIGURE 29.17
On the Property Pages dialog box, you can specify the report file and output destination.

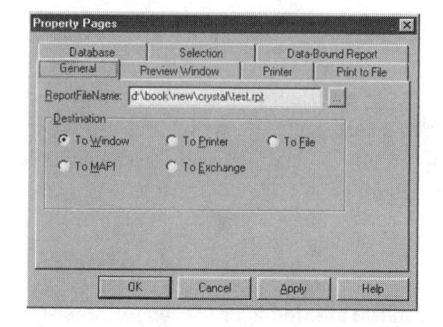

Selecting the ReportFileName is the minimum setup for Crystal Reports. At this point, you can write the single line of code necessary to run the report and test it by running your program.

Setting Optional Properties Although only the ReportFileName is required for a report, you might want to use several optional properties with the report. The first of these properties is the SelectionFormula property. This property enables you to limit the number of records that are included in the report. The SelectionFormula property is similar to the Where clause of a SQL statement but uses its own particular format to enter the information. (This format is the same as that described in the earlier section "Customizing Your Report.") The following is an example of setting this property from code:

```
CrystalReport1.SelectionFormula = "{Authors.Year Born} >= 1955"
```

You also can use multiple expressions by including the And or Or operators.

> **CAUTION**
> If you enter a SelectionFormula when you're designing your report, any formula you enter in the SelectionFormula property of the Crystal Reports control provides an additional filter on the records.

Another optional property is `CopiesToPrinter`. This property enables you to print multiple copies of your report easily at one time. You can set this property to any integer value.

The final property you might need to set at runtime is `DataFiles`. This property is not available at designtime. It specifies the name of the database file to be used with the report. Now you might be thinking, "I told the report what file to use when I created it." That is true, but when you created the report, the database file was stored with a path based on your directory structure. And your path might not be the same as the directory structure of your users.

The `DataFiles` property is actually an array with the first element number of 0. If you're using more than one database in your report, you need to set the value of each `DataFiles` array element. For most of your reports, however, you will be using only a single database. The following line of code shows you how to set the value of the `DataFiles` property for the database; this line assumes that the database file is in the same folder as your application:

```
rptMember.DataFiles(0) = App.Path & "\Members.mdb"
```

Displaying the Report Even after you add the Crystal Reports control to your form and set its properties, you still have to tell Crystal Reports when to print or display the report by adding a line of code. The report then prints using the report file and other properties that you set. If you have your report set up to preview onscreen, it appears in a window similar to the one shown in Figure 29.18. The following line of code uses the `PrintReport` method to run a report:

```
CrystalReport1.PrintReport
```

Note that even though the name of the method is `PrintReport`, it is sent to the destination you specified earlier.

NOTE You can also print a report by setting the `Action` property of the Crystal Reports control to 1.

FIGURE 29.18
The desired report has been printed to the screen.

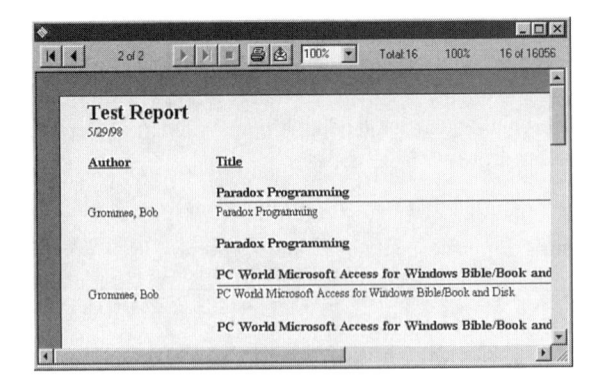

From Here...

In this chapter, you took a brief look at a new feature of Visual Basic 6.0, the Data Report. You walked through a simple report, examined some of the enhancements you can make to a report's appearance, and reviewed a few methods used to automate report printing and exporting. You also looked at an old favorite reporting tool, Crystal Reports. For more related information, see the following chapters:

- To learn how you can create reports by using Excel or Word, see Chapter 22, "Using OLE to Control Other Applications."
- If you want to learn more about databases in general, see Chapter 24, "Database Basics."
- For an introduction to retrieving data with ADO, see Chapter 28, "Using ActiveX Data Objects (ADO)."

PART VII

Visual Basic and the Internet

30 Using VBScript 665

31 Active Server Pages 687

32 ActiveX Documents 719

33 Visual Basic and Other Uses of the Internet 741

CHAPTER 30

Using VBScript

In this chapter

Introduction to VBScript 666

Tools Used with VBScript 671

The VBScript Language 673

Using VBScript in Internet Explorer 676

The Windows Scripting Host 682

This chapter begins a section on Visual Basic and the Internet. The Internet is one of the most talked-about topics in computers today. Although the Internet has been around a long time, until just a few years ago, it remained out of the public eye, used mostly by the academic world. However, today everyone seems to have an e-mail address and a Web site. In this book, you learn several methods of applying your VB knowledge to the Internet. This chapter serves as an overview of VBScript, a subset of Visual Basic that can be used to program the Internet.

Introduction to VBScript

The Visual Basic language comes in several flavors besides the "traditional" standalone development tool it has always been. One of those flavors is Visual Basic for Applications (VBA). Another flavor, not to be confused with VBA, is the Visual Basic scripting language, or VBScript. Descriptions of all three appear in Table 30.1.

Table 30.1 VB Versus VBA Versus VBScript

Language	Description
Visual Basic	Standalone development environment that allows you to compile executable files, ActiveX Controls, and DLLs.
VBA	The version of Visual Basic designed to be used within an application, such as Excel, Access, or Visio. Starting with Microsoft Office 97, VBA and VB share the same IDE.
VBScript	Small subset of the VB language interpreted by Internet Explorer, Internet Information Server, Microsoft Outlook, and the Windows Scripting Host.

The VBScript language itself does not have anywhere near the power of VB or VBA, nor does it have its own development environment. These limitations are by design, however. The strength of VBScript is not in the language itself, but how and where it can be used, such as the following:

- **Web pages**—Client-side VBScript code can be embedded in standard HTML, allowing Web pages to contain application-like functionality.
- **Active Server Pages**—Server-side VBScript code can be used in Active Server Pages, allowing Web pages to be generated and altered before returning content to a browser.
- **The Windows Scripting Host**—Visual Basic script code can be run from the DOS command line like a batch file, allowing you to automate certain tasks.

Enhancing the Internet with VBScript

VBScript was first introduced for use with the Internet. The Internet itself is a physical network of computers. However, when most people think of the Internet, they do not think about the network but about specific applications used with it. The following are some examples of these applications:

- **World Wide Web**—Interactive documents viewed in a Web browser. They can contain news, information, and programs to download to your computer.
- **E-mail**—Electronic mail, used to send messages to a specific individual.
- **Newsgroups**—Bulletin-board style discussion groups in which you can post questions and answers about a wide variety of topics.
- **Chat**—Live communication with others connected to the Internet in the form of typed messages, audio, or video.
- **File Transfer and Terminal Access**—Transfer of files (FTP) and remote access (Telnet) to a computer.

By far, the most popular use of the Internet is the World Wide Web. The idea for the World Wide Web come from Tim Berners-Lee as a way to aid his memory by inserting links into his documents. He eventually proposed a "global hypertext space" which would lead to today's web of millions of linked documents. A link not only provides a reference to a supporting document, it also allows the reader to "jump" directly to the supporting document—hence the term *hyperlink*. The hyperlinked documents form a "web" of information accessible to everyone on the Internet.

VBScript on the Web Server

You probably know from experience that the Web of today has evolved quite a bit from just a series of linked documents. Web sites contain rich multimedia elements and database-driven content, and can behave almost like standard applications. Arguably the most powerful improvements to the Web have been added to the Web server.

The Web server is the computer that delivers the requested Web pages to the browser. The concept of *requesting* a Web page is key to understanding what a Web server does. Many people make the mistake of thinking of Web pages as documents stored on file servers; this is not how the system works! The role of the Web server is pictured in Figure 30.1.

FIGURE 30.1
The Web server sends an HTML stream back to the browser in response to a request for a Web page.

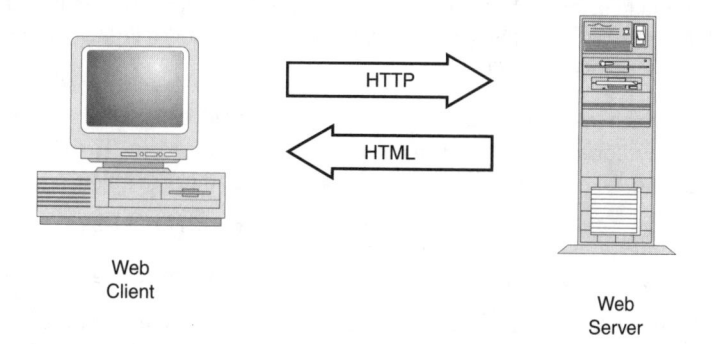

To further illustrate the difference, consider the real-world example of researching William Shakespeare at your local library. Upon entering the library, you can just go to the Shakespeare section and pick up a book, or you can ask the librarian to help you.

If you go get a book yourself, the library is acting like a file server in that you are simply accessing a file (book) stored in it. On the other hand, if you request that the librarian help you, he or she will use his or her own expertise by asking questions and offering suggestions. In this case, the librarian is acting like a Web server because he or she is controlling your access to the files (books).

> **NOTE** The method by which browsers and Web servers talk to each other is known as the Hypertext Transfer Protocol, or HTTP.

Because all requests go through the Web server, the Web server can modify the information returned to the browser however it sees fit. One typical example is including database information in a Web page. This can be accomplished by executing a program on the server that handles database access and returns information in a format that the browser can understand. The way that Microsoft provides this technology to VB programmers is known as Active Server Pages, or ASP. ASP is illustrated in Figure 30.2.

FIGURE 30.2
Active Server Pages are HTML with script code that is executed on the server before the user sees the results.

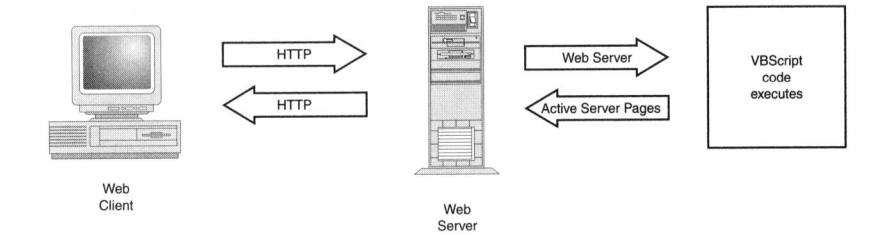

ASP is an exciting and powerful Web technology, so much so that it has its own chapter in this book—Chapter 31, "Active Server Pages."

VBScript in the Browser

In addition to using VBScript on the Web server, VBScript code can be executed on the user's desktop. To understand how this works, you have to know a little about the language in which Web pages are written: HTML.

HTML, which stands for Hypertext Markup Language, consists of some formatting codes that allow an author to create hyperlinks and format the document. The HTML language is fairly easy to understand, even for newcomers, as illustrated in the following example:

```
<FONT SIZE = "+2"> This is a sample web Page! </FONT> <BR>
<B> I hope you enjoy it! </B> <BR><BR>
The following is a hyperlink:   <A HREF = "http://www.que.com"> Click me! </A>
```

HTML includes both the document text and formatting codes. A special viewer, known as a browser, interprets the formatting codes and displays the Web page. A browser displaying the preceding lines of HTML is shown in Figure 30.3.

FIGURE 30.3
If you have used a personal computer in the last year or two, you have certainly encountered a Web browser.

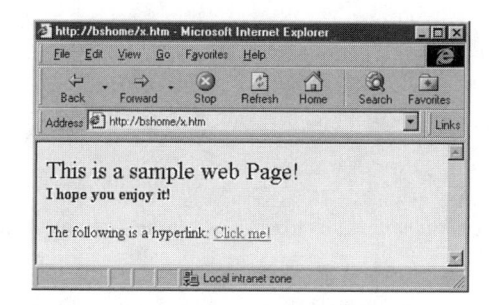

A good VB programmer should have no trouble picking up HTML basics. The preceding example uses several formatting codes, or *HTML tags*. Most HTML elements have a starting point and an ending point, indicated by corresponding tags. For example, the `<B>` and `</B>` tags tell the browser that the text between them should be displayed in boldface format.

> **TIP**
> Learn more about HTML by viewing the HTML code behind your favorite Web pages. To do so in Internet Explorer, right-click in an empty area of the page and choose View Source.

Many books and online references are available to help you learn more about HTML. For the purposes of this chapter, Table 30.2 lists some commonly used HTML elements.

Table 30.2 Common HTML Tags

Tag	Description
`<HR>`	Horizontal separator bar
` `	Line break
`<B>` and `</B>`	Boldface
`<I>` and `</I>`	Italics
`<U>` and `</U>`	Underline
`<CENTER>` and `</CENTER>`	Centers text
`<A HREF=url> linktext </A>`	Inserts a hyperlink (or "anchor")
`<IMG SRC=imagefile ALT=tooltip text>`	Inserts a GIF or JPEG image
`<HTML>` and `</HTML>`	Denotes start and end of a document
`<HEAD>` and `</HEAD>`	Start and end of document header
`<TITLE>` and `</TITLE>`	Page title located in the header
`<BODY>` and `</BODY>`	Denotes start and end of the body
`<TABLE>` and `</TABLE>`	Denotes start and end of a table

continues

Table 30.2 Continued

Tag	Description
`<TR>` and `</TR>`	Within the `<TABLE>` tag, indicates a row
`<TD>` and `</TD>`	Within the `<TR>` tag, indicates a column
`<FORM action=url method=method name=name>` and `</FORM>`	Denotes start and end of a form
`<INPUT type=type value=value name=name>`	Form Input element
`<FONT>` and `</FONT>`	Controls many aspects of the current font, including typeface and size

> **NOTE** Internet Explorer 4.0 also includes support for DHTML, or *dynamic HTML,* which makes Web pages even more programmable by providing programmatic access to HTML tags. ∎

The HTML codes listed in Table 30.2 are a small fraction of those available for use. In addition, codes can be nested in different ways to produce different results. Although HTML can do a lot of interesting things by itself, it lacks the power of a programming language. Other than jumping from one document to another and submitting forms, there are no real actions that you can take with standard HTML. However, you can script code to HTML to make Web pages a little more functional. Scripting languages such as VBScript and JScript are embedded in HTML and indicated by a special `<SCRIPT>` tag. The following example uses VBScript to display a message box:

```
<SCRIPT Language = "VBScript">
<!--
Dim nAnswer
nAnswer = MsgBox ("Would you like to visit my site?" ,vbYesNo,"Hello!")

If nAnswer = vbNo Then
    MsgBox "Well, then I will send you somewhere else!"
    Window.Location = "http://www.nowhere.com"
end if
-->
</SCRIPT>

<FONT SIZE = "+2"> This is a sample web Page! </FONT> <BR>
<B> I hope you enjoy it! </B> <BR><BR>
The following is a hyperlink:   <A HREF = "http://www.que.com"> Click me! </A>
```

The preceding HTML example contains a section of VBScript code added at the beginning. When the browser begins to parse the HTML in the Web page, it encounters the VBScript code and executes it. You will learn more details about using VBScript in your pages later in the chapter.

Tools Used with VBScript

To use VBScript, you need to have the right tools. The following sections provide a brief rundown of some items that make working with VBScript easier.

The VB Scripting Engine

The Script code is interpreted and executed by a *scripting engine*. The scripting engine for VBScript is a file named VBSCRIPT.DLL, located in the \Windows\System directory. VBScript is installed with one of the applications that use it, such as Internet Explorer, Outlook, Internet Information Server, or the Windows Scripting Host. However, a few different versions of VBScript have been released, and some of the examples in this chapter may not work with VBScript versions prior to 3.0. To determine the version you have installed, right-click the VBSCRIPT.DLL file in Explorer and choose P_r_operties, as shown in Figure 30.4.

FIGURE 30.4
Make sure that you are using the latest VBScript engine by checking the properties of VBSCRIPT.DLL.

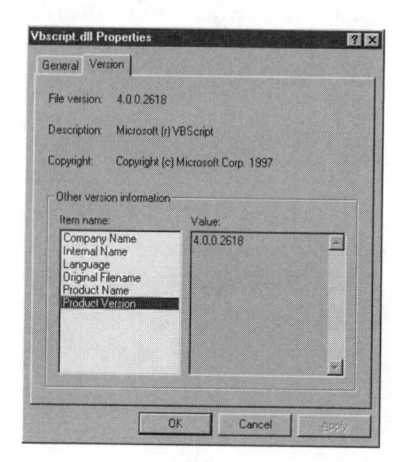

Another indication that your version of VBScript is old is an error when you attempt to use an intrinsic constant (such as vbYesNo in the earlier example), because these constants were not included in the first version. If you want to upgrade to the latest version of VBScript, visit the Web site at http://www.microsoft.com/vbscript. This site contains downloadable files for the latest scripting engines that you can place on your Web site, as well as documentation for the VBScript language.

Host Application

The applications with which you can use VBScript are also known as *hosts* for VBScript. The most common hosts are Internet Explorer and Internet Information Server. Outlook also uses VBScript as its macro language. In addition, Microsoft recently introduced the Windows Scripting host, which allows you to run VBScript code from a regular Windows platform such as Windows NT or Windows 95.

> **N O T E** Internet Explorer hosts VBScript that runs on the user's desktop. VBScript does not currently run in Netscape Navigator. However, VBScript in Active Server Pages runs on Internet Information Server, allowing you to use VBScript to create browser-independent HTML or generate browser-specific pages on the fly.

Although the VBScript language works the same everywhere, each host application exposes a different set of objects to VBScript. So some of the statements that work in IE do not work in IIS and vice versa.

Text Editor

Many people who use VBScript with Web pages use a simple text editor to enter VBScript code because VBScript does not (yet) have its own integrated development environment. This means all the great IDE features you are used to in regular VB are not available. You have to be careful that what you enter is spelled and formatted correctly. Some more advanced text editors, such as HomeSite, help you with VBScript code entry by providing automatic color-coding and toolbar buttons for commonly used statements.

Although a text editor as simple as Notepad will work, I recommend one that shows you line numbers. When an error occurs in your code, Internet Explorer returns the line number, as shown in Figure 30.5.

FIGURE 30.5
When an error occurs in your VBScript code, Internet Explorer displays the offending line number, which you can use to track down the error.

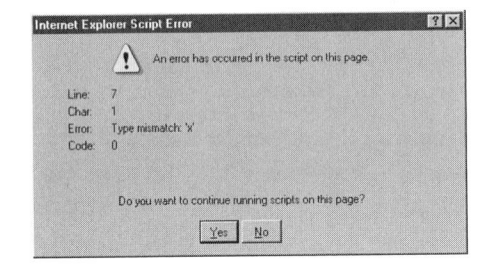

By leaving the text editor and browser open at the same time, you can easily switch back and forth between them. This is one way to debug VBScript: Edit and save the code, and then click the Refresh button on the browser to try again.

Advanced Web Tools

If you get tired of just using a text editor, you may want to try some of the more advanced Web tools, such as the following:

- **ActiveX Control Pad**—A free tool from Microsoft, really not that advanced, but it does provide a way to get class IDs for ActiveX controls.
- **Microsoft FrontPage**—A Web page creation application. FrontPage includes a Script Wizard, which creates VBScript code for you and makes working with ActiveX controls and events easy.

- **Visual InterDev**—Another Microsoft product, aimed more at developers of database-driven Web pages; it generates VBScript code for you.
- **Internet Client SDK**—Software development kit available for downloading from Microsoft; it provides samples, documentation, and utilities for working with the Internet.

The VBScript Language

When compared to standard VB, VBScript could almost be called "VB-Stripped" because it lacks so many functions. However, this is by design; the power of VBScript is in where it can be used and the objects it can access rather than in the language itself. Therefore, using VBScript will take some adjusting if you are used to Visual Basic.

Working with Variants Only

Perhaps the most striking difference between VB and VBScript is that all variables in VBScript are variants. The following statements are valid VBScript declarations:

```
Dim sLastName
Dim nCounter
Dim myArray(2,5)
```

VBScript does not allow a standard VB declaration with the As keyword. If you attempt to include one, you receive an error. The variant-only rule also applies to all variables used in subs and functions:

```
Function CalcInterest(P,R,T)
    CalcInterest = P * R * T
End Function
```

In the CalcInterest sample function, all the parameters and the return value are variants. The calling code could legally assign the string "Hello" to one of the parameters, although a type mismatch error would occur in the multiplication statement. For this reason, I strongly suggest adhering to the variable naming conventions you use in regular Visual Basic. You can also use the Option Explicit statement in the header of your Web page to require variable declarations.

Several functions in VBScript also can be used to determine the type of variable being stored in a variant. They are summarized in Table 30.3.

Table 30.3 Determining a Variable Type in VBScript

Function(s)	Purpose
VarType(varname)	Returns a constant
TypeName(varname)	Returns a description
Is()... functions	Checks for specific types and conditions

The following VBScript code displays the description of the type of each element in a variant array:

```
Dim varArray(5)
Dim i
varArray(1) = "This is a string"
varArray(2) = 123.456
varArray(3) = #12/25/1999#
varArray(4) = 10
varArray(5) = Null

For  i  = 1 to 5
  Msgbox "Array element " & i & " is of type " & TypeName(varArray(i))
Next
```

Notice also that the array example makes use of a For loop. In VBScript, a variable name cannot be placed after a Next statement in a For loop. Doing so causes an error.

Using Objects for Added Power

Although the VBScript language has definite limitations, keep in mind that you can use VBScript to communicate with external objects. These objects can be ActiveX DLLs that you write in regular Visual Basic or other automation objects installed on your system, such as Microsoft Excel or Word.

First, you create an instance of the object by using the CreateObject method:

```
Set objWord = CreateObject("Word.Application")
```

Next, you call methods and reference properties in the object:

```
objWord.Visible = True
objWord.Activate
objWord.Documents.Add
objWord.WordBasic.Insert "Here is some text"
```

Finally, when you are finished with the object, destroy the reference to it:

```
Set objWord = Nothing
```

> **NOTE** In Chapter 31, "Active Server Pages," you discover Server.CreateObject(), which is used to create objects in an Active Server Page.

Learn more about creating your own custom objects in Chapter 16, "Classes: Reusable Components." After you create these objects, you can use them with the CreateObject function.

▶ **See** "Creating an ActiveX DLL," **p. 368**

When using your own objects with VBScript, you have to handle certain return values carefully because VBScript uses only variants. Most return values such as Integer or String work as you would expect with VBScript, but arrays require special attention. Examples of returning arrays and recordsets are described in Chapter 27.

Accessing the File System

To prevent harmful scripts from damaging the host computer, VBScript offers some special functions that replace the normal VB functions or perform the same activity in a different way. One major area of difference is in the handling of file access. The standard Visual Basic File input and output commands, as discussed in Chapter 21, "Working with Files," are not available in VBScript. Instead, all file access is provided through the methods and properties of special objects. The objects used in dealing with files are listed in Table 30.4.

Table 30.4 VBScript Objects Used for Working with Files

Object	Description
File	A file on the local machine
Folder	A folder (directory) on the local machine
Drive	A drive on the local machine
TextStream	An object that provides sequential read/write capability
FileSystemObject	An object that represents the entire file system, used to reference all the above objects

To perform file and disk operation, use a method or property of an object listed in Table 30.4. The most important object is the `FileSystemObject` object. You use VBScript's `CreateObject` function to create a reference to it, as in the following line of code:

```
Set objFs = CreateObject("Scripting.FileSystemObject")
```

Obviously, this object gives a malicious programmer a way to damage your system. For this reason, Internet Explorer displays a warning message when VBScript accesses external objects, as shown in Figure 30.6.

FIGURE 30.6
Internet Explorer has several security settings to prevent harmful scripts or controls from running on your computer.

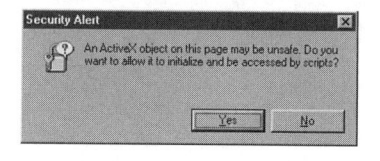

The code in Listing 30.1 displays the last time a user visited a particular Web page. It keeps track of this information by creating a text file called LASTVISIT.TXT in the WINDOWS directory. Open the file in Internet Explorer and click the Refresh button several times to test it.

Listing 30.1 VBSFILES.HTM—Accessing the File System in Internet Explorer 4.0

```
<HTML>
<HEAD>

<SCRIPT Language = "VBScript">
<!--OPTION EXPLICIT
    Dim objfs       'FileSystemObject Object
    Dim objfile     'File Object
    Dim objTs       'TextStream Object

    Dim sInfoFile   'Path to the info file
    Dim sInfo       'Variable used to store information

    'Create a reference to the local file system
    Set objFs = CreateObject("Scripting.FileSystemObject")

    'Determine path to file in the windows directory
    sInfoFile = objFS.GetSpecialFolder(0) & "\LASTVISIT.TXT"

    'If file exists then read a line of text
    If objfs.FileExists(sInfoFile) Then
        Set objfile = objfs.GetFile(sInfoFile)
        Set objts = objfile.OpenAsTextStream(1) 'Reading = 1, Writing = 2
        sInfo = objts.ReadLine()
        objts.close
    Else
        sInfo = "You haven't visited this web site before!"
    End If

    'Write message to the browser window
    Document.Write sInfo & "<BR>"

    'Store new message in the file for next time
    sInfo = "Your last visit was <B>" & Now & "</B>. Welcome back!"
    Set objts = objfile.OpenAsTextStream(2) 'Reading = 1, Writing = 2
    objts.WriteLine(sInfo)
    objts.close

    Set objfs = Nothing

-->
</SCRIPT>
</HEAD>
</HTML>
```

Using VBScript in Internet Explorer

The following sections describe how to use client-side VBScript in your Web pages. VBScript can also be used on the server, as discussed in Chapter 27. Although server-side VBScript can be browser independent, client-side VBScript requires that the user have Microsoft Internet Explorer. Currently, Netscape users cannot run VBScript code. Remember to keep your audience in mind when using VBScript.

Events and Procedures

In standard Visual Basic, you respond to events by placing code in event procedures. You can also use event procedures in VBScript, although writing them is not as easy because the event procedure declarations are not provided for you.

As an example, consider the following HTML code, which creates two form elements, an input box and a button:

```
<INPUT Type="text" Name="txtLastName" Value="Smith" Size=20>
<INPUT Type="Button" Name="cmdCalculate" Value="Perform Calculation">
```

Because the preceding two form elements are named, all you have to do to create an event procedure is write a VBScript subroutine with the appropriate name and parameters. For example, by creating a VBScript subroutine called cmdCalculate_OnClick(), you can get IE to execute code in response to the button's Click event. The code in Listing 30.2 uses VBScript events in a simple interest calculator.

Listing 30.2 SIMPLEVBS.ZIP—Using VBScript to Access Web Page Elements

```
<HTML>
<HEAD><TITLE>Simple example of VBScript</TITLE></HEAD>

<SCRIPT Language = "VBScript">
<!--

Function CalcInterest(P,R,T)
    CalcInterest = P * R * T
End Function

Sub cmdCalculate_OnClick()
    Dim lPrincipal
    Dim dblRate
    Dim nYears
    Dim cInterest

    lPrincipal = CLng(txtPrincipal.value)
    dblRate = CDbl(txtRate.value)
    nYears = CInt(txtTime.value)

    cInterest = CalcInterest(lPrincipal, dblRate, nYears)

    MsgBox "Your Interest is " & FormatCurrency(cInterest)
End Sub
Sub txtRate_OnChange()
    If CDbl(txtRate.Value) > 1 Then txtRate.Value = txtRate.Value / 100
End Sub

-->
</SCRIPT>
<BODY>
<BR>

Enter Principal: <INPUT Type="Text" Name="txtPrincipal" Value="100000"><BR>
Enter Int. Rate: <INPUT Type="Text" Name="txtRate" Value="0.08"><BR>
```

continues

Listing 30.2 Continued

```
Time in Years: <INPUT Type="text" Name="txtTime" Value="20"><BR>
<INPUT Type="Button" Name="cmdCalculate" Value="Calculate Interest">
</BODY>
</HTML>
```

> **NOTE** Listing 30.2 uses HTML form elements, which have a different set of events and properties. Note, for example, the use of the `Value` property instead of the `Text` property. However, as you will see in an upcoming example, you can also insert controls onto Web pages, which have a more familiar set of properties and events.

In the sample Web page in Listing 30.2, Internet Explorer knows which event procedure to run because the event procedure is named appropriately. However, you could just as easily specify a different `Click` event procedure by naming it in the button's HTML:

```
<INPUT Type="Button" Name="myButton" Value="Calculate" OnClick="MyProcedure">
```

This syntax is useful with images in Web pages. Consider the standard method of creating an image hyperlink:

```
<A HREF="http://www.newsite.com/"> <IMG SRC="myimage.gif"></A>
```

This approach works, but your only option is to jump to a new page. A more versatile method is to specify a `Click` event in the `IMG` tag. The `Click` event procedure could use VBScript code to move to the new site or perform whatever action you wanted:

```
<SCRIPT Language = "VBScript">
<!--
Sub ImageClicked()
   Window.Navigate ("http://www.newsite.com/")
End Sub
-->
</SCRIPT>
<IMG SRC="myimage.gif" OnClick="ImageClicked">
```

One easy way to find out the available events is to use the Script Wizard in Microsoft FrontPage. Simply insert the element you want in FrontPage and bring up the Script Wizard, which is shown in Figure 30.7.

In the previous example, you examined the `Navigate` method of Internet Explorer's `Window` object. This method causes Internet Explorer to open the specified URL. Another useful function is `document.write`, which writes HTML to the browser window:

```
<SCRIPT Language = "VBScript">
<!--
document.write "The current date and time is " & Now
-->
</SCRIPT>
```

FIGURE 30.7
The Script Wizard provides a hierarchical view of events.

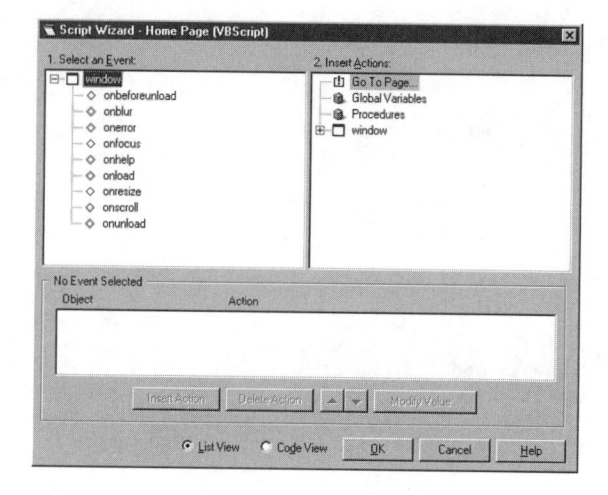

Look on the Microsoft Web site for a complete list of the objects and methods available in Internet Explorer.

Forms

Forms are HTML elements used to send information back to the Web server. The following is an example of an HTML form with two text boxes:

```
<FORM Action="formproc.asp" METHOD="POST" NAME="frmTest">
 Please enter your name and E-Mail address below:<BR>
 Name:   <INPUT Type=Text size=40 name=txtName>    <BR>
 Email: <INPUT Type=Text size=30 name=txtEmail>   <BR>
 <INPUT Type=Submit Name=cmdSend Value="Send Values to Server">
</FORM>
```

The Submit button tells the browser to send all the <INPUT> fields between the <FORM> tags to the Web server. The Web server (in this case, the Active Server Page formproc.asp) can then access each of these elements and put them in a database. However, before you submit the form to the server, you might want to use VBScript to validate or change the information. Listing 30.3 shows an example of validating form data with VBScript.

Listing 30.3 VBSFORM.ZIP—Modifying and Submitting a Form with VBScript

```
<HTML>
<HEAD><TITLE>Simple example of Forms</TITLE></HEAD>
<SCRIPT Language = "VBScript">
<!--
Sub submitform()
```

continues

Listing 30.3   Continued

```vbscript
    Dim nPos
    Dim sUserType
    Dim f

    Set f = Document.frmMain

    'Make sure name is not blank
    If Trim(f.txtName.Value) = "" Then
        Msgbox "Please enter your name and try again!"
        Exit Sub
    End if

    'Validate E-Mail Address Format
    nPos = Instr(f.txtEmail.Value,"@")
    If nPos = 0 Then
        Msgbox "Please use the format user@server.domain"
        Exit Sub
    End If

    'Classify user as business or other
    nPos = Instr(LCase(f.txtEmail.Value),".com")
    If nPos <> 0 Then '.com = commercial domain
        sUserType = "BUSINESS"
    Else
        sUserType = "OTHER"
    End If

    'Put user type in hidden form field
    f.txtUserType.Value = sUserType

    'Submit the form
    f.Method = "POST"
    f.Action = "formproc.asp"
    f.submit

End Sub
-->
</SCRIPT>

<BODY>

 Please fill out all fields below:<BR><BR>

<FORM NAME=frmMain>

 Name:  <INPUT Type=Text maxlength=20 size=20 name=txtName>    <BR>
 Email: <INPUT Type=Text maxlength=30 size=30 name=txtEmail>   <BR>

 <INPUT Type=Hidden name=txtUserType>

 <INPUT Type=Button OnClick=submitform Value="Continue">
</FORM>

</BODY>
</HTML>
```

> **CAUTION**
> Remember, VBScript does not run in Netscape Navigator, so you may want to perform validation tasks on the server.

In Listing 30.3, many of the form tasks are handled in VBScript instead of HTML. For example, the ACTION and METHOD parameters are left out of the form declaration. No submit button was provided because the form was submitted from VBScript code. Also, notice the hidden form field, which stores a value that the user did not enter. A sample run of the page in Listing 30.3 is shown in Figure 30.8.

FIGURE 30.8
VBScript validates form data before submitting it to the Web server.

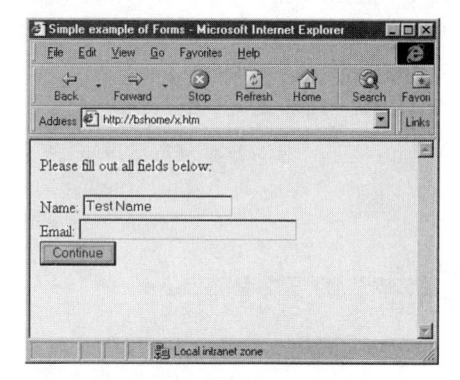

Using ActiveX Controls

In addition to creating objects with the CreateObject method, you can embed objects in your Web page by using the <OBJECT> tag. The <OBJECT> tag allows you to place ActiveX controls in a Web page. Your VBScript code can then access these objects, as in the list box example here:

```
<HTML>
<BODY>
<OBJECT id=lstmain classid=clsid:8BD21D20-EC42-11CE-9E0D-00AA006002F3
width=152 height=164>
<PARAM name=ScrollBars value=3>
<PARAM name=DisplayStyle value=2>
</OBJECT>

<SCRIPT Language = "VBScript">
<!--
    Dim i
    For i = 1 to 10
        lstMain.AddItem "Item " & i
    Next

    Sub lstMain_Click()
        Msgbox "You Clicked " & lstMain.List(lstMain.ListIndex)
    End Sub
```

```
-->
</SCRIPT>
</BODY>
</HTML>
```

The different parts of the <OBJECT> tag are as follows:

- ID—Indicates the name VBScript uses to identify the object, like the Name property in Visual Basic.
- CLASSID—Acts as a unique identifier from the Windows Registry that identifies the object.
- CODEBASE—Provides the URL for the OCX or CAB file used to download the object. In the example, the ListBox control is built into Internet Explorer, so the CODEBASE parameter is not needed.
- height and width—Indicate the size of the object.
- PARAM tags—Control behavior of an object, like the Properties window in Visual Basic.

The best way to insert ActiveX controls into a Web page is to do so in FrontPage and then copy the resulting HTML into your Web page. Figure 30.9 shows the list of ActiveX controls in FrontPage.

FIGURE 30.9
Class IDs can be determined by using FrontPage. The controls that begin with "Microsoft Forms" are built in, or intrinsic to, Internet Explorer and do not require downloading.

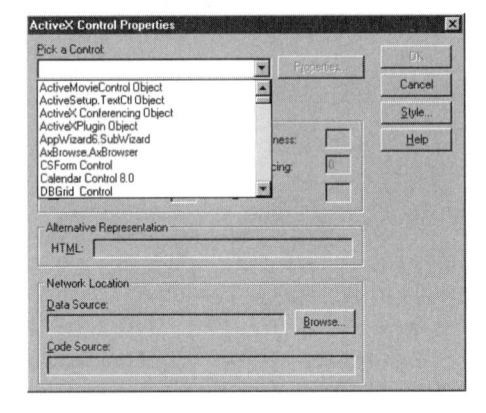

In Chapter 14, "Creating ActiveX Controls," you learned how to create your own ActiveX controls, which can be placed on a Web page. Using your own controls offers several advantages over plain VBScript and HTML, including the following:

- Full VB functionality is available.
- Your code cannot be easily viewed by the user, as with script code.

The Windows Scripting Host

In addition to VBScript's multiple uses on the Internet, Microsoft has also recently touted VBScript as a replacement for batch files. By installing the Windows Scripting Host, available for free at http://www.microsoft.com/scripting, you can run VBScript commands from an MS-DOS Prompt window or the Windows Explorer. The VBScript code itself is created in a text editor and stored in a file with a VBS extension.

Running Scripts

The Windows Scripting Host actually installs two hosts that can run VBScript code: CSCRIPT.EXE, which is designed for use in an MS-DOS Prompt window, and WSCRIPT.EXE, which is designed for execution from Windows.

To demonstrate the difference, create a VBS file that uses the `WScript.Echo` method, as in the following example:

```
WScript.Echo "Hello, world!"
```

Executing the preceding statement with CScript causes `"Hello, world!"` to be printed in the MS-DOS Prompt window. WScript, on the other hand, presents the text in a message box.

The simplest way of executing a script is to supply the script file name as a parameter to either of the preceding executables:

```
CScript.exe d:\scripts\test.vbs
```

You can also just double-click a script file in the Windows Explorer. However, several command-line options are available for the Scripting host, as listed in Table 30.5. These options must be preceded by two forward slashes (//) in the command line.

Table 30.5 Scripting Host Parameters

Parameters	Description
//B and //I	Selects batch or interactive mode. Batch mode does not display any prompts.
//logo and //nologo	Controls display of Microsoft copyright information.
//T:nn	Determines a script timeout in seconds. The script is stopped if execution time exceeds the timeout value.
//H:CScript	Makes CScript the host associated with your script files.
//H:WScript	Makes WScript the host associated with your script files.
//S	Saves these options (for the current Windows user only).

You can also place the options in Table 30.5 in a WSH file. A WSH file is like a PIF file for batch files; it contains the options in INI file format:

```
[ScriptFile]
Path=D:\scripts\test.vbs

[Options]
Timeout=10
```

```
DisplayLogo=0
BatchMode=0
```

Any arguments passed to the script itself are included after the scripting host options and script filename. You can retrieve them by using the `Arguments` collection of the `Wscript` object:

```
Dim nCount
nCount = WScript.Arguments.Count
WScript.Echo "There are " & nCount & " arguments."

For i = 0 to nCount - 1
 Wscript.Echo WScript.Arguments(i)
Next
```

Useful Objects and Methods

The usefulness of any object library depends on the types of objects and methods it exposes to the programmer. Since the Windows Scripting Host is intended to replace or supplement batch files, it includes many useful features for accessing the operating system, including the following:

- Creating desktop shortcuts
- Mapping network drives
- Accessing the Registry
- Working with automation objects
- Working with NT 5.0 user accounts

You can download sample code to perform all the tasks in the preceding list, along with complete documentation for the Windows Scripting Host, from the Microsoft Web Site. Three main objects let you perform these tasks. You have already seen the `WScript` object in sample code. The `WScript` object is available directly from VBScript.

ON THE WEB

The Windows Scripting Host, along with documentation and examples, can be downloaded from the Microsoft Scripting Technology Web page at http://www.microsoft.com/scripting.

Two other objects, `Shell` and `Network`, must be referenced through `WScript` by using the `CreateObject` function. For example, the following script uses the `Run` method of the `Shell` object to run a program and wait for it to finish:

```
Dim WshShell
Set WshShell = WScript.CreateObject("WScript.Shell")
'first parameter is Window Style, second is Wait
WshShell.Run "notepad",1,True
MsgBox "Done!"
```

As you work with the Windows Scripting Host, you will see that it contains tremendous power to automate Windows-based tasks.

From Here...

This chapter introduced you to a way to extend your Visual Basic skills to the Internet. You can learn more about related topics in the following chapters:

- To see how to use VBScript on Web servers to activate your Web pages, see Chapter 31, "Active Server Pages."
- For more information on how to Web-enable your standalone Visual Basic applications, see Chapter 33, "Visual Basic and Other Uses of the Internet."

CHAPTER 31

Active Server Pages

In this chapter

Introduction to Active Server Pages **688**

Creating ASP Files **693**

Database Access with Active Server Pages **697**

The ASP Objects **704**

Using Your Own ActiveX DLL with ASP **711**

The IIS Application Project **711**

As you move from page to page on the World Wide Web, you may wonder what sort of intelligence exists on the other end. For example, how does that online music store process orders submitted from its Web pages? How does the shipping company display your package status? The answer is that some type of program is running on the Web server, accepting input from you and dynamically generating Web pages with the results. In the UNIX world, these programs might be CGI scripts or C programs. However, Microsoft has recently entered this area with Active Server Pages, a Web-server component that allows you to use your Visual Basic knowledge to create powerful Web server scripts. This chapter introduces you to Active Server Pages and some of its many features.

Introduction to Active Server Pages

If you are developing an intranet or Internet application, Active Server Pages is definitely worth investigating. Active Server Pages (ASP) is a component of Microsoft's Web server software that allows you to embed server-side script code in Web pages. As you know, the Hypertext Markup Language (HTML), used to created pages on the World Wide Web, is by itself static content. You can enhance this content on the client side through the use of client-side script, Java applets, Dynamic HTML, or ActiveX controls. However, Active Server Pages is a server-side enhancement, because all the script code (usually VBScript) runs on the server. This means you can create Web sites that are dynamic and database-driven, yet return only standard HTML that is viewable in all browsers. A solution that uses Active Server Pages is ideal when your audience includes both Netscape and IE users or you want to avoid the issues associated with downloading applets or other client-side controls.

NOTE Microsoft's Web server product for the Windows NT operating system is called Internet Information Server (IIS). In addition, Microsoft Personal Web Server is available as a "lightweight" Web server for a desktop PC. The Active Server Pages component is built-in to both Web servers, which at the time of this writing were available for download in the NT/95 Option Pack. For a glimpse at some of the differences between these products, see the upcoming section "Virtual Directories."

Active Server Pages Versus Standard HTML

Internet Information Server identifies an Active Server Page by its .ASP extension. To create a new ASP file, you simply change the extension on an existing .HTM file or start a new text file in a text editor. The ASP file can contain either standard HTML or script code, but usually contains some of both. The script code is what makes an Active Server Page different from a standard HTML page.

Consider the URL, or Universal Resource Locator, that identifies documents on the Web. Here are two URLs, one for a standard Web page and the other for an Active Server Page:

`http://www.mysite.com/mypage.htm`

`http://www.mysite.com/mypage.asp`

A conventional URL (the first line) represents only a single static Web page. On the other hand, one Active Server Page (the second line) can produce many different Web pages in a user's browser, all from a single URL.

Think about how browsing works: through request-and-response communication between the browser and the Internet server. No matter what the Web server does, the end result is that a stream of HTML is returned to the browser in response to a request. When that request is for a standard .HTM file, it simply reads the file from the disk drive and passes it back to the browser. However, when the Internet server processes an .ASP file, it executes any embedded code during the process. This embedded script code can take different actions on the server, including generate the HTML that is returned to the browser.

For example, suppose you want to create a Web page that displays the time of day when it is requested. The time of day is dynamic and cannot easily be placed in a standard static HTML page. However, you can do this easily with an Active Server Page, such as the one shown in Listing 31.1.

Listing 31.1 ASPDEMO.ZIP—A Simple Active Server Page Displays the Date and Time

```
<HTML>
<BODY>

The Current date and time is
<%
   Dim sTime
   sTime = Now
   Response.Write(sTime)
%>

</BODY>
</HTML>
```

This ASP file in Listing 31.1 displays the current date and time. It contains a mixture of standard HTML and VBScript code. If you access the ASP file on your Web server, each time you press the browser's Refresh button, the server will execute the VBScript code, updating the date and time. However, if a user chooses to view the source in his browser, he will only see the resulting HTML:

```
<HTML>
<BODY>

The Current date and time is
7/5/1998 12:30:00

</BODY>
</HTML>
```

Notice that the server-side VBScript code is hidden from the user, because it is never sent back to the browser. Because the code runs on the server, it can access databases or use custom components, as shown in Figure 31.1.

FIGURE 31.1
Server-side scripting allows you to create powerful Web sites.

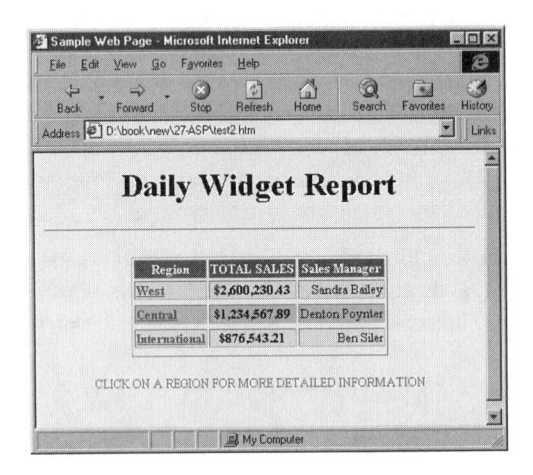

Virtual Directories

Before you can jump right in and use Active Server Pages, you have to do a little Web server administration. As you know, the files on your Web site are located in a directory on the Web server hard drive—for example, C:\InetPub\wwwroot\financeinfo\. This path is known as the *physical directory*, because it points to an actual location on the server's hard drive. However, when a user on the Internet wants to access files in this directory, he uses an URL like http://myserver/finance/Monthlyreport.htm. How does Internet Information Server map the address in the URL to the appropriate physical directory? The answer is through the use of *virtual directories*.

In our example, the Web server knows that the virtual directory /finance is really the financeinfo subdirectory. Virtual directories act as an alias to real directories. Virtual directories, as well as many other important aspects of the Web server, are controlled with the Internet Service Manager. (Similarly, Personal Web Server is managed with Personal Web Manager.) Screenshots of Internet Service Manager and Personal Web Manager are shown in Figure 31.2.

Creating Virtual Directories for ASP Files The process of creating a virtual directory is simple. Follow these steps:

1. Use Windows Explorer or the MS-DOS prompt to create a new physical directory (for example, \Inetpub\wwwroot\test).

2. Open the Internet Service Manager, which should have been installed in a program group on your server.

   NOTE IIS can be managed remotely if you have administrative authority on the Web server.

Introduction to Active Server Pages

3. The process of creating a virtual directory differs slightly in different versions of the Internet Service Manager: Each version of this software is pictured in Figure 31.2.
   - Directories tab, and click the New button.
   - If you have IIS 4.0, right-click your Web site and choose New Virtual directory.
   - If you are using Personal Web Manager, click the Advanced icon and then the Add button.

FIGURE 31.2
Internet Information Server 3.0, 4.0, and Personal Web Server have different administration tools.

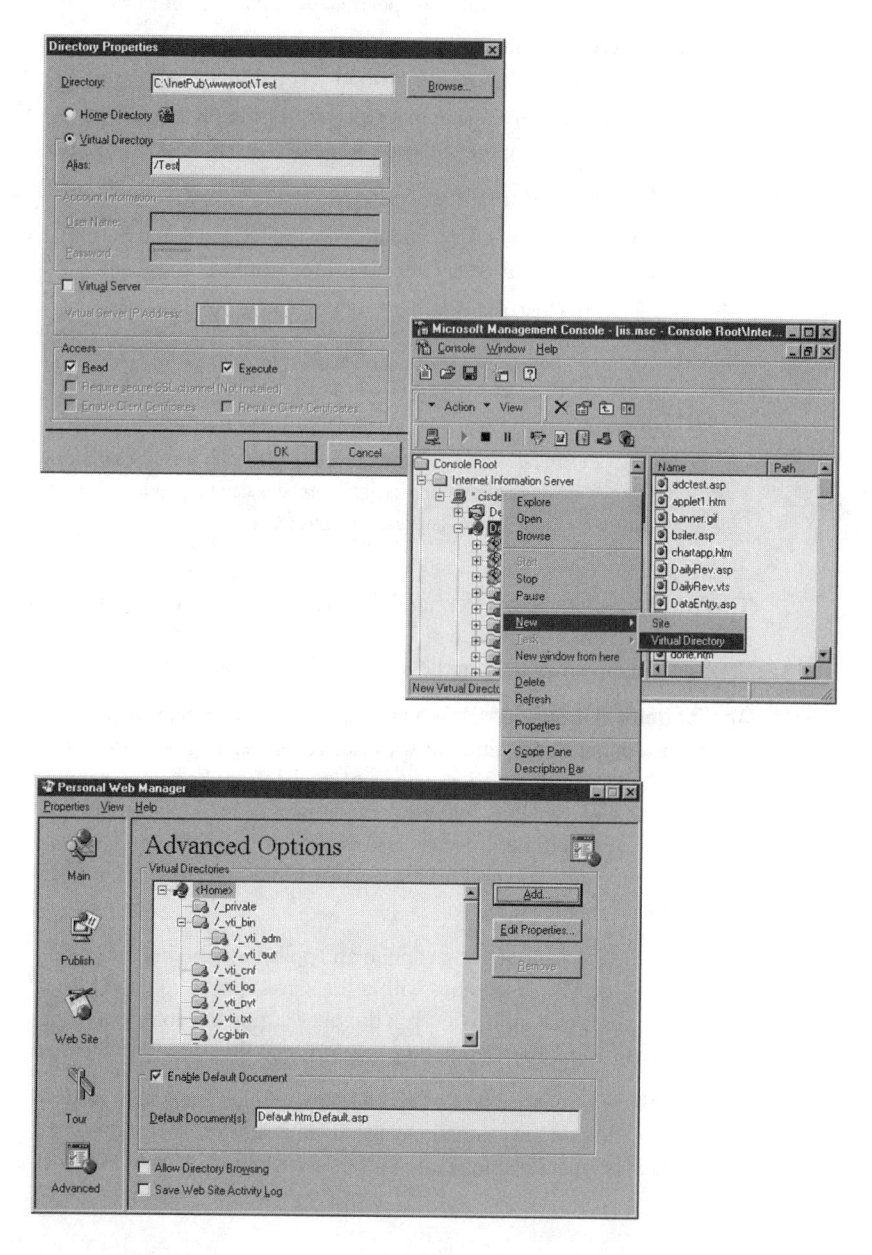

4. Specify the physical directory (which you can find with the Browse button) and the virtual directory (also known as the *alias*). For your sample, enter /test as the alias for the new directory.

5. The next step is to set the appropriate permissions for the new directory. You should see several choices available:

   - Read permission allows users to read files from the virtual directory. In general, you should enable this permission on all of your virtual directories.
   - Script permission means that scripts can be executed from the virtual directory. You need to check this option if you intend to use ASP files in the directory.
   - Execute permission is script permission plus the ability to execute other programs. (Script permission was not a separate choice in IIS 3.0.)
   - Write permission allows users to upload files to a directory.

   For this sample directory, you need to enable Read and Script permissions. (If you are using IIS 3.0, enable Read and Execute permissions.)

6. Press OK to close the new directory window. You are now ready to begin placing ASP files in the directory.

> **CAUTION**
> Because ASP code executes on your server, think very carefully about directory permissions. If you give a virtual directory Write and Execute permission, potentially anyone on the Internet could upload his own .ASP file and execute it on your server—a very dangerous situation!

That's it! Now that you have created the /test virtual directory, you can place ASP files in it and execute them from a browser. You create your first sample ASP file and use it with the /test virtual directory later in the section "Creating a Simple ASP File."

Applications and Sessions   When designing a Web site, directory layout is important from an organizational standpoint, but with Active Server Pages it becomes even more important because the virtual directories represent *applications*. In our previous example, the /test directory and the files contained within it are considered to be an ASP application. Subdirectories underneath virtual directories are also part of the application. For example, if you use Windows Explorer to create a subdirectory underneath the /test directory, then the new directory is part of the test application.

When a user first accesses any page in an application, he initiates a new *session* with the application. As long as the user stays within the same application and keeps loading Web pages, he is "in" the same session. However, if the user jumps to another application, closes the browser, or stops browsing for an extended period of time then the Web server ends the session.

Why are these semantics important? As you will see, Active Server Pages contain objects and events that allow you to maintain state within a session. In other words, you can store session- and application-specific information on the server and share it between multiple ASP files.

Creating ASP Files

To create ASP files, you can use a text editor such as Notepad or a more advanced tool like Visual InterDev. In any case, your ASP file can consist of any mix of HTML and code. However, some of your pages will probably contain all code, while others will have only standard HTML. The code you write in an ASP file is script code, like the VBScript code discussed in Chapter 30, "Using VBScript."

In the following section, you create and experiment with a simple ASP file. Subsequent sections explore more involved issues in creating ASP files.

Creating a Simple ASP File

Using the same code shown earlier in Listing 31.1 and the virtual /test directory you created in the preceding section, you can create a basic ASP file and experiment with using it. Follow these steps:

1. Enter the following code in Notepad or another text editor:

   ```
   <HTML>
   <BODY>
   
   The Current date and time is
   <%
      Dim sTime
      sTime = Now
      Response.Write(sTime)
   %>
   
   </BODY>
   </HTML>
   ```

2. Name the file THETIME.ASP and save it to the /test directory.

3. Open the file in your browser using the URL `http://myserver/test/thetime.asp`, where *myserver* is the name of your NT server or PC.

   If your code does not run but is instead displayed on the screen, make sure that the file has an .ASP extension and the virtual directory has the correct permissions.

> **NOTE** Microsoft's Web server software allows you to specify default document names (usually DEFAULT.ASP and DEFAULT.HTM). This means a user does not have to carry the URL out to the file level—for example, `http://myserver/test/` automatically displays the DEFAULT.ASP or DEFAULT.HTM file, if it exists in the /test directory.

Using Server-Side Scripting Tags

When processing an ASP file, the Web server only executes the code designated as server-side script. All other parts of an ASP file are sent directly back to the browser. In your ASP files, the server-side code can be marked in a couple of different ways:

- Use the HTML `<SCRIPT>` tag with the `RUNAT=SERVER` option.
- Use `<%` and `%>` to mark the beginning and end of the server-side script. This syntax is shorter and is the one I recommend.

However you decide to mark the script, make sure to place it *within* the script delimiters, as in the following examples:

```
<SCRIPT LANGUAGE="VBSCRIPT" RUNAT="SERVER">
Dim i
For i = 1 to 10
    Response.Write ("This is line " & i & "<BR>")
Next
</SCRIPT>
```

The same code can also be marked with the shorter tags:

```
<%
Dim i
For i = 1 to 10
    Response.Write ("This is line " & i & "<BR>")
Next
%>
```

Notice that you do not need to specify a scripting language in the second example. This is because the default scripting language for ASP files is VBScript. However, the default scripting language is a configurable option, so you might want to place the following line at the beginning of each of your ASP files:

```
<%@ LANGUAGE="VBSCRIPT" %>
```

This line is a directive to the script engine that sets the default language to VBScript for the current ASP page. Although your script tags can be placed anywhere in the ASP file, there are a few restrictions:

- Certain directives and options, like the previous line of code and the `Option Explicit` statement, must be placed at the very beginning of the file, even before the `<HTML>` tag.
- If your page is used to redirect the user to another side, you cannot send any HTML back to the browser. (You get a demonstration of this in an upcoming section.)
- You cannot enter straight HTML inside the script tags, unless you use the `Response.Write` statement.

Also, keep in mind that the code you are entering is VBScript, not the full-featured Visual Basic language. There are some differences and limitations, as discussed in Chapter 30, "Using VBScript."

▶ See "Introduction to VBScript," **p. 666**
▶ See "The VBScript Language," **p. 673**

Simple but Dynamic Web Pages

Now that you know the basics, let's write another simple ASP file. At my office there is a computer named `cdtower` which, as you might have guessed, is attached to a tower of CD-ROM drives. The purpose of the machine is to allow people on the LAN to connect and install software. However, because people are always swapping and borrowing CD-ROMs, it is hard to know at a given time which CD is in each drive. It would be great if there was a way to automatically keep track of the CDs on a Web page. Fortunately, with Personal Web Server and Active Server Pages, this task is very easy to accomplish.

You use VBScript's `FileSystemObject` to determine the volume labels of each drive on a computer. By placing this VBScript code in an ASP file where the code executes on the server, you can have the volume labels of the server's CD drives displayed on a remote browser. The code, shown in Listing 31.2, is fairly straightforward.

Listing 31.2 ASPDEMO.ZIP—VOLLABEL.ASP

```
<HTML>
<BODY>
<H1>Drive List</H1><HR>
<%
        Dim objFileSys
        Dim objDrives
        Dim objDrive

    'IGNORE DISK NOT READY ERRORS
    On Error Resume Next

        'CREATE REFERENCES TO FILE SYSTEM AND DRIVES COLLECTION
        Set objFileSys = Server.CreateObject("Scripting.FileSystemObject")
        Set objDrives = objFileSys.Drives

        'DISPLAY VOLUME LABELS
        For Each objDrive in objDrives
            if objDrive.DriveLetter > "C" Then
                Response.Write ("The CD in Drive " & objDrive.DriveLetter)
                Response.Write (" is " & objDrive.VolumeName & ". <BR> ")
            End If
        Next

        'CLEAN UP!
        Set objDrives = Nothing
        Set objFileSys = Nothing
%>
</BODY>
</HTML>
```

When a user accesses this page, the section of VBScript code executes on the Web server. The Web page in Listing 31.2 accomplishes its purpose, but leaves a lot to be desired in terms of formatting. It would appear neater if you used some HTML formatting codes, such as the <TABLE> tag. This can be easily accomplished by modifying the Response.Write statements. (As you probably have gathered by now, Response.Write is used in an ASP file to send HTML back to the browser.)

In your example, you display the `VolumeID` property of the `Drive` object. It would be nice to also display a more informative description. You can accomplish this by creating a custom function, `sDescription`, that returns a description for a given volume:

```
Function sDescription(sVolID)
  Select Case UCase(sVolID)
    Case "BACKUP0398"
      sDescription = "Backup of critical files 3/98"
    Case "DN_60ENUD2"
      sDescription = "Developer's Network CD #2"

    ' Add more descriptions here

    Case Else
      sDescription = "Unknown"
  End Select
End Function
```

You can create your own subroutines and functions in ASP files, just like Visual Basic. To create the `sDescription` function, simply enter the function at the top of the section of VBScript code. The scope of the function will be for the current ASP page; you can call it just like a standard VB function:

```
Response.Write sDescription(objDrive.VolumeName)
```

The final ASP page, with table and description enhancements, is shown in Figure 31.3.

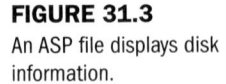

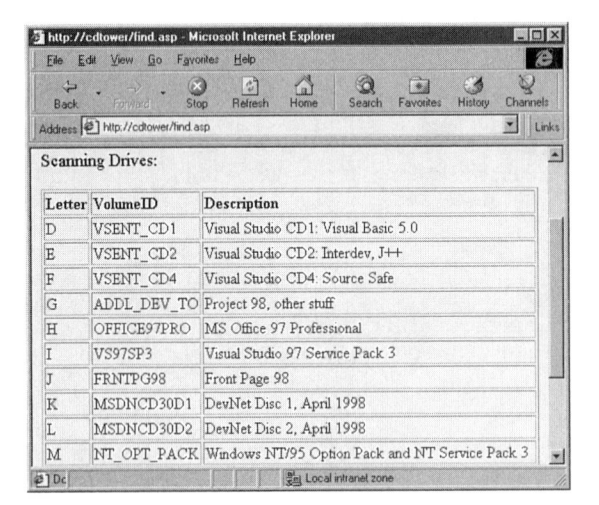

FIGURE 31.3
An ASP file displays disk information.

Using Include Files

When you write VBScript code in Active Server Pages, you can create functions and subroutines at the beginning of your page and call them throughout the Active Server Page. You might, for example, create a subroutine that accepts a number and generates HTML based on the number:

```
Sub DisplayAmount(nAmount)
    Dim sHTML

    sHTML = "<FONT "
    If nAmount < 2000 Then sHTML = sHTML & "COLOR=RED"
    If nAmount > 4000 Then sHTML = sHTML & "COLOR=GREEN"
    sHTML = sHTML & ">"

    sHTML = sHTML & FormatCurrency(nAmount)
    sHTML = sHTML & "</FONT>"
    Response.Write sHTML
End Sub
```

The `DisplayAmount` subroutine accepts a numeric value and then colors and formats it based on the value itself. Procedures like this one would be very useful in many ASP files, but there is no way to declare this subroutine as public to all ASP files. You could cut and paste it into each file, but maintaining all the copies of it would become a chore. The answer to this problem is to move the function to a separate file and include it where necessary. To include other files in the current ASP file, use the `#INCLUDE` statement. Two example files are as follows:

```
<!—#INCLUDE VIRTUAL = "/test/formatfuncs.asp"—>
```

```
<!— #INCLUDE FILE="C:\Inetpub\wwwroot\test\formatfuncs.asp" —>
```

The first line of code uses the virtual directory to specify an include file. The next statement uses the physical directory. Either way, the end result is that the contents of `formatfuncs.asp` are inserted into the current ASP file before script execution. Some common uses of the `#INCLUDE` directive are to add footers at the bottom of each Web page, such as the company name or e-mail address.

Database Access with Active Server Pages

Suppose you want to publish the contents of a database on the Web. With ASP, you can use ADO objects in your VBScript code to access databases. As discussed in Chapter 28, "Using ActiveX Data Objects (ADO)," to access a database you first need to identify a *data source*. The actual database can be located on the Web server itself or on another machine, as long as you can connect to it via a data source.

When setting up data sources for use with ASP, you generally should use a System Data Source Name (DSN) rather than a User DSN. The System DSN allows the data source to be available to the Web server at all times, not just when a certain user is logged in.

▶ **See** "Setting Up a Data Source," **p. 613**

> **N O T E** You can also use a DSN-less connection that does not require you to set up a data source. This is also discussed in Chapter 28. ■

In this section, the examples assume that the BIBLIO data source has been set up as described in Chapter 26, "Using Data Access Objects (DAO)."

▶ **See** "Setting Up a DAO Project," **p. 567**

> **NOTE** If you have problems connecting to a Microsoft SQL Server data source using standard security on a different machine from the Web server, you might receive an error like `Connection Open error` in the function `CreateFile()`. This means that the NT account making the connection (usually the `I_USR` account) does not have sufficient authority on the NT SQL server.

Querying a Database

With what you have read up to this point, you have all of the knowledge necessary to run an ADO database query and display the results in a Web page. However, even a small database like BIBLIO.MDB has many records. Therefore, you need to provide some way to query the database for just the records that the user wants to see, which of course means you need to accept user input.

Setting Up a Sample Query Page The `<FORM>` tag built in to the HTML language allows user input to be sent to the Web server. Let's set up an HTML form, DBQUERY.HTM, that allows the user to enter an author's name to search for. Simply enter the HTML code in Listing 31.3 and save it on the Web server.

Listing 31.3 ASPDEMO.ZIP—DBQUERY.HTM is a Standard HTML Form

```
<HTML><BODY>
<H1>Biblio Database Search</H1><HR>

<FORM ACTION=dbsearch.asp METHOD=POST>

Enter Author to search for:
<INPUT TYPE=TEXT NAME=txtSearch>
<INPUT TYPE=SUBMIT VALUE="Begin Search">

</FORM>

</BODY></HTML>
```

> **NOTE** An HTML form consists of different types of `<INPUT>` tags, which appear in the user's browser as data entry fields. The contents of these fields are sent to the Web server when the user "submits" a form.

Note that the code in Listing 31.3 is not an ASP page. It contains no VBScript statements and has the standard .HTM extension. It simply submits an HTML form to an ASP page called DBSEARCH.ASP. The purpose of DBSEARCH.ASP, shown in Listing 31.4, is to perform the actual search.

Writing DBSEARCH.ASP is fairly easy, as well. You basically have three things to do:

1. Retrieve the value the user wants to search for from the form field `txtSearch` and use it to build a query.

2. Execute the query using ADO to obtain a recordset.
3. Send the contents of the recordset back to the user's browser.

The code for DBSEARCH.ASP, shown in Listing 31.4, uses the Like statement in the SQL query.

Listing 31.4 ASPDEMO.ZIP—DBSEARCH.ASP Performs the Database Search

```
<HTML><BODY>
<%
   Dim cn
   Dim rs
   Dim sSQL
   Dim sSearchString

   'GET THE SEARCH STRING FROM THE FORM
   sSearchString = Request.Form("txtSearch")

   If sSearchString = "" Then
      Response.Write ("No search string entered!")
      Response.End
   End If

   'CONNECT TO THE DATABASE AND PERFORM THE SEARCH
   Set cn = Server.CreateObject("ADODB.Connection")
        cn.Open "DSN=BIBLIO"

   sSQL = "SELECT * FROM AUTHORS WHERE AUTHOR LIKE "
   sSQL = sSQL & "'" & sSearchString & "%' ORDER BY AUTHOR"

   Set rs = cn.Execute(sSQL)

%>
<TABLE BORDER=1>
<TR>Author's Name</TR>
<%

   'DISPLAY THE RESULTS IN A TABLE
   While Not rs.EOF
      Response.Write ("<TR><TD>")
      Response.Write rs.Fields("Author")
      Response.Write ("<TD></TR>")
            rs.MoveNext
   Wend

   rs.Close
   cn.Close
   Set rs = Nothing
   Set cn = Nothing
%>
</TABLE>
</BODY></HTML>
```

After you have created DBQUERY.HTM and DBSEARCH.ASP, you should be able to open the URL for DBQUERY.HTM, enter a few letters of the alphabet, and have the matching records displayed in the browser (see Figures 31.4 and 31.5).

FIGURE 31.4.
This page contains a standard HTML form that allows the user to enter a value and post it to an ASP page for processing.

FIGURE 31.5
VBScript code on the server returns the contents of a recordset in the form of an HTML table.

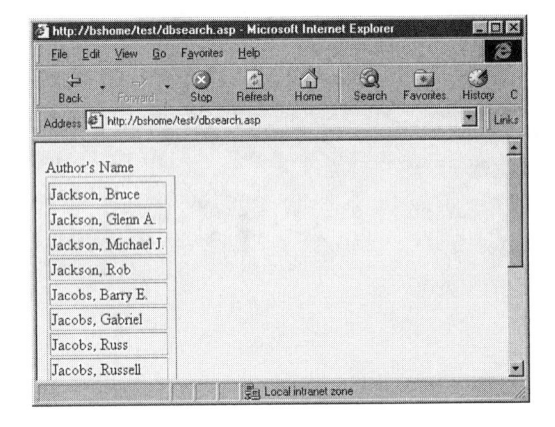

> **NOTE** In your database search example, you used separate ASP and HTM files. You could have just as easily combined the two files into a single ASP file. The only change you would need to make would be to have the form action refer to the same page. You might also want to use an `if` statement to check for the form value to see if you need to display the results:
>
> ```
> <% If Request.Form("txtSearch") <> "" Then DisplayResults %>
> ```
>
> The preceding line of code assumes that you have written a custom function, `DisplayResults`, to execute the query.

Displaying Data with Drill-Down Links   The code in Listings 31.3 and 31.4 uses an HTML form field to retrieve the search criteria from the user. The user must first type a value into a text box and press a button. However, many times it is more convenient to use hyperlinks to perform database navigation. For example, suppose you want to allow the user to click an author's name in the list of authors to display the books by that author. You can do this very easily by generating hyperlinks for each author. To generate these hyperlinks, modify the `While` loop code from Listing 31.4 as follows:

```
'DISPLAY THE RESULTS IN A TABLE
While Not rs.EOF
   Response.Write ("<TR><TD><A HREF=author.asp?id=")
   Response.Write rs.fields("AU_ID") & ">"
   Response.Write rs.Fields("Author")
   Response.Write ("</A><TD></TR>")
         rs.MoveNext
Wend
```

Run a search, and each author's name in the resulting list should appear as a hyperlink to a new ASP file, AUTHOR.ASP. If you choose View Source in your browser, you will see that each hyperlink is unique:

`<A HREF=author.asp?id=16061>Jackson, Bruce</A>`

The preceding line of HTML passes a parameter `id` to the ASP page AUTHOR.ASP. If you click the hyperlink, the browser will ask the server for this URL:

`http://bshome/test/author.asp?id=16061`

Note that the URL includes the `id` parameter, which is separated from the base (or target) URL by a question mark. If there were additional parameters, they would be separated by an ampersand (&). The syntax for using parameters in a URL is as follows:

`http://targetURL ? parm1name=parm1value & parm2name=parm2value & parm3name=parm3value etc...`

The collection of parameters in an URL is also known as the query string and can be retrieved with the `QueryString` collection of the `Request` object:

`If Request.QueryString("id") = "" Then Response.Write "No ID entered!"`

As with the `Request.Form` example in Listing 31.4, the value passed to an ASP page in the query string can be retrieved and used in a database query:

```
    sSQL = "SELECT Title FROM [Title Author], [Titles] "
sSQL = sSQL & " WHERE [Title Author].ISBN = [Titles].ISBN "
sSQL = sSQL & " and [Title Author].AU_ID=" & Request.QueryString("id")
```

As an exercise, create AUTHOR.ASP using the preceding query. Except for the database field names, the structure of the ASP file should be identical to that in Listing 31.4.

Updating Information in a Database

Displaying data with ASP is useful, but at some point you also need to add or edit information. The previous section described two ways to get input from a client's browser to an ASP page:

- Posting with HTML forms
- Adding parameters to the URL querystring

Both of these methods are useful and appropriate in certain cases, but using the POST method with HTML forms is much more versatile. In the examples shown so far, you have only used the TEXT input field. However, there are many types of HTML form elements that can be used, such as radio buttons, drop-down boxes, and free-form text areas. One type of field that is very useful when dealing with database updates is a HIDDEN form field. A hidden form field is like a text field, but the user cannot see it or change its value. This type of field can be generated from an ASP page and sent down to the browser. When the user submits a form, the value of a hidden form field is sent back to the server with the other form fields.

Revisit the example in Listings 31.3 and 31.4 and add edit capability for the author's name and birth year. In addition, you will consolidate all of the functionality from the previous example into subroutines in a single ASP page:

- AskForAuthors takes the place of DBQUERY.HTM.
- GetAuthorList replaces DBSEARCH.ASP.
- DisplayEditScreen is a new procedure, which displays a form that allows you to edit an author's information.
- UpdateDBInfo changes the database.

The code for the new ASP page, AUTHOREDIT.ASP, is shown in Listing 31.5.

Listing 31.5 ASPDEMO.ZIP—ASP Page Allowing Searching and Editing

```
<HTML><BODY>
<%
Dim cn
Dim rs
Dim sSQL
Const MYASPNAME="authoredit.asp"

Sub AskForAuthors()

    Response.Write ("<H1>Biblio Database Search</H1><HR>")
    Response.Write ("<FORM ACTION=" & MYASPNAME & "?mode=search METHOD=POST>")
    Response.Write ("Enter Author to search for:")
    Response.Write ("<INPUT TYPE=TEXT NAME=txtSearch>")
    Response.Write ("<INPUT TYPE=SUBMIT VALUE=""Click to Search"">")
    Response.Write ("</FORM>")

End Sub

Sub GetAuthorList()

    'CONNECT TO THE DATABASE AND PERFORM THE SEARCH
    Set cn = Server.CreateObject("ADODB.Connection")
        cn.Open "DSN=BIBLIO"

    sSQL = "SELECT * FROM AUTHORS WHERE AUTHOR LIKE "
    sSQL = sSQL & "'" & Request.Form("txtSearch")
    sSQL = sSQL & "%' ORDER BY AUTHOR"
    Set rs = cn.Execute(sSQL)
```

```
    'DISPLAY THE RESULTS IN A TABLE
    Response.Write("<TABLE BORDER=1><TR>Author's Name</TR>")
    While Not rs.EOF
        Response.Write ("<TR><TD><A HREF=" & MYASPNAME & "?id=")
        Response.Write rs.fields("AU_ID") & "&mode=dispedit>"
        Response.Write rs.Fields("Author")
        Response.Write ("</A><TD></TR>")

                rs.MoveNext
    Wend

    rs.Close
    cn.Close
End Sub

Sub DisplayEditScreen()

    'CONNECT TO THE DATABASE AND GET THIS AUTHOR'S INFO
    Set cn = Server.CreateObject("ADODB.Connection")
        cn.Open "DSN=BIBLIO"

    sSQL = "SELECT * FROM AUTHORS WHERE AU_ID= " & Request.QueryString("id")
    Set rs = cn.Execute(sSQL)

    'GENERATE THE HTML FORM
    Response.Write ("<H1>Edit Author Information</H1><HR>")
    Response.Write ("<FORM ACTION=" & MYASPNAME & "?mode=updatedata
METHOD=POST>")

    Response.Write ("Name:<INPUT TYPE=TEXT NAME=txtName")
    Response.Write (" VALUE='" & rs.Fields("Author") & "'><BR>")
    Response.Write ("Year Born:<INPUT TYPE=TEXT NAME=txtYear")
    Response.Write (" VALUE='" & rs.Fields("Year Born") & "'><BR>")
    Response.Write ("<INPUT TYPE=HIDDEN NAME=AuthorID VALUE=")
    Response.Write (rs.Fields("AU_ID") & ">")

    Response.Write ("<INPUT TYPE=SUBMIT VALUE=""Update Info"">")
    Response.Write ("</FORM>")

End Sub

Sub UpdateDBInfo()

    'CONNECT TO THE DATABASE
    Set cn = Server.CreateObject("ADODB.Connection")
        cn.Open "DSN=BIBLIO"

    'BUILD SQL UPDATE STATEMENT
    sSQL = "UPDATE AUTHORS SET Author='" & Request.Form("txtName") & "',"
    sSQL = sSQL & "[Year Born]=" & Request.Form("txtYear")
    sSQL = sSQL & " WHERE AU_ID=" & Request.Form("AuthorID")
    cn.Execute(sSQL)
```

continues

Listing 31.5   Continued

```
        'DISPLAY A MESSAGE
        Response.Write ("<H1> Information Updated!</H1>")
        AskForAuthors
End Sub


Select Case Request.QueryString("mode")
    Case "search"
        GetAuthorList
    Case "dispedit"
        DisplayEditScreen
    Case "updatedata"
        UpdateDBInfo
    Case Else
        AskForAuthors
End Select

Set rs = Nothing
Set cn = Nothing
%>
</TABLE>
</BODY></HTML>
```

> **NOTE** When working with user input, be wary of the quote character. You might need to write a function to manipulate quotes in a form field before using the field value in a SQL statement.

Listing 31.5 is a single ASP file, yet it generates four distinct HTML screens. The query string parameter `mode` determines what action the ASP page performs.

The ASP Objects

Active Server Pages has several built-in objects accessible from script code. So far, you have seen some examples of the `Response` and the `Server` objects. In this section, you explore these objects in a little more detail and give examples of their uses. The objects are as follows:

- Session
- Response
- Request
- Server
- Application

Managing Security with the *Session* Object

As alluded to earlier, IIS has features that allow your ASP application to retain information between pages. You can, for example, have a form where the user selects a country from a list and then submits that value to an ASP page. The ASP page can store this value on the server so it is available to other ASP pages. This is accomplished through the use of *Session variables*. Session variables are declared and accessed like a collection. To create a session variable, simply give it a name and value:

```
Session("Country")="United States"
```

One frequent use of ASP session variables is to manage security. When database information is on the Internet, you probably do not want everyone in the world to be able to update it. Additionally, you might want to restrict access so that only certain people can see certain information. If you want to add security to your Web site, the obvious solution is to display some type of login page so that only valid users can get into your site. Your login page can be a simple HTML form with fields for user name and password. The form submits these values to an ASP file that checks the user name and password for validity.

But even if you add such a login page, how do you prevent users from simply entering the URL they want and bypassing the login screen? The answer is to use session variables. Suppose you have an ASP file, REPORT.ASP, that you want to secure. You can add a simple If statement at the top of the page to verify that a session variable has been set:

```
<%
    If Session("UserName")="" Then
        Response.Write "You are not logged in!<BR>"
        Response.End
    End If

    Response.Write ("Welcome, " & Session("UserName"))
%>
```

The If statement checks the contents of a session variable called UserName and ends the response from the Web server if the value is empty. In other words, the contents of REPORT.ASP after the If statement are available only to users who have the session variable UserName set to a value.

> **TIP** If you have multiple pages that you want to secure, use an include file to make the security check easier to maintain.

To validate a user login and set the UserName session variable, you need to write some ASP code. This code, shown in Listing 31.6, checks the information from the login form and sets the session variable if the user's password is correct.

Listing 31.6 ASPDEMO.ZIP—CHECKUSER.ASP Verifying Logins Against a Database

```asp
<%
   Dim cn
   Dim rs
   Dim sCheckName
   Dim sCheckPW

   'CLEAR SESSION VARIABLE
   Session("UserName")=""

   'GET USERNAME AND PASSWORD FROM THE FORM
   sCheckName = Request.Form("txtusername")
   sCheckPW = Request.Form("txtpassword")

   'IF THEY DIDN'T ENTER ANYTHING THEN RETURN TO LOGIN PAGE
   If sCheckName = "" then Response.Redirect "login.html"

   'CHECK USER PASSWORD IN THE DATABASE
   Set cn = Server.CreateObject("ADODB.Connection")
        cn.Open "Driver=Microsoft Access Driver
(*.mdb);DBQ=C:\data\security.mdb"
   sSQL = "SELECT * FROM UserList WHERE UserName='" & sCheckName & "'"
   Set rs = cn.Execute(sSQL)

   'IF THEY AREN'T IN DATABASE THEN RETURN TO LOGIN PAGE
   If rs.EOF Then
      rs.Close
      cn.Close
      Response.Redirect "login.html"
   End If

   'IF PASSWORD DOESN'T MATCH THEN RETURN TO LOGIN PAGE
   If UCase(rs.Fields("Password")) <> UCase(sCheckPW) Then
      rs.Close
      cn.Close
      Response.Redirect "login.html"
   End If

   rs.Close
   cn.Close

   'PASSWORD IS VALID! - SET SESSION VARIABLE
   Session("UserName")=sCheckName

   'GO ON TO REPORT PAGE
   response.redirect "report.asp"

%>
```

The code in Listing 31.6 makes use of the Response.Redirect command, which redirects the user's browser to a new URL. Unless he or she enters a valid user name and password, he or she is continuously redirected back to the login page. If this were a real application, you might want to have a counter that alerts an administrator after a certain number of failed attempts.

> **CAUTION**
> The type of security described here can be thought of as *application-level* security. It does not provide *network-level* security. For example, someone could use specialized hardware to listen to the network transmissions to and from the Web server—much like tapping a telephone line—to determine your password. To prevent this kind of spying, you need to investigate a secure connection using the `https` protocol.

Because a browser operates on a request-and-response basis, the user does not really establish a continuous connection with the Web server. Therefore, the server has no real way of knowing when the connection is broken, so a session will timeout after a certain number of minutes. You control this with the `TimeOut` property of the `Session` object:

```
Session.TimeOut = 60
```

Executing the previous statement causes the timeout to be set to 60 minutes. After 60 minutes of inactivity, the server ends the user's session, destroying any session variables. You can also purposely end a session with the `Abandon` method, as in the following line of code:

```
Session.Abandon
```

Controlling Output with the *Response* Object

Another useful object in Active Server Pages is the `Response` object. You have already been introduced to `Response.Write`, which is used to send HTML or other text back to the browser.

The *Response.Write* Statement   You can build a string in the `Response.Write` statement by using the string concatenation operator (&), as in the following example:

```
<%
Response.Write ("Hello, " & Session("USERID") & "<BR>")
%>
```

> **NOTE**   You can also use the short script tags and the equals sign (=) to send the contents of a variable back to the browser, as in the following example:
>
> ```
> Hello, <% =Session("USERID") %><BR>
> ```
>
> I prefer using the `Response.Write` method, but this short form is good when you need to embed a simple value in your HTML.

In addition to standard HTML, you can use `Response.Write` to generate client-side script from the server. For example, consider the following segment of ASP code:

```
<%
sString = "This is an ASP variable"
Response.Write (vbCrLf & "<SCRIPT LANGUAGE=VBScript>" & vbCrLf)
```

```
Response.Write ("Msgbox " & Chr(34) & sString & Chr(34) & vbCrLf)
Response.Write ("</SCRIPT>" & vbCrLf )
%>
```

The preceding code actually generates VBScript statements that will be executed by the browser. The `Response.Write` statements execute on the server, causing `<SCRIPT>` tags and code to be sent back to the browser. In other words, you use code in an ASP page to generate code for the browser. This might seem confusing at first, but if you type in the example and view the source in the browser, it will make more sense. Also, note that you paid particular attention to quotes and carriage returns in the client code, just as if you had entered it manually.

One use of server-generated client script is to control an ActiveX object embedded in a Web page. For example, your ASP page could contain the `<OBJECT>` tag for a list box or other control, plus the dynamically generated statements to add specific data items to it.

The *Response* Object and Other Methods   In the security example, you learned about two other methods of the `Response` object: `Redirect` and `End`. The `End` is used to end the current response to the client, as in this example:

```
<H1> Here is some HTML the browser will see! </H1>
<% Response.End %>
<H1> but the browser will never see this! </H1>
```

The `Redirect` method is used to ask the browser to move to a new URL, as in the following example:

```
<% Response.Redirect ("http://www.callsomeonewhocares.com/" %>
```

The previous line of code only works if no HTML has been returned. In other words, if you attempt to use `Response.Redirect` after a `Response.Write`, an error occurs.

One property of the `Response` object that you should have mentioned in the security section is the `Expires` property. As you might know, the browser stores everything it reads from the Internet temporarily on your hard drive. This group of temporary files is known as the *cache*. Certain files, such as graphic images, are ideal for storing in the cache. Others, such as the login page (with name and password), are not. You set the `Expires` property to the number of minutes you want the page to remain in the cache. For the security page, you would probably want to set it to zero, as in the following example:

```
Response.Expires = 0
```

The `Response` object is also used to send cookies to the user's browser. Cookies work like session variables but are stored on the client PC. (IIS actually uses cookies to help maintain the session IDs.) Cookies are useful when you want to save personal settings on a user's hard drive and retrieve them later. However, cookies are not guaranteed to be available—a lot of users consider them an invasion of privacy so they disable them. To send a cookie to the user's browser, simply assign a value as you would with a session variable:

```
Response.Cookies("MYCOOKIE") = 1234
```

A similar `Cookies` collection used with the `Request` object is used to retrieve cookie values.

Retrieving Data with the *Request* Object

The `Request` object allows ASP code to access everything about an incoming browser request. You already know that you can use the `Request` object to get the value of a parameter in an URL by using the parameter name with the `QueryString` property. Like many other collections, `QueryString` has a `Count` property and an index which allow you to iterate through the values:

```
Dim n
For n = 1 to Request.QueryString.Count
   Response.Write ("Parameter " & n & "Value = " & Request.QueryString(n) & "<BR>")
Next
```

You can also receive information from HTML forms with the `Form` collection of the `Request` object. For example, if you have a form field name `txtLastName`, you can display the value submitted with the following code:

```
Response.Write "You entered " & Request.Form("txtLastName")
```

As you can see, a lot of the information in the `Request` object is accessed through collections. You can use a `For Each` loop to list all of the objects in a collection. Listing 31.7 displays all of the information in the `Request.Servervariables` collection.

Listing 31.7 ASPDEMO.ZIP—VARIABLES.ASP Lists the Contents of the *ServerVariables* Collection

```
<%@ LANGUAGE="VBSCRIPT" %>
<HTML>
<HEAD><TITLE>Variables</TITLE></HEAD>
<BODY>
<HR>
<H1 align="center">Server Variables</H1>
<%
For Each item in Request.ServerVariables
%>
<STRONG><%=item%></STRONG>=<%=Request.ServerVariables(item)%><BR>
<%
Next
%>
</BODY>
</HTML>
```

Create a new ASP file on your Web server, VARIABLES.ASP. Enter the code from Listing 31.7 and load the page in your browser. You should see a list of all the server variables, as shown in Figure 31.6.

> **NOTE** You could add more `For...Each` loops to Listing 31.2 to show what is contained in other collections, such as the `Request.Form` collection, and use it as a debugging tool.

FIGURE 31.6
The Server variable HTTP_USER_AGENT allows you to determine a user's browser type.

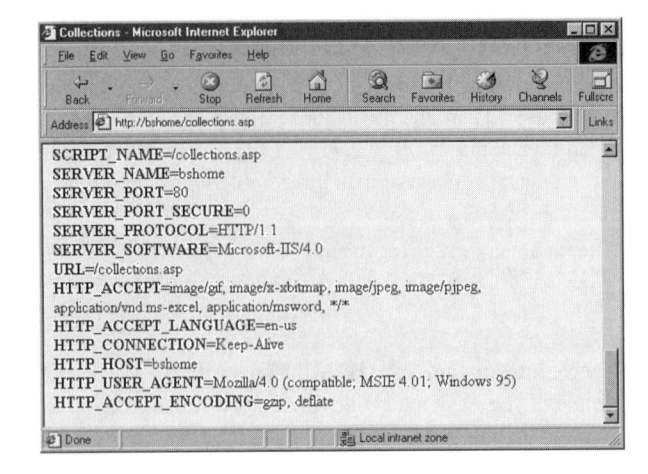

```
SCRIPT_NAME=/collections.asp
SERVER_NAME=bshome
SERVER_PORT=80
SERVER_PORT_SECURE=0
SERVER_PROTOCOL=HTTP/1.1
SERVER_SOFTWARE=Microsoft-IIS/4.0
URL=/collections.asp
HTTP_ACCEPT=image/gif, image/x-xbitmap, image/jpeg, image/pjpeg,
application/vnd.ms-excel, application/msword, */*
HTTP_ACCEPT_LANGUAGE=en-us
HTTP_CONNECTION=Keep-Alive
HTTP_HOST=bshome
HTTP_USER_AGENT=Mozilla/4.0 (compatible; MSIE 4.01; Windows 95)
HTTP_ACCEPT_ENCODING=gzip, deflate
```

The *Server* Object

The primary use of the ASP `Server` object is to create objects on the Web server so your ASP application can access them. You have already seen how to create an ADO connection object:

```
Set cn = Server.CreateObject("ADODB.Connection")
```

You can also create objects from classes that you compile into an ActiveX DLL, as you will see shortly.

As an alternative to the `Server.CreateObject` statement, you can embed an `<OBJECT>` tag in your ASP file with the RUNAT option set to Server:

```
<OBJECT RUNAT="Server" ID=cn PROGID="ADODB.Connection"></OBJECT>
```

Either syntax creates an `ADODB.Connection` object on the Web server. However, the `<OBJECT>` tag cannot be used inside the script tags.

The *Application* Object and GLOBAL.ASA

Earlier in this chapter, you discovered how the directory layout is used to identify ASP applications. This is important if you want to program the Start and End events associated with applications and sessions. To write procedure code for these events, you place a special file called GLOBAL.ASA in the ASP application's root directory. The GLOBAL.ASA can contain code for these events, as in the following example:

```
Sub Session_OnStart()
   Dim x
   Set x = Server.CreateObject("ADODB.Connection")
   Set Session("CONNECTION") = x

End Sub
```

You can use the GLOBAL.ASA file to add a Web page hit counter, close and open databases, or any other activity that needs to occur when a user starts and exits your application.

Using Your Own ActiveX DLL with ASP

You can do a lot by using VBScript code in an Active Server Page, but VBScript of course lacks the power of full-blown Visual Basic, not to mention all of the IDE features you may be used to. However, by using the `Server.CreateObject` function, you can create instances of your own ActiveX DLL's on an ASP page.

First, create and test your ActiveX DLL in a normal Visual Basic environment. Then, you need to install and register the DLL on the Web server so it can be used from an ASP page. Creating an ActiveX DLL is covered in more detail in Chapter 16, "Classes: Reusable Components."

▶ **See** "Creating an ActiveX DLL," **p. 368**

Once you have created your ActiveX DLL, install it on the Web server. If you already have the Visual Basic runtime files installed on the Web server, installation of your DLL may be as simple as copying the DLL over and running REGSVR32 to register it.

After the DLL is installed and registered, you can create an object from a class in the DLL with the `Server.CreateObject` statement:

```
Set objVariable = Server.CreateObject("MyProject.MyClass")
```

After an object has been created, you can access it from the current ASP page. To pass it along to another page, you can store it in a session variable, like the GLOBAL.ASA example in the previous section.

Using ActiveX DLLs with ASP is very simple, just access the methods and properties from VBScript:

```
Response.Write objVariable.GetUserData("Smith")
```

VBScript only uses variants, so be careful when declaring functions in your DLL. Arrays and other data types do not always work the same as they would in standard Visual Basic. You should create a small test function in your DLL so that you will be familiar with the VBScript limitations.

The IIS Application Project

A new project type in Visual Basic 6.0 is the IIS Application. An IIS Application is a special type of ActiveX DLL that works on a Web server to process requests from the client and return HTML to the user's browser. Does this sound similar to what an ASP page does? Well it should. IIS applications allow you to access many of the same objects (Server, Response, Request, and so on) as an ASP page and are themselves hosted in an ASP page. As a matter of fact, an IIS application works in a similar way to what was covered in the last section regarding calling an ActiveX DLL from an ASP page. The difference is that an IIS Application is set up specifically to deal with the Web; although an ActiveX DLL project contains a standard VB class module, an IIS Application project contains a *WebClass*.

Creating an IIS Application

To start an IIS application, open Visual Basic and choose IIS Application from the list of available project types. A new project is created with a single object, `WebClass1`, shown in Figure 31.7.

FIGURE 31.7
An IIS application is a specialized type of ActiveX DLL that runs on the Web server.

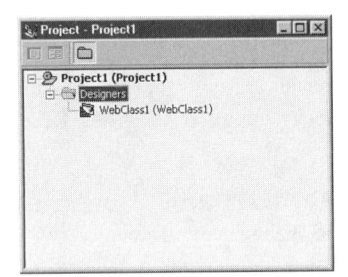

Notice that `WebClass1` is not a form or standard class module, but an *ActiveX Designer*. ActiveX Designers help you create specific kinds of ActiveX components and are integrated right into the VB development environment. In an IIS application, the WebClass designer takes care of a lot of "low level" work for you in working with HTML. In fact, when you finally compile your IIS Application DLL, much of the VB code you write will be talking to the WebClass DLL.

Because the Web is inherently document-based, an IIS application depends on files being in their proper locations. Therefore, it is very important to save the IIS project before you start doing anything. Go ahead and create a separate directory for the application, such as C:\IISDemo, and save the project files.

As with forms, `WebClass1` has both a code view and a design view. Open the design view by right-clicking the WebClass and selecting View Object. You then see the screen shown in Figure 31.8.

FIGURE 31.8
A WebClass can contain two types of WebItems.

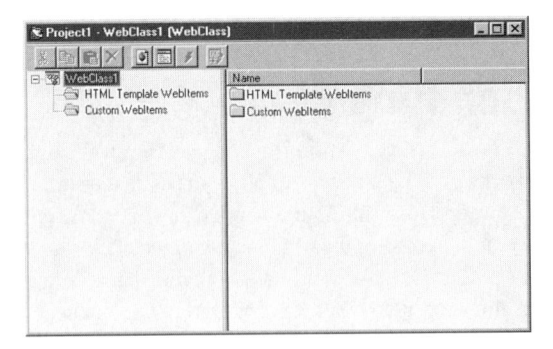

As you can see, a WebClass contains *WebItems*. There are two different types of WebItems, which you'll learn about shortly:

- HTML Template WebItems—A WebItem based on an HTML template file that already exists
- Custom WebItems—A WebItem created totally in code

So what is a WebItem? Well, it is nothing but code (remember this is just an ActiveX DLL) and because this is a server-based application there is no visual interface. WebItems provide a way to connect Visual Basic program events to the document-based world of HTML.

Running an IIS Application

Before you go any further, look at the code for the WebClass. Right-click the class name in the Project Explorer window and choose View code. You should see the default code for the WebClass's Start event, as shown in Figure 31.9.

FIGURE 31.9
The WebClass' Start event provides an initial HTML screen via the familiar Response object.

Go ahead and run the project by clicking the VB Start button or pressing F5. Remember, because IIS applications are Web server-based like ASP, you need to have a Web server running to use and debug them.

> **NOTE** The examples discussed in this chapter were created with Visual Basic, Personal Web Server, and Transaction Server (included with PWS) running on the same machine.

Each time you run your IIS Application in the VB IDE, Visual Basic generates an ASP file and attempts to launch it in Internet Explorer. The first time you run a new IIS Application, you will see a message like that in Figure 31.10, which asks you for the virtual directory name.

FIGURE 31.10
Visual Basic automatically creates a virtual directory and ASP file to host your WebClass.

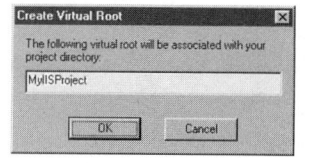

When the application runs, you should see the HTML screen provided by the WebClass's `Start` event. If you look in the project directory, you might notice that Visual Basic has created an ASP file that creates an instance of your WebClass. By now, you should understand a little bit more about how an IIS application works—kind of like an ASP file but with all of the Web activity accessible through the Visual Basic environment. In the next section, you learn more about what a WebClass can do by adding WebItems to it. For now, stop the project in Visual Basic and return to design mode.

WebClass Instancing

Open the Code window again and note the standard events available for a WebClass. Put `Debug.Print` *eventname* statements in each of them and run the project again. Watch the sequence of events:

1. When you start the project, the browser is launched. The ASP file loaded by the browser contains a `Server.CreateObject` statement, which creates an instance of the WebClass, causing the `Initialize` event to fire.
2. The ASP file also makes a request for a Web page to the WebClass, causing the `BeginRequest` event to fire.
3. The WebClass's `Start` event fires (much like the `Form_Load` event) causing HTML to be sent back to the browser.
4. When all the HTML has been sent to the browser, the request has been satisfied so the `EndRequest` event fires.
5. The `Terminate` event fires, causing the instance of the WebClass to be destroyed.

Step 5 in the preceding list should have at least caused you to raise an eyebrow. Why was the WebClass created and then immediately destroyed? The answer is because the `StateManagement` property of the WebClass was set to `wcNoState`. This means if you set a local variable or property in the `Start` event of the WebClass, it would not be available on successive calls. If the `StateManagement` property was set to `wcRetainInstance` then each call to the WebClass from the ASP page would be to the same instance, and you could store state information.

However, there is a deeper issue here than just setting a property. It is more a philosophy of how you write applications. The connection-less nature of the Web is more suited to transaction-based processing instead of state-based processing. When working with transactions, you really don't care about communicating with the same instance of an object because you pass all the information needed to complete a transaction along with each call to the object.

Most of us tend to write code that depends on an object's being in a certain state—for example, you will set a bunch of properties on an object and then later call a method on the object that uses those properties:

```
x.AccountID = 123456
x.AccountHolder = "Stephanie and Brent"
```

```
x.Amount = "$20.00"
x.DepositMoney
```

In these lines of code, x represents an instance of an ActiveX component that handles bank account functions. The last line is a method call to `DepositMoney`, which presumably requires the other account information to work. This code depends on repeated access to the same object. Another way to write this, in which all of the information is passed to the object, is as follows:

```
x.DepositMoney(123456,"Stephanie and Brent","$20.00")
```

Of course, this example is very simple, but think about a more complex example where you were repeatedly calling functions on the object. In the first example, you would have to have access to the same instance of the object x, but in the second example it does not matter. Although the second example looks like more work, if you can write code that is state-independent, you can use tools like Microsoft Transaction Server to pool object connections and create a very "scalable" application.

Using an HTML Template WebItem

To learn how HTML templates work with a WebClass, first create the following simple HTML template, TEST.HTM:

```
<HTML>
<BODY>
<H1> This is a test page </H1>
<BR>
<A HREF=http://www.somewhere.com> Link to somewhere! </A>

<IMG SRC=guestbook.gif>

</BODY>
</HTML>
```

There is nothing special about TEST.HTM, until you import it into the project. To do this, open the Designer window for `WebClass1`, right-click `WebClass1`, and choose Add HTML Template. Select TEST.HTM from the File dialog box. Your Designer window should now look like the one in Figure 31.11.

> **NOTE** It is a good idea to import an HTML template from *outside* the project directory, because Visual Basic will automatically save a copy of the template (with subsequent changes) in the project directory. ■

After importing an HTML file, it becomes a WebItem.

Creating a Template Event   In the right pane of the Designer window, you see a list of all the HTML tags in the template file that can be connected to Visual Basic events. The new WebItem itself is also given a name, `Template1`.

FIGURE 31.11
When you add an HTML template to a WebClass, you are presented with all of the HTML tags in the template that can be connected to VB events.

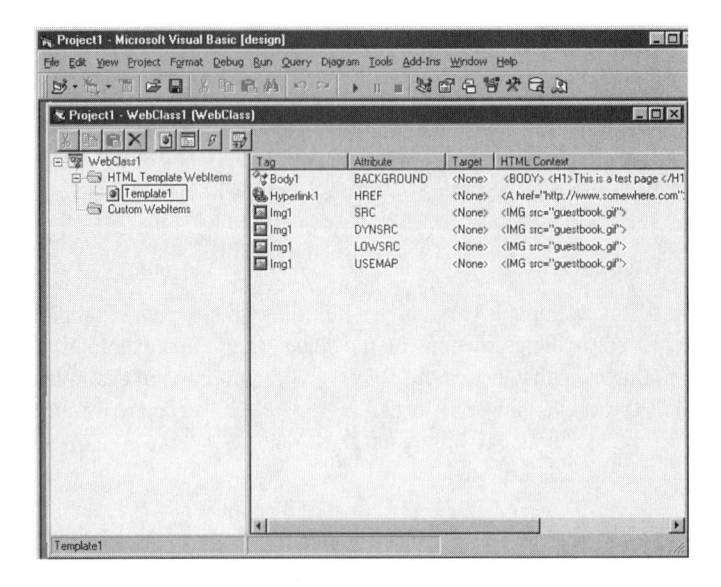

By way of comparison, think about what happens when you add a TextBox control to a standard Visual Basic form. You are in effect placing an object (the text box) in a container (the form). After you draw the text box, you can access all of its properties and events from the form's Code window. Similarly, `Template1` is an object in your WebClass, much like the text box object on a form.

The only difference between the events in a text box and those in a WebItem is that WebItem events are not automatically available from the Code window. You first have to go through the process of connecting HTML tags to program events.

Try it with your sample program. Remember the hyperlink in the template to www.somewhere.com? When you imported the template, it was given the name `Hyperlink1`. Right-click it and choose Connect to Custom Event. A new event appears in the Designer window, also called `Hyperlink1`. Double-click the event name and the Code window opens in the `Template1_HyperLink1` event. This new event is fired whenever a user clicks the hyperlink. Enter the following `Response.Write` statement so that the event procedure looks like this:

```
Private Sub Template1_Hyperlink1()
    Response.Write "<BR> You clicked me!<BR>"
End Sub
```

Next, run the project. When the first page loads, change the filename at the end of the URL (something like `Project1_WebClass1.ASP`) to the template filename, TEST.HTM, and press Enter. The template page loads. If you choose View Source, you might notice that the hyperlink no longer points to www.somewhere.com but instead to an event in the WebClass. Click the hyperlink and you should see the words *You Clicked Me* displayed in the browser. You have just seen how a hyperlink in an HTML file can be connected to a Visual Basic program event.

Sending a Template to the Browser By default, a WebClass's Start event sends a few lines of HTML back to the browser. You can also send templates back to the browser, such as the sample just created, by using the WriteTemplate method. Open the Start event of the WebClass and replace the default lines of code with the following line:

```
Me.Template1.WriteTemplate
```

Run the application and the template based on the file TEST.HTM should be the first thing you see. Notice that the browser is not redirected to TEST.HTM, but instead the HTML from the template file is passed back during the Start event.

The WriteTemplate method can be very useful when combined with the ProcessTag event. This event can be used to dynamically generate HTML content, similar to the way you use Response.Write statements in an ASP page to generate HTML on-the-fly. It works by searching for tags within your template (much like HTML tags but with a special prefix) and replacing them with whatever information you choose.

To demonstrate this, again bring up the template file TEST.HTM. (Make sure to bring up the file in the project directory, not the original import file.) Add the following line to the template somewhere in the body of the document and save it:

```
<WC@mytag>My Information</WC@mytag>
```

The preceding line of code contains a "customized" tag, <WC@mytag>. During execution of the WriteHTMLTemplate method, each time the WebClass encounters a tag with the wc@ prefix, the ProcessTag event is fired. The tag name (mytag) and contents (My Information) are passed to the event and can be modified before being sent to the browser:

```
Private Sub Template1_ProcessTag(ByVal TagName As String, TagContents As String, SendTags As Boolean)

If TagName = "WC@mytag" Then

    TagContents = "<B> Here is some new information </B>"

End If

End Sub
```

Using a Custom WebItem

The other type of WebItem that can be added to the WebClass is a *custom WebItem*. The events in a custom WebItem are just like the ones in an HTML Template WebItem, and you have the option to add your own custom events that can be raised from a Web page. However, there is no template in a Custom WebItem. It exists only in your VB code, as a set of event procedures. You can connect items in an HTML Template WebItem to a Custom WebItem with a few simple steps:

1. Right-click the WebClass's name in the Project Explorer window and choose View Object. The Designer window appears.

2. Again, right-click the WebClass name in the Designer window and choose Add Custom WebItem.
3. Select an HTML tag name in an HTML Template WebItem and connect it to the custom WebItem.
4. Write code for the events as described in the previous section.

As you might have realized from the examples, using WebClasses is a little more complex than standard ASP pages. However, they exist in the Visual Basic environment, which opens up a new realm of possibilities.

From Here...

In this chapter you learned about Active Server Pages, one way to apply your knowledge of Visual Basic to the Internet. To read about other Internet topics, see the following chapters:

- To learn how to create ActiveX controls that can be used on a Web page, see Chapter 14, "Creating ActiveX Controls."
- If you want to quickly migrate a Visual Basic program to the Internet, see Chapter 32, "ActiveX Documents."
- To find out about other Internet topics, see Chapter 33, "Visual Basic and Other Uses of the Internet."

CHAPTER 32

ActiveX Documents

In this chapter

Understanding ActiveX Documents **720**

Creating Your First ActiveX Document **722**

Exploring the UserDocument Object **729**

Using the Hyperlink Object in Your Document **733**

Using the ActiveX Document Migration Wizard **733**

Creating a More Complex Document **737**

You probably are aware that many things are happening with the Internet these days. In particular, the World Wide Web has gained enormous popularity. It seems that everywhere you turn, everyone has a Web site—from car manufacturers to charitable organizations to the guy next door. Internet stuff is everywhere. And although just having a static Web page used to be acceptable, more and more people and organizations are providing dynamic content on their pages. These interactive Web pages do a lot more than just display fixed information. Seeing Web pages that act like applications is commonplace now, and several tools are available to help you create such pages.

When you first look at creating interactive content, the process can appear daunting. I know it did for me. More often than not, the concern I hear is not "Can I do this?" but "What's the best way to do this?" When you try to think of ways to program for the Web, dozens of terms may come to mind: Perl, CGI, Active Server Pages, VBScript, and Java, to name a few. The ActiveX documents discussed in this chapter are not necessarily the best choice for all occasions, but they do make Internet programming accessible to VB programmers.

Understanding ActiveX Documents

Because ActiveX documents are perfect for use on the World Wide Web, this chapter will begin with a quick refresher course. You probably have become familiar enough with Web pages to know that they are basically just document files. Web files are similar to Word documents except that they are written in a special format: HTML (which stands for Hypertext Markup Language). Just as Word is the viewer for DOC files, a Web browser (such as Netscape or Internet Explorer) is used to view HTML files. HTML files on the Internet have an address, or *URL* (Uniform Resource Locator), that is used to locate a specific document.

The Web began as just a bunch of linked documents. However, a static document cannot produce the level of interactivity you see today. Two things about the Web have made this change possible:

- The way Web pages are retrieved
- Browser enhancements

The Hypertext Transfer Protocol, or HTTP, is the means by which your browser and the Web server communicate. The browser simply requests an URL and then displays the returned HTML stream.

Notice that I use the word "requests"; this is an important concept. Requesting a file is very different from opening one on your hard drive—hence the need to have a protocol. Think of this process as being similar to your asking a friend to send you a document via e-mail. With this process, unlike your opening a document on your hard drive, your friend could edit the document before sending it or send you a completely different document. In a similar manner, logic can be placed on the Web server to modify the returned document based on any number of criteria, including information from user.

On the browser side, the returned HTML stream has evolved quite a bit since the Web's first days. In addition to formatted text and graphics, Web pages can include script code and Java applets. These advances were made possible by the increasing complexity of the Internet browser, which has evolved to support all these embedded objects. ActiveX documents, discussed in this chapter, are applications downloaded to the client's desktop by Internet Explorer (IE).

What Is an ActiveX Document?

Put in simplest terms, an ActiveX document is an application that runs inside a container, such as Internet Explorer, instead of running as a standalone program. An example of such an application is shown in Figure 32.1.

> **NOTE** Even though you can use an ActiveX document inside Internet Explorer, you must have all the required runtime DLLs installed on the client machine.

FIGURE 32.1
This simple ActiveX document is running in Internet Explorer.

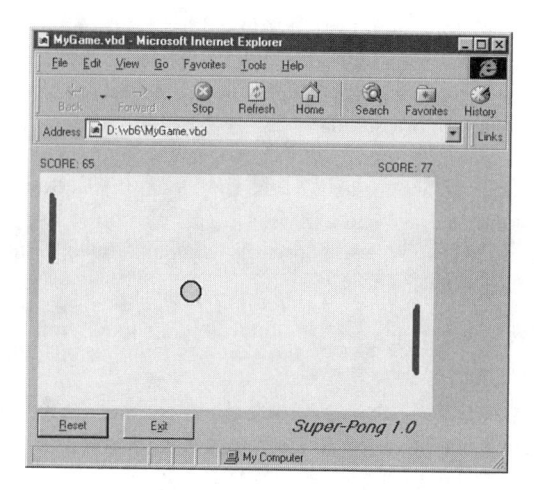

The "document" portion of the name comes from the analogy to word processing documents or spreadsheets. These files contain data but must be accessed by a program in order to be viewed or edited. For example, you can create a document in Word and store it in a file. If you pass the file along to another user, that user can't do anything with it unless he or she has a copy of Word. An ActiveX document works much the same way. You can create an ActiveX document and store it in a file. If you pass the file to someone else, that person must have a program capable of supporting ActiveX documents before being able to use the file.

Fortunately, several containers support ActiveX documents, including Internet Explorer, Microsoft Office 97 binders, and the Visual Basic IDE. Your users can run your program inside one of these container applications.

What Are the Advantages of Using ActiveX Documents?

The primary reason to use ActiveX documents in Visual Basic is to create Internet-enabled applications. Creating ActiveX documents provides a number of advantages over creating Internet applications by other means. Some of these advantages include the following:

- You do not have to learn another programming language to create the documents. All your Visual Basic expertise can be applied to ActiveX documents.
- You can design your Internet application by using the Visual Basic design environment. This process is much simpler than the code-and-test method that you have to use with some other languages.
- You also have access to Visual Basic's rich debugging environment for testing your code and fixing any problems that arise.
- By using the Hyperlink object, you can easily navigate to other pages from the browser. These pages can be other ActiveX documents or any Web address.

So, Visual Basic makes creating an ActiveX document easy, but why would you want to create one in the first place? Why not just create a standard application? The answer, in a word, is "Internet." ActiveX frees you of the complications involved with the older means of distributing an application. If your program is a standard EXE, then you must send installation diskettes to all the users. ActiveX documents, on the other hand, can be set up on a Web server so that they are downloaded automatically when a user opens the Web page. Codes embedded in the Web page tell Internet Explorer to download a cabinet (CAB) file containing your application and all necessary components. This Web-based approach makes it simpler to maintain your code and to keep everyone running the same version.

Of course, using ActiveX documents over the Internet does have some disadvantages. The main disadvantages are as follows:

- At the time of this writing, only Microsoft's browser, Internet Explorer, supports ActiveX. Therefore, if your audience is the whole Internet (versus a corporate intranet, for example), you may want to investigate a server-side approach, such as using Active Server Pages.
- Even though Internet Explorer handles downloading your application, it still has to be "installed" on the client PC—with all the proper support files. Every time you create a new version of your ActiveX document, the users need to update a local copy, which may be time consuming on a slow Internet connection.

Creating Your First ActiveX Document

Creating an ActiveX document is similar to creating standard applications in Visual Basic. In this chapter, you will re-create the loan payment calculator example from Chapter 2, "Creating Your First Program," but this time as an ActiveX document. To create a document, follow this basic sequence of events:

1. Start a new ActiveX document project.
2. Create the user interface for the application.
3. Write the code to perform the application's tasks.
4. Test and debug the application.
5. Use the Package and Deployment Wizard to create an Internet download setup.

Obviously, several details are involved in each of these steps, but you can see that the process is something you are familiar with. To walk through the process of creating an ActiveX document, you will create a mortgage calculator like the one you created in Chapter 2. Using this same application will illustrate the similarities between creating an ActiveX document and a standard Visual Basic program.

NOTE The preceding steps refer to creating an *application*. Because an ActiveX document is an interactive application as opposed to a static file, such as a word processing document, the term *application* is often used to refer to an ActiveX document.

Starting an ActiveX Document Project

The first step toward creating an ActiveX document is to start your project. You do so by selecting New Project from the File menu. The New Project dialog box then appears (see Figure 32.2). From this dialog box, select the option to create an ActiveX Document EXE by double-clicking the icon. This action starts a new project containing a single User Document, UserDocument1. Double-click the object in the Project Explorer window and you should see the blank designer screen, as shown in Figure 32.3.

FIGURE 32.2
The New Project dialog, which can be displayed by pressing Ctrl+N, sets up the initial project configuration.

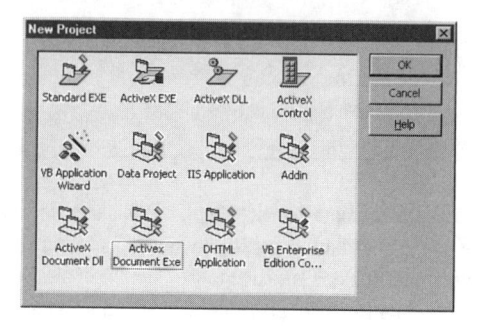

NOTE If the UserDocument is not displayed automatically, double-click the UserDocument object in the Project window to display it.

Notice that the UserDocument designer looks a lot like a form designer without a border. As a matter of fact, it is also like the UserControl object that you use to create ActiveX controls. You create the user interface for the ActiveX document here, just like with a form. (For more information about creating ActiveX controls, see Chapter 14, "Creating ActiveX Controls.")

FIGURE 32.3
ActiveX documents run inside a container and therefore do not have title bars, borders, and other features of independent windows.

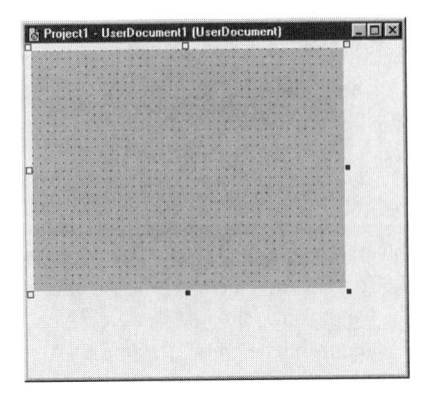

After you create the project, you can change the properties of the project and the UserDocument to descriptive names, as listed in Table 32.1. To access the properties of the project, choose Properties from the Project menu. You can access the properties of the UserDocument from the Properties window (by choosing View, Properties Window). After you set the properties, save the files of the project by clicking the Save button on the toolbar. You then have to specify names for each of the new files.

Table 32.1 Project and UserDocument Properties

Property	Setting
Project Type	ActiveX EXE
Project Name	ActXCalc
Project Description	ActiveX Document Loan Calculator
UserDocument Name	CalcDoc

Document Filenames

You save the source code of ActiveX documents in a text file much the same way you save a form. The description of the UserDocument object and any controls is stored along with the code of the document in a file with the extension .DOB. This is similar to the FRM file of a form. If the interface has any graphical components, they are stored in a DOX file, similar to the FRX file for forms. When you compile your ActiveX document, you create either an EXE or DLL file, along with a VBD file. The VBD file is the one accessed by Internet Explorer. This VBD file is the "document" part of the file, similar to a DOC file from Microsoft Word.

Creating the Interface of the Document

You create the interface of your ActiveX document by drawing controls on the UserDocument object, just as you would draw them on the form of a standard program. You can use almost any

Visual Basic control in the creation of your document. The only exception is that you cannot use the OLE container control as part of an ActiveX document. Another restriction is that an ActiveX document cannot contain embedded objects, such as Word or Excel documents.

> **CAUTION**
>
> If you use custom controls in your document, you need to check licensing and royalty requirements before distributing the controls.

To create the interface of the sample application, you need to add four Label controls, four TextBox controls, and one CommandButton to the UserDocument.

The Label controls should have the following settings for the Name and Caption properties:

Name	Caption
lblPrincipal	Principal:
lblTerm	Term (Years):
lblInterest	Interest Rate (%):
lblPayment	Monthly Payment:

All four text boxes should have their Text properties deleted so that the text boxes appear empty when the document is first shown. The text boxes should be named txtInterest, txtPayment, txtPrincipal, and txtTerm.

The command button of the document should have the Name property set to cmdCalculate and the Caption property set to Calculate Payment.

After you add the controls to the document, your UserDocument should look like the one in Figure 32.4.

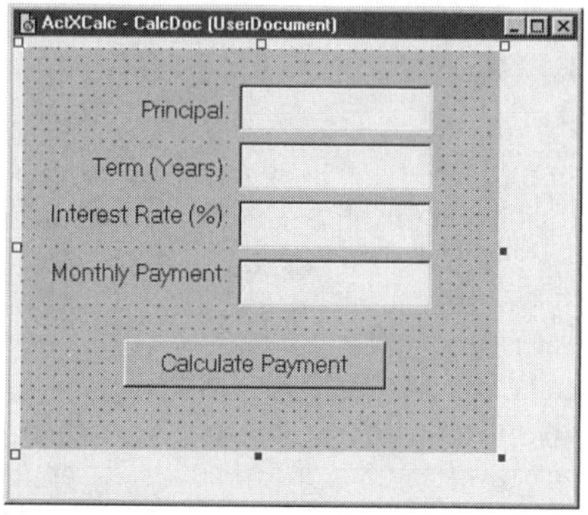

FIGURE 32.4
The Document calculator looks similar to the LoanCalc program created earlier.

Adding Code to the Document

After you create the interface of the document by using Visual Basic controls, you are ready to write the code that makes the document perform a task. As with the forms in a standard program, you write code for events of the controls in the document. All code work is done in the Code window. You can access the Code window by double-clicking a control or by clicking the View Code button in the Project window. For the sample application, you need to enter the code from Listing 32.1 in the Click event of the command button.

Listing 32.1 CALCDOC.DOB—Placing Code in the *Click* Event to Run the Calculation

```
Private Sub cmdCalculate_Click()

    Dim m_Principal As Single, m_Interest As Single
    Dim m_Payment As Single, m_Term As Integer
    Dim m_fctr As Single

    m_Principal = Val(txtPrincipal.Text)
    m_Interest = Val(txtInterest.Text) / 1200
    m_Term = Val(txtTerm.Text)
        m_fctr = (1 + m_Interest) ^ (m_Term * 12)
    m_Payment = m_Interest * m_fctr * m_Principal / (m_fctr - 1)
    txtPayment.Text = Format(m_Payment, "Fixed")

End Sub
```

Although the code in Listing 32.1 exists in a UserDocument object, it works just like code inside a form. First the values entered by the user are retrieved from the text boxes and stored in local variables. Next the code calculates the payment and displays the results in the text box txtPayment.

Testing Your ActiveX Document

After entering the code and saving your document, you are ready to test the code. Testing an ActiveX document is a little different than testing a standard program because the document must run inside another application. To determine what type of application runs when you start the project, display the Debugging tab of the Properties dialog box. This dialog box has several options, as you can see in Figure 32.5.

The default option in the Debugging tab, Start Component, allows the code in the component to determine the manner in which it starts. If you have Internet Explorer installed, and you start an ActiveX Document project, this default setting causes the application to be loaded automatically into Internet Explorer. Try it now with the sample project. Simply press F5 or click the VB Start button, and you should see the Web version of the Loan Calculator appear, as shown in Figure 32.6.

FIGURE 32.5
Use the Debugging tab of the Properties dialog box to select whether an ActiveX document starts in the browser or another application.

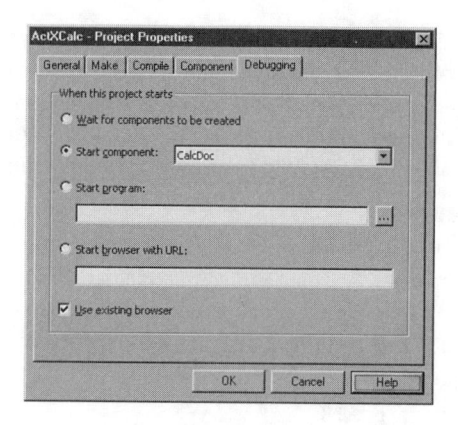

If you want to open the ActiveX document manually, choose Wait for Components to Be Created from the Debugging tab. In this case, Visual C`sic only starts the project; you must open the document in Internet Explorer. To open an ActiveX document manually, follow these steps:

1. Run your document by pressing F5 or clicking the VB Start button on the toolbar. (Note that Visual Basic does not display the user interface of your program.)
2. Minimize Visual Basic and start Internet Explorer.
3. From IE's File menu, choose Open. In the resulting Open dialog box, you can enter the name of the file to be opened by IE.
4. Specify the path and name of your ActiveX document. The name is the value of the Name property of the UserDocument object, followed by a .VBD extension. If you are running your document within VB, the file is located in the same folder as Visual Basic. For a typical installation, the path is C:\Program Files\DevStudio\Vb.
5. Click the OK button in the Open dialog box to load your document. The CalcDoc document is shown running in Internet Explorer in Figure 32.6.

> **NOTE** If you click the Browse button in the Open dialog box to find the file, remember to change the Files of Type selection from HTML files to All Files. ■

FIGURE 32.6
Internet Explorer can host an ActiveX document.

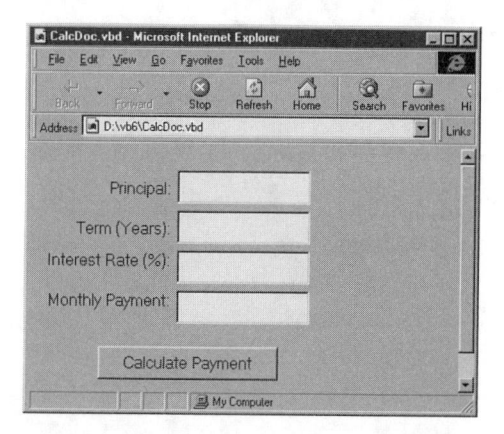

You can also open your ActiveX documents inside your own custom Web page. If you want to see how your HTML looks with the ActiveX document, simply choose Start Browser with URL and enter the URL of your Web page. (Note that if you select this option you must ensure that your Web page includes the necessary code to display the ActiveX document.) In addition, you can use the Start Program option if you want to test your ActiveX document in another application.

If your code doesn't perform like it should, you can use all of Visual Basic's debugging tools to track down and eliminate errors. (Debugging is discussed in detail in Chapter 9, "Visual Basic Programming Fundamentals.") You can set breakpoints in your code, set "Watches" to observe the values of variables, and step through the code line by line to locate an error. Figure 32.7 shows a typical debugging session.

▶ See "Debugging Your Programs," p. 173

> **CAUTION**
> Terminating your program without closing Internet Explorer may cause errors in IE. Therefore, you should close and restart IE each time you run your document. Note that closing IE does not stop the ActiveX document project in Visual Basic.

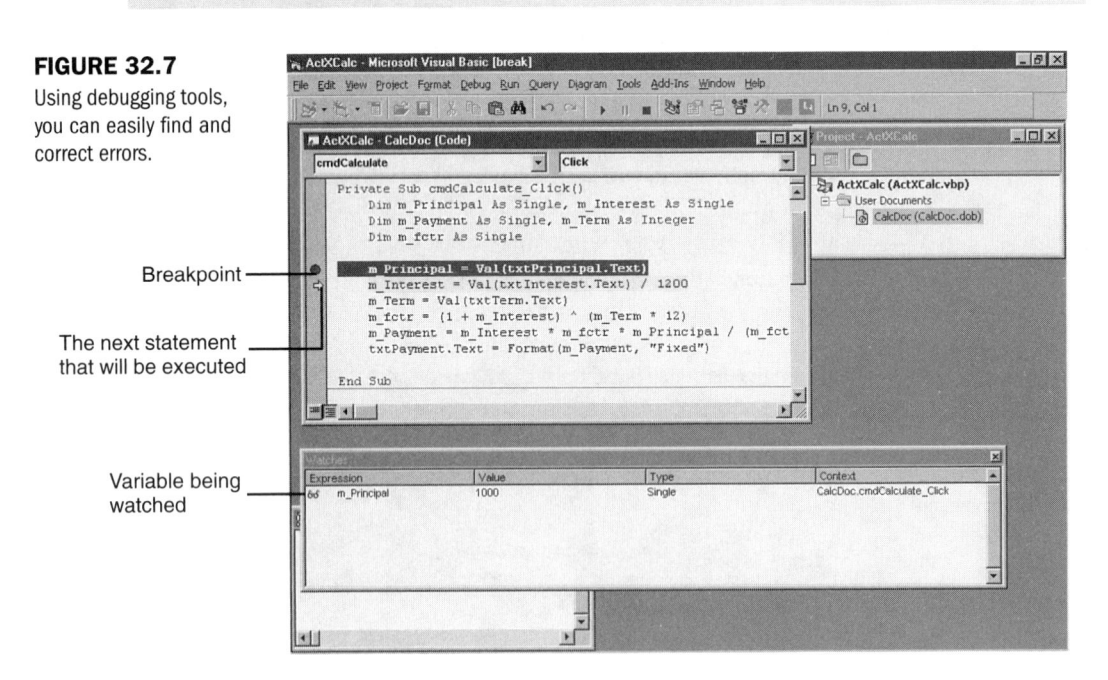

FIGURE 32.7
Using debugging tools, you can easily find and correct errors.

Compiling Your Document

After you finish testing and debugging your document, you can compile the document for distribution. To start the compilation process, select Make from Visual Basic's File menu. In the resulting Make dialog box, you can specify the name and location of the EXE or DLL file. The name of the VBD file is based on the Name property of the UserDocument object. This file is placed in the same folder that you specified for the EXE file.

After compilation, your document can be used in any of the programs that handle ActiveX documents. As you learned previously, Internet Explorer is one such program; the Office 97 Binder is another. To access an ActiveX document with the Binder, start the Binder and then select Add from File from the Section menu. This action opens a dialog box that enables you to specify the file to be loaded. Here, you specify the name and location of your VBD file and then click the OK button to load the document.

If you want to put your ActiveX document on the Internet, you first need to run the Packaging and Deployment Wizard with the Internet Package option. The wizard creates a Package subdirectory that contains the following:

- A CAB file containing all the required components and DLL files
- The VBD file that is used to open the document in Internet Explorer
- A Support directory in case you need to rebuild the CAB file manually
- A sample HTML file, pictured in Figure 32.7, that shows you how to include your document on a Web page

▶ **See** "Packaging ActiveX Components" **p. 788**

FIGURE 32.8
You can copy the HREF line from the sample HTML file to your own Web pages.

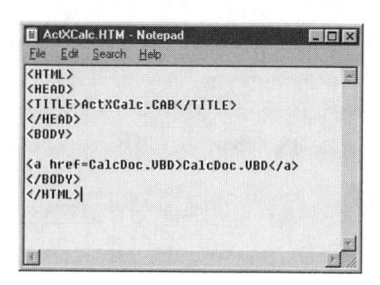

```
<HTML>
<HEAD>
<TITLE>ActXCalc.CAB</TITLE>
</HEAD>
<BODY>

<a href=CalcDoc.VBD>CalcDoc.VBD</a>
</BODY>
</HTML>
```

Exploring the UserDocument Object

Just as a form is the main part of a standard program, the UserDocument object is the key part of an ActiveX document. The UserDocument provides the canvas for all the controls that make up the user interface of the document. As you can do with a form, you can place controls on the UserDocument, or you can use graphics methods and the Print method to display other information directly on the document. This capability provides great flexibility in the design of your documents and the manner in which you present information to the user.

Understanding the Key Events of a UserDocument

Although the UserDocument is similar to a form in many respects, it also has some key differences. For example, several key properties, methods, and events are supported by a UserDocument but are not supported by a form, and vice versa. The reason for these differences is the different nature of the objects themselves: A form is independent, whereas a UserDocument is always in a container.

The main events of a form that are not supported by the UserDocument object are the `Activate`, `Deactivate`, `Load`, and `Unload` events. The UserDocument, on the other hand, supports the following events that are not supported by a form:

- `AsycReadComplete`. Occurs when the container holding the document has finished an asynchronous read request.
- `EnterFocus`. Occurs when the ActiveX document receives focus.
- `ExitFocus`. Occurs when the ActiveX document loses focus.
- `Hide`. Occurs when the user navigates from the current ActiveX document to another document.
- `InitProperties`. Occurs when the document is first loaded. However, if any properties have been saved using the `PropertyBag` object, the `ReadProperties` event occurs instead.
- `ReadProperties`. Occurs in place of the `InitProperties` event if items are stored in a `PropertyBag` object. This event also occurs as the document is first loaded.
- `Scroll`. Occurs when the user uses the scrollbar of the container in which the ActiveX document is running.
- `Show`. Occurs when the user navigates from another document to the ActiveX document.
- `WriteProperties`. Occurs as the program is about to be terminated. This event happens right before the `Terminate` event, but it occurs only if the `PropertyChanged` statement has been used to indicate that a change has occurred in a property's value.

Creating and Storing Properties for a UserDocument

Despite the similarities between the UserDocument and a form, in some ways the UserDocument is much more similar to a UserControl than a form. All three objects—the form, the UserControl, and the UserDocument—enable you to create properties and methods to extend their capabilities. However, only the UserControl and the UserDocument have the capability to use the `PropertyBag` object. The `PropertyBag` object, along with some special events, is used to store values of public properties so that settings are preserved between sessions.

Because the process for creating and saving properties was discussed in detail in the coverage of ActiveX controls, I won't repeat the details here (see Chapter 14, "Creating ActiveX Controls"). However, a quick recap may help you remember the steps involved. To create and store properties for the UserDocument, you need to do the following:

1. Create a property by using the `Property Let` and `Property Get` procedures. You can create the shell of the property by using the Add Procedure dialog box, which you can access from the Tools menu of Visual Basic.
2. To indicate that the value of a property has changed, place the `PropertyChanged` statement in the `Property Let` procedure of each property whose value you want to store.
3. To store the values of the property, use the `WriteProperty` method of the `PropertyBag` object to output the values of the changed properties. The code for this method is placed in the `WriteProperties` event of the UserDocument.
4. To retrieve the values of the property, use the `ReadProperty` method of the `PropertyBag` object to output the values of the changed properties. The code for this method is placed in the `ReadProperties` event of the UserDocument.

▶ **See** "Adding Properties" **p. 331**

The result of the code for handling these tasks in a sample document is shown in Figure 32.9.

FIGURE 32.9
Use the ReadProperty and WriteProperty methods to retrieve and store public properties of the UserDocument.

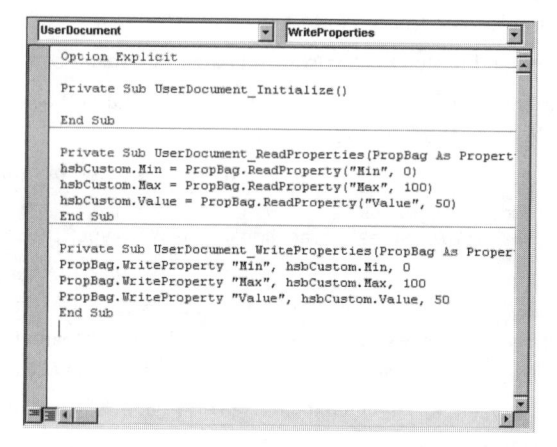

```
Option Explicit

Private Sub UserDocument_Initialize()

End Sub

Private Sub UserDocument_ReadProperties(PropBag As Propert
hsbCustom.Min = PropBag.ReadProperty("Min", 0)
hsbCustom.Max = PropBag.ReadProperty("Max", 100)
hsbCustom.Value = PropBag.ReadProperty("Value", 50)
End Sub

Private Sub UserDocument_WriteProperties(PropBag As Proper
PropBag.WriteProperty "Min", hsbCustom.Min, 0
PropBag.WriteProperty "Max", hsbCustom.Max, 100
PropBag.WriteProperty "Value", hsbCustom.Value, 50
End Sub
```

Working with the Methods of the UserDocument

In addition to the different events that UserDocument supports, the UserDocument also supports two key methods that a form does not: `AsyncRead` and `CancelAsyncRead`. The `AsyncRead` method enables the document to request that its container read in data from a file or URL. As the name implies, the read is performed asynchronously. As you can imagine, the ability to read a file asynchronously comes in handy when you're working with the Internet. For example, you might write a data viewer application that retrieves information from a server. The `AsyncRead` method requires that you specify the file (or information) to be read and the type of information that is being read. The three supported data types are summarized in Table 32.2.

Table 32.2 Types of Data Supported by the *AsyncRead* Method

Constant	Description
vbAsyncTypeFile	The data is contained in a file created by Visual Basic.
vbAsyncTypeByteArray	The data is a byte array containing retrieved data.
vbAsyncTypePicture	The data is stored in a Picture object.

The `CancelAsyncRead` method is used to terminate an asynchronous read prior to its completion.

As an example, add an asynchronous read to the ActiveX Document Loan Calculator. Before adding code for the `AsyncRead` method, set up the project as follows:

1. If you have not already done so, create the sample project described in the preceding sections.
2. Open the `CalcDoc` UserDocument object, and add two new controls to the form: a second command button and an Image control.
3. Name the command button `cmdGetPic`, and name the Image control `imgMain`.
4. Find the path to a picture file on your hard drive or intranet that you can use for this test. In the example, I use D:\Pictures\Brian.BMP.
5. Add the `AsyncRead` code to the `Click` event of the command button, as follows:
   ```
   Private Sub CmdGetPic_Click()
       AsyncRead "d:\pictures\brian.bmp", vbAsyncTypePicture, "MyPicture"
   End Sub
   ```
   The code simply initiates a download of the picture BRIAN.BMP to the client machine. In this case, I specified an exact file path on a local hard drive, but you can also use a URL just as easily—for example, `http://myserver/mypicture.gif`.
6. Add the following code to the `AsyncReadComplete` event of the user document to put the downloaded picture into the Image control:
   ```
   Private Sub UserDocument_AsyncReadComplete(AsyncProp As AsyncProperty)

   MsgBox "The picture download has finished with status " &
   AsyncProp.StatusCode
   Set imgMain.Picture = AsyncProp.Value

   End Sub
   ```
   The `AsyncReadComplete` event fires after the picture is downloaded, in which case a message box is displayed and the picture (stored in the parameter `AsyncProp`) is displayed in the Image control.

   NOTE   If you are loading an image from the Web (with the `http://` syntax), Internet Explorer may cache it locally. To make the most of the cache, you can add an optional parameter to the end of the `AsyncRead` call to control when and if the cache image is used. For a list of the settings of this parameter, see the `AsyncRead` method topic in the online help file.

In the sample, note that only one asynchronous download is happening. If you initiate multiple downloads, you can use the `PropertyName` property to determine which object is passed to the `AsyncReadComplete` event. In this case, the value of that property is `MyPicture`.

In addition to starting an asynchronous read and detecting when it completes, Visual Basic 6 now allows you to monitor its progress through the `AsyncReadProgress` event. Several properties are passed to this event, allowing you to display the download progress to the user. For example, you may want to display a status bar with the number of bytes downloaded or inform the user as connections are made and downloads are started.

Using the Hyperlink Object in Your Document

One object of extreme importance in ActiveX documents is the Hyperlink object. This object is accessed through the `HyperLink` property of the UserDocument object. It has no properties and only three methods. However, the Hyperlink object is what enables an ActiveX document to call another ActiveX document or to navigate to a Web site. The three methods of the Hyperlink object are the following:

- `NavigateTo`. This method causes the container that holds the ActiveX document to jump to a file or URL specified in the method. You use this method to move from one ActiveX document to another.
- `GoBack`. This method performs a hyperlink jump to the previous document in the history list of a container. If the container does not support hyperlinking or no items appear in the history list, an error occurs.
- `GoForward`. This method is the counterpart of the `GoBack` method. `GoForward` causes the container to move to the next document in the history list. If no more documents are available, an error occurs.

> **NOTE** A container such as Internet Explorer, which supports hyperlinking, executes on its own the jump specified in a `NavigateTo` method. A container such as Office 97 Binder, which does not support hyperlinking, starts a hyperlink-capable program to process the jump.

The following lines of code show example uses of the `Navigate` method:

```
UserDocument.Hyperlink.NavigateTo "MyDoc.VBD"
UserDocument.Hyperlink.NavigateTo "http://www.mysite.com"
```

The first line of code loads another ActiveX document in the same directory, while the second example directs the container to an Internet site.

Using the ActiveX Document Migration Wizard

So far, you have learned how to create an ActiveX document from scratch. But, if you are like me, you have a lot of time and effort invested in creating standard Visual Basic applications. Can you capitalize on the work you have already done, short of using cut and paste to bring in pieces of a program?

Fortunately, the answer is yes. Visual Basic provides a tool called the ActiveX Document Migration Wizard that can help you convert forms from an existing application to UserDocument objects for an ActiveX document. The key word here is "help." The wizard does not create a complete ActiveX document directly from your standard application. Instead, the wizard does the following:

- Copies the properties of the forms to new user documents.
- Copies menu items from the source forms to the new user documents.
- Copies all controls from the source forms, retaining their relative positions on the forms. All control properties are retained. Note that OLE container controls and embedded OLE objects are not copied.
- Copies the code from the form event procedures to the corresponding procedures in the user document, including all event procedures associated with the component controls.
- Comments out code statements that are not supported by ActiveX documents, such as Load, Unload, and End.

Although the ActiveX Document Migration Wizard can do a lot of the work of converting a document for you, it cannot handle some processes. Therefore, you have to do some coding work before you can compile and distribute your document.

First, you need to remove unsupported events, such as Load and Unload. Although the wizard comments out the Load and Unload statements, it does not do anything with the event procedures code. If you use these events to initialize the properties of a form or its controls, you may want to move some of the code from the Load event to the Initialize event of the UserDocument. Likewise, you may want to move some of the code from the Unload event to the Terminate event of the UserDocument.

You also need to make sure that you do not reference any nonexistent objects. For example, if you migrate a form to a UserDocument, any references to the form by name (for example, Form1) are invalid.

Running the ActiveX Document Migration Wizard

To run the ActiveX Document Migration Wizard, you need to make sure that it is available in Visual Basic. You make the wizard available by selecting it from the Add-In Manager dialog box, which you can access by choosing Add-In Manager from the Add-Ins menu. After you add the wizard to the Visual Basic IDE, you can run it by choosing ActiveX Document Migration Wizard from the Add-Ins menu.

The following steps describe the process of converting the forms of a project into ActiveX documents:

1. Open the project whose forms you want to convert. The wizard works correctly only from within the project.
2. Start the ActiveX Document Migration Wizard. You first see the introductory screen, which explains a little of what the wizard will and will not do for you. Click the Next button to proceed.

3. From the screen shown in Figure 32.10, select the forms from the current project that you want to convert to ActiveX documents. All the forms of the current project are shown in the forms list. You can select any form by clicking the check box next to the form name. Multiple selections are allowed. After you make your selections, click the Next button to move to the next part of the process.

FIGURE 32.10
Select your forms from the list in the wizard.

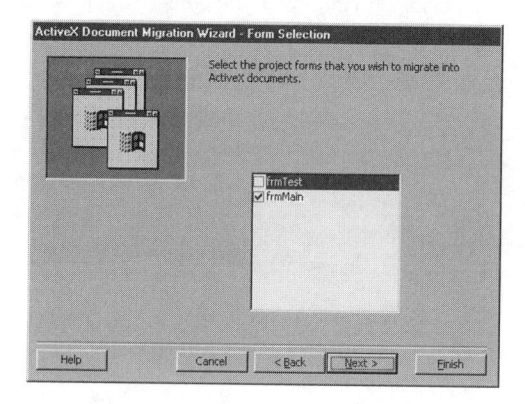

4. Use the Options page of the ActiveX Document Migration Wizard (shown in Figure 32.11) to control how the wizard processes the forms you have selected. The three options enable you to do the following:

   - Choose to comment out invalid code. This option comments out statements such as Load, Unload, or End that are not supported by ActiveX documents.
   - Remove original forms after conversion. This option removes the forms from the current project after the conversion is made. Typically, you do not check this option because you want to keep your original project intact.
   - Choose whether to convert your project to an ActiveX EXE or ActiveX DLL project. The option defaults to ActiveX EXE. (ActiveX DLLs are used for creating shared components rather than applications.)

FIGURE 32.11
Select the options that are appropriate to your needs.

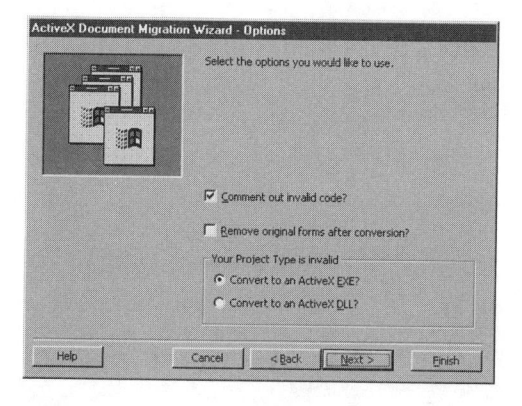

After you make your choices, click the Next button to proceed to the final page of the wizard.

5. Choose whether you would like to see a summary report after the wizard's part in the conversion is completed. After you make your selection, click the Finish button to begin the conversion. The summary report, shown in Figure 32.12, describes which additional activities you need to perform to complete the conversion process.

FIGURE 32.12
The ActiveX Document Migration Wizard uses a summary report to guide you through the rest of the conversion process.

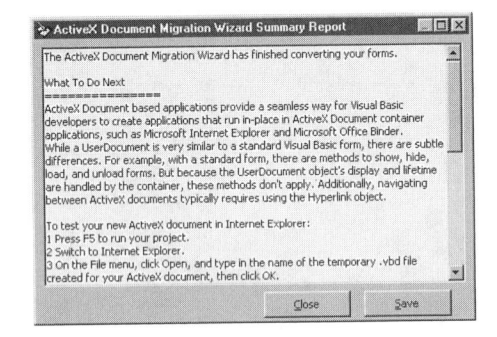

Looking at the Results of the Wizard's Work

After the ActiveX Document Migration Wizard finishes its work, it places the newly created UserDocument objects in the same project as the original forms. The document source files are stored in the same folder as the original form files and are given similar names, with the appropriate extension. For example, a form stored in the file FRMTEST1.FRM would create a UserDocument stored in the file DOCTEST1.DOB. As you learned previously, the controls of the form are copied to the UserDocument, and their relative positions are preserved. Figure 32.13 shows both the original form and the resulting UserDocument.

FIGURE 32.13
The UserDocument and the original form have the same user interface.

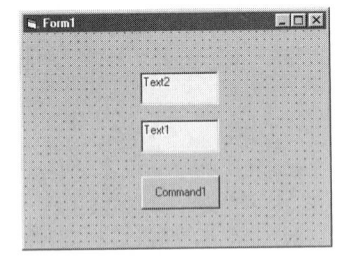

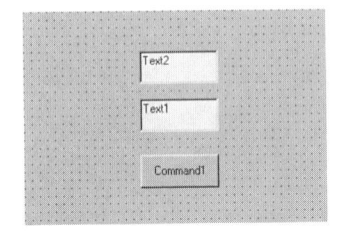

Also, as I stated previously, most of the code from your original form is copied over to the UserDocument. Invalid code is commented out and identified by the ActiveX Document Migration Wizard. (This result assumes that you chose to comment out invalid code on the Options page of the wizard.) Figure 32.14 shows an example of this process.

FIGURE 32.14
Invalid code is identified by the [AXDW] mark in a comment statement.

```
Private Sub Command1_Click()
'[AXDW] The following line was commented out by the ActiveX Document Migration Wizard
'       Unload Me
End Sub
```

Invalid code line

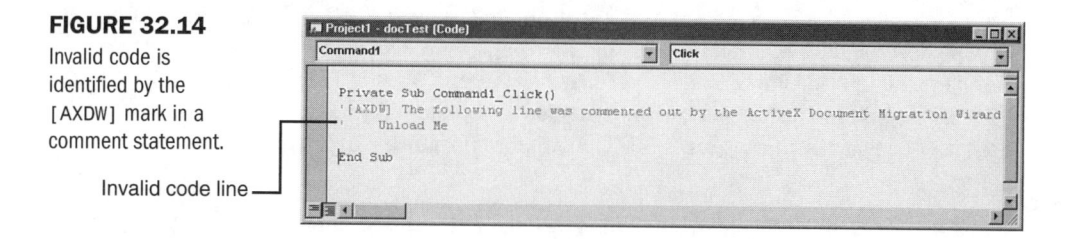

Creating a More Complex Document

Obviously, only so much room is available on a UserDocument object. Therefore, you are limited in the amount of information that can be displayed in a single document. In this regard, a single document is like an application with a single form. However, you can create additional documents as part of your project and then navigate among the various documents. You can also include standard forms in the applications that you create with ActiveX documents. In the following sections, you look at the details involved in using multiple documents and forms in your ActiveX document–based application.

Programming Additional Documents

To use additional documents in your ActiveX application, you need to create the additional documents and then provide a mechanism for moving back and forth between the documents. This process is somewhat different than moving between forms in a standard program because the UserDocument object does not support the `Load` and `Unload` statements, or the `Show` and `Hide` methods that are available to forms.

To add another document to your project, you first need to add another UserDocument object to the project. You do so by choosing Add User Document from the Project menu. This action places a second (or third, fourth, and so on) document in your project, under the UserDocuments folder. As with the first document you created, you need to specify a name for the document.

The next step requires you to draw the interface of the additional document and add the code that enables it to perform its tasks. This process is the same as the one you used to create the original document.

Now for the tricky part. Because you cannot use the `Show` method to display a document (as you can with forms), how do you get back and forth between the various documents in your application? The answer is to use the `NavigateTo` method of the Hyperlink object. The `NavigateTo` method instructs a container application to go to a particular file or URL and load the page. If the file is an ActiveX document, it gets processed just like your original page.

To move from your first document to your second, you need to run the `NavigateTo` method as shown in the following line of code:

```
Hyperlink.NavigateTo App.Path & "\docnav2.vbd"
```

The `App.Path` property specifies the path to the current document. By using this path as the basis for locating the second document, the document can be loaded without incident, provided that the documents are stored in the same directory. Figures 32.15 and 32.16 show the two pages of a sample document loaded in Internet Explorer. To get from the second document back to the first, you use the `NavigateTo` method again. For both documents, the method is used in code that responds to an event. The event is typically the `Click` event of a command button.

When you move to the second document of the application, notice that the Back button of Internet Explorer is enabled. You can use this button to move back to the first document. However, you should provide a direct link using the `NavigateTo` method because the first document may not always be the previous document in the history list. Also, if the first document has scrolled out of the history list, using the `NavigateTo` method is the only way to get to the document again.

Using and Displaying Forms from the Document

In addition to working with more than one document, you can work with standard forms in your ActiveX document applications. To use a form in a project, you create it the same way you would create a form for a standard project—draw the interface of the form and write the code to perform tasks. To display the form from your document, use the `Show` method. Then, to remove the form, use the `Unload` statement.

▶ **See** "Visual Basic Building Blocks," **p. 39**

Although forms can be part of your application, they are not handled the same way as documents. Forms are not contained within the application that contains the ActiveX document. Forms are independent of the container, as shown in Figure 32.17.

From Here...

This chapter introduced you to the world of ActiveX documents. You learned how these documents enable you to easily create applications that can run inside Internet Explorer or other ActiveX-enabled container applications. You also learned about the similarity between the UserDocument object and the forms of a standard application.

This chapter also touched on some other topics related to the creation of ActiveX documents that are covered in more detail in other chapters. To learn more about these topics, see the following chapters:

- To learn more about designing and creating forms, see Chapter 3, "Visual Basic Building Blocks."
- To learn more about debugging your programs, see Chapter 9, "Visual Basic Programming Fundamentals."
- To learn more about creating ActiveX controls, see Chapter 14, "Creating ActiveX Controls" and Chapter 15, "Extending ActiveX Controls."
- To find an alternative way to create an Internet application, see Chapter 31, "Active Server Pages."

CHAPTER 33

Visual Basic and Other Uses of the Internet

In this chapter

Adding Browser Functionality to Your Application **742**

Programming E-Mail **747**

Using the Internet Transfer Control **751**

Most chapters in the Internet portion of this book focus on how you can use Visual Basic to take Web pages beyond standard HTML. Although Web pages might be the most popular way to use the Internet, you can do a lot more with Visual Basic and the Internet, such as the following:

- Integrate the Web browser into your application
- Send and receive e-mail messages
- Transfer files with the Internet Transfer Control

Although this list in no way exhausts the ways you can use Visual Basic with the Internet, these topics are relevant and useful to many developers. This chapter provides a practical introduction to each of the topics.

Adding Browser Functionality to Your Application

Often you might want to integrate Internet browsing into an otherwise standard Visual Basic program. For example, you might provide a list of links to documentation and other support Web pages. By adding just a few lines of code, you can have your application automatically launch the user's browser and open the correct page. You can also add a browser control to your application, which allows the user to peruse Web pages inside a window contained on a Visual Basic form. Either method provides an easy way to use the functionality of a Web browser in your VB applications.

Creating a Browser on a Form

The simplest way to add the contents of a Web site to your application is to use the WebBrowser control, which is installed with Internet Explorer 4.0. First, add the control to a Standard EXE project by choosing Components from the Project menu and selecting Microsoft Internet Controls. Next, draw a WebBrowser control on a form at the size you want.

To make the WebBrowser control work, you only need to write a single line of code, as in the following example:

```
WebBrowser1.Navigate "http://www.quecorp.com/"
```

The WebBrowser control's Navigate method causes the WebBrowser control to connect to the specified URL and retrieve a Web page, as shown in Figure 33.1.

Because the WebBrowser is a control inside your Visual Basic program, it does not automatically contain all of the toolbars and other controls associated with Microsoft Internet Explorer. However, you can easily add your own command buttons or custom functions to make the WebBrowser control navigate to the sites you want.

Adding Browser Functionality to Your Application | 743

FIGURE 33.1
With the WebBrowser control, you can add a live Web page to your form.

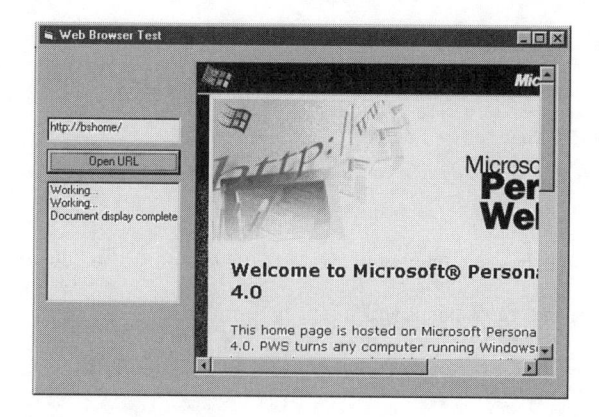

As you know, Web pages can contain graphics and other items, which can take a while to download. All of this happens asynchronously within the browser control while the rest of your VB program continues as normal. However, it would be nice to know when the Web page has been completely displayed. Notice that the sample form in Figure 33.1 includes a list box that displays the status of the browser. This was coded by using a just a few properties and events of the WebBrowser control:

- The `Busy` property is a Boolean property that is `True` if the browser is in the process of communicating with the Web server. The sample in Figure 33.1 used a Timer control to repeatedly check this property and update the list box.
- The `Stop` method is just like the Stop button on Internet Explorer. It could be used to stop the WebBrowser control from displaying the page if it is taking too long.
- The `DocumentComplete` event is fired by the WebBrowser control when the Web site is completely displayed. This event does not fire if the WebBrowser control's `Visible` property is set to `False`.

Listing 33.1 provides the code necessary to create the sample shown in Figure 33.1.

Listing 33.1 BROWSER.ZIP—Using a WebBrowser Control

```
Private Sub cmdNavigate_Click()

    WebBrowser1.Visible = False
    WebBrowser1.Navigate txtURL.Text
    tmrMain.Enabled = True

End Sub

Private Sub tmrMain_Timer()

    If WebBrowser1.Busy = True Then
        lstStatus.AddItem "Working..."
```

continues

Listing 33.1 Continued

```
    Else
        WebBrowser1.Visible = True
        tmrMain.Enabled = False
    End If

End Sub

Private Sub WebBrowser1_DocumentComplete(ByVal pDisp As Object, URL As Variant)

    lstStatus.AddItem "Document display completed."

End Sub
```

Launching the Browser from Your Application

In addition to using the WebBrowser control, you can launch the Web browser as a separate program. This allows the user more freedom because he can resize the browser window and use all of its built-in features. An additional advantage is that you do not have to take up screen real estate on your own forms with an embedded browser control.

Creating an Internet Shortcut   The first step to launching Web sites from an application is to understand the simple concept of an URL (Uniform Resource Locator) file, also known as an Internet shortcut. Internet shortcuts are like regular Windows shortcuts, but they point to a Web site rather than an executable file. Double-clicking an Internet shortcut opens your browser and navigates to the Web site represented by the shortcut.

An Internet shortcut is just a plain text file (actually it's an INI file) containing the URL of the Web site. The structure is as follows:

```
[InternetShortcut]
URL=http://www.que.com/
```

The Favorites list in Microsoft Internet Explorer is actually just a bunch of URL files. If you find the Favorites directory on your hard drive, you should be able to see these .URL files. Because the structure of a URL file is so simple, it is very easy to create one from Visual Basic. You can use the INI file functions discussed in Chapter 21, "Working with Files," or just create a standard text file:

```
Open "C:\TEMP.URL" For Output As #1
Print #1, "[InternetShortcut]"
Print #1, "URL=http://www.somewhere.com"
Close #1
```

These four lines of code create an Internet shortcut called TEMP.URL. After it's created, you should be able to click the shortcut icon to launch a Web site.

▶ **See** "Using INI Files," **p. xxx** (Ch 21)

Adding Browser Functionality to Your Application

Launching an Internet Shortcut   There are a couple of ways to launch an Internet shortcut from Visual Basic. You can use an API call or shell out to another program, which opens the browser for you.

The Windows API call `ShellExecute` executes the program associated with the .URL extension. If everything has been set up properly, the associated program should be your default browser. As with all API calls, you first have to declare them.

▶ **See** "Using API Calls in Visual Basic," **p. 452**

The following code segment launches the site using the `ShellExecute` API and the file C:\TEMP.URL:

```
Const SW_SHOWNORMAL = 1
Dim lRetVal As Long 'RETURN VALUE
Dim lWindow As Long 'BROWSER HWND
lRetVal = ShellExecute(lWindow, "open", "C:\Temp.URL", "", "", SW_SHOWNORMAL)
```

> **NOTE** `ShellExecute` and `FindExecutable` are API calls that can be used to determine which program is associated with a certain file extension and then launch the program. They are not limited to use with Internet shortcuts, which is why many of the parameters in the example are left blank.

Using the `ShellExecute` API to launch a Web site is easy, but there is even an easier method. Windows has a program called RUNDLL32.EXE, which is used to call functions in a DLL. To demonstrate, go to an MS-DOS Window (or the Start menu, Run prompt) and enter the following command line:

```
rundll32.exe shdocvw.dll,OpenURL c:\temp.url
```

This command has the same effect as double-clicking the Internet shortcut file. You can easily use Visual Basic's `Shell` function to call the command from code:

```
Shell "rundll32.exe shdocvw.dll,OpenURL c:\temp.url", vbNormalFocus
```

Although the API method seems like a more elegant solution, using RUNDLL32 works just as well. As a matter of fact, if you examine the `InternetShortcut` key in the Windows Registry (under `HKEY_CLASSES_ROOT`), you'll find that this is exactly how Windows launches Internet shortcuts.

An Enhanced About Box   To demonstrate how launching a Web site can work, we will create an About box with a Web site link. An About Box is a form (usually accessed through the About menu) that displays information about your program. Visual Basic includes an About box template, which is the basis for our project.

Follow these steps to create the About box example:

1. Create a new Standard EXE project in Visual Basic.
2. Click the Add Form button, or choose Project, Add Form. The Add Form dialog box appears.

3. Select About dialog and click Open. A new form should be added to your program that looks like the one shown in Figure 33.2.

FIGURE 33.2
Visual Basic includes a standard About Box form.

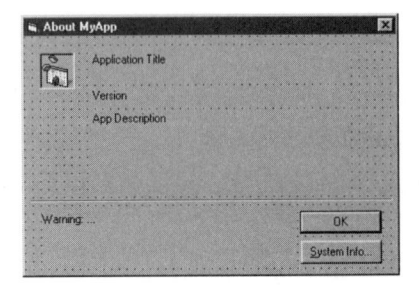

4. Decrease the size of the App Description label, lblDescription, so that you can fit an additional Label control on the form. (Changing the Height property to about 550 should do it for this example.)
5. Draw the new Label control beneath lblDescription and call it lblURL.
6. Open the Properties window for lblURL and make the following changes:
   - Set the ForeColor property to light blue.
   - Open the Font dialog box and turn on the Underline property.
   - Set the Caption property to the URL of a Web site—www.quecorp.com for this example.

After you perform the preceding steps, your label should look like an Internet hyperlink.

7. Add the code shown in Listing 33.2 in the label's Click event. This code opens the URL.

Listing 33.2 INETDEMO.ZIP—Launching a Web Site from a Form

```
Private Sub lblURL_Click()
    Dim nFile As Integer

    'WRITE A TEMP URL FILE
    nFile = FreeFile
    Open App.Path & "\TEMP.URL" For Output As #nFile
    Print #nFile, "[InternetShortcut]"
    Print #nFile, "URL=" & lblURL.Caption
    Close #nFile

    'LAUNCH THE BROWSER
    Shell "rundll32.exe shdocvw.dll,OpenURL " & App.Path & "\temp.url", _
          vbNormalFocus

    'DELETE THE TEMP FILE
    Kill App.Path & "\TEMP.URL"

End Sub
```

To test this program, you need to display the About form and click the URL. Traditionally, an About box is displayed when the user selects the About menu item. However, for testing purposes, you can put the following statement in the Load event of Form1:

frmAbout.Show

The enhanced About box is shown in Figure 33.3.

FIGURE 33.3
A properly formatted label control acts as a "fake" hyperlink.

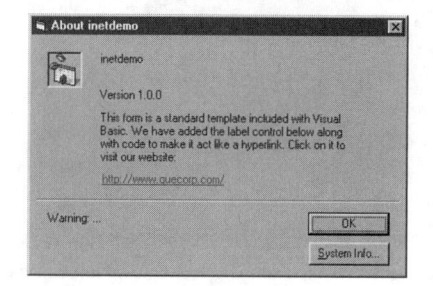

Programming E-Mail

It seems as though almost everyone these days has an e-mail address. Although e-mail is ideal for the type of personal communications used in regular mail, it has the added benefit of being able to transfer files and other information. For example, a Visual Basic program where I work pulls information from a database, stores it in a spreadsheet, and then sends the spreadsheet to the appropriate people. All of this happens automatically every morning without any human intervention. To perform such automation tasks, you need a method of interacting with e-mail from Visual Basic.

One such method is OLE Messaging (also known as Microsoft Active Messaging and Collaboration Data Objects). OLE Messaging is an object-oriented interface to Windows Messaging. When you install some versions of Microsoft Outlook or Exchange, a file called OLEMSG32.DLL is installed in your Windows System directory.

> **NOTE** The e-mail tools included with Visual Basic are the MAPI controls and the MAPI API. These are still available, but they are not as easy to use as OLE Messaging.

To use OLE Messaging, you have to add a reference to this DLL by selecting the Active Messaging Object Library on the References dialog box (choose Properties, References) as shown in Figure 33.4.

After adding the reference, press F2 to bring up Visual Basic's Object Browser. You can view all of the objects, properties, and methods included with the reference.

FIGURE 33.4
To use Active Messaging, you must have OLEMSG32.DLL installed on your system.

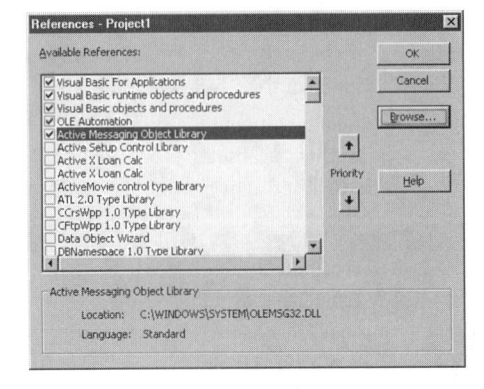

ON THE WEB

The examples in this section were created using Microsoft Outlook. Documentation for Active Messaging is available on Microsoft's Web site:

www.microsoft.com/ithome/resource/exchange/active/default.htm

Microsoft also has expanded Active Messaging functionality in Microsoft Exchange Server 5.5 well beyond messaging and has renamed it *Collaboration Data Objects* (*CDO*). For more information, visit the following Web site:

www.microsoft.com/exchange/guide/papers/cdo.asp

Logging on to E-Mail

The first step in working with e-mail from Visual Basic is to start a messaging *session*. The session represents a connection between your Visual Basic program and the e-mail system. To start a session, you have to create a new session object and then call the Logon method, as in the following example:

```
Dim objSession As Object
Set objSession = CreateObject("MAPI.Session")
objSession.Logon
```

When you start Microsoft Exchange or Outlook interactively, you might have to enter a user name, profile name, or password, depending on how your PC is configured. In the previous code example, we did not provide any of these parameters, so executing these statements would cause the e-mail system to prompt for any necessary logon information.

To create any kind of automated e-mail processing program, you need to avoid having dialog boxes appear. To do this, you must provide additional parameters to the Logon method:

```
objSession.Logon "Your Profile Name", , False, False
```

The first two parameters in the previous line of code are the profile name and profile password. If your profile is set up so that it does not need a password, you can leave the password parameter blank, as in the example.

NOTE You can create a profile in the Mail and Fax Control Panel applet or from the Tools, Services menu in Outlook.

The third parameter, `ShowDiag`, is a boolean value which determines whether any dialog boxes should be shown during e-mail logon. If this parameter is set to `True`, the user will see the logon prompt even if you have provided all of the necessary parameters. For automatic, unattended logon, you need to set this property to `False`.

The final optional parameter, `NewSession`, determines whether a new session is created during the logon process even if one already exists. By setting this parameter to `False`, you can cause Active Messaging to share an existing e-mail session. In other words, if you already have Outlook open, then Active Messaging does not have to repeat the logon process.

Sending a Message

The great thing about Active Messaging is that messages and other objects are represented using the familiar collections syntax. We have already discussed collections in several other chapters, so you should be familiar with adding and removing objects in a collection. As with many other collections, the collection's `Add` method can be used to create objects in two ways: to return an object reference or with parameters specifying object properties.

▶ **See** "Creating Classes That Contain Collections," **p. 373**

To send a message with Active Messaging, you need to perform the following steps:

1. Add a new Message object to the Messages collection of the Inbox.
2. Set the message text, subject, and add files to the `Attachments` collection.
3. Add the recipients' names (and/or addresses) to the `Recipients` collection.
4. Resolve recipients' names to determine their actual addresses.
5. Call the `Send` method to send the message.

The code to perform all of the preceding steps is both short and easy to understand:

```
' ... Assume we have already logged on

  'Add a new message to the Inbox
  Set objMessage = objSession.Inbox.Messages.Add

  'Set the subject and body text
  objMessage.Subject = "Test Message"
  objMessage.Text = "This is a test, repeat only a test message!"

  'Add an attachment
  objMessage.Attachments.Add "Monthly Report", , ActMsgFileData, _
      "C:\MyReport.XLS"

  'Add a recipient to the list
  objMessage.Recipients.Add "bsiler@bigfoot.com", , ActMsgTo
  objMessage.Recipients.Resolve
```

```
'Send The Message
objMessage.Send
```

As you can see from the example, Active Messaging uses collections to manage `Message`, `Recipient`, and `Attachment` objects. The code sample first sets up a new `Message` object and then invokes the `Send` method to send the message. All of the methods and properties of these objects are listed in the OLEMSG32.DLL file and can be viewed in the Object Browser.

The only thing that might be somewhat confusing is the concept of resolving the recipient names. In your e-mail system you have an address book. Resolving simply means taking a friendly name from the address book (for example, "Dad at Work") and converting it to the actual address that the e-mail server uses (`SMTP:jsmith@somewhere.com`).

Accessing the Contents of a Message

We have just seen how to send an e-mail message with Active Messaging. You can also use the `Messages` collection to access unread (or read) messages with Visual Basic code. One possible use for this feature would be to send out an e-mail with a specific subject and then have a program automate replies to the e-mail or store the responses in a database. For example, consider the following code:

```
For Each objMessage In objSession.Inbox.Messages
    If objMessage.Unread = True Then
        If Instr(objMessage.Subject, "Catalog Request") Then
             ProcessMessage objMessage.Text
        End If
    End If
Next objMessage
```

The sample code uses a `For Each` loop to iterate through each message in the `Messages` collection. If a message has not been read (indicated by the `Unread` property) and the subject contains some specific words, a user-defined function `ProcessMessage` is called. The `ProcessMessage` function, which accepts the message text as a parameter, can do any number of things with the message, including initiate a reply or add the contents of the message to a database table.

Working with e-mail messages is easy, because each message is represented as an independent object with properties and methods. You can use a `For Each` loop to browse the `Messages` collection and process them as desired. The following few lines of code print the subjects of all unread messages that were sent after 7/4/1998:

```
For Each objMessage In objSession.Inbox.Messages
        If objMessage.Unread = True And objMessage.Submitted = False Then
            If objMessage.TimeSent >= "7/4/98" Then
                 Debug.Print objMessage.Sender, objMessage.Subject
            End If
        End If
Next objMessage
```

The code sample uses a series of `If` statements to determine if the current message is unread, has been submitted, and has been sent on or later than July 4, 1998.

> **TIP** Using an interface such as Active Messaging might make your program more error prone because of the uncontrollable user interaction. For this reason, I suggest creating user-defined functions with error handling for each task you want to perform (logging on, sending a message, and so on).

In this section, we have given you a glimpse into the Active Messaging Library. To discover the full list of available properties and methods, use Visual Basic's Object Browser or see the help file ACTMSG.HLP included in the download file.

Using the Internet Transfer Control

Another Internet feature of Visual Basic is the Internet Transfer control. This control allows you to establish a connection to another computer and transfer files. It is Microsoft's attempt to make it easy to use two Internet protocols: HTTP and FTP. HTTP, or Hypertext Transfer Protocol, is the means by which a Web browser communicates with a Web server. If you have transferred information across the Internet, you may already be familiar with the File Transfer Protocol (FTP). In this section, we'll look at a sample use of both protocols.

Retrieving HTML

When you access a Web page normally, the browser uses the `GET` command (defined by the HTTP protocol) to ask the Web server for a document. For example, if you open the URL `http://www.food.com/peanuts.html`, the browser establishes a connection with the machine at the address `www.food.com` and then sends the command `GET /peanuts.html`. The HTML is returned to the browser over the connection as plain text, and the browser uses its own logic to parse and format it appropriately.

When you use the Internet Transfer control with the HTTP protocol, you can retrieve HTML for processing by your own program. For example, you could periodically query a Web site for stock information. Your VB program could then save the stock information in a SQL database for other users to view. In other words, the Internet Transfer control can be used to automatically collect data from a Web site.

As an example, we will use the Internet Transfer control to retrieve HTML and print it on a form. To create the sample project, perform the following steps:

1. Open Visual Basic and create a new Standard EXE project.
2. Display the Project Components dialog box and add a reference to Microsoft Internet Transfer Control 6.0.
3. Draw an instance of the Internet Transfer control on the form. Note that this control will appear as an icon no matter how large you draw it.
4. Add a text box named `txtURL` and a command button named `cmdRetrieve`.

After completing these steps, your form should look like the one shown in Figure 33.5. You are now ready to add code to the sample project.

FIGURE 33.5
The Internet Transfer control does not appear automatically in the Visual Basic Toolbox.

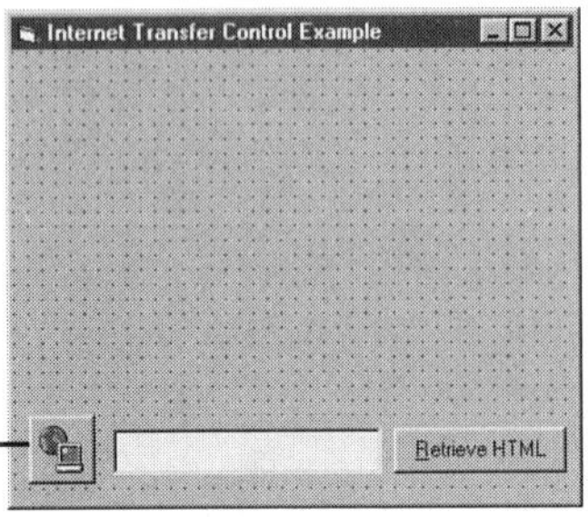

The Internet Transfer control has one event, the `StateChanged` event. The purpose of this event is to notify your program when different activities are happening. For example, the control is in one state when it is connecting to the Web server and in another when it is retrieving HTML. The current state is indicated by the `State` parameter of the event procedure. Enter the code for our sample program's `StateChanged` event, which is shown in Listing 33.3.

Listing 33.3   INETDEMO.ZIP— Retrieving Raw HTML from a Web Server

```
Private Sub Inet1_StateChanged(ByVal State As Integer)

    Select Case State

        Case 12 'icResponseCompleted
            stemp = Inet1.GetChunk(100)
            While stemp <> ""
                Me.Print stemp;
                stemp = Inet1.GetChunk(100)
            Wend
            Me.Print

        Case 11 'icError
            MsgBox Inet1.ResponseInfo, vbCritical, "ERROR!"

    End Select

End Sub
```

Our code only handles two states, the `icResponseCompleted` state and the error state. The `icResponseCompleted` state indicates that the control has finished receiving a response from the Web server. The Internet Transfer control's `GetChunk` method is used to retrieve the response text from the buffer 100 bytes at a time and print it on the form.

> **N O T E** A complete list of states and their meanings is in the online documentation article entitled "StateChanged Event."

Although the `StateChanged` event contains the main portion of code for this sample program, you still need to add code to the `Click` event of `cmdRetrieve` to initiate the request. The code in Listing 33.4, uses the `Execute` method of the Internet Transfer control to issue an HTTP command.

Listing 33.4 INETDEMO.ZIP—The *Execute* Method

```
Private Sub cmdRetrieve_Click()

    Inet1.protocol = icHTTP
    Inet1.Execute CStr(txtURL), "GET /"

    While Inet1.StillExecuting
        DoEvents
    Wend

    MsgBox "Done!"

End Sub
```

After entering the code in Listing 33.4, run the program and enter a test URL in the text box. Click the button and the HTML should be displayed on the form, as shown in Figure 33.6.

FIGURE 33.6
The Internet Transfer control can be used to retrieve HTML from a Web site.

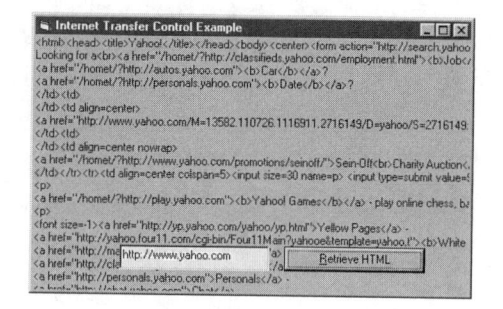

In our sample program, we just printed the results on the form. To work with the HTML as a string, you need to store it in a string variable or label control. When the download is complete, you can easily search the HTML for the information you want using standard string functions.

Transferring Files

FTP, the Internet's File Transfer Protocol, has been around a lot longer than the World Wide Web. As with the Web, FTP involves both a client and a server machine. Although in recent years FTP clients have become graphical, the standard implementation of the FTP client is text based, like the one shown in Figure 33.7.

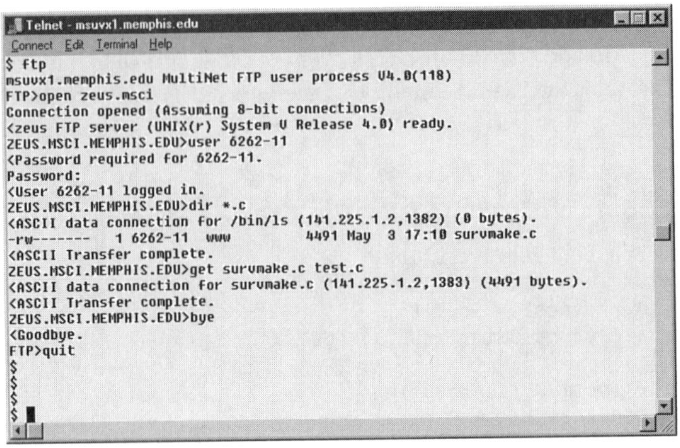

FIGURE 33.7
A sample FTP session on the Vax VMS system.

If you have used a DOS prompt, then you can understand how FTP works. FTP allows you to change the current directory, display a file list, and copy files—just like you would at a DOS prompt. The major difference is that you are browsing a directory structure on a remote machine. The commands are also slightly different. FTP's get and put commands are used to retrieve and send files to and from the remote machine.

Because FTP is a standard protocol used on many platforms (UNIX, Windows, AS/400, and so on), it is ideal for transferring data between machines. The Internet Transfer control provides an easy way to do this from Visual Basic. In this section, we will create a simple program that retrieves a file from an FTP server.

To begin, let's build on the example from the previous section. Create the sample project as described, adding an additional command button, cmdGetFile. The code for cmdGetFile is shown in Listing 33.5.

Listing 33.5 INETDEMO.ZIP—Using FTP with the Internet Transfer Control

```
Private Sub cmdGetFile_Click()
    Me.Cls
    Inet1.protocol = icFTP
    Inet1.UserName = "anonymous"
    Inet1.Password = "guest@"
    Inet1.Execute "ftp.microsoft.com", "pwd"
    While Inet1.StillExecuting
        DoEvents
    Wend
    
    Inet1.Execute , "dir *.txt"
    While Inet1.StillExecuting
        DoEvents
    Wend
    
    Inet1.Execute , "GET dirmap.txt c:\dirmap.txt"
    While Inet1.StillExecuting
```

```
        DoEvents
    Wend

    MsgBox "Done!"

End Sub
```

The code in Listing 33.5 uses the Internet Transfer control to perform three FTP commands:

- `pwd`—Prints the current working directory on the remote machine
- `dir`—Lists files on the remote machine
- `get`—Downloads a file from the remote machine to the client machine

Notice that after each of these commands we use a `While` loop to determine if the Internet control has finished executing the command before attempting to executing a new command. The code in the `StateChanged` event should cause the responses from the `pwd` and `dir` commands to be printed on the form. The final command, `get`, transfers a text file from the FTP server to the local hard drive. This example could be used for performing automated data retrieval from a remote system, or pulling a daily weather map or other image from your favorite Web site.

From Here...

In this chapter, we have given you a small taste of a few Internet topics outside of the usual Web arena. The best place to learn about the Internet is of course on the Internet, but if you want to find out more about the Visual Basic concepts used in this chapter see the following other chapters:

- If you want to learn the basics of using the Windows API, see Chapter 20, "Accessing the Windows API."
- To learn more about INI and text files, see Chapter 21, "Working with Files."
- To find out about controlling other OLE interfaces like Active Messaging, see Chapter 22, "Using OLE to Control Other Applications."

PART VIII

Appendixes

- **A** Introduction to the Development Environment 759
- **B** Packaging Your Applications 775
- **C** SQL Summary 793

APPENDIX A

Introduction to the Development Environment

In this chapter

Understanding the Environment's Key Features **760**

Starting Up **761**

The Visual Basic Work Area **762**

Visual Basic's *Integrated Development Environment* (*IDE*), which is the interface of Visual Basic itself, contains a number of tools that you can use as you develop your applications. The IDE underwent a major overhaul between versions 4.0 and 5.0 of Visual Basic; however, the interface for Visual Basic 6.0 is much the same as its predecessor. In this appendix, you'll take a quick look around the interface and learn about some of its features.

Understanding the Environment's Key Features

Since version 5.0, Visual Basic has sported a Multiple Document Interface (MDI) environment. If you are unfamiliar with MDI, you can compare it to having multiple documents open in Microsoft Word. Each document is contained in a child window, which is, in turn, contained within the main parent window. As with other MDI applications, such as Word or Excel, you can choose to have the child document fill the whole window or have multiple windows visible simultaneously.

TIP If you are not already using a big monitor (17 inches or larger) at high resolution, get one. You need a lot of screen space to use Visual Basic's interface most effectively. I recommend a screen resolution of 800×600 as a minimum, or 1024×768 if your video card (and eyes) can support it.

You can edit more than one project in the same Visual Basic session. Therefore, you don't have to close one project in order to open and make changes to another. This capability is convenient if you are developing projects that interact with each other because you can save and compile all projects in a group with a single menu option.

Another relatively new feature is dockable toolbars and windows. Now a window can be floating in the middle of the screen or docked along one of the edges. Dockable windows include the toolbars and windows with small title bars, such as the Toolbox.

In addition to the window management enhancements, Visual Basic offers some useful tools to make code entry easier. Microsoft calls them *Auto List Member* and *Auto Quick Info*; you will call them *fantastic*. If you have trouble remembering, for example, MessageBox constants, control properties, or even the parameters to your own functions, the code editor assists you with completing the information automatically while you type. For example, as soon as you press the Spacebar after a `MsgBox` function call, you are presented with the parameters in a ToolTip-like format with a drop-down box of the available constants.

TIP When you are presented with the drop-down box mentioned in the preceding paragraph, you don't have to use the mouse to select an item. Just keep typing (or use the arrow keys) until the list item you want is highlighted; then press the spacebar, comma (,), Enter, or Tab, and continue with your program.

Starting Up

When you start Visual Basic, you see the New Project dialog box, shown in Figure A.1. This dialog box has the following three tabs:

- **New.** Lets you choose one of several types of projects to create.
- **Existing.** Allows you to browse for a project that's already been created and saved.
- **Recent.** Presents you with a list of projects that have been worked on previously. The most recent projects are listed first.

FIGURE A.1
The New Project dialog box's New tab lets you select from several types of projects to create.

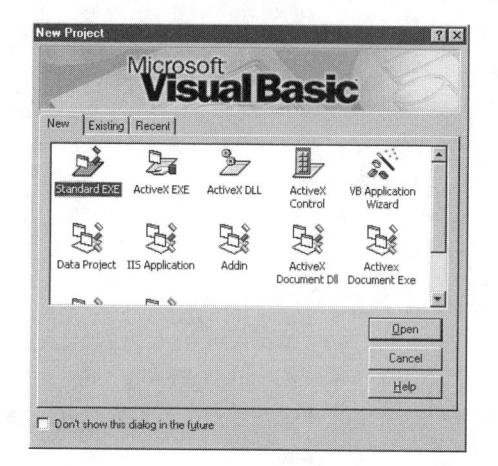

> **N O T E** There is another version of the New Project dialog box. You'll see this version when Visual Basic is already running and you select File, New Project from the menu system. This version of the New Project dialog box is similar to the one pictured in Figure A.1, but does not have the Existing and Recent tabs.

If you choose to create a new project, Visual Basic creates the appropriate project template for you, based on your selection from the New Project dialog box. You can choose to create one of these project types:

- **Standard EXE.** You use this type of project to create a standard Windows program (EXE file). You will probably use this type of project most often.
- **ActiveX EXE.** This automation server performs tasks as part of a multiple-tier application. The end result is a program that contains public classes that can be accessed by other programs or can run by itself. This server previously was called an *OLE automation server*.
- **ActiveX DLL.** This remote automation program is created as a DLL. ActiveX DLLs cannot run alone; however, because an ActiveX DLL runs in-process, it is faster than an out-of-process ActiveX EXE.
- **ActiveX Control.** With this option, you can create your own custom controls (OCXs). You can use them in your Visual Basic programs or in any ActiveX-capable application.

- **VB Application Wizard.** If you want something quick and generic, this option builds the skeleton of an application (similar to a word processor template). You can then customize the application to suit your needs.
- **Data Project.** This type of project includes the shell of a data-enabled application. You can customize the components to quickly develop a program that works with databases.
- **IIS Application.** This option creates a project that can be used in conjunction with Windows NT's Internet Information Server (IIS) to run in a Web-based environment.
- **Add-in.** This type of program provides additional functionality to Visual Basic itself. An example of an add-in is the Visual Data Manager.
- **ActiveX Document DLL.** This type of project creates a DLL that can be used by applications running within Microsoft Internet Explorer.
- **ActiveX Document EXE.** This type of project creates an application that can run inside Microsoft Internet Explorer.
- **DHTML Application.** This option creates the framework of a Dynamic HTML application, which can be run in a Web browser.

The Visual Basic Work Area

After you select the project type from the New Project dialog box, you are presented with the design environment. Here you do the work of actually creating your masterpiece application. The basic design environment is shown in Figure A.2. Visual Basic probably looked like this figure when you started it for the first time.

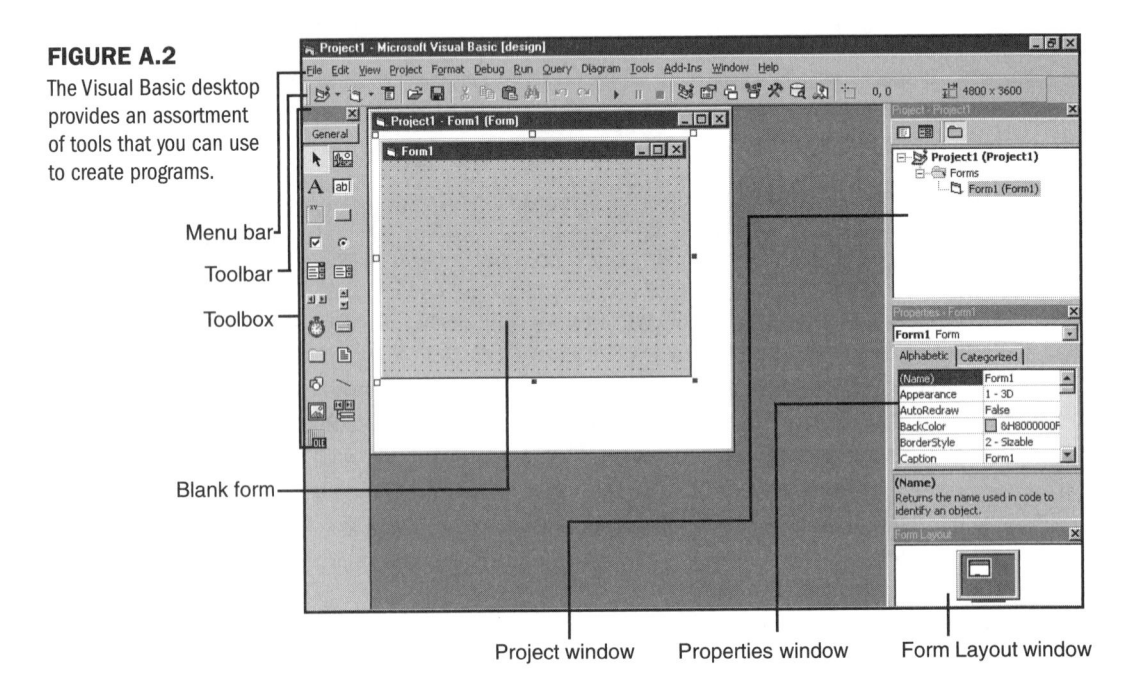

FIGURE A.2
The Visual Basic desktop provides an assortment of tools that you can use to create programs.

As you can see, Visual Basic shares a lot of elements with other Windows programs. The toolbars and menus look similar to those in Office 97. A few of the menu items are the same: File, Edit, Help, and others.

Using the Menu Bar

Many programmers want to find quick keyboard shortcuts for frequently used tasks. As with other Windows programs, the menus at the top of the Visual Basic screen can be displayed by holding down the Alt key while pressing the appropriate underlined character in the menu bar. After the initial menu is displayed, you can simply press the underlined character of a menu item to select it. For example, press Alt+F to open the File menu, and then press P to choose the Print command.

Visual Basic also offers several shortcut keys that let you bypass the menu entirely. Most of them are listed to the right of their respective menu items. For example, in the View menu, you might notice F2 to the right of Object Browser. This means that you can see the Object Browser by pressing F2. Although I have listed some quick shortcuts in Table A.1, a quick perusal of the menus would definitely be worth your while.

Table A.1 Shortcut Keys

Menu Item	Shortcut Key	Description
Edit, Cut	Ctrl+X	Removes the selected text or control from its current location and copies it to the Clipboard.
Edit, Copy	Ctrl+C	Makes a copy of the selected text or control on the Clipboard, but does not remove it from its original location.
Edit, Paste	Ctrl+V	Pastes the contents of the Clipboard to the active form or code window.
Edit, Undo	Ctrl+Z	Undoes the last change.
Edit, Find	Ctrl+F	Finds a piece of text. (You must be in an edit window to use this command.)
File, Open	Ctrl+O	Opens a project.
File, Save	Ctrl+S	Saves the current file.
File, Print	Ctrl+P	Displays the Print dialog box, from which you can print the current form or module or the entire application.
View, Project Explorer	Ctrl+R	Shows the Project Explorer window (if it's not already displayed).
View, Properties Window	F4	Shows the Properties window (if it's not already displayed).

> **TIP** Experimentation is encouraged. In addition to the preceding list, Visual Basic includes some not-so-obvious tricks such as Ctrl+Y (to delete a line of code), which is apparently an homage to WordStar.

Accessing Functions with the Toolbars

Visual Basic's *toolbars* provide you with quick access to some of the functions you will use most often. Four toolbars are available (see Figure A.3):

- **Standard.** The Standard toolbar is displayed by default and offers quick access to frequently used functions.
- **Debug.** The Debug toolbar has buttons for use when you're debugging your programs.
- **Edit.** The Edit toolbar's buttons are handy when you're writing code.
- **Form Editor.** The Form Editor toolbar contains buttons that help you tweak the appearance of controls on your forms.

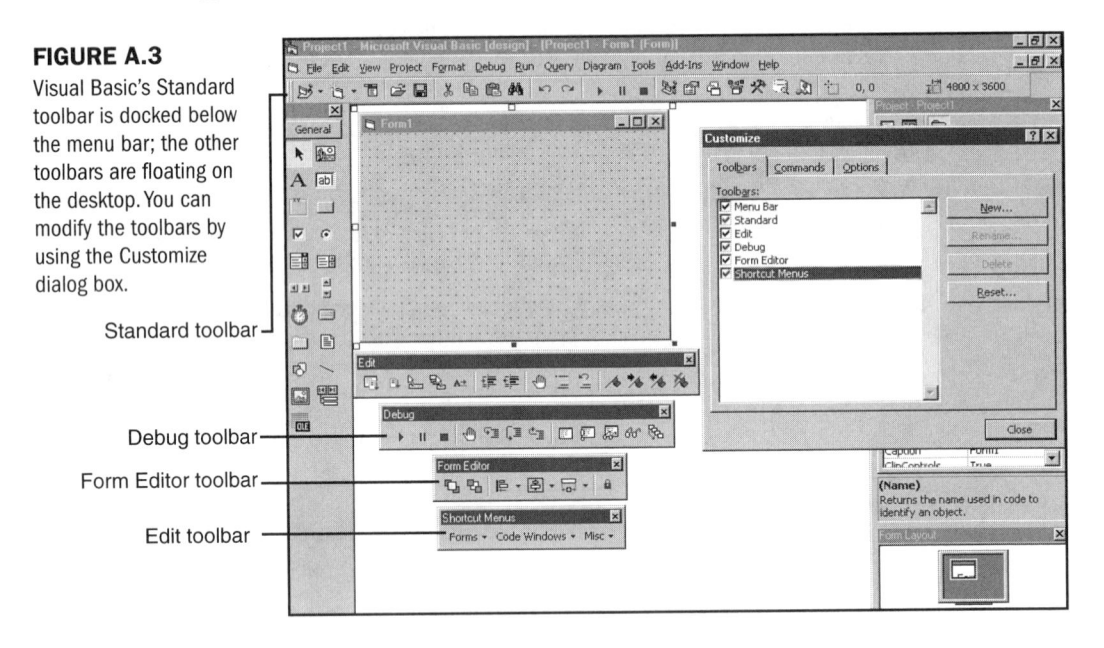

FIGURE A.3
Visual Basic's Standard toolbar is docked below the menu bar; the other toolbars are floating on the desktop. You can modify the toolbars by using the Customize dialog box.

Standard toolbar
Debug toolbar
Form Editor toolbar
Edit toolbar

The Standard toolbar is the only one displayed the first time you start Visual Basic. You can specify which toolbars are displayed by choosing View, Toolbars or by right-clicking any visible toolbar. Any of them can be free-floating or "docked" just below the menu bar; their startup positions will be the same as the last time you exited Visual Basic. Choosing View, Toolbars, Customize allows you to modify the existing toolbars, or even create your own.

Visual Basic's toolbars follow the standard used by the latest generation of programs in that they provide you with *ToolTips*. A ToolTip is a little yellow box that pops up if you let the mouse pointer hover over a button for a few seconds; it contains a description of the underlying button's function.

> **TIP** ToolTips can also display the value of a variable in a code window. Use this feature by letting the mouse pointer hover over a variable name while in break mode. This feature is a real time-saver if you are used to setting up a watch or printing values in the Immediate window.

Display all the toolbars as explained in the preceding paragraph, and move the pointer over the buttons to familiarize yourself with them. Remember that you can always use the ToolTip feature when you're unsure which button is which.

Two of these buttons require special attention. The Add Project button and the Add Form button both invoke drop-down lists of items (see Figure A.4). If you select one of these items, the default item for the button changes to the type of item that you selected.

FIGURE A.4
Drop-down buttons allow you to specify the type of project or file to be added.

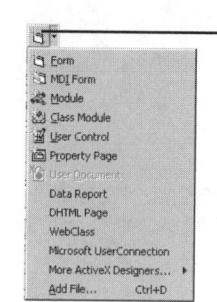

The Add Project button allows you to add a project to the desktop. It can be one of the following four types:

- Standard EXE
- ActiveX EXE
- ActiveX DLL
- ActiveX Control

The Add Form button lets you add any of the following pieces to your current project:

- Form
- MDI form
- Module
- Class module
- User control
- Property page
- Existing files

You learn about most of the other buttons on the toolbar a little later. However, two special areas on the toolbar deserve mentioning. At the far right of the toolbar are two blocks, with each containing a pair of numbers. These two blocks show the position and size of the form or control with which you are working. The two numbers in the first block indicate the horizontal and vertical positions, respectively, of the upper-left corner of the current object, as measured from the upper-left corner of the screen (if the current object is a form), or of the current form (if the current object is a control). The two numbers in the second block show the horizontal and vertical dimensions, respectively, of the current object. These numbers are not visible, however, when you are editing in a code window.

NOTE Both the position and dimension information are given in *twips*. A twip is a unit of measure that Visual Basic uses to ensure that placement and sizing of objects is consistent on different types of screens. A twip is equal to 1/20 of a printer's point; approximately 1,440 twips make up a logical inch (the amount of screen space that would take up one inch when printed).

Let me add one final note about the toolbars. If you don't like having them located at the top of the screen, you can move any of them by clicking the double bars at the left edge and dragging to a new location. You can park a toolbar against any other edge of the desktop or leave them floating in the middle, as shown in Figure A.5.

FIGURE A.5
Even the standard toolbar can float freely on the desktop.

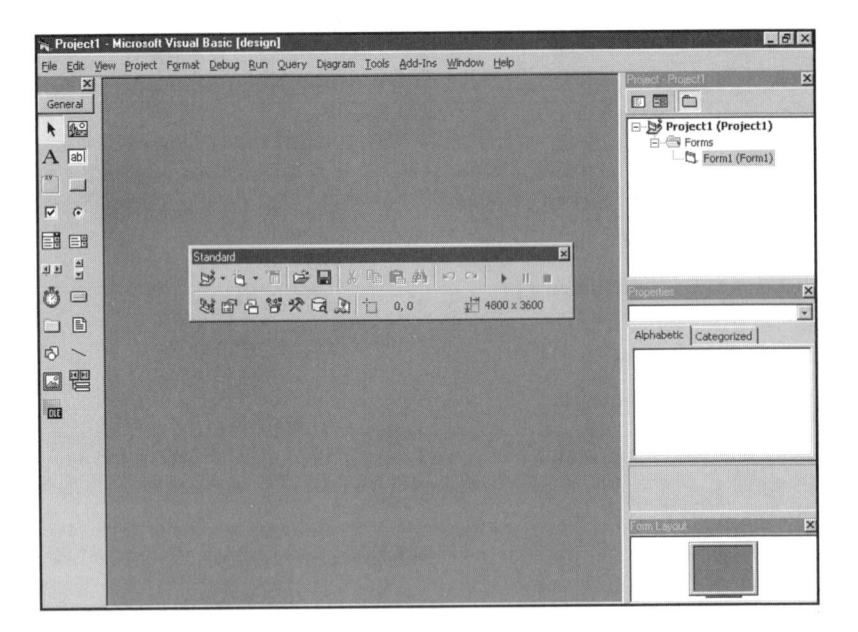

Organizing Visual Basic's Controls

The controls that are used in Visual Basic are the heart and soul of the programs that you create. The controls allow you to add functionality to your program quickly and easily. You can find controls that allow you to edit text, connect to a database, retrieve file information from a user, or display and edit pictures.

Obviously, with all these controls available, you need a way to keep them organized. This is the function of the *Toolbox* (see Figure A.6). This Toolbox contains buttons representing the controls that are available for use in your program. (A list of the basic set of Visual Basic 6 controls is contained in Table A.2.) Clicking one of the control "tools" allows you to draw a control of that type on a form. Double-clicking a tool places a default-sized control of that type in the center of the current form. Clicking the Pointer tool in the upper-left of the Toolbox cancels a pending control-drawing function and restores the mouse pointer's normal functionality.

FIGURE A.6
The basic control set is available when you first start Visual Basic. The Toolbox can be moved around onscreen to a location that is convenient for you.

— Pointer tool

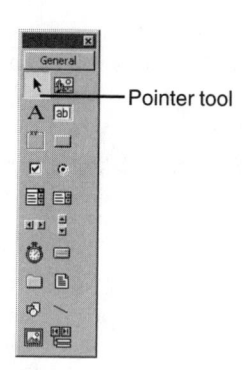

Table A.2 Standard Visual Basic Controls

Control Name	Function
PictureBox	Displays a graphic image.
Label	Displays text that the users cannot directly modify.
TextBox	Displays text that the users can edit.
Frame	Provides a method for grouping controls. (To group controls in a frame, select the frame with a single-click first; then draw a control in it.)
CommandButton	Allows the users to initiate a program action. Can include an icon, caption, and ToolTips.
CheckBox	Displays or allows input of a two-part choice, such as Yes/No or True/False.
OptionButton	Displays or allows a choice among multiple items. (Also known as a radio button.)
ComboBox	Allows the users to select an entry from a list or enter a new value.

continues

Table A.2 Continued

Control Name	Function
ListBox	Displays a list of items from which the users can select one or more entries.
HscrollBar (Horizontal Scrollbar)	Produces a numerical value based on the scrollbar's horizontal position.
VscrollBar (Vertical Scrollbar)	Same as above but vertical. Note the scrollbars behave like standard Windows scrollbars.
Timer	Provides a means for an action to be taken after passage of a certain amount of time.
DriveListBox	Displays and allows users to choose from available disk drives on the computer.
Dir ListBox	Displays and allows users to choose from available subdirectories on a drive.
FileListBox	Displays and allows users to choose from available files in a directory.
Shape	Displays geometric shapes on the form.
Line	Displays lines on the form.
Image	Displays a graphic image. Similar in appearance to the picture control but different functionality.
Data	Provides a link to database files.
OLE	Provides a way to link to OLE servers.

You can add other controls to the Toolbox by choosing Project, Components. This action brings up the Components dialog box (see Figure A.7). In this dialog box, you can choose any additional controls (OCXs) that have been installed on your system. If you choose to add a control to the Toolbox, it appears in the Toolbox after you click the OK or Apply button.

FIGURE A.7
You can add controls to the Toolbox by using the Components dialog box.

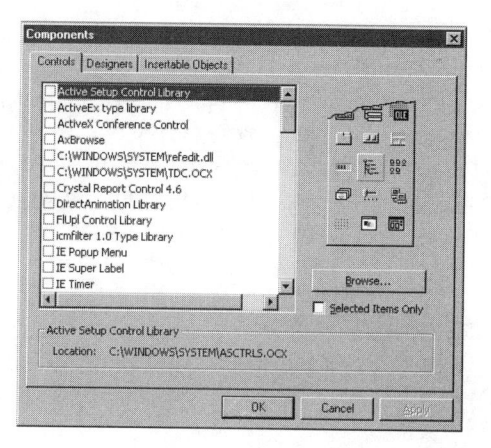

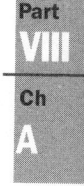

> **TIP** You can also access the Components dialog box by right-clicking the Toolbox and then selecting the Components item from the pop-up context-sensitive menu.

By default, all the components for your project appear in the Toolbox in one big group. However, if you use a lot of controls, managing all of them can be very difficult. To help with this problem, Visual Basic allows you to add tabs to the Toolbox. (It has one tab, General, by default.) To add a tab, right-click the Toolbox, select <u>A</u>dd Tab from the pop-up context-sensitive menu, and give the new tab a name. You can then move controls from one tab to another and group your controls in the way that is most convenient to you. Figure A.8 shows the Toolbox with a Grid Controls tab added to it.

FIGURE A.8
A handy feature in Visual Basic 6 enables you to group control tools using custom tabs in the Toolbox.

The Canvas of Your Programs

The windows you design in your Visual Basic programs are known as *forms*. You can think of the form as an artist's canvas. You use elements in the Toolbox to "draw" your user interface on a form.

The form is part of the desktop and is your primary work area for creating the user interface. If you look closely at the form in Figure A.9, you might notice that the form has dots on it. These dots form a grid whose purpose is to help you position controls on the form; it is invisible when your program is running. You can control the spacing of the grid dots by choosing Tools, Options and selecting the appropriate options on the General tab of the resulting dialog box. You can also choose not to display the grid at all. The default grid is 120 by 120 twips. I prefer to make the grid smaller (60 by 60 twips), which allows me more precise control over the placement of objects on my form. This tighter grid is illustrated in Figure A.10.

FIGURE A.9
When you are designing a form in Visual Basic, a grid is available to help you easily line up controls.

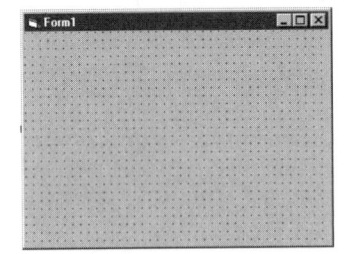

FIGURE A.10
Making the grid smaller gives you tighter control over the way objects are placed on your forms.

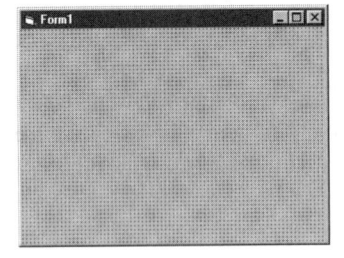

Controlling Your Forms and Controls

The *Properties window* is an important part of the Visual Basic desktop. It shows all the available properties for the currently selected form, control, or module (see Figure A.11). If the Properties window isn't visible, first select the object(s) whose properties you want to view or change, and then press F4. You can also view this window by choosing View, Properties Windows, or by right-clicking an object and choosing Properties from the context-sensitive menu that pops up.

Properties determine how a form or control looks and how it behaves in a program. The Properties window lists all of the currently selected object's properties that can be changed at *designtime,* as opposed to *runtime* properties, which can be changed only during program execution. Many properties can be changed either at designtime or at runtime.

FIGURE A.11
The Properties window, shown here in its undocked state, provides an easy way to change the properties that govern the appearance and behavior of objects.

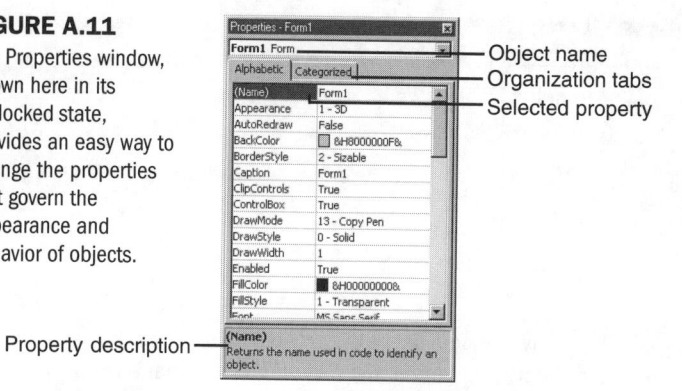

- Object name
- Organization tabs
- Selected property
- Property description

An example of a property is the `Caption` property of a Label control. You can change it by simply typing `Hello World` in the `Caption` field in the Properties window (a designtime change) or by adding a statement in your code like `Form1.Label1.Caption = "Hello World"` (a runtime change).

The Properties window has two tabs on it. These tabs allow you to group the properties either alphabetically or by logical categories. Another improvement to the Properties window is that it now includes a description of the selected property in a pane at the bottom. Having this information helps you avoid much of the need to look up properties in the Help system.

> **NOTE** For convenience, the `Name` property of any object appears at the top of the list of properties rather than in its proper alphabetical order. ■

> **NOTE** Many controls have an entry labeled (Custom) in the Properties window. Clicking the ellipsis (…) next to this entry brings up a special Property Page dialog box containing all the designtime properties for that control in an easy-to-modify format. ■

Using the Project Window

Another window on the desktop is the *Project window*, as shown in Figure A.12. This window shows a list of all the forms, code modules, and other components that are used in your program. If you want to view a form or code module, double-click it here during designtime, or click it once and click the View Object or View Code button.

> **NOTE** One way to think of a project is as a group of related files. The project brings together all the files needed to create your program. ■

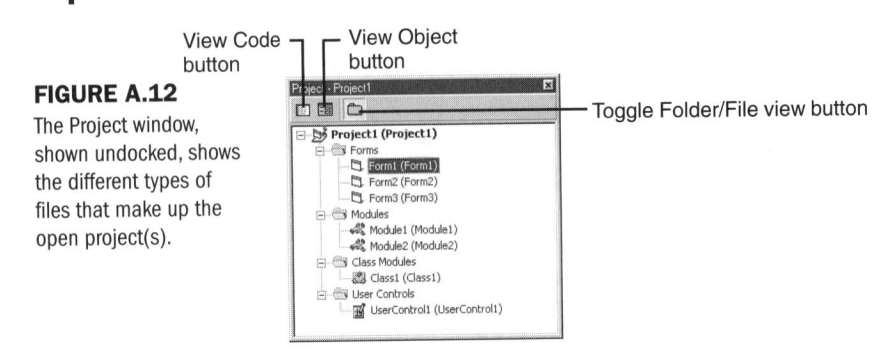

FIGURE A.12
The Project window, shown undocked, shows the different types of files that make up the open project(s).

View Code button
View Object button
Toggle Folder/File view button

When you save a project, you're basically saving a list of the various files that make up a project. The project file itself is stored with a default extension of *.VBP* (Visual Basic Project). Several other types of files make up the components of the projects. Some of the more common types are listed in Table A.3.

Table A.3 Visual Basic File Types

File Type	Extension
Visual Basic Form	.FRM
Code Module	.BAS
Class Module	.CLS
User-Created Control	.CTL
ActiveX Document Form File	.DOB

The Project window uses an outline list to show you not only the forms and code modules in the open project(s), but also any class modules, user-defined controls, or property pages. You can view your project in two ways. The folder view, which you can access by clicking the left button, displays the parts of your project organized by category. On the other hand, clicking the rightmost button lists the elements of your project based on their associated filenames.

Where Work Gets Done

The final piece of the desktop is one or more *Code windows*. In Code windows, you do all the entry and editing of program code that allows your programs to actually perform tasks (see Figure A.13). Each form has its own associated Code window. A project can also contain a couple of types of standalone Code windows known as *modules*. To access a Code window, you can double-click a form or one of its objects, or you can click the View Code button in the Project window while the appropriate object is highlighted.

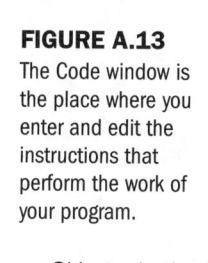

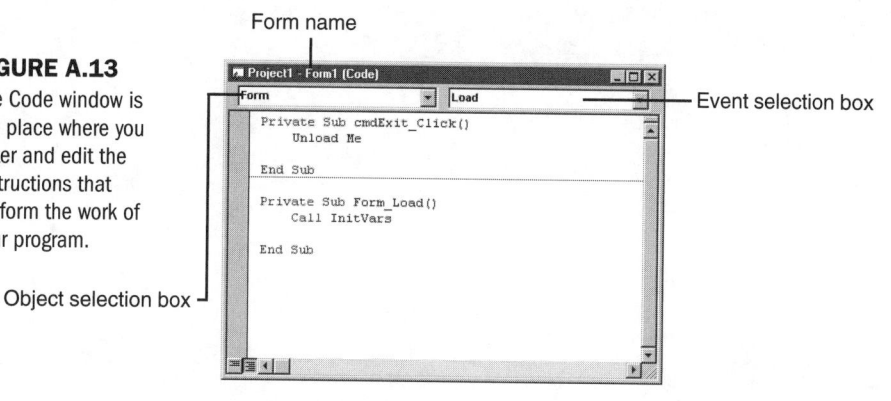

The Visual Basic Work Area

FIGURE A.13
The Code window is the place where you enter and edit the instructions that perform the work of your program.

Customizing Your Environment

As you've learned, the Visual Basic development environment is highly customizable. Most of the windows and toolbars in Visual Basic can be placed at the edges of the main program window, or they can float anywhere on the screen. You can position and resize the windows to fit your preferences; the next time you start Visual Basic, the environment will be as you left it. Figure A.14 shows you one way the development environment can be rearranged.

FIGURE A.14
The various pieces of Visual Basic's development environment can be arranged in many ways.

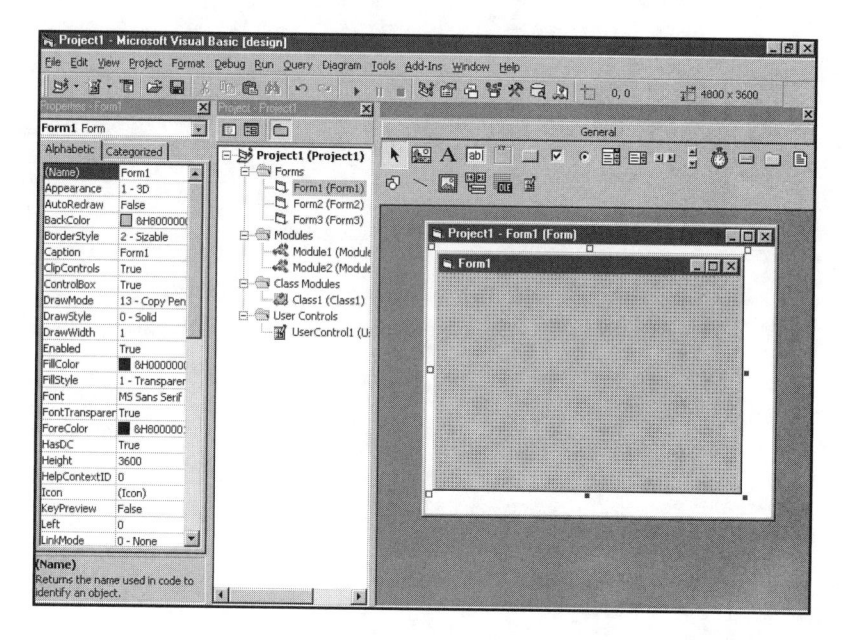

APPENDIX B

Packaging Your Applications

In this chapter

Compiling Your Program **776**

Packaging a Standard EXE Project **778**

Packaging ActiveX Components **788**

After you complete your program, it is time to move it out of the VB development environment so that others can use it. The first step is to compile the source code. The objective here is to create an EXE file (or DLL/OCX depending on the project type) that can be distributed to other machines. After compiling, you can create installation files for the program by using the Package and Deployment Wizard. The purpose of this wizard is to package your program and all necessary support files so that it will run on a machine that does not have Visual Basic installed. If your program is a Standard EXE project, the Package and Deployment Wizard provides a setup program that the users can execute. Typically, they can insert a CD or diskette and run SETUP.EXE. In addition to creating installs for Standard EXE projects, the Package and Deployment Wizard can also be used with ActiveX controls or other ActiveX components. This appendix discusses compiling your program and then steps you through the process of using the wizard to create an application package.

> **NOTE** The Package and Deployment Wizard replaces the Application Setup Wizard from earlier versions of Visual Basic.

Compiling Your Program

The first step toward distributing your program is to compile it. All you have to do is select File, Make. This menu item lists the project name and the proper file extension for the type of program you are creating. For a Standard EXE or ActiveX EXE, the file extension is .EXE. For an ActiveX DLL, the file extension is .DLL, and for the ActiveX control, the file extension is .OCX. After you select Make, the Make Project dialog box appears; this dialog box allows you to specify the name and location of the target file. Visual Basic then does the rest of the work.

If any errors that prevent a successful compile are encountered, you have to correct them and compile again. Any time you make changes to the program code after you have compiled it, you need to compile and distribute your project again. Although Visual Basic handles the actual compilation with no intervention, you do need to make a few decisions in the *projectname* Project Properties dialog box. The Compile and Make tabs of this dialog box are also available through the Options button on the Make Project dialog box.

Optimizing Your Code

The first choice to make is whether to compile to P-code or native code. P-code is the way Visual Basic programs have been compiled since version 1, whereas compiling to native code was a new option with Visual Basic 5.0. Native code is optimized for the processor chip and runs faster than P-code, but it produces a larger executable file. If you choose to compile to native code, you also need to make a decision about compiler optimization. You can choose to have the compiler try to create the smallest possible code, the fastest possible code, or not perform any optimization. You also have the option of compiling your program specifically for the Pentium Pro processor.

> **TIP** You should compile using native code, since speed is more of a concern than using up a few extra bytes of hard disk space.

To choose the compiler options, you need to click the Compile tab of the Project Properties dialog box (see Figure B.1). To squeeze every last bit of speed out of VB, you may want to also look at the Advanced Optimizations dialog box, also shown in Figure B.1. As you can see, Microsoft put these options in here with a "use at your own risk" warning. However, I usually check Remove Array Bounds Checks—because the program code itself should do this—and Remove Safe Pentium™ FDIV Checks—which turns off software correction for the infamous Pentium chip bug. If you want to play safe, making choices in the Advanced Options dialog box should probably be the last thing you do.

FIGURE B.1
To optimize the output of the Visual Basic compiler, visit the Advanced Optimizations dialog box.

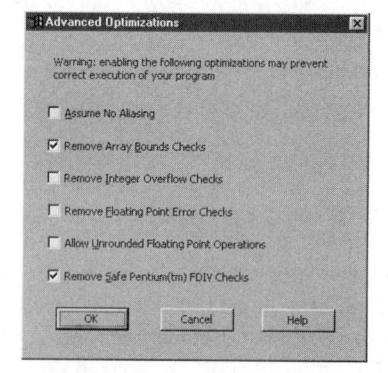

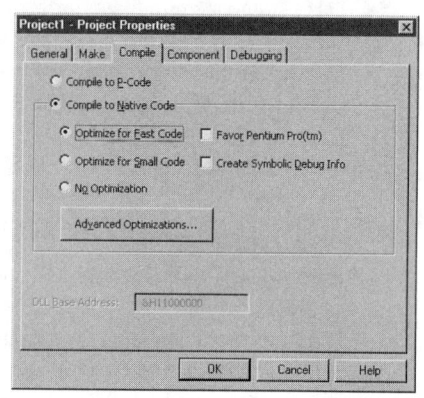

Setting the Project Name, Title, and Icon

Another important step when compiling your code is to make sure that the project name and title are set to meaningful values. By default, Visual Basic assigns a generic name to your project, such as Project1. Even if you change the target filename from the Make Project dialog box, you still need to change the project name and title internally. If you have written an ActiveX component, such as an ActiveX DLL with a public class, you already know the importance of the project name and have probably already set it to a meaningful value. The project title is also important because it may appear in the Windows task list or an error dialog box. These name and title fields are located in the General and Make tabs of the Project Properties dialog box, respectively.

> **NOTE** Generally, there is no reason why you need the project title and name to be different. If no project title is specified, VB automatically changes the project title to match the project name. ■

Before distributing an application, you should also select an icon from the Make tab of the Project Properties dialog box. Although an icon is not critical, using one is an easy way to make your application appear more professional. All you have to do is assign an icon to a form and then select the form name from the Icon drop-down box.

Preparing to Create a Setup Program

After you successfully compile your application, test the compiled version on your own computer to make sure that it runs outside the Visual Basic IDE. For a Standard EXE project, run the executable from the Windows Explorer. For an ActiveX component, attempt to use the component in a Visual Basic project or Web page. Before distributing the application to multiple users, you also need to perform more thorough testing on a PC other than your own.

I also suggest compiling your project to a different directory than the one you have been using. Doing so may help you discover any additional files (for example, INI files or bitmaps) that you have programmed the application to access. After you have made a note of these files and created a working compiled application, you are ready for the next step—using the Package and Deployment Wizard.

Packaging a Standard EXE Project

Even though you may have just compiled your code into an executable file, that executable file cannot run on its own. Users of your program must have some VB runtime files (for example, DLLs) properly installed first. In the days of VB 3.0, sometimes copying the file VBRUN300.DLL and copying your EXE were the only steps required. Today, the mere presence of a required DLL file is usually not enough; more often than not, it must also be registered in the Windows Registry.

On the bright side, the setup utility included with Visual Basic has improved in quality with each successive release. The latest incarnation of this utility, now known as the Package and Deployment Wizard, is the best yet. It has a totally redesigned interface that includes some additional customization features not present in previous versions. The purpose of this wizard is to "package" your program with the required support files so that it can be installed from a disk, directory, or the Internet—just like any off-the-shelf program.

Creating a Standard EXE Package

A shortcut to the Package and Deployment Wizard should have been installed with VB. The main screen, pictured in Figure B.2, is the starting point for creating installation routines for any type of Visual Basic project. This section focuses on the steps for a Standard EXE project. If you want to use this section as a step-by-step example, you first need to create a simple Standard EXE project and then save and compile it. Then start the Package and Deployment Wizard.

Packaging a Standard EXE Project

FIGURE B.2
The most important option on the first screen of the Package and Deployment Wizard is the Package button, which builds an installation package for your application.

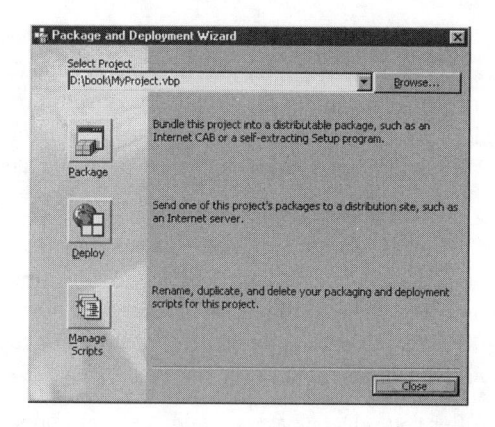

Select a Project File The first thing you have to do in the Package and Deployment Wizard is select a project file (.VBP file) by using the Browse button. Then click the Package button to begin the process.

> **N O T E** If you have not yet compiled your project, you get a message asking whether you would like the wizard to compile it for you. You cannot proceed unless you have a compiled file. I usually compile in the Visual Basic IDE because compiling here adds an extra step.

Select a Package Type After reading information from your VBP file, the wizard presents the Package Type screen, shown in Figure B.3. From this dialog box, you can select the Package Type to create. Remember that *package* is just another word for a set of files used to install your application.

> **N O T E** If you see the Packaging Script screen instead of the Package Type screen, simply choose None and click Next. This screen only appears if you have previously saved a set of package instructions.

FIGURE B.3
The valid package types for a Standard EXE project are a standard setup package and a dependency file.

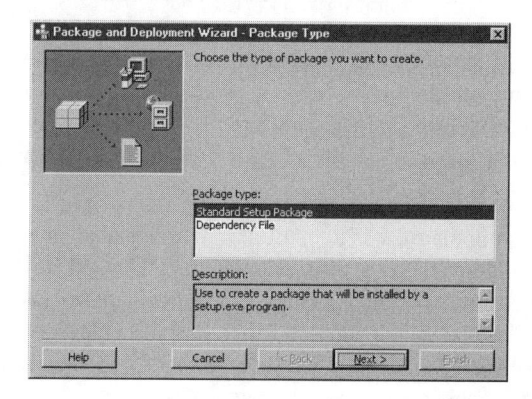

Note that if you choose the dependency file package type, the wizard does not actually create a working installation program. A dependency file holds information about all the files required by your program, for the purpose of including the installation of your project within the installation of another project. Unless you are creating a single setup for a bunch of projects, you should select the Standard Setup Package Option. If you are following along, do that now and click Next.

Assign a Package Folder The next thing the Package and Deployment Wizard needs from you is the location of a package folder. The package folder is the directory in which the wizard creates your installation files. You can enter the name of a new directory if you do not want to place installation files in an existing directory. By default, a new folder called Package is created in the same directory as your project file.

Select Files to Include After you select a package folder, you are presented with the Included Files screen, shown in Figure B.4. The Included Files screen lists the files that will be part of the installation package and allows you to add additional files. If you have additional files to distribute, such as INI or BMP files used by your program, you can add them to the list by using the Add button. ToolTips indicate whether a specific file was manually added or is required by another file.

FIGURE B.4
The check box indicates that an item (and its dependent files, if known) will be included in the installation package.

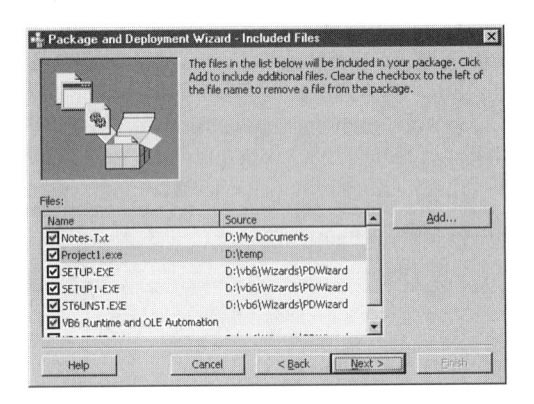

Suppose you want to add another Visual Basic EXE, DLL, or OCX file to your project. Perhaps you have separated your application into multiple projects; for example, you may have created an "Administration module" EXE for managing login IDs. If you have not created a package for each of the other projects, you may see the Missing Dependency Information dialog box, which is shown in Figure B.5.

The reason for the warning message is to make sure your installation works. For example, if you decide to include additional EXEs, you also need the DLLs and OCXs required by those EXEs. You can either generate the dependency information with the Package and Deployment Wizard or just ignore this message if you know that no special files are required. If you click any check boxes on this screen (which I do not recommend), the wizard does not ask you about that file's dependency information ever again.

FIGURE B.5
This warning message indicates that the wizard could not find a dependency (DEP) file for the selected item.

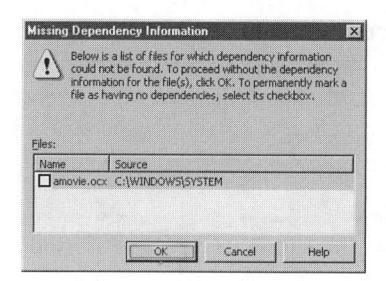

Select Cab Options The next step in the Package and Deployment Wizard is to choose the type of CAB files you wish to create. The Cab Options screen, shown in Figure B.6, allows you to group the installation CAB files according to your distribution media. If you plan to install from a network server or CD-ROM, choose the Single cab option. Choose Multiple cabs if you plan to use floppy diskettes.

> **N O T E** In previous versions of Visual Basic, installation files were compressed and renamed with an underscore to save space. The latest version of Visual Basic uses the CAB format (short for cabinet). CAB files (which are similar to ZIP files) contain compressed versions of your installation files. You can manipulate these compressed files from the MS-DOS command prompt by using the EXTRACT utility or from Windows with the CabView utility.

FIGURE B.6
You can compress all the installation files into a huge CAB file or multiple smaller CAB files.

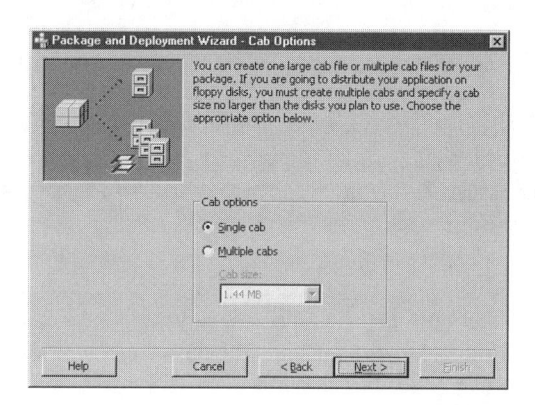

At this point, you have given the Package and Deployment Wizard the most critical information for installing a Standard EXE project. The remaining screens, which were not available in earlier versions of Visual Basic, allow you to further customize the installation routine.

Assign an Installation Title Click the Next button on the Cab Options screen, and you see the Installation Title screen. The Installation Title screen, not pictured here, allows you to specify a title for the installation program, such as Executive Reporting System. The title is then displayed in the background as the setup program runs.

Set Up Shortcuts and Program Groups   Another new setup feature in Visual Basic 6 is the Start Menu Items screen, pictured in Figure B.7. The Start Menu Items screen gives you control over the shortcut icons and program groups created by the setup routine. In previous versions of Visual Basic, the wizard simply created a single shortcut to your project's main executable.

FIGURE B.7
Your installation routine can create multiple shortcuts and program groups.

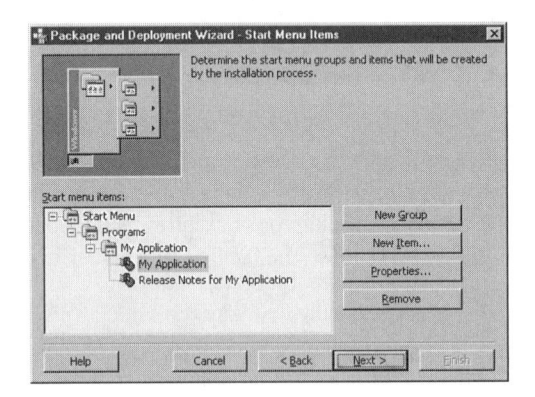

Use the New Group and New Item buttons to add additional program groups and shortcuts to your installation. Each button presents a dialog box for you to enter a description and other information. For example, you might want to create a shortcut to the application release notes or a URL file that takes the users to your Web site. In this case, click the New Item button. Select the target file from the list of included files and enter the title for the new shortcut icon.

> **N O T E**   The Properties button performs a different function depending on whether you have a group or item selected. For items, you can edit the file, title, and working directory. For NT program groups, you can determine whether they are created as Common (available from the Start Menu of all user accounts) or Private (available to the current user only).

Assign Installation Locations   After you finish setting up Start menu items for your application, click Next and another customization dialog box, Install Locations, appears. Use this screen, shown in Figure B.8, to view and change the directories in which application files are installed.

Some files, such as DLL and OCX files, are traditionally placed in the Windows System directory. Likewise, the application executable file is usually copied to a directory that users choose during installation. Because these directories vary from machine to machine, the Package and Deployment Wizard uses macros to represent them.

FIGURE B.8
You can customize the location of any installed file.

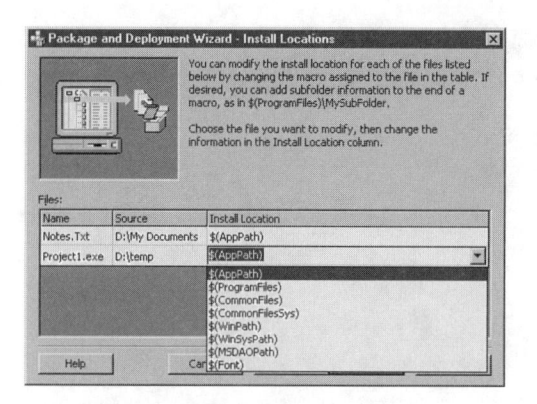

You can think of macros, indicated by the $(macroname)$ syntax, like tokens that the setup routine replaces with the actual directory path for a given machine. Consider, for example, the Windows System directory, which is usually C:\Windows\System in Windows 95 and C:\WINNT\SYSTEM32 in Windows NT. In addition, selecting a custom path during Windows setup causes the Windows System directory to be something unusual like D:\MyWin95\System. However, the $(WinSysPath)$ macro locates the system directory on any PC.

Mark Any Shared Components   The next dialog box, Shared Files, allows you to mark certain files in your installation as shared components. Shared components are typically DLLs or other files used by multiple programs. For example, if you have 10 Visual Basic programs installed on a user's machine, they all "share" the MSVBVM60.DLL runtime file. If a file is marked as shared, it is not removed during the uninstall process, unless no other applications are using the file. Visual Basic takes care of selecting shared files, and the Windows Registry keeps track of the applications that use them. Generally, you should accept the default settings on the Shared Files screen (see Figure B.9).

> **NOTE**   Setting the main executable file as shared, although not its intended purpose, removes two warning messages regarding replacing an existing file. The messages are contradictory (such as `Cancel Setup?` followed by `Continue Setup?`) and probably would confuse some users. By marking the file as a shared component, you tell the setup program that the users do not need to be prompted before overwriting the file.

> **NOTE**   You can remove (or uninstall) applications by choosing Add/Remove programs from the Windows Control Panel.

FIGURE B.9
Shared files can be left behind after an application is removed.

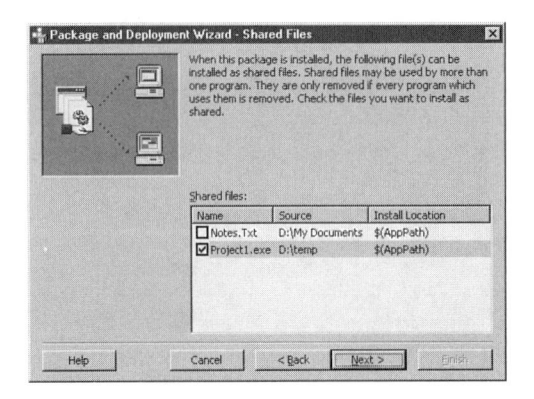

Save Your Script Finally, after the Package and Deployment Wizard has all the information it needs, you see the Finished screen. If you have made many changes to the standard options, you can name your packaging script something meaningful for future use. Otherwise, just click Finish, and your installation files are created.

> **TIP**
> After you save a script file, the next time you package an application, you will see the Packaging Script screen. You can load an existing script or select None to start fresh. To delete or rename a script, choose Manage Scripts from the initial screen.

After installation files have been created, you see a Packaging Report, as shown in Figure B.10.

FIGURE B.10
The Packaging Report lets you know where the wizard put the installation files.

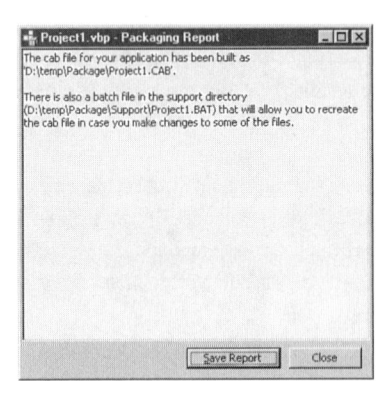

Finish the Packaging Process When you close the Packaging Report window, you return to the main screen. The packaging process is now complete, and you should be able to test your installation by running SETUP.EXE from the Build Folder.

When you're creating a setup for several different users, test your installation thoroughly to make sure that all the necessary components are included. Testing on your own PC is not sufficient because you already have the required DLLs and OCXs.

> **TIP**
> One method of ensuring that your installation includes all the right parts is to try it on a test machine that contains nothing but the operating system. This situation can be tricky because each test of the installation changes the test machine. I suggest getting software that allows you to restore a PC from an image file so that you can test with a variety of software configurations.

A Closer Look at the Setup Process

You've just seen the process by which you create a set of setup files, also known as a *package*. It is probably a safe bet to assume that most computer users are already familiar with the concept of installing, or setting up, an application. Who hasn't spent 30 minutes watching the bar graph crawl by during a slow setup routine? From a user's viewpoint, the setup program performs a simple function. However, for troubleshooting purposes, the developer needs to realize that a lot more is going on than just copying files to the destination PC. In the following sections, you will look at the files created by the Package and Deployment Wizard and at what happens during the setup process.

Installation Files The steps you used to create a Standard EXE setup package in the previous sections create two new folders on your hard drive:

- **Package folder.** Contains the compressed installation files in CAB format, the Setup Executable, the dependency file, and a setup control file, SETUP.LST. You copy (or deploy) the contents of the Package folder to your distribution location.

- **Support folder.** Contains the decompressed installation files. You do not need to distribute this folder with your application.

> **NOTE** If you are creating an ActiveX component setup, additional files are created. You learn about ActiveX in later sections.

One of the files created by the Setup Wizard, SETUP.LST, is the controlling file for the entire setup process. You can view SETUP.LST in a text editor, as shown in Figure B.11.

The SETUP.LST File Don't let the cryptic lines of text in the SETUP.LST file intimidate you; the structure of the file is actually fairly straightforward. It contains all the information necessary to control the installation of a Standard EXE project. Take a brief step-by-step look now at how SETUP.LST is used:

1. When SETUP.EXE is executed by a user, the files in the [BootStrap Files] section of SETUP.LST are copied, decompressed, and registered on the destination machine. This process may require rebooting if certain critical files are out of date. Because the VB runtime files may not be present, SETUP.EXE must be written in a language capable of running without them.

FIGURE B.11
The choices you made in the Packaging and Deployment Wizard are reflected in the SETUP.LST file.

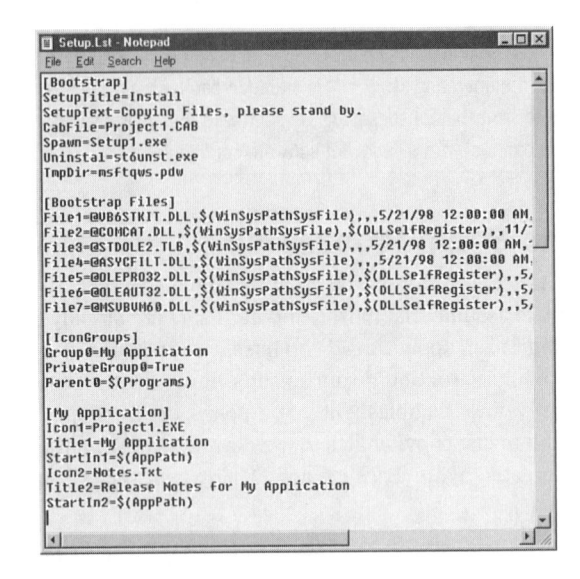

```
[Bootstrap]
SetupTitle=Install
SetupText=Copying Files, please stand by.
CabFile=Project1.CAB
Spawn=Setup1.exe
Uninstal=st6unst.exe
TmpDir=msftqws.pdw

[Bootstrap Files]
File1=@VB6STKIT.DLL,$(WinSysPathSysFile),,,5/21/98 12:00:00 AM,
File2=@COMCAT.DLL,$(WinSysPathSysFile),$(DLLSelfRegister),,11/
File3=@STDOLE2.TLB,$(WinSysPathSysFile),,,5/21/98 12:00:00 AM,
File4=@ASYCFILT.DLL,$(WinSysPathSysFile),,,5/21/98 12:00:00 AM,
File5=@OLEPRO32.DLL,$(WinSysPathSysFile),$(DLLSelfRegister),,5,
File6=@OLEAUT32.DLL,$(WinSysPathSysFile),$(DLLSelfRegister),,5,
File7=@MSVBVM60.DLL,$(WinSysPathSysFile),$(DLLSelfRegister),,5,

[IconGroups]
Group0=My Application
PrivateGroup0=True
Parent0=$(Programs)

[My Application]
Icon1=Project1.EXE
Title1=My Application
StartIn1=$(AppPath)
Icon2=Notes.Txt
Title2=Release Notes for My Application
StartIn2=$(AppPath)
```

These few files are the minimum files necessary to run a Visual Basic program, specifically SETUP1.EXE, which does most of the work in setting up your application. This is the main purpose for SETUP.EXE, which is basically a "wrapper" for SETUP1.EXE. SETUP1.EXE comes with VB and is included automatically by the wizard in your CAB file.

2. SETUP1.EXE displays a welcome screen and asks the user to choose a destination directory for the application, as you can see in Figure B.12.

FIGURE B.12
The user can choose a destination folder for your application.

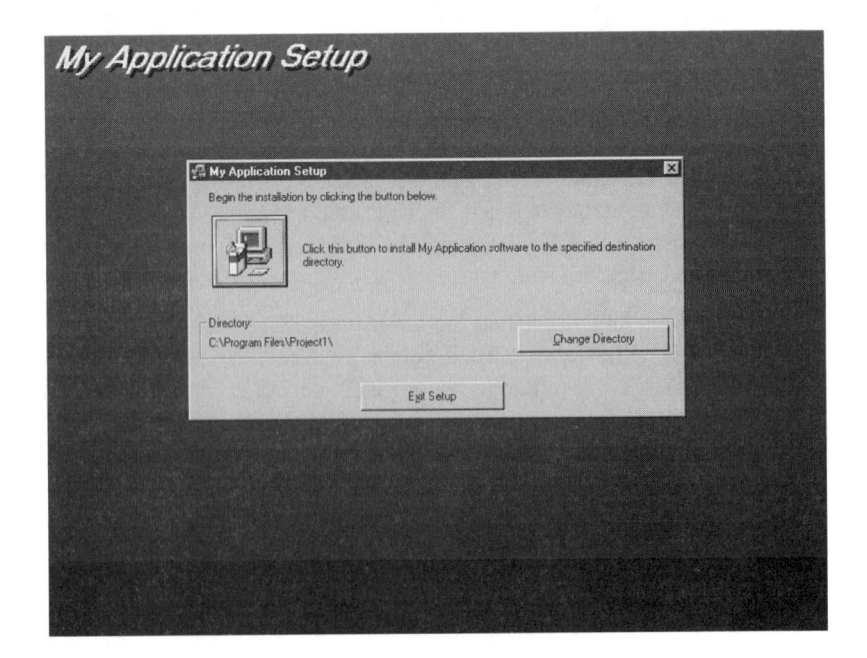

> **NOTE** If you do not want the user to have the option of specifying a destination folder, add the line `ForceUseDefDir=1` to the `[Setup]` section of SETUP.LST. To specify a different default directory, change the `DefaultDir` line.

3. If the user chooses to continue, the program creates the application directory and begins copying files. The files to be copied are listed in the [Setup1 Files] section of SETUP.LST. You may notice that for each file in the [Setup1 Files] section there is a long list of parameters. These parameters give the setup routine information about each individual file, such as the destination directory and version number.

> **CAUTION**
> The version number of your program is very important. If you do not increment the version number in the Project Properties dialog box, Setup assumes the user already has the correct version, so it does not need to copy over it. If you are having problems, view the installation log file to see which files were actually copied.

4. When SETUP1.EXE finishes copying files, it attempts to register some of them. Whether a file needs to be registered is determined by one of the SETUP.LST parameters, typically (`DLLSelfRegister`) or `$(EXESelfRegister)`.

> **NOTE** If you need to register a file manually, use the REGSVR32 utility included with Visual Basic. You can register ActiveX EXEs with Windows by running them with the command-line parameter `/REGSERVER`.

5. SETUP1.EXE creates the shortcut icons for your program. The program group names are listed in the `[IconGroups]` section.
6. The major actions taken by the setup program (copying, registering, and so on) are saved in a log file in the application directory. This log file is used by the uninstall program but can also be a useful troubleshooting tool.

Rebuilding a CAB File As you may have noticed, all your installation files are compressed into one or more CAB files. If you make even a minor change to your program, you need to recompile the project and place the new executable in the CAB file. For this reason, the Package and Deployment Wizard places a second, decompressed, copy of the installation files in the Support directory. It also creates a batch file named after your project, such as PROJECT1.BAT. If you want to update your installation package without going through the wizard again, you can use this batch file.

To rebuild your CAB file, place the new EXE in the Support directory. Then double-click the batch file. A new CAB file is built in the Support directory and must be copied over the existing CAB file in the Package directory.

Customizing Setup Even though you can customize SETUP.LST to a great extent, a standard Setup Wizard installation still might not be suitable for your needs. For example, you may want to create your own "wrapper" program around SETUP.EXE to perform other functions. You could temporarily map a network drive to the installation server, run SETUP.EXE, and then disconnect the drive after installation. If you emailed this program to the users, they would not have to worry about connecting to the right network drive. Another possibility would be storing each user's date of installation in a database. As with SETUP.EXE, you might have to write this program so that it would run without the VB6 runtime files.

If you want to run a setup program other than SETUP1.EXE, you can still use Microsoft's SETUP.EXE to install the VB6 runtime DLLs. To do so, replace the SETUP1.EXE program in the Support directory with your own program and rebuild the CAB file. You can also remove the [Setup1 Files] section from SETUP.LST entirely if your setup program doesn't need it.

NOTE Microsoft includes the source code for SETUP1.EXE with Visual Basic. If you want view this code, open the project SETUP1.VBP in the Wizards\PDWizard\setup1 directory. If you need to make any changes, first make a backup copy of the original files.

Successful Setups

Installing a Visual Basic application can become a real headache if you have a lot of users. For a client/server application, chances are you will also need to install database drivers and set up data sources, which is an extra step. Even Internet setups, which are supposed to be handled automatically by Internet Explorer, may run into complications and require tinkering with the security settings.

I think that most people would agree that users of an application should not be forced to jump through hoops just to install it. A good goal to have is a single setup process that does everything as quickly and efficiently as possible. To reach this goal, you may have to get creative and go beyond the standard Setup Wizard approach, but your application will look more professional in the end.

The way to save yourself troubleshooting time later is to thoroughly test your installation. As mentioned earlier, a test machine that can be reset from a file image is a useful tool. You should test your application with different operating systems, test upgrades versus fresh installations, and test the interaction of your application with other software packages.

Packaging ActiveX Components

In the preceding sections, you learned about using the Package and Deployment Wizard with a Standard EXE project. For ActiveX components, such as an ActiveX control (OCX file) or an ActiveX DLL, the process is similar, but some options are specific to these project types.

Internet Download

With an ActiveX component, you still have the option of creating a Standard installation that can be executed explicitly by the users. However, you also can create a package for Internet download. In this case, the Internet Explorer browser handles installation. To specify an Internet installation package, choose Internet Package from the Package Type screen, as shown in Figure B.13.

Another important decision to make is which of the required files to include in your CAB file.

FIGURE B.13
If you are creating an ActiveX control for Internet Explorer, you need to create an Internet installation package.

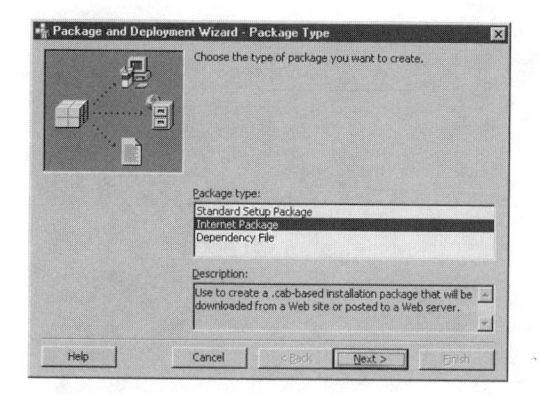

For users to install your ActiveX component, they also need to have all the necessary Visual Basic DLL files. By default, the wizard creates a package that tells the browser to download VB runtime files from a Microsoft Web site. In other words, when users hit your Web site, your ActiveX component is copied from the CAB file on the site, but the remaining DLLs come from Microsoft.

If your Internet connection is unreliable, slow, or not connected all the time, you may want to include the Visual Basic runtime files in your CAB file. You can also specify multiple smaller CAB files on your own server for speed purposes. You can select these options in the Components dialog box, as pictured in Figure B.14.

FIGURE B.14
You can specify the download location for a file by single-clicking it and entering the URL or network path.

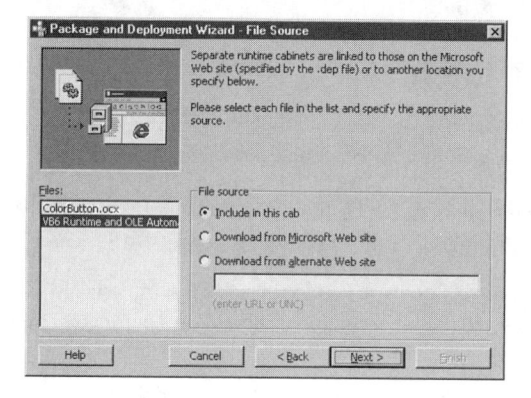

Scripting Options

If you are creating a package for an ActiveX component that will be used on a Web page, you need to make sure it is marked Safe for Scripting and Initialization, as shown in Figure B.15.

FIGURE B.15
The Safety Settings dialog box determines the safety level at which an object is registered on users' PCs.

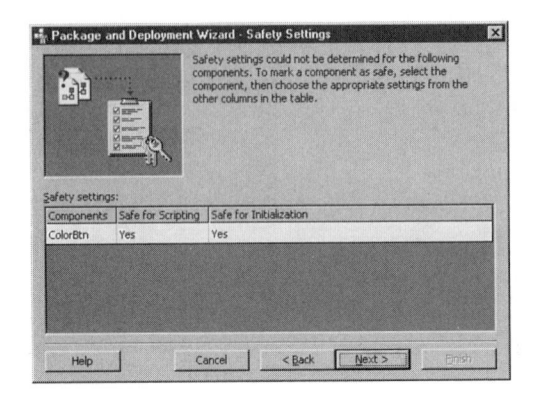

Safe for Scripting means that the object can be accessed from a scripting language, such as VBScript, without harming the user's computer. Safe for initialization means that someone can create an instance of your object without harming the user's computer. As an example, suppose you created an ActiveX control with a method that deletes files. Your Web pages might use this method responsibly, but someone else could use your control with their own VBScript code to perform malicious activities. Of course, in order for you to use your own control, these options need to be enabled, so make sure and put a lot of thoughts into the methods and properties you make available.

▶ **See** "Installing Your Control over the Internet" **p. 316**

▶ **See** "Using VBScript," **p. 665**

Files Created for the Internet

The Package and Deployment Wizard creates a different kind of CAB file for Internet packages. As you may recall, a Standard installation package includes a SETUP.EXE file for the users to run. An Internet package, however, does not include a setup program because Internet Explorer handles the installation. Inside the CAB file is an INF file that tells Internet Explorer which files to install. A sample INF file is shown in Figure B.16.

If you are creating an ActiveX control, IE also creates a sample HTM file. This file includes HTML code that you use to place the ActiveX control on one of your own Web pages:

```
<OBJECT ID="UserControl1"
CLASSID="CLSID:9A15C6AE-CB22-11D1-BE62-10005A75B6DB"
CODEBASE="Project1.CAB#version=1,0,0,0">
</OBJECT>
```

These few lines of HTML code are all you need to embed your ActiveX object in a Web page. Note that the object's unique class ID and version number are provided. Internet Explorer uses this information and the information in the INF file to determine whether it needs to download and install the ActiveX component. This is one of the strengths of ActiveX and Internet Explorer: You can place updated controls on your Web server and have them installed automatically on client PCs.

FIGURE B.16
The INF file tells Internet Explorer which project files to install and where to get them.

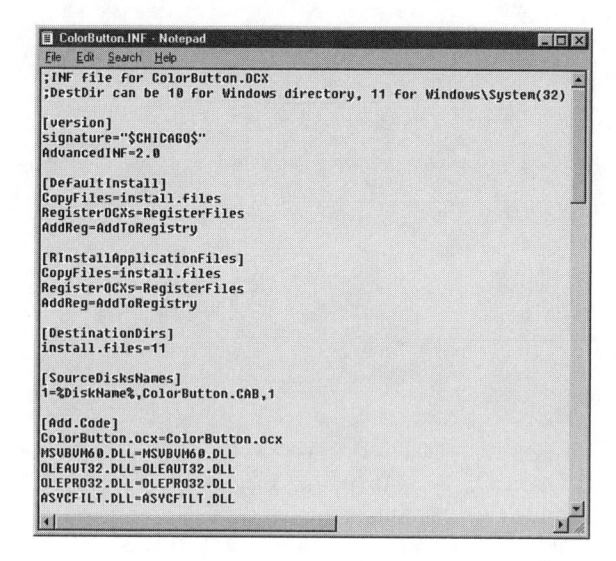

From Here...

In this appendix, you explored how to use the Setup Wizard to create an installation program for your users. You also looked behind the scenes to find out what happens when an application setup executes and how to customize it. For additional information about setup-related topics, see the following chapters:

- To learn about creating ActiveX Controls, see Chapter 14, "Creating ActiveX Controls."
- To find out how to create an ActiveX document, see Chapter 32, "ActiveX Documents."

APPENDIX C

SQL Summary

In this chapter

Defining SQL   794

Using *SELECT* Statements   796

SQL Action Statements   816

Using Data-Definition-Language Statements   818

Using SQL   820

Creating SQL Statements   823

Optimizing SQL Performance   825

Passing SQL Statements to Other Database Engines   827

In several of the earlier chapters on working with databases, you saw how SQL statements were used to determine what information would be available in a recordset. This chapter explains how to create those SQL statements and how to do much more with SQL. The examples in this chapter all use an Access database, but the techniques of using SQL are applicable to many database formats. In fact, SQL statements are the cornerstone of working with many database servers, such as Oracle or SQL Server.

There are two basic types of SQL statements that are covered in this chapter: data-manipulation language (DML) and data-definition language (DDL). Most of the chapter deals with DML statements, and, unless a statement is identified otherwise, you should assume that it is a DML statement.

Defining SQL

Structured Query Language (SQL) is a specialized set of programming commands that enable the developer (or end user) to do the following kinds of tasks:

- Retrieve data from one or more tables in one or more databases.
- Manipulate data in tables by inserting, deleting, or updating records.
- Obtain summary information about the data in tables, such as totals; record counts; and minimum, maximum, and average values.
- Create, modify, or delete tables in a database (Access databases only).
- Create or delete indexes for a table (Access databases only).

SQL statements enable the developer to perform functions in one line or a few lines of code that would take 50 or 100 lines of standard BASIC code to perform.

What SQL Does

As the name implies, Structured Query Language statements create a query that is processed by the database engine. The query defines the fields to be processed, the tables containing the fields, the range of records to be included, and, for record retrieval, the order in which the returned records are to be presented.

When retrieving records, a SQL statement usually returns the requested records in a *dynaset*. Recall that a dynaset is an updatable recordset that actually contains a collection of pointers to the base data. Dynasets are temporary and are no longer accessible after they are closed. SQL does have a provision for the times when permanent storage of retrieved records is required.

NOTE The Microsoft SQL syntax used in this chapter is designed to work with the Jet database engine and is compatible with ANSI SQL (there are, however, some minor differences between Microsoft SQL and ANSI SQL). In addition, if you use SQL commands to query an external database server such as SQL Server or Oracle, read the documentation that comes with the server to verify that the SQL features you want to use are supported and that the syntax of the statements is the same.

The Parts of the SQL Statement

A SQL statement consists of three parts:

- **Parameter declarations**—These are optional parameters that are passed to the SQL statement by the program.
- **The manipulative statement**—This part of the statement tells the Query engine what kind of action to take, such as `SELECT` or `DELETE`.
- **Options declarations**—These declarations tell the Query engine about any filter conditions, data groupings, or sorts that apply to the data being processed. These include the `WHERE`, `GROUP BY`, and `ORDER BY` clauses.

These parts are arranged as follows:

`[Parameters declarations] Manipulative statement [options]`

The parameters declaration section is where you define any parameters used in the SQL statement. Any values defined in the parameters declaration section are assigned before the SQL statement is executed.

Most of this chapter uses only the manipulative statement and the options declarations. Using these two parts of the SQL statement, you can create queries to perform a wide variety of tasks. Table C.1 lists four of the manipulative clauses and their purposes.

Table C.1 Parts of the Manipulative Statement

Statement	Function
`DELETE FROM`	Removes records from a table
`INSERT INTO`	Adds a group of records to a table
`SELECT`	Retrieves a group of records and places the records in a dynaset or table
`UPDATE`	Sets the values of fields in a table

Although manipulative statements tell the database engine what to do, the options declarations tell it what fields and records to process. The discussion of the optional parameters makes up the bulk of this chapter. In this chapter, you first look at how the parameters are used with the `SELECT` statement and then you apply the parameters to the other manipulative statements. Many of the examples in this chapter are based on the sales-transaction table of a sample database that might be used to manage an aquarium business.

The following discussions of the different SQL statements show just the SQL statement syntax. Be aware that these statements can't be used alone in Visual Basic. The SQL statement is always used to create a `QueryDef`, to create a dynaset or snapshot using the Execute method, or as the `RecordSource` property of a data control. This section explains the part of a SQL statement. Later in the appendix, the "Using SQL" section explains how these statements are actually used in code.

> **NOTE** A QueryDef is a part of the database that stores the query definition. This definition is the SQL statement that you create.

Using *SELECT* Statements

The SELECT statement retrieves records (or specified fields from records) and places the information in a dynaset or table for further processing by a program. The SELECT statement follows this general form:

```
SELECT [predicate] fieldlist FROM tablelist [table relations]
    [range options] [sort options] [group options]
```

> **NOTE** In my demonstrations of code statements, words in all caps are SQL keywords, and italicized words or phrases are used to indicate terms that a programmer would replace in an actual statement—for example, *fieldlist* would be replaced with Lastname, Firstname. Phrases or words inside square brackets are optional terms.

The various components of the preceding statement are explained in this chapter. Although a SQL statement can be greatly complex, it also can be fairly simple. The simplest form of the SELECT statement is shown here:

```
SELECT * FROM Sales
```

Defining the Desired Fields

The fieldlist part of the SELECT statement is used to define the fields to be included in the output recordset. You can include all fields in a table, selected fields from the table, or even calculated fields based on other fields in the table. You can also choose the fields to be included from a single table or from multiple tables.

The fieldlist portion of the SELECT statement takes the following form:

```
[tablename.]field1 [AS alt1][,[tablename.]field2 [AS alt2]]
```

Selecting All Fields from a Table The *, or wild-card parameter, is used to indicate that you want to select all the fields in the specified table. The wild card is used in the fieldlist portion of the statement. The statement SELECT * FROM Sales, when used with the sample database you are developing, produces the output recordset shown in Figure C.1.

Selecting Individual Fields from a Table Frequently, you need only a few fields from a table. You can specify the desired fields by including a field list in the SELECT statement. Within the field list, the individual fields are separated by commas. In addition, if the desired field has a space in the name, as in Order Quantity, the field name must be enclosed within square brackets, [].The recordset that results from the following SELECT statement is shown in Figure C.2. A recordset created with fields specified is more efficient than one created with the wild card (*), both in terms of the size of the recordset and speed of creation. As a general rule, you should limit your queries to the smallest number of fields that can accomplish your purpose.

```
SELECT [Item Code], Quantity FROM Sales
```

FIGURE C.1
Using * in the `fieldlist` parameter selects all fields from the source table.

FIGURE C.2
This recordset results from specifying individual fields in the SELECT statement.

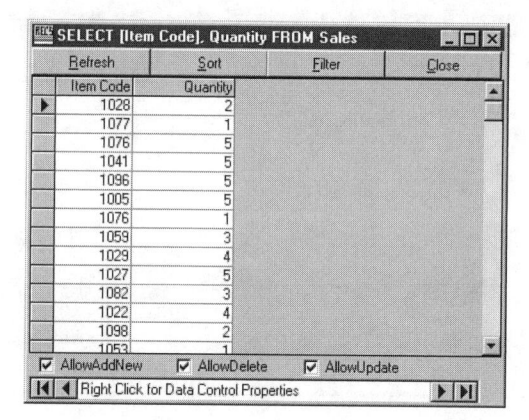

Selecting Fields from Multiple Tables As you might remember from the discussions on database design in Chapter 24, "Database Basics," you normalize data by placing it in different tables to eliminate data redundancy. When you retrieve this data for viewing or modification, you want to see all the information from the related tables. SQL lets you combine information from various tables into a single recordset.

To select data from multiple tables, you specify three things:

- The table from which each field is selected
- The fields from which you are selecting the data
- The relationship between the tables

Specify the table for each field by placing the table name and a period in front of the field name (for example, `Sales.[Item Code]` or `Sales.Quantity`). (Remember, square brackets must enclose a field name that has a space in it.) You also can use the wild-card identifier (*) after the table name to indicate that you want all the fields from that table.

To specify the tables you're using, place multiple table names (separated by commas) in the `FROM` clause of the `SELECT` statement.

The relationship between the tables is specified either by a `WHERE` clause or by a `JOIN` condition. These elements are discussed later in this chapter.

The statement in Listing C.1 is used to retrieve all fields from the Sales table and the Item Description and Retail fields from the Retail Items table. These tables are related by the Item Code field. Figure C.3 shows the results of the statement.

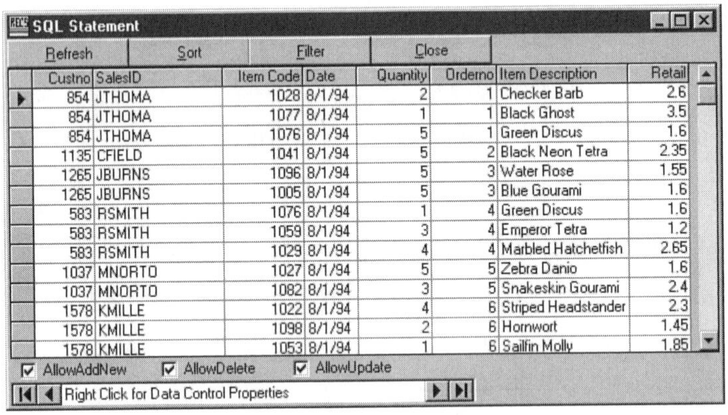
SQL Statement
Refresh
Sort
Filter
Close
Custno SalesID Item Code Date Quantity Orderno Item Description Retail
854 JTHOMA 1028 8/1/94 2 1 Checker Barb 2.6
854 JTHOMA 1077 8/1/94 1 1 Black Ghost 3.5
854 JTHOMA 1076 8/1/94 5 1 Green Discus 1.6
1135 CFIELD 1041 8/1/94 5 2 Black Neon Tetra 2.35
1265 JBURNS 1096 8/1/94 5 3 Water Rose 1.55
1265 JBURNS 1005 8/1/94 5 3 Blue Gourami 1.6
583 RSMITH 1076 8/1/94 1 4 Green Discus 1.6
583 RSMITH 1059 8/1/94 3 4 Emperor Tetra 1.2
583 RSMITH 1029 8/1/94 4 4 Marbled Hatchetfish 2.65
1037 MNORTO 1027 8/1/94 5 5 Zebra Danio 1.6
1037 MNORTO 1082 8/1/94 3 5 Snakeskin Gourami 2.4
1578 KMILLE 1022 8/1/94 4 6 Striped Headstander 2.3
1578 KMILLE 1098 8/1/94 2 6 Hornwort 1.45
1578 KMILLE 1053 8/1/94 1 6 Sailfin Molly 1.85
AllowAddNew
AllowDelete
AllowUpdate
Right Click for Data Control Properties

FIGURE C.3
Selecting fields from multiple tables produces a combined recordset.

NOTE The listing shows an underscore character at the end of each of the first three lines. This is used to break the lines for the purpose of page-width in the book. When you enter the expressions, they need to be on a single line.

Listing C.1 SALES.TXT—Selecting Fields from Multiple Tables in a SQL Statement

```
SELECT Sales.*, [Retail Items].[Item Description], _
    [Retail Items].Retail  _
    FROM Sales, [Retail Items]  _
    WHERE Sales.[Item Code]=[Retail Items].[Item Code]
```

NOTE You can leave out the table name when specifying fields as long as the requested field is present only in one table in the list. However, it is very good programming practice to include the table name, both for reducing the potential for errors and for readability of your code.

Creating Calculated Fields The example in Listing C.1 has customer-order information consisting of the item ordered, quantity of the item, and the retail price. Suppose that you also want to access the total cost of the items. You can achieve this by using a *calculated field* in the SELECT statement. A calculated field can be the result of an arithmetic operation on numeric fields (for example, Price * Quantity) or the result of string operations on text fields (for example, Lastname & Firstname). For numeric fields, you can use any standard arithmetic operation (+, -, *, /, ^). For strings, you can use the concatenation operator (&). In addition, you can use Visual Basic functions to perform operations on the data in the fields (for example, you can use the MID$ function to extract a substring from a text field, the UCASE$ function to place text in uppercase letters, or the SQR function to calculate the square root of a number). Listing C.2 shows how some of these functions can be used in the SELECT statement.

Listing C.2 TOTPRICE.TXT—Creating a Variety of Calculated Fields with the *SELECT* Statement

```
'*******************************************
'Calculate the total price for the items
'*******************************************
SELECT [Retail Items].Retail * Sales.Quantity FROM _
    [Retail Items],Sales _
    WHERE Sales.[Item Code]=[Retail Items].[Item Code]
'******************************************************************
'Create a name field by concatenating the Lastname and
'Firstname fields
'******************************************************************
SELECT Lastname & ', ' & Firstname FROM Customers
'******************************************************************
'Create a customer ID using the first 3 letters of the Lastname
' and Firstname fields and make all letters uppercase.
'******************************************************************
SELECT UCASE$(MID$(Lastname,1,3)) & UCASE$(MID$(Firstname,1,3)) _
    FROM Customers
'******************************************************************
'Determine the square root of a number for use in a data report.
'******************************************************************
SELECT Datapoint, SQR(Datapoint) FROM Labdata
```

In the listing, no field name is specified for the calculated field. The Query engine automatically assigns a name such as Expr1001 for the first calculated field. The next section, "Specifying Alternative Field Names," describes how you can specify a name for the field.

Calculated fields are placed in the recordset as read-only fields—they can't be updated. In addition, if you update the base data used to create the field, the changes are not reflected in the calculated field.

> **N O T E** If you use a calculated field with a data control, it is best to use a label control to show the contents of the field. This prevents the user from attempting to update the field and causing an error. You could also use a text box with the locked property set to `True`. (You can learn more about the Data control and bound controls by reviewing Chapter 25, "The Data Control and Data-Bound Controls.") If you use a text box, you might want to change the background color to indicate to the user that the data cannot be edited.

Specifying Alternative Field Names Listing C.2 created calculated fields to include in a recordset. For many applications, you will want to use a name for the field other than the one automatically created by the query engine.

You can change the syntax of the `SELECT` statement to give the calculated field a name. You assign a name by including the `AS` clause and the desired name after the definition of the field (refer to the second part of Listing C.3). If you want, you can also use this technique to assign a different name to a standard field.

Listing C.3 CUSTNAME.TXT—Accessing a Calculated Field's Value and Naming the Field

```
'**************************************************
'Set up the SELECT statement without the name
'**************************************************
Dim NewDyn As RecordSet
SQL = "SELECT Lastname & ', ' & Firstname FROM Customers"
'**********************************************
'Create a dynaset from the SQL statement
'**********************************************
NewDyn = OldDb.OpenRecordset(SQL)
'**********************************
'Get the value of the created field
'**********************************
Person = NewDyn.Recordset(0)
'*********************************************************
'Set up the SELECT statement and assign a name to the field
'*********************************************************
SQL = "SELECT Lastname & ', ' & Firstname As Name FROM Customers"
'**********************************************
'Create a dynaset from the SQL statement
'**********************************************
NewDyn = OldDb.OpenRecordset(SQL)
'**********************************
'Get the value of the created field
'**********************************
Person = NewDyn.Recordset("Name")
```

Specifying the Data Sources

In addition to telling the database engine what information you want, you must tell it in which table to find the information. This is done with the FROM clause of the SELECT statement. Here is the general form of the FROM clause:

```
FROM table1 [IN data1] [AS alias1][,table2 [IN data2] [AS alias2]]
```

Various options of the FROM clause are discussed in the following sections.

Specifying the Table Names   The simplest form of the FROM clause is used to specify a single table. This is the form of the clause used in this statement:

```
SELECT * FROM Sales
```

The FROM clause can also be used to specify multiple tables (refer to Listing C.1). When specifying multiple tables, separate the table names with commas. Also, if a table name has an embedded space, the table name must be enclosed in square brackets, [] (refer to Listing C.1).

Using Tables in Other Databases   As you develop more applications, you might have to pull data together from tables in different databases. For example, you might have a ZIP code database that contains the city, state, and ZIP code for every postal code in the United States. You do not want to have to duplicate this information in a table for each of your database applications that requires it. The SELECT statement lets you store that information once in its own database and then pull it in as needed. To retrieve the information from a database other than the current one, you use the IN portion of the FROM clause. The SELECT statement for retrieving the ZIP code information along with the customer data is shown in Listing C.4.

Listing C.4   GETCUST.TXT—Retrieving Information from More than One Database

```
'****************************************************************
'We are working from the TRITON database which is already open.
'****************************************************************
SELECT Customers.Lastname, Customers.Firstname, Zipcode.City, _
    Zipcode.State  FROM Customers, Zipcode IN USZIPS  _
    WHERE Customers.Zip = Zipcode.Zip
```

Assigning an Alias Name to a Table   Notice the way the table name for each of the desired fields was listed in Listing C.4. Because these table names are long and there are a number of fields, the SELECT statement is fairly long. The statement gets much more complex with each field and table you add. In addition, typing long names each time increases the chances of making a typo.

To alleviate this problem, you can assign the table an alias by using the AS portion of the FROM clause. Using AS, you can assign a unique, shorter name to each table. This alias can be used in all the other clauses in which the table name is needed. Listing C.5 is a rewrite of the code from Listing C.4, using the alias CS for the Customers table and ZP for the Zipcode table.

Listing C.5   ALIAS.TXT   Using a Table Alias to Cut Down on Typing

```
'*******************************************************
'We use aliases to make the statement easier to enter.
'*******************************************************
SELECT CS.Lastname, CS.Firstname, ZP.City, ZP.State    _
    FROM Customers AS CS, Zipcode IN USZIPS AS ZP      _
    WHERE CS.Zip = ZP.Zip
```

Using *ALL*, *DISTINCT*, or *DISTINCTROW* Predicates

In most applications, you select all records that meet specified criteria. You can do this by specifying the ALL predicate in front of your field names or by leaving out any predicate specification (ALL is the default behavior). Therefore, the following two statements are equivalent:

```
SELECT * FROM Customers
SELECT ALL * FROM Customers
```

There might be times, however, when you want to determine the unique values of fields. For these times, use the DISTINCT or DISTINCTROW predicate. The DISTINCT predicate causes the database engine to retrieve only one record with a specific set of field values—no matter how many duplicates exist. For a record to be rejected by the DISTINCT predicate, its values for all the selected fields must match those of another record. For example, if you are selecting first and last names, you can retrieve several people with the last name Smith, but you can't retrieve multiple occurrences of Adam Smith.

If you want to eliminate records that are completely duplicated, use the DISTINCTROW predicate. DISTINCTROW compares the values of all fields in the table, whether or not they are among the selected fields. For the sample database, you can use DISTINCTROW to determine which products have been ordered at least once. DISTINCTROW has no effect if the query is on only a single table.

Listing C.6 shows the uses of DISTINCT and DISTINCTROW.

Listing C.6   DISTINCT.TXT—Obtaining Unique Records with the *DISTINCT* or *DISTINCTROW* Predicates

```
'*******************************
'Use of the DISTINCT predicate
'*******************************
SELECT DISTINCT [Item Code] FROM Sales
```

```
'********************************
'Use of the DISTINCTROW predicate
'********************************
SELECT DISTINCTROW [Item Code] FROM [Retail Items], Sales _
      [Retail Items] INNER JOIN Sales _
      ON [Retail Items].[Item Code]=Sales.[Item Code]
```

Setting Table Relationships

When you design a database structure, you use key fields so that you can relate the tables in the database. For example, you use a salesperson ID in the Customers table to relate to the salesperson in the Salesperson table. You do this so that you don't have to include all the salesperson data with every customer record. You use these same key fields in the SELECT statement to set the table relationships so that you can display and manipulate the related data. That is, when you view customer information, you want to see the salesperson's name, not his or her ID.

You can use two clauses to specify the relationships between tables:

- JOIN—This combines two tables, based on the contents of specified fields in each table and the type of JOIN.
- WHERE—This usually is used to filter the records returned by a query, but it can be used to emulate an INNER JOIN. You will take a look at the INNER JOIN in the following section.

N O T E Using the WHERE clause to join tables creates a read-only recordset. To create a modifiable recordset, you must use the JOIN clause. ■

Using a *JOIN* Clause   The basic format of the JOIN clause is as follows:

```
table1 {INNER¦LEFT¦RIGHT} JOIN table2 ON table1.key1 = table2.key2
```

The Query engine used by Visual Basic (also used by Access, Excel, and other Microsoft products) supports three JOIN clauses: INNER, LEFT, and RIGHT. Each of these clauses returns records that meet the JOIN condition, but each behaves differently in returning records that do not meet that condition. Table C.2 shows the records returned from each table for the three JOIN conditions. For this discussion, *table1* is the left table and *table2* is the right table. In general, the left table is the first one specified (on the left side of the JOIN keyword) and the right table is the second table specified (on the right side of the JOIN keyword).

N O T E You can use any comparison operator (<, <=, =, >=, >, or <>) in the JOIN clause to relate the two tables. ■

Appendix C SQL Summary

Table C.2 Records Returned Based on the Type of JOIN Used

JOIN Type Table	Records from Left Table	Records from Right Table
INNER	Only records with corresponding record in right table	Only records with corresponding record in left table
LEFT	All records	Only records with corresponding record in left table
RIGHT	Only records with corresponding record in right table	All records

To further understand these concepts, consider the sample database with its Customers and Salesperson tables. In that database, you created a small information set in the tables consisting of ten customers and four salespeople. Two of the customers have no salesperson listed, and one of the salespeople has no customers (he's a new guy!). You select the same fields with each JOIN but specify an INNER JOIN, LEFT JOIN, and RIGHT JOIN (see Listing C.7). Figure C.4 shows the two base-data tables from which this listing is working. Figure C.5 shows the resulting recordsets for each of the JOIN operations.

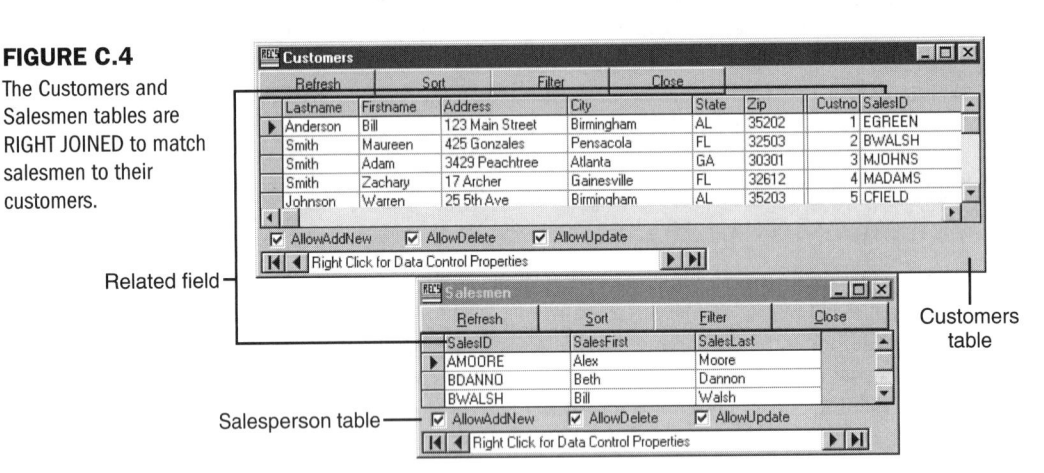

FIGURE C.4
The Customers and Salesmen tables are RIGHT JOINED to match salesmen to their customers.

Listing C.7 JOIN.TXT—Examples of the Three JOIN Types

```
'***************************
'Select using an INNER JOIN
'***************************
SELECT CS.Lastname, CS.Firstname, SL.Saleslast, SL.Salesfirst _
    FROM Customers AS CS, Salesmen AS SL, _
```

```
        CS INNER JOIN SL ON CS.SalesID=SL.SalesID
'***************************
'Select using an LEFT JOIN
'***************************
SELECT CS.Lastname, CS.Firstname, SL.Saleslast, SL.Salesfirst _
    FROM Customers AS CS, Salesmen AS SL, _
    CS LEFT JOIN SL ON CS.SalesID=SL.SalesID
'***************************
'Select using an RIGHT JOIN
'***************************
SELECT CS.Lastname, CS.Firstname, SL.Saleslast, SL.Salesfirst _
    FROM Customers AS CS, Salesmen AS SL, _
    CS RIGHT JOIN SL ON CS.SalesID=SL.SalesID
```

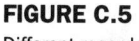

FIGURE C.5
Different records are returned with the different JOIN types.

INNER JOIN

LASTNAME	FIRSTNAME	SALESLAST	SALESFIRST
Evans	Wanda	Burns	John
Hawthorne	Wanda	Burns	John
Moore	Paula	Burns	John
Hawthorne	Lisa	Green	Elizabeth
Thompson	Frank	Green	Elizabeth
Walters	Lisa	Green	Elizabeth
Evans	Lisa	Green	Elizabeth
Hawthorne	Michele	Green	Elizabeth

LEFT JOIN

LASTNAME	FIRSTNAME	SALESLAST	SALESFIRST
Anderson	Bill		
Smith	Maureen	Walsh	Bill
Smith	Adam	Johnson	Mary
Smith	Zachary	Adams	Max
Johnson	Warren	Fields	Carol
Williams	Stephanie	Moore	Alex
Taylor	Lisa	Dannon	Beth
Davis	David	Smith	Robyn
Miller	Catherine		
Roberts	Judy	Evans	Lisa

RIGHT JOIN

LASTNAME	FIRSTNAME	SALESLAST	SALESFIRST
Smith	Zachary	Adams	Max
Johnson	Warren	Fields	Carol
Williams	Stephanie	Moore	Alex
Taylor	Lisa	Dannon	Beth
Davis	David	Smith	Robyn
		Thomas	Jim
Roberts	Judy	Evans	Lisa
		Reid	Sam

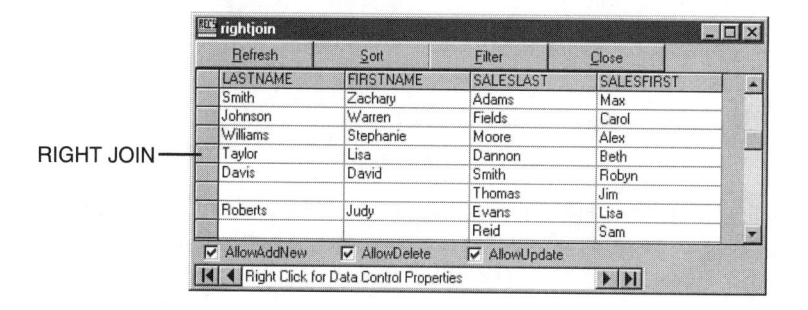

Note that, in addition to returning the salesperson with no customers, the RIGHT JOIN returned all customer records for each of the other salespeople, not just a single record. This is because a RIGHT JOIN is designed to return all the records from the right table, even if they have no corresponding record in the left table.

Using the *WHERE* Clause You can use the WHERE clause to relate two tables. The WHERE clause has the same effect as an INNER JOIN. Listing C.8 shows the same INNER JOIN as Listing C.7, this time using the WHERE clause instead of the INNER JOIN.

Listing C.8 WHERE.TXT—A *WHERE* Clause Performing the Same Function as an *INNER JOIN*

```
'*****************************************
'Select using WHERE to relate two tables
'*****************************************
SELECT CS.Lastname, CS.Firstname, SL.Saleslast, SL.Salesfirst _
    FROM Customers AS CS, Salesmen AS SL, _
    WHERE CS.SalesID=SL.SalesID
```

Setting the Filter Criteria

One of the most powerful features of SQL commands is that you can control the range of records to be processed by specifying a filter condition. You can use many types of filters, such as Lastname = "Smith", Price < 1, or birthday between 5/1/94 and 5/31/94. Although the current discussion is specific to the use of filters in the SELECT command, the principles shown here also work with other SQL commands, such as DELETE and UPDATE.

Filter conditions in a SQL command are specified using the WHERE clause. The general format of the WHERE clause is as follows:

```
WHERE logical-expression
```

There are four types of *predicates* (logical statements that define the condition) that you can use with the WHERE clause. These are shown in the following table:

Predicate	Action
Comparison	Compares a field to a given value
LIKE	Compares a field to a pattern (for example, A*)
IN	Compares a field to a list of acceptable values
BETWEEN	Compares a field to a range of values

Using the Comparison Predicate As its name suggests, the *comparison predicate* is used to compare the values of two expressions. There are six comparison operators (the symbols that describe the comparison type) that you can use; the operators and their definitions are summarized in Table C.3.

Table C.3 Comparison Operators Used in the WHERE Clause

Operator	Definition
<	Less than
<=	Less than or equal to
=	Equal to
>=	Greater than or equal to
>	Greater than
<>	Not equal to

Here is the generic format of the comparison predicate:

`expression1 comparison-operator expression2`

For all comparisons, both expressions must be of the same type (for example, both must be numbers or both must be text strings). Several comparisons of different types are shown in Listing C.9. The comparison values for strings and dates require special formatting. Any strings used in a comparison must be enclosed in single quotes (for example, 'Smith' or 'AL'). Likewise, dates must be enclosed between pound signs (for example, #5/15/94#). The quotes and the pound signs tell the Query engine the type of data that is being passed. Note that numbers do not need to be enclosed within special characters.

Listing C.9 COMPARE.TXT—Comparison Operators Used with Many Types of Data

```
'*********************************************************
'Comparison of text data using customer table as source
'*********************************************************
SELECT * FROM Customers WHERE Lastname='Smith'
'*********************************************************
'Comparison of numeric data using Retail Items table
'*********************************************************
SELECT * FROM [Retail Items] WHERE Retail<2
'*****************************************************
'Comparison of date data using Sales table
'*****************************************************
SELECT * FROM Sales WHERE Date>#8/15/94#
```

Using the *LIKE* Predicate With the LIKE predicate, you can compare an *expression* (that is, a field value) to a pattern. The LIKE predicate lets you make comparisons such as last names starts with *S*, titles containing *SQL*, or five-letter words starting with *M* and ending with *H*. You use the wild cards * and ? to create the patterns. The actual predicates for these comparisons would be `Lastname LIKE 'S*'`, `Titles LIKE '*SQL*'`, and `Word LIKE 'M???H'`, respectively.

The LIKE predicate is used exclusively for string comparisons. The format of the LIKE predicate is as follows:

expression LIKE *pattern*

The patterns defined for the LIKE predicate make use of wild-card matching and character-range lists. When you create a pattern, you can combine some of the wild cards and character lists to allow greater flexibility in the pattern definition. When used, character lists must meet three criteria:

- The list must be enclosed within square brackets.
- The first and last characters must be separated by a hyphen.
- The range of the characters must be defined in ascending order (for example, a z, and not z a).

In addition to using a character list to match a character in the list, you can precede the list with an exclamation point to indicate that you want to exclude the characters in the list. Table C.4 shows the type of pattern matching you can perform with the LIKE predicate. Listing C.10 shows the use of the LIKE predicate in several SELECT statements.

Table C.4 The *LIKE* Predicate Using a Variety of Pattern Matching

Wild Card	Used to Match	Example Pattern	Example Results
*	Multiple characters	S*	Smith, Sims, sheep
?	Single character	an?	and, ant, any
#	Single digit	3524#	35242, 35243
[list]	Single character in list	[c-f]	d, e, f
[!list]	Single character not in list	[!c-f]	a, b, g, h
combination	Specific to pattern	a?t*	art, antique, artist

Listing C.10 LIKE.TXT—Use the *LIKE* Predicate for Pattern-Matching

```
'****************************
'Multiple character wild card
'****************************
SELECT * FROM Customers WHERE Lastname LIKE 'S*'
'****************************
'Single character wild card
'****************************
SELECT * FROM Customers WHERE State LIKE '?L'
'****************************
```

```
'Character list matching
'***********************
SELECT * FROM Customers WHERE MID$(Lastname,1,1) LIKE '[a-f]'
```

Using the IN Predicate The IN predicate lets you determine whether the expression is one of several values. Using the IN predicate, you can check state codes for customers to determine whether the customer's state matches a sales region. This example is shown in the following sample code:

```
SELECT * FROM Customers WHERE State IN ('AL', 'FL', 'GA')
```

Using the BETWEEN Predicate The BETWEEN predicate lets you search for expressions with values within a range of values. You can use the BETWEEN predicate for string, numeric, or date expressions. The BETWEEN predicate performs an *inclusive search*, meaning that if the value is equal to one of the endpoints of the range, the record is included. You can also use the NOT operator to return records outside the range. The form of the BETWEEN predicate is as follows:

expression [NOT] BETWEEN *value1* AND *value2*

Listing C.11 shows the use of the BETWEEN predicate in several scenarios.

Listing C.11 BETWEEN.TXT—Using the *BETWEEN* Predicate to Check an Expression Against a Range of Values

```
'*****************
'String comparison
'*****************
SELECT * FROM Customers WHERE Lastname BETWEEN 'M' AND 'W'
'******************
'Numeric comparison
'******************
SELECT * FROM [Retail Items] WHERE Retail BETWEEN 1 AND 2.5
'***************
'Date comparison
'***************
SELECT * FROM Sales WHERE Date BETWEEN #8/01/94# AND #8/10/94#
'***********************
'Use of the NOT operator
'***********************
SELECT * FROM Customers WHERE Lastname NOT BETWEEN 'M' AND 'W'
```

Combining Multiple Conditions The WHERE clause can also accept multiple conditions so that you can specify filtering criteria on more than one field. Each individual condition of the multiple conditions is in the form of the conditions described in the preceding sections on using predicates. These individual conditions are then combined using the logical operators AND and OR. By using multiple-condition statements, you can find all the Smiths in the Southeast, or you can find anyone whose first or last name is Scott. Listing C.12 shows the statements for these examples. Figure C.6 shows the recordset resulting from a query search for Scott.

Listing C.12—ANDOR.TXT—Combining Multiple WHERE Conditions with AND or OR

```
'**********************************
'Find all Smiths in the Southeast
'**********************************
SELECT * FROM Customers WHERE Lastname = 'Smith' AND  _
    State IN ('AL', 'FL', 'GA')
'********************************************************
'Find all occurrences of Scott in first or last name
'********************************************************
SELECT * FROM Customers WHERE Lastname = 'Scott' _
    OR Firstname = 'Scott'
```

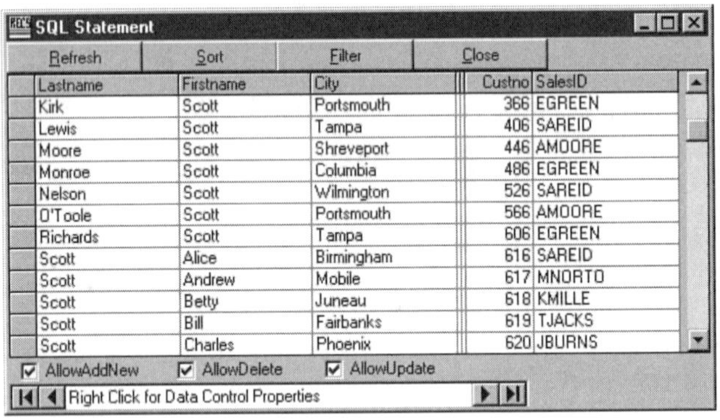

FIGURE C.6
You can use multiple conditions to enhance a WHERE clause.

Lastname	Firstname	City	Custno	SalesID
Kirk	Scott	Portsmouth	366	EGREEN
Lewis	Scott	Tampa	406	SAREID
Moore	Scott	Shreveport	446	AMOORE
Monroe	Scott	Columbia	486	EGREEN
Nelson	Scott	Wilmington	526	SAREID
O'Toole	Scott	Portsmouth	566	AMOORE
Richards	Scott	Tampa	606	EGREEN
Scott	Alice	Birmingham	616	SAREID
Scott	Andrew	Mobile	617	MNORTO
Scott	Betty	Juneau	618	KMILLE
Scott	Bill	Fairbanks	619	TJACKS
Scott	Charles	Phoenix	620	JBURNS

Setting the Sort Conditions

In addition to specifying the range of records to process, you can also use the SELECT statement to specify the order in which you want the records to appear in the output dynaset. The SELECT statement controls the order in which the records are processed or viewed. Sorting the records is done by using the ORDER BY clause of the SELECT statement.

You can specify the sort order with a single field or with multiple fields. If you use multiple fields, the individual fields must be separated by commas.

The default sort order for all fields is ascending (that is, A-Z, 0-9). You can change the sort order for any individual field by specifying the DESC keyword after the field name (the DESC keyword affects only the one field, not any other fields in the ORDER BY clause). Listing C.13 shows several uses of the ORDER BY clause. Figure C.7 shows the results of these SELECT statements.

> **NOTE** When you're sorting records, the presence of an index for the sort field can significantly speed up the SQL query.

FIGURE C.7
The ORDER BY clause specifies the sort order of the dynaset.

Note that first names are out of order.

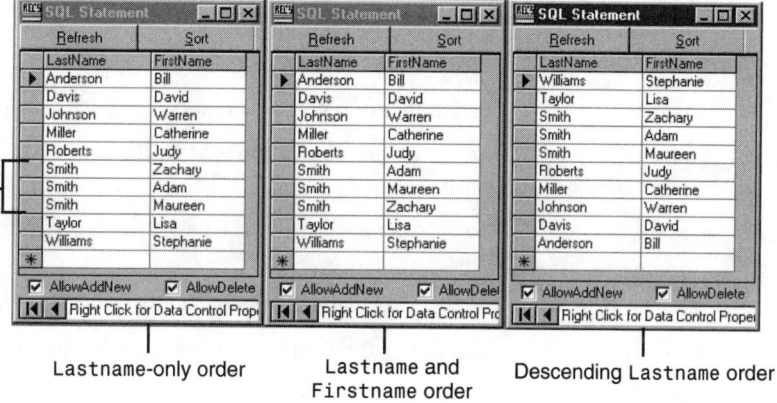

Lastname-only order | Lastname and Firstname order | Descending Lastname order

Listing C.13 SORT.TXT—Specifying the Sort Order of the Output Dynaset

```
'*****************
'Single field sort
'*****************
SELECT * FROM Customers ORDER BY Lastname
'*******************
'Multiple field sort
'*******************
SELECT * FROM Customers ORDER BY Lastname, Firstname
'**********************
'Descending order sort
'**********************
SELECT * FROM Customers ORDER BY Lastname DESC, Firstname
```

Using Aggregate Functions

You can use the SELECT statement to perform calculations on the information in your tables by using the SQL *aggregate functions*. To perform the calculations, define them as a field in your SELECT statement, using the following syntax:

function(expression)

The expression can be a single field or a calculation based on one or more fields, such as Quantity * Price or SQR(Datapoint). The Count function can also use the wild card * as the expression, because Count returns only the number of records. Table C.5 shows the 11 aggregate functions available in Microsoft SQL.

Table C.5 Aggregate Functions Provide Summary Information About Data in the Database

Function	Returns
Avg	The arithmetic average of the field for the records that meet the WHERE clause
Count	The number of records that meet the WHERE clause
Min	The minimum value of the field for the records that meet the WHERE clause
Max	The maximum value of the field for the records that meet the WHERE clause
Sum	The total value of the field for the records that meet the WHERE clause
First	The value of the field for the first record in the recordset
Last	The value of the field for the last record in the recordset
StDev	The standard deviation of the values of the field for the records that meet the WHERE clause
StDevP	The standard deviation of the values of the field for the records that meet the WHERE clause
Var	The variance of the values of the field for the records that meet the WHERE clause
VarP	The variance of the values of the field for the records that meet the WHERE clause

NOTE In Table C.5, StDev and StDevP seem to perform the same function. The same is true of Var and VarP. The difference between the functions is that the StDevP and VarP evaluate populations where StDev and Var evaluate samples of populations.

As with other SQL functions, these aggregate functions operate only on the records that meet the filter criteria specified in the WHERE clause. Aggregate functions are unaffected by sort order. Aggregate functions return a single value for the entire recordset unless the GROUP BY clause (described in the following section) is used. If GROUP BY is used, a value is returned for each record group. Listing C.14 shows the SELECT statement used to calculate the minimum, maximum, average, and total sales amounts, as well as the total item volume from the Sales table in the sample case. Figure C.8 shows the output from this query.

FIGURE C.8
The table shows the summary information from aggregate functions.

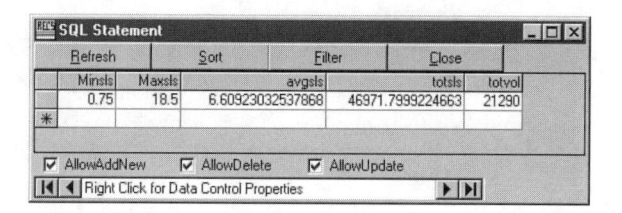

Listing C.14 SUMMARY.TXT—Using Aggregate Functions to Provide Summary Information

```
SELECT Min(SL.Quantity * RT.Retail) AS Minsls, _
    Max(SL.Quantity * RT.Retail) AS Maxsls, _
    Avg(SL.Quantity * RT.Retail) AS Avgsls, _
    Sum(SL.Quantity * RT.Retail) AS Totsls, _
    Sum(SL.Quantity) AS Totvol _
    FROM Sales AS SL, [Retail Items] AS RT _
    WHERE SL.[Item Code]=RT.[Item Code]
```

Creating Record Groups

Creating record groups lets you create a recordset that has only one record for each occurrence of the specified field. For example, if your group the Customers table by state, you have one output record for each state. This arrangement is especially useful when combined with the calculation functions described in the preceding sections. When groups are used in conjunction with aggregate functions, you can easily obtain summary data by state, salesperson, item code, or any other desired field.

Most of the time, you want to create groups based on a single field. You can, however, specify multiple fields in the GROUP BY clause. If you do, a record is returned for each unique combination of field values. You can use this technique to get sales data by salesperson and item code. Separate multiple fields in a GROUP BY clause with commas. Listing C.15 shows an update of Listing C.14, adding groups based on the salesperson ID. Figure C.9 shows the results of the query.

Listing C.15 GROUP.TXT—Using the *GROUP BY* Clause to Obtain Summary Information for Record Groups

```
SELECT SL.SalesID, Min(SL.Quantity * RT.Retail) AS Minsls, _
    Max(SL.Quantity * RT.Retail) AS Maxsls, _
    Avg(SL.Quantity * RT.Retail) AS Avgsls, _
    Sum(SL.Quantity * RT.Retail) AS Totsls, _
    Sum(SL.Quantity) AS Totvol _
    FROM Sales AS SL, [Retail Items] AS RT _
    WHERE SL.[Item Code]=RT.[Item Code] _
    GROUP BY SL.SalesID
```

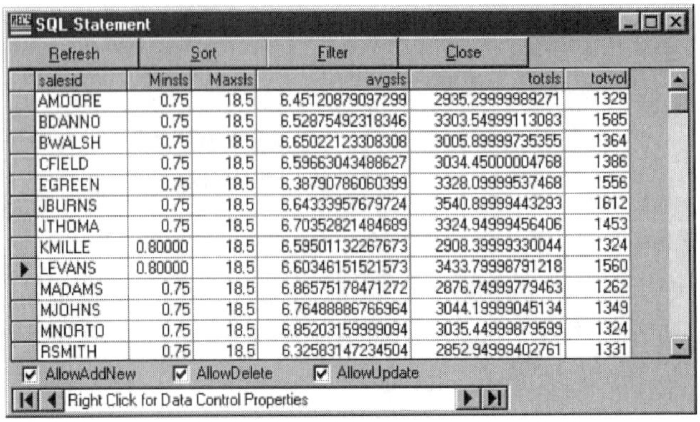
SQL Statement

Refresh Sort Filter Close

salesid	Minsls	Maxsls	avgsls	totsls	totvol
AMOORE	0.75	18.5	6.45120879097299	2935.29999989271	1329
BDANNO	0.75	18.5	6.52875492318346	3303.54999113083	1585
BWALSH	0.75	18.5	6.65022123308308	3005.89999735355	1364
CFIELD	0.75	18.5	6.59663043488627	3034.45000004768	1386
EGREEN	0.75	18.5	6.38790786060399	3328.09999537468	1556
JBURNS	0.75	18.5	6.64333957679724	3540.89999443293	1612
JTHOMA	0.75	18.5	6.70352821484689	3324.94999456406	1453
KMILLE	0.80000	18.5	6.59501132267673	2908.39999330044	1324
LEVANS	0.80000	18.5	6.60346151521573	3433.79998791218	1560
MADAMS	0.75	18.5	6.86575178471272	2876.74999779463	1262
MJOHNS	0.75	18.5	6.76488886766964	3044.19999045134	1349
MNORTO	0.75	18.5	6.85203159999094	3035.44999879599	1324
RSMITH	0.75	18.5	6.32583147234504	2852.94999402761	1331

AllowAddNew AllowDelete AllowUpdate

Right Click for Data Control Properties

FIGURE C.9
Using GROUP BY creates a summary record for each defined group.

The `GROUP BY` clause can also include an optional `HAVING` clause. The `HAVING` clause works similarly to a `WHERE` clause but examines only the field values of the returned records. The `HAVING` clause determines which of the selected records to display; the `WHERE` clause determines which records to select from the base tables. You can use the `HAVING` clause to display only those salespeople with total sales exceeding $3,000 for the month. Listing C.16 shows this example; Figure C.10 shows the output from this listing.

Listing C.16 HAVING.TXT—The *HAVING* Clause Filters the Display of the Selected Group Records

```
SELECT SL.SalesID, Min(SL.Quantity * RT.Retail) AS Minsls,  _
     Max(SL.Quantity * RT.Retail) AS Maxsls,  _
     Avg(SL.Quantity * RT.Retail) AS Avgsls,  _
     Sum(SL.Quantity * RT.Retail) AS Totsls,  _
     Sum(SL.Quantity) AS Totvol  _
     FROM Sales AS SL, [Retail Items] AS RT  _
     SL INNER JOIN RT ON SL.[Item Code]=RT.[Item Code]  _
     GROUP BY SL.SalesID  _
     HAVING Sum(SL.Quantity * RT.Retail) > 3000
```

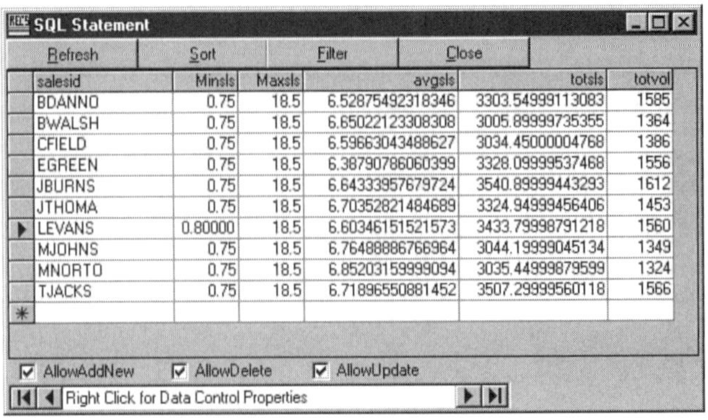
SQL Statement

Refresh Sort Filter Close

salesid	Minsls	Maxsls	avgsls	totsls	totvol
BDANNO	0.75	18.5	6.52875492318346	3303.54999113083	1585
BWALSH	0.75	18.5	6.65022123308308	3005.89999735355	1364
CFIELD	0.75	18.5	6.59663043488627	3034.45000004768	1386
EGREEN	0.75	18.5	6.38790786060399	3328.09999537468	1556
JBURNS	0.75	18.5	6.64333957679724	3540.89999443293	1612
JTHOMA	0.75	18.5	6.70352821484689	3324.94999456406	1453
LEVANS	0.80000	18.5	6.60346151521573	3433.79998791218	1560
MJOHNS	0.75	18.5	6.76488886766964	3044.19999045134	1349
MNORTO	0.75	18.5	6.85203159999094	3035.44999879599	1324
TJACKS	0.75	18.5	6.71896550881452	3507.29999560118	1566

AllowAddNew AllowDelete AllowUpdate

Right Click for Data Control Properties

FIGURE C.10
The HAVING clause limits the display of group records.

Creating a Table

In all the examples of the SELECT statement used earlier in this chapter, the results of the query were output to a dynaset or a snapshot. Because these recordsets are only temporary, their contents exist only as long as the recordset is open. After a close method is used or the application is terminated, the recordset disappears (although any changes made to the underlying tables are permanent).

Sometimes, however, you might want to permanently store the information in the recordset for later use. Do so with the INTO clause of the SELECT statement. With the INTO clause, you specify the name of an output table (and, optionally, the database for the table) in which to store the results. You might want to do this to generate a mailing-list table from your customer list. This mailing-list table can then be accessed by your word processor to perform a mail-merge function or to print mailing labels. Listing C.4, earlier in this chapter, generated such a list in a dynaset. Listing C.17 shows the same basic SELECT statement as was used in Listing C.4, but the new listing uses the INTO clause to store the information in a table.

Listing C.17—INTO.TXT—Using the *INTO* Clause to Save Information to a New Table

```
SELECT CS.Firstname & ' ' & CS.Lastname, CS.Address, ZP.City, _
    ZP.State, CS.ZIP INTO Mailings FROM Customers AS CS, _
    Zipcode IN USZIPS AS ZP WHERE CS.Zip = ZP.Zip
```

> **CAUTION**
> The table name you specify should be that of a new table. If you specify the name of a table that already exists, that table is overwritten with the output of the SELECT statement.

Using Parameters

So far in all of the clauses, you have seen specific values specified. For example, you specified 'AL' for a state of 1.25 for a price. But what if you don't know in advance what value you want to use in comparison? Well, this is precisely what parameters are used for in a SQL statement. The parameter is to the SQL statement what a variable is to a program statement. The parameter is a placeholder whose value is assigned by your program before the SQL statement is executed.

To use a parameter in your SQL statement, you first have to specify the parameter in the PARAMETERS declaration part of the statement. The PARAMETERS declaration comes before the SELECT or other manipulative clause in the SQL statement. The declaration specifies both the name of the parameter and its data type. The PARAMETERS clause is separated from the rest of the SQL statement by a semicolon.

After you have declared the parameters, you simply place them in the manipulative part of the statement where you want to be able to substitute a value. The following code line shows how a parameter would be used in place of a state ID in a SQL statement:

```
PARAMETERS StateName String; SELECT * FROM Customers
    WHERE State = StateName
```

When you go to run the SQL statement in your program, each parameter is treated like a property of the QueryDef. Therefore, you need to assign a value to each parameter before you use the Execute method. The following code shows you how to set the property value for the preceding SQL statement and open a recordset:

```
Dim OldDb As Database, Qry As QueryDef, Rset As Recordset
Set OldDb = DBEngine.Workspaces(0).OpenDatabase("C:\Triton.Mdb")
Set Qry = OldDb.QueryDefs("StateSelect")
Qry!StateName = "AL"
Set Rset = Qry.OpenRecordset()
```

As you can see, using parameters makes it easy to store your queries in the database and still maintain the flexibility of being able to specify comparison values at runtime.

SQL Action Statements

In the previous section, you saw how the SELECT statement can be used to retrieve records and place the information in a dynaset or table for further processing by a program. This was just one of the four manipulative statements that you defined earlier in this chapter. The three remaining statements are as follows:

- DELETE FROM—An action query that removes records from a table
- INSERT INTO—An action query that adds a group of records to a table
- UPDATE—An action query that sets the values of fields in a table

In the following sections, you take a look at how to use these statements to further refine that data that you are manipulating in a database via a SQL function.

Using the *DELETE* Statement

The DELETE statement is used to create an *action query*. The DELETE statement's purpose is to delete specific records from a table. An action query does not return a group of records into a dynaset as SELECT queries do. Instead, action queries work like program *subroutines*. That is, an action query performs its functions and returns to the next statement in the calling program.

The syntax of the DELETE statement is as follows:

```
DELETE FROM tablename [WHERE clause]
```

The WHERE clause is an optional parameter. If it is omitted, all the records in the target table are deleted. You can use the WHERE clause to limit the deletions to only those records that meet specified criteria. In the WHERE clause, you can use any of the comparison predicates defined in the earlier section "Using the Comparison Predicate." Following is an example of the DELETE statement used to eliminate all customers who live in Florida:

```
DELETE FROM Customers WHERE State='FL'
```

> **CAUTION**
> After the DELETE statement is executed, the records are gone and can't be recovered. The only exception is if transaction processing is used. If you're using transaction processing, you can use a ROLLBACK statement to recover any deletions made since the last BEGINTRANS statement was issued.

Using the *INSERT* Statement

Like the DELETE statement, the INSERT statement is another action query. The INSERT statement is used in conjunction with the SELECT statement to add a group of records to a table. The syntax of the statement is as follows:

```
INSERT INTO tablename SELECT rest-of-select-statement
```

You build the SELECT portion of the statement exactly as explained in the first part of this chapter in the section "Using *SELECT* Statements." The purpose of the SELECT portion of the statement is to define the records to be added to the table. The INSERT statement defines the action of adding the records and specifies the table that is to receive the records.

One use of the INSERT statement is to update tables created with the SELECT INTO statement. Suppose that you're keeping a church directory. When you first create the directory, you create a mailing list for the current member list. Each month, as new members are added, you either can rerun the SELECT INTO query and re-create the table, or you can run the INSERT INTO query and add only the new members to the existing mailing list. Listing C.18 shows the creation of the original mailing list and the use of the INSERT INTO query to update the list.

Listing C.18 INSERT.TXT—Using the *INSERT INTO* Statement to Add a Group of Records to a Table

```
'********************************
'Create a new mailing list table
'********************************
SELECT CS.Firstname & ' ' & CS.Lastname, CS.Address, ZP.City, _
    ZP.State, CS.ZIP INTO Mailings FROM Members AS CS, _
    Zipcode IN USZIPS AS ZP WHERE CS.Zip = ZP.Zip
'********************************
'Update the mailing list each month
'********************************
INSERT INTO Mailings SELECT CS.Firstname & ' ' & CS.Lastname, _
    CS.Address, ZP.City, ZP.State, CS.ZIP _
    FROM Customers AS CS, Zipcode IN USZIPS AS ZP _
    WHERE CS.Zip = ZP.Zip AND CS.Memdate>Lastmonth
```

Using the *UPDATE* Statement

The UPDATE statement is another action query. It is used to change the values of specific fields in a table. The syntax of the UPDATE statement is as follows:

UPDATE *tablename* SET *field* = *newvalue* [WHERE *clause*]

You can update multiple fields in a table at one time by listing multiple *field* = *newvalue* clauses, separated by commas. The inclusion of the WHERE clause is optional. If it is excluded, all records in the table are changed.

Listing C.19 shows two examples of the UPDATE statement. The first example changes the salesperson ID for a group of customers, as happens when a salesperson leaves the company and his or her accounts are transferred to someone else. The second example changes the retail price of all retail sales items, as can be necessary to cover increased operating costs.

Listing C.19   UPDATE.TXT—Using the *UPDATE* Statement to Change Field Values for Many Records at Once

```
'**********************************************
'Change the SalesID for a group of customers
'**********************************************
UPDATE Customers SET SalesID = 'EGREEN' WHERE SalesID='JBURNS'
'***************************************************************
'Increase the retail price of all items by five percent
'***************************************************************
UPDATE [Retail Items] SET Retail = Retail * 1.05
```

Using Data-Definition-Language Statements

Data-definition-language statements (DDLs) let you create, modify, and delete tables and indexes in a database with a single statement. For many situations, these statements take the place of the data-access-object methods described in Chapter 24, "Database Design and Normalization." However, there are some limitations to using the DDL statements. The main limitation is that these statements are supported only for Jet databases (remember that data-access objects can be used for any database accessed with the Jet engine). The other limitation of DDL statements is that they support only a small subset of the properties of the table, field, and index objects. If you need to specify properties outside of this subset, you must use the methods described in Chapter 24.

Defining Tables with DDL Statements

Three DDL statements are used to define tables in a database:

- CREATE TABLE—Defines a new table in a database
- ALTER TABLE—Changes a table's structure
- DROP TABLE—Deletes a table from the database

Creating a Table with DDL Statements To create a table with the DDL statements, you create a SQL statement containing the name of the table and the names, types, and sizes of each field in the table. The following code shows how to create the Orders table of the sample case:

```
CREATE TABLE Orders (Orderno LONG, Custno LONG, SalesID TEXT (6), _
    OrderDate DATE, Totcost SINGLE)
```

Notice that when you specify the table name and field names, you do not have to enclose the names in quotation marks. However, if you want to specify a name with a space in it, you must enclose the name in square brackets (for example, [Last name]).

When you create a table, you can specify only the field names, types, and sizes. You can't specify optional parameters such as default values, validation rules, or validation error messages. Even with this limitation, the DDL CREATE TABLE statement is a powerful tool that you can use to create many of the tables in a database.

Modifying a Table By using the ALTER TABLE statement, you can add a field to an existing table or delete a field from the table. When adding a field, you must specify the name, type, and (when applicable) the size of the field. You add a field using the ADD COLUMN clause of the ALTER TABLE statement. To delete a field, you only need to specify the field name and use the DROP COLUMN clause of the statement. As with other database-modification methods, you can't delete a field used in an index or a relation. Listing C.20 shows how to add and then delete a field from the Orders table created in the preceding section.

Listing C.20 ALTERTAB.TXT—Using the *ALTER TABLE* Statement to Add or Delete a Field from a Table

```
'***************************************************
'Add a shipping charges field to the "Orders" table
'***************************************************
ALTER TABLE Orders ADD COLUMN Shipping SINGLE
'***********************************
'Delete the shipping charges field
'***********************************
ALTER TABLE Orders DROP COLUMN Shipping
```

Deleting a Table You can delete a table from a database using the DROP TABLE statement. The following simple piece of code shows how to get rid of the Orders table. Use caution when deleting a table; the table and all its data are gone forever after the command has been executed.

```
DROP TABLE Orders
```

Defining Indexes with DDL Statements

Two DDL statements are designed especially for use with indexes:

- CREATE INDEX—Defines a new index for a table
- DROP INDEX—Deletes an index from a table

Creating an Index   You can create a single-field or multi-field index with the CREATE INDEX statement. To create the index, you must give the name of the index, the name of the table for the index, and at least one field to be included in the index. You can specify ascending or descending order for each field. You can also specify that the index is a primary index for the table. Listing C.21 shows how to create a primary index on customer number and a two-field index with the sort orders specified. These indexes are set up for the Customers table of the sample case.

Listing C.21   CREATEIND.TXT—Create Several Types of Indexes with the CREATE INDEX Statement

```
'*******************************************
'Create a primary index on customer number
'*******************************************
CREATE INDEX Custno ON Customers (Custno) WITH PRIMARY
'*****************************************************************
'Create a two field index with ascending order on Lastname and
'    descending order on Firstname.
'*****************************************************************
CREATE INDEX Name2 ON Customers (Lastname ASC, Firstname DESC)
```

Deleting an Index   Getting rid of an index is just as easy as creating one. To delete an index from a table, use the DROP INDEX statement as shown in the following example. These statements delete the two indexes created in Listing C.21. Notice that you must specify the table name for the index that you want to delete:

```
DROP INDEX Custno ON Customers
DROP INDEX Name2 ON Customers
```

Using SQL

As stated at the beginning of the chapter, you can't place a SQL statement by itself in a program. It must be part of another function. This part of the chapter describes the various methods used to implement the SQL statements.

Executing an Action Query

The Jet engine provides an execute method as part of the database object. The execute method tells the engine to process the SQL query against the database. An action query can be executed by specifying the SQL statement as part of the execute method for a database. An action query can also be used to create a QueryDef. Then the query can be executed on its own. Listing C.22 shows how both of these methods are used to execute the same SQL statement.

Listing C.22 EXECUTE.TXT—Run SQL Statements with the *DatabaseExecute* or *QueryExecute* Method

```
Dim OldDb AS Database, NewQry AS QueryDef
'*******************************************************
'Define the SQL statement and assign it to a variable
'*******************************************************
SQLstate = "UPDATE Customers SET SalesID = 'EGREEN'"
SQLstate = SQLstate + " WHERE SalesID='JBURNS'"
'*********************************************
'Use the database execute to run the query
'*********************************************
OldDb.Execute SQLstate
'*********************************************
'Create a QueryDef from the SQL statement
'*********************************************
Set NewQry = OldDb.CreateQueryDef("Change Sales", SQLstate)
'*********************************************
'Use the query execute to run the query
'*********************************************
NewQry.Execute
'*******************************************************
'Run the named query with the database execute method
'*******************************************************
OldDb.Execute "Change Sales"
```

Creating a *QueryDef*

Creating a QueryDef lets you name your query and store it in the database with your tables. You can create either an action query or a *retrieval query* (one that uses the SELECT statement). After the query is created, you can call it by name for execution (shown in a listing in the previous section "Executing an Action Query") or for creation of a dynaset (as described in the following section). Listing C.22 showed how to create a QueryDef called Change Sales that is used to update the salesperson ID for a group of customers.

Creating Dynasets and Snapshots

To use the SELECT statement to retrieve records and store them in a dynaset or snapshot, you must use the SELECT statement in conjunction with the OpenRecordset method. Using the OpenRecordset method, you specify the type of recordset with the options parameter. With this method, you either can use the SELECT statement directly or use the name of a retrieval query that you have previously defined. Listing C.23 shows these two methods of retrieving records.

Listing C.23 CREATEMETH.TXT—Using the Create Methods to Retrieve the Records Defined by a *SELECT* Statement

```
Dim OldDb As Database, NewQry As QueryDef, NewDyn As Recordset
Dim NewSnap As Recordset
'**********************************************************
'Define the SELECT statement and store it to a variable
'**********************************************************
SQLstate = "SELECT RI.[Item Description], SL.Quantity,"
SQLstate = SQLstate & " RI.Retail, _
    SL.Quantity * RI.Retail AS Subtot"
SQLstate = SQLstate & "FROM [Retail Items] AS RI, Sales AS SL"
SQLstate = SQLstate & "WHERE SL.[Item Code]=RI.[Item Code]"
'************************
'Create dynaset directly
'************************
Set NewDyn = OldDb.OpenRecordset(SQLstate, dbOpenDynaset)
'***************
'Create QueryDef
'***************
Set NewQry = OldDb.CreateQueryDef("Get Subtotals", SQLstate)
NewQry.Close
'******************************
'Create snapshot from querydef
'******************************
Set NewSnap = OldDb.OpenRecordset("Get Subtotals", dbOpenSnapshot)
```

You have seen how SELECT statements are used to create dynasets and snapshots. But, the comparison part of a WHERE clause and the sort list of an ORDER BY clause can also be used to set dynaset properties. The filter property of a dynaset is a WHERE statement without the WHERE keyword. When setting the filter property, you can use all the predicates described in the section "Using the *WHERE* Clause," earlier in this chapter. In a like manner, the sort property of a dynaset is an ORDER BY clause without the ORDER BY keywords.

Using SQL Statements with the Data Control

The data control uses the RecordSource property to create a recordset when the control is loaded. The RecordSource can be a table, a SELECT statement, or a predefined query. Therefore, the entire discussion on the SELECT statement (in the section "Using *SELECT* statements") applies to the creation of the recordset used with a data control.

N O T E When you specify a table name for the RecordSource property, Visual Basic uses the name to create a SELECT statement such as this:

SELECT * FROM *table*

Creating SQL Statements

When you create and test your SQL statements, you can program them directly into your code and run the code to see whether they work. This process can be very time-consuming and frustrating, especially for complex statements. There are, however, three easier ways of developing SQL statements that might be available to you:

- The Visual Data Manager Add-in that comes with Visual Basic
- Microsoft Access (if you have a copy)
- Microsoft Query

NOTE Users of Microsoft Excel or Microsoft Office also have access to Microsoft Query, the tool in Access.

The Visual Data Manager and Access both have query builders that can help you create SQL queries. They provide dialog boxes for selecting the fields to include, and they help you with the various clauses. When you have finished testing a query with either application, you can store the query as a `QueryDef` in the database. This query can then be executed by name from your program. As an alternative, you can copy the code from the query builder into your program, using standard cut-and-paste operations.

Using the Visual Data Manager

The Visual Data Manager is a Visual Basic add-in that allows you to create and modify databases for your Visual Basic programs. The Visual Data Manager also has a window that allows you to enter and debug SQL queries. And if you don't want to try to create the query yourself, VDM has a query builder that makes it easy for you to create queries by making choices in the builder.

NOTE If you want to learn about the inner workings of the Visual Data Manager, it is one of the sample projects installed with Visual Basic. The project file is VISDATA.VBP and is found in the VISDATA folder of the Samples folder.

To start the Visual Data Manager, simply select the Visual Data Manager item from the Add-Ins menu of Visual Basic. After starting the program, open the File menu and select the Open Database item; then select the type of database to open from the submenu. You are presented with a dialog box that allows you to open a database. After the database is opened, a list of the tables and queries in the database appears in the left window of the application. The Visual Data Manager with the Triton.Mdb database open is shown in Figure C.11.

FIGURE C.11
You can use the Visual Data Manager Add-In to develop SQL queries.

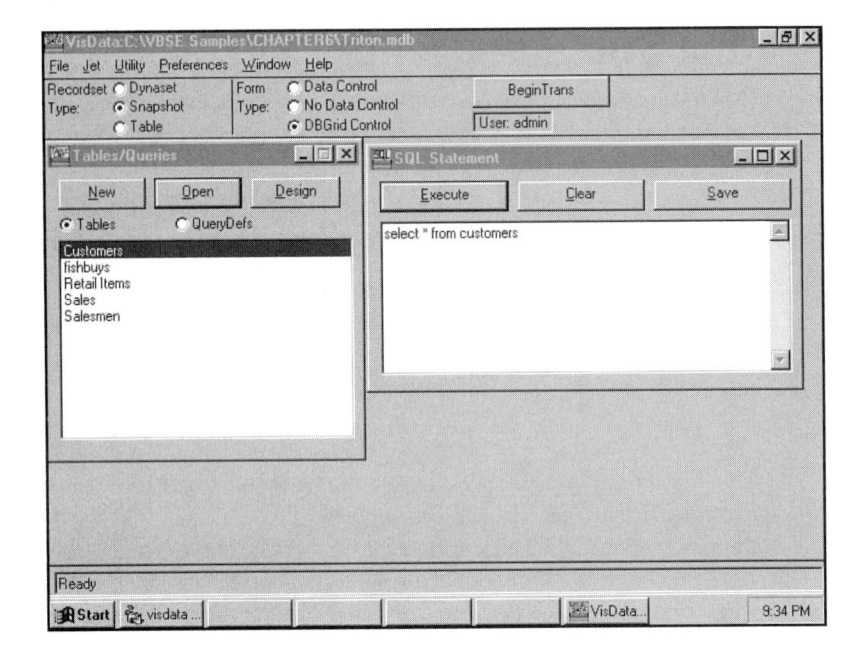

To develop and test SQL statements, first enter the statement in the text box of the SQL dialog box (the one on the right in Figure C.11). When you're ready to test the statement, click the Execute SQL button. If you're developing a retrieval query, a dynaset is created and the results are displayed in a data entry form (or a grid) if the statement has no errors. If you're developing an action query, a message box appears, telling you that the execution of the query is complete (again, assuming that the statement is correct). If you have an error in your statement, a message box appears informing you of the error.

The Visual Data Manager Add-In also includes a Query Builder. You can access the Query Builder (shown in Figure C.12) by choosing Query Builder from the Utilities menu of the Visual Data Manager. To create a query with the Query Builder, follow these steps:

1. Select the tables to include from the Tables list.
2. Select the fields to include from the Fields to Show list.
3. Set the WHERE clause (if any) using the Field Name, Operator, and Value drop-down lists at the top of the dialog box.
4. Set the table JOIN conditions (if any) by clicking the Set Table Joins command button.
5. Set a single-field ORDER BY clause (if any) by selecting the field from the Order By Field drop-down box and selecting either the Asc or Desc option.
6. Set a single GROUP BY field (if any) by selecting the field from the Group By Field drop-down box.

FIGURE C.12
The Query Builder makes it easy to build SQL statements.

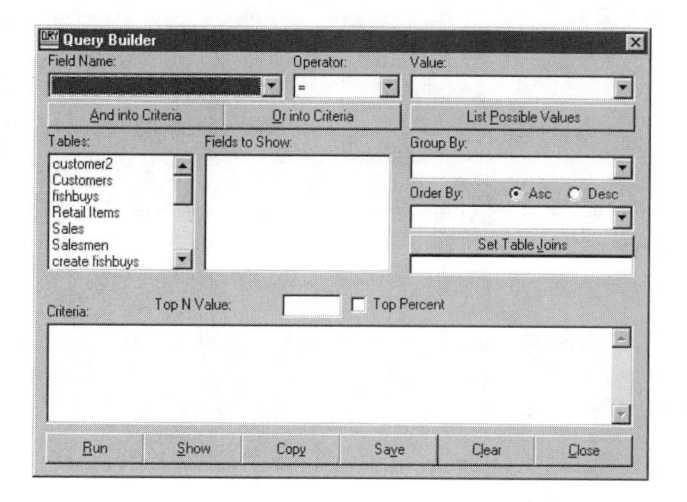

After you have set the Query Builder parameters, you can run the query, display the SQL statement, or copy the query to the SQL statement window. The Query Builder provides an easy way to become familiar with constructing SELECT queries.

When you have developed the query to your satisfaction (either with the Query Builder or by typing the statement directly), you can save the query as a QueryDef in your database. In your Visual Basic code, you can then reference the name of the query you created. Alternatively, you can copy the query from Visual Data Manager and paste it into your application code.

Using Microsoft Access

If you have a copy of Microsoft Access, you can use its query builder to graphically construct queries. You can then save the query as a QueryDef in the database and reference the query name in your Visual Basic code.

One of more creative uses for Access is to reverse-engineer a QueryDef. Microsoft Access allows you to build a graphical representation of the tables and databases for a particular QueryDef entered in SQL format. This reverse-engineering process gives you a unique way to debug or make modifications graphically to an existing query.

Optimizing SQL Performance

Developers always want to get the best possible performance from every aspect of their applications. Wanting high performance out of SQL queries is no exception. Fortunately, there are several methods you can use to optimize the performance of your SQL queries.

Using Indexes

The Microsoft Jet database engine uses an optimization technology called Rushmore. Under certain conditions, Rushmore uses available indexes to try to speed up queries. To take maximum advantage of this arrangement, you can create an index on each of the fields you typically use in a WHERE clause or a JOIN condition. This is particularly true of key fields used to relate tables (for example, the Custno and SalesID fields in the sample database). An index also works better with comparison operators than with the other types of WHERE conditions, such as LIKE or IN.

> **NOTE** Only certain types of queries are optimizable by Rushmore. For a query to use Rushmore optimization, the WHERE condition must use an indexed field. In addition, if you use the LIKE operator, the expression should begin with a character, not a wild card. Rushmore works with Jet databases and FoxPro and dBase tables. Rushmore does not work with ODBC databases.

Compiling Queries

Compiling a query refers to creating a QueryDef and storing it in the database. If the query already exists in the database, the command parser does not have to generate the query each time it is run, and this increases execution speed. If you have a query that is frequently used, create a QueryDef for it.

Keeping Queries Simple

When you're working with a lot of data from a large number of tables, the SQL statements can become quite complex. Complex statements are much slower to execute than simple ones. Also, if you have a number of conditions in WHERE clauses, this increases complexity and slows execution time.

Keep statements as simple as possible. If you have a complex statement, consider breaking it into multiple smaller operations. For example, if you have a complex JOIN of three tables, you might be able to use the SELECT INTO statement to create a temporary table from two of the three and then use a second SELECT statement to perform the final JOIN. There are no hard-and-fast rules for how many tables are too many or how many conditions make a statement too complex. If you're having performance problems, try some different ideas and find the one that works best.

Another way to keep things simple is to try to avoid pattern-matching in a WHERE clause. Because pattern-matching does not deal with discrete values, pattern-matching is hard to optimize. In addition, patterns that use wild cards for the first character are much slower than those that specifically define that character. For example, if you're looking for books about SQL, finding ones with *SQL* anywhere in the title (pattern = "*SQL*") requires looking at every title in the table. On the other hand, looking for titles that start with *SQL* (pattern = "SQL*") lets you skip over most records. If you had a Title index, the search would go directly to the first book on SQL.

Passing SQL Statements to Other Database Engines

Visual Basic has the capability of passing a SQL statement through to an ODBC database server such as SQL Server. When you pass a statement through, the Jet engine does not try to do any processing of the query, but it sends the query to the server to be processed. Remember, however, that the SQL statement must conform to the SQL syntax of the host database.

To use the pass-through capability, set the options parameter in the `OpenRecordset` or the execute methods to the value of the `dbSQLPassThrough` constant.

The project file, SQLDEMO.VBP, available from the Que Web site, contains many of the listings used in this chapter. Each listing is assigned to a command button. Choosing the command button creates a dynaset by using the SQL statement in the listing; the results are displayed in a data-bound grid. The form containing the grid also has a text box that shows the SQL statement. Download the file from www.mcp.com/info.

From Here...

This chapter has taught you the basics of using SQL in your database program. You have seen how to select records and how to limit the selection using the WHERE clause. You have also seen how SQL statements can be used to modify the structure of a database and how to use aggregate functions to obtain summary information.

Index

Symbols

' (single quotation marks), 580
#INCLUDE statement, ASP include files, 697
& (ampersand)
    access keys, 67
    concatenation, Response.Write statement (ASP), 183, 707
    menu access keys, 116
    Menu controls, 110
* (asterisk), fixed-length string declarations, 165
+ (addition operator), 177
- (subtraction operator), 177
\ (integer division operator), 179
/ (division operator), 178
... (ellipsis), Menu controls, 114
^ (exponentiation operator), 181
| (pipe symbol), 152
16-bit API functions, 452
32-bit functions, 452

A

About box
    with Web site link, 745
    form template, 240
AbsolutePosition property, 584
Access (Microsoft), 543
    Data control, 546
    sample database application, 513
access keys, 116
    command buttons, 67
    menu Click event, 119
access mode
    dynaset options, 572
    snapshot options, 574
action queries, 589
    SQL, 820-821
action SQL statements, 816-818
    DELETE, 816-817
    INSERT, 817
    UPDATE, 818
Activate event, child forms, 391
activated objects, 498
Active Messaging, 747
    sending messages, 749
Active Server Pages, *see* ASP
ActiveConnection object, disconnected recordsets, 638
ActiveConnection property, RecordSet object, 630
ActiveForm keyword, 391
ActiveX controls, 306
    Address control, 307
        adding properties, 310
        resize code, 309
    Ambient object, 342
        colors, 343
        properties, 343
    Calculator, 345
        interface, 346
        methods/events, 348
        operation property, 347
        testing, 349
    compiling
        distributing, 315-316
        OCX file, 315
        testing, 315
    development strategies, 307
    DLLs, 368-371
        enums, 372
        IIS Application, 712
        instancing property, 371
        project, 761
    DLLs with ASP, 711
    enhancing, 317
    error handling, 355-356
    Extender object, 344
    installing, 316

Interface Wizard, 323
  properties, 324-327
packaging projects
  Internet download, 788
  Internet files, 790
  scripting options, 789
SIGNCODE utility, 317
testing
  Internet Explorer, 313
  project group, 311-313
user-drawn, 333
  button events, 337
  button properties, 335-336
  button property pages, 337
  testing button, 338
  user interface, 333-335
VBScript, 681-682
see also ADO

ActiveX Designers, IIS Application, 712

ActiveX documents, 720-722
  Binder, 729
  coding, 726
  compiling, 729
  containers, 721
  creating, 722
  displaying forms, 738
  Hyperlink object, 733
  interface, 724
  Migration Wizard, 733-737
  multiple documents, 737-738
  opening, 727
  projects, 723-724, 762
  testing, 726-728
  UserDocument object, 729
    key events, 730
    methods, 731-733
    properties, 730

actmsg.hlp, 751

Add Field dialog box, 539

Add File dialog box, 239

Add Form button (IDE), 765

Add Form dialog box, 158

Add In Manager dialog box, 557

Add Index dialog box, 541

Add Ins, Migration Wizard, 734

Add MDI Form dialog box, 384

Add method
  Active Messaging, 749
  Buttons collection, 134
  ListImages collection, 249
  ToolBar control collections, 134

Add Procedure dialog box, 226, 363

Add Project button (IDE), 765

Add Properties dialog box, 331

Add Watch dialog box, 218

Add-In Manager, 323

add-ins, 762

AddItem method, 70

addition, 177

AddNew method, 590

Address control, 307
  adding properties, 310
  resize code, 309

AddressText property, 310

ADO (ActiveX Data Objects), 612
  ASP, 697
  Command object, 636
  data connection methods, 612
  Data control, 614
    connecting to data source, 616-617
    displaying data, 618
    record source, 619
    setting up, 615
  data sources, setting up, 613
  DataGrid control, 619-620
    customizing layout, 624-626
    setting up, 621-622
    splitting up, 623-624
  declaring objects, 627
  disconnected recordsets, 637
    reconnecting, 638
    uses of, 639
  installation, 612
  Recordset object
    adding new data, 635
    displaying field values, 631
    updating data, 634
  recordsets, 630-631
    navigating, 632-634

ADONAV.ZIP, 633

ADOTEST.ZIP, 631, 636

Advanced Optimizations dialog box, 777

aggregate functions (SELECT SQL statements), 811-813

alias names, assigning to tables (SELECT SQL statements), 801-802

Alias.txt (code listing), table aliases, 802

Align button, 88

Align property, StatusBar control, 280

Alignment property, 65
  Label control, 28

ALL predicates (SELECT SQL statements), 802-803

AllowArrows property, DataGrid control, 622

AllowColumnReorder property, 256

AllowCustomize property, 135

ALTER TABLE statement, defining tables with DDLs, 819

Altertab.txt (code listing), ALTER TABLE statement, 819

Ambient object, 342
  colors, 343
  properties, 343
AmbientChanged event, 343
ampersand (&)
  access keys, 67, 116
  concatenation,
    Response.Write statement
      (ASP), 183, 707
  Menu controls, 110
Andor.txt (code listing), combining multiple WHERE conditions, 810
Animation control, 285-287
animations
  screen saver application, 511
  Timer control, 83
API calls
  API Text Viewer, 452-453
  callbacks, 463
  calls
    caller ID application
      sounds, 503
    controlling other
      windows, 458-460
    null characters, 460
    ShellExecute, 745
    sndPlaySound, 457
    SystemParametersInfo, 457
    transparent images, 519, 523
  subclassing, 464
    event handlers, 465-467
  wrapper functions, 454-457
APIDEMO.ZIP, 457-459
APIWRAP.ZIP, 454
App.Path property, 738
  locating files, 476
Appearance property, 621
  Frame control, 84
append mode, 481
Application object (ASP), 710
Application object (Word), 492

application-level security, 707
applications, 12
  ASP, 692
  customized, 12
  definition of, 12
  designing, 14-15
  exiting event, 32
  running, 36
  user interfaces, 18
ApplyChanges event procedure, Property Pages, 353
Arguments collection, Wscript object, 684
arguments, *see* **properties**
Arrange method, 392
arrays
  comp to collections, 134
  compared to collections, 250
  menu item, 298
  parallel, 297
  variable arrays, 166
As keyword, 34
Asc function, 194
ASCII character codes, 193
ASP (Active Server Pages), 668, 688, 693
  ActiveX DLLs, 711
  Application object, 710
  apps/sessions, 692
  database access, 697
    queries, 698-701
    updating, 701, 704
  dynamic Web pages, 694
  example file, 693
  include files, 696
  objects, 704
  Request object, 709
  Response object, 708
  Server object, 710
  server-side scripting tags, 693
  Session object, 705-707
    Response.Write
      statement, 707

  virutal directories, 690-692
  vs HTML, 688
ASPDEMO.ZIP, 689
assignment statement, 36
assignment statements, 175
asterisk (*), fixed-length string declarations, 165
AsyncRead method, 731
AT#CID=1 command (HyperTerminal), 502
Auto List Member, 760
  classes, 372
Auto List Members, 47
Auto Quick Info, 760
AutoShowChildren property, 385
AutoSize property, 431
  Label control, 63
  StatusBar control, 282
AVI file format, Animation control, 285

B

BackColor property, 335
Band objects, CoolBar control, 136
batch optimistic, 638
BeginTrans command, 592
BETWEEN predicates, filter criteria, 809
Between.txt (code listing), BETWEEN predicate, 809
BIBLIO.MDB database, 613
  DAO, 568
Binder, ActiveX documents, 729
binding, DataGrid control, 620
Binding Type setting, 560
bitmaps, ImageList control, 125

block If statements, 205
Bookmark property, 578
Bookmarks collection, 495
Boolean type, toggling values, 122
BorderStyle property
    Frame control, 84
    labels, 64
    Line control, 427
    settings, 53
bound controls, 550
    adding to forms, 551
    ADO Data control, 615
    displaying data, 552-553
    RemoteData control, 607
branches, 258
break mode, 215
breakpoints, setting, 217
BROWSER.ZIP, 743
browsers, 668
    cache files, 708
    integrating into apps, 742
        launching the browser, 744-747
    see also ASP
BuddyControl property, 269
buttons
    colored, 333
    Image property, 129
    Key property, 129
    Style property, 129
    toolbars, 129-131
        coding, 132
        properties, 129-131
buttons argument, 141
Buttons collection, 134
    Key property, 134
ByRef keyword, 230

C

CAB files
    packaging Standard EXE projects, 781
    ActiveX controls, 316
    Standard EXE projects, 787
cache, browser files, 708
CALC.ZIP, 347-349, 355
CALCDOC.DOB, 726
CalcGeneral Property Page, 353
Calculate Button, variable declarations, 34
Calculate Payment button, 33
Calculate procedure, variables, 34
calculation queries, 589
Calculator control, 345
    interface, 346
    methods/events, 348
    operation property, 347
    testing, 349
Call statement, running procedures, 227
CALLBACK.ZIP, 464
callbacks, 463
caller ID, 502-503
    checking for calls, 507-509
    Communications control, 505-507
    INI file, 504
    intervals, 503
    modem messages, 507
    playing sounds, 503
    Sub Main procedure, 505
CALLID.ZIP, 505-507
calling procedures, 229
cancel button, 68
canvas (IDE), 769
Caption property, 28, 110
    ADO Data control, 615
    ampersand (&), 67
    CommandButton control, 30
    Data control, 547
    DataGrid control, 621
    Frame control, 84
    Label control, 63

carriage returns
    Caption property, Label control, 64
    input boxes, 147
Case Else statement, 208
Case statement, 207
CASECONV.ZIP, 185
CausesValidation property, 66
CDate function, 200
cdlCFEffects flag, 153
Cells collection, 497
Change event, 79
Change event procedure, Property Pages, 352
CharAccept property, 319, 328
characters
    replacing in strings, 191-193
    strings, specific strings, 193
ChDir command, 474
ChDrive command, 474
check boxes, 68
CheckBoxes property, 257
CheckCommandLine function, 512
Checked property, 111, 121
child forms, 382
    automatic organization, 392
    Form Resize event, 406
    initializing, 391
    menus, 391
    setting up, 386
    window arrangement, 393
    window lists, 393
    window methods, 405
Child property, 260
child tables, 532
Children property, 260
ChildWindowCount property, 402
Chr function, 193

Circle method, 434
Class Builder, 376
class modules, 362
　methods, 365
　objects, 366
　　binding, 366
　　destroying, 367
　　events, 367
　properties
　　Property Get procedure, 365
　　property procedures, 363
　　public variables, 362
classes, 360-361
　collections, 373
　grouped actions, 374
　properties/methods, 373
　OOP, 360
　see also class modules
Clear method, 71
Click event, menu items, 119
Click event procedure
　Exit button, 32
　VBScript, 678
client/server applications, installing, 788
client/server databases, ODBC, 596
Cls method, 437
cmdGetFile command button, 754
code, 31
　optimizing for compiling, 776
　writing, 34
　see also Code window
code modules, adding to projects, 236
Code window, 32
　comments, 35
　indenting code, 34
　Object box, 33
　pop-up menus, 123
　Procedure box, 33

procedures, creating new, 226
Code windows, 100
　event procedures, 98
Code windows (IDE), 772
coding
　break mode, 215
　control arrays, 294
　　handling events, 294
　　Index property, 295
　Data control, 555
　events, 100
　ImageList control, 249
　panels, 283
　toolbars, 133
Collaboration Data Objects (CDO), 748
COLLECT.ZIP, 373
collections
　Active Messaging, 750
　Bookmarks, 495
　Buttons, 134
　Cells, 497
　classes, 373
　ColumnHeaders, 251
　ComboItems, 268
　compared to arrays, 249
　grouped actions, 374
　ImageList control, 249
　ListImages, 133
　managing, Excel/Word, 497
　Messages, 750
　Printers, 214
　properties/methods, 373
　Tables, 495
　toolbars, 133
　user-defined, 373
　Variables, 495
　Words, 494
Color Blender project, 276
Color dialog boxes, 154
Color list, 443
Color Palette, 443
COLORBTN.ZIP, 334-336
colored buttons, drawing, 333

colors, Ambient object, 343
ColumnHeaders collection, 251
ColumnHeaders property, 621
Columns property, 72
combo boxes, 75-76
　choices not in list, 77
　choices not it list, 76
　drop-down lists, 76
　initial choices, 76
ComboItems collection, 268
command buttons, 67
　Click Event procedure, 32
　default button, 144
　message boxes, 140
　MsgBox function, 143
Command object, 636
CommandButton control, 30, 67, 110
　Caption property, 30
　access keys, 67
CommandDialog control, Flags property, 152
commands
　ChDir, 474
　ChDrive, 474
　FileCopy, 473
　Get, 483
　If statement, 205
　Input, 479
　Kill, 474
　Name, 474
　Open, 478
　Put, 483
　Seek, 484
comments, 35
Common controls, 246-248
　Animation control, 285-287
　ImageList, 248
　　setting up at design time, 248
　　setting up with code, 249
　ListView control, 251-257
　organizing data, 250
　progress bar, 284

Common controls

status bars, 279-283
status/progress reporting, 278
TabStrip control, 261-266
TreeView control, 258
    Child property, 260
    Children property, 260
    nodes, 258
    Parent property, 259
    Root property, 259
user input, 266
    DTPicker control, 274
    ImageCombo control, 266-268
    MonthView control, 271-273
    Slider control, 275-278
    UpDown control, 269-270

CommonDialog control, 148-149
    Color dialog box, 154
    File dialog box, 150
    Filter property, 151
    Font dialog box, 152
    Help dialog box, 157
    Print dialog box, 155
    ShowFont method, 153
    ShowOpen method, 151
    ShowPrinter method, 156
    ShowSave method, 151

Communications control, 505-507

Compare.txt (code listing), comparison operators, 807

comparison operators, Seek method, 581

comparison predicates, filter criteria, 806

comparisons, Case statement, 208

compiling, 776
    ActiveX controls
        distributing, 315-316
        OCX file, 315
        testing, 315
    ActiveX documents, 729

optimizing code, 776
project info, 777
setup program, 778

COMPNAME.ZIP, 455-456

components, saving projects, 21

Components dialog box, 238

ComputeControlSize method, 273

computer programs, languages, 13

ComputerInfo class, API calls, 455

concatenation operator (&), 183

conditions, combining multiple (filter criteria), 809-810

Connection object, ADO, 627

connections, Execute method, 628

ConnectionString property, 616, 627
    connecting without DSN, 629

Const keyword, 172

constants, 171
    API functions, 451
    color, 443
    creating, 172
    intrinsic, 171
    string constants, 141

constituent controls, 307

Contact Manager application, 395-400

Container control, 497
    embedded objects
        designtime, 498
        runtime, 499
    linked objects, 499

container controls
    Frame, 83
    option buttons, 69

containersActiveX documents, 721

context menu, DataGrid control, 623

control arrays, 290
    adding to forms, 291-293
    coding, 294
        handling events, 294
        Index property, 295
    creating, 291
    For...Next loop, 295
    loading/unloading at runtime, 299
    parallel arrays, 297
    removing elements, 296

Control Panel, ODBC Data Source Administrator, 598

control statements, 204
    Case, 207
    Case Else statement, 208
    debugging, 214-216
        stepping through code, 216-217
        tracking variable values, 218
    Do loops, 211
        Do Until, 213
        Do While, 211-213
    Else, 206
    ElseIf, 206
    End Select, 208
    enumeration loops, 214
    error trapping, 219
        controlling flow after errors, 220
        types of errors, 221
    Exit For, 211
    False condition, Not operator, 205
    For Each, 214
    For loops, 210-211
    If, 204
        multiple commands, 205
        multiple If, 206
        single-line, 204

controls | 835

Loop, 211
Next, 210
Select Case, 207-209
controls, 14, 23, 41
   adding at runtime, 300
   adding by double-clicking, 25
   adding to forms, 24
   Address control, 307
      adding properties, 310
      resize code, 309
   aligning, 88
   aligning on form, 770
   Ambient object, 342
      colors, 343
      properties, 343
   bound, 550
      adding to forms, 551
      displaying data, 552-553
   Calculator, 345
      interface, 346
      methods/events, 348
      operation property, 347
      testing, 349
   CommandButton, 30, 67, 110
   common events, 99
   CommonDialog, 148-149
   Communications, 505-507
   compiling
      distributing, 315-316
      OCX file, 315
      testing, 315
   CoolBar, 136
   Crystal Reports, 658-660
   custom icons, 323
   Data, 546
   Data Report, 645
   DataGrid, 619-620
      customizing grid, 626
      customizing layout, 624
      setting up, 621-622
      splitting up, 623-624
   development strategies, 307
   DLLs, 368-371
      enums, 372
      IIS Application, 712
      instancing property, 371
      project, 761
   DLLs with ASP, 711
   drawing multiple on form, 27
   Enabled property, 48
   enhancing, 317
   error handling, 355-356
   events, 32
   Extender object, 344
   form design, 412
   Form Editor toolbar, 88
   Frame, 83-85
   function of, 42
   horizontal spacing, 89
   HScrollBar, 78
   IDE, organizing controls, 766
   IDE Toolbox, 767
   Image, 430
   ImageList, 125
   installing, 316
   Interface Wizard, 323
      properties, 324-327
   Internet transfer
      retrieving HTML, 751-753
      transferring files, 753-755
   intrinsic, 60-62
   labeling, 28
   labels, 27
   Line/Shape, 426-428
   ListBox, 70
   ListView, 437
   loading/unloading at runtime, 299
   making choices, 66
      check boxes, 68
      combo boxes, 75-77
      command button, 67
      list boxes, 70-73
      option buttons, 68
   managing, 238
   Menu, 110
   moving, 27
   multiple, 86
      Form Editor toolbar, 87-89
      Format menu, 89
      frames, 90
      Properties window, 87
   Name property, 25
   naming, 25
   opening Code window, 33
   organizing on forms, 410
   packaging projects
      Internet download, 788
      Internet files, 790
      scripting options, 789
   PictureBox, 431
   placing in frames, 84
   ProgressBar, 422
   properties
      assignment statements, 175
      setting, 25
   Property Pages, 351
   referencing with properties, 49-50
   RemoteData, 607
      setting up, 608
   removing at runtime, 301
   resizing, 27
   RichTextBox, 445
   rptFunction, 652
   scrollbars, 78-81
   selecting, 25
   selecting multiple, 28
   SIGNCODE utility, 317
   special-purpose, 78
   TabStrip, 410
   testing
      Internet Explorer, 313
      project group, 311-313
   text, 62
      appearance, 64
      Label control, 63
      text boxes, 65-66
   text boxes, adding, 26
   TextBox, 23, 65
      properties, 26
   Timer, 81-83
   ToolBar, 125
   unbound, 575
   user-drawn, 333
      button events, 337
      button properties, 335-336
      button property pages, 337

testing button, 338
user interface, 333-335
user input, 23
Visible property, 48
VBScript, 681-682
VScrollBar, 78
WebBrowser, 742
see also ADO; ActiveX Controls; Control arrays; Data control

Controls collection, 90

cookies, ASP Response object, 708

CoolBar control, 136

CopiesToPrinter property, 660

copying files, FileCopy command, 473

core-level capabilities, 597

Count property, recordset fields, 632

counter loops, 210

Create Custom Interface Members dialog box, 325

CREATE INDEX statement, defining indexes with DDLs, 820

Create New Data Source dialog box, 600

Create Report Expert, 655

CreateEmbed method, 499

Createind.txt (code listing), creating indexes, 820

CreateIndex function, 586

CreateLink method, 500

CreateLocalFile function, 519

Createmeth.txt (code listings), retrieving records with Create methods, 822

CreateObject function, late binding, 366

CreateObject method (VBScript), 674

CRW32.EXE, 654

Crystal Reports, 653-654
Create Report Expert, 655
Crystal Reports control, 658-660
field types, 657
selection formula, 657

CSCRIPT.EXE, 683

CurDir$ function, 474

cursor types, 632

CursorLocation property, disconnected recordsets, 637

CursorType property, navigating recordsets, 632

custname.txt (code listing), accessing field values, 800

custom controls, third-party, 413

custom dialog boxes, 157
form templates, 157

custom programs, 12

customizing IDE, 773

D

DAO (Data Access Objects), 566
AbsolutePosition property, 584
Bookmark property, 578
compared to RDO, 603-605
displaying data, 575
Filter property, 585
Find methods, 579
indexes, creating new, 586
modifying multiple records, 589
    loops, 587
Move methods, 577
navigating records, 576
NoMatch property, 579
ODBC Source, 602
opening existing database, 568
PercentPosition property, 584
projects, 567

Recordset objects, 569
    dynasets, 571-573
    forward-only, 574
    snapshots, 573
    tables, 570
Seek method, 581-583
Sort property, 586
tables, setting current index, 581

DAOSAMPL.TXT, 606

Data control, 546-547
adding to forms, 547
ADO, 614
    connecting to data source, 616-617
    displaying data, 618
    navigating recordsets, 618
    record source, 619
    setting up, 615
coding, 555
navigating databases, 554
properties, 548-549
properties compared to RemoteData control, 607
sample application, 553
SQL statements, 822
see also bound controls; DAO; DataGrid control

data entry forms, 411
Data Form Wizard, 558
types, 560

data files, Do Until statement, 213

Data Form Wizard, 557-558
command buttons, 561
form fields, 560
Form screen, 559

data normalization, see normalization

data organization, 529

Data Project, 762

Data Report, 642
controls, 645
graphics, 649
predefined fields, 648
printing/exporting

ExportReport method, 651
PrintReport method, 651
setting up, 644-646
Show method, 647

Data Reports
function fields, 652
see also Crystal Reports

data reports, *see* reports

Data Source (ODBC), 597

Data Source Administrator, 598

Data Source Administrator dialog box, 598-599

data sources
ADO, 613
connecting to Data control, 616-617
reports, 642

data types
returned values, 148
user-defined, 162
variables, 162
Variant, 35

data validation, 231
MaxLength property, 440

Data-Definition-Language statements, *see* DDLs

DatabaseName property, 549

databases
Access, 543
access philosophies, 596
accessing field info, 575
ADO
Command object, 636
connecting without DSN, 629
connection methods, 612
Data control, 615
data sources, 613
DataGrid control, 619-626
opening connections, 627
recordsets, 630-631
ASP, 697
navigating with hyperlinks, 700
queries, 698-701
updating, 701, 704
bound controls, 550
adding to forms, 551
displaying data, 552-553
DAO, 566-568
Recordset objects, 569-574
Data control, 546-547
adding to forms, 547
properties, 548-549
Data Form Wizard, 557-558
designing, 528-529
implementation, 537
indexes, 534
normalization, 530
objectives, 528
queries, 536
tables, 530
disconnected recordsets, 637
reconnecting, 638
uses of, 639
displaying data, 575
navigating with Data control, 554
queries, Execute method, 628
RDO
accessing databases, 605-606
compared to DAO, 603-605
RemoteData control, 607-608
recordsets, cursor type, 632
sample application, form, 553
third-party, 543
transaction processing, 592
transactions, WebClass, 714
Visual Data Manager, 537
adding tables, 539
copying tables, 542
creating database file, 538
field changes, 540
indexes, 541
renaming/deleting tables, 542
table structure, 542
see also recordsets

DATACNTL.ZIP, 556

DataField property, 552
adding fields, 645
function fields, 652
sample application, 553

DataFiles property, 660

DataGrid control, 619-620
customizing grid, 626
customizing layout, 624
properties, 621-622
setting up, 621-622
splits, 623
splitting up, 623-624

DataReport object, 643

DataSource property, 552
sample application, 553

DataSpace object, 639

Date data type, 200

DateAdd function, 200-201

dates
formatting, 200-201
Year 2000, 201
formatting functions, 196
MonthView/DTPicker controls, 271

DBEngine object, 567

DBQUERY.HTM, 698

DDLs (Data-Definition-Language) statements, 818-820
defining indexes, 819-820
CREATE INDEX statement, 820
DROP INDEX statement, 820
defining tables, 818-819
ALTER TABLE statement, 819
DROP TABLE statement, 819

Debug toolbar, 764

debugging
  ActiveX documents, 728
  ActiveX with Internet
    Explorer, 314
  between multiple instances
    of VB, 370
  control statements, 214-216
    stepping through code,
      216-217
    tracking variable values,
      218
decision statements, 204
**Declare statement, API
  functions, 450**
declaring
  ADO objects, 627
  API functions, 450
  functions, 231
  variables, 34
    implicit, 164
    scope, 167
**declaring variables, Dim
  statement, 160**
default buttons, 67, 144
  command buttons, 67
defining
  fields, SELECT SQL
    statements, 796-800
  indexes, with DDLs, 819-820
  tables, with DDLs, 818-819
**DELETE FROM statement,
  manipulative statements,
  795**
Delete method, 592
**DELETE SQL action
  statement, 816-817**
DELETE statement, 590
deleting
  files, Kill command, 474
  records, 592
dependency files, 780
design
  databases, 528-529
    indexes, 534
    normalization, 530
    queries, 536

  tables, 530
  forms, 410-411
    controls, 412
    data entry, 411
    multiple, 413-414
    graphics, 426
    PC differences, 415-416
    user expectations, 417
      list boxes, 417
      menus, 420
      multiple instances of
        application, 420-421
      perceived speed, 422-423
Design mode, 20
designing
  user interface, 41
  programs, 14
    programming process, 15
designtime
  embedded objects, 498
  list box contents, 71
  properties, 770
desktop, *see* **IDE**
destroying objects, 367
Detail section
  adding fields, 645
  adding headers, 646
**Details section (Crystal
  Reports), 655**
Development Environment,
  see **IDE**
device context, 439
DeviceName property, 214
DHTML, 670
**DHTML Application project,
  762**
dialog boxes
  Add Field, 539
  Add File, 239
  Add In Manager, 557
  Add Index, 541
  Add MDI Form, 384
  Add Procedure, 226, 363
  Add Properties, 331
  Add Watch, 218
  Advanced Optimizations,
    777

  Color, 154
  CommonDialog control,
    148-149
  Components, 238
  Create Custom Interface
    Members, 325
  Create New Data Source,
    600
  custom, 157
    form templates, 157
  default button, 144
  File, 150-152
  Font, 152-154
  Help, 157
  InputBox function, 146
    return values, 147
  Insert Database Field, 655
  Insert Object, 498
  message boxes, 140
    modality, 145
    MsgBox function,
      141-146
  Method Builder, 377
  Missing Dependency
    Information, 780
  New Project, 18, 723
  Open, 150
  Print, 155
  Project Properties, 241
  Record Selection Formula,
    657
  References, 238
  Safety Settings, 790
  Save As, 150
  Save File As, 21
  Save Project As, 22
  Select Interface Members,
    324
  Select Picture, 249
  Select the Property Pages,
    330
  Set Mapping, 326
  SQL Server, 602
  Table Structure, 539
Dim keyword, 34
  dynasets, 572
  multiple form instances, 390
  snapshots, 574
Dir$ function, 470-472

event procedures **839**

directories
   ASP, layout of, 692
   setting current, 474
disconnected recordsets, 637
   reconnecting, 638
   uses of, 639
Display Properties dialog box, Screen Saver tab, 512
DisplayCurrentRecord function, 634
displaying
   data
      bound controls, 552-553
      drill-down links, 701
      pop-up menus, 123
      reports, 647
         Crystal Reports, 660
DISTINCT predicates, SELECT SQL statements, 802-803
Distinct.txt (code listing), DISTINCT predicates, 802-803
DISTINCTROW predicates, SELECT SQL statements, 802-803
distributing ActiveX controls, 315
   over Internet, 316
   setup program, 316
division, 178-181
DLLs (Dynamic Link Libraries)
   ActiveX, 368-371
      enums, 372
         instancing property, 371
   ActiveX with ASP, 711
   installing ActiveX projects, 789
   referencing, 370
   Standard EXE projects, 778
   type libraries, 163
Do loops, 211
   Do Until, 213
   Do While, 211-213

Do Until statement, 213
Do While statement, 211-213
DOB extension, 724
dockable toolbars, 760
Document object (Word), 492
documents, *see* ActiveX documents
dot notation, 46
   specifying properties, 63
double-clicking, 417
downlading, ADO, 612
DownPicture property, 68
DRAWAPI.ZIP, 438
drill-down links, displaying database data, 701
Drive object, VolumeID property, 696
drivers, ODBC, 597
DROP INDEX statement, defining indexes with DDLs, 820
DROP TABLE statement, defining tables with DDLs, 819
drop-down lists, 76
DSN (Data Source Name), 598
   ASP, 697
   connecting without, 629
DTPicker control, 274
dwReserved parameter, 451
dynamic Web pages, 694
dynasets, 547
   access mode options, 572
   advantages, 571
   creating with SQL, 821-822
   DAO, 571-573
   Filter condition, 586
   limitations, 571
   subset dynasets, 573

E

e-mail applications, 747
   accessing messages, 750
   logging on, 748
   sending messages, 749
early binding, 366
Edit menu, 109
   hiding, 120
   visibility, 121
Edit method, 591
Edit toolbar, 764
ellipsis (...), 114
Else statement, 206
ElseIf statement, 206
embedding, *see* OLE
Enabled property, 48, 111, 119-121
   DataGrid control, 622
encapsulation, 360
   procedures, 233
End Sub statement, creating new procedures, 226
enumeration loops, 214
enumerations, 372
EnumWindows API function, 463
EOF function, 479
   Loop statement, 212
error handling controls, 355-356
error trapping, 219
   controlling flow after errors, 220
   labeling code lines, 219
   On Error statement, 219
   types of errors, 221
ErrorTrap procedure, 356
Esc key, cancel button, 68
event handlers, subclassing, 465-467
event procedures, 31, 367
   erro handling, 356
   menu items, coding, 119

events, 51, 96
  AmbientChange, 343
  Calculator control, 348
  Change, 79
  class modules, 367
  coding, 100
  control arrays, 294
  GotFocus, 99
  handling
    calling events, 101
    detecting, 97
    procedures, 100-101
    types of, 98-99
  Initialize, 104
  KeyDown, 71
  LostFocus, 99
  menu items, 119
  MouseDown, 100
  MouseUp, pop-up menus, 124
  Resize, 105
  responding to, 31
  Screen Saver application, 510
  sequences, 102
    determining order, 103-106
    multiple events, 102
  specifying procedures, 33
  StateChanged, 752
  Timer, 81
  toolbars, coding, 132
  user-drawn ActiveX controls, 337
  UserDocument object, 730
  Validate, 66
  VBScript, 677-679
  WebItem template, 715
EVENTS.FRM, 97
Excel objects, 496-497
  cell/range values, 497
executable files, packaging, 778
Execute method, 628
Execute.txt (code listing), executing action queries, 821

Exit button, Click event procedure, 32
Exit For statement, 211
Exit Sub statement, 230
explicit declaration, variables, 163
exponentiation operator (^), 181
exporting reports, ExportReport method, 651
ExportReport method, 651
expressions, operator precedence, 182
Extender object, 344
extender properties, 344
extensions, 772
  ASP, 688
  compiling programs, 776
  DOB, 724
  file type filter, 152
  FRM, 43
  FRX, 43
  HTM, 688
  VBP, 22

F

False condition, Not operator, 205
Favorites list (Internet Explorer), 744
fields
  adding to reports, Crystal Reports, 657
  defining, SELECT SQL statements, 796-800
  displaying values, 631
Fields collection
  accessing field info, 575
  Count property, 632
File dialog boxes, 152
file formats, graphics, 428
file functions, 470
  Dir$, 470-472
  file manipulation, 473-474

finding files, 475-476
  Shell, 475
File menu, 109
  visibility, 121
file system, VBScript, 675
file types, 772
  filtering for display, 151
FileCopy command, 473
FileName property, 151
filenames, DOB extension, 724
files
  locating, 475
  Open dialog box, 404
  opening/saving, 151
FileSystemObject object (VBScript), 675, 695
filter criteria, SELECT SQL statements, 806-810
  BETWEEN predicate, 809
  combining multiple conditions, 809-810
  comparison predicate, 806
  IN predicate, 809
  LIKE predicate, 807-809
Filter property, 151, 585
Find methods, 579
FindFirst method, 398, 580
finding files, 470
FINDTEST.TXT, 580
FindWindow function, 458
fixed-length strings, variables, 165
flags, cdlCFEffects, 153
Flags property, 152
  colors, 155
  Font dialog box, 153
FlatScrollBars property, 257
floating-point division, 178
flow control, *see* control statements
focus, shelled programs, 475

Font dialog boxes, 154
Font object, 442
Font property, 55
  Label control, 153
fonts, RichTextBox control, 445
For Each loop, 214
For loops, 210-211
For...Next loop, 210
  control arrays, 295
ForeColor property, 434
Form Editor toolbar, 87-89, 764
form templates, custom dialog boxes, 157
form-level variables, 168
Form_Load event procedure, disconnected recordsets, 637
Form_Resize event, child forms, 406
Format function, 197-200
Format menu, 89
FormatCurrency function, 196
FormatDateTime function, 196
formatting output, 195
  date values, 200-201
    Year 2000, 201
  Format function, numbers, 197-200
  functions, 195
    date format, 196
    rounding numbers, 197
  numeric formats, 198
forms, 20, 40
  About box, with Web site link, 745
  accessing, 236
  ActiveForm keyword, 391
  adding color, 443
  adding controls, 24
  adding pictures, 429

adding standard toolbar, 127
adding toolbars, 125
bound controls, 551
child
  automatic organization, 392
  initializing, 391
  window lists, 393
command buttons, Data Form Wizard, 561
control arrays, 291-293
controls, moving/resizing, 27
converting to ActiveX documents, 734
Data controls, 547
data fields, 561
Data Form Wizard, 557-558
databases, sample application, 553
designing, 410-411
  controls, 412
  data entry, 411
  multiple forms, 413-414
displaying, 55-57
displaying in ActiveX documents, 738
drawing multiple controls, 27
drawing user interface, 769
events, 104
MDI
  child, 384
  child forms, 384
  framework, 402-407
  multiple instances, 388-390
  parent forms, 383
message boxes, 140
modal/modeless, 56
multiple, adding new forms, 235
naming, 30
parts of, 40
PopUpMenu method, 124
procedures, 234
properties
  changing, 30
  key properties, 53

referencing with properties, 49-50
resizing user events, 416
search, 398
startup, 241
subclassing, 464
Width property, 30
forms (HTML), VBScript, 679-681
forward-only recordsets, 574
Frame control, 83-85
frames, muliple controls, 90
FreeFile function, 479
FRM extension, 43
FromPage property, 156
FrontPage, VBScript, 672
FRX extension, 43
FTP (File Transfer Protocol), transferring files, 753
FullRowSelect property, 256
Function control, 652
  Data Reports, 652
function fields, 652
Function keyword, 231
functional specification, 529
functions, 231-232
  aggregate, SELECT SQL statements, 811-813
  Asc, 194
  callbacks, 463
  CDate, 200
  CheckCommandLine, 512
  Chr, 193
  comp to statements, 141
  CreateIndex, 586
  CreateLocalFile, 519
  CreateObject, late binding, 366
  CurDir$, 474
  database sample application, 513
  DateAdd, 200-201
  DisplayCurrentRecord, 634

EnumWindows API, 463
EOF, 479
FindWindow, 458
Format, 197-200
FormatCurrency, 196
FormatDateTime, 196
formatting, 195
    parameters, 196
FreeFile, 479
Input, 480
InputBox, 146
    return values, 147
InsrRev, 188
InStr, 187
LCase, 185
Left, 189
Len, 147, 185
Mid, 190
MsgBox, 141-142, 146
    return value, 143-145
Open, 150
ProcessMessage, 750
QBColor, 444
Replace, 193
RGB, 444
RGB( ), 278
Right, 189
Right$, 476
Round, 197
Save As, 150
scope, 232
Shell, 461, 745
ShowWindow, 460
sndPlaySound, 457
Str, 194
StrConv, 186
string manipulation, 183
SUM, 589
SystemParametersInfo, 457
Timer, 82
TransparentPaint, 519
Trim, 191
UCase, 185
Val, 148, 194
Val( ), 36
WeekDayName, 197
see also file functions

FunctionType property, 652

G

GDIs, 519
GENDATA.FRM, 302
General Property Page, 331
Get command
    Internet Transfer control, 751
    random access files, 483
GetChunk method, 752
Getcust.txt (code listing), retrieving information from multiple databases, 801
GetDiskFreeSpace function, 453
Global keyword, 167
GotFocus event, 99
GotFocus event procedure
    control arrays, 297
    menu visibility, 392
graphics, 426
    adding to reports, 649
    controls
        Image, 430
        Line/Shape, 426-428
        loading pictures on form, 429-430
        Picture property, 428
        PictureBox, 431
        pictures/images, 428
        formats compatible, 428
        ImageList control, 248
    methods, 432
        Line, 433
        PaintPicture, 436-437
        Print, 435
        PSet, 435
grid (IDE form), 770
GridLines property, 256
Group Footer sections, Function controls, 652
Group.txt (code listing), GROUP BY clause, 813
GUID, 317
GUIs, *see* user interfaces

H

handling events
    calling events, 101
    detecting, 97
    procedures, 100-101
    types of, 98
        system initiated, 99
        user-initiated, 98
Having.txt (code listing), HAVING clause, 814
headers, adding to reports, 646
Help button, message boxes, 144
Help dialog box, 157
Help menu, 109
HelpCommand property, 157
HelpContextID property, 111
HelpFile property, 157
HIDDEN form field, 702
Hide method, 56
hierarchies
    nodes, 258
    TreeView control, 258
Horizontal Spacing option, 89
hosts (VBScript), 671
hot keys, Menu controls, 110
HotTracking property, 257
HoverSelection property, 257
HScrollBar control, 78
HTML files, 668
    ActiveX documents, 720
    ASP, query page, 698
    exporting reports to, 651
    forms
        Post method, 702
        user input quotes, 704

Internet Transfer control, 751-753
  retrieving automatically, 753
  tags, 669-670
  vs ASP, 688
  WebItem template, 715-717
HTTP (Hypertext Transfer Protocol), 668, 720
  Internet Transfer control, 751
Hyperlink object, 733
hyperlinks, 667
  navigating databases, 700
HyperTerminal, Caller ID application, 502

I

icons
  assigning to forms, 778
  message boxes, 142
icResponseCompleted state, 752
IDE (Integrated Development Environment), 760
  canvas, 769
  Code windows, 772
  controls, adding by double clicking, 25
  customizing, 773
  debugging control statements, 215
  Design mode, 20
  drawing on forms, 769
  Environment options, auto saving projects, 21
  Label control, 28
  menu bar, 763
  organizing controls, 766
  Project Explorer, 20
  Project window, 771
  Properties window, 25, 770
  Run mode, 20
  saving projects, 21
  Start command, 37
  start up, 761

TextBox control, 23
toolbars, 764-766
Toolbox, 767
  adding CommanDialog control, 149
  adding ToolBar control, 125
  intrinsic controls, 60
ToolTips, 764
twips, 766
work area, 762
If statement, 204
  ASP login page, 705
  multiple commands, 205
  multiple If, 206
  single-line, 204
IIS (Internet Information Server)
  ASP, 688
    Session object, 705
  directory permissions, 692
  IIS Application, 712-713
    custom WebItem, 717
    HTML template WebItem, 715-717
    WebClass instancing, 714
  virtual directories, 690
Image control, 430
  Stretch property, 430
Image property, 129
ImageCombo control, 266-268
ImageList control, 125, 248
  adding images, 127
  setting up at designtime, 248
  setting up with code, 249
images, 428
  toolbars, 126
  transparent, 519, 523
implicit declaration, variables, 164
implied loops, multiple records, 588
IN predicates, filter criteria, 809

inactivated objects, 498
include files (ASP), 696
Indentation property, 268
index, 250
Index parameter, 72
Index property, 110, 581
  control arrays, 295
indexes
  creating new, 586
  database design, 534
  defining, with DDLs, 819-820
  multiple-key, 535
  optimizing SQL performance, 826
  setting, 581
  single-key, 535
  Visual Data Manager, 541-542
INETDEMO.ZIP, 746, 752-754
INF files, installing ActiveX projects, 790
information hiding, 233
inheritance, 360
INI files, 484, 487
  caller ID application, 504
INIEXAMPLE.ZIP, 486
INIFUNC.BAS, 485
Initialize event, 104
InitProperties event, extender properties, 345
InitProperties() event procedure, matching control colors, 343
Input command, 479
input boxes, 146
  word-wrapping, 147
Input function, 480
Input keyword, 479
InputBox function, 146
  return values, 147

InputLen property, caller ID application, 507
Insert Database Field dialog box, 655
INSERT INTO statement, manipulative statements, 795
Insert Object dialog box, 498
INSERT SQL action statement, 817
Insert.txt (code listing), INSERT INTO SQL action statement, 817
installation files, Standard EXE projects, 785
installing
    ActiveX controls, 316
    Crystal Reports, 653
instances
    classes, 360
    MDI forms, 390
Instancing property, 371
instancing property, ActiveX, 371
InStr function, 187
INSTREX.ZIP, 188-190
InstrRev function, 188
integer division, 178
integer division (), 179
Interface Wizard, 323
    properties, 324-327
    summary page, 327
interfaces
    ActiveX documents, 724
    Calculator control, 346
    Loan Calculator program, 37
Internet
    ActiveX documents, 720
    disconnected recordsets, 637

e-mail apps, 747
    accessing messages, 750
    logging on, 748
    sending messages, 749
    VBScript, 666
Internet Explorer
    ActiveX controls, testing, 313
    ActiveX documents, 721
    Favorites list, 744
    security settings, 675
    VBScript
        ActiveX controls, 681-682
        events/procedures, 677-679
        forms, 679-681
        VBScript errors, 672
Internet Information Server, see IIS
Internet servers, ASP, 689
Internet Service Manager, 690
Internet shortcuts, 744
    launching from other apps, 745
Internet Transfer control
    retrieving HTML, 751-753
    transferring files, 753-755
Interval property, 82
Into.txt (code listing), INTO clause, 815
intrinsic conrols, 60
intrinsic constants, 141, 171
    vbCrLf, 141
intrinsic constants (VBScript), 671
intrinsic controls, 60-62
inventory database, transaction processing, 592
ItemData property, 74
iteration, For/Next loops, 210

J - K

Jet engine, 537
    DAO, 567
    Data control, properties, 548
    DatabaseName property, 548
    selecting databases, 548
JOIN clause, table relationships, SELECT SQL statements, 803
Join.txt (code listing), JOIN clause, 804-805
key events, 100
Key property, 129, 134
    collections, 250
keyboard commands
    command button events, 67
    menu access keys, 116
    shortcuts, 412
KeyDown event, 71
KeyPress event
    code listing, 321
    limited character text box, 321
keywords
    ActiveForm, 391
    ByRef, 230
    Const, 172
    Function, 231
    Input, 479
    Me, 390
    New, 366, 390
    Private, procedures, 233
    Public, procedures, 232
    Static, 169, 233
    WithEvents, 368
Kill command, 474

L

Label control, 28
    Alignment property, 65
    compared to TextBox, 28
    text, 63
        appearance, 64
        AutoSize property, 63

listings

WordWrap property, 63
text appearance, 28
labeling
code lines (error trapping), 219
controls, 28
labels, updating testing forms, 48
languages, 13
Large Icon view, 255
LargeChange property, 80, 275
late binding, 366
launching programs
Shell function, 475
startup time, 422
LCase function, 185
Left function, 189
Left property, 44
Len function, 147, 185
LIKE predicates, filter criteria, 807-809
Like.txt (code listing), LIKE predicates, 808-809
limited character text box, KeyPress event, 321
Limited Character TextBox control, Interface Wizard, 324
limited character textbox control, 318
LIMITED.ZIP, 319-320
Line control, 426
line feeds
Caption property, Label control, 64
input boxes, 147
Line method, 433
linked objects, OLE Container control, 499
list boxes, 70-72
appearance, 72
controlling choices, 70
list array, 72

multiple selections, 73
multiple-selection, 73
sorting items, 72
user expectations, 417
ListBox control, 70
LISTBOX.ZIP, 417
LISTFILL.ZIP, 478
ListImages collection, 133, 249
ListIndex property, 73
listings
ADONAV.ZIP, 633
ADOTEST.ZIP, 631, 636
Alias.txt, table aliases, 802
Altertab.txt (code listing), ALTER TABLE statement, 819
Andor.txt, combining multiple WHERE conditions, 810
APIDEMO.ZIP, 457-459
APIWRAP.ZIP, 454
ASPDEMO.ZIP, 689-709
Between.txt, BETWEEN predicate, 809
CALC.ZIP, 347-349, 355
CALCDOC.DOB, 726
CALLBACK.ZIP, 464
CALLID.ZIP, 505-507
CASECONV.ZIP, 185
Code to Calculate the Monthly Payment, 36
COLLECT.ZIP, 373
COLORBTN.ZIP, 334-336
Compare.txt, comparison operators, 807
COMPNAME.ZIP, 455-456
Createind.txt, creating indexes, 820
Createmeth.txt, retrieving records with Create methods, 822
Custname.txt, accessing field values, 800
DAOSAMPL.TXT, 606
DATACNTL.ZIP, 556
Distinct.txt (code listing),

DISTINCT predicates, 802-803
DRAWAPI.ZIP, 438
EVENTS.FRM, 97
Execute.txt, executing action queries, 821
FINDTEST.TXT, 580
For Each to handle collections, 375
GENDATA.FRM, 302
Getcust.txt, retrieving information from multiple databases, 801
Group.txt, GROUP BY clause, 813
Having.txt, HAVING clause, 814
INETDEMO.ZIP, 746, 752-754
INIEXAMPLE.ZIP, 486
INIFUNC.BAS, 485
Insert.txt, INSERT INTO SQL action statement, 817
INSTREX.ZIP, 188-190
Into.txt (code listing), INTO clause, 815
Join.txt, JOIN clause, 804-805
Like.txt, LIKE predicates, 808-809
LIMITED.ZIP, 319-320
LISTBOX.ZIP, 417
LISTFILL.ZIP, 478
LISTVIEW.ZIP, 253-255
LOGPRINT.ZIP, 480
MAILING.ZIP, 184
MAINMDI.TXT, 397
MATHEX.ZIP, 180
MDICHILD.TXT, 405
MDICHILD2.TXT, 406
MDIDEMO2.FRM, 389
MDIPARENT.TXT, 402
MDIPARENT2.TXT, 403
MDIPARENT3.TXT, 404
MDIPROCS.TXT, 399
MDIPROCS2.TXT, 399
OPTIONARRAY.TXT, 297
PREVINST.ZIP, 421
RDOSAMPL.TXT, 606
REPLACE.ZIP, 192

RPTDEMO, 647
RPTDEMO.ZIP, 643
Sales.txt, selecting fields from multiple tables, 798
SCRLDEMO.ZIP, 80
SEARCH.TXT, 398
SEEKTEST.TXT, 581
SELCASE.ZIP, 209
SHELLWAIT.ZIP, 462
SIMPLEVBS.ZIP, 677
SLIDERS.ZIP, 277-278
Sort.txt (code listing), specifying sort order of output dynaset, 811
SQLXPORT.ZIP, 514
STATUS.ZIP, 283-284
SUBCLASS.ZIP, 465-466
Summary.txt, aggregate functions, 813
TBRDEMO.TXT, 132
TIMEREX.ZIP, 82
Totprice.txt, creating calculated fields, 799
TRANSACT.TXT, 593
TRANSPAR.ZIP, 520, 523
TREEVIEW.ZIP, 263-265
Update.txt, UPDATE SQL action statement, 818
VBSFILES.HTM, 676
VBSFORM.ZIP, 679
Where.txt, WHERE clause, 806
WORDDEMO.TXT, 492

ListItems collection, Add method, 254

ListView control, 251-257, 437
   new features, 256
   properties, 252

LISTVIEW.ZIP, 253-255

Load event, TabStrip control, 264

Load event procedure, MDI child forms, 389

Load statement, 56, 300

LoadPicture method, 429

Loan Calculator program, 18
   adding controls, 24
   as an ActiveX document, 722
   Calculate Payment button, 33
   CommandButton controls, Name/Caption properties, 30
   Label controls, Name/Caption properties, 29
   Name/Caption properties, 30
   procedure code, 35
   saving projects, 22
   user interface, 18

local variables, 168

Locked property, 439

locking records, 634

LockType property, 634

log files, sequential text files, 480

logging on, e-mail, 748

logical order, 534

login page, ASP Session object, 705

Logon method, 748

LogPrint procedure, 228

LOGPRINT.ZIP, 480

lookup tables, 533

looping statements
   Do, 211
      Do Until, 213
      Do While, 211-213
   debugging, 214-216
      stepping through code, 216-217
      tracking variable values, 218
   enumeration, 214
   For, 210-211
   For Each, 214
   modifying multiple records, 587

LostFocus event procedure, 99
   coding, 294
   menu invisibility, 392

low-level languages, 13

M

machine language, 13

MAILING.ZIP, 184

MAINMDI.TXT, 397

Make Same Size button, 88

manipulative statements, SQL, 795

mapping, 326
   Calculator control properties, 346

MarshallOptions property, 639

math operations, 176
   addition/subtraction, 177
   exponentiation, 181
   multiplication/division, 178-181
   precedence, 181-182

MATHEX.ZIP, 180

MaxLength property, 65, 440

MDI, 382
   child forms, 384
      automatic organization, 392
      window lists, 393
   Contact Manager application, 395-400
   framework
      child template, 405-407
      parent template, 402-405
   menus, 391
   multiple instances, 388
      creating with object variables, 390
   optimizing, 400
   parent forms, 383
   setting up child forms, 386

setting up parent forms, 384-385
VB IDE, 760
window list, 395
MDI (Multiple Document Interface) applications, form positioning, 45
MDIChild property, 386
MDICHILD.TXT, 405
MDICHILD2.TXT, 406
MDIDEMO2.FRM, 389
MDIPARENT.TXT, 402
MDIPARENT2.TXT, 403
MDIPARENT3.TXT, 404
MDIPROCS.TXT, 399
MDIPROCS2.TXT, 399
Me keyword, MDI child forms, 390
measurements, twips, 47
memory, Nothing property, 367
menu bar (IDE), 763
menu bars, 108-110
Menu control property, 120
Menu controls, 110
Menu Editor, 110, 298, 391
  modifying menu structure, 115
  pop-up menus, 123
menu item arrays, 298
menus
  access keys, 116
  blocking access, 120
  Checked property, 121
  coding items, 119
  design, user expectations, 420
  Enabled property, 119-121
  grayed out, 120
  grouping, 114
  MDI, 391
  menu bars, 109
  modifying structure, 115

multiple-level, 112
NegotiatePosition property, 122
pop-up, 122
  activating, 124
separator bars, 114
shortcut keys, 117-118
Visible property, 119-121
WindowList property, 122
see also toolbars
message boxes, 140
  default buttons, 144
  Help button, 144
  icons, 142
  modality, 145
  MsgBox function, 141-142, 146
    return value, 143-145
Messages collection, 750
Method Builder dialog box, 377
methods, 50
  Add
    Buttons collection, 134
    ListImages collection, 249
  AddItem, 70
  AddNew, 590
  Arrange, 392
  AsyncRead, 731
  Auto List Members, 50
  Calculator control, 348
  Circle, 434
  class modules, 365
  Clear, 71
  Cls, 437
  collections, 373
  comp to properties, 51
  ComputeControlSize, 273
  CreateEmbed, 499
  CreateLink, 500
  CreateObject (VBScript), 674
  Delete, 592
  Edit, 591
  Execute, 628
  ExportReport, 651
  Find, 579
  FindFirst, 398, 580

GetChunk, 752
graphics, 432
Hide, 56
Hyperlink object, 733
Line, 433
LoadPicture, 429
Logon, 748
Move, 577
NavagateTo, 737
Navigate, Hyperlink object, 733
Navigate (VBScript), 678
Open, 628
OpenDatabase, 568
PaintPicture, 436-437
Point, 437
PopUpMenu, 124
Print, 435
PrintReport, 651
PropertyChanged, 321
PSet, 435
RDO, 604
Redirect, 708
RegisterDatabase, 602
RemoveItem, 71
SaveAs, 494
Seek, 581-583
Show, 56
ShowFont, 153
ShowOpen, 151
ShowPrinter, 156
ShowSave, 151
transaction processing, 593
Update, 591
UpdateBatch, 638
UserDocument object, 731-733
ValidateEntries, 348
VBScript, 684
WriteTemplate, 717
see also functions
microprocessor, machine code, 13
Microsoft Access, creating SQL statements, 825
Mid function, 190
Mid statement, 191
Migration Wizard, 733-737

Missing Dependency Information dialog box, 780
MixedState property, 135
mnuFileItems_Click event, child forms, 407
modal forms, 56
modality
  forms, 56
  message boxes, 145
modeling applications, 529
modems, Caller ID application, 502
  messages, 507
module files, procedures, 234
module-level variables, 168
modules, 772
  accessing, 236
  naming, 236
modulus division, 178
monitor resolutions, 415
MonthCols property, 272
MonthRows property, 272
MonthView control, 271-273
mouse clicks, 417
Mouse events, user-drawn control buttons, 337
MouseDown event, 100
MouseMove event, Screen Saver application, 511
MouseUp event, pop-up menus, 124
Move method, arguments, 52
Move methods, 577
MS Comm control, 505
MsgBox function, 141-142, 146
  command buttons, 143
  return value, 143-145
MSVBVM60.DLL, 315
MultiLine property, 65
multiple conditions, combining, filter criteria, 809-810
multiple controls, 86
multiple-key indexes, 535
multiple-tier drivers, 597
multiplication, 178-181
MultiSelect property, 73, 273

N

Name command, 474
Name property, 25, 110
  Data control, 547
  forms, 30
  Properties window, 26
  report objects, 646
naming
  class modules, 362
  controls, 25
  forms, 30
  modules, 236
  objects, 49
  table
    alias (SELECT SQL statements), 801-802
    specifying (SELECT SQL statements), 801
  variables, 34, 160
native code, 776
natural order, 534
Navigate method (VBScript), 678
  Hyperlink object, 733
  WebBrowser control, 742
NavigateTo method (VBScript), 737
navigating recordsets, 618, 632-634
NegotiatePosition property, 111, 122
network-level security, 707
New keyword, 366, 390
New Project dialog box, 18, 723
  VB IDE, 761
NewIndex property, 74
Next statement, 210
nodes, 258
NoMatch property, 579
normalization, database design, 530
Not keyword, Checked menu property, 122
Not operator, 205
Notepad, sequential files, 477
null characters, API calls, 460
numbers
  formatting, 197-200
  in strings, 194
numeric formats, defining, 198
numerical data, math operations, 176

O

Object box, 33, 98
Object Browser
  constant values, 171
  Word Object Library, 491
OBJECT tag
  ASP Server object, 710
  installing ActiveX controls, 317
OBJECT tag (HTML), 681-682
objects, 14
  activated, 498
  Application (ASP), 710
  ASP, 704
  class modules, 366
    binding, 366
    destroying, 367
    events, 367
  collections, 134

toolbars, 133
Connection, ADO, 627
DataReport, 643
DataSpace, 639
Excel, 496-497
   cell/range values, 497
FileSystemObject
   (VBScript), 675
Font, 442
Hyperlink, 733
methods, 50
multiple form instances, 390
naming, 49
   prefixes, 49
OLE Container control, 498
properties, specifying, 63
Property Pages, 350
PropertyBag, 320, 730
Recordset, 630
Request (ASP), 709
Response (ASP), 708
Selection, 493
Server (ASP), 710
Session (ASP), 705-707
   Response.Write
      statement, 707
setting properties, 25
UserDocument, 729
VBScript, 674, 684
   file access, 675
see also DAO

OCX files, installing, 316

ODBC, 596
Data Source, 597
data sources
   creating with DAOs, 602
   RemoteData control, 607
drivers, 597-603
   ADO data sources, 613
servers, 573

ODBC Data Source Administrator, 598

ODBC Manager, ODBC Source, 600

OLE (Object Linking and Embedding)
Container control, 497
   embedded objects at
      designtime, 498
   embedded objects at
      runtime, 499
   linked objects, 499
Excel objects, 496-497
   cell/range values, 497
Word objects, 490-491
   Application/Document, 492
   saving/opening/printing, 494
   text, 494
   Word.Basic, 496

OLE automation server, 761

OLE DB, 612

OLE Messaging, 747

OLEMSG32.DLL, 747

On Error statement, 219
Resume statement, 220

OOP (object oriented programming)
classes, 360
wrapper classes, 455

Open command, 478

Open dialog box, 404

Open function, 150

Open method, 628

OpenDatabase method, 568

opening
   ActiveX documents, 727
   connections (ADO
      Connection object), 627
   databases, DAO, 568
   random access files, 483
   tables, 570
   Word documents, 494

opening files, 151

OpenRecordset method
dynasets, 572
snapshots, 574

operating systems, differences, 415

Operation property, Calculator control, 347

operator precedence, 181-182

operators
addition (+), 177
division (/), 178
exponentiation (^), 181
mod, 179
multiplication (x), 178
subtraction (-), 177

option buttons, 68-69

Option Explicit statement, variables, 169

OPTIONARRAY.TXT, 297

options declarations, 795

Outlook, Active Messaging, 748

P

P-code, 776

Package and Deployment Wizard, Standard EXE project, 778-785
CAB files, 787
installation files, 785
SETUP.LST file, 785

package folder, 780

packaged programs, 12

packaging
   ActiveX components
      Internet download, 788
      Internet files, 790
      scripting options, 789
   Standard EXE projects, 778-785
      CAB files, 787
      installation files, 785
      SETUP.LST file, 785

Packaging and Deployment Wizard, 729

PaintPicture method, 436-437

panels, 280
coding, 283
status bars, 281
styles, 281

Panels collection, 281
parallel arrays, 297
parameters
  API functions, 451
  declarations, SQL
    statements, 795
  Index, 72
  passing to procedures, 230
  SELECT SQL statements,
    815-816
parent forms, 382
  setting up, 384-385
Parent property, 259
parent relationship, 260
parent tables, 532
parsing strings, 187
pasing by value, 230
passing by reference, 230
PasswordChar property,
  440
Path property, locating files,
  476
paths, Dir$ function, 470
PC differences, 415-417
PercentPosition property,
  584
performance
  MDI apps, 401
  SQL, 825-826
    compiling queries, 826
    indexes, 826
    simplifying queries, 826
  table organization, 534
permissions, IIS virtual
  directories, 692
Personal Web Manager,
  691
physical directory, 690
physical order, 534
Picture property, 68, 428
PictureAlignment property,
  257
PictureBox control, 431

pictures, 428
pipe symbol, 152
Play method, Animation
  control, 287
Point method, 437
Pointer tool (IDE), 767
polymorphism, 361
pop-up menus, 122-123
  activating, 124
  Code window, 123
PopUpMenu method, 124
positioning objects, 44
POST method, ASP HTML
  forms, 702
PostMessage API, 461
precedence (operator),
  181-182
predicates, SELECT SQL
  statements, 802-803
prefixes, 49
  variable names, 34, 161
PREVINST.ZIP, 421
PrevInstance property, 421
Print dialog boxes, 155
Print method, 435
PrinterDefault property,
  156
Printers collection, 214
printing
  reports, 651
    ExportReport method,
      651
    PrintReport method, 651
  Word documents, 494
PrintReport method, 651
Private declarations, API
  Viewer, 453
Private keyword, 168
private procedures, 232
Private Sub, 32
private varibles, 168
Procedure box, 33, 98

procedure code, 35
procedures, 224-225
  ErrorTrap, 356
  LogPrint, 228
  module files, 234
  passing data to, 228
  Property Get, 310
  public, 365
  reusing, 233-234
  running, 227
  scope, 232
  Sub Main, 241
  TransferTable, 519
  types of, 227
  VBScript, 677-679
  see also methods; functions
ProcessMessage function,
  750
productivity tools, 12
program commands, DAO,
  566
programming languages, 13
programming systems, 12
programs
  customized, 12
  definition of, 12
  designing, 14-15
  exiting event, 32
  running, 36
  user interfaces, 18
  see also applications
progress bar, 284
progress information, 279
ProgressBar control, 284,
  422
Project Explorer, 20
  saving projects, 22
project groups, 369
  multiple instances of VB,
    370
  test projects, 311
Project Properties dialog
  box, 241
  Compile tab, 777
Project window (IDE), 771

properties | 851

projects, 18
ActiveX, 368
ActiveX controls, adding with Property Pages Wizard, 332
ActiveX document, 723
adding code modules, 236
adding reports, 643
automatically saving, 21
Color Blender, 276
compiling info, 777
DAO, 567
forms, accessing, 236
IIS Application, 711
managing
controls, 238
program references, 238
MDI forms, 388
multiple, 368
multiple forms, 235
naming, 777
program design, 15
resaving, 31
samples, baseball statistics, 251
saving, 20-23
templates, 240
testing, 47
types, 761

prompt parameter, 147

proper case, 294

properties, 43
AbsolutePosition, 584
ActiveX documents, 724
adding to classes, 362
Address control, 310
AddressText, 310
ADO Data control, 615
Align, StatusBar control, 280
Alignment, Label control, 65
AllowArrows, DataGrid control, 622
AllowColumnReorder, 256
AllowCustomize, 135
Ambient object, 343
App.Path, 738
AutoShowChildren, 385
AutoSize, 63, 431
StatusBar control, 282

BackColor, 335
Bookmark, 578
BorderStyle, labels, 64
Caption, 28
Label control, 63
CausesValidation, 66
changing at runtime, 45
form resize program, 46-48
CharAccept, 319, 328
CheckBoxes, 257
Checked, 121
Child, 260
Children, 260
ChildWindowCount, 402
class modules
Property Get procedure, 365
property procedures, 363
public variables, 362
collections, 373
Columns, 72
CommonDialog control, 149
Communications control, 505
comp to methods, 51
ConnectionString, 616, 627
controlling object position, 44
controlling object size, 44
controlling user interaction, 48
CopiesToPrinter, 660
CursorType, 632
Data controls, 548-549
DatabaseName, 549
DataField, 552
DataFiles, 660
DataGrid control, 621
DataSource, 552
designtime, 770
DeviceName, 214
dot notation, 46
DownPicture, 68
drawing, 433
Enabled, 48, 119-121
extender, 344
FileName, 151
FIleter, 585
Filter, 151

Flags, 152
Font dialog box, 153
FlatScrollBars, 257
Font, 55
Label control, 153
font attributes, 154
Font object, 442
ForeColor, 434
forms
changing, 30
key properties, 53
FromPage, 156
FullRowSelect, 256
FunctionType, 652
GridLines, 256
HelpCommand, 157
HelpFile, 157
HotTracking, 257
HoverSelection, 257
Image, 129
Indentation, 268
Index, 581
Instancing, 371
Interface Wizard, 324-327
Interval, 82
ItemData, 74
Key, 129, 134
collections, 250
LargeChange, 80, 275
Left, 44
ListIndex, 73
ListView control, 252
Locked, 439
LockType, 634
loop processing (records), 588
MarshallOptions, 639
MaxLength, 65, 440
MDIChild, 386
Menu controls, 110
message boxes
MixedState, 135
MonthCols, 272
MonthRows, 272
MonthView control, 271
MultiLine, 65
MultiSelect, 73, 273
Name, 25
NegotiatePosition, 122
NewIndex, 74

properties

NoMatch, 579
Operation, Calculator control, 347
Parent, 259
PasswordChar, 440
PercentPosition, 584
Picture, 68, 428
PictureAlignment, 257
PrevInstance, 421
PrinterDefault, 156
Property Pages Wizard, 331
Public variables, 167
Range, 497
RecordSource, 549
referencing forms/controls, 49-50
RemoteData control compared to Data control, 607
ReportFileName, 658
Root, 259
Screen Saver application, 510
ScrollBars, 385
SelectedItem, 268
SelectionFormula, 659
SelImage, 267
SelLength, 441
setting, 25
Slider control, 275
SmallChange, 79, 275
Sort, 586
Sorted, 72
specifying, 63
splits, 624
StateManagement, 714
StillConnecting, 606
Stretch, 430
Style, 129
 list boxes, 72
SubItems, 251
SyncBuddy, 270
TabAction, 622
Text, 26, 71
TextBackGround, 257
TimeOut, 707
ToolBar control, 128
toolbars, 128
ToolboxBitmap, 323
ToolTipText property, 134

Top, 45
ToPage, 156
user-drawn ActiveX controls, 335-337
user-drawn controls, values, 338
UserDocument object, 730
View, 252
Visible, 48, 119-121
VolumeID, 696
WebBrowser control, download status, 743
Width, forms, 30
WindowList, 122
WordWrap, 63
WrapText, 626

Properties dialog box, Debugging tab, 726

Properties window (IDE), 87, 770
setting properties, 25

Property Get procedure, 310, 363
class modules, 365

Property Let procedure, 363
TextBox control, 320

Property Pages, 350
ApplyChanges event procedure, 353
Change event procedure, 352
connecting to control, 353
controls, 351
multiple control selections, 355
objects, 350
SelectionChanged event procedure, 352

Property Pages dialog box, Crystal Reports, 659

Property Pages Wizard, 330-332
adding properties, 331

property procedures
class modules, 363
types of, 363

Property Set procedure, 365
PropertyBag object, 320, 730
PropertyChanged method, 321
PSet method, 435
Public declarations, API Viewer, 453
Public keyword, procedures, 232
public members, mapping, 326
public procedures, 232, 365
public variables, 167
 class modules, 362
Put command, random access files, 483

Q

QBColor function, 444
queries
 action, 589
  SQL, 820-821
 ADO Data control, 619
 ASP, 698-701
 calculation, 589
 compiling, optimizing SQL performance, 826
 database design, 536
 Execute method, 628
 simplifying, optimizing SQL performance, 826
QueryDefs
 creating with SQL, 821
 Data control properties, 549
 SQL statements, 796
QueryString collection, ASP, displaying data, 701
quotation mark ('), comments, 35
 user input (HTML forms), 704

R

RAD (Rapid Application Development) tools, 14
radio buttons, 68
random access files
  Get command, 483
  opening, 483
  Put command, 483
  record type, 482
  Seek command, 484
Random mode, 482
Range property, 497
RDO (Remote Data Objects)
  accessing databases, 605-606
  compared to DAO, 603-605
  methods, 604
  RemoteData control, 607
  setting up, 608
rdoResultset object, recordset types, 603
RDOSAMPL.TXT, 606
reading sequential text files, 478
receiving the focus, 66
record groups, creating with SELECT SQL statements, 813-814
Record Selection Formula dialog box, 657
record sources, 616
  setting up, 617
record types, random access files, 482
records
  adding to recordsets, 590
  adding/deleting, 555
  deleting, 592
  editing, 591
  locking, 634
    batch optimistic, 638
  multiple, modifying
    loops, 587
    SQL, 589
  updating, 591

Recordset object, 569, 630
  adding new data, 635
  creating, 630
  CursorType property, 632
  displaying field values, 631
  dynasets, 571-573
  forward-only, 574
  LockType property, 634
  navigating recordsets, 632
  snapshots, 573
  tables, 570
  updating data, 634
recordsets, 630-631
  AbsolutePosition property, 584
  accessing field info, 575
  adding records, 590
  Bookmark property, 578
  Data control, 546
    properties, 547
  disconnected, 637
    reconnecting, 638
    uses of, 639
  Filter property, 585
  Find methods, 579
  modifying multiple records
    loops, 587
    SQL, 589
  multiusers, 635
  navigating, 618, 632-634
  navigating records, 576
  NoMatch property, 579
  PercentPosition property, 584
  Seek method, 581-583
  Sort property, 586
  types of, 569
RecordSource property, 549
Redirect method, 708
references, 238
References dialog box, 238
  Word Object Library, 491
Regional Settings Control Panel, 416
RegisterDatabase method, 602
remainder division, 178

Remote Data Services (RDS), disconnected recordsets, 639
RemoteData control, 607
  setting up, 608
RemoveItem method, 71
repetitive tasks, 209
Replace function, 193
REPLACE.ZIP, 192
Report Footer section, function fields, 652
Report view, 255
report-style list, 251
ReportFileName property, 658
reports
  adding fields, 645
  adding to projects, 643
  creating, 642
    with Crystal Reports, 655
  Data Report, setting up, 644-646
  data source, 642
  displaying report, 647
  exporting to HTML files, 651
  function fields, 652
  graphics, 649
  predefined fields, 648
  printing/exporting, 651
    ExportReport method, 651
    PrintReport method, 651
  see also Crystal Reports
Request object (ASP), 709
Require Variable Declaration option, 169
Resize event, 105
  ActiveX controls, 309
  limited character textbox control, 319
  Line control, 426
resizing ActiveX controls, 309
Response object (ASP), 708

Response.Write statement (ASP), 707
Resume statement, 220
retrieving records, Get command, 483
return values
    data types, checking, 148
    message boxes, 143
reusability
    classes, 360
    procedures, 233-234
RGB( ) function, 278, 444
RichTextBox control, 445
Right$ function, 189, 476
Root property, 259
Round function, 197
RowDividerStyle property, 622
RPTDEMO, 647
RPTDEMO.ZIP, 643
rptFunction control, 652
RTF template file, 445
rubber-band boxes, 28
Run mode, 20
RUNDLL32.EXE, 745
running programs, 36
runtime
    embedded objects, 499
    menu properties, setting, 120
    SendKeys statement, 66

S

Safety Settings dialog box, 790
Sales.txt (code listing), selecting fields from multiple tables, 798
Save As function, 150
Save File As dialog box, 21
Save Project As dialog box, 22
SaveAs method, 494
saving
    files, 151
    projects, 20-23
        folder locations, 22
    Word documents, 494
scope (variable), 166, 232
screen resolutions, 415
    IDE, 760
screen saver, 509
    animation, 511
    Windows interaction, 512
SCRIPT tag, 670
scripting
    ASP, server-side tags, 693
    accessing file system, 675
    ActiveX controls, 681-682
    ADO, FileSystemObject object, 695
    advanced tools, 672
    ASP, 689
        ActiveX DLLs, 711
        include files, 696
        server-side tags, 694
    events/procedures, 677-679
    forms, 679-681
    host application, 671
    Internet, 666
    objects, 674
    server-side, 690
    text editors, 672
    variants, 673
    VB scripting engine, 671
    Web server, 667-670
scripting engine, 671
SCRLDEMO.ZIP, 80
scrollbars, 78-81
    Columns property, 72
    labels, 80
    list boxes, 70
    scrolling values, 79
ScrollBars property, 385
SDIs (Single Document Interface), forms, 413
search form, 398

SEARCH.TXT, 398
searching strings, 187-188
security
    application-level, 707
    ASP session variables, 705
    network-level, 707
Seek command, random access files, 484
Seek method, 581-583
SEEKTEST.TXT, 581
SELCASE.ZIP, 209
Select Case statement, 207-209
Select Interface Members dialog box, 324
Select Picture dialog box, 249
SELECT statement, manipulative statements, 795
SELECT statements, SQL, 796-816
    aggregate functions, 811-813
    assigning alias names to tables, 801-802
    defining fields, 796-800
    filter criteria, 806-810
    parameters, 815-816
    predicates, 802-803
    record groups, 813-814
    sort conditions, 810-811
    specifying table names, 801
    table relationships, 803-806
    tables, creating, 815
    tables in other databases, 801
Select the Property Pages dialog box, 330
SelectedControls object, Property Pages, 355
SelectedItem property, 268
selecting controls, 25
Selection object, 493

SelectionChanged event procedure, Property Pages, 352
SelectionFormula property, 659
SelImage property, 267
SelLength property, 441
Send To menu, 113
SendKeys statement, 66
separator bars, 114
  reorganizing menus, 115
sequential text files, 477
  reading, 478-480
  writing, 480
Server object (ASP), 710
servers, ASP, 688
Servervariables collection, 709
Session object (ASP), 705-707
  Response.Write statement, 707
  TimeOut property, 707
Session variables, 705
sessions (ASP), 692
  messaging, 748
Set Mapping dialog box, 326
Set Next Statement, 216
Set statement, 365
  Word documents, 494
setup program, compiling, 778
SETUP.EXE program, 316
SETUP.LST file, Standard EXE projects, 785
Shape control, 426
shared network files, sequential files, 478
Shell function, 461, 475, 745
ShellExecute API call, 745

SHELLWAIT.ZIP, 462
shortcut icons, packaging Standard EXE projects, 782
shortcut keys, 117-118
  commonly used, 118
  menu Click event, 119
  VB IDE, 763
Shortcut property, 110
Show method, 56
  Data Report, 647
ShowFont method, 153
ShowOpen method, 151
ShowPrinter method, 156
ShowSave method, 151
ShowWindow function, 460
SIGNCODE utility, 317
SIMPLEVBS.ZIP, 677
single quotation marks ('), 580
single-clicking, 417
single-key indexes, 535
single-tier drivers, 597
sizing
  MDI child forms, 389
  objects, 44
  handles, controls, 27
Slider control, 275-278
SLIDERS.ZIP, 277-278
SmallChange property, 79, 275
snapshots
  access mode options, 574
  creating with SQL, 821-822
  Recordset objects, 573
sndPlaySound function, 457
software, see programs
sort conditions, SELECT SQL statements, 810-811
Sort property, 586
Sort.txt (code listing),

specifying sort order of output dynaset, 811
Sorted property, 72
SourceSafe, 23
Spacebar events, 103
spaces, removing from strings, 191
special-purpose controls, 78
splash screens, 422
splits (DataGrid control), 623
  properties, 624
SQL (Structured Query Language), 794-796, 820-822
  action queries, executing, 820-821
  dynasets, 821-822
  modifying multiple records, 589
  optimizing performance, 825-826
    compiling queries, 826
    indexes, 826
    simplifying queries, 826
  QueryDefs, creating, 821
  RecordSource property, 549
  snapshots, 821-822
  statements, 795-796
    action, 816-818
    creating, 823-825
    Data Control usage, 822
    DDLs (Data-Definition-Language), 818-820
    passing to other databases, 827
    SELECT, 796-816
SQL Server, sample application, 513
SQL Server dialog box, 602
SQLXPORT.ZIP, 514
standard controls, see common controls

Standard EXE projects, 761
  packaging, 778-785
    CAB files, 787
    installation files, 785
    installation location, 782
    SETUP.LST file, 785
    shared components, 783
Standard toolbar, 764
Standard toolbar control, 127-128
Start command (IDE), 37
Startup Form, 55, 241
  child forms, 387
Startup Object, 55
Startup Project, 313, 369
StartupPosition property, settings, 55
StateChanged event, 752
StateManagement property, 714
statements
  assignment, 175
  Case, 207
  Case Else, 208
  comp to functions, 141
  Declare, API functions, 450
  Exit For, 211
  Exit Sub, 230
  Load, 56
  Loop, 211
  Mid, 191
  On Error, 219
  Option Explicit, 169
  Response.Write (ASP), 707
  Select Case, 207-209
  SendKeys, 66
  Set, 365
  SQL, 795-796
    action, 816-818
    creating, 823-825
    Data Control usage, 822
    DDLs (Data-Definition-Language), 818-820
    passing to other databases, 827
    SELECT, 796-816
  TypeOf, 91

Unload, 57
writing, 174
see also commands
Static keyword, 169
  procedures, 233
static variables, 168
status bars, 279-283
status information, 279
STATUS.ZIP, 283-284
Step value, 210
stepping through code, 216
StillConnecting property, 606
Stop method, Animation control, 287
stored queries, 536
Str function, 194
StrConv function, 186
Stretch property, 430
string constants, 141
string variables, 141
strings, 182
  changing case, 185-186
  concatenation, 183
  determining length, 185
    Len function, 147
  extracting pieces, 189-190
  fixed-length, 165
  numeric digits, 194
  removing spaces, 191
  replacing characters, 191-193
  searching, 187-188
  specific characters, 193
Style property, 129
  drop-down lists, 76
  list boxes, 72
Sub Main procedure, 241
Sub statement
  Private procedures, 233
  procedures, starting position, 225
SUBCLASS.ZIP, 465-466

subclassing, 464
  event handlers, 465-467
SubItems property, 251
subprocedures, see procedures
subtraction, 177
SUM function, 589
Summary.txt (code listing), aggregate functions, 813
SyncBuddy property, 270
system events, 99
system modal option, 145
SystemParamtersInfo function, 457

T

TabAction property, 622
Table Structure dialog box, 539
tables
  access mode options, 571
  adding with Visual Data Manager, 539
  assigning alias names, SELECT SQL statements, 801-802
  child, 532
  creating, SELECT SQL statements, 815
  database design, 530
  defining, with DDLs, 818-819
  dynasets, 571
  indexes, 534
  lookup, 533
  normalization, 531
  opening, 570
  organization rules, 533
  parent, 532
  queries, 536
  RDO, 604
  recordsets, 570
  setting relationships, SELECT SQL statements, 803-806

specifying names, SELECT
   SQL statements, 801
topical organization, 530
using in other databases,
   SELECT SQL statements,
   801
Visual Data Manager
   copying, 542
   field changes, 540
   indexes, 541
   renaming/deleting, 542
   table structure, 542

Tables collection, 495

**TabStrip control, 261-266,
410**

tags
   HTML, 669-670
   server-side scripting (ASP),
   693
   see also ASP; HTML files

TBRDEMO.TXT, 132

**tbrDropDown style button,
131**

templates
   child forms, 388
   MDI child forms, 405-407
   MDI parent forms, 402-405
   projects, 240
   RichTextbox control, 445

testing
   Calculator control, 349
   projects, 778
   user-drawn ActiveX
   controls, 338

text, 62
   editing in text boxes, 440
   Label control, 63
      appearance, 64
      AutoSize property, 63
      WordWrap property, 63
   text boxes, 65
      validating input, 66
   validating, 66
   Word documents, 494

text boxes, 65, 439
   adding, 26
   as variables, declaring, 176
   editing text, 440
   labeling, 27
   locking out users, 439
   MaxLength property, 440
   naming, 25
   PasswordChar property, 440
   receiving the focus, 66
   validating input, 66
   word-wrapping, 147

**text controls, enhancing,
318**

text editors, VBScript, 672

text files, sequential, 477
   reading, 478-480
   writing, 480

Text property, 26, 71
   accessing, 36

**TextBackGround property,
257**

TextBox control, 23, 65
   adding to Loan Calculator,
   24
   compared to Label, 28
   enhancing, 319
   MultiLine property, 65
   properties, 26
   Text property, accessing, 36

third-party controls, 41

time formats, 199

TimeOut property, 707

Timer control, 81-83
   Caller ID application, 503
   Screen Saver application
   animations, 511

Timer event, 81

Timer function, 82

TIMEREX.ZIP, 82

title argument, 141

**toggling Boolean values,
122**

ToolBar control, 125
   collections, 134
   standard, 127

toolbars, 124-125
   AllowCustomize property,
   135
   buttons, 129-131
      properties, 129-131
   coding, collections, 133
   coding buttons, 132
   CoolBar control, 136
   example, 131
   images, 126
   properties, 128
   standard button, 129
   standard control, 127-128
   ToolTips, 131
   user customization, 135

toolbars (IDE), 764-766
   form size/position
   coordinates, 765
   moving, 766

Toolbox (IDE), 767
   CommandButton control, 29
   CommanDialog control, 149
   Common controls, 247
   controls, 42
   controls, 768
   Crystal Report control, 658
   custom icons, 323
   Data Report Designer
   window, 644
   intrinsic controls, 60
   ToolBar control, 125

**ToolboxBitmap property,
323**

tools
   Auto List Members, 47
   Crystal Reports, 653
   IDE, 760
   scripting engine, 671

Tools menu, 109

ToolTips, 24
   IDE, 764
   toolbars, 131

ToolTipText property, 134

Top property, 45

ToPage property, 156

**Totprice.txt (code listing),
   creating calculated fields,
   799**

TRANSACT.TXT, 593

transaction processing, 592
transactions, WebClass, 714
transferrring files, Internet Transfer control, 753-755
TransferTable procedure, 519
TRANSPAR.ZIP, 520, 523
transparent images, 519, 523
TransparentPaint function, 519
TreeTab project, 261
TreeView control, 258
- Child property, 260
- Children property, 260
- nodes, 258
- Parent property, 259
- root property, 259

TREEVIEW.ZIP, 263-265
Trim function, 191
troubleshooting ActiveX controls, 317
twips, 47, 766
txtArray control array, 295
txtArray_LostFocus event procedure, 295
TxtCharLimit control, testing, 322
type libraries, 163
TypeOf statement, 91

U

UCase function, 185
uFlags parameter, 451
unbound controls, 575
Unload statement, 57, 301
Update method, 591
UPDATE SQL action statement, 818

UPDATE statement
- manipulative statements, 795
- updating fields, 590

Update.txt (code listing), UPDATE SQL action statement, 818
UpdateBatch method, 638
updating databases with ASP, 701, 704
updating records, 591
UpDown control, 269-270
URLs (Uniform Resource Locator), ASP, 688, 744
user actions, 51
user controls, Ambient object, 342
user-defined types, 162
user-drawn ActiveX controls, 333
- button events, 337
- button properties, 335-336
- button property pages, 337
- testing button, 338
- user interface, 333-335

user events, 98
user interaction
- choice making controls, 66
- Color dialog boxes, 154
- command buttons, 67
- CommonDialog control, 148-149
- controlling interaction with properties, 48
- custom dialog boxes, 157
  - form templates, 157
- dialog boxes, default button, 144
- exit click event procedure, 32
- File dialog box, 150
- File dialog boxes, 152
- Font dialog box, 152
- Font dialog boxes, 154
- Help dialog boxes, 157
- list boxes, 70

- message boxes, 140
- MsgBox function, 141-146
- Print dialog boxes, 155
- ToolTips, 131
- user input, 23
  - Common controls, 266
  - DTPicker, 274
  - ImageCombo control, 266-268
  - input boxes, 146
  - InputBox function, 146-147
  - MonthView, 271-273
  - Slider, 275-278
  - UpDown control, 269-270
- validating input, 66

user interfaces
- controls, 14
- converting forms to UserDocument, 736
- creating, 18
- drawing on forms, 769
- form design, 410
- forms, 40
- Frame control, 83-85
- PC differences, 415-416
- saving projects, 20-23
- scrollbars, 78-81
- Timer control, 81-83
- user-drawn ActiveX controls, 333-335
- user expectations, 417
  - list boxes, 417
  - menus, 420
  - multiple instances of application, 420-421
  - perceived speed, 422-423
- user input, 23
- UserDocument object, 729

UserControl object, 308
- Resize event, ActiveX controls, 309
- user-drawn controls, 333

UserDocument object, 729
- filenames, 724
- interface controls, 724
- key events, 730
- methods, 731-733

properties, 730
users
events, 31
menu bars, 108
text boxes, locking out users, 439
toolbars, user customization, 135

V

Val( ) function, 36, 148, 194
returned types, 148
Validate event, 66
ValidateEntries method, 348
validating data, VBScript forms, 681
validating input, 66
Value property
MonthView control, 273
ProgressBar control, 285
variable arrays, 166
variables, 34, 160
assignment statements, 36, 175
debugging, tracking values, 218
declaring, 34
Dim keyword, 34
explicit declaration, 163
fixed-length strings, 165
implicit declaration, 164
input boxes, 146
local, 168
looping limits, 210
message boxes, return values, 143
naming, 34, 160
Option Explicit statement, 169
public, 167
scope, 166
Session object, 705
static, 168, 233

string variables, 141
types of, 161
user-drawn controls, 335
Variant data type, 35
VBScript, 673
Word documents, 495
Variables collection, 495
VARIABLES.ASP, 709
Variant data type, 35
VB Application Wizard, 762
VBA (Visual Basic for Applications), compared to VB and VBScript, 666
vbCrLf constant, 141
VBP extension, 22
VBScript, 666, 673
accessing file system, 675
ActiveX controls, 681-682
ADO, FileSystemObject object, 695
advanced tools, 672
ASP, 689
ActiveX DLLs, 711
include files, 696
server-side tags, 694
events/procedures, 677-679
forms, 679-681
host application, 671
Internet, 666
methods, 684
objects, 674, 684
running, 683
text editors, 672
variants, 673
VB scripting engine, 671
Web server, 667-670
VBSCRIPT.DLL, 671
VBSFILES.HTM, 676
VBSFORM.ZIP, 679
version numbers, 787
vertical-market software developers, 13
video resolution, IDE, 760
View menu, 109
View property, 252

views, indexes, 535
virtual directories, WebClass, 714
virtual directories (ASP), 690-692
Visible property, 48, 111, 119-121
pop-up menus, 123
Visual Data Manager, 537
adding tables, 539
copying tables, 542
creating database file, 538
creating SQL statements, 823-825
field changes, 540
indexes, 541
reasons for using, 543
renaming/deleting tables, 542
table structure, 542
VolumeID property, 696
VScrollBar control, 78

W - Z

WAV files, Caller ID application, 504
waveform (.WAV) sound files, sndPlaySound function, 457
Web pages
ActiveX controls, 682
ASP, 694
Web servers
ActiveX DLLs with ASP, 711
ASP, 688
IIS Application project, 711
VBScript, 667-670
Web sites, ASP, 688
WebBrowser control, 742
download status, 743
WebClass, 712
HTML WebItem template, 715
instancing, 714

templates, sending to browser, 717
WebItems, 712
  custom, 717
  template event, 715
WeekDayName function, 197
WHERE clause, table relationships, SELECT SQL statements, 806
Where.txt (code listing), JOIN clause, 806
While statement, 211
white board, 34
Widen Form command button, 47
Width property, forms, 30
Win32 API, *see* Windows API
Window menu, 109
WindowList property, 111, 122
Windows
  Code, 32
  controlling with API calls, 458
    window handles, 458-460
  modality, 145
  properties, 43
  toolbars, 124

Windows API, 450-451
  API Text Viewer, 452-453
  callbacks, 463
  calls
    controlling other windows, 458-460
    sndPlaySound, 457
    SystemParametersInfo, 457
  subclassing, 464
    event handlers, 465-467
  wrapper functions, 454-457
Windows dialog boxes, CommonDialog control, 148
Windows Explorer, *see* **ListView control**
Windows ODBC Data Source Administrator, 598
Windows Scripting Host
  running VBScript, 683
  VBScript methods, 684
  VBScript objects, 684
Windows Scripting host, 671
WINHLP32.EXE, 157
With statement, Worksheet object, 497
WithEvents keyword, 368
Wizards
  Packaging and Deployment, 729
  Property Pages, 330

WM_CLOSE message, 461
Word Object Library, 491
Word objects, 490-491
  Application/Document, 492
  saving/opening/printing, 494
  text, 494
  Word.Basic, 496
word-wrapping, input boxes, 147
Word.Basic, 496
WORDDEMO.TXT, 492
Words collection, 494
WordWrap property, Label control, 63
work area (IDE), 762
Worksheet object, Range property, 497
wrapper functions, Windows API, 454-457
WrapText property, 626
WriteCIDData routine, 507
WriteTemplate method, 717
writing sequential text files, 480
Wscript object, 684
WSCRIPT.EXE, 683
x (multiplication operator), 178
Year 2000, date values, 201

VISUAL BASIC®

PROGRAMMER'S JOURNAL

101 TECH TIPS

AND

MABRY SOFTWARE, INC.

VISUAL BASIC® 6 ACTIVEX CONTROL REFERENCE

Contents

Section I
VBPJ 101 Tech Tips

Welcome to the Seventh Edition of the VBPJ Technical Tips Supplement! 3
Deleting an Array Element 3
Invoke "Open With ..." Dialog Box 3
SSTAB Vs. Option Buttons 4
Change the Appearance Property of a Text Box at Run Time 4
Dealing With Null Values Returned From RDO Resultsets 5
In Search of Sample Code 5
Floating an Edit Box 5
Yet Another CenterForm Routine 6
Tie a Message Box to Debug.Assert for Advanced Debugging 6
Modernize Your Toolbar Look 7
Force an MDI Window Refresh 7
Take Advantage of Related Documents Area in Project Window 8
Copy Drawn Picture to Clipboard 8
Erase a Variant Array 9
Force a Single Select For a Grid 9
Ragged Arrays 10
Adjust Combo Box Drop-Down Width 10
MessageBox Advantage 11
Enum API Constants Save Time Coding 11
Type-o-Matic Text Box 12
ReDim the Right Array! 12
Set the ListIndex Without the Click Event 13
Cleaning Up After a Crash 13
Send Mail From VB5 13
Avoid the Flickering 14
Adding Full Paths to a TreeView 14
Replacement for Now() and Timer() 15
Tile an Image Onto a Form 15
Zap Expired Docs 15
Quick Class Tests 16
A Quicker "Next/Previous Weekday" 16
Remove Min/Max Buttons From MDI Form 16
Make Buttons Appear 17
Add a New Number Format 17
Live Action Captions 18

IsMissing Behavior Changed in VB5 18
Set Default Font for New Controls 18
Reduce Filtering Frustration 19
Rotate an Object About a Point 19
Use OLE Automation to Call 16-Bit DLLs From VB5 (or VB4 32) 19
Yeah, But Which Common Controls? 20
Disable Easily 20
Determine List Item by Coordinates 21
Custom Menu Accelerators 21
Menu Properties Shortcut 22
Taking a Form in Front of Another Form 22
Add Remarks to Your Procedures 22
Reduce the Clutter in Your VB IDE 23
Hide Enumerations for Validation 23
Browse VB Command as You Type 23
Find Your Constant or Enum Values 24
Watch Out for "()" When Calling Subroutines 24
Use the Same Name for Your Error Handlers 24
View the Names of Your Database Fields Directly From the IDE 24
Collect User Requirements With Scenarios 25
Put Your Check-Box Value Into Your Database 25
Be Careful When Mimicking Tool-Tip Help 25
Watch How You Use Your Booleans 25
Use Refresh, Not DoEvents 26
Form-Level Variables Won't Clear 26
Forms Not Showing Up in Taskbar 26
RTFM 27
Don't Forget That Mouse Pointer 27
Working With Collections 27
Simplify Boolean Variable Updates 28
KeyPress Won't Fire When Pasting Into Text Box 28
Limit Selected Check Boxes With Collection Logic 28
Numeric Conversion of Strings 28
SQL Trick to Join Multiple Select Statements 29
Debugger Isn't Invoked 29
Where Did It Go? 29
VB Hijacks the Registry 30
Consistent Project Descriptions 30
Roll Your Own 30
Use RDO to Access Stored Functions and Procedures on a Server 30
Use OLE Automation to Print Access Reports 31
Find Out Who Is Connected to an Access Database 31

Perform Some Common Database Chores 32
Password Protect an Access Database 33
Generate Random Strings 34
Make Sure All Access QueryDef Objects are Closed 34
Use Name Parameters With Oracle Stored Procedures 35
Declare Your Objects Properly 35
Use the Object Library Name When Dimming Object Variables 35
A Better Use for StrConv 35
Load a Grid From a SQL Statement 36
Invisible Control Placement on MDIForm Client Area .36
Q&D Zoom Using Forms 2.0 Designer 37
Scrollbars and 3-D Effects on Non-MDI Forms 37
Special Effects With Forms 2.0 Designer 37
Easy Updates of Property Window for Multiple Controls 38
Roll-Your-Own Decimal Entry Filter 38
Repeat Performance 38
Transport a List 39
Find Text Between Two Strings 39
Tell Me It's True 39
Make One Form Parent of Another 40
Do Easy Form-Level Keystroke Trapping 40
Avoid Binary Compatibility Problems 40
Emulate a Click Event for Right-Clicks Over CommandButton Controls 40
Q&D Sort Using Hidden List Box 41
A Generic Routine to Fill Unbound Lists 42

Section II

Mabry ActiveX Controls

DFInfo Control Reference   45
Indic Control Reference   61
JoyStk Control Reference   75
LED Control Reference   91
Mail Control Reference   103
Slider Control Reference   165
Time Control Reference   187
ZipInf Control Reference   203

VISUAL BASIC®
PROGRAMMER'S JOURNAL
INCLUDES WINDOWS PROGRAMMING & VISUAL PROGRAMMING

101
TECH TIPS

SEVENTH EDITION

for Visual Basic Developers

SUBSCRIBE

To the **Ultimate Add-on Tool** for Microsoft **Visual Basic**®

Get the nuts and bolts programming information and advice you can utilize right away. More Windows® programmers turn to *VBPJ* each month for practical pointers, in-depth technical articles, and solid information. Get twelve information-packed issues with your paid subscription. Plus you'll also receive:

- **TWO BONUS ISSUES**
  The annual *VBPJ* Buyer's Guide and the Enterprise Computing issues.*

- **101+ TECH TIPS**
  Companion booklet mailed with our February and August issues of *VBPJ*.

- **PREMIER CLUB DISCOUNT**
  25% off to *VBPJ* and *Java™ Pro* subscribers.

*Buyer's Guide is mailed in April; the Enterprise Issue is mailed in September.

WHAT YOU CAN **EXPECT** EACH MONTH **FROM *VBPJ*:**

- Access data faster, better from your VB apps
- Use OOP to create more efficient, maintainable code
- Find and use the best database tools and libraries
- Build Web sites and Web apps with VB
- Integrate multiple databases and technologies
- Learn how to use Visual Studio tools in your Windows apps
- Write tight, fast code
- Get the most out of VBA and Office
- Manage your code more efficiently
- Optimize resource and memory use

FULL MONEY-BACK GUARANTEE!

For **FASTER** Service Call:
1-800-848-5523
(Monday through Friday 9:00am-5:00pm PST)
INTERNATIONAL: 650-833-7100

FTP FAWCETTE TECHNICAL PUBLICATIONS

www.devx.com
or email us at **customerservice@fawcette.com**

Please allow four weeks for delivery of first issue. International subscriptions must be payable in U.S.Dollars plus postage; Canada/Mexico add $18 per year for surface delivery; all other countries add $44 per year for airmail. Visual Basic, ActiveX and C++ are trademarks of Microsoft Corporation. Java is a trademark of Sun Microsystems. All other trademarks are the property of their respective owners.

101 TECH TIPS
For VB Devleopers

For even more tricks and tips go to
HTTP://www.devx.com

Welcome to the Seventh Edition of the VBPJ Technical Tips Supplement!

These tips and tricks were submitted by professional developers using Visual Basic 3.0, Visual Basic 4.0, Visual Basic 5.0, Visual Basic for Applications (VBA), and Visual Basic Script (VBS). The tips were compiled by the editors at Visual Basic Programmer's Journal. Special thanks to VBPJ Technical Review Board members.

If you'd like to submit a tip to Visual Basic Programmer's Journal, please send it to User Tips, Fawcette Technical Publications, 209 Hamilton Avenue, Palo Alto, California, USA, 94301-2500. You can also fax it to 650-853-0230 or send it electronically to vbpjedit@fawcette.com or 74774.305@compuserve.com. Please include a clear explanation of what the technique does and why it's useful, and indicate if it's for VBA, VBS, VB3, VB4 16- or 32-bit, or VB5. Please limit code length to 20 lines. Don't forget to include your e-mail and mailing address. If we publish your tip, we'll pay you $25 or extend your VBPJ subscription by one year.

VB3, VB4 16/32, VB5
Level: Beginning

Deleting an Array Element

Conventional wisdom suggests that to delete an array element, you must move up all the subsequent elements to close the "gap" left by the deleted item. However, if the sequence of the elements isn't significant (as in an unsorted array), this algorithm quickly deletes an item:

```
' Element to delete
iDelete = 5
' Number of elements before deletion
nElements = UBound(Array)
' Replace iDelete with last item in array
Array(iDelete) = Array(nElements)
' Use ReDim Preserve to shrink array by one
ReDim Preserve Array(LBound(Array) _
      To nElements - 1)
```

—*Basil Hubbard, Hamilton, Ontario, Canada*

VB4 32, VB5, VBA
Level: Intermediate

Invoke "Open With ..." Dialog Box

When launching a data file with the ShellExecute() function, Windows tries to find the associated application and open the data file with this application. But what happens if no association exists? ShellExecute() simply returns error code 31 (no association) and nothing happens. Wouldn't it be nice if your program invoked the "Open with ..." dialog box so you can choose which application you want to associate with your data file? Here's a solution—call the ShellDoc routine and pass a fully qualified path/file name of the data file you wish to open:

```
Option Explicit

Declare Function GetDesktopWindow Lib "user32" () As Long
Declare Function ShellExecute Lib _
    "shell32.dll" Alias "ShellExecuteA" _
    (ByVal hWnd As Long, ByVal lpOperation _
    As String, ByVal lpFile As String, _
```

continues

```
        ByVal lpParameters As String, _
        ByVal lpDirectory As String, _
        ByVal nShowCmd As Long) As Long
Declare Function GetSystemDirectory Lib _
        "kernel32" Alias "GetSystemDirectoryA" _
        (ByVal lpBuffer As String, ByVal nSize _
        As Long) As Long
Private Const SE_ERR_NOASSOC = 31
Public Sub ShellDoc(strFile As String)
    Dim lngRet As Long
    Dim strDir As String
    lngRet = ShellExecute(GetDesktopWindow, _
         "open", strFile, _
         vbNullString, vbNullString, vbNormalFocus)
    If lngRet = SE_ERR_NOASSOC Then
        ' no association exists
        strDir = Space(260)
        lngRet = GetSystemDirectory(strDir, _
            Len(strDir))
        strDir = Left(strDir, lngRet)
        ' show the Open with dialog box
        Call ShellExecute(GetDesktopWindow, _
            vbNullString, "RUNDLL32.EXE", _
            "shell32.dll,OpenAs_RunDLL " & _
            strFile, strDir, vbNormalFocus)
    End If
End Sub
```

—Thomas Weidmann, received by e-mail

VB4 32, VB5
Level: Beginning

SSTAB Vs. Option Buttons

Although VB's SSTab control behaves as if each tab page is a container, it actually uses a single container for all tab pages. This can cause unexpected behavior if you have groups of option buttons on different pages. Clicking on an option button on one page clears all the uncontained option buttons on the other, seemingly unrelated, pages. Solve this problem by adding your own containers (frames or picture boxes) for each group of options you want to be mutually exclusive.

—Steve Cisco and Roland Southard, Franklin, Tennessee

VB4 32, VB5
Level: Beginning

Change the Appearance Property of a Text Box at Run Time

Sorry, you can't change the Appearance property of a text box at run time—but you can make it look like you have! If set to none, a 3-D picture box has a flat BorderStyle property. Put your text box (with a flat appearance) inside a picture box (with a 3-D appearance) and change the picture box's border style. Use this complete code—be sure you place Text1 inside Picture1:

```
Private m_Text1_Appearance As Long

Private Sub Form_Load()
    With Text1
        Picture1.Width = .Width
        Picture1.Height = .Height
        .Move 0, 0
    End With
    Text1_Appearance = 1  '3D
End Sub

Public Property Let _
    Text1_Appearance(nAppearance As Long)
    With Picture1
        Select Case nAppearance
            Case 0  'Flat
                .BorderStyle = nAppearance
            Case 1  '3D
                .BorderStyle = nAppearance
        End Select
        m_Text1_Appearance = .BorderStyle
    End With
End Property

Public Property Get Text1_Appearance() As Long
    Text1_Appearance = m_Text1_Appearance
End Property
```

—Jim Deutch, Cazenovia, New York

101 TECH TIPS
For VB Devleopers

VB4 32, VB5
Level: Beginning

Dealing With Null Values Returned From RDO Resultsets

If you're assigning the values of columns you return from RDO queries into string variables, you'll get an "Invalid use of Null" error if one of the columns has a Null value. For most purposes, I'd rather have the value as an empty string anyway. Rather than code for that each time I access a column, I've written a function called Clean that turns Null values into empty strings. I call it like this:

```
strMyString=Clean(rdoResultset("MyVarCharColumn"))
```

I also convert Empty values as well, for use with Variants:

```
Public Function Clean(ByVal varData As Variant) As String

If IsNull(varData) Then
        Clean = ""
ElseIf IsEmpty(varData) Then
        Clean = ""
Else
        Clean = CStr(varData)
End If

End Function
```

—*James T. Stanley, Muncie, Indiana*

VB3, VB4 16/32, VB5
Level: Beginning

In Search of Sample Code

I'm always looking for sample code, and the setup1.vbp file is an excellent source of reusable code. It comes with VB and is part of the VB setup kit. The contents vary, depending on what version of VB you have, but you'll find useful examples in each version. For example, the VB5 file sample code does these things:

- Gets the Windows directory.
- Gets the Windows System directory.
- Determines if a file or directory exists.
- Determines if you're running WinNT or Win95.
- Determines drive type.
- Checks disk space.
- Creates a new path.
- Reads from an INI file.
- Parses date and time.
- Retrieves the short path name of a file containing long file names.

Plus, a whole module works to log errors to an error file. This code is well-commented and can easily be cut and pasted into your project.

—*Carole McCluskey, Seattle, Washington*

VB4 16/32, VB5
Level: Intermediate

Floating an Edit Box

To minimize the number of controls on my forms, I use a text box as a floating input control that I either overlay onto a grid or swap with a label. Here is my swap subroutine:

```
Public Sub SwapControls(cHide As Control, _
    cShow As Control, Optional Value)
    With cHide
        .Visible = False
        cShow.Move .Left, .Top, .Width, .Height
    End With
    If IsMissing(Value) Then
        If TypeOf cShow Is TextBox Or _
            TypeOf cShow Is Label Then
                cShow = cHide
        End If
    Else
        cShow = Value
    End If

    With cShow
        .Visible = True
        .ZOrder
        If TypeOf cShow Is TextBox Then
            .SelStart = 0
            .SelLength = Len(cShow)
            If .Visible Then
                .SetFocus
            End If
```

continues

```
        End If
    End With
End Sub
```

When I enter the statement "SwapControls lblData, txtData," lblData disappears and txtData appears in its place with the value of lblData selected and the focus set to it. After you make your entry, execute the statement "SwapControls txtData, lblData."

—Calogero S. Cumbo, Waterloo, Ontario, Canada

VB4 32, VB5
Level: Intermediate

Yet Another CenterForm Routine

In the April 1997 issue of VBPJ, you published a tip called "Consider the Taskbar When Centering Forms." You can center forms more easily with the SystemParametersInfo API call:

```
Private Declare Function _
     SystemParametersInfo Lib "user32" Alias _
     "SystemParametersInfoA" (ByVal uAction _
     As Long, ByVal uParam As Long, R As Any, _
     ByVal fuWinIni As Long) As Long
Private Type RECT
     Left As Long
     Top As Long
     Right As Long
     Bottom As Long
End Type
Private Const SPI_GETWORKAREA = 48
Public Sub CenterForm(frm As Form)
     Dim R As RECT, lRes As Long,
     Dim lW As Long, lH As Long
     lRes = SystemParametersInfo( _
          SPI_GETWORKAREA, 0, R, 0)
     If lRes Then
          With R
               .Left = Screen.TwipsPerPixelX * .Left
               .Top = Screen.TwipsPerPixelY * .Top
               .Right = Screen.TwipsPerPixelX * .Right
               .Bottom = Screen.TwipsPerPixelY * .Bottom
               lW = .Right - .Left
               lH = .Bottom - .Top
               frm.Move .Left + (lW - frm.Width) \ 2, _
                    .Top + (lH - frm.Height) \ 2
          End With
     End If
End Sub
```

—Nicholas Sorokin, Sarasota, Florida

VB5
Level: Intermediate

Tie a Message Box to Debug.Assert for Advanced Debugging

Placing a message box in an error trap can provide useful debugging information, but it doesn't allow you to return to the subroutine or function to poke around and further debug the code. This version of a message box expedites design-time debugging by breaking execution if the developer presses OK:

```
Private Function MyDebugMsg(ByVal aMessage _
     As String) As Boolean
     ' This function is used for expediting
     ' development
     If MsgBox(aMessage, vbOKCancel, _
          "OK puts you into the Error Trap") = vbOK Then
               MyDebugMsg = False
     Else
          MyDebugMsg = True
     End If
End Function

' Sample sub
Public Sub SetColor()
On Error GoTo SetColorError

' body of the subroutine would go here,
' force an error to demonstrate
Error 5

SetColorErrorExit:
     Exit Sub

SetColorError:
     ' In an error trap place this line in addition to any
     ' other error handling code
     Debug.Assert MyDebugMsg(Err.Description & " in SetColor")

     'other error handling code
     Resume SetColorErrorExit
End Sub
```

—Stan Mlynek, Burlington, Ontario, Canada

101 TECH TIPS
For VB Devleopers

For even more tricks and tips go to
HTTP://www.devx.com

VB4 32, VB5
Level: Intermediate

Modernize Your Toolbar Look

Using only a few Windows API calls, you can change the standard VB5 toolbar into an Office 97 look-alike. I've implemented two display styles for the toolbar. The first allows you to change the toolbar to an Office 97-style toolbar (similar to the one used by VB5), and the second allows you to change the toolbar to the Internet Explorer 4.0-style toolbar. If you want to use the second style, you must supply each button with some text in order to achieve the effect. In both cases, the button edges are flat and only appear raised when the mouse passes over the button. To implement it, add this code to a BAS module:

```
Private Declare Function SendMessage Lib "user32" Alias _
    "SendMessageA" (ByVal hwnd As Long, ByVal wMsg As Long, _
    ByVal wParam As Integer, ByVal lParam As Any) As Long
Private Declare Function FindWindowEx Lib "user32" Alias _
    "FindWindowExA" (ByVal hWnd1 As Long, ByVal hWnd2 _
    As Long, ByVal lpsz1 As String, ByVal lpsz2 As _
    String) As Long

Private Const WM_USER = &H400
Private Const TB_SETSTYLE = WM_USER + 56
Private Const TB_GETSTYLE = WM_USER + 57
Private Const TBSTYLE_FLAT = &H800
Private Const TBSTYLE_LIST = &H1000

Public Sub Office97Toolbar(tlb As Toolbar, _
    tlbToolbarStyle As Long)
    Dim lngStyle As Long
    Dim lngResult As Long
    Dim lngHWND As Long

    ' Find child window and get style bits
    lngHWND = FindWindowEx(tlb.hwnd, 0&, _
        "ToolbarWindow32", vbNullString)
    lngStyle = SendMessage(lngHWND, _
        TB_GETSTYLE, 0&, 0&)

    ' Use a case statement to get the effect
    Select Case tlbToolbarStyle
    Case 1:
        ' Creates an Office 97 like toolbar
        lngStyle = lngStyle Or TBSTYLE_FLAT
    Case 2:
        ' Creates an Explorer 4.0 like toolbar,
        ' with text to the right
        ' of the picture. You must provide text
        ' in order to get the effect.
        lngStyle = lngStyle Or TBSTYLE_FLAT _
            Or TBSTYLE_LIST
    Case Else
        lngStyle = lngStyle Or TBSTYLE_FLAT
    End Select

    ' Use the API call to change the toolbar
    lngResult = SendMessage(lngHWND, _
        TB_SETSTYLE, 0, lngStyle)

    ' Show the effects
    tlb.Refresh
End Sub

    Call this routine while a form with a toolbar is loading:

Private Sub Form_Load()
    Call Office97Toolbar(Me.Toolbar1, 2)
    ' whatever…
End Sub
```

—**Michiel Leij, The Netherlands**

VB3, VB4 16/32, VB5
Level: Intermediate

Force an MDI Window Refresh

I sometimes want an MDI parent window to be repainted. For example, if a modal dialog is displayed over the MDI form and you click on OK, the dialog is hidden and an operation occurs, which takes a few seconds to complete. In the meantime, remnants of the dialog are still visible because Windows doesn't have time to complete the paint operation, and the screen looks messy. MDI forms don't have a Refresh method, and I don't want to throw a DoEvents into my code because it's dangerous. This code gives my MDI form a Refresh method:

```
Public Sub Refresh()
    Call RedrawWindow(Me.hWnd, 0&, 0&, _
        RDW_ALLCHILDREN Or RDW_UPDATENOW)
End Sub

    You need to declare these API constants:

Public Const RDW_ALLCHILDREN = &H80
Public Const RDW_UPDATENOW = &H100

' Note: The data type of the lprcUpdate
```

continues

```
' parameter has been changed
' from RECT to Any so 0& (NULL) can be passed.
#If Win32 Then
    Declare Function RedrawWindow Lib _
        "user32" (ByVal hwnd As Long, _
        lprcUpdate As Any, ByVal hrgnUpdate _
        As Long, ByVal fuRedraw As Long) As Long
#ElseIf Win16 Then
    Declare Function RedrawWindow Lib "User" _
        (ByVal hWnd As Integer, lprcUpdate As Any, _
        ByVal hrgnUpdate As Integer, ByVal fuRedraw As _
        Integer) As Integer
#End If
```

—Thomas Weiss, Buffalo Grove, Illinois

VB5
Level: Beginning

Take Advantage of Related Documents Area in Project Window

If you use a resource file in your application, you can see the RES file appear in the project window under "Related Documents." This is the only type of file that VB automatically adds to this node of the project tree. You can add any type of file you like to this area manually, though. From the Project menu, select Add File, or right-click on the project window and select Add File from the context menu. In the dialog box, select All Files for the file type and check the Add As Related Document option.

Adding additional related files here helps organize your project and gives you quick access to useful items, including design documents, databases, resource scripts, help-project files, and so on. Once a file has been added, double-click on it in the project window to open it with the appropriate application.

—Joe Garrick, Coon Rapids, Minnesota

VB4 32, VB5
Level: Advanced

Copy Drawn Picture to Clipboard

The VB Picture control can hold several different formats of pictures: BMP, DIB, ICO, CUR, WMF, and others under VB5. Additionally, you can use graphics methods to "draw" on the control. The only native method that converts the image on the picture control, including the drawn graphics, to a bitmap and transfers the bitmap to the system clipboard requires you to use AutoRedraw.

However, this technique causes problems. This code shows the declarations and functions required to transfer the image on a VB picture control to the system clipboard as a bitmap. Add this code to a BAS module, call PicToClip, and pass the picture box as the only parameter:

```
'       #
'       # API Declarations
'       #
'       Bitmap
Private Declare Function BitBlt Lib "gdi32" _
    (ByVal hDestDC As Long, ByVal x As Long, _
    ByVal y As Long, ByVal nWidth As Long, _
    ByVal nHeight As Long, ByVal hSrcDC As _
    Long, ByVal xSrc As Long, ByVal ySrc As _
    Long, ByVal dwRop As Long) As Long
Private Declare Function _
    CreateCompatibleBitmap Lib "gdi32" (ByVal hDC As Long, _
    ByVal nWidth As Long, ByVal nHeight As Long) As Long
Private Declare Function CreateCompatibleDC _
    Lib "gdi32" (ByVal hDC As Long) As Long
Private Declare Function DeleteDC Lib _
    "gdi32" (ByVal hDC As Long) As Long
Private Declare Function GetDC Lib "user32" _
    (ByVal hWnd As Long) As Long
Private Declare Function ReleaseDC Lib "user32" _
    (ByVal hWnd As Long, ByVal hDC As Long) As Long
Private Declare Function SelectObject Lib "gdi32" _
    (ByVal hDC As Long, ByVal hObject As Long) As Long
' Clipboard
Private Declare Function OpenClipboard Lib _
    "user32" (ByVal hWnd As Long) As Long
Private Declare Function CloseClipboard Lib _
    "user32" () As Long
Private Declare Function EmptyClipboard Lib _
    "user32" () As Long
```

101 TECH TIPS
For VB Devleopers

For even more tricks and tips go to
HTTP://www.devx.com

```
Private Declare Function SetClipboardData Lib "user32" _
    (ByVal wFormat As Long, ByVal hMem As Long) As Long
'   #
'   # API Constants
'   #
'   Clipboard formats
Private Const CF_BITMAP = 2
' ROP
Private Const SRCCOPY = &HCC0020

Public Sub PicToClip(pic As PictureBox)
    Dim hSourceDC As Long
    Dim hMemoryDC As Long
    Dim lWidth As Long
    Dim lHeight As Long
    Dim hBitmap As Long
    Dim hOldBitmap As Long
'       #
'       # NOTE: Error trapping has been removed
'         for the sake of clarity
'       #
    With pic
        ' Determine bitmap size
        lWidth = .Parent.ScaleX(.ScaleWidth, _
            .ScaleMode, vbPixels)
        lHeight = .Parent.ScaleY(.ScaleHeight, _
            .ScaleMode, vbPixels)

        ' Get hBitmap loaded with image on
        ' Picture control
        hSourceDC = GetDC(.hWnd)
        hMemoryDC = CreateCompatibleDC(.hDC)
        hBitmap = CreateCompatibleBitmap( _
            .hDC, lWidth, lHeight)
        hOldBitmap = SelectObject(hMemoryDC, _
            hBitmap)
        Call BitBlt(hMemoryDC, 0, 0, lWidth, _
            lHeight, pic.hDC, 0, 0, SRCCOPY)
        hBitmap = SelectObject(hMemoryDC, _
            hOldBitmap)

        ' Copy to clip board
        Call OpenClipboard(.Parent.hWnd)
        Call EmptyClipboard
        Call SetClipboardData(CF_BITMAP, _
            hBitmap)
        Call CloseClipboard

        ' Clean up GDI
        Call ReleaseDC(.hWnd, hSourceDC)
        Call SelectObject(hMemoryDC, hBitmap)
        Call DeleteDC(hMemoryDC)
    End With
End Sub
```

—**Tom McCormick, Bedford, Massachusetts**

VB4 16/32, VB5
Level: Beginning

Erase a Variant Array

You'll find the IsArray() function helpful when you use Variant arrays that you can set or unset through your code and need to test often. However, once you declare the array, IsArray() returns True, even if the array has been erased using the Erase keyword. To solve this, reset a Variant array by assigning zero or null, so the IsArray() function returns the proper value:

```
Dim myVar As Variant
Debug.Print IsArray(myVar)       'Returns False
ReDim myVar(0 To 5)
Debug.Print IsArray(myVar)       'Returns True
Erase myVar
Debug.Print IsArray(myVar)       'Returns True
myVar = 0
Debug.Print IsArray(myVar)       'Returns False
```

To avoid this kind of tricky problem, use an Erase subroutine like this one:

```
Public Sub vErase(ByRef pArray As Variant)
    Erase pArray
    pArray = 0
End Sub
```

—**Nicolas Di Persio, Montreal, Quebec, Canada**

VB5
Level: Intermediate

Force a Single Select For a Grid

Setting the SelectionMode property of the MSFlexGrid to flexSelectionByRow forces all columns in a row to be selected rather than a single cell. It also allows selection of multiple rows simultaneously. To force a single row selection for a grid, I have a function called UpdateGrid that ensures only one row is selected, regardless of a drag on the rows or if the Shift and the Up and Down arrow keys are used. This is useful if you want to present a list of items in a grid format and only want one highlighted:

```
Sub UpdateGrid(grdInput As MSFlexGrid)
    If grdInput.Rows = (grdInput.FixedRows + 1) Then
        ' only one row in the grid and it
        ' it a fixed one: don't do anything
        Exit Sub
    Else
        ' more than one row in the grid
        If grdInput.RowSel <> grdInput.Row Then
            ' user selected a different row in the grid
            ' than the current row:
            ' set it to the highlighted row
            grdInput.RowSel = grdInput.Row
        End If
    End If
End Sub
```

In the SelChange event for a grid, put in this code:

```
Private Sub myGrid_SelChange
    UpdateGrid myGrid
End Sub
```

—Mike Peters, received by e-mail

VB4 16/32, VB5
Level: Intermediate

Ragged Arrays

Who said arrays in VB can't change all dimensions while preserving data? I call this the "variable dimensions array," and I use it when applications need data arrays with more flexible sizes in all dimensions. This variable prevents your apps from having empty elements in arrays (even if the Variant data type takes a lot of memory). For example, take a look at this two-dimensional array. Instead of declaring the variables with the two dimensions from the beginning, simply declare a Variant:

```
Dim myVar as Variant
' Then 'redim' the first dimension only (2
' elements):
redim myVar(0 to 1)
' You can now use the Array() function for
' each element of the array:
myVar(0) = Array(0, 10, 50)
myVar(1) = Array("test1", "test2", "test3", "test4")
```

Use this code to get the data:

```
myVar(0)(1) = 10
myVar(1)(2) = "test3"
```

You can use as many parentheses as you want, and you can still use the Redim Preserve statement with each element and all dimensions. Simple! Note that you can also use a subroutine to resize one element of the array if you don't want to use the Array() function:

```
Public Sub sbDeclare(ByRef pItem As Variant, _
        pLower As Integer, pUpper As Integer)
    ReDim Preserve pItem(pLower To pUpper)
End Sub

Call sbDeclare(myVar(0), 0, 1)
```

—Nicolas Di Persio, Montreal, Quebec, Canada

VB4 32, VB5
Level: Intermediate

Adjust Combo Box Drop-Down Width

Due to limited space on a form, you sometimes must keep the width of combo boxes small. Because a combo box lacks a horizontal scrollbar, some text might remain hidden. Use these functions to retrieve the current size of a drop-down and to resize the drop-down portion of the combo box as needed at run time. Add this code to a BAS module and call it from wherever convenient—perhaps during your Form_Load procedure:

```
Private Declare Function SendMessage Lib _
    "USER32" Alias "SendMessageA" _
    (ByVal hwnd As Long, ByVal Msg As Long, _
    ByVal wParam As Long, ByVal lParam As _
    Long) As Long
Private Const CB_GETDROPPEDWIDTH = &H15F
Private Const CB_SETDROPPEDWIDTH = &H160
Private Const CB_ERR = -1

Public Function GetDropdownWidth(cboHwnd As Long) As Long
    Dim lRetVal As Long
    '*** To get the combo box drop-down width.
    '*** You may use this function if you want
    '*** to change the width in proportion
    '*** i.e. double, half, 3/4 of existing width.
    lRetVal = SendMessage(cboHwnd, CB_GETDROPPEDWIDTH, 0, 0)
    If lRetVal <> CB_ERR Then
        GetDropdownWidth = lRetVal
        'Width in pixels
    Else
```

```
            GetDropdownWidth = 0
        End If
End Function

Public Function SetDropdownWidth(cboHwnd As _
        Long, NewWidthPixel As Long) As Boolean
    Dim lRetVal As Long
    ' *** To set combo box drop-down width ***
    lRetVal = SendMessage(cboHwnd, _
            CB_SETDROPPEDWIDTH, NewWidthPixel, 0)
    If lRetVal <> CB_ERR Then
            SetDropdownWidth = True
    Else
            SetDropdownWidth = False
        End If
End Function
```

—Rajeev Madnawat, Sunnyvale, California

VB3, VB4 16/32
Level: Intermediate

MessageBox Advantage

You've probably noticed that the display time stops when an application pops up VB's built-in MsgBox. Although the system timer continues to tick, the timer control isn't updated every second, nor do other events (such as painting) process. To update the timer, replace VB's built-in MsgBox with the MessageBox API function. MessageBox-generated dialogs don't stop the timer from updating, and they allow other normal processing, such as form painting:

```
' General Declarations in BAS module
Public Declare Function MessageBox Lib _
        "user32" Alias "MessageBoxA" (ByVal _
        hWnd As Long, ByVal lpText As String, _
        ByVal lpCaption As String, ByVal wType _
        As Long) As Long

' Call from within any form like this:
Call MessageBox(Me.hWnd, _
        "This is a test in API Message Box", _
        "API Message Box", vbInformation)
```

To use this technique in VB3, declare all parameters in the API call as integer. While calling, pass MB_ICONINFORMATION as the last parameter, instead of vbInformation. You can find the constant value for MB_ICONINFORMATION in the CONSTANT.txt file. Note that many of the intrinsic VB constants used with MsgBox also work with the MessageBox API. Now for the best news about this workaround—it's totally unnecessary under VB5! Timer (and other) events are never blocked by a MsgBox call when run from an EXE. It's important to understand that they'll still be blocked in the IDE, but take a look next time you compile and you'll see your clock just keeps on ticking.

—Vasudevan Sampath, San Jose, California

VB5
Level: Intermediate

Enum API Constants Save Time Coding

You can simplify Win32 APIs by using enumerated types instead of constants. When you use enumerated types, VB provides you with a list of values when you define the API in your application:

```
Option Explicit

' define scrollbar constants as enumerations
Enum sb
        SB_BOTH = 3
        SB_CTL = 2
        SB_HORZ = 0
        SB_VERT = 1
End Enum

Enum esb
        ESB_DISABLE_BOTH = &H3
        ESB_DISABLE_DOWN = &H2
        ESB_DISABLE_LEFT = &H1
        ESB_ENABLE_BOTH = &H0
        ESB_DISABLE_RIGHT = &H2
        ESB_DISABLE_UP = &H1
End Enum
```

Note that you need to change the Declares to match the new Enums:

```
Private Declare Function EnableScrollBar Lib _
        "user32" (ByVal hWnd As Long, ByVal _
        wSBflags As sb, ByVal wArrows As esb) As _
        LongPrivate Declare Function _
        ShowScrollBar Lib "user32" (ByVal hWnd _
        As Long, ByVal wBar As sb, ByVal bShow _
        As Boolean) As Long
```

When coding up these API calls, VB displays enumerated lists for both the wSBflags and wArrows parameters to EnableScrollBar, and displays both the wBar and bShow parameters to ShowScrollBar:

```
Call EnableScrollBar(Me.hWnd, SB_BOTH, _
     ESB_ENABLE_BOTH)
Call ShowScrollBar(Me.hWnd, SB_BOTH, True)
```

—Tom Domijan, Aurora, Illinois

VB3, VB4 16/32, VB5
Level: Intermediate

Type-o-Matic Text Box

This code creates a smart input box. Every time you type something into this text box, the first letters of your string are compared against the members of a hidden list box. The code guesses how your string should be completed and finishes it for you, similar to how the latest versions of Microsoft Excel and Internet Explorer behave.

To use this technique, add a list box to your form and set its Visible property to False. This example fills the list at Form_Load with some likely selections. In a real app, you'd add a new element to the list after each user entry is completed. Add this code to the form containing the text and list boxes:

```
Option Explicit

#If Win32 Then
    Private Const LB_FINDSTRING = &H18F
    Private Declare Function SendMessage Lib _
        "User32" Alias "SendMessageA" (ByVal _
        hWnd As Long, ByVal wMsg As Long, _
        ByVal wParam As Long, lParam As Any) _
        As Long
#Else
    Private Const WM_USER = &H400
    Private Const LB_FINDSTRING = (WM_USER + 16)
    Private Declare Function SendMessage Lib _
        "User" (ByVal hWnd As Integer, ByVal _
        wMsg As Integer, ByVal wParam As _
        Integer, lParam As Any) As Long
#End If

Private Sub Form_Load()
    List1.AddItem "Orange"
    List1.AddItem "Banana"
    List1.AddItem "Apple"
    List1.AddItem "Pear"
End Sub

Private Sub Text1_Change()
    Dim pos As Long
    List1.ListIndex = SendMessage( _
        List1.hWnd, LB_FINDSTRING, -1, ByVal _
        CStr(Text1.Text))
    If List1.ListIndex = -1 Then
        pos = Text1.SelStart
    Else
        pos = Text1.SelStart
        Text1.Text = List1
        Text1.SelStart = pos
        Text1.SelLength = Len(Text1.Text) - pos
    End If
End Sub

Private Sub Text1_KeyDown(KeyCode As _
    Integer, Shift As Integer)
    On Error Resume Next
    If KeyCode = 8 Then 'Backspace
        If Text1.SelLength <> 0 Then
            Text1.Text = Mid$(Text1, 1, _
                Text1.SelStart - 1)
            KeyCode = 0
        End If
    ElseIf KeyCode = 46 Then 'Del
        If Text1.SelLength <> 0 And _
            Text1.SelStart <> 0 Then
            Text1.Text = ""
            KeyCode = 0
        End If
    End If
End Sub
```

—Paolo Marozzi, Ascoli Piceno, Italy

VB3, VB4 16/32, VB5
Level: Beginning

ReDim the Right Array!

Many VB programmers use the Option Explicit statement to make sure each variable has been explicitly declared before using it. This means you'll always notice a misspelled variable, which if not caught might cause your application to behave erratically. However, when you use the ReDim statement (documented, albeit ambiguously), Option Explicit can't save you. Consider this procedure:

```
Sub DisplayDaysInThisYear
    Dim iDaysInYear(365)
    ' Initially dimension array
```

101 TECH TIPS
For VB Devleopers

For even more tricks and tips go to
HTTP://www.devx.com

```
        If ThisIsLeapYear() Then
        ' Is this year a leap year?
                ReDim iDaysInYr(366)
                ' Extra day this year!
        End If

        MsgBox "This year has " & _
                UBound(iDaysInYear) & " days in it!"
End Sub
```

This ReDim statement creates a new variable called iDaysInYr, even though you really wanted to reallocate the storage space of the iDaysInYear() array. So the message box displays the incorrect number of days in the year. You can't prevent this from happening, other than being careful when coding the ReDim statement. However, if you use ReDim Preserve, Option Explicit makes sure the variable was previously declared.

—Frank Masters, Grove City, Ohio

VB4 32, VB5
Level: Intermediate

Set the ListIndex Without the Click Event

If you set the ListIndex property of a list-box or combo-box control, VB might generate an unwanted Click event. Instead of writing code to bypass the Click event, use SendMessage to set the ListIndex without generating the event. Call the SetListIndex function below, passing the list (either a list box or combo box) and the desired new index value. SetListIndex attempts to set the value and returns the current index so you can confirm whether your request "took." For example, this code should set the index to the tenth element:

```
Debug.Print SetListIndex(List1, 9)
```

If an error occurred (if there were only eight elements, for example), the previous index value is returned. Code the SetListIndex function in a standard module:

```
Private Declare Function SendMessage Lib _
    "user32" Alias "SendMessageA" (ByVal _
```

```
    hWnd As Long, ByVal wMsg As Long, ByVal _
    wParam As Long, lParam As Any) As Long

Public Function SetListIndex(lst As Control, _
    ByVal NewIndex As Long) As Long
    Const CB_GETCURSEL = &H147
    Const CB_SETCURSEL = &H14E
    Const LB_SETCURSEL = &H186
    Const LB_GETCURSEL = &H188

    If TypeOf lst Is ListBox Then
        Call SendMessage(lst.hWnd, _
            LB_SETCURSEL, NewIndex, 0&)
        SetListIndex = SendMessage(lst.hWnd, _
            LB_GETCURSEL, NewIndex, 0&)
    ElseIf TypeOf lst Is ComboBox Then
        Call SendMessage(lst.hWnd, _
            CB_SETCURSEL, NewIndex, 0&)
        SetListIndex = SendMessage(lst.hWnd, _
            CB_GETCURSEL, NewIndex, 0&)
    End If
End Function
```

—Greg Ellis, St. Louis, Missouri

VB3, VB4 16/32, VB5, VBA
Level: Intermediate

Cleaning Up After a Crash

If your app uses temporary files, store the file name(s) in the Registry as you create them. When you exit the program, delete the temporary file and its related Registry entry. However, if you shut off the machine, Windows crashes, or your program crashes, your temporary file will stay in the Registry. This leads to wasted space, and you must then delete the files from their temporary directory. Because you stored the temporary file name in the Registry, you can check for it when your program starts up again and delete it if it still exists.

—Brian Hutchison, Seattle, Washington

VB3, VB4 16/32, VB5
Level: Beginning

Send Mail From VB5

If Microsoft Outlook is installed, you have an easy way to send e-mail from VB5. To use this technique with VB3, remove the With construct and fully qualify each object property reference:

```
Dim olapp As Object
Dim oitem As Object

Set olapp = CreateObject("Outlook.Application")
Set oitem = olapp.CreateItem(0)
With oitem
    .Subject = "VBPJ RULES"
    .To = "MONTEZUMA;other Names;"
    .Body = "This message was sent from VB5"
    .Send
End With
```

—Jim Griffith, Montezuma, Georgia

VB3, VB4 16/32, VB5
Level: Beginning

Avoid the Flickering

Developers often need to load forms with information, which is time-consuming. The form is often a list box filled from an outside source, and this causes the list-box contents to flash annoyingly as the information goes into it. Solve this by bringing in the declaration of the LockWindowUpdate API call:

```
#If Win16 Then
    Declare Function LockWindowUpdate Lib _
        "User" (ByVal hWndLock As Integer) As Integer
#Else
    Declare Function LockWindowUpdate Lib _
        "user32" (ByVal hWndLock As Long) As Long
#End If
```

The hWndLock variable refers to the hWnd property of the form where you don't want to have screen updates shown. When you reissue the LockWindowUpdate with a value of 0 for hwndLock, you'll free up the screen and all updates will be shown instantly:

```
Dim lErr as Long
Dim x as Integer

'No list box flicker, it will appear blank for
'just a moment…
Screen.MousePointer = vbHourglass
lErr = LockWindowUpdate(Me.hWnd)

For x = 1 to 5000
    lstMyListbox.AddItem CStr(x)
Next
```

Now all the information is there:

```
lErr = LockWindowUpdate(0)
Screen.MousePointer = vbDefault
```

—Bruce Goldstein, Highlands Ranch, Colorado

VB4 32, VB5
Level: Intermediate

Adding Full Paths to a TreeView

Have you ever wanted to add nodes to a TreeView control using a full path instead of adding a node at a time? You can do it with this code:

```
Public Sub AddPathToTree(Tree As TreeView, Path As String)
    Dim PathItem As String
    Dim NewItem As String
    Dim PathLen As Integer
    Dim c As String * 1
    Dim i As Integer
    
    'ADD A BACKSLASH AS A TERMINATOR
    If Right$(Path, 1) <> "\" Then Path = Path & "\"
    
    PathLen = Len(Path)
    
    'RUN THROUGH THE PATH LOOKING FOR BACKSLASHES
    For i = 1 To PathLen
        c = Mid$(Path, i, 1)
        If c = "\" Then
            If PathItem = "" Then
                'ADD THE ROOT ITEM TO THE TREE
                On Error Resume Next
                Tree.Nodes.Add , , "\" & NewItem, _
                    NewItem
                PathItem = "\" & NewItem
            Else
                'ADD THE NEXT CHILD TO THE TREE
                Tree.Nodes.Add PathItem, tvwChild, _
                    PathItem _
                    & "\" & NewItem, NewItem
                PathItem = PathItem & "\" & NewItem
            End If
            NewItem = ""100
        Else
            NewItem = NewItem & c
```

101 TECH TIPS
For VB Devleopers

For even more tricks and tips go to
HTTP://www.devx.com

```
            End If
    Next i
End Sub
```

Simply call this routine passing the TreeView control and the full path as parameters. All the necessary nodes will be added if they don't already exist:

```
AddPathToTree TreeView1, _
        "RootLevel\Child1\Child2\Child3\Child4"
```

—Tom Stock, St. Petersburg, Florida

VB3, VB4 16/32, VB5
Level: Beginning

Replacement for Now() and Timer()

The simple BetterNow() function, shown here, replaces the built-in Now() function. It's faster (10 microseconds vs. 180 microseconds on a Pentium 166MMX) and more accurate, potentially supplying one-millisecond resolution, instead of 1000 milliseconds.

Because it's also faster and more accurate than Timer(), which clocks at 100 microseconds and provides 55 milliseconds resolution, it should also replace Timer, especially when Timer() is used to measure elapsed times. Besides, Timer() rolls over at midnight, and BetterNow() doesn't:

```
#If Win16 Then
    Private Declare Function timeGetTime Lib _
          "MMSYSTEM.DLL" () As Long
#Else
    Private Declare Function timeGetTime Lib "winmm.dll" _
          () As Long
#End If

Function BetterNow() As Date
    Static offset As Date
    Static uptimeMsOld As Long
    Dim uptimeMsNew As Long
    Const oneSecond = 1 / (24# * 60 * 60)
    Const oneMs = 1 / (24# * 60 * 60 * 1000)
    uptimeMsNew = timeGetTime()
    ' check to see if it is first time function called or
    ' if timeGetTime rolled over (happens every 47 days)
    If offset = 0 Or uptimeMsNew < uptimeMsOld Then
        offset = Date - uptimeMsNew * oneMs + CDbl(Timer) * _
                        oneSecond
        uptimeMsOld = uptimeMsNew
    End If
    BetterNow = uptimeMsNew * oneMs + offset
End Function
```

—Andy Rosa, received by e-mail

VB4 16/32, VB5
Level: Beginning

Tile an Image Onto a Form

Adding this code to a form causes it to tile the image stored in Picture1 across the entire form whenever the form requires a refresh:

```
Private Sub Form_Load()
    With Picture1
        .AutoSize = True
        .BorderStyle = 0
        .Visible = False
    End With
End Sub

Private Sub Form_Paint()
    Dim i As Long, j As Long
    With Picture1
        For i = 0 To Me.ScaleWidth Step .Width
            For j = 0 To Me.ScaleHeight Step .Height
                PaintPicture .Picture, i, j
            Next j
        Next i
    End With
End Sub

Private Sub Form_Resize()
    Me.Refresh
End Sub
```

—Devin Coon, Pittsburgh, Pennsylvania

VBA
Level: Beginning

Zap Expired Docs

This VBA Microsoft Word routine purges a document when it's opened after a predefined expiration date. I've only tested this macro with Word 97:

```
Sub Purge()
    Dim ExpirationDate As Date
    ExpirationDate = #4/1/98#
```

```
            'This particular document expires on 1 April 1998
            If Date >= ExpirationDate Then
                'Purge the document
                With Selection
                    .WholeStory
                    .Delete Unit:=wdCharacter, Count:=1
                    .TypeText Text:= _
                            "This document expired on" & _
                            Str(ExpirationDate) & "."
                    .TypeParagraph
                End With
                ActiveDocument.Save
                'Alert the user
                MsgBoxResult = MsgBox("This document has expired. " _
                            & "Please acquire an updated copy.", , _
                            "Document Purge")
            End If
End Sub
```

In order to work, you should call this macro from a document's AutoOpen macro.

—Dorin Dehelean, Dollard des Ormeaux, Quebec, Canada

VB4 16/32, VB5
Level: Intermediate

Quick Class Tests

When testing properties and methods of an object that you're writing, you don't have to run a test project or form to test it. Instead, open the Immediate window and begin typing and executing code:

```
Set c = new Class1
? c.TestProperty
```

—Trey Moore, San Antonio, Texas

VB3, VB4 16/32, VB5
Level: Advanced

A Quicker "Next/Previous Weekday"

In the latest tips supplement ["101 Tech Tips for VB Developers," Supplement to the February 1998 issue of VBPJ], I noticed a tip titled "Determine Next/Previous Weekday." This code is shorter and accomplishes the same task with no DLL calls:

```
Public Function SpecificWeekday(ByVal D As Date, Optional _
        ByVal WhatDay As VbDayOfWeek = vbSaturday, _
        Optional GetNext As Boolean = True) As Date
    SpecificWeekday = (((D - WhatDay + GetNext) \ 7) - _
            GetNext) * 7 + WhatDay
End Function
```

This code averages about 10 times faster in VB3 and up to 30 times faster in VB5. It works because VB keeps dates internally as the number of days since Saturday, December 30, 1899. A date of 1 represents Sunday, December 31, 1899, which is also its own weekday. This means the WeekDay function is equivalent to the expression (Date - 1) Mod 7 + 1. This is coded for VB5, but by altering the way the Optional parameters are handled, you can make it work in either VB3 or VB4.

—Phil Parsons, Newmarket, Ontario, Canada

VB3, VB4 16/32, VB5
Level: Intermediate

Remove Min/Max Buttons From MDI Form

Unlike other forms, MDI forms don't have MinButton and MaxButton properties to enable or disable the form's Minimize and Maximize buttons. If you add this code to an MDI parent form's Load event, it disables the Minimize and Maximize buttons on the MDI form. If you just want to disable one or the other, comment out the appropriate line, based on which constant you don't need:

```
Sub MDIForm_Load()
    Dim lWnd as Long
    lWnd = GetWindowLong(Me.hWnd, GWL_STYLE)
    lWnd = lWnd And Not (WS_MINIMIZEBOX)
    lWnd = lWnd And Not (WS_MAXIMIZEBOX)
    lWnd = SetWindowLong(Me.hWnd, GWL_STYLE, lWnd)
End Sub
```

Add this code (which includes the required API declarations) to a BAS module:

```
#If Win32 Then
    Private Declare Function SetWindowLong Lib "user32" _
        Alias "SetWindowLongA" (ByVal hwnd As Long, ByVal _
        nIndex As Long, ByVal dwNewLong As Long) As Long
    Private Declare Function GetWindowLong Lib "user32" _
```

```
            Alias "GetWindowLongA" (ByVal hwnd As Long, ByVal _
            nIndex As Long) As Long
#Else
    Declare Function SetWindowLong Lib "User" (ByVal hwnd _
            As Integer, ByVal nIndex As Integer, ByVal _
            dwNewLong As Long) As Long
    Declare Function GetWindowLong Lib "User" (ByVal hwnd _
            As Integer, ByVal nIndex As Integer) As Long
#End If

Const WS_MINIMIZEBOX = &H20000
Const WS_MAXIMIZEBOX = &H10000
Const GWL_STYLE = (-16)
```

—Joselito Ogalesco, Morton, Pennsylvania

VB4 32, VB5
Level: Intermediate

Make Buttons Appear

VB doesn't display the Min and Max buttons in a form's caption area when you specify BorderStyle Fixed Dialog. If you set the MinButton and MaxButton properties on the form to True, the Minimize and Maximize entries in the context menu are visible—but the buttons are still invisible! To fix this, add this code to a standard module:

```
Private Declare Function GetWindowLong Lib "user32" Alias _
    "GetWindowLongA" (ByVal hWnd As Long, ByVal nIndex As _
    Long) As Long
Private Declare Function SetWindowLong Lib "user32" Alias _
    "SetWindowLongA" (ByVal hWnd As Long, ByVal nIndex As _
    Long, ByVal dwNewLong As Long) As Long

Private Const GWL_STYLE = (-16)
Private Const WS_MINIMIZEBOX = &H20000
Private Const WS_MAXIMIZEBOX = &H10000

Public Sub SetCaptionButtons(Frm As Form)
    Dim lRet As Long
    lRet = GetWindowLong(Frm.hWnd, GWL_STYLE)
    SetWindowLong Frm.hWnd, GWL_STYLE, lRet Or _
        WS_MINIMIZEBOX * (Abs(Frm.MinButton)) Or _
        WS_MAXIMIZEBOX * (Abs(Frm.MaxButton))
End Sub
```

You must call the subroutine SetCaptionButtons from the Form_Load event, passing a reference to your form. This should work in VB3 and VB4 16 with the proper 16-bit API declarations (see "Remove Min/Max Buttons From MDI Form").

—Geir A. Bergsløkken, Grinder, Norway

VB4 16/32, VB5
Level: Intermediate

Add a New Number Format

A client needed the numbers to show up in certain data files in the "x100" format to accommodate interchanging data with a legacy system. That is, if the number is "23.56," it shows up as "2356," and "23" becomes "2300." Because I didn't want to create a special case throughout my code to manage this, and the VB Format function doesn't support such a format, I subclassed the Format function and added the new format myself:

```
Public Function Format(Expression As Variant, Optional _
    sFormat As Variant, Optional FirstDayOfWeek As _
    Variant, Optional FirstWeekOfYear As Variant) As String
    If IsMissing(sFormat) Then
        Format = VBA.Format(Expression)
    ElseIf sFormat = "x100" Then
        ' handle the special x100 case
        Expression = Expression * 100
        Format = VBA.Format(Expression, "0.")
        Format = Left$(Format, InStr(1, Format, ".") - 1)
    Else
        ' wasn't my special format, so pass through to the
        ' real format function
        If IsMissing(FirstWeekOfYear) And _
            IsMissing(FirstDayOfWeek) Then
            Format = VBA.Format(Expression:=Expression, _
                Format:=sFormat)
        ElseIf IsMissing(FirstDayOfWeek) Then
            Format = VBA.Format(Expression:=Expression, _
                FirstWeekOfYear:=FirstWeekOfYear)
        ElseIf IsMissing(FirstWeekOfYear) Then
            Format = VBA.Format(Expression:=Expression, _
                FirstDayOfWeek:=FirstDayOfWeek)
        End If
    End If
End Function
```

This allows me to simply call the Format function as I normally would everywhere in my code, have my "x100" format, and still support all the normal Format parameters and options. Note the use of VBA.Format in the routine to reference the built-in format function.

—Jon Pulsipher, Bellevue, Washington

VB5
Level: Intermediate

Live Action Captions

When building a TextBox or Label UserControl, the Caption or Text property sometimes doesn't work well with the standard controls, as the control's appearance doesn't change when you type the value into the Properties window.

To make your UserControl behave the way you want, go to the UserControl's code window and select Procedure Attributes from the Tools menu. Find your Caption or Text property on the combo box and click on Advanced. On the Procedure ID combo box, select Text. Test it by putting an instance of your control on a form and changing the Text or Caption property at design time. The Property Let procedure will fire with each keystroke, allowing your update routine to reflect what the user has typed.

—Leonardo Bosi, Buenos Aires, Argentina

VB5
Level: Intermediate

IsMissing Behavior Changed in VB5

In VB5, you can assign a default value to a typed optional argument. But you must then use the IsMissing function carefully, because when the optional argument is typed, IsMissing always returns False. Only when using an untyped (Variant) optional argument will IsMissing be accurate in determining whether a value was passed. If no default value is assigned and the argument is typed, VB automatically assigns the default value normally assigned to such a type—typically 0 or an empty string.

Under this condition, you shouldn't use IsMissing to detect whether the argument has been set. You can detect it with two methods. The first method is to not give the argument a type when you declare, so you can use the IsMissing function to detect it. The second method is to give a default value when you declare, but you won't have to set that value when you call it. This code gives some examples about using optional arguments and the IsMissing function:

```
Private Sub fun1(..., Optional nVal)
'- Without type (Variant)
    ...
    If IsMissing(nVal) Then
        '- You can use IsMissing here
    Else
    End If
End Sub

Private Sub fun2(..., Optional nVal As Integer)
'- With type but no default value
    ...
    If IsMissing(nVal) Then
        '- You cannot use IsMissing here to detect is
        '- nVal been set, always return true
        '- VB will give nVal a default value 0 because
        '- its type is Integer
    End If
End Sub

Private Sub fun3(..., Optional nVal As Integer = -1)
    If nVal = -1 Then
        '- You can use this to detect , in function equals to
        '- IsMissing
        '- But you must sure the the value -1 will not be
        '- used when the procedure is called
    Else
    End If
End Sub
```

—Henry Jia, received by e-mail

VB3, VB4 16/32, VB5
Level: Beginning

Set Default Font for New Controls

When you place controls on a form, the Font properties of all the controls default to a sans serif font rather than a default font that you specify. To avoid this annoyance, set the Font property for the form to

101 TECH TIPS
For VB Devleopers

For even more tricks and tips go to
HTTP://www.devx.com

the value you'd like the controls to use before placing controls on the form.

—Trey Moore, San Antonio, Texas

VB3, VB4 16/32, VB5
Level: Intermediate

Reduce Filtering Frustration

This code works wonders to reduce flicker and lessen your frustration. Place a timer on the form (tmr_Timer) and set the Interval to 1000. Set Enabled to False, then place this code in the txt_Filter_Change event:

```
Private Sub txtFilter_Change()
    Timer1.Enabled = False
    Timer1.Enabled = True
End Sub
```

In the Timer event, call this routine that refreshes your recordset:

```
Private Sub Timer1_Timer()
    Timer1.Enabled = False
    Call MyUpdateRecordsetRoutine
End Sub
```

The recordset will only be updated if you haven't pressed a key for a full second. Each time you press a key, the timer is reset and the one-second countdown starts all over again.

—Tom Welch, received by e-mail

VB3, VB4 16/32, VB5
Level: Intermediate

Rotate an Object About a Point

You can rotate any object about a center using polar coordinates. Simply define your center Xo and Yo, which in this case is the center of a form. The amount of rotation is determined by direction, one degree:

```
Private Direction As Long
Private Xo As Long, Yo As Long
```

```
Private Sub Form_Click()
    If Direction = 1 Then
        Direction = 359        'counterclockwise
    Else
        Direction = 1          'clockwise
    End If
End Sub

Private Sub Form_Load()
        Direction = 1          'clockwise
End Sub

Private Sub Form_Resize()
    Xo = Me.ScaleWidth \ 2
    Yo = Me.ScaleHeight \ 2
End Sub

Private Sub Timer1_Timer()
    Dim i  As Byte
    Dim r As Single
    Dim Pi As Single
    Dim theta As Single
    Dim plotx, ploty, dx, dy As Integer

    Xo = Form1.Width / 2
    'get center, image is to rotate about
    Yo = Form1.Height / 2
    Pi = 4 * Atn(1)
    dx = Image1.Left - Xo
    'get horizontal distance from center
    dy = Image1.Top - Yo
    '  ""    vertical   ""
    theta = Atn(dy / dx)
    'get angle about center
    r = dx / Cos(theta)
    'get distance from center
    plotx = r * Cos(theta + Direction * Pi / 180) + Xo
    'get new x rotate about center
    ploty = r * Sin(theta + Direction * Pi / 180) + Yo
    '       ""       y       ""
    Image1.Left = plotx
    Image1.Top = ploty
End Sub
```

—David A. Sorich, Countryside, Illinois

VB4 16/32, VB5
Level: Intermediate

Use OLE Automation to Call 16-Bit DLLs From VB5 (or VB4 32)

First, create a VB4-16 project and call it VB16Project. In the project, create a class module that includes a function that calls your 16-bit DLL in the usual way. Name the class VB16Class and the function VB16DLLCall. In your VB4-16 project, remove the default form and add a standard module with a Main subroutine or function.

Under the Tools/Options/Project/StartMode section, click on the OLE Server radio button. Make sure your class module's Instancing Property is set to 1 (CreateableSingleUse) or 2 (CreateableMultiUse). Compile and save your project as an Executable. Now create a 32-bit application using VB4-32 or VB5. To call the 16-bit DLL in your 32-bit project, use this code:

```
Dim MyObj as Object
Set MyObj = CreateObject("VB16Project.VB16Class")
Call MyObj.VB16DLLCall()
```

—Jim Miles, Thousand Oaks, California

VB4 32, VB5
Level: Advanced

Yeah, But Which Common Controls?

This fragment of code from the VB standard module shows the GetComCtlVersion function that retrieves the major and minor version numbers of the Comctl32.dll installed on the local system. Use this function when you subclass toolbar or listview controls from Comctl32.ocx and implement hot-tracking toolbar or full-row select in the listview. It's also useful when checking the DLL version in your setup application:

```
VersionDistribution Platform
4.00       Microsoft Windows 95/Windows NT 4.0
4.70       Microsoft Internet Explorer 3.0x
4.71       Microsoft Internet Explorer 4.00
4.72       Microsoft Internet Explorer 4.01

Option Explicit

Private Const S_OK = &H0

Private Declare Function LoadLibrary Lib "kernel32" _
    Alias "LoadLibraryA" (ByVal lpLibFileName As String) _
    As Long
Private Declare Function GetProcAddress Lib "kernel32" _
    (ByVal hModule As Long, ByVal lpProcName As String) As _
    Long
Private Declare Function FreeLibrary Lib "kernel32" ( _
    ByVal hLibModule As Long) As Long
Private Declare Function DllGetVersion Lib "comctl32.dll" _
    (pdvi As DLLVERSIONINFO) As Long

Private Type DLLVERSIONINFO
    cbSize As Long
    dwMajorVersion As Long
    dwMinorVersion As Long
    dwBuildNumber As Long
    dwPlatformID As Long
End Type

Public Function GetComCtlVersion(nMajor As Long, nMinor As _
    Long) As Boolean
    Dim hComCtl As Long
    Dim hResult As Long
    Dim pDllGetVersion As Long
    Dim dvi As DLLVERSIONINFO
    
    hComCtl = LoadLibrary("comctl32.dll")
    If hComCtl <> 0 Then
    hResult = S_OK
    pDllGetVersion = GetProcAddress(hComCtl, _
        "DllGetVersion")
        If pDllGetVersion <> 0 Then
            dvi.cbSize = Len(dvi)
            hResult = DllGetVersion(dvi)
            If hResult = S_OK Then
                nMajor = dvi.dwMajorVersion
                nMinor = dvi.dwMinorVersion
            End If
        End If
        Call FreeLibrary(hComCtl)
        GetComCtlVersion = True
    End If
End Function
```

—Lubomir Bruha, Czech Republic

VB3, VB4 16/32, VB5
Level: Beginning

Disable Easily

You can easily give your check-box control a Locked property without making your own custom control. First, create a frame large enough to contain your check boxes. Clear the caption and set the border style to None. Put as many check boxes as needed on this frame, setting their captions and so on. When

101 TECH TIPS
For VB Devleopers

For even more tricks and tips go to
HTTP://www.devx.com

you're done, set the frame's Enabled property to False. You can use the same trick to make other controls, such as option buttons and text boxes, appear enabled but not respond.

—Dexter Jones, received by e-mail

VB3, VB4 16/32, VB5
Level: Intermediate

Determine List Item by Coordinates

I wanted users to be able to get a definition for each item in a list box by right-clicking on the item. Unfortunately, right-clicking doesn't automatically select the item, so you need some other way of knowing your location in the list box. Simply reading the Y value from the MouseDown event and converting that value to a line number will work, unless the user scrolls the list. I used the SendMessage API, which can get information from controls, to solve the problem. Here's the code:

```
'Declarations section
Private Declare Function SendMessage Lib "user32" _
    Alias "SendMessageA" (ByVal hWnd As Long, _
        ByVal wMsg As Long, ByVal _
        wParam As Long, lParam As _
        Any) As Long
Const LB_GETITEMHEIGHT = &H1A1
'value to get height of one line in listbox

    'listbox code
Private Sub List1_MouseDown(Button As Integer, Shift As _
    Integer, X As Single, Y As Single)
    Dim msg As String
    Dim TopIndex As Long
    Dim CharHeight As Long
    Dim CurIndex As Long

    With List1
        'find height of one line in listbox
        CharHeight = SendMessage(.hWnd, LB_GETITEMHEIGHT, _
            0, 0)
        'function returns height in pixels so convert to
        'twips
        CharHeight = CharHeight * Screen.TwipsPerPixelY

        If Button = 2 Then 'right click
            'find index number of item that received right
            'click
            CurIndex = Y \ CharHeight + .TopIndex
            'If index number is valid then display
            'information
            If CurIndex < .ListCount Then
                'Code to retrieve and display item
                'definition
                'goes here. Mine looks like this.
                msg = GetMessage(.List(CurIndex))
                frmInfo.Label1.Caption = msg
                frmInfo.Show
            End If
        End If
    End With
End Sub
```

If the items in your list box are always displayed in the same order and no deletions occur, then all you need is an array of definitions that correspond to each item in the list box. To retrieve the appropriate definition, use this code:

```
msg = DefinitionArray(CurIndex)
```

After displaying the definition in a window, you only need code for the list-box MouseUp event:

```
If Button = 2 Then frmInfo.Hide
```

—Kevin W. Williams, Oklahoma City, Oklahoma

VB3, VB4 16/32, VB5
Level: Intermediate

Custom Menu Accelerators

To set the shortcut key of a menu item to something other than what the VB menu editor displays, use this code in the Form_Load event of a form:

```
Private Sub Form_Load()
    mnuExit.Caption = mnuExit.Caption & vbTab & "ALT+F4"
End Sub
```

This adds the text "ALT+F4" to the caption of the mnuExit menu item and right-justifies it with any other shortcuts on the menu. ALT+F4 is already supported by Windows to close a window, so this shortcut needs no additional code for an exit menu choice. If you add shortcuts that Windows doesn't internally support, then set the KeyPreview property of the form to True and check the KeyUp event on the form to see if the shortcut was selected.

—Dave Kinsman, Renton, Washington

VB3, VB4 16/32, VB5
Level: Beginning
Menu Properties Shortcut

You can set the properties of any menu item by selecting the menu item in the Properties window drop-down list. This is often faster than selecting the Menu Editor menu choice and has the added benefit of showing you the changes to the menu choice immediately. It's also the only way to access the Tag property of the menu item at design time.

—Dave Kinsman, Renton, Washington

VB5
Level: Beginning
Taking a Form in Front of Another Form

When building a floating toolbar, you might need to keep it in front of the main form of your application. This took time to do in VB3 and VB4, because you had to resort to API functions. In VB5, you can take advantage of a new, optional argument of the Show method:

```
' within the main form
frmFloating.Show 0, Me
```

The second argument sets the owner form for the window being displayed. The "owned" form will always be in front of its owner, even when it doesn't have the input focus. Moreover, when the owner form is closed, all its owned forms are automatically closed also.

—Francesco Balena, Bari, Italy

VB5
Level: Intermediate
Add Remarks to Your Procedures

You can make your code more readable by always adding a remark on top of all your procedures. Create an add-in that makes it fast and easy. First, run New Project under the File menu and select Addin from the project gallery that appears. In the Project Properties dialog, change the project name to RemBuilder. In the AddToIni procedure (contained in the AddIn.bas module), change the MyAddin.Connect string to RemBuilder.Connect.

Press F2 to show the Object Browser, select the RemBuilder project in the upper combo box, then right-click on the Connect class in the left-most pane and select the Properties menu command. In the dialog that appears, change the description into Automatic Remark Builder (or whatever you want).

In the IDTExtensibility_OnConnection procedure (in the Connect.cls module), search for the My Addin string and modify it to &Remark Builder. This is the caption of the menu item that will appear in the Add-Ins menu. In the Immediate window, type AddToIni and press Enter to register the add-in in the VBADDIN.ini file. In the MenuHandler_Click procedure in Connect.cls, delete the only executable line (Me.Show) and insert this code instead:

```
SendKeys "'" & String$(60, "-") & vbCrLf _
    & "' Name:" & vbCrLf _
    & "' Purpose:" & vbCrLf _
    & "' Parameters:" & vbCrLf _
    & "' Date: " & Format$(Now, "mmmm,dd yy") _
    & "' Time: " & Format$(Now, "hh:mm") & vbCrLf _
    & "'" & String$(60, "-") & vbCrLf
```

Compile this program into an EXE or a DLL ActiveX component, then install the add-in as usual from the Add-In Manager. Before you create a procedure, select the Remark Builder menu item from

101 TECH TIPS
For VB Devleopers

For even more tricks and tips go to
HTTP://www.devx.com

the Add-Ins menu to insert a remark template in your code window, and you'll never again have to struggle against an under-documented program listing.

—Francesco Balena, Bari, Italy

VB5
Level: Intermediate
Reduce the Clutter in Your VB IDE

Here's another simple but useful add-in you can add to your arsenal. Follow the directions given in the previous tip "Add Remarks to Your Procedures," with only minor differences. Use the project name CloseWindows rather than RemBuilder. Also, change the description to "Close All IDE Windows." Finally, type a suitable caption for the menu command, such as Close IDE &Windows. Insert this code in the MenuHandler_Click procedure:

```
Dim win As VBIDE.Window
For Each win In VBInstance.Windows
    If win Is VBInstance.ActiveWindow Then
        ' it's the active window, do nothing
    ElseIf win.Type = vbext_wt_CodeWindow Or _
           win.Type = vbext_wt_Designer Then
        ' code pane or designer window
        win.Close
    End If
Next
```

When you select the add-in from the Add-Ins menu, it closes all the forms and code windows currently open, except the one you're working with.

—Francesco Balena, Bari, Italy

VB5
Level: Intermediate
Hide Enumerations for Validation

VB5 introduced support for enumerations, which are related sets of constants. Although you can declare a property as an enumerated type, VB lets you assign any long integer value to the property. Were you able to determine the lowest and highest values in the enumeration, you could easily validate an enumerated property, but the language doesn't support it. Instead, you can inspect the minimum and maximum values by creating hidden members in the enumeration:

```
Public Enum MyAttitudeEnum
    [_maMin] = 1
    maHappy = 1
    maSad = 2
    maIndifferent = 3
    [_maMax] = 3
End Enum
```

Inspecting the values of [_maMin] and [_maMax] makes it easy for you to validate against an enumerated type.

—Jeffrey McManus, San Francisco, California

VB5
Level: Beginning
Browse VB Command as You Type

When you refer to an object in VB5, you get a drop-down list of that object's properties and methods. But, did you know that the statements and functions of the VB language itself are just a big list of properties and methods? You can view this list at any time in a VB code window by typing the name of the library in which this code resides:

VBA.

Once you type the dot after VBA, the bulk of the VB language drops down. You can then select the language element you want from the list. This is a great help when you're trying to remember the name of a VB language element that you don't often use.

—Jeffrey McManus, San Francisco, California

VB5
Level: Beginning

Find Your Constant or Enum Values

I use constants for things like control-array index numbers, but it's a hassle to keep scrolling to the top of the module to remember the constant names. If you name all the constants with the same first few letters, you can use the new IntelliSense features of VB5 to obtain the list any time you need it. Simply type in the first few letters and press Ctrl+Space. A selection list then appears.

—Deborah Kurata, Pleasanton, California

VB3, VB4 16/32, VB5
Level: Beginning

Watch Out for "()" When Calling Subroutines

To call a subroutine, you can use the Call statement or simply the name of the subroutine:

```
Call MyRoutine(firstParameter)
'Or
MyRoutine firstParameter
```

Notice you don't include the parentheses in the second case. If you do, VB assumes you mean them as an operator. VB then determines the value of the parameter and passes the value to the routine, instead of passing the reference as expected. This is apparent in this example:

```
Call MyRoutine(Text1)
```

This passes the text-box control to MyRoutine. If you did it without the Call statement, VB evaluates Text1, which returns the default property value of the text box:

```
MyRoutine(Text1)
```

This default property is the text-box text. So, if the routine expects a control, you pass the text string from the control instead and will receive a type-mismatch error. To prevent this, always use the Call statement or don't put parentheses in when calling a subroutine.

—Deborah Kurata, Pleasanton, California

VB5
Level: Beginning

Use the Same Name for Your Error Handlers

Older versions of VB required a unique name for your error-handler labels in order to use On Error GoTo <label>. You had to concatenate the module name and routine name to ensure a unique error-handler label. This is no longer true. You can now use something standard, such as ERR_HANDLER, to identify every error handler. This makes them easier to find when reviewing your error handling.

—Deborah Kurata, Pleasanton, California

VB5
Level: Beginning

View the Names of Your Database Fields Directly From the IDE

When developing code that maps to database fields, you often need to look back at the tables to determine the correct database fields. With VB5, you can now do this without leaving the comfort of the Integrated Development Environment (IDE). Start by setting a breakpoint after the code that populates the recordset, then run the application. When VB breaks at that line, drag your recordset object variable onto the Watches window, or open the Locals window. Click on the plus sign to open the recordset. You can look at any recordset properties, including the field names.

—Deborah Kurata, Pleasanton, California

101 TECH TIPS
For VB Devleopers

For even more tricks and tips go to
HTTP://www.devx.com

VB3, VB4 16/32, VB5
Level: Beginning
Collect User Requirements With Scenarios

When talking to the user or subject-matter expert about an application's requirements, write the requirements in the form of scenarios. A scenario both defines the requirement and provides a list of steps detailing how the resulting feature will be used. For example, instead of writing a requirement to "process payroll," your scenario might be to select an employee from a list of existing employees, to enter the time allocated to the project for each employee, and so on. This clarifies requirements and helps you better visualize how users will use the feature. Once you understand the reasoning behind the request, you might even find a better way to meet the requirement. You can then use these scenarios as the test plan for the feature.

—Deborah Kurata, Pleasanton, California

VB3, VB4 16/32, VB5
Level: Beginning
Put Your Check-Box Value Into Your Database

Jeremy Boschen pointed out an easy way to load a Boolean into a check-box control in the tip, "Use Boolean Variables for Check-Box Values" [101 Tech Tips for VB Developers, Supplement to the February 1998 issue of VBPJ, page 1]. Conversely, you might want to put the value of the check box into a database as a number. To do so, use this code:

```
!db_field = Abs(Check1.Value = vbChecked)
```

This puts 1 into your database field. To make the value −1, change the Abs in the line to CInt. For VB3, you can't use the constant vbChecked and must use the value 1.

—Joe Karbowski, Traverse City, Michigan

VB3, VB4 16/32, VB5
Level: Intermediate
Be Careful When Mimicking Tool-Tip Help

Be careful about tips to easily duplicate tool-tip help with only tip control and mouse events. If your "tip" control doesn't have the same parent as the control you're moving over, you'll put your tip control in the wrong spot! The coordinates for a control refer to its parent, so trying to position it against the wrong parent (as opposed to the form) results in an (x, y) position different than you want. Also, make sure your tip control has the highest z-order, or it might show up "behind" a nearby control. Lastly, be careful about relying on the Form_MouseMove event to "turn off" your tip, because the event might not get fired as you move between two frames or move quickly over the form.

—Joe Karbowski, Traverse City, Michigan

VB4 32, VB5
Level: Beginning
Watch How You Use Your Booleans

With the introduction of the Boolean data type in VB4, you might be tempted to convert it to a numeric value using the Val function for storage in a database table. Watch out! Val won't convert a Boolean into -1 (or 1) as you might expect. Use the Abs or CInt functions, depending on the format you need:

```
Val(True) gives 0
CInt(True) gives -1
Abs(True) gives 1
```

—Joe Karbowski, Traverse City, Michigan

VB3, VB4 16/32, VB5
Level: Beginning

Use Refresh, Not DoEvents

When executing code and tying up the system, developers often use a label or status bar to display messages. If you simply assign your text or message to the control (for example, lblMsg.Caption = "Still working…"), you won't see the text because your code loop isn't allowing the form to respond to the message. To make the message visible, use the Refresh method of the control. Don't use the DoEvents command to refresh the text to the user—this introduces re-entrancy issues. Note that displaying messages slows down performance, so use them intelligently:

```
Private Sub Command1_Click()
    Dim J As Long
    For J = 1 To 1000
        Label1.Caption = "Message " & J
        Label1.Refresh
    Next J
End Sub
```

—Joe Karbowski, Traverse City, Michigan

VB3, VB4 16/32, VB5
Level: Beginning

Form-Level Variables Won't Clear

When you use multiple forms in a project, make sure you explicitly set a form to Nothing after you unload it. If you don't, simply unloading the form won't necessarily clear out variables from the form. Setting it to Nothing does reset form-level variables:

```
Private Sub ShowNewForm()
    Load Form2
    Form2.Show vbModal
    Unload Form2
    Set Form2 = Nothing
End Sub
```

To see how the problem occurs, create a new standard executable project, with a form and a command button. Use this code:

```
Option Explicit
Private Sub Command1_Click()
    Load Form2
    Form2.Show vbModal
    Unload Form2
    'Set Form2 = Nothing
End Sub
```

Add a second form with a label and a command button on it, and paste in this code:

```
Option Explicit
Private msStuff As String
Private Sub Command1_Click()
    Hide
End Sub
Private Sub Form_Load()
    Label1.Caption = "value is " & msStuff
End Sub
Private Sub Form_Unload(Cancel As Integer)
    msStuff = "hey!"
End Sub
```

Press the command button on Form 1 to show Form 2. The label control shows that the msStuff variable is empty. Hide Form 2 by pressing the button, then pressing the button on Form 1 again. This time, Form 2 will have a value in the msStuff variable, showing that it doesn't clear out.

—Joe Karbowski, Traverse City, Michigan

VB3, VB4 16/32, VB5
Level: Beginning

Forms Not Showing Up in Taskbar

In VB3 you can set up an executable project to start up in the main subroutine, and it shows up in the Windows 95 taskbar:

```
Public Sub Main()
    Load frmFoo
    frmFoo.Show 1
    Unload frmFoo
End Sub
```

However, if you show a form modally in VB5, no matter if it's the first form in the program or not, it won't show up in the taskbar. If you want to see the item in the taskbar, you must show it nonmodally.

—Joe Karbowski, Traverse City, Michigan

VB3, VB4 16/32, VB5, VBA, VBS
Level: All
RTFM

Read The Fawcette Magazines.

—VBPJ Staff

VB3, VB4 16/32, VB5
Level: Beginning
Don't Forget That Mouse Pointer

If you turn the mouse pointer into an hourglass (and back to normal) in a routine with error handling, don't forget to turn the mouse pointer back to normal in the error-handler section. Otherwise, the program might look busy, but actually be done:

```
Private Function CalcTotal() As Long
    On Error GoTo ProcErr

    Screen.MousePointer = vbHourglass
    '
    'Code that may raise error
    '
    Screen.MousePointer = vbNormal
    Exit Function 'Don't go into error handler

ProcErr:
    Screen.MousePointer = vbNormal
    '
    'Error handling code
    '
End Function
```

—Joe Karbowski, Traverse City, Michigan

VB4 32, VB5
Level: Beginning
Working With Collections

When working with collections, use an error handler to easily determine if a given key exists in the collection. If you try to access an item from a collection where the key doesn't exist, you'll get an error. Likewise, if you try to add an item that exists, you'll also get an error. This example shows an error handler for adding an item to a collection. To trap for errors where an item exists, trap error code 457:

```
Private Function BuildCustCol(CustList As ListBox) As _
        Collection
    On Error GoTo ProcError
    Dim colCust As Collection
    Dim lngCustCnt As Long
    Dim J As Long

    Set colCust = New Collection
    For J = 0 To CustList.ListCount - 1
            lngCustCnt = colCust(CStr(CustList.List(J))) + 1
            colCust.Remove (CStr(CustList.List(J)))
            colCust.Add Item:=lngCustCnt, _
                    Key:=CStr(CustList.List(J))
    Next J
    Set BuildCustCol = colCust
    Set colCust = Nothing
    Exit Function

ProcError:
    Select Case Err
            Case 5 'collection item doesn't exist, so add it
                    colCust.Add Item:=0, _
                            Key:=CStr(CustList.List(J))
                    Resume
            Case Else
            'untrapped error
    End Select

End Function
```

—Joe Karbowski, Traverse City, Michigan

VB3, VB4 16/32, VB5, VBA, VBS
Level: Beginning

Simplify Boolean Variable Updates

Instead of using an If construct to set a Boolean variable, you can assign a Boolean variable to the result of any logical comparison. For example, instead of this code:

```
If MyNumber > 32 Then
        BooleanVar = True
Else
        BooleanVar = False
End If
```

Use this code:

```
BooleanVar = (MyNumber > 32)
```

—Joe Karbowski, Traverse City, Michigan

VB3, VB4 16/32, VB5
Level: Intermediate

KeyPress Won't Fire When Pasting Into Text Box

Don't put rules for validating text values or formats in the KeyPress event—use the Change event instead. If you "paste" into a text box, the KeyPress event isn't fired and all your validation goes out the window. Also, if you don't carefully put code in the Change event that sets the value of a text box, you'll create an infinite loop:

```
Private Sub Text1_Change()
      'Append asterisk to text
      Text1.Text = Text1.Text & "*"
End Sub
```

Here's a better way:

```
Private Sub Text2_Change()
      Dim lCurr As Long
      'Append asterisk to text
      lCurr = Text2.SelStart
      If Right$(Text2.Text, 1) <> "*" Then
            Text2.Text = Text2.Text & "*"
            'Be kind and don't put the cursor at the front of the
            'text
            Text2.SelStart = lCurr
      End If
End Sub
```

—Joe Karbowski, Traverse City, Michigan

VB4 32, VB5
Level: Intermediate

Limit Selected Check Boxes With Collection Logic

Use the Count property to determine exactly how many controls are loaded. You can also use the For Each loop to perform code on each control. For instance, if you have a control array of check boxes and you don't want more than three checked, use this code:

```
Private Sub Check1_Click(Index As Integer)
      Dim chk As CheckBox
      Dim lCnt As Long
      Const cMAX = 3
      
      For Each chk In Check1
            If chk.Value = vbChecked Then
                  lCnt = lCnt + 1
                  If lCnt > cMAX Then
                        Check1(Index).Value = vbUnchecked
                        MsgBox "Too many checked!"
                        Exit For
                  End If
            End If
      Next chk
End Sub
```

—Joe Karbowski, Traverse City, Michigan

VB4 32, VB5
Level: Beginning

Numeric Conversion of Strings

When dealing with numerics and strings, be advised of a couple "gotchas." The Val() function isn't internationally aware and will cause problems if you have users overseas. But you can't just blindly switch to

101 TECH TIPS
For VB Devleopers

For even more tricks and tips go to
HTTP://www.devx.com

CLng, CInt, and so on, which are internationally aware. These functions don't support an empty string (vbNullString or "") or strings that fail the IsNumeric test and will raise an error if used as such. Consider wrapping your own function around these calls to check for an empty text string before converting:

```
Public Function CInt(IntValue as Variant) as Integer
    If IsNumeric(IntValue) Then
            MyCInt = CInt(IntValue)
    Else
            MyCInt = 0
    End If
End Function
```

—Joe Karbowski, Traverse City, Michigan

VB3, VB4 16/32, VB5
Level: Intermediate
SQL Trick to Join Multiple Select Statements

Don't overlook the UNION keyword in SQL as a way to simplify selections from multiple tables. For instance, to select the customer with the highest sales from three tables with basically the same layout, use the UNION keyword to allow your VB code to open only one resultset with the answer:

```
Private Function MaxCustSales() As Long
    Dim sSql as string

    sSql =          "select max(cust_sales) max_sales from " & _
                    "sales.dbo.sales_east " & "UNION " & _
                    "select max(cust_sales) max_sales from " & _
                    "sales.dbo.sales_west " & _"UNION " & _
                    "select max(cust_sales) max_sales from " & _
                    "sales.dbo.sales_intl " & _
                    "ORDER BY max_sales DESC"
```

Do this to open the resultset:

```
    If NOT IsNull(!max_sales) Then
                MaxCustSales = !max_sales
        End If

End Function
```

—Joe Karbowski Traverse City, Michigan

VB5
Level: Intermediate
Debugger Isn't Invoked

When working on developing or debugging an app created by automation (for example, by ActiveX DLL), if you normally invoke that app from a calling program (EXE), leave the calling program running and run the app you're debugging in the VB Integrated Development Environment (IDE)—gotcha! Your debug and breakpoints won't get hit. The calling program still has the "real" automation project in memory and isn't using the version from the VB IDE. You must close down the calling program that's running and restart it to use your VB IDE version. You'll see an example of this when you try to make your automation project into a DLL and it balks, saying "Permission Denied." You need to close down any calling programs.

—Joe Karbowski, Traverse City, Michigan

VB4 32, VB5
Level: Intermediate
Where Did It Go?

Have you ever wondered why your ActiveX DLL with a form doesn't show up in the taskbar? Because you're showing the form modally (.Show vbModal). VB4 only allows DLLs with a user interface to be shown modally. VB5, however, has no such limitation. If you want your VB5 DLL to show up in the taskbar, you need to change your code to support showing it nonmodally.

—Joe Karbowski, Traverse City, Michigan

VB5
Level: Intermediate
VB Hijacks the Registry

Be aware that VB's Integrated Development Environment (IDE) hijacks the Registry settings for your public classes when working on projects such as ActiveX DLLs and Controls. The IDE temporarily replaces (in the Registry) the existing InProcServer32 for your class to a LocalServer32 entry pointing to the VB IDE version being run. Should VB crash, that Registry entry won't return to its proper state. Then, when you try to run your program "normally," you'll get various messages that the item can't run in multi-instance mode—or other cryptic errors. You must restart the project inside the VB IDE and stop it again.

—Joe Karbowski, Traverse City, Michigan

VB5
Level: Beginning
Consistent Project Descriptions

Always set the Description property of your ActiveX projects (found in Properties) to be prefixed with your company name or initials. That way, all your internal objects and components will be grouped together alphabetically, and you won't have to search for them in the list.

—Joe Karbowski, Traverse City, Michigan

VB5
Level: Advanced
Roll Your Own

If you roll your own controls in VB5 to support database applications, consider putting a Valid property, a Validation event, and a Required property on your controls. The Required property helps you determine whether a text box (for example) can be left blank, and it updates the Valid property. The Validation event should be fired by your control, allowing the developers to put their custom checks or links to the business-rules layer. Then, the developers can set the Valid property of your control accordingly. At the appropriate time, developers can check a control's Valid property to see if they can continue.

—Joe Karbowski, Traverse City, Michigan

VB4 32, VB5
Level: Intermediate
Use RDO to Access Stored Functions and Procedures on a Server

This code illustrates a VB5 routine that calls a given server's stored functions or procedures. The first parameter is the stored function procedure name that resides on the server (ORACLE, SQL Server, and so on). The second parameter is a dynamic array that takes an arbitrary number of input arguments for the stored function or procedure. It returns data from the server:

```
Public db As rdoEngine
Public en As rdoEnvironment
Public cn1 As rdoConnection

Public Function Get_STOREDFUN(sFun As String, ParamArray _
    sColumns() As Variant) As Variant [rdoResultset]

    Dim sSQL As String
    Dim Rs As rdoResultset
    Dim Qry As rdoQuery
    Dim X As Integer

    sSQL = "{ ? = Call " & sFun
    If UBound(sColumns) = -1 Then
        'Do Nothing here
    Else
        sSQL = sSQL & " ("
        For X = 0 To UBound(sColumns)
            sSQL = sSQL & "?,"
        Next
        sSQL = Left(sSQL, Len(sSQL) - 1) & ")"
    End If
```

```
        sSQL = sSQL & " }"

        Set Qry = cn1.CreateQuery("doFunction", sSQL)
        Qry(0).Direction = rdParamReturnValue

        For X = 0 To UBound(sColumns)
            Qry(X + 1).Direction = rdParamInput
            Qry.rdoParameters(X + 1) = sColumns(X)
        Next

        Set Rs = Qry.OpenResultset(rdOpenForwardOnly, _
            rdConcurReadOnly)

        Get_STOREDFUN = Qry(0)
  [Set Get_STOREDFUN = Rs]

  End Function
```

If you have three stored functions in a server, each one takes a different number of input arguments. You can call the same VB5 routine to get returning data:

```
        sPrdPlant = Get_STOREDFUN("ZIP_2PLANT", CStr(txtZip))
        sControl  = Get_STOREDFUN("CONTRNUM")
        fItemPrice = Get_STOREDFUN("GET_UnitPrice", Cstr(prd), _
            Clng(qty))
```

—Kevin Shieh, Milton, Washington

VB4 32, VB5
Level: Intermediate

Use OLE Automation to Print Access Reports

You can print canned reports in an Access database from VB in different ways. I created this routine to print any report with any criteria or filter from any database. It opens Access with the user- or program-controlled database, then opens the report in the mode specified. In order for this to work with Access constants, you must select Access from the References dialog box (accessed from References under the Tools menu in VB4 and under the Project menu in VB5).

The PrintReport subroutine has the same parameters as the Access Docmd.OpenReport command with the exception of DBPath. I didn't use IsMissing to test for missing parameters because Access handles it for you, but you can add it to supply your own default values for any missing parameters. Note: In VB4, any optional parameter must be a Variant data type. When you want to print a report from code, call the routine like this:

```
        PrintReport MyDBPath, MyReportName, acPreview, _
            MyCriteria

Sub PrintReport(ByVal DBPath As String, ByVal ReportName _
    As String
Optional OpenMode As Integer, Optional Filter As String, _
    Optional
Criteria As String)

        Dim appAccess As Object
        Set appAccess = CreateObject("Access.Application")
        appAccess.OpenCurrentDatabase (DBPath)
'**********************************************************
        'Access constants for OpenMode are
        'acNormal  - Print (default)
        'acPreview - Print Preview
        'acDesign  - Design Edit Mode
'**********************************************************
        appAccess.DoCmd.OpenReport ReportName, OpenMode, _
            FilterName
Criteria
'**********************************************************
        'if open mode is Preview then don't quit Access this can
        'also be deleted if you do not want Access to quit after
        'printing a report
'**********************************************************
        If OpenMode <> acPreview Then
                appAccess.Quit
        End If
        Set appAccess = Nothing

End Sub
```

—James Kahl, St. Louis Park, Minnesota

VB4 32, VB5
Level: Intermediate

Find Out Who Is Connected to an Access Database

If you're creating a Jet-based multiuser database system, you'll sometimes need to know who is currently connected to the shared database. To get this information in situations where you don't want to integrate a full Access security system, you have two choices. First, you can code in your own "connected users" table and require users to log on with a simple form on startup. Second, and better, you can use the simple msldbusr.dll. This is probably the best "power toy" ever created for multiuser Jet developers. It tells you the computer names connected by accessing the LDB of the database file. You can rename the MDB with any extension, but the LDB is what counts and it works fine.

Once you get the data from the DLL, you can integrate it with Mauro Mariz's tip, "Send Messages to WinPopUp from Your Application" [101 Tech Tips for VB Developers, Supplement to the February 1998 issue of VBPJ, page 18] to tell the remote user to finish up and shut down the remote app so you can perform maintenance with an exclusive connection.

If you want to integrate your own security system based on connected users without forcing manual logons, you can let the remote apps connect, then run the connections against a list of allowed computer names and take action before allowing them full access. Although this DLL is listed as "currently unsupported," it does only what it's supposed to. You can get it, along with a few other Jet locking utilities, at http://support.microsoft.com/support/kb/articles/q176/6/70.asp.

—Robert Smith, San Francisco, California

VB4 32, VB5
Level: Intermediate

Perform Some Common Database Chores

These several database functions work together and perform various utility functions, such as checking if fields and tables exist, creating fields and tables, and so on. The interface hides all the code and returns True or False to report the status of the functions:

```
Function CreateDatabase(DatabasePath As String, dbLanguage _
        As String, JetVersion As Integer) As Boolean
    Dim TempWs As Workspace
    Dim TempDB As Database

    On Error GoTo Errors:
            Set TempWs = DBEngine.Workspaces(0)
            Set TempDB = TempWs.CreateDatabase(DatabasePath, _
                    dbLanguage, JetVersion)
            CreateDatabase = True
    Exit Function
Errors:
    CreateDatabase = False
End Function

Function CreateTable(DatabasePath As String, NewTableName _
        As String) As Boolean
    Dim dbsTarget As Database
    Dim tdfNew As TableDef

    On Error GoTo Errors:
            If TableExists(DatabasePath, NewTableName) = False _
            Then
                'This table does not exist on the target
                'database, so it is ok to add it.
                Set dbsTarget = OpenDatabase(DatabasePath)
                Set tdfNew = _
                    dbsTarget.CreateTableDef(NewTableName)
                With tdfNew
                    .Fields.Append .CreateField("Temp", _
                            dbInteger)
                End With

                'The new table has been created, append it to
                'the database
                dbsTarget.TableDefs.Append tdfNew
                dbsTarget.TableDefs(NewTableName).Fields. _
                    Delete ("Temp")
                dbsTarget.Close

                CreateTable = True
            Else
                'This table does exist on the target
                'database, so do not add it.
            End If
    Exit Function
Errors:
    CreateTable = False
End Function

Function CreateField(DatabasePath As String, _
        TargetTableName As String, NewFieldName As String, _
        FieldDataType As Integer) As Boolean
    Dim dbsTarget As Database
    Dim tdfTarget As TableDef
```

101 TECH TIPS
For VB Devleopers

For even more tricks and tips go to
HTTP://www.devx.com

```
        On Error GoTo Errors:
            CreateField = False
            Set dbsTarget = OpenDatabase(DatabasePath)
            If TableExists(DatabasePath, TargetTableName) Then
                'The table exists, assign the table to the
                'tabledef and proceed.
                Set tdfTarget = _
                        dbsTarget.TableDefs(TargetTableName)
                If Not FieldExists(DatabasePath, _
                    TargetTableName, NewFieldName) Then
                    'The Field doesn't exist, so create it.
                    With tdfTarget
                        .Fields.Append _
                            .CreateField(NewFieldName, _
                                FieldDataType)
                    End With
                    CreateField = True
                Else
                    'Field exists, we cannot create it.
                End If
            Else
                'The table does not exist, so we cannot add a
                'new field to it.
            End If
        Exit Function
Errors:
        CreateField = False
End Function

Function TableExists(DatabasePath As String, TableName As _
        String) As Boolean
        Dim dbsSource As Database
        Dim tdfCheck As TableDef

        On Error GoTo Errors:
            TableExists = False
            Set dbsSource = OpenDatabase(DatabasePath)
            With dbsSource
                ' Enumerate TableDefs collection.
                For Each tdfCheck In .TableDefs
                    If tdfCheck.Name = TableName Then
                        TableExists = True
                        Exit For
                    Else
                    End If
                Next tdfCheck
            End With
        Exit Function
Errors:
    TableExists = False
End Function

Function FieldExists(DatabasePath As String, TableName As _
        String, FieldName As String) As Boolean
        Dim dbsSource As Database
        Dim tdfSource As TableDef
        Dim fldCheck As Field

        On Error GoTo Errors:
            FieldExists = False
```

```
            If TableExists(DatabasePath, TableName) Then
                Set dbsSource = OpenDatabase(DatabasePath)
                Set tdfSource = dbsSource.TableDefs(TableName)
                With tdfSource
                    ' Enumerate TableDefs collection.
                    For Each fldCheck In .Fields
                        If fldCheck.Name = FieldName Then
                            FieldExists = True
                            Exit For
                        End If
                    Next fldCheck
                End With
            Else
                'The Table doesn't exist, so neither
                'can the field.
                FieldExists = False
            End If
        Exit Function
Errors:
        FieldExists = False
End Function
```

If you do frequent lookups, it's more productive to open and close your database externally to the functions. Because this code opens and closes the database each time, it's not meant for intensive or constant calling.

—Marc Mercuri, Somerville, Massachusetts

VB5
Level: Beginning

Password Protect an Access Database

For simple Microsoft Access security, set the database password from the Security item under the Tools menu in Access, select Set Database Password, and enter a password. To use the database in VB, pass a value along with the "pwd" keyword to the SOURCE value of the OpenDatabase method:

```
Dim db as Database
Dim Wkspc as WorkSpaces
Dim strPass as STRING

strPass = ";pwd=PASSWORD"

Set Wkspc = Workspaces(0)
Set db = Wkspc.OpenDatabase(DBName, False, False, strPass)
```

—Danny Valentino, Brampton, Ontario, Canada

VB4 32, VB5
Level: Beginning

Generate Random Strings

This code helps test SQL functions or other string-manipulation routines so you can generate random strings. You can generate random-length strings with random characters and set ASCII bounds, both upper and lower:

```
Public Function RandomString(iLowerBoundAscii As _
    Integer, iUpperBoundAscii As Integer, _
    lLowerBoundLength As Long, _
    lUpperBoundLength As Long) As String

    Dim sHoldString As String
    Dim lLength As Long
    Dim lCount As Long

    'Verify boundaries
    If iLowerBoundAscii < 0 Then iLowerBoundAscii = 0
    If iLowerBoundAscii > 255 Then iLowerBoundAscii = 255
    If iUpperBoundAscii < 0 Then iUpperBoundAscii = 0
    If iUpperBoundAscii > 255 Then iUpperBoundAscii = 255
    If lLowerBoundLength < 0 Then lLowerBoundLength = 0

    'Set a random length
    lLength = Int((CDbl(lUpperBoundLength) - _
        CDbl(lLowerBoundLength) + _
        1) * Rnd + lLowerBoundLength)

    'Create the random string
    For lCount = 1 To lLength
        sHoldString = sHoldString & _
            Chr(Int((iUpperBoundAscii - _
                iLowerBoundAscii _
                + 1) * Rnd + iLowerBoundAscii))
    Next
    RandomString = sHoldString
End Function
```

—Eric Lynn, Ballwin, Missouri

VB4 32, VB5
Level: Intermediate

Make Sure All Access QueryDef Objects are Closed

When you're working with QueryDef (SQL instructions stored on an MDB database) and open it, DAO loads all the QueryDefs. For example, if you have an MDB with five QueryDefs named qryCustomers, qryOrders, qryContacts, qrySales, and qryPersons, and you want to use the qryCustomers, do this:

```
Dim qdCustomer as QueryDef
Dim rsCustomer as RecordSet

    Set qdCustomer= Db.QueryDefs("qryCustomers")
    qdCustomer.Parameters![Custom ID]= 195
    Set rsCustomer= qdCustomer.OpenRecordSet(dbReadOnly)
        While not rsCustomer.Eof
            txtCustomerName= rsCustomer!Name
            ...........
            rsCustomer.MoveNext
        Wend

    rsCustomer.Close 'Close it
    set rsCustomer=Nothing
    'Free the reference to rsCustomer

    qdCustomer.Close 'Close it
    set qdCustomer = Nothing
    'Free the reference to qdCustomer
```

The problem is that DAO only closes the qdCustomer, but the other four QueryDefs (qryOrders, qryContacts, qrySales, and qryPersons) remain open. To solve the problem, use this subroutine:

```
Public Sub ToNothing()
Dim qdGeneric as QueryDef

    'Surf the QueryDefs Collection
    For each qdGeneric in Db.QueryDefs
        qdGeneric.close 'Close it
        Set qdGeneric = Nothing
    Next

End Sub
```

Now put the call to the subroutine ToNothing:

```
    .
    .
    .
rsCustomer.Close
Set rsCustomer = Nothing
ToNothing
```

—Gonzalo Medina Galup, Miami, Florida

101 TECH TIPS
For VB Devleopers

For even more tricks and tips go to
HTTP://www.devx.com

VB4 32, VB5
Level: Intermediate

Use Name Parameters With Oracle Stored Procedures

When executing an Oracle stored procedure, use the named parameter convention. In place of this code:

```
OraDatabase.ExecuteSQL _
     ("Begin Employee.GetEmpName (:EMPNO, :ENAME); end;")
```

Use this code:

```
OraDatabase.ExecuteSQL ("Begin Employee.GetEmpName _
     (empno=>:EMPNO, ename=>:ENAME); end;")
```

The second example still works even if you change the positions of the stored-procedure arguments. Also, with this convention, you can write a generic routine to assemble the SQL statement without worrying about positioning the stored-procedure arguments.

—Arnel J. Domingo, Hong Kong, China

VB3, VB4 16/32, VB5
Level: Intermediate

Declare Your Objects Properly

Never declare an Object variable as New. If you do, you'll always increment the reference count of the object, regardless of whether you use it. Also, remember to set your objects to Nothing when finished. For instance, instead of this way:

```
Private Sub Foo()
      Dim oCust as New clsCust
      'do stuff with oCust

End Sub
```

Do it this way:

```
Private Sub Foo()
      Dim oCust as clsCust
      Set oCust = New clsCust
      'do stuff with oCust
      Set oCust = Nothing
End Sub
```

—Joe Karbowski, Traverse City, Michigan

VB4 32, VB5
Level: Beginning

Use the Object Library Name When Dimming Object Variables

I always put the word DAO in front of all references to DAO objects. Here are some examples:

```
Dim Db  As DAO.DataBase
Dim rs  As DAO.Recordset
```

This way, VBA knows what library to look in for the definition of DBEngine (the top object). If you don't do this, VBA surfs the references collections to find it. You can also use the word VBA in front of functions (Left$, Mid$, MsgBox, and so on) and write the subroutine or function like this:

```
Public Sub MsgBox ()
VBA.Msgbox "The new way to use VBA :-)", vbInformation + _
      vbOkonly, "VBPJ TechTip Section"

End Sub

Private Sub  Form_Load()
      'Call the MsgBox Sub
      MsgBox

End Sub
```

—Gonzalo Medina Galup, Miami, Florida

VB4 16/32, VB5
Level: Beginning

A Better Use for StrConv

When using proper names, you sometimes need to capitalize the first letter of each word. For example, you need to convert "john smith" into "John

Smith." With VB3, you had to write a custom function to do the job; VB4's versatile StrConv routine, on the other hand, lets you do it with one statement:

```
properName = StrConv(text, vbProperCase)
```

However, be aware that this variant of StrConv also forces a conversion to lowercase for all the characters not at the beginning of a word. In other words, "seattle, USA," is converted to "Seattle, Usa," which you don't want. You still need to write a custom routine, but you can take advantage of StrConv to reduce the amount of code in it:

```
Function ProperCase(text As String) As String
    Dim result As String, i As Integer
    result = StrConv(text, vbProperCase)
    ' restore all those characters that
    ' were uppercase in the original string
    For i = 1 To Len(text)
        Select Case Asc(Mid$(text, i, 1))
            Case 65 To 90            ' A-Z
                Mid$(result, i, 1) = Mid$(text, i, 1)
        End Select
    Next
    ProperCase = result
End Function
```

—Francesco Balena, Bari, Italy

VB4 32, VB5

Level: Beginning

Load a Grid From a SQL Statement

Use this code for a generic routine to load a grid from a SQL statement. The example is for Remote Data Objects (RDO) and Sheridan Software Systems' grid, but it works with minor modification for any grid and resultset type. Also, you can load combo boxes in a similar fashion:

```
Public Sub LoadGridFromSQL(TargetGrid As SSDBGrid, rdoConn _
        As rdoConnection, Sql As String, Optional ClearGrid As _
        Boolean = True)
    Dim J As Integer
    Dim rsResult As rdoResultset
    Dim sAddItem As String

    If ClearGrid Then
        TargetGrid.RemoveAll
    End If
    
    TargetGrid.Redraw = False
    
    Set rsResult = rdoConn.OpenResultset(Sql, _
            rdOpenForwardOnly, rdConcurReadOnly, rdExecDirect)
    With rsResult
        Do Until .EOF
            
            'Build add item string
            sAddItem = vbNullString
            For J = 1 To .rdoColumns.Count
                If IsNull(.rdoColumns.Item(J - 1)) Then
                    sAddItem = sAddItem & _
                            vbNullString & vbTab
                Else
                    sAddItem = sAddItem & _
                            .rdoColumns.Item(J - 1) & _
                            vbTab
                End If
            Next J
            
            'Remove extra tab from end
            TargetGrid.AddItem Left$(sAddItem, _
                    Len(sAddItem) - 1)
            .MoveNext
            
        Loop
        .Close
    End With   'rsResult
    
    TargetGrid.Redraw = True
    Set rsResult = Nothing
    
End Sub
```

—Joe Karbowski, Traverse City, Michigan

VB4 16/32, VB5

Level: Beginning

Invisible Control Placement on MDIForm Client Area

With VB4 or higher, you can place invisible controls—such as the standard Timer and CommonDialog or UserControls built with VB5 that have their InvisibleAtRuntime property set—directly on an MDIForm. In previous versions of VB, you could only put controls with an Align property on an MDIForm.

Because CommonDialog and Timer controls are often necessary, programmers previously had to hide "container" forms or use a PictureBox as a ToolBar

101 TECH TIPS
For VB Devleopers

For even more tricks and tips go to
HTTP://www.devx.com

and cash in on its container functionality to hide the invisible controls. This is no longer necessary, though it's not widely known.

—Ron Schwarz, Mt. Pleasant, Michigan

VB5
Level: Intermediate
Q&D Zoom Using Forms 2.0 Designer

How would you like to be able to make a form automatically resize and reposition all its controls and fonts whenever you resize the form? How would you like to do that using only two lines of executable code and no third-party controls? It's easy, using one of VB5's little-explored features: the Forms 2.0 Designer.

To place a Forms 2.0 Designer in your project, open the Components window (hit Control T; select Components from the Project menu; or right-click on the toolbox and select Components). Click on the Designers tab.

A few caveats: You can only use the Forms 2.0 control set—it appears in its own toolbox when you're in the designer—and ActiveX controls. Only the Forms 2.0 controls scale their fonts. You can't use control arrays in a Forms 2.0 Designer. And you're not allowed to distribute the Forms 2.0 engine, so users need to have Office or Internet Explorer installed on their machines.

Here's all you need to do:

```
Option Explicit
Private w As Long

Private Sub UserForm_Initialize()
    w = Me.Width
End Sub

Private Sub UserForm_Resize()
    Me.Zoom = (Me.Width / w) * 100
End Sub
```

—Ron Schwarz, Mt. Pleasant, Michigan

VB5
Level: Intermediate
Scrollbars and 3-D Effects on Non-MDI Forms

Standard VB forms don't support a scrollable client area. Normally, when one is needed, programmers resort to convoluted solutions such as filling the client area with a picture box, placing another picture box inside the first, manually adding two scrollbars, and placing the actual form content inside the nested picture box. Then programmers add code to handle the scrolling when the scrollbars are changed.

VB5's Forms 2.0 Designer provides the ability to automatically place scrollbars on a form and have them appear only when required. Place a Forms 2.0 Designer into your project and examine the Properties window. Click on the Categorized tab, and look at the Scrolling section for information on the scrolling properties and their usage.

For information on how to add a Forms 2.0 Designer and caveats on usage, see the "Q&D Zoom Using Forms 2.0 Designer" tip.

—Ron Schwarz, Mt. Pleasant, Michigan

VB5
Level: Intermediate
Special Effects With Forms 2.0 Designer

Forms 2.0 Designer provides a variety of special visual effects. Your forms can have flat, raised, sunken, etched, or bumpy background textures. You can also have the background picture tile, zoom, or stretch (zoom without distortion) to the form size. For background effects, check out the SpecialEffect property in the Appearance section of the Properties window. Picture properties are covered in the Picture section.

For information on how to add a Forms 2.0 Designer and caveats on usage, see the "Q&D Zoom Using Forms 2.0 Designer" tip.

—Ron Schwarz, Mt. Pleasant, Michigan

VB5
Level: Beginning

Easy Updates of Property Window for Multiple Controls

When you're editing a series of controls, you can multiselect them either by clicking while holding down the Control button or by "lassoing" them with the mouse, then enter the appropriate data in the Properties window, and apply it to all selected controls.

But what about those times when you need to edit the properties for several controls, but each needs different data? You're in for a tedious session of clicking on the controls one by one and hopping back and forth between the Form window and Properties window.

Unless, of course, you're in on a dirty little secret: When you click on a control—or a form—you can simply start typing! As soon as you type the first key, VB automatically switches focus to the Properties window and starts entering your keystrokes into the same property that you edited in the previous control.

—Ron Schwarz, Mt. Pleasant, Michigan

VB3, VB4-16/32, VB5
Level: Beginning

Roll-Your-Own Decimal Entry Filter

Here's an easy method for making sure your users enter only numeric data, and only one decimal point. First, place two Public procedures in a standard module. You can use Private procedures in a form if you're only using it there, but you'll lose easy portability for future projects.

The first procedure makes sure the decimal point is only entered once. The second procedure filters out all non-numeric characters except the decimal point:

```
Public Sub DecCheck(Target As String, ByRef KeyStroke As _
    Integer)
    If InStr(Target, ".") And KeyStroke = 46 Then
        KeyStroke = 0
    End If
End Sub

Public Sub NumCheck(ByRef KeyStroke As Integer)
    If (KeyStroke < 48 Or KeyStroke > 57) And (KeyStroke _
        <> 46 And KeyStroke <> 8) Then
        KeyStroke = 0
    End If
End Sub
```

Then invoke the code from your TextBox's KeyPress event:

```
Private Sub txtUnitPrice_KeyPress(KeyAscii As Integer)
    DecCheck txtUnitPrice, KeyAscii
    NumCheck KeyAscii
End Sub
```

One caveat: This code doesn't prevent text characters from being pasted in via the clipboard.

—Ron Schwarz, Mt. Pleasant, Michigan

VB3, VB4 16/32, VB5, VBA
Level: Beginning

Repeat Performance

A simple loop through your main string lets you count the occurrences of a specified character or string. This function is useful for determining if enough commas appear in your comma-delimited string:

```
Function Tally(sText As String, sFind As String) As Long
    Dim lFind As Long
    Dim lLast As Long

    Do
        lFind = InStr(lLast + 1, sText, sFind)
```

101 TECH TIPS
For VB Devleopers

```
            If lFind Then
                lLast = lFind
                Tally = Tally + 1
            End If
    Loop Until lFind = 0
End Function
```

—Jeffrey Renton, Spring, Texas

VB5
Level: Intermediate

Transport a List

The typical way of entering user-specified data into a list box is one entry at a time; however, you can accept multiple delimited entries at once and add them to a list box with a call to this function. Passing the function a delimited string fills the list box with the values; the list box can be cleared first if requested in the bClear parameter. If you pass an empty string, the values from the list box are used to create a delimited string:

```
Function ConvertList(cList As Control, ByVal sText As _
        String, ByVal sDelimiter As String, Optional bClear As _
        Boolean = False) As String
    Dim lLoop As Long
    Dim lFind As Long

    If Len(sText) Then
        If bClear Then cList.Clear
        Do
            lFind = InStr(sText, sDelimiter)
            If lFind Then
                cList.AddItem Left$(sText, lFind - 1)
                sText = Mid$(sText, lFind + 1)
            End If
        Loop Until lFind = 0
        If Len(sText) Then cList.AddItem sText
    Else
        For lLoop = 0 To cList.ListCount - 1
            If lLoop = cList.ListCount - 1 _
                Then sDelimiter = vbNullString
            ConvertList = ConvertList & cList.List(lLoop) _
                & sDelimiter
        Next lLoop
    End If
End Function
```

Here's how you can call it to fill a list, then output the same list using a different delimiter:

```
Call ConvertList(List1, "yellow¦green¦red", "¦", True)
Debug.Print ConvertList(List1, "", "/")
```

—Jeffrey Renton, Spring, Texas

VB3, VB4 16/32, VB5, VBA
Level: Beginning

Find Text Between Two Strings

This function is useful for returning a portion of a string between two points in the string. You could, for example, extract a range name returned by Excel found between parentheses:

```
Function Between(sText As String, sStart As _
        String, sEnd As String) As String
    Dim lLeft As Long, lRight As Long

    lLeft = InStr(sText, sStart) + (Len(sStart) - 1)
    lRight = InStr(lLeft + 1, sText, sEnd)

    If lRight > lLeft Then Between = _
        Mid$(sText, lLeft + 1, ((lRight - 1) - lLeft))
End Function
```

Note that it only works for the first occurrences of the start and stop delimiters.

—Jeffrey Renton, Spring, Texas

VB5
Level: Beginning

Tell Me It's True

The typical method of validating multiple expressions is to string together a series of If statements separated with an equal number of And statements. Shorten that process by passing one or more comma-delimited equations to return a True or False result:

```
Function IsTrue(ParamArray paOptions()) As Boolean
    Dim lLoop As Long

    IsTrue = True
    For lLoop = LBound(paOptions) To UBound(paOptions)
        IsTrue = IsTrue And paOptions(lLoop)
```

continues

```
            If paOptions(lLoop) = False Then Exit For
    Next lLoop
End Function
```

—Jeffrey Renton, Spring, Texas

VB5
Level: Beginning

Make One Form Parent of Another

Prior to VB5, when you wanted to make a form appear on top of another form, you either made it modal or used an MDIForm with children. If you wanted to go beyond that, you had to use API calls. Starting with VB5, you can use the Show method's optional ownerform parameter to set one form as the parent of another. This means you always place the child form—not an MDI child—on top of the parent form, even though the parent form remains active. You can also use the style vbModal parameter to force modality, but that defeats any reason to use ownerform. Here's how you invoke the ownerform parameter, making a form a nonmodal child of a non-MDIForm:

```
Private Sub Command1_Click()
        Form2.Show , Me
End Sub
```

—Ron Schwarz, Mt. Pleasant, Michigan

VB3, VB4 16/32, VB5
Level: Intermediate

Do Easy Form-Level Keystroke Trapping

If you set a form's KeyPreview property to True, all keystrokes for items on that form first trigger the form's events. This makes it easy to do form-level filtering and keystroke trapping. For example, if you want to make all text boxes on a form force uppercase entry, you can do it with three lines of executable code:

```
Private Sub Form_KeyPress(KeyAscii As Integer)
    If KeyAscii >= 97 And KeyAscii <= 122 _
        Then 'a-z
            KeyAscii = KeyAscii - 32
    End If
End Sub
```

—Ron Schwarz, Mt. Pleasant, Michigan

VB4 32, VB5
Level: Advanced

Avoid Binary Compatibility Problems

To prevent losing the ability to maintain binary compatibility with compiled object code, take the first compiled build and move it into a separate directory, then tell VB to maintain compatibility with it. It makes intuitive sense to maintain compatibility with each previous version, but it leaves lots of room for breaking compatibility. Maintaining a separate version that is used solely as a compatibility master protects you.

—Ron Schwarz, Mt. Pleasant, Michigan

VB3, VB4 16/32, VB5
Level: Intermediate

Emulate a Click Event for Right-Clicks Over CommandButton Controls

Sometimes it's useful to trap the right click over controls such as CommandButton. Unfortunately, the Click event only fires for left button clicks. The MouseDown and MouseUp events fire for both buttons, and even report which button was clicked, but nothing in life could ever be that simple, right?

The first problem is that if you use the MouseDown event, you trap the click when the user clicks down on the key, which is counter to the way things normally work in Windows. For instance, when you

101 TECH TIPS
For VB Devleopers

click the left button, the control's Click event won't fire until you release, giving you the ability to slide off the control before releasing. A fire-on-downstroke event gives no such safety net.

So you're probably thinking, "Well, then just use the MouseUp event!" This solution creates another gotcha: Even if you slide off the control before releasing, the MouseUp event fires anyway!

Fortunately, the MouseUp event reports the mouse cursor's X and Y positions, and using simple math comparing them to the control's placement and size, it's easy to determine whether the mouse was over the control at the instant it was released. Here's how you do it:

```
Option Explicit
Private Sub Command1_MouseUp(Button As Integer, _
      Shift As Integer, X As Single, Y As Single)
Dim OffMe As Boolean
         If Button = 2 Then      'right button
               X = X + Command1.Left
               Y = Y + Command1.Top
               OffMe = False
               Select Case X
                     Case Is < Command1.Left, Is > _
                     (Command1.Left + Command1.Width)
                           OffMe = True
               End Select
               Select Case Y
                     Case Is < Command1.Top, Is > _
                     (Command1.Top + Command1.Height)
                           OffMe = True
               End Select
               If Not OffMe Then
                     '****************
                     'Your code goes here
                     '****************
               End If
         End If
End Sub
```

—Ron Schwarz, Mt. Pleasant, Michigan

VB3, VB4 16/32, VB5
Level: Intermediate

Q&D Sort Using Hidden List Box

VB has no built-in Sort function. Although lots of sort routines of varying complexity and performance are available, there's a simple "cheat" that you might find useful. The standard VB ListBox control has a Sorted property. Anything you add to a list box will automatically be placed in its proper rank, if you set Sorted to True before running the program. (Sorted is read-only at run time.)

Then simply use the AddItem method to insert items, and the ListBox maintains them in sorted order. A couple things to watch out for: list boxes store everything as strings. Although you can use Evil Type Coercion (ETC) to load numbers into them, keep in mind that as strings, they're sorted according to string rules. That means that 900 are perceived as greater than 1,000. This code uses random numbers and adds leading zeros to them as needed after ETCing them to strings. This code uses two CommandButtons, one ListBox, and one TextBox with its MultiLine property set to True. Click on Command1 to load up the ListBox, and click on Command2 to extract the data one element at a time and display it in Text1.

Don't forget to set the ListBox's Visible property to False for your real applications:

```
Option Explicit
Dim c As Long
Dim i As String
Private Sub Command1_Click()
      List1.Clear
      For c = 1 To 10
            i = Int(Rnd * 10000)
            While Len(i) < 4
                  i = "0" + i
            Wend
```

continues

```
            List1.AddItem i
        Next
End Sub
Private Sub Command2_Click()
    Text1 = ""
    For c = 0 To List1.ListCount
        Text1 = Text1 & List1.List & vbCrLf
    Next
End Sub
```

—Ron Schwarz, Mt. Pleasant, Michigan

VB4 32, VB5
Level: Intermediate

A Generic Routine to Fill Unbound Lists

A common need in database processing is retrieving a list of the values of a particular column field for every record in a table. This function takes arguments for a database name, table name, field name, and optional SQL criteria string, and it returns a collection that contains the list of all row values for the specified column field:

```
Public Function GetColumnData(ByVal DbName As String, _
    ByVal TableName As String, ByVal DataFieldName As _
    String, Optional WhereCriteria As String) As Collection

    Dim WS As Workspace
    Dim DB As Database
    Dim RS As Recordset
    Dim SQLQuery As String
    Dim Results As Collection
    Dim FieldValue As String
    Dim Count As Integer

    Set WS = CreateWorkspace("", "admin", "", dbUseJet)
    Set DB = WS.OpenDatabase(DbName)
    SQLQuery = "SELECT " & TableName & _
        "." & DataFieldName & " FROM " & TableName
    If WhereCriteria <> "" Then _
        SQLQuery = SQLQuery & " WHERE " & WhereCriteria
    Set Results = New Collection
    Set RS = DB.OpenRecordset(SQLQuery, dbOpenForwardOnly)
    If Not RS Is Nothing Then
        Count = 0
        'this count will be a unique key
        'in the collection
        Do While Not RS.EOF
            FieldValue = RS.Fields(DataFieldName)
            Results.Add FieldValue, CStr(Count)
            Count = Count + 1
            RS.MoveNext
        Loop
        RS.Close
        Set RS = Nothing
    End If
    DB.Close
    Set DB = Nothing
    WS.Close
    Set WS = Nothing
    Set GetColumnData = Results
    Set Results = Nothing

End Function
```

This procedure is great for filling unbound lists and combo boxes or for driving other database processing based on the returned list. Here's a simple example:

```
' get a list of Social Security numbers
' for all employees over age 65
Dim lst As Collection
    Dim i As Integer

    Set lst = GetColumnData("employee.mdb", _
        "tblEmployees", "SSNum", "Age>65")

    If Not lst Is Nothing Then
        For i = 1 To lst.Count
            'do something with lst(i)
        Next i
        Set lst = Nothing
    End If
```

In this code, efficiency is traded for ease of use. The procedure opens a connection to the database each time it's called, which is an expensive operation, especially if used inside a loop. As an alternative, you could pass an optional database object. Another efficiency enhancement would be to declare the GetColumnData function as Recordset. After the recordset is open, simply Set GetColumnData = RS. By doing this, you can dispense with the collection altogether. It would also save an iteration through the recordset/collection within the GetColumnData function to assign it to the collection.

Also, note that duplicate values are allowed in the returned collection. I left out error checking intentionally to keep the code as short as possible.

—Allen Broadman, received by e-mail

Mabry Software, Inc.

Visual Basic® 6 ActiveX Control Reference

Visit us online to check out over fifty **ActiveX + COM** controls!

Barcode VBX/OCX

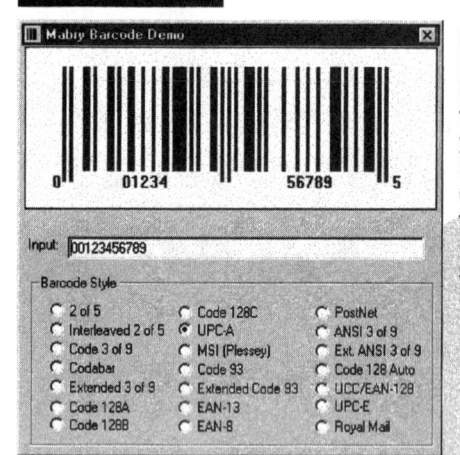

Make Barcode display and printing a snap! Twenty-one barcode styles to choose from. Have vertical or horizontal orientation. Just pick the Barcode style, set the size and fill the caption property with the information you want to be displayed as a Barcode. You can allow Barcode to fill the space you have designated or you can control the width yourself by setting the width of the narrowest bar in pixels.

See our website for more information on this popular control!

Mabry Mail is fully MIME, POP3 and SMTP compliant! Get four controls in one. Send and receive MIME compliant messages with unlimited attachments. Mail can also be used independently as an all purpose encoder and decoder control, or in combination with other controls. It supports encoding and decoding of Base64, Binhex40, UU and Quoted-Printable.

The Mail control comes with a sample program written in VB that is nearly a complete mail client!

Mail VBX/OCX

Mail VBX/OCX

HTTP:// www.mabry.com

We Sell C++ Source Code For Our Controls!

Mabry Software Inc
503 316th St NW
Stanwood, WA 98292
Phone + Fax 360.629.9278 or 800.99.mabry

Prices subject to change without notice.

DFInfo

Description
DFInfo OCX is an OLE custom control that gives convenient access to disk and file information. VB programmers are able to read and modify miscellaneous information about files (date, time, size, attribute flags, date and time of last modification, and so on). Information about the computer's drives is available through a second set of properties.

File Name
DFINFO32.OCX

ActiveX/OCX Object Name
Mabry.DFInfoCtrl/Mabry.DiskInfoCtrl

ActiveX Compatibility
VB 4.0 (32-bit), 5.0 and 6.0

ActiveX Built With
Microsoft Visual C++ v4

ActiveX—Required DLLs
MFC40.DLL (October 6th, 1995 or later)

OLEPRO32.DLL (October 6th, 1995 or later)

MSVCRT40.DLL (September 29th, 1995 or later)

Distribution Note
When you develop and distribute an application that uses this control, you should install the control file into the user's Windows SYSTEM directory. The control file has version information built into it. So, during installation, you should ensure that you are not overwriting a newer version.

DFInfo DiskInfo Control Properties
Properties that have special meaning for this control or that only apply to this control are marked with an asterisk (*).

   *ClusterSize Property
   *DefaultDrive Property
   *Disk Property

*FreeClusters Property
*FreeSpace Property
*Network Property
*NumFloppies Property
*SectorSize Property
*StartupDrive Property
*TotalClusters Property
*TotalSpace Property
*Version Property
*VolumeName Property

DFInfo FileInfo Control Properties

Properties that have special meaning for this control or that only apply to this control are marked with an asterisk (*).

*FileDate Property
*Filename Property
*FileTime Property
*IsArchived Property
*IsHidden Property
*IsReadOnly Property
*IsSystem Property
*SerialNumber Property
*Size Property
*Version Property

Frequently Asked Questions

How do I make SerialNumber property match the serial number that the DOS DIR command displays?

The DOS DIR command displays the serial number in hex format. Use the following code to format the SerialNumber property:

```
SerialNumberText = Hex$( DFInfo1.SerialNumber )
```

ClusterSize Property

Description
Number of sectors per cluster.

Syntax
object.**ClusterSize**

The syntax of the **ClusterSize** property has these parts:

DFInfo

Part	Description
object	A DFInfo control.

Remarks

This is the number of sectors in each cluster on the drive specified by the Disk property.

This property is read-only at runtime only.

Data Type

Long

DefaultDrive Property

Description

Drive letter of the current default drive.

Syntax

`object.DefaultDrive [= drive ]`

The syntax of the **DefaultDrive** property has these parts:

Part	Description
object	A DFInfo control.
drive	A string expression that specifies the default drive.

Remarks

This is the drive letter of current default drive. Setting this property changes the default drive to the drive letter specified.

This property is only available at runtime.

Data Type

String

Disk Property

Description

Drive letter of the disk to examine.

Syntax

`object.Disk [= disk ]`

The syntax of the **Disk** property has these parts:

Part	Description
object	A DFInfo control.
disk	A string expression that specifies the drive to examine.

Remarks
This is the drive letter of drive to examine with the other properties (that is, ClusterSize, FreeSpace, VolumeName, after).

This property is only available at runtime.

Data Type
String

FileDate Property

Description
Reads or sets the date of the selected file.

Syntax
object.**FileDate** [= date]

The syntax of the **FileDate** property has these parts:

Part	Description
object	A DFInfo control.
date	A string expression that specifies the file's date.

Remarks
This property represents the date of the file specified by Filename. This property is kept in "MM-DD-YYYY" format. For example, June 23, 1994 would be "06-23-1994".

When this property is set, the date of the file is changed.

This property is only available at runtime.

Data Type
String

Filename Property

Description
Determines the file that DFInfo reads/modifies.

Syntax
object.**Filename** [= filename]

The syntax of the **Filename** property has these parts:

Part	Description
object	A DFInfo control.
filename	A string expression that specifies the file to examine.

DFInfo

Remarks

This is the first property you should set when dealing with files. Set it to the name (and path, if needed) of the file. If the file exists, all the other properties will be set with the current information. If not, Size will be set to −1.

This is only available at runtime.

Data Type
String

FileTime Property

Description
Reads or sets the time of the selected file.

Syntax
`object.FileTime [= time ]`

The syntax of the **FileTime** property has these parts:

Part	Description
object	A DFInfo control.
time	A string expression that specifies the file's time.

Remarks

This property represents the date of the file specified by Filename. This property is kept in HH:MM:SS format. For example, 4:15pm would be "16:15:00".

When this property is set, the time of the file is changed.

This property is only available at runtime.

Data Type
String

FreeClusters Property

Description
Number of free clusters.

Syntax
`object.FreeClusters`

The syntax of the **FreeClusters** property has these parts:

Part	Description
object	A DFInfo control.

Remarks

This is the number of free clusters available on the drive specified by the Disk property.

This property is read-only at runtime only.

Data Type
Long

FreeSpace Property

Description
Number of free bytes on the drive.

Syntax
`object.FreeSpace`

The syntax of the **FreeSpace** property has these parts:

Part	Description
object	A DFInfo control.

Remarks
This is the number of free bytes available on the drive specified by the Disk property.

This property is read-only and only available at runtime.

Data Type
Long

IsArchived Property

Description
Reads, sets, or clears the file's archive bit.

Syntax
`object.IsArchived [= archive ]`

The syntax of the **IsArchived** property has these parts:

Part	Description
object	A DFInfo control.
archive	A Boolean expression that determines the value of the file's archive flag.

Remarks

This property determines the archive bit of the file specified by Filename. When this property is set, the system bit of the file is changed to reflect the new value.

DFInfo

This property is only available at runtime.

Data Type
Boolean

IsHidden Property

Description
Reads, sets, or clears the file's hidden bit.

Syntax
object.**IsHidden** [= hidden]

The syntax of the **IsHidden** property has these parts:

Part	Description
object	A DFInfo control.
hidden	A Boolean expression that determines the value of the file's hidden flag.

Remarks
This property determines the hidden bit of the file specified by Filename. When this property is set, the hidden bit of the file is changed to reflect the new value.

This property is only available at runtime.

Data Type
Boolean

IsReadOnly Property

Description
Reads, sets, or clears the file's read-only bit.

Syntax
object.**IsReadOnly** [= readonly]

The syntax of the **IsReadOnly** property has these parts:

Part	Description
object	A DFInfo control.
readonly	A Boolean expression that determines the value of the file's read-only flag.

Remarks
This property determines the read-only bit of the file specified by Filename. When this property is set, the read-only bit of the file is changed to reflect the new value.

This property is only available at runtime.

Data Type
Boolean

IsSystem Property

Description
Reads, sets, or clears the file's system bit.

Syntax
object.**IsSystem** [= *system*]

The syntax of the **IsSystem** property has these parts:

Part	Description
object	A DFInfo control.
system	A Boolean expression that determines the value of the file's system flag.

Remarks
This property determines the system bit of the file specified by Filename. When this property is set, the system bit of the file is changed to reflect the new value.

This property is only available at runtime.

Data Type
Boolean

Network Property

Description
Flag determining whether drive is local or on a network.

Syntax
object.**Network**

The syntax of the **Network** property has these parts:

Part	Description
object	A DFInfo control.

Remarks
If this property is True, the drive, specified by the Disk property, is a network drive. Otherwise, this drive is local.

This property is read-only and only available at runtime.

DFInfo

Data Type
Boolean

NumFloppies Property

Description
Number of floppy drives in the system.

Syntax
`object.NumFloppies`

The syntax of the **NumFloppies** property has these parts:

Part	Description
object	A DFInfo control.

Remarks
This property tells the number of floppy drives in this computer.

This property is read-only and only available at runtime.

Data Type
Integer

SectorSize Property

Description
Number of bytes in a sector.

Syntax
`object.SectorSize`

The syntax of the **SectorSize** property has these parts:

Part	Description
object	A DFInfo control.

Remarks
This is the number of bytes per sector on the drive specified by the Disk property.

This property is read-only and only available at runtime.

Data Type
Long

SerialNumber Property

Description
Media ID/serial number of the drive.

Syntax
object.SerialNumber

The syntax of the **SerialNumber** property has these parts:

Part	Description
object	A DFInfo control.

Remarks
This is the serial number of the drive specified by the Disk property.

This property is read-only at runtime only.

Data Type
Long

Size Property

Description
Reads or sets the file's size.

Syntax
object.Size [= *size*]

The syntax of the **Size** property has these parts:

Part	Description
object	A DFInfo control.
size	A long integer that specifies the size of the file.

Remarks
This property reads or sets the size of the file specified by Filename. When this property is set, the size of the file is changed to reflect the new value.

This property is only available at runtime.

Data Type
Long

DFInfo

StartupDrive Property

Description
Drive letter of the startup (boot) drive.

Syntax
object.`StartupDrive`

The syntax of the **StartupDrive** property has these parts:

Part	Description
object	A DFInfo control.

Remarks
This is the drive letter of the drive from which DOS is booted.

This property is read-only and only available at runtime.

> Note
>
> This property is present in all DFInfo controls, but only contains valid data in the VBX version.

Data Type
String

TotalClusters Property

Description
Total number of clusters on the drive.

Syntax
object.`TotalClusters`

The syntax of the **TotalClusters** property has these parts:

Part	Description
object	A DFInfo control.

Remarks
This is the total number of clusters on the drive specified by the Disk property.

This property is read-only and only available at runtime.

Data Type
Long

TotalSpace Property

Description
Total number of bytes on the drive.

Syntax
`object.TotalSpace`

The syntax of the **TotalSpace** property has these parts:

Part	Description
object	A DFInfo control.

Remarks
This is the total number of bytes on the drive specified by the Disk property.

This property is read-only and only available at runtime.

Data Type
Long

Version Property

Description
Returns the version of the control.

Syntax
`object.Version`

The syntax of the **Version** property has these parts:

Part	Description
object	A DFInfo control.

Remarks
This property holds the current version of the control. It is read-only and available at both design time and runtime.

Data Type
String

VolumeName Property

Description
Volume name of the drive.

DFInfo

Syntax
object.**VolumeName** [= *name*]

The syntax of the **VolumeName** property has these parts:

Part	Description
object	A DFInfo control.
name	A string expression that specifies the drive's volume name.

Remarks
This is the volume name of the drive specified by the Disk property. When this property is set, the volume name of the drive is changed.

This property is only available at runtime.

Data Type
String

How to Buy the Source Code for This Control

CREDITS
DFInfo was written by James Shields.

CONTACT INFORMATION
Orders, inquiries, technical support, questions, comments, and so on, can be sent to mabry@mabry.com on the Internet. Our mailing address/contact information is

Mabry Software, Inc.
503 316th Street Northwest
Stanwood, WA 98292

Sales: 1-800-99-MABRY (U.S. Only)
Voice: 360-629-9278
Fax: 360-629-9278
Web: http://www.mabry.com

COST
The cost of DFInfo and the C/C++ source code (of the control itself) is US$50 (US$55 for International orders).

Prices are subject to change without notice.

DELIVERY METHODS
We can ship this software to you via air mail or email.

Mabry Software, Inc. HTTP://www.mabry.com

Air Mail—you will receive disks, a printed manual, and printed receipt if you choose this delivery method. The costs are

US$10.00	US Priority Mail
US$15.00	Airborne Express 2nd Day (US deliveries only)
US$20.00	Airborne Express Overnight (US deliveries only)
US$20.00	Global Priority Mail (Int'l deliveries only; Western Europe, Pacific Rim and Canada only)
US$45.00	International Airborne Express (Int'l deliveries only)

Email—We can ship this package to you via email. You need to have an email account that can accept large file attachments (which includes CompuServe, AOL, and most Internet providers). If you choose this option, please note: a printed manual is not included. We will, however, email a receipt to you.

Be sure to include your full mailing address with your order. Sometimes (on the Internet) the package cannot be emailed, so we are forced to send it through normal mail.

CompuServe Email—CompuServe members can use the software registration forum (GO SWREG) to register this package. DFInfo's SWREG ID number is 1069. The source code version's ID number is 1070. PLEASE NOTE: When you order through SWREG, we send the registered package to your CompuServe account (not your Internet or AOL account) within a few hours.

ORDER/PAYMENT METHODS

You can order this software by phone, fax, email, mail. Please note that orders must include all information that is requested on our order form. Your shipment WILL BE DELAYED if we have to contact you for additional information (such as phone number, street address, and so on).

You can pay by credit card (VISA, MasterCard, American Express, Discover, NOVUS), check (U.S. dollars drawn on a U.S. bank), cash, International Money Order, International Postal Order, Purchase Order (established business entities only—terms net 30), or wire transfer.

WIRE TRANSFER INFORMATION

Here is the information you need regarding our account for a wire funds transfer:

Bank Name:	SeaFirst—Stone Way Branch
Bank Address:	3601 Stone Way North
	Seattle, WA 98103
Bank Phone:	206-585-4951
Account Name:	Mabry Software, Inc.
Routing Number:	12000024
Account Number:	16311706

DFInfo

If you are paying with a wire transfer of funds, please add US$25.00 to your order. This is the fee that SeaFirst Bank charges Mabry Software. Also, please ADD ANY ADDITIONAL FEES THAT YOUR BANK MIGHT CHARGE for wire transfer service. If you are paying with a wire transfer, we must have full payment deposited to our account before we can ship your order.

Copyright © 1993–1998 by Mabry Software, Inc.

DFInfo Order Form

Mail this form to

Mabry Software, Inc.
503 316th Street Northwest
Stanwood, WA 98292

Phone: 360-629-9278
Fax: 360-629-9278
Internet: mabry@mabry.com
Web: www.mabry.com

Where did you get this copy of DFInfo? _____

Name: _____

Ship to: _____

_____

_____

Phone: _____

Fax: _____

Email: _____

Credit Card #: _____ exp. _____

P.O. # (if any): _____

Signature _____

Qty ordered____ SOURCE CODE AND REGISTRATION

$50.00 ($55.00 international). Check or money order in U.S. currency drawn on a U.S. bank. Add $10.00 per order for shipping and handling.

Indic

Description
Horizontal and vertical Indicator OCX custom controls allow you to create professional VU segmented meters. This custom control was specially designed to allow you to easily create state-of-the-art graphic LED VU meters. Three separate colored segment sections can be defined with up to twenty LED segments per section. A comprehensive set of 3-D bevel properties allows for flexible visual control.

- Horizontal and vertical indicator (otherwise known as a VU meter).
- Display information (such as volume, balance, and so on)
- A comprehensive set of 3-D bevel properties allows for flexible visual control.
- Three separate colored segment sections can be defined with up to twenty LED segments per section.

A Visual Basic sample project, VU Meter, is included to show off some of the properties of VINDIC. It allows you to play with the VU Indicator properties to see how cool you can make a VU meter look.

File Name
HINDIC32.OCX, VINDIC32.OCX

ActiveX/OCX Object Name
Mabry.HIndicCtrl/Mabry.VIndicCtrl

ActiveX Compatibility
VB 4.0 (32-bit), 5.0 and 6.0

ActiveX Built With
Microsoft Visual C++ v4

ActiveX—Required DLLs
MFC40.DLL (October 6th, 1995 or later)

OLEPRO32.DLL (October 6th, 1995 or later)

MSVCRT40.DLL (September 29th, 1995 or later)

Mabry Software, Inc.

HTTP://www.mabry.com

Distribution Note

When you develop and distribute an application that uses this control, you should install the control file into the user's Windows SYSTEM directory. The control file has version information built into it. So, during installation, you should ensure that you are not overwriting a newer version.

Indic Properties

Properties that have special meaning for this control or that apply only to this control are marked with an asterisk (*).

BackColor Property	*ItemForeColor1 Property
*BevelInner Property	*ItemForeColor2 Property
*BevelOuter Property	*ItemForeColor3 Property
*BevelWidth Property	Left Property
*Border Property	*Max Property
*BorderWidth Property	*Min Property
Enabled Property	Name Property
Height Property	Parent Property
hWnd Property	Tag Property
Index Property	Top Property
*ItemBackColor Property	*Value Property
*ItemCount1 Property	*Version Property
*ItemCount2 Property	Visible Property
*ItemCount3 Property	Width Property

Indic Events

Events that have special meaning for this control or that apply only to this control are marked with an asterisk (*).

Click Event

DblClick Event

Bevel Properties Example

In this example, the program shows what happens when you vary the bevels on the controls. To try this example, paste the code into the Declarations section of a form that contains a horizontal indicator and a horizontal scroll bar. Press F5. Play with the scroll bar.

```
Sub Form_Load ()
    Form1.BackColor = &HC0C0C0
```

```
    HScroll1.Min = 0
    HScroll1.Max = 3
    HScroll1.Value = 0

    HIndicator1.BackColor = &HC0C0C0
End Sub

Sub HScroll1_Scroll ()
    HIndicator1.BevelInner = HScroll1.Value
    HIndicator1.BevelOuter = HScroll1.Value
End Sub
```

ItemBackColor Property Example

In this example, the program shows what happens when you vary the gap. To try this example, paste the code into the Declarations section of a form that contains a horizontal scroll bar, a label, and a horizontal slider control. Press F5. Play with the horizontal scroll bar.

```
Sub Command1_Click ()
    CMDialog1.Color = HIndicator1.ItemBackColor
    CMDialog1.Flags = 1
    CMDialog1.Action = 3

    HIndicator1.ItemBackColor = CMDialog1.Color
End Sub

Sub Form_Load ()
    Form1.BackColor = &HC0C0C0

    Command1.Top = 240
    Command1.Left = 240
    Command1.Width = 1800
    Command1.Height = 360
    Command1.Caption = "Change Color"

    HIndicator1.Top = 720
    HIndicator1.Left = 240
    HIndicator1.Width = 3600
    HIndicator1.Height = 900
    HIndicator1.BevelInner = 3
    HIndicator1.BevelOuter = 1
    HIndicator1.BackColor = &HC0C0C0

    HIndicator1.ItemBackColor = &HC0C0C0
End Sub
```

ItemForeColor and ItemCount Properties Example

In this example, the program shows what happens when you vary the color and count of the items in an indicator. To try this example, paste the code into the Declarations section of a form that contains three horizontal scroll bars, three labels, three command buttons, a common dialog box control, and a horizontal indicator control. Press F5. Play with the command buttons and the scroll bars.

```
Sub Command1_Click ()
    CMDialog1.Color = HIndicator1.ItemForeColor1
    CMDialog1.Flags = 1
    CMDialog1.Action = 3

    HIndicator1.ItemForeColor1 = CMDialog1.Color
End Sub

Sub Command2_Click ()
    CMDialog1.Color = HIndicator1.ItemForeColor2
    CMDialog1.Flags = 1
    CMDialog1.Action = 3

    HIndicator1.ItemForeColor2 = CMDialog1.Color
End Sub

Sub Command3_Click ()
    CMDialog1.Color = HIndicator1.ItemForeColor3
    CMDialog1.Flags = 1
    CMDialog1.Action = 3

HIndicator1.ItemForeColor3 = CMDialog1.Color
End Sub

Sub Form_Load ()
    Form1.BackColor = &HC0C0C0

    HIndicator1.Top = 1680
    HIndicator1.Left = 240
    HIndicator1.Width = 6000
    HIndicator1.Height = 600
    HIndicator1.BevelInner = 3
    HIndicator1.BevelOuter = 1
    HIndicator1.Value = 100
    HIndicator1.BackColor = &HC0C0C0
    HIndicator1.ItemBackColor = &HC0C0C0

    Command1.Top = 240
    Command1.Left = 240
    Command1.Width = 1800
    Command1.Height = 360

Command1.Caption = "Change Color 1"

    HScroll1.Top = 240
    HScroll1.Left = 2160
    HScroll1.Width = 900
```

```
    HScroll1.Min = 0
    HScroll1.Max = 20
    HScroll1.Value = HIndicator1.ItemCount1

    Label1.Top = 240
    Label1.Left = 3180
    Label1.Width = 2000
    Label1.BackColor = &HC0C0C0

    Command2.Top = 720
    Command2.Left = 240
    Command2.Width = 1800
    Command2.Height = 360
    Command2.Caption = "Change Color 2"

    HScroll2.Top = 720
    HScroll2.Left = 2160
    HScroll2.Width = 900
    HScroll2.Min = 0
    HScroll2.Max = 20
    HScroll2.Value = HIndicator1.ItemCount2

    Label2.Top = 720
    Label2.Left = 3180
    Label2.Width = 2000
    Label2.BackColor = &HC0C0C0

    Command3.Top = 1200
    Command3.Left = 240
    Command3.Width = 1800
    Command3.Height = 360
    Command3.Caption = "Change Color 3"

    HScroll3.Top = 1200
    HScroll3.Left = 2160
    HScroll3.Width = 900
    HScroll3.Min = 0
    HScroll3.Max = 20
    HScroll3.Value = HIndicator1.ItemCount3

    Label3.Top = 1200
    Label3.Left = 3180
    Label3.Width = 2000
    Label3.BackColor = &HC0C0C0
End Sub

Sub HScroll1_Change ()
    HIndicator1.ItemCount1 = HScroll1.Value
    Label1.Caption = "ItemCount1: " & HScroll1.Value
End Sub
Sub HScroll1_Scroll ()
```

```
        Call HScroll1_Change
    End Sub

    Sub HScroll2_Change ()
        HIndicator1.ItemCount2 = HScroll2.Value
        Label2.Caption = "ItemCount2: " & HScroll2.Value
    End Sub

    Sub HScroll2_Scroll ()
        Call HScroll2_Change
    End Sub

    Sub HScroll3_Change ()
        HIndicator1.ItemCount3 = HScroll3.Value
        Label3.Caption = "ItemCount3: " & HScroll3.Value
    End Sub

    Sub HScroll3_Scroll ()
        Call HScroll3_Change
    End Sub
```

BevelInner Property

Description
Determines the 3-D style of the border immediately surrounding the control.

Syntax
object.**BevelInner** [= *bevel*]

The syntax of the **BevelInner** property has these parts:

Part	Description
object	An Indic control.
bevel	An integer that determines the style of bevel.

Remarks
The value of this property determines the style of the inner border. This property might be one of four values:

Constant	Value	Description
bcNone	0	Normal frame
bcRaised	1	Raised frame (3-D)
bcInset	2	Inset frame (3-D)
bcLowered	3	Lowered frame (3-D)

Data Type
Integer (enumerated)

BevelOuter Property

Description
Determines the 3-D style of the border (if any) surrounding the control.

Syntax
`object.BevelOuter [= bevel ]`

The syntax of the **BevelOuter** property has these parts:

Part	Description
object	An Indic control.
bevel	An integer that determines the style of bevel.

Remarks
The value of this property determines the style of the outer bevel. This property might be one of four values:

Constant	Value	Description
bcNone	0	Normal frame
bcRaised	1	Raised frame (3-D)
bcInset	2	Inset frame (3-D)
bcLowered	3	Lowered frame (3-D)

Data Type
Integer (enumerated)

BevelWidth Property

Description
Determines the width of the inner and outer bevels.

Syntax
`object.BevelWidth [= width ]`

The syntax of the **BevelWidth** property has these parts:

Part	Description
object	An Indic control.
width	An integer that determines the width of the inner and outer bevels (in pixels).

Remarks
The value of this property determines the width of the inner border (if any, see BevelInner) and the outer border (if any, see Border and BevelOuter). This is always measured in pixels.

Data Type
Integer

Border Property

Description
Determines if a border is used.

Syntax
`object.Border [= border ]`

The syntax of the **Border** property has these parts:

Part	Description
object	An Indic control.
border	An integer that determines if a border is present.

Remarks
The value of this property determines if a border is present. If this property is set to None, no border (inner bevel or outer bevel) is displayed. This property might be one of the following values:

Constant	Value	Description
bNone	0	None
bSingle	1	Single width

Data Type
Integer (enumerated)

BorderWidth Property

Description
Determines the distance between the inner border and the outer border.

Syntax
`object.BorderWidth [= width ]`

The syntax of the **BorderWidth** property has these parts:

Part	Description
object	An Indic control.
width	An integer that determines the distance between the inner and outer bevels (in pixels).

Indic

Remarks
The value of this property determines the distance between the inner border (if any, see the BevelInner property) and the outer border (if any, see the BevelOuter property). This property is always measured in pixels.

Data Type
Integer

ItemBackColor Property

Description
Determines the color of the background of the items.

Syntax
`object.ItemBackColor [= background ]`

The syntax of the **ItemBackColor** property has these parts:

Part	Description
object	An Indic control.
background	A color expression that determines the color of an indicator "light" when "off."

Remarks
This property specifies the color of the item backgrounds. The items are filled with this color when not "on" (that is, filled with one of the ItemForeColors).

Data Type
Color

ItemCount1, ItemCount2 and ItemCount3 Properties

Description
Determines the number of items in the indicator.

Syntax
`object.ItemCount1 [= count ]`
`object.ItemCount2 [= count ]`
`object.ItemCount3 [= count ]`

The syntax of the **ItemCount1**, **ItemCount2** and **ItemCount3** properties has these parts:

Part	Description
object	An Indic control.
count	An integer that determines the number of items in each segment of the indicator.

Remarks

This property specifies the number of the items in the control. These properties must be greater than or equal to zero. If all three are zero, no items are displayed.

The first ItemCount1 items are painted with ItemForeColor1. The next ItemCount2 items are painted with ItemForeColor2. And, the remaining ItemCount3 items are painted with ItemForeColor3.

Data Type
Integer

ItemForeColor1, ItemForeColor2 and ItemForeColor3 Properties

Description
Determines the color of the selected items.

Syntax
```
object.ItemForeColor1 [= item ]
object.ItemForeColor2 [= item ]
object.ItemForeColor3 [= item ]
```

The syntax of the **ItemForeColor1**, **ItemForeColor2** and **ItemForeColor3** properties has these parts:

Part	Description
object	An Indic control.
item	A color expression that determines the color of the segments in the indicator.

Remarks
This property specifies the color of the items when they are selected (this is dependent upon the Min, Max, Value, and ItemCount properties).

The first ItemCount1 items are painted with ItemForeColor1. The next ItemCount2 items are painted with ItemForeColor2. And the remaining ItemCount3 items are painted with ItemForeColor3.

Data Type
Color

Max and Min Properties

Description
Determines the range of values for this control.

Indic

Syntax
```
object.Max [= value ]
object.Min [= value ]
```

The syntax of the **Max** and **Min** properties has these parts:

Part	Description
object	An Indic control.
value	An integer that determins the outside range of the value.

Remarks
These properties determine the range of values for the control in question. If Max is set to less than Min, the range of values is swapped.

Data Type
Integer

Value Property

Description
Specifies the current position of the indicator.

Syntax
```
object.Value [= value ]
```

The syntax of the **Value** property has these parts:

Part	Description
object	An Indic control.
value	An integer that determines the current position of the control.

Remarks
This property determines the current value of the control. This is the default property.

This property must range from Max to Min.

Data Type
Integer

Version Property

Description
Returns the version of the control.

Syntax
```
object.Version
```

Mabry Software, Inc.

HTTP://www.mabry.com

The syntax of the **Version** property has these parts:

Part	Description
object	An Indic control.

Remarks

This property holds the current version of the control. It is read-only and available at both design time and runtime.

Data Type

String

How to Buy the Source Code for This Control

CREDITS

Indic was written by James Shields.

CONTACT INFORMATION

Orders, inquiries, technical support, questions, comments, and so on can be sent to mabry@mabry.com on the Internet. Our mailing address/contact information is

Mabry Software, Inc.
503 316th Street Northwest
Stanwood, WA 98292

Sales: 1-800-99-MABRY (U.S. only)
Voice: 360-629-9278
Fax: 360-629-9278
Web: http://www.mabry.com

COST

The cost of Indic and the C/C++ source code (of the control itself) is US$60 (US$65 for International orders).

Prices are subject to change without notice.

DELIVERY METHODS

We can ship this software to you via air mail or email.

Air Mail—you will receive disks, a printed manual, and printed receipt if you choose this delivery method. The costs are

US$10.00	US Priority Mail
US$15.00	Airborne Express 2nd Day (US deliveries only)
US$20.00	Airborne Express Overnight (US deliveries only)
US$20.00	Global Priority Mail (Int'l deliveries only; Western Europe, Pacific Rim and Canada only)
US$45.00	International Airborne Express (Int'l deliveries only)

Email—We can ship this package to you via email. You need to have an email account that can accept large file attachments (which includes CompuServe, AOL, and most Internet providers). If you choose this option, please note: a printed manual is not included. We will, however, email a receipt to you.

Be sure to include your full mailing address with your order. Sometimes (on the Internet) the package cannot be emailed, so we are forced to send it through normal mail.

CompuServe Email—CompuServe members can use the software registration forum (GO SWREG) to register this package. Indic's SWREG ID number is 10289. The source code version's ID number is 10291. PLEASE NOTE: When you order through SWREG, we send the registered package to your CompuServe account (not your Internet or AOL account) within a few hours.

ORDER/PAYMENT METHODS

You can order this software by phone, fax, email, mail. Please note that orders must include all information that is requested on our order form. Your shipment WILL BE DELAYED if we have to contact you for additional information (such as phone number, street address, and so on).

You can pay by credit card (VISA, MasterCard, American Express, Discover, NOVUS), check (U.S. dollars drawn on a U.S. bank), cash, International Money Order, International Postal Order, Purchase Order (established business entities only—terms net 30), or wire transfer.

WIRE TRANSFER INFORMATION

Here is the information you need regarding our account for a wire funds transfer:

Bank Name:	SeaFirst—Stone Way Branch
Bank Address:	3601 Stone Way North
	Seattle, WA 98103
Bank Phone:	206-585-4951
Account Name:	Mabry Software, Inc.
Routing Number:	12000024
Account Number:	16311706

If you are paying with a wire transfer of funds, please add US$25.00 to your order. This is the fee that SeaFirst Bank charges Mabry Software. Also, please ADD ANY ADDITIONAL FEES THAT YOUR BANK MIGHT CHARGE for wire transfer service. If you are paying with a wire transfer, we must have full payment deposited to our account before we can ship your order.

Copyright © 1996–1998 by Mabry Software, Inc.

Mabry Software, Inc.

HTTP://www.mabry.com

Indic Order Form

Mail this form to
Mabry Software, Inc.   Phone: 360-629-9278
503 316th Street Northwest   Fax: 360-629-9278
Stanwood, WA 98292   Internet: mabry@mabry.com
                              Web: www.mabry.com

Where did you get this copy of Indic? _____

Name: _____

Ship to: _____

_____

_____

_____

Phone: _____

Fax: _____

Email:_____

Credit Card #: _____ exp. _____

P.O. # (if any): _____

Signature _____

Qty ordered____ SOURCE CODE AND REGISTRATION

$60.00 ($65.00 international). Check or money order in U.S. currency drawn on a U.S. bank. Add $10.00 per order for shipping and handling.

JoyStk

Description
JoyStk gives joystick information (movement, buttons) for your programs. It supports two joysticks, one 4-button joystick or one 3-D joystick.

File Name
JOYSTK32.OCX

ActiveX / OCX Object Name
Mabry.JoyStkCtrl

ActiveX Compatibility
VB 4.0 (32-bit), 5.0 and 6.0

ActiveX Built With
Microsoft Visual C++ v4

ActiveX—Required DLLs
MFC40.DLL (October 6th, 1995 or later)

OLEPRO32.DLL (October 6th, 1995 or later)

MSVCRT40.DLL (September 29th, 1995 or later)

Remarks
JoyStk requires that a Windows joystick driver is installed.

When using JoyStk, be sure to set the Enabled property to True at runtime. If this is not done, the control will not function. Merely making sure that the Enabled property is True at design time is not enough. Also, you should ensure that Enabled is set to False prior to exiting.

Distribution Note
When you develop and distribute an application that uses this control, you should install the control file into the user's Windows SYSTEM directory. The control file has version information built into it. So, during installation, you should ensure that you are not overwriting a newer version.

JoyStk Properties
Properties that have special meaning for this control or that apply only to this control are marked with an asterisk (*).

Align Property
*Button1 Property
*Button2 Property
*Button3 Property
*Button4 Property
*Buttons Property
*Devices Property
Enabled Property
HelpContextID Property
hWnd Property
Index Property
Left Property
*Manufacturer Property
Name Property
*Period Property
*PeriodMax Property
*PeriodMin Property

*Port Property
*Product Property
*ProductName Property
Tag Property
*Threshold Property
Top Property
*Version Property
*XMax Property
*XMin Property
*XPos Property
*YMax Property
*YMin Property
*YPos Property
*ZMax Property
*ZMin Property
*ZPos Property

JoyStk Events

Events that have special meaning for this control or that apply only to it are marked with an asterisk (*).

*ButtonDown Event

*ButtonUp Event

*Move Event

Button Event Example

In this example, the labels show which buttons are down and which are up. To try this example, paste the code into the Declarations section of a form that contains two labels and a JoyStk control. Press F5.

```
Sub Form_Load ()
    Joystick1.Enabled = True

    Call JoystickCheck
End Sub

Sub Form_Unload (Cancel As Integer)
```

JoyStk

```
        Joystick1.Enabled = False
End Sub

Sub Joystick1_ButtonDown (Button As Integer)
    Call JoystickCheck
End Sub

Sub Joystick1_ButtonUp (Button As Integer)
    Call JoystickCheck
End Sub

Sub JoystickCheck ()
    Dim Up As String
    Dim Down As String

    If Not Joystick1.Button1 Then
        Up = Up + "1"
    Else
        Down = Down + "1"
    End If

    If Joystick1.Buttons >= 2 Then
        If Not Joystick1.Button2 Then
            Up = Up + "2"
        Else
            Down = Down + "2"
        End If
    End If

    If Joystick1.Buttons >= 3 Then
        If Not Joystick1.Button3 Then
            Up = Up + "3"
        Else
            Down = Down + "3"
        End If
    End If

    If Joystick1.Buttons >= 4 Then
         If Not Joystick1.Button4 Then
            Up = Up + "4"
        Else
            Down = Down + "4"
        End If
    End If

    Label1.Caption = "Up: " & Up
    Label2.Caption = "Down: " & Down
End Sub
```

Information Properties Example

In this example, the program shows the informational properties. To try this example, paste the code into the Declarations section of a form that contains seven labels and a JoyStk control. Make sure that the Port property of the JoyStk control is set properly. Press F5. You'll see the settings of all the informational properties.

```
Sub Form_Load ()
    Joystick1.Enabled = True

    Label1.Caption = "Buttons: " & Joystick1.Buttons
    Label2.Caption = "Devices: " & Joystick1.Devices
    Label3.Caption = "Manufacturer: " & Joystick1.Manufacturer
    Label4.Caption = "PeriodMin: " & Joystick1.PeriodMin
    Label5.Caption = "PeriodMax: " & Joystick1.PeriodMax
    Label6.Caption = "Product: " & Joystick1.Product
    Label7.Caption = "ProductName: " & Joystick1.ProductName

    Joystick1.Enabled = False
End Sub
```

Period Property Example

In this example, the program shows the effects of different settings for the Period property. To try this example, paste the code into the Declarations section of a form that contains a horizontal scroll bar, two labels, and a JoyStk control. Press F5. Play with the horizontal scroll bar, and then try the joystick, the scroll bar again, and so on

```
Sub Form_Load ()
    Joystick1.Enabled = True

    HScroll1.Min = Joystick1.PeriodMin
    HScroll1.Max = Joystick1.PeriodMax
    HScroll1.Value = (Joystick1.PeriodMax + Joystick1.PeriodMin) / 2

    Call HScroll1_Change
End Sub

Sub Form_Unload (Cancel As Integer)
    Joystick1.Enabled = False
End Sub

Sub HScroll1_Change ()
    Label1.Caption = "Period: " & HScroll1.Value & " milliseconds"

    ' need to disable the joystick while doing this
    Joystick1.Enabled = False
    Joystick1.Period = HScroll1.Value
    Joystick1.Enabled = True
End Sub

Sub HScroll1_Scroll ()
```

JoyStk

```
        Call HScroll1_Change
End Sub

Sub Joystick1_Move (X As Integer, Y As Integer, Z As Integer)
    Label2.Caption = "Position: " & X & "," & Y
End Sub
```

Positional Properties Example

In this example, the program shows the changes in the position of the joystick when run. It also shows the relative amount (as compared to XMin, XMax, YMin, and YMax). To try this example, paste the code into the Declarations section of a form that contains two labels and a JoyStk control. Press F5. Then play with the joystick.

```
Sub Form_Load ()
    Joystick1.Enabled = True
End Sub

Sub Form_Unload (Cancel As Integer)
    Joystick1.Enabled = False
End Sub

Sub Joystick1_Move (X As Integer, Y As Integer, Z As Integer)
    Dim XP As Integer
    Dim YP As Integer

    Label1.Caption = "Position: " & X & "," & Y

    XP = (100 * (X - Joystick1.XMin)) / (Joystick1.XMax - Joystick1.XMin)
    YP = (100 * (Y - Joystick1.YMin)) / (Joystick1.YMax - Joystick1.YMin)
    Label2.Caption = "Relative: X " & XP & "%   Y " & YP & "%"
End Sub
```

Threshold Property Example

In this example, the program shows the effects of different settings for the Threshold property. To try this example, paste the code into the Declarations section of a form that contains a horizontal scroll bar, two labels, and a JoyStk control. Press F5. Play with the horizontal scroll bar, and then try the joystick, the scroll bar again, and so on

```
Sub Form_Load ()
    Joystick1.Enabled = True

    HScroll1.Min = 1
    HScroll1.Max = 32000
    HScroll1.Value = 100

    Call HScroll1_Change
End Sub

Sub Form_Unload (Cancel As Integer)
    Joystick1.Enabled = False
```

```
    End Sub

    Sub HScroll1_Change ()
        Label1.Caption = "Threshold: " & HScroll1.Value & " units"

        ' need to disable the joystick while doing this
        Joystick1.Enabled = False
        Joystick1.Threshold = HScroll1.Value
        Joystick1.Enabled = True
    End Sub

    Sub HScroll1_Scroll ()
        Call HScroll1_Change
    End Sub

    Sub Joystick1_Move (X As Integer, Y As Integer, Z As Integer)
        Label2.Caption = "Position: " & X & "," & Y
    End Sub
```

Button1, Button2, Button3, and Button4 Properties

Description
Returns the current state of the joystick's buttons.

Syntax
object.**Button1**
object.**Button2**
object.**Button3**
object.**Button4**

The syntax of the **Button1**, **Button2**, **Button3**, and **Button4** properties has these parts:

Part	Description
object	A JoyStk control.

Remarks
These properties tell you which button(s) were pressed at the last time the joystick was polled (see the Period property). They are read-only at runtime only. They are valid only after the joystick has been enabled.

Data Type
Integer (Boolean)

ButtonDown Event

Description
Occurs when the user pushes one or more of the joystick's buttons.

JoyStk

Syntax
`Sub object_ButtonDown([index As Integer,] button As Integer)`

The syntax of the **ButtonDown** event has these parts:

Part	Description
object	A JoyStk control.
index	An integer that identifies a control if it's in a control array.
button	An integer that specifies the button pressed.

Remarks
This event only occurs when a button is pressed. The joystick must be enabled for this event to happen.

button represents the button pressed.

Buttons Property

Description
Returns the number of buttons on the joystick.

Syntax
`object.Buttons`

The syntax of the **Buttons** property has these parts:

Part	Description
object	A JoyStk control.

Remarks
This property returns the number of buttons on the joystick.

This property is read-only at runtime only. It is valid only after the joystick has been enabled.

Data Type
Integer

ButtonUp Event

Description
Occurs when the user releases one or more of the joystick's buttons.

Syntax
`Sub object_ButtonUp([index As Integer,] button As Integer)`

The syntax of the **ButtonUp** event has these parts:

Part	Description
object	A JoyStk control.
index	An integer that identifies a control if it's in a control array.
button	An integer that specifies the joystick button released.

Remarks
This event only occurs when a button is released. The joystick must be enabled for this event to happen.

button represents the button pressed.

Devices Property

Description
Returns the number of joysticks supported by the current driver.

Syntax
object.**Devices**

The syntax of the **Devices** property has these parts:

Part	Description
object	A JoyStk control.

Remarks
This property tells you how many joysticks are supported in the system.

This property is read-only at runtime only. It is valid only after the joystick has been enabled.

Data Type
Integer

Manufacturer Property

Description
Returns the manufacturer's ID of the joystick.

Syntax
object.**Manufacturer**

The syntax of the **Manufacturer** property has these parts:

Part	Description
object	A JoyStk control.

JoyStk

Remarks
This represents the manufacturer of the driver. The values returned are

Value	Description
1	Microsoft

This property is read-only at runtime only. It is valid only after the joystick has been enabled.

Data Type
Integer

Move Event

Description
Occurs when the user moves the joystick.

Syntax
`Sub object_Move([index As Integer,] X As Long, Y As Long, Z As Long)`

The syntax of the **Move** event has these parts:

Part	Description
object	A JoyStk control.
index	An integer that identifies a control if it's in a control array.
X	A long integer that specifies the joystick's new X position.
Y	A long integer that specifies the joystick's new Y position.
Z	A long integer that specifies the joystick's new Z position.

Remarks
This event occurs when the joystick's position changes. The change must be larger than the current setting of the Threshold property. The joystick must be enabled for this event to happen.

X, Y, and Z represent the joystick's new position (Z is only valid for 3-D joysticks).

Period Property

Description
Sets the polling interval for the joystick.

Syntax
`object.Period [= integer ]`

The syntax of the **Period** property has these parts:

Part	Description
object	A JoyStk control.
integer	An integer that specifies the polling rate of the joystick driver, in milliseconds.

Remarks
This property determines the polling rate (in milliseconds) of the joystick.

When changing this property at runtime, the control should be disabled prior to changing it, and then re-enabled afterwards.

Data Type
Integer

PeriodMax and PeriodMin Properties

Description
Returns the minimum and maximum times between polling that this joystick supports.

Syntax
`object.PeriodMax`
`object.PeriodMin`

The syntax of the **PeriodMax** and **PeriodMin** properties has these parts:

Part	Description
object	A JoyStk control.

Remarks
These properties specify the minimum and maximum times between polling that the joystick driver supports (see the Period property).

This property is read-only at runtime only. It is valid only after the joystick has been enabled.

Data Type
Integer

Port Property

Description
Determines which joystick port to use.

Syntax
`object.Port [= integer ]`

The syntax of the **Port** property has these parts:

Part	Description
object	A JoyStk control.
integer	An integer that determines the joystick port to use.

JoyStk

Remarks
This property determines which joystick to use. The allowable values are

Value	Description
1	Joystick 1, 3-D joystick, or 4-button joystick
2	Joystick 2

This property must be set at design time.

Data Type
Integer

Product Property

Description
Returns the product ID for the joystick driver.

Syntax
`object.Product`

The syntax of the **Product** property has these parts:

Part	Description
object	A JoyStk control.

Remarks
This represents the product ID of the driver. The values returned are

Value	Description
1	Microsoft MIDI Mapper
2	Microsoft Wave Mapper
3	Sound Blaster MIDI output port
4	Sound Blaster MIDI input port
5	Sound Blaster internal synthesizer
6	Sound Blaster waveform output port
7	Sound Blaster waveform input port
9	AdLib-compatible synthesizer
10	MPU401 MIDI output port
11	MPU401 MIDI input port
12	IBM Game Control Adapter

This property is read-only at runtime only. It is valid only after the joystick has been enabled.

Data Type
Integer

ProductName Property

Description
Returns the product name of the joystick driver.

Syntax
object.`ProductName`

The syntax of the **ProductName** property has these parts:

Part	Description
object	A JoyStk control.

Remarks
This property specifies the product name of the joystick driver.

This property is read-only at runtime only. It is valid only after the joystick has been enabled.

Data Type
String

Threshold Property

Description
Determines the amount the joystick must move for an event to be fired.

Syntax
object.`Threshold` [= *threshold*]

The syntax of the **Threshold** property has these parts:

Part	Description
object	A JoyStk control.
threshold	An integer that specifies the distance the joystick must move before JoyStk fires a Move event.

Remarks
This property determines how much the joystick must move for a Move event to be fired.

When changing this property at runtime, the control should be disabled prior to changing it and re-enabled afterwards.

Data Type
Integer

JoyStk

Version Property

Description
Returns the version of the control.

Syntax
`object.Version`

The syntax of the **Version** property has these parts:

Part	Description
object	A JoyStk control.

Remarks
This property holds the current version of the control. It is read-only and available at both design time and runtime.

Data Type
String

XMax, XMin, YMax, YMin, ZMax, and ZMin Properties

Description
Returns the full range of the joystick's position.

Syntax
`object.XMax`
`object.XMin`
`object.YMax`
`object.YMin`
`object.ZMax`
`object.ZMin`

The syntax of the **XMax, XMin, YMax, YMin, ZMax,** and **ZMin** properties has these parts:

Part	Description
object	A JoyStk control.

Remarks
These properties tell you the full range of the joystick's position. They are read-only at runtime only. They are valid only after the joystick has been enabled.

Data Type
Integer (long)

XPos, YPos, and ZPos Properties

Description
Returns the current position of the joystick.

Syntax
object.XPos
object.YPos
object.ZPos

The syntax of the **XPos, YPos,** and **ZPos** properties has these parts:

Part	Description
object	A JoyStk control.

Remarks
These properties tell you where the joystick was the last time it was polled (see the Period property). They are read-only at runtime only. They are valid only after the joystick has been enabled.

Data Type
Integer (long)

How to Buy the Source Code for This Control

CREDITS
JoyStk was written by Zane Thomas.

CONTACT INFORMATION
Orders, inquiries, technical support, questions, comments, and so on can be sent to mabry@mabry.com on the Internet. Our mailing address/contact information is

Mabry Software, Inc.
503 316th Street Northwest
Stanwood, WA 98292

Sales: 1-800-99-MABRY (U.S. Only)
Voice: 360-629-9278
Fax: 360-629-9278
Web: http://www.mabry.com

COST
The cost of JoyStk and the C/C++ source code (of the control itself) is US$60 (US$65 for International orders).

Prices are subject to change without notice.

DELIVERY METHODS
We can ship this software to you via air mail or email.

Air Mail—you will receive disks, a printed manual, and printed receipt if you choose this delivery method. The costs are

US$10.00	US Priority Mail
US$15.00	Airborne Express 2nd Day (US deliveries only)
US$20.00	Airborne Express Overnight (US deliveries only)
US$20.00	Global Priority Mail (Int'l deliveries only; Western Europe, Pacific Rim and Canada only)
US$45.00	International Airborne Express (Int'l deliveries only)

Email—We can ship this package to you via email. You need to have an email account that can accept large file attachments (which includes CompuServe, AOL, and most Internet providers). If you choose this option, please note: a printed manual is not included. We will, however, email a receipt to you.

Be sure to include your full mailing address with your order. Sometimes (on the Internet) the package cannot be emailed, so we are forced to send it through normal mail.

CompuServe Email—CompuServe members can use the software registration forum (GO SWREG) to register this package. JoyStk's SWREG ID number is 1340. The source code version's ID number is 1341. PLEASE NOTE: When you order through SWREG, we send the registered package to your CompuServe account (not your Internet or AOL account) within a few hours.

ORDER/PAYMENT METHODS

You can order this software by phone, fax, email, or mail. Please note that orders must include all information that is requested on our order form. Your shipment WILL BE DELAYED if we have to contact you for additional information (such as phone number, street address, and so on).

You can pay by credit card (VISA, MasterCard, American Express, Discover, NOVUS), check (U.S. dollars drawn on a U.S. bank), cash, International Money Order, International Postal Order, Purchase Order (established business entities only—terms net 30), or wire transfer.

WIRE TRANSFER INFORMATION

Here is the information you need regarding our account for a wire funds transfer:

Bank Name:	SeaFirst—Stone Way Branch
Bank Address:	3601 Stone Way North
	Seattle, WA 98103
Bank Phone:	206-585-4951
Account Name:	Mabry Software, Inc.
Routing Number:	12000024
Account Number:	16311706

Mabry Software, Inc.   HTTP://www.mabry.com

If you are paying with a wire transfer of funds, please add US$25.00 to your order. This is the fee that SeaFirst Bank charges Mabry Software. Also, please ADD ANY ADDITIONAL FEES THAT YOUR BANK MIGHT CHARGE for wire transfer service. If you are paying with a wire transfer, we must have full payment deposited to our account before we can ship your order.

Copyright © 1993–1998 by Mabry Software, Inc.

JoyStk Order Form

Mail this form to

Mabry Software, Inc.
503 316th Street Northwest
Stanwood, WA 98292

Phone: 360-629-9278
Fax: 360-629-9278
Internet: mabry@mabry.com
Web: www.mabry.com

Where did you get this copy of JoyStk? _____

Name: _____

Ship to: _____

_____

_____

Phone: _____

Fax: _____

Email: _____

Credit Card #: _____ exp. _____

P.O. # (if any): _____

Signature _____

Qty ordered____ SOURCE CODE AND REGISTRATION

$60.00 ($65.00 international). Check or money order in U.S. currency drawn on a U.S. bank. Add $10.00 per order for shipping and handling.

LED

Description
A Visual Basic custom control that behaves like an LED. 3-D effects and colors are all user definable.

File Name
LED32.OCX

ActiveX/OCX Object Name
Mabry.LED

ActiveX Compatibility
VB 4.0 (32-bit), 5.0, and 6.0

ActiveX Built With
Microsoft Visual C++ v4

ActiveX—Required DLLs
MFC40.DLL (October 6th, 1995 or later)

OLEPRO32.DLL (October 6th, 1995 or later)

MSVCRT40.DLL (September 29th, 1995 or later)

Distribution Note
When you develop and distribute an application that uses this control, you should install the control file into the user's Windows SYSTEM directory. The control file has version information built into it. So, during installation, you should ensure that you are not overwriting a newer version.

LED Properties
Properties that have special meaning for this control or that only apply to this control are marked with an asterisk (*).

*BevelInner Property   *BevelWidthInner Property

*BevelOuter Property   *BevelWidthOuter Property

*BevelShapeInner Property   *BorderWidth Property

*BevelShapeOuter Property   *DisabledColor Property

Mabry Software, Inc.

HTTP://www.mabry.com

Enabled Property
Height Property
hWnd Property
Index Property
Left Property
Name Property
*OffColor Property
*OnColor Property

Parent Property
Tag Property
Top Property
*Value Property
*Version Property
Visible Property
Width Property

LED Events

Events that have special meaning for this control or that apply only to this control are marked with an asterisk (*).

Click Event
DblClick Event
DragDrop Event
DragOver Event
MouseDown Event
MouseMove Event
MouseUp Event

Bevel Properties Example

In this example, the program changes styles of the bevels used. To try this example, paste the code into the Declarations section of a form that contains two horizontal scroll bars (one for BevelInner, and one for BevelOuter), two labels (which show the properties), and an LED control. Press F5. Play with the scroll bars to see things change.

```
Sub Form_Load ()
    Me.BackColor = RGB(192, 192, 192)

    HScroll1.Value = 0
    HScroll1.Min = 0
    HScroll1.Max = 3

    HScroll2.Value = 0
    HScroll2.Min = 0
    HScroll2.Max = 3

    Call HScroll1_Change
    Call HScroll2_Change
End Sub
```

LED

```
Sub HScroll1_Change ()
    LED1.BevelInner = HScroll2.Value
    Label1.Caption = "BevelInner:" & Format$( HScroll1.Value )
End Sub

Sub HScroll1_Scroll ()
    Call HScroll1_Change
End Sub

Sub HScroll2_Change ()
    LED1.BevelOuter = HScroll3.Value
    Label2.Caption = "BevelOuter:" & Format$( HScroll2.Value )
End Sub

Sub HScroll2_Scroll ()
    Call HScroll2_Change
End Sub
```

Width Properties Example

In this example, the program varies the width of bevels. To try this example, paste the code into the Declarations section of a form that contains three horizontal scroll bars, three labels, and an LED control. Press F5. Play with the scroll bars to see things change.

```
Sub Form_Load ()
    HScroll1.Value = LED1.BevelWidthOuter
    HScroll1.Min = 0
    HScroll1.Max = 10

    HScroll2.Value = LED1.BevelWidthInner
    HScroll2.Min = 0
    HScroll2.Max = 10

    HScroll3.Value = LED1.BorderWidth
    HScroll3.Min = 0
    HScroll3.Max = 10

    Call HScroll1_Change
    Call HScroll2_Change
    Call HScroll3_Change
End Sub

Sub HScroll1_Change ()
    LED1.BevelWidthOuter = HScroll1.Value
    Label1.Caption = "BevelWidthOuter:" & Format$( HScroll1.Value )
End Sub

Sub HScroll1_Scroll ()
    Call HScroll1_Change
End Sub
```

```
Sub HScroll2_Change ()
    LED1.BevelWidthInner = HScroll3.Value
    Label2.Caption = "BevelWidthInner:" & Format$( HScroll2.Value )
End Sub

Sub HScroll2_Scroll ()
    Call HScroll2_Change
End Sub

Sub HScroll3_Change ()
    LED1.BorderWidth = HScroll3.Value
    Label3.Caption = "BorderWidth:" & Format$( HScroll3.Value )
End Sub

Sub HScroll3_Scroll ()
    Call HScroll3_Change
End Sub
```

BevelInner Property

Description
Determines the 3-D style of the border immediately surrounding the LED area.

Syntax
object.**BevelInner** [= *integer*]

The syntax of the **BevelInner** property has these parts:

Part	Description
object	An LED control.
integer	An integer that determines the bevel style.

Remarks
The value of this property determines the style of the LED's border. This property might be one of five values:

Constant	Value	Description
msBevelNone	0	No frame
msBevelRaised	1	Raised frame (3-D)
msBevelInset	2	Inset frame (3-D)
msBevelLowered	3	Lowered frame (3-D)
msBevelSolid	4	Solid frame

Data Type
Integer (enumerated)

BevelOuter Property

Description
Determines the 3-D style of the border (if any) surrounding the control.

Syntax
object.BevelOuter [= integer]

The syntax of the **BevelOuter** property has these parts:

Part	Description
object	An LED control.
integer	An integer that determines the bevel style.

Remarks
The value of this property determines the style of the control's border. This property might be one of five values:

Constant	Value	Description
msBevelNone	0	No frame
msBevelRaised	1	Raised frame (3-D)
msBevelInset	2	Inset frame (3-D)
msBevelLowered	3	Lowered frame (3-D)
msBevelSolid	4	Solid frame

Data Type
Integer (enumerated)

BevelShapeInner Property

Description
Determines the shape of the 3-D style of the border immediately surrounding the LED area.

Syntax
object.BevelShapeInner [= integer]

The syntax of the **BevelShapeInner** property has these parts:

Part	Description
object	An LED control.
integer	An integer that determines the shape of the inner bevel.

Remarks
The value of this property determines the shape of the LED's border. If the BevelShapeOuter property is set to 1 (Ellipse), this property is automatically set to 1.

This property might be one of two values:

Constant	Value	Description
msShapeRectangle	0	Rectangle
msShapeEllipse	1	Ellipse

Data Type
Integer (enumerated)

BevelShapeOuter Property

Description
Determines the shape of the 3-D style of the border surrounding the control.

Syntax
object.**BevelShapeOuter** [= *integer*]

The syntax of the **BevelShapeOuter** property has these parts:

Part	Description
object	An LED control.
integer	An integer that determines the shape of the outer bevel.

Remarks
The value of this property determines the shape of the control's border. If the BevelShapeInner property is set to 0 (Rectangle), this property is automatically set to 0.

This property might be one of two values:

Constant	Value	Description
msShapeRectangle	0	Rectangle
msShapeEllipse	1	Ellipse

Data Type
Integer (enumerated)

BevelWidthInner and BevelWidthOuter Properties

Description
Determines the width of the inner and outer borders (bevels).

Syntax
object.**BevelWidthInner** [= *integer*]
object.**BevelWidthOuter** [= *integer*]

LED

The syntax of the **BevelWidthInner** and **BevelWidthOuter** properties has these parts:

Part	Description
object	An LED control.
integer	An integer that specifies the width of a bevel, in pixels.

Remarks
These properties determine the width of the inner border (if any, see the BevelInner property) and the outer border (if any, see the BevelOuter property). These properties are always measured in pixels.

Data Type
Integer

BorderWidth Property

Description
Determines the distance between the inner border and the outer border.

Syntax
object.**BorderWidth** [= *integer*]

The syntax of the **BorderWidth** property has these parts:

Part	Description
object	An LED control.
integer	An integer that specifies the gap between the inner and outer bevels, in pixels.

Remarks
The value of this property determines the distance between the inner border (if any, see the BevelInner property) and the outer border (if any, see the BevelOuter property). This property is always measured in pixels.

Data Type
Integer

DisabledColor Property

Description
Determines the color of the LED when the control is disabled.

Syntax
object.**DisabledColor** [= *color*]

The syntax of the **DisabledColor** property has these parts:

Part	Description
object	An LED control.
color	A color expression that determines the color of the LED when disabled.

Remarks
This property determines what color the LED is when the control is disabled.

Data Type
Color

OffColor Property

Description
Sets the color of the LED when the control is off.

Syntax
`object.OffColor [= color ]`

The syntax of the **OffColor** property has these parts:

Part	Description
object	An LED control.
color	A color expression that determines the color of the LED when it is off.

Remarks
This property determines what color the LED is when the control is off (that is, Value = False).

Data Type
Color

OnColor Property

Description
Sets the color of the LED when the control is on.

Syntax
`object.OnColor [= color ]`

LED

The syntax of the **OnColor** property has these parts:

Part	Description
object	An LED control.
color	A color expression that determines the color of the LED when it is on.

Remarks
This property determines what color the LED is when the control is on (that is, Value = True).

Data Type
Color

Value Property

Description
Turns the LED on or off.

Syntax
object.**Value** [= *boolean*]

The syntax of the **Value** property has these parts:

Part	Description
object	An LED control.
Boolean	A Boolean flag that determines the state of the LED (on or off).

Remarks
This property determines whether the LED is on or off. If the control is disabled, the LED is painted using the DisabledColor property. If Value is True, the LED is painted using the OnColor property. And, if Value is False, the LED is painted using the OffColor property.

This property is the default value of the control.

Data Type
Integer (Boolean)

Version Property

Description
Returns the version of the control.

Syntax
object.**Version**

Mabry Software, Inc.

HTTP://www.mabry.com

The syntax of the **Version** property has these parts:

Part	Description
object	An LED control.

Remarks
This property holds the current version of the control. It is read-only and available at both design time and runtime.

Data Type
String

How to Buy the Source Code for This Control

CREDITS
LED was written by James Shields.

CONTACT INFORMATION
Orders, inquiries, technical support, questions, comments, and so on can be sent to mabry@mabry.com on the Internet. Our mailing address/contact information is

Mabry Software, Inc.
503 316th Street Northwest
Stanwood, WA 98292

Sales: 1-800-99-MABRY (U.S. only)
Voice: 360-629-9278
Fax: 360-629-9278
Web: http://www.mabry.com

COST
The cost of LED and the C/C++ source code (of the control itself) is US$50 (US$55 for International orders).

Prices are subject to change without notice.

DELIVERY METHODS
We can ship this software to you via air mail or email.

Air Mail—you will receive disks, a printed manual, and printed receipt if you choose this delivery method. The costs are

US$10.00	US Priority Mail
US$15.00	Airborne Express 2nd Day (US deliveries only)
US$20.00	Airborne Express Overnight (US deliveries only)
US$20.00	Global Priority Mail (Int'l deliveries only; Western Europe, Pacific Rim and Canada only)
US$45.00	International Airborne Express (Int'l deliveries only)

Email—We can ship this package to you via email. You need to have an email account that can accept large file attachments (which includes CompuServe, AOL, and most Internet providers). If you choose this option, please note: a printed manual is not included. We will, however, email a receipt to you.

Be sure to include your full mailing address with your order. Sometimes (on the Internet) the package cannot be emailed, so we are forced to send it through normal mail.

CompuServe Email—CompuServe members can use the software registration forum (GO SWREG) to register this package. LED's SWREG ID number is 3380. The source code version's ID number is 3381. PLEASE NOTE: When you order through SWREG, we send the registered package to your CompuServe account (not your Internet or AOL account) within a few hours.

ORDER/PAYMENT METHODS

You can order this software by phone, fax, email, mail. Please note that orders must include all information that is requested on our order form. Your shipment WILL BE DELAYED if we have to contact you for additional information (such as phone number, street address, and so on).

You can pay by credit card (VISA, MasterCard, American Express, Discover, NOVUS), check (U.S. dollars drawn on a U.S. bank), cash, International Money Order, International Postal Order, Purchase Order (established business entities only—terms net 30), or wire transfer.

WIRE TRANSFER INFORMATION

Here is the information you need regarding our account for a wire funds transfer:

Bank Name:	SeaFirst—Stone Way Branch
Bank Address:	3601 Stone Way North
	Seattle, WA 98103
Bank Phone:	206-585-4951
Account Name:	Mabry Software, Inc.
Routing Number:	12000024
Account Number:	16311706

If you are paying with a wire transfer of funds, please add US$25.00 to your order. This is the fee that SeaFirst Bank charges Mabry Software. Also, please ADD ANY ADDITIONAL FEES THAT YOUR BANK MIGHT CHARGE for wire transfer service. If you are paying with a wire transfer, we must have full payment deposited to our account before we can ship your order.

Copyright © 1994–1998 by Mabry Software, Inc.

Mabry Software, Inc.

HTTP://www.mabry.com

LED Order Form

Mail this form to

Mabry Software, Inc.　　　Phone: 360-629-9278
503 316th Street Northwest　Fax: 360-629-9278
Stanwood, WA 98292　　　Internet: mabry@mabry.com
　　　　　　　　　　　　Web: www.mabry.com

Where did you get this copy of LED? _____

Name: _____

Ship to: _____

_____

_____

_____

Phone: _____

Fax: _____

Email:_____

Credit Card #: _____ exp. _____

P.O. # (if any): _____

Signature _____

Qty ordered _____ SOURCE CODE AND REGISTRATION

$50.00 ($55.00 international). Check or money order in U.S. currency drawn on a U.S. bank. Add $10.00 per order for shipping and handling.

Mail

Description
Mail OCX is the only control in the VB market that is fully MIME compliant, and it's really four controls in one. It provides SMTP and POP3. It also can send and receive MIME compliant messages with unlimited attachments. And, it supports encoding/decoding of Base64, Binhex40, UU, and Quoted-Printable.

Mabry Software's Mail meets the complete specifications for MIME (RFC1521 and 1522), POP3 (RFC1725), and SMTP (RFC0821).

Mail can also be used independently as a general purpose encoder and decoder control, or in combination with other controls that need encoding/decoding capability.

The Mail control comes with a sample program written in VB that is nearly a complete mail client. The sample program shows how to use all the major features (and most of the minor ones) of Mail.

File Name
MMAIL32.OCX

ActiveX/OCX Object Name
Mabry.MailCtrl

ActiveX Compatibility
VB 4.0 (32-bit, 5.0, 6.0, Access 95, Access 97, Visual FoxPro 5.0, and Delphi)

ActiveX Built With
Microsoft Visual C++ v4

ActiveX—Required DLLs
MFC40.DLL (October 6th, 1995 or later)

OLEPRO32.DLL (October 6th, 1995 or later)

MSVCRT40.DLL (September 29th, 1995 or later)

About Error Handling
There are two types of errors. The first type of error is thrown when a property is set or during the time between calling a method and the time the call returns. The second type of error is thrown only when Blocking is False and an error occurs during the asynchronous operation of a method.

The first type of error must be handled using On Error trapping. The second type of error results in firing the AsyncError event.

So, complete error handling when Blocking is False requires On Error trapping during all method invocations and responding to firings of the AsyncError event. When Blocking is True, only On Error trapping is required.

Despite the extra work required to handle errors when Blocking is False, it is recommended that this approach be taken with any application that has a user interface.

Important Note
The Blocking property must not be changed while a connection is established. You should only change the Blocking property when the control is not connected to a server. Changing the Blocking property while connected could cause some strange behavior in the control.

Distribution Note
When you develop and distribute an application that uses this control, you should install the control file into the user's Windows SYSTEM directory. The control file has version information built into it. So, during installation, you should ensure that you are not overwriting a newer version.

Mail Properties

Properties that have special meaning for this control or that apply only to it are marked with an asterisk (*).

*Action Property	*ContentType Property
*AuthenticationType Property	*Date Property
*BCC Property	*Debug Property
*Blocking Property	*DstFilename Property
*Body Property	*EMailAddress Property
*BodyCount Property	*Flags Property
*Buffer Property	*From Property
*CC Property	*Headers Property
*ConnectType Property	*HeadersCount Property
*ContentDescription Property	*HeaderText Property
*ContentDisposition Property	*Host Property
*ContentID Property	*LastError Property
*ContentSubtype Property	*Lines Property
*ContentSubtypeParameters Property	*LogonName Property
*ContentTransferEncoding Property	*LogonPassword Property

Mail

*MessageClass Property
*MessageID Property
*MultipartBoundary Property
*Part Property
*Parts Property
*PopMessageCount Property
*PopMessageSizes Property
*PopPort Property
*ReadData Property
*SmtpPort Property
*SrcFilename Property
*Subject Property
*Timeout Property
*To Property
*Version Property
*WriteData Property

Mail Events
Events that have special meaning for this control or that apply only to it are marked with an asterisk (*).

*AsyncError Event
*Debug Event
*Done Event
*Progress Event

Mail Methods
Methods that have special meaning for this control or that apply only to it are marked with an asterisk (*).

*Abort Method
*AboutBox Method
*Ascend Method
*Connect Method
*CreatePart Method
*Decode Method
*DeletePart Method
*Descend Method
*Disconnect Method
*Encode Method
*HostDelete Method
*NewMessage Method
*Read Method
*ReadMessage Method
*Write Method
*WriteMessage Method

Frequently Asked Questions
How do I retrieve only the headers from a message (TOP functionality)?

There is a value for Flags that is used when MailSrcIsHost is also set as part of the Flags value. The value is MailReadHeaderOnly (= 256). When it is set along with MailSrcIsHost, only the message headers are retrieved. Everything normally associated with an email message will be as it is without the MailReadHeaderOnly flag, except that the message will contain no body of any kind.

How do I send the same message to a list of 100 people?

The Mabry Mail control conforms to RFC 821, which allows multiple recipients to be specified.

To do this, create a comma-delimited string of valid addresses and assign the entire string to either the To, CC, or BCC property (note—all recipients are shown in the To and CC property, but the BCC hides the mail list from each user—see the To, CC, and BCC Properties in the Help file for further details).

You could create the string by looping through the contents of a ListBox, a populated array, or Collection object that you create.

When the email is sent, the communication between the client (your app.) and the server allows the client side to inform the server of all the intended recipients. Then a single copy of the mail is transmitted to the server, resulting in reduced network traffic.

Why do I get an error that says "Busy executing asynchronous command" when I try to send a message?

The Mail control is still performing another command. You need to either key off of the Done event before executing subsequent mail commands, or set Blocking = True. See the Blocking property in the Help file for details of blocking versus nonblocking modes.

Also, you might be able to utilize the CC or BCC properties if sending the same file to multiple recipients. You can specify multiple recipients in each property by separating the email addresses with commas. The Help file contains details of these two properties.

How do I retrieve the cc: header line from an email message? Can I just read the CC property?

The CC property is used for sending a CC to someone. You'd have to retrieve the address(es) of those who were CC'ed on a received email by reading through the Headers property. This is a string array (the size is contained in HeadersCount) that contains each header line. Simply run through the Headers property array looking for lines that begin with CC:.

What is the general procedure for sending mail?

The control is capable of creating multipart messages and encoding messages. Refer to the ENCODE and MAIL samples that come with the control for encoding/decoding messages.

Here are the basic steps for sending mail:

1. Instruct the control that you want to create a new message by issuing the NewMessage method (or set the Action property to MailActionNewMessage).
2. Set the To property to the email address of the intended recipient (note: multiple recipients can be used by separating the email addresses with commas).
3. Set the CC and BCC properties to valid email addresses if you want to CC or blind CC this email to others (note: multiple recipients can be used by separating the email addresses with commas).
4. Set the Host property.
5. Set the From property (this is the user-friendly name of who is sending the message).
6. Set the EMailAddress property (this is the email address of the sender, so the recipient knows to whom to respond).

Mail

7. Set the Subject.
8. Set the Headers property as desired. Something similar to the following is sufficient:
   ```
   Mail1.Headers(Mail1.HeadersCount) = "X-Mailer: Mabry "
   ```
9. Set the MessageID property. Each mail message must have a world-unique ID. Something similar to the following is sufficient:
   ```
   Mail1.MessageID = Year(Now) & Month(Now) & Day(Now) & Fix(Timer) &
   "_MabryMail"
   ```
10. Set the first element of the Body property:
    ```
    Mail1.Body(0) = "blah blah blah"
    ```
11. Set the ConnectType property to MailConnectTypeSMTP.
12. Issue the Connect method (or set the Action property to MailActionConnect).
13. Use the Flags property to instruct the control that the source of the message is the Body and the destination is to be the host:
    ```
    Mail1.Flags = MailSrcIsBody + MailDstIsHost
    ```
14. Write the message with the WriteMessage method (or set the Action property to MailActionWriteMessage).
15. Repeat steps 1–14 as desired.

What is the general procedure for receiving mail?

The control is capable of handling multipart messages and decoding messages. Refer to the ENCODE and MAIL samples that come with the control for encoding/decoding messages.

Here are the basic steps for retrieving mail from a host and writing messages to a disk:

1. Set the Host property.
2. Set the LogonName property.
3. Set the LogonPassword.
4. Set the ConnectType property to MailConnectTypePOP3.
5. Issue the Connect method (or set the Action property to MailActionConnect).
6. Instruct the control in which you want the source of the message to be the host by using the setting Flags = MailSrcIsHost.
7. If the PopMessageCount property is greater than zero, there is mail to retrieve.
8. Select a message to receive by setting the MessageID property to a valid value (a value between 1 and PopMessageCount).
9. Issue the ReadMessage method (or set the Action property to MailActionReadMessage).
10. Instruct the control that you want the destination of the message to be a file by using the setting Flags = MailDstIsFile.

11. Determine where you want to store the message by setting the DstFilename property, that is, Mail1.DstFilename = "C:\email\in\mail.msg". Note: if multiple messages are to be received, a naming scheme is needed to prevent previous messages from being overwritten.
12. Write the message with the WriteMessage method (or set the Action property to MailActionWriteMessage).
13. Repeat steps 6 through 12 as desired.
14. Disconnect from the server by issuing the Disconnect method (or set the Action property to MailActionDisconnect).

Do you have a separate control for encoding/decoding?

No, we do not have a separate control for encoding/decoding, but the Mail control can be easily adapted for such functionality. Just use the SrcFilename and DstFilename properties and the Decode/Encode methods. These methods are not dependent on any of the mail-specific methods like Connect, ReadMessage, and so on

Is there a property that lets you add custom extra fields like x-mailer, Reply-to, Priority, and others?

Use the EMailAddress property for the Reply-to, and then use the Headers property for creating custom headers. The property is a string array, so you would do something like:

```
Mail1.Headers(0) = "X-Mailer: Mabry"
Mail1.Headers(1) = "X-Priority: 3"
```

How do I recover parts (attachments) from forwarded mail? If Mail1.parts was 2 on the original, then, after forwarding, Mail1.parts is 1. As a result, I cannot recover the attachment. What do I do?

The control can handle recursive parts—when a message has multiple parts embedded within parts, you need to Descend into a Part to access its multiple parts.

In other words, if an original message has two parts and it's forwarded, the new message has one part. If you descend into that one part, the Parts property will be 2 (the two original parts) and you can access them.

If the user cancels Dial–up-Networking, is there a way to reset the Mabry Mail control? Disconnect or Abort will not work because the socket was never connected.

The only thing you can do in that case is wait for the Winsock to timeout and then trap the error.

Alternatively, you could use the latest version of the Mabry RAS control to see if the connection exists, and, if not, attempt to establish the connection. If the user aborts the connection, you can prevent the Mail control from attempting to connect by checking the RAS.EntryConnected property before issuing the Mail.Connect method.

Why does the Mabry Mail control strip quotes (") out of email addresses in the To, CC and BCC properties?

Quotes should be stripped out. The quote character is a special character and gets stripped out unless preceded by a "\" character.

Mail

For example, if you use Netscape to send a message and the From in Netscape is "Joe Blow" (in quotes), the source header gets converted to "\"Joe Blow"\"

You could put the quotes back in, but our tests indicated that some mail clients (that is, Pegasus) might have problems if the mail is sent with quotes in From.

If I send a message to my normal SMTP server, the message arrives OK. But, if I send the message specifying another SMTP server, I find two boundary lines in the body message. Do you know why?

If you are setting the Host property, the message should be the same regardless of the server—unless the SMTP server is a re-mailer that forwards the message on to the final destination. If this is the case, the problem is the intermediate mail server (and it's really not a problem—it is common for forwarded messages).

When this happens, check the Content-Type of the final message. If it is "message" or "message/RFC821", the intermediate mail server is forwarding (and altering) the message. The control can't do anything to correct that.

When I attempt to connect to a server that is unavailable, the operation times out and an "Operation Timed Out" message box pops up. How can I prevent the message box from displaying?

Establish the connection asynchronously (Blocking = False).

Why do current messages sent by my program include headers from previous messages?

The Headers property accumulates headers until it is cleared. When creating a new message, use the NewMessage method (or set the Action property to MailActionNewMessage) to clear the Headers property.

How can I shorten the Timeout period during a Connect? My program waits for 2 minutes (in the case of no connection) before returning.

The Timeout property is only to be used after connecting to the server (to handle server timeouts vs. WinSock timeouts). WinSock is controlling the connect timeout.

To abort a connect and unload your application if a connection doesn't occur within 15 seconds, set Blocking to False and use a standard Timer control set to 15 seconds to unload the form when it fires. Note—don't forget to disable the timer if the connect is successful!

I'm using nonblocking (asynchronous) mode, but the Done event never fires for some methods, like NewMessage. Why is this?

The Done event only fires when the method invoked involves a call to the Winsock interface. Because blocking is a function of the Winsock interface, if an action of the control doesn't involve WinSock, the blocking function is not applicable and the Done event doesn't fire.

How can I send email when Blocking = False?

It is difficult to write nonblocking in an **email** because code needs to be in various subroutines. Here is a simple sample of sending in nonblocking mode:

In the Declarations section, define a Boolean flag (if using VB3, make it an integer and change the True/False as necessary):

```
Dim fBusy as Boolean
```

In the Done event, set the fBusy flag = False:

```
Private Sub Mail1_Done()
    'this clears the fBusy flag
    fBusy = False
End Sub
```

Then, use the following code to send your mail:

```
    Mail1.Blocking = False
    Mail1.Action = 11 'MailActionNewMessage
    Mail1.To = "somebody@somewhere.com"
    Mail1.From = "My Name"
    Mail1.EMailAddress = "me@mydomain.com"
    Mail1.Subject = "This is the subject"
    Mail1.Body(0) = "This is the message."
    Mail1.Host = "smtp.mydomain.com"
    Mail1.ConnectType = 0 'MailConnectTypeSMTP

    fBusy = True 'set the busy flag — the Done event will clear it
    Mail1.Action = 3 'MailActionConnect
    Do While (fBusy)
        DoEvents
    Loop

    Mail1.Flags = 64 'MailDstIsHost

    fBusy = True
    Mail1.Action = MailActionWriteMessage
    Do While (fBusy)
        DoEvents
    Loop
    Mail1.Action = MailActionDisconnect
```

Note: you might want to enable a timer to prevent an endless loop in the Do/Loop code.

What is the difference between Buffer and Body properties in the Mail control?

The buffer is just a temporary string variable that is useful when encoding/decoding attachments. The actual body of the message is in the Body property, which is a string array (the OCX does not have the size limitation, so you can use only the first element of the array).

Do you know of any SMTP servers that have known problems with your control?

MAIL doesn't work with a server called IMS Pop3 when the mailbox is empty, and it is clearly the server failing to follow the RFC. This server does not terminate a multiline response as specified in the RFC and so the control's method times out.

The RFCs define the protocols and, thus, anyone who creates an application that conforms to the RFC should be able to communicate with anyone else who conforms. The Mabry Mail control conforms with RFC 821 (SMTP) and RFC 1725 (POP3). It is also MIME compatible and complies with RFC 1521 and 1522.

Can the Mabry Mail control be used with Microsoft Exchange?

The Mail control complies with POP3 and SMTP protocols. Microsoft Exchange supports these, but Microsoft's Knowledge Base indicates that some versions of Exchange might have problems routing certain SMTP messages. It will accept:

```
techsupport@mabry.com
```

but not

```
Techical Support Staff <techsupport@mabry.com>
```

See http://www.microsoft.com/kb/ for updated information and Exchange Service Pack information.

Can the Mail control be used to write a mail server?

No, the Mabry Mail control supports the POP3 and SMTP protocols from the perspective of the client side, not the server side. However, the Mabry ASocket control, which provides direct access to the WinSock interface, could be used as a building block in a mail server.

Can I use MMAIL32.OCX to create an Active Server Object that can be called (no GUI) from an ASP script?

Generally, you can't because controls require a container, but there is a clever workaround. Use VB5 to create an ActiveX control and place the Mabry control in the ActiveX control. Using the ActiveX interface wizard, map all the Mabry tool's properties and methods to the ActiveX component.

Then you should be able to create the control and reference the control using your custom ActiveX control. For example, to use a Mail control on an .ASP page:

```
set myMail = server.createobject("MyProject.MyForm")

myMail.connecttype=0
myMail.host=" ...... "
etc.
```

> **Note**
>
> The Mabry License Agreement explicity states that you cannot use a Mabry control to create an ActiveX control to be marketed as an ActiveX control. You can, however, use the previous method to create an ActiveX control to be used in server-side Web pages or in your applications.

I need to send very large files (3 megabytes) using Microsoft Access. How can I do this?

If you're using the ActiveX (OCX-32) version, it shouldn't be a problem. The Body(0) property can handle the entire encoded file.

Can I create Confirm Delivery and Confirm Reading receipts to verify that the end user received and read the message?

Yes. Return receipts are simply specialized headers. These receipt headers are not part of the official RFC, which means the mail client that receives the messages does not HAVE to recognize nor respond to receipt headers.

Here is an example using the same format that Pegasus mail uses for receipts:

```
Dim lpRead As String
Dim lpRcv As String

'create the "confirm read" receipt
lpRead = "X-Confirm-Reading-To: ""Someone"" <someone@domain.com>"

'create the "confirm received" receipt
lpRcv = "Return-receipt-to: ""Someone"" <someone@domain.com>"

'add the custom headers to the header array
mMail1.Headers(mMail1.HeadersCount) = lpRead
mMail1.Headers(mMail1.HeadersCount) = lpRcv
```

I have been unable to use the Abort method without getting socket errors. Why?

The Abort method is only valid after you've been authenticated by the mail server and are in the Transaction state—it aborts transactions but not connections.

I don't understand the Flags property. How do I use it?

When you want to send a message, you really need two flags, one to indicate the source of the message and one to indicate the destination. The Flag property in the Help file describing the values and the relevancy of the flags varies depending upon whether you are sending or receiving a message.

In a nutshell, when sending a message, the host is usually the destination and the source is usually the Body, a file, or the control's buffer.

Why doesn't the server accept my command when using the Write method?

All strings must be terminated with a CR/LF (Chr[13] & Chr[10]). You must add a CRLF at the end of your string.

Why do I get a GPF when I try to unload my form (or control) from the Done event?

This is not uncommon in many controls. If the form containing the control is unloaded but the control's C++ code for the event has to reference the control, the GPF occurs because the control is no longer available after it is has been unloaded. The solution is to enable a timer in the Done event and have the Timer unload the form (or control).

With which TCP/IP stacks have your Internet controls been tested?

The majority of our internal testing is done on either Windows NT's or Windows 95's standard stacks. We also utilize a 3.1 machine running Trumpet Winsock.

Mail

As part of our beta program, the controls wind up on a variety of stacks like Novell (known to have differences in Winsock, but should be OK with the latest patches from Novell), WFWG (also has a known problem that can cause FTP trouble, but Microsoft has a patch for that product as well [article ID Q122544]).

The controls support the standard Winsock interface, so, in general, the 16-bit environments that do not come with a default stack (That is, Windows 3.x) might involve a bit more setup, but as long as some reputable stack is used, there shouldn't be any problems.

How do I enable/disable the Windows 95 Dial-Up Networking connect prompt when my application issues a Connect method?

The fact that the DUN pops up when attempting to establish a network connection is a Windows 95 OS setting. To change this behavior, choose Dial-Up Networking from My Computer, and select Settings… from the Connections menu. Set the desired value in the "When establishing a network connection" frame.

How do I convert my code from BLOCKING (Synchronous) to NONBLOCKING (Asynchronous)?

Check out the simple, nonblocking samples available on our sample code page at `http://www.mabry.com/sampcode.htm`

Also, a quick fix for converting Blocking code to nonblocking code is as follows:

```
Blocking=False
```

In the Declarations of the Form, add

```
Private fDone as Boolean
```

In the Done event of the control set the fDone flag as shown:

```
Private Sub mMail1_Done()
    fDone = True
End Sub
```

Then, when invoking a method, loop until the Done event sets the fDone flag.

```
fDone = False
mMail1.Connect
Do
    DoEvents
    'here is where your application
    'can do other things
Loop Until (fDone)
```

Notes

> You might want to set a timer in the loop so it won't loop endlessly should some problem occur. Also, depending upon your code, you might want to conditionally set the fDone flag in the AsyncError event.
>
> This method is not recommended for the FTP control because the DoEvents might result in packets arriving out of sequence.

How can I detect whether someone has entered an IP or host name?

Use the following function to check for a host name or IP address:

```
' This Function receives a string argument and
' validates whether the string is a valid IP value,
' by verifying that it is in the format of w.x.y.z and
' that each octet is between 0 and 255
'
' Returns True if IP there are 4 octets and each is
' between 0 and 255.
'
' Returns False in all other cases
'
' Disclaimer — this function will not detect certain
' values such as netmasks like 255.255.255.255,
' which meet the criteria but are not valid IPs.
'
Private Function Valid_IP(IP As String) As Boolean
    Dim i As Integer
    Dim dot_count As Integer
    Dim test_octect As String

    IP = Trim$(IP)

    ' make sure the IP long enough before
    ' continuing
    If Len(IP) < 8 Then
        Valid_IP = False
        Exit Function
    End If

    i = 1
    dot_count = 0
    For i = 1 To Len(IP)
        If Mid$(IP, i, 1) = "." Then
            ' increment the dot count and
            ' clear the test octet variable
            dot_count = dot_count + 1
            test_octet = ""
            If i = Len(IP) Then
                ' we've ended with a dot
                ' this is not good
                Valid_IP = False
                Exit Function
            End If
        Else
            test_octet = test_octet & Mid$(IP, i, 1)
            On Error Resume Next
            byte_check = CByte(test_octet)
```

```
            If (Err) Then
                ' either the value is not numeric
                ' or exceeds the range of the byte
                ' data type.
                Valid_IP = False
                Exit Function
            End If
        End If
    Next i
    ' so far, so good
    ' did we get the correct number of dots?
    If dot_count <> 3 Then
        Valid_IP = False
        Exit Function
    End If
    ' we have a valid IP format!
    Valid_IP = True
End Function
```

What is the meaning of Error 20002 "unexpected server response"?

The control has issued some command and the server didn't accept it. It could be anything from an improperly formatted email address to an unimplemented command on the server. You'll have to enable debugging to see what the command and reply are.

I'm unclear on blocking. Can you explain it to me?

When your application requests data from a network connection, it's hard to predict how long it will take before the data arrives and the call can complete. As a programmer, you have to determine whether to wait for the outcome of the call, or return immediately to your application and get the data *when* the data arrives.

Calls that wait, are called *blocking* calls. Because the call must complete before the application continues, blocking calls are also referred to as synchronous calls.

Calls that return control to your application immediately are called *nonblocking* calls. Because your application can perform tasks while the call is retrieving the data, nonblocking calls are also referred to as asynchronous calls.

Mabry Internet controls support both blocking and nonblocking calls.

Important to note is that even when using blocking calls, Windows can send event messages (such as Timer events, mouse clicks, and so on) to your application and it can respond to them. This can result in errors. It's the responsibility of the programmer to minimize the likelihood of these situations (such as disabling any Timers or command buttons that interrupt the call) and handle any errors should such conditions arise.

Error handling is very important when issuing calls to a network. Always use some method of On Error handling when invoking blocking calls. For nonblocking calls, normal On Error handling is required in addition to responding to the AsyncError event.

Should I use blocking or nonblocking calls?

It depends on your application. See the explanation on blocking calls for a complete description of blocking versus nonblocking.

Why do I keep getting the error "Busy executing asynchronous command"?

A call has been invoked, but a previous call hasn't been completed yet. Either set Blocking mode to True or wait for the Done event before issuing subsequent commands.

Important to note is that even when using blocking calls, Windows can send event messages (such as Timer events, mouse clicks, and so on) to your application and it can respond to them. This can result in errors. It's the responsibility of the programmer to minimize the likelihood of these situations (such as disabling any Timers or command buttons that will interrupt the call) and handle any errors should such conditions arise.

How do I tell what's happening when the control is talking to a server?

The Internet Pack controls have debugging support built in. Set the Debug property on the control to 1, and then add the following code to the Debug event of the control:

```
Debug.Print Message
```

Error Codes

Constant	Value	Description
	0	No error.
WSAEINTR	10004	System level interrupt interrupted socket operation.
WSAEBADF	10009	Generic error for invalid format, bad format.
WSAEACCES	10013	Generic error for access violation.
WSAEFAULT	10014	Generic error for fault.
WSAEINVAL	10022	Generic error for invalid format, entry, and so on
WSAEMFILE	10024	Generic error for file error.
	10025	The IP address provided is not valid or the host specified by the IP doesn't exist.
WSAEWOULDBLOCK	10035	The socket is marked as nonblocking and the operation would block. You will be notified when the operation completes. This is just a warning, your operation will complete successfully. It is safe to ignore this error code.
WSAEINPROGRESS	10036	This error is returned if any Windows Sockets function is called while a blocking function is in progress.

Constant	Value	Description
WSAEALREADY	10037	The asynchronous routine being canceled has already completed.
WSAENOTSOCK	10038	Invalid socket or not connected to remote.
WSAEDESTADDRREQ	10039	A destination address is required.
WSAEMSGSIZE	10040	The socket is of type ASocketDatagram, and the datagram is larger than the maximum supported by the Windows Sockets implementation.
WSAEPROTOTYPE	10041	The specified port is the wrong type for this socket.
WSAENOPROTOOPT	10042	The option is unknown or unsupported.
WSAEPROTONOSUPPORT	10043	The specified port is not supported.
WSAESOCKTNOSUPPORT	10044	The specified socket type is not supported in this address family.
WSAEOPNOTSUPP	10045	The referenced socket is not a type that supports connection-oriented service.
WSAEAFNOSUPPORT	10047	Addresses in the specified family cannot be used with this socket.
WSAEADDRINUSE	10048	The specified address is already in use.
WSAEADDRNOTAVAIL	10049	The specified address is not available.
WSAENETDOWN	10050	The connected network is not available.
WSAENETUNREACH	10051	The connected network is not reachable.
WSAENETRESET	10052	The connected network connection has been reset.
WSAECONNABORTED	10053	The current connection has been aborted by the network or intermediate services.
WSAECONNRESET	10054	The current socket connection has been reset.
WSAENOBUFS	10055	No buffer space is available. The socket cannot be connected.
WSAEISCONN	10056	The socket is already connected.
WSAENOTCONN	10057	The current socket has not been connected.
WSAESHUTDOWN	10058	The connection has been shutdown.
WSAETIMEDOUT	10060	The current connection has timed out.
WSAECONNREFUSED	10061	The requested connection has been refused by the remote host.
WSAENAMETOOLONG	10063	Specified host name is too long.
WSAEHOSTDOWN	10064	Remote host is currently unavailable.
WSAEHOSTUNREACH	10065	Remote host is currently unreachable.

continues

Constant	Value	Description
WSASYSNOTREADY	10091	Remote system is not ready.
WSAVERNOTSUPPORTED	10092	Current socket version isn't supported by application.
WSANOTINITIALISED	10093	Socket API is not initialized.
WSAEDISCON	10101	Socket has been disconnected.
WSAHOST_NOT_FOUND	11001	Remote host could not be found.
WSATRY_AGAIN	11002	Remote host could not be found, try again.
WSANODATA	11004	Remote host could not be found.
	20001	Internal control state error.
	20002	Unexpected server response.
	20003	Login required.
	20004	Login failed.
	20005	Already connected to server.
	20006	Busy executing asynchronous command.
	20007	Can't change blocking mode, busy, or connected to server.
	20008	Operation timed out.
	20009	Cannot Ascend, already at top level of message.
	20010	Cannot Descend, message has no parts.
	20011	Invalid user name.
	20012	Invalid password.
	20013	Could not open file.
	20014	Could not close file.

Simple Message Send Example

The following example shows how to send a simple message using an SMTP server:

```
' Enable blocking mode
mMail1.Blocking = True

' Set header properties
mMail1.To = "someone@somewhere.com"
mMail1.From = "Your Name <you@wherever.com>"
mMail1.Host = "smtphost.wherever.com"
mMail1.EMailAddress = Chr(34) & "Your Name" & Chr(34) &
[ic:ccc]"<you@wherever.com.com>"

' Put text of message in body
mMail1.Body(0) = "E-Mail Message"

' Connect to server
mMail1.Action = MailActionConnect
```

```
' Send e-mail message to server
mMail1.Flags = MailDstIsHost
mMail1.Action = MailActionWriteMessage

' Disconnect
mMail1.Action = MailActionDisconnect
```

Abort Method

Description
Aborts the current POP3 connection. Not valid for SMTP connections.

Syntax
`object.Abort`

The syntax of the **Abort** method has these parts:

Part	Description
object	Required. A Mail control.

Remarks
When you connect to a POP3 server, a transaction is started. During the transaction you might delete messages using the HostDelete method. A transaction is terminated by using either the Disconnect or Abort methods. Using Abort terminates the current transaction and begins another transaction (it doesn't disconnect from the server). When a transaction is terminated this way, all messages deleted with the HostDelete method aren't deleted by the server.

AboutBox Method

Description
Displays the About Box for the control.

Syntax
`object.AboutBox`

The syntax of the **AboutBox** method has these parts:

Part	Description
object	Required. A Mail control.

Remarks
This method displays the About Box for this control which includes copyright information.

Action Property

Description
Causes control to initiate a command or method.

Syntax
`object.Action [= integer ]`

The syntax of the **Action** property has these parts:

Part	Description
object	A Mail control.
integer	An integer that specifies the action to perform.

Remarks
Setting this property makes the Mail control perform an action. The action depends on the value set. Mail accepts the following:

Constant	Value	Description
MailActionNoAction	0	No action
MailActionAbort	1	Abort POP3 Transaction (Abort)
MailActionAscend	2	Ascend out of message part (Ascend)
MailActionConnect	3	Connect to host system (Connect)
MailActionCreatePart	4	Create a new message part (CreatePart)
MailActionDecode	5	Decode data (Decode)
MailActionDeletePart	6	Delete current message part (DeletePart)
MailActionDescend	7	Descend into current message part (Descend)
MailActionDisconnect	8	Disconnect from host system (Disconnect)
MailActionEncode	9	Encode data (Encode)
MailActionHostDelete	10	Delete received message from POP3 server (HostDelete)
MailActionNewMessage	11	Create new message (NewMessage)
MailActionRead	12	Read data from server (Read)
MailActionReadMessage	13	Read a message (ReadMessage)
MailActionWrite	14	Write data to a server (Write)
MailActionWriteMessage	15	Write a message (WriteMessage)

Data Type
Integer

Ascend Method

Description
Ascends out of the current message part.

Syntax
`object.Ascend`

The syntax of the **Ascend** method has these parts:

Mail

Part	Description
object	Required. A Mail control.

Remarks

Ascends from the current message up to the previous message in a multipart message. All properties are set to the current message after the ascend operation is completed.

When Ascend is executed, all relevant properties are saved and associated with the message part from which you are ascending. To create parts (attachments), use the CreatePart method. Descend into the part with Descend. Assign message contents and properties as required and then Ascend out of the part.

AsyncError Event

Description

Fired when an error occurs during asynchronous operations.

Syntax

Sub *object*_AsyncError([*index* As Integer,] *errornumber* As Integer, *errormessage* As String)

The syntax of the **AsyncError** event has these parts:

Part	Description
object	A Mail control.
index	An integer that identifies a control if it's in a control array.
errornumber	An integer that holds the current error number.
errormessage	A string expression that holds text describing the current error.

Remarks

If an error occurs during the execution of asynchronous commands (only possible when Blocking is set to False) the program is notified by firing the AsyncError event.

AuthenticationType Property

Description

Specifies type of authentication to use.

Syntax

object.AuthenticationType

The syntax of the **AuthenticationType** property has these parts:

Part	Description
object	A Mail control.

Remarks

This property determines the type of authorization to perform when connecting to an ESMTP server. Currently, this control supports the following constants:

Constant	Value	Description
	0	None
MailAuthentication	1	"auth login"
TypeAuthLogin		style
		authentication
		(current de
		facto standard)

About ESMTP Auth Login Authentication

A de facto standard for ESMTP login authentication has evolved. The Mabry Mail control now supports this nonstandard standard. To enable the Mail control to successfully invoke the authentication protocol, you must do the following:

```
Mail1.LogonName = UserName
Mail1.LogonPassword = UserPassword
Mail1.ConnectType = MailConnectTypeESMTP
Mail1.AuthenticationType = MailAuthenticationTypeAuthLogin
Mail1.Connect
```

Your users must know whether or not their server supports auth login and, if so, their login name and password.

Data Type
Integer (enumerated)

BCC Property

Description
Blind Carbon Copy recipients of current message.

Syntax
object.**BCC** [= *string*]

The syntax of the **BCC** property has these parts:

Part	Description
object	A Mail control.
string	A string expression that contains a list of email addresses.

Remarks
Three properties are used to specify the recipients of any given email message, the To, CC, and BCC properties. All recipients see the list of recipients in the To and CC properties in the header of the copy of the email message they receive. Recipients listed in the BCC field won't be known to other recipients.

Mail

Multiple recipients might be specified and, if so, they must be separated by commas. The following are examples of valid addresses:

```
zane@mabry.com
zane@mabry.com
Zane Thomas <zane@mabry.com>
```

If you choose to include a full name as well as an email address, as done in the third example, you must enclose the actual email address in angle brackets.

You shouldn't use other formats for specifying an email address. The Mail control attempts to extract the actual email address from the string specified. You might find, however, that the Mail control doesn't recognize them.

Data Type
String

Blocking Property

Description
Determines if methods or actions are blocking.

Syntax
object.**Blocking** [= *boolean*]

The syntax of the **Blocking** property has these parts:

Part	Description
object	A Mail control.
Boolean	A Boolean flag that determines if the control waits for completion of an operation (True) or returns control to the program immediately (False).

Remarks
If this property is set to True, commands using either the Action property or any of the methods won't return to your code until the command completes. In other words, the command is handled synchronously.

If this property is False, any commands are handled asynchronously. They return to you immediately. You are notified of completion with the Done event. When the user-interface requires that the user be able to cancel file transfers, it is recommended that Blocking be set to False so that your program can respond quickly to user actions.

Important Note

> The Blocking property must not be changed while a connection is established. You should only change the Blocking property when the control is not connected to a server. Changing the Blocking property while connected could cause some strange behavior in the control.

Data Type
Integer (Boolean)

Body Property

Description
An array containing the body of an email message.

Syntax
`object.Body( index ) [= body ]`

The syntax of the **Body** property has these parts:

Part	Description
object	A Mail control.
index	An integer that identifies a part of the Body array.
body	A variant that specifies the text for the body piece identified by index.

Remarks
The Body property is an array. The OCX version of Mail puts the entire body of received email messages in element number zero of the array.

When using the OCX, there is no practical restriction on the number of bytes you assign to the first element of the array.

The BodyCount property tells you how many elements are in the Body array.

Note that the data type for this property is Variant, so you might store strings containing null (&h00) characters in the body of a message. This is usually followed by encoding the body contents into Base64 (or one of the other supported formats) prior to transmission.

Also note that any message or message part containing a multipart message has no body. The body of a multipart message is the parts which must be accessed using the Descend method.

Data Type
Variant

BodyCount Property

Description
The number of elements in the Body property array.

Syntax
`object.BodyCount`

The syntax of the **BodyCount** property has these parts:

Mail

Part	Description
object	A Mail control.

Remarks

Some email messages have text in their bodies that contains more bytes than can be returned as the value of a string by the VBX version of the Mail control. For that reason, the Body property is an array and the BodyCount property tells you how many elements are in the array.

This property is read-only and only available at runtime.

Data Type
Integer

Buffer Property

Description
A general-purpose buffer.

Syntax
object.**Buffer** [= *string*]

The syntax of the **Buffer** property has these parts:

Part	Description
object	A Mail control.
string	A string expression.

Remarks

A few methods, such as Encode and Decode, require both a source and destination. The Buffer property can be used as either the source or the destination under some circumstances. Note that the utility of the Buffer property is somewhat limited in the VBX because of the limitation on the length of the string it might contain. However, because the Buffer property is provided merely as a convenience and all mail-related tasks can be accomplished without it, the VBX limitation is not significant.

Data Type
String

CC Property

Description
List of message recipients who should receive copies of the email message.

Syntax
object.**CC** [= *string*]

The syntax of the **CC** property has these parts:

Part	Description
object	A Mail control.
string	A string expression that contains a list of email addresses.

Remarks
Three properties are used to specify the recipients of any given email message, the To, CC, and BCC properties. All recipients will see the recipients in the To and CC properties in the header of the copy of the email message they receive. Recipients listed in the BCC field won't be known to other recipients.

Multiple recipients might be specified and, if so, they must be separated by commas. The following are examples of valid addresses:

    zane@mabry.com
    zane@mabry.com
    Zane Thomas <zane@mabry.com>

If you choose to include a full name as well as an email address, as is done in the third example, you must enclose the actual email address in angle brackets.

You should not use other formats for specifying an email address. The Mail control attempts to extract the actual email address from the string specified. You might find, however, that the Mail control doesn't recognize them.

Data Type
String

Connect Method

Description
Connects to a mail server.

Syntax
object.**Connect**

The syntax of the **Connect** method has these parts:

Part	Description
object	Required. A Mail control.

Remarks
Connects to either an SMTP or POP3 server, depending upon the setting of the ConnectType property. Before executing the Connect method you must first set the Host property. When connecting to a POP3 server, you must also set the LogonName and LogonPassword properties.

Mail

Important Note

The Blocking property must not be changed while a connection is established. You should only change the Blocking property when the control isn't connected to a server. Changing the Blocking property while connected could cause some strange behavior in the control.

ConnectType Property

Description
Specifies type of server to use.

Syntax
object.**ConnectType** [= *integer*]

The syntax of the **ConnectType** property has these parts:

Part	Description
object	A Mail control.
integer	An integer that specifies the type of connection to use.

Remarks
The Mail control supports POP3 and SMTP servers. Before using the Connect method to connect to a server, you should set the ConnectType property as shown in the following table. After executing the Disconnect method, you can change the ConnectType property if required.

Constant	Value	Description
MailConnectTypeSMTP	0	Connect to SMTP server
MailConnectTypePOP3	1	Connect to POP3 server
MailConnectTypeESMTP	2	Connect to ESMTP (authenticated SMTP) server (see Authorization Property)

About ESMTP Auth Login Authentication
A de facto standard for ESMTP login authentication has evolved. The Mabry Mail control now supports this nonstandard standard. To enable the Mail control to successfully invoke the authentication protocol you must do the following:

```
Mail1.LogonName = UserName
Mail1.LogonPassword = UserPassword
Mail1.ConnectType = MailConnectTypeESMTP
Mail1.AuthenticationType = MailAuthenticationTypeAuthLogin
Mail1.Connect
```

Your users will need to know whether or not their server supports auth login and, if so, their login name and password.

Data Type
Integer (enumerated)

ContentDescription Property

Description
User-friendly description of an email message.

Syntax
object.**ContentDescription** [= *string*]

The syntax of the **ContentDescription** property has these parts:

Part	Description
object	A Mail control.
string	A string that describes the content of an email message (or part, in a multipart message).

Remarks
A user-friendly description of the content of an email message (or part of a multipart message) might be provided. For instance, you could assign "This is an image in Gif89a format" as the value of this property when emailing a GIF file.

Data Type
String

ContentDisposition Property

Description
Provides a recommended disposition to the message recipient.

Syntax
object.**ContentDisposition** [= *string*]

The syntax of the **ContentDisposition** property has these parts:

Part	Description
object	A Mail control.
string	A string that contains the recommended disposition for an email message (or part, in a multipart message).

Remarks
MIME messages might have a ContentDisposition header. ContentDisposition is used to indicate two things: whether a message part should be displayed as an attachment or inline, and the suggested name of a file for storing the message.

Examples:

ContentDisposition = "attachment; filename=foo.zip" indicates that the contents should be displayed as an attachment and the suggested filename for storing the contents is foo.zip.

Mail

ContentDisposition = "inline; filename=me.gif" indicates that the contents should be displayed inline and that the suggested filename is me.gif.

Note that you would expect to find the first example only in a body part, which is application/zip or application/x-zip-compressed; while the second example might appear in a body part which is image/gif.

Data Type
String

ContentID Property

Description
An arbitrary unique content identifier.

Syntax
`object.ContentID [= string ]`

The syntax of the **ContentID** property has these parts:

Part	Description
object	A Mail control.
string	A string that specifies a unique content identifier.

Remarks
In constructing a high-level user agent, it might be desirable to allow one body to make reference to another. Accordingly, bodies might be labeled using the ContentID property. Note that ContentID has special meaning in the case of the multipart/alternative content type. Refer to RFC1521 for the details of constructing such messages.

Data Type
String

ContentSubtype Property

Description
Specifies a message's subtype.

Syntax
`object.ContentSubtype [= string ]`

The syntax of the **ContentSubtype** property has these parts:

Part	Description
object	A Mail control.
string	A string that specifies the subtype for a message or message part (in a multipart message).

Remarks

Each part of a MIME message has a type and subtype. The ContentSubtype property specifies the subtype corresponding to a particular message part. The following table lists the most common types and subtypes.

Type	Subtype	Description
text	plain	Text/plain is the default format for Internet mail messages.
multipart	mixed	Used for independent body parts that don't need to be bundled in any particular order. Unrecognized multipart SubTypes are treated as mixed, as specified by RFC1521.
	alternative	Used when alternative views of the same message are bundled in a multipart message. For instance, a multipart/alternative message might contain a plain-text version and a rich-text version of the same message body.
	parallel	A message whose parts are intended to be displayed simultaneously. For instance, a parallel message might contain an audio part and a text part. In that case, the intent of the sender is that the audio is played while the text is displayed.
	digest	Similar to the multipart/mixed type except that the bundled messages default to type message/rfc822 instead of text/plain. The control makes this detail largely irrelevant but for completeness, multipart/digest messages are indicated as being so.
Message	rfc822	Indicates that the body of the message is an encapsulated message. Unlike top-level RFC 822 messages, it isn't required that each message/rfc822 body must include a From, Subject, and at least one destination header. Also note that the encapsulated message might itself be a MIME message and it's necessary to use the Descend method to access the headers and body of the encapsulated message.
	partial	Mail transports or mail programs might arbitrarily break large messages into multiple partial messages. The application (the program using this

Mail

Type	Subtype	Description
		control) must locate the pieces of a partial message, reassemble them into a complete message, and then use either the MessageFromFile or MessageFromBuffer methods to create a complete (decoded if necessary) message.
	external-body	Indicates that the body of the message is stored external to the message. The ContentsSubtypeParameters property provides further information on how to retrieve the message body.
application	octet-stream	Indicates that the body contains binary data.
	zip	Indicates that the body contains a ZIP file
	x-zip-compressed	Indicates that the body contains a ZIP file
	x-uuencode	A wrapped UUencoded message
	mac-binhex40	A BinHex message
	x-*	Any other subtype of application beginning with x-.
image	jpeg	The message body is a JPEG graphic.
	gif	The message body is a GIF graphic.
audio	basic	The message body is 8bit ISDN mu-law [PCM] data, a single channel recorded at 8000hz.
video	mpeg	The message body is an MPEG animation.

Data Type
String

ContentSubtypeParameters Property

Description
Specifies parameters used with various ContentSubtypes.

Syntax
`object.ContentSubtypeParameters [= string ]`

The syntax of the **ContentSubtypeParameters** property has these parts:

Part	Description
object	A Mail control.
string	A string that specifies the subtype parameters for a message or message part (in a multipart message).

Remarks

Many of the ContentType/ContentSubtype combinations also require one or more parameters. The following table lists the parameters specified in RFC1521.

Type / Subtype	Parameter	Description
text/plain	charset	Specifies the character set that should be used when displaying the message.
multipart/*	boundary	All the parts of a multipart message are separated by the character string given as the value of the boundary parameter. Usually you don't need to parse the individual parts of a multipart message because the control does it automatically. If you need to parse the message yourself, read RFC1521 for the details on using the boundary parameter.
message/partial	number	Partial message parts are numbered 1 through the total number of parts. Although it is recommended that all partial messages give both the current number and total number parameters, RFC1521 only requires the last part of a set of partial messages to specify the total number.
	total	Total number of parts in the partial message. Required only for the last part, but might be present in other parts.
	id	A world unique identifier used to associate the parts of a partial message with each other.
Message/external-body	access-type name expiration size permission site directory mode server subject	Access-type and the other message/external-body parameters have numerous uses. Read RFC1521 for a complete understanding of these parameters.

Mail

Type / Subtype	Parameter	Description
application/octet-stream	type	General type of data, intended for user viewing and not for automatic processing.
	padding	Number of bits of padding appended. Used only for bit-stream data.
application/zip	name	Recommended filename for zip file.

Data Type
String

ContentTransferEncoding Property

Description
Describes how the message data was (or should be) encoded prior to transmission.

Syntax
object.**ContentTransferEncoding** [= *string*]

The syntax of the **ContentTransferEncoding** property has these parts:

Part	Description
object	A Mail control.
string	A string expression that specifies an encoding method.

Remarks
The original SMTP specification, RFC821, restricts mail messages to 7-bit US-ASCII data formatted into lines of no more than 1000 characters. Many of the content types might be used to send data that is not 7-bit ASCII and that might not reasonably be broken up into lines of no more than 1000 characters. To provide for the transmission of such data, the MIME standard (RFC1521) defines the following transfer encoding types:

```
quoted-printable
base64
8bit
binary
7bit
```

Of these standard types, only quoted-printable and Base64 indicate that the message body contains data that has actually been encoded. The other types (8-bit, binary, and 7-bit) indicate the kind of data contained in the message.

The MIME standard also allows extensions to the ContentTransferEncoding header. Such extensions are specified with the prefix 'x-'. For instance, x-uuencode is often used to indicate UUencoding. Message parts with ContentTransferEncoding x-uuencode and mac-binhex40 are sometimes received. The mail control supports decoding and encoding message parts using these formats in addition to the standard MIME encoding formats listed above.

The contents of the ContentTransferEncoding property are used by the Encode and Decode methods to determine how to encode/decode data. For this purpose, the following are the only valid values for ContentTransferEncoding:

```
Base64
quoted-printable
mac-binhex40
x-uuencode
```

You can extend the functionality of your email client by recognizing nonstandard ContentTransferEncoding values in received messages (such as x-binhex) and modifying the value of the property appropriately before invoking the Decode method.

Data Type
String

ContentType Property

Description
Describes the data contained in a message or message part.

Syntax
object.**ContentType** [= *string*]

The syntax of the **ContentType** property has these parts:

Part	Description
object	A Mail control.
string	A string expression that specifies the content type for a message or message part.

Remarks
ContentType categorizes the contents of a message into one of a number of broad groups. The specific type of data in a message is further specified by the ContentSubtype and ContentSubtypeParameters properties. It's possible that a received message is of a type not described in the following. Any such messages are nonstandard, and if not specific to your email implementation, you can probably do no better than to allow the user to save the contents to a file.

Type	Description
text	Simple text message containing textual information in one of a number of character sets (as specified by the ContentSubtypeParameters property).
multipart	Message is a multipart MIME message. Used to combine several body parts, possibly of differing types of data, into a single message.

Mail

Type	Description
application	Application specific message.
message	Encapsulates another mail message, most often seen in forwarded messages.
image	Still images such as gif and jpeg.
audio	Audio or voice data.
video	Video or moving image data.

Data Type
String

CreatePart Method

Description
Creates a new part in a MIME multipart message.

Syntax
object.**CreatePart**

The syntax of the **CreatePart** method has these parts:

Part	Description
object	Required. A Mail control.

Remarks
The new part is created with the following defaults:

```
ContentDescription  = ""
ContentID = ""
ContentSubtype = "plain"
ContentSubtypeParameters = "charset=us-ascii"
ContentType = "text"
```

When the new part is created, the Parts property is one greater than it was before CreatePart was executed, and Part is set to select the newly created part. Before adding content to the new part or modifying any of its headers, you must use Descend to move into the new part.

Date Property

Description
Date message sent.

Syntax
object.**Date** [= *string*]

The syntax of the **Date** property has these parts:

Part	Description
object	A Mail control.
string	A string expression that specifies the date and time a message was created.

Remarks
The date and time an email message was sent in standard RFC822 format:

    Wed, 30 Oct 1996 00:58:56 -0500

The -0500 indicates that the local time (00:58:56) where the message is sent from is 5 hours earlier than Greenwich Mean Time (GMT).

Data Type
String

Debug Property

Description
Enables and disables the Debug event.

Syntax
object.**Debug** [= *debugflag*]

The syntax of the **Debug** property has these parts:

Part	Description
object	A Mail control.
debugflag	An integer that determines if Debug events are fired.

Remarks
Setting Debug to one (1) enables the Debug event. Setting it to zero (0) disables the Debug event. All other values are invalid at this time.

Data Type
Integer (enumerated)

Debug Event

Description
Fired when the control has debugging information for the program.

Syntax
Sub *object*_**Debug**([*index* As Integer,] *message* As String)

The syntax of the **Debug** event has these parts:

Mail

Part	Description
object	A Mail control.
index	An integer that identifies a control if it's in a control array.
message	A string expression that holds a debugging message from the control.

Remarks
The Debug event is enabled by setting the Debug property to a non-zero value (1 is the only permitted non-zero value at this time). When the Debug property is non-zero, the Debug event fires as messages are sent to and received from the server. Printing the Message argument string to Visual Basic's debug window will help you understand what is happening as you debug your application.

Decode Method

Description
Decodes data encoded with Base64, BinHex40, quoted-printable or UUencoding.

Syntax
object.**Decode***encoding,flags,source,destination*

The syntax of the **Decode** method has these parts:

Part	Description
object	Required. A Mail control.
encoding	Optional. A string expression that specifies the encoding format.
flags	Optional. An integer expression that specifies the source and destination locations.
source	Optional. A string expression that holds the source data (if flags includes MailSrcIsBuffer).
destination	Optional. A string expression that receives the decoded data, if the flags parameter includes MailDstIsBuffer.

Remarks
When using the VBX version of Mail, the encoding format is specified by the ContentTransferEncoding property. When using the Decode method with the OCX version, you might override the ContentTransferEncoding property by supplying a value for the encoding parameter. Acceptable values for the ContentTransferEncoding property (or the encoding parameter) are:

```
base64
binhex40
quoted-printable
x-uuencode
```

The Flags property (*flags* parameter) specifies the source for data to decode and its destination. The following flag values are acceptable:

Flag	Meaning
MailSrcIsBuffer	Decode contents of Buffer
MailSrcIsFile	Decode contents of file named by the SrcFilename property
MailSrcIsBody	Decode contents of the current message part's body
MailDstIsBuffer	Decoded contents are placed in the Buffer property
MailDstIsFile	Decoded contents are written to a file named by the DstFilename property
MailDstIsBody	Decoded contents are written to the current message part's body

When using the OCX version, buffers and filenames can be used as the optional source and destination parameters. The Flags property determines how these optional parameters are used.

DeletePart Method

Description
Deletes the current part.

Syntax
`object.DeletePart`

The syntax of the **DeletePart** method has these parts:

Part	Description
object	Required. A Mail control.

Remarks
Deletes the part currently selected by the Part property. This can be useful if the user decides to delete an attachment.

Descend Method

Description
Descends into the current message part.

Syntax
`object.Descend`

The syntax of the **Descend** method has these parts:

Part	Description
object	Required. A Mail control.

Mail

Remarks
When a message has multiple MIME parts, the Parts property is greater than zero. When this is the case, a part can be selected by using the Descend method. After the method executes, the control's properties are set to reflect the contents of the part into which you descend.

Disconnect Method

Description
Performs a normal disconnect from the mail server.

Syntax
object.**Disconnect**

The syntax of the **Disconnect** method has these parts:

Part	Description
object	Required. A Mail control.

Remarks
When connected to an SMTP server, the Disconnect method simply disconnects. Disconnect has special semantics when you're connected to a POP3 server. Messages that are marked for deletion using the HostDelete method are deleted from the POP3 user's mailbox by the server upon the successful completion of the Disconnect method.

Important Note
The Blocking property must not be changed while a connection is established. You should only change the Blocking property when the control is not connected to a server. Changing the Blocking property while connected could cause some strange behavior in the control.

Done Event

Description
This event procedure is fired when the control completes an action or method.

Syntax
Sub *object*_**Done**([*index* As Integer])

The syntax of the **Done** event has these parts:

Part	Description
object	A Mail control.
index	An integer that identifies a control if it's in a control array.

Remarks

Fired when a method has finished executing without error. If an error occurs during execution of any method and Blocking is True, then an error is thrown by the control and must be handled by On Error.

When Blocking is False, an error might be thrown during execution of a method as it is when Blocking is True. However, errors that occur during background execution of methods when Blocking is False result in firing of the AsyncError event.

DstFilename Property

Description
The destination filename for certain methods.

Syntax
`object.DstFilename [= filename ]`

The syntax of the **DstFilename** property has these parts:

Part	Description
object	A Mail control.
filename	A string expression that specifies a filename.

Remarks
Some of the methods, such as Encode and Decode, might use a destination file. When that is the case, the destination filename is given by the DstFilename property.

Data Type
String

EMailAddress Property

Description
Email address of the message sender.

Syntax
`object.EMailAddress [= address ]`

The syntax of the **EMailAddress** property has these parts:

Part	Description
object	A Mail control.
address	A string expression that specifies the email address of the message sender.

Mail

Remarks
SMTP servers like to know who is sending email. The EMailAddress Property is used to set the email address given to the SMTP server prior to sending mail. The simplest form of the required email address is:

```
zane@mabry.com
```

However, you should provide a user-friendly version, as in the following:

```
"Zane Thomas" <zane@mabry.com>
```

Data Type
String

Encode Method

Description
Encodes data using either Base64, quoted-printable, BinHex40, or UUencoding.

Syntax
object.**Encode***encoding,flags,source,destination*

The syntax of the **Encode** method has these parts:

Part	Description
object	Required. A Mail control.
encoding	Optional. A string expression that specifies the encoding format.
flags	Optional. An integer expression that specifies the source and destination locations.
source	Optional. A string expression that holds the source data (if the flags parameter includes MailSrcIsBuffer).
destination	Optional. A string expression that receives the encoded data, if the flags parameter includes MailDstIsBuffer.

Remarks
When using the VBX version of Mail, the encoding format is specified by the ContentTransferEncoding property. When using the Encode method with the OCX version, you might override the ContentTransferEncoding property by supplying a value for the encoding parameter. Acceptable values for the ContentTransferEncoding property (or the encoding parameter) are:

```
base64
binhex40
quoted-printable
x-uuencode
```

The Flags property (*flags* parameter) specifies the source for data to encode and its destination. The following flag values are acceptable:

Flag	Meaning
MailSrcIsBuffer	Encode contents of Buffer
MailSrcIsFile	Encode contents of file named by the SrcFilename property
MailSrcIsBody	Encode contents of the current message part's body
MailDstIsBuffer	Encoded contents are placed in the Buffer property
MailDstIsFile	Encoded contents are written to file named by the DstFilename property
MailDstIsBody	Encoded contents are written to the current message part's body

When implementing the OCX version, buffers and filenames can be used as the optional source and destination parameters. The Flags property determines how these optional parameters are used.

Flags Property

Description
Used to specify options for some methods.

Syntax
object.**Flags** [= *flags*]

The syntax of the **Flags** property has these parts:

Part	Description
object	A Mail control.
flags	A long integer that specifies options.

Remarks
The Encode, Decode, WriteMessage, and ReadMessage methods require both a source and a destination. The Flags property is used to select the source and destination for these methods. The following table lists the possible values that might used:

Constant	Value	Description
MailSrcIsBuffer	1	Source is Buffer.
MailSrcIsFile	2	Source is a file named by the SrcFilename property.
MailSrcIsHost	4	Source is mail host
MailSrcIsBody	8	Encode/decode source is message body
MailDstIsBuffer	16	Destination is Buffer.
MailDstIsFile	32	Destination is file named by DstFilename property.

Mail

Constant	Value	Description
MailDstIsHost	64	Destination is mail host
MailDstIsBody	128	Encode/decode destination is message body
MailReadHeaderOnly	256	Download only the message headers from the POP server (useful for scanning mail). When this flag is set, only the headers are retrieved. Everything normally associated with an email message will be as it is without the MailReadHeaderOnly flag, except that the message contains no body text of any kind.

All uses of the Flags property require that values from the table be OR'ed together. One value specifies the source data for a method and the other specifies the destination. For instance, if the ReadMessage method is used, an email message can be retrieved from the host and stored in a file as shown in the following code fragment:

```
Mail1.Flags = MailSrcIsHost Or MailDstIsFile
    Mail1.DstFilename = "c:\foo"
    Mail1.Action = MailActionReadMessage
```

Data Type
Integer (long)

From Property

Description
The sender of an email message.

Syntax
object.**From** [= *string*]

The syntax of the **From** property has these parts:

Part	Description
object	A Mail control.
string	A string expression that specifies the data for the From: header line.

Remarks
Normal email messages contain a From: header that contains the email address of the message sender. However, email advertisers and other spam-o-gram generators often place invalid email addresses in this header field.

Data Type
String

Headers Property

Description
Contents of an email message's header lines.

Syntax
`object.Headers( index ) [= string ]`

The syntax of the **Headers** property has these parts:

Part	Description
object	A Mail control.
index	An integer that identifies a particular header line.
string	A string expression that specifies the name and data for a header line.

Remarks
When receiving messages, the Mail control parses the message headers and assigns the common headers (such as To, From, and Subject) to their respective properties. In addition to this, all headers are placed in the Headers array, one header in each element of the array. The HeadersCount property tells you how many headers are in the array at any time.

> **Note**
>
> As with all other message-related properties, the Headers array changes when you Descend into, or Ascend out of, part of a multipart message.

Data Type
String

HeadersCount Property

Description
Number of elements in the Headers property array.

Syntax
`object.HeadersCount [= count ]`

The syntax of the **HeadersCount** property has these parts:

Part	Description
object	A Mail control.
count	A long integer that specifies the number of header line entries.

Remarks
This property tells you how many headers were received for a message (or the current part of a multipart message). The headers are stored in the Headers property.

Mail

Data Type
Integer (long)

HeaderText Property

Description
Contains the entire header for a message.

Syntax
`object.HeaderText [= string ]`

The syntax of the **HeaderText** property has these parts:

Part	Description
object	A Mail control.
string	A string expression that specifies the entire set of headers for a message or message part.

Remarks
You might access all the headers for a message at once by using the HeaderText property. This is functionally equivalent to iterating over the Headers array and concatenating all the elements of that array.

Data Type
String

Host Property

Description
Name or IP address of the SMTP or POP3 host.

Syntax
`object.Host [= string ]`

The syntax of the **Host** property has these parts:

Part	Description
object	A Mail control.
string	A string expression that specifies the name or IP address of the host.

Remarks
Used to specify the name (or IP address directly) of the SMTP or POP3 host to use during execution of the next Connect method.

Data Type
String

HostDelete Method

Description
Deletes a message from the POP3 mailbox (on the server/host).

Syntax
object.`HostDelete`

The syntax of the **HostDelete** method has these parts:

Part	Description
object	Required. A Mail control.

Remarks
When you connect to a POP3 server, a transaction is started. During the transaction, you might mark messages for deletion by storing the message ID in the MessageID property and invoking the HostDelete method.

There are two ways to terminate a POP3 connection: Abort and Disconnect. Abort terminates the current transaction without actually deleting any messages and starts a new transaction. Disconnect performs a normal disconnect and any messages marked for deletion by the HostDelete command are deleted from the POP3 user's mailbox.

LastError Property

Description
Holds the last error number reported.

Syntax
object.`LastError`

The syntax of the **LastError** property has these parts:

Part	Description
object	A Mail control.

Remarks
This property contains the result of the last method executed. It is zero if the last method completed without error. Otherwise, it contains an error code.

This property is read-only and only available at runtime.

Data Type
Integer

Mail

Lines Property

Description
Number of lines in the current email message.

Syntax
`object.Lines [= long ]`

The syntax of the **Lines** property has these parts:

Part	Description
object	A Mail control.
long	A long integer that specifies the number of lines of text in the message body.

Remarks
Some email programs provide a Lines: header to tell you how many lines of text are contained in the current email message.

Data Type
Integer (long)

LogonName Property

Description
User name on the server.

Syntax
`object.LogonName [= string ]`

The syntax of the **LogonName** property has these parts:

Part	Description
object	A Mail control.
string	A string expression that specifies the user name to implement when connecting.

Remarks
Most POP3 hosts require that connecting clients be known to them, so they require a logon name and password. The LogonName and LogonPassword properties must be set before attempting to connect to a POP3 host that requires authentication.

Data Type
String

LogonPassword Property

Description
Host logon password.

Syntax
object.**LogonPassword** [= *string*]

The syntax of the **LogonPassword** property has these parts:

Part	Description
object	A Mail control.
string	A string expression that specifies the password to use when connecting.

Remarks
Most POP3 hosts require that connecting clients be known to them, so they require a logon name and password. The LogonName and LogonPassword properties must be set before attempting to connect to a POP3 host that requires authentication.

Data Type
String

MessageClass Property

Description
The email message type.

Syntax
object.**MessageClass** [= *string*]

The syntax of the **MessageClass** property has these parts:

Part	Description
object	A Mail control.
string	A string expression that specifies the general classification of the current message.

Remarks
Defines the general classification of an email message.

Value	Description
Generic	A generic email message not identified as belonging to any other MessageClass category.

Mail

Value	Description
MIMEVersion 1.0	A MIME version 1.0 email message that might have multiple parts. The ContentType and ContentSubtype properties further identify the contents of a MIME email message. Parts are set appropriately for the current message. See the Part and Parts properties, and the Ascend, Descend, CreatePart and DeletePart methods for further discussion of multipart message handling.

Data Type
String

MessageID Property

Description
An email message's world-unique identification.

Syntax
`object.MessageID [= string ]`

The syntax of the **MessageID** property has these parts:

Part	Description
object	A Mail control.
string	A string expression that uniquely identifies a message.

Remarks
RFC821 requires that all email messages have a world-unique message ID. Exactly how a developer can guarantee that a unique message ID is generated is not specified. However, a reasonably long MessageID composed of the user's name and something similar to TimeSerial should work under most circumstances.

> Note
> Most SMTP servers generate a MessageID header line for you if one isn't supplied. However, you should not rely on this.

Data Type
String

MultipartBoundary Property

Description
Message-unique string that separates message parts.

Syntax

`object.MultipartBoundary [= string ]`

The syntax of the **MultipartBoundary** property has these parts:

Part	Description
object	A Mail control.
string	A string expression that specifies the string used to separate parts in a multipart message.

Remarks

The parts of a multipart message are separated by the string in the MultipartBoundary property. This string must be chosen so that it doesn't occur in the body of any message part. The underscore character ('_') doesn't appear in Base64 encoded data, so if you use that character somewhere in your boundary, don't be concerned about what is in the body of a Base64 encoded message part.

Data Type

String

NewMessage Method

Description

Creates a new, empty message.

Syntax

`object.NewMessage`

The syntax of the **NewMessage** method has these parts:

Part	Description
object	Required. A Mail control.

Remarks

Discards the contents of the current message and all its parts, if any, and creates a new empty email message.

Part Property

Description

Selected part of a multipart message.

Syntax

`object.Part [= long ]`

Mail

The syntax of the **Part** property has these parts:

Part	Description
object	A Mail control.
long	A long integer that specifies an individual part of a multipart message.

Remarks
This property is used to select one part of a multipart message. Typically, you set this property before using the CreatePart method or the Descend method to move into one part of a multipart message.

Data Type
Integer (long)

Parts Property

Description
Number of parts in the current multipart message.

Syntax
object.`Parts`

The syntax of the **Parts** property has these parts:

Part	Description
object	A Mail control.

Remarks
A MIME message might contain multiple parts. The Parts property tells you how many parts are contained in the current message.

This property is read-only and only available at runtime.

Data Type
Integer (long)

PopMessageCount Property

Description
Number of new messages available from the POP3 server.

Syntax
object.`PopMessageCount`

The syntax of the **PopMessageCount** property has these parts:

Part	Description
object	A Mail control.

Remarks
After the Mail control connects to a POP3 server, this property tells you how many new messages are contained in the user's POP3 mailbox.

This property is read-only and only available at runtime.

Data Type
Integer

PopMessageSizes Property

Description
Number of bytes in each POP3 message.

Syntax
object.**PopMessageSizes** [= *index*]

The syntax of the **PopMessageSizes** property has these parts:

Part	Description
object	A Mail control.
index	An integer that identifies a message.

Remarks
After you have connected to a POP3 server, the PopMessageCount property tells you how many email messages are in the user's POP3 mailbox. The PopMessageSizes array then has one element for each message. Each element tells you how many bytes are in each email message. When downloading messages, you can use this information together with the information provided in the Progress event to display a progress bar.

This property is read-only and only available at runtime.

Data Type
Integer (long)

PopPort Property

Description
Specifies POP server's port on the Host.

Syntax
object.**PopPort** [= *port*]

Mail

The syntax of the **PopPort** property has these parts:

Part	Description
object	A Mail control.
port	A long integer that specifies the POP server's port number.

Remarks
This property determines the port number to use when accessing your POP server. Normally you can use the default setting.

Sometimes security measures (firewalls, wormholes, and so on) require you to use a different port. This property allows you to change the port number that the Mail control uses to accommodate the security.

PopPort is used when the ConnectType property is MailConnectTypePOP3 (1).

Data Type
Integer (long)

Progress Event

Description
Fired as lengthy operations progress.

Syntax
Sub *object*_**Progress**([*index* As Integer,] *bytecount* As Long, *bytestotal* As Long)

The syntax of the **Progress** event has these parts:

Part	Description
object	A Mail control.
index	An integer that identifies a control if it's in a control array.
bytecount	A long integer that specifies the number of bytes sent or received.
bytestotal	A long integer that specifies the total number of bytes to send or receive.

Remarks
The Progress event is fired while email is being sent or received. This event lets you know how close to completion the operation is and might be used to display a progress bar or other status indicator.

Read Method

Description
Used to do raw reads of server responses.

Syntax
object.`Read`

The syntax of the **Read** method has these parts:

Part	Description
object	Required. A Mail control.

Remarks
This control has a pair of methods, Read and Write, and corresponding properties, ReadData and WriteData, that can be used to communicate directly with the server. These methods and properties are provided so you can handle nonstandard protocols that might be implemented on special-purpose servers.

Used to read the server's response after a command has been sent using the Write method. The Done event is fired when data arrives from the server after the Write method has been invoked if the control is in nonblocking mode (see Blocking).

ReadData Property

Description
Data received from the Read method or its Action equivalent.

Syntax
object.`ReadData`

The syntax of the **ReadData** property has these parts:

Part	Description
object	A Mail control.

Remarks
This control has a pair of methods, Read and Write, and corresponding properties, ReadData and WriteData, that can be used to communicate directly with the server. These methods and properties are provided so you can handle nonstandard protocols that might be implemented on special-purpose servers.

In some circumstances, you might have to interact directly with the server. This can happen if a particular server has nonstandard extensions you choose to use. The Read method lets you directly retrieve data sent by the server. Upon successful completion of the Read method (or the Action property equivalent) the ReadData property contains whatever the server sent.

Data Type
String

ReadMessage Method

Description
Reads a message and makes it available through the control's properties.

Syntax
`object.ReadMessage flags, filenameOrID`

The syntax of the **ReadMessage** method has these parts:

Part	Description
object	Required. A Mail control.
flags	Optional. An integer that specifies the source of the message.
filenameOrID	Optional. A string expression that contains either a filename or a message ID (depending on the flags parameter).

Remarks
The Flags property (or the *flags* parameter) specifies the source of the email message to be read. You can read messages from files, buffers, or from a POP3 host.

Flag	Description
MailSrcIsBuffer	Buffer contains a message to read
MailSrcIsFilename	SrcFilename has the name of a file containing the message to read
MailSrcIsHost	Host server is used to retrieve a message specified by MessageID
MailReadHeaderOnly	Only the header lines are read from a message. When this flag is set, only the headers are retrieved. Everything normally associated with an email message will be as it is without the MailReadHeadersOnly flag, except that the message contains no body text of any kind.

Important Note for Mail
For most commands that interact with either a POP or SMTP server, the Timeout property specifies the total time to wait for the command to complete. Note that timeout values are specified in seconds, not milliseconds.

With either the ReadMessage or WriteMessage commands, the Timeout property specifies an inactivity time. If data doesn't arrive (or cannot be sent) within the time specified by the Timeout property, the command is aborted.

If you set some reasonable value for Timeout, 30 seconds for instance, it will most likely work for connecting, sending and retrieving messages, and all other mail commands.

SmtpPort Property

Description
Specifies SMTP server's port on the Host.

Syntax
`object.SmtpPort [= port ]`

The syntax of the **SmtpPort** property has these parts:

Part	Description
object	A Mail control.
port	A long integer that specifies the SMTP server's port number.

Remarks
This property determines the port number to use when accessing your SMTP server. Normally you can use the default setting.

Sometimes security measures (firewalls, wormholes, and so on) require you to use a different port. This property allows you to change the port number that the Mail control uses to accommodate the security.

SmtpPort is used when the ConnectType property is MailConnectTypeSMTP (0).

Data Type
Integer (long)

SrcFilename Property

Description
Source filename for some methods.

Syntax
`object.SrcFilename [= string ]`

The syntax of the **SrcFilename** property has these parts:

Part	Description
object	A Mail control.
string	A string expression that specifies a filename.

Remarks
A number of operations, such as Encode and Decode, might use a source file. When that is the case, the source filename is given by the SrcFilename property.

Data Type
String

Mail

Subject Property

Description
Subject of the email message.

Syntax
`object.Subject [= string ]`

The syntax of the **Subject** property has these parts:

Part	Description
object	A Mail control.
string	A string expression that specifies the subject of a message.

Remarks
Email messages typically have a Subject: header line. When email is received, the Subject: header is parsed and the subject itself is stored in the Subject property. Before sending email, you might set the Subject property.

Data Type
String

Timeout Property

Description
Time, in seconds, it takes to wait for an operation to complete.

Syntax
`object.Timeout`

The syntax of the **Timeout** property has these parts:

Part	Description
object	A Mail control.

Remarks
Methods that require interaction with a server might hang indefinitely due to a slow or nonresponsive server. You can set the maximum time to wait for any operation to complete by assigning a non-zero number of seconds to the Timeout property. When the Timeout property is set to zero, there is no timeout.

Data Type
Integer

To Property

Description
Intended message recipient(s).

Syntax
object.**To** [= *string*]

The syntax of the **To** property has these parts:

Part	Description
object	A Mail control.
string	A string expression that contains the receipient(s) of the current message.

Remarks
Three properties are used to specify the recipients of any given email message, the To, CC, and BCC properties. All recipients will see the recipients in the To and CC properties in the header of the copy of the email message that they receive. Recipients listed in the BCC field won't be known to other recipients.

Multiple recipients might be specified and, if so, they must be separated by commas. The following are examples of valid addresses:

    zane@mabry.com
    zane@mabry.com
    Zane Thomas <zane@mabry.com>

If you choose to include a full name as well as an email address, as shown in the third line of the previous example, you must enclose the actual email address in angle brackets.

You shouldn't use other formats for specifying an email address. The Mail control attempts to extract the actual email address from the string specified. You might find, however, that the Mail control does not recognize them.

Data Type
String

Version Property

Description
Returns the version of the control.

Syntax
object.**Version**

Mail

The syntax of the **Version** property has these parts:

Part	Description
object	A Mail control.

Remarks
This property holds the current version of the control. It is read-only and available at both design time and runtime.

Data Type
String

Write Method

Description
Sends a string to the server.

Syntax
`object.Write`

The syntax of the **Write** method has these parts:

Part	Description
object	Required. A Mail control.

Remarks
This control has a pair of methods, Read and Write, and corresponding properties, ReadData and WriteData, that can be used to communicate directly with the server. These methods and properties are provided so that you can handle nonstandard protocols that might be implemented on special-purpose servers.

This method is used to write a string to the server and is useful for sending nonstandard commands or for invoking some of the more obscure or nonstandard commands. When the server's response comes back, the Done event is fired if the control is in nonblocking mode.

All strings must be terminated with a CR/LF (Chr[13] & Chr[10]) as part of the string.

WriteData Property

Description
Data to send to server

Syntax
`object.WriteData [= string ]`

The syntax of the **WriteData** property has these parts:

Part	Description
object	A Mail control.
string	A string expression that holds data to send to the FTP server.

Remarks

This control has a pair of methods, Read and Write, and corresponding properties, ReadData and WriteData, that can be used to communicate directly with the server. These methods and properties are provided so you can handle nonstandard protocols that might be implemented on special-purpose servers.

This control handles all aspects of the usual protocols. However, there might be circumstances where you need to interact directly with a server. When this is the case, you can send commands directly to the server by assigning a command string to the WriteData property and using the Write method (or its Action property equivalent).

All strings must be terminated with a CR/LF (Chr[13] & Chr[10]) as part of the string.

Data Type
String

WriteMessage Method

Description
Writes an email message either to a file, buffer, or an SMTP server.

Syntax
`object.WriteMessageflags,filename`

The syntax of the **WriteMessage** method has these parts:

Part	Description
object	Required. A Mail control.
flags	Optional. An integer that specifies the destination of the message.
filename	Optional. A string expression that holds the filename (only used if flags contains MailDstIsFilename).

Remarks

Writes a fully formatted MIME message to the destination specified by the Flags property (or by the optional *flags* parameter when using the OCX version).

The Flags property (or optional *flags* parameter when using the OCX version) determines the destination of the message:

Mail

Flag	Meaning
MailDstIsBuffer	Formatted message is written to the Buffer property
MailDstIsFilename	Formatted message is written to the file named by the DstFilename property
MailDstIsHost	Formatted message is written to the mail host.

Important Note for Mail

For most commands that interact with either a POP or SMTP server, the Timeout property specifies the total time to wait for the command to complete. Note that timeout values are specified in seconds, not milliseconds.

With either the ReadMessage or WriteMessage commands, the Timeout property specifies an inactivity time. If data doesn't arrive (or cannot be sent) within the time specified by the Timeout property, the command is aborted.

If you set some reasonable value for Timeout, 30 seconds for instance, it will most likely work for connecting, sending and retrieving messages, and all other mail commands.

How to Buy the Source Code for This Control

CREDITS
Mail was written by Zane Thomas.

CONTACT INFORMATION
Orders, inquiries, technical support, questions, comments, etc. can be sent to mabry@mabry.com on the Internet. Our mailing address/contact information is

Mabry Software, Inc.
503 316th Street Northwest
Stanwood, WA 98292

Sales: 1-800-99-MABRY (U.S. only)
Voice: 360-629-9278
Fax: 360-629-9278
Web: http://www.mabry.com

COST
The cost of Mail and the C/C++ source code (of the control itself) is US$199 (US$204 for International orders).

Prices are subject to change without notice.

Mabry Software, Inc.

HTTP://www.mabry.com

DELIVERY METHODS

We can ship this software to you via air mail or email.

Air Mail—you will receive disks, a printed manual, and printed receipt if you choose this delivery method. The costs are:

US$10.00	US Priority Mail
US$15.00	Airborne Express 2nd Day (US deliveries only)
US$20.00	Airborne Express Overnight (US deliveries only)
US$20.00	Global Priority Mail (Int'l deliveries only; Western Europe, Pacific Rim and Canada only)
US$45.00	International Airborne Express (Int'l deliveries only)

Email—We can ship this package to you via email. You need to have an email account that can accept large file attachments (which includes CompuServe, AOL, and most Internet providers). If you choose this option, please note: a printed manual is not included. We will, however, email a receipt to you.

Be sure to include your full mailing address with your order. Sometimes (on the Internet) the package cannot be emailed, so we are forced to send it through normal mail.

CompuServe Email—CompuServe members can use the software registration forum (GO SWREG) to register this package. DFInfo's SWREG ID number is 1069. The source code version's ID number is 1070. PLEASE NOTE: When you order through SWREG, we send the registered package to your CompuServe account (not your Internet or AOL account) within a few hours.

ORDER/PAYMENT METHODS

You can order this software by phone, fax, email, mail. Please note that orders must include all information that is requested on our order form. Your shipment WILL BE DELAYED if we have to contact you for additional information (such as phone number, street address, and so on).

You can pay by credit card (VISA, MasterCard, American Express, Discover, NOVUS), check (U.S. dollars drawn on a U.S. bank), cash, International Money Order, International Postal Order, Purchase Order (established business entities only—terms net 30), or wire transfer.

Mail

WIRE TRANSFER INFORMATION
Here is the information you need regarding our account for a wire funds transfer:

Bank Name:	SeaFirst—Stone Way Branch
Bank Address:	3601 Stone Way North
	Seattle, WA 98103
Bank Phone:	206-585-4951
Account Name:	Mabry Software, Inc.
Routing Number:	12000024
Account Number:	16311706

If you are paying with a wire transfer of funds, please add US$25.00 to your order. This is the fee that SeaFirst Bank charges Mabry Software. Also, please ADD ANY ADDITIONAL FEES THAT YOUR BANK MIGHT CHARGE for wire transfer service. If you are paying with a wire transfer, we must have full payment deposited to our account before we can ship your order.

Copyright © 1996-1998 by Mabry Software, Inc.

Mail Order Form

Mail this form to

Mabry Software, Inc.
503 316th Street Northwest
Stanwood, WA 98292

Phone: 360-629-9278
Fax: 360-629-9278
Internet: mabry@mabry.com
Web: www.mabry.com

Where did you get this copy of Mail? _____

Name: _____

Ship to: _____

_____

_____

_____

Phone: _____

Fax: _____

Email: _____

Credit Card #: _____ exp. _____

P.O. # (if any): _____

Signature _____

Qty ordered ____ SOURCE CODE AND REGISTRATION

$199.00 ($204.00 international). Check or money order in U.S. currency drawn on a U.S. bank. Add $10.00 per order for shipping and handling.

Slider

Slider

Description
The Slider OCX custom control is similar in function to a scroll bar, but has a different appearance. It is actually two controls in one—a horizontal slider and a vertical slider. You can easily create a cool looking audio mixer with these custom controls. A complete set of bevel properties allows you to quickly get that 3-D look. Four different thumb styles add to the flexibility of this control:

- Complete set of bevel properties.
- Slider is similar in function to a scroll bar, but looks better.
- Pro audio mixer fader style thumbs.
- Up, down, left, and right thumb properties.
- Left, right, and both tick properties with tickcolor, tickcount, tickwidth, ticklength, and gap control.
- Horizontal and vertical slider custom controls.
- Control of the 3-D style of the track.

A Visual Basic sample project is included, so you can quickly see the wide range of great looking sliders you can create with the Slider control.

File Name
HSLIDE32.OCX, VSLIDE32.OCX

ActiveX/OCX Object Name
Mabry.HSlideCtrl/Mabry.VSlideCtrl

ActiveX Compatibility
VB 4.0 (32-bit), 5.0, and 6.0

ActiveX Built With
Microsoft Visual C++ v4

ActiveX—Required DLLs
MFC40.DLL (October 6th, 1995 or later)

OLEPRO32.DLL (October 6th, 1995 or later)

MSVCRT40.DLL (September 29th, 1995 or later)

Mabry Software, Inc.

HTTP://www.mabry.com

Distribution Note

When you develop and distribute an application that uses this control, you should install the control file into the user's Windows SYSTEM directory. The control file has version information built into it. So, during installation, you should ensure that you are not overwriting a newer version.

Slider Properties

Properties that have special meaning for this control or that apply only to this control are marked with an asterisk (*).

BackColor Property	Tag Property
*BevelInner Property	*ThumbHeight Property
*BevelOuter Property	*ThumbStyle Property
*BevelWidth Property	*ThumbWidth Property
*BorderWidth Property	*TickColor Property
Enabled Property	*TickCount Property
*Gap Property	*TickLength Property
Height Property	*TickMarks Property
hWnd Property	*TickWidth Property
Index Property	Top Property
*LargeChange Property	*TrackBevel Property
Left Property	*TrackWidth Property
*Max Property	*Value Property
*Min Property	*Version Property
Name Property	Visible Property
Parent Property	Width Property

Slider Events

Events that have special meaning for this control or that apply only to this control are marked with an asterisk (*).

*Change Event	MouseMove Event
GotFocus Event	MouseUp Event
LostFocus Event	*Scroll Event
MouseDown Event	

Slider

Bevel Properties Example
In this example, the program shows what happens when you vary the bevels on the controls. To try this example, paste the code into the Declarations section of a form that contains a knob, a horizontal indicator, and a horizontal slider control. Press F5. Play with the knob.

```
Sub Form_Load ()
    Form1.BackColor = &HC0C0C0

    Knob1.Width = 3000
    Knob1.Height = 2000
    Knob1.Radius = 500
    Knob1.TickCount = 4
    Knob1.Min = 0
    Knob1.Max = 3
    Knob1.Value = 0
    Knob1.FontSize = 7
    Knob1.FontBold = False
    Knob1.FontName = "Arial"
    Knob1.FontSize = 7
    Knob1.TickCaption(0) = "None"
    Knob1.TickCaption(1) = "Raised"
    Knob1.TickCaption(2) = "Inset"
    Knob1.TickCaption(3) = "Lowered"

    HIndicator1.BackColor = &HC0C0C0

    HSlider1.TrackBevel = 0

    HSlider1.TrackWidth = 5
    HSlider1.BorderWidth = 4
End Sub

Sub Knob1_Scroll ()
    HSlider1.BevelInner = Knob1.Value
    HSlider1.BevelOuter = Knob1.Value
    HIndicator1.BevelInner = Knob1.Value
    HIndicator1.BevelOuter = Knob1.Value
End Sub
```

Gap Property Example
In this example, the program shows what happens when you vary the gap. To try this example, paste the code into the Declarations section of a form that contains a horizontal scroll bar, a label, and a horizontal slider control. Press F5. Play with the horizontal scroll bar.

```
Sub Form_Load ()
    Form1.BackColor = &HC0C0C0

    Label1.BackColor = &HC0C0C0
    Label1.Top = 240
    Label1.Left = 2840
    Label1.Height = 255
```

```
    HSlider1.Height = 1000
    HSlider1.Width = 2000

    HScroll1.Top = 240
    HScroll1.Left = 720
    HScroll1.Width = 2000
    HScroll1.Min = 0
    HScroll1.Max = 20
    HScroll1.Value = 2

    HSlider1.BevelOuter = 1
    HSlider1.BevelInner = 3
    HSlider1.TickMarks = 3
    HSlider1.TickCount = 11
    HSlider1.Height = 1000
    HSlider1.Width = 2000
    HSlider1.ThumbHeight = 360
    HSlider1.ThumbWidth = 120
    HSlider1.Gap = HScroll1.Value
    HSlider1.Value = 50
End Sub

Sub HScroll1_Change ()
    Call HScroll1_Scroll
End Sub

Sub HScroll1_Scroll ()
    HSlider1.Gap = HScroll1.Value
    Label1.Caption = "Gap: " & HScroll1.Value
End Sub
```

Thumb Properties Example

In this example, the program shows what happens when you vary the size of the thumb. To try this example, paste the code into the Declarations section of a form that contains a horizontal slider, a horizontal scroll bar, a vertical scroll bar, a knob, and two label controls. Press F5. Play with the scroll bars and the knob.

```
Sub Form_Load ()
    Form1.BackColor = &HC0C0C0
    Form1.Height = 4880
    Form1.Width = 4000

    Knob1.Left = 204
    Knob1.Top = 2400
    Knob1.Width = 3400
    Knob1.Height = 2000
    Knob1.Radius = 500
    Knob1.Min = 0
    Knob1.Max = 3
    Knob1.TickCount = 4
    Knob1.TickCaption(0) = "Normal"
```

Slider

```
        Knob1.TickCaption(1) = "Pointed Up"
        Knob1.TickCaption(2) = "Pointed Down"
        Knob1.TickCaption(3) = "Lined"

        Label1.BackColor = &HC0C0C0
        Label1.Top = 240
        Label1.Left = 2840
        Label1.Height = 255

        Label2.BackColor = &HC0C0C0
        Label2.Top = 1840
        Label2.Left = 240
        Label2.Height = 255

        HSlider1.Height = 1000
        HSlider1.Width = 2000

        HScroll1.Top = 240
        HScroll1.Left = 720
        HScroll1.Width = 2000
        HScroll1.Min = 90
        HScroll1.Max = 500
        HScroll1.Value = 120

        VScroll1.Top = 720
        VScroll1.Left = 240
        VScroll1.Height = 1000
        VScroll1.Min = 90
        VScroll1.Max = 500
        VScroll1.Value = 240

        HSlider1.Height = 1000
        HSlider1.Width = 2000
        HSlider1.ThumbHeight = VScroll1.Value
        HSlider1.ThumbWidth = HScroll1.Value
        HSlider1.Value = 50
    End Sub

    Sub HScroll1_Change ()
        Call HScroll1_Scroll
    End Sub

    Sub HScroll1_Scroll ()
        HSlider1.ThumbWidth = HScroll1.Value
        Label1.Caption = HScroll1.Value
    End Sub

    Sub Knob1_Change ()
        Call Knob1_Scroll
    End Sub
```

```
Sub Knob1_Scroll ()
    HSlider1.ThumbStyle = Knob1.Value
End Sub

Sub VScroll1_Change ()
    Call VScroll1_Scroll
End Sub

Sub VScroll1_Scroll ()
    HSlider1.ThumbHeight = VScroll1.Value
    Label2.Caption = VScroll1.Value
End Sub
```

Tick Properties Example

In this example, the program shows what happens when you change the look of the tick marks. To try this example, paste the code into the Declarations section of a form that contains a horizontal slider, a knob, two command buttons, four horizontal scroll bars, four labels, and a common dialog control. Press F5. Play with the scroll bars and the command buttons.

```
Sub Command1_Click ()
    CMDialog1.Color = HSlider1.TickColor
    CMDialog1.Flags = 1
    CMDialog1.Action = 3

    HSlider1.TickColor = CMDialog1.Color
    Knob1.TickColor = CMDialog1.Color
End Sub

Sub Command2_Click ()
    CMDialog1.Color = Knob1.TickCaptionColor
    CMDialog1.Flags = 1
    CMDialog1.Action = 3

    Knob1.TickCaptionColor = CMDialog1.Color
End Sub

Sub Form_Load ()
    Form1.BackColor = &HC0C0C0

    HSlider1.Top = 1680
    HSlider1.Left = 240
    HSlider1.Width = 6000

    HSlider1.Height = 600
    HSlider1.Value = 100
    HSlider1.BackColor = &HC0C0C0

    Knob1.Top = 2400
    Knob1.Left = 240
    Knob1.Width = 1800
    Knob1.Height = 1800
```

Slider

```
Knob1.Radius = 400
Knob1.TickCount = 5

Command1.Top = 240
Command1.Left = 240
Command1.Width = 1800
Command1.Height = 360
Command1.Caption = "Change TickColor"

Command2.Top = 720
Command2.Left = 240
Command2.Width = 1800
Command2.Height = 360
Command2.Caption = "Change TickCaptionColor"

HScroll1.Top = 240
HScroll1.Left = 2160
HScroll1.Width = 900
HScroll1.Min = 0
HScroll1.Max = 20
HScroll1.Value = Knob1.TickCount

Label1.Top = 240
Label1.Left = 3180
Label1.Width = 2000
Label1.BackColor = &HC0C0C0

HScroll2.Top = 600
HScroll2.Left = 2160
HScroll2.Width = 900
HScroll2.Min = 0
HScroll2.Max = 20
HScroll2.Value = Knob1.TickGap

Label2.Top = 600
Label2.Left = 3180
Label2.Width = 2000
Label2.BackColor = &HC0C0C0

HScroll3.Top = 960
HScroll3.Left = 2160
HScroll3.Width = 900
HScroll3.Min = 0
HScroll3.Max = 20
HScroll3.Value = Knob1.TickLength

Label3.Top = 960
Label3.Left = 3180
Label3.Width = 2000
Label3.BackColor = &HC0C0C0
```

```vb
        HScroll4.Top = 1320
        HScroll4.Left = 2160
        HScroll4.Width = 900
        HScroll4.Min = 0
        HScroll4.Max = 20
        HScroll4.Value = Knob1.TickWidth

        Label4.Top = 1320
        Label4.Left = 3180
        Label4.Width = 2000
        Label4.BackColor = &HC0C0C0
    End Sub

    Sub HScroll1_Change ()
        Dim I As Integer

        HSlider1.TickCount = HScroll1.Value
        Knob1.TickCount = HScroll1.Value
        Label1.Caption = "TickCount: " & HScroll1.Value

        For I = 0 To HScroll1.Value - 1
            Knob1.TickCaption(I) = Chr$(I + 65)
        Next I
    End Sub

    Sub HScroll1_Scroll ()
        Call HScroll1_Change
    End Sub

    Sub HScroll2_Change ()
        HSlider1.Gap = HScroll2.Value
        Knob1.TickGap = HScroll2.Value
        Label2.Caption = "TickGap: " & HScroll2.Value

    End Sub

    Sub HScroll2_Scroll ()
        Call HScroll2_Change
    End Sub

    Sub HScroll3_Change ()
        HSlider1.TickLength = HScroll3.Value
        Knob1.TickLength = HScroll3.Value
        Label3.Caption = "TickLength: " & HScroll3.Value
    End Sub

    Sub HScroll3_Scroll ()
        Call HScroll3_Change
    End Sub

    Sub HScroll4_Change ()
        HSlider1.TickWidth = HScroll4.Value
```

Slider

```
    Knob1.TickWidth = HScroll4.Value
    Label4.Caption = "TickWidth: " & HScroll4.Value
End Sub

Sub HScroll4_Scroll ()
    Call HScroll4_Change
End Sub
```

TrackBevel Property Example

In this example, the program shows what happens when you vary the track bevel. To try this example, paste the code into the Declarations section of a form that contains a knob and a horizontal slider control. Press F5. Play with the knob.

```
Sub Form_Load ()
    Form1.BackColor = &HC0C0C0

    Knob1.Width = 3000
    Knob1.Height = 2000
    Knob1.Radius = 500
    Knob1.TickCount = 4
    Knob1.Min = 0
    Knob1.Max = 3
    Knob1.Value = 0
    Knob1.FontSize = 7
    Knob1.FontBold = False
    Knob1.FontName = "Arial"
    Knob1.FontSize = 7
    Knob1.TickCaption(0) = "Normal"
    Knob1.TickCaption(1) = "Raised"
    Knob1.TickCaption(2) = "Inset"
    Knob1.TickCaption(3) = "Lowered"

    HSlider1.TrackBevel = 0
    HSlider1.TrackWidth = 5
End Sub

Sub Knob1_Scroll ()
    HSlider1.TrackBevel = Knob1.Value
End Sub
```

TrackWidth Property Example

In this example, the program shows what happens when you vary the track width. To try this example, paste the code into the Declarations section of a form that contains a label, a vertical scroll bar, and a horizontal slider control. Press F5. Play with the scroll bar.

```
Sub Form_Load ()
    Label1.Caption = "0"

    HSlider1.TrackBevel = 3

    VScroll1.Min = 0
```

```
        VScroll1.Max = 20
End Sub

Sub VScroll1_Scroll ()
    Label1.Caption = VScroll1.Value
    HSlider1.TrackWidth = VScroll1.Value
End Sub
```

BevelInner Property

Description
Determines the 3-D style of the border immediately surrounding the control.

Syntax
object.**BevelInner** [= *bevel*]

The syntax of the **BevelInner** property has these parts:

Part	Description
object	A Slider control.
bevel	An integer that determines the style of bevel to use.

Remarks
The value of this property determines the style of the inner border. This property might be one of four values:

Constant	Value	Description
bcNone	0	Normal frame
bcRaised	1	Raised frame (3-D)
bcInset	2	Inset frame (3-D)
bcLowered	3	Lowered frame (3-D)

Data Type
Integer

BevelOuter Property

Description
Determines the 3-D style of the border (if any) surrounding the control.

Syntax
object.**BevelOuter** [= *bevel*]

The syntax of the **BevelOuter** property has these parts:

Slider

Part	Description
object	A Slider control.
bevel	An integer that determines the style of bevel to use.

Remarks

The value of this property determines the style of the control's border. This property might be one of four values:

Constant	Value	Description
bcNone	0	Normal frame
bcRaised	1	Raised frame (3-D)
bcInset	2	Inset frame (3-D)
bcLowered	3	Lowered frame (3-D)

Data Type

Integer

BevelWidth Property

Description

Determines the width of the inner and outer borders (bevels).

Syntax

object.**BevelWidth** [= *width*]

The syntax of the **BevelWidth** property has these parts:

Part	Description
object	A Slider control.
width	An integer that determines the width of the bevels.

Remarks

The value of this property determines the width of the inner border (if any, see BevelInner) and the outer border (if any, see BevelOuter). This property is always measured in pixels.

Data Type

Integer

BorderWidth Property

Description

Determines the distance between the inner border and the outer border.

Syntax

object.**BorderWidth** [= *width*]

The syntax of the **BorderWidth** property has these parts:

Part	Description
object	A Slider control.
width	An integer that determines the distance between the inner and outer bevels.

Remarks
The value of this property determines the distance between the outer border (if any, see BevelOuter) and the inner border (if any, see BevelInner). This property is always measured in pixels.

Data Type
Integer

Change Event

Description
Occurs when the value has changed.

Syntax
Sub *object*_Change([*index* As Integer])

The syntax of the **Change** event has these parts:

Part	Description
object	A Slider control.
index	An integer that identifies a control if it's in a control array.

Remarks
This event occurs when the value of the control has changed (usually through user interaction). When this event occurs, the control also updates the control specified by the link properties.

Gap Property

Description
Determines the distance between the inside of the border and the tick marks.

Syntax
object.**Gap** [= *width*]

The syntax of the **Gap** property has these parts:

Part	Description
object	A Slider control.
width	An integer that determines the distance between the outer bevel and the tick marks.

Slider

Remarks

The value of this property determines the distance between the inner border and the tick marks. This property is measured in pixels.

Data Type

Integer

LargeChange Property

Description

Determines how far the slider moves when clicked outside the thumb.

Syntax

`object.LargeChange [= change ]`

The syntax of the **LargeChange** property has these parts:

Part	Description
object	A Slider control.
change	An integer that determines the amount to change.

Remarks

The value of this property determines how far the thumb moves when the control is clicked outside the thumb and near the track.

Data Type

Integer

Max and Min Properties

Description

Determines the range of values for this control.

Syntax

`object.Max`
`object.Min`

The syntax of the **Max** and **Min** properties has these parts:

Part	Description
object	A Slider control.

Remarks

These properties determine the range of values for the control in question. If Max is set to less than Min, the range of values is swapped.

Data Type

Integer

Scroll Event

Description
Occurs while a user changes the value.

Syntax
Sub *object*_Scroll([*index* As Integer])

The syntax of the **Scroll** event has these parts:

Part	Description
object	A Slider control.
index	An integer that identifies a control if it's in a control array.

Remarks
You can use this event to perform calculations or to manipulate controls that must be coordinated with changes in these controls. Use the Change event when you want an update to occur after the change is complete.

ThumbHeight and ThumbWidth Properties

Description
Determines the size of the thumb.

Syntax
object.ThumbHeight [= *size*]
object.ThumbWidth [= *size*]

The syntax of the **ThumbHeight** and **ThumbWidth** properties has these parts:

Part	Description
object	A Slider control.
size	A single-precision floating point number that determines the height/width of the thumb.

Remarks
The values of these properties determine the size of the thumb. These properties are measured in twips.

Data Type
Single

ThumbStyle Property

Description
Determines the style of the thumb.

Slider

Syntax
`object.ThumbStyle [= style ]`

The syntax of the **ThumbStyle** property has these parts:

Part	Description
object	A Slider control.
style	An integer that determines the style of the thumb.

Remarks
The value of this property determines the style of the control's border. This property might be one of four values:

Constant	Value	Description
tscNormal	0	Normal
tscPointedUp / tscPointedLeft	1	Pointer up/left
tscPointedDown / tscPointedRight	2	Pointed down/right
tscLined	3	Lined

Data Type
Integer

TickColor Property

Description
Determines what color the ticks are.

Syntax
`object.TickColor [= color ]`

The syntax of the **TickColor** property has these parts:

Part	Description
object	A Slider control.
color	A long integer that determines the color of the tick marks.

Remarks
This property specifies the color of the tick marks.

Data Type
Long

TickCount Property

Description
Determines the total number of tick marks.

Syntax
object.TickCount [= count]

The syntax of the **TickCount** property has these parts:

Part	Description
object	A Slider control.
count	An integer that determines the number of tick marks.

Remarks
This property determines the total number of tick marks.

Data Type
Integer

TickLength Property

Description
Determines the length of the tick marks.

Syntax
object.TickLength [= length]

The syntax of the **TickLength** property has these parts:

Part	Description
object	A Slider control.
length	An integer that determines the length of the tick marks.

Remarks
This property specifies the length, in pixels, of the tick marks.

Data Type
Integer

TickMarks Property

Description
Determines the location of the tick marks.

Slider

Syntax
`object.TickMarks [= style ]`

The syntax of the **TickMarks** property has these parts:

Part	Description
object	A Slider control.
style	An integer that determines the location of the tick marks.

Remarks
This property determines the location of the tick marks. The legitimate values are:

Constant	Value	Description
vtmcNone/htmcNone	0	No tick marks
vtmcLeft/htmcTop	1	Left for VSlider/Top for HSlider
vtmcRight/htmcBottom	2	Right for VSlider/Bottom for HSlider
vtmcBoth/htmcBoth	3	Both

Data Type
Integer

TickWidth Property

Description
Determines the width of the tick marks.

Syntax
`object.TickWidth [= width ]`

The syntax of the **TickWidth** property has these parts:

Part	Description
object	A Slider control.
width	An integer that determines the width of the tick marks.

Remarks
This property determines the width of the tick marks, and it is measured in pixels.

Data Type
Integer

TrackBevel Property

Description
Determines the 3-D style of the track.

Syntax

`object.TrackBevel [= style ]`

The syntax of the **TrackBevel** property has these parts:

Part	Description
object	A Slider control.
style	An integer that determines the style of the track's bevel.

Remarks

The value of this property determines the style of the control's track. This property might be one of four values:

Constant	Value	Description
bcNone	0	Normal
bcRaised	1	Raised (3-D)
bcInset	2	Inset (3-D)
bcLowered	3	Lowered (3-D)

Data Type
Integer

TrackWidth Property

Description
Determines the width of the track.

Syntax

`object.TrackWidth [= width ]`

The syntax of the **TrackWidth** property has these parts:

Part	Description
object	A Slider control.
width	An integer that determines the width of the bevel.

Remarks
The value of this property determines the width of the track, and it is measured in pixels.

Data Type
Integer

Slider

Value Property

Description
Specifies the current position of the control's thumb.

Syntax
`object.Value [= value ]`

The syntax of the **Value** property has these parts:

Part	Description
object	A Slider control.
value	An integer that determines the current position of the thumb.

Remarks
This property determines the current value of the control (that is, the position of the thumb). This is the default property of these controls.

Data Type
Integer

Version Property

Description
Returns the version of the control.

Syntax
`object.Version`

The syntax of the **Version** property has these parts:

Part	Description
object	A Slider control.

Remarks
This property holds the current version of the control. It is read-only and available at both design time and runtime.

Data Type
String

Mabry Software, Inc.

HTTP://www.mabry.com

How to Buy the Source Code for This Control

CREDITS
Slider was written by James Shields.

CONTACT INFORMATION
Orders, inquiries, technical support, questions, comments, and so on can be sent to mabry@mabry.com on the Internet. Our mailing address/contact information is

Mabry Software, Inc.
503 316th Street Northwest
Stanwood, WA 98292

Sales: 1-800-99-MABRY (U.S. only)
Voice: 360-629-9278
Fax: 360-629-9278
Web: http://www.mabry.com

COST
The cost of Slider and the C/C++ source code (of the control itself) is US$60 (US$65 for International orders).

Prices are subject to change without notice.

DELIVERY METHODS
We can ship this software to you via air mail or email.

Air Mail—you will receive disks, a printed manual, and printed receipt if you choose this delivery method. The costs are

US$10.00	US Priority Mail
US$15.00	Airborne Express 2nd Day (US deliveries only)
US$20.00	Airborne Express Overnight (US deliveries only)
US$20.00	Global Priority Mail (Int'l deliveries only; Western Europe, Pacific Rim and Canada only)
US$45.00	International Airborne Express (Int'l deliveries only)

Email—We can ship this package to you via email. You need to have an email account that can accept large file attachments (which includes CompuServe, AOL, and most Internet providers). If you choose this option, please note: a printed manual is not included. We will, however, email a receipt to you.

Be sure to include your full mailing address with your order. Sometimes (on the Internet) the package cannot be emailed, so we are forced to send it through normal mail.

CompuServe Email—CompuServe members can use the software registration forum (GO SWREG) to register this package. DFInfo's SWREG ID number is 1069. The source code version's ID number is 1070. PLEASE NOTE: When you order through SWREG, we send the registered package to your CompuServe account (not your Internet or AOL account) within a few hours.

ORDER/PAYMENT METHODS

You can order this software by phone, fax, email, mail. Please note that orders must include all information that is requested on our order form. Your shipment WILL BE DELAYED if we have to contact you for additional information (such as phone number, street address, and so on).

You can pay by credit card (VISA, MasterCard, American Express, Discover, NOVUS), check (U.S. dollars drawn on a U.S. bank), cash, International Money Order, International Postal Order, Purchase Order (established business entities only—terms net 30), or wire transfer.

WIRE TRANSFER INFORMATION

Here is the information you need regarding our account for a wire funds transfer:

Bank Name:	SeaFirst—Stone Way Branch
Bank Address:	3601 Stone Way North
	Seattle, WA 98103
Bank Phone:	206-585-4951
Account Name:	Mabry Software, Inc.
Routing Number:	12000024
Account Number:	16311706

If you are paying with a wire transfer of funds, please add US$25.00 to your order. This is the fee that SeaFirst Bank charges Mabry Software. Also, please ADD ANY ADDITIONAL FEES THAT YOUR BANK MIGHT CHARGE for wire transfer service. If you are paying with a wire transfer, we must have full payment deposited to our account before we can ship your order.

Copyright © 1996-1998 by Mabry Software, Inc.

Mabry Software, Inc.

HTTP://www.mabry.com

Slider Order Form

Mail this form to

Mabry Software, Inc.
503 316th Street Northwest
Stanwood, WA 98292

Phone: 360-629-9278
Fax: 360-629-9278
Internet: mabry@mabry.com
Web: www.mabry.com

Where did you get this copy of Slider? _____

Name: _____

Ship to: _____

_____

_____

_____

Phone: _____

Fax: _____

Email: _____

Credit Card #: _____ exp. _____

P.O. # (if any): _____

Signature _____

Qty ordered _____ SOURCE CODE AND REGISTRATION

$199.00 ($204.00 international). Check or money order in U.S. currency drawn on a U.S. bank. Add $10.00 per order for shipping and handling.

Time

Description

The Time control allows you to retrieve the current Greenwich Mean Time (GMT) from time servers on the Internet. The time servers usually have the correct time because they all talk among themselves to keep things accurate. Our favorite server is the one at MIT (mit.edu). Another good server is at "tock.usno.navy.mil".

You can use the Time control in any application where you need to have accurate time/date stamps. This includes financial transactions, medical data, long-term data collection, or anywhere else that a reliable time stamp is needed. You can even use this control to update the time of day on your systems and servers.

The Time control requests the time from time servers that use the Network Time Protocol (RFC 1305) to synchronize themselves.

File Name
TIME32.OCX

ActiveX/OCX Object Name
Mabry.TimeCtrl

ActiveX Compatibility
VB 4.0 (32-bit), 5.0, and 6.0

ActiveX Built With
Microsoft Visual C++ v4

ActiveX—Required DLLs
MFC40.DLL (October 6th, 1995 or later)

OLEPRO32.DLL (October 6th, 1995 or later)

MSVCRT40.DLL (September 29th, 1995 or later)

Distribution Note

> When you develop and distribute an application that uses this control, you should install the control file into the user's Windows SYSTEM directory. The control file has version information built into it. So, during installation, you should ensure that you are not overwriting a newer version.

Mabry Software, Inc.

HTTP://www.mabry.com

Time Properties

Properties that have special meaning for this control or that apply only to this control are marked with an asterisk (*).

*Action Property

*Blocking Property

*GMTTime Property

*Host Property

*LastError Property

*LocalTime Property

*Version Property

Time Events

Events that have special meaning for this control or that apply only to this control are marked with an asterisk (*).

*AsyncError Event

*Done Event

Time Methods

Methods that have special meaning for this control or that apply only to this control are marked with an asterisk (*).

*AboutBox Method

*GetTime Method

How do I set the system time using the Mabry Time control?

Use the LocalTime property to set Visual Basic's Time statement, as in the following example:

```
Time = Time1.LocalTime
```

If you want to do a bit of validation first:

```
If IsDate(Time1.LocalTime) Then
    Time = Time1.LocalTime
End If
```

How do I enable/disable the Windows 95 Dial-Up Networking connect prompt when my application issues a Connect method?

The fact that the DUN pops up when attempting to establish a network connection is a Win95 OS setting. To change this behavior, choose Dial-Up Networking from "My Computer," and select "Settings…" from the "Connections" menu. Set the desired value in the "When establishing a network connection" frame.

How do I convert my code from BLOCKING (Synchronous) to NONBLOCKING (Asynchronous)?

Check out the simple, nonblocking samples available on our sample code page at `http://www.mabry.com/sampcode.htm`.

Also, a quick fix for converting blocking code to nonblocking code is as follows:

```
Blocking=False
```

In the Declarations of the Form, add

```
Private fDone as Boolean
```

In the Done event of the control, set the fDone flag as shown:

```
Private Sub mMail1_Done()
    fDone = True
End Sub
```

Then, when invoking a method, just loop until the Done event sets the fDone flag:

```
fDone = False
mMail1.Connect
Do
    DoEvents
    'here is where your application
    'can do other things
Loop Until (fDone)
```

Notes:

You might want to set a timer in the loop so it won't loop endlessly if some problem occurs. Also, depending upon your code, you might want to conditionally set the fDone flag in the AsyncError event.

This method isn't recommended for the FTP control because the DoEvents might result in packets arriving out of sequence.

How can I detect whether someone has entered an IP or host name?

You can use the following function to check for a host name or IP address.

```
' This Function receives a string argument and
' validates whether the string is a valid IP value,
' by verifying that it is in the format of w.x.y.z and
' that each octet is between 0 and 255
'
' Returns True if IP there are 4 octets and each is
' between 0 and 255.
'
' Returns False in all other cases
'
' Disclaimer — this function will not detect certain
' values such as netmasks like 255.255.255.255,
' which meet the criteria but are not valid IPs.
'
Private Function Valid_IP(IP As String) As Boolean
    Dim i As Integer
    Dim dot_count As Integer
    Dim test_octect As String

    IP = Trim$(IP)
```

```
    ' make sure the IP long enough before
    ' continuing
    If Len(IP) < 8 Then
        Valid_IP = False
        Exit Function
    End If

    i = 1
    dot_count = 0
    For i = 1 To Len(IP)
        If Mid$(IP, i, 1) = "." Then
            ' increment the dot count and
            ' clear the test octet variable
            dot_count = dot_count + 1
            test_octet = ""
            If i = Len(IP) Then
                ' we've ended with a dot
                ' this is not good
                Valid_IP = False
                Exit Function
            End If
        Else
            test_octet = test_octet & Mid$(IP, i, 1)
            On Error Resume Next
            byte_check = CByte(test_octet)
            If (Err) Then
                ' either the value is not numeric
                ' or exceeds the range of the byte
                ' data type.
                Valid_IP = False
                Exit Function
            End If
        End If
    Next i
    ' so far, so good
    ' did we get the correct number of dots?
    If dot_count <> 3 Then
        Valid_IP = False
        Exit Function
    End If
    ' we have a valid IP format!
    Valid_IP = True
End Function
```

What is the meaning of Error 20002 "unexpected server response"?

The control has issued some command and the server didn't accept it. It could be anything from an improperly formatted email address to an unimplemented command on the server. You'll have to enable debugging to see what the command and reply are.

Time

I'm unclear on blocking. Can you explain it to me?

When your application requests data from a network connection, it is hard to predict how long it takes before the data arrives and the call completes. As a programmer, you have to determine whether to wait for the outcome of the call or return immediately to your application and get the data *when* the data arrives.

Calls that wait are called *blocking* calls. Because the call must complete before the application continues, blocking calls are also referred to as synchronous calls.

Calls that return control to your application immediately are called *nonblocking* calls. Because your application can perform tasks while the call is retrieving the data, nonblocking calls are also referred to as asynchronous calls.

Mabry Internet controls support both blocking and nonblocking calls.

It is important to note that even when using blocking calls, Windows can send event messages (such as Timer events, mouse clicks, and so on) to your application and it can respond to them. This can result in errors. It is the responsibility of the programmer to minimize the likelihood of these situations (such as disabling any Timers or command buttons that interrupt the call) and handle any errors if such conditions arise.

Error handling is very important when issuing calls to a network. Always use some method of On Error handling when invoking blocking calls. For nonblocking calls, normal On Error handling is required in addition to responding to the AsyncError event.

Should I use blocking or nonblocking calls?

It depends on your application. See a later section, "Blocking Property," for a complete description of blocking versus nonblocking.

Why do I keep getting the error "Busy executing asynchronous command"?

A call has been invoked, but a previous call hasn't completed yet. Either set Blocking mode to true or wait for the Done event before issuing subsequent commands.

It is important to note that even when using blocking calls, Windows can send event messages (such as Timer events, mouse clicks, and so on) to your application and it can respond to them. This can result in errors. It is the responsibility of the programmer to minimize the likelihood of these situations (such as disabling any Timers or command buttons that interrupt the call) and handle any errors if such conditions arise.

How do I tell what's happening when the control is talking to a server?

The Internet Pack controls have debugging support built-in. Simply set the Debug property on the control to 1 and then add the following code to the Debug event of the control:

```
Debug.Print Message
```

Error Codes

Constant	Value	Description
	0	No error.
WSAEINTR	10004	System level interrupt interrupted socket operation.
WSAEBADF	10009	Generic error for invalid format, bad format.
WSAEACCES	10013	Generic error for access violation.
WSAEFAULT	10014	Generic error for fault.
WSAEINVAL	10022	Generic error for invalid format, entry, and so on
WSAEMFILE	10024	Generic error for file error.
	10025	The IP address provided is not valid or the host specified by the IP does not exist.
WSAENOTSOCK	10038	Invalid socket or not connected to remote.
WSAEADDRINUSE	10048	The specified address is already in use.
WSAEADDRNOTAVAIL	10049	The specified address is not available.
WSAENETDOWN	10050	The connected network is not available.
WSAENETUNREACH	10051	The connected network is not reachable.
WSAENETRESET	10052	The connected network connection has been reset.
WSAECONNABORTED	10053	The current connection has been aborted by the network or intermediate services.
WSAECONNRESET	10054	The current socket connection has been reset.
WSAENOTCONN	10057	The current socket has not been connected.
WSAESHUTDOWN	10058	The connection has been shutdown.
WSAETIMEDOUT	10060	The current connection has timed out.
WSAECONNREFUSED	10061	The requested connection has been refused by the remote host.
WSAENAMETOOLONG	10063	Specified host name is too long.
WSAEHOSTDOWN	10064	Remote host is currently unavailable.

Time

Constant	Value	Description
WSAEHOSTUNREACH	10065	Remote host is currently unreachable.
WSASYSNOTREADY	10091	Remote system is not ready.
WSAVERNOTSUPPORTED	10092	Current socket version not supported by application.
WSANOTINITIALISED	10093	Socket API is not initialized.
WSAEDISCON	10101	Socket has been disconnected.

AboutBox Method

Description
Displays the About Box for the control.

Syntax
object.**AboutBox**

The syntax of the **AboutBox** method has these parts:

Part	Description
object	Required. A Time control.

Remarks
This method displays the About Box for this control, which includes copyright information.

Action Property

Description
Causes control to initiate a command/method.

Syntax
object.**Action** [= *action*]

The syntax of the **Action** property has these parts:

Part	Description
object	A Time control.
action	An integer that determines the action to take.

Remarks
Setting this property makes the time control perform an action. The action depends on the value set. Time accepts the following:

Value	Description
1	Retrieves the time. This works the same as the GetTime method.

Data Type
Integer (enumerated)

AsyncError Event

Description
Fired when an error occurs during asynchronous operations.

Syntax
Sub *object*_AsyncError([*index* As Integer,] *errornumber* As Integer, *errormessage* As String)

The syntax of the **AsyncError** event has these parts:

Part	Description
object	A Time control.
index	An integer that identifies a control if it's in a control array.
errornumber	An integer that holds the current error number.
errormessage	A string expression that holds text describing the current error.

Remarks
If an error occurs during the execution of asynchronous commands (only possible when Blocking is set to False), the program is notified by firing the **AsyncError** event.

Blocking Property

Description
Determines if methods or actions are blocking.

Syntax
object.Blocking [= *boolean*]

The syntax of the **Blocking** property has these parts:

Part	Description
object	A Time control.
Boolean	A *Boolean* flag that determines whether the control waits for completion of an operation (True) or returns control to the program immediately (False).

Remarks
If this property is set to True, any commands using either the Action property or any of the methods won't return to your code until the command completes. In other words, the command is handled synchronously.

Time

If this property is False, any commands are handled asynchronously. They return to you immediately. You are notified of completion with the Done event. When the user interface requires that the user be able to cancel file transfers, it is recommended that Blocking be set to False so that your program can respond quickly to user actions.

Data Type
Integer (*Boolean*)

Done Event

Description
This event procedure is fired when the control retrieves the current time.

Syntax
Sub *object*_Done([*index* As Integer,] *errornumber* As Integer)

The syntax of the **Done** event has these parts:

Part	Description
object	A Time control.
index	An integer that identifies a control if it's in a control array.
errornumber	An integer that is always zero. This can be ignored.

Remarks
This event fires when an asynchronous time retrieval operation completes (when Blocking is set to False). The current time will be found in the GMTTime and LocalTime properties. They are formatted as follows:

mon-dd-yyyy hh:mm:ss

For example:
    Feb-26-1995 08:25:22
    Aug-14-1996 10:30:58

GetTime Method

Description
Gets current time from specified server.

Syntax
object.**GetTime***host,blocking*

The syntax of the **GetTime** method has these parts:

Part	Description
object	Required. A Time control.
host	Optional. A string that holds either the name of the time host or the IP address of the time host.
blocking	Optional. A *Boolean* flag that determines if the method returns immediately (False) or if the control waits until completion to return (True).

Remarks

This method requests the current time from the host. If no host is specified, the Host property is used.

This method can be called in one of two ways: blocking or nonblocking. This is determined by the *Blocking* parameter or, if the Blocking parameter is not specified, the Blocking property.

If blocking, the Time control doesn't return control to your program until it retrieves the time from the host specified or until it times out.

With nonblocking, the control returns immediately. The control fires the Done event upon completion (good or bad). Sometimes, with the nonblocking method, a warning is reported (10035) immediately. This is only a warning from the WinSock layer letting you know that transmission to the host needs to wait, briefly, and can be treated as normal.

GMTTime Property

Description
Holds the last time retrieved from a time server (Greenwich Mean Time).

Syntax
`object.GMTTime`

The syntax of the **GMTTime** property has these parts:

Part	Description
object	A Time control.

Remarks
This property is valid only after a GetTime method or Action property command retrieves the time from a time server. GMTTime is formatted as follows:

    mon-dd-yyyy hh:mm:ss

For example:

    Feb-26-1995 08:25:22
    Aug-14-1996 10:30:58

Time

GMTTime's format is compatible with Visual Basic's CDate, CVDate, IsTime and related functions. This property is only available at runtime and is read-only.

Data Type
String

Host Property

Description
Time requests information from the host with this address.

Syntax
object.**Host** [= *hostname*]

The syntax of the **Host** property has these parts:

Part	Description
object	A Time control.
hostname	A string expression that holds the name or IP address of a time server.

Remarks
This property determines which server that the Time control polls for the Greenwich Mean Time. The time is retrieved when you use either the Action property or the GetTime method.

Data Type
String

LastError Property

Description
Holds the last error number reported.

Syntax
object.**LastError**

The syntax of the **LastError** property has these parts:

Part	Description
object	A Time control.

Remarks
This property contains the result of the last method executed. It is zero if the last method completed without error. Otherwise, it contains an error code.

This property is read-only and only available at runtime.

Data Type
Integer

LocalTime Property

Description
Holds the last time retrieved from a time server (based on your local time zone).

Syntax
object.`LocalTime`

The syntax of the **LocalTime** property has these parts:

Part	Description
object	A Time control.

Remarks
This property is valid only after a GetTime method or Action property command retrieves the time from a time server. LocalTime is formatted as follows :

```
mon-dd-yyyy hh:mm:ss
```

For example:
```
Feb-26-1995 08:25:22
Aug-14-1996 10:30:58
```

LocalTime's format is compatible with Visual Basic's CDate, CVDate, IsTime and related functions. This property is only available at runtime and is read-only.

Data Type
String

Version Property

Description
Returns the version of the control.

Syntax
object.`Version`

The syntax of the **Version** property has these parts:

Part	Description
object	A Time control.

Remarks
This property holds the current version of the control. It is read-only and available at both design time and runtime.

Time

Data Type
String

How to Buy the Source Code for This Control

CREDITS
Time was written by Zane Thomas.

CONTACT INFORMATION
Orders, inquiries, technical support, questions, comments, and so on can be sent to mabry@mabry.com on the Internet. Our mailing address/contact information is

Mabry Software, Inc.
503 316th Street Northwest
Stanwood, WA 98292

Sales: 1-800-99-MABRY (U.S. only)
Voice: 360-629-9278
Fax: 360-629-9278
Web: http://www.mabry.com

COST
The cost of Time and the C/C++ source code (of the control itself) is US$50 (US$55 for International orders).

Prices are subject to change without notice.

DELIVERY METHODS
We can ship this software to you via air mail or email.

Air Mail—you will receive disks, a printed manual, and printed receipt if you choose this delivery method. The costs are

US$10.00	US Priority Mail
US$15.00	Airborne Express 2nd Day (US deliveries only)
US$20.00	Airborne Express Overnight (US deliveries only)
US$20.00	Global Priority Mail (Int'l deliveries only; Western Europe, Pacific Rim and Canada only)
US$45.00	International Airborne Express (Int'l deliveries only)

Email—We can ship this package to you via email. You need to have an email account that can accept large file attachments (which includes CompuServe, AOL, and most Internet providers). If you choose this option, please note: A printed manual is not included. We will, however, email a receipt to you.

Be sure to include your full mailing address with your order. Sometimes (on the Internet) the package cannot be emailed, so we are forced to send it through normal mail.

CompuServe Email—CompuServe members can use the software registration forum (GO SWREG) to register this package. Time's SWREG ID number is 6524. The source code version's ID number is 9063. PLEASE NOTE: When you order through SWREG, we send the registered package to your CompuServe account (not your Internet or AOL account) within a few hours.

Mabry Software, Inc.

HTTP://www.mabry.com

ORDER/PAYMENT METHODS

You can order this software by phone, fax, email, mail. Please note that orders must include all information that is requested on our order form. Your shipment WILL BE DELAYED if we have to contact you for additional information (such as phone number, street address, and so on).

You can pay by credit card (VISA, MasterCard, American Express, Discover, NOVUS), check (U.S. dollars drawn on a U.S. bank), cash, International Money Order, International Postal Order, Purchase Order (established business entities only—terms net 30), or wire transfer.

WIRE TRANSFER INFORMATION

Here is the information you need regarding our account for a wire funds transfer:

Bank Name:	SeaFirst—Stone Way Branch
Bank Address:	3601 Stone Way North
	Seattle, WA 98103
Bank Phone:	206-585-4951
Account Name:	Mabry Software, Inc.
Routing Number:	12000024
Account Number:	16311706

If you are paying with a wire transfer of funds, please add US$25.00 to your order. This is the fee that SeaFirst Bank charges Mabry Software. Also, please ADD ANY ADDITIONAL FEES THAT YOUR BANK MIGHT CHARGE for wire transfer service. If you are paying with a wire transfer, we must have full payment deposited to our account before we can ship your order.

Copyright © 1996-1998 by Mabry Software, Inc.

Time

Time Order Form

Mail this form to

Mabry Software, Inc.
503 316th Street Northwest
Stanwood, WA 98292

Phone: 360-629-9278
Fax: 360-629-9278
Internet: mabry@mabry.com
Web: www.mabry.com

Where did you get this copy of Time? _____

Name: _____

Ship to: _____

_____

_____

_____

Phone: _____

Fax: _____

Email: _____

Credit Card #: _____ exp. _____

P.O. # (if any): _____

Signature _____

Qty ordered _____ SOURCE CODE AND REGISTRATION

$50.00 ($55.00 international). Check or money order in U.S. currency drawn on a U.S. bank. Add $10.00 per order for shipping and handling.

ZipInf

Description
ZipInf OCX is a Visual Basic custom control that lets you determine the number of files in a ZIP file plus many items of useful information about each file, including the compressed size of each file, its 32-bit CRC, its date stamp, time stamp, associated comment, name, method of compression, and full uncompressed size,

ZipInf doesn't compress or decompress data.

File Name
ZIPINF32.OCX

ActiveX/OCX Object Name
Mabry.ZipInfCtrl

ActiveX Compatibility
VB 4.0 (32-bit), 5.0, and 6.0

ActiveX Built With
Microsoft Visual C++ v4

ActiveX—Required DLLs
MFC40.DLL (October 6th, 1995 or later)

OLEPRO32.DLL (October 6th, 1995 or later)

MSVCRT40.DLL (September 29th, 1995 or later)

Distribution Note
> When you develop and distribute an application that uses this control, you should install the control file into the user's Windows SYSTEM directory. The control file has version information built into it. So, during installation, you should ensure that you are not overwriting a newer version.

Mabry Software, Inc.

HTTP://www.mabry.com

ZipInf Properties

Properties that have special meaning for this control or that apply only to this control are marked with an asterisk (*).

Align Property
*DateFormat Property
Enabled Property
*FileComment Property
*FileName Property
*ItemCompressed Property
*ItemCRC Property
*ItemDate Property
*ItemFileComment Property
*ItemFileName Property

*ItemMethod Property
*ItemTime Property
*ItemUncompressed Property
Left Property
*ListCount Property
Name Property
Tag Property
Top Property
*Version Property

ZipInf Methods

Methods that have special meaning for this control or that apply only to this control are marked with an asterisk (*).

Clear Method

DateFormat Property Example

In this example, the program shows how the DateFormat property affects the ItemDate property. To try this example, paste the code into the Declarations section of a form that contains two text boxes, a command button, and a ZipInf control. Press F5. Fill in the first text box with a legitimate ZIP file name (with full path). Fill in the second text box with a date format string (such as "MM-DD-YY" or "D-M-YYYY"). Then, press the command button.

```
Sub Command1_Click ()

Dim I As Integer

List1.Clear
ZipInfo1.FileName = Text1.Text
ZipInfo1.DateFormat = Text2.Text
For I = 0 To ZipInfo1.ListCount - 1
List1.AddItem ZipInfo1.ItemFileName(I) & " " & ZipInfo1.ItemDate(I)
Next I

End Sub
```

ZipInf

File Properties Example

In this example, the program shows the ListCount and FileComment properties. To try this example, paste the code into the Declarations section of a form that contains two labels, a text box, a command button, and a ZipInf control. Press F5. Fill in the text box with the filename (including full path) of a ZIP file. Then, press the command button.

```
Sub Command1_Click ()

ZipInfo1.FileName = Text1.Text
If Len(ZipInfo1.FileComment) = 0 Then
Label1.Caption = "FileComment: (none)"
Else
Label1.Caption = "FileComment: " & ZipInfo1.FileComment      End If
Label2.Caption = "ListCount: " & ZipInfo1.ListCount

End Sub
```

Item Properties Example

In this example, the program shows the various ZIP file item properties. To try this example, paste the code into the Declarations section of a form that contains seven labels (make these somewhat wide), a text box, a command button, a list box, and a ZipInf control. Press F5. Fill in the text box with the filename (including full path) of a ZIP file. Then, click on various file names in the list box.

```
Sub Command1_Click ()

Dim I As Integer

ZipInfo1.FileName = Text1.Text
List1.Clear
For I = 0 To ZipInfo1.ListCount - 1
List1.AddItem
ZipInfo1.ItemFileName(I)
Next I

End Sub
Sub List1_Click ()

Dim I As Integer

I = List1.ListIndex
Label1.Caption = "ItemCompressed: " & ZipInfo1.ItemCompressed(I)
↳Label2.Caption = "ItemCRC: " & Hex$(ZipInfo1.ItemCRC(I))
↳Label3.Caption = "ItemDate: " & ZipInfo1.ItemDate(I)
Label4.Caption = "ItemFileComment: " & ZipInfo1.ItemFileComment(I)
↳Label5.Caption = "ItemMethod: " & ZipInfo1.ItemMethod(I)
↳Label6.Caption = "ItemTime: " & ZipInfo1.ItemTime(I)
Label7.Caption = "ItemUncompressed: " & ZipInfo1.ItemUncompressed(I)
End Sub
```

DateFormat Property

Description
Determines the format of the date used by the ItemDate property.

Syntax
object.DateFormat

The syntax of the **DateFormat** property has these parts:

Part	Description
object	A ZipInf control.

Remarks
Setting this property determines the format of the date used with the ItemDate property. This can be used to override the international settings found in WIN.INI. By using this property, you can ensure that you always get a date formatted in a specific fashion. If you leave it to the format found in WIN.INI, you'll have to figure out what format (that is, MM/DD/YY, DD/MM/YY, or YY/MM/DD) it is.

This string can consist of punctuation and symbols. The symbols are

Symbol	Meaning
d	Day of the month: 1–31
dd	Day of the month: 01–31
m	Month of the year: 1–12
mm	Month of the year: 01–12
yy	Year: 00–99
yyyy	Year: 1970–2099

More information about this format can be found in the Windows Resource Kit under **[intl] Section**, and in the VB Programmer's Guide under **Format$**.

Data Type
String

FileComment Property

Description
Holds the comment field from the ZIP file.

Syntax
object.FileComment

ZipInf

The syntax of the **FileComment** property has these parts:

Part	Description
object	A ZipInf control.

Remarks
This property holds the comment string loaded from the ZIP file (specified by the FileName property).

This property is read-only.

Data Type
String

FileName Property

Description
Specifies the ZIP file to examine.

Syntax
object.**FileName** [= filename]

The syntax of the **FileName** property has these parts:

Part	Description
object	A ZipInf control.
filename	A string expression that holds the full path and filename to a ZIP file.

Remarks
Setting this property causes ZipInf to load the various properties with information from the ZIP file specified. If the file specified is not found, ZipInf causes a File Not Found (7) error. If the file specified isn't a ZIP file, ZipInf causes a Not a ZIP File (29999) error. If the ZIP file is corrupt, ZipInf causes a Corrupt ZIP File (29998) error.

Data Type
String

ItemFileComment Property

Description
Contains the comment associated with a file in the ZIP file.

Syntax
object.**ItemFileComment**(FileIndex)

The syntax of the **ItemFileComment** property has these parts:

Part	Description
object	A ZipInf control.
FileIndex	An integer that identifies a file contained with the ZIP file.

Remarks

This property returns the comment associated with the file specified by *FileIndex*. *FileIndex* must be between 0 and ListCount –1.

This property is read-only and only available at runtime.

Data Type
String

ItemFileName Property

Description
Contains the names of the files in a ZIP file.

Syntax
`object.ItemFileName( FileIndex )`

The syntax of the **ItemFileName** property has these parts:

Part	Description
object	A ZipInf control.
FileIndex	An integer that identifies a file contained with the ZIP file.

Remarks
This property returns the name of the file specified by *FileIndex*. *FileIndex* must be between 0 and ListCount –1.

This property is read-only and only available at runtime.

Data Type
String

ItemCompressed Property

Description
Contains the compressed size of a file in the ZIP file.

Syntax
`object.ItemCompressed( FileIndex )`

ZipInf

The syntax of the **ItemCompressed** property has these parts:

Part	Description
object	A ZipInf control.
FileIndex	An integer that identifies a file contained with the ZIP file.

Remarks

This property returns the compressed size (that is, how much space it takes up in the ZIP file) of the file specified by *FileIndex*. *FileIndex* must be between 0 and ListCount –1. The format of this property is determined by the short date format in WIN.INI and by the DateFormat property (which takes precedence).

This property is read-only and only available at runtime.

Data Type
Integer (long)

ItemCRC Property

Description
Contains the 32-bit CRC of a file in the ZIP file.

Syntax
`object.ItemCRC( FileIndex )`

The syntax of the **ItemCRC** property has these parts:

Part	Description
object	A ZipInf control.
FileIndex	An integer that identifies a file contained with the ZIP file.

Remarks

This property returns the 32-bit cyclic redundancy check (CRC) of the file specified by *FileIndex*. *FileIndex* must be between 0 and ListCount –1. The format of this property is determined by the short date format in WIN.INI and by the DateFormat property (which takes precedence).

This property is read-only and only available at runtime.

Data Type
Integer (long)

ItemDate Property

Description
Contains the date stamp of a file in the ZIP file.

Syntax

object.**ItemDate**(*FileIndex*)

The syntax of the **ItemDate** property has these parts:

Part	Description
object	A ZipInf control.
FileIndex	An integer that identifies a file contained with the ZIP file.

Remarks

This property returns the date stamp on the file specified by *FileIndex*. *FileIndex* must be between 0 and ListCount –1. The format of this property is determined by the short date format in WIN.INI and by the DateFormat property (which takes precedence).

This property is read-only and only available at runtime.

Data Type
String

ItemMethod Property

Description
Contains the compressed method used for a file in the ZIP file.

Syntax

object.**ItemMethod**(*FileIndex*)

The syntax of the **ItemMethod** property has these parts:

Part	Description
object	A ZipInf control.
FileIndex	An integer that identifies a file contained with the ZIP file.

Remarks

This property returns the compressed method used on the file specified by *FileIndex*. *FileIndex* must be between 0 and ListCount –1. The compression methods are

Value	Description
0	No compression—stored.
1	Shrunk
2	Reduced
3	Reduced
4	Reduced
5	Reduced
6	Imploded
7	Tokenized (not used)
8	Deflated

This property is read-only and only available at runtime.

Data Type
Integer

ItemTime Property

Description
Contains the time stamp of a file in the ZIP file.

Syntax
`object.ItemTime( FileIndex )`

The syntax of the **ItemTime** property has these parts:

Part	Description
object	A ZipInf control.
FileIndex	An integer that identifies a file contained with the ZIP file.

Remarks
This property returns the time stamp on the file specified by *FileIndex*. *FileIndex* must be between 0 and ListCount −1. This property's format is HH:MM:SS (that is, similar to the default Time$ format).

This property is read-only and only available at runtime.

Data Type
String

ItemUncompressed Property

Description
Contains the full size of a file in the ZIP file.

Syntax
`object.ItemUncompressed( FileIndex )`

The syntax of the **ItemUncompressed** property has these parts:

Part	Description
object	A ZipInf control.
FileIndex	An integer that identifies a file contained with the ZIP file.

Remarks
This property returns the full size (that is, uncompressed, in bytes) of the file specified by FileIndex. FileIndex must be between 0 and ListCount −1.

This property is read-only and only available at runtime.

Data Type
Integer (long)

ListCount Property

Description
Specifies the number of files within the ZIP file.

Syntax
`object.ListCount`

The syntax of the **ListCount** property has these parts:

Part	Description
object	A ZipInf control.

Remarks
This property gets set when the FileName property is set. This property tells how many files are in the ZIP file. The information about the individual files can be accessed through the following properties: ItemCRC, ItemCompressed, ItemDate, ItemFileName, ItemFileComment, ItemMethod, ItemTime, and ItemUncompressed.

If the file currently selected isn't a ZIP file or if the file specified doesn't exist, this property is set to –1.

This property is read-only.

Data Type
Integer

Version Property

Description
Returns the version of the control.

Syntax
`object.Version`

The syntax of the **Version** property has these parts:

Part	Description
object	A ZipInf control.

Remarks
This property holds the current version of the control. It is read-only and available at both design time and runtime.

Data Type
String

ZipInf

How to Buy the Source Code for This Control

CREDITS
ZipInf was written by James Shields.

CONTACT INFORMATION
Orders, inquiries, technical support, questions, comments, and so on can be sent to mabry@mabry.com on the Internet. Our mailing address/contact information is

Mabry Software, Inc.
503 316th Street Northwest
Stanwood, WA 98292

Sales: 1-800-99-MABRY (U.S. only)
Voice: 360-629-9278
Fax: 360-629-9278
Web: http://www.mabry.com

COST
The cost of ZipInf and the C/C++ source code (of the control itself) is US$50 (US$55 for International orders).

Prices are subject to change without notice.

DELIVERY METHODS
We can ship this software to you via air mail or email.

Air Mail—you will receive disks, a printed manual, and printed receipt if you choose this delivery method. The costs are

US$10.00	US Priority Mail
US$15.00	Airborne Express 2nd Day (US deliveries only)
US$20.00	Airborne Express Overnight (US deliveries only)
US$20.00	Global Priority Mail (Int'l deliveries only; Western Europe, Pacific Rim and Canada only)
US$45.00	International Airborne Express (Int'l deliveries only)

Email—We can ship this package to you via email. You need to have an email account that can accept large file attachments (which includes CompuServe, AOL, and most Internet providers). If you choose this option, please note: A printed manual is not included. We will, however, email a receipt to you.

Be sure to include your full mailing address with your order. Sometimes (on the Internet) the package cannot be emailed, so we are forced to send it through normal mail.

CompuServe Email—CompuServe members can use the software registration forum (GO SWREG) to register this package. ZipInf's SWREG ID number is 1595. The source code version's ID number is 1596. PLEASE NOTE: When you order through SWREG, we send the registered package to your CompuServe account (not your Internet or AOL account) within a few hours.

Mabry Software, Inc.

HTTP://www.mabry.com

ORDER/PAYMENT METHODS

You can order this software by phone, fax, email, or mail. Please note that orders must include all information that is requested on our order form. Your shipment WILL BE DELAYED if we have to contact you for additional information (such as phone number, street address, and so on).

You can pay by credit card (VISA, MasterCard, American Express, Discover, NOVUS), check (U.S. dollars drawn on a U.S. bank), cash, International Money Order, International Postal Order, Purchase Order (established business entities only—terms net 30), or wire transfer.

WIRE TRANSFER INFORMATION

Here is the information you need regarding our account for a wire funds transfer:

Bank Name:	SeaFirst—Stone Way Branch
Bank Address:	3601 Stone Way North
	Seattle, WA 98103
Bank Phone:	206-585-4951
Account Name:	Mabry Software, Inc.
Routing Number:	12000024
Account Number:	16311706

If you are paying with a wire transfer of funds, please add US$25.00 to your order. This is the fee that SeaFirst Bank charges Mabry Software. Also, please ADD ANY ADDITIONAL FEES THAT YOUR BANK MIGHT CHARGE for wire transfer service. If you are paying with a wire transfer, we must have full payment deposited to our account before we can ship your order.

Copyright © 1993-1998 by Mabry Software, Inc.

ZipInf

ZipInf Order Form

Mail this form to

Mabry Software, Inc.
503 316th Street Northwest
Stanwood, WA 98292

Phone: 360-629-9278
Fax: 360-629-9278
Internet: mabry@mabry.com
Web: www.mabry.com

Where did you get this copy of ZipInf? _____

Name: _____

Ship to: _____

_____

_____

_____

Phone: _____

Fax: _____

Email: _____

Credit Card #: _____ exp. _____

P.O. # (if any): _____

Signature _____

Qty ordered ____ SOURCE CODE AND REGISTRATION

$50.00 ($55.00 international). Check or money order in U.S. currency drawn on a U.S. bank. Add $10.00 per order for shipping and handling.

What's on the CD-ROM

What's on the CD-ROM

The companion CD-ROM contains full versions of eight Mabry Software Controls: DFInfo, Indic, Joystk, Led, Mail, Slider, Time, and ZipInf.

Windows 95 Installation Instructions

1. Insert the CD-ROM into your CD-ROM drive.
2. From the Windows 95 desktop, double-click the My Computer icon.
3. Double-click the icon representing your CD-ROM drive.
4. Double-click the icon titled START.EXE to run the CD-ROM interface. You can install any or all of the Mabry controls from the interface.

Note

If Windows 95 is installed on your computer, and you have the AutoPlay feature enabled, the START.EXE program starts automatically whenever you insert the disc into your CD-ROM drive.

Windows NT Installation Instructions

1. Insert the CD-ROM into your CD-ROM drive.
2. From File Manager or Program Manager, choose Run from the File menu.
3. Type <drive>\START.EXE and press Enter, where <drive> corresponds to the drive letter of your CD-ROM. For example, if your CD-ROM is drive D:, type D:\START.EXE and press Enter. This will run the CD-ROM interface. You can install any or all of the Mabry controls from the interface.

FREE ISSUE!

FREE CD-ROM GIFT

The Ultimate Add-on Tool for Microsoft Visual Basic

As part of your purchase, you are eligible to receive a free issue of ***Visual Basic Programmer's Journal***, the leading magazine for Visual Basic programmers.

There's a lot to know about Visual Basic and its improved development tools. And ***VBPJ*** is the only magazine devoted to giving you the timely information you need with articles on subjects like:
- When—and how—to use the latest data access technologies
- How DHTML and the Web affect the way you develop and deploy apps
- Which new Visual Basic features save time—and which to avoid
- Creating reusable code with Visual Basic classes

But don't let the development information stop with your free issue. When you subscribe to ***VBPJ***, we'll also send you a **FREE** CD-ROM – with three issues of ***VBPJ*** in electronically readable format, plus all the source code & sample apps from each issue.

Filled with hands-on articles and indispensable tips, tricks and utilities, *Visual Basic Programmer's Journal* will save your hours of programming time. And, ***VBPJ*** is the only magazine devoted to making VB programmers more productive.

A single tip can more than pay for a year's subscription.

Send for your free issue today.

MY GUARANTEE

If at any time I do not agree that *Visual Basic Programmer's Journal* is the best, most useful source of information on Visual Basic, I can cancel my subscription and receive a full refund.

☐ ***YES!*** Please rush me the next issue of ***Visual Basic Programmer's Journal*** to examine without obligation. If I like it, I'll pay the low rate of $22.95,* for a full year—eleven additional issues plus the annual ***Buyers Guide*** and ***Enterprise*** issue, (for a total of fourteen). Also, with my paid subscription, I'll receive a **FREE** gift—three issues (with sample apps and code) of ***VBPJ*** on CD-ROM! If I choose not to subscribe, I'll simply write cancel on my bill and owe nothing. The free issue is mine to keep with your compliments.

Name: _____

Company: _____

Address: _____

_____

City: _____ State: _____ Zip: _____

* Basic annual subscription rate is $34.97. Your subscription is for 12 monthly issues plus two bonus issues. Canada/Mexico residents please add $18/year for surface delivery. All other countries please add $44/year for air mail delivery. Canadian GST included. Send in this card or fax your order to 415.853.0230. Microsoft and Visual Basic are registered trademarks and ActiveX is a trademark of Microsoft Corporation.

8035

FREE ISSUE!

Find out for yourself what *Visual Basic Programmer's Journal* can do for you.

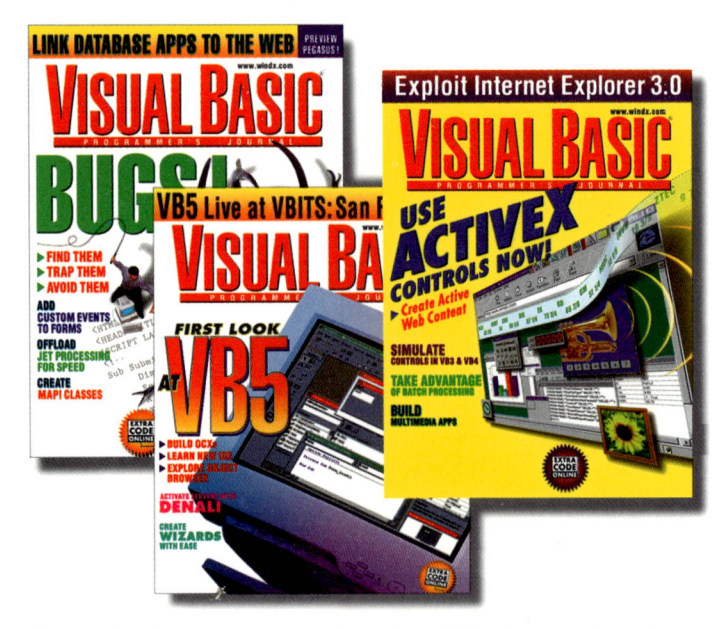

Visual Basic is the most productive Windows development environment. Get the most out of it by learning from the experts that write for ***Visual Basic Programmer's Journal.***

BUSINESS REPLY MAIL
FIRST CLASS MAIL   PERMIT NO. 317   PALO ALTO

POSTAGE WILL BE PAID BY ADDRESSEE

Visual Basic Programmer's Journal
P.O. Box 58872
Boulder, CO 80323-8872

NO POSTAGE
NECESSARY
IF MAILED
IN THE
UNITED STATES

Check out select articles online at http://www.devx.com